DETECTING MEN

Author's Note

Any good reference is a work in progress and *Detecting Men* is no exception. From the first keystroke of data entry in March 1996, until January 1998 when two Zip disks were delivered to our printer, constant changes were a fact of life. New series were announced, books were dropped, titles were changed, pub dates came and went, while spellings, locations and details were in a perpetual state of flux. No sooner were errors corrected than new ones popped up to take their places among the 100,000 facts presented in this first edition of *Detecting Men*. We would like to say you'll find perfect consistency among the various chapters in this book, but we know that is not the case. The most current and up-to-date information is always presented in Chapter 1, The Master List. If you find conflicting information elsewhere in the book, you should always assume the Master List, including profile text, character description, title list and awards information, is the most current and accurate data we have collected. A wise friend once suggested a few errors be scattered about so as not to disappoint those who take great pleasure in finding them. We have happily obliged.

DETECTING MEN

A Reader's Guide and Checklist
for Mystery Series Written by Men

Willetta L. Heising

PURPLE
MOON
PRESS

For information address: Purple Moon Press, 3319 Greenfield Road, Suite 317, Dearborn, Michigan 48120-1212.

Phone 313-593-1033
Fax 313-593-4087
E-mail <purplemoon@prodigy.net> or <willetta@purplemoonpress.com>

Excerpts from Barry Gardner's reviews of *Detecting Women* and *Detecting Women 2* are reprinted with the kind permission of George Easter, Editor and Publisher, *Deadly Pleasures*.

ISBN: 0-9644593-3-7

Printed on recycled paper and bound in the USA by
Malloy Lithographing, Inc. of Ann Arbor, Michigan

Cover design, electronic prepress and text design by
Jacqué Consulting & Design of Dearborn, Michigan

The paper used in this publication meets the minimum requirements of American National Standard for Information Sciences—Permanence of Paper for Printed Library Materials.
ANSI Z39.48-1984

First printing February 1998

Publisher's Cataloging-in-Publication
(Provided by Quality Books, Inc.)

Heising, Willetta L.
 Detecting men : a reader's guide and checklist for mystery series written by men / Willetta L. Heising. – 1st ed.
  p. cm.
  Includes bibliographical references and index.
  ISBN: 0-9644593-3-7

 1. Detective and mystery stories, English—Bibliography.
 2. Detective and mystery stories, American—Bibliography.
 3. Detective and mystery stories—Miscellaneous.   I. Title

    Z2014.F4H45 1998   016.823'0872
                             QBI97-41483

DEDICATION

Barry Wilson Gardner
(1939-1996)

Brilliant critic and big-hearted man
Lover of mystery reference books

Acknowledgments

On several fronts I have been blessed with two experts for the price of one. To them I owe the largest debt. First and foremost, my senior partners and lead investors, who have been my strongest supporters from the beginning; Alice Ann Carpenter and John Leininger of Grave Matters, who've heard it all; my market research firm, Feldman & Fairstein, for their special touch; publicity experts, Kate and Doug Bandos of KSB Promotions, for their continuing support; and Linda and Dick Eddy, hawkeyed proofreaders, intrepid indexers and wonderful friends. I am so very lucky to have you guys on my team.

The list of people who have helped with *Detecting Men* is a long one. Among those who gave most generously of their time and careful attention are Janis Brown, Bill Deeck, Susan Eggers, Geraldine Galentree, Barry Gardner, Claudia Gordon, Dick Higgins, Al Hubin, Marv Lachman, Joan Martin, Doris Ann Norris, Anne Petersen, Thalia Proctor, Don Sandstrom, Ron Serduik, Sharon Villines, Judith Wainright and John Wallace.

To the heroic team at Jacqué Consulting & Design who outdid themselves, especially in the 4th quarter, my heartfelt thanks. Jackie McClure, Molly Williams, Carol Romano, Sue Stoker, Michael Tripodi, Katie Maguire and Pat Ostella—we'll start earlier next time. I promise. And to Patrice Smith, Lynn Rohkohl and the production staff at Malloy Lithographing, a very special hurrah for making this book a reality.

Thank you one and all.

CONTENTS

Lists, lists and more lists

Extras

BARRY W. GARDNER
a personal tribute

I first met Barry Gardner at EyeCon in June of 1995, although I'd been reading his reviews in *Mystery News* and *Deadly Pleasures* since early 1993. I liked his reviewing style and his taste in mysteries and I knew he was retired from the Dallas Fire Department where he'd been deputy chief. I naturally assumed he'd been a fixture in the mystery community for a very long time.

The first day at EyeCon, George Easter (*Deadly Pleasures* editor and publisher) told me Barry had reviewed **Detecting Women** for the current issue, proudly adding that a copy was included with everyone's convention registration material. "Isn't that wonderful?" George asked. I was sick. THE

Barry Gardner had reviewed **Detecting Women**. Surely he would find my first efforts lacking, and worse yet, my private-eye-writer heroes would be the first to know. I was going to crash and burn in Milwaukee. It promised to be a very long weekend. But what I didn't know was that Barry Gardner was a freak for mystery reference books. He owned them all.

Panicked at the prospect of a bad review, I didn't open my copy of *Deadly Pleasures* until late Friday night. After putting it off as long as I could, I asked friends to stand by, just in case a 911 call was needed. Imagine my surprise, relief, and sheer delight to learn that Barry Gardner approved of

DETECTING WOMEN, by Willetta L. Heising (Large-size paperback, Purple Moon Press, $19.95, March 1995). This appeared unexpected and unannounced at the Mystery Bookstore here in Dallas, and being the reference book-loving fool that I am I snapped it up. Paid real money, too.

The book is devoted to women writers' series; not to female series characters, and not to books by women in general. So you'll find Hercule Poirot but not Modesty Blaise, and no listings for Dorothy B. Hughes or Minette Walters. Given its deliberately limited scope, however, there's a lot of useful information here. It's presented in very usable form—at least for my uses—and I think it's a superb job of desktop publishing in appearance and readability. Annual updates are planned, and that's good—there are of course a number of errors, inevitable with the first edition of any reference work, and the author has already identified many books left out.

It's broken down into sections, with the largest one being an alphabetical-by-author listing of all the books in series order. There are also sections on (listings by) mystery types, series characters, settings, and a chronology that lists each book in year order. There's also a brief section on anthologies that shows each author's appearance in those covered, and sections on periodicals and awards. I like the format a lot; I wish I had the expertise and resources to do similar books on PI and police novels, and I hope someone else does and will. It won't replace any reference book on your shelf, but it's a valuable addition for anyone, and an invaluable one for those whose interest lies primarily in gender-specific reading.

Quibbles? Sure. . .I would have liked to have had publishers noted, and an indication of paperback originals. The bibliography section omits both Hubin's Crime Fiction II and **Twentieth Century Crime & Mystery Writers** (inexplicable omissions of the standard reference works on crime fiction, unless there were some criteria for inclusion not stated), and *Deadly Pleasures* (ditto). All told, though, this is a book that any real aficionado should have on her or his reference shelf.

The author states in the introduction, "I am no apologist for gender-specific interests. We read what we like." Well, yes. She obviously isn't, and we do. Having in the past been labeled sexist for having the temerity to point out that there are rather fundamental differences not only in men and women but in the kinds of books they write, I do wonder what kind of reaction a man might provoke by making the exact same comment. Sorry. I just couldn't help myself.

Barry Gardner's review is reprinted with permission from Deadly Pleasures, Issue 13, Summer 1996

Detecting Women. He actually LIKED it. (Barry's reviews of **Detecting Women** are printed below.)

And 24 hours later I was sitting at the top of the Hyatt with Les Roberts, Noreen Ayres and Barry, talking private-eye-fiction talk with the pros. Actually, they talked and I listened, for fear of saying something that would remove any doubt about my qualifications. It was the beginning of a fine friendship with Barry Gardner, however brief.

Barry was on my case about **Detecting Men** from that first meeting, but I didn't think he was serious. I told him what I told everyone who asked—"Not my book. Not my job. Not my problem. Call a man." I told Barry if he was so hot for the book, he should do it himself. In those soft Texas gentleman tones of his, he said, "Darlin' I'm plum out of ambition. You do the book. I'll help."

Overwhelmed by the size of the project, I asked Barry if he'd pick 50 books for me to read to make sure I had a good overview of contemporary series mysteries written by men. Barry's list is reprinted on page 11, along with the letter that accompanied it (page 10). The last time we talked, the afternoon of July 14, I was leaving the Cluefest hotel, on my way to the airport. He chastised me for not having brought the first stack of material for him to look over and I promised to put something in the mail within the week. His final admonition was "Don't wait too long." And Friday afternoon, July 19, he died at his desk.

This would have been a better book if Barry had lived to oversee it. But I like to think he would be pleased with we accomplished in round one. This one's for you Barry. And, yes, I'm still reading.

DETECTING WOMEN 2, by Willetta L. Heising (Large-size Trade Paperback, $24.95 Purple Moon Press, February 1996). This book is devoted to women writers' series; not to female series characters, and not to books by women in general. So you'll find Hercule Poirot but not Modesty Blaise, and no lists for Dorothy B. Hughes or Minette Walters. What you will find is a listing for just about every female author of a crime/mystery/detective series from before the turn of the century through 1995.

Chapter 1 includes each of these authors alphabetically, with a brief biographical note and comment on the series character(s), and then a chronological book-by-book listing of the series with year, and awards winners and nominees noted. Chapter 2 breaks the series down by type, listing under each grouping the author, character, date of first book, number of books in the series, sleuth's occupation, and the setting. Chapter 3 lists the series characters alphabetically by first name, providing the same information as Chapter 2. Chapter 4 groups the series by settings, with the same information. Chapter 5 offers an interesting chronology (limited to authors covered in the book) that includes each title published in each year, with a notation for first books in series. There are also some very interesting graphics. Chapter 6 is an

alphabetical list of titles with 1st in series noted, Chapter 7 deals with pseudonyms, Chapter 8 with short stories. Chapter 9 with awards and organizations (does not list award winners by year, however). Chapter 10 with resources, Chapter 11 is a glossary, Chapter 12 a bibliography, and Chapter 13 the index. Whew!

What this is, is quite simply the most useful reference book for the scope it encompasses that I've ever seen. If you are interested in series crime fiction by women authors, I cannot imagine you wanting information it fails to provide. I read a relatively small percentage of the authors included, but I nevertheless find myself browsing through DW2 just for the sheer pleasure of doing so. If you are anything more than a casual reader of crime fiction, you need this book. (And no, I don't get a commission.) The **Detecting Women 2 Pocket Guide** (which for arcane publishing reasons preceded the full-size work) is also a marvel of utility.

Detecting Men is in progress, and will cover series characters written by male authors, with the further limitation that only living authors will be included. While I bemoan the limitations, I understand the reasons for them, and I would much rather have the limited books than none like them at all. Heising deserves all our thanks, and she certainly has mine.

Barry Gardner's review is reprinted with permission from Deadly Pleasures, Issue 13, Summer 1996

Barry W. Gardner

May 27, 1996

Dear Willetta,

Herewith the list of 50 male authors who write series characters and are still alive—and as far as I know are all still actively writing. As I told you it would be, the list is shy on serial killers, cozies, thrillers, and Big Lawyer books; it mostly reflects my own tastes, though there are a couple of authors included I'm not that fond of but thought you ought to be familiar with. With some authors which book you read is of little or no importance (though I've always listed my choice of one of the best), but with others it is. Any title with an asterisk is one that I think is important; any without one can be substituted for with little impact. The name of the series character follows the title, and without further ado:

(Barry's list is reprinted on the facing page.)

Looking back over the list, I can say two things: a) it's idiosyncratic as all hell but includes at least *most* of the male series writers who would be considered important, and b) if you read all fifty books you'll be better acquainted with male series writers than are most people. Hope it's of help to you, and holler if you need more.

Best,

Barry

BARRY'S LIST
50 Picks for Detecting Men

Robert Barnard: **Death By Sheer Torture** (Perry Trethowan)
Lawrence Block: **When the Sacred Ginmill Closes*** (Matt Scudder)
James Lee Burke: **Heaven's Prisoners*** (Dave Robicheaux)
W. J. Burley: **Wycliffe and the Tangled Web** (Inspector Wycliffe)
Michael Connelly: **The Concrete Blonde*** (Harry Bosch)
K. C. Constantine: **The Man Who Liked Slow Tomatoes*** (Mario Balzic)
Thomas H. Cook: **Night Secrets** (Frank Clemmons) (But his best books are non-series)
Robert Crais: **The Monkey's Raincoat** (Elvis Cole)
James Crumley: **The Last Good Kiss*** (C. W. Sughrue)
Loren D. Estleman: **Motor City Blue** (Amos Walker)
Dick Francis: **Odds Against*** (Sid Halley)
Brian Freemantle: **Charlie M*** (Charlie Muffin)
Jonathan Gash: **The Sleepers of Erin** (Lovejoy)
Bartholomew Gill: **The Death of a Joyce Scholar*** (Peter McGarr)
Joe Gores: **Dead Skip*** (DKA)
Stephen Greenleaf: **Toll Call*** (John Marshal Tanner)
John Harvey: **Wasted Years*** (Charlie Resnick)
Jeremiah Healy: **Yesterday's News** (John Francis Cuddy)
Reginald Hill: **Bones and Silence** (Dalziel and Pascoe)
Stuart M. Kaminsky: **A Cold Red Sunrise** (Porfiry Rostnikov)
Jonathan Kellerman: **Over the Edge** (Alex Delaware)
Dennis Lehane: **A Drink Before the War** (Kenzie and Gennaro)
Elmore Leonard: **Stick** (Stick) (But his best books are non-series)
David L. Lindsey: **In the Lake of the Sun** (Stuart Haydon)
Dick Lochte: **Sleeping Dog*** (Dahlquist and Bloodworth)
Peter Lovesey: **The Last Detective*** (Peter Diamond)
Arthur Lyons: **All God's Children** (Jacob Asch)
John Malcolm: **The Goodwin Sideboard** (Tim Simpson)
Archer Mayor: **Fruits of the Poisonous Tree*** (Joe Gunther)
Ed McBain: **Killer's Wedge** (87th Precinct)
James McClure: **The Song Dog** (Tromp and Zondi)
Gregory McDonald: **Fletch*** (Fletch)
James Melville: **A Sort of Samurai** (Superintendent Otani)
Walter Mosley: **Devil in a Blue Dress** Easy Rawlins)
Jack O'Connell: **Box 9** (Quinsigamond {a town})
Robert B. Parker: **Early Autumn*** (Spenser)
Thomas Perry: **The Butcher's Boy*** (Butcher's Boy)
David M. Pierce: **Down in the Valley** (Vic Daniel)
Bill Pronzini: **Shackles** ("nameless")
John R. Riggs: **Let Sleeping Dogs Lie** (Garth Ryland)
Les Roberts: **The Cleveland Connection*** (Milan Jacovich)
Jonathan Ross: **Here Lies Nancy Frail** (George Rogers)
James Sallis: **The Long-Legged Fly** (Lew Griffin)
John Sandford: **Rules of Prey** (Lucas Davenport)
Steven Saylor: **Roman Blood** (Gordianus the Finder)
Mickey Spillane: **I, the Jury*** (Mike Hammer)
Jonathan Valin: **The Lime Pit*** (Harry Stoner)
Richard Whittingham: **State Street** (Joe Morrison)
Don Winslow: **A Cool Breeze on the Underground** (Neal Carey)
Daniel Woodrell: **Muscle for the Wing** (Rene Shade)

HOW TO USE THIS BOOK

No matter what your preference for hunting mysteries—by author, character, type, background, setting, title, date or awards won—*Detecting Men* has a list for you. Complete with boxes to check for every series title, the Master List is designed to keep track of books you've read, books you own, books you intend to buy, books you especially like, or anything about mystery series written by men that you'd like to keep track of.

Chapter 1—Master List

In the Master List, more than 600 author entries appear in alphabetical order by last name, according to the name under which a mystery series is published. You will find P.C. Doherty listed under five different names, four of which are pseudonyms identified with a **[P]**. Each listing shows the series titles published under that name. For example, Dennis Lynds is listed as Michael Collins, the pseudonym under which his Dan Fortune series is published. An author profile with information about the author's life and work is followed by his series character(s) and book titles in order of publication. The date following the title is intended to be the *earliest* date of publication.

For books first published in Britain, Canada or Australia, you should expect the U.S. edition to lag behind at least a year or more. Also, the U.S. title might differ from the British, Canadian or Australian title, or the book may not be published in the United States. There may also be differences between hardcover and paperback editions. But whenever more than one title is known, both titles will be listed, with a notation indicating whether the second title is U.S., British or an alternate title. APA is used to indicate "also published as."

When an author has more than one series detective, the characters are listed in alphabetical order by first name. A short character description, including the primary series setting, follows the character's name. This may not be the setting for every book in the series, but it is typically the home base of the protagonist.

Whenever a book has been nominated or received recognition for a major prize or award in the mystery field, the book title appears in bold type followed by the specific nomination or award and a star. If you're interested in reading award-winning authors, just scan the pages of Chapter 1 looking for bold, starred titles. Solid stars ★ indicate award winners and open stars ☆ identify nominations. Because these awards are a fairly recent phenomenon, you should not overlook titles which predate awards. A description of the various mystery awards can be found following Awards List 3 at the back of Chapter 8, Mystery Book Awards.

In this first edition, for the most part, we have included only those male series writers who were alive in 1995. After the data base had been closed, we learned of the death of several authors and rather than remove them we chose to leave them in.

Chapter 2—Mystery Types

For the purpose of organization, the 813 mystery series presented in *Detecting Men* have been subdivided into four basic groups based on standard classifications for police procedurals, private eye novels, espionage, and traditional mysteries featuring amateur detectives. Rather than restricting the last group solely to amateur detectives, we have applied the 69 mystery backgrounds for traditional mysteries to police and private eye series as well. You'll find historical police and private eye series from ancient Rome to 21st century, as well as black, gay, disabled, ethnic and environmental series, among others.

We have tried to cross-reference as many as possible, especially when the background is important to the series. For example, historical private eye series appear in the P.I. section and again in the appropriate historical section. Thus, you will find Steven Saylor's Gordianus the Finder listed with other private eyes and again in the 'Historical, ancient' section.

Mystery backgrounds include:
    Academic
    Advertising & Public Relations
    Animals, cats
    _____, dogs
    _____, horses
    _____, other
    Architecture & Engineering
    Art & Antiques
    Assassins & Avengers
    Authors & Writers
    Black Detectives
    Books & Libraries
    Botanical
    Business & Finance
    Computers & Technology
    Criminals
    Cross Genre
    Disabled Detectives
    Domestic & Family
    Ecclesiastical & Religious
    Environment & Wilderness
    Ethnic & Native American
    Film Making (see Movies & Film Making)
    Gardening (see Botanical)
    Gay & Lesbian Detectives
    Gourmet & Food
    Government & Politics
    Historical, ancient
    _____, medieval
    _____, 16th century
    _____, 17th century
    _____, 18th century
    _____, 19th century
    _____, 1920s
    _____, 1930s
    _____, 1940s
    _____, 1950s
    _____, 1960s
    _____, 1970s
    Hotels & Inns
    Humor
    Journalism, magazine
    _____, newspaper
    _____, photography
    _____, radio & television
    Legal, attorney
    _____, judge
    _____, other
    Medical
    Military
    Movies & Film Making
    Music
    Psychological & Paranormal
    Security & Protective Services
    Senior Sleuths
    Small Town
    Sports, agents & writers
    _____, auto racing
    _____, baseball
    _____, diving
    _____, fishing & hunting
    _____, football
    _____, golf
    _____, horse racing
    _____, sailing & yachting
    _____, soccer
    _____, tennis
    Suburban
    Theatre & Performing Arts
    Toys & Games
    Travel

We have identified black, gay & lesbian and disabled sleuths, but these are never the only categories in which they are listed. Black cops and private eyes are listed first as cops and P.I.s and secondly as black detectives.

The 'Cross Genre' category includes fantasy, science fiction, horror and western private eyes. This is not meant to be an exhaustive list of cross genre detective fiction, but rather a sampling of series you might not be familiar with.

In Chapters 2-4 we use a series shorthand for date of the first book in the series and number of books in the series. When you see '56-47, for example, you will know the series begins in 1956 and currently stands at 47 books, as does Ed McBain's 87th Precinct series. This two-part column, included in all table-format lists (types, series characters and settings), makes it easy to spot the long-running series.

Whenever a collection of short stories featuring a series character appears in the series list, it will appear in the order in which it was published, but will not be numbered. Anthologies are not considered to be series installments. For example, *Always Outnumbered, Always Outgunned* (1997)—Walter Mosely's short story collection introducing Socrates Forthlow—is listed as 'ss' rather than #1 in the series. The shortand for this series is '97-ss.

Chapter 3—Series Characters

This list will prove useful for those who know a character's first name but not the author's. Whenever the series character is a pair, each of the partners is listed separately. For example, both Elvis Cole and Joe Pike from Robert Crais' private eye series appear in the character listing, first under Elvis and later under Joe. The partner's name is always attached so you know the character is part of a series pair.

Chapter 4—Settings

Settings identified in the Master List and Chapter 4 are not necessarily the setting for each book in the series, but typically the home base of the series character(s). When world travel is part of the story line, we attempt to classify the series as such. When the setting changes from book to

book, we choose what appears to be the most frequent setting. When there are several books in a series, each with different settings, we try to specify the current location. States of the U. S. are listed in alphabetical order, according to their two-letter state abbreviation. Within each state, cities and towns appear in alphabetical order, with fictional towns included as if they were real. Unspecified locations are grouped together at the beginning of each section. Locations outside the United States are presented alphabetically by country and further by city, province or region alphabetically.

Chapter 5—Title Chronology

Within the chronological list, all 4,531 series titles are arrayed by year—presented in alphabetical order according to the author's last name. Whenever a title is the first in a series, it is marked with a **1** in front of the title. Black header bars separate the decades and beginning in 1990, underscores are provided between letters of the alphabet according to the author's last name for each year's titles. Titles nominated or receiving mystery book awards are marked with open and solid stars. Because these prizes are a fairly recent phenomenon, stars do not appear until 1961.

Chapter 6—Alphabetical List of Titles

In the alphabetical list of titles, all 4,531 series titles are listed in alphabetical order. Whenever the first word in the title is an article (a, an, the), it is dropped and the second word controls the title's placement. When a title is the first in a series, it is identified by a **1**. Alternate titles are listed as part of the entry for first appearance of a particular work. Titles are also starred to indicate award winners and nominees.

Chapter 7—Pseudonyms

A discussion of how pseudonyms are presented appears at the beginning of Chapter 7.

Chapter 8—Mystery Book Awards

More than 400 awards and nominations are presented in Chapter 8 in three formats. Only those awards and nominations given to series mysteries written by men are included here. You will not find awards or nominations for nonseries novels or for authors not included in this data base. List 1 shows winners and nominees in alphabetical order by conferring agency and award name. List 2 reconfigures the same information year by year for each award category, starting with Best First Novel, from the most recent awards to the earliest. List 3 is an alphabetical list of the same awards and nominations by author's last name.

Index

The index includes authors (last name first) and series characters (first name first). Index entries for authors included in the Master List are marked with a black square bullet ■. The first index entry for each author will be his location in the Master List. Multiple mentions of an author on a single page are not separately identified.

How You Can Help

The first edition of any new reference is bound to contain errors, some of which come from errors in earlier reference sources. Without reading at least one book in each of the 813 series identified in this data base, it's doubtful we could be entirely certain of each character's occupation, the series setting, or even the correct mystery type and background. It's surprising how often a book's dust jacket will contain misinformation about the story. Furthermore, many out of print titles are hard to find.

If you have personal knowledge you'd be willing to share, we hope you'll get in touch with us and help correct omissions or errors you find. Please provide documentation when you contact us about errors. A photocopy of a book's copyright page is often the best documentation for certain errors. When you suggest authors for inclusion, please provide a title list or tell us how to get in touch with the author. If you are the editor, publisher or family member of the author, it is also helpful to know this.

If you are one of the more than 100 authors in our 'overflow' box, we sincerely regret leaving you out of this edition. We ran out of time and space in this first edition. However, we look forward to including you in the second edition of *Detecting Men*, planned for release in October 1999. It is not too early to send your title list, character descriptions, awards and biographical information now, so that we can properly include your work.

A special thank you to all who continue to provide information, support and enthusiasm for our *Detecting* series of mystery readers guides. We couldn't do it without you.

About the Author

Willetta L. Heising is the author and publisher of the Macavity Award-winning *Detecting Women, A Reader's Guide and Checklist for Mystery Series Written by Women* (1995) and its popular successor, *Detecting Women 2* (1996), the 1997 Agatha, Anthony and Macavity Award winner for nonfiction, as well as an Edgar nominee. Purple Moon Press will launch two new publishing ventures in 1998 with the arrival of *Detecting News* and the introduction of a Purple Moon Press web site. In October, along with the third edition of *Detecting Women*, Purple Moon Press will sponsor its first Mystery Series Week (October 4-10) which Willetta hopes will become an annual event at bookstores and libraries.

Before establishing Purple Moon Press in 1994, Willetta spent 20 years in the business world, chiefly at Michigan's largest bank where she held positions in facilities planning, market research, product management and private banking. A former Certified Financial Planner and one-time instructor in economic geography at Wayne State University, Willetta earned a B.A. degree in geography and sociology from Valparaiso University. She also worked briefly as a Detroit city planner and site location analyst for a Michigan supermarket chain.

A popular speaker, workshop leader and panel moderator, she is a member of Great Lakes Booksellers Association, Publishers Marketing Association, Sisters in Crime, Small Press Association of North America and the Women's National Book Association. She is also a life member of the St. Louis (MO) Genealogical Society. Born in Coronado, California and growing up in a large Navy family, she attended schools in six states, Norway and France, before moving to Michigan where she has lived since graduate school days.

You can reach her at:

Purple Moon Press
3319 Greenfield Road, Suite 317
Dearborn MI 48120-1212
phone 313-593-1033 or fax 313-593-4087
e-mail <purplemoon@prodigy.net> or <willetta@purplemoonpress.com>
and on the Worldwide Web at <www.purplemoonpress.com>

■ **ABBOTT, Jeff**

Dallas native Jeff Abbott is the creator of what he describes as "non-traditional traditional mysteries." Featuring small town librarian Jordan Poteet of Mirabeau, Texas, the series opener won both the Agatha and Macavity awards for best first novel. Abbott sees Jordan as an Everyman for the '90s—devoted to his family, loyal to his friends, but far from perfect in his efforts to deal with the dark side of human nature. The author admits that a difficult personal situation inspired him to write *Distant Blood* (1996), the longest and darkest book in the series. A graduate of Rice University with degrees in english and history, Abbott lives in Austin where he previously worked as a computer software interface designer. He credits his grandmother with the launch of his writing career. She provided the Big Chief tablets on which he wrote his first short stories.

Jordan Poteet...small-town librarian in Mirabeau, Texas
- ❑ ❑ 1 - **Do Unto Others (1994) Agatha & Macavity winner** ★★
- ❑ ❑ 2 - The Only Good Yankee (1995)
- ❑ ❑ 3 - Promises of Home (1996)
- ❑ ❑ 4 - Distant Blood (1996)

■ **ADAMS, Harold**

Shamus award winning author Carl Adams is the creator of Depression-era sign-painter and ex-con in Carl Wilcox, who's got an appetite for pretty women and a talent for uncovering the truth in what is now a 14-book series. His parents own the Wilcox Hotel in their South Dakota town of 1,300 and Carl often returns there to help out his father with whom his relationship could best be described as negative. Adams recently told St. James Press that his first Kyle Adams book, *When Rich Men Die* (1987), may yet become a series. This contemporary character shares the author's personal experience working for the Minneapolis Better Business Bureau. Unlike Adams, Kyle has both investigative and on-air experience in television. In two as yet unpublished books, Kyle goes to France and later northern Minnesota. Adams' novels typically run 200 pages or less—a perfect length for those who like to start and finish their mysteries in an evening.

Carl Wilcox...Depression era sign-painter in Cordon, South Dakota
- ❑ ❑ 1 - Murder (1981)
- ❑ ❑ 2 - Paint the Town Red (1982)
- ❑ ❑ 3 - The Missing Moon (1983)
- ❑ ❑ 4 - **The Naked Liar (1985) Shamus nominee** ☆
- ❑ ❑ 5 - The Fourth Widow (1986)
- ❑ ❑ 6 - The Barbed Wire Noose (1987)
- ❑ ❑ 7 - The Man Who Met the Train (1988)

❑ ❑   8 - The Man Who Missed the Party (1989)
❑ ❑   9 - **The Man Who Was Taller Than God (1992) Shamus winner ★**
❑ ❑ 10 - A Perfectly Proper Murder (1993)
❑ ❑ 11 - A Way With Widows (1994)
❑ ❑ 12 - The Ditched Blond (1995)
❑ ❑ 13 - Hatchet Job (1996)
❑ ❑ 14 - The Ice Pick Artist (1997)

■ ADAMSON, Lydia [P]

The prolific Lydia Adamson, author of more than two dozen titles in three series featuring women amateur sleuths who love animals, turns out to be New York cat lover Frank King. Since 1990 he's been regularly turning out series installments featuring Off Off Broadway actress and cat-sitter Alice Nestleton, small-town New York veterinarian Deidre Quinn Nightingale and retired New York City librarian and eccentric bird-watcher Lucy Wayles. With more than 1.5 million copies of the Adamson books in print, the publisher plans to continue releasing two new installments in each series every year. The intrepid veterinarian's next appearance (#8) is *Dr. Nightingale Meets Puss in Boots* (1997). Under his own name, the author previously published a pair of mysteries featuring an unemployed New York actress with five dogs.

Alice Nestleton...part-time actress and cat-sitter in New York, New York
❑ ❑   1 - A Cat in the Manger (1990)
❑ ❑   2 - A Cat of a Different Color (1990)
❑ ❑   3 - A Cat in Wolf's Clothing (1991)
❑ ❑   4 - A Cat by Any Other Name (1992)
❑ ❑   5 - A Cat in the Wings (1992)
❑ ❑   6 - A Cat with a Fiddle (1993)
❑ ❑   7 - A Cat with No Regrets (1994)
❑ ❑   8 - A Cat in a Glass House (1993)
❑ ❑   9 - A Cat on the Cutting Edge (1994)
❑ ❑ 10 - The Cat in Fine Style (1995)
❑ ❑ 11 - A Cat on a Winning Streak (1995)
❑ ❑ 12 - A Cat in a Chorus Line (1996)
❑ ❑ 13 - A Cat Under the Mistletoe (1996)
❑ ❑ 14 - A Cat on a Couch (1996)
❑ ❑ 15 - A Cat on a Beach Blanket (1997)

Deidre Nightingale, Dr....young woman veterinarian in New York
❑ ❑   1 - Dr. Nightingale Comes Home (1994)
❑ ❑   2 - Dr. Nightingale Rides the Elephant (1994)
❑ ❑   3 - Dr. Nightingale Goes to the Dogs (1995)
❑ ❑   4 - Dr. Nightingale Goes the Distance (1995)
❑ ❑   5 - Dr. Nightingale Enters the Bear Cave (1996)
❑ ❑   6 - Dr. Nightingale Chases Three Little Pigs (1996)
❑ ❑   7 - Dr. Nightingale Rides to the Hounds (1997)

Lucy Wayles...ex-librarian birdwatcher in New York, New York
❑ ❑ 1 - Beware the Tufted Duck (1996)
❑ ❑ 2 - Beware the Butcher (1997)°

■ ADCOCK, Thomas

Born and raised in Detroit, Adcock got his start covering the police beat and city politics for the *Detroit Free Press*. His first book under his own name was *Precinct 19* (1984), a nonfiction look at his year spent with officers of Manhattan's Upper East Side. From his current neighborhood in Hell's Kitchen, Adcock reviews novels for *The New York Times*, writes radio dramas for broadcast in central Europe and teaches

creative writing at the New School for Social Research. He also writes an Edgar-award winning series featuring NYPD street crimes detective Neil "Hock" Hockaday, shamrock Catholic and recovering alcoholic. Adcock once worked in advertising, wrote scripts for TV soaps and penned a dozen paperback novels under three pseudonyms—all with the initials BS. He is married to New York actress Kim Sykes.

Neil Hockaday...NYPD street crimes detective in New York, New York
- ❏ ❏ 1 - Sea of Green (1989)
- ❏ ❏ 2 - **Dark Maze (1991) Edgar winner ★**
- ❏ ❏ 3 - Drown All the Dogs (1994)
- ❏ ❏ 4 - Devil's Heaven (1995)
- ❏ ❏ 5 - Thrown Away Child (1996)
- ❏ ❏ 6 - Grief Street (1997)

■ ADLER, Warren

Brooklyn-born Warren Adler spent 20 years as president of an advertising and public relations firm in Washington DC before writing the best-selling *War of the Roses* (1981), which later became a Hollywood film starring Michael Douglas and Kathleen Turner directed by Danny DeVito. It was Adler's 10th novel that launched his Washington DC police series featuring rich-girl-turned-homicide-detective Fiona Fitzgerald first seen in *American Quartet* (1981). After 23 published novels, Adler says he's still excited by new stories and new ways of telling them and has never wanted to be anything but a writer of novels and short stories. One of the founders of the Jackson Hole Writer's Conference, he writes five or six hours a day on his computer from his Wyoming study cum library. His latest novel is titled *Jackson Hole, Uneasy Eden* (1997).

Fiona Fitzgerald...homicide detective in Washington, D.C.
- ❏ ❏ 1 - American Quartet (1981)
- ❏ ❏ 2 - American Sextet (1983)
- ❏ ❏ 3 - Immaculate Deception (1991)
- ❏ ❏ 4 - Senator Love (1991)
- ❏ ❏ 5 - The Witch of Watergate (1992)
- ❏ ❏ 6 - The Ties That Bind (1994)

■ ALBERT, Marvin H.

Marvin H. Albert (1924-1996) authored more than 100 westerns, mysteries, spy novels, film novelizations, biographies and works of history before his 1996 death in the south of France where he had lived for 20 years. His unique private eye creation was a French-speaking American name Pete Sawyer, son of a U.S. pilot shot down over France and a beautiful, brilliant World War II resistance fighter. Raised by his Chicago grandparents, Sawyer spoke fluent French thanks to summers spent with his mother. As a screenwriter, Albert adapted nine of his novels for film, including *Apache Rising*, which became *Duel at Diablo* with Sidney Poitier, and *Miami Mayhem*, which became *Tony Rome* with Frank Sinatra. Among his many pseudonyms was J. D. Christilian which he used for the best-selling *Scarlet Women* (1996), a mystery set in New York City in 1871.

Pierre-Ange "Pete" Sawyer...French-speaking American P.I. in Paris, France
- ❏ ❏ 1 - **Stone Angel (1986) Shamus nominee ☆**
- ❏ ❏ 2 - Back in the Real World (1986)
- ❏ ❏ 3 - Get Off at Babylon (1987)
- ❏ ❏ 4 - Long Teeth (1987)
- ❏ ❏ 5 - The Last Smile (1988)
- ❏ ❏ 6 - The Midnight Sister (1989)
- ❏ ❏ 7 - **Bimbo Heaven (1990) Shamus nominee ☆**
- ❏ ❏ 8 - The Zig-Zag Man (1991)
- ❏ ❏ 9 - The Riviera Contract (1992)

■ ALBERT, Neil

Oregon native Neil Albert is a Pennsylvania trial lawyer who wrote his first full-length adventure novel in longhand at the age of 13. He still keeps the journal he started in college, but he says it wasn't until he'd spent an entire year reading good modern fiction that he was able to write his first private eye novel. The Shamus-nominated series opener *January Corpse* (1991) introduces disbarred Philadelphia attorney Dave Garrett, who barely makes ends meet. *Cruel April* (1996), in which his girlfriend Kate disappears from the airport, has been optioned for a TV movie. Dave's most recent case-of-the-month, *A Tangled June* (1997), is a fictionalized account of the Albert's own search for his birth parents. Home is a 53-acre farm in the Amish country of Lancaster where he keeps horses, rides bicycles and target shoots. He's currently writing a nonfiction book about a local murder case.

Dave Garrett...disbarred lawyer turned private eye in Lancaster County, Pennsylvania
- ❑ ❑ 1 - **The January Corpse (1991) Shamus nominee** ☆
- ❑ ❑ 2 - The February Trouble (1992)
- ❑ ❑ 3 - Burning March (1994)
- ❑ ❑ 4 - Cruel April (1995)
- ❑ ❑ 5 - Appointment in May (1996)
- ❑ ❑ 6 - Tangled June (1997)

■ ALDING, Peter [P]

Peter Alding is one of half a dozen pen names used by Roderic Jeffries for his more than 100 mysteries and 25 books for children (some crime-related). Under the Alding name he wrote 14 police novels featuring Constable Kerr and Inspector Fusil beginning with *The C.I. D. Room* (1967), published in the U.S. as *All Leads Negative*. The likable young detective and his hard-to-please superior work in the seatown of Fortrow. According to Carol Simpson Stern in *St. James Guide* (4th ed.), "Kerr and Fusil work on cases where the evidence is misleading, the public unreliable as witnesses, and the criminals brilliant in their cunning." "Often it is poetic justice, not legal, justice that reigns," she says. Jeffries writes under his own name as well as Jeffrey Ashford, Hastings Draper, Roderic Graeme and Graham Hastings.

Kerr, Constable & Fusil, Insp...young police detective & his superior in Fortrow, England
- ❑ ❑ 1 - The C. I. D. Room (1967) U.S.-All Leads Negative
- ❑ ❑ 2 - Circle of Danger (1968)
- ❑ ❑ 3 - Murder Among Thieves (1969)
- ❑ ❑ 4 - Guilt Without Proof (1970)
- ❑ ❑ 5 - Despite the Evidence (1971)
- ❑ ❑ 6 - Call Back to Crime (1972)
- ❑ ❑ 7 - Field of Fire (1973)
- ❑ ❑ 8 - The Murder Line (1974)
- ❑ ❑ 9 - Six Days to Death (1975)
- ❑ ❑ 10 - Murder is Suspected (1977)
- ❑ ❑ 11 - Ransom Town (1979)
- ❑ ❑ 12 - A Man Condemned (1981)
- ❑ ❑ 13 - Betrayed by Death (1982)
- ❑ ❑ 14 - One Man's Justice (1983)

■ ALDYNE, Nathan [P]

Nathan Aldyne was the shared pseudonym of Michael McDowell and Dennis Schuetz, whose humorous mysteries featured gay bartender Dan Valentine and his straight friend Clarisse Lovelace. In book three they open a gay bar named Slate across the street from a police station in Boston's South End. Recent word from St. Martin's Press is that the early books in the series will be re-released, with more to follow from McDowell writing alone after the death of Dennis Schuetz. Under the pen name Axel Young, the Aldyne team also co-wrote *Blood Rubies* (1982) and *Wicked Stepmother* (1983). McDowell started writing fiction while at Harvard and finished six novels before selling the seventh, which became his first published work, *The Amulet* (1979). Armed with a Ph.D. from Brandeis, he teamed with Warren Skaaren to write the screenplay for the 1988 comedy film *Beetlejuice*.

Dan Valentine & Clarisse Lovelace...gay and straight bar owners in Boston, Massachusetts
- ❏ ❏ 1 - Vermilion (1980)
- ❏ ❏ 2 - Cobalt (1982)
- ❏ ❏ 3 - Slate (1984)
- ❏ ❏ 4 - Canary (1986)

■ ALEXANDER, Bruce [P]

Bruce Alexander is the pseudonym of Bruce Cook, former *Los Angeles Daily News* book editor and prolific author of both fiction and nonfiction. As Bruce Alexander he writes an 18th-century London series featuring Sir John Fielding, blind magistrate and founder of the first police force and his 13-year-old orphan sidekick, Jeremy Proctor. In the series opener, the boy is arrested for a crime he did not commit and becomes Sir John's eyes out of gratitude when Fielding clears his name. Their next exploit is *Person or Persons Unknown* (1997). The series has been optioned for film by Penny Marshall's Parkway Productions and Britain's Picture Palace. As Bruce Cook he has written everything from a mystery series about a Chicano detective to a study of the Beat Generation and a country music and travel guide, *The Town That Country Built: Welcome to Branson, Missouri* (1993).

John Fielding, Sir...blind magistrate and founder of first police force in London, England
- ❏ ❏ 1 - Blind Justice (1994)
- ❏ ❏ 2 - Murder in Grub Street (1995)
- ❏ ❏ 3 - Watery Grave (1996)

■ ALEXANDER, Gary

Washington state native Gary Alexander is the creator of two mystery series and the author of more than 80 short stories which have appeared in a variety of periodicals. His longer-running series features Superintendent Bamsan Kiet of the fictional kingdom of Luong and his adjutant Captain Binh who have now appeared in six installments beginning with *Pigeon Blood* (1988). In their most recent adventure, they travel to Seattle in *Kiet Goes West* (1992). Alexander's newer series, set in the Yucatan, features an erstwhile tour guide and souvenir retailer who just happens to be an ex-cop. Kirkus called *Dead Dinosaurs* "a giddy gallimaufry of fraud, paranoia, [and] corruption high and low." It seems a con artist named Dugdale is trying to sell a Dead Dinosaur exhibit in Luis' home village of Ho-Keh as a front for slot machines to fleece blue-haired cruise-ship vacationers.

Bamsan Kiet, Supt.....police supt. in an imaginary country in the Far East
- ❏ ❏ 1 - Pigeon Blood (1988)
- ❏ ❏ 2 - Unfunny Money (1989)
- ❏ ❏ 3 - Kiet and the Golden Peacock (1989)
- ❏ ❏ 4 - Kiet and the Opium War (1990)
- ❏ ❏ 5 - Deadly Drought (1991)
- ❏ ❏ 6 - Kiet Goes West (1992)

Luis Balam...ex-traffic cop turned tour operator in Yucatan, Mexico
- ❏ ❏ 1 - Blood Sacrifice (1993)
- ❏ ❏ 2 - Dead Dinosaurs (1994)

■ ALEXANDER, Lawrence

Former television story editor and scriptwriter Lawrence Alexander is the creator of a three-book historical mystery series starring Teddy Roosevelt during his days as New York City police commissioner at the turn of the century. The series opens with *The Big Stick* (1986), released exactly 90 years after

Roosevelt was first appointed police commissioner in 1896. The former Rough Rider returns in *Speak Softly* (1987) followed by *The Strenuous Life* (1991). Some of Lawrence Alexander's television writing credits include scripts for such well-known nightime dramas of the 1970s as *Charlie's Angels*, *Barnaby Jones*, *Cannon*, *Matt Houston* and *Baretta*. His *Dear Tony* episode of *Baretta* won this New York City native an Edgar Allen Poe Award in 1978 for best television episode.

Teddy Roosevelt...1890s police commissioner in New York, New York
- ❏ ❏ 1 - The Big Stick (1986)
- ❏ ❏ 2 - Speak Softly (1987)
- ❏ ❏ 3 - The Strenuous Life (1991)

■ ALLBEURY, Ted

Former British Intelligence officer Ted Allbeury began writing novels in 1970 at the age of 54, after the kidnapping of his four-year-old daughter. With his first book, *A Choice of Enemies* (1972), he said he wanted his daughter to know that he tried to find her. In the novel, a working-class spy from Birmingham defects to Poland after learning his missing daughter is there under the control of a Belgian double agent. In his review of *The Judas Factor*, Robin Winks suggested that Allbeury has not become as popular as Ian Fleming or le Carré because he "tells it like it is." With a belief that all wars inevitably end in disaster, Allbeury doesn't see the world as black and white; as a result his stories are often quite sad. Former creative director of a London advertising agency, Theodore Edward le Bouthillier Allbeury has also written under the names Richard Butler and Patrick Kelly.

Tad Anders...Polish-British agent in England
- ❏ ❏ 1 - Snowball (1974)
- ❏ ❏ 2 - Palomino Blonde (1975)
       U.S.-Omega-Minus
- ❏ ❏ 3 - The Judas Factor (1984)

■ ALLEGRETTO, Michael

Shamus award winner Michael Allegretto is the author of five private eye novels featuring ex-Denver cop Jacob Lomax, introduced in *Death on the Rocks* (1987), named Best First P.I. Novel by Private Eye Writers of America and nominated for an Anthony the same year. In their review of *Blood Relative* (1992), *Kirkus* described Jake as "quick with his fists, dead accurate with his gun, [and] sometimes personable." *The Buffalo News* pronounced him "the type of sardonic, sassy companion you'd like to have a beer with." In addition to his Jake Lomax books, Allegretto has written at least four neo-Gothic suspense novels including *Shadow House* (1994), *The Suitor* (1993), *The Watchmen* (1991) and *Night of Reunion* (1990). He lives in Denver (CO).

Jacob Lomax...ex-cop turned P.I. in Denver, Colorado
- ❏ ❏ 1 - **Death on the Rocks (1987) Shamus winner ★ Anthony nominee** ☆
- ❏ ❏ 2 - Blood Stone (1988)
- ❏ ❏ 3 - The Dead of Winter (1989)
- ❏ ❏ 4 - Blood Relative (1992)
- ❏ ❏ 5 - Grave Doubt (1995)

■ ALLEN, Garrison [P]

Garrison Allen is the pseudonym of Gary Amo, Edgar-nominated for his first novel, *Come Nightfall* (1990). As Garrison Allen he writes a series set in *Empty Creek* (AZ), featuring ex-Marine mystery bookstore owner Penelope Warren and her wily feline sidekick Big Mike. The cat is a 25-lb. Abyssinian named after

Sherlock Holmes' older brother Mycroft. In book 4, *Baseball Cat* (1997), Mycroft and Penelope suspect foul play when Empty Creek's minor league team owner is found dead in the visitors' dugout. Other nonseries titles written as Gary Amo (featuring women protagonists) are *Come Darkness* (1993), *Creeping Shadows* (1992) and *Silent Night* (1991). A Peace Corps volunteer in Malawi and English instructor in Ethiopia, Amo works as a newspaper editor in southern California.

Penelope Warren...ex-Marine mystery bookstore owner in Empty Creek, Arizona
- ❏ ❏ 1 - Desert Cat (1994)
- ❏ ❏ 2 - Royal Cat (1995)
- ❏ ❏ 3 - Stable Cat (1996)

■ ALLEN, Steve

Author of more than 40 books and over 4000 songs (some say 7000), Steve Allen was born Stephen Valentine Patrick William Allen to vaudeville performers who took him on tour. Called television's Renaissance man, he is the creator and original host of *The Tonight Show* (starting in 1954), as well as the PBS series *Meeting of the Minds* which ran for 5 years starting in the late '70s. Original scripts from these programs, where historical figures such as Elizabeth Barrett Browning, Einstein and Machiavelli were Allen's "talk show" guests, are now available in book form. The history of his five decades in broadcasting, *Hi-Ho Steverino!* (1992), was his 38th book. His 49th, *Die Laughing*, is due out in early '98. Since 1982, Allen has written 8 mysteries where he and his wife Jayne Meadows are amateur detectives in a variety of show business settings.

Steve Allen & Jayne Meadows...celebrity crime-solving duo in Los Angeles, California
- ❏ ❏ 1 - The Talk Show Murders (1982)
- ❏ ❏ 2 - Murder in Hollywood (1988)
- ❏ ❏ 3 - Murder on the Glitter Box (1989)
- ❏ ❏ 4 - Murder in Manhattan (1990)
- ❏ ❏ 5 - Murder in Vegas (1991)
- ❏ ❏ 6 - The Murder Game (1993)
- ❏ ❏ 7 - Murder on the Atlantic (1995)
- ❏ ❏ 8 - Wake Up to Murder (1996)

■ ALLYN, Doug

Doug Allyn writes two Michigan mystery series—one with a tough Latino cop from Detroit and the other a single mother and deepwater diver on Michigan's Huron Bay. The earlier series features Lupe Garcia, fed up with the Detroit Police Department in *The Cheerio Killings* (1989) and *Motown Underground* (1993). Underwater welder Michelle "Mitch" Mitchell is working on an oil rig in the Gulf of Mexico when her father's suspicious death sends her back to Michigan. Once there, she inherits more than a dive shop. Nominated no less than 5 times for Edgar awards for his short stories, this author has also received a Shamus nomination in that category. Allyn, who speaks Chinese, makes his primary living as a musician, traveling the Midwest with his wife and their rock band Devil's Triangle. They live in Montrose (MI).

Lupe Garcia...tough Latino cop in Detroit, Michigan
- ❏ ❏ 1 - The Cheerio Killings (1989)
- ❏ ❏ 2 - Motown Underground (1993)

Michelle Mitchell...single mother and dive shop owner in Huron Harbor, Michigan
- ❏ ❏ 1 - Icewater Mansions (1995)
- ❏ ❏ 2 - Black Water (1996)
- ❏ ❏ 3 - Dance In Deep Water (1997)

■ AMBLER, Eric

Grand Master Eric Ambler won the first Gold Dagger ever presented (1959) for *Passage of Arms* and collected several other Daggers from the Crime Writers' Association. His novels were "the well into which everybody has dipped," said John le Carré at a lunch held in Ambler's honor. Reported by Julian Symons for the London Times, Graham Greene cabled a greeting: "To the master from one of his disciples." The son of music hall performers, Ambler had careers in engineering, vaudeville, advertising, educational films and screenwriting. He won a 1953 Academy Award nomination for his screenplay of *The Cruel Sea* and at least 6 of his novels became major motion pictures. At the age of 75, after a near-fatal spin-out on a Swiss mountain road, he decided to write his autobiography. The result earned him an Edgar award for best critical/biographical (*Here Lies: An Autobiography*, 1985).

Arthur Abdel Simpson...comic rogue and petty crook in England
- ❏ ❏ 1 - **The Light of Day (1962) Edgar winner & Gold Dagger runner-up ★★ U.S.-Topkapi**
- ❏ ❏ 2 - Dirty Story (1967)

Charles Latimer...British university lecturer turned detective novelist in Turkey
- ❏ ❏ 1 - The Mask of Dimitrios (1939) U.S.-A Coffin for Dimitrios
- ❏ ❏ 2 - The Intercom Conspiracy (1969)

■ ANAYA, Rudolfo

Rudolfo Anaya is the creator of Sonny Baca, part-time rodeo rider and Nuevos Mexican private eye. Struggling to follow in the footsteps of his legendary lawman grandfather, Sonny works the mean streets of Albuquerque (NM). Aided and abetted by coyotes and a curendera, or healer, he battles against forces that include evil brujas or witches such as Raven, who appears in both *Zia Summer* (1995) and *Rio Grande Fall* (1996). These are modern private eye novels laced with mysticism and magic of Chicana culture. Anaya's best known work is *Bless Me, Ultima*, his coming of age novel that has been hailed as a masterpiece of Hispanic literature. Other writing from Anaya includes *Albuquerque* (1993), *The Anaya Reader* (1994) and *Jalamanta: A Message from the Desert* (1996).

Sonny Baca...part-time rodeo rider private eye in Albuquerque, New Mexico
- ❏ ❏ 1 - Zia Summer (1995)
- ❏ ❏ 2 - Rio Grande Fall (1996)

■ ANDRUS, Jeff

Jeff Andrus has been writing for television since winning first place in the 1972 Samuel Goldwyn Writing Competition. His TV dramas include the Humanitas Prize-nominated movie *Proud Men* (1987), starring Charlton Heston and Peter Strauss, and *The Jeweler's Shop*, adapted from a play by Pope John Paul II. Andrus' mystery series features Monterey family man and out-of-work personnel manager John Tracer, who starts a private investigations business in book 2 when he's hired by a next-door neighbor to locate the man's sister, Princess Ariel from Zartov, a colony on the planet Venus. The cast includes in-laws, wife, kids, Dog, and a pig named Alfred, who may yet star in their own TV series being developed by Andrus. A Stanford University graduate, he previously taught screenwriting at UCLA.

John Tracer...family-man sleuth in Monterey, California
- ❏ ❏ 1 - Tracer, Inc. (1994)
- ❏ ❏ 2 - Neighborhood Watch (1996)

■ ANTHONY, Michael David

Michael David Anthony has written a pair of ecclesiastical mysteries featuring Richard Harrison, an Anglican church official introduced in *The Becket Factor* (1990), a mystery which exhumed the bones of Thomas a Becket. The *Houston Post* called it "quite remarkable," while the *Los Angeles Times* pronounced

the atmosphere "vividly musty." Returning in *Dark Provenance* (1994), with a radical new archdeacon bent on costcutting and a mysterious death from his own past cause, Harrison has need for more than prayerful concern. Son of an Anglican clergy, Anthony has been a lecturer, teacher, freelance journalist and radio scriptwriter. He lives in London.

Richard Harrison...Anglican church official in England
- ❏ ❏   1 - The Becket Factor (1990)
- ❏ ❏   2 - Dark Provenance (1994)

■ ARDEN, William [P]

William Arden is one of the pseudonyms of Dennis Lynds, author of 5 crime and mystery series under 5 different names. As William Arden he produced 5 books about Kane Jackson, industrial spy and private eye specializing in big business clients, primarily drug and chemical companies. Writing in *1001 Midnights* (1986), Francis M. Nevins called *A Dark Power* (1968) "one of the best P.I.novels of the Sixties." After 35 years in the chemical industry, first as a chemist and later as a trade-publications editor, Lynds knows something about what goes on in that business. Past president of Private Eye Writers of America, he was awarded the PWA Lifetime Achievement Award in 1988. Born in St. Louis and raised in Brooklyn, he lives in Santa Barbara (CA) with his wife, mystery writer Gayle Lynds.

Kane Jackson...industrial espionage specialist in New Jersey
- ❏ ❏   1 - A Dark Power (1968)
- ❏ ❏   2 - Deal in Violence (1969)
- ❏ ❏   3 - The Goliath Scheme (1970)
- ❏ ❏   4 - Die to a Distant Drum (1972)
     Brit.-Murder Underground
- ❏ ❏   5 - Deadly Legacy (1973)

■ ARDIES, Tom

Seattle native Tom Ardies began his writing career at the *Vancouver Sun* in Vancouver, British Columbia where he worked as a reporter, columnist and editorial writer for 15 years from 1950 to 1964. After transferring to the *Honolulu Star Bulletin* as telegraph editor, Ardies later served as special assistant to the governor of Guam from 1965 to 1967. His trio of espionage novels from the early '70s stars a handsome American spy named Charlie Sparrow, introduced in *Their Man in the White House* (1971). Sparrow returns in the delighfully-titled *This Suitcase Is Going to Explode* (1972) and again in *Pandemic* (1973). Ardies wrote the screenplay *Russian Roulette* based on his 1974 novel *Kosygin is Coming*. A veteran of the U.S. Air Force, he attended Daniel McIntyre Collegiate Institute in Winnipeg, Canada.

Charlie Sparrow...handsome American spy in the United States
- ❏ ❏   1 - Their Man in the White House (1971)
- ❏ ❏   2 - This Suitcase is Going to Explode (1972)
- ❏ ❏   3 - Pandemic (1973)

■ ARDIN, William

British author William Ardin is the creator of Charles Ramsay, Chelsea antiques dealer and shop owner introduced in *Plain Dealer* (1992). In his most recent adventure (book 4), Ramsay must determine the true provenance of the Mary Medallion before arranging a sale that could destroy his reputation. Although the series is not yet published in the U.S., the books are available in U.K. paperback editions. Brought up in Kent and Norfolk, Ardin was educated at the Royal Grammar School (Worcester), and later won a scholarship to Oxford University. Formerly a market research expert in the petrochemical industry, he now lives in a hillside village in Galloway, a historic region in the southwest of Scotland, overlooking the ruins of Sweetheart Abbey, built by Devorgilla in the 13th Century.

Charles Ramsay...Chelsea antiques dealer in London, England
- ❏ ❏   1 - Plain Dealer (1992)
- ❏ ❏   2 - Some Dark Antiquities (1994)
- ❏ ❏   3 - Light at Midnight (1995)
- ❏ ❏   4 - The Mary Medallion (1996)

■ ARMISTEAD, John

Alabama-born John Armistead spent 25 years as a Baptist pastor until a head deacon told him, "You publish another book and you're out of here!" He resigned two weeks later and began a new career as religion editor of the *Tupelo* (MS) *Daily Journal*. Set in Mississippi hill country, the offending series opener introduced Sheriff Grover Bramlett, a doting grandfather with a Jack Daniel's-drinking mother. While battling to keep his weight under 275, the sheriff finds time for watercolor painting, even in the midst of dealing with snake-handling preachers. A one-time kindergarten teacher who later taught high school, Armistead is the proud owner of a blue Electra Glide Harley. A rider since the age of 14, he is a member of the Harley Owners Group (HOG), the American Academy of Religion (AAR) and Mystery Writers of America (MWA). He also paints and fly fishes.

Grover Bramlett...small-town sheriff in Sheffield, Mississippi
- ❏ ❏   1 - A Legacy of Vengeance (1994)
- ❏ ❏   2 - A Homecoming for Murder (1995)
- ❏ ❏   3 - Cruel as the Grave (1996)

■ ASHFORD, Jeffrey [P]

Jeffrey Ashford is one of half a dozen pen names used by Roderic Jeffries for his more than 100 mysteries and 25 books for children. Under the Ashford name he has produced a new book practically every year since 1960, many of them legal mysteries and all but two nonseries. Next under the Ashford name is *The Price of Failure* (1998), featuring a young police officer blackmailed by a kidnapper of the daughter of an English lord. Ashford wrote only two books featuring Det. Insp. Don Kerry, described in *Detectionary*, as "the epitome of the hard-working underpaid English police inspector [who] despite several difficult colleagues, a religious fanatic among them, loves his work." In addition to his work as Jeffrey Ashford, he writes under his own name, Peter Alding, Hastings Draper, Roderic Graeme and Graham Hastings.

Don Kerry, Det. Insp.....British detective inspector in England
- ❏ ❏   1 - Investigations Are Proceeding (1961) U.S.-The D. I.
- ❏ ❏   2 - Enquiries Are Continuing (1964) U.S.-The Superintendent's Room

■ ASPLER, Tony

As wine columnist for *The Toronto Star*, Tony Aspler knows his grapes. And it's no surprise his amateur detective is a Toronto wine journalist. Each book features a diffferent wine region, allowing readers to sniff clues in France, Italy and most recently, along the Douro River in Portugal (*Death on the Douro*, 1997). In his nonseries novel *Titanic* (1990), the ship's wine waiter meets a previous employer accused of murder. With Gordon Pape, Aspler has written several political thrillers including *Chain Reaction* (1978), *The Scorpion Sanction* (1980) and *The Music Wars* (1982). A former London radio producer and Canadian Broadcasting Corporation executive producer, Aspler was a graduate student at Trinity College in Dublin. His non-fiction work includes *Vintage Canada*, *Tony Aspler's International Guide to Wine* and *The Wine Lover Dines*.

Ezra Brant...wine journalist in Toronto, Ontario
- ❏ ❏   1 - Blood Is Thicker Than Beaujolais (1993)
- ❏ ❏   2 - The Beast of Barbaresco (1996)
- ❏ ❏   3 - Death on the Douro (1997)

■ AVALLONE, Michael

Michael Avallone has written more than 200 paperback novels in the last 45 years, including private eye stories, gothics, espionage thrillers, erotica, movie and television tie-ins and books for juveniles (*Keith Partridge, Master Spy*, 1972). Self-proclaimed "King of the Paperbacks" and "Fastest Typewriter in the East," Avallone is best known for 31 P.I. novels featuring Ed Noon, a certifiable character who loves baseball, old movies and dumb jokes. His better similes, metaphors and wacky prose have come to be known as "Noonisms" and among those singled out in Bill Pronzini's *Gun in Cheek* (1982) is the following from *The Case of the Violent Virgin*: "Her hips were beautifully arched and her breasts were like proud flags waving triumphantly. She carried them high and mighty." Avallone has used more than a dozen pseudonyms for his fiction.

Ed Noon...movie-nut private eye in New York, New York
- ❑ ❑ 1 - The Tall Dolores (1953)
- ❑ ❑ 2 - The Spitting Image (1953)
- ❑ ❑ 3 - Dead Game (1954)
- ❑ ❑ 4 - Violence in Velvet (1956)
- ❑ ❑ 5 - The Case of the Bouncing Betty (1957)
- ❑ ❑ 6 - The Case of the Violent Virgin (1957)
- ❑ ❑ 7 - The Crazy Mixed Up Corpse (1957)
- ❑ ❑ 8 - The Voodoo Murders (1957)
- ❑ ❑ 9 - Meanwhile Back at the Morgue (1960)
- ❑ ❑ 10 - The Alarming Clock (1961)
- ❑ ❑ 11 - The Bedroom Bolero (1963)
     Brit.-The Bolero Murders
- ❑ ❑ 12 - The Living Bomb (1963)
- ❑ ❑ 13 - There is Something About a Dame (1963)
- ❑ ❑ 14 - Lust is No Lady (1964)
     Brit.-The Brutal Kook
- ❑ ❑ 15 - The Fat Death (1966)
- ❑ ❑ 16 - The February Doll Murders (1966)
- ❑ ❑ 17 - Assassins Don't Die in Bed (1968)
- ❑ ❑ 18 - The Horrible Man (1968)
- ❑ ❑ 19 - The Flower-Covered Corpse (1969)
- ❑ ❑ 20 - The Doomsday Bag (1969)
     Brit.-Killer's Highway
- ❑ ❑ 22 - Little Miss Murder (1971)
     Brit.-The Ultimate Client
- ❑ ❑ 23 - Shoot It Again, Sam (1972)
- ❑ ❑ 24 - The Girl in the Cockpit (1972)
- ❑ ❑ 25 - Kill Her—You'll Like It (1973)
- ❑ ❑ 26 - The Hot Body (1973)
- ❑ ❑ 27 - Killer on the Keys (1973)
- ❑ ❑ 28 - The X-Rated Corpse (1973)
- ❑ ❑ 29 - The Big Stiffs (1977)
- ❑ ❑ 30 - Dark on Monday (1978)
- ❑ ❑ 31 - High Noon at Midnight (1988)

■ AXLER, Leo [P]

Leo Axler is the pseudonym of former funeral director and horror writer Gene Lazuta whose amateur sleuth is Cleveland funeral director Bill Hawley. Like his creator, Hawley joined the family mortuary business right out of college. Although Bill doesn't mind dealing with caskets and mourners, he's always looking for something more exciting. Once typed as a 'splatter punk' novelist after turning out such titles as *Blood Flies*, *Bleeder*, and *Vyrmin*, Lazuta says he only wrote horror because he thought it was a niche he might fit into. Having worked for an ambulance service as a teenager and being a longtime amateur student of forensic pathology, his switch to murder mysteries seems preordained. But he's quick to caution that the work of a real life funeral director is nothing like Bill Hawley's undertakings. "You stand around in a suit a lot and count carnations," he says.

Bill Hawley...undertaker sleuth in Cleveland, Ohio
- ❑ ❑   1 - Final Viewing (1994)
- ❑ ❑   2 - **Double Plot (1994) Shamus nominee** ☆
- ❑ ❑   3 - Grave Matters (1995)
- ❑ ❑   4 - Separated at Death (1996)

■ AYRES, E. C.

Eugene C. Ayres worked as a writer/producer in film and animation for television and newspapers for 20 years before winning the 1992 PWA/SMP contest by adapting one of his old screenplays as a novel. St. Martin's published *Hour of the Manatee* in 1994, introducing laid-back Florida photographer/P.I. Tony Lowell and his friend and occasional adversary, police detective Lena Bedrosian. Up next is book 4, *Lair of the Lizard* (1998). Ayres is also working on *Red Tide*, what he hopes will be the first in a series of eco-thrillers, environmental suspense thrillers without all the right-wing politics and military paraphernalia. Ayres spent 10 years in New York writing and producing for *Sesame Street*, ABC, and Time-Life TV before moving to Los Angeles where he helped create and develop children's series such as *Smurfs*, *Kissyfur* and *Scooby Doo*. He lives in St. Petersburg.

Tony Lowell...photographer private eye in Florida
- ❑ ❑   1 - **Hour of the Manatee (1994) SMP/PWA winner** ★
- ❑ ❑   2 - Eye of the Gator (1995)
- ❑ ❑   3 - Night of the Panther (1997)

■ BABULA, William

Shakespeare scholar and prize-winning playwright, William Babula, is the creator of San Franciso private eye Jeremiah St. John, introduced in the aptly-named *St. John's Baptism* (1988). Dean of the School of Arts and Humanities at Sonoma State University since 1981, Babula started his teaching career at the University of Miami in Coral Gables, where he was English department chair for six years. A Phi Beta Kappa at Rutgers, Babula earned both his M.A. and Ph.D. at the University of California at Berkeley. Born in Stamford, Connecticut, he is a frequent contributor of short stories and articles to various language and literature journals. When asked about making the transition from scholarly writing to the writing of fiction and drama, Babula says, 'the latter is certainly a lot more enjoyable, and quite frankly, the research is easier."

Jeremiah St. John...private investigator in San Francisco, California
- ❑ ❑   1 - St. John's Baptism (1988)
- ❑ ❑   2 - According to St. John (1989)
- ❑ ❑   3 - St. John and the Seven Veils (1991)
- ❑ ❑   4 - St. John's Bestiary (1994)
- ❑ ❑   5 - St. John's Bread (1997)

⊗ ■ BAILEY, Jo

Minnesota mystery writer Jo(seph) Bailey writes a series featuring a female security guard in a big-city Midwestern hospital. Single mother Jan Gallagher is introduced in *Bagged* (1991), where a body hidden in the hospital morgue turns out to be a much-disliked staff surgeon. In book 2 (*Recycled*, 1993), Jan is shuffled off to a do-nothing job after suing the hospital for sex discrimination and winning. She's assigned as staff liaison with the DEA and ends up playing decoy when a paid assassin comes after the federal witness awaiting a liver transplant. Just when she thinks things can't get worse, a race riot breaks out and one of the hospital's black guards is kidnapped in book 3 (*Erased*, 1996). With over 15 years' experience working in an inner-city public hospital, this author keeps an otherwise low profile in Minneapolis (MN).

Jan Gallagher...hospital security guard in Minnesota
- ❑ ❑ 1 - Bagged (1991)
- ❑ ❑ 2 - Recycled (1993)
- ❑ ❑ 3 - Erased (1996)

DONE **■ BAKER, John**

John Baker has worked as a social worker, shipbroker, truck driver, milkman and recently in the computer industry. His first novel, which introduces private detective Sam Turner, takes its title from Bob Dylan who "heard the song of a poet who died in the gutter." Sam hadn't given any thought to becoming a detective until he found himself fabricating his credentials at a men's discussion group he attended just to escape his cold flat. The delightful cast of characters includes teenager Geordie and his dog Barney, rescued by Sam from a life on the streets, and Celia Allison, a little old lady and retired English teacher who becomes Sam's office manager and Geordie's tutor after she's interviewed as a witness in book one. The whole gang returns in *Death Minus Zero*, which features an escaped convict who's lusting after a female prison psychiatrist. Married with five children, Baker lives in York.

Sam Turner...newly-sober private eye in York, England
- ✓ ❑ ❑ 1 - Poet in the Gutter (1995)
- – ❑ ❑ 2 - Death Minus Zero (1996)

⊗ ■ BARNAO, Jack [P]

Jack Barnao is a pseudonym used by Ted Wood for his series featuring John Locke, ex-Grenadier guard turned private security agent. Locke is Canadian-born and lives in Toronto, but served in both the Grenadier guards and the SAS. Although Toronto is home base for Locke, he travels widely in his security business. In the series opener, he heads to Florence (Italy); book 2 takes him to Mexico; book 3 to France. The author was born in England, where his father was a Grenadier, and emigrated to Canada in his early 20s after serving 3 years in the Royal Air Force. Following a short police career in Toronto, Wood spent more than 15 years in advertising before turning to writing full-time. He lives in Whitbey, Ontario where he owns and operates a bed and breakfast.

John Locke...ex-Grenadier guard turned private security agent in Toronto, Ontario
- ❑ ❑ 1 - Hammerlocke (1987)
- ❑ ❑ 2 - Lockestep (1988)
- ❑ ❑ 3 - Timelocke (1991)

■ BARNARD, Robert

Author of more than 30 mysteries, many of which are nonseries, Agatha Award winner Robert Barnard has created two Scotland Yard detectives. First came Insp. Perry Trethowan, who must investigate the death of his own father, found dead in spangled tights in a medieval torture machine, in *Sheer Torture*

(1981), one of Barnard's personal favorites among all his titles. Later he gave Charlie Peace, a young black constable appearing in two of the Trethowan books, his own series. Charlie's 5th appearance is *No Place of Safety* (1997). Among Barnard's numerous awards for short stories are the 1988 Agatha for "More Final Than Divorce". When asked if any of his characters resemble individuals from his everyday life, Barnard said no. "People can be so much nastier, can act so much meaner, than they are usually allowed to do in books," he added.

Charlie Peace...young black Scotland Yard detective in London, England
- ❑ ❑ 1 - Death and the Chaste Apprentice (1989) √
- ❑ ❑ 2 - A Fatal Attachment [incl Oddie] (1992)
- ❑ ❑ 3 - A Hovering of Vultures [incl Oddie] (1993)
- ❑ ❑ 4 - The Bad Samaritan [incl Oddie] (1995)

Oddie...inner city schoolteacher in London, England
- ❑ ❑ 1 - A City of Strangers (1990)

Perry Trethowan, Insp.....Scotland Yard inspector in London, England
- ❑ ❑ 1 - Sheer Torture (1981) U.S.-Death by Sheer Torture
- ❑ ❑ 2 - Death and the Princess (1982)
- ❑ ❑ 3 - The Missing Bronte (1983) U.S.-The Case of the Missing Bronte
- ❑ ❑ 4 - Bodies [incl Charlie Peace] (1986)
- ❑ ❑ 5 - Death in Purple Prose [incl Charlie Peace] (1987) U.S.-The Cherry Blossom Corpse

■ BARNES, Trevor

Trevor Barnes is the creator of a three-book series featuring Scotland Yard Superintendent Blanche Hampton whose final appearance was in *Taped*. Narrated by the superintendent's black assistant, this book was published only in England. A former senior news and current affairs producer with the BBC, Barnes has written frequently on espionage for both newspapers and academic publications. According to the U.S. edition of *Midsummer Night's Killing*, his pioneering research on Western intelligence during the Cold War forms some of the background of this novel, where a headless corpse is found on Hampstead Heath. A graduate of Cambridge University and a Harvard University Kennedy Scholar, Barnes lives in London with his wife and daughter. Born in Suffolk, he currently makes his living as a solicitor.

Blanche Hampton, Det. Supt.....Scotland Yard detective superintendent in London, England
- ❑ ❑ 1 - A Midsummer Killing (1989)
- ❑ ❑ 2 - A Pound of Flesh (1993)

■ BARNETT, James

Scotland Yard detective James Barnett published six books featuring a Scotland Yard troublemaker and bad boy named Owen Smith. In his first case, *Head of the Force*, the chief superintendent must handle an investigation where the head has been removed from the body—and it's the Commissioner's. In book 2 a young female RAF flight lieutenant is murdered and that's just one of the strange things happening at Cladenham RAF base when Smith is called to investigate. He goes to the Caribbean in *Palmprint* (1980) and ends up in Canada trailing an international assassin. After being transferred to a quiet borough on his final case, Smith's inadequate supervision leads to the death of a young detective. Born and raised in Scotland, James Barnett spent 30 years with the Metropolitan Police of London

Owen Smith, Chief Supt.....chief superintendent in England
- ❑ ❑ 1 - Head of the Force (1978)
- ❑ ❑ 2 - Backfire is Hostile! (1979)
- ❑ ❑ 3 - Palmprint (1980)
- ❑ ❑ 4 - The Firing Squad (1981)
- ❑ ❑ 5 - Marked for Destruction (1982)
- ❑ ❑ 6 - Diminished Responsibility (1984)

■ BARRE, Richard

Shamus award winner Richard Barre is the creator of Wil Hardesty—Vietnam survivor, greybeard surfer and California private eye mourning the loss of his young son. Wil's first appearance in *The Innocents* (1995) was a Shamus award winner and Anthony nominee for best first novel. Barre admits to surfing experience, but says his exploits are not in Hardesty's league. Wil is bigger, badder and more fearless than his creator, according to Barre, who spent his military tour of duty at a Coast Guard office in San Francisco. The ambush scene in *The Innocents* is based on a real event, but it was Barre's C.O. who lived to tell about it. A graduate of California State University, Barre spent 15 years as creative director of his own advertising agency. From his Santa Barbara home office, he works as a travel writer and editor while plotting Wil's next challenge.

Wil Hardesty...Vietnam vet and greybeard surfer turned P.I. in Southern California
- ❏ ❏ 1 - **The Innocents (1995) Shamus winner ★ Anthony nominee ☆**
- ❏ ❏ 2 - Bearing Secrets (1996)
- ❏ ❏ 3 - The Ghosts of Morning (1998)

■ BARRETT, Neal, Jr.

Author of more than 30 novels, many of them science fiction, Neal Barrett, Jr. has recently turned to mysteries. He is the creator of a new series featuring Washington DC graphic artist, Wiley Moss, ace illustrator of insects for the Smithsonian and *National Geographic*. Wacky Wiley is introduced in *Skinny Annie Blues* (1996) where he's summoned to Galveston when the father he hasn't seen in 19 years turns up dead. In book 2 Wiley is kidnapped by thugs and dragged to a brothel in Idaho where a minor mobster named Spuds wants Wiley to sketch his 18 resident cuties, the Spudettes. Among Barrett's nonseries novels are *Dead Dog Blues* (1994) and *Pink Vodka Blues* (1992). Author of the film novelization of *Judge Dredd* (1995), he's also written Spider Man and Babylon 5 novels. Born in San Antonio, he lives in Austin (TX).

Wiley Moss...graphic artist for the Smithsonian in Washington, D.C.
- ❏ ❏ 1 - Skinny Annie Blues (1996)
- ❏ ❏ 2 - Bad Eye Blues (1997)

■ BARRETT, Robert G.

Australian author Robert G. Barrett has written 7 humorously-titled books featuring Les Norton, a hillbilly from Queensland, hired as a Sydney nightclub bouncer. He makes his first appearance in *You Wouldn't Be Dead for Quids* (1985), at the Kelly Club, Kings Cross. Book 4 takes Norton to Canberra, where he plays minder to a young member of a royal family. In book 6 he's back in the minding business—this time in Surfers Paradise. But he hits the jackpot in book 7, winning a raffle which takes him to the U.S.A. in *Les Norton's Back In and de Fun Don't Done* (1993). Barrett was raised in Bondi where he worked primarily as a butcher. He has appeared in a number of Australian films and television commercials but prefers writing. He lives in Terrigal.

Les Norton...nightclub bouncer in Sydney, Australia
- ❏ ❏ 1 - You Wouldn't Be Dead for Quids (1985)
- ❏ ❏ 2 - The Real Thing (1986)
- ❏ ❏ 3 - The Boys from Binjiwunyawunya (1987)
- ❏ ❏ 4 - The Godson (1989)
- ❏ ❏ 5 - Between the Devlin and the Deep Blue Seas (1991)
- ❏ ❏ 6 - White Shoes, White Lines and Blackie (1992)
- ❏ ❏ 7 - Les Norton's Back In and de Fun Don't Done (1993)

■ BARTH, Richard

Richard Barth is the creator of a seven-book series featuring septuagenarian sleuth Margaret Binton and her gaggle of senior cohorts who have no trouble getting involved in just causes. Their latest case (*Deathics*, 1993) involves a young writer who was Margaret's buddy in a quit-smoking program. He was stabbed to death on his doorstep, but Margaret is convinced it wasn't random violence and she sets out to prove it. With an undergraduate degree with honors from Amherst College (MA), Barth earned an MFA from Pratt Institute and later taught at the Fashion Institute of Technology. A goldsmith and sculptor, he has had solo and group shows in the United States and England.

Margaret Binton...70-something little old lady in New York, New York
- ❑ ❑ 1 - The Rag Bag Clan (1978)
- ❑ ❑ 2 - A Ragged Plot (1981)
- ❑ ❑ 3 - One Dollar Death (1982)
- ❑ ❑ 4 - The Condo Kill (1985)
       Brit.-The Co-Op Kill
- ❑ ❑ 5 - Deadly Climate (1988)
- ❑ ❑ 6 - Blood Doesn't Tell (1989)
- ❑ ❑ 7 - Deathics (1993)

■ BASS, Milton R.

Shamus award nominee Milton Bass is the creator of two California private eye series. His San Diego P.I. Benny Freedman appeared in 4 books in the late '80s before Bass introduced Vinnie Altobelli. An ex-San Bernadino cop recovering from a heart attack, Vinnie first appears in *The Half-Hearted Detective* (1993), a Shamus nominee for best paperback original. According to a *Boston Globe* reviewer, "Bass lets it all hang out when he writes; a nice mix of stylish suspense, sex, and slapdash action. He scares you too..." In *The Broken-Hearted Detective* (1994) Vinnie and his cop pal Brady land in Tucson in search of Bernie's nurse/girlfriend who's gone missing. It's 106 degrees when they arrive and that's the least of their problems.

Benny Freedman...private eye in San Diego, California
- ❑ ❑ 1 - The Moving Finger (1986)
- ❑ ❑ 2 - Dirty Money (1986)
- ❑ ❑ 3 - The Bandini Affair (1987)
- ❑ ❑ 4 - The Belfast Connection (1988)

Vinnie Altobelli...ex-cop coronary survivor P.I. in San Bernadino, California
- ❑ ❑ 1 - **The Half-Hearted Detective (1993) Shamus nominee** ☆
- ❑ ❑ 2 - **The Broken-Hearted Detective (1994) Edgar nominee** ☆

■ BASTABLE, Bernard [P]

Bernard Bastable is the pseudonym used by Agatha award winner Robert Barnard for his historical series featuring Wolfgang Mozart and Princess Victoria. Educated at Oxford, he started writing novels in the late 1960s after teaching most of his life at universities in Norway and Australia. When asked to name his favorite mystery writers, he picked Christie and Allingham. From his own list of over 30 titles, he picked *Sheer Torture* (written as Robert Barnard) and *Dead, Mr. Mozart* as his personal favorites. About his Mozart series he said, "Most of the characters...were historical personages. Many of them, however, have little more than a shadowy existence in diaries and memoirs of the period, and where this is the case, I have felt at liberty to endow them with personalities that suited my story." The author lives in England.

Wolfgang Mozart & Princess Victoria...19th century composer-teacher & British princess in London
- ❑ ❑ 1 - Dead, Mr. Mozart (1995)
- ❑ ❑ 2 - Too Many Notes, Mr. Mozart (1995)

■ BATESON, David

During the 1950s, British thriller writer David Bateson wrote six novels featuring British private eye Larry Vernon, who makes his first appearance in *It's Murder, Senorita* (1954). Two of Vernon's cases take him to Australia. In book 5, *I'll Go Anywhere* (1959), he gets an assignment in Sydney which eventually leads him to Cairns. It's back to Sydney in book 6, *I'll Do Anything* (1960), where the murder trail which starts in the city ends up in the Outback. Other crime fiction titles from Bateson include *Insomnia Street* (1953), *Night Is for Violence* (1958) and *This Side of Terror* (1959).

Larry Vernon...British private eye in England
- ❏ ❏   1 - It's Murder, Senorita (1954)
- ❏ ❏   2 - The Man from the Rock (1955)
- ❏ ❏   3 - The Big Tomorrow (1956)
- ❏ ❏   4 - The Soho Jungle (1958)
- ❏ ❏   5 - I'll Go Anywhere [Australia] (1959)
- ❏ ❏   6 - I'll Do Anything [Australia] (1960)

■ BATTEN, Jack

Canadian author Jack Batten has written 4 books featuring a Toronto lawyer and jazz buff named Crang, who first appears in *Crang Plays the Ace* (1987). In book 3, *Riviera Blues* (1990), Crang travels to Monaco. In addition to the Crang series, Batten has co-written, with Michael Bliss, a Sherlockian pastiche titled "Sherlock Holmes' Great Canadian Adventure." When called on by Canada's first and greatest Prime Minister, Holmes saves the Dominion of Canada from a takeover by the United States. The piece first appeared in *Weekend Magazine* (May 28, 1977) and was later reprinted in several larger works. Batten graduated from the University of Toronto Law School and practiced law in Toronto for 4-5 years before becoming a full-time writer and reviewer. He lives in Toronto.

Crang...lawyer and jazz buff in Toronto, Ontario
- ❏ ❏   1 - Crang Plays the Ace (1987)
- ❏ ❏   2 - Straight No Chaser (1989)
- ❏ ❏   3 - Riviera Blues (1990)
- ❏ ❏   4 - Blood Count (1991)

■ BAXT, George

Brooklyn native George Baxt has written more than 25 novels, including the Edgar-nominated *A Parade of Cockeyed Creatures* (1967) starring a high school teacher and missing persons detective. Presently Baxt is best known for his (now 12) celebrity murder cases, where the protagonists are Hollywood legends. According to Jeff Banks and Don Sandstrom in *St. James Guide* (4th ed.), the first 3 books are laugh riots, owing to the wealth of anecdotes and witticisms about Parker, Hitchcock and Bankhead. Writing about his series with Pharoah Love, they call Baxt one of the finest of modern satirists, likening his portrayal of New York City's homosexual underground to "juggling while walking on eggshells." After a 26-year hiatus, Pharoah returns in book 4 as a black supercop, but it's the first 3 that Banks and Sandstrom say are stunners.

Jacob Singer...1940s Hollywood private eye in Los Angeles, California
- ❏ ❏   1 - The Dorothy Parker Murder Case (1984)
- ❏ ❏   2 - The Alfred Hitchcock Murder Case (1986)
- ❏ ❏   3 - The Tallulah Bankhead Murder Case (1987)
- ❏ ❏   4 - The Talking Pictures Murder Case (1990)
- ❏ ❏   5 - The Greta Garbo Murder Case (1992)
- ❏ ❏   6 - The Noel Coward Murder Case (1992)
- ❏ ❏   7 - The Marlene Dietrich Murder Case (1993)

❑ ❑ 8 - The Mae West Murder Case (1993)
❑ ❑ 9 - The Bette Davis Murder Case (1994)
❑ ❑ 10 - The Humphrey Bogart Murder Case (1995)
❑ ❑ 11 - The William Powell and Myrna Loy Murder Case (1996)
❑ ❑ 12 - The Fred Astaire and Ginger Rogers Murder Case (1997)

Pharoah Love...gay black NYPD detective in New York, New York
❑ ❑ 1 - A Queer Kind of Death (1966)
❑ ❑ 2 - Swing Low, Sweet Harriett (1967)
❑ ❑ 3 - Topsy and Evil (1968)
❑ ❑ 4 - A Queer Kind of Love (1994)
❑ ❑ 5 - A Queer Kind of Umbrella (1995)

Sylvia Plotkin & Max Van Larsen...author-teacher & police detective in New York
❑ ❑ 1 - **A Parade of Cockeyed Creatures (1967) Edgar nominee** ☆
❑ ❑ 2 - "I!" Said the Demon (1969)
❑ ❑ 3 - Satan is a Woman (1987)

■ BAYER, William

Edgar award winner William Bayer (pronounced BUY-er) is the creator of NYPD homicide detective Frank Janek, well known to TV movie audiences as Richard Crenna. Janek's first case was *Peregrine*, named best novel by Mystery Writers of America in 1982. Bayer's lawyer father and playwright mother, writing together as Oliver Weld Bayer, wrote 4 mysteries during the '40s, making him a second generation mystery writer. In addition to the Janek books, he has written at least 9 other novels and 2 nonfiction books. Writing as David Hunt, he is the author of *The Magician's Tale* (1997) and with Nancy Harmon (writing together as Leonie St. John) author of *Love with a Harvard Accent* (1962). A former U.S.I.A. foreign service officer and documentary filmmaker in Washington DC, New York and Saigon, Bayer writes full-time from his home in San Francisco. Among other projects, he is writing a sequel to *The Magician's Tale.*

Frank Janek, Lt....NYPD homicide detective in New York
❑ ❑ 1 - **Peregrine (1981) Edgar winner** ★
❑ ❑ 2 - Switch (1984)
❑ ❑ 3 - Wallflower (1991)
❑ ❑ 4 - Mirror Maze (1994)

■ BEAN, Gregory

Award-winning newspaper columnist and editor Gregory Bean is the creator of a new series featuring Harry Starbranch, burned out Denver homicide detective turned small-town police chief in Victory, Wyoming. A former Casper (WY) police reporter, he clearly knows the beat and the landscape. Born and raised in Wyoming, Bean was an honors graduate of the University of Wyoming where he earned both his B.A. and M.A. degrees. He has been a reporter and editor for more than 15 years, with newspapers and magazines in Wyoming, Illinois, Massachusetts and New Jersey. He currently lives in East Brunswick (NJ), where he is executive editor for Greater Media Newspapers.

Harry Starbranch...burned-out Denver cop turned small-town police chief in Victory, Wyoming
❑ ❑ 1 - No Comfort in Victory (1995)
❑ ❑ 2 - Long Shadows in Victory (1996)
❑ ❑ 3 - A Death in Victory (1997)

■ BEINHART, Larry

Edgar award winner Larry Beinhart has written three books featuring hardboiled private eye Tony Cassella, born and bred New Yorker and Yale Law School dropout. In book 1, a best-first-novel Edgar winner and Shamus nominee, Tony is hired by a wealthy law firm who fears one of their former lawyers will spill his guts to the SEC in a plea bargain. Book 2 starts with a simple skip trace but heats up quickly. Tony's enjoying fatherhood and an anonymous life in the Austrian Alps in book 3, until a wealthy businessman turns up dead and the CIA, IRS and KGB get involved. Married to actor and mystery writer Gillian Farrell, Beinhart spent 1994 in Oxford, England, as the recipient of the Raymond Chandler Fulbright Fellowship. He is also the author of *How To Write a Mystery* (1996) and *American Hero* (1993), adapted for film as the 1997 Dustin Hoffman-Robert DeNiro movie *Wag the Dog*.

Tony Casella...family-man private eye in New York, New York
- ❏ ❏ 1 - **No One Rides for Free (1986) Edgar winner ★ Shamus nominee ☆**
- ❏ ❏ 2 - You Get What You Pay For (1988)
- ❏ ❏ 3 - Foreign Exchange (1991)

■ BELSKY, Dick

Working journalist Dick Belsky has written 6 novels featuring New York journalists who happen to be women. His primary character is 40-something Jenny McKay, a TV news reporter who is bright, aggressive and dogged in her pursuit of a story. Featured in 4 Berkley paperbacks, Belsky says she's a lot of fun. New in 1997 is *Loverboy*, a hardcover thriller which brings back Lucy Shannon, last seen 12 years ago in the papberback *One for the Money* . Belsky was metro editor at the *New York Post* before signing on as news editor at *STAR Magazine*, just in time to catch the story of a prostitute and sleazy presidential adviser Dick Morris. In 1977 Belsky wrote two nonfiction juvenile books—*Tom Seaver: Baseball Superstar* and *The Juice: The O.J. Simpson Story*. An Ohio University graduate and native of Cleveland, he lives in New York City.

Jenny McKay...TV news reporter in New York
- ❏ ❏ 1 - South Street Confidential (1989) APA-Broadcast Clues
- ❏ ❏ 2 - Live from New York (1993)
- ❏ ❏ 3 - The Mourning Show (1994)
- ❏ ❏ 4 - Summertime News (1995)

Lucy Shannon...newspaper reporter in New York, New York
- ❏ ❏ 1 - One For the Money (1985)
- ❏ ❏ 2 - Loverboy [as by R. G. Belsky] (1997)

■ BENISON, C. C. [P]

C. C. Benison is the pseudonym of Canadian author Douglas Whiteway, whose first published novel revolves around Jane Bee, a young Canadian housemaid in the service of the Queen of England. In *Death at Buckingham Palace* (1995), Jane and Her Majesty team up to solve a murder after Jane stumbles over the body of a footman in one of the palace corridors. Whiteway began work on the book in 1991 and researched it almost entirely in Winnipeg where he lives, except for a brief trip to London in 1993 to walk his characters through the mystery. Although it's a work of fiction, he set the book in real time (Fall '93) and included actual events that took place at Buckingham Palace. A journalist and freelance writer with a degree in journalism from Carleton University in Ottawa, Whiteway has worked for both the *Winnipeg Tribune* and the *Winnipeg Free Press*.

Jane Bee...housemaid at Buckingham Palace in London, England
- ❏ ❏ 1 - Murder at Buckingham Palace (1996)
- ❏ ❏ 2 - Death at Sandringham House (1996)
- ❏ ❏ 3 - Death at Windsor Castle (1997)

■ BERGER, Bob

NetGuide magazine columnist Bob Berger wrote a pair of mysteries featuring newspaper columnist James Denny, also known as Dr. Risk. His crime-solving tools are a mix of probability, life expectancy, chemistry, statistics and good old common sense. In *The Risk of Heaven* (1996) Dr. Risk wakes up alone on an East River dock and every man's worst nightmare. He's arrested for molesting the young daughter of an old friend and the first person he has to convince of his innocence is himself. A risk theorist by training, Berger is the author of *Beating Murphy's Law, the Amazing Science of Risk* (1994), a Dell trade paperback that explains how anyone can use the secrets of probability theory and the 2-by-2 box matrix to get the edge in decision-making. Berger says he's a guy who takes risks. He drove a New York City cab, was a stock broker during the '87 crash, wrote a play that actually got produced and after years of confirmed bachelorhood, married a woman he met at a bus stop.

James Denny aka Dr. Risk...risk theorist and newspaper columnist in New York, New York
- ❑ ❑ 1 - The Risk of Murder (1995)
- ❑ ❑ 2 - The Risk of Heaven (1996)

■ BERLINSKI, David

David Berlinski is best known in academic circles for his 1995 book *A Tour of the Calculus*, which launched what have been dubbed the Berlinski debates. An accomplished poet, this university professor has taught philosophy, mathematics and English at Stanford. According to Forbes magazine Berlinski is "the most controversial challenger to the dogma of modern science in our time." He is also the creator of cynical San Francisco private eye Aaron Asherfeld, first appearing in *A Clean Sweep* (1993). Asherfeld is a cynical fellow with three ex-wives. He's been described by *Kirkus Reviews* as "a resourceful pipsqueak whose don't-tread-on-me attitude is equally offensive to gays...frat rats, sensitivity trainers, politically incorrect hired goons, the police, and his frantic, hilariously venal employees." Berlinski lives in San Francisco.

Aaron Asherfeld...cynical P.I. with 3 ex-wives in San Francisco, California
- ❑ ❑ 1 - A Clean Sweep (1993)
- ❑ ❑ 2 - Less Than Meets the Eye (1994)
- ❑ ❑ 3 - The Body Shop (1996)

■ BERNHARDT, William

Oklahoma native William Bernhardt has written 7 books in the series featuring Tulsa trial lawyer Ben Kincaid, introduced in *Primary Justice* (1992), Bernhardt's first novel. Book 4 takes Ben to the backwoods of Arkansas for a case involving a white supremacy group harassing a group of Vietnamese. Staunchly-liberal Ben finds himself representing the supremacist. His newest case is *Extreme Justice* (1998). In addition to the Kincaid series, Bernhardt has 2 nonseries titles, *The Code of Buddyhood* (1993) and *Double Jeopardy* (1995). Describing his writing practices in an on-line interview for Amazon, Bernhardt says his wireless keyboard and 31-inch monitor allow him to sit in a recliner on the opposite side of the room and still see his work, which he says "looks a lot better blown up on a 31-inch screen." Bernhardt lives in Tulsa where he is a director of the Arts and Humanities Council.

Ben Kincaid...attorney in Tulsa, Oklahoma
- ❑ ❑ 1 - Primary Justice (1991)
- ❑ ❑ 2 - Blind Justice (1992)
- ❑ ❑ 3 - Deadly Justice (1993)
- ❑ ❑ 4 - Perfect Justice (1994)
- ❑ ❑ 5 - Cruel Justice (1996)
- ❑ ❑ 6 - Naked Justice (1997)

■ BICKHAM, Jack

Oklahoma newspaper editor and journalism professor Jack Bickham has written more than 60 books, including westerns, mysteries and comedy. His part-time CIA agent and tennis player Brad Smith is featured in 6 books, starting with a trip to Belgrade in *Tiebreaker* (1989). As John Miles he wrote 2 titles featuring a Colorado woman sheriff and 3 set in an Oklahoma retirement center. Under the name Jeff Clinton he penned at least 10 Wildcat books. Several of his earlier works were made into movies, including the 1975 Disney film *The Apple Dumpling Gang*, starring Bill Bixby and Don Knotts. For many years Bickham taught journalism at the University of Oklahoma and was a guiding force behind their Professional Writing Program. A licensed private pilot, he has recently retired from teaching and moved to Alaska.

Charity Ross...1890s widowed frontier ranch owner in Oklahoma City, Oklahoma
- ❏ ❏ 1 - The War Against Charity Ross (1967)
- ❏ ❏ 2 - Target: Charity Ross (1968)

Brad Smith...championship tennis player and part-time CIA agent in the United States
- ❏ ❏ 1 - Tiebreaker (1989)
- ❏ ❏ 2 - Dropshot (1990)
- ❏ ❏ 3 - Overhead (1991)
- ❏ ❏ 4 - Breakfast at Wimbledon (1991)
- ❏ ❏ 5 - Double Fault (1993)
- ❏ ❏ 6 - The Davis Cup Conspiracy (1994)

■ BIDERMAN, Bob

Mystery author Bob Biderman is the creator of San Francisco investigative journalist Joseph Radkin who makes his first appearance in *Strange Inheritance* (1985), followed by *The Genesis Files* (1988). In *Judgement of Death* (1989), Radkin travels to London to inquire about two sensational poison cases after the death of his predecessor. And in book 4, *Paper Cuts* (1990), he travels to Oregon. In addition to these four mysteries, Biderman has written *Koba* (1988) which was published only in England.

Joseph Radkin...investigative journalist in San Francisco, California
- ❏ ❏ 1 - Strange Inheritance (1985)
- ❏ ❏ 2 - The Genesis Files (1988)
- ❏ ❏ 3 - Judgement of Death (1989)
- ❏ ❏ 4 - Paper Cuts (1990)

■ BIGGLE, Lloyd, Jr.

Science fiction and mystery writer Lloyd Biggle, Jr., has written a 3-book series featuring private detectives J. Pletcher and Raina Lambert, whose strangest case is their third. The P.I.s travel to Napolean Corners (GA), where the town is named after a Civil War cannon and quirkiness abounds. They discover a community of monks, a self-proclaimed witch and a wealthy grandfather who thinks he's a Confederate general. Biggle's science fiction includes 5 books in the Jan Darzek series and at least 7 other titles. He has also written more than 75 mystery and science fiction stories for magazines and anthologies. After completing his Ph.D. in musicology at the University of Michigan, Biggle taught music there for several years. Founder and president of the Science Fiction Oral History Association, Biggle lives in Ypsilanti (MI).

J. Pletcher & Raina Lambert...pair of private eyes in the United States
- ❏ ❏ 1 - Interface for Murder (1987)
- ❏ ❏ 2 - A Hazard of Losers (1991)
- ❏ ❏ 3 - Where Dead Soldiers Walk (1994)

■ BIRKETT, John

Two-time Shamus Award nominee John Birkett has written a pair of private eye novels featuring Michael Rhineheart of Louisville (KY). Rhineheart is a man who knows his bourbon and takes it with branch water. First appearing in the Shamus-nominated *The Last Private Eye* (1988), he is joined by his sleuthing secretary Sally McGuire and a crusty old pro named Farnsworth. Sally will do anything to learn the ropes; Rhineheart hopes she doesn't hang herself. In the series opener, the trio is working to solve a mysterious disappearance at the Kentucky Derby racetrack. Later, Rhineheart is hired to deliver the ransom for a kidnapped horse, but not to recover the horse, when the trio returns in *The Queen's Mare* (1990). Book 2 was another Shamus nominee, a paperback original from Avon, like its predecessor.

Michael Rhineheart...private eye in Louisville, Kentucky
- ❏ ❏ 1 - **The Last Private Eye (1988) Shamus nominee** ☆
- ❏ ❏ 2 - **The Queen's Mare (1990) Shamus nominee** ☆

■ BISHOP, Paul

Paul Bishop heads the Sex Crimes and Major Assault Crimes units of the West Los Angeles Detective Division. His 20 years with the LAPD include three with the Anti-Terrorist Divsion, where he was assigned to a federal task force working with the LA Sheriff's Department, FBI, CIA and Secret Service. He credits his several female detective partners with being the inspiration for series detective Fey Croaker. She's a smart-talking, hard-bitten, 40-something homicide supervisor, who coincidentally has her creator's current day job. A former second division soccer player in England, Bishop writes another series featuring a one-eyed former world class soccer player turned private eye. *Sporting Press* magazine editor Ian Chapel goes undercover in the opener when he joins the team to find a killer after the goalie is murdered in Bishop's personal favorite of all his novels.

Calico Jack Walker & Tina Tamiko...ex-patrol cop & his former rookie partner in Los Angeles, California
- ❏ ❏ 1 - Citadel Run (1988)
- ❏ ❏ 2 - Sand Against the Tide (1990)
- ❏ ❏ 3 - Dark of the Heart (1998)

Fey Croaker...40-something homicide unit supervisor in Los Angeles, California
- ❏ ❏ 1 - Kill Me Again (1994)
- ❏ ❏ 2 - Twice Dead (1996)
- ❏ ❏ 3 - Tequila Mockingbird (1997)
- ❏ ❏ 4 - Chalk Whispers (1998)

Ian Chapel...one-eyed pro soccer goalie turned P.I. in Los Angeles, California
- ❏ ❏ 1 - Chapel of the Ravens (1991)
- ❏ ❏ 2 - Criminal Tendencies (1998)

■ BLATTY, William Peter

Director, screenwriter and novelist William Peter Blatty won both an Academy Award and Golden Globe for the screenplay of his own 1971 novel *The Exorcist*. Among his 9 books and 11 screenplays are his latest book, *Demons Five, Exorcists Nothing* (1996), which he calls a realistic fable of towering ambition and Hollywood cross and doublecross. The screenplay of another of his books, *The Ninth Configuration*, won him another Golden Globe. Blatty also directed the film (starring Stacy Keach and Moses Gunn) about a military base psychiatrist who becomes the object of hate pranks which turn serious. Other Blatty screenplays include *John Goldfarb, Please Come Home* and *What Did You Do in the War, Daddy?* Blatty makes his home in Montecito (CA).

Bill Kinderman, Lt.....police lieutenant in Washington, D.C.
- ❏ ❏ 1 - The Exorcist (1971)
- ❏ ❏ 2 - Legion (1983)

■ **BLOCK, Lawrence**

Grand Master Lawrence Block is the author of more than 40 novels. A 3-time winner of the Edgar Award, he has won 4 Shamus Awards, several Maltese Falcon Awards and was the first recipient of the Nero Wolfe Award. His best-known series characters are a melancholy, alcoholic, unlicensed P.I. named Matt Scudder, and a burglar/bibliophile named Bernie Rhodenbarr, hailed by *Newsday* as "the kind of crook Dickens would have created: smart, witty, and with a nice sense of self-irony." Block launched his fiction career with short stories for *Manhunt* and other crime magazines, along with more than a few paperback sex novels written pseudonymously. It was a *Chicago Tribune* reviewer who noted that Block is "the rare pro who survived a hack apprenticeship without becoming one." Arriving in early 1998 is *Hitman*, the first book-length appearance of the wistful hitman Keller, who appeared previously in the short story "Answers to Soldier."

Bernie Rhodenbarr...professional burglar and bibliophile in New York, New York
- ❑ ❑ 1 - Burglars Can't Be Choosers (1977)
- ❑ ❑ 2 - The Burglar in the Closet (1978)
- ❑ ❑ 3 - **The Burglar Who Liked to Quote Kipling (1979) Nero Wolfe winner ★**
- ❑ ❑ 4 - The Burglar Who Studied Spinoza (1981)
- ❑ ❑ 5 - The Burglar Who Painted Like Mondrian (1983)
- ❑ ❑ 6 - The Burglar Who Traded Ted Williams (1994)
- ❑ ❑ 7 - The Burglar Who Thought He Was Bogart (1995)
- ❑ ❑ 8 - The Burglar in the Library (1997)

Evan Tanner...government agent with permanent insomnia in the United States
- ❑ ❑ 1 - The Thief Who Couldn't Sleep (1966)
- ❑ ❑ 2 - The Cancelled Czech (1966)
- ❑ ❑ 3 - Tanner's Twelve Swingers (1967)
- ❑ ❑ 4 - Two for Tanner (1967)
- ❑ ❑ 5 - Here Comes a Hero (1968)
- ❑ ❑ 6 - Tanner's Tiger (1968)
- ❑ ❑ 7 - Me Tanner, You Jane (1970)

Leo Haig...private investigator in New York, New York
- ❑ ❑ 1 - No Score [as by Chip Harrison] (1970)
- ❑ ❑ 2 - Chip Harrison Scores Again [as by C. Harrison] (1971)
- ❑ ❑ 3 - Make Out With Murder [as by C. Harrison] (1974)
  - APA-The Five Little Rich Girls [as by Lawrence Block]
- ❑ ❑ 4 - The Topless Tulip Caper (1975)

Matt Scudder...unlicensed reformed alcoholic P.I. in New York, New York
- ❑ ❑ 1 - The Sins of the Fathers (1976)
- ❑ ❑ 2 - In the Midst of Death (1976)
- ❑ ❑ 3 - **Time to Murder and Create (1976) Edgar nominee ☆**
- ❑ ❑ 4 - **A Stab in the Dark (1978) Shamus nominee ☆**
- ❑ ❑ 5 - **Eight Million Ways to Die (1982) Shamus winner ★ Edgar nominee ☆**
- ❑ ❑ ss - Like a Lamb to the Slaughter [short stories] (1984)
- ❑ ❑ 6 - **When the Sacred Ginmill Closes (1986) Shamus nominee ☆**
- ❑ ❑ 7 - **Out on the Cutting Edge (1989) Shamus nominee ☆**
- ❑ ❑ 8 - **A Ticket to the Boneyard (1990) Shamus nominee ☆**
- ❑ ❑ 9 - **A Dance at the Slaughterhouse (1991) Edgar winner ★ Shamus nominee ☆**
- ❑ ❑ 10 - A Walk Among the Tombstones (1992)
- ❑ ❑ 11 - **The Devil Knows You're Dead (1993) Shamus winner ★**
- ❑ ❑ ss - Sometimes You Get the Bear [short stories] (1993)
- ❑ ❑ 12 - **A Long Line of Dead Men (1994) Edgar Winner ★ Shamus nominee ☆**
- ❑ ❑ 13 - Even the Wicked (1997)

■ BOGART, Stephen Humphrey

Author and television producer Stephen Bogart is one of three children of movie icons Humphrey Bogart and Lauren Bacall. He is also the author of fiction and nonfiction about his famous father. With Gary Provost he wrote *Bogart: In Search of My Father* (1995) and the same year published *Play It Again*, the first in his series with a character not unlike himself. However, R.J. Brook makes his living as a private detective specializing in evidence pictures of cheating marital partners. In book 1 his estranged mother is murdered and R.J. tries to solve the case. In his review for *Washington Post Book World*, Kinky Friedman said: "The characters feel real, the dialogue is killer bee, and, for better or worse, the book smells like New York." A graduate of the University of Hartford (CT), Bogart was previously the producer of *Court TV*.

R. J. Brook...celebrity-son private eye in New York, New York
- ❑ ❑ 1 - Play It Again (1995)
- ❑ ❑ 2 - The Remake (1997)

■ BOLAND, John C.

A former senior editor at *Barrons*, John C. Boland writes about the world of high finance from an insider's perspective. The lighter of his two series is set on Wall Street and features low-key stockbroker Donald McCarry. Another series (not listed here) introduces Baltimore investment banker Richard Welles who nearly loses his life trying to discover who's destroying a client company in *Rich Man's Blood* (1993). A casual favor for a grateful father sends Welles to Las Vegas in the complicated real estate scam of *The Margin* (1995). In addition to his financial fiction, Boland wrote *Wall Street's Insiders: How You Can Profit With the Smart Money* (1985) and managed a hedge fund in the early '90s. A resident of Baltimore, the American Boland is not related to former British CWA chairman John B(ertram) Boland (1913-1976), who wrote more than 30 suspense novels and hundreds of short stories between 1955 and 1975.

Donald McCarry...Wall Street stockbroker in New York, New York
- ❑ ❑ 1 - Brokered Death (1991)
- ❑ ❑ 2 - The Seventh Beaver (1993)
- ❑ ❑ 3 - Death in Jerusalem (1994)

■ BOLTON, Melvin

Wildlife management consultant Melvin Bolton has written 3 espionage novels featuring a 1980s British spy named Peter Lawson, first in hardcover British editions, followed two years later by publication in the U.S. Following book 1, *The Softener* (1984), Lawson returns in *The Testing* (1987). Later his intelligence work takes him to Afghanistan in *The Offering* (1988). According to Hubin, the author was born in England and earned his M.S. degree from London University in wildlife management consulting. Among his professional publications are *Management of Crocodiles in Captivity, FAO Conservation Guide No.22* (1990) and *Ethiopian Wildlands*. New in hardcover is *Conservation and the Use of Wildlife Resources, Conservation Biology Series No. 8*, (1997) edited by Bolton. He lives in Australia.

Peter Lawson...British spy in England
- ❑ ❑ 1 - The Softener (1984)
- ❑ ❑ 2 - The Testing (1987)
- ❑ ❑ 3 - The Offering (1988)

■ BOND, Michael

Michael Bond, O.B.E., is best known around the world as the creator of the beloved children's character Paddington Bear who has his own corner in the London Toy Museum and books in 20 languages. For adults, Bond has written a series of wonderfully bizarre gastronomic mysteries featuring Monsieur Pamplemousse (literal translation: Mr. Grapefruit) and his bloodhound Pommes Frites (French Fries). Pamplemouse is a food inspector and gourmet test-eater with Pommes Frites serving as his doggy Dr.

Watson. In an interview with *Contemporary Authors*, Bond says he got the idea for a food detective while dining in a restaurant near Lyons where the house specialty was a chicken cooked in a pig's bladder. It was brought to the table and cut open by the headwaiter with a great flourish, prompting Bond to ask himself, "What if it weren't a chicken inside?"

Aristide Pamplemousse & Pommes Frites...gourmet test-eater & his bloodhound in La Douce, France
- ❏ ❏ 1 - Monsieur Pamplemousse (1983)
- ❏ ❏ 2 - Mr. Pamplemousse en Fete (1984)
- ❏ ❏ 3 - Mr. Pamplemousse and the Secret Mission (1985)
- ❏ ❏ 4 - Mr. Pamplemousse on the Spot (1986)
- ❏ ❏ 5 - Mr. Pamplemousse Takes the Cure (1987)
- ❏ ❏ 6 - Mr. Pamplemousse Aloft (1989)
- ❏ ❏ 7 - Mr. Pamplemousse Investigates (1990)
- ❏ ❏ 8 - Mr. Pamplemousse Stands Firm (1993)

■ BOURGEAU, Art

Edgar nominee Art Bourgeau is the owner of Whodunit?, a mystery bookstore in Philadelphia (PA). He is also a mystery writer of both nonfiction and fiction, including his 4-book series featuring Claude "Snake" Kirlin and F.T. Zevich, a Tennessee magazine freelancer and his sidekick buddy, whom the author is to said to have compared to "free love versions of Tom Sawyer and Huckleberry Finn." These two make their first appearance in *A Lonely Way to Die* (1980), followed by *The Most Likely Suspects* (1981), *The Elvis Murders* (1985) and *Murder at the Cheatin' Heart Motel* (1985). Bourgeau also wrote two nonseries mysteries set in Philadelphia—*Wolfman* (1989) and *The Seduction* (1988). His best critical/biographical Edgar nomination was for *The Mystery Lover's Companion* (1986). Along with his wife, author Patricia MacDonald, Bourgeau lives in Cape May (NJ).

Claude "Snake" Kirlin & F.T. Zevich...magazine freelancer & sidekick in Tennessee
- ❏ ❏ 1 - A Lonely Way to Die (1980)
- ❏ ❏ 2 - The Most Likely Suspects (1981)
- ❏ ❏ 3 - The Elvis Murders (1985)
- ❏ ❏ 4 - Murder at the Cheatin' Heart Motel (1985)

■ BOWEN, Michael

Michael Bowen is a practicing trial attorney in Milwaukee (WI) and author of two mystery series. Foreign Service officer Richard Michaelson is featured in 4 books set in Washington DC, where his next assignment is tentatively titled *Comedy of Manors*. Bowen's other series features a '60s New York husband-and-wife detective team last seen in *Act of Faith* (1993). In addition to his mysteries, Bowen has written *Can't Miss* (1987), a mainstream novel about the first woman to play major league baseball. In an interview with *Contemporary Authors*, he disclosed that his two driving ambitions are to make it to the U.S. Supreme Court and appear on the French television program *Apostrophes*. A cum laude graduate of Harvard Law, Bowen is married to another Harvard lawyer. Together they are parents of 5 children, none of whom are yet Harvard Law graduates.

Richard Michaelson...retired Foreign Service officer in Washington, D.C.
- ❏ ❏ 1 - Washington Deceased (1990)
- ❏ ❏ 2 - Faithfully Executed (1992)
- ❏ ❏ 3 - Corruptly Procured (1994)
- ❏ ❏ 4 - Worst Case Scenario (1996)

Thomas & Sandrine Cadette Curry...1960s husband & wife detective team in New York, New York
- ❏ ❏ 1 - Badger Game (1989)
- ❏ ❏ 2 - Fielder's Choice (1991)
- ❏ ❏ 3 - Act of Faith (1993)

■ BOWEN, Peter

Peter Bowen has written 4 books featuring Gabriel Du Pré, Montana cattle brand inspector, Metis Indian, gifted fiddler and reluctant sheriff, introduced in *Coyote Wind* (1994). Marilyn Stasio of *The New York Times Book* Review called his work "truly mysterious—informed by Western legend, steeped in Indian superstition, peopled with characters who communicate by reading one another's minds...riding with Du Pré is some kind of enchantment." His 5th appearance is *Thunder Horse* (1998) where the action takes place following an earthquake. The tremblor halts the plans of a Japanese corporation to develop a trout farm and uncovers an ancient burial ground. When a snomobiler turns up dead, he's carrying a large fossil tooth, perhaps from a T. Rex skeleton. Du Pré knows there are only four known T. Rex skeletons ever located and he expects a fifth would be worth killing for.

Gabriel Du Pré...Metis Indian cattle inspector and sometimes sheriff in Montana
- ❑ ❑ 1 - Coyote Wind (1994)
- ❑ ❑ 2 - Specimen Song (1995)
- ❑ ❑ 3 - Wolf, No Wolf (1996)
- ❑ ❑ 4 - Notches (1997)

■ BOX, Edgar [P]

Edgar Box is the pseudonym used by Gore Vidal for three books written in the early '50s featuring a New York public relations consultant named Peter Cutler Sargeant II, once described as pleasantly pig-faced (*1001 Midnights*). Ghostwriter for a New York drama critic, the 30-something publicist opens his own firm when his previous job is eliminated. Peter's adventures begin with *Death in the Fifth Position* (1952), where he is hired to provide favorable publicity for a visiting Russian ballet company. As Gore Vidal, the author provided his own blurb(s) for a series he is said to have dashed off in three weeks' time. Writing in *1001 Midnights*, Marvin Lachman and Francis M. Nevins found Vidal's self-testimonial "surprisingly accurate." On the paperback editions of all 3 books was printed the following: "The work that Dr. Kinsey began with statistics, Edgar Box has completed with wit in the mystery novel."

Peter Cutler Sargeant, II...public relations consultant in New York, New York
- ❑ ❑ 1 - Death in the Fifth Position (1952)
- ❑ ❑ 2 - Death Before Bedtime (1953)
- ❑ ❑ 3 - Death Likes It Hot (1954)

■ BOYER, Rick

Rick Boyer is the byline used by Richard Lewis Boyer for his mysteries featuring Concord (MA) oral surgeon Charlie "Doc" Adams, first appearing in the Edgar award-winning *Billingsgate Shoal* which took best novel honors in 1983. In book 8, *Pirate Trade* (1995), Doc gets more than he bargained for when he buys an ivory-decorated purse for his wife. Boyer says his first novel, *The Giant Rat of Sumatra* (1976), was a serious attempt (6 years' worth) to continue the Sherlockian saga as Conan Doyle himself might have. Writing with David Savagu for Rand McNally, Boyer produced several books in their 'Places Rated' series, including volumes on the best places to live ('81 and '85) and the best places to retire ('83 and '87). A graduate of Denison University (B.A.) and the University of Iowa (M.F.A.), Boyer is currently associate professor of English at Western Carolina University.

Charlie "Doc" Adams...oral surgeon in Concord, Massachusetts
- ❑ ❑ 1 - **Billingsgate Shoal (1982) Edgar winner ★**
- ❑ ❑ 2 - The Penny Ferry (1984)
- ❑ ❑ 3 - The Daisy Ducks (1986)
- ❑ ❑ 4 - Moscow Metal (1987)
- ❑ ❑ 5 - The Whale's Footprints (1988)
- ❑ ❑ 6 - Gone to Earth (1990)
- ❑ ❑ 7 - Yellow Bird (1991)
- ❑ ❑ 8 - Pirate Trade (1995)

■ BOYLE, Gerry

Done

Gerry Boyle is the creator of Jack McMorrow, ex-New York Times metro reporter turned editor of a small-town weekly in Maine whose 5th appearance is *Borderline* (1998). As noted in the *Washington Post Book World* review, "this is hardworking Maine, poverty Maine, where the local economy is ruled by the paper mill...The rhythms of the weekly newspaper work a wonderful counterpoint to the building tension of McMorrow's investigation." Boyle has been in the news business since his 1978 graduation from Colby College (ME), except for short stints in book publishing and mail delivery. Currently a columnist and formerly a reporter and editor for the *Cental Maine Morning Sentinel* in Waterville, he has received ten awards from the Maine and New England Press Associations, including 3 firsts. Married with 3 children, Boyle lives in a rambling 1827 house in China, Maine.

Jack McMorrow...ex-NY Times reporter turned small-town editor in Androscoggin, Maine
- ☑ ❑ 1 - Deadline (1993)
- ☑ ❑ 2 - Bloodline (1995)
- ☑ ❑ 3 - Lifeline (1996)
- ☑ ❑ 4 - Potshot (1997)

■ BRADBERRY, James

Done

Award-winning architect and academic James Bradberry is a former Fulbright Fellow with master's degrees from Cambridge University and the University of Pennsylvania. He's taught architecture at Penn, Yale, Temple and the Technical University of Nova Scotia. Jamie Ramsgill, fictional Princeton professor and architect, is introduced as the advisor to an architectural competition for a chapel that will serve as the tomb for Italy's richest man. In a starred review *Publishers Weekly* called it "an old-fashioned mystery in a gleaming new dress." Book two takes Jamie to Cambridge for reserarch and a visit with his mentor, who is retiring as the head of the architecture school. In book three Jamie's back in Philadelphia and next time out he'll be renovating his new digs—a 12-story former grain elevator. Bradberry lives in Villanova (PA), but not in a grain elevator.

Jamie Ramsgill, Prof....architect and Princeton professor in Princeton, New Jersey
- ☑ ❑ 1 - The Seventh Sacrament (1994)
- ☒ ❑ 2 - Ruins of Civility (1996)
- ☑ ❑ 3 - Eakins' Mistress (1997)

■ BRADY, John

done

Dublin-born author John Brady emigrated to Canada after graduating from Trinity College with a degree in sociology. His series detective, Inspector Matt Minogue of the Dublin CID, is introduced in *A Stone of the Heart* (1988), winner of the Ellis Award for Best First Novel. When a gunman from the North kills a Garda officer, Minogue finds himself involved in Irish-American gun-running. The *San Francisco Chronicle* called the series opener "a mordant and moving story of Irish terrorism and political cynicism with a Dublin police officer of uncommon wit and sensitivity." Minogue is an "archetypal Irishman," said the *St. Louis Post-Dispatch*, "a wonderful blend of urban cynicism and hopeless optimism." A former elementary school teacher, the author currently lives in Bradford, Ontario.

Matt Minogue, Sgt....Irish police detective in Dublin, Ireland
- ☑ ❑ 1 - **Stone of the Heart (1988) Ellis winner ★**
- ☑ ❑ 2 - Unholy Ground (1989)
- ☒ ❑ 3 - Kaddish in Dublin (1990)
- ☒ ❑ 4 - All Souls (1993)
- ☒ ❑ 5 - **The Good Life (1994) Ellis nominee ☆**

■ BREEN, Jon

Librarian, college professor, reviewer, scholar, mystery writer, parodist—all apply to Jon Breen, winner of 2 Edgars, 2 Anthonys and a Macavity for nonfiction mystery writing. He is also the author of 6 mystery novels, including the Dagger-nominated *Touch of the Past* (1988), more than 80 short stories and over 200 review columns for *Ellery Queen's Mystery Magazine* and *The Armchair Detective*. Breen lists his interests as spectator sports (thoroughbred racing his favorite), reading detective fiction, trials both real and fanciful, and musical comedy. By his own estimate, roughly half his fictional output has had some athletic connection, including his 4-book series featuring track announcer Jerry Brogan. Breen's second series opens with a bookshop mystery (*The Gathering Place*) and the woman (Rachel Hemmings) who inherits it. Professor of English at Rio Hondo College in Whittier (CA), Breen lives in Fountain Valley.

Jerry Brogan...track announcer at Surfside Meadows in California
- ❏ ❏ 1 - Listen for the Click (1983)
         Brit.-Vicar's Roses
- ❏ ❏ 2 - Triple Crown (1985)
- ❏ ❏ 3 - Loose Lips (1990)
- ❏ ❏ 4 - Hot Air (1991)

Rachel Hennings...bookstore owner in Los Angeles, California
- ❏ ❏ 1 - The Gathering Place (1984)
- ❏ ❏ 2 - **Touch of the Past (1988) Dagger nominee** ☆

■ BRETT, John Michael [P]

John Michael Brett is the pseudonym of Miles Tripp for his books featuring British adventurer Hugo Baron, introduced in *Diecast* (1963). The series opener was published under the name Michael Brett, but the byline was changed slightly to John Michael Brett for books 2 and 3. *A Plague of Dragons* (1965) takes the adventuring hero to Africa. This author is past Chairman of the Crime Writers' Association (1968-69) and under his real name has written more than 30 novels, including 12 in the series featuring British private investigator John Samson. His autobiography, *The Eighth Passenger: A Flight of Recollection and Discover*, was published in 1969. A trained solicitor, Tripp spent 30 years as a member of the legal staff of London's Charity Commission.

Hugo Baron...British adventurer in England
- ❏ ❏ 1 - Diecast [as by Michael Brett] (1963)
- ❏ ❏ 2 - A Plague of Dragons (1965)
- ❏ ❏ 3 - A Cargo of Spent Evil (1965)

■ BRETT, Michael

Michael Brett is the creator of a 60's New York private eye named Pete McGrath, who was featured in 10 books starting with *Kill Him Quickly, It's Raining* (1966). According to Art Scott (writing in *1001 Midnights*), these paperback originals were intended as Pocket Books' answer to better-known and better-selling P.I. characters Shell Scott and Mike Shayne among others. But McGrath never quite came into his own in Scott's estimation, and was most identifiable by his penchant for talking to himself. One of the McGrath installments (*Live a Little, Die a Little*) was filmed (with liberal changes) as a mildly pornographic detective spoof titled *Cry Uncle*, which Scott says attained modest cult status.

Pete McGrath...wise-cracking private eye in New York, New York
- ❏ ❏ 1 - Kill Him Quickly, It's Raining (1966)
- ❏ ❏ 2 - Another Day, Another Stiff (1967)
- ❏ ❏ 3 - Dead, Upstairs in a Tub (1967)
- ❏ ❏ 4 - An Ear for Murder (1967)
- ❏ ❏ 5 - The Flight of the Stiff (1967)
- ❏ ❏ 6 - Turn Blue, You Murderers (1967)
- ❏ ❏ 7 - We the Killers (1967)
- ❏ ❏ 8 - Death of a Hippie (1968)
- ❏ ❏ 9 - Lie a Little, Die a Little (1968) APA-Cry Uncle!
- ❏ ❏ 10 - Slit My Throat, Gently (1968)

■ **BRETT, Simon**

Simon Brett is the author of more than 50 books, including the Charles Paris series starring a middle-aged alcoholic actor who stumbles across mysteries while going about his work in show business. Brett's own career as a radio, television and stage producer, writer and occasional actor provides authentic background to the Paris novels, which are wry and humorous looks at the world of British entertainment. Vaudeville buffs will especially enjoy *A Comedian Dies* (1979) where funny radio gags are provided as chapter headings. Brett's Mrs. Pargeter series features the widow of a thief who uses her dead husband's connections to her considerable advantage. Much darker in tone than any of his series novels is Brett's psychological thriller, *A Shock to the System* (1984), which was filmed starring Michael Caine as a businessman turned murderous when his career is threatened.

Charles Paris...charming alcoholic actor in England
- ❏ ❏ 1 - Cast, In Order of Disappearance (1975)
- ❏ ❏ 2 - So Much Blood (1976)
- ❏ ❏ 3 - Star Trap (1977)
- ❏ ❏ 4 - An Amateur Corpse (1978)
- ❏ ❏ 5 - A Comedian Dies (1979)
- ❏ ❏ 6 - The Dead Side of the Mike (1980)
- ❏ ❏ 7 - Situation Tragedy (1981)
- ❏ ❏ 8 - Murder Unprompted (1982)
- ❏ ❏ 9 - Murder in the Title (1983)
- ❏ ❏ 10 - Not Dead, Only Resting (1984)
- ❏ ❏ 11 - **A Shock to the System (1984) Edgar nominee** ☆
- ❏ ❏ 12 - Dead Giveaway (1985)
- ❏ ❏ 13 - What Bloody Man Is That? (1987)
- ❏ ❏ 14 - A Series of Murders (1989)
- ❏ ❏ 15 - Corporate Bodies (1991)
- ❏ ❏ 16 - A Reconstructed Corpse (1993)
- ❏ ❏ 17 - Sicken and So Die (1995)

Melita Pargeter...widow of a thief in England
- ❏ ❏ 1 - A Nice Class of Corpse (1986)
- ❏ ❏ 2 - Mrs., Presumed Dead (1988)
- ❏ ❏ 3 - Mrs. Pargeter's Package (1990)
- ❏ ❏ 4 - Mrs. Pargeter's Pound of Flesh (1992)
- ❏ ❏ 5 - Mrs. Pargeter's Plot (1996)

■ BREWER, James D.

Civil War expert and retired Army officer James D. Brewer is the creator of a Mississippi River series set during the days of Reconstruction. Hard-drinking, crippled Southern veteran Masey Baldridge saves the livelihood of Yankee riverboat captain Luke Williamson and by book 3, they've formed the Big River Detective Agency with Salina Tyner who once worked the river as a lady of the evening. The action continues in *No Escape* (1998) which takes place during the Memphis yellow fever epidemic of 1873. Brewer once taught English at West Point and served as editor-in-chief of *Armor* magazine. Currently working on a new series featuring retired military intelligence officer Vance Rider, Brewer has also written *The Raiders of 1862* (1997)—an in-depth study of the pivotal campaigns of three Southern cavalry commanders, including diary accounts and other never-before-published information.

Luke Williamson & Masey Baldridge...Yankee riverboat captain & Confederate veteran
- ❏ ❏   1 - No Bottom (1994)
- ❏ ❏   2 - No Virtue (1995)
- ❏ ❏   3 - No Justice (1996)
- ❏ ❏   4 - No Remorse (1997)

■ BREWER, Steve

Veteran journalist Steve Brewer is the creator of comedic Albuquerque investigator Bubba Mabry, a fumbling good ol' boy with a social conscience. When Bubba's hired by the living Elvis in *Lonely Street*, he meets a tough little newspaper gal named Felicia who returns with him in *Baby Face*. In *Witchy Woman*, Felicia infiltrates a female pagan cult outside Taos and by the time they're chasing mobster developers in *Shaky Ground*, Bubba's facing matrimony. Next he'll be up against a group of racist skinheads in *Dirty Pool* (1998). Like his fictional private eye, Brewer is a Southerner transplanted to the Southwest. Raised in his parents' home state of Arkansas, he worked for the *Arkansas Gazette* in Little Rock starting in high school. After an 8-year AP tour of four states and 10 years at the *Albuquerque Journal*, he's currently on sabbatical writing fiction full time from a backyard studio.

Bubba Mabry...low-rent P.I. in Albuquerque, New Mexico
- ❏ ❏   1 - Lonely Street (1994)
- ❏ ❏   2 - Baby Face (1995)
- ❏ ❏   3 - Witchy Woman (1996)
- ❏ ❏   4 - Shaky Ground (1997)

■ BRIODY, Thomas Gately

Award-winning television journalist, Thomas Gately Briody, is the creator of rogue reporter Michael Carolina, whose beat is Rhode Island, the tiniest, crookedest state in the nation. The reporter says he relies on only one bedrock truth—everybody in Rhode Island is covering up for someone else. In Carolina's third investigation, *Rogue's Wager* (1997), a clamdigger with dynamite sets off a crazy chain of events and it's Carolina's job to figure out what's really going on. The author is a criminal defense lawyer who lives in Providence where he once worked as a television reporter. He says he started writing a novel while waiting for the phone to ring after first opening his law practice. Briody's 10 years in TV journalism included assignments in Boston and several towns in the Midwest. A graduate of Pomona College and the University of Iowa, he is working on a legal mystery and several other writing projects.

Michael Carolina...former TV investigative reporter in Providence, Rhode Island
- ❏ ❏   1 - Rogue's Isles (1995)
- ❏ ❏   2 - Rogue's Justice (1996)

■ **BRUNO, Anthony**

Done

Avowed "mob watcher" Anthony Bruno has written 6 books showcasing the exploits of FBI agents Gibbons and Tozzi, tagged by *People* magazine as "the best fictional cop duo around." More recently he introduced an overweight parole officer who goes undercover at a weight-loss spa in *Devil's Food* (1997). As reserach for his nonfiction book *The Iceman* (1994), he once spent several hours locked in an interview room with the 6'4", 260-lb. mass murderer who claimed to have killed over 100 people, dubbed the Iceman when police discovered he'd kept one of his victims frozen in an ice-cream truck for over 2 years. A second-degree black belt student and instructor of aikido, Bruno holds an M.A. degree in medieval studies and has worked as a New York book editor and an archivist of rare books in Boston. Married to author Judith Sachs, he lives in New Jersey.

Bert Gibbons & Mike Tozzi...FBI agents undercover with the Mob in New York, New York
- ☐ ☐ 1 - Bad Guys (1988)
- ☐ ☐ 2 - Bad Blood (1989)
- ☐ ☐ 3 - Bad Luck (1990)
- ☐ ☐ 4 - Bad Business (1991)
- ☐ ☐ 5 - Bad Moon (1992)
- ☐ ☐ 6 - Bad Apple (1994)

Loretta Kovacs & Frank Marvelli...parole officer and partner in New Jersey
- ☐ ☐ 1 - Devil's Food (1997)

■ **BUCKLEY, William F.**

Done

American conservative William F. Buckley is well-known for his television program *Firing Line* and *National Review*, the magazine he founded. It is less well-known that he is the author of a series of best-selling espionage novels based on his personal experience working for the CIA during the 1950s. Blackford Oakes shares Buckley's experience in English public schools, his years at Yale University and his CIA training which Buckley says is exact in every detail. Each novel takes readers behind the scenes of the political crises of the '50s and '60s, with the actual historical figures who become his characters. An avid yachtsman, Buckley is also the author of several sailing books chronicling his sailing expeditions, including *Airborne* (1976), *Atlantic High* (1982) and *Racing Through Paradise* (1987).

Blackford "Blacky" Oakes...CIA agent recruited from Yale in Washington, D.C.
- ☐ ☐ 1 - Saving the Queen (1976)
- ☐ ☐ 2 - Stained Glass (1978)
- ☐ ☐ 3 - Who's on First (1980)
- ☐ ☐ 4 - Marco Polo, If You Can (1982)
- ☐ ☐ 5 - The Story of Henri Tod (1984)
- ☐ ☐ 6 - See You Later, Alligator (1986)
- ☐ ☐ 7 - High Jinx (1986)
- ☐ ☐ 8 - Mongoose, R.I.P. (1988)
- ☐ ☐ 9 - Tucker's Last Stand (1990)
- ☐ ☐ 10 - A Very Private Plot (1994)
- ☐ ☐ 11 - Brothers No More (1995)

■ BURKE, James Lee

Dave

Edgar award winner James Lee Burke is the creator of Dave Robicheaux (pronounced ro-bo-show), ex-New Orleans cop, Vietnam vet and recovering alcoholic. Book 2 in this series (*Heaven's Prisoners*) made its movie debut in 1997 starring Alec Baldwin, who holds film rights to at least 3 Robicheaux books. Also new this year is Burke's 15th novel, introducing Texas attorney and former Texas Ranger Billy Bob Holland, in his series debut (*Cimarron Rose*). In a 1997 *CBS Sunday Morning* interview, Burke read from the actual Civil War journals of his great-grandfather Sam, material which Burke used in developing the story. He also talked about the record he holds for the most thoroughly rejected manuscript in American publishing history (*The Lost Get Back Boogie*). Turned down by 111 editors, this book went on to earn a Pulitzer Prize nomination after publication by Louisiana State University Press, the year before *The Neon Rain* (1987) and the start of Dave Robicheaux.

Dave Robicheaux...deputy sheriff in Louisiana
- ☑ ❑ 1 - The Neon Rain (1987)
- ☑ ❑ 2 - Heaven's Prisoners (1988)
- ☑ ❑ 3 - **Black Cherry Blues (1989) Edgar winner ★**
- ☑ ❑ 4 - A Morning for Flamingoes (1990)
- ☑ ❑ 5 - A Stained White Radiance (1992)
- ☑ ❑ 6 - In the Electric Mist with Confederate Dead (1993)
- ☑ ❑ 7 - **Dixie City Jam (1994) Hammett nominee ☆**
- ☑ ❑ 8 - Burning Angel (1995)
- ☑ ❑ 9 - **Cadillac Jukebox (1996) Dagger nominee ☆**

■ BURLEY, W. J.

Dave

W. J. Burley is William James Burley, creator of Chief Superintendent Wycliffe who has appeared in more than 20 cozy procedurals as a good copper in a quiet Cornish village. The Wycliffe books and stories based on the characters have been serialized on British network television. Although Burley's first novel was not published until he was 52, his Wycliffe series is one of the longer-running crime series still in publication, with book 21 (*Wycliffe and the Redhead*) published in Britain in September 1997, one month after the author's 83rd birthday. A graduate of Oxford University with a degree in zoology, he began his professional career as a gas engineer and later spent 20 years as head of the biology department and sixth form tutor at a school in Cornwall.

Charles Wycliffe, Supt.....area CID superintendent in West Country, England
- ✗ ❑ ❑ 1 - Three-Toed Pussy (1968)
- ✗ ❑ ❑ 2 - To Kill a Cat (1970)
- ☑ ❑ 3 - Guilt Edged (1971)
- ☑ ❑ 4 - Death in a Salubrious Place (1973)
- ✗ ❑ ❑ 5 - Death in Stanley Street (1974)
- ✗ ❑ ❑ 6 - Wycliffe and the Pea-Green Boat (1975)
- ✗ ❑ ❑ 7 - Wycliffe and the Schoolgirls (1976)
- ☑ ❑ 8 - Wycliffe and the Scapegoat (1978)
- ☑ ❑ 9 - Wycliffe in Paul's Court (1980)
- ☑ ❑ 10 - Wycliffe's Wild Goose Chase (1982)
- ☑ ❑ 11 - Wycliffe and the Beales (1983)
- ☑ ❑ 12 - Wycliffe and the Four Jacks (1985)
- ☑ ❑ 13 - Wycliffe and the Quiet Virgin (1986)
- ☑ ❑ 14 - Wycliffe and the Windsor Blue (1987)
- ☑ ❑ 15 - Wycliffe and the Tangled Web (1988)

☑ ☐ 16 - Wycliffe and the Cycle of Death (1990)
☑ ☐ 17 - Wycliffe and the Dead Flautist (1991)
☑ ☐ 18 - Wycliffe and the Last Rites (1992)
☑ ☐ 19 - Wycliffe and the Dunes Mystery (1993)
☑ ☐ 20 - Wycliffe and the House of Fear (1995)

■ BURNS, Rex [P]

Rex Burns is the pseudonym of mystery writer Raoul Stephen Sehler, winner of the 1976 best first novel Edgar award for *The Alvarez Journal*, which introduced Denver cop Gabe Wager. The Chicano cop calls himself Hispano—part Hispanic, part police. Burns has also written at least 3 books about ex-Secret Service agent and Stanford law school dropout, Devlin Kirk, owner of a Denver surveillance company specializing in high tech security. The suicide which starts the *Suicide Season* (1987) is that of Kirk's father, a successful Denver businessman. Professor of American literature at the University of Colorado at Denver, Burns is a regular newspaper reviewer and serves as advisor to the forthcoming Oxford Companion to Mystery. Born in San Diego, he earned his undergraduate degree in English and creative writing from Stanford University and his M.A. and Ph.D. from the University of Minnesota.

Devlin Kirk...owner of industrial surveillance company in Denver, Colorado
☑ ☐ 1 - Suicide Season (1987)
☑ ☐ 2 - Parts Unknown (1990)
☑ ☐ 3 - Body Guard (1991)
☑ ☐ 4 - Body Slam (1997)

Gabe Wagner...homicide detective in Denver, Colorado
☑ ☐ 1 - **The Alvarez Journal (1975) Edgar winner ★**
☑ ☐ 2 - The Farnsworth Score (1977)
☑ ☐ 3 - Speak for the Dead (1978)
☑ ☐ 4 - Angle of Attack (1979)
☑ ☐ 5 - The Avenging Angel (1983)
☑ ☐ 6 - Strip Search (1984)
☑ ☐ 7 - Ground Money (1986)
☑ ☐ 8 - The Killing Zone (1988)
☑ ☐ 9 - Endangered Species (1993)
☑ ☐ 10 - Bloodline (1995)
☑ ☐ 11 - The Leaning Land (1997)

■ BURNS, Ron

Historical novelist Ron Burns has written 2 books in a new mystery series with frontier Army captain Harrison Hull who first appears in *The Mysterious Death of Meriwether Lewis* (1993). Historians are still puzzled by the circumstances surrounding the famous explorer's death. On his way to meet President Madison, Lewis died violently outside Nashville. In book 2, Hull is asked by Thomas Jefferson to locate slaves who've disappeared from his nephew's KY plantation. Both books are based on fact and rich with historical detail. Burns has also written 2 mysteries set in 180 A.D. with a well-connected Roman lawyer who debuts in *Roman Nights* (1991) and returns in *Roman Shadows* (1992). Gaius Livinius Severus marries into one of Rome's wealthiest families, becomes a senator and goes spying for Cicero. Born in Detroit (MI), Burns lives in Santa Monica (CA).

Harrison Hull, Capt.....18th century frontier Army captain in Virginia
☑ ☐ 1 - The Mysterious Death of Meriwether Lewis (1993)
☑ ☐ 2 - Enslaved (1994)

■ BUSBY, Roger

British journalist and police information officer Roger Busby has written 8 books in 2 series featuring Scotland Yard detective inspectors. Introduced in *Robbery Blue* (1969), DI Leric appeared in a total of 5 titles until 1973 when Busby left the Birmingham newspaper where he'd been working and joined the Devon and Cornwall Constabulary as police information and public relations officer. In 1985 he launched a new series with DI Tony Rowley whose second appearance in *Snow Man* (1987) earned Busby a Police Review Award from Crime Writers' Assocation (sponsored by *The Police Review* 1985-87) for the crime novel that best portrayed police work and procedure. Busby says writing helps him relax after a hard day at work. Among his nonseries novels are *Garvey's Code* (1978) and *New Face in Hell* (1976).

Leric, Det. Insp.....Scotland Yard inspector in London, England
- ❑ ❑ 1 - Robbery Blue (1969)
- ❑ ❑ 2 - The Frighteners (1970)
- ❑ ❑ 3 - Deadlock (1971)
- ❑ ❑ 4 - A Reasonable Man (1972)
- ❑ ❑ 5 - Pattern of Violence (1973)

Tony Rowley, Det. Insp.....Scotland Yard inspector in London, England
- ❑ ❑ 1 - The Hunter (1985)
- ❑ ❑ 2 - **Snow Man (1987) Police Review Winner ★**
- ❑ ❑ 3 - Crackshot (1990)

■ BUTLER, Richard [P]

Richard Butler is the pseudonym used by Ted Allbeury for his pair of espionage novels featuring Max Farne, a luxury boat salesman and spy in Santa Margherita, Italy. A former British Intelligence officer himself, Allbeury has said he tries to show that people employed in espionage or intelligence work have private lives and their work affects their lives. Paraphrasing H.R.F. Keating (in *20th Century Crime & Mystery Writers, 2nd ed.*)...Allbeury's people are real...so that by the time you finish one of his books, you've not only lived excitingly and even wept inward tears for the sadness of things, you've learned about individuals and even about national consciousness. Former creative director of a London advertising agency, Theodore Edward le Bouthillier Allbeury has written as Ted Allbeury as well as Richard Butler and Patrick Kelly.

Max Farne...luxury boat salesman and spy in Santa Margherita, Italy
- ❑ ❑ 1 - Where All the Girls are Sweeter (1975)
- ❑ ❑ 2 - Italian Assets (1976)

■ BYRD, Max

Shamus award winner Max Byrd wrote 3 books in the early '80s featuring transplanted Boston P.I. Mike Haller, specializing in missing persons in San Francisco. Introduced in the Shamus-award winning first novel, *California Thriller* (1981), Mike hunts for a missing journalist who was on the trail of private bacteriological-warfare tests. This author is a scholarly investigator of 18th century language, and has published critical essays on Defoe and two book-length studies of images of the city of London. His nonseries fiction includes *Target of Opportunity* (1988), *Fuse Time* (1991) and *Jefferson* (1993). A native of Atlanta (GA), Byrd is presently a professor of English at the University of California, Davis. He taught previously at Yale University.

Mike Haller...P.I. specializing in missing persons in San Francisco, California
- ❑ ❑ 1 - **California Thriller (1981) Shamus winner ★**
- ❑ ❑ 2 - Fly Away, Jill (1981)
- ❑ ❑ 3 - **Finders Weepers (1983) Shamus nominee ☆**

■ CAINE, Hamilton [P]

Hamilton Caine is the pseudonym used by Stephen (Lee) Smoke for his series featuring Los Angeles private eye Ace Carpenter, introduced in *Carpenter, Detective* (1981), nominated for a Shamus award for best paperback original the first year these awards were given by Private Eye Writers of America (PWA). The sequel, *Hollywood Heroes* (1986) appeared five years later. Smoke also wrote several novels in the Ninja Master series featuring series character Brett Wallace published during the 1980s under the Warner house name Wade Barker.

Ace Carpenter...private eye in Los Angeles, California
- ❑ ❑ 1 - **Carpenter, Detective (1981)**
- ❑ ❑ 2 - Hollywood Heroes (1986)

■ CAMPBELL, Harlen

Harlen Campbell is the creator of Rainbow Porter, a Vietnam veteran turned detective, introduced in *Monkey on a Chain* (1993), when Porter comes down from his isolated mountain home above Albuquerque to investigate the suspicious death of one of his wartime buddies. The sequel, *Coin Trick*, has been written but not sold. Campbell attended New Mexico State University where he earned B.A. degrees in both English and journalism and an M.A. in English literature. Along with a brief stint as a journalist in the Army and an even briefer one teaching college English, he has worked in computer programming, satellite tracking, property management and bar tending. He lives in the foothills of the Sandia Mountains of New Mexico where he is a self-employed web site developer and internet content writer.

Rainbow Porter...Vietnam veteran turned detective in New Mexico
- ❑ ❑ 1 - Monkey on a Chain (1993)

■ CAMPBELL, Robert

Robert Campbell's first novel, *The Spy Who Sat and Waited*, was nominated for an American Book Award in 1976 and 10 years later his first Jimmy Flannery title won both the Edgar and Anthony for best paperback original. Book 11 in this animal-titled series is *Pigeon Pie*, coming in 1998. His Hollywood P.I. series debuted with a Shamus best-novel nomination in 1987 and in 1988 the first of his 2 Jake Hatch novels introduced the railroad detective from Omaha (NE) who later appeared in *Red Cent* (1989). Campbell, who lives in northern California, also wrote a number of nonseries novels as R. Wright Campbell and F.G. Clinton. Born and raised in Newark (NJ), he attended Pratt Institute where he earned a certificate in illustration. During his days as a Hollywood screenwriter he was nominated for an Academy Award for *Man of a Thousand Faces*.

Jake Hatch...railroad detective in the United States
- ❑ ❑ 1 - Plugged Nickel (1988)
- ❑ ❑ 2 - Red Cent (1989)

Jimmy Flannery...sewer inspector & Democratic precinct captain in Chicago, Illinois
- ❑ ❑ 1 - **The Junkyard Dog (1986) Anthony & Edgar winner ★★**
- ❑ ❑ 2 - The 600-Pound Gorilla (1987)
- ❑ ❑ 3 - Hip-Deep in Alligators (1987)
- ❑ ❑ 4 - Thinning the Turkey Herd (1988)
- ❑ ❑ 5 - The Cat's Meow (1988)
- ❑ ❑ 6 - Nibbled to Death by Ducks (1989)
- ❑ ❑ 7 - The Gift Horse's Mouth (1990)
- ❑ ❑ 8 - In a Pig's Eye (1991)
- ❑ ❑ 9 - Sauce for the Goose (1995)
- ❑ ❑ 10 - The Lion's Share (1996)

Whistler...sentimental private eye in Hollywood, California
- ☑ ❑ 1 - **In La-La Land We Trust (1986) Shamus nominee** ☆
- ☑ ❑ 2 - Alice in La-La Land (1987)
- ☑ ❑ 3 - Sweet La-La Land (1990)
- ☑ ❑ 4 - The Wizard of La-La Land (1995)

■ CASLEY, Dennis

Dennis Casley is a native of Cornwall, England who has travelled extensively on assignment for the World Bank. His mystery series featuring Kenyan Chief Inspector James Odhiambo blends Casley's considerable knowledge of Africa with his personal experience in international banking and civil service bureaucracies. In the series opener, the charismatic black detective is faced with the murder of a well-to-do expatriate woman at a chic game resort. The Chief Inspector travels to Cornwall in book 2 for a Commonwealth conference marred by two deaths at a haunted Cornish lake. When the local police refuse his help Odhiambo teams up with a clever female administrative officer to investigate. Casley, who has lived all over the world, including Washington DC and Nairobi, currently makes his home in Cornwall.

James Odhiambo...chief inspector in Kenya
- ☑ ❑ 1 - Death Underfoot (1994)
- ☑ ❑ 2 - Death Undertow (1995)
- ☑ ❑ 3 - Death Understates (1995)

■ CHAMBERS, Peter

Peter Chambers has written more than 50 novels under his own name and as Peter Chester and Philip Daniels. This former Chairman of the Crime Writers' Association (1984-85) is best known for his 36-book series featuring a hard-nosed California P.I. who first appeared in *Murder Is for Keeps* (1961). According to June Thomson in *St. James Guide* (4th edition), this P.I. is "as American as bourbon on the rocks," and although he's armed with "wise-cracking assurance" and a specialist knowledge of guns, Preston is "not foul-mouthed." In contrast, writing as Philip Daniels, the author is "as English as tea in the vicarage," says Thomson. According to the *St. James Guide*, the Black Dagger series of reprinted crime classics was his brain child. A former professional jazz musician, Chambers lives in Berkshire, England.

Mark Preston...hard-nosed private eye in Monkton City, California
- ☑ ❑ 1 - Murder is for Keeps (1961)
- ☑ ❑ 2 - Wreath for a Redhead (1962)
- ☑ ❑ 3 - The Big Goodbye (1962)
- ☑ ❑ 4 - Dames Can Be Deadly (1963)
- ☑ ❑ 5 - Down-Beat Kill (1963)
- ☑ ❑ 6 - Lady, This is Murder (1963)
- ☑ ❑ 7 - This'll Kill You (1964)
- ☑ ❑ 8 - Nobody Lives Forever (1964)
- ☑ ❑ 9 - You're Better Off Dead (1965)
- ☑ ❑ 10 - Always Take the Big Ones (1965)
- ☑ ❑ 11 - No Gold When You Go (1966)
- ☑ ❑ 12 - Don't Bother to Knock (1966)
- ☑ ❑ 13 - The Bad Die Young (1967)
- ☑ ❑ 14 - The Blonde Wore Black (1968)
- ☑ ❑ 15 - No Peace for the Wicked (1968)
- ☑ ❑ 16 - Speak Ill of the Dead (1968)
- ☑ ❑ 17 - They Call It Murder (1973)
- ☑ ❑ 18 - Somebody Has to Lose (1975)
- ☑ ❑ 19 - The Deadlier They Fall (1979)
- ☑ ❑ 20 - Lady, You're Killing Me (1979)

❑ ❑ 21 - The Day of the Big Dollar (1979)
❑ ❑ 22 - The Beautiful Golden Frame (1980)
❑ ❑ 23 - Nothing Personal (1980)
❑ ❑ 24 - The Deep Blue Cradle (1980)
❑ ❑ 25 - A Long Time Dead (1981)
❑ ❑ 26 - The Lady Who Never Was (1981)
❑ ❑ 27 - Female—Handle With Care (1981)
❑ ❑ 28 - Murder Is Its Own Reward (1982)
❑ ❑ 29 - The Highly Explosive Case (1982)
❑ ❑ 30 - A Miniature Murder Mystery (1982)
❑ ❑ 31 - Jail Bait (1983)
❑ ❑ 32 - Dragons Can Be Dangerous (1983)
❑ ❑ 33 - Bomb-Scare Flight 147 (1984)
❑ ❑ 34 - The Moving Picture Writes (1984)
❑ ❑ 35 - The Vanishing Holes Murders (1985)
❑ ❑ 36 - The Hot Money Caper (1992)

■ CHAMPION, David

David Champion is the creator of ace trial lawyer Bomber Hanson and his amiable son and investigator Tod, who make their first appearance in *The Mountain Massacres* (1995). The Hansons live in Angleton, a resort town of 50,000 on the central coast of California. *Kirkus* said their opening had an "agreeably goofy charm" with "a grudge, a murder, an investigation, a trial, and a surprise ending all in 161 pages." In book 2 Bomber takes on big tobacco with a blind Pennsylvania Dutch father of 12 daughters for a client. The ace trial lawyer will be back in court in 1998 with *Celebrity Trouble*. Champion's first novel was *The Snatch* (1994), a kidnapping-revenge story featuring an off-the-wall Los Angeles cop named Harry Schlacter, his cop's-daughter girlfriend, and a memorable cast of South Central gang characters.

Bomber Hanson...ace trial lawyer in California
❑ ❑ 1 - The Mountain Massacres (1995)
❑ ❑ 2 - Nobody Roots for Goliath (1996)

■ CHARYN, Jerome

Jerome Charyn is the creator of a New York series featuring deputy police commissioner Isaac Sidel, whose first 4 cases are collected as *The Isaac Quartet*, published in 1984. Twelve years after book 4, Charyn returned to the commissioner in 1990 with *The Good Policeman* which became a French TV pilot in 1996. The story features an exclusive Manhattan brotherhood (the Christy Mathewson Club) of pre-World War II baseball memorabilia collectors. Phi Beta Kappa from Columbia University, Charyn has taught at New York's School of the Performing Arts, Stanford, Rice and Princeton Universities, City College of New York, and since 1995 has been adjunct professor of film studies at The American University of Paris. Founding editor of *Dutton Review*, he is a former executive editor of *Fiction* and has written at least a dozen nonseries novels in addition to the Sidel books.

Isaac Sidel...former police commissioner in New York, New York
❑ ❑ 1 - Blue Eyes (1975)
❑ ❑ 2 - Marilyn the Wild (1976)
❑ ❑ 3 - The Education of Patrick Silver (1976)
❑ ❑ 4 - Secret Isaac (1978)
❑ ❑ 5 - The Good Policeman (1990)
❑ ❑ 6 - Maria's Girls (1992)
❑ ❑ 7 - Montezuma's Man (1993)
❑ ❑ 8 - Little Angel Street (1994)
❑ ❑ 9 - El Bronx (1997)

■ CHESBRO, George

George C. Chesbro was a special education teacher for 15 years before introducing Dr. Robert Frederickson, Ph.D. criminologist, black belt karate expert, former circus headliner and private investigator who just happens to be a dwarf, nicknamed Mongo from his circus days. By book 7, Mongo has left academia and formed Frederickson and Frederickson with his normal-sized brother Garth, ex-NYPD detective. *Playboy* described their adventures as "Raymond Chandler meets Stephen King by way of Alice's looking glass," as the brothers deal with sorcerers, shapeshifting, psychic phenomena and other fantasy and science fiction elements. As David Cross, Chesbro has written 3 books featuring renegade super ninja, John "Chant" Sinclair. Thanks to crossover action, book 10 in the Mongo series wraps up the 3 Chant books and Veil Kendry appears in several of the Mongo books.

Robert "Mongo" Frederickson, Dr.....dwarf criminology prof and former circus gymnast in New York
- ❏ ❏   1 - Shadow of a Broken Man (1977)
- ❏ ❏   2 - City of Whispering Stone (1978)
- ❏ ❏   3 - An Affair of Sorcerors (1979)
- ❏ ❏   4 - The Beasts of Valhalla (1985)
- ❏ ❏   5 - Two Songs This Archangel Sings
       [incl Veil Kendry] (1986)
- ❏ ❏   6 - The Cold Smell of Sacred Stone (1988)
- ❏ ❏   7 - Second Horseman Out of Eden (1989)
- ❏ ❏   8 - The Language of Cannibals (1990)
- ❏ ❏   ss - In the House of Secret Enemies [short stories] (1990)
- ❏ ❏   9 - The Fear in Yesterday's Rings (1991)
- ❏ ❏ 10 - Dark Chant in a Crimson Key [incl John "Chant" Sinclair as by David Cross] (1992)
- ❏ ❏ 11 - An Incident at Blood Tide (1993)
- ❏ ❏ 12 - Bleeding in the Eye of a Brainstorm (1995)
- ❏ ❏ 13 - Dream of a Falling Eagle (1996)

Veil Kendry...painter and adventurer in New York, New York
- ❏ ❏   1 - Veil (1986)
- ❏ ❏   2 - Jungle of Steel and Stone (1988)

■ CLANCY, Tom

Best-selling thriller writer Tom Clancy made headlines in 1997 when he signed the first nine-figure deal in publishing history for a 5-year multi-media deal. New in December 1997 is the nonseries novel *Politika* accompanied by PC games (in multi-player and single player format) from Red Storm Entertainment plus a Politika website. The first printing of book 8 in his Jack Ryan series was 2 million copies of the 847-page *Executive Orders* (1996). A former insurance agent, Clancy has been called "king of the techno-thriller" (*New York Times Magazine*) and "poet laureate of the military-industrial complex" (Ross Thomas in *Washington Post Book World*). In a 1988 interview with *Contemporary Authors*, Clancy said he does not play war games, has never had access to classified material of any kind and never spent more than three weeks researching any of his books.

Jack Ryan...CIA analyst in Washington, D.C.
- ❏ ❏   1 - The Hunt for Red October (1984)
- ❏ ❏   2 - Patriot Games (1987)
- ❏ ❏   3 - The Cardinal of the Kremlin (1988)
- ❏ ❏   4 - Clear and Present Danger (1989)
- ❏ ❏   5 - The Sum of All Fears (1991)
- ❏ ❏   6 - Without Remorse (1993)
- ❏ ❏   7 - Debt of Honor (1994)
- ❏ ❏   8 - Executive Orders (1996)

■ **CLARK, Douglas**

During his long career as a pharmaceutical executive, Douglas Clark gathered enough toxicological fact to produce more than two dozen ingenious murders to test his Scotland Yard team of Masters and Green. In a St. James Press interview, Clark noted that his books are intended for readers who prefer stories with little or no bad language, violence or torrid sex. What readers will find is strict reliance on medical and scientific fact. Masters carries a virtual library of toxicology books which are put to good use for uncovering plots involving everything from arsine in *The Monday Theory* (1983) to zinc sulphate in *Sick to Death* (1971). According to *Detectionary*, Masters is tall, athletic, handsome, well-dressed and wealthy; he is fond of beautiful women and they in turn are attracted to the distinguished, pipe-smoking chief inspector. His subordinate, Inspector Green, dislikes him intensely.

George Masters, C.S. & Bill Green, C.I.....Scotland Yard detective team in London, England
- ❏ ❏ 1 - Nobody's Perfect (1969)
- ❏ ❏ 2 - Death After Evensong (1969)
- ❏ ❏ 3 - Deadly Pattern (1970)
- ❏ ❏ 4 - Sweet Poison (1970)
- ❏ ❏ 5 - Sick to Death (1971)
- ❏ ❏ 6 - Premedicated Murder (1975)
- ❏ ❏ 7 - Dread and Water (1976)
- ❏ ❏ 8 - Table d'Hote (1977)
- ❏ ❏ 9 - The Gimmel Flask (1977)
- ❏ ❏ 10 - The Libertines (1978)
- ❏ ❏ 11 - Heberden's Seat (1979)
- ❏ ❏ 12 - Poacher's Bag (1980)
- ❏ ❏ 13 - Golden Rain (1980)
- ❏ ❏ 14 - Roast Eggs (1981)
- ❏ ❏ 15 - The Longest Pleasure (1981)
- ❏ ❏ 16 - Shelf Life (1982)
- ❏ ❏ 17 - Doone Walk (1982)
- ❏ ❏ 18 - Vicious Circle (1983)
- ❏ ❏ 19 - The Monday Theory (1983)
- ❏ ❏ 20 - Bouquet Garni (1984)
- ❏ ❏ 21 - Dead Letter (1984)
- ❏ ❏ 22 - Jewelled Eye (1985)
- ❏ ❏ 23 - Performance (1985)
- ❏ ❏ 24 - Storm Center (1986)
- ❏ ❏ 25 - The Big Grouse (1986)
- ❏ ❏ 26 - Plain Sailing (1987)
- ❏ ❏ 27 - Bitter Water (1990)

■ **CLARKSON, John**

John Clarkson has written 3 books featuring a security firm operative named Devlin, once an NYPD cop for all of 6 months. Former Secret Service and Vietnam veteran, Devlin was first in his class at the police academy. Set amidst New York's after-hours club scene, Devlin's brother George is savagely beaten in book 1, on a boozy night of bar-hopping after their father's funeral. In avenging his brother's brutal attack, Devlin calls up the considerable resources of his employer, William Chow of Pacific Rim Security Company. A citizen of the East, but comfortable in the West, Chow and Pacific Rim go anywhere in the world for multi-billion dollar conglomerates and a small roster of wealthy individuals. Book 2 takes Devlin to Hawaii while book 3 sends him to London. These books are "dark, sexy, tough and fast," according to *Kirkus Reviews*. Clarkson lives in New York City.

Jack Devlin...ex-Secret Service turned security firm investigator in the United States
- ❑ ❑ 1 - And Justice for One (1992)
- ❑ ❑ 2 - One Man's Law (1994)
- ❑ ❑ 3 - One Way Out (1996)

■ CLEARY, Jon

Edgar award winning author Jon Cleary became the first recipient of the Australian Crime Writers Association Lifetime Achievement Award (Ned Kelly Award) in 1996. Creator of Inspector Scobie Malone of Sydney, Australia, Cleary has written more than 40 books, including 13 in the Malone series. A family man with a sense of drama, Malone thinks police interrogations should be like night club acts. "Always leave them wanting more," he says. Perhaps best known for his nonmystery novel *The Sundowners* (1952), Cleary has seen at least 7 of his books made into movies and he has written the scripts for several. His Edgar award was for *Peter's Pence* (1974), a non-Malone mystery novel. After leaving school at 15 to become a commercial artist, he won second prize in an Australian literary contest and launched his writing career at the age of 28.

Scobie Malone...family-man police inspector in Sydney, Australia
- ❑ ❑ 1 - The High Commissioner (1966)
- ❑ ❑ 2 - Helga's Web (1970)
- ❑ ❑ 3 - Ransom (1973)
- ❑ ❑ 4 - Dragons at the Party (1987)
- ❑ ❑ 5 - Now and Then, Amen (1988)
- ❑ ❑ 6 - Babylon South (1989)
- ❑ ❑ 7 - Murder Song (1990)
- ❑ ❑ 8 - Pride's Harvest (1991)
- ❑ ❑ 9 - Dark Summer (1991)
- ❑ ❑ 10 - Bleak Spring (1993)
- ❑ ❑ 11 - Autumn Maze (1994)
- ❑ ❑ 12 - Winter Chill (1995)
- ❑ ❑ 13 - Endpeace (1996)

■ CLEEVE, Brian

Irish-born author Brian Cleeve is the author of at least 7 nonfiction books and more than 20 novels, including 4 in his series with Sean Ryan, ex-Irish revolutionary turned British Intelligence agent, starting with *Vote X for Treason* (1964) where Ryan is recruited from prison to infiltrate groups who threaten British security. In a 1982 interview with *Contemporary Authors* Cleeve noted a distinct shift in his writing starting in 1980 when he began producing books of mysticism that he says he had been working towards all his writing life. These include The *House on the Rock* (1980), *The Seven Mansions* (1980), *The Fourth Mary* (1982) and *A Woman of Fortune* (1993). After 5 years in the British Merchant Navy and 6 years as a freelance journalist in South Africa, he returned to Ireland in 1955 to earn his Ph.D. at the national University of Ireland. He lives in Dublin, Ireland.

Sean Ryan...ex-Irish revolutionary turned British Intelligence in England
- ❑ ❑ 1 - Vote X for Treason (1964) APA-Counterspy
- ❑ ❑ 2 - Dark Blood, Dark Terror (1965)
- ❑ ❑ 3 - The Judas Goat (1966)
      U.S.-Vice Isn't Private
- ❑ ❑ 4 - Violent Death of a Bitter Englishman (1967)

■ **CLUSTER, Dick**

Dick Cluster has written a pair of mysteries featuring Alex Glauberman, auto repair shop owner and chemotherapy patient with a fantasy about being a Jewish Sherlock Holmes. In *Return to Sender* (1988) he's hired to go to Europe to stop the delivery of a package and when his client is murdered, Alex is in real danger himself. In *Repulse Monkey* (1989) it's the babysitter who's in trouble, suspected of killing a former boyfriend. Alex and his ladylove Professor Meredith Phillips are on the case. A Harvard University graduate, Cluster is a former editor of *Dollars and Sense* where 5 years of research on the economy became *Shrinking Dollars, Vanishing Jobs* (1980) which he co-wrote with Nancy Rutter. Cluster also wrote *They Should Have Served That Cup of Coffee: Seven Radicals Remember the Sixties* (1979).

Alex Glauberman...auto repair shop owner in Boston, Massachusetts
- ❏ ❏ 1 - Return to Sender (1988)
- ❏ ❏ 2 - Repulse Monkey (1989)

■ **CLYNES, Michael [P]**

Michael Clynes is the pseudonym used by P.C. Doherty for his 16th century series featuring Sir Roger Shallot (a raffish fellow) who is servant to Benjamin Daunbey, the nephew of Cardinal Wolsey. As described in a *Kirkus* review, these tales represent "Sir Roger's recounting of his past exploits—some wily, others lecherous, most dishonest." Not only does Shallot say he slept with Elizabeth I, he claims to have suggested plot ideas to Shakespeare. Each entry in the series has a detailed subtitle similar to the following for book 2—The Poisoned Chalice: Being the Second Journal of Sir Roger Shallot Concerning Wicked Conspiracies and Horrible Murders Perpetrated in the Reign of Henry VIII. For other historical series from this author, see P.C. Doherty, Ann Dukthas, C.L. Grace and Paul Harding.

Roger Shallot, Sir...agent of Cardinal Wolsey in England
- ❏ ❏ 1 - The White Rose Murders (1991)
- ❏ ❏ 2 - The Poisoned Chalice (1992)
- ❏ ❏ 3 - The Grail Murders (1993)
- ❏ ❏ 4 - A Brood of Vipers (1994)
- ❏ ❏ 5 - The Gallows Murders (1995)
- ❏ ❏ 6 - Relic Murders (1996)

■ **COBEN, Harlan**

Award-winning author Harlan Coben has bagged Anthony, Edgar and Shamus awards for his paperback originals featuring ex-basketball player and Yoo-Hoo drinker Myron Bolitar. After an injury sent him to law school, Myron launched a second career with his own sports agency, where he gets by with a little help from his friends, Windsor Horne Lockwood III (Win, for short) and Esperanza (she's his secretary, taking night classes at NYU law school). Despite Win's blond, Waspy good looks, he's an artist at tae kwon do. After 4 years as roommates at Duke, Myron now rents office space for MB SportsReps from Win, top producer at his family's Park Avenue securities firm. Win handles money matters (and sometimes muscle) for Myron's clients. An Amherst grad, Coben lives in New Jersey with his pediatrician wife, their two perfect children and his large collection of loud ties.

Myron Bolitar...injured basketball player turned sports agent in New York, New York
- ❏ ❏ 1 - **Deal Breaker (1995) Anthony winner ★ Edgar winner** ☆
- ❏ ❏ 2 - Dropshot (1996)
- ❏ ❏ 3 - **Fade Away (1996) Edgar & Shamus winner ★★ Anthony nominee** ☆
- ❏ ❏ 4 - Backspin (1997)

■ COBURN, Andrew

New Hampshire native Andrew Coburn saw his first novel (*The Trespassers*, 1974) published at the age of 42. During his almost 20 years as a newspaper writer and editor, his closest friends were criminals, cops and trial lawyers, "a breed apart from the rest of us," he told *St. James Guide* in an interview. He went on to say that his female characters intrigue him the most, because "they face the facts of life and death with more fortitude than men. To a man, mortality is not natural," he said. "To a woman, it's simply one more thing to cope with." Coburn's latest book is not part of his Boston police series but a big what-if about the Lindbergh baby. In *Kidnapping* (1997), Coburn tells the tale of David Shellenbach and his dying father's stunning revelation that David is the kidnapped child of Charles Lindbergh. Coburn lives in Massachusetts.

James Morgan...chief of police in a Boston suburb in Massachusetts
- ❑ ❑ 1 - No Way Home (1992)
- ❑ ❑ 2 - Voices in the Dark (1994)

■ COE, Tucker [P]

Tucker Coe is one of the pseudonyms of Grand Master Donald E. Westlake, 4-time Edgar winner and author of more than 40 novels under his own name and dozens more under several pseudonyms. The Tucker Coe creation is ex-NYPD cop Mitch Tobin, "in many ways Westlake's most fascinating creation," according to Bill Pronzini (*1001 Midnights*). Tobin is thrown off the force after his partner is shot and killed while covering for him, while Tobin was in bed with a woman other than his wife. Tobin withdraws to his home in Queens where he starts building a high wall in the backyard but occasionally takes simple detecting jobs. In book 5, "the other woman" reappears and Tobin is forced to sort out his feelings for her while pursuing a murder investigation he wants no part of. Pronzini called the ending "violent, powerful, ironic and appropriate," labeling these 5 books a "perfect quintology."

Mitch Tobin...ex-cop P.I. in Queens, New York
- ❑ ❑ 1 - Kinds of Love, Kinds of Death (1966)
- ❑ ❑ 2 - Murder Among Children (1968)
- ❑ ❑ 3 - Wax Apple (1970)
- ❑ ❑ 4 - A Jade in Aries (1971)
- ❑ ❑ 5 - Don't Lie to Me (1972)

■ COLLINS, Max Allan, Jr.

Max Allan Collins has been called the "Renaissance Man of mystery fiction" with 5 series to his credit and an unprecedented 7 Shamus nominations (winning twice) for the first 8 Nate Heller novels. Twice nominated for an Edgar (fiction and non-fiction), he directed, wrote and executive-produced *Mommy* starring Patty McCormack and scripted the HBO film *The Expert*. A rock musician and songwriter, Collins wrote the internationally syndicated *Dick Tracy* comic strip from 1977 to 1993, co-created the comic book feature *Ms. Tree*, wrote *Batman* comic books and newspaper strips, and is currently developing the *Mike Danger* comics project with Mickey Spillane, simultaneously under development as a Miramax motion picture. Among his movie and TV novelizations are *Air Force One* (1997), *NYPD Blue: Blue Beginning* (1995), and *NYPD Blue: Blue Blood* (1997), covering the missing time between the 2nd and 3rd seasons.

Eliot Ness...1930s public safety officer in Cleveland, Ohio
- ❑ ❑ 1 - The Dark City (1987)
- ❑ ❑ 2 - Butcher's Dozen (1988)
- ❑ ❑ 3 - Bullet Proof (1989)
- ❑ ❑ 4 - Murder by the Numbers (1993)

Frank Nolan...aging thief in Iowa
- ❑ ❑ 1 - Bait Money (1973)
- ❑ ❑ 2 - Blood Money (1973)
- ❑ ❑ 3 - Fly Paper (1981)

❏ ❏   4 - Hush Money (1981)
❏ ❏   5 - Hard Cash (1981)
❏ ❏   6 - Scratch Fever (1982)
❏ ❏   7 - Spree (1987)

Mallory...small-town student mystery writer in Iowa
❏ ❏   1 - No Cure for Death (1983)
❏ ❏   2 - The Baby Blue Rip-Off (1983)
❏ ❏   3 - Kill Your Darlings (1984)
❏ ❏   4 - A Shroud for Aquarius (1985)
❏ ❏   5 - Nice Weekend for a Murder (1986)

Nate Heller...1930s ex-cop turned private eye in Chicago, Illinois
❏ ❏   1 - **True Detective (1983) Shamus winner ★**
❏ ❏   2 - **True Crime (1984) Shamus nominee ☆**
❏ ❏   3 - **The Million Dollar Wound (1986) Shamus nominee ☆**
❏ ❏   4 - **Neon Mirage (1988) Shamus nominee ☆**
❏ ❏   5 - **Stolen Away (1991) Shamus winner ★**
❏ ❏   6 - **Carnal Hours (1994) Shamus nominee ☆**
❏ ❏   7 - **Blood and Thunder [Huey Long] (1995)**
❏ ❏   8 - **Damned in Paradise [Clarence Darrow] (1996) Shamus nominee ☆**

Quarry...psychotic Vietnam vet and hired killer in Iowa
❏ ❏   1 - The Broker (1976)
        APA-Quarry (1985)
❏ ❏   2 - The Broker's Wife (1976)
        APA-Quarry's List (1985)
❏ ❏   3 - The Dealer (1976)
        APA-Quarry's Deal (1986)
❏ ❏   4 - The Slasher (1977)
        APA-Quarry's Cut (1986)
❏ ❏   5 - Primary Target (1987)

■ COLLINS, Michael [P]

Michael Collins is one of the pseudonyms of Dennis Lynds, author of 5 crime and mystery series under 5 different names. His primary series is the one written as Michael Collins for which he won an Edgar for best first novel. Spanning 25 years, these books feature a one-armed New York private eye named Dan Fortune who moves to Santa Barbara in book 14. Well-read and self-educated, Fortune lost his arm in an accident while looting a docked ship in his misspent youth. *The Cadillac Cowboy* (1995) introduces a new series character for Collins—ex-Green Beret, ex-CIA Langford Morgan who emerges from a self-imposed exile in the mountains of Costa Rica to settle some old scores. A past president of Private Eye Writers of America, Lynds was awarded the PWA Lifetime Achievement Award in 1988. Married to mystery writer Gayle Lynds, he lives in Santa Barbara (CA).

Dan Fortune...one-armed Polish-Lithuanian P.I. in New York, New York
❏ ❏   1 - **Act of Fear (1967) Edgar winner ★**
❏ ❏   2 - The Brass Rainbow (1969)
❏ ❏   3 - Night of the Toads (1970)
❏ ❏   4 - Walk a Black Wind (1971)
❏ ❏   5 - Shadow of a Tiger (1972)
❏ ❏   6 - The Silent Scream (1973)
❏ ❏   7 - Blue Death (1975)
❏ ❏   8 - The Blood-Red Dream (1976)
❏ ❏   9 - The Night Runners (1978)
❏ ❏ 10 - The Slasher (1980)

   ❏ ❏ 11 - Freak (1983)
   ❏ ❏ 12 - Minnesota Strip (1987)
   ❏ ❏ 13 - Red Rosa (1988)
   ❏ ❏ 14 - Castrato (1989)
   ❏ ❏ 15 - Chasing Eights (1990)
   ❏ ❏ 16 - The Irishman's Horse (1991)
   ❏ ❏ 17 - **Cassandra in Red (1992) Shamus nominee** ☆
   ❏ ❏ ss - Crime, Punishment and Resurrection
          [novella & short stories] (1992)

■ CONNELLY, Michael

Former crime reporter Michael Connelly introduced LAPD homicide detective Harry Bosch in *Black Echo* (1992), winner of the 1993 Edgar award for best first novel. Harry is short for Hieronymus (Bosch), son of a murdered prostitute who named him for the 16th century Dutch painter because she liked one of his paintings. Harry had a tough childhood in foster homes and an even tougher time as a tunnel rat in Vietnam. He often runs afoul of his superiors at work. His first 4 cases with Harry earned Connelly 7 award nominations after the intial Edgar win, and his nonseries novel *The Poet* (1996) netted him an Anthony award in 1997. Coming in 1998 will be a standalone thriller about a former FBI agent. A graduate of the University of Florida (Gainesville), Connelly spent 13 years as a reporter, earning a shared Pulitzer Prize for staff reporting his last year at the *Los Angeles Times*.

Harry Bosch...homicide detective in Los Angeles, California
   ❏ ❏ 1 - **The Black Echo (1992) Edgar winner** ★
   ❏ ❏ 2 - **The Black Ice (1993) Anthony & Hammett nominee** ☆☆
   ❏ ❏ 3 - **The Concrete Blonde (1994) Anthony & Macavity nominee** ☆☆
   ❏ ❏ 4 - **The Last Coyote (1995) Anthony, Hammett & Macavity nominee** ☆☆☆
   ❏ ❏ 5 - Trunk Music (1997)

■ CONROY, Richard Timothy

Former Smithsonian Foreign Affairs official Richard Timothy Conroy has created a series sleuth with experience not unlike his own. Miss Manners herself called book one a "delicious romp through the improprieties of Washington." Book two is actually a prequel, relating how Henry was nudged off the Foreign Service fast track and detoured into the backwater known as the Nation's Attic. Henry's typical day might include tracking down lost shipments or giving guided tours to low-level dignitaries, a routine that allows for late starts, long lunches, plenty of gossip and time for sleuthing. *Our Man in Belize* (1997) tells the story of Conroy's time as American vice consul during the last days of British Honduras, before Hurricane Hattie blew what is now a snorkeling paradise out of the 19th century and into the 20th. He is married to *Washington Post* columnist Sarah Booth.

Henry Scruggs...40-something Smithsonian official in Washington, D.C.
   ❏ ❏ 1 - The India Exhibition (1992)
   ❏ ❏ 2 - Mr. Smithson's Bones (1993)
   ❏ ❏ 3 - Old Ways in the New World (1994)

■ CONSTANTINE, K. C. [P]

K. C. Constantine is the pseudonym used by Carl Kosak for his Edgar-nominated Rocksburg series featuring small-town police chief Mario Balzic, once called the crankiest cop in western Pennsylvania. He's also been described as boozing, profane, compassionate, understanding, and a better than even match for any state investigator who invades his territory. Nominated for a best-novel Edgar for book 8, the series was scheduled to close with Balzic's retirement in book 11 where he faces armed commandos, in addition to the 25 cops and 15,000 civilians he normally watches over. Although the torch is passed in book 12, Balzic is back in book 13, complete with his name on the cover proclaiming *Family Values* (1997) A Mario Balzic Novel. A Pittsburgh native and former minor league baseball player, the author also served in the Marine Corps.

Mario Balzic...small-town police chief in Rocksburg, Pennsylvania
- ❑ ❑ 1 - The Rocksburg Railroad Murders (1972)
- ❑ ❑ 2 - The Man Who Liked to Look at Himself (1973)
- ❑ ❑ 3 - The Blank Page (1974)
- ❑ ❑ 4 - A Fix Like This (1975)
- ❑ ❑ 5 - The Man Who Liked Slow Tomatoes (1982)
- ❑ ❑ 6 - Always a Body to Trade (1983)
- ❑ ❑ 7 - Upon Some Midnights Clear (1985)
- ❑ ❑ 8 - **Joey's Case (1988) Edgar nominee** ☆
- ❑ ❑ 9 - Sunshine Enemies (1990)
- ❑ ❑ 10 - Bottom Liner Blues (1993)
- ❑ ❑ 11 - Cranks and Shadows (1995)
- ❑ ❑ 12 - Good Sons (1996)
- ❑ ❑ 13 - Family Values (1997)

■ CONWAY, Peter [P]

Peter Conway is the pseudonym of Peter Claudius Gautier-Smith, born 1929, who wrote more than 20 crime fiction titles from 1972 to 1985. Among these were three books featuring female sleuth Lucy Beck, introduced in *Motive for Revenge* (1972). This series was published in hardcover editions in England from Hale. Also using the Peter Conway pseudonym was the prolific George Alexis Milkomanovich, who wrote more than 120 books (fiction and nonfiction), including 5 crime novels during the early '40s. Born in 1903 to a Russian general and a countess living in Baku , Russia, this Peter Conway was a plastic surgeon who lectured in the U.S., Italy, England and Australia. He lived primarily in Australia but maintained an office in Oakland (CA). He also wrote under the names George Alexis Bankoff, George Borodin, George Braddon, Alec Redwood and George Sava.

Lucy Beck...female sleuth in England
- ❑ ❑ 1 - Motive for Revenge (1972)
- ❑ ❑ 2 - The Padded Cell (1973)
- ❑ ❑ 3 - Escape to Danger (1974)

■ COOK, Bob

British author Bob Cook has written at least 3 books featuring London philosophy professor and MI6 agent Michael Wyman, introduced in *Disorderly Elements* published by in the U.K. by Gollancz in 1985 and in the U.S. by St. Martin's Press the following year. Although St. Martin's did not publish book 2, *Questions of Identity* (1987) set in Italy, or the 3rd in the Wyman series, they did release two other titles from Cook, *Paper Chase* (1990) and *Fire and Forget* (1990).

Michael Wyman...philosophy professor and MI6 agent in London, England
- ❑ ❑ 1 - Disorderly Elements (1985)
- ❑ ❑ 2 - Questions of Identity (1987)
- ❑ ❑ 3 - Faceless Mortals (1988)

■ **COOK, Bruce**

Former *Los Angeles Daily News* book editor Bruce Cook is the creator of Mexican-American P.I. Chico Cervantes, who sometimes tilts at windmills like the fictional creation of his namesake. A prolific author of both fiction and non-fiction, Cook wrote *The Beat Generation: The Tumultuous '50s Movement and Its Impact on Today* (1971), re-released in 1994 with his new preface and afterword, following the sale of 100,000 copies of the first edition. After graduating from Loyola University, Cook worked as a German translator for the U.S. Army and later wrote a biography of the German dramatist and poet, *Brecht in Exile* (1983). As Bruce Alexander, he writes a London historical series featuring blind magistrate Sir John Fielding. As co-author with the late William Coughlin, Cook completed *The Last Judgment* (1997) after the Detroit judge's death in 1993.

Antonio "Chico" Cervantes...Mexican-American private eye in Los Angeles, California
- ❑ ❑   1 - Mexican Standoff (1988)
- ❑ ❑   2 - Rough Cut (1990)
- ❑ ❑   3 - Death as a Career Move (1992)
- ❑ ❑   4 - The Sidewalk Hilton (1994)

■ **COOK, Glen**

Best known as a science fiction and fantasy writer, Glen Cook is the author of more than 35 novels. This veteran General Motors assembly worker, once labeled "the working man's fantasy writer," typically writes about the common folk in his various series, including Dread Empire, Black Company, Darkwar, and Starfishers. His private eye series features Garrett, a hardboiled human P.I. described by one reviewer as Chandler meets J. R. Tolkien. The 6'2" ex-Marine private eye with a passion for redheads hires himself out to fantasy creatures in need of a private investigator. In book 5, he must find the Book of Shadows before it falls into the wrong hands. This book of magic is 100 sheets of paper thin brass bound in tooled mammoth leather, with each page containing a powerful spell. Born in New York City, Cook lives in St. Louis.

Garrett...30-something fantasy private eye in TunFaire
- ❑ ❑   1 - Sweet Silver Blues (1987)
- ❑ ❑   2 - Cold Copper Tears (1988)
- ❑ ❑   3 - Bitter Gold Hearts (1988)
- ❑ ❑   4 - Old Tin Sorrows (1989)
- ❑ ❑   5 - Dread Brass Shadows (1990)
- ❑ ❑   6 - Red Iron Nights (1991)
- ❑ ❑   7 - Deadly Quicksilver Lies (1994)
- ❑ ❑   8 - Petty Pewter Gods (1995)

■ **COOK, Stephen**

A working journalist for more than 25 years, British author Stephen Cook has written a pair of police procedurals featuring CID Detective Sergeant Judy Best, first seen in *Dead Fit* (1993). While pumping iron at her favorite club, Judy attracts the attention of an arrogant investment banker who ends up dead, and her black boyfriend is arrested. In *One Dead Tory* (1994), the recently-promoted Judy has to contend with a difficult new boss and a murdered Tory leader. A journalist for the *Guardian* since 1978, Cook wrote two earlier novels, *Upperdown* (1985) and *Empire Born* (1986). *Upperdown* is a satire on British public schools in the '60s, while *Empire Born* is a serious book about race relations in Kenya, based on the author's personal experience growing up there between 1952 and 1961. Cook lives in London.

Judy Best...weight-lifting police officer in England
- ❑ ❑   1 - Dead Fit (1993)
- ❑ ❑   2 - One Dead Tory (1994)

■ COOK, Thomas H.

Edgar award winner Thomas H. Cook has written 16 books since 1979, including detective fiction, true crime and literary novels. His first two novels, published by Playboy Press, included *Blood Innocents* (1980), which earned him an Edgar nomination for best paperback original. Four years later, with the introduction of his series detective, Atlanta private eye Frank Clemons, Cook received another Edgar nomination, this time for best novel (*Sacrificial Ground*, 1988). His third nomination, in the fact crime category, was for BLOOD ECHOES (1992), and 4 years later *The Chatham School Affair* (1996) won him the best novel Edgar. An Alabama native, Cook earned his B.A. at Georgia State College, M.A. at Hunter College and M.Phil. from Columbia University. He previously taught college English and history, and spent 4 years as contributing editor of *Atlanta* magazine. He lives in New York City.

Frank Clemons...private eye in Atlanta, Georgia
- ❏ ❏ 1 - **Sacrificial Ground (1988) Edgar nominee** ☆
- ❏ ❏ 2 - Flesh and Blood (1989)
- ❏ ❏ 3 - Night Secrets (1990)

■ COOPER, Brian

English author Brian Cooper's first work of crime fiction, *Where the Fresh Grass Grows*, was published in the U.K. in 1955 and the U.S. (retitled as *Maria*) the following year. He wrote at least 8 other books before introducing his World War II era DCI from Norfolk. By book 2, John Spencer Lubbock is retired and pursuing his hobby of windmills. According to Carol Harper (*Deadly Pleasures #12*), the retired DCI has extensive files on the architecture, workings and history of windmills all over Norfolk, but it is his local knowledge and thorough investigating style that makes him so helpful to the former sergeant (Michael Bruce Tench) who Lubbock accurately predicted would one day be DCI himself. Much of book 4 takes place in a bird sanctuary on the coast north of Norfolk and like the earlier books contains lots of Norfolk dialect which Harper says can be confusing at times.

John Spencer Lubbock...retired World War II D.C.I. in Norfolk, England
- ❏ ❏ 1 - The Cross of San Vincente (1991)
- ❏ ❏ 2 - The Singing Stones (1993)
- ❏ ❏ 3 - Covenant with Death (1994)
- ❏ ❏ 4 - Shadows on the Sand (1995)

■ COPPER, Basil

Long-time journalist Basil Copper has written more than 70 books, including 52 in the series featuring Mike Faraday, a hard-boiled Los Angeles private eye who quotes 17th century poet Robert Herrick ("Gather ye rosebuds while ye may"). Faraday and his powder-blue Buick are introduced in *The Dark Mirror* (1966) and last seen in *Print-Out* (1988). As part of his considerable writing of fantasy, occult and macabre works, Copper has also published serious studies of the vampire and Dracula legends. His 6 collections of Solar Pons stories are the result of his being commissioned during the '70s to continue the series started by August Derleth during the '20s. A past chairman of the Crime Writer's Association, Copper is one of England's leading collectors of film and is considered an authority on silent films and early talkies.

Mike Faraday...hard-boiled private eye who quotes Herrick in Los Angeles, California
- ❏ ❏ 1 - The Dark Mirror (1966)
- ❏ ❏ 2 - Night Frost (1966)
- ❏ ❏ 3 - No Flowers for the General (1967)
- ❏ ❏ 4 - Scratch on the Dark (1967)
- ❏ ❏ 5 - Die Now, Live Later (1968)

❑ ❑   6 - Don't Bleed on Me (1968)
❑ ❑   7 - The Marble Orchard (1969)
❑ ❑   8 - Dead File (1970)
❑ ❑   9 - No Letters from the Grave (1971)
❑ ❑ 10 - The Big Chill (1972)
❑ ❑ 11 - Strong-Arm (1972)
❑ ❑ 12 - A Great Year for Dying (1973)
❑ ❑ 13 - Shock-Wave (1973)
❑ ❑ 14 - The Breaking Point (1973)
❑ ❑ 15 - A Voice from the Dead (1974)
❑ ❑ 16 - Feedback (1974)
❑ ❑ 17 - Ricochet (1974)
❑ ❑ 18 - The High Wall (1975)
❑ ❑ 19 - Impact (1975)
❑ ❑ 20 - A Good Place to Die (1975)
❑ ❑ 21 - The Lonely Place (1976)
❑ ❑ 22 - Crack in the Sidewalk (1976)
❑ ❑ 23 - Tight Corner (1976)
❑ ❑ 24 - The Year of the Dragon (1977)
❑ ❑ 25 - Death Squad (1977)
❑ ❑ 26 - Murder One (1978)
❑ ❑ 27 - A Quiet Room in Hell (1979)
❑ ❑ 28 - The Big Rip-Off (1979)
❑ ❑ 29 - The Caligari Complex (1980)
❑ ❑ 30 - Flip-Side (1980)
❑ ❑ 31 - The Long Rest (1981)
❑ ❑ 32 - The Empty Silence (1981)
❑ ❑ 33 - Dark Entry (1981)
❑ ❑ 34 - Hang Loose (1982)
❑ ❑ 35 - Shoot-Out (1982)
❑ ❑ 36 - The Far Horizon (1982)
❑ ❑ 37 - Trigger-Man (1983)
❑ ❑ 38 - Pressure Point (1983)
❑ ❑ 39 - Hard Contract (1983)
❑ ❑ 40 - The Narrow Corner (1983)
❑ ❑ 41 - The Hook (1984)
❑ ❑ 42 - You Only Die Once (1984)
❑ ❑ 43 - Tuxedo Park (1985)
❑ ❑ 44 - The Far Side of Fear (1985)
❑ ❑ 45 - Snow-Job (1986)
❑ ❑ 46 - Jet-Lag (1986)
❑ ❑ 47 - Blood on the Moon (1986)
❑ ❑ 48 - Heavy Iron (1987)
❑ ❑ 49 - Turn Down an Empty Glass (1987)
❑ ❑ 50 - Bad Scene (1987)
❑ ❑ 51 - House-Dick (1988)
❑ ❑ 52 - Print-Out (1988)

■ **CORK, Barry**

Barry Cork is the creator of a golf-loving Scottish police inspector named Angus Struan, introduced in *Deadball* (1988) where the inspector is faced with the death of a greenskeeper just before an important tournament. In book 2 the play shifts to a course in the Hebrides and moves on to stockbroker country in book 3. In *Winter Rules* (1991), book 4, published in the U.S. in 1993, Inspector Struan plays host to a visiting African head of state and then travels to Africa where he gets involved with building the first golf course in his host country. Smuggled cars and Third World politics become part of the game.

Angus Struan, Insp.....golfing police inspector in Scotland
- ❏ ❏ 1 - Deadball (1988)
- ❏ ❏ 2 - Unnatural Hazard (1989)
- ❏ ❏ 3 - Laid Dead (1990)
- ❏ ❏ 4 - Winter Rules (1991)

■ **CORMANY, Michael**

Michael Cormany is the creator of Dan Kruger, ex-cop turned private investigator from Chicago (IL), introduced in *Lost Daughter* (1988), a Shamus nominee for best first novel. Kruger, who plays guitar in a band called Full Frontal Nudity when the P.I. business is slow, is described by Dick Higgins as pretty hardboiled, a little noir, and slightly offbeat. In book 4, *Polaroid Man* (1991), Kruger risks his own life trying to find out who murdered a beautiful young woman with a past that others want to keep hidden. In a 1992 interview with *Contemporary Authors* Cormany describes himself as a bluecollar worker with no college education who writes P.I. fiction for the love of it. He lives in Aurora (IL).

Dan Kruger...private investigator in Chicago, Illinois
- ❏ ❏ 1 - **Lost Daughter (1988) Shamus nominee** ☆
- ❏ ❏ 2 - Red Winter (1989)
- ❏ ❏ 3 - Rich or Dead (1990)
- ❏ ❏ 4 - Polaroid Man (1991)

■ **CORRIS, Peter**

Australian author Peter Corris has written more than 50 books, including at least 36 works of crime fiction. His longest-running series features Sydney private eye Cliff Hardy introduced in 1980, with 15 novels and at least 4 collections of short stories. According to Maxim Jakubowski (*St. James Guide*) the best of the series is book 4, *The Empty Beach* (1983), which was filmed with Bryan Brown in Hardy's beat-up leather jacket and blue jeans. "Amid the mayhem...[of] ingenious plots," says Jakubowski, "Corris offers grim social descriptions of modern Sydney with wry asides and the right amount of whimsy." With a Ph.D. in history from Australian National University, Corris has also written a historical saga (*The Gulliver Fortune*, 1989), a social history of prizefighting (*Lords of the Ring*, 1980), and has coauthored several autobiographies.

Cliff Hardy...Aussie private eye in Sydney, Australia
- ❏ ❏ 1 - The Dying Trade (1980)
- ❏ ❏ 2 - White Meat (1981)
- ❏ ❏ 3 - The Marvellous Boy (1982)
- ❏ ❏ 4 - The Empty Beach (1983)
- ❏ ❏ ss - Heroin Annie [short stories] (1984)
- ❏ ❏ 5 - Make Me Rich (1985)
- ❏ ❏ ss - The Big Drop [short stories] (1985)
- ❏ ❏ 6 - Deal Me Out (1986)

❑ ❑ 7 - The Greenwich Apartments (1986)
❑ ❑ 8 - The January Zone (1987)
❑ ❑ ss - The Man in the Shadows [short stories] (1988)
❑ ❑ 9 - O'Fear (1989)
❑ ❑ 10 - Wet Graves (1991)
❑ ❑ 11 - Aftershock (1991)
❑ ❑ 12 - Beware of the Dog (1992)
❑ ❑ 13 - Matrimonial Causes (1993)
❑ ❑ ss - Burn and Other Stories (1993)
❑ ❑ 14 - Casino (1994)
❑ ❑ 15 - The Washington Club (1997)

Luke Dunlop...ex-cop working witness protection in Sydney, Australia
❑ ❑ 1 - Set Up (1992)
❑ ❑ 2 - Cross Off (1993)

Ray Crawley...Federal Security Agency director in Sydney, Australia
❑ ❑ 1 - Pokerface (1985)
❑ ❑ 2 - The Baltic Business (1988)
❑ ❑ 3 - The Kimberly Killing (1988)
❑ ❑ 4 - The Cargo Club (1990)
❑ ❑ 5 - The Azanian Action (1991)
❑ ❑ 6 - The Japanese Job (1992)
❑ ❑ 7 - The Time Trap (1994)

Richard Browning...Aussie private eye with Hollywood ties in Sydney, Australia
❑ ❑ 1 - "Box Office" Browning (1987)
❑ ❑ 2 - "Beverly Hills" Browning (1987)
❑ ❑ 3 - Browning Takes Off (1989)
❑ ❑ 4 - Browning in Buckskin (1991)
❑ ❑ 5 - Browning P.I. (1992)
❑ ❑ 6 - Browning Battles On (1993)
❑ ❑ 7 - Browning Sahib (1994)
❑ ❑ 8 - Browning Without a Cause (1995)

■ CORY, Desmond [P]

Desmond Cory is a pseudonym of Shaun Lloyd McCarthy, ex-Marine Commando, Oxford graduate, former university lecturer and one-time journalist and translator. A fellow of the Institute of Linguists and honorary member of the Institute of Swiss Psychiatrists, he has written more than 35 novels since his first book in 1951—the series opener with British agent Johnny Fedora. Books 12-16, known as the Feramontov Quintet, feature the former Soviet agent Feramontov turned renegade. In the '90s Cory has been writing about the comic misadventures of eccentric Welsh math professor John Dobie. As McCarthy he wrote a Hamlet parody, *Lucky Ham* (1977), which Mary Helen Becker in *St. James Guide* calls "a brilliant takeoff on practically everybody." Born in Sussex, England, he currently lives on Cyprus where he teaches English at Eastern Mediterranean University.

John Dobie...math professor in Cardiff, Wales
❑ ❑ 1 - Strange Attractor (1991)
          U.S.-The Catalyst
❑ ❑ 2 - The Mask of Zeus (1992)
❑ ❑ 3 - The Dobie Paradox (1993)

Johnny Fedora...British agent in England
- ❏ ❏ 1 - Secret Ministry (1951)
- ❏ ❏ 2 - This Traitor, Death (1952)
- ❏ ❏ 3 - Dead Man Falling (1953)
- ❏ ❏ 4 - Intrigue (1954)
- ❏ ❏ 5 - Height of Day (1955)
- ❏ ❏ 6 - High Requiem (1956)
- ❏ ❏ 7 - Johnny Goes North (1956)
- ❏ ❏ 8 - Johnny Goes East (1958)
- ❏ ❏ 9 - Johnny Goes West (1959)
- ❏ ❏ 10 - Johnny Goes South (1959)
- ❏ ❏ 11 - The Head (1960)
- ❏ ❏ 12 - Undertow (1962)
- ❏ ❏ 13 - Hammerhead (1963)
- ❏ ❏ 14 - Feramontov (1966)
- ❏ ❏ 15 - Timelock (1967)
- ❏ ❏ 16 - Sunburst (1971)

Linda Grey...British female in England
- ❏ ❏ 1 - Begin, Murderer! (1951)
- ❏ ❏ 2 - This is Jezebel (1952)
- ❏ ❏ 3 - Lady Lost (1953)
- ❏ ❏ 4 - The Shaken Leaf (1955)

Mr. Dee...Englishman in England
- ❏ ❏ 1 - Stranglehold (1961)
- ❏ ❏ 2 - The Name of the Game (1964)

■ CRAIG, David [P]

David Craig is a pseudonym of Allan James Tucker, better known for his writing as Bill James with the Harpur and Iles police series. As David Craig he has written two short series from the late '60s and early '70s. First came 3 books featuring London Home Office administrator Roy Rickman introduced in *The Alias Man* (1968), and later a pair of novels with British intelligence agents Stephen Bellecroix & Sheila Roath, first seen in *Young Men May Die* (1970). In addition to these 5 series books, Tucker wrote at least 7 nonseries novels under the name David Craig during the '70s. He has recently revived the David Craig pseudonym for a new series set in the Cardiff dockland (*Forget It*, 1995). Born in Wales and educated at University College in Cardiff, the author has worked as both a newspaper and magazine journalist as well as in radio and TV.

Roy Rickman...Home Officer Administrator in London, England
- ❏ ❏ 1 - The Alias Man (1968)
- ❏ ❏ 2 - Message Ends (1969)
- ❏ ❏ 3 - Contact Lost (1970)

Stephen Bellecroix & Sheila Roath...British agents in England
- ❏ ❏ 1 - Young Men May Die (1970)
- ❏ ❏ 2 - A Walk at Night (1971)

■ **CRAIG, Philip**

Philip R. Craig grew up on a small cattle ranch near Durango, Colorado and rode horseback to a one-room school for eight years. At Boston University he was an All-American fencer, earned a degree in religion and philosophy and played a lot of bridge. He studied poetry with Robert Lowell who convinced him he had no future as a poet, but after earning an MFA in prose fiction at the University of Iowa Writers' Workshop, he saw his first novel published in 1969 when he was 35. During the 20 years between his first book and the start of his Martha's Vineyard series, Craig says he submitted numerous novels no one wanted to publish. His fictional ex-Boston cop Jefferson "J.W." Jackson now has eight solved cases to his credit. The author spends his summers on Martha's Vineyard and winters in Hamilton, Massachusetts, where he is associate professor of English at Wheelock College.

Jefferson "J.W." Jackson...30-something ex-Boston cop in Martha's Vineyard, Massachusetts
- ❏ ❏ 1 - A Beautiful Place to Die (1989)
- ❏ ❏ 2 - The Woman Who Walked into the Sea (1991)
- ❏ ❏ 3 - The Double-Minded Men (1992)
- ❏ ❏ 4 - Cliff Hanger (1993)
- ❏ ❏ 5 - Off Season (1994)
- ❏ ❏ 6 - A Case of Vineyard Poison (1995)
- ❏ ❏ 7 - Death on a Vineyard Beach (1996)
- ❏ ❏ 8 - A Deadly Vineyard Holiday (1997)

■ **CRAIS, Robert**

Former television writer Robert Crais has won all 4 mystery-writing awards for his Elvis Cole novels and a 1981 Emmy nomination for *Hill Street Blues*. Other TV credits include *JAG*, *L.A. Law*, *Cagney & Lacey*, *Miami Vice*, *Quincy* and *Baretta* (to which he sold the 2nd script he ever wrote). P.I. Elvis Cole survived Ranger training, Vietnam and studio security work to open his own detective agency with ex-LAPD officer Joe Pike, who also owns a gun shop. Elvis drives a '66 yellow 'Vette and decorates his office with Disney memorabilia, but he never shrinks from a fight. Says Crais, "Elvis is the man I try to be." According to his press kit bio, Crais is an active marksman, aerobatic pilot, gourmet cook, distance runner and collector of objets d'art. After growing up in Louisiana and working the circus midway at 15, he currently lives in the Santa Monica mountains with his family, 2 cats and 14,000 books.

Elvis Cole & Joe Pike...pair of Hollywood private eyes in Los Angeles, California
- ❏ ❏ 1 - **The Monkey's Raincoat (1987) Edgar, Anthony & Macavity winner ★★★ Shamus nominee ☆**
- ❏ ❏ 2 - Stalking the Angel (1989)
- ❏ ❏ 3 - **Lullaby Town (1992) Shamus nominee ☆**
- ❏ ❏ 4 - **Free Fall (1993) Edgar nominee ☆**
- ❏ ❏ 5 - Vodoo River (1995)
- ❏ ❏ 6 - **Sunset Express (1996) Shamus winner ★**
- ❏ ❏ 7 - Indigo Slam (1997)

■ **CRIDER, Bill**

Anthony award winner Bill Crider writes 3 mystery series—one amateur detective (college professor Carl Burns), one sheriff (Dan Rhodes) and a private eye (Truman Smith). In 1996 he published the first 3 Mike Gonzo books, which are humorous adventure stories for middle readers (ages 8-12). New in 1997 are book 5 in the Truman Smith series, *Murder Takes a Break*, and Crider's first collaboration with former *Today Show* regular Willard Scott. *Murder Under Blue Skies* launches their Virginia bed and breakfast series featuring a retired weatherman sleuth. Crider chairs the English and Fine Arts Department at Alvin (TX) Community College. His doctoral dissertation at the University of Texas at Austin was on private eye fiction and he has written several horror novels as Jack MacLane and westerns under his own name.

Carl Burns...college professor in Texas
- ❏ ❏ 1 - One Dead Dean (1988)
- ❏ ❏ 2 - Dying Voices (1989)
- ❏ ❏ 3 - ...A Dangerous Thing (1994)

Dan Rhodes...laid-back sheriff with a motley crew of deputies in Blacklin County, Texas
- ❏ ❏ 1 - **Too Late to Die (1986) Anthony winner ★**
- ❏ ❏ 2 - Shotgun Saturday Night (1987)
- ❏ ❏ 3 - Cursed to Death (1988)
- ❏ ❏ 4 - Death on the Move (1989)
- ❏ ❏ 5 - Evil at the Root (1990)
- ❏ ❏ 6 - Booked for a Hanging (1992)
- ❏ ❏ 7 - Murder Most Fowl (1994)
- ❏ ❏ 8 - Winning Can Be Murder (1996)
- ❏ ❏ 9 - Death by Accident (1997)

Truman Smith...private eye in Galveston, Texas
- ❏ ❏ 1 - **Dead on the Island (1991) Shamus nominee** ☆
- ❏ ❏ 2 - Gator Kill (1992)
- ❏ ❏ 3 - When Old Men Die (1994)
- ❏ ❏ 4 - The Prairie Chicken Kill (1996)

■ CROSS, David [P]

David Cross is the pseudonym used by George C. Chesbro for 3 paperback originals featuring ex-Special Forces soldier John Sinclair turned renegade super ninja hero (Chant). Thanks to shared characters and crossover action between the Chesbro and Cross books, book 10 in the Mongo series actually wraps up the action of the 3 Chant books. The dwarf detective searches for Chant in *Dark Chant in a Crimson Key* (1992) and should probably be read after the Chant series. The author was a special education teacher for 15 years before his first novel was published in 1976, a non-mystery titled *King's Gambit*. The following year he launched the Mongo series and has since written 21 books and numerous shorts stories. One of his nonseries mysteries, *Bone* (1989), features a homeless New York City man with double amnesia.

John "Chant" Sinclair...renegade super ninja in New York, New York
- ❏ ❏ 1 - Chant (1986)
- ❏ ❏ 2 - Silent Killer (1986)
- ❏ ❏ 3 - Code of Blood (1987)

■ CROWE, John [P]

John Crowe is one of the pseudonyms of Dennis Lynds, author of 5 crime and mystery series under 5 different names. The series written as John Crowe is more appropriately described as the Buena Costa County series, taking its name from a fictional jurisdiction along the southern California coast north of Los Angeles. Although there are various continuing characters, each book has a different primary investigator. Books 1, 3 and 6 are police procedurals, while book 4 is a private eye novel and book 5 features an amateur detective. Book 2 is also a law enforcement novel, but Border Patrol instead of police. A past president of Private Eye Writers of America, the author was awarded the 1998 PWA Lifetime Achievement Award.

Lee Beckett...private eye in Buena Costa Co., California
- ❏ ❏ 1 - Another Way to Die (1972)
- ❏ ❏ 2 - A Touch of Darkness (1972)
- ❏ ❏ 3 - Bloodwater (1974)
- ❏ ❏ 4 - Crooked Shadows (1975)
- ❏ ❏ 5 - When They Kill Your Wife (1977)
- ❏ ❏ 6 - Close to Death (1979)

■ CRUMLEY, James

Hammett award winner James Crumley is the creator of several colorful series characters, including Milodragovitch, the cocaine addict and womanizing drunk, and Sughrue, the Vietnam criminal and Army spy, also a boozer. As Crumley noted in an interview with *St. James Guide*, his detectives are more comfortable around criminals than in the company of solid, middle-class citizens, so his "vision of justice is less clear-cut." In *The Wrong Case* (1975), Milo says, "I have neither character nor morals, no religion, no purpose in life...so is it any wonder I drink?" Milo's forte is self-destruction, according to Elmore Leonard in his review of *Dancing Bear* (1983). After earning an M.F.A. from the University of Iowa, Crumley spent almost 20 years as a professor of English and creative writing at universities in 6 states from Pennsylvania to Oregon. Born in Texas, he currently lives in Montana.

C. W. Sughrue...ex-Army spy turned P.I. in Montana
- ❏ ❏ 1 - The Last Good Kiss (1978)
- ❏ ❏ 2 - **The Mexican Tree Duck (1993) Hammett winner ★**
- ❏ ❏ 3 - Bordersnakes [incl Milo] (1996)

Milo Milodragovitch...ex-Army spy and hard drinking P.I. in Montana
- ❏ ❏ 1 - The Wrong Case (1975)
- ❏ ❏ 2 - **Dancing Bear (1983) Shamus nominee ☆**

■ CUNNINGHAM, E. V. [P]

E. V. Cunningham is a pseudonym of Howard (Melvin) Fast, author of more than 80 books, including 20 mysteries written between 1960 and 1986 as E. V. Cunningham. Among these are several police detective stories set in New York City and Beverly Hills (CA). In at least 5 books (titled with a woman's first name), a plucky heroine is caught in a bizarre situation. One of these (*Samantha*, 1967) introduces a Japanese-American detective who later gets his own series. A Zen Buddhist, like his creator, Sgt. Masuto is "aloof in philosophy but socially involved as detective and family man; a karate expert, lover of roses, and possessor of caustic wit," according to Frank Campenni (*St. James Guide*). Jailed for contempt of Congress in 1947, the author was awarded the Soviet International Peace prize in 1954 and won an Emmy award in 1976 for his television play 21 Hours at Munich.

Harvey Krim...NYPD detective in New York, New York
- ❏ ❏ 1 - Lydia (1964)
- ❏ ❏ 2 - Cynthia (1968)

John Comaday & Larry Cohen...police commissioner & Manhattan DA's 1st assistant in New York
- ❏ ❏ 1 - Penelope (1965)
- ❏ ❏ 2 - Margie (1966)

Masao Masuto, Sgt.....Japanese-American police detective in Beverly Hills, California
- ❏ ❏ 1 - Samantha (1967) APA-The Case of the Angry Actress
- ❏ ❏ 2 - The Case of the One-Penny Orange (1977)
- ❏ ❏ 3 - The Case of the Russian Diplomat (1978)
- ❏ ❏ 4 - The Case of the Poisoned Eclairs (1979)
- ❏ ❏ 5 - The Case of the Sliding Pool (1981)
- ❏ ❏ 6 - The Case of the Kidnapped Angel (1982)
- ❏ ❏ 7 - The Case of the Murdered Mackenzie (1984)

■ CUSSLER, Clive

Former advertising creative director and Edgar nominee Clive Cussler has written more than a dozen Dirk Pitt novels with 70 million books in print in 40 languages, available in over 100 countries around the world, according to *Publishers Weekly*. With his royalties he has created a nonprofit organization to discover and preserve historic shipwrecks, National Underwater & Marine Agency (NUMA). Like his hero

Dirk Pitt, Cussler has assembled an amazing record. With his NUMA crew of volunteers, he has discovered more than 60 lost ships of historic significance, donating the artifacts to museums. In *The Sea Hunters* (1996), coauthored with Craig Dirago, he describes 12 of the real-life NUMA expeditions. Like Pitt, Cussler's collection of classic automobiles (he owns at least 80) is one of the finest in the world. He divides his time between Arizona and Colorado.

Dirk Pitt...special projects director of national underwater-marine agency in the United States
- ❑ ❑   1 - **The Mediterranean Caper (1973) Edgar nominee** ☆ Brit.-Mayday!
- ❑ ❑   2 - Iceberg (1975)
- ❑ ❑   3 - Raise the Titanic! (1976)
- ❑ ❑   4 - Vixen 03 (1978)
- ❑ ❑   5 - Night Probe! (1981)
- ❑ ❑   6 - Pacific Vortex! (1983)
- ❑ ❑   7 - Deep Six (1984)
- ❑ ❑   8 - Cyclops (1986)
- ❑ ❑   9 - Treasure (1988)
- ❑ ❑   10 - Dragon (1990)
- ❑ ❑   11 - Sahara (1992)
- ❑ ❑   12 - Inca Gold (1994)
- ❑ ❑   13 - Shock Wave (1996)

▪ CUTLER, Stan

Television writer and producer Stan Cutler is the creator of the Goodman and Bradley Hollywood series featuring a 50-something, jaded, macho private eye and a 30-something gay writer of celebrity biographies. Their stories are told in alternating chapters, beginning with the Shamus-nominated *Best Performance by a Patsy* (1991), where Bradley signs on to ghost Goodman's tell-all autobiography. During the writing, it becomes clear that the wrong guy may have been put away by one of Goodman's early investigations. Cutler has a long list of TV credits, including associate producer of the *Farmer's Daughter* ('66-'67) and writer for *That Girl*, *The Danny Thomas Show*, *The Courtship of Eddie's Father*, *9 to 5* and other programs. Born in Newark (NJ) where his father was a corporation president, Cutler lives in Los Angeles.

Rayford Goodman & Mark Bradley...jaded macho P.I. & gay writer of celebrity biographies in Hollywood, California
- ❑ ❑   1 - **Best Performance by a Patsy (1991) Shamus nominee** ☆
- ❑ ❑   2 - The Face on the Cutting Room Floor (1991)
- ❑ ❑   3 - Shot on Location (1993)
- ❑ ❑   4 - Rough Cut (1994)

▪ DALY, CONOR

Conor Daly is the creator of a three-book series of golf mysteries featuring Kieran Lanahan, a lawyer turned county club golf pro in Westchester County (NY). In the opening title, *Local Knowledge* (1995), Kieran is pulled right off the course in the middle of a championship match, and hauled away by police for questioning in the murder of a millionaire country club owner. The cops don't really suspect Kieran but they're very interested in an ex-juvenile delinquent who's now his pro shop assistant. Finally qualifying for the PGA championship at Winged Foot, Kieran is threatened in book 2 by the arson destruction of his pro shop, the death of one of the firefighters and the suspicious death of his caddy. *Booklist* called it "the best golfing mystery on the market."

Kieran Lanahan...lawyer turned country club golf pro in Westchester County, New York
- ❑ ❑   1 - Local Knowledge (1995)
- ❑ ❑   2 - Buried Lies (1996)
- ❑ ❑   3 - Outside Agency (1997)

■ DANIEL, David

Boston-born David Daniel is department chair of communications and media at Newbury College in Massachusetts, where he teaches film studies. He has published several thrillers, including *The Tuesday Man* (1990) and over 50 short stories in addition to the series featuring private eye Alex Rasmussen who walks the mean streets of rundown mill town Lowell, Massachusetts, hometown of Jack Kerouac and current home to the second-largest Cambodian community in the U.S., outside of Los Angeles. This series opener about the clash of a town's newest immigrants with Yankee tradition won the St. Martin's Press/PWA Best First Private Eye Novel competition. Daniel recently collaborated with CNN broadcaster Chris Carpenter to write *Murder at the Baseball Hall of Fame* (1996) and *Murder at the Tennis Hall of Fame* (1997).

Alex Rasmussen...private investigator in Lowell, Massachusetts
- ❑ ❑ 1 - **The Heaven Stone (1994) SMP/PWA winner ★ Shamus nominee ☆**
- ❑ ❑ 2 - The Skelly Man (1995)

■ DANIEL, David & Chris Carpenter

Mystery author David Daniel and baseball broadcaster Chris Carpenter are collaborating on a new series featuring ex-cop turned private eye Frank Branco. In the series opener Branco witnesses the death of a former major league player while visiting the Baseball Hall of Fame. Hired by the dead player's ex-wife, Branco investigates what turns into a 30-year-old mystery from a bygone era of baseball. David Daniel teaches film studies at Newbury College in Brookline (MA) where he is department chair of communications and media. He is the author of more than 50 short stories and several thrillers in addition to a private eye series set in Lowell (MA). Chris Carpenter is a broadcaster for CNN in Boston where he produces a nationally syndicated baseball program. He too lives in the Boston area.

Frank Branco...ex-cop turned private eye in Boston, Massachusetts
- ❑ ❑ 1 - Murder at the Baseball Hall of Fame (1996)
- ❑ ❑ 2 - Murder at the Tennis Hall of Fame (1997)

■ DAVIS, J. Madison

J. Madison Davis has written a pair of mysteries featuring a white and black investigative pair in New Orleans who work for a woman from an old Creole family. In *White Rook* (1990) they deal with an extremist militia group and in *Red Knight* (1992) they're caught up in the attempted assassination of a former civil rights organizer. His nonseries novel, *The Murder of Frau Schuetz* (1988), was an Edgar nominee for best first novel. Currently a professor of fiction and film writing at the University of Oklahoma, Davis has written and compiled criticism on Edward Albee (1986), Dick Francis (1989), Robertson Davies (1989) and Stanislaw Lem (1990). Having started college intent on becoming an archaeologist, he has a degree in anthropology and has taken part in three digs. Born in Charlottesville, Virginia, he holds a Ph.D. from the University of Southern Mississippi.

Delbert "Dub" Greenert & Vonna Saucier...white & black investigator pair in New Orleans, Louisiana
- ❑ ❑ 1 - White Rook (1990)
- ❑ ❑ 2 - Red Knight (1992)

■ DAVIS, Kenn

Kenn Davis was the *San Francisco Chronicle* artist from 1959 until 1985, so it's no surprise his P.I. is suave and streetwise with an artistic eye and love of classical music. Black poet and private eye Carver Bascombe moves to San Francisco from Detroit and befriends an art dealer who becomes his mentor. Book 1, for which they shared an Edgar nomination, was co-written with John Stanley. Writing alone, Davis was Edgar-nominated for book 3 and Shamus-nominated for book 4. While still a teenager he penned comic strips, but an interest in photography and journalism led him to the *Chronicle*. With John Stanley, he wrote a series of short film scripts and a book about Humphrey Bogart titled *Bogart '48* (1979). His individual shows have been mounted in galleries from San Francisco to New York, Los Angeles, Boston, Denver and Orlando.

Carver Bascombe...suave black poet private eye in San Francisco, California
- ❑ ❑   1 - **The Dark Side (1976) [w/John Stanley] Edgar nominee** ☆
- ❑ ❑   2 - The Forza Trap (1979)
- ❑ ❑   3 - **Words Can Kill (1984) Edgar nominee** ☆
- ❑ ❑   4 - **Melting Point (1986) Shamus nominee** ☆
- ❑ ❑   5 - Nijinsky is Dead (1987)
- ❑ ❑   6 - As October Dies (1987)
- ❑ ❑   7 - Acts of Homicide (1989)
- ❑ ❑   8 - Blood of Poets (1990)

■ DAVIS, Thomas D.

Shamus-award winner Thomas D. Davis has worked as an insurance claims investigator, bar musician and college philosophy professor. He is the author of a philosophy textbook (now in its third edition) which introduces philosophical problems through his own short stories. Having written three brooding private eye novels with philosophical themes, Davis says he's now working on a much lighter mystery set in Italy. Since 1993, he and his wife have spent three months each year in a medieval Tuscan hill town about 30 minutes south of Florence. Since they have many Italian friends who speak no English, Davis gets a lot of practice on his Italian which he says is not nearly as good as his wife's. Their U.S. home base is in northern California where she works as a marriage and family counselor.

Dave Strickland...private eye in Azalea, California
- ❑ ❑   1 - **Suffer Little Children (1991) Shamus winner** ★
- ❑ ❑   2 - Murdered Sleep (1994)
- ❑ ❑   3 - Consuming Fire (1996)

■ DEANDREA, William L.

Three-time Edgar winner William DeAndrea (1952-1996) won consecutive Edgar awards in 1979 and 1980, one of only 3 writers to accomplish such a feat for adult fiction. DeAndrea won a third Edgar for nonfiction with *Encyclopedia Mysteriosa* (1994). His primary series featured New York television troubleshooter, Matt Cobb, whose first appearance won an Edgar for best first novel. Under the punning pseudonym Philip DeGrave (say it out loud), he wrote a pair of light mysteries, *Unholy Moses* (1985) and *Keep the Baby, Faith* (1986). His two historical mysteries were *The Lunatic Fringe* (1980) and *Five O'Clock Lightning* (1982) with its plot to kill Mickey Mantle in 1953. A longtime columnist for *The Armchair Detective*, DeAndrea once worked at Murder Ink bookstore in Manhattan where he met his wife Orania Papazoglou, who writes mysteries as Jane Haddam.

Clifford Driscoll...no-name American spy in New York, New York
- ❑ ❑   1 - Cronus (1984)
- ❑ ❑   2 - Snark (1985)
- ❑ ❑   3 - Azreal (1987)
- ❑ ❑   4 - Atropos (1990)

Lobo Blacke & Quinn Booker...crippled ex-frontier lawman & his biographer in Le Four, Wyoming
- ❑ ❑   1 - Written in Fire (1995)
- ❑ ❑   2 - The Fatal Elixir (1997)

Matt Cobb...network television executive in New York, New York
- ❑ ❑   1 - **Killed in the Ratings (1978) Edgar winner** ★
- ❑ ❑   2 - Killed in the Act (1981)
- ❑ ❑   3 - Killed with a Passion (1983)
- ❑ ❑   4 - Killed on the Ice (1984)
- ❑ ❑   5 - Killed in Paradise (1988)
- ❑ ❑   6 - Killed on the Rocks (1990)
- ❑ ❑   7 - Killed in Fringe Time (1995)
- ❑ ❑   8 - Killed in the Fog (1996)

Niccolo Benedetti, Prof.....world-renowned criminologist-professor in Sparta, New York
- ❏ ❏ 1 - **The HOG Murders (1979) Edgar winner ★**
- ❏ ❏ 2 - The Werewolf Murders (1992)
- ❏ ❏ 3 - The Manx Murders (1994)

■ DEAVER, Jeffery

Former Wall Street attorney Jeffery Wilds Deaver lived in the fast lane of $900-million-dollar financing deals in the 1980s while writing unpublished thrillers in his spare time. He says one was so bad he destroyed it in the law firm's document shredder. A full-time novelist since his 1990 Edgar nomination for *Manhattan Is My Beat*, he now divides his time between northern Virginia, Carmel (CA) and New York City. Editor of his high school literary magazine in suburban Chicago, he holds a journalism degree from the University of Missouri and has worked as a folk singer, songwriter, music teacher and magazine editor, all before graduating from Fordham University School of Law. His nonseries bestseller, *A Maiden's Grave* (1995), became an HBO original movie starring James Garner and Marlee Matlin.

Lincoln Rhyme & Amelia Sachs...disabled ex-head of NYPD forensics & rookie beat cop in New York
- ❏ ❏ 1 - The Bone Collector (1997)

Rune...NYPD detective in New York, New York
- ❏ ❏ 1 - **Manhattan is My Beat (1989) Edgar nominee ☆**
- ❏ ❏ 2 - Death of a Blue Movie Star (1990)
- ❏ ❏ 3 - Hard News (1991)

■ DEBROSSE, Jim

Newspaper reporter Jim DeBrosse has written a 3-book series featuring Cincinnati (OH) newspaper reporter Rick Decker who is, "brash, irreverent, and so personable that even criminals can't resist spilling their guts to him," said *Publishers Weekly* of *Hidden City* (1991). After suffering a romantic setback with his longtime girlfriend, Rick welcomes the distraction of a trip to the Caribbean in book 3, as he and his investigative partner Rebo Johnson set out to cover the disappearance of Justin Grammer, 22-year-old scion of one of Cincinnati's wealthiest families. Traveling incognito, Rick and Rebo book passage on the Southern Cross, the cruise ship where Justin was last seen, only to find that like the two of them, no one is who he seems to be. DeBrosse does his reporting in his hometown of Dayton (OH).

Rick Decker...investigative reporter in Cincinnati, Ohio
- ❏ ❏ 1 - The Serpentine Wall (1988)
- ❏ ❏ 2 - Hidden City (1991)
- ❏ ❏ 3 - Southern Cross (1994)

■ DEE, Ed

Former New York City police officer Ed Dee retired as a lieutenant in 1982 after 20 years in the department. He completed his undergraduate degree at Fordham University and attended law school while still on the force, later earning an M.F.A. in creative writing at Arizona State University. Dee says he "wanted to write about the department in a way that no one had done before...get to the heart of the experience of being a cop in a city like New York." In the series opener, Detectives Ryan and Gregory discover a body floating in a barrel off Peck Slip at South Street Seaport. Later they find it's the corpse of a murdered cop missing for 10 years. In a starred review of *Little Boy Blue* (1997), *Publishers Weekly* calls Ryan "a poet of his personal New York...captured by Dee as if he were Hopper painting it for *Police Gazette*."

Anthony Ryan & Joe Gregory...NYPD detective partners in New York
- ❏ ❏ 1 - 14 Peck Slip (1994)
- ❏ ❏ 2 - Bronx Angel (1995)
- ❏ ❏ 3 - Little Boy Blue (1997)

■ DEIGHTON, Len

Len Deighton was an immediate success with his first novel, *The Ipcress File* (1962), which introduced the working-class hero, his most original contribution to spy fiction. Although his protagonist had no name, Harry Palmer was assigned for the film adaptations and the name stuck. Extensive travel around the world was always part of Deighton's painstaking research. According to a *Contemporary Authors* interview, he once made half a million words of notes before beginning a novel. Highly praised as a writer of military history, he once worked as an assistant pastry cook at the Royal Festival Hall in London and wrote a French cookbook titled *Ou est le garlic* (1965), later reprinted as *Basic French Cooking* (1979). In 1977 he and Peter Mayle collaborated on *How To Be a Pregnant Father*.

Bernard Samson...middle-aged British spy in London, England
- ❏ ❏ 1 - Berlin Game (1983)
- ❏ ❏ 2 - Mexico Set (1984)
- ❏ ❏ 3 - London Match (1985)
- ❏ ❏ 4 - Spy Hook (1988)
- ❏ ❏ 5 - Spy Line (1989)
- ❏ ❏ 6 - Spy Sinker (1990)
- ❏ ❏ 7 - Faith (1994)
- ❏ ❏ 8 - Hope (1995)
- ❏ ❏ 9 - Charity (1996)

Harry Palmer...lazy cynical British agent with no name in London, England
- ❏ ❏ 1 - The Ipcress File (1962)
- ❏ ❏ 2 - Horse Under Water (1963)
- ❏ ❏ 3 - **Funeral in Berlin (1964) Edgar nominee** ☆
- ❏ ❏ 4 - The Billion Dollar Brain (1966)
- ❏ ❏ 5 - An Expensive Place to Die (1967)
- ❏ ❏ 6 - Spy Story (1974)
- ❏ ❏ 7 - Twinkle, Twinkle, Little Spy (1976)
  - U.S.-Catch a Falling Spy

■ DEMILLE, Nelson

After dropping out of Hofstra University in 1966, Nelson DeMille went to Vietnam as an infantry officer where he started keeping a combat diary. In 1997 he published an article about his first trip back, and plans to explore Vietnam (for the second time) in his next novel. DeMille says he told the officer's side of the war experience in *Word of Honor* (1985). Author of the 1997 bestseller *Plum Island*, DeMille also wrote a pair of trilogies featuring NYPD homicide detectives Joe Keller and Joe Ryker. Under the name Ellen Kay, he authored a biography of Barbara Walters and has also written under the names Jack Cannon, Kurt Ladner, Brad Matthews and Michael Weaver. DeMille completed his undergraduate degree from Hofstra in 1970 and worked as an insurance fraud investigator before launching his writing career.

Joe Keller, Det. Sgt.....NYPD homicide detective in New York
- ❏ ❏ 1 - The Smack Man (1975)
- ❏ ❏ 2 - The Cannibal (1975)
- ❏ ❏ 3 - Night of the Phoenix (1975)

Joe Ryker, Det. Sgt.....NYPD homicide detective in New York
- ❏ ❏ 1 - The Sniper (1974)
- ❏ ❏ 2 - The Hammer of God (1974)
- ❏ ❏ 3 - The Agent of Death (1975)

■ DEXTER, Colin

When Colin Dexter was named Diamond Dagger Award winner at the Palace of Westminster in 1997, CWA members wanted to know if book 12 would really be the last appearance of Inspector Morse, but Dexter wasn't letting on. Former British national crosswords champion ('60s-'70s), Dexter spent 13 years teaching Latin and Greek before retiring because of his profound hearing loss. On a 1973 Welsh holiday with nothing to do, he created Inspector Morse and gave the Inspector his own personal interests— Wagner, crosswords, the classics and beer. Brilliant and eccentric, Morse is well-known to TV audiences thanks to 31 programs filmed in Britain and shown on PBS. With a record rivaling that of Alfred Hitchcock, Dexter has appeared in 28 of 31. In what was billed as his farewell gesture, Dexter finally disclosed Morse's first name on the last page of *Death Is Now My Neighbour* (1996).

Morse, Chief Insp.....chief inspector in England
- ❑ ❑ 1 - Last Bus to Woodstock (1975)
- ❑ ❑ 2 - Last Seen Wearing (1976)
- ❑ ❑ 3 - The Silent World of Nicholas Quinn (1977)
- ❑ ❑ 4 - **Service of All the Dead (1979) Silver Dagger winner ★**
- ❑ ❑ 5 - **The Dead of Jericho (1981) Silver Dagger winner ★**
- ❑ ❑ 6 - The Riddle of the Third Mile (1983)
- ❑ ❑ 7 - The Secret of Annexe 3 (1986)
- ❑ ❑ 8 - **The Wench is Dead (1989) Gold Dagger winner ★**
- ❑ ❑ 9 - The Jewel That Was Ours (1991)
- ❑ ❑ 10 - **The Way Through the Woods (1992) Gold Dagger winner ★**
- ❑ ❑ 11 - The Daughters of Cain (1994)
- ❑ ❑ 12 - **Death Is Now My Neighbor (1996) Dagger nominee ☆**

■ DIBDIN, Michael

Gold Dagger winner Michael Dibdin is the creator of Italian police inspector Aurelio Zen introduced in *Ratking*, the CWA pick for best novel published in England in 1988. The complex plot deals with the kidnapping of a rich industrialist in Perugia where Dibdin once lived. By book 5, Zen's commitment to work is at an all-time low, and he finds himself disgraced in Naples—having the time of his life. New in the U.S. in 1996 is a Dibdin thriller set in Seattle with police detective Kristine Kjarstad (*Dark Specter*). After attending schools in England and Scotland, Dibdin later earned degress in English literature from British (Sussex) and Canadian (Alberta) universities. During his 4 years in Italy he taught English at the University of Perugia, and after living in Oxford for a number of years, he is now in Seattle (WA).

Aurelio Zen, Insp.....Italian police inspector in Rome, Italy
- ❑ ❑ 1 - **Ratking (1988) Gold Dagger winner ★**
- ❑ ❑ 2 - **Vendetta (1990) CWA '92 winner ★**
- ❑ ❑ 3 - Cabal (1992)
- ❑ ❑ 4 - Dead Lagoon (1994)
- ❑ ❑ 5 - Cosi Fan Tutti (1996)

■ DICKINSON, Peter

Two-time Gold Dagger winner Peter Dickinson is the author of 20 adult novels and 27 children's books. Among his 17 mysteries are the two Gold Dagger winners in the Supt. Pibble series. Published in the U.S. as *The Glass-Sided Ants' Nest*, book 1 has Pibble solving a case involving an entire New Guinea tribe brought to England by an anthropologist. Living in a retirement home and preparing to kill himself in the last book in the series, Pibble stumbles onto a murder. The *LA Times Book Review* called it "just possibly a masterpiece". In his first children's books (*The Changes: A Trilogy*, 1975), Dickinson created a modern England where the wizard Merlin has been revived, and under the influence of a mad chemist, hurls

Britain back to the 5th century in a dramatic anti-technology statement. Former assistant editor of *Punch* magazine ('52-'69), Dickinson was born in Zambia (formerly Northern Rhodesia) where his father was a colonial civil servant.

James Pibble, Supt.....Scotland Yard superintendent in London, England
- ❏ ❏ 1 - **Skin Deep (1968) Gold Dagger winner ★**
    U.S.-The Glass-Sided Ants' Nest
- ❏ ❏ 2 - **A Pride of Heroes (1969) Gold Dagger winner ★**
    U.S.-The Old English Peep Show
- ❏ ❏ 3 - The Seals (1970)
    U.S.-The Sinful Stones
- ❏ ❏ 4 - Sleep and His Brother (1971)
- ❏ ❏ 5 - The Lizard in the Cup (1972)
- ❏ ❏ 6 - One Foot in the Grave (1979)

■ DISHER, Garry

Australian born Garry Disher attended Stanford University on a creative writing fellowship in the late '70s and began writing crime novels as a result of his love for contemporary North American fiction. His Aussie bank robber Wyatt has appeared in 5 books since *Kickback* (1991) introduced the series. Among more than 15 other titles Disher has written are several books for children, including *The Bamboo Flute*, 1993 winner of the Australian Children's Book Council Book-of-the-Year Award. This coming of age novel set during the Depression grew out of a heartache in his father's childhood. It tells of a 12-year-old boy's longing to restore his family to the happiness missing since money problems forced the sale of the mother's piano. Disher grew up in rural South Australia, travelled widely and now lives on the Victorian coast.

Wyatt...Aussie bank robber in Melbourne, Australia
- ❏ ❏ 1 - Kickback (1991)
- ❏ ❏ 2 - Paydirt (1992)
- ❏ ❏ 3 - Deathdeal (1993)
- ❏ ❏ 4 - Crosskill (1994)
- ❏ ❏ 5 - Port Villa Blues (1995)

■ DOBYNS, Stephen

Stephen Dobyns is a published poet and novelist, with 9 collections of poetry, 18 novels and one nonfiction book, including 9 Saratoga mysteries featuring ex-cop and ex-stable security guard Charlie Bradshaw. Son of an Episcopal minister, Dobyns was briefly a reporter at the *Detroit News*, and has been teaching English, creative writing and poetry at various universities for almost 30 years. *People* magazine said of *The Church of Dead Girls* (1997), "Picture *Our Town* as retold by Stephen King." King himself is reported to have written a 3-page letter heaping praise on Dobyns' thriller, linking its theme of collective hysteria to one of Dobyns's own poems ("The Town" from *Cemetery Nights*, 1987). The King quote chosen for the [*Dead Girls*] cover..."If ever there was a tale for a moonless night, a high wind, and a creaking floor, this is it."

Charlie Bradshaw...ex-cop ex-stable security guard turned detective in Saratoga Springs, New York
- ❏ ❏ 1 - Saratoga Longshot (1976)
- ❏ ❏ 2 - Saratoga Swimmer (1981)
- ❏ ❏ 3 - Saratoga Headhunter (1985)
- ❏ ❏ 4 - Saratoga Snapper (1986)
- ❏ ❏ 5 - Saratoga Bestiary (1988)
- ❏ ❏ 6 - Saratoga Hexameter (1990)
- ❏ ❏ 7 - Saratoga Haunting (1993)
- ❏ ❏ 8 - Saratoga Backtalk (1994)
- ❏ ❏ 9 - Saratoga Fleshpot (1995)

■ DOHERTY, P. C.

Since 1986 Oxford history scholar and school headmaster P.C. Doherty has written more than 36 books in at least 7 historical mystery series with settings from Chaucer's time to the 16th century. His books appear under the names Michael Clynes, Ann Dukthas, C.L. Grace, Paul Harding and his own, P.C. Doherty. It is suspected that a new series published under the name Anna Apostolou (*Murder in Macedon*, 1997) is his 8th historical mystery series. There are 3 Doherty series beginning with the 10 books featuring Hugh Corbett, trusted clerk and frequent spy for Edward I. The other Doherty series feature Matthew Jenkyn, 15th century double-agent spy, in 2 books, and Nicholas Chirke, a young lawyer who narrates at least 4 Canterbury Tales. Doherty, who has a doctorate in history from Oxford, lives in Essex, England.

Hugh Corbett...spy for King Edward I in England
- ❏ ❏ 1 - Satan in St. Mary's (1986)
- ❏ ❏ 2 - The Crown in Darkness (1988)
- ❏ ❏ 3 - Spy in Chancery (1988)
- ❏ ❏ 4 - The Angel of Death (1989)
- ❏ ❏ 5 - The Prince of Darkness (1992)
- ❏ ❏ 6 - Murder Wears a Cowl (1992)
- ❏ ❏ 7 - The Assassin in the Greenwood (1993)
- ❏ ❏ 8 - The Song of a Dark Angel (1994)
- ❏ ❏ 9 - Satan's Fire (1995)
- ❏ ❏ 10 - The Devil's Hunt (1996)

Matthew Jenkyn...15th century soldier, double agent spy in England
- ❏ ❏ 1 - The Whyte Hart (1988)
- ❏ ❏ 2 - The Serpent Among the Lilies (1990)

Nicholas Chirke...young medieval lawyer in England
- ❏ ❏ 1 - An Ancient Evil (1994)
- ❏ ❏ 2 - A Tapestry of Murders (1995)
- ❏ ❏ 3 - A Tournament of Murders (1996)
- ❏ ❏ 4 - Ghostly Murders (1997)

■ DOLD, Gaylord

Former law professor Gaylord Dold has written a 9-book series featuring '50s Wichita P.I. Mitch Roberts, a guy who loves the St. Louis Cardinals, chess, Rita Hayworth and cats. The first 6 were Fawcett paperbacks, with books 3, 4 and 5 earning Shamus nominations in that category. At the start of book 9, Mitch is temporarily living in London where he's hired by an insurance company to deliver the ransom that will free a kidnapped woman doctor in Zaire. Dold's new character is a young Chinese-American woman cop named Grace Wu, who goes under cover in the San Francisco drug trade in *Schedule Two* (1996). Dold studied for two years at the London School of Economics after receiving both his M.A. and J.D. degrees from the University of California. He lives in Wichita (KS), where he is managing editor of Watermark Press, a small publishing house specializing in literary fiction.

Grace Wu...undercover agent for the SFPD and DEA in San Francisco, California
- ❏ ❏ 1 - Schedule Two (1996)

Mitch Roberts...1950s private eye in Wichita, Kansas
- ❑ ❑ 1 - Hot Summer, Cold Murder (1987)
- ❑ ❑ 2 - Cold Cash (1987)
- ❑ ❑ 3 - **Snake Eyes (1987) Shamus nominee** ☆
- ❑ ❑ 4 - **Bone Pile (1988) Shamus nominee** ☆
- ❑ ❑ 5 - **Muscle and Blood (1989) Shamus nominee** ☆
- ❑ ❑ 6 - Disheveled City (1990)
- ❑ ❑ 7 - A Penny for the Old Guy (1991)
- ❑ ❑ 8 - Rude Boys (1992)
- ❑ ❑ 9 - The World Beat (1993)

■ DONALDSON, D. J.

Donald J. Donaldson lasted 6 months as a 9th grade science teacher before being lured into a Ph.D. program in human anatomy by a master teacher who used detective stories to make his points. These days Donaldson teaches microscopic anatomy and does research on wound healing at the University of Tennessee Medical School in Memphis. His mystery series features plenty of forensic science, as he amply demonstrated to the American Academy of Forensic Sciences in a 1996 presentation on his mysteries. Donaldson's continuing characters are Andy Broussard, Chief Medical Examiner for Orleans Parish, and his suicide investigator Kit Franklyn, who also does psychological profiling for the New Orleans Police Department. A man who always has lemon drops in his pockets, Broussard owns six 1957 T-birds. In his words, "Six is abundance. Seven would be eccentricity."

Kit Franklyn & Andy Broussard...criminal psychologist & medical examiner in New Orleans, Louisiana
- ❑ ❑ 1 - Cajun Nights (1988)
- ❑ ❑ 2 - Blood on the Bayou (1991)
- ❑ ❑ 3 - No Mardi Gras for the Dead (1992)
- ❑ ❑ 4 - New Orleans Requiem (1994)
- ❑ ❑ 5 - Louisiana Fever (1996)
- ❑ ❑ 6 - Sleeping with the Crawfish (1997)

■ DOOLITTLE, Jerome

Former Carter presidential speechwriter Jerome Doolittle is the author of a 6-book series featuring a political consultant and one-time wrestler turned private eye in Cambridge (MA). The series opener, *Body Scissors* (1990), was nominated for a Shamus award. After serving as U.S. embassy spokesman in Casablanca and Vientiane from 1966 to 1970, he opened a restaurant in the Laotian capital, but returned to the States to work for Carter during the 1976 presidential campaign. In addition to his Tom Bethany mysteries, Doolittle has written a novel about the secret air war in Laos (*The Bombing Officer*) and two books on the American wilderness. He once worked as a feature writer, columnist and editor at *The Washington Post* and later taught writing at Harvard. A Middlebury College (VT) graduate, he lives in Connecticut.

Tom Bethany...political consultant and former wrestler in Cambridge, Massachusetts
- ❑ ❑ 1 - **Body Scissors (1990) Shamus nominee** ☆
- ❑ ❑ 2 - Strangle Hold (1991)
- ❑ ❑ 3 - Bear Hug (1992)
- ❑ ❑ 4 - Head Lock (1993)
- ❑ ❑ 5 - Half Nelson (1994)
- ❑ ❑ 6 - Kill Story (1995)

■ DOSS, James D.

James D. Doss is the creator of a new mystery series blending Native American mysticism with the modern crime scene of southwestern Colorado. Shaman Daisy Perika joins forces with Ute police sergeant Charlie Moon and his Anglo colleague Scott Parris in tales of equal parts science and magic, ghosts and police work. Doss lives in northern New Mexico where during the week he works as a member of the technical staff at the Los Alamos National Laboratory and on weekends writes mystery novels from a small log cabin in the Sangre de Cristo mountains above Taos. He credits his electrical engineering background with giving him the eye for detail necessary in plotting a good mystery. In addition to continuing his Shaman series, he plans to develop a new series for young adults.

Charlie Moon & Scott Parris...Ute police sergeant & Anglo colleague in Granite Creek, Colorado
- ❏ ❏ 1 - The Shaman Sings (1994)
- ❏ ❏ 2 - The Shaman Laughs (1995)
- ❏ ❏ 3 - The Shaman's Mistake (1996)
- ❏ ❏ 4 - The Shaman's Dream (1997)

■ DOUGLAS, Arthur [P]

Under the pseudonym Arthur Douglas, Gerald Hammond wrote 3 suspense thrillers during the 1980s, starring British Army major Jonathan Craythorne. Although the Major makes an appearance in *The Goods* (1985), also published under the Douglas name, he is only a minor character. Hammond's military experience includes service in the Queen's Royal Regiment and two years as architect for the Navy, Army, Air Force Institute. Former resident architect at St. Andrews University, Hammond has been writing full-time since 1983 from his home in Scotland. Best known for his long-running series featuring small-town gunsmith Keith Calder, he writes another sporting series with a dog breeder named John Cunningham, whose partners in detection include Isobel Kitts (vet) and Beth Catrell (kennelmaid).

Jonathan Craythorne, Major...British Army major in England
- ❏ ❏ 1 - Last Rights (1986)
- ❏ ❏ 2 - A Very Wrong Number (1987)
- ❏ ❏ 3 - A Worm Turns (1988)

■ DOUGLAS, John [P]

Shamus nominee John Douglas is the author of two private eye novels featuring a West Virginia photographer named Jack Reese. *Shawnee Alley Fire* (1987), which introduced the series, was nominated for Best First Private Eye Novel in 1988. Other best -first nominees that year were Les Roberts, Parnell Hall, Robert Bowman and Michael Allegretto, who won for his first Jacob Lomax novel. Douglas's intrepid journalist returns in *Haunts* (1990). Born in Maryland, the author is a journalist living in West Virginia, according to Hubin in *Crime Fiction II*.

Jack Reese...photographer in Shawnee, West Virginia
- ❏ ❏ 1 - **Shawnee Alley Fire (1987) Shamus nominee** ☆
- ❏ ❏ 2 - Haunts (1990)

■ DOWLING, Gregory

After graduating from Oxford, Gregory Dowling went to Italy to teach for a year and continues to live there. In a 4-book series beginning with *Double Take* (1985), his American sleuth, January Esposito, has a nice steady job teaching English in Verona. Along with interesting tie-ins with Italian art history, Dowling excels at funny minor characters. In their review of book 2, Kirkus called it "a cosy thriller...skewering Neapolitans, stuffy Brits, pomposities of all persuasions." Dowling was the translator of Christina Comencini's first novel, *The Missing Pages* (1994), the story of a rich man and his 19-year-old daughter who becomes mute without explanation. Missing pages from her diary hold the key. Born and educated in Bristol, England, he makes his home in Venice.

January Esposito...American teacher of English in Tuscany, Italy
- ❑ ❑ 1 - Double Take (1985)
- ❑ ❑ 2 - Neapolitan Reel (1988)
  U.S.-See Naples and Kill
- ❑ ❑ 3 - Every Picture Tells a Story (1991)
- ❑ ❑ 4 - A Nice Steady Job (1994)

■ DOWNING, Warwick

Former Denver assistant U.S. attorney, Warwick Downing says he was born into the law. His father and grandfather were lawyers, his brother is a lawyer and his sister is married to one. He's written 3 paperback originals featuring a Denver defense attorney and 3 private eye novels with a Denver setting. More recently, he wrote a legal thriller, *Choice of Evils* (1994 pbo), featuring a 40-something woman attorney from the Denver office of the National Association of Special Prosecutors. Slated to join the prosecution team on a highly controversial murder case, she's bumped in favor of an Arab prosecutor with American connections. On trial is an ex-Marine, all-American golden boy accused of killing a subject of the Arab kingdom of Rashidi. Before she knows it, Frances "Frankie" Rommel is the defense lawyer trying to save him.

Jack S. Bard...defense attorney in Denver, Colorado
- ❑ ❑ 1 - A Clear Case of Murder (1990)
- ❑ ❑ 2 - The Water Cure (1992)
- ❑ ❑ 3 - A Lingering Doubt (1993)

Joe Reddman...private investigator in Denver, Colorado
- ❑ ❑ 1 - The Player (1974)
- ❑ ❑ 2 - The Mountains West of Town (1975)
- ❑ ❑ 3 - The Gambler, the Minstrel & the Dance Hall Queen (1976)

■ DRUMMOND, Ivor [P]

Ivor Drummond is one of the pseudonyms of Roger Erskine Longrigg who writes horror as Domini Taylor, general fiction as Longrigg and mysteries as Ivor Drummond and Frank Parrish. Drummond's wealthy adventuring trio, introduced in *The Man With the Tiny Head* (1969), includes Lady Jennifer Norrington, Count Alesandro Di Ganzarello and Coleridge Tucker, III, also known as Jenny, Sandro and Colly. Writing in *St. James Guide* (4th edition), George Kelley picks *The Necklace of Skulls* (1977) as the best in the series. Author of more than 40 books, Longrigg has a degree in modern history from Oxford. During the '70s he also published 4 nonfiction books on the history of horse racing, foxhunting and the sport of English squires.

Jennifer Norrington, Alesandro Di Ganzarello & Coleridge Tucker, III...James Bond-like adventuring trio in London, England
- ❑ ❑ 1 - The Man with the Tiny Head (1969)
- ❑ ❑ 2 - The Priests of the Abomination (1970)
- ❑ ❑ 3 - The Frog in the Moonflower (1972)
- ❑ ❑ 4 - The Jaws of the Watchdog (1973)
- ❑ ❑ 5 - The Power of the Bug (1974)
- ❑ ❑ 6 - A Tank of Sacred Eels (1976)
- ❑ ❑ 7 - The Necklace of Skulls (1977)
- ❑ ❑ 8 - A Stench of Poppies (1978)
- ❑ ❑ 9 - The Diamonds of Loreta (1980)

■ DUBOIS, Brendan

Former newspaper reporter Brendan DuBois is the creator of the Lewis Cole mysteries featuring a magazine writer from Tyler Beach, New Hampshire. Cole is a former Department of Defense research analyst who investigates things mysterious in and around the Granite State. The third book in this series, *Shattered Shell*, is scheduled for 1998. Author of more than 30 short stories that have been widely anthologized, DuBois has won a Shamus award and twice been nominated for an Edgar award in the short story category. His short fiction has been published in *Playboy*, *Ellery Queen's Mystery Magazine* and *Alfred Hitchcock's Mystery Magazine*. DuBois is also at work on what publishers call a high-concept thriller—this one with a Castro connection. Specifically, the book will answer the question "What if the Cuban missile crisis had turned into a full-fledged war?" DuBois is a lifelong resident of the New Hampshire coast.

Lewis Cole...magazine writer in Tyler Beach, New Hampshire
- ❏ ❏ 1 - Dead Sand (1994)
- ❏ ❏ 2 - Black Tide (1995)

■ DUKTHAS, Ann [P]

Ann Dukthas is one several pseudonyms used by the prolific P.C. Doherty, Oxford scholar and school headmaster. In the Dukthas series, published only in the U.S. and only in hardcover, Nicholas Segalla is condemned to travel through time solving the great mysteries of history. He tells his tales to Oxford lecturer Ann Dukthas. The big question in book 1—did Mary Queen of Scots murder her husband? In book 2 Segalla uncovers the mysterious fate of Marie Antoinette's young son, left behind when his mother was beheaded in 1793. History says he died, but rumors persist that he escaped. Book 3 moves to 1889 Vienna to uncover the truth about the supposed murder/suicide of Archduke Randolph, heir to the Hapsburg throne, and his beautiful young mistress. It's back to 16th century England in book 4, amidst rumors of a plot to poison Queen Mary Tudor (*In the Time of the Poisoned Queen*, 1998).

Nicholas Segalla...time-traveling scholar in England
- ❏ ❏ 1 - A Time for the Death of a King (1994)
- ❏ ❏ 2 - The Prince Lost to Time (1995)
- ❏ ❏ 3 - The Time of Murder at Mayerling (1996)

■ DUNBAR, Tony

In addition to his legal duties, Tony Dunbar's fictional sleuth, New Orleans attorney Tubby Dubonnet, manages to find time to referee the romantic entanglements of his ex-wife and their three daughters. Good thing he has college wrestling experience. The only thing crazier than Tubby's family life is the parade of bizarre clients marching through his office. "For all the eccentric characters and bizarre events that Mr. Dunbar stuffs into his colorful narrative, the story still holds up in court," said the *NYTBR* of book three. Fried oyster po-boy-lovin' Tubby returns in *Shelter from the Storm* (1998) when a deluge (of rain) threatens Mardi Gras. A graduate of Brandeis University and Tulane University School of Law, Dunbar is also the author of four nonfiction books. He is not related to mystery writer Sophie Dunbar who writes about sexy New Orleans hairdresser Claire Claiborne.

Tubby Dubonnet...bon vivant defense attorney in New Orleans, Louisiana
- ❏ ❏ 1 - Crooked Man (1994)
- ❏ ❏ 2 - City of Beads (1995)
- ❏ ❏ 3 - Trick Question (1997)

■ DUNCAN, W. Glenn

Shamus award-winning author, W. Glenn Duncan, wrote 6 Gold Medal paperbacks with an ex-Dallas cop turned private eye known as Rafferty, who's as comfortable in big bucks Dallas as he is on the violent prairies five minutes out of town. As noted on the cover of the series opener, *Rafferty's Rules* (1987), this P.I. has a rule against killing for hire, but doesn't mind stirring up a little trouble. His steady date is a sexy antique dealer named Hilda Gardner. His good buddy is Cowboy, the "most dangerous man on earth." Duncan's Shamus award was for book 6, *Fatal Sisters* (1990). A former newsman and professional pilot, Duncan has lived in California, Florida, Iowa, Ohio, Oregon and Texas. He currently lives with his wife and family in Australia.

Rafferty...ex-cop private eye in Dallas, Texas
- ❏ ❏ 1 - Rafferty's Rules (1987)
- ❏ ❏ 2 - Last Seen Alive (1987)
- ❏ ❏ 3 - Poor Dead Cricket (1988)
- ❏ ❏ 4 - Wrong Place, Wrong Time (1989)
- ❏ ❏ 5 - Cannon's Mouth (1990)
- ❏ ❏ **6 - Fatal Sisters (1990) Shamus winner ★**

■ DUNDEE, Wayne

Six-time Shamus nominee Wayne Dundee wrote 3 novels featuring Joe Hannibal, a blue-collar private eye from Rockford (IL). The *Houston Chronicle* called Joe sexy and sensitive, praising book 1 for its "sexuality minus violence and brutality, and strongly independent men and women." Each of the three Hannibal books was nominated for a Shamus award in a different category—book 1 for Best First P.I. Novel, book 2 for Best P.I. Novel, and book 3 for Best P.I. Paperback Original. In 1987 Dundee earned an Edgar nomination in the short story category for "Body Count" (*Mean Streets*, Mysterious Press). The same short story was also nominated for a Shamus award, as were two of Dundee's other short stories (1986, 1991). A former editor of *Hardboiled* magazine, he lives in Rockford (IL).

Joe Hannibal...blue-collar P.I. in Rockford, Ilinois
- ❏ ❏ **1 - The Burning Season (1988) Shamus nominee** ☆
- ❏ ❏ **2 - The Skintight Shroud (1990) Shamus nominee** ☆
- ❏ ❏ **3 - The Brutal Ballet (1992) Shamus nominee** ☆

■ DUNNING, John

Denver author and renowned book hunter John Dunning rents storage for his 8,000 volumes, mostly mysteries saved from the Old Algonquin Book Store which he closed in 1994. His storage space is pristine and climate controlled, with oriental rugs on the floor of his reading area. According to Dunning, book collecting is the second greatest game in the world. "The greatest game is writing them yourself," he told *People* magazine in a 1995 interview. His best known work is the Nero Wolfe Award winner *Booked To Die* (1992), which introduces Denver cop Cliff Janeway and the fascinating world of book collecting. Despite having dropped out of school in the 10th grade to join the Army, Dunning has taught college courses in journalism, written for the *Denver Post* and *Christian Science Monitor*, and served as press secretary for one of Congresswoman Pat Schroder's political campaigns in the '70s.

Cliff Janeway...cop and rare book expert in Denver, Colorado
- ❏ ❏ **1 - Booked to Die (1992) Nero Wolfe winner ★**
- ❏ ❏ **2 - Bookman's Wake (1995) Dagger, Edgar & Macavity nominee** ☆☆☆

■ EDDENDEN, A. E.

Arthur Edward Eddenden spent 40 years in Canadian advertising, specializing in graphic design, art direction and rendering, before he saw his first mystery published at the age of 60. He has since written two others featuring '40s policemen, Insp. Albert V. Tretheway (pronounced tre-THOO-ey) and Constable Jonathan (Jake) Small, from Fort York (read Hamilton), Ontario. Regulars at their local movie house, these two police officers see about 150 movies a year, helping them make the connection when local pranks seem to be inspired by films being shown during book 3, *Murder at the Movies* (1996). Scenes from a Laurel and Hardy comedy and *Wizard of Oz* progress to murders à la *Gunga Din* and *Beau Geste*. Realizing *Gone With the Wind* is coming next, Tretheway and Small fear that someone wants to burn Fort York to the ground.

Albert V. Tretheway, Insp. & Jake Small, Constable...1940s Canadian police officers in Fort York, Ontario
- ❑ ❑   1 - A Good Year for Murder (1988)
- ❑ ❑   2 - Murder on the Thirteenth (1992)
- ❑ ❑   3 - Murder at the Movies (1996)

■ EDWARDS, Martin

Martin Edwards is a Liverpool solicitor, as is his fictional creation Harry Devlin who has appeared in 5 novels and numerous short stories featured in British anthologies and *Ellery Queen's Mystery Magazine*. The series has also been optioned for British television. Starting with *All the Lonely People* (1991), which was short-listed for the CWA Creasey Award, Edwards' series titles are taken from '60s pop songs. Scheduled for U.S. publication in the spring of 1998 is book 5, *Eve of Destruction*. Edwards read law at Balliol College, Oxford, the alma mater of Lord Peter Wimsey, Captain Hook and Dr. Gideon Fell, as well as almost 30 modern crime writers, including Robert Barnard. In addition to 5 nonfiction books on legal topics, Edwards has written essays and reviews for such magazines as *CADS* and *Deadly Pleasures*.

Harry Devlin...solicitor in Liverpool, England
- ❑ ❑   1 - All the Lonely People (1991)
- ❑ ❑   2 - Suspicious Minds (1992)
- ❑ ❑   3 - I Remember You (1993)
- ❑ ❑   4 - Yesterday's Papers (1994)
- ❑ ❑   5 - Eve of Destruction (1996)

■ EGLETON, Clive

Clive Egleton is a recognized master of the spy thriller who has written dozens of nonseries titles, as well as 5 Peter Ashton books and 3 novels featuring resistance fighter David Garnett. Under the names Patrick Blake and John Tarrant he has written at least 5 other works of espionage fiction. The exploits of Egleton's British agents are drawn from his own experience as an agent in Cyprus, the Persian Gulf and East Africa during the late '50s and early '60s. After retiring from a 30-year military career, he began work for the Ministry of Defence as a civil servant in 1981. In an interview with *Contemporary Authors* shortly thereafter, he told about writing his books on the train from Portsmouth Harbor to Waterloo Station (London) during his daily commute.

David Garnett...resistance fighter in England
- ❑ ❑   1 - A Piece of Resistance (1970)
- ❑ ❑   2 - Last Post for a Partisan (1971)
- ❑ ❑   3 - The Judas Mandate (1972)

Peter Ashton...British spy in England
- ❑ ❑   1 - Hostile Intent (1993)
- ❑ ❑   2 - A Killing in Moscow (1994)
- ❑ ❑   3 - Death Throes (1995)
- ❑ ❑   4 - A Lethal Involvement (1995)
- ❑ ❑   5 - Warning Shot (1996)

■ **ELKINS, Aaron**

Multiple-award winning author Aaron Elkins launched his mystery writing career with "the skeleton detective," an anthropology professor who moved around Europe teaching at U.S. military bases. Elkins himself taught anthropology for the University of Maryland's Overseas Division with assignments that took him to NATO installations in England, Germany, Holland, Spain, Sicily and Sardinia. He kept a journal and made good use of his notes, winning a best novel Edgar for book 4, *Old Bones* (1987). New in '98 will be another Gideon Oliver book. His shorter series features art museum curator Chris Norgren in 3 books with more to follow. With wife Charlotte, he writes a golf series featuring a struggling woman golfer named Lee Ofsted and her cop boyfriend Graham Sheldon, appearing in *Wicked Slice* (1989), *Rotten Lies* (1995), and *Cutting Strokes* (1997). The Elkins live on the coast of Rhode Island.

Chris Norgren...art museum curator in Seattle, Washington
- ❏ ❏ 1 - A Deceptive Clarity (1987)
- ❏ ❏ 2 - A Glancing Light (1991)
- ❏ ❏ 3 - **Old Scores (1993) Nero Wolfe winner ★ Agatha nominee ☆**

Gideon Oliver...anthropology professor in Port Angeles, Washington
- ❏ ❏ 1 - Fellowship of Fear (1982)
- ❏ ❏ 2 - The Dark Place (1983)
- ❏ ❏ 3 - Murder in the Queen's Armes (1985)
- ❏ ❏ 4 - **Old Bones (1987) Edgar winner ★**
- ❏ ❏ 5 - Curses! (1989)
- ❏ ❏ 6 - Icy Clutches (1990)
- ❏ ❏ 7 - Make No Bones (1991)
- ❏ ❏ 8 - Dead Men's Hearts (1994)
- ❏ ❏ 9 - Twenty Blue Devils (1997)

■ **ELLROY, James**

James Ellroy has been described as dark, dense, sex obsessed and emotionally complex—tags he says he hopes to live up to. Once a golf caddy at the Bel Air Country Club, he was a drunk and a petty burglar until double pneumonia nearly killed him in 1977. He joined AA, got sober, and spent 10 months writing *Brown's Requiem* (1981) in longhand. His 2nd book, *Clandestine* (1982), earned him an Edgar nomination and freedom to quit his caddy job. Among his early books were 3 featuring Lloyd Hopkins, a detective sergeant in the Rampart Division. Then came the L.A. Quartet—*The Black Dahlia* (1987), *The Big Nowhere* (1988), *L.A. Confidential* (1990) and *White Jazz* (1992). In a '92 interview with *Contemporary Authors*, Ellroy talked about his plans to produce a series (perhaps 10 novels) tracing 20th century America through crime—all part of his plan to be the greatest crime writer of all time.

Lloyd Hopkins...detective sergeant in the Rampart Division in Los Angeles, California
- ❏ ❏ 1 - Blood on the Moon (1984)
- ❏ ❏ 2 - Because the Night (1984)
- ❏ ❏ 3 - Suicide Hill (1986)

■ **ELY, Ron**

Ron Ely is best known as the film actor who once played Tarzan and later hosted the Miss America pageant. He also starred as '60s cult hero Doc Savage in *Doc Savage: Man of Bronze*, producer George Pal's last film. And now it seems he's writing California mysteries featuring Jake Sands, retired salvage agent and reluctant recoverer of lost things. Think "Travis McGee meets Baywatch," suggested one enthusiastic reviewer. *East Beach* (1995) is set in the world of Santa Barbara beach volleyball and Jake buys himself the neon shorts and cool shades required to play. Seems he's already got the body and the skill.

Jake Sands...professional recoverer of lost things in Santa Barbara, California
- ❏ ❏ 1 - Night Shadows (1994)
- ❏ ❏ 2 - East Beach (1995)

■ EMERSON, Earl

Lt. Earl Emerson of the Seattle Fire Department is the creator of Mac Fontana, formerly a big city arson investigator, now fire chief and acting sheriff in the small town of Staircase, Washington, a widower raising a young son. The author is a married father of three who's been fighting big city fires for 20 years. He also writes private eye fiction featuring ex-cop Thomas Black in a series that has earned five nominations and a Shamus award for best private eye novel. Black, who drives a pickup truck and share the author's enthusiasm for bicycling, makes his 10th appearance in *Deception Pass* (1997), named for a stunning natural landmark on the Puget Sound coast. Emerson, who says he wrote a dozen full-length novels before selling his first book, was the 1996 recipient of the Spotted Owl award from Friends of Mystery for the best Pacific Northwest mystery.

Mac Fontana...ex-firefighter and arson investigator in Staircase, Washington
- ❏ ❏ 1 - Black Hearts and Slow Dancing (1988)
- ❏ ❏ 2 - Help Wanted: Orphans Preferred (1990)
- ❏ ❏ 3 - **Morons and Madmen (1993) Anthony nominee** ☆
- ❏ ❏ 4 - Going Crazy in Public (1996)
- ❏ ❏ 5 - Dead Horse Paint Company (1997)

Thomas Black...bicycling enthusiast P.I. in Seattle, Washington
- ❏ ❏ 1 - **The Rainy City (1985)) Shamus nominee** ☆
- ❏ ❏ 2 - **Poverty Bay (1985) Shamus winner ★ Edgar nominee** ☆
- ❏ ❏ 3 - Nervous Laughter (1985)
- ❏ ❏ 4 - Fat Tuesday (1987)
- ❏ ❏ 5 - **Deviant Behavior (1988) Shamus nominee** ☆
- ❏ ❏ 6 - Yellow Dog Party (1991)
- ❏ ❏ 7 - The Portland Laugher (1994)
- ❏ ❏ 8 - **The Vanishing Smile (1995) Shamus nominee** ☆
- ❏ ❏ 9 - The Million-Dollar Tattoo (1996)
- ❏ ❏ 10 - Deception Pass (1997)

■ ENGEL, Howard

Ellis Award winner Howard Engel is the creator of a kinder, gentler detective—a witty Jewish private eye who loves egg salad on white bread, and has no stomach for violence. Benny Cooperman walks the quiet streets of small-town Grantham (read St. Catherines), Ontario, not far from Niagara Falls, where there are few guns and lots of space. In addition to his 9 books and a novella (*The Whole Megillah*, 1991) featuring Benny, Engel has written a nonseries novel titled *Murder in Montparnasse* (1992), 2 screenplays and a pair of radio plays. Writing with Janel Hamilton (under the joint pseudonym of F.X. Woolf) he wrote a TV script novelization of *Murder in Space* (1985). A former CBC broadcaster in Europe, Engel once worked as a high school teacher of English and history, and for 5 years was executive producer of *Anthology*, CBC's flagship literary program.

Benny Cooperman...small-town Jewish private eye in Grantham, Ontario
- ❏ ❏ 1 - The Suicide Notice (1980)
  U.S.-The Suicide Murders
- ❏ ❏ 2 - The Ransom Game (1981)
- ❏ ❏ 3 - Murder on Location (1982)
- ❏ ❏ 4 - **Murder Sees the Light (1984) Ellis winner ★**
- ❏ ❏ 5 - A City Called July (1986)
- ❏ ❏ 6 - A Victim Must Be Found (1988)
- ❏ ❏ 7 - Dead and Buried (1990)
- ❏ ❏ 8 - There Was an Old Woman (1993)
- ❏ ❏ 9 - Getting Away with Murder (1995)

■ **ENGLEMAN, Paul**

Shamus award winner Paul Engleman is the creator of two Chicago mystery series. Prematurely "retired" (for political reasons) firefighter Phil Moony is introduced in *The Man With My Name* (1993), where his namesake turns up dead. Private eye Mark Renzler figures in 5 cases, including the Shamus award-winning opener, *Dead in Centerfield* (1983). Engleman co-authored with Dick Clark *Murder on Tour: A Rock 'n Roll Mystery* (1989). A graduate of Beloit College in Wisconsin, Engleman has worked as a postal employee, Kelly Girl clerk, watch repairman and national publicity director for *Playboy* magazine. He lives with his wife and two sons in Chicago, where he writes a weekly column for the *Chicago Sun-Times* called "Diary of a Dad Housewife."

Mark Renzler...ex-baseball player private eye in Chicago, Illinois
- ❑ ❑ 1 - **Dead in Centerfield [1961] (1983) Shamus winner ★**
- ❑ ❑ 2 - Catch a Fallen Angel [1969] (1986)
- ❑ ❑ 3 - Murder-in-Law (1987)
- ❑ ❑ 4 - Who Shot Longshot Sam? [1974] (1989)
- ❑ ❑ 5 - Left for Dead [1972] (1995)

Phil Moony...ex-firefighter private eye in Chicago, Illinois
- ❑ ❑ 1 - The Man With My Name (1993)
- ❑ ❑ 2 - The Man With My Cat (1997)

■ **ESTABROOK, Barry**

Barry Estabrook has written two books featuring veteran cop Garwood Plunkett, whose job it is to preserve the tranquility of one cozy little Adirondack Mountain town in upstate New York. In *Whirlpool* (1995), Plunkett investigates the death of a real estate developer found at the wrong end of a fish hook, as toxic dumping and multi-million-dollar business scams invade Wilmington (NY). *Kirkus Reviews* called *Bahama Heat* (1991), "feisty, goofy and unputdownable." An editor at Chapters Publishing Company, Estabrook has written articles for *The New York Times*, *Reader's Digest* and *Eating Well* magazine. Born in Plainfield, New Jersey, he lives in the Green Mountains of Vermont.

Garwood Plunkett, Sheriff...veteran cop in Adirondack Mountains, New York
- ❑ ❑ 1 - Bahama Heat (1991)
- ❑ ❑ 2 - Whirlpool (1995)

■ **ESTLEMAN, Loren D.**

Since the 1976 publication of his first novel, Michigan author Loren D. Estleman has produced 40 books in a variety of genres—private eye novels, Westerns, fictionalized history, contract killer books and Sherlock Holmes pastiches. His out-of-sequence 20th century history known as the Detroit Chronicles includes *Whiskey River* (1990), *Motown* (1991), *King of the Corner* (1992), *Edsel* (1995) and *Stress* (1996). Next are *Jitterbug* (1998) and *The Ponchartrain Club* (1999) which will recount the earliest days of the auto industry. In 1998 Detroit's favorite P.I. Amos Walker will make his 12th appearance in *The Witchfinder*. A legend in the P.I. short story arena, Estleman has earned 8 nominations and two Shamus Awards during the past 15 years. And he pounds out two books a year on his favorite manual typewriter, a 25-year-old Olympia. But the oldest machine in his collection is an 1892 Blickensderfer which he restored himself.

Amos Walker...6'1" Vietnam vet private eye in Detroit, Michigan
- ❑ ❑ 1 - Motor City Blue (1980)
- ❑ ❑ 2 - Angel Eyes (1981)
- ❑ ❑ 3 - The Midnight Man (1982)
- ❑ ❑ 4 - **The Glass Highway (1983) Shamus nominee ☆**
- ❑ ❑ 5 - **Sugartown (1984) Shamus winner ★**
- ❑ ❑ 6 - Every Brilliant Eye (1986)

❑ ❑ 7 - **Lady Yesterday (1987) Shamus nominee** ☆
❑ ❑ 8 - Downriver (1988)
❑ ❑ ss - General Murders [10 short stories] (1988)
❑ ❑ 9 - Silent Thunder (1989)
❑ ❑ 10 - Sweet Women Lie (1990)
❑ ❑ 11 - Never Street (1997)

Peter Macklin...hit man for the mob in Detroit, Michigan
❑ ❑ 1 - Kill Zone (1984)
❑ ❑ 2 - Roses Are Dead (1985)
❑ ❑ 3 - Any Man's Death (1986)

Sherlock Holmes...19th century consulting detective in London, England
❑ ❑ 1 - Sherlock Holmes versus Dracula (1978)
❑ ❑ 2 - Dr. Jekyll and Mr. Holmes (1978)

■ **EVERS, Crabbe [P]**

Crabbe Evers is the shared pseudonym of William Brashler and Reinder Van Til for their present day baseball mysteries featuring ex-sportswriter Duffy House and his hubba-hubba niece Petey. Retired from journalism, Duffy works as a special investigator for the Commissioner of Baseball, with each book mixing real events and personalities with a fictional plot. The first 3 were paperback originals. Brashler has been producing baseball books for adults and juveniles since the late '70s, including *The Story of Negro League Baseball* (1994) and *The Bingo Long Traveling All-Stars & Motor Kings* (1993). Van Til's latest book is *Lost Daughters: Recovered Memory Therapy and the People It Hurts* (1997) with 5 personal accounts of how RMT has led to false accusations by daughters of sexual abuse by their fathers. The first story is Van Til's own.

Duffy House...ex-sportswriter turned investigator in Chicago, Illinois
❑ ❑ 1 - Murder in Wrigley Field (1991)
❑ ❑ 2 - Murderer's Row (1991)
❑ ❑ 3 - Bleeding Dodger Blue (1992)
❑ ❑ 4 - Fear in Fenway (1993)
❑ ❑ 5 - Tigers Burning (1994)

■ **EVERSON, David H.**

Two-time Shamus Award nominee David H. Everson (pronounced EE-ver-son) is the creator of a 7-book series featuring Robert Miles, a minor league baseball player turned private eye and chief troubleshooter for the Speaker of the Illinois House of Representatives. According to letters in a dead congressman's files, Joseph X. Smith is in possession of a 19th century diary proving that Lincoln was involved in the assassination of Mormon leader Joseph Smith. Along with his cigar-smoking sidekick Mitch, and Mitch's history professor friend Rachel, Bobby is surrounded by vengeful Mormons, dead bodies, and thugs making drug drops in ice cream trucks (*False Profits*, 1992). Political scientist Everson is also the author of *The Making of a Primary: The Illinois Presidential Primary, 1912-1992* (1996).

Robert Miles...baseball minor leaguer turned P.I. in Springfield, Illinois
❑ ❑ 1 - **Recount (1987) Shamus nominee** ☆
❑ ❑ 2 - **Rebound (1988) Shamus nominee** ☆
❑ ❑ 3 - Rematch (1989)
❑ ❑ 4 - Instant Replay (1989)
❑ ❑ 5 - A Capital Killing (1990)
❑ ❑ 6 - False Profits (1992)
❑ ❑ 7 - Suicide Squeeze (1995)

■ **EVERSZ, Robert**

Robert Eversz spent more than 10 years in Los Angeles studying at UCLA Film School and working as a Hollywood screenwriter and filmmaker. But in 1992 he put his worldly goods in storage, packed two suitcases and fled to Prague to join the YAWPs (Young American Writers in Prague). Although he has abandoned his previous series, Eversz says he may bring back Cantini or someone like her in the future. While living the experience needed to create *Gypsy Hearts* (1997), he wrote *Shooting Elvis* (1996) which he calls his sabbatical novel. In her *Manchester Evening News* column, Val McDermid picked *Shooting Elvis* (published in 12 countries around the world) as the best humorous crime novel published in England in 1996. *Kirkus* called *Gypsy Hearts* "hilarious storytelling, with brainy send-ups of vampiric Europeans and idiotic Americans on the dark side of the post-Cold War Grand Tour."

Paul Marston & Angel Cantini...private eye & female prize fighter in Los Angeles, California
- ❑ ❑ 1 - The Bottom Line is Murder (1988)
- ❑ ❑ 2 - False Profit (1990)

■ **FAHERTY, Terence**

Terence Faherty is the creator of two mystery series, including the first-novel Edgar nominee, *Deadstick* (1991), which introduces failed seminarian turned law firm researcher Owen Keane. Owen's next appearance is book 6, *The Ordained* (Dec. '97). Although the *New York Times* called the Keane books "metaphysical mysteries," Faherty thinks of them as psychological mysteries. His newer series features Scott Elliot, a World War II veteran and former B-movie supporting player who's now hanging around Hollywood doing legwork for a one-time studio security chief. Faherty readily admits he started this series to indulge his passion for old movies. An Indiana native, he lives in Indianapolis (IN), home of the poet James Whitcomb Riley and birthplace of John Dillinger. Faherty is not a failed seminarian.

Owen Keane...ex-seminarian and law firm researcher in Boston, Massachusetts
- ❑ ❑ 1 - **Deadstick (1991) Edgar nominee** ☆
- ❑ ❑ 2 - Live to Regret (1992)
- ❑ ❑ 3 - The Lost Keats [prequel] (1993)
- ❑ ❑ 4 - Die Dreaming (1994)
- ❑ ❑ 5 - Prove the Nameless (1996)

Scott Elliott...1940s failed actor turned private eye in Hollywood, California
- ❑ ❑ 1 - Kill Me Again (1996)
- ❑ ❑ 2 - Come Back Dead (1997)
- ❑ ❑ 3 - Passage to Lisbon (1998)

■ **FALLON, Martin [P]**

Martin Fallon is one of several pseudonyms of Harry Patterson, the English-Irish teacher and thriller writer best known as Jack Higgins. Under the Fallon name he wrote 6 books about Paul Chavasse, a globe-trotting British spy first seen in *The Testament of Caspar Schultz* (1962). It was 1975 when Higgins hit the international bestseller lists with *The Eagle Has Landed*, a suspense thriller about a 1943 Nazi plot to kidnap Winston Churchill. According to George Kelley, writing in *1001 Midnights*, book 2 in the Chavasse series was rewritten by the author in 1996 and promptly became a best seller. This author is now published in 56 languages. Among his other pseudonyms are James Graham (named after James Graham College in Yorkshire where the author had taught) and Hugh Marlowe.

Paul Chavasse...globe-trotting British spy in London, England
- ❑ ❑ 1 - The Testament of Caspar Schultz (1962)
- ❑ ❑ 2 - Year of the Tiger (1963)
- ❑ ❑ 3 - The Keys of Hell (1965)
- ❑ ❑ 4 - Midnight Never Comes (1966)
- ❑ ❑ 5 - Dark Side of the Street (1967)
- ❑ ❑ 6 - A Fine Night for Dying (1969)

■ FELDMEYER, Dean

Edgar nominee Dean Feldmeyer has written a pair of small town mysteries featuring Methodist minister Dan Thompson, sent to Baird (KY) for rehabilitation after what his ex-wife called "the big crash." The preacher's downfall involved booze, debts and the third-grade Sunday School teacher. But two years after the revocation of his ordination, the bishop called with an offer Dan couldn't refuse. Take the church in Appalachian Hillbilly country, stay out of trouble for a couple of years and you can be back where you were in no time. The series opener, *Viper Quarry* (1994), was Edgar-nominated for best paperback original in 1995. Feldmeyer is the author of several nonfiction titles including *Beating Burnout in Youth Ministry* (1989), *Fixing Your Frazzled Family* (1990) and *Just This Once* (1990).

Dan Thompson...small-town Methodist minister in Baird, Kentucky
- ❏ ❏ 1 - **Viper Quarry (1994) Edgar nominee** ☆
- ❏ ❏ 2 - Pitchfork Hollow (1995)

■ FINK, John

Former Chicago police reporter John Fink has written two books featuring Windy City television reporter and weekend anchor Jimmy Gillespie, introduced in *The Leaf Boats* (1991). In *Painted Leaves* (1995), Jimmy gets involved when an old classmate is found dead of an apparent suicide and circumstances are strangely similar to mysterious killings in Jimmy's own family. Fink's nonseries mystery, *Libel the Dead* (1992), is set in the world of magazine publishing. For more than 20 years he worked at the *Chicago Tribune* as reporter, copy editor and magazine editor before switching to *Chicago* magazine for a decade as editor. A former instructor at Northwestern University, Fink holds degrees from Millikin University (B.A.) and University of Illinois at Urbana-Champaign (M.A.). He continues to consult for publications in Chicago (IL).

Jimmy Gillespie...TV reporter and weekend anchor in Chicago, Illinois
- ❏ ❏ 1 - The Leaf Boats (1991)
- ❏ ❏ 2 - Painted Leaves (1995)

■ FINKELSTEIN, Jay

Jay Finkelstein has written two mysteries featuring New York literary agent and part-time sleuth Leo Gold, introduced in *See No Evil* (1996). Leo and his girlfriend Lizzie run off to Egypt for a romantic getaway, but she mysteriously disappears from a Cairo perfume shop and Leo investigates. After nearly failing freshman composition, Finkelstein graduated from George Washington University in Washington, DC with a degree in public affairs. He earned an M.A. in public administration from Indiana University and has worked as a software engineer, computer systems analyst and technical writer. After spending 8 years in Israel, Finkelstein now lives in New York City. He was born in New Rochelle (NY), not far from the home of Rob and Laura Petrie.

Leo Gold...30-something Jewish P.I. in New York, New York
- ❏ ❏ 1 - See No Evil (1996)
- ❏ ❏ 2 - Idle Gossip (1997)

■ FLIEGEL, Richard

Richard Fliegel has written 7 books in a series featuring Shelly Lowenkopf, a Jewish cop from New York's Allerton Avenue precinct, who leaves the force in book 6, *A Minyan for the Dead* (1993), and starts making a killing as a private eye. Coincidentally, Fliegel earned a Shamus nomination for best private eye paperback original with this title. In his private eye inaugural, Lowenkopf and his partner Max Pfeiffer are attending a memorial service when the rabbi is arrested during the prayers, on the suspicion he murdered the woman being prayed for. In *The Man Who Murdered Himself* (1994), the ex-cop and a former Bronx detective go to a private clinic looking for a loyal patient.

Shelly Lowenkopf, Sgt.....Allerton Avenue precinct cop in New York, New York
- ❏ ❏ 1 - The Art of Death (1988)
- ❏ ❏ 2 - The Next to Die (1989)
- ❏ ❏ 3 - The Organ Grinder's Monkey (1989)
- ❏ ❏ 4 - Time to Kill (1990)
- ❏ ❏ 5 - A Semiprivate Doom (1991)
- ❏ ❏ **6 - A Minyan for the Dead (1993) Shamus nominee** ☆
- ❏ ❏ 7 - The Man Who Murdered Himself (1994)

■ FLYNN, Don

Playwright, journalist and television writer Donald Robert Flynn is the author of 5 newspaper mysteries published during the 1980s under the byline Don Flynn. Starting with *Murder Isn't Enough* (1983), these books feature Ed "Fitz" Fitzgerald, a *New York Daily Tribune* reporter. Flynn's own newspaper experience took him to St. Joseph and Kansas City (MO), Topeka (KS), Chicago (IL) and New York City, where he worked at the *Journal-American*, *Herald Tribune*, and *Daily News* starting in the early '60s. Between 1969 and 1983, nine of his plays were produced at Off-Off Broadway theaters and other New York, Long Island and Connecticut playhouses. With his wife Charlotte J. Bayton, under the pseudonym Kate Williams, he also wrote 4 books in the Sweet Valley High series during 1983 and 1984.

Ed "Fitz" Fitzgerald...Daily Tribune reporter in New York, New York
- ❏ ❏ 1 - Murder Isn't Enough (1983)
- ❏ ❏ 2 - Murder on the Hudson (1985)
- ❏ ❏ 3 - Ordinary Murder (1987)
- ❏ ❏ 4 - Murder in A-Flat (1988)
- ❏ ❏ 5 - A Suitcase in Berlin (1989)

■ FOLLETT, Ken

British thriller writer Ken Follett became one of the world's youngest millionaire authors when he wrote his first bestseller before the age of 30. This Edgar-award winning title, *Eye of the Needle* (1978), reportedly sold 10 million copies in its first 10 years in print. Worldwide sales of all his titles have since surpassed 40 million books. Follett's earliest fiction was published pseudonymously and the first books appearing under his own name were two titles featuring industrial spy Piers Roper, the James Bond of the board room. By his own estimation, the two Roper novels mark a place "half way between bad and good" in his development as a writer. His earliest work (under the names Simon Myles and Zachary Stone) he describes as "crudely sensational, full of sex, violence and conspicuous consumption, all more or less gratuitous."

Piers Roper...industrial spy in London, England
- ❏ ❏ 1 - The Shakeout (1975)
- ❏ ❏ 2 - The Bear Raid (1976)

■ FORBES, Colin

The more than 20 international thrillers written by Colin Forbes have been translated into more than 20 languages, including his 9 books featuring the British Secret Service second-in- command known as Tweed, and freelance foreign correspondent Bob Newman. Paula Grey is also a continuing character. According to Greg Goode writing in *St. James Guide* (4th edition), Colin Forbes is NOT a pseudonym of Raymond H. Sawkins, and Forbes himself has stated that all his books carry his own byline. Goode picks *Terminal* (1984) as the standout in this series and remarks on Forbes's choice of themes in the Tweed books: a murder combined with a possible defection in *Cover Story* (1985); the hunt for an SIS mole in *The Janus Man* (1988); risk of war with the Soviets in *Deadlock* (1988); rescue of Tweed and a computer in *Shockwave* (1990).

Tweed...British Secret Service 2nd-in-command in London, England
- ❑ ❑ 1 - Double Jeopardy (1982)
- ❑ ❑ 2 - Terminal (1984)
- ❑ ❑ 3 - Cover Story (1985)
- ❑ ❑ 4 - The Janus Man (1988)
- ❑ ❑ 5 - Deadlock (1988)
- ❑ ❑ 6 - The Greek Key (1989)
- ❑ ❑ 7 - Shockwave (1990)
- ❑ ❑ 8 - Whirlpool (1991)
- ❑ ❑ 9 - Precipice (1996)

■ FORD, G. M.

G.M. Ford is the creator of wisecracking Seattle P.I. Leo Waterman, introduced in the Anthony and Shamus-nominated *Who in Hell Is Wanda Fuca?* (1995). Thanks to Leo's father, Wild Bill Waterman, who served 11 terms on the Seattle city council, Leo has connections everywhere. He also has the help of a very unusual bunch of assistants—a group of homeless men he calls "The Boys." They make great operatives, Leo has learned, because they are almost invisible. They can hang out on a street corner for hours and no one sees them. With master's degrees in English (Adelphi University) and political science (University of Washington, Seattle), Ford taught creative writing and communications for 20 years before turning to writing full-time. Writing every day from 6 AM to 2 PM, he says he makes it up as he goes along.

Leo Waterman...wisecracking private eye in Seattle, Washington
- ❑ ❑ 1 - **Who in Hell is Wanda Fuca? (1995) Anthony & Shamus nominee** ☆☆
- ❑ ❑ 2 - Cast in Stone (1996)
- ❑ ❑ 3 - The Bum's Rush (1997)
- ❑ ❑ 4 - A Steak in the Action (1998)

■ FORREST, Richard

Richard Forrest's mysteries have been described as socially conscious and emotionally satisfying. His sleuthing pair of Lyon and Bea Wentworth are an English professor turned children's book author and his feisty, feminist wife, a Connecticut state senator. Lyon's Korean wartime buddy is now the local chief of police. The professor's doctoral dissertation on violence in children's literature supplies an important thread in this series where Lyon pilots his hot air balloon over a crime scene in book one. After an 8-year absence, Lyon and Bea return in 1997 to find themselves investigating the Piper family curse. Peyton Piper, munitions manufacturer and senatorial hopeful, fears for his lovely daughter as she turns 18. Winner of a special Edgar award in 1975, Forrest is a former insurance executive who wrote 3 novels as Stockton Woods during the 1980s. He lives in Old Saybrook (CT).

Lyon & Bea Wentworth...children's book author & state senator in Connecticut
- ❑ ❑ 1 - A Child's Garden of Death (1975)
- ❑ ❑ 2 - The Wizard of Death (1977)
- ❑ ❑ 3 - Death Through the Looking Glass (1978)
- ❑ ❑ 4 - The Death in the Willows (1979)
- ❑ ❑ 5 - The Death at Yew Corner (1980)
- ❑ ❑ 6 - Death Under the Lilacs (1985)
- ❑ ❑ 7 - Death on the Mississippi (1989)
- ❑ ❑ 8 - The Pied Piper of Death (1997)

■ FOXX, Jack [P]

Jack Foxx is a pseudonym used by Bill Pronzini for 4 novels written during the 1970s. Two of these feature Singapore bush pilot Dan Connell who flies freelance charters in *The Jade Figurine* (1972) and *Dead Run* (1975). Another Foxx title is the nonseries *Wildfire* (1978), a California thriller about a small logging town menaced by bad guys and a forest fire. The remaining Foxx is a 19th century historical novel (*Freebooty*, 1976) featuring Pinkerton agent Fergus O'Hara and his wife Hattie, who board the steamer *Freebooty* for the trip inland from San Francisco to Stockton (CA). Writing in *1001 Midnights*, Marcia Muller calls this one "entertaining, well plotted and full of engaging characters." Pronzini was the first president of Private Eye Writers of America (PWA) and received their Life Achievement award in 1987.

Dan Connell...freelance charter pilot in Southeast Asia
- ❏ ❏ 1 - The Jade Figurine (1972)
- ❏ ❏ 2 - Dead Run (1975)

■ FRANCIS, Dick

Retired steeplejockey Richard Stanley Francis is known to the world as Dick Francis. After retiring from horseracing at 36, he worked for 6 years as a racing correspondent and published his first mystery at 42. Since 1962 he has written a book a year and is currently writing #37 from his home in the Cayman Islands. Named Grand Master in 1996, he has won a Silver Dagger (in 1965 with *For Kicks*) and 2 Edgars (for *Forfeit* in 1969 and *Whip Hand* in 1980). He rode the Grand National 8 times and suffered 12 fractured collar bones and 5 broken noses before losing the race of a lifetime, riding the Queen Mother's horse. With the race virtually won, the horse fell 10 strides from the winning post. To this day Francis says he hasn't a clue what happened. But as he told *Contemporary Authors*, "If that mystery hadn't happened, I might never have written all these other ones."

Kit Fielding...jockey in England
- ❏ ❏ 1 - Break-in (1985)
- ❏ ❏ 2 - Bolt (1986)

Sid Halley...injured steeplechase jockey turned P.I. in England
- ❏ ❏ 1 - **Odds Against (1965) Edgar nominee** ☆
- ❏ ❏ 2 - **Whip Hand (1979) Edgar & Gold Dagger winner** ★★
- ❏ ❏ 3 - **Come to Grief (1995) Edgar winner** ★ **Shamus nominee** ☆

■ FRASER, James [P]

James Fraser is one of two pseudonyms of Yorkshire-born fiction writer Alan White, who published 30 novels between 1965 and 1985, including the 9-book series featuring Inspector Superintendent Bill Aveyard released under the name James Fraser. Described as young, ambitious and tough, Aveyard is a gourmet cook who enjoys dazzling women in the kitchen as well as the bedroom. In book 2, Aveyard finds himself a suspect and things are not what they seem. Writing under his own name of Alan White, the author produced 17 war and adventure novels, 8 of which employed the word 'Long' in the title (*Long Watch*, *Long Drop*, *Long Fuse*, *Long Summer*, etc.). He wrote 4 other novels using the name Alec Whitney.

William Aveyard, Insp.....ambitious village police inspector in England
- ❏ ❏ 1 - The Evergreen Death (1968)
- ❏ ❏ 2 - A Cock-Pit of Roses (1969)
- ❏ ❏ 3 - Deadly Nightshade (1970)
- ❏ ❏ 4 - Death in a Pheasant's Eye (1971)
- ❏ ❏ 5 - Blood on a Widow's Cross (1972)
- ❏ ❏ 6 - The Five-Leafed Clover (1973)
- ❏ ❏ 7 - A Wreath of Lords and Ladies (1974)
- ❏ ❏ 8 - Who Steals My Name? (1974)
- ❏ ❏ 9 - Hearts Ease in Death (1977)

■ FREELING, Nicolas

London-born Nicolas Freeling, author of 35 mystery novels, worked as a professional cook in various European hotels and restaurants from 1948 to 1960. He began writing his first book, *Love in Amsterdam* (1962), while serving a 3-week jail sentence for stealing food. Retitled *Death in Amsterdam* (1964) in the U.S., the novel introduced Dutch police detective Van der Valk whose widow Arlette takes over the series beginning with book 12, *The Widow*. The second of Freeling's long-running police series features Inspector Henri Castang of Brussels, described as a "cop at heart, a bureaucrat by circumstance" and a man forged in the fires of war-torn Europe." Freeling's cooking memoirs appear as *The Kitchen: A Delicious Account of the Author's Years as a Grand Hotel Cook* (1970), reissued in 1991 as *The Kitchen Book*. The author, who describes himself as the most European of English writers, lives near Strasbourg, France.

Henri Castang...French policeman in Brussels, Belgium
- ❑ ❑ 1 - A Dressing of Diamond (1974)
- ❑ ❑ 2 - What Are the Bugles Blowing For? (1975)
  U.S.-The Bugles Blowing
- ❑ ❑ 3 - Lake Isle (1976)
  U.S.-Sabine
- ❑ ❑ 4 - The Night Lords (1978)
- ❑ ❑ 5 - Castang's City (1980)
- ❑ ❑ 6 - Wolfnight (1982)
- ❑ ❑ 7 - The Back of the North Wind (1983)
- ❑ ❑ 8 - No Part in Your Death (1984)
- ❑ ❑ 9 - A City Solitary (1985)
- ❑ ❑ 10 - Cold Iron (1986)
- ❑ ❑ 11 - Lady Macbeth (1988)
- ❑ ❑ 12 - Not as Far as Velma (1989)
- ❑ ❑ 13 - The Pretty How Town (1992)
  U.S.-The Flanders Sky
- ❑ ❑ 14 - You Know Who (1993)
- ❑ ❑ 15 - The Seacoast of Bohemia (1995)
- ❑ ❑ 16 - A Dwarf Kingdom (1996)

Van der Valk, Insp.....intellectual Dutch police inspector in Amsterdam, Netherlands
- ❑ ❑ 1 - Love in Amsterdam (1962)
  U.S.-Death in Amsterdam
- ❑ ❑ 2 - Because of the Cats (1963)
- ❑ ❑ 3 - **Gun Before Butter (1963) Gold Dagger runnerup ★**
  U.S.-Question of Loyalty
- ❑ ❑ 4 - Double-Barrel (1964)
- ❑ ❑ 5 - Criminal Conversation (1965)
- ❑ ❑ 6 - **The King of the Rainy Country (1966) Edgar winner ★**
- ❑ ❑ 7 - The Dresden Green (1966)
- ❑ ❑ 8 - Strike Out Where Not Applicable (1967)
- ❑ ❑ 9 - Tsing-Boum (1969)
  U.S.-Tsing-Boom!
- ❑ ❑ 10 - Over the High Side (1971)
  U.S.-The Lovely Ladies
- ❑ ❑ 11 - A Long Silence [incl Arlette] (1972)
  U.S.-Aupres de ma Blonde
- ❑ ❑ 12 - The Widow [Arlette alone] (1979)
- ❑ ❑ 13 - One Damn Thing After Another (1981)
  U.S.-Arlette
- ❑ ❑ 14 - Sand Castles [prequel] (1989)

■ **FREEMANTLE, Brian**

Brian Freemantle has written more than 36 novels published around the world since leaving his 30-year career as a foreign press correspondent in 1975 to write spy thrillers. His best known creation is working class British agent Charlie Muffin, described by mystery critic Newgate Callendar as "a slob who breaks all the rules; the best in the business." An expert in Russian affairs, Charlie has been jailed, exiled and marked for death by his own government, but he's survived the Cold War, outlasted the Soviet Union and outsmarted the KGB by the time he's sent to Beijing in book 10 to rescue his new apprentice. Many of Charlie's adventures have been filmed for international television and films. He has written at least 6 novels as Jonathan Evans and Jack Winchester; a biography of Sean Connery as Richard Gant; and other nonfiction under his own name and as John Maxwell.

Charlie Muffin...working-class British agent in London, England
- ❏ ❏ 1 - Charlie Muffin (1977)
  U.S.-Charlie M
- ❏ ❏ 2 - Clap Hands, Here Comes Charlie (1978)
  U.S.-Here Comes Charlie M
- ❏ ❏ 3 - The Inscrutable Charlie Muffin (1979)
- ❏ ❏ 4 - Charlie Muffin's Uncle Sam (1980)
  U.S.-Charlie Muffin USA
- ❏ ❏ 5 - Madrigal for Charlie Muffin (1981)
- ❏ ❏ 6 - Charlie Muffin and the Russian Rose (1985)
- ❏ ❏ 7 - Charlie Muffin San (1987)
  U.S.-See Charlie Run
- ❏ ❏ 8 - The Runaround (1988)
- ❏ ❏ 9 - Comrade Charlie (1989)
- ❏ ❏ 10 - Charlie's Apprentice (1993)

William Cowley & Dimitri Danilov, Col.....FBI agent & Russian investigator in Washington, D.C.
- ❏ ❏ 1 - The Button Man (1992)
- ❏ ❏ 2 - No Time for Heroes (1994)

■ **FRIEDMAN, Kinky**

Richard Friedman, better known as Kinky, is a recording artist and leader of the country and western band Kinky Friedman and the Texas Jewboys. He is also the author of 10 comic mysteries featuring a cigar-chomping, cat-loving, wise-cracking country singer/amateur sleuth named Kinky. While pronouncing the books "outrageously funny," a *People* magazine reviewer said "the conventional mystery plot is nothing more than an excuse for Friedman to deliver one-liners, puns, gratuitous insults, smutty innuendo and X-rated jokes." After earning a B.A. from the University of Texas where he studied the classics, Friedman joined the Peace Corps and worked in Borneo for 2 years—experience he puts to use in book 4, *Frequent Flyer* (1989). This son of a psychology professor and speech therapist counts among his fans Nelson Mandela, Bill Clinton, Joseph Heller, Jackie Collins and Bob Dylan.

Kinky Friedman...country & western singer turned sleuth in New York, New York
- ❏ ❏ 1 - Greenwich Killing Time (1986)
- ❏ ❏ 2 - A Case of Lone Star (1987)
- ❏ ❏ 3 - When the Cat's Away (1988)
- ❏ ❏ 4 - Frequent Flyer (1989)
- ❏ ❏ 5 - Musical Chairs (1991)
- ❏ ❏ 6 - Elvis, Jesus & Coca Cola (1993)
- ❏ ❏ 7 - Armadillos & Old Lace (1994)
- ❏ ❏ 8 - God Bless John Wayne (1995)
- ❏ ❏ 9 - The Love Song of J. Edgar Hoover (1996)
- ❏ ❏ 10 - Roadkill (1997)

■ FROST, Mark

Twin Peaks writer and co-creator Mark Frost received an Edgar nomination for best first novel for *The List of 7* (1993) which became a runaway national best seller and a 1994 film from Universal Pictures. In his fiction debut, Frost presents a theory about the origins of Holmes and Watson. Could Sherlock Holmes be based on a man named Jack Sparks? Could Conan Doyle actually be Dr. Watson? The book opens with a seance and an anonymous letter sent to the struggling young physician and writer, Arthur Conan Doyle. Soon he is on the trail of a dangerous group of elite Satanists called the Brotherhood of the Dark, and reluctantly allied with Jack Sparks, a special agent to the Queen. Together they must prevent this diabolical group from destroying Victorian society. In book 2, *The 6 Messiahs* (1996), Conan Doyle and his brother are on a book tour across America.

Conan Doyle & Jack Sparks...historical figure and special agent to the Queen in London, England
- ❑ ❑ 1 - **The List of 7 (1993) Edgar nominee** ☆
- ❑ ❑ 2 - The 6 Messiahs (1996)

■ FULLER, Dean

Dean Fuller has been for many years a composer and arranger in musical theatre. He is also the creator of charismatic French detective, Alex Grismolet, a 6' 10", red-headed tuba player who lives on a Paris houseboat. Standard attire for this Chief Inspector of the Sûreté is jeans, anorak and running shoes. Not so for his dimunitive assistant, the 5' 4" Alphonsas Varnas, once a pig farmer in Germany who now favors three-piece black suits. A Lithuanian national 20 years Alex's senior, Inspector Varnas is fluent in Litvak, Russian, German and Polish. He also speaks a sort of French, and English without articles or with unnecessary ones. "So, Alex, how are the things," he is likely to ask. Varnas attributes this to learning French and English in a rush. "I learn French on VE Day when I walk through French sector of Germany. English I learn in American sector next day."

Alex Grismolet, Chief-Insp.....Chef-Insp. of the Sûreté in Paris, France
- ❑ ❑ 1 - A Death in Paris (1992)
- ❑ ❑ 2 - Death of a Critic (1996)

■ FULLER, Timothy

Timothy Fuller published his first mystery, *Harvard has a Homicide* (1936), at the age of 22 while still an undergraduate student at Harvard University. His amateur sleuth Edmund "Jupiter" Jones, charming klutz and instructor in Harvard's fine arts department, is joined by his girlfriend Helen, who later becomes his wife. According to Bill Pronzini, writing in *1001 Midnights* (1986), *Three Thirds of a Ghost* (1941) may be the most appealing of Fuller's books, owing to its setting in a Boston bookshop, where a local author is shot dead during his speech to a crowd of 200 guests at the bookstore's 150th birthday party. Said Pronzini, "If your taste runs to the humorous, sophisticated, slightly screwball type of storytelling popular in the 1930s, this bibliomystery (and any of the other Jupiter Jones romps) is definitely your sort of Boston tea party."

Edmund "Jupiter" Jones...grad student in fine arts in Massachusetts
- ❑ ❑ 1 - Harvard Has a Homicide (1936) Brit.-J for Jupiter
- ❑ ❑ 2 - Three Thirds of a Ghost (1941)
- ❑ ❑ 3 - Reunion with Murder (1941)
- ❑ ❑ 4 - This Is Murder, Mr. Jones (1943)
- ❑ ❑ 5 - Keep Cool, Mr. Jones (1950)

■ FURUTANI, Dale

Dale Furutani is a 3-time nominee for best first novel for *Death in Little Tokyo* (1996), the first mystery to feature an Asian-American sleuth written by an Asian-American author. Nominated for the Agatha, Anthony and Macavity awards, this book introduces amateur detective, Ken Tanaka, a 40-something computer programmer from the Little Tokyo neighborhood of Los Angeles. To make good use the mountain of research material he collected for *The Toyotomi Blades* (1997), Furutani wrote the first book (not yet published) in a new historical series set in 1603 Japan among the non-nobility. Like his protagonist, Furutani is a third generation Japanese-American, born in Hawaii and raised in southern California. He holds a B.A. in creative writing and an M.B.A. in marketing and information systems from UCLA. Former owner of an automotive consulting firm, he is currently director of information technology for Nissan Motor Corp. in the U.S.

Ken Tanaka...Asian American computer programmer in Los Angeles, California
- ❏ ❏ 1 - **Death in Little Tokyo (1996) Anthony & Macavity winner ★★ Agatha nominee ☆**
- ❏ ❏ 2 - The Toyotomi Blades (1997)

■ GAITANO, Nick [P]

Nick Gaitano was a pseudonym of the Edgar-nominated Eugene John "Guy" Izzi (1953-1996) whose strange death in December was something right out of one of his novels. Although ruled a suicide by the Chicago police department, some still believe foul play was involved. Found hanging from a rope outside his 14th floor office window, he was wearing a bullet-proof vest, carrying brass knuckles and chemical spray. Three computer disks in his pockets contained an 800-page story of a Chicago writer who infiltrates Indiana-based militia groups and is later hanged by them from his 14th story office window. On the disk, the author survives the fall, climbs back up the rope and kills the militia members in a shootout. Izzi published 6 novels under his own name between 1987 and 1990, in addition to the Edgar-nominated *The Booster* (1989).

Jake Phillips...homicide detective in Chicago, Illinois
- ❏ ❏ 1 - Mr. X (1995)
- ❏ ❏ 2 - Jaded (1996)

■ GALWAY, Robert Conington [P]

Robert Conington Galway is a pseudonym of Philip Donald McCutchan, past Chairman of the Crime Writers' Association (1965-66), and author of more than 115 books starting in 1957 with a one-off titled *Whistle and I'll Come*. Under the Galway name he has written a 12-book espionage series featuring British spy James Packard, first appearing in *The Timeless Sleep* (1963). With the exception of the first and last book in the series, all were titled with the name of Packard's assignment, such as *Assignment Sydney* (1970), for example. As Duncan MacNeil he has written 14 military novels set on frontier of India during the 1890s, featuring Capt. James Ogilvie of the 114th Highlanders. His best-known work includes the 22 books featuring Commander Esmonde Shaw and 11 with D.C.S. Simon Shard which are published under his own name.

James Packard...British spy in London, England
- ❏ ❏ 1 - The Timeless Sleep (1963)
- ❏ ❏ 2 - Assignment New York (1963)
- ❏ ❏ 3 - Assignment London (1963)
- ❏ ❏ 4 - Assignment Andalusia (1965)
- ❏ ❏ 5 - Assignment Malta (1966)
- ❏ ❏ 6 - Assignment Gaolbreak (1968)
- ❏ ❏ 7 - Assignment Argentina (1969)
- ❏ ❏ 8 - Assignment Fenland (1969)
- ❏ ❏ 9 - Assignment Sea Bed (1969)
- ❏ ❏ 10 - Assignment Sydney (1970)
- ❏ ❏ 11 - Assignment Death Squad (1970)
- ❏ ❏ 12 - The Negative Man (1971)

■ GARDNER, John

John Gardner's many occupations have included American Red Cross entertainer (he was an illusionist), Commando Service in the Far and Middle East during World War II, ordained Episcopal priest, Royal Air Force chaplain, theatre reviewer for the *Stratford upon Avon Herald* and accomplished thriller writer. Chosen by the estate of Ian Fleming to continue the James Bond novels, Gardner has written 14 of them since 1981. He has also written 8 books with an anti-Bond-imitator character, the cowardly Boysie Oakes, first seen in *The Liquidator* (1964). Boysie is "afraid to fly and can't stand the sight of blood, but he's handsome, cultivated and a devil with women," according to *Detectionary*. Gardner lists as his main passions politics, crime, police agencies and security services and said recently he intended to write next a classic suspense style novel set in Shanghai during the early '30s.

Boysie Oakes...cowardly British agent for Special Security in London, England
- ❑ ❑ 1 - The Liquidator (1964)
- ❑ ❑ 2 - The Understrike (1965)
- ❑ ❑ 3 - Amber Nine (1966)
- ❑ ❑ 4 - Madrigal (1967)
- ❑ ❑ 5 - Founder Member (1969)
- ❑ ❑ 6 - Traitor's Exit (1970)
- ❑ ❑ 7 - The Airline Pirates (1970)
- ❑ ❑ 8 - A Killer for a Song (1975)

Derek Torry...British spy in England
- ❑ ❑ 1 - A Complete State of Death (1969)
  - U.S.-The Stone Killer
- ❑ ❑ 2 - The Corner Men (1974)

Herbie Kruger...British Intelligence senior operative in England
- ❑ ❑ 1 - The Nostradamus Traitor (1979)
- ❑ ❑ 2 - The Garden of Weapons (1980)
- ❑ ❑ 3 - The Quiet Dogs (1982)
- ❑ ❑ 4 - The Secret Houses (1987)
- ❑ ❑ 5 - The Secret Families (1989)
- ❑ ❑ 6 - Maestro (1993)
- ❑ ❑ 7 - Confessor (1995)

James Bond...British agent in London, England
- ❑ ❑ 1 - Licence Renewed (1981)
- ❑ ❑ 2 - For Special Services (1982)
- ❑ ❑ 3 - Icebreaker (1983)
- ❑ ❑ 4 - Role of Honour (1984)
- ❑ ❑ 5 - Nobody Lives Forever (1986)
- ❑ ❑ 6 - No Deals Mr. Bond (1987)
- ❑ ❑ 7 - Win, Lose, or Die (1989)
- ❑ ❑ 8 - Brokenclaw (1990)
- ❑ ❑ 9 - The Man from Barbarossa (1991)
- ❑ ❑ 10 - Death is Forever (1992)
- ❑ ❑ 11 - Never Send Flowers (1993)
- ❑ ❑ 12 - Seafire (1994)
- ❑ ❑ 13 - Goldeneye (1995)
- ❑ ❑ 14 - Cold Fall (1996)

James Moriarty, Prof.....archenemy of Sherlock Holmes in London, England
- ❑ ❑ 1 - The Return of Moriarty (1974) APA-Moriarty
- ❑ ❑ 2 - The Revenge of Moriarty (1975)

■ **GARFIELD, Brian**

Edgar-award winner Brian Garfield has written more than 65 novels, but is best known as the author of *Death Wish* (1972), made famous by the 1974 movie starring Charles Bronson. In a 1981 interview with *Contemporary Authors*, Garfield noted his dislike for the film and his resentment of the distorted image of his work that resulted, noting he much prefers creating suspense without the use of violence. His Edgar award winning novel *Hopscotch* (1975), which became a 1981 film starring Walter Matthau, is a good example of suspense without brutality. Garfield grew up in Arizona with lots of writers around the house, thanks to his mother's work as *Saturday Review* cover artist, requiring her to paint numerous author portraits. He has written more than 40 westerns under the names Bennett Garland, Alex Hawk, John Ives, Drew Malloy, Frank O'Brian, Jonas Ward, Brian Wynne and Frank Wynne.

Paul Benjamin...vigilante murderer in Arizona
- ❏ ❏ 1 - Death Wish (1972)
- ❏ ❏ 2 - Death Sentence (1975)

Sam Watchman...part Navajo State trooper in Arizona
- ❏ ❏ 1 - Relentless (1972)
- ❏ ❏ 2 - The Threepersons Hunt (1974)

■ **GARFIELD, Henry**

Henry Garfield is the great-great-grandson of James A. Garfield (1831-1881), 20th President of the United States and the last to be born in a log cabin. A San Diego newspaper editor and freelance writer, this author is the creator of a new series that blends elements of werewolf legends with a small-town mystery, beginning with *Moondog* (1995), set in the southern California mountain community of Julian. The amateur detective is Cyrus "Moondog" Nygerski, a reclusive writer and school bus driver who befriends the new English teacher in book 2 when she finds herself in a classroom with students who seem possessed by characters from classical literature. Originally from Philadelphia, Garfield grew up in Blue Hill, Maine, spent his high school years at a stuffy New Hampshire prep school and attended the same college as Stephen King.

Cyrus "Moondog" Nygerski...reclusive writer in Southern California
- ❏ ❏ 1 - Moondog (1995)
- ❏ ❏ 2 - Room 13 (1997)

■ **GASH, Jonathan [P]**

Jonathan Gash is the pseudonym of Dr. John Grant, whose 40-year medical career has included work as a private consultant in infectious diseases, university professor, general practitioner and clinical pathologist. He is also the creator of Lovejoy, that irascible antiques dealer from East Anglia who is loved in spite of himself. Introduced in *The Judas Pair*, winner of the 1977 Creasey award for best first novel, Lovejoy has now made 19 appearances in book form and more than 90 episodes on BBC television. As noted in the *St. James Guide* (4th edition), "the Gash mysteries are fascinating for their special focus on antique lore. They are also fascinating for their way of being nasty and horrible in a pleasant sort of way." In 1997 Gash began a new series featuring hospital physician Dr. Clare Burtonall, first seen in *Different Women Dancing*.

Clare Burtonall, Dr.....hospital physician in England
- ❏ ❏ 1 - Different Women Dancing (1997)

Lovejoy...antiques expert and forger in East Anglia, England
- ❏ ❏ 1 - **The Judas Pair (1977) Creasey winner** ★
- ❏ ❏ 2 - Gold from Gemini (1978)
       U.S.-Gold by Gemini
- ❏ ❏ 3 - The Grail Tree (1979)

  ❏ ❏ 4 - Spend Game (1980)
  ❏ ❏ 5 - The Vatican Rip (1981)
  ❏ ❏ 6 - Firefly Gadroon (1982)
  ❏ ❏ 7 - The Sleepers of Erin (1983)
  ❏ ❏ 8 - The Gondola Scam (1984)
  ❏ ❏ 9 - Pearlhanger (1985)
  ❏ ❏ 10 - The Tartan Ringers (1986)
          U.S.-The Tartan Sell
  ❏ ❏ 11 - Moonspender (1986)
  ❏ ❏ 12 - Jade Woman (1988)
  ❏ ❏ 13 - The Very Last Gambado (1989)
  ❏ ❏ 14 - The Great California Game (1990)
  ❏ ❏ 15 - The Lies of Fair Ladies (1991)
  ❏ ❏ 16 - Paid and Loving Eyes (1992)
  ❏ ❏ 17 - The Sin Within Her Smile (1993)
  ❏ ❏ 18 - The Grace in Older Women (1995)
  ❏ ❏ 19 - The Possessions of a Lady (1996)

■ GAT, Dimitri

Dimitri Gat is the creator of a two-book series featuring a Pittsburgh information specialist named Yuri Nevsky who first appeared in *Nevsky's Return* (1982). After having been nominated for a Shamus award for book one, Gat was accused of plagiarism following the publication of book 2, *Nevsky's Demon* (1983), thought to contain material taken from a work of John D. MacDonald (according to George Easter, *Deadly Pleasures* #3). As a result, Gat adopted the pen name C. K. Cambray for the psychological novels he began writing. More recently, he has resumed publishing under his real name with the nonseries thriller *Child's Cry* (1995) which involves a young mother falsely accused of murder at a day care center where she worked. Gat is a former cataloger and administrator at the Harvard University Library.

Yuri Nevsky...information specialist in Pittsburgh, Pennsylvania
  ❏ ❏ 1 - **Nevsky's Return (1982) Shamus nominee** ☆
  ❏ ❏ 2 - Nevsky's Demon (1983)

■ GIBBS, Tony

Tony Gibbs was born Wolcott Gibbs, Jr., son of a pair of writers in New York City where he grew up and joined the publishing world, first as publicity manager and later book editor. A former senior editor of *The New Yorker*, *Yachting* and *Islands* magazines, Gibbs has written 11 nonfiction books, mostly on sailing and yachting. His fiction includes 3 series which involve both the publishing and sailing worlds. Diana Speed, book publisher and savvy investigator, is featured in 2 books, as are Harbormaster Neal Donahoe and Coast Guard Lt. Tory Lennox. Another 3 titles involve the owner of a racing yacht named *Glory*, her skipper, and the ship's cook and bottle-washer. Gibbs lives in Santa Barbara (CA) with his wife Elaine St. James, author of *Simplify Your Life* (1994) and *Simplify Your Life with Kids* (1997).

Diana Speed...publishing company chief financial officer in New York, New York
  ❏ ❏ 1 - Shadow Queen (1992)
  ❏ ❏ 2 - Capitol Offense (1995)

Gillian Verdean, Jeremy Barr & Patrick O'Mara...yacht owner, skipper & mate in Long Island, New York
  ❏ ❏ 1 - Dead Run (1988)
  ❏ ❏ 2 - Running Fix (1990)
  ❏ ❏ 3 - Land Fall (1992)

Neal Donahoe & Victoria "Tory" Lennox...harbor cop and Coast Guard Lt. in Santa Barbara, California
  ❏ ❏ 1 - Shot in the Dark (1996)
  ❏ ❏ 2 - Fade to Black (1997)

■ **GILBERT, Michael**

Michael Gilbert is one of the 12 founding members of the British Crime Writers' Association. Named Grand Master by the Mystery Writers of America in 1987, he has been knighted as a Commander in the Order of the British Empire. Once a London solicitor, Gilbert has produced 28 novels, more than 300 short stories and numerous plays for stage, television and radio. Written in 1938, his debut novel introduced Inspector Hazelrigg in *Close Quarters*, appearing first in London (1947) and later in New York (1963). On the 50th anniversary of *Close Quarters* comes *Into Battle* (1997), where Gilbert brings back Luke Pagan, the London cop first seen in Roller Coaster and pairs him with Joe Narrabone for a World War I tale of the early days of modern intelligence. No high-tech spy toys here, just dogged effort.

Hazelrigg, Insp.....British police inspector in London, England
- ❑ ❑ 1 - Close Quarters (1947)
- ❑ ❑ 2 - They Never Looked Inside (1948)
    U.S.-He Didn't Mind Danger
- ❑ ❑ 3 - The Doors Open (1949)
- ❑ ❑ 4 - Smallbone Deceased (1950)
- ❑ ❑ 5 - Death Has Deep Roots (1951)
- ❑ ❑ 6 - Fear To Tread (1953)

Joe Narrabone...WWI policeman turned British Secret agent in London, England
- ❑ ❑ 1 - Ring of Terror (1995)
- ❑ ❑ 2 - Into Battle (1997)

Patrick Petrella...Metropolitan Police inspector in London, England
- ❑ ❑ ss - Blood and Judgment (1959)
- ❑ ❑ ss - Amateur in Violence [incl 3 w/Hazelrigg] (1973)
- ❑ ❑ ss - Petrella at Q (1977)
- ❑ ❑ ss - Young Petrella [incl 2 w/Hazelrigg] (1988)
- ❑ ❑ 1 - Roller Coaster (1993)

■ **GILL, Bartholomew [P]**

Bartholomew Gill is the pseudonym of Mark McGarrity whose story-telling maternal grandfather was the real Bartholomew Gill. Not to slight the other side of his family tree, the author named his protagonist, Peter McGarr, after his paternal grandfather, Peter McGarrity. Each of the McGarr books featuring the chief superintendent of Ireland's Special Crimes Unit pays homage to a special aspect of Irish history or culture. In book 13 it's the tinkers, or travelers as they prefer to be called (*Death of an Irish Tinker*, 1997). After earning a B.A. at Brown University (MA), McGarrity went to Dublin where he earned his M.Litt. at Trinity College. He also lived in Sienna, Italy, and has worked as a speech writer, public relations and annual report writer and financial reporter. Under his own name he has written *A Passing Advantage* (1980) and *Neon Caesar* (1989).

Peter McGarr, Chief Insp.....Irish chief of detectives in Ireland
- ❑ ❑ 1 - McGarr and the Politician's Wife (1977)
- ❑ ❑ 2 - McGarr and the Sienese Conspiracy (1977)
- ❑ ❑ 3 - McGarr on the Cliffs of Moher (1978)
- ❑ ❑ 4 - McGarr at the Dublin Horse Show (1980)
- ❑ ❑ 5 - McGarr and the P.M. of Belgrave Square (1983)
- ❑ ❑ 6 - McGarr and the Method of Descartes (1984)
- ❑ ❑ 7 - McGarr and the Legacy of a Woman Scorned (1986)
- ❑ ❑ **8 - The Death of the Joyce Scholar (1989) Edgar nominee** ☆
- ❑ ❑ 9 - The Death of Love (1992)
- ❑ ❑ 10 - Death on a Cold, Wild River (1993)
- ❑ ❑ 11 - Death of an Ardent Bibliophile (1995)
- ❑ ❑ 12 - Death of an Old Sea Wolf (1996)

■ GODDARD, Ken

Former director of a California police crime lab, Ken Goddard currently heads the nation's only wildlife forensics laboratory. From their Ashland, Oregon headquarters, his 30 forensic scientists support federal, state and international wildlife law enforcement. But he swears the 'real' Fish & Wildlife Service is nothing like his novels. Fictional wildlife investigator Henry Lightstone is an ex-San Diego homicide detective who works undercover in Anchorage, Alaska, in book 1 (*Prey*), deals with eco-terrorists in the Bahamas in book 2 (*Wildfire*), and heads into the mountains of Oregon in book 3 (*Double Blind*). The most recent supporting cast includes a duck-poaching Congressman, the FBI, a sexy witch with a pet panther, a blind soothsayer, Bigfoot, and a warehouse stocked with crocodiles, poisonous Australian snakes and 750 giant red-kneed tarantulas. *Kirkus* called Goddard "the *Field & Stream* Tom Clancy."

Henry Lightstone...National Fish and Wildlife Investigator in Oregon
- ❏ ❏ 1 - Prey (1992)
- ❏ ❏ 2 - Wildfire (1994)
- ❏ ❏ 3 - Double Blind (1997)

■ GODDARD, Robert

British author Robert Goddard was nominated for the Booker Prize with his first novel, *Past Caring* (1986), the story of a young history graduate who struggles to uncover information about a controversial political figure of Edwardian England. Goddard's fourth book, *Into the Blue* (1990), is the first of a pair featuring middle-aged Harry Barnett, an Englishman working as a caretaker on an island in Greece. Harry goes searching for clues after the disappearance of a beautiful young woman who vanishes while sightseeing. Still reeling from the loss of his friend the missing tourist, Harry learns in book 2 that he has a 33-year-old son, recently fired from a research job and now in a coma from an insulin overdose. Harry's back in the investigations business in *Out of the Sun* (1996).

Harry Barnett...middle-aged Englishman caretaker in Greece
- ❏ ❏ 1 - Into the Blue (1990)
- ❏ ❏ 2 - Out of the Sun (1996)

■ GOLDBERG, Lee

Television scriptwriter and producer Lee Goldberg has written 2 installments of a series featuring Charlie Willis, ex-cop turned TV cop turned studio security agent. Book one, *My Gun Has Bullets* (1995), "is apt to make you cackle like a sitcom laugh track," according to *Entertainment Weekly*. Currently co-executive producer of *Diagnosis Murder*, Goldberg has scripted episodes of *SeaQuest*, *Cosby Mysteries*, *Baywatch*, *Spenser: For Hire*, *Likely Suspects* and *Cobra*, among others. His nonfiction work includes 2 volumes of *Unsold Television Pilots* and *The [New] Jewish Student's Guide to American Colleges*. During the mid-'80s he wrote a men's action adventure series for Pinnacle (*.357 Vigilante* #1 through #4) under the name Ian Ludlow (so the books would be shelved next to Robert Ludlum). He describes these as "sleazy paperbacks that are mercifully out of print."

Charlie Willis...ex-cop turned TV cop turned studio security agent in Los Angeles, California
- ❏ ❏ 1 - My Gun Has Bullets (1995)
- ❏ ❏ 2 - Beyond the Beyond (1997)

■ GOLDBERG, Leonard S.

Leonard Goldberg MD has written 4 books featuring Los Angeles forensic pathologist Joanna Blalock and police detective Jake Sinclair, introduced in *Deadly Medicine* (1992). In book 4 Joanna's archaeologist sister needs a liver transplant after catching a killer disease in Guatemala and Joanna learns some deadly facts about organ procurement. Goldberg also wrote the nonseries novel *Transplant* (1980). A consulting physician in Los Angeles, Goldberg is affiliated with the UCLA Medical Center where he is a clinical professor. A leading forensic authority, he serves regularly as an expert witness in medical malpractice trials. A native of South Carolina, he attended the Citadel before earning his bachelor's degree at the College of Charleston and his M.D. at the Medical College of South Carolina. He lives in Los Angeles.

Joanna Blalock, Dr. & Jake Sinclair...forensic pathologist & police detective in Los Angeles, California
- ❏ ❏ 1 - Deadly Medicine (1992)
- ❏ ❏ 2 - Deadly Practice (1994)
- ❏ ❏ 3 - Deadly Care (1996)
- ❏ ❏ 4 - Deadly Harvest (1997)

■ GOODRUM, Charles A.

Former Library of Congress assistant director Charles A. Goodrum is the creator of Dr. Edward George, retired Yale librarian, featured in the 4-book series of Werner-Bok Library mysteries, starting with *Dewey Decimated* (1977), a best first novel Edgar nominee. In book 4, the scholarly detective squad includes Betty Creighton Jones, Werner-Bok CEO, her persistent suitor the Williamsburg archaeologist, retired Yale librarian Dr. George, and student intern Kit Chang. They're on the trail of clues in Chinatown and the Library of Congress Rare Book Room. Goodrum spent 30 years at the Library of Congress after earning an M.A. at Columbia and attending Princeton University and Wichita State. His humorous memoir, *I'll Trade You a Moose* (1967), was produced by Walt Disney Studios as a TV movie. A native of Kansas, Goodrum lives in northern Virginia.

Edward George, Dr.....retired Yale librarian in Washington, D.C.
- ❏ ❏ **1 - Dewey Decimated (1977) Edgar nominee** ☆
- ❏ ❏ 2 - Carnage of the Realm (1979) Brit.-Dead for a Penny
- ❏ ❏ 3 - The Best Cellar (1987)
- ❏ ❏ 4 - A Slip of the Tong (1992)

■ GORES, Joe

Three-time Edgar winner Joe Gores (rhymes with doors) has written 5 books featuring Daniel Kearney Associates, a San Francisco auto repo and skip-tracing agency modeled after one of the firms Gores worked for during 12 years as a private eye. His Edgar-nominated *32 Cadillacs* (1992) is an uproarious tale of DKA's attempt to repossess a fleet of pink Cadillacs stolen by Bay Area gypsies who intend to drive them to Iowa for the funeral of the King of the Gypsies. The 3 Edgars won by Gores include one for best short story and another for best first novel (*A Time of Predators*) which he collected the same night in 1970. His third was for TV drama, won in 1976 for an episode of *Kojak*. Gores also wrote scripts for *Magnum P.I.*, *Remington Steele*, *Mike Hammer*, *T. J. Hooker* and *Columbo*, among others. He once taught English in Kenya and later managed an auto auctioneering company in San Francisco.

Daniel Kearney Associates...auto repo & skip-tracing firm in San Francisco, California
- ❏ ❏ 1 - Dead Skip (1972)
- ❏ ❏ 2 - Final Notice (1973)
- ❏ ❏ 3 - Gone, No Forwarding (1978)
- ❏ ❏ **4 - 32 Cadillacs (1992) Edgar nominee** ☆
- ❏ ❏ 5 - Contract Null & Void (1996)

■ GORMAN, Ed

Shamus award winner Ed Gorman spent 20 years in advertising before he sobered up (literally) and started writing fiction in 1985. His writing is "strong, fast and sleek as a bullet," says Dean Koontz, who calls Gorman "one of the best." His has created such diverse characters as an 1890s bounty hunter (Leo Guild) and an alcoholic New York theatre critic (Tobin). His Iowa detectives include a 50-something P.I. (Walsh), an ex-cop turned actor and security guard (Jack Dwyer), and an ex-FBI profiler (Robert Payne) appearing next in *Harlot's Moon* (1998). He has recently written several political thrillers as E. J. Gorman, including *The Marilyn Tapes* (1995), *The First Lady* (1995) and *Senatorial Privilege* (1997). A four-time Shamus nominee for his private eye fiction, Gorman publishes *Mystery Scene* magazine and is a prolific editor of original anthologies. He lives in Cedar Rapids (IA).

Jack Dwyer...ex-cop part-time actor and security guard in Cedar Rapids, Iowa
- ❑ ❑ 1 - Roughcut (1985)
- ❑ ❑ 2 - **New, Improved Murder (1985) Shamus nominee** ☆
- ❑ ❑ 3 - Murder Straight Up (1986)
- ❑ ❑ 4 - Murder in the Wings (1986)
- ❑ ❑ 5 - **The Autumn Dead (1987) Shamus nominee** ☆
- ❑ ❑ 6 - A Cry of Shadows (1990)

Leo Guild...1890s bounty hunter in Western United States
- ❑ ❑ 1 - Guild (1987)
- ❑ ❑ 2 - Death Ground (1988)
- ❑ ❑ 3 - Blood Game (1989)
- ❑ ❑ 4 - Dark Trail (1990)

Robert Payne...psychological profile investigator in New Hope, Iowa
- ❑ ❑ 1 - Blood Moon (1994) Brit.-Blood Red Moon
- ❑ ❑ 2 - Hawk Moon (1996)

Tobin...hot-tempered movie critic in New York, New York
- ❑ ❑ 1 - Murder on the Aisle (1987)
- ❑ ❑ 2 - Several Deaths Later (1988)

Walsh...50-something private eye in Cedar Rapids, Iowa
- ❑ ❑ 1 - The Night Remembers (1991)

■ **GOUGH, Laurence**

Two-time Ellis award winner Laurence Gough (pronounced Goff) has written 9 books featuring Jack Willows and Claire Parker, a pair of Vancouver, British Columbia, police detectives. The series opener, *The Goldfish Bowl* (1987) was named best first novel by Crime Writers of Canada, with book 3, *Hot Shots* (1989) taking best novel honors two years later. Toronto author Peter Robinson describes Claire Parker as his "detective dream date" and praises Gough's "spare, economic prose and vivid sense of Vancouver." He also credits Gough with "great wit and muscle," along with "special insight into the minds of narcissistic, not-very-bright, young wannabe criminals." A published poet and scriptwriter for CBC Radio, Gough lives in Vancouver. He has also written a Middle East thriller titled *Sandstorm* (1990).

Jack Willows & Claire Parker...police detective partners in Vancouver, Canada
- ❑ ❑ 1 - **The Goldfish Bowl (1987) Ellis winner** ★
- ❑ ❑ 2 - Death on a No. 8 Hook (1988) U.S.-Silent Knives
- ❑ ❑ 3 - **Hot Shots (1989) Ellis winner** ★
- ❑ ❑ 4 - Serious Crimes (1990)
- ❑ ❑ 5 - Accidental Deaths (1991)
- ❑ ❑ 6 - Fall Down Easy (1992)
- ❑ ❑ 7 - Killers (1994)
- ❑ ❑ 8 - Heartbreaker (1995)
- ❑ ❑ 9 - Memory Lane (1996)

■ **GRACE, C. L. [P]**

C.L. Grace is the pseudonym used by P.C. Doherty for his 15th century series featuring Kathryn Swinbrooke, Canterbury's City physician, apothecary, herbalist and death investigator. She is frequently assisted by soldier Colum Murtagh, the King's Commissioner who is her love but not her lover, according to a *Kirkus* review. The author is said to have based the character of Kathryn on the fact that women doctors played vital roles in medieval medicine, only to be excluded from the profession later on. This series is published only in the United States, and only in hardcover. It is not released in England and not yet reprinted in mass market paperback. For other historical series from this author, see Michael Clynes, P.C. Doherty, Ann Dukthas, and Paul Harding.

Kathryn Swinbrooke...15th century physician, apothecary, death investigator in Canterbury, England
- ❏ ❏   1 - A Shrine of Murders (1993)
- ❏ ❏   2 - The Eye of God (1994)
- ❏ ❏   3 - The Merchant of Death (1995)
- ❏ ❏   4 - The Book of Shadows (1996)

■ GRADY, James

A former investigative reporter for Jack Anderson and U.S. Senate aide to Lee Metcalf, James Grady has written 11 novels, numerous short stories and movie scripts for Paramount, Universal and Twentieth Century Fox. He is perhaps best known for his pair of espionage thrillers featuring CIA agent Richard Malcolm, immortalized by Robert Redford in *Three Days of the Condor*, inexplicably three days shorter than Grady's original novel. *Six Days of the Condor* (1974) was republished in 1975 under the three-day title as a movie tie-in. Grady's other series pairs feature a Baltimore police detective and a Washington DC private investigator. The Black Lizard anthology *Unusual Suspects* (1996), which he edited, raised funds for hunger and illiteracy programs worldwide. A native of Montana, Grady lives in Washington (DC) with his wife, ABC *PrimeTime Live* producer Bonnie Goldstein.

Devlin Rourke, Sgt.....police detective sergeant in Baltimore, Maryland
- ❏ ❏   1 - Razor Game (1985)
- ❏ ❏   2 - Just a Shot Away (1987)

John Rankin...private investigator in Washington, D.C.
- ❏ ❏   1 - Runner in the Street (1984)
- ❏ ❏   2 - Hard Bargains (1985)

Richard Malcolm...CIA analyst and grad student in Washington, D.C.
- ❏ ❏   1 - Six Days of the Condor (1974)
     - APA-Three Days of the Condor
- ❏ ❏   2 - Shadow of the Condor (1975)

■ GRAEME, Roderic [P]

Roderic Graeme is one of half a dozen pen names used by Roderic Jeffries for more than 100 mysteries and 25 books for children (some crime-related). As Roderic Graeme he continued the Blackshirt series started by his father Bruce Graeme (1900-1982), who with at least 4 pseudonyms of his own, set a fine example of productivity, longevity and numerous interesting characters. Blackshirt was a well-known and respected mystery writer named Richard Verrel, who became a gentleman thief by night, dressing all in black and stealing for the thrill and excitement. Jeffries added 20 more titles to the ones written by his father, giving the series a run of 46 years (1923-1969). He writes under his own name as well as Jeffrey Ashford, Hastings Draper, Roderic Graeme, Graham Hastings.

Richard Verrel as Blackshirt...romantic thief and best-selling author in England
- ❏ ❏   1 - Concerning Blackshirt (1952)
- ❏ ❏   2 - Blackshirt Wins the Trick (1953)
- ❏ ❏   3 - Blackshirt Passes By (1953)
- ❏ ❏   4 - Salute to Blackshirt (1954)
- ❏ ❏   5 - The Amazing Mr. Blackshirt (1955)
- ❏ ❏   6 - Blackshirt Meets the Lady (1956)
- ❏ ❏   7 - Paging Blackshirt (1957)

   ❑ ❑   8 - Blackshirt Helps Himself (1958)
   ❑ ❑   9 - Double for Blackshirt (1958)
   ❑ ❑ 10 - Blackshirt Sets the Pace (1959)
   ❑ ❑ 11 - Blackshirt Sees It Through (1960)
   ❑ ❑ 12 - Blackshirt Finds Trouble (1961)
   ❑ ❑ 13 - Blackshirt Takes the Trail (1962)
   ❑ ❑ 14 - Blackshirt on the Spot (1963)
   ❑ ❑ 15 - Call for Blackshirt (1963)
   ❑ ❑ 16 - Blackshirt Saves the Day (1964)
   ❑ ❑ 17 - Danger for Blackshirt (1965)
   ❑ ❑ 18 - Blackshirt at Large (1966)
   ❑ ❑ 19 - Blackshirt in Peril (1967)
   ❑ ❑ 20 - Blackshirt Stirs Things Up (1969)

■ GRANGER, Bill

Chicago journalist Bill Granger is the creator of three series, including his best known work about a field agent for R Section named Devereaux. Tucked inside the Agriculture Department, R Section was created by President Kennedy to provide an independent audit of intelligence operations following the Bay of Pigs fiasco. Code-named November Man, Devereaux first appeared in a 1979 novel that strangely paralleled the IRA bomb-assassination of Britain's Lord Mountbatten in August of that same year. His two Chicago series feature a pair of police detectives, Terry Flynn and Karen Kovac, and ex-sportswriter Jimmy Drover. Granger's newspaper coverage of courts, cops and Chicago politics for both major dailies and UPI earned numerous journalism awards. Born and raised in the Chicago area, he is a graduate of DePaul University and writes other fiction under the names Joe Gash and Bill Griffiths.

Devereaux aka November Man...field intelligence agent for R Section in New York, New York
   ❑ ❑   1 - The November Man [Edinburg] (1979)
   ❑ ❑   2 - Schism [Florida] (1981)
   ❑ ❑   3 - The Shattered Eye [France] (1982)
   ❑ ❑   4 - The British Cross [Helsinki] (1983)
   ❑ ❑   5 - The Zurich Numbers (1984)
   ❑ ❑   6 - Hemingway's Notebook [Caribbean] (1986)
   ❑ ❑   7 - There Are No Spies (1986)
   ❑ ❑   8 - The Infant of Prague (1987)
   ❑ ❑   9 - Henry McGee Is Not Dead [Alaska] (1988)
   ❑ ❑ 10 - The Man Who Heard Too Much (1989)
   ❑ ❑ 11 - League of Terror (1990)
   ❑ ❑ 12 - The Last Good German (1991)
   ❑ ❑ 13 - Burning the Apostle (1993)

Jimmy Drover...ex-sportswriter in Chicago, Illinois
   ❑ ❑ 1 - Drover (1991)
   ❑ ❑ 2 - Drover and the Zebras (1992)
   ❑ ❑ 3 - Drover and the Designated Hitter (1994)

Terry Flynn & Karen Kovac...Special Squad detectives in Chicago, Illinois
   ❑ ❑ 1 - **Public Murders (1980) Edgar winner ★**
   ❑ ❑ 2 - Priestly Murders [as by Joe Gash] (1984)
   ❑ ❑ 3 - Newspaper Murders [as by Joe Gash] (1985)
   ❑ ❑ 4 - The El Murders (1987)

■ GRANT, Maxwell [P]

Maxwell Grant is one of the pseudonyms of Dennis Lynds, author of 5 crime and mystery series under 5 different names. The first book-length mysteries he wrote were published under the house name Maxwell Grant as part of an attempt to revive The Shadow adventure series in the mid-'60s. Conceived as a radio character in the '30s, there was later a *Shadow* magazine and the full-length novels. As Dennis Lynds, he wrote two nonseries novels, two short story collections, including *Why Girls Ride Sidesaddle* (1980) and a novella, *Talking to the World* (1995). Past president of the Private Eye Writers of America, he was awarded the PWA Lifetime Achievement Award in 1988. Married to mystery writer Gayle Lynds, he lives in Santa Barbara (CA). The Shadow...P.I. of unknown identity in the United States

   ❏ ❏ 1 - The Shadow Strikes (1964)
   ❏ ❏ 2 - Shadow Beware (1965)
   ❏ ❏ 3 - Cry Shadow (1965)
   ❏ ❏ 4 - The Shadow's Revenge (1965)
   ❏ ❏ 5 - Mark of the Shadow (1966)
   ❏ ❏ 6 - Shadow—Go Mad! (1966)
   ❏ ❏ 7 - The Night of the Shadow (1966)
   ❏ ❏ 8 - The Shadow—Destination Moon (1967)

■ GRAY, A. W.

Former professional poker player and jazz musician, Albert William Gray, is the creator of 6'6" Dallas attorney Bino Phillips, introduced in *Bino* (1988). The name on his office door is W. A. Phillips for Wendell Arthur Phillips. His father the Baptist deacon had named him for a old-time circuit-riding preacher, but he'd been called Bino (pronounced BY-no) since he was a kid—short for albino because of his white hair. The supporting cast includes his secretary Dodie (Dora Annette) and investigator Half-a-Point Harrison, who used to run a bookmaking operation with his father Pop Harrison. Also known for his true crime books, Gray is the author of *The Cadet Murder Case* (1997) and *Poisoned Dreams* (1994). As Sarah Gregory he writes legal thrillers starring a beautiful and brainy Texas attorney. A lifelong Texas resident, Gray lives in Fort Worth.

Bino Phillips...6'6" attorney in Dallas, Texas
   ❏ ❏ 1 - Bino (1988)
   ❏ ❏ 2 - In Defense of Judges (1990)
   ❏ ❏ 3 - Killings (1993)
   ❏ ❏ 4 - Bino's Blues (1995)

■ GRAYSON, Richard [P]

Richard Grayson is a nom de plume for Richard Grindal, a consultant to the Scotch Whisky Association in London. As Grayson, he writes 2 mystery series, including the 9-book historical series featuring French police Inspector Jean-Paul Gautier from turn-of-the-century Paris. Book 9 is not a food mystery. The 'gratin' here refers to upper-crust Parisiennes, as they were called during the glamorous Belle Epoque era. When a chambermaid bitten by a cobra is found dead in the bed of a notorious millionaire, Insp. Gautier investigates. During the '50s Grayson wrote 4 books featuring British businessman John Bryant, last seen in *Dead So Soon* (1960). Under his own name he has penned several mysteries set in the Scotland, including *The Tartan Conspiracy* (1993). A graduate of Cambridge University, he lives in London.

Jean-Paul Gautier, Insp...fin-de-siécle French police inspector in Paris, France
   ❏ ❏ 1 - The Murders at Impasse Louvain (1978)
   ❏ ❏ 2 - The Monterant Affair (1980)
   ❏ ❏ 3 - The Death of the Abbe Didier (1981)
   ❏ ❏ 4 - The Montmarte Murders (1982)
   ❏ ❏ 5 - Crime Without Passion (1983)

❑ ❑ 6 - Death en Voyage (1986)
❑ ❑ 7 - Death on the Cards (1988)
❑ ❑ 8 - Death off Stage (1991)
❑ ❑ 9 - Death au Gratin (1994)

John Bryant...British businessman, England
❑ ❑ 1 - The Spiral Path (1955)
❑ ❑ 2 - Death in Melting (1957)
❑ ❑ 3 - Madman's Whisper (1958)
❑ ❑ 4 - Dead So Soon (1960)

■ GREELEY, Andrew M.

Andrew M. Greeley has written more than 120 books with over 15 million copies in print, primarily on topics of religion and sociology. His 30 novels include the Blackie Ryan series, most recently *The Bishop at Sea* (1997), and his newer series with Nuala (pronounced NEW-la) Ann McGrail, a young Irish immigrant appearing next in *Irish Whiskey* (1998). Greeley spent 10 years as a Chicago parish priest, later joining the National Opinion Research Center after earning a Ph.D. in sociology from the University of Chicago. More than slightly controversial, Greeley has been accused of writing steamy bestsellers for money. When he tried to pledge a million dollars of book royalties to inner-city Chicago schools, [then] Cardinal Bernardin turned the money down, without giving a reason, according to Greeley "arguably the first time in history the Catholic Church has turned down money from anyone."

John Blackwood "Blackie" Ryan...Catholic priest in Chicago, Illinois
❑ ❑ 1 - Happy Are the Meek (1985)
❑ ❑ 2 - Happy Are the Clean of Heart (1986)
❑ ❑ 3 - Happy Are Those Who Thirst for Justice (1987)
❑ ❑ 4 - Happy Are the Merciful (1992)
❑ ❑ 5 - Happy Are the Peacemakers (1993)
❑ ❑ 6 - Happy Are the Poor in Spirit (1994)
❑ ❑ 7 - Happy Are Those Who Mourn (1995)
❑ ❑ 8 - Happy Are the Oppressed (1996)

Nuala Ann McGrail...young Irish immigrant psychic and singer in Chicago, Illinois
❑ ❑ 1 - Irish Gold (1994)
❑ ❑ 2 - Irish Lace (1996)

■ GREENLEAF, Stephen

Like his fictional San Francisco private eye John Marshall Tanner, Stephen Greenleaf is a non-practicing attorney. While Tanner doesn't like the institution, Greenleaf says his reasons are more personal—he found himself too anxiety-prone to work as a litigator, the only area of the law that really appealed to him. Back in the days when he thought he might be a country lawyer, he wrote the first Tanner novel waiting to take the Iowa bar exam. After taking a writer's workshop to use up his G.I. Bill money, he never looked back. While most private eye writers collect their nominations early in a series, Greenleaf picked up his first with book 11, where Tanner goes to Seattle on a case for his former secretary Peggy Nettleton, who is about to marry another man. Born in Washington, DC, Greenleaf grew up in Iowa and has lived in San Francisco, Monterey (CA), Portland (OR), Seattle (WA) and now Ashland, Oregon.

John Marshall Tanner...non-practicing attorney P.I. in San Francisco, California
❑ ❑ 1 - Grave Error (1979)
❑ ❑ 2 - Death Bed (1980)
❑ ❑ 3 - State's Evidence (1982)
❑ ❑ 4 - Fatal Obsession (1983)
❑ ❑ 5 - Beyond Blame (1986)
❑ ❑ 6 - Toll Call (1987)

❑ ❑   7 - Book Case (1991)
❑ ❑   8 - Blood Type (1992)
❑ ❑   9 - Southern Cross (1993)
❑ ❑ 10 - False Conception (1994)
❑ ❑ 11 - **Flesh Wounds (1996) Shamus nominee** ☆
❑ ❑ 12 - Past Tense (1997)

■ GREER, Robert O.

Robert O. Greer has written three books featuring black Denver bail bondsman and bounty hunter C. J. Floyd, introduced in *The Devil's Hatband* (1996). Continuing characters include a pair of ex-rodeo cowboys down on their luck and Floyd's girlfriend Mavis. Greer is the founder and editor-in-chief of the *High Plains Literary Review* and holds a master's degree in creative writing from Boston University. He also holds degrees in dentistry, medicine and pathology. He specializes in head and neck pathology and cancer reserach at Colorado Health Sciences Center, where he is a professor of pathology, medicine, surgery and dentistry. In 1983 his cancer research group was the first to report a link between smokeless tobacco and certain cancers of the mouth. He also reviews books for Denver's NPR affiliate and raises Black Baldy cattle on his ranch near Steamboat Springs (CO).

C. J. Floyd...bail bondsman and bounty hunter in Denver, Colorado
❑ ❑   1 - The Devil's Hatband (1996)
❑ ❑   2 - The Devil's Red Nickel (1997)
❑ ❑   3 - The Devil's Backbone (1998)

■ GREGORY, Sarah [P]

Sarah Gregory is a pseudonym of former professional poker player and jazz musician, Albert William Gray, who also writes as William Gray and A. W. Gray. His Bino Phillips series, written as A. W. Gray, includes 4 books featuring a 6'6" Dallas attorney with white hair. Also known for his true crime books, Gray is the author of *The Cadet Murder Case* (1997) and *Poisoned Dreams* (1994). As Sarah Gregory he writes legal thrillers which outsell his other crime fiction by a wide margin. The Gregory books feature Sharon Hays, a beautiful and brainy Texas attorney, who in book 2 finds herself representing an innocent death row inmate after a pro bono case turned up evidence of another man's guilt. The accused had been railroaded by his very powerful father-in-law and Sharon is forced to ruffle some dangerous political feathers. A lifelong Texas resident, Gray lives in Fort Worth.

Sharon Hays...defense attorney in Dallas, Texas
❑ ❑   1 - In Self Defense (1996)
❑ ❑   2 - Public Trust (1997)

■ GRISSOM, Ken

Houston Post reporter Ken Grissom has worked at newspapers all across the Texas and Louisiana Gulf Coast, no doubt collecting material for his mysteries featuring a one-eyed Creole salvager named John Rodrigue. Although the series opener, *Drop-Off* (1988), takes Rodgrique to the Caribbean, he is later based in Galveston (TX). Trying to keep away from demon Jamaican run and beautiful women, he lets a pretty face (she's a Venezuelan anthropologist) involve him in an international spy ring that is plotting to sabotage a NASA space shuttle with an all-women crew. In their review of *Drowned Man's Key* (1992), Kirkus called Rodrigue "one very appealing Creole." A native of Corpus Christi, Grissom is also the author of *Buckskins and Black Powder: A Mountain Man's Guide to Muzzleloading* (1983).

John Rodrigue...one-eyed Creole salvager in the Caribbean
❑ ❑   1 - Drop-Off (1988)
❑ ❑   2 - Big Fish (1991)
❑ ❑   3 - Drowned Man's Key (1992)

■ HACKLER, Micah S.

Micah S. Hackler has written 4 paperback mysteries featuring single father and part-time New Mexico rancher and sheriff Cliff Lansing and his deputy Gabe Hanna. When first seen in *Legend of the Dead* (1995), the sheriff has an unsolved murder on his hands after a local is killed in the desert digging up Indian artifacts to sell on the black market and a Zuni shaman and U.S. senator become assassins' targets. In *Coyote Returns* (1996), Cliff has to contend with the FBI, a high-stakes power struggle over timber and a gunshot girlfriend in a coma. A serial killer is collecting scalps and leaving feathers with the bodies in *The Shadow Catcher* (1997), while a rare emerald amulet is uncovered by archaeologists in *The Dark Canyon* (1997). Strangely, an entry in the journal of Cliff's great grandfather provides a clue to the amulet's power. Hackler traces his own ancestry to Cherokee survivors of the Trail of Tears.

Cliff Lansing & Gabe Hanna...single-father part-time rancher-sheriff & his deputy in New Mexico
- ❏ ❏ 1 - Legend of the Dead (1995)
- ❏ ❏ 2 - Coyote Returns (1996)
- ❏ ❏ 3 - The Shadow Catcher (1997)
- ❏ ❏ 4 - The Dark Canyon (1997)

■ HAILEY, J. P. [P]

J. P. Hailey is the pseudonym used by Parnell Hall for his Steve Winslow courtroom mysteries, beginning with *The Baxter Trust* (1988). In *The Anonymous Client* (1989), the New York City actor-turned-lawyer becomes the prime suspect in a murder investigation after receiving $10,000 in the mail with an unsigned note. Under his own name, this author writes the Stanley Hastings private eye series, beginning with *Detective* (1987), winner of the Edgar and Shamus nominations for best first novel. He once worked as a private detective and has several screenplays to his credit. In 1969 he spoke the immortal words "Come back with my chariot!" (wearing a leopard skin) in *Hercules in New York* (1969), Arnold Schwartznegger's first movie. Hall has never seen the movie, but he knows it plays occasionally, and whenever it does he receives a $40 (pretax) residual check.

Steve Winslow...courtroom attorney in New York, New York
- ❏ ❏ 1 - The Baxter Trust (1988)
- ❏ ❏ 2 - The Anonymous Client (1989)
- ❏ ❏ 3 - The Underground Man (1990)
- ❏ ❏ 4 - The Naked Typist (1990)
- ❏ ❏ 5 - The Wrong Gun (1992)

■ HALL, James W.

Hammett Award nominee James W. Hall has written 6 books featuring an avenging South Florida private eye named Thorn. Literate and fierce at the same time, these novels are strongly tied to environmental, medical and animal rights issues. Thorn's most recent case, *Red Sky at Night* (1997), involves 11 murdered dolphins who were part of a Florida Keys healing experiment. In the Hammett-nominated *Buzz Cut* (1996) a cruise ship is hijacked by a homidical maniac, while poachers and orangutan kidnappers from the jungles of Borneo murder the daughter of a friend in *Gone Wild* (1995). Born in Kentucky, Hall once lived in Bilbao, Spain. He currently writes novels, poetry, short stories and screenplays from his home in a South Florida avocado grove. He holds an M.A. from Johns Hopkins and a Ph.D. from the University of Utah.

Thorn...eco-avenger P.I. in Key Largo, Florida
- ❏ ❏ 1 - Under Cover of Daylight (1987)
- ❏ ❏ 2 - Tropical Freeze (1989) Brit.-Squall Line

❏ ❏ 3 - Mean High Tide (1994)
❏ ❏ 4 - Gone Wild (1995)
❏ ❏ 5 - **Buzz Cut (1996) Hammett nominee** ☆
❏ ❏ 6 - Red Sky at Night (1997)

■ **HALL, Parnell**

Parnell Hall is the creator of Stanley Hastings, owner of a one-man detective agency, whose first case received best-first-novel Edgar and Shamus nominations for *Detective* (1987). Hall uses some of his own experience from 2 years as a New York City P.I. for cases he assigns Stanley and his wife Alice, who becomes more involved in the business as the series progresses. A part-time actor, Hall has worked in summer stock, regional theater and interactive dinner theater events. In *Juror* (1990) he loans one of his movie experiences to Stanley, who plays 'Skinny Hercules' in Arnold Schwartzenegger's first film (*Hercules in New York*, 1969). Attired in a leopard skin, Stanley has to chase his runaway chariot down Broadway, waving a hotdog. Writing as J. P. Hailey he is the author of the Steve Winslow courtroom mysteries.

Stanley Hastings...married actor and private eye in New York, New York
❏ ❏ 1 - **Detective (1987) Edgar & Shamus nominee** ☆☆
❏ ❏ 2 - Murder (1988)
❏ ❏ 3 - Favor (1988)
❏ ❏ 4 - Strangler (1989)
❏ ❏ 5 - Client (1990)
❏ ❏ 6 - Juror (1990)
❏ ❏ 7 - Shot (1992)
❏ ❏ 8 - Actor (1993)
❏ ❏ 9 - Blackmail (1994)
❏ ❏ 10 - **Movie (1995) Shamus nominee** ☆
❏ ❏ 11 - Trial (1996)
❏ ❏ 12 - Scam (1997)
❏ ❏ 13 - Suspense (1998)

■ **HALL, Robert Lee**

California artist and teacher Robert Lee Hall is the author of numerous mystery novels including the witty historical series featuring oh-so-clever American inventor Benjamin Franklin, introduced in *Benjamin Franklin Takes the Case* (1998). In his latest adventure, a tale told in *London Blood* (1997), a killer is stalking young women, leaving an ancient coin inscribed with the words "do what you will" by his victims' bodies. A native of San Francisco (CA), Hall earned both his BFA and MFA from the California College of Arts and Crafts. During a sabbatical to study etching he first began writing short stories and wrote his first novel from a short story that got out of hand. His other fiction includes *Murder at San Simeon* (1988), *The King Edward Plot* (1980) and *Exit Sherlock Holmes* (1977).

Benjamin Franklin...18th century American inventor in London, England
❏ ❏ 1 - Benjamin Franklin Takes the Case (1988)
❏ ❏ 2 - Benjamin Franklin & a Case of Christmas Murder (1990)
❏ ❏ 3 - Murder at Drury Lane (1992)
❏ ❏ 4 - Benjamin Franklin and the Case of Artful Murder (1994)
❏ ❏ 5 - Murder by the Waters (1995)
❏ ❏ 6 - London Blook (1997)

■ HALLINAN, Timothy

Timothy Hallinan is the creator of a 4-degreed Los Angeles P.I. named Simeon Grist. Book 1, the author's first novel, was written in just 6 weeks after his house burned to the ground and everything he owned was lost, including all the fragments of books he'd started and abandoned. He said the fire was a defining moment. He knew that part of his life wasn't working, so he left the country and wrote like a man possessed. With a graduate thesis on Shakespeare to prove it, Hallinan is compulsive about the Bard's great theme of restoration of order. And he shares his various degrees with Grist so the P.I.'s mental process can include a wide range of material without it seeming forced or pretentious. A former rock lyricist and vocalist, Hallinan founded his own upscale PR and consulting firm. He divides his time among Manhattan, Los Angeles and Bangkok, Thailand.

Simeon Grist...four-degreed P.I. in Los Angeles, California
- ❏ ❏ 1 - The Four Last Things (1989)
- ❏ ❏ 2 - Everything but the Squeal (1990)
- ❏ ❏ 3 - Skin Deep (1991)
- ❏ ❏ 4 - Incinerator (1992)
- ❏ ❏ 5 - A Man With No Time (1993)
- ❏ ❏ 6 - The Bone Polisher (1995)

■ HAMILTON, Donald

The Edgar-nominated Don Hamilton has been writing about American superspy Matt Helm over a period of four decades. As described by Robert Skinner (*St. James Guide*), Helm is a "curious amalgam of average guy, sportsman, patriot and ruthless killer...sentimental about dogs, and almost maudlin in love." He usually has to solve a rather complex mystery before he can "make the touch." According to Skinner, Helm idealizes the frontier hero, his own rigid code of honor a blend of chivalry and Code of the West. Interestingly, Hamilton had some success as a writer of westerns during the '50s. His novel *The Big Country* (1957), considered one of this century's great western novels, became an award-winning 1958 movie starring Gregory Peck, Jean Simmons, Burl Ives, Charlton Heston and Chuck Connors.

Matt Helm...American superspy in the United States
- ❏ ❏ 1 - Death of a Citizen (1960)
- ❏ ❏ 2 - The Wrecking Crew (1960)
- ❏ ❏ 3 - The Removers (1961)
- ❏ ❏ 4 - Murderer's Row (1962)
- ❏ ❏ 5 - The Silencers (1962)
- ❏ ❏ 6 - The Ambushers (1963)
- ❏ ❏ 7 - The Shadowers (1964)
- ❏ ❏ 8 - The Ravagers (1964)
- ❏ ❏ 9 - The Devastators (1965)
- ❏ ❏ 10 - The Betrayers (1966)
- ❏ ❏ 11 - The Menacers (1968)
- ❏ ❏ 12 - The Interlopers (1969)
- ❏ ❏ 13 - The Poisoners (1971)
- ❏ ❏ 14 - The Intriguers (1972)
- ❏ ❏ 15 - The Intimidators (1974)
- ❏ ❏ 16 - The Terminators (1975)
- ❏ ❏ 17 - **The Retaliators (1976) Edgar nominee** ☆
- ❏ ❏ 18 - The Terrorizers (1977)
- ❏ ❏ 19 - The Revengers (1982)
- ❏ ❏ 20 - The Annihilators (1983)
- ❏ ❏ 21 - The Infiltrators (1984)

❑ ❑ 22 - The Detonators (1985)
❑ ❑ 23 - The Vanishers (1986)
❑ ❑ 24 - The Demolishers (1987)
❑ ❑ 25 - The Frighteners (1989)
❑ ❑ 26 - The Threateners (1992)
❑ ❑ 27 - The Damagers(1993)

■ HAMMOND, Gerald

Gerald Hammond lives in the Scottish Highlands where he hunts, fishes and writes two mystery series. One features the world of sport shooting, the other the world of dogs. Gunsmith Keith Calder is a shooting instructor and former poacher who marries, opens a gunshop and becomes more respectable as the series progresses. And the daughter who's a baby in book 6 becomes a sleuth in her own right and a gun club steward by book 14. In the newer series, dog breeder John Cunningham's sleuthing partners are veterinarian Isobel Kitts and kennelmaid Beth Catrell. As Arthur Douglas, he has written 3 books with a British Army major. Hammond's own military experience includes service in the Queen's Royal Regiment and 2 years as architect for the Navy, Army, Air Force Institute. Former resident architect at St. Andrews University, he has been writing full-time since 1983.

John Cunningham...war hero and hunting dog trainer in Scotland
❑ ❑ 1 - Dog in the Dark (1989)
❑ ❑ 2 - Doghouse (1989)
❑ ❑ 3 - Whose Dog Are You? (1990)
❑ ❑ 4 - Give a Dog a Name (1992)
❑ ❑ 5 - The Curse of the Cockers (1993)
❑ ❑ 6 - Sting in the Tail (1994)
❑ ❑ 7 - Mad Dogs and Scotsmen (1995)
❑ ❑ 8 - Bloodlines (1996)

Keith Calder...gunsmith and sport shooter in Newton Lauder, Scotland
❑ ❑ 1 - Dead Game (1979)
❑ ❑ 2 - The Reward Game (1980)
❑ ❑ 3 - The Revenge Game (1981)
❑ ❑ 4 - Fair Game (1982)
❑ ❑ 5 - The Game (1982)
❑ ❑ 6 - Cousin Once Removed (1984)
❑ ❑ 7 - Sauce for the Pigeon (1984)
❑ ❑ 8 - Pursuit of Arms (1985)
❑ ❑ 9 - Silver City Scandal (1986)
❑ ❑ 10 - The Executor (1986)
❑ ❑ 11 - The Worried Widow (1987)
❑ ❑ 12 - Adverse Report (1987)
❑ ❑ 13 - Stray Shot (1988)
❑ ❑ 14 - A Brace of Skeet (1989)
❑ ❑ 15 - Let Us Prey (1990)
❑ ❑ 16 - Home to Roost (1990)
❑ ❑ 17 - In Camera (1991)
❑ ❑ 18 - Snatch Crop (1991)
❑ ❑ 19 - Thin Air (1993)
❑ ❑ 20 - Hook or Crook (1994)
❑ ❑ 21 - Carriage of Justice (1995)
❑ ❑ 22 - Follow That Gun (1996)
❑ ❑ 23 - Sink or Swim (1997)

■ HANDBERG, Ron

Ron Handberg spent 30 years in broadcasting and television journalism, retiring in 1989 as vice president and general manager of WCCO-TV, the CBS affiliate in Minneapolis-St. Paul (MN). With much of his career spent in the news department, he has collected lots of story ideas for mystery thrillers involving a television newsroom crew. In *Savage Justice* (1992), the Channel 7 Twin Cities newest anchor gets a hot tip from an old flame about a judge who's got a very dirty secret. In *Cry Vengeance* (1993), one of the newsroom's rookie reporters discovers a group of sexual assault victims who are taking the law into their own hands. The police and Channel 7 lawyers order her to drop the story. When last seen, in *Malice Intended* (1997), news anchor and single mother Maggie Lawrence is facing blackmail and hit-and-run. Just your average day behind the television news cameras

TV newsroom series...newsroom crew in Minneapolis, Minnesota
- ❏ ❏ 1 - Savage Justice (1992)
- ❏ ❏ 2 - Cry Vengeance (1993)
- ❏ ❏ 3 - Malice Intended (1997)

■ HANDLER, David

Edgar award winner David Handler is the creator of celebrity ghostwriter Stewart "Hoagy" Hoag and his faithful, but neurotic, cat-food-eating basset hound Lulu, who accompanies him on his travels. As the one-time "It Boy" of modern fiction, Hoagy is forced to dig up dirt and schmooze with celebrities ever since the dismal failure of his second book. Joining Lulu as a supporting cast member is Merilee Nash, Hoagy's long-time love and ex-wife. In book 8, he's writing the story of New York's hottest celebrity, a cold-blooded serial killer who calls himself "The Answer Man." A former journalist and sometime ghostwriter and producer, Handler writes extensively for television. With an M.S. from Columbia University, he has also worked as a syndicated columnist and Broadway critic. Born in Los Angeles, he currently lives in a 200-year-old carriage house in Old Lyme (CT).

Stewart "Hoagy" Hoag...celebrity ghostwriter in the United States
- ❏ ❏ 1 - The Man Who Died Laughing (1988)
- ❏ ❏ 2 - The Man Who Lived By Night (1989)
- ❏ ❏ **3 - The Man Who Would Be F. Scott Fitzgerald (1990) Edgar winner ★**
- ❏ ❏ 4 - The Woman Who Fell From Grace (1991)
- ❏ ❏ 5 - The Boy Who Never Grew Up (1993)
- ❏ ❏ 6 - The Man Who Cancelled Himself (1995)
- ❏ ❏ 7 - The Girl Who Ran Off With Daddy (1996)
- ❏ ❏ 8 - The Man Who Loved Women to Death (1997)

■ HANSEN, Joseph

When Lambda award winner and Shamus nominee Joseph Hansen published his first Dave Brandstetter mystery in 1970, the gay insurance investigator (and his creator) broke new ground in popular fiction. It took 3 years to convince a publisher that Hansen's matter-of-fact, nonapologetic approach to homosexuality could sell. Brandstetter was shrewd, cool, tough-minded, and in spite of this, a gay man. According to Hansen, the message that gays are no different from other people hardly seems earth-shaking, but he felt gay characters had been treated shabbily in detective fiction and his mission was to change that. As Rose Brock he wrote a pair of Gothic novels, one of which (*Longleaf*, 1974) was set in New Orleans. Hansen says he hated every day of the 18 months it took to research the book, which promptly sold more copies than anything he'd ever done. A native of Aberdeen (SD), he lives in Los Angeles (CA). He has also written fiction as James Colton.

Dave Brandstetter...gay death-claims investigator in Los Angeles, California
- ❏ ❏   1 - Fadeout (1970)
- ❏ ❏   2 - Death Claims (1973)
- ❏ ❏   3 - Troublemaker (1975)
- ❏ ❏   4 - The Man Everybody Was Afraid Of (1978)
- ❏ ❏   5 - Skinflick (1979)
- ❏ ❏   **6 - Gravedigger (1982) Shamus nominee** ☆
- ❏ ❏   7 - Nightwork (1984)
- ❏ ❏   ss - Brandstetter and Others [short stories] (1984)
- ❏ ❏   8 - The Little Dog Laughed (1986)
- ❏ ❏   9 - Obedience (1988)
- ❏ ❏ 10 - The Boy Who Was Buried This Morning (1990)
- ❏ ❏ 11 - **Country of Old Men (1991) Lambda winner** ★

■ HANSON, Rick

Rick Hanson is the creator of a humorous mystery series featuring Oregon sculptor Adam McCleet, an ex-Marine and former Portland cop. In the series opener, McCleet investigates the disappearance of his big sister's 4th husband, who vanished from a Seattle orthodontist's convention. A vicious, karate-kicking dentist turns out to be the Yuppie Ripper, stealing vital organs from young professionals in the Pacific Northwest. In book 4, McCleet stands to inherit a fortune if he can find the killer of the eccentric "Salmon King of Oregon" within 30 days. The Salmon King was fairly certain the killer would be present, so he hires the ex-cop post mortem, during the viewing of his videotaped will. After touring Southeast Asia as a Marine combat photographer, Hanson worked as an aerial photographer in Denver (CO).

Adam McCleet...ex-cop turned sculptor in Portland, OR
- ❏ ❏ 1 - Spare Parts (1994)
- ❏ ❏ 2 - Mortal Remains (1995)
- ❏ ❏ 3 - Still Life (1996)
- ❏ ❏ 4 - Splitting Heirs (1997)

■ HARDING, Paul [P]

Paul Harding is one of the pseudonyms of Oxford history scholar and school headmaster P.C. Doherty, author of at least 36 books in seven historical mystery series with settings from Chaucer's time to the 16th century. His books appear under the names Michael Clynes, Ann Dukthas, C.L. Grace, Paul Harding and his own, P.C. Doherty. And it is suspected that a new series published under the name Anna Apostolou (*Murder in Macedon*, 1997) is another of his. The Paul Harding books are subtitled the "*Sorrowful Mysteries of Brother Athelstan*" and feature a 14th century Dominican monk and London's coroner. The pair is described by a *Kirkus* reviewer as the "loud-mouthed, wine-swilling, softhearted Lord Coroner (John Cranston) and his clever aide Friar Athelstan of down-at-the-heels St. Erconwald's church."

Athelstan, Brother & John Cranston...14th century Dominican monk & coroner in London, England
- ❏ ❏ 1 - The Nightingale Gallery (1991)
- ❏ ❏ 2 - The House of the Red Slayer (1992) U.S.-The Red Slayer
- ❏ ❏ 3 - Murder Most Holy (1992)
- ❏ ❏ 4 - The Anger of God (1993)
- ❏ ❏ 5 - By Murder's Bright Light (1994)
- ❏ ❏ 6 - The House of Crows (1995)
- ❏ ❏ 7 - An Assassins's Riddle (1996)

■ HARKNETT, Terry

By the time he turned 50, British author Terry Harknett had published more than 150 novels, including a pair of mystery series. A trilogy featuring Chief Supt. John Crown starts with a story set in Macao, while his longer series focuses on private investigator Steve Wayne, with cases throughout the Far East. Harknett has written widely under at least 15 pen names, often as a ghost writer. According to *Hawk's Authors' Pseudonyms* (1995), Harknett has written as Frank Chandler (ghosted *A Fistful of Dollars*, 1972), David Ford, George G. Gilman, Peter Haining, Adam Hardy, Jane Harman, Joseph Hedges (12 Sphere novels), William M. James, Alex Peters, Charles R. Pike, William Pine, James Russell, Thomas H. Stone, Thomas P. Stone and William Terry. In a *Contemporary Authors* interview in the mid '80s, he described his work in progress as "One new book every two months."

John Crown, Chief Supt.....chief superintendent in China
- ❏ ❏ 1 - Crown: Macao Mayhem (1974)
- ❏ ❏ 2 - Crown: The Sweet and Sour Kill (1974)
- ❏ ❏ 3 - Crown: Bamboo Shoot-Out (1975)

Steve Wayne...private investigator in the Far East
- ❏ ❏ 1 - The Benevolent Blackmailer (1962)
- ❏ ❏ 2 - The Scratch on the Surface (1962)
- ❏ ❏ 3 - Invitation to a Funeral (1963)
- ❏ ❏ 4 - Dead Little Rich Girl (1963)
- ❏ ❏ 5 - The Evil Money (1964)
- ❏ ❏ 6 - The Man Who Did Not Die (1964)
- ❏ ❏ 7 - The Two-Way Frame (1967)
- ❏ ❏ 8 - Death of an Aunt (1967)
- ❏ ❏ 9 - The Softcover Kill (1971)

■ HARPER, Richard

During the 1980s Richard Harper wrote at least four paperback mysteries featuring Arizona police detectives, including at least two books with Tom Ragnon, a cop who lives in a trailer. Ragnon is introduced in *Death Raid* (1986), which takes place mostly in Mexico, but he's back in Arizona for book 2, *Kinderkill* (1989). One of Harper's earlier novels, *The Kill Factor* (1984), features the investigative team of Det. Sgt. Doug Roberts and his new Chicano partner, "Rabbit" Gomez. Their partnership starts with a prickly distrust but gradually develops into respect and rapport in a novel praised as "first-rate" by Marcia Muller (*1001 Midnights*). According to Muller, Harper's earlier police novel (featuring different detectives), *Death to the Dancing Masters* (1980), is "equally good." Both nonseries books are set in fictional Mimbres County (AZ).

Tom Ragnon...cop who lives in a trailer in Arizona
- ❏ ❏ 1 - Death Raid (1986)
- ❏ ❏ 2 - Kinderkill (1989)

■ HARRINGTON, William

William Harrington spent more than 20 years practicing law—governmental, corporate and private— before turning to full-time writing. Since 1963 he has produced more than 20 books under his own name, ghostwritten at least 14 for celebrities and penned another 17 or more pseudonymously. He is currently best known for his Columbo series, numbering 6 books since 1993. *New York Daily News* said of the latest, "That rumpled raincoat is as convincing in the mind's eye as it is on the small screen," while *Booklist* praised Harrington's "attention to forensic detail that matches any of the more serious procedurals." It has long been assumed Harrington ghostwrites the Elliott Roosevelt mysteries, based on acknowledgments in the early books. After completing an M.A. at Duke, Harrington earned his law degree at Ohio State. A Phi Beta Kappa from Marietta College (OH), he is a licensed pilot.

Columbo, Lt....rumpled police detective in Los Angeles, California
- ❑ ❑ 1 - Columbo: The Grassy Knoll (1993)
- ❑ ❑ 2 - Columbo: The Helter Skelter Murders (1994)
- ❑ ❑ 3 - Columbo: The Hoffa Connection (1995)
- ❑ ❑ 4 - Columbo: The Game Show Killer (1996)
- ❑ ❑ 5 - Columbo: The Glitter Murder (1997)
- ❑ ❑ 6 - Columbo: The Hoover Files (1998)

■ HARRISON, Ray

Ray(mond Vincent) Harrison is the creator of a police series set in Victorian England, featuring an unlikely pair of coppers. According to an interview with *Contemporary Authors*, Sgt. Bragg comes from the bottom of the pile, a countryman with only basic formal education, a cynical attitude to the upper class and a view of right and wrong that only loosely accords with justice under the law. Constable Morton, on the other hand, is a wealthy young man from an influential family, armed with a university degree and a conviction that he ought to do something useful with his life. Before turning to full-time writing in 1983, Harrison spent 30 years in business and finance working as a tax inspector, fraud squad investigator, managing director of an insurance group and director of a financial consulting group. He earned both his B.A. (with honors) and M.A. at Cambridge University. He lives in County Cork, Ireland.

Joseph Bragg, Sgt. & James Morton, Constable...Victorian police officers in England
- ❑ ❑ 1 - French Ordinary Murder (1983)
    U.S.-Why Kill Arthur Potter?
- ❑ ❑ 2 - Death of an Honourable Member (1984)
- ❑ ❑ 3 - Death of a Dancing Lady (1985)
- ❑ ❑ 4 - Deathwatch (1985)
- ❑ ❑ 5 - Counterfeit of Murder (1987)
- ❑ ❑ 6 - A Season for Death (1987)
- ❑ ❑ 7 - Harvest of Death (1988)
- ❑ ❑ 8 - Tincture of Death (1989)
- ❑ ❑ 9 - Sphere of Death (1990)
- ❑ ❑ 10 - Patently Murder (1990)
- ❑ ❑ 11 - Akin to Murder (1992)
- ❑ ❑ 12 - Murder in Petticoat Square (1993)
- ❑ ❑ 13 - Hallmark of Murder (1995)
- ❑ ❑ 14 - Murder by Design (1996)

■ HARRISS, Will

In his first published novel Will Harriss begins with the murder of a librarian found with a copy of *The Bay Psalm* Book in his hand. Cliff suspects the book, thought to be the first printed in the American colonies, was a forgery. But it was donated to the library by a candidate for governor of California who claimed a $300,000 tax deduction. The mystery was inspired by the career of Thomas J. Wise, famous English bibliographer and forger who concocted stories about his forgeries which many unwitting professors incorporated into their lectures for decades. In *Noble Rot* (1993), Harriss introduces a new amateur sleuth who, after blowing his inheritance, goes to work in his uncle's Napa Valley winery, only to find a dead body in the fermentation tank. A former senior research editor at the Rand Corporation, Harriss is an avid fly fisherman who has published short stories and articles and sold both television and movie scripts.

Cliff Dunbar...former English professor turned detective in Los Angeles, California
- ❑ ❑ 1 - **The Bay Psalm Book Murder (1983) Edgar winner ★**
- ❑ ❑ 2 - Timor Mortis (1986)

■ HART, Roy

Roy Hart has written a series of English village mysteries featuring Detective Superintendent Douglas Roper, frequently sent from County headquarters to outlying Dorset communities when local crimes need his investigative attention. In the series opener, *Seascape With Dead Figures* (1987), a killer New Year's Eve party turns into just that for the wealthy host, whose body is found at the foot of a seaside cliff. Shortly after, the man who found the body becomes a corpse himself. But Roper has a theory. When last seen in *A Deadly Schedule* (1994), Roper is vacationing in Crete when the body of a rich Englishman turns up bludgeoned in his hotel. Back at home, a murder and seeming suicide appear to be linked. Roper's 20 years of police experience lead him to question if the killer from Crete has come to Dorsey.

Douglas Roper, Chief Insp.....detective superintendent in Dorset, England
- ❏ ❏ 1 - Seascape with Dead Figures (1987)
- ❏ ❏ 2 - A Pretty Place for a Murder (1987)
- ❏ ❏ 3 - A Fox in the Night (1988)
- ❏ ❏ 4 - Remains to be Seen (1989)
- ❏ ❏ 5 - Robbed Blind (1990)
- ❏ ❏ 6 - Breach of Promise (1991)
- ❏ ❏ 7 - Final Appointment (1993)
- ❏ ❏ 8 - A Deadly Schedule (1994)

■ HARVEY, Clay

Clay Harvey is the creator of Tyler Vance, former special operative turned family man who'd like to devote himself to parenting and outdoors writing, but just can't seem to avoid trouble. In the series opener, our hero pulls into a North Carolina bank parking lot just as an armed robber is exiting the bank. Vance reacts the only way he knows how (as a trained killer) and invokes the wrath of organized crime. All hell breaks loose (literally). Six months later in book 2, lots of money ($2 million) from an earlier gun deal turns up in Mexico. But the Bosnian Muslims who say it's theirs want it back and Vance ends up in the middle. Great supporting cast and more laughs than you'd expect, but there are lots of guns here folks. No big surprise Harvey has written several gun manuals including *Popular Sporting Rifle Cartridges* (1984) and *The Rifles, the Cartridges and the Game* (1991)

Tyler Vance...ex-operative turned family man in NC, United States
- ❏ ❏ 1 - A Flash of Red (1996)
- ❏ ❏ 2 - A Whisper of Black (1997)

■ HARVEY, James Neal

James Neal Harvey is the creator of Lt. Ben Tolliver, a tall, rangy ex-Marine turned NYPD homicide detective. Not particularly suited to working indoors, he's one of those cops prone to swimming against the tide. By book 4 he's assigned to the Special Investigations Unit of the Manhattan DA's Office, thanks to his impressive record with high-profile cases as head of the Sixth Precinct detective squad. In a story described by one reviewer as *Listening to Prozac* meets *Invasion of the Body Snatchers*, Tolliver matches wits with a brilliant shrink whose posh office/residence on East 80th Street has a basement laboratory full of large Norway brown rats (research subjects). The evil psychiatrist is bent on developing a drug for mind control. A full-time writer and married father of 5, Harvey divides his time between Palm Beach (FL) and Martha's Vineyard (MA).

Ben Tolliver, Lt.....NYPD lieutenant in New York, New York
- ❏ ❏ 1 - By Reason of Insanity (1991)
- ❏ ❏ 2 - Painted Ladies (1994)

  ❏ ❏   3 - Flesh & Blood (1994)
  ❏ ❏   4 - Mental Case (1996)
  ❏ ❏   5 - Dead Game (1997)

■ **HARVEY, John**

"If John Harvey's novels were songs," said the *New York Times Book Review*, "Charlie Parker would play them. [Harvey] sings the blues for people too bruised to carry the tune themselves." Print credits for this London-born novelist and poet include more than 90 books, with 9 western series totaling at least 53 novels. He has written TV and radio scripts, novelizations from other media and books for juveniles. With an M.A. in American Studies from the University of Nottingham, he has lectured at university and taught high school English and drama. An ardent and informed jazz aficionado, he even finds time for critical work (his essay on James Crumley is included in *Criminal Proceedings*, 1997). An exhaustive (and exhausting!) bibliography can be found at his website <www.mellotone.co.uk>, along with his literate and funny newsletter, *In a Mellotone*.

Charlie Resnick, Det. Insp.....40-something jazz fan police detective in Nottingham, England
  ❏ ❏   1 - Lonely Hearts (1989)
  ❏ ❏   2 - **Rough Treatment (1990) Dagger nominee** ☆
  ❏ ❏   3 - Cutting Edge (1991)
  ❏ ❏   4 - Off Minor (1992)
  ❏ ❏   5 - Wasted Years (1993)
  ❏ ❏   6 - Cold Light (1994)
  ❏ ❏   7 - Living Proof (1995)
  ❏ ❏   8 - Easy Meat (1996)
  ❏ ❏   9 - Still Water (1997)
  ❏ ❏   10 - Last Rites (1998)

Scott Mitchell...private eye in England
  ❏ ❏   1 - Amphetamines and Pearls (1976)
  ❏ ❏   2 - The Geranium Kiss (1976)
  ❏ ❏   3 - Junkyard Angel (1977)
  ❏ ❏   4 - Neon Madmen (1977)

■ **HAUTMAN, Pete**

Pete(r Murray) Hautman published his first adult mystery in 1993. The *Wall Street Journal* thought the dialogue was "terrific and the descriptions laugh-out-loud funny." The *New York Times Book Review* suggested "whatever Pete Hautman was doing before he wrote *Drawing Dead*, he was wasting his time." Turns out he'd been working in graphic design and illustration until he decided in 1991 to write full time. Since then he has produced 3 mysteries about a group of small-town gamblers and more than 50 non-fiction books for kids. Writing as Peter Murray for The Child's World, he has covered everything from *Your Bones* (1992) to *Science Tricks With Air* (1994), as well as biographies of Sitting Bull, Marie Curie, Thomas Edison and Martin Luther King, Jr. Married to mystery writer and poet Mary Logue, he lives in Minneapolis (MN).

Joe Crow, Sam O'Gara, Axel Speeter & Tommy Fabian...small-town professional gamblers in Minnesota
  ❏ ❏   1 - Drawing Dead (1994)
  ❏ ❏   2 - Short Money (1995)
  ❏ ❏   3 - The Mortal Nuts (1996)

■ **HAVILL, Steven F.**

Steven F. Havill is the creator of Bill Gastner, the 60-something insomniac undersheriff of Posadas County, New Mexico, introduced in *Heartshot* (1991). *Publishers Weekly* called book 2 "an evocative tale of hard lives on the edge of society. The portly detective is a genuine low-key pleasure." *Washington Times* praised the "very liberated relationship between Gastner and the woman (deputy Estelle Reyes-Guzman) he not only likes as a person but respects as an officer of the law." In addition to his 6 mysteries, Havill has written 4 westerns. His first novel, *The Killer* (1991), was a finalist for the Medicine Pipe Bearers Award from Western Writers of America. A teacher of high school biology and English, Havill earned both his B.A. and M.A. from the University of New Mexico. He lives near Albuquerque (NM).

Bill Gastner...insomniac undersheriff in Posadas County, New Mexico
- ❏ ❏ 1 - Heartshot (1991)
- ❏ ❏ 2 - Bitter Recoil (1992)
- ❏ ❏ 3 - Twice Buried (1994)
- ❏ ❏ 4 - Before She Dies (1996)
- ❏ ❏ 5 - Privileged to Kill (1997)
- ❏ ❏ 6 - Prolonged Exposure (1998)

■ **HAYWOOD, Gar Anthony**

Los Angeles native Gar Anthony Haywood writes two mystery series featuring black detectives—one a wise-guy private eye and the other a retired couple who plan to see America in their Airstream trailer. The tough, wise-guy is Aaron Gunner, introduced in *Fear of the Dark* (1988), winner of the St. Martin's Press/PWA Best First Private Eye Novel contest and a best-first-novel Shamus. *Publishers Weekly* found "the flash and funk of L.A. vivid and the cast of characters quirky and memorable." Joe and Dottie Loudermilk are the retired cop and former schoolteacher who leave their 5 grown kids behind when they hitch the Airstream to their pickup and hit the road. Nobody was more surprised than the author when he discovered the "voice" of these comic mysteries was Dottie's. Haywood, who lives in Venice (CA), has also written for the *Los Angeles Times* and the *New York Times Book Review*.

Aaron Gunner...black wise-guy P.I. in Los Angeles, California
- ❏ ❏ 1 - **Fear of the Dark (1988) Shamus & SMP/PWA winner ★★**
- ❏ ❏ 2 - Not Long for This World (1990)
- ❏ ❏ 3 - You Can Die Trying (1993)
- ❏ ❏ 4 - It's Not a Pretty Sight (1996)
- ❏ ❏ 5 - When Last Seen Alive (1998)

Dottie & Joe Loudermilk...traveling retired black couple in the United States
- ❏ ❏ 1 - Going Nowhere Fast (1994)
- ❏ ❏ 2 - Bad News Travels Fast (1995)

■ **HEALD, Tim**

Tim(othy Villiers) Heald is the creator of Simon Bognor, special investigator to the British Board of Trade, featured in 10 mysteries. Simon's inquiries delve into the English stately home business, Fleet Street, dogbreeding, food, Toronto, Oxford village life and middle England—all of which Heald knows from personal experience. He has also written several biographies, including one of fictional Avenger John Steed (*John Steed: An Authorized Biography*, 1977), Prince Philip (*Philip: A Portrait of the Duke of Edinburgh*, 1991) and Barbara Cartland (*Life of Love*, 1995). Former chairman of the Crime Writers' Association, Heald served as editor and contributor to *A Classic English Crime* (1990), a tribute from CWA members in honor of the 100th year of Agatha Christie. With three added contributors, this same group has reconvened for *A Classic Christmas Crime* (1997). A former associate editor of Toronto's *Weekend Magazine*, Heald has worked as a columnist and feature writer for several London publications. His Oxford degree, with honors, is in modern history.

Simon Bognor...special investigator to the British Board of Trade in England
- ❏ ❏ 1 - Unbecoming Habits (1973)
- ❏ ❏ 2 - Blue Blood Will Out (1974)
- ❏ ❏ 3 - Deadline (1975)
- ❏ ❏ 4 - Let Sleeping Dogs Lie (1976)
- ❏ ❏ 5 - Just Desserts (1977)
- ❏ ❏ 6 - Murder at Moose Jaw (1981)
- ❏ ❏ 7 - Masterstroke (1982)
  - U.S.-A Small Masterpiece
- ❏ ❏ 8 - Red Herrings (1985)
- ❏ ❏ 9 - Brought to Book (1988)
- ❏ ❏ 10 - Business Unusual (1989)

■ HEALY, Jeremiah

Nine-time Shamus nominee Jeremiah Healy is the creator of John Francis Cuddy, U.S. Army police lieutenant turned private investigator, first seen in *Blunt Darts* (1984), a Shamus nominee for best first novel. While still mourning a dead wife (he visits her grave to talk to her), Cuddy has an ongoing relationship with a woman assistant DA. Healy uses his own experience as an Army captain of military police for Cuddy's knowledge of investigative technique and his years of practicing and teaching law for recognizing how the legal system works. A graduate of Rutgers College and Harvard Law School, he is a former professor at the New England School of Law. His latest book is a legal thriller, *The Stalking of Sheilah Quinn* (1998), where a criminal defense attorney becomes the quarry for a murder defendent she got out on bail. Healy is past president of Private Eye Writers of America.

John Francis Cuddy...Army police lieutenant turned private investigator in Boston, Massachusetts
- ❏ ❏ 1 - **Blunt Darts (1984) Shamus nominee** ☆
- ❏ ❏ 2 - **The Staked Goat (1986) Shamus winner** ★
  - Brit.-The Tethered Goat
- ❏ ❏ 3 - So Like Sleep (1987)
- ❏ ❏ 4 - **Swan Dive (1988) Shamus nominee** ☆
- ❏ ❏ 5 - Yesterday's News (1989)
- ❏ ❏ 6 - Right To Die (1991)
- ❏ ❏ 7 - **Shallow Graves (1992) Shamus nominee** ☆
- ❏ ❏ 8 - **Foursome (1993) Shamus nominee** ☆
- ❏ ❏ 9 - Act of God (1994)
- ❏ ❏ 10 - Rescue (1995)
- ❏ ❏ 11 - **Invasion of Privacy (1996) Shamus nominee** ☆

■ HEALY, R. Austin

Former newspaper journalist R. Austin Healy is the author of a new horseracing mystery series featuring ex-CIA and former NYPD detective Mike Flint transplanted to Saratoga, New York, and introduced in *The Ninth Race* (1995). Flint and the horses return in *Sweetfeed* (1996) and are scheduled to race again in *Casino Saratoga*. Healy says his Mike Flint is no relation to Wendy Hornsby's LAPD detective of the same name (significant other to filmmaker Maggie MacGowen). After his 6 kids got him started on the Internet, Healy says he enjoys using the computer for research. A resident of Clifton Park (NY), he lists skiing as his favorite sport but is partial to the Caribbean island of Anguilla, near St. Maarten. He grew up in Albany (NY) and later attended Siena College in Loudenville (NY). He has written for various regional and national magazines.

Mike Flint...ex-CIA and NYC cop in Saratoga, New York
- ❏ ❏ 1 - The Ninth Race (1995)
- ❏ ❏ 2 - Sweetfeed (1996)

■ HECK, Peter J.

Former science fiction editor Peter J. Heck is the creator of a historical mystery series featuring Mark Twain and his secretary Wentworth Cabot, introduced in *Death on the Mississippi* (1995). Cabot plays Watson to Twain's Holmes and each adventure is served up with an entertaining dose of 19th century local color, including the best restaurants and entertainment of the day. A former advertising copy editor and creative director, Heck later edited a newsletter for Waldenbooks, which led to the job where he was Lynn Hightower's science fiction editor. After seeing firsthand how successful novels are pitched, he decided to try his own hand at fiction. Heck's leisure interests include motorcycle racing and playing lead guitar and singing with the Don't Quit Your Day Job Players, a blues-rock-folk band of science fiction writers and editors.

Mark Twain & Wentworth Cabot...19th century American author and his secretary in the United States
- ❏ ❏ 1 - Death on the Mississippi (1995)
- ❏ ❏ 2 - A Connecticut Yankee in Criminal Court (1996)

■ HEFFERNAN, William

Edgar award winner William Heffernan is the author of a series of paperback novels featuring NYPD detective Paul Devlin, introduced in *Ritual* (1988). Edgar award-winning book 4, *Tarnished Blue* (1995), concerns the brutal murder of a highly regarded police captain who was betrayed at every turn by those he trusted. Heffernan's most recent novel is *The Dinosaur Club* (1997), a downsizing story about some 50-50 club members (over 50 making $50,000) who have some fun fighting back. Warner Brothers paid a cool $1 million for the movie rights and John Wells, writer/producer of *ER*, will write the screenplay. A former investigative reporter and 3-time Pulitzer Prize nominee during his days in Buffalo and New York City, Heffernan now lives in Vermont, where the family household includes a cat named Kitty and an enormous Bouvier named Babar.

Paul Devlin...NYPD detective in New York, New York
- ❏ ❏ 1 - Ritual (1988)
- ❏ ❏ 2 - Blood Rose (1991)
- ❏ ❏ 3 - Scarred (1993)
- ❏ ❏ 4 - **Tarnished Blue (1995) Edgar winner ★**
- ❏ ❏ 5 - Winter's Gold (1997)

■ HELLER, Keith

Minnesota native Keith Heller is the creator of the George Man mystery series featuring an early 18th century parish watchman in London, whose duties were similar to those of the early police. After his introduction in *Man's Illegal Life* (1984), George returns in *Man's Storm* (1985), where he is busy putting out fires, rescuing the injured and investigating the murder of a woman who refused to close her husband's shop during the great storm of November 27, 1703. Former assistant professor of English in Nagoya, Japan, Heller has also lived in Spain. He holds an M.A. from North Dakota State University and spent 6 years teaching and doing graduate study at the University of Nebraska. Writing as K. J. Heller he is the author of *How to Find Work Abroad: Teaching English as a Foreign Language* (1983).

George Man...early 18th century parish watchman in London, England
- ❏ ❏ 1 - Man's Illegal Life (1984)
- ❏ ❏ 2 - Man's Storm (1985)
- ❏ ❏ 3 - Man's Loving Family (1985)

■ **HEMLIN, Tim**

Tim Hemlin has written a series of paperback mysteries featuring Neil Marshall, a Houston (TX) graduate student in creative writing, struggling poet, part-time chef-caterer and about-to-be divorced man. In the series opener, our hero is apparently not busy enough, so he moonlights as a private eye when his oldest friend, racehorse breeder Jason Keys, is murdered. In book 2 he witnesses the near-fatal shooting of a legendary Houston private eye and puts his own life at risk. Things are only slightly less complicated in book 3 when Neil caters a fundraiser for a local thug who wants to be mayor. For 12 years Hemlin was a chef for a gourmet catering company in Houston. These days he teaches high school English and lives with his wife and children near Houston (TX).

Neil Marshall...graduate student poet in Houston, Texas
- ❏ ❏ 1 - If Wishes Were Horses... (1996)
- ❏ ❏ 2 - A Whisper of Rage (1997)
- ❏ ❏ 3 - People in Glass Houses (1997)

■ **HENDERSON, Laurence**

British author Laurence Henderson has written four police novels featuring detective sergeant Arthur Milton, first seen in *With Intent* (1968). Book 2, *Sitting Target* (1970), became an MGM-EMI film of the same title in 1972, directed by Douglas Hickox. Book 3, *Cage Until Tame* (1972), was followed by *Major Enquiry* (1976) and the entire series was published in the U.S. by St. Martin's Press. More recently Henderson has written *The Final Glass* (1990), a nonseries novel set in Ireland.

Arthur Milton...detective sergeant in England
- ❏ ❏ 1 - With Intent (1968)
- ❏ ❏ 2 - Sitting Target (1970)
- ❏ ❏ 3 - Cage Until Tame (1972)
- ❏ ❏ 4 - Major Enquiry (1976)

■ **HENSLEY, Joe L.**

Former 5th Judicial Circuit judge and past president of the Indiana Judges Association, Joe L. Hensley writes about the law and people who become involved in it. He says his retirement from the bench in 1989 has not ended his fascination with courtrooms, trials and lawyers. According to Mike Bowen, Hensley is "the only judge I've ever seen in fiction who talks to lawyers the way judges really talk to lawyers and uses the kind of language judges use when the reporter has her fingers off the keys." Educated at Indiana University, Hensley has worked as a private attorney, a county prosecutor, one-term Indiana legislator, circuit judge, and law firm partner. While most of his books feature crusading defense attorney Donald Robak, *Grim City* (1994) introduces Mexican-American lawyer, part-time parole officer and judicial assistant Jim Carlos Singer of Grimsley City (KY), Grim City for short.

Donald Robak...crusading defense attorney and state legislator in Bington, Indiana
- ❏ ❏ 1 - Deliver Us to Evil (1971)
- ❏ ❏ 2 - Legislative Body (1972)
- ❏ ❏ 3 - Song of Corpus Juris (1974)
- ❏ ❏ 4 - A Killing in Gold (1978)
- ❏ ❏ 5 - Minor Murders (1979)
- ❏ ❏ 6 - Outcasts (1981)
- ❏ ❏ 7 - Robak's Cross (1985)
- ❏ ❏ 8 - Robak's Fire (1986)
- ❏ ❏ ss - Robak's Firm [short stories] (1987)
- ❏ ❏ 9 - Robak's Run (1990)
- ❏ ❏ 10 - Robak's Witch (1997)

■ HERVEY, Evelyn [P]

Evelyn Hervey is a pseudonym of Diamond Dagger recipient Henry Reymond Fitzwalter Keating, best known for his Inspector Ghote series set in Bombay, India. The Hervey books feature a 19th century spinster governess named Harriet Unwin, first seen in *The Governess* (1994). Keating's most recent fiction is a collection of stories *In Kensington Gardens* (1997) beautifully illustrated by Gwen Mandley. From 1967 to 1983 he was the chief mystery reviewer for the *London Times* where he was noted for his friendly encouragement of new talent. Past Chairman of the Crime Writers' Association and President of The Detection Club since 1985, Keating occupies the office once held by G. K. Chesteron, Agatha Christie and Dorothy L. Sayers. He shares his Halloween birthday with mystery writers Dick Francis, Kinky Friedman and Janet Dawson.

Harriet Unwin...19th century spinster governess in England
- ❏ ❏ 1 - The Governess (1984)
- ❏ ❏ 2 - The Man of Gold (1985)
- ❏ ❏ 3 - Into the Valley of Death (1986)

■ HIGGINS, George V.

Ex-prosecutor George V. Higgins has published 21 novels with courtroom settings, most recently *A Change of Gravity* (1997) which involves a Massachusetts grand jury looking to indict the ex-chairman of the State House Ways and Means Committee. In Dilys Winn's *Murder Ink* (1977), he is at the top of a short list of books to be read aloud. According to Winn, "if you try to read these to yourself you wind up moving your lips." Although his dialogue may look unintelligible on the page, "it comes to life when you actually repeat the words." A former journalist for several New England newspapers, Higgins has worked as an attorney on both sides of criminal practice. Former assistant attorney general for the Commonwealth of Massachusetts, he holds an M.A. from Stanford University and a law degree from Boston College. His first novel, *The Sins of Eddie Coyle* (1972), was his first bestseller.

Jerry Kennedy...criminal defense attorney in Boston, Massachusetts
- ❏ ❏ 1 - Kennedy for the Defense (1980)
- ❏ ❏ 2 - The Rat on Fire (1981)
- ❏ ❏ 3 - Penance for Jerry Kennedy (1985)
- ❏ ❏ 4 - Defending Billy Ryan (1992)

■ HIGGINS, Jack [P]

Every Jack Higgins novel since *The Eagle Has Landed* (1975) has become an international best seller with several adapted for the big screen. This suspense thriller, about a 1943 plot to kidnap Winston Churchill, introduced IRA hero Liam Devlin who appeared in 3 additional books. Now published in 56 languages, Higgins reportedly occupied 5 of the top 10 spots on the Warsaw list of best sellers in 1995. Jack Higgins is actually a pseudonym of Harry Patterson, but many of his Patterson novels were later re-released as by Jack Higgins. Before entering college at the age of 27, he worked as a circus roustabout, factory worker and laborer. With degrees in sociology, social psychology and economics from the University of London, he later worked as a teacher. An expert scuba diver and marksman, he lives on Jersey in the Channel Islands.

Dougal Munro & Jack Carter...1940s brigadier & captain in Ireland
- ❏ ❏ 1 - Night of the Fox (1986)
- ❏ ❏ 2 - Cold Harbor (1990)

Liam Devlin...1940s IRA hero in Ireland
- ❏ ❏ 1 - The Eagle Has Landed (1975)
- ❏ ❏ 2 - Touch the Devil (1982)

  ❑ ❑ 3 - Confessional (1985)
  ❑ ❑ 4 - The Eagle Has Flown (1991)

Nick Miller, Sgt.....Central Division detective in London, Engalnd
  ❑ ❑ 1 - The Graveyard Shift (1965)
  ❑ ❑ 2 - Brought in Dead (1967)

Sean Dillon...IRA enforcer turned British special agent in Ireland
  ❑ ❑ 1 - Eye of the Storm (1992)
  ❑ ❑ 2 - Thunder Point (1993)
  ❑ ❑ 3 - On Dangerous Ground (1994)
  ❑ ❑ 4 - Angel of Death (1995)
  ❑ ❑ 5 - Drink with the Devil (1996)
  ❑ ❑ 6 - The President's Daughter (1997)

■ HILARY, Richard [P]

Richard Hilary is the pseudonym used by Richard Bodino and Hilary Connors for their four-book series featuring Ezell "Easy" Barnes, an ex-prize fighter and cop turned private eye in Newark (NJ). Easy makes his first appearance in *Snake in the Grasses* (1987), followed by *Pieces of Cream* (1987), *Pillow of the Community* (1988) and *Behind the Fact* (1989).

Ezell "Easy" Barnes...ex-prize fighter and cop turned P.I. in Newark, New Jersey
  ❑ ❑ 1 - Snake in the Grasses (1987)
  ❑ ❑ 2 - Pieces of Cream (1987)
  ❑ ❑ 3 - Pillow of the Community (1988)
  ❑ ❑ **4 - Behind the Fact (1989) Shamus nominee** ☆

■ HILL, John Spencer

John Spencer Hill is a scholar of Milton, Coleridge and the Bible, and the creator of Italian Det. Insp. Carlo Arbati, a published poet. Rich with Florentine opera and history, the series opener won the Ellis Award for best first novel and the 1995-96 Critic's Choice Award from the *San Francisco Chronicle Review of Books*. Praise for *The Last Castrato* (1995) called it a "complex, literate and disturbing novel." In book 2 an American is murdered with an ancient bronze spear at the home of a patron of the arts who is a friend of Insp. Arbati's. A professor of English at the University of Ottawa, Hill lives 50 miles from the city in an 1843 stone house situated on 3 acres where he has planted 200 trees. After earning a Ph.D. from the University of Toronto, Hill spent 6 years as a lecturer in English at the University of Western Australia in Perth.

Carlo Arbati...policeman poet in Florence, Italy
  ❑ ❑ **1 - The Last Castrato (1995) Ellis winner** ★
  ❑ ❑ 2 - Ghirlandaio's Daughter (1997)

■ HILL, Reginald

Diamond Dagger recipient Reginald Hill has written more than 40 books since introducing police detectives Dalziel (pronounced dee-ell) and Pascoe in 1970. With 15 novels and 2 short story collections in print, the series has also become popular on BBC television, winning a Gold Dagger and Edgar and Anthony best-novel nominations. A 1996 short story collection tells how Dalziel and Pascoe met and looks to the future where Commissioner Pascoe of Eurofed Justice investigates murder on the moon. Hills newer series features black private detective Joe Sixsmith, whose first appearance was nominated for a Last Laugh Award. Under a variety of pseudonyms, Hill writes historical adventure (Charles Underhill), science fiction (Dick Morland), and other mystery and adventure (Patrick Ruell). After earning a B.A. (with honors) from Oxford, he spent 20 years teaching before turning to full-time writing in 1982.

Andrew Dalziel, Supt. & Peter Pascoe, Sgt.....pair of police inspectors in Yorkshire, England
- ❑ ❑ 1 - A Clubbable Woman (1970)
- ❑ ❑ 2 - An Advancement of Learning (1971)
- ❑ ❑ 3 - Ruling Passion (1973)
- ❑ ❑ 4 - An April Shroud (1975)
- ❑ ❑ 5 - A Pinch of Snuff (1978)
- ❑ ❑ 6 - A Killing Kindness (1980)
- ❑ ❑ ss - Pascoe's Ghost [short stories] (1979)
- ❑ ❑ 7 - Deadheads (1983)
- ❑ ❑ 8 - Exit Lines (1984)
- ❑ ❑ 9 - Child's Play (1987)
- ❑ ❑ 10 - Underworld (1988)
- ❑ ❑ 11 - **Bones and Silence (1990) Gold Dagger winner ★ Edgar nominee ☆**
- ❑ ❑ 12 - One Small Step [novella] (1990)
- ❑ ❑ 13 - Recalled to Life (1992)
- ❑ ❑ 14 - **Pictures of Perfection (1994) Anthony nominee ☆**
- ❑ ❑ 15 - The Wood Beyond (1995)
- ❑ ❑ ss - Asking for the Moon [4 long stories] (1996)

Joe Sixsmith...black private detective in England
- ❑ ❑ 1 - **Blood Sympathy (1993) Last Laugh nominee ☆**
- ❑ ❑ 2 - Born Guilty (1995)
- ❑ ❑ 3 - Killing the Lawyers (1997)

■ HILLERMAN, Tony

Tony Hillerman was 45 years old when his Edgar-nominated first novel, *The Blessing Way* (1970), was published. The former working journalist and UPI Santa Fe (NM) bureau chief was teaching journalism at the University of New Mexico, where he chaired the department from 1966-73. Since then, his name has become synonymous with Southwestern history and culture, particularly the Navajo. He has won Edgar, Anthony, Macavity and Nero Wolfe awards, as well as policewriting awards in France and the Navajo Tribes Special Friend Award. In 1994 he received Lifetime Achievement honors at the World Mystery Convention. His recent fiction includes the non-Leaphorn/Chee novel *Finding Moon* (1995), the story of a Colorado newspaper editor's return to Vietnam in search of his dead brothers lost daughter. Phi Beta Kappa at the University of Oklahoma, Hillerman earned an M.A. at the University of New Mexico. He lives in Albuquerque (NM).

Jim Chee, Sgt.....Navajo tribal police officer in Arizona
- ❑ ❑ 1 - People of Darkness (1980)
- ❑ ❑ 2 - The Dark Wind (1982)
- ❑ ❑ 3 - The Ghostway (1984)
- ❑ ❑ 4 - **Skinwalkers [incl Leaphorn] (1987) Anthony winner ★**
- ❑ ❑ 5 - **A Thief of Time [incl Leaphorn] (1988) Macavity winner ★ Edgar nominee ☆**
- ❑ ❑ 6 - Talking God [incl Leaphorn] (1989)
- ❑ ❑ 7 - **Coyote Waits [incl Leaphorn] (1990) Nero Wolfe winner ★**
- ❑ ❑ 8 - **Sacred Clowns [incl Leaphorn] (1993) Anthony nominee ☆**
- ❑ ❑ 9 - The Fallen Man [incl Leaphorn] (1996)

Joe Leaphorn, Lt.....Navajo tribal police officer in Arizona
- ❑ ❑ 1 - **The Blessing Way (1970) Edgar nominee ☆**
- ❑ ❑ 2 - **Dance Hall of the Dead (1973) Edgar winner ★**
- ❑ ❑ 3 - **Listening Woman (1978) Edgar nominee ☆**

■ HOCH, Edward D.

Edgar award winner Edward D. Hoch (rhymes with coke) published his first short story in 1955 and since then more than 800 others. For 20 years he edited *The Year's Best Mystery* and *Suspense Stories* and since 1973 has had a story in every single issue of *Ellery Queen's Mystery Magazine*. Among his many series characters are the 2000-year old Simon Ark, his only series character to appear in a novel-length work; a cipher expert with British Intelligence named Rand; a turn-of-the-century westerner named Ben Snow; Dr. Sam Hawthorne, small-town doctor from the '20s and '30s; professional thief Nick Velvet; and Capt. Leopold, an upstate New York detective. His 1968 Edgar was for a Leopold short story *"The Oblong Room."* More than a dozen of Hoch's stories have been adapted for television, including at least three for the series *McMillan and Wife*.

Simon Ark...ancient hounder of Satan in New York, New York
- ❏ ❏ 1 - The Judges of Hades [5 novellas] (1971)
- ❏ ❏ 2 - City of Brass [short novel w/2 novellas] (1971)
- ❏ ❏ 3 - The Quests of Simon Ark [short stories] (1984)

■ HOLTON, Hugh

Commander Hugh Holton has served in every division of the Chicago Police Department. Currently the highest ranking active duty police officer writing novels, he is watch commander of one of the most dangerous districts (Wentworth) in Chicago. Frequently seen on television, he has appeared on *The Oprah Winfrey Show* and been written up in a front page piece for *The New York Times*. He writes a regular column (Cop's Corner) for *Mystery Scene* magazine and has published short stories in *Detective Story* magazine. A Vietnam veteran, he has spent more than 25 years with the Chicago police department, where his father also served for 33 years and rose to command rank. VP of the Midwest chapter of Mystery Writers of America, Holton earned bachelor's and master's degrees in history and journalism from Roosevelt University in Chicago.

Larry Cole...black police commander in Chicago, Illinois
- ❏ ❏ 1 - Presumed Dead (1994)
- ❏ ❏ 2 - Windy City (1995)
- ❏ ❏ 3 - Chicago Blues (1996)
- ❏ ❏ 4 - Violent Crimes (1997)

■ HONE, Joseph

Joseph Hone has written four novels featuring an incompetent British spy named Peter Marlow, whose second appearance in *The Sixth Directorate* (1975) was named one of the best suspense novels of the last 10 years by *The New York Times*. Reviewer Anatole Broyard said the work has "elegance, wit, sympathy, irony, surprise, action, a rueful love affair and a melancholy Decline of the West mood." Author of several travel books, he has written radio scripts for BBC, worked as a freelance broadcaster and taught English in Heliopolis and Suez. A former radio and television officer for the Office of Public Relations at the UN, he produced radio programs for the World Bank and later served as writer-in-residence at the College of William and Mary and Sweet Briar College. Born in London, he lives near Banbury (England).

Peter Marlow...incompetent British spy in England
- ❏ ❏ 1 - The Private Sector (1971)
- ❏ ❏ 2 - The Sixth Directorate (1975)
- ❏ ❏ 3 - The Flowers of the Forest (1980) U.S.-The Oxford Gambit
- ❏ ❏ 4 - The Valley of the Fox (1982)

■ HONIG, Donald

Donald Honig has written more than 50 books, many of them having to do with baseball. Early in his career he edited *Blue and Gray: Great Writings of the Civil War* (1961) and *Short Stories of Stephen Crane* (1962). More recently, he has written a pair of mysteries featuring Capt. Thomas Maynard, a Civil War veteran introduced in *The Sword of General Englund* (1995). In book 2, he is hired to investigate a case of possible desertion after a Montana Territory gold miner thinks he's seen a decorated commanding officer supposedly killed in battle. *Publishers Weekly* says Honig greatly expands his hero's character in this tale, "demonstrating his mastery of time and place." Under the name Donald Martin, Honig writes short stories for *Alfred Hitchcock Mystery Magazine*. Born on Long Island (NY), he lives in Connecticut.

Thomas Maynard, Capt.....Civil War Army captain in Dakota Territory
- ❏ ❏ 1 - The Sword of General Englund (1996)
- ❏ ❏ 2 - The Ghost of Major Pryor (1997)

■ HORNIG, Doug

Doug Hornig has created two Charlottesville (VA) series characters—a laid-back Vietnam veteran P.I. whose first appearance received an Edgar nomination (followed by a best-novel Shamus nomination for book 2) and a burned-out government agent introduced in *Waterman* (1987). With Peter Caine, he has written the medical thriller *Virus* (1989), described as part police procedural, part suspense/horror. In addition to his screenplay *Reunion*, which won first prize in the 1990 Virginia Governor's Screenwriting Competition, Hornig has published poetry, written another screenplay and had a song commerically recorded. Among his many past jobs are factory worker, journalist, taxi driver, computer programmer, bar singer, bookstore clerk and photographer. Born in New York City, he earned a bachelor's degree from George Washington University.

Loren Swift...Vietnam vet private eye in Charlottesville, Virginia
- ❏ ❏ 1 - **Foul Shot (1984) Edgar nominee** ☆
- ❏ ❏ 2 - **Hardball (1985) Shamus nominee** ☆
- ❏ ❏ 3 - The Dark Side (1986)
- ❏ ❏ 4 - Deep Dive (1988)

Steven Kirk...burned-out government agent in Charlottesville, Virginia
- ❏ ❏ 1 - Waterman (1987)
- ❏ ❏ 2 - Stinger (1990)

■ HORWITZ, Merle

Merle Horwitz is the creator of Harvey Ace, a retired Los Angeles private investigator who plays the horses. Introduced in *Bloody Silks* (1990), Harvey makes his only return appearance in *Dead Heat* (1990). More recently Horwitz has written *The Great Deli Cookbook: An Adventure Not Equaled in Modern Gastronomy* (1995). The author is a practicing attorney in Los Angeles (CA).

Harvey Ace...retired P.I. who plays the horses in Los Angeles, California
- ❏ ❏ 1 - Bloody Silks (1990)
- ❏ ❏ 2 - Dead Heat (1990)

■ **HOUSEWRIGHT, David**

David Housewright won a best-first-novel Edgar award for his first mystery featuring Holland Taylor, a former homicide detective turned private investigator in St. Paul (MN). Also nominated for a Shamus award, *Penance* (1995) has Taylor helping a female gubernatorial candidate. When a pivotal figure from his past is murdered, he is called in for questioning. In *Practice to Deceive*, our P.I. hero really gets rolling. After provoking a hit man, he gets shot, smarts off with the cops and ends up in jail, while trying to recover stolen pension funds from a crooked investment manager. In addition to writing for the *Minneapolis Star Tribune* and the *Grand Forks* (ND) *Herald*, Housewright has worked in advertising and started his own agency. His journalism assignments included sportswriting and police and court beats, as well as politics and health care.

Holland Taylor...ex-cop turned private investigator in St. Paul, Minnesota
- ❏ ❏ 1 - **Penance (1995) Edgar winner ★ Shamus nominee ☆**
- ❏ ❏ 2 - Practice to Deceive (1997)

■ **HOYT, Richard**

Former Army Intelligence agent Richard Hoyt is the creator of two series characters—ex-CIA agent James Burlane and softboiled Seattle private eye John Denson, whose second outing was a Shamus nominee for best novel. In *30 for a Harry* (1981) Denson goes undercover at the *Seattle Star* to find a blackmailer. Like his creator, Denson is a former journalist, ex-intelligence agent. With Congressman Neil Abercrombie of Hawaii, Hoyt has written another Burlane novel, *Blood of Patriots* (1996), where gunmen storm the House of Representatives, decimating the Democratic ranks. Hoyt holds a journalism degree from the University of Oregon and a doctorate in American studies from the University of Hawaii. After 2 years in Army Intelligence, he spent 5 years as a newspaper reporter and 10 as a college professor. An Oregon native, he lives in Portland (OR).

James Burlane...ex-CIA operative turned private eye in the United States
- ❏ ❏ 1 - Trotsky's Run (1982)
- ❏ ❏ 2 - Head of State (1985)
- ❏ ❏ 3 - The Dragon Portfolio (1986)
- ❏ ❏ 4 - Siege (1987)
- ❏ ❏ 5 - Marimba (1992)
- ❏ ❏ 6 - Red Card (1994)
- ❏ ❏ 7 - Japanese Game (1995)
- ❏ ❏ 8 - Tyger! Tyger! (1996)

John Denson...flaky private eye in Seattle, Washington
- ❏ ❏ 1 - Decoys (1980)
- ❏ ❏ 2 - **30 for a Harry (1982) Shamus nominee ☆**
- ❏ ❏ 3 - The Siskiyou Two-Step (1983)
  APA-**Siskiyou**
- ❏ ❏ 4 - Fish Story (1985)
- ❏ ❏ 5 - Whoo? (1991)
- ❏ ❏ 6 - Bigfoot (1993)
- ❏ ❏ 7 - Snake Eyes (1995)

■ HUEBNER, Frederick D.

Seattle attorney Frederick D. Huebner (pronounced HEEB-ner) says he uses "crime and detective fiction to explore legal issues and to present a contemporary description of the Pacific Northwest." His series character, Matt Riordan, is a burned-out lawyer turned investigator, seen first in *The Joshua Sequence* (1986). Riordan continues to work as an attorney until book 3 when he defends an old friend on charges of murder and arson. After the trial, Riordan gives up the lawyering. Born in Harvey (IL), Huebner earned his undergraduate degree at Macalester College (magna cum laude) and his law degree (with honors) at the University of Washington. A contributor to both the *Washington Law Review* and *Washington State Bar News*, he practices law in Seattle (WA).

Matt Riordan...burned-out lawyer turned investigator in Seattle, Washington
- ❑ ❑ 1 - The Joshua Sequence (1986)
- ❑ ❑ 2 - The Black Rose (1987)
- ❑ ❑ 3 - **Judgment by Fire (1988) Edgar nominee** ☆
- ❑ ❑ 4 - Picture Postcard (1990)
- ❑ ❑ 5 - Methods of Execution (1994)

■ HUNT, Richard

Richard Hunt is the creator of Det. Chief Insp. Sidney Walsh, who has been called Cambridge's answer to Insp. Morse, starting with *Death of a Merry Widow* (1993). Hunt, who says he likes to include the local color of a university town and modern high technology in his crime investigations, is himself an associate member of the Chartered Institute of Management Accountants and director of a shoe manufacturing company. *Kirkus* has praised his "sharp eye for procedural detail, as well as the usual British literacy and warmth in handling the police." In *Murder Benign* (1995), an archaeologist is killed in his home and a clay tablet is stolen. Walsh has no shortage of suspects, including the archaeologist's wife, who benefits from her husband's death and whose alibi is not convincing. Raised and educated in Cambridge, Hunt lives in Norfolk, England.

Sidney Walsh, Det. Chief Insp.....detective chief inspector in Cambridge, England
- ❑ ❑ 1 - Death of a Merry Widow (1993)
- ❑ ❑ 2 - Deadlocked (1994)
- ❑ ❑ 3 - Murder Benign (1995)
- ❑ ❑ 4 - The Man Trap (1996)

■ HUNTER, Alan

Since his debut in 1955 with *Gently Does It*, Alan Hunter has written more than 40 mysteries featuring Chief Supt. George Gently of Scotland Yard. In an interview with St. James Press, Hunter disclosed that he built the superintendent from information he found in a book about real life police detectives. *Crime and the Police* by Anthony Martienssen provided thumbnail sketches of four top-ranking detectives which Hunter says he blended into his own concept. Like his father before him, the author was once a poultry farmer. He also worked as an antiquarian bookseller (later owning his own bookshop) and was a regular contributor and crime fiction review for the *Eastern Daily Press* in Norwich. Author of several plays and a collection of poetry, Hunter has a deep interest in Zen Buddhism and 20th century French literature. He lives in Norwich (England).

George Gently, Chief Supt.....chief superintendent of Scotland Yard in Norchester, East Anglia, England
- ❑ ❑ 1 - Gently Does It (1955)
- ❑ ❑ 2 - Gently By the Shore (1956)

❏ ❏ 3 - Gently Down the Stream (1957)
❏ ❏ 4 - Landed Gently (1957)
❏ ❏ 5 - Gently Through the Mill (1958)
❏ ❏ 6 - Gently in the Sun (1959)
❏ ❏ 7 - Gently with the Painters (1960)
❏ ❏ 8 - Gently to the Summit (1961)
❏ ❏ 9 - Gently Go Man (1961)
❏ ❏ 10 - Gently Where the Roads Go (1962)
❏ ❏ 11 - Gently Floating (1963)
❏ ❏ 12 - Gently Sahib (1964)
❏ ❏ 13 - Gently with the Ladies (1965)
❏ ❏ 14 - Gently North-West (1967)
          U.S.-Gently in the Highlands
❏ ❏ 15 - Gently Continental (1967)
❏ ❏ 16 - Gently Coloured (1969)
❏ ❏ 17 - Gently with the Innocents (1970)
❏ ❏ 18 - Gently at a Gallop (1971)
❏ ❏ 19 - Vivienne: Gently Where She Lay (1972)
❏ ❏ 20 - Gently French (1973)
❏ ❏ 21 - Gently in Trees (1974)
          U.S.-Gently Through the Woods
❏ ❏ 22 - Gently With Love (1975)
❏ ❏ 23 - Gently Where the Birds Are (1976)
❏ ❏ 24 - Gently Instrumental (1977)
❏ ❏ 25 - Gently to a Sleep (1978)
❏ ❏ 26 - The Honfleur Decision (1980)
❏ ❏ 27 - Gabrielle's Way (1981)
          U.S.-The Scottish Decision
❏ ❏ 28 - Fields of Heather (1981)
          U.S.-Death on the Heath
❏ ❏ 29 - Gently Between Tides (1982)
❏ ❏ 30 - Amorous Leander (1983)
          U.S.-Death on the Broadlands
❏ ❏ 31 - The Unhung Man (1983)
          U.S.-The Unhanged Man
❏ ❏ 32 - "Once a Prostitute" (1984)
❏ ❏ 33 - The Chelsea Ghost (1985)
❏ ❏ 34 - Goodnight, Sweet Prince (1986)
❏ ❏ 35 - Strangling Man (1987)
❏ ❏ 36 - Traitor's End (1988)
❏ ❏ 37 - Gently with the Millions (1989)
❏ ❏ 38 - Gently Scandalous (1990)
❏ ❏ 39 - Gently to a Kill (1991)
❏ ❏ 40 - Gently Tragic (1992)
❏ ❏ 41 - Gently in the Glens (1993)
❏ ❏ 42 - Bomber's Moon (1994)
❏ ❏ 43 - Jackpot! (1995)
❏ ❏ 44 - The Love of Gods (1997)

■ HUNTER, Fred W.

Fred W. Hunter writes two Chicago series—one a more traditional police series, with a grandmotherly Watson to assist the homicide detective; the other an espionage series with a twist. "Imagine *North by Northwest* with the man of your choice in the Eva Marie Saint role," says Hunter. Or picture Tommy and Tuppence Beresford as a gay married couple. The espionage tales are told in first person, while the police novels are third person point of view. The Ransom mysteries (except book 1) include his name in the title, with *Ransom for Killing* (1998) coming next, followed by *Unpaid Ransom* (1999). Hunter writes in longhand with a fine-point pen on orchid-colored legal pads and transfers his work to the computer at the end of the day. Writing directly to the monitor screen interrupts his flow. His downtown Chicago hi-rise home is shared with several cats and way too many video movies.

Alex Reynolds...accidental spy in Chicago, IL
- ❏ ❏ 1 - Government Gay (1997)
- ❏ ❏ 2 - Federal Fag (1998)

Jeremy Ransom & Emily Charters...homicide detective & his adopted grandmother in Chicago, IL
- ❏ ❏ 1 - Presence of Mind (1994)
- ❏ ❏ 2 - Ransom for an Angel (1995)
- ❏ ❏ 3 - Ransom for Our Sins (1996)
- ❏ ❏ 4 - Ransom for a Holiday (1997)

■ HUNTER, Stephen

Stephen Hunter spent 15 years as movie critic for *The Baltimore Sun*, but recently moved to *The Washington Post* where he occupies the same spot. A gun buff and techno-thriller writer, he has written two books featuring a Vietnam vet master sniper whose Arizona state trooper father was gunned down in 1955. The experience of having his father murdered is something the author shares with Swagger, although the circumstances differ. Based on his collected reviews from the *Sun*, Hunter wrote *Violent Screen: A Critic's 13 Years (1981-94) on the Front Lines of Movie Mayhem* (1995). One hundred reviews are arranged by genre and type of violence with film noir, sexual obsession, horror, and domestic violence among the headings. Hunter's other fiction includes *Time to Hunt* (1998), *Dirty White Boys* (1994) and *Tapestry of Spies* (first published as *The Spanish Gambit*).

Bob "the Nailer" Swagger...master sniper in the United States
- ❏ ❏ 1 - Point of Impact (1993)
- ❏ ❏ 2 - Black Light (1996)

■ IRVINE, Robert

During the late '60s Robert Irvine was news director at one of the country's biggest television stations (KABC-TV, Los Angeles) and his Edgar-nominated series features a Los Angeles TV reporter. While *The Face Out Front* (1977) is set at the same station, Robert Christopher does not appear. Another of Irvine's series features a reporter named Vicki Garcia (who he says was inspired by Connie Chung) coming next in *Flat Cats*. His Moroni (pronounced Mor-OH-nye) Traveler series shows great affection for Utah and its people, and although his great-grandparents were Mormon pioneers, Irvine was not raised Mormon. With his wife Angie, he is one half of Val Davis, author of *Track of the Scorpion* (1996) featuring archaeologist Nicolette Scott, scheduled to return in *Flight of the Serpent*. While his wife has degrees in English literature and computer engineering, Irvine was the archaeology student.

Kevin Manwaring & Vicki Garcia...field producer & television reporter in Los Angeles, California
- ❏ ❏ 1 - Barking Dogs (1994)

Moroni Traveler...non-Morman ex-football player private eye in Salt Lake City, Utah
   ❑ ❑ 1 - Baptism for the Dead (1988)
   ❑ ❑ 2 - The Angel's Share (1989)
   ❑ ❑ 3 - Gone to Glory (1990)
   ❑ ❑ 4 - Called Home (1991)
   ❑ ❑ 5 - The Spoken Word (1992)
   ❑ ❑ 6 - The Great Reminder (1993)
   ❑ ❑ 7 - Hosanna Shout (1994)
   ❑ ❑ 8 - Pillar of Fire (1995)

Robert Christopher...television reporter in Los Angeles, California
   ❑ ❑ 1 - **Jump Cut (1974) Edgar nominee** ☆
   ❑ ❑ 2 - **Freeze Frame (1976) Edgar nominee** ☆
   ❑ ❑ 3 - Horizontal Hold (1978)
   ❑ ❑ 4 - Ratings are Murder (1985)

■ JACKSON, Jon A.

Michigan native Jon A. Jackson is the creator of Detroit homicide detective Fang Mulheisen, introduced in *The Diehard* (1977), returning for his 7th appearance in *Man With an Axe* (1998). A favorite character in this series is Joe Service, first seen in *Hit on the House* (1993) when he's killing off the bosses of organized crime. The womanizing hit man takes a bullet himself in *Dead Man*, one of *Publishers Weekly's* 10 Best Books of 1994, and is on the run from Sgt. Mulheisen and the Detroit mob (who thinks Joe has some of their drug money) in *Dead Folks* (1996). Born in Royal Oak (MI), Jackson attended Wayne State University in Detroit and later earned a B.A. from the University of Montana and an MFA from the University of Iowa. He lives in Montana where he combines writing, carpentry, fishing and white-water canoeing.

Fang Mulheisen, Sgt.....police detective sergeant in Detroit, Michigan
   ❑ ❑ 1 - The Diehard (1977)
   ❑ ❑ 2 - The Blind Pig (1978)
   ❑ ❑ 3 - Grootka (1990)
   ❑ ❑ 4 - Hit on the House (1993)
   ❑ ❑ 5 - Deadman (1994)
   ❑ ❑ 6 - Dead Folks (1996)

■ JAHN, Michael

Edgar award winner Michael Jahn is the creator of NYPD detective Bill Donovan, who talks an old girlfriend (a black undercover cop named Marcie) into working as a decoy to catch a psycho killer in the series opener (*Night Rituals*, 1982). Donovan marries his longtime love in book 5 and becomes a new father in *Murder on Fifth Avenue* (1998). Because Jahn himself is having so much fun being a father again in his early 50's, he says he didn't want Donovan to miss the experience. In addition to his best-paperback-Edgar-winning *The Quark Maneuver* (1977), Jahn has written novelizations for the TV series *Switch* and *The Rockford Files* and a film novelization for *The Frighteners* (1996). A former reporter for *The New York Times* and current newsletter editor for Mystery Writers of America, Jahn says he likes the distraction of CNN playing in the background while he writes.

Bill Donovan, Capt.....chief of special investigations in New York, New York
   ❑ ❑ 1 - Night Rituals (1982)
   ❑ ❑ 2 - Death Games (1987)
   ❑ ❑ 3 - City of God (1992)
   ❑ ❑ 4 - Murder at the Museum of Natural History (1994)
   ❑ ❑ 5 - Murder on Theater Row (1997)

■ **JAMES, Bill [P]**

Bill James is the pseudonym used by (Allan) James Tucker for his chilling and bleak police series featuring a pair of relatively high-ranking detectives, D.C.S. Colin Harpur and D.C. Desmond Iles. James says his books are about the impossibility of controlling crime by strictly legitimate means. Described by one reviewer as perhaps the "darkest and least optimistic crime writer in Britain today," James wrote a dozen crime novels under the name David Craig during the late '60s and '70s and at least five others during the same period as James Tucker. He recently revived his David Craig pseudonym for a new series set in the modernizing Cardiff dockland beginning with *Forget It* (1995). Born in Cardiff (Wales) and educated at University College (Cardiff), he has worked as a newspaper, magazine, radio and TV journalist, and as a university lecturer.

Colin Harpur, D.C.S. & Desmond Iles, D.C.....detective chief superintendent & detective constable in an English seaport
- ❑ ❑ 1 - You'd Better Believe It (1985)
- ❑ ❑ 2 - The Lolita Man (1986)
- ❑ ❑ 3 - Halo Parade (1987)
- ❑ ❑ 4 - Protection (1988) APA-Harpur and Iles
- ❑ ❑ 5 - Come Clean (1989)
- ❑ ❑ 6 - Take (1990)
- ❑ ❑ 7 - Club (1991)
- ❑ ❑ 8 - Astride a Grave (1991)
- ❑ ❑ 9 - Gospel (1992)
- ❑ ❑ 10 - Roses, Roses (1993)
- ❑ ❑ 11 - In Good Hands (1994)
- ❑ ❑ 12 - The Detective is Dead (1995)
- ❑ ❑ 13 - Top Banana (1996)

■ **JANES, J. Robert**

Canadian author J. Robert Janes has written more than 20 books, including 8 in his series set in occupied France during 1942 and 1943. Beginning with *Mayhem* (1992), retitled *Mirage* in the U.S., a French chief inspector (Jean-Louis St-Cyr) is shadowed by a maverick Gestapo officer (Hermann Kohler) ordered to follow the French detective's progress. In the series opener, an unidentified body found in the Fontainebleau Forest leads to a rich aristocratic family, the not-so-holy Abbey of St. Gregory and back to the Gestapo general who ordered Kohler to follow the investigation. Set in Antwerp is *The Alice Factor* (1991), a story of diamonds and espionage in 1937. A former mining engineer, geologist, high school teacher and geology professor, Janes has has written 4 geology textbooks, a 5-book juvenile mystery series and at least 4 other adult mysteries. Born in Toronto, he lives in Niagara-on-the-Lake.

Jean-Louis St-Cyr & Hermann Kohler...1940s French police inspector & Gestapo agent in Paris, France
- ❑ ❑ 1 - Mayhem (1992) U.S.-Mirage
- ❑ ❑ 2 - Carousel (1992)
- ❑ ❑ 3 - Kaleidoscope (1993)
- ❑ ❑ 4 - Mannequin (1994)
- ❑ ❑ 5 - Salamander (1994)
- ❑ ❑ 6 - Dollmaker (1995)
- ❑ ❑ 7 - Stonekiller (1995)
- ❑ ❑ 8 - Sandman (1996)

Richard Hagen...1940s diamond dealer in Antwerp, Belgium
- ❑ ❑ 1 - The Alice Factor (1991)

■ **JARDINE, Quintin**

Quintin Jardine is the creator of Robert Skinner, head of Edinburgh's CID, introduced in *Skinner's Rules* (1993), which was shortlisted for the John Creasey Award for Britain's best first crime novel. Described as both literate and gritty, this series includes graphic violence and sex, as well as a sympathetic side to Skinner, who marries in book 2 (an American physician with forensic experience) after being widowed for many years. His 20-year-old daughter gets a baby brother in book 3. A former journalist, Jardine spent almost 10 years working for the Government Information Service advising Ministers and senior civil servants as well as handling media coverage for Royal visits and other public relations. Since 1986 he has been working as an independent public relations consultant as well as writing fiction. Born and raised in the West of Scotland, he lives in East Lothian.

Robert Skinner...high-ranking cop in Edinburgh, Scotland
- ❑ ❑ 1 - **Skinner's Rules (1993) Creasey nominee** ☆
- ❑ ❑ 2 - Skinner's Festival (1994)
- ❑ ❑ 3 - Skinner's Trail (1994)
- ❑ ❑ 4 - Skinner's Round (1995)
- ❑ ❑ 5 - Skinner's Ordeal (1996)

■ **JASPERSOHN, William**

Shamus award-winner William Jaspersohn has written more than 20 books, most of which are for young readers, including A Day in the Life series (*A Day in the Life of a Television News Reporter*, ... *Marine Biologist*, ... *Veterinarian*, ... *Airline Pilot*). He is also the creator of Peter Boone, ex-Red Sox pitcher turned private eye, introduced in *Native Angels* (1995), winner of a best paperback Shamus award. The Vermont private eye discovers the country roads of the Green Mountain State can be as gritty as the mean streets of Boston when searching for a missing wife in book 1 and a teenager who's disappeared in book 2. A graduate of Dartmouth College, Jaspersohn worked briefly as a high school English teacher in Maine. His books for kids, many of which are photo essays, are ones he says he wishes had been there when he was growing up. Born in Connecticut, he currently lives in Vermont.

Peter Boone...ex-Red Sox pitcher turned P.I. in Vermont
- ❑ ❑ 1 - **Native Angels (1995) Shamus winner** ★
- ❑ ❑ 2 - Lake Effect (1996)

■ **JECKS, Michael**

Michael Jecks is the creator of a 14th century mystery series featuring Simon Puttock, bailiff of Lydford Castle and Sir Baldwin Furnshill, Keeper of the King's Peace, master of the local Manor and former Templar Knight. They are introduced in *The Last Templar* (1995) in the year 1316, a time of booming trade but also widespread violence, cruelty and abuse of privilege. In book 2 a local midwife and healer, regarded by some as a witch, is found frozen and mutilated, while a tin miner on the moors is found hanged in book 3 after putting himself in the protection of the King. In addition to the first 5 books, Jecks says he has synopses for another 5, all set in the early 1320s, with all but one taking place in Crediton or Dartmoor. After studying actuarial science at university, Jecks held 13 jobs in as many years, selling computers, software and leasing, before throwing away his television and starting to write fiction.

Simon Puttock & Sir Baldwin Furnshill...medieval West County bailiff & ex-Templar Knight in Devon, England
- ❑ ❑ 1 - The Last Templar (1995)
- ❑ ❑ 2 - The Merchant's Partner (1995)
- ❑ ❑ 3 - A Moorland Hanging (1996)
- ❑ ❑ 4 - The Crediton Killings (1997)
- ❑ ❑ 5 - The Abbot's Gibbet (1998)

■ JEFFERS, H. Paul

New York author H. Paul Jeffers has written more than 30 books including mysteries, westerns, historical and celebrity biographies, true crime and other nonfiction. His 3 mystery series feature a female investigator for the DA's office, a '30s ex-cop P.I. who'd rather be playing clarinet in a jazz band, and the aide to a chief of detectives faced with murder scenes recreated from classic mysteries. An expert on Teddy Roosevelt, Jeffers is the author of *Commissioner Roosevelt, 1895-1897* (1994), *Colonel Roosevelt, 1897-1898* (1996) and *The Bully Pulpit: A Teddy Roosevelt Book of Quotations* (1998). His crime related nonfiction includes *Bloody Business: Scotland Yard's Most Famous and Bloody Cases* (1994); *Gentleman Gerald: The Crimes and Times of Gerald Chapman, America's First Public Enemy No. 1* (1995); and *A Spy in Canaan: My Life as a Jewish-American Businessman Spying for Israel in Arab Lands* (1993).

Arlene Flynn...chief investigator for the District Attorney in New York, New York
- ❑ ❑ 1 - What Mommy Said (1997)

Harry MacNeil...1930s ex-cop private eye in New York
- ❑ ❑ 1 - The Rubout at the Onyx (1981)
- ❑ ❑ 2 - Murder on Mike (1984)
- ❑ ❑ 3 - The Ragdoll Murder (1987)

John Bogdanovic, Sgt.....aide-de-camp to NYPD Chief of Detectives in New York
- ❑ ❑ 1 - A Grand Night for Murder (1995)
- ❑ ❑ 2 - Reader's Guide to Murder (1996)
- ❑ ❑ 3 - Corpus Corpus (1998)

■ JEFFRIES, Ian [P]

Ian Jeffries is the pseudonym of British author Peter Hays, who produced three police novels featuring Sgt. Craig during the late 1950s and early 1960s. The sergeant is introduced in *Thirteen Days* (1959) and reappears in *Dignity and Purity* (1960) and *It Wasn't Me!* (1961). Jeffries later wrote a nonseries crime novel titled *House-Surgeon* (1966). All four titles were published only in England by Jonathan Cape.

Sgt. Craig...police sergeant in England
- ❑ ❑ 1 - Thirteen Days (1959)
- ❑ ❑ 2 - Dignity and Purity (1960)
- ❑ ❑ 3 - It Wasn't Me! (1961)

■ JEFFRIES, Roderic

Published in 15 languages, Roderic Jeffries has written 100 mysteries and another 25 books for children (mostly mysteries) under his own name and several pseudonyms. As Roderic Graeme he wrote 20 Blackshirt novels between 1952 and 1969 continuing the series begun by his father Graham Montague Jeffries (1900-1982). As Peter Alding and Jeffrey Ashford he writes two series about English police detectives, and when he moved to Mallorca for health reasons in 1972 he began writing a series featuring a Spanish police detective named Alvarez. Introduced in *Mistakenly in Mallorca* (1974), Insp. Alvarez makes his 21st appearance in *A Maze of Murders* (1998). Calling him "sleepy on the outside, sharp as a tack within," *Publishers Weekly* described Alvarez "as complicated and admirable as his detective work." Jeffries spent 6 years in the British Merchant Navy and later practiced law for several years.

Enrique Alvarez, Insp.....Spanish police inspector in Mallorca, Spain
- ❑ ❑ 1 - Mistakenly in Mallorca (1974)
- ❑ ❑ 2 - Two-Faced Death (1976)
- ❑ ❑ 3 - Troubled Deaths (1977)
- ❑ ❑ 4 - Murder Begets Murder (1979)

❑ ❑   5 - Just Desserts (1980)
❑ ❑   6 - Unseemly End (1981)
❑ ❑   7 - Deadly Petard (1983)
❑ ❑   8 - Three and One Make Five (1984)
❑ ❑   9 - Layers of Deceit (1985)
❑ ❑ 10 - Almost Murder (1986)
❑ ❑ 11 - Relatively Dangerous (1987)
❑ ❑ 12 - Death Trick (1988)
❑ ❑ 13 - Dead Clever (1989)
❑ ❑ 14 - Too Clever by Half (1990)
❑ ❑ 15 - A Fatal Fleece (1991)
❑ ❑ 16 - Murder's Long Memory (1991)
❑ ❑ 17 - Murder Confounded (1993)
❑ ❑ 18 - Death Takes Time (1994)
❑ ❑ 19 - An Arcadian Death (1995)
❑ ❑ 20 - An Artistic Way to Go (1996)

■ **JENKINS, Geoffrey**

Geoffrey Jenkins spent more than 20 years as a working journalist in Salisbury (now Zimbabwe), Pretoria (South Africa) and London and later wrote radio and television scripts, screenplays, novels and magazine features for American, British and South African publications. Among his 15 books, most of which are crime fiction, are a pair of mysteries featuring Commander Geoffrey Peace of the British Navy. The commander is first seen in *A Twist of Sand* (1959), set in South Africa, filmed in 1967 with a screenplay written by mystery author Marvin H. Albert. Other Jenkins books to make it to the big screen were *River of Diamonds* (1964) released in 1990, and *In Harm's Way* (1986). Born in Port Elizabeth, South Africa, where his father was an editor, Jenkins lives in Pretoria.

Geoffrey Peace...British naval commander in England
❑ ❑   1 - A Twist of Sand (1959)
❑ ❑   2 - Hunter Killer (1966)

■ **JENKINS, Jerry**

Author of more than 100 books, Jerry Jenkins has been writing sports biographies for more than 20 years, with heroes ranging from Hank Aaron (*Bad Henry*, 1974) to Meadowlark Lemon (*Meadowlark*, 1987) and Brett Butler (*A Field of Hope*, 1997). His 6 juvenile mystery series number 40 books and he currently tops the Christian best-seller charts with the first two books in his Left Behind series, co-written with Tim LaHaye—*Left Behind* (1995) and *Tribulation Force* (1996). During the '80s Jenkins wrote 2 Chicago mystery series, one featuring a woman reporter and the other a waitress/artist pair who become private eyes. His interest in detective fiction seems to be genetic, as his father was a chief of police and his two brothers are career law enforcement officers. Writer in residence at Chicago's Moody Bible Institute, Jenkins also teaches and writes marriage and family books.

Jennifer Grey...newspaper reporter and columnist in Chicago, Illinois
❑ ❑   1 - Gateway (1983)
❑ ❑   2 - Heartbeat (1983)
❑ ❑   3 - Three Days in Winter (1983)
❑ ❑   4 - Too Late to Tell (1984)
❑ ❑   5 - The Calling (1984)
❑ ❑   6 - Veiled Threat (1985)

Margo Franklin & Philip Spence...pair of private eyes in Chicago, Illinois
- ❏ ❏ 1 - Margo (1979)
  APA-The Woman at the Window
- ❏ ❏ 2 - Hilary (1980)
  APA-Murder Behind Bars
- ❏ ❏ 3 - Karlyn (1980)
  APA-The Daylight Intruder
- ❏ ❏ 4 - Paige (1981)
  APA-The Meeting at Midnight
- ❏ ❏ 5 - Allyson (1981)
  APA-The Silence is Broken
- ❏ ❏ 6 - Shannon (1982)
  APA-Thank You, Good-Bye
- ❏ ❏ 7 - Courtney (1983)
- ❏ ❏ 8 - Erin (1983)
  APA-Gold Medal Murder
- ❏ ❏ 9 - Janell (1983)
- ❏ ❏ 10 - Lindsey (1983)
  APA-Dying to Come Home
- ❏ ❏ 11 - Megham (1983)
- ❏ ❏ 12 - Lyssa (1984)
- ❏ ❏ 13 - Margo's Reunion (1984)

■ JEVONS, Marshall [P]

Marshall Jevons is the shared pseudonym of William Breit (rhymes with light) and Kenneth G. Elzinga for their mysteries featuring a Milton-Friedman-lookalike economics professor. In book 1 a retired general and a former Supreme Court justice are murdered in the Caribbean and the Harvard professor uses economic theory to solve the case. Both Breit and Elzinga received their PhDs at the University of Michigan and were teaching at the University of Virginia at the time they started their fiction-writing collaboration. Breit now teaches at Trinity University in San Antonio (TX), while Elzinga is still on the faculty at UVA in Charlottesville. Born in New Orleans (LA), Breit earned his B.A. at the University of Texas, while Michigan native Elzinga started his academic career at Kalamazoo College (MI). Together they have also written several books on antitrust law and public policy.

Henry Spearman...Harvard professor in Cambridge, Massachusetts
- ❏ ❏ 1 - Murder at the Margin (1978)
- ❏ ❏ 2 - The Fatal Equilibrium (1985)
- ❏ ❏ 3 - A Deadly Indifference (1995)

■ JOHNSON, E. Richard

Edgar award winner E. Richard Johnson was an inmate at the Stillwater State Prison (MN) when he wrote his first crime novel introducing police detective Tony Lonto. Winner of the best first novel Edgar in 1969, *Silver Street* (1968) was reissued in 1997 by International Polygonics. The book has been described as "savagely fascinating, uncompromising, revealing and hard as nails." Bill Pronzini (*1001 Midnights*) called it a "must-*not*-read for those who like their...fictional detectives polite, well educated, and witty." Of the dozen books Johnson has produced since, only one other has featured Tony Lonto. Most take place in unspecified midwestern citites. Johnson's more recent work includes *Dead Flowers* (1990) and *Case Load* (1991). He spent 4 years in Army Intelligence and later worked as a logger, forester, ranch hand and well-driller.

Tony Lonto...police detective in the United States
- ❏ ❏ 1 - **Silver Street (1968) Edgar winner ★**
  Brit.-The Silver Street Killer
- ❏ ❏ 2 - The Inside Man (1969)

■ **JUDD, Bob**

Ohio native Bob Judd started his advertising career as a copywriter for J. Walter Thompson in New York and later spent 5 years as creative director of their London office. Author of a mystery series set in the world of international auto racing, Judd sees the sport as a metaphor for life, with drivers going round and round, faster and faster, on the leading edge of technology, taking prodigious risks. In an interview with *Contemporary Authors*, he said, "Add the conflicting forces of the largest corporations on earth and a devoted following of 4 billion fans, and you will find the novel fills a larger screen than a film ever dreamed of." In book 2, which appeared first as *Monza* (1991) and later as *Curve* (1994), Evers is the leading contender in Italy's Formula One Grand Prix, racing against a rich, young Italian whose wife had asked for Evers' help just before she was murdered.

Forrest Evers...former international race car driver
- ❏ ❏ 1 - Formula One (1989)
- ❏ ❏ 2 - Monza (1991)
  - APA-Curve
- ❏ ❏ 3 - Burn (1992)
  - Brit.-Phoenix
- ❏ ❏ 4 - Race (1992)
- ❏ ❏ 5 - Spin (1994)

■ **KAHN, Michael A.**

Amherst graduate Michael A. Kahn shares his Harvard Law School background with his series detective Rachel Gold, featured in five legal thriller mysteries. They're both St. Louis natives who started their careers as junior associates in large Chicago firms and later returned to St. Louis. While Rachel opened a solo practice in a trendy neighborhood, Kahn became a partner in a large firm in a more staid part of town, but they're both trial lawyers specializing in civil litigation. Although Kahn says he's not yet given Rachel one of his real cases, he always puts her in legal practice situations. A former elementary school teacher who got his literary start writing offbeat feature articles for *Chicago Magazine*, Kahn is a full-time trial attorney and married father of five who writes from ten to midnight on his laptop computer at the kitchen table.

Rachel Gold...defense attorney in St. Louis, Missouri
- ❏ ❏ 1 - Canaan Legacy (1988)
  - APA-Grave Designs
- ❏ ❏ 2 - Death Benefits (1993)
- ❏ ❏ 3 - Firm Ambitions (1994)
- ❏ ❏ 4 - Due Diligence (1995)
- ❏ ❏ 5 - Sheer Gall (1996)

■ **KAKONIS, Tom**

Tom Kakonis explores the world of gamblers, grifters, hookers and cons in his series featuring English professor turned gambler Tom Waverly, jailed for seven years when a tragic overreaction turned fatal. Set in Traverse City (MI), the series opener takes its title from a large bankroll of mostly one dollar bills with a large denomination bill on the outside. Born in California at the start of the Depression, Kakonis is the son of a Greek immigrant and a South Dakota farm girl who went west in search of adventure. Currently an English professor at a Michigan university, he has worked as a railroad laborer, pool hall and beach idler, army officer and technical writer. But he says his prison teaching experience has been the most useful in creating fictional villains and heroes. As Adam Barrow he has written a paperback thriller (*Flawless*, 1997) about a handsome serial killer.

Timothy Waverly...would-be professor turned card sharp ex-con in Palm Beach, Florida
- ❏ ❏ 1 - Michigan Roll (1988)
- ❏ ❏ 2 - Double Down (1991)
- ❏ ❏ 3 - Shadow Counter (1993)

■ KAMINSKY, Stuart M.

Edgar award winner Stuart M. Kaminsky has written more than 35 detective novels in 3 series, recently adding novelizations of *The Rockford Files* to his line-up. His Hollywood series, launched in 1977, stars 1940s P.I. Toby Peters, whose clients range from Errol Flynn (book 1) to W.C. Fields (book 20). Much darker is his Edgar-award-winning series featuring Inspector Rostnikov of the Moscow police, up against all the frustrations of life in Russia. His Chicago police detective is 60-ish insomniac Abe Lieberman, addicted to crosswords and old movies. Abe and Toby's creator knows his movies. A distinguished professor of film, Kaminsky has written screenplays, film biographies, and books on film theory and film making. A Chicago native who now lives in Sarasota (FL), he is currently writing 4 novels a year. His newest character, a Florida law firm investigator, so far appears only in short stories.

Abe Lieberman...60-something Jewish police detective in Chicago, Illinois
- ❏ ❏ 1 - Lieberman's Folly (1990)
- ❏ ❏ 2 - Lieberman's Choice (1993)
- ❏ ❏ 3 - Lieberman's Day (1995)
- ❏ ❏ 4 - Lieberman's Thief (1995)
- ❏ ❏ 5 - Lieberman's Law (1996)

James Rockford...low-rent private eye in Los Angeles, California
- ❏ ❏ 1 - The Rockford Files: The Green Bottle (1996)
- ❏ ❏ 2 - The Rockford Files: Devil on My Doorstep (1998)

Porfiry Rostnikov, Insp.....Russian police inspector in Moscow, Russia
- ❏ ❏ 1 - Death of a Dissident (1981) Brit.-Rostnikov's Corpse
- ❏ ❏ 2 - **Black Knight in Red Square (1983) Edgar nominee** ☆
- ❏ ❏ 3 - Red Chameleon (1985)
- ❏ ❏ 4 - A Fine Red Rain (1987)
- ❏ ❏ 5 - **A Cold Red Sunrise (1988) Edgar winner** ★
- ❏ ❏ 6 - The Man Who Walked Like a Bear (1990)
- ❏ ❏ 7 - Rostnikov's Vacation (1991)
- ❏ ❏ 8 - Death of a Russian Priest (1992)
- ❏ ❏ 9 - Hard Currency (1995)
- ❏ ❏ 10 - Blood and Rubles (1996)
- ❏ ❏ 11 - Tarnished Icons (1997)

Toby Peters...1940s Hollywood private investigator in Los Angeles, California
- ❏ ❏ 1 - Bullet for a Star (1977)
- ❏ ❏ 2 - Murder on the Yellow Brick Road (1978)
- ❏ ❏ 3 - You Bet Your Life (1979)
- ❏ ❏ 4 - The Howard Hughes Affair (1979)
- ❏ ❏ 5 - Never Cross a Vampire (1980)
- ❏ ❏ 6 - High Midnight (1981)
- ❏ ❏ 7 - Catch a Falling Clown (1982)
- ❏ ❏ 8 - He Done Her Wrong (1983)
- ❏ ❏ 9 - The Fala Factor (1984)
- ❏ ❏ 10 - Down for the Count (1985)
- ❏ ❏ 11 - The Man Who Shot Lewis Vance (1986)
- ❏ ❏ 12 - Smart Moves (1987)
- ❏ ❏ 13 - Think Fast, Mr. Peters (1988)
- ❏ ❏ 14 - Buried Caesars (1989)
- ❏ ❏ 15 - **Poor Butterfly (1990) Shamus nominee** ☆
- ❏ ❏ 16 - The Melting Clock (1991)
- ❏ ❏ 17 - The Devil Met a Lady (1993)
- ❏ ❏ 18 - Tomorrow is Another Day (1995)
- ❏ ❏ 19 - Dancing in the Dark (1996)
- ❏ ❏ 20 - A Fatal Glass of Beer (1997)

■ KANTNER, Rob

While some consultants and corporate types are giving up the structured work life to write fiction, Detroiter Rob Kantner has gone the other way. After 9 novels in as many years, 5 of which were Shamus nominees, including 3 best paperback award winners, Kantner is now buzzing around the country consulting on quality improvement issues. His newest book is *OS-9000 Answer Book: 101 Questions and Answers about the Automotive Quality System Standard* (1997). This is not good news for fans of Ben Perkins, Detroit private eye, last seen in *Concrete Hero* (1994). In addition to his paperback award winners, Kantner earned 4 Shamus short story nominations, including a win for "*Fly Away Home*" which he collected along with his first best paperback award in 1987—a pretty impressive quality achievement by any industry's standard.

Ben Perkins...ex-union strike buster turned P.I. in Detroit, Michigan
- ❏ ❏ 1 - **The Back-Door Man (1986) Shamus winner ★**
- ❏ ❏ 2 - The Harder They Hit (1987)
- ❏ ❏ 3 - **Dirty Work (1988) Shamus winner ★**
- ❏ ❏ 4 - **Hell's Only Half Full (1989) Shamus winner ★**
- ❏ ❏ 5 - **Made in Detroit (1990) Shamus nominee ☆**
- ❏ ❏ 6 - **The Thousand-Yard Stare (1991) Shamus nominee ☆**
- ❏ ❏ 7 - The Quick and the Dead (1992)
- ❏ ❏ 8 - The Red, White and Blues (1993)
- ❏ ❏ 9 - Concrete Hero (1994)

■ KATZ, Jon

Media critic Jon Katz wears at least 3 hats and writes under all of them. He's a carpooling dad and creator of suburban detective Kit DeLeeuw (pronounced de-LOO), who makes his 5th appearance in *Death Row* (1998). Former media critic for *Rolling Stone* and *New York* magazine, Katz currently holds that position at *Wired* magazine. An interactive journalist who's been actively online for 6 years, his *Media Rants* (1997) is a collection of essays on media and online issues from his columns for *The Netizen* (Hotwired). He has also written *Virtuous Reality: How America Surrendered Discussion of Moral Values to Opportunists, Nitwits and Blockheads like William Bennett* (1997), a book that has provoked strong reactions from critics (*The Washington Post*) and supporters (NPR). Former executive producer of the *CBS Morning News*, he lives in suburban New Jersey.

Kit DeLeeuw...Wall Street shark turned surburban detective in Rochambeau, New Jersey
- ❏ ❏ 1 - Death by Station Wagon (1992)
- ❏ ❏ 2 - The Family Stalker (1994)
- ❏ ❏ 3 - The Last Housewife (1995)
- ❏ ❏ 4 - The Father's Club (1996)

■ KATZ, Michael J.

Michael J. Katz is the creator of a 3-book series featuring soft-boiled Chicago private eye Murray Glick and his sportscaster buddy Andy Sussman, introduced in *Murder Off the Glass* (1987), a basketball mystery in which Andy does the legwork and Murray does the thinking. In book 2, *Last Dance in Redondo Beach* (1989), the action moves back and forth between the Windy City and Los Angeles in the bizarre world of professional wrestling. A Chicago native, Katz now lives in Los Angeles. He has also written *Congratulations...Your Girlfriend's Engaged! The Ultimate Survival Guide for Grooms To Be* (1992), a book he says fills a void in the socialization of a generation of American males. The publisher says she loved the book so much she married the author, who she claims is as funny in real life as he is in print.

Murray Glick & Andy Sussman...P.I. & sportscaster buddy in Chicago, Illinois
- ❏ ❏ 1 - Murder Off the Glass (1987)
- ❏ ❏ 2 - Last Dance in Redondo Beach (1989)
- ❏ ❏ 3 - The Big Freeze (1991)

■ KAUFELT, David A.

Former advertising copywriter David A. Kaufelt wrote 9 novels before launching his mystery series featuring a female real estate attorney on Long Island (NY), introduced in *The Fat Boy Murders* (1993). In book 3, praised for its eccentric characters and sexy dialogue, Wyn may have to use herself as bait to catch whoever's killing realtor/developers. Kaufelt's mainstream novels include *Silver Rose* (1982), *American Tropic* (1986), and *Six Months with an Older Woman* (1973), which was made into a CBS television movie. A former creative writing instructor at Upsala College (NJ), he earned an undergraduate degree in engineering at the University of Pennsylvania and an M.A. from New York University. Co-founder of the Key West Literary Festival, he lives half the year in Key West with his wife and son. They spend their summers in Sag Harbor, Long Island.

Wynsome "Wyn" Lewis...ex-Manhattan real estate attorney in Wagg's Neck Harbor, New York
- ❏ ❏ 1 - The Fat Boy Murders (1993)
- ❏ ❏ 2 - The Winter Women Murders (1994)
- ❏ ❏ 3 - The Ruthless Realtor Murders (1997)

■ KAVANAGH, Dan [P]

Dan Kavanagh is the pseudonym used by British novelist Julian Barnes for his 4-book series about a bisexual ex-cop private eye in London, last seen in *Going to the Dogs* (1987). The cynical, neurotic, street-smart Duffy gets called away from his low-life London beat to a country mansion in book 4, where darned if there isn't a body in the library. But this is not Agatha Christie. It's "on-the-make-Britain of the 1980s, where new money talks loud but old vices flourish." The dust jacket bio says Kavanagh was born in County Sligo, Ireland, and left home at 19 to roam the world, serving as an entertainment officer on a Japanese supertanker and working as a baggage handler at Toronto International Airport. As Julian Barnes he often appears in the pages of *The Washington Post Book World*. His recent fiction includes *Cross Channel* (1996) and *Letters from London* (1995).

Nick Duffy...bisexual ex-cop P.I. in London, England
- ❏ ❏ 1 - Duffy (1980)
- ❏ ❏ 2 - Fiddle City (1981)
- ❏ ❏ 3 - Putting the Boot In (1985)
- ❏ ❏ 4 - Going to the Dogs (1987)

■ KEATING, H. R. F.

1996 Cartier Diamond Dagger recipient for lifetime achievement, Henry Reymond Fitzwalter Keating is the creator of Insp. Ganesh Ghote (pronounced GO-tay), Bombay's crack Hindu police inspector, appearing in the Gold Dagger winner *The Perfect Murder* (1964) and 19 subsequent books. Keating's second Gold Dagger was awarded to *The Murder of the Maharajah* (1980), a 1930 mystery set in the Maharajah's palace with Insp. Ghote's father-to-be appearing as one of the minor characters. Keating has written at least 15 other books, including his most recent collection of stories *In Kensington Gardens* (1997) beautifully illustrated by Gwen Mandley. Past Chairman of the Crime Writers' Association and President of The Detection Club since 1985, Keating occupies the office once held by G. K. Chesteron, Agatha Christie and Dorothy L. Sayers. He shares his Halloween birthday with mystery writers Dick Francis, Kinky Friedman and Janet Dawson.

Ganesh Ghote, Insp.....Indian police inspector in Bombay, India
- ❏ ❏ 1 - **The Perfect Murder (1964) Gold Dagger winner ★ Edgar nominee** ☆
- ❏ ❏ 2 - Inspector Ghote's Good Crusade (1966)
- ❏ ❏ 3 - Inspector Ghote Caught in Meshes (1967)
- ❏ ❏ 4 - Inspector Ghote Hunts the Peacock (1968)
- ❏ ❏ 5 - Inspector Ghote Plays a Joker (1969)
- ❏ ❏ 6 - Inspector Ghote Breaks an Egg (1970)
- ❏ ❏ 7 - Inspector Ghote Goes by Train (1971)
- ❏ ❏ 8 - Inspector Ghote Trusts the Heart (1972)

❑ ❑ 9 - Bats Fly Up for Inspector Ghote (1974)
❑ ❑ 10 - Filmi, Filmi, Inspector Ghote (1976)
❑ ❑ 11 - Inspector Ghote Draws a Line (1979)
❑ ❑ 12 - Go West, Inspector Ghote (1981)
❑ ❑ 13 - The Sheriff of Bombay (1984)
❑ ❑ 14 - Under a Monsoon Cloud (1986)
❑ ❑ 15 - The Body in the Billiard Room (1987)
❑ ❑ 16 - Dead on Time (1988)
❑ ❑ ss - Insp. Ghote, His Life and Crimes [short stories] (1989)
❑ ❑ 17 - The Iciest Sin (1990)
❑ ❑ 18 - Cheating Death (1991)
❑ ❑ 19 - Doing Wrong (1993)
❑ ❑ 20 - Asking Questions (1996)

■ KEEGAN, Alex

After surviving the Clapham (London) Rail Disaster in December 1988, Alex Keegan dropped out of business and became a house husband. Four years later he decided to take up fiction writing, so he wrote a 5-year plan. Several short stories and a mystery series featuring a young woman detective constable are the result. Book 1, *Cuckoo* (1993), was nominated for a 1995 Anthony for best first novel after its U.S. publication in 1994. Brighton D.C. Kathy "Caz" Flood is scheduled to make her 5th appearance in *Robin* (1997, U.K. edition). Keegan has worked for the RAF, in direct selling and as a computer consultant and television engineer. A committed runner, he is a U.K. top-thirty veteran sprinter and holds a degree in psychology from Liverpool University. He currently lives in Southampton with his wife and their two young children.

Kathy "Caz" Flood, D.C.....detective constable in Brighton, England
❑ ❑ **1 - Cuckoo (1993) Anthony nominee** ☆
❑ ❑ 2 - Vulture (1994)
❑ ❑ 3 - Kingfisher (1995)
❑ ❑ 4 - Razorbill (1996)

■ KELLERMAN, Jonathan

Jonathan Kellerman won both the Edgar and Anthony best first novel awards for the opener to his Alex Delaware series, now in its 12th installment. The murder of the daughter of an Israeli consul in *Survival of the Fittest* (1997) brings back police detective Daniel Sharavi, first seen in *The Butcher's Theater* (1988), a nonseries best seller about serial killings in Jerusalem. Kellerman spent 10 years as a practicing psychologist, working with young cancer patients, the subject of his *Psychological Aspects of Childhood Cancer* (1980) and *Helping the Fearful Child* (1981). He uses the experience gained in his practice as the basis for the Delaware series. A former freelance illustrator, teacher and youth director, Kellerman holds a Ph.D. from the University of Southern California. He is married to mystery novelist Faye Kellerman.

Alex Delaware...child psychologist in Los Angeles, California
❑ ❑ **1 - When the Bough Breaks (1985) Anthony & Edgar winner** ★★ Brit.-Shrunken Heads
❑ ❑ 2 - Blood Test (1986)
❑ ❑ 3 - Over the Edge (1987)
❑ ❑ 4 - Silent Partner (1989)
❑ ❑ 5 - Time Bomb (1990)
❑ ❑ 6 - Private Eyes (1992)
❑ ❑ 7 - Devil's Waltz (1993)
❑ ❑ 8 - Bad Love (1994)
❑ ❑ 9 - Self-Defense (1995)
❑ ❑ 10 - The Web (1996)
❑ ❑ 11 - The Clinic (1997)
❑ ❑ 12 - Survival of the Fittest (1997)

■ KELLEY, Patrick A.

Patrick A. Kelley is the creator of a five-book series from the 1980s featuring a professional magician named Harry Colderwood, first seen in *Slightly Murder* (1985). In book 3, *Slightly Invisible* (1987) Harry's taken his act on the road in Ohio, where a beautiful college coed has disappeared. A psychic's been called in to find her, and a friend of Harry's is being framed for the kidnapping. What's more, Harry is convinced the psychic is a fraud. All he has to do is prove it, and demonstrate his friend's innocence at the same time. In the midst of it all, Harry has to go on stage in a mind-reading act, or risk what could turn into his unscheduled entry into the spirit world. Like his fictional creation, Patrick A. Kelley is also a professional magician.

Harry Colderwood...professional magician in Pennsylvania
- ❑ ❑ 1 - Slightly Murder (1985)
- ❑ ❑ 2 - Slightly Lethal (1986)
- ❑ ❑ 3 - Slightly Invisible (1987)
- ❑ ❑ 4 - Slightly Deceived (1987)
- ❑ ❑ 5 - Slightly Guilty (1988)

■ KEMELMAN, Harry

Harry Kemelman (1908-1996) was the creator of Rabbi David Small of Barnard's Crossing, a town based on his own Marblehead (MA). A local resident since the '40s, Kemelman had written a book about the building of Marblehead's synagogue. According to an early 1996 interview with Michele Slung of *The Washington Post Book World*, the manuscript was rejected by an editor at Crown who suggested Kemelman rework it as a crime novel. He said he remembered thinking when he arrived home that evening how the synagogue parking lot looked like a good place to hide a body. After 12 days of nonstop typing and a year of revisions, *Friday the Rabbi Slept Late* was born, winning Kemelman a best-first-novel Edgar in 1965. Three weeks before his death in December 1996 Kemelman celebrated his 88th birthday. His 11th Rabbi Small novel was published just 9 months earlier.

David Small, Rabbi...rabbi sleuth in Barnard's Crossing, Massachusetts
- ❑ ❑ 1 - **Friday the Rabbi Slept Late (1964) Edgar winner ★**
- ❑ ❑ 2 - Saturday the Rabbi Went Hungry (1966)
- ❑ ❑ 3 - Sunday the Rabbi Stayed Home (1969)
- ❑ ❑ 4 - Monday the Rabbi Took Off (1972)
- ❑ ❑ 5 - Tuesday the Rabbi Saw Red (1974)
- ❑ ❑ 6 - Wednesday the Rabbi Got Wet (1976)
- ❑ ❑ 7 - Thursday the Rabbi Walked Out (1978)
- ❑ ❑ 8 - Someday the Rabbi Will Leave (1985)
- ❑ ❑ 9 - One Fine Day the Rabbi Bought a Cross (1987)
- ❑ ❑ 10 - The Day the Rabbi Resigned (1992)
- ❑ ❑ 11 - That Day the Rabbi Left Town (1996)

■ KEMPRECOS, Paul

Paul Kemprecos has written a 6-book series featuring Aristotle Plato Socarides (pronounced sock-a-REE-dees), ex-cop and part-time fisherman private eye, introduced in *Cool Blue Tomb* (1991), a Shamus award winner for best paperback original. In the series opener, it's a killer whale at a marine park who's the prime suspect when the orca trainer is found dead in the pool. The supporting cast includes Soc's 17-pound Maine coon cat and a crusty Greek uncle who sails a rickety old boat from Florida to Cape Cod in search of sunken treasure. Former editor of the *Cape Cod Business Journal*, Kemprecos once wrote a popular weekly column on commercial fishing. After earning a degree in journalism from Boston University, he worked as a reporter and managing editor of *The Cape Codder* newspaper.

Aristotle Plato Socarides...ex-cop part-time fisherman P.I. in Cape Cod, Massachusetts
- ❑ ❑ 1 - **The Cool Blue Tomb (1991) Shamus winner ★**
- ❑ ❑ 2 - Neptune's Eye (1991)
- ❑ ❑ 3 - Death in Deep Water (1992)
- ❑ ❑ 4 - Feeding Frenzy (1993)
- ❑ ❑ 5 - The Mayflower Murder (1995)
- ❑ ❑ 6 - Rock Bottom (1996)
- ❑ ❑ 7 - Bluefin Blues (1997)

■ KENNEALY, Jerry

Two-time Shamus nominee and former San Francisco police officer Jerry Kennealy has been a licensed private investigator in the San Francisco Bay Area since 1971. And he's been writing about P.I. Nick Polo since 1987. While fictional private eyes range from hardboiled to soft, Kennealy describes his investigator as al dente. In the series opener, Polo is serving a prison term for theft when he's offered his freedom and a P.I. license in exchange for uncovering a blackmail scheme directed at the city's female mayor. Sexually incriminating photographs are involved. Kennealy says part of the fun of writing books is that Polo gets to do all those illegal things that Kennealy the private investigator shies away from, like breaking and entering and tapping phones. A resident of San Francisco, Kennealy is also the author of *The Conductor* (1996) and *The Suspect* (1998).

Nick Polo...private eye in San Francisco, California
- ❑ ❑ 1 - Polo Solo (1987)
- ❑ ❑ 2 - Polo, Anyone? (1988)
- ❑ ❑ 3 - Polo's Ponies (1988)
- ❑ ❑ 4 - Polo in the Rough (1989)
- ❑ ❑ 5 - **Polo's Wild Card (1990) Shamus nominee** ☆
- ❑ ❑ 6 - Green With Envy (1991)
- ❑ ❑ 7 - **Special Delivery (1992) Shamus nominee** ☆
- ❑ ❑ 8 - Vintage Polo (1993)
- ❑ ❑ 9 - Beggars Choice (1994)
- ❑ ❑ 10 - All That Glitters (1997)

■ KENT, Bill

Bill Kent is the creator of an Atlantic City police series featuring an impossibly idealistic vice detective, Louis Monroe, introduced in *Under the Boardwalk* (1989), a *New York Times* notable crime book that year. In book 2, Det. Monroe prepares to marry while trying to gather evidence on a corrupt partner. Meanwhile he has to deal with a beached whale, an amazing slot machine payoff and fistfights with a 300-pound dominatrix. There's wheeling and dealing and deception galore. Titles in this series are all part of the refrain from the popular song *Under the Boardwalk*. A recognized authority on Atlantic City, Kent has been covering the gambling mecca as a journalist for more than 20 years. He has also written a travel guide, *Fodor's Vacations on the Jersey Shore, With an Insider's Look at Atlantic City and Cape May* (1991). He lives with his family in Philadelphia (PA).

Louis Monroe...Don Quixote-style cop in Atlantic City, New Jersey
- ❑ ❑ 1 - Under the Boardwalk (1989)
- ❑ ❑ 2 - Down by the Sea (1993)
- ❑ ❑ 3 - On a Blanket with my Baby (1995)

■ KENYON, Michael

Michael Kenyon is the creator of the witty, bawdy Detective Chief Inspector Henry Peckover, known as the Bard of the Yard, a fellow who loves his beer, his sweet wife and brown hats. Sadly, his uproarious verse is not appreciated at the Yard. Chosen for inclusion in *100 Great Detectives*, Peckover and his creator are lauded by Peter Lovesey who thoughtfully provides a sample of the Bard's poetry. In *Kitchen Catastrophe*, Peckover writes: O action-painted kitchen! O decorated me! O living, panchromatic art! O flying potpourri! O hot and fishy particles! Of aubergine and squid! The day I took my finger Off our blender's airborne lid! In addition to his mysteries, Kenyon is the author of *A French Affair*, an account of the years his family spent in France. Born in England, he now lives in Southampton (NY), where he is a frequent contributor to *Gourmet* magazine.

Henry Peckover, Chief Insp.....Scotland Yard's cockney poet in London, England
- ❏ ❏ 1 - Zigzag [incl O'Malley] (1981) U.S.-The Elgar Variation
- ❏ ❏ 2 - The God Squad Bod (1982) U.S.-The Man at the Wheel
- ❏ ❏ 3 - A Free-Range Wife (1983)
- ❏ ❏ 4 - A Healthy Way to Die (1986)
- ❏ ❏ 5 - Peckover Holds the Baby (1988)
- ❏ ❏ 6 - Kill the Butler (1991)
- ❏ ❏ 7 - Peckover Joins the Choir (1993)
- ❏ ❏ 8 - Peckover and the Bog Man (1994)

O'Malley, Supt.....comic Irish cop in Ireland
- ❏ ❏ 1 - The 100,000 Welcomes (1970)
- ❏ ❏ 2 - The Shooting of Dan McGrew (1972)
- ❏ ❏ 3 - A Sorry State (1974)

■ KERR, Philip

British author Philip Kerr has written 3 books featuring a German ex-cop turned private eye in Berlin during the 1930s. Bernie Gunther makes his first appearance in *March Violets* (1989). He is sent to a concentration camp, but survives and turns up in postwar Vienna. Retitled *Berlin Noir* (1993), these three books were later published as a trilogy. Kerr's next novel, *A Philosophical Investigation* (1992), was praised by Ruth Rendell as "quite the best crime novel this year." Set in the early 21st century, it features a woman detective, Chief Inspector Jakowicz, in charge of the hunt for a serial killer threatening national security. In his most recent work of fiction, *Gridiron* (1995), Kerr has an electronic building animate itself. This thriller was published in the U.S. as *The Grid* (1996).

Bernie Gunther...1930s German private eye in Berlin, Germany
- ❏ ❏ 1 - March Violets (1989)
- ❏ ❏ 2 - The Pale Criminal (1990)
- ❏ ❏ 3 - A German Requiem (1991)

■ KIENZLE, William X.

William X(avier) Kienzle (pronounced KIN-zell) is the creator of Father Robert Koesler, the sleuthing priest of a 19-book series set in Detroit where Kienzle himself was a parish priest for 20 years. In an interview with *St. James Guide* (4th edition) Kienzle says his priests are human, but strong in their calling, a reflection of the respect he has for the vocation he was once privileged to exercise. Editor of the *Michigan Catholic* for a dozen years, Kienzle left the priesthood in 1974 and became editor of *MPLS* magazine in Minneapolis. He later served as director of the Center for Contemplative Studies at the University of

Dallas, but has since returned to the Detroit area where he lives with his wife of more than 20 years. His series opener, *The Rosary Murders* (1979), became a major motion picture in 1987 starring Donald Sutherland as Father Koesler. The screenplay was written by Elmore Leonard and Fred Walton.

Robert Koesler, Father...Catholic priest in Detroit, Michigan
- ❏ ❏ 1 - The Rosary Murders (1979)
- ❏ ❏ 2 - Death Wears a Red Hat (1980)
- ❏ ❏ 3 - Mind Over Murder (1981)
- ❏ ❏ 4 - Assault with Intent (1982)
- ❏ ❏ 5 - Shadow of Death (1983)
- ❏ ❏ 6 - Kill and Tell (1984)
- ❏ ❏ 7 - Sudden Death (1985)
- ❏ ❏ 8 - Deathbed (1986)
- ❏ ❏ 9 - Deadline for a Critic (1987)
- ❏ ❏ 10 - Marked for Murder (1988)
- ❏ ❏ 11 - Eminence (1989)
- ❏ ❏ 12 - Masquerade (1990)
- ❏ ❏ 13 - Chameleon (1991)
- ❏ ❏ 14 - Body Count (1992)
- ❏ ❏ 15 - Dead Wrong (1993)
- ❏ ❏ 16 - Bishop as Pawn (1994)
- ❏ ❏ 17 - Call No Man Father (1995)
- ❏ ❏ 18 - Requiem for Moses (1996)
- ❏ ❏ 19 - The Man Who Loved God (1997)

■ **KILMER, Nicholas**

A playwright, painter, and former college dean, Nicholas Kilmer has also been a teacher of art, English and Latin, and a translator of Dante, de Ronsard and Petrarch. He currently makes his living buying and selling old paintings and writing art mysteries featuring a Vietnam vet turned art hunter for a rich collector in Cambridge (MA). Fred Taylor and his boss Clayton Reed are last seen in *O Sacred Head* (1997) where Fred is called out in the middle of the night to identify a 17th century painting of Christ in Agony. The painting has been used to decorate a murder scene with a headless John Doe found in a vacant luxury condo near Harvard. While vacationing in Tuscany several years ago, Kilmer says he was approached about a cache of old masters in a Swiss bank vault, much like the ones offered to Clayton in book 3. The author lives in Cambridge (MA).

Fred Taylor...Vietnam veteran turned art hunter in Cambridge, Massachusetts
- ❏ ❏ 1 - Harmony in Flesh and Black (1995)
- ❏ ❏ 2 - Man With a Squirrel (1996)
- ❏ ❏ 3 - O Sacred Head (1997)

■ **KINCAID, D. [P]**

D. Kincaid is the pseudonym of Bert Fields, author of a pair of legal mysteries featuring unorthodox Los Angeles trial attorney Harry Cain, introduced in *The Sunset Bomber* (1986), and later seen in *The Lawyer's Tale* (1992). According to George Easter (*Deadly Pleasures #3*, Fall 1993), Fields employed the pseudonym to protect his professional reputation as a practicing attorney.

Harry Cain...unorthodox trial lawyer in Los Angeles, California
- ❏ ❏ 1 - The Sunset Bomber (1986)
- ❏ ❏ 2 - The Lawyer's Tale (1992)

■ KING, Frank

Frank King is the creator of part-time actress and waitress Sally Tepper, known around her Hell's Kitchen neighborhood as the 'dog lady' because she keeps strays. Sally and her five dogs (Bernstein, Heineken, Molson, Budweiser and Stout) head into the subway tunnels after the killer of a homeless friend in book two. *Kirkus* called Sally a "quirky but likable yo-yo" in the book dedicated to "that homeless woman on West 51st who told [King] her dog had been kidnapped by the Mayor." Best known for his series mysteries written as Lydia Adamson, King currently has more than 1.5 million books in print in three series featuring female amateur sleuths. A former copywriter, he wrote three earlier mystery-thrillers, *Down and Dirty* (1978), *Night Vision* (1979), and *Raya* (1980) set in Cairo in 1942. He is also credited with the first baseball horror novel ever written, *Southpaw* (1988).

Sally Tepper...unemployed actress with five dogs in New York, New York
- ❑ ❑ 1 - Sleeping Dogs Die (1988)
- ❑ ❑ 2 - Take the D Train (1990)

■ KING, Peter

Peter King is a retired Cordon Bleu chef whose series detective Goodwin Harper is a food consultant to Scotland Yard, specializing in ancient recipes, obscure ingredients and rare spices. He gets drafted by the Yard after being a guest at the luncheon where a muckraking journalist keels over in the roast pork perigourdine. *People* magazine picked this series opener as a Beach Book of the Week in 1996. Book 2 finds the Gourmet Detective trying to authenticate the rare "Celestial Spice." When book 3 takes him to the wine country of Provence, an attempted buyout of a large vineyard leaves a badly mutilated corpse on the grounds, and our sleuth goes undercover as a working journalist. Each of these books features real recipes and cooking techniques. The author lives in Florida.

Goodwin Harper...food consultant to Scotland Yard in London, England
- ❑ ❑ 1 - The Gourmet Detective (1996)
- ❑ ❑ 2 - Spiced to Death (1997)
- ❑ ❑ 3 - Dying on the Vine (1998)

■ KIRTON, Bill

British author Bill Kirton has written two police procedurals featuring Detective Chief Inspector Carston introduced in *Material Evidence* (1995), and seen again in *Rough Justice* (1996). The two books have been published only in Great Britain.

Carston, D.C.I....detective chief inspector in England
- ❑ ❑ 1 - Material Evidence (1995)
- ❑ ❑ 2 - Rough Justice (1996)

■ KNIEF, Charles

Charles Knief (pronounced NEEF) is the creator of John Caine, Navy SEAL turned P.I., introduced in *Diamond Head* (1996), winner of the St. Martin's Press/PWA Best First Private Eye Novel contest in 1995. An admiral in Pearl Harbor asks Caine to find his daughter's killer and when the P.I. discovers the daughter had been involved in Hawaii's snuff film industry, he knows he has to save his former commanding officer from scandal. The action in book 2 moves to San Diego (CA), much like the author, who was previously working with the Department of Defense on Oahu and has since relocated to southern California. Knief is a consulting engineer, an expert marksman and a black belt in Kwan Cho Fa. Part of the realism in book 1 is his personal experience with a Pearl Harbor drug smuggling case that he decided to turn into fiction.

John Caine...Navy SEAL turned P.I. in Pearl Harbor, Hawaii
- ❑ ❑   1 - **Diamond Head (1996) SMP/PWA winner ★**
- ❑ ❑   2 - Sand Dollars (1998)

■ KNIGHT, J. D.

First published as a poet, J. D. Knight likes to say he has moved from free verse to the freely perverse with his creation of bounty hunter and private eye Virgil Proctor, introduced in *Zero Tolerance* (1995), a Shamus award nominee for best paperback original. Joining the P.I. in his first case is defense attorney Andrea Faber, as they work to find the missing son of Virgil's new client. Virgil knows he's getting close to something unpleasant when his house is torched and one of his friends is murdered. *Publishers Weekly* and the *San Francisco Chronicle* raved, while Richard North Patterson called *Zero Tolerance* "an impressive debut." Look for Virgil's return in *One-Way Ticket* (1998). Knight, who lives in northern California, is currently writing book 3 in this series.

Virgil Proctor...bounty hunter P.I. in the United States
- ❑ ❑   1 - **Zero Tolerance (1995) Shamus nominee** ☆
- ❑ ❑   2 - One-Way Ticket (1998)

■ KNOX, Bill

Author of more than 70 books, Bill Knox is best known for his two longest-running series; one featuring Scottish Crime Squad officers Colin Thane and his sidekick Phil Moss; the other Scottish Fishery Protection Service officer Webb Carrick. Last seen in the U.K. edition of *Blood Proof* (1997), the two Glasgow detectives were making their 22nd appearance since 1957. Under the pen name Robert MacLeod he wrote 22 books in 3 more crime series—10 books with Scottish Treasury investigator Jonathan Gaunt, 6 books featuring marine-claims investigator Andrew Laird; and 6 more with UN troubleshooter Talos Cord. The Gaunt series was published in the U.S. as by Noah Webster, while the Laird series was released here under the name Michael Kirk. Knox spent more than 40 years working in print and broadcast journalism, including a dozen years as host of a weekly Scottish television program called *Crime Desk*.

Colin Thane & Phil Moss...Scottish Crime Squad officers in Glasgow, Scotland
- ❑ ❑   1 - Deadline for a Dream (1957) U.S.-In at the Kill
- ❑ ❑   2 - Death Department (1959)
- ❑ ❑   3 - Leave it to the Hangman (1960)
- ❑ ❑   4 - Little Drops of Blood (1962)
- ❑ ❑   5 - Sanctuary Isle (1962) U.S.-The Gray Sentinels
- ❑ ❑   6 - The Man in the Bottle (1963) U.S.-The Killing Game
- ❑ ❑   7 - The Taste of Proof (1965)
- ❑ ❑   8 - The Deep Fall (1966) U.S.-The Ghost Car
- ❑ ❑   9 - Justice on the Rocks (1967)
- ❑ ❑ 10 - The Tallyman (1969)
- ❑ ❑ 11 - Children of the Mist (1970) U.S.-Who Shot the Bull?
- ❑ ❑ 12 - To Kill a Witch (1971)
- ❑ ❑ 13 - Draw Batons! (1973)
- ❑ ❑ 14 - Rally to Kill (1975)
- ❑ ❑ 15 - Pilot Error (1977)
- ❑ ❑ 16 - Live Bait (1978)
- ❑ ❑ 17 - A Killing in Antiques (1981)
- ❑ ❑ 18 - The Hanging Tree (1983)
- ❑ ❑ 19 - **The Crossfire Killings (1986) Police Review ★**
- ❑ ❑ 20 - The Interface Man (1989)
- ❑ ❑ 21 - The Counterfeit Killers (1996)

Webb Carrick...chief officer of the Scottish Fishery Protection Service in Scotland
  ❑ ❑ 1 - The Scavengers (1964)
  ❑ ❑ 2 - Devilweed (1966)
  ❑ ❑ 3 - Blacklight (1967)
  ❑ ❑ 4 - The Klondyker (1968) U.S.-A Figurehead
  ❑ ❑ 5 - Blueback (1969)
  ❑ ❑ 6 - Seafire (1970)
  ❑ ❑ 7 - Stormtide (1972)
  ❑ ❑ 8 - Whitewater (1974)
  ❑ ❑ 9 - Hellspout (1976)
  ❑ ❑ 10 - Witchrock (1977)
  ❑ ❑ 11 - Bombship (1980)
  ❑ ❑ 12 - Bloodtide (1982)
  ❑ ❑ 13 - Wavecrest (1985)
  ❑ ❑ 14 - Dead Man's Mooring (1987)
  ❑ ❑ 15 - The Drowning Nets (1991)

■ KOHLER, Vince

Newspaper staff writer Vince Kohler is the creator of Eldon Larkin, reporter for a small-town Oregon newspaper, in a series optioned for television. Introduced in *Rainy North Woods* (1990), Eldon was last seen in *Raven's Widows* (1996), taking a much-deserved Alaskan fishing vacation to get away from his romantic troubles and a cranky, demanding editor. Instead he discovers the body of an unpopular local Indian artist, crushed under one of his own totem poles. Eldon wants the story almost as much as he wants to impress the attractive woman editor of the local paper. Kohler writes about aerospace and other topics for the daily *Oregonian* where he also reviews mysteries. A resident of Portland (OR), he grows roses, reads classical, medieval and Civil War history, and occasionally teaches writing classes.

Eldon Larkin...small-town newspaper reporter in Port Jerome, Oregon
  ❑ ❑ 1 - Rainy North Woods (1990)
  ❑ ❑ 2 - Rising Dog (1992)
  ❑ ❑ 3 - Banjo Boy (1994)
  ❑ ❑ 4 - Raven's Widows (1996)

■ KUHLKEN, Ken

Ken Kuhlken is the creator of Tom Hickey, a San Diego private eye in the '40s, said to have been inspired by Kuhlken's father. Introduced in *The Loud Adios* (1991), winner of the SMP/PWA contest for best first P.I. novel, the action shifts back to 1942 in *The Venus Deal* (1993) when Tom was still part owner of their San Diego bar with suspected mobster Paul Castillo. *The Angel Gang* (1994) finds Tom retired in Tahoe until somebody kidnaps his wife and rival gangsters compete for his attention in San Diego. This wild ride completes the trilogy. Kuhlken's short stories have appeared in *Esquire* and many literary magazines and his novel *Midheaven* was a finalist for the PEN Hemingway prize for best first fiction of 1980. The following year he won an NEA Literature Fellowship and now holds degrees in literature and fiction writing from San Diego State and The University of Iowa. A professor at San Diego State University, he lives in Costa Mesa (CA).

Tom Hickey...1940s P.I. and restaurateur in San Diego, California
  ❑ ❑ 1 - **The Loud Adios (1991) SMP/PWA winner ★**
  ❑ ❑ 2 - The Venus Deal [prequel] (1993)
  ❑ ❑ 3 - The Angel Gang (1994)

■ KURLAND, Michael

Edgar nominee Michael Kurland is the author of over 30 books, including two historical mystery series and three crime-related reference books. His most recent mysteries feature columnist and radio personality Alexander Brass, the voice of Manhattan nightlife during the Depression. In book 2, *The Girls in High-Heeled Shoes* (1998), Brass investigates the disappearance of a colorful Broadway character named Two-Headed Mary. Kurland's nonfiction work includes *How to Solve a Murder: The Forensic Handbook* (1995) and *How To Try a Murder: The Handbook for Armchair Lawyers* (1997), showing the inner workings of a murder trial and how prosecutors, defense attorneys and judges do their jobs. Also from MacMillan Reference is Kurland's *Gallery of Rogues: Portraits in True Crime* (1994) with profiles of more than 500 lawmen, criminals and con artists.

Alexander Brass...1930s newspaper columnist in New York, New York
- ❑ ❑ 1 - Too Soon Dead (1997)

James Moriarty, Prof.....archenemy of Sherlock Holmes in London, England
- ❑ ❑ 1 - **The Infernal Device (1979) Edgar nominee** ☆
- ❑ ❑ 2 - Death by Gaslight (1982)

■ LAKE, M. D. [P]

Agatha award winnner M.D. Lake is the pseudonym of Allen Simpson, former Professor of Scandinavian Studies at the University of Minnesota, who writes the Peggy O'Neill series about a campus cop. Although Peggy is based on the experience of a real Minnesota campus security officer, Lake says he puts a lot of himself in the character, along with his wife and daughter. When asked why a Scandinavian Studies professor would immerse himself in a world of mayhem and murder he said, "There are a lot of people I'd like to see dead or behind bars, but I can only make them that way in mysteries." In Peggy's most recent appearance, *Midsummer Malice* (1997) the author introduces multiple points of view and the two nastiest bad guys he's ever created. Lake's 1993 Agatha award was for his short story *"Kim's Game."*

Peggy O'Neill...university campus cop in Minnesota
- ❑ ❑ 1 - Amends for Murder (1989)
- ❑ ❑ 2 - Cold Comfort (1990)
- ❑ ❑ 3 - Poisoned Ivy (1991)
- ❑ ❑ 4 - A Gift for Murder (1991)
- ❑ ❑ 5 - Murder by Mail (1993)
- ❑ ❑ 6 - Once Upon a Crime (1994)
- ❑ ❑ 7 - Grave Choices (1995)
- ❑ ❑ 8 - Flirting with Death (1996)
- ❑ ❑ 9 - Midsummer Malice (1997)

■ LANSDALE, Joe R.

Texas native Joe R. Lansdale is the creator of two unlikely East Texas buddies, one white and straight, the other black and gay, introduced in *Savage Season* (1990). This series is "sometimes profane, crude, tasteless, violent and hilariously funny in roughly equal parts," according to Bill Crider (*St. James Guide*), who thinks Lansdale doesn't just break taboos; he tears them into tiny pieces." Winner of Bram Stoker and British Fantasy awards, Landsdale has written westerns, dark fantasy, horror, science fiction, comics, young adult and animated scripts for Batman series, in addition to his work in crime fiction. Recently back in print are his horror classics, *Drive-In: A B-Movie with Blood and Popcorn* (World Fantasy award nominee for best novel) and *Drive-In 2*, from 1988-89, repackaged as *The Drive-In: A Double-Feature Omnibus* (1997).

Hap Collins & Leonard Pine...straight white & gay black good ol' boys in East Texas
- ❑ ❑ 1 - Savage Season (1990)
- ❑ ❑ 2 - Mucho Mojo (1994)
- ❑ ❑ 3 - The Two-Bear Mambo (1995)
- ❑ ❑ 4 - Bad Chili (1997)

■ LASHNER, William

Philadelphia lawyer William Lashner used his own experience to write his first novel, *Hostile Witness* (1995), which introduced hard-boiled Philadelphia lawyer Victor Carl, whose exploits have since been translated into nine languages. Lashner says he wasn't quite as down and out as Victor, whose two-man office seems to be on a permanent losing streak. Drug dealers, corrupt politicians, a Hasidic detective and a love interest are all part of the action in book 1. A trial attorney in the Criminal Division of the Justice Department during the Reagan administration, Lashner also worked in the Narcotic and Dangerous Drug Section and the Office of Special Investigations, which is the U.S. government's Nazi hunting unit. A graduate of New York University School of Law and the Iowa Writers Workshop, he lives in Philadelphia with his wife and two children.

Victor Carl...hard-boiled lawyer in Philadelphia, Pennsylvania
- ❑ ❑ 1 - Hostile Witness (1995)
- ❑ ❑ 2 - Veritas (1997)

■ LE CARRÉ, John [P]

Diamond Dagger award winner and Grand Master John le Carré has won two Gold Daggers, an Edgar and a Silver Dagger for his espionage fiction, much of which features his sad superspy George Smiley, introduced in *Call for the Dead* (1961). Although physically unimposing (he's short and fat and wears really bad clothes), Smiley is a brilliant agent. Le Carré is a pseudonym of David (John Moore) Cornwell, a working diplomat in the British Foreign Office in London (and later in Bonn) when his first novels were published. Because of his diplomatic position, he was not allowed to publish under his own name. In a *Washington Post* interview, he says he has told so many lies about where the name (French for square) came from that he has long since forgotten. Many of these novels have been adapted for feature films and television miniseries.

George Smiley...British Intelligence agent and scholar in London, England
- ❑ ❑ **1 - Call for the Dead (1961) Gold Dagger runnerup ★**
- ❑ ❑ 2 - A Murder of Quality (1962)
- ❑ ❑ **3 - The Spy Who Came in from the Cold (1963) Edgar & Gold Dagger winner ★★**
- ❑ ❑ 4 - The Looking Glass War (1965)

❑ ❑   5 - Tinker, Tailor, Solider, Spy (1974)
❑ ❑   6 - **The Honourable Schoolboy (1977) Gold Dagger winner** ★
❑ ❑   7 - Smiley's People (1980)
❑ ❑   8 - The Secret Pilgrim (1991)

■ LEE, Christopher

British author Christopher Lee is the creator of a new police series set in Bath, England, featuring Inspector James Boswell Hodge Leonard, introduced in *The Bath Detective* (1995). Book 2 with the Bath inspector is *The Killing of Sally Keemer* (1997). According to Crime In Store, London's crime and mystery bookstore, these are police stories with a gritty, underworld edge. So far they are published only in Britain, but the first title is available in paperback.

James Boswell Hodge Leonard, Insp.....police inspector in Bath, England
❑ ❑   1 - The Bath Detective (1995)
❑ ❑   2 - The Killing of Sally Keemer (1996)

■ LEHANE, Dennis

Shamus award winner Dennis Lehane is the creator of Boston detective duo Patrick Kenzie and Angie Gennaro, first seen in *A Drink Before the War* (1994). Describing himself as a post-Watergate, post-Vietnam, Generation X-er who never bought the good-will-out theory, Lehane thinks it far more interesting to write about very flawed men and women trying to do the best they can in a very flawed world. With an undergraduate degree from Eckerd College and a master's from Florida International University, he has worked as a therapeutic counselor for mentally handicapped and emotionally disturbed children, a college English instructor and a chauffeur for the Boston Ritz-Carlton Hotel. He has written, produced and directed an independent film titled *Neighborhoods*, a romantic comedy he plans to enter in the Sundance film competition.

Patrick Kenzie & Angela Gennaro...private detectives in Boston, Massachusetts
❑ ❑   1 - **A Drink Before the War (1994) Anthony & Shamus winner** ★★
❑ ❑   2 - Darkness, Hold My Hand (1996)
❑ ❑   3 - Sacred (1997)

■ LEITZ, David

Former advertising creator David Lietz is now creating mysteries for his amateur sleuth Max Addams, proprietor of Whitefork Lodge, a trout-fishing paradise in nothern Vermont. Starting with *Casting in Dead Water* (1996), Max gives a guided tour of his favorite fishing spots and plenty of tips about fly fishing. The supporting cast includes Max's assistant Red Crosley, his housekeeper and cook, Stormy Bryant, and an elderly Setter-Retriever mix named Spotter. In book 2 a hotshot ad agency comes to the lodge to shoot a beer commercial and the arrogant producer turns up dead. Leitz spent 30 years creating television commercials but now concentrates on fly fishing and writing fiction. He divides his time between a 250-year-old farmhouse on the northern Massachusetts coast and a rustic cabin in the woods of southern Vermont.

Max Addams...proprietor of trout-fishing lodge in Northern Vermont
❑ ❑   1 - Casting in Dead Water (1996)
❑ ❑   2 - Dying to Fly Fish (1996)
❑ ❑   3 - Fly Fishing Can Be Fatal (1997)

■ LEJEUNE, Anthony [P]

Anthony Lejeune is a pseudonym used by London-born journalist Edward Anthony Thompson for 2 mystery series. During the early '60s he wrote 3 books featuring crime reporter Adam Gifford, who ends up working with a hush-hush figure in the War Office. The series provides an authentic picture of London newspaper life (old Fleet Street) in the '50s, says Lejeune, "now gone like lost Atlantis." He is particularly proud of his clue structure in *Key Without a Door* (1988), featuring professor James Glowery. Set in post-independence Congo, Lejeune's nonseries novel, *Glint of Spears* (1963), sets up a dramatic rescue attempt (complete with cannibals) for a missionary whose station has been destroyed. Carol Simpson Stern (*St. James Guide*) says, "The tale is gripping; the landscape hot, wooded and fly-infested; the people cunning and desperate."

Adam Gifford...crime reporter in London, England
- ❏ ❏ 1 - News of Murder (1961)
- ❏ ❏ 2 - Duel in the Shadows (1962)
- ❏ ❏ 3 - The Dark Trade (1965) U.S.-Death of a Pornographer

James Glowery...British professor in England
- ❏ ❏ 1 - Professor in Peril (1987)
- ❏ ❏ 2 - Key Without a Door (1988)

■ LEONARD, Elmore

Having his novels made into movies is what Elmore Leonard wanted all along, so he started with westerns. While writing Chevrolet advertising copy for Campbell-Ewald during the 1950s, he sold 30 short stories and 5 novels before the market for westerns peaked. His first crime novel, *The Big Bounce* (1969), was rejected by 84 publishers and film producers before Gold Medal bought it for a paperback original. When the film rights sold for $50,000 it was goodbye westerns, hello crime fiction. Since then, 32 of his 34 novels have been optioned or bought by Hollywood and 5 are currently in production, including a sequel to *Get Shorty* (1990) for John Travolta to reprise his 1995 Chili Palmer role, and a TV pilot for ABC with Beau Bridges starring as the hard-line judge in the Hammett Prize winner *Maximum Bob* (1991). Named Grand Master in 1992, Leonard is a 3-time Edgar nominee with *La Brava* taking best novel honors for 1983. Born in New Orleans, he vacations in Florida and calls a northern Detroit (MI) suburb home.

Frank Ryan...process server in Detroit, Michigan
- ❏ ❏ 1 - Swag (1976) APA-Ryan's Rules
- ❏ ❏ 2 - Unknown Man No. 89 (1977)

Raylan Givens...federal marshall in Florida
- ❏ ❏ 1 - Pronto (1993)
- ❏ ❏ 2 - Riding the Rap (1995)

■ LESCROART, John T.

It took John T. Lescroart (LES-kwah) 11 years to get his first novel published, but since then he's written almost one book a year, while earning Shamus and Anthony nominations for best novel. That first book, *Son of Holmes* (1986), introduced the literary link between Holmes and Nero Wolfe, a British secret service agent carrying an American passport. Lescroart's newer crime fiction, set in San Francisco, features a failed cop-lawyer who ends up practicing law again, first as a prosecutor, then as a defense attorney. His former partner and long-time friend, a black Jewish cop named Abe Glitsky, is chief of SFPD homicide in *A Certain Justice* (1995). Born and raised in Texas, Lescroart once worked in Europe as a singer and guitar player and later as editor and advertising director at *Guitar Player* magazine, a word processor and a law firm adminstrator. He lives in Davis (CA).

Abe Glitsky...black Jewish cop in San Francisco, California
- ❏ ❏ 1 - A Certain Justice (1995)
- ❏ ❏ 2 - Guilt (1997)

Auguste Lupa...British Secret Service agent with U.S. passport
- ❏ ❏ 1 - Son of Holmes (1986)
- ❏ ❏ 2 - Rasputin's Revenge [1916] (1987)

Dismas Hardy...ex-cop bartender and ex-ADA turned defense attorney in San Francisco, California
- ❏ ❏ 1 - **Dead Irish (1989) Shamus nominee** ☆
- ❏ ❏ 2 - The Vig (1990)
- ❏ ❏ 3 - Hard Evidence (1993)
- ❏ ❏ 4 - **The 13th Juror (1994) Anthony nominee** ☆

■ LESLIE, John

John Leslie is the creator of 50-something, piano-playing, Key West private eye, Gideon "Bud" Lowry, first seen in *Killing Me Softly* (1994). At 57, Bud is an ex-Marine, Korean War veteran who spent two years as a Key West cop while racking up 3 marriages and 3 divorces. He plays piano bar 4 nites a week, owns a cat named Tom and has an ex-prizefighter buddy named Sweets who once fought Ernest Hemingway. Bud's most recent case, *Love for Sale* (1997), opens with the news that his sometime lover Cassie is marrying someone else. After spending the evening with a local escort named Katy, he ends up with a new client, soon dead, and a mysterious salvaged chalice. Leslie's nonseries fiction includes *Havanna Hustle* (1994), *Damaged Goods* (1993), *Killer in Paradise* (1990), *Bounty Hunter Blues* (1990) and *Blood on the Keys* (1988).

Gideon Lowry...private eye in Key West, Florida
- ❏ ❏ 1 - Killing Me Softly (1994)
- ❏ ❏ 2 - Night and Day (1995)
- ❏ ❏ 3 - Love For Sale (1997)

■ LEVINE, Paul

Former Miami trial lawyer Paul Levine is the creator of ex-linebacker turned lawyer Jake Lassiter, who made his television debut in the 1995 NBC movie, *Lassiter: Justice on the Bayou*, adapted from the series opener. Jake's supporting cast includes his moonshine-guzzling braintrust, Granny Lassiter, cranky retired coroner Charlie Riggs and precocious nephew Kip. His most recent client (*Flesh and Bones*) shot a man on the next bar stool while Lassiter was enjoying a drink in a South Beach bar. Then she fainted in his arms. A recognized authority on First Amendment issues, Levine has taught communications law at the University of Miami and written both a syndicated TV show (*You & the Law*, 1977-82) and a nationally-syndicated column. A graduate of Penn State University and the University of Miami School of Law, he lives in Coconut Grove (FL).

Jake Lassiter...ex-linebacker turned lawyer in Miami, Florida
- ❏ ❏ 1 - To Speak for the Dead (1990)
- ❏ ❏ 2 - Night Vision (1992)
- ❏ ❏ 3 - False Dawn (1993)
- ❏ ❏ 4 - Mortal Sin (1994)
- ❏ ❏ 5 - Slashback (1995)
- ❏ ❏ 6 - Fool Me Twice (1996)
- ❏ ❏ 7 - Flesh and Bones (1997)

■ **LEVITSKY, Ronald**

Ronald Levitsky is the creator of Nate Rosen, a Washington DC civil rights lawyer whose work for the Committee to Defend the Constitution takes him to a new locale in each book. Musket Shoals (VA) hosts the series opener where Rosen's obnoxious client is on trial for the murder of a young Vietnamese woman. Religious issues are prominent in books 2 and 3, beginning with Rosen's trip to Earlyville (TN) where the use of poisonous snakes during religious services gets the Rev. Gideon McCrae in serious trouble. Rosen's third case features an elderly Indian holy man on trial for murder in Bear Coat (SD). Indian artifacts, gambling casinos and greedy developers all play a part. As a caring divorced father, the civil rights lawyer is often drawn to Chicago where his daughter lives with her mother and new stepfather. His own unresolved issues, Jewish ones in particular, play a continuing role in the series.

Nate Rosen...civil rights lawyer in Washington, D.C.
- ❏ ❏ 1 - The Love That Kills (1991)
- ❏ ❏ 2 - The Wisdom of Serpents (1992)
- ❏ ❏ 3 - Stone Boy (1993)
- ❏ ❏ 4 - The Innocence That Kills (1994)

■ **LEWIN, Michael Z.**

Most of Edgar-nominee Michael Z(inn) Lewin's crime fiction is set in his hometown of Indianapolis (IN), although he has not lived there since 1971. His Hoosier series characters include a middle-aged private eye, his cop buddy, and a female social worker. In 1994 Lewin published the first in a new series with a 3-generational family from Bath, England. Coming next is *Rover's Tales: A Four-Legged Good Samaritan and his Travels in the Dog World* (1998), published in England as *Underdog*. *Booklist* praised Lewin's "unerring ear for dialogue and poignant empathy for the world's underdogs," while *Publishers Weekly* called it "a story that will keep readers in stitches." After majoring in physics and chemistry at Harvard, where he graduated cum laude, Lewin spent a year reading chemistry at Cambridge University. He has lived in England since 1971.

Albert Samson...middle-age low-key P.I. in Indianapolis, Indiana
- ❏ ❏ 1 - **Ask the Right Question (1971) Edgar nominee** ☆
- ❏ ❏ 2 - The Way We Die Now (1973)
- ❏ ❏ 3 - The Enemies Within (1974)
- ❏ ❏ 4 - The Silent Salesman (1978)
- ❏ ❏ 5 - Missing Woman (1981)
- ❏ ❏ 6 - Out of Season, Out of Time (1984) Brit.-Out of Time
- ❏ ❏ 7 - And Baby Will Fall [Adele Buffington narrates] (1988) Brit.-Child Proof
- ❏ ❏ 8 - Called by a Panther (1991)
- ❏ ❏ 9 - Underdog (1994)

Leroy Powder...cop friend of Albert Samson's in Indianapolis, Indiana
- ❏ ❏ 1 - Night Cover (1976)
- ❏ ❏ 2 - Hard Line (1982)
- ❏ ❏ 3 - Late Payments (1986)

Lunghi family...3-generation private eye family in Bath, England
- ❏ ❏ 1 - Family Business (1994)

■ **LEWIS, Roy**

British author Roy Lewis is (John) Roy(ston) Lewis, who began writing detective fiction in order to use his legal knowledge more creatively. He has written more than 35 novels and at least 20 other books, primarily law-related nonfiction under the name J. R. Lewis. His crime fiction includes 3 series beginning with 8 books featuring Inspector John Crow. In 1980 Lewis launched a legal series with former policeman turned solicitor Eric Ward, whose many personal problems include dealing with glaucoma. Medieval architectural expert Arnold Landon is Lewis' most recent creation. In book 7, *A Secret Dying* (1992), Landon takes a job with the Department of Antiquities and Museums to finish a research project for a colleague who has disappeared. *Booklist* called it "an understated marvel of breathless economy." Lewis lives in Cumbria, England.

Arnold Landon...medieval architecture expert & researcher in England
❑ ❑   1 - A Gathering of Ghosts (1982)
❑ ❑   2 - Most Cunning Workmen (1984)
❑ ❑   3 - A Trout in the Milk (1986)
❑ ❑   4 - Men of Subtle Craft (1987)
❑ ❑   5 - The Devil is Dead (1989)
❑ ❑   6 - A Wisp of Smoke (1991)
❑ ❑   7 - A Secret Dying (1992)
❑ ❑   8 - Bloodeagle (1993)
❑ ❑   9 - The Crossbearer (1994)
❑ ❑ 10 - A Short-Lived Ghost (1995)
❑ ❑ 11 - Angel of Death (1995)

Eric Ward...policeman turned solicitor in England
❑ ❑   1 - A Certain Blindness (1980)
❑ ❑   2 - Dwell in Danger (1982)
❑ ❑   3 - A Limited Vision (1983)
❑ ❑   4 - Once Dying, Twice Dead (1984)
❑ ❑   5 - Blurred Reality (1985)
❑ ❑   6 - A Premium on Death (1986)
❑ ❑   7 - The Salamander Chill (1988)
❑ ❑   8 - A Necessary Dealing (1989)
❑ ❑   9 - A Kind of Transaction (1991)

John Crow, Insp.....British police inspector in England
❑ ❑   1 - A Lover Too Many (1969)
❑ ❑   2 - Error of Judgement (1971)
❑ ❑   3 - A Secret Singing (1972)
❑ ❑   4 - Blood Money (1973)
❑ ❑   5 - A Question of Degree (1974)
❑ ❑   6 - A Part of Virtue (1975)
❑ ❑   7 - Nothing but Foxes (1977)
❑ ❑   8 - A Relative Distance (1981)

■ LEWIS, Roy H.

Roy H(arley) Lewis is the creator of antiquarian book dealer Matthew Coll, formerly of British military intelligence, now living in a Dorset village where he and his bookshop occupy a 6-bedroom Queen Anne house built in 1703. In book 1, the Antiquarian Booksellers Association asks Coll to investigate a series of rare book thefts from libraries and private collectors. While book 2 deals with book auctions and a 16th century manuscript, book 3 has Matthew acting as a consultant to a large conglomerate buying valuable books. Another bibliomystery from Lewis, *Where Agents Fear to Tread* (1984), features rare Arabic manuscripts stolen from British libraries, smuggled back into Pakistan. Along with his wife, the author operates an antiquarian book search service in London where he also writes for film, theatre and television.

Matthew Coll...antiquarian book dealer in Dorset, England
- ❏ ❏ 1 - A Cracking of Spines (1980)
- ❏ ❏ 2 - The Manuscript Murders (1981)
- ❏ ❏ 3 - A Pension for Death (1983)
- ❏ ❏ 4 - Miracles Take a Little Longer (1986)
- ❏ ❏ 5 - Death in Verona (1989)

■ LEWIS, Ted

British author Ted Lewis is the creator of Jack Carter, an employee of the London rackets organization, introduced in *Jack's Return Home* (1970), also published as *Get Carter* (1971) and adapted for film, first as the MGM movie *Get Carter* and again for MGM as *Hit Man* (1972), also for MGM. Book 2, *Jack Carter's Law* (1974), was published in the U.S. as *Jack Carter and the Law* (1975). In addition to the Carter series, Lewis has written at least 5 other titles including *Grievous Bodily Harm* (1980), *Boldt* (1976), *Billy Rags* (1973), *Plender* (1971) and *All the Way Home and All the Night Through* (1965). According to *Hubin's Crime Fiction II* (1994), Ted Lewis has worked in advertising and as an animation specialist in television and films.

Jack Carter...employee of rackets organization in London, England
- ❏ ❏ 1 - Jack's Return Home (1970 APA-Get Carter
- ❏ ❏ 2 - Jack Carter's Law (1974) APA-Jack Carter and the Law
- ❏ ❏ 3 - Jack Carter and the Mafia Pigeon (1977)

■ LINDSAY, Paul

Ex-Marine and bad-boy agent Paul Lindsay spent 20 years in the FBI's Detroit office before retiring to New Hampshire in 1993. His last case was a big one. While heading up the Highland Park Strangler investigation, Lindsay was himself being investigated by the paper-pushing suits at the Hooverdome (his words). With the publication of his first novel, this hump from the streets (his words again) launched an open act of rebellion no former agent had dared—a book critical of the agency by someone still on the job. Rather than waiting until retirement, Lindsay says he forced the showdown and risked his job and lifetime pension, so no one could say he was a disgruntled former employee. According to a Detroit reviewer, "Lindsay mixes a fine and tasty brew from his own street experience with a gung-ho imagination and great gobs of breathtaking flair. Devlin is one righteously rogue agent."

Mike Devlin...FBI agent in Detroit, Michigan
- ❏ ❏ 1 - Witness to the Truth (1992)
- ❏ ❏ 2 - Codename: Gentkill (1995)
- ❏ ❏ 3 - Freedom to Kill (1997)

■ **LINDSEY, David L.**

Edgar nominee David L. Lindsey is the creator of Houston homicide detective Stuart Haydon, first seen in *A Cold Mind* (1983). "This is not a book for the squeamish," says Newell Dunlap in *1001 Midnights* (1986), "as scenes of death, autopsy and animal dissection are recorded in explicit detail." Someone is killing Houston call girls by infecting them with rabies. As Haydon sets out to do something about it, he uncovers a Brazilian slave trade connection. The author has obviously traveled to Central America, as most of book 5 takes place in Guatemala City, where the detective has gone in search of the missing daughter of a prominent Houston family. The book contains lots of information about actual hotels, streets and neighborhoods and CIA involvement in recent politics. Lindsey is a book editor living in Austin (TX).

Stuart Haydon, Sgt.....homicide detective in Houston, Texas
- ❏ ❏ 1 - A Cold Mind (1983)
- ❏ ❏ 2 - Heat From Another Sun (1984)
- ❏ ❏ 3 - Spiral (1986)
- ❏ ❏ 4 - **In the Lake of the Moon (1988) Edgar nominee** ☆
- ❏ ❏ 5 - **Body of Truth (1992) Edgar nominee** ☆

■ **LIPINSKI, Thomas**

Pittsburgh native Thomas Lipinski is the creator of private eye Carroll Dorsey, former basketball star and law-school dropout, whose first appearance was a runner-up in the St. Martin's Press/Private Eye Writers Association Best First Novel contest as well as a Shamus nominee for Best First Private Eye Novel. *Drood Review* called the series opener "Stone solid...he does everything right." After the notoriety of his first big case, the P.I.'s business is failing and his romance with Dr. Gretchen Keller is more off than on at the start of book two. Adding to his troubles, Dorsey must confront his politically powerful father and some skeletons in his own family closet in book three. A lifelong Pittsburgh resident, Lipinski has worked as a prison administrator, social worker, insurance claims investigator and college instructor. He earned an MFA in creative writing from the University of Pittsburgh.

Carroll Dorsey...ex-basketball star law-school dropout P.I. in Pittsburgh, Pennsylvania
- ❏ ❏ 1 - **The Fall-Down Artist (1994) Shamus nominee** ☆
- ❏ ❏ 2 - A Picture of Her Tombstone (1996)
- ❏ ❏ 3 - The Dust on God's Breath (1998)

■ **LIVINGSTON, Jack [P]**

Twice-nominated for a Shamus award, Jack Livingston is the creator of Joseph Francis Binney, the genre's first deaf private eye, introduced in *A Piece of the Silence* (1982). After losing his hearing in an underwater demolition accident in the Navy, Binney talks and lipreads so skillfully he rarely fumbles his communications. He also drinks like a fish, smokes like a chimney and is an easy mark for a pretty woman. The distinctive quarter-sized scar, just below his right eye, is from a rat bite he got while trapped in a warehouse elevator shaft. In addition to its Shamus nomination, *Die Again, Macready* (1984) was also nominated for best novel by the British Crime Writers' Association. According to *Hawk's Authors' Pseudonyms*, Livingston is the pen name of James L. Nusser, former merchant seaman and medical editor from upstate New York.

Joe Binney...hearing-impaired private eye in New York, New York
- ❏ ❏ 1 - **A Piece of the Silence (1982) Shamus nominee** ☆
- ❏ ❏ 2 - **Die Again, Macready (1984) Shamus & Dagger nominee** ☆☆
- ❏ ❏ 3 - The Nightmare File (1986)
- ❏ ❏ 4 - Hell-Bent for Election (1988) APA-Hell-Bent for Homicide

■ LOCHTE, Dick

Dick Lochte is the creator of an unlikely detective duo—a wise-cracking teenage girl and a grumpy P.I. One reviewer called them "Hepburn at 14 and Bogart at his middle-aged best." The series opener, written in alternating his-and-her points of view, earned Lochte best-first-novel Edgar, Anthony and Shamus nominations and the 1986 Nero Wolfe Award. A native of New Orleans with an English degree from Tulane, Lochte also writes a Shamus-nominated series set in his hometown. For more than 25 years he has lived and worked in Los Angeles where he reviews books, audio, film and theatre for newspapers and national magazines. In collaboration with former LA prosecutor Christopher Darden, he is writing a new series featuring a young black woman prosecutor who will debut in *The Trials of Nikki Hill* (1998). Although fictional, this prosecutor will still be dealing with legal fallout from the OJ Simpson trial.

Serendipity Dahlquist & Leo Bloodworth...gum-snapping 15-yr-old girl & grumpy 50-something P.I. in L.A.
- ❏ ❏ 1 - **Sleeping Dog (1985) Nero Wolfe winner ★ Anthony, Edgar & Shamus nominee** ☆☆☆
- ❏ ❏ 2 - Laughing Dog (1988)

Terry Manion...private eye in New Orleans, Louisiana
- ❏ ❏ 1 - Blue Bayou (1992)
- ❏ ❏ 2 - **Neon Smile (1995) Shamus nominee** ☆

■ LOGUE, John

When John Logue was writing about sports for *The Atlanta Journal*, he sat across from Ed Miles, some say the greatest golf writer in America. Logue proudly admits he patterned his Edgar-nominated series character after Ed Miles, at least in his devotion to golf. In book 5, sportswriter John Morris and his love interest Julia Sullivan are off to St. Andrews for the British Open. When an American golfer is found strangled, an antique ball (a Feathery) has been stuffed in his throat. Up next is *A Rain of Death* (1998), set at the 1974 Bing Crosby Pro-Am tournament. In addition to his time with *The Atlanta Journal*, Logue spent 25 years writing for *Southern Living* magazine, often about golf, which he finds irresistible as a metaphor for murder. He says he loves the wonderful contradiction of golf—played over an immaculate surface, yet contested with all the deadliness of nature itself.

John Morris...Associated Press sportswriter in Atlanta, Georgia
- ❏ ❏ 1 - **Follow the Leader [golf] (1979) Edgar nominee** ☆
- ❏ ❏ 2 - Replay: Murder [football] (1983)
- ❏ ❏ 3 - Flawless Execution [football] (1986)
- ❏ ❏ 4 - Murder on the Links [golf] (1996)
- ❏ ❏ 5 - The Feathery Touch of Death [golf] (1997)

■ LOVESEY, Peter

Peter Lovesey created his first series character for a Macmillan Publishing contest. When *Wobble to Death* (1970) won first place, his mystery writing career and the Cribb and Thackeray series were launched, later earning him a Silver Dagger and two book awards in France. Although there are no more books planned, six stories written with his wife appeared as TV originals. Lovesey's Bath detective Peter Diamond is even more highly-decorated, having won 2 Silver Daggers, as well as Anthony and Macavity awards. His Gold Dagger winner was *The False Inspector Dew* (1982), set aboard an ocean liner bound for New York in 1921. Written under the name Peter Lear is *Goldengirl* (1977), the story of a woman bred to win 3 Gold medals at the 1980 Moscow Olympics. Susan Anton and James Coburn starred in the 1979 movie. Past Chairman of the Crime Writers' Association, Lovesey lives in Stratford-upon-Avon.

Albert Edward, Prince of Wales...19th century heir to the British throne in London, England
- ❏ ❏ 1 - Bertie and the Tinman (1987)
- ❏ ❏ 2 - Bertie and the Seven Bodies [1890] (1990)
- ❏ ❏ 3 - Bertie and the Crime of Passion (1993)

Peter Diamond...ex-cop in Bath, England
- ❏ ❏ 1 - **The Last Detective (1991) Anthony winner ★**
- ❏ ❏ 2 - Diamond Solitaire (1992)
- ❏ ❏ 3 - **The Summons (1995) Silver Dagger winner ★ Edgar nominee ☆**
- ❏ ❏ 4 - **Bloodhounds (1996) Silver Dagger & Macavity winner ★★**
- ❏ ❏ 5 - Upon a Dark Night (1997)

Richard Cribb, Sgt. & Edward Thackeray, Constable...Victorian policemen in London, England
- ❏ ❏ 1 - Wobble to Death (1970)
- ❏ ❏ 2 - The Detective Wore Silk Drawers (1971)
- ❏ ❏ 3 - Abracadaver (1972)
- ❏ ❏ 4 - **Mad Hatter's Holiday (1973) Dagger nominee ☆**
- ❏ ❏ 5 - Invitation to a Dynamite Party (1974)
  U.S.-The Tick of Death
- ❏ ❏ 6 - A Case of Spirits (1975)
- ❏ ❏ 7 - Swing, Swing Together (1976)
- ❏ ❏ 8 - **Waxwork (1978) Silver Dagger winner ★**

■ LUBER, Philip

Forensic psychologist Philip Luber has spent more than 15 years evaluating and treating violent mentally ill patients and criminal offenders. He has also written a series featuring widowed psychiatrist Harry Kline and Special Agent Veronica Pace, introduced in *Forgive Us Our Sins* (1994). Luber describes Harry as smarter, richer, better-looking and with more hair than his creator. Both men have young daughters, but Luber's has not been kidnapped, nor has he been attacked, almost murdered, or found it necessary to kill. Just about everything else he's seen firsthand. Harry and Veronica return in book 3, *Pray for Us Sinners* (1998) and are expected back in 1999. Born in Philadelphia, Luber has degrees from Tufts, Temple and the University of Texas. An accomplished pianist and singer-songwriter, he lives near Boston with his wife and daughter.

Harry Kline & Veronica Pace...psychiatrist & FBI special agent in Concord, Massachusetts
- ❏ ❏ 1 - Forgive Us Our Sins (1994)
- ❏ ❏ 2 - Deliver Us From Evil (1997)

■ LUPICA, Mike

Sports columnist Mike Lupica writes a column for *Newsday* which is syndicated by the *Los Angeles Times*. In addition to his *Sporting Life* column for *Esquire* magazine, he is also a regular on ESPN's Sunday morning program *The Sports Reporters* and serves as sports essayist for the *MacNeil-Lehrer NewsHour*. Lupica's first Peter Finley mystery *Extra Credit* (1988) earned him an Edgar nomination for best first novel. And New York's hippest investigative reporter has since made several return appearances with his Channel A cohorts, ace cameraman and wisecracking sidekick Marty Pearl and the lovely Natalie, Finley's brave and helpful assistant. Their third outing, *Limited Partners* (1990), became the CBS movie *Money, Power and Murder*, for which Lupica wrote the teleplay. He divides his time between Connecticut and Florida.

DiMaggio...private eye in the sports world in New York, New York
- ❏ ❏ 1 - Jump (1996)

Peter Finley...investigative TV reporter in New York, New York
- ❏ ❏ 1 - **Dead Air (1986) Edgar nominee ☆**
- ❏ ❏ 2 - Extra Credits (1988)
- ❏ ❏ 3 - Limited Partner (1990)

■ LUPOFF, Richard A.

Richard A. Lupoff received his very first rejection letter from none other than Anthony Boucher, for stories submitted to *The Magazine of Fantasy and Science Fiction* when Lupoff was 16. Since then he has written science fiction, fantasy, horror, mystery and adventure novels and worked in radio, television and film, earning nominations for both Hugo and Nebula awards. His short story *12:01 PM* has been filmed 3 times—as an Oscar-nominated short feature, a Fox-TV movie of the week, and (in a plagiarized version) a box-office hit. He describes his Hobart Lindsay-Marvia Plum series as a single mega-novel of 8 volumes in length, with each volume a long chapter in a complete murder mystery. A career retrospective of his short stories, *Before...12:01...After* (1996), includes the classic title story, a Marvia Plum mystery and more than 20 other mystery, science fiction, fantasy and horror stories.

Hobart Lindsay & Marvia Plum...insurance claims adjuster & Berkeley detective in California
- ❑ ❑ 1 - The Comic Book Killer (1988)
- ❑ ❑ 2 - The Classic Car Killer (1992)
- ❑ ❑ 3 - The Bessie Blue Killer (1994)
- ❑ ❑ 4 - The Sepia Siren Killer (1994)
- ❑ ❑ 5 - The Cover Girl Killer (1995)
- ❑ ❑ 6 - The Silver Chariot Killer (1996)
- ❑ ❑ 7 - The Radio Red Killer (1997)
- ❑ ❑ 8 - The Tinpan Tiger Killer (1998)

■ LUSBY, Jim

Jim Lusby is the creator of a new police series set in Ireland, featuring Detective Inspector Carl McCadden of the Waterford Garda and his sergeant Liam de Burgh, introduced in *Making the Cut* (1995). McCadden has been pulled off a murder case by his superior officer in the series opener, but just can't let it go. He returns in *Flashback* (1996), a prequel to the series action. These books have not been published in the U.S., but book 1 is available as a paperback reprint in Ireland.

Carl McCadden, D.I.....unconventional Irish police inspector in Waterford, Ireland
- ❑ ❑ 1 - Making the Cut (1995)
- ❑ ❑ 2 - Flashback [prequel] (1996)

■ LUTZ, John

Two-time Shamus winner John Lutz published his first short story in 1966 and since then has produced more than 30 novels and 200 short stories, becoming "one of the most reliable pros of American P.I. writing," according to *The Washington Post*. It has been suggested he created his unconventional St. Louis private eye as a fictional backlash to super macho P.I.s like Mike Hammer. If Spillane's tough guy hammers every case, Alo Nudger can be expected to nudge his to conclusion, but not before everything goes wrong for him. Ex-Orlando cop Fred Carver, involuntarity retired from the force after being kneecapped by a street punk, is Lutz's more conventional private eye. Past president of both MWA and PWA, he was awarded Lifetime Achievement honors from PWA in 1995. His *SWFSeeks Same* (1990) was the basis for the 1992 movie *Single White Female* starring Bridget Fonda. He lives in Webster Groves (MO) where he once worked as a switchboard operator for the St. Louis Metropolitan Police Department.

Alo Nudger...antacid-chewing bad-luck P.I. in St. Louis, Missouri
- ❑ ❑ 1 - Buyer Beware (1976)
- ❑ ❑ 2 - **Nightlines (1985) Shamus nominee** ☆
- ❑ ❑ 3 - The Right to Sing the Blues (1986)
- ❑ ❑ 4 - **Ride the Lightning (1987) Shamus nominee** ☆
- ❑ ❑ 5 - Dancer's Debt (1988)
- ❑ ❑ 6 - Time Exposure (1989)
- ❑ ❑ 7 - Diamond Eyes (1990)

❏ ❏ 8 - Thicker Than Blood (1993)
❏ ❏ 9 - Death By Jury (1995)
❏ ❏ 10 - Oops! (1997)

E. L. Oxman & Art Tobin...pair of investigators in the United States
❏ ❏ 1 - The Eye [with Bill Pronzini] (1984)
❏ ❏ 2 - Shadowtown (1988)

Fred Carver...crippled ex-cop P.I. in Del Moray, Florida
❏ ❏ 1 - Tropical Heat (1986)
❏ ❏ 2 - Scorcher (1987)
❏ ❏ **3 - Kiss (1988) Shamus winner ★**
❏ ❏ 4 - Flame (1990)
❏ ❏ 5 - Bloodfire (1991)
❏ ❏ 6 - Hot (1992)
❏ ❏ 7 - Spark (1993)
❏ ❏ 8 - Torch (1994)
❏ ❏ 9 - Burn (1995)
❏ ❏ 10 - Lightning (1996)

■ LYNCH, JACK

Twice nominated for a Shamus award, Jack Lynch's Peter Bragg series has also been nominated for an Edgar for best paperback original. Starting with *Bragg's Hunch* (1982), these books feature a Korean War veteran and former newspaper reporter (in Seattle, Kansas City and San Francisco), who sometimes tends bar in Sausalito where he lives. After doing some part-time work for a lawyer buddy, Bragg finds himself a fifth-floor office on Market and hangs out his shingle. A Seattle native with a B.A. in journalism from the University of Washington, Lynch has worked for *TV Guide* magazine and newpapers in Seattle and San Francisco. A former Sausalito bartender, he also clerked for a year at a San Francisco brokerage house. According to *Private Eyes: 101 Knights* (1985), he's a shirttail relative of General George Armstrong Custer.

Peter Bragg...private eye in San Francisco, California
❏ ❏ 1 - Bragg's Hunch (1982)
❏ ❏ **2 - The Missing and the Dead (1982) Edgar nominee** ☆
❏ ❏ **3 - Pieces of Death (1982) Shamus nominee** ☆
❏ ❏ 4 - Sausalito (1984)
❏ ❏ **5 - San Quentin (1984) Shamus nominee** ☆
❏ ❏ 6 - Seattle (1985)
❏ ❏ 7 - Monterey (1985)

■ LYONS, Arthur

Shamus nominee Arthur Lyons has written 10 books featuring private eye Jacob Asch, whose first two cases use material from Lyons' nonfiction book *The Second Coming: Satanism in America* (1970), later reprinted as *Satan Wants You: The Cult of Devil Worship in America* (1989). Owing to his research experience, Lyons has consulted with several law enforcement agencies on murder cases where occult involvement was suspected. With former Los Angeles medical examiner Thomas Noguchi, he has collaborated on both fiction and nonfiction and with Marcell Truzzi he has written *The Blue Sense: Psychic Detectives and Crime* (1991). A Los Angeles native with a B.A. in political science from the University of California at Santa Barbara, Lyons lives in Palm Springs where he owns Lyons' English Grille.

Jacob Asch...Jewish-Episcopal ex-reporter P.I. in Los Angeles, California
❏ ❏ 1 - The Dead Are Discreet (1974)
❏ ❏ 2 - All God's Children (1975)
❏ ❏ 3 - The Killing Floor (1976)

    ❏ ❏ 4 - Dead Ringer (1977)
    ❏ ❏ 5 - Castles Burning (1980)
    ❏ ❏ 6 - **Hard Trade (1982) Shamus nominee** ☆
    ❏ ❏ 7 - At the Hands of Another (1983)
    ❏ ❏ 8 - Three With a Bullet (1985)
    ❏ ❏ 9 - Fast Fade (1987)
    ❏ ❏ 10 - Other People's Money (1989)
    ❏ ❏ 11 - False Pretenses (1993)

■ MACKENZIE, Donald

Canadian Donald MacKenzie (1918-1993) was a jewel thief and confidence man who launched a literary career from prison. A thief from the age of 12, he was able to write realistic fictional accounts of jewel thefts, con games, forgeries and safecracking. Among his more than 40 books are the autobiographical *Occupation: Thief* (1955) and *Gentleman at Crime* (1956). His series detective, tough Scotland Yard inspector John Raven, is first seen in Zaleski's *Percentage* (1974) and gets his own series starting with *Raven in Flight* (1976). After leaving the Yard, the somewhat bohemian Raven turns freelance and works from his Thames houseboat. Born in Toronto where his father was a writer, MacKenzie attended prep schools in England, Canada and Switzerland before gaining proficiency in languages at Upper Canada College. At the age of 20 he returned to Europe and began his 10-year run as a playboy and jewel thief.

John Raven...unorthodox detective inspector in London, England
    ❏ ❏ 1 - Raven in Flight (1976)
    ❏ ❏ 2 - Raven and the Ratcatcher (1977)
    ❏ ❏ 3 - Raven and the Kamikaze (1977)
    ❏ ❏ 4 - Raven Settles a Score (1978)
    ❏ ❏ 5 - Raven Feathers His Nest (1979) Brit.-Raven After Dark
    ❏ ❏ 6 - Raven and the Paperhangers (1980)
    ❏ ❏ 7 - Raven's Revenge (1980)
    ❏ ❏ 8 - Raven's Longest Night (1983)
    ❏ ❏ 9 - Raven's Shadow (1984)

■ MACLEOD, Robert [P]

Under the name Robert MacLeod, Scottish author Bill Knox published three mystery series dating from the mid '60s. United Nations troubleshooter Talos Cord appeared 6 times and starting in 1970 there were 10 titles featuring Jonathan Gaunt, an external auditor with the Queen's and Lord Treasurer's Remembrancer. The Gaunt titles were published under the name Noah Webster in the U.S. To further complicate the Knox bibliography, his series with marine insurance claims investigator Andrew Laird appeared in the U.S. under the name Michael Kirk, except for the last volume which came out under the Webster pen name. Among his more than 70 titles, Knox is best known for two long-running series under his own name. his more than 40 years in print and broadcast journalism includes 10 as host of a weekly TV program called Crime Desk.

Andrew Laird...international marine insurance claim investigator
    ❏ ❏ 1 - All Other Perils (1974)
    ❏ ❏ 2 - Dragonship (1976)
    ❏ ❏ 3 - Salvage Job (1978)
    ❏ ❏ 4 - Cargo Risk (1980)
    ❏ ❏ 5 - Mayday from Malaga (1983)
    ❏ ❏ 6 - Witchline (1988)

Jonathan Gaunt...external auditor for the Queen in Edinburgh, Scotland
- ❑ ❑ 1 - A Property in Cyprus (1970) U.S.-A Flickering Death
- ❑ ❑ 2 - A Killing in Malta (1972)
- ❑ ❑ 3 - A Burial in Portugal (1973)
- ❑ ❑ 4 - A Witchdance in Bavaria (1975)
- ❑ ❑ 5 - A Pay-Off in Switzerland (1977)
- ❑ ❑ 6 - An Incident in Iceland (1979)
- ❑ ❑ 7 - A Problem in Prague (1981)
- ❑ ❑ 8 - A Legacy from Tenarife (1984)
- ❑ ❑ 9 - The Money Mountain (1987) U.S.-A Flight from Paris
- ❑ ❑ 10 - The Spanish Maze Game (1990)

Talos Cord...United Nations troubleshooter in New York, New York
- ❑ ❑ 1 - Cave of Bats (1964)
- ❑ ❑ 2 - Lake of Fury (1966) U.S.-The Iron Sanctuary
- ❑ ❑ 3 - Isle of Dragons (1967)
- ❑ ❑ 4 - Place of Mists (1969)
- ❑ ❑ 5 - Path of Ghosts (1971)
- ❑ ❑ 6 - Nest of Vultures (1973)

■ MAHONEY, Dan

Former NYPD captain and son of a police officer, Dan Mahoney published his first Brian McKenna novel in 1993. While *Detective First Grade* tells the story of a 5-day war between the detective and a group of terrorists, book 2 opens with him enjoying early retirement in Florida, until the funeral of a close friend sends him back to New York. In their review of *Edge of the City*, *People* magazine said "Memo to Bruce Willis: here's your next Die Hard." McKenna's 4th appearance, *Once In, Never Out* (1998), opens in Reyjavik, Iceland where a British diplomat and his wife are killed by bombs and McKenna arrives in search of an Irish-born waitress whose brother the priest is an aide to the Cardinal of the New York Archdiocese. As a private investigator, Mahoney has provided security services for Yoko Ono and other celebrities, including his brother, rock singer Eddie Money.

Brian McKenna...police detective in New York, New York
- ❑ ❑ 1 - Detective First Grade (1993)
- ❑ ❑ 2 - Edge of the City (1995)
- ❑ ❑ 3 - Hyde (1997)

■ MAITLAND, Barry

Barry Maitland's Creasey-nominated debut novel, *The Marx Sisters* (1994), tells the story of three elderly sisters living in Jerusalem Lane, a little piece of Dickensian London real estate where pre-War emigres from Central Europe are barely hanging on against the threats of redevelopment. Det. Sgt. Kathy Kolla and Det. Chief Insp. David Brock from Scotland Yard's Serious Crime Branch are called to investigate when the first sister turns up dead. Book 2 in this series, *The Malcontenta*, won the Ned Kelly award for best novel in Australia in 1995. Born in Scotland and brought up in London, Maitland studied architecture at the University of Cambridge. He practiced and taught in the U.K. before moving to Australia, where he is now professor of architecture at the University of Newcastle. He previously published a number of books on architecture.

Kathy Kolla, Det. Sgt. & David Brock, D.C.I.....young Scotland Yard detective & her mentor in London, England
- ❑ ❑ 1 - **The Marx Sisters (1994) Creasey nominee** ☆
- ❑ ❑ 2 - **The Malcontenta (1995) Ned Kelly winner** ★
- ❑ ❑ 3 - All My Enemies (1996)

■ MALCOLM, John [P]

John Malcolm is the pseudonym of John (Malcolm) Andrews, antiques expert and past chairman of the British Crime Writers' Association. As John Andrews he has published numerous guides to antiques and has used his background in fine arts and international business to create a mystery series where each book highlights a different 19th or 20th century artist. These are novels of fraud or other art crime where events or artefacts from the past affect the present. In each case, the basis of the art history is factually correct. Financial consultant turned art investment specialist, Tim Simpson, has been described as "clean, classy and tough" (*The New Yorker*) and "urbane as Peter Wimsey,...but more virile" (*Publishers Weekly*). Born in Manchester, the author lives in Sussex where he and his wife are founders of the British Antique Collectors Club.

Tim Simpson...financial consultant turned art investment specialist in London, England
- ❏ ❏ 1 - A Back Room in Somers Town (1984)
- ❏ ❏ 2 - The Godwin Sideboard (1984)
- ❏ ❏ 3 - The Gwen John Sculpture (1985)
- ❏ ❏ 4 - Whistler in the Dark (1986)
- ❏ ❏ 5 - Gothic Pursuit (1987)
- ❏ ❏ 6 - Mortal Ruin (1988)
- ❏ ❏ 7 - The Wrong Impression (1990)
- ❏ ❏ 8 - Sheep, Goats and Soap (1991)
- ❏ ❏ 9 - A Deceptive Appearance (1992)
- ❏ ❏ 10 - The Burning Ground (1993)
- ❏ ❏ 11 - Hung Over (1994)
- ❏ ❏ 12 - Into the Vortex (1996)

■ MALLETT, Lyndon

Lyndon Mallett is the creator of a fast-with-his-fists debt collector named Taffin, who works in the small Irish coastal town of Lasherham. In the series opener, Taffin is teaching a young fellow named Albert the collection business. While collecting debts at the standard rate of 20% Taffin retrieves a child for its distraught mother and teaches the wayward father a lesson about responsibility. When crooked business interests behind a proposed chemical plant hire toughs to rough up local protestors, a former teacher of Taffin's hires him to provide protection for the protesters. An affair with a local barmaid and conflict with his teacher-mentor round out the action for Taffin, who was played by Pierce Brosnan in the 1987 Irish film of the same name. Two more books complete the series.

Taffin...fast-with-his-fists debt collector in Lasherham, Ireland
- ❏ ❏ 1 - Taffin (1980)
- ❏ ❏ 2 - Taffin's First Law (1980)
- ❏ ❏ 3 - Ask Taffin Nicely (1989)

■ MALONE, Paul [P]

Paul Malone is a pseudonym used by Michael Newton for 3 novels featuring DEA agent Jack Fowler, introduced in *Trigger Pull* (1991). Under his own name are 2 books with an LAPD homicide detective and 9 with a pair of FBI agents assigned to the Violent Criminal Apprehension Program (VICAP). He has also written 70 books in the Executioner series, featuring ex-Green Beret Mack Bolan whose family is killed by gangsters. Other of Newton's pseudonyms are Mark Kozlow, John Cannon and Vince Robinson. In total he has written more than 140 books during the past 20 years, primarily action-adventure and true crime. His newest titles are *Waste Land* (1998), a Charles Starkweather biography from Pocket Books and *Killer Cops* (1998) from Loompanics. A native of Bakersfield (CA), he lives in Nashville (IN).

Jack Fowler...DEA agent in the United States
- ❏ ❏ 1 - Trigger Pull (1991)
- ❏ ❏ 2 - Pipeline (1991)
- ❏ ❏ 3 - Shakedown (1992)

■ **MANESS, Larry**

Playwright Larry Maness is the creator of a new series featuring private eye Jake Eaton and his superdog Watson, introduced in *Nantucket Revenge* (1995). A millionaire's daughter is being threatened by a kook who closes down the Nantucket airport, runs the local ferry aground, harpoons a bank president and spreaguns a dock manager. Jake is hired to investigate. In book 2, *A Once Perfect Place* (1996), involves another rich client, this time a Boston widow has given the state of New Hampshire 20,000 acres of pristine forest as a memorial to her late husband, a Nobel laureate and environmentalist. Why is a New Hampshire sheriff dead and the aerial surveyor missing? Book 3, *Strangler* (1998) opens with a murder that bears an eerie resemblance to the work of the Boston Strangler of 30 years ago.

Jake Eaton & Watson...P.I. & his superdog in Cambridge, Massachusetts
- ❏ ❏ 1 - Nantucket Revenge (1995)
- ❏ ❏ 2 - A Once Perfect Place (1996)

■ **MANN, Paul**

Paul Mann is the creator of blue-eyed Anglo-Indian attorney, George Sansi of Bombay, India, who, when last seen, was hired by a minister of the environment in *The Burning Ghats* (1996) to investigate a chemical spill into the Ganges. His previous case had taken him to the Ganja coast, a decadent beach community of Western dropouts, drugs and money. Mann once told *Contemporary Authors* that he grew up in England with a working class Tory/police officer father and a manic-depressive alcoholic mother who worked as a nurse in a lunatic asylum. His acute sense of the absurd he said was "inevitable." For 25 years he traveled the world writing for leading newspapers and magazines in London, New York, Montreal and Sydney. He now lives in Maine. His thriller titles include *The Libyan Contract* (1988), *The Beirut Contract* (1989), *The Traitor's Contract* (1990) and *The Britannia Contract* (1993)

George Sansi...Anglo-Indian attorney in Goa, India
- ❏ ❏ 1 - Season of the Monsoon (1993)
- ❏ ❏ 2 - The Ganja Coast (1995)
- ❏ ❏ 3 - The Burning Ghats (1996)

■ **MARGOLIS, Seth**

Seth Margolis is the creator of Joe DiGregorio, an ex-Long Island cop turned Manhattan P.I., introduced in *False Faces* (1991). When Joe returns in *Vanishing Act* (1993), he is asked by a mysterious tycoon to help fake his death. Although Joe could use the work, he declines to take the case and several days later the businessman turns up dead for real. Margolis has also written *Perfect Angel* (1997), a serial killer novel that starts with hypnosis at a 35th birthday party, and *Losing Isaiah* (1993), the story of a custody battle between two mothers over a 3-year old crack baby. Academy award winner Jessica Lange and Halle Berry played the mothers in the 1993 film. After earning an M.B.A. from New York University, Margolis wrote his first book (*False Faces*) in longhand while working for a Big 8 accounting firm. He now writes full-time.

Joe DiGregorio...ex-Long Island cop turned Manhattan P.I. in New York, New York
- ❏ ❏ 1 - False Faces (1991)
- ❏ ❏ 2 - Vanishing Act (1993)

■ MARLOWE, Stephen

Ex-FBI agent Chester Drum often ends up a long way from his F Street office in Washington DC, but his best friend works for the State Dept. and can usually get him home safely. Drum's adventures are always part travelogue as he moves with ease around the world. His creator had been successfully writing science fiction under his own name of Milton Lesser until the mid-'50s, when he switched to crime novels. After choosing the Marlowe pseudonym for mysteries, Lesser changed his name legally to Stephen Marlowe in 1958. Having written 60 books, including several as Jason Ridgway, Andrew Frazer and C. H. Thames, he is now writing action thrillers and alternative biographies such as *The Lighthouse at the End of the World: A Tale of Edgar Allan Poe* (1995). A graduate of the College of William and Mary, where he was previously writer-in-residence, he lives in New York City.

Chester Drum...ex-FBI agent turned P.I. in Washington, D.C.
- ❏ ❏ 1 - The Second Longest Night (1955)
- ❏ ❏ 2 - Murder is My Dish (1956)
- ❏ ❏ 3 - Mecca for Murder (1956)
- ❏ ❏ 4 - Trouble is My Name (1957)
- ❏ ❏ 5 - Killers are My Meat (1957)
- ❏ ❏ 6 - Violence is My Business (1958)
- ❏ ❏ 7 - Terror is My Trade (1958)
- ❏ ❏ 8 - Homicide is My Game (1959)
- ❏ ❏ 9 - Peril is My Pay (1960)
- ❏ ❏ 10 - Danger is My Line (1960)
- ❏ ❏ 11 - Death is My Comrade (1960)
- ❏ ❏ 12 - Manhunt is My Mission (1961)
- ❏ ❏ 13 - Jeopardy is My Job (1962)
- ❏ ❏ 14 - Francesca (1963)
- ❏ ❏ 15 - Drum Beat—Berlin (1964)
- ❏ ❏ 16 - Drum Beat—Dominique (1965)
- ❏ ❏ 17 - Drum Beat—Madrid (1966)
- ❏ ❏ 18 - Drum Beat—Erica (1967)
- ❏ ❏ 19 - Drum Beat—Marianne (1968)

■ MARQUIS, Max

Max Marquis (pronounced mar-KEE) has created a new police series featuring London D. I. Harry Timberlake, first seen in *The Twelfth Man* (1991) where the ax murder of an important barrister leads the inspector to a string of seemingly unrelated killings. In a starred review *Publishers Weekly* praised the book's "sardonic tone" and "riveting, edge-of-the seat climax." In book 2 Harry travels to the underworld of Marseilles in search of a killer. Having also written as Edward F. Barnes and Michael Meath, Marquis has co-written a screenplay (*Strongroom*) written with Richard Harris. His nonseries fiction includes *Deadly Doctors* (1992) and *Vengeance* (1990). Previously he has worked as a soccer referee and commentator in French for Swiss television, newspaper columnist, sports editor and writer for television. Based in London, he summers in France.

Harry Timberlake, Det. Insp.....aloof detective inspector in London, England
- ❏ ❏ 1 - The Twelfth Man (1991)
- ❏ ❏ 2 - Undignified Death (1993)
- ❏ ❏ 3 - Written In Blood (1995)

■ MARSHALL, William

Born in Sydney, Australia, William Marshall has lived all over the world, including the U.S., Europe and the Far East. He has worked as a playwright, journalist, proofreader, morgue attendant and teacher in an Irish prison. But he is best known for his hapless Hong Kong cops of Yellowthread Street Station, whose

15th appearance (*Nightmare Syndrome*) coincided with the reversion of Hong Kong to Chinese rule July 1, 1997. Although the series was adapted for 13 episodes on British television in 1990, Marshall says they didn't use the characters, the plots or the book titles. His other police novels feature Lt. Felix Elizalde, detective of the Western District Bureau in the Philippines and Tillman and Muldoon, a turn-of-the-century cop pair in New York City. Marshall has also written a number of noncrime novels and several works of nonfiction.

Felix Elizalde, Lt.....detective of the Western District Bureau in the Philippines
- ❏ ❏ 1 - Manila Bay (1986)
- ❏ ❏ 2 - Whisper (1988)

Harry Feiffer, Chief Insp.....chief inspector of Yellowthread Street station in Hong Kong, China
- ❏ ❏ 1 - Yellowthread Street (1975)
- ❏ ❏ 2 - The Hatchet Man (1976)
- ❏ ❏ 3 - Gelignite (1976)
- ❏ ❏ 4 - Thin Air (1977)
- ❏ ❏ 5 - Skulduggery (1979)
- ❏ ❏ 6 - Sci Fi (1981)
- ❏ ❏ 7 - Perfect End (1981)
- ❏ ❏ 8 - War Machine (1982)
- ❏ ❏ 9 - The Far Away Man (1984)
- ❏ ❏ 10 - Road Show (1985)
- ❏ ❏ 11 - Head First (1986)
- ❏ ❏ 12 - Frogmouth (1987)
- ❏ ❏ 13 - Out of Nowhere (1988)
- ❏ ❏ 14 - Inches (1994)

Tillman & Muldoon...turn-of-the-century policemen in New York, New York
- ❏ ❏ 1 - Out of Nowhere (1988)
- ❏ ❏ 2 - Faces in the Crowd (1991)

■ MARSTON, Edward [P]

Edward Marston is a pseudonym of Keith Miles who started writing golf mysteries under his own name in the late '80s. Author of more than 40 books, as well as a playwright with a lifelong interest in theater, he writes an Edgar-nominated series featuring a stage manager for an Elizabethan theater troupe. While Nicholas Bracewell handles backstage politics and actors' egos with equal skill and daring, "the tragedies being performed onstage pale in comparison to all the blood and thunder offstage," according to *The Washington Post Book World*. In another historical series, Marston directs an 11th century soldier and lawyer who investigate land claims for William the Conqueror's Domesday Book. His newest series, written as Keith Miles, features a 1920s Welsh architect who comes to the U.S. to work with Frank Lloyd Wright. Miles lives in rural Kent, England.

Nicholas Bracewell...stage manager for Elizabethan acting company in London, England
- ❏ ❏ 1 - The Queen's Head (1988)
- ❏ ❏ 2 - The Merry Devils (1989)
- ❏ ❏ 3 - The Trip to Jerusalem (1990)
- ❏ ❏ 4 - The Nine Giants (1991)
- ❏ ❏ 5 - The Mad Courtesan (1992)
- ❏ ❏ 6 - The Silent Woman (1992)
- ❏ ❏ **7 - The Roaring Boy (1995) Edgar nominee** ☆
- ❏ ❏ 8 - The Laughing Hangman (1996)
- ❏ ❏ 9 - The Fair Maid of Bohemia (1997)

Ralph Delchard & Gervase Bret...11th century soldier & lawyer in England
- ❏ ❏ 1 - The Wolves of Savernake (1993)
- ❏ ❏ 2 - The Ravens of Blackwater (1994)
- ❏ ❏ 3 - The Dragons of Archenfield (1995)
- ❏ ❏ 4 - The Lions of the North (1996)
- ❏ ❏ 5 - The Serpents of Harbledown (1996)

■ MARTIN, James E.

James E. Martin is the creator of a private eye from Cleveland (OH) cast completely against type. Gil Disbro is a young, conservative, divorced non-drinker living with an older woman (a college professor, no less). "He's one of the most straight-ahead, ungimmicky private eyes around," said a *Booklist* reviewer. Owing to affirmative action quotas and departmental cutbacks, Disbro's plans to become a cop have been permanently sidelined. With a degree in English and history from Ohio State University, Martin taught junior and senior high school for five years before joining the Norwalk (OH) police force where he rose to the rank of captain. For several years after his police retirement he worked as a special investigator for the State of Ohio and continued writing feature stories for the *Lorain Journal*. After being sidelined by major heart surgery he turned to writing mysteries.

Gil Disbro...teetotaler private eye in Cleveland, Ohio
- ❏ ❏ 1 - The Mercy Trap (1989)
- ❏ ❏ 2 - The Flip Side of Life (1990)
- ❏ ❏ 3 - And Then You Die (1992)
- ❏ ❏ 4 - A Fine and Private Place (1994)

■ MARTINI, Steve

Steve(n Paul) Martini is widely-known for his courtroom scenes featuring criminal defense attorney Paul Madriani, supported by a long-suffering wife and young daughter, along with good friend and sometimes co-counsel Harry Hinds, who wears bow ties with his pinstripes. Martini's recent thriller, *The List* (1997), is a pseudonym caper about a best-selling novelist who had been an attorney going nowhere at her Seattle law firm. *Kirkus* called it "absolutely irresistible balderdash." A former private practice lawyer and state attorney for various California agencies, Martini was born in San Francisco. During law school he worked as a journalist and State House correspondent for the *Los Angeles Daily Journal*. He once served as special counsel for California Victims of Violent Crimes Program. A full-time writer since 1991, he lives in Seattle (WA). His 1998 book, *Critical Mass*, is another standalone thriller.

Paul Madriani...defense attorney in California
- ❏ ❏ 1 - Compelling Evidence (1992)
- ❏ ❏ 2 - Prime Witness (1993)
- ❏ ❏ 3 - Undue Influence (1994)
- ❏ ❏ 4 - The Judge (1995)

■ MASTERS, J. D.

J. D. Masters has written six paperback original mysteries featuring Lt. Donovan Steele of the New York City police department. Beginning with *Steele* (1989), each of the ensuing titles includes the rugged NYPD lieutenant's name—*Cold Steele* (1989), *Jagged Steele* (1990), *Killer Steele* (1990), *Renegade Steele* (1990) and *Target Steele* (1990). All six were published by Charter.

Donovan Steele, Ltd.....police lieutenant in New York
- ❑ ❑ 1 - Steele (1989)
- ❑ ❑ 2 - Cold Steele (1989)
- ❑ ❑ 3 - Jagged Steele (1990)
- ❑ ❑ 4 - Killer Steele (1990)
- ❑ ❑ 5 - Renegade Steele (1990)
- ❑ ❑ 6 - Target Steele (1990)

■ MASUR, Harold Q.

Former New York attorney Harold Q. Masur started writing for pulp magazines in the '40s and produced the first of 11 Scott Jordan mysteries in 1947. An attorney like his creator, Jordan narrates his cases in first person, functioning more like a private detective than a courtroom lawyer. Although he is described as relaxed and non-cynical, Jordan is capable of fast action and quick thinking, according to Art Scott (*St. James Guide*). In between books 10 and 11 of the Jordan series, Masur produced two nonseries novels. *The Attorney* (1973) is an elaborate account of a sensational sex murder trial, while *The Broker* (1981) deals with financial plots behind a proxy fight for control of a film studio. Past president of Mystery Writers of America, Masur also served as the organization's general counsel. He was honored with The Raven Award in 1992 for his years of service to MWA.

Scott Jordan...criminal defense attorney in New York, New York
- ❑ ❑ 1 - Bury Me Deep (1947)
- ❑ ❑ 2 - Suddenly a Corpse (1949)
- ❑ ❑ 3 - You Can't Live Forever (1951)
- ❑ ❑ 4 - So Rich, So Lovely, and So Dead (1952)
- ❑ ❑ 5 - The Big Money (1954)
- ❑ ❑ 6 - Tall, Dark, and Deadly (1956)
- ❑ ❑ 7 - The Last Gamble (1958)
    - Brit.-The Last Breath
    - APA-Murder on Broadway
- ❑ ❑ 8 - Send Another Hearse (1960)
- ❑ ❑ ss - The Name is Jordan [short stories] (1962)
- ❑ ❑ 9 - Make a Killing (1964)
- ❑ ❑ 10 - The Legacy Lenders (1967)
- ❑ ❑ 11 - The Mourning After (1981)

■ MATTHEWS, Lew [P]

Lew Matthews is the pseudonym used by Matthew Z. Lewin for a new mystery series featuring Horatio T. Parker, introduced in *Unseen Witness* (1992). Crime reporter for a Hampstead weekly newspaper, Parker is assigned the story of a lifetime—the murder of a female film star. And quite unexpectedly, he inherits 52 million pounds. What happens next is one great story, according to George Easter in his rave review (4 out of 5 stars) in *Deadly Pleasures* #14. Unfortunately, the book was a HarperCollins paperback printed only in England. Most of Lewin's crime fiction is set in his hometown of Indianapolis (IN), although he has not lived there since 1971. After majoring in physics and chemistry at Harvard, where he graduated cum laude, Lewin spent a year reading chemistry at Cambridge University. He has lived in England since 1971. In 1994 he introduced a series with a 3-generational detecting family from Bath.

Horatio T. Parker...crime reporter for a weekly newspaper in Hampstead, England
- ❑ ❑ 1 - Unseen Witness (1992)
- ❑ ❑ 2 - A Conviction of Guilt (1993)
- ❑ ❑ 3 - A Picture of Innocence (1996)

■ MAXIM, John

In the late '70s, marketing executive John R. Maxim took a sabbatical from his international consulting career to see if he could write a novel. The result was *Platforms* (1980) and he has since written 10 others, including four titles in the Bannerman series, featuring a Westport, Connecticut agency of investigators. Maxim says he'll be writing more Bannerman books after Avon re-releases the earlier titles. His newest series character is retired Israeli intelligence agent Elizabeth Stride, an American known professionally as the Black Angel, who retreats to Hilton Head Island in *Haven* (1997). The high-octane thriller action is scheduled to continue in *Mosaic* (1998). A former Procter & Gamble product manager, Maxim once served as consultant to several world cruise lines and handled North American marketing for the Orient Express. Having traveled to almost everywhere on the globe that isn't polar, he now lives on Hilton Head Island.

Paul Bannerman...private investigations firm owner in Westport, Connecticut
- ❏ ❏ 1 - The Bannerman Solution (1989)
- ❏ ❏ 2 - The Bannerman Effect (1990)
- ❏ ❏ 3 - Bannerman's Law (1991)
- ❏ ❏ 4 - A Matter of Honor (1993)

■ MAYO, J. K.

J. K. Mayo writes about the exploits of British Intelligence officer Col. Harry Seddall, introduced in *The Hunting Season* (1985), where a successful London playwright innocently witnesses a murder and quickly becomes a target of incompetent hitmen and shadowy government officials. "Tense, involving, emotional and romantic in the true sense," said Val McDermid in her review column for the *Manchester Evening News*. She called Mayo "le Carré with an attitude." Under old English law, 'Wolf's Head' was the cry for pursuit of an outlaw, as one to be hunted down like a wolf, yet in book 2 Harry finds himself developing sympathy for the hunted assassin. While *Cry Havoc* (1990) finds Harry pitted against assassins in the U.S., Mexico and France, the first explosion in book 5 kills a colleague in the office directly above him at Whitehall.

Harry Seddall, Col.....British Intelligence officer in England
- ❏ ❏ 1 - The Hunting Season (1985)
- ❏ ❏ 2 - Wolf's Head (1987)
- ❏ ❏ 3 - Cry Havoc (1990)
- ❏ ❏ 4 - A Shred of Honour (1995)
- ❏ ❏ 5 - The Masterless Men (1995)
- ❏ ❏ 6 - The Interloper (1996)

■ MAYOR, Archer

Archer Mayor is the creator of Brattleboro (VT) police officer Joe Gunther who first appears in *Open Season* (1988), when jurors who convicted a black Vietnam vet of rape and murder are systematically being attacked. As one reviewer pointed out, Gunther is no Andy of Mayberry. His most recent case (book 8) takes him to neighboring *Bellows Falls* (1997) where he is asked to conduct a minor Internal Affairs investigation. Spousal abuse and police corruption quickly turn murderous. Mayor's nonfiction work includes *Southern Timberman: The Legacy of William Buchanan* (1988). A graduate of Yale University, he has worked as a medical illustrator, theatre photographer, newspaper reporter and editor, researcher and political campaign staffer and emergency medical technician. Born in Mt. Kisco (NY), he lives in Vermont where he writes full-time.

Joe Gunther, Lt.....homicide detective in Brattleboro, Vermont
- ❏ ❏ 1 - Open Season (1988)
- ❏ ❏ 2 - Borderlines (1990)
- ❏ ❏ 3 - Scent of Evil (1992)
- ❏ ❏ 4 - The Skeleton's Knee (1993)
- ❏ ❏ 5 - Fruits of the Poisonous Tree (1994)
- ❏ ❏ 6 - The Dark Root (1995)
- ❏ ❏ 7 - The Ragman's Memory (1996)
- ❏ ❏ 8 - Bellows Falls (1997)

■ MCBAIN, Ed [P]

Ed McBain is a pseudonym of Evan Hunter. Born Salvatore Lambino, this Grand Master assembled his name from his high school (John Evan High School) and college (Hunter College). As Hunter and McBain, his more than 90 books have sold over 100 million copies worldwide, with his 87th Precinct novels the longest-running series in contemporary crime fiction. In early 1998 he will publish book 13 in the Matthew Hope series, *The Last Best Hope*. The reason for the McBain pseudonym was that mysteries were in such disfavor in the '50s, it was thought they would tarnish his reputation as a real writer. Yet as Evan Hunter he wrote the script for *The Birds*, giving rise to one of his favorite inside jokes—having fictional characters refer to the script as if it were written by Hitchcock himself. During his employ at Scott Meredith Literary Agency he once counseled P.G. Wodehouse on how to trim his books.

87th Precinct...thinly-disguised NYPD cops in Isola, New York

- ❑ ❑ 1 - Cop Hater (1956)
- ❑ ❑ 2 - The Mugger (1956)
- ❑ ❑ 3 - The Pusher (1956)
- ❑ ❑ 4 - The Con Man (1957)
- ❑ ❑ 5 - Killer's Choice (1957)
- ❑ ❑ 6 - Killer's Payoff (1958)
- ❑ ❑ 7 - Killer's Wedge (1958)
- ❑ ❑ 8 - Lady Killer (1958)
- ❑ ❑ 9 - 'Til Death (1959)
- ❑ ❑ 10 - King's Ransom (1959)
- ❑ ❑ 11 - Give the Boys a Great Big Hand (1960)
- ❑ ❑ 12 - The Heckler (1960)
- ❑ ❑ 13 - See Them Die (1960)
- ❑ ❑ 14 - Lady, Lady, I Did It! (1961)
- ❑ ❑ 15 - The Empty Hours (1962)
- ❑ ❑ 16 - Like Love (1962)
- ❑ ❑ 17 - Ten Plus One (1963)
- ❑ ❑ 18 - Ax (1964)
- ❑ ❑ 19 - He Who Hesitates (1965)
- ❑ ❑ 20 - Doll (1965)
- ❑ ❑ 21 - Eighty Million Eyes (1966)
- ❑ ❑ 22 - Fuzz (1968)
- ❑ ❑ 23 - Shotgun (1969)
- ❑ ❑ 24 - Jigsaw (1970)
- ❑ ❑ 25 - Hail, Hail, The Gang's All Here! (1971)
- ❑ ❑ 26 - Sadie When She Died (1972)
- ❑ ❑ 27 - Let's Hear It for the Deaf Man (1972)
- ❑ ❑ 28 - Hail to the Chief (1973)
- ❑ ❑ 29 - Bread (1974)
- ❑ ❑ 30 - Blood Relatives (1975)
- ❑ ❑ 31 - So Long as You Both Shall Live (1976)
- ❑ ❑ 32 - Long Time No See (1977)
- ❑ ❑ 33 - Calypso (1979)
- ❑ ❑ 34 - Ghosts (1980)
- ❑ ❑ 35 - Heat (1981)
- ❑ ❑ 36 - Ice (1983)
- ❑ ❑ 37 - Lightning (1984)
- ❑ ❑ 38 - Eight Black Horses (1985)
- ❑ ❑ 39 - Poison (1987)
- ❑ ❑ 40 - Tricks (1987)
- ❑ ❑ 41 - Lullaby (1989)
- ❑ ❑ 42 - Vespers (1990)

    ❑ ❑ 43 - Widows (1991)
    ❑ ❑ 44 - Kiss (1992)
    ❑ ❑ 45 - Mischief (1993)
    ❑ ❑ 46 - Romance (1995)
    ❑ ❑ 47 - Nocturne (1997)

Matthew Hope...attorney in Florida
    ❑ ❑ 1 - Goldilocks (1977)
    ❑ ❑ 2 - Rumplestiltskin (1981)
    ❑ ❑ 3 - Beauty and the Beast (1983)
    ❑ ❑ 4 - Jack and the Beanstalk (1984)
    ❑ ❑ 5 - Snow White and Rose Red (1985)
    ❑ ❑ 6 - Cinderella (1986)
    ❑ ❑ 7 - Puss in Boots (1987)
    ❑ ❑ 8 - The House That Jack Built (1988)
    ❑ ❑ 9 - Three Blind Mice (1990)
    ❑ ❑ 10 - Mary, Mary (1993)
    ❑ ❑ 11 - There Was a Little Girl (1994)
    ❑ ❑ 12 - Gladly the Cross-Eyed Bear (1996)

■ MCCALL, Thomas

Thomas McCall has written two police mysteries featuring one-legged Chicago cop Nora Callum, introduced in *A Wide and Capable Revenge* (1993), where she investigates the shooting of a seemingly innocent mother of three in a cathedral. Nora uncovers a trail that leads from present-day Chicago back to World War II Russia. In book 2 Nora is under investigation by Internal Affairs for killing an unarmed suspect she thinks shot her prostitute friend's bail-jumping boyfriend. The background romance is not Nora's, but involves a NASA physicist and his lover Irina Varonyev, a Russian programmer, who are collaborating on a Mars space probe. "Nora and the police work both have a welcome edge," says *Kirkus* and "there's real tenderness in the doomed romance." McCall lives in Chicago (IL).

Nora Callum...one-legged cop in Chicago, Illinois
    ❑ ❑ 1 - A Wide and Capable Revenge (1993)
    ❑ ❑ 2 - Beyond Ice, Beyond Death (1995)

■ MCCALL, Wendell [P]

Wendell McCall is a pseudonym used by Ridley Pearson for two books featuring Chris Klick, a 6' 4" dropout songwriter turned private eye, introduced in *Dead Aim* (1988). The Idaho P.I. makes a second appearance in *Aim for the Heart* (1990). That same year Pearson became the first American to be awarded the Raymond Chandler Fulbright Fellowship in detective fiction in association with Oxford University, where he researched and outlined two new books in a series that has been optioned by HBO for a three-film deal to star Jamie Lee Curtis. While writing songs for a touring bar band in the '70s, he worked as a dishwasher and a housekeeper in a hospital surgery suite. A former Seattle resident, Pearson lives in a high mountain valley in Idaho. He plays bass guitar for the Rock Bottom Remainders—a literary garage band with Dave Barry, Amy Tan and Stephen King.

Chris Klick...6'4" dropout-songwriter turned P.I. in Idaho
    ❑ ❑ 1 - Dead Aim (1988)
    ❑ ❑ 2 - Aim for the Heart (1990)

■ MCCLURE, James

Gold and Silver Dagger award winner James McClure is the author of more than a dozen books, including 8 in the Kramer and Zondi series featuring an Afrikaner cop and his Bantu detective assistant in Trekkersburg, South Africa. These books span the final 20-some years of apartheid yet somehow manage to maintain a strong sense of humor. Only one of the books was ever banned (according to *St. James Guide*) and that was *The Sunday Hangman* (1977), which supposedly contained forbidden information about hanging and prisons. Although *The Song Dog* (1991) is the latest to be published, it could actually be read first, as it is a prequel to the rest of the series. McIlvanney's nonfiction work includes *Spike Island: Portrait of a Police Division* (1980) about Liverpool, and *Copworld: Policing the Streets of San Diego, California* (1985). Born in Johannesburg, he lives in Oxford.

Tromp Kramer, Lt. & Mickey Zondi, Sgt.....Africaner cop and Bantu detective assistant in South Africa
- ❏ ❏ 1 - **The Steam Pig (1971) Gold Dagger winner ★**
- ❏ ❏ 2 - The Caterpillar Cop (1972)
- ❏ ❏ 3 - The Gooseberry Fool (1974)
- ❏ ❏ 4 - Snake (1975)
- ❏ ❏ 5 - The Sunday Hangman (1977)
- ❏ ❏ 6 - The Blood of an Englishman (1980)
- ❏ ❏ 7 - The Artful Egg (1984)
- ❏ ❏ 8 - The Song Dog (1991)

■ MCCONNELL, Frank

Frank (DeMay) McConnell is the creator of an unlikely pair of private eyes introduced in an ecology-based mystery titled *Murder Among Friends* (1983). Bridge O'Toole is an ex-nun who runs a Chicago detective agency she took over from her sick father. Harry Garnish is her smart-aleck chief detective. While book 2, *Blood Lake* (1987), takes them to Wisconsin, and book 3, *The Frog King* (1990), to California, they're back in Chicago in book 4. *Liar's Poker* (1993) has them checking out the work of a religious guru who may be having an unhealthy influence on the wife of their client Professor Browder. During the investigation, lucky Harry is seduced by a lovely young woman named Lisa.

Harry Garnish & Bridget O'Toole...private investigators in Chicago, Illinois
- ❏ ❏ 1 - Murder Among Friends (1983)
- ❏ ❏ 2 - Blood Lake (1987)
- ❏ ❏ 3 - The Frog King (1990)
- ❏ ❏ 4 - Liar's Poker (1993)

■ MCCUTCHAN, Philip

Former Chairman of the Crime Writers' Association, Philip McCutchan has written more than 115 books since 1957. His longest-running series features Commander Esmonde Shaw who is seconded to the Foreign Office from Scotland Yard, introduced in 1960 and last seen in book 22, *Burn-Out* (1995). His second series under his own name features D.C.S. Simon Shard in 11 novels starting with *Call for Simon Shard* (1974). Shard's last appearance was in *The Abbott of Stockbridge* (1992). Under the name Robert Conington Galway he has written a 12-book espionage series featuring British spy James Packard. With the exception of the first and last book in the series, all were titled with the name of Packard's assignment. As Duncan MacNeil he has written 14 military novels set on the frontier of India during the 1890s, featuring Capt. James Ogilvie of the 114th Highlanders.

Esmonde Shaw, Commander...Naval Intelligence turned anti-intelligence in London, England
- ❏ ❏ 1 - Gibralter Road (1960)
- ❏ ❏ 2 - Redcap (1961)
- ❏ ❏ 3 - Bluebolt One (1962)
- ❏ ❏ 4 - The Man from Moscow (1963)
- ❏ ❏ 5 - Warmaster (1963)
- ❏ ❏ 6 - Moscow Coach (1964)
- ❏ ❏ 7 - The Dead Line (1966)
- ❏ ❏ 8 - Skyprobe (1966)
- ❏ ❏ 9 - The Screaming Dead Ballons (1968)
- ❏ ❏ 10 - The Bright Red Businessmen (1969)

❑ ❑ 11 - The All-Purpose Bodies (1969)
❑ ❑ 12 - Hartinger's Mouse (1970)
❑ ❑ 13 - This Drakotny (1971)
❑ ❑ 14 - Sunstrike (1979)
❑ ❑ 15 - Corpse (1980)
❑ ❑ 16 - Werewolf (1982)
❑ ❑ 17 - Rollerball (1984)
❑ ❑ 18 - Greenfly (1987)
❑ ❑ 19 - The Boy Who Liked Monsters (1989)
❑ ❑ 20 - The Spatchcock Plan (1990)
❑ ❑ 21 - Polecat Brennan (1994)
❑ ❑ 22 - Burn-Out (1995)

Simon Shard, Det. Chief Supt.....Scotland Yard supt. 2nd to the Foreign Office in London, England
❑ ❑ 1 - Call for Simon Shard (1974)
❑ ❑ 2 - A Very Big Bang (1975)
❑ ❑ 3 - Blood Run East (1976)
❑ ❑ 4 - The Eros Affair (1977)
❑ ❑ 5 - Blackmail North (1978)
❑ ❑ 6 - Shard Calls the Tune (1981)
❑ ❑ 7 - The Hoof (1983)
❑ ❑ 8 - Shard at Bay (1985)
❑ ❑ 9 - The Executioners (1986)
❑ ❑ 10 - The Logan File (1991)
❑ ❑ 11 - The Abbot of Stockbridge (1992)

■ MCDONALD, Gregory

Two-time Edgar award winner Gregory McDonald is the author of two dozen books, including 11 Fletch novels, 3 Flynn mysteries and a pair with Skylar Whitfield. Fletch is Irwin M. Fletcher, a smug investigative reporter who ends up with $3 million on a South American beach in book 1, enabling him to adopt a beach-bum-socialite sleuth role for future novels. McDonald's cop, Francis Xavier Flynn first appeared in book 2 of the Fletch series but was such a hit with readers that his publisher demanded a sequel. The newest series features a 20-something doofus from Tennessee who visits Connecticut kin in book 2. After graduating from Harvard, McDonald's first job was marine insurance underwriter. He later worked as a reporter, arts and humanities editor and critic-at-large at the *Boston Globe*. Past president of Mystery Writers of America, he lives on a farm in Tennessee.

Francis Xavier Flynn...tenacious police inspector in Boston, Massachusetts
❑ ❑ 1 - Flynn (1977)
❑ ❑ 2 - The Buck Passes Flynn (1981)
❑ ❑ 3 - Flynn's In (1984)

Irwin M. Fletcher...reporter turned beach bum socialite in the United States
❑ ❑ 1 - **Fletch (1974) Edgar winner ★**
❑ ❑ 2 - **Confess Fletch [incl Flynn] (1976) Edgar winner ★**
❑ ❑ 3 - Fletch's Fortune (1978)
❑ ❑ 4 - Fletch and the Widow Bradley (1981)
❑ ❑ 5 - Fletch's Moxie (1982)
❑ ❑ 6 - Fletch and the Man Who (1983)
❑ ❑ 7 - Carioca Fletch (1984)
❑ ❑ 8 - Fletch Won (1985)
❑ ❑ 9 - Fletch, Too [prequel] (1986)
❑ ❑ 10 - Son of Fletch (1993)
❑ ❑ 11 - Fletch Reflected (1994)

Skylar Whitfield...small-town good-ol'-boy in Tennessee
- ❏ ❏   1 - Skylar (1995)
- ❏ ❏   2 - Skylar in Yankeeland (1997)

■ **MCELDOWNEY, Eugene**

Eugene McEldowney is the creator of hard-drinking Irish police superintendent, Cecil Megarry, the kind of cop who clears his throat in the morning with a shot of Bushmills. According to the Irish Independent, Megarry "rivals [Inspector] Morse for angst and integrity." While working a double murder in book one, he fortifies himself with caffeine, nicotine and alcohol as he grills informers in grimy pubs and quizzes little old ladies over tea. In the end he finds the answer in a public library. Although weary of brutality and corruption, he lets himself be called back from suspension in book two to solve what seems like a modest bank robbery. Evidence leads to the Catholic ghetto of West Belfast and things heat up quickly. By book three, he's on holiday in Dublin recovering from a mild heart attack. A member of the editorial staff at the *Irish Times*, McEldowney lives in a fishing village on the outskirts of Dublin.

Cecil Megarry...hard-drinking Irish cop in Belfast, Ireland
- ❏ ❏   1 - A Kind of Homecoming (1994)
- ❏ ❏   2 - A Stone of the Heart (1995)
- ❏ ❏   3 - The Strange Case of Harpo Higgins (1995)

■ **MCGARRITY, Michael**

Michael McGarrity is an ex-Santa Fe cop who has worked as a ranch hand, college teacher, corporate consultant, psychotherapist in private practice, investigator for the New Mexico public defender's office, and held key positions in the New Mexico Department of Health. He entered law enforcement in his 40s as a deputy sherif for Santa Fe County, where he established the department's first sex crimes unit and led it to award-winning status, personally breaking many of their most difficult cases. He's now putting all this experience to use writing the Kevin Kerney Santa Fe mysteries. Following the Anthony-nominated series opener, Tularosa (Spanish for the place of reddish willows), each book promises to be a mystery in today's New Mexico with roots in the rich past. The Tularosa book jacket was done by Peter de la Fuente, a Santa Fe artist and great-grandson of N.C. Wyeth, "The Great Illustrator."

Kevin Kerney...ex-chief of detectives in Sante Fe, New Mexico
- ❏ ❏   1 - **Tularosa (1996) Anthony nominee** ☆
- ❏ ❏   2 - Mexican Hat (1997)

■ **MCGAUGHEY, Neil**

Novelist and reviewer Neil McGaughey (rhymes with McCoy) spent 16 years in California and Mississippi state government before turning to writing full time. The best of his many book reviews published by *The Clarion-Ledger* (Jackson MS) became part of his series of books featuring syndicated mystery reviewer Stokes Moran, the pen name of Kyle Malachi. McGaughey says he'll be ending the series with *A Corpse By Any Other Name* (1998) when he and Kyle kill off Stokes Moran. In these mysteries written for afficionados, McGaughey presents a mystery without a murder (book 1), suspects interviewed before the murder is committed (book 2), the victim solving his own murder (book 3) and a murder with no suspects at all (book 4). From his home in Mississippi, he is working on a big thriller involving a triple murder, an illusionist and a $25 million-dollar heist from a riverboat casino.

Stokes Moran aka Kyle Malachi...syndicated mystery critic in Tipton, Connecticut
- ❏ ❏   1 - Otherwise Known as Murder (1994)
- ❏ ❏   2 - And Then There Were Ten (1995)
- ❏ ❏   3 - The Best Money Murder Can Buy (1996)
- ❏ ❏   4 - A Corpse By Any Other Name (1998)

■ MCILVANNEY, William

William McIlvanney is perhaps the only mystery writer to have ever won a Silver Dagger and an Edgar nomination for two consecutive books in a series, which is what he accomplished with *Laidlaw* (1977) and *The Papers of Tony Veitch* (1983). Set in Glasgow, these police novels begin the series featuring Insp. Jack Laidlaw, a philosophical and anguished policeman. When his novel *Docherty* was published in 1975, winner of a Whitbread Literary Award, McIlvanney was hailed as the most important novelist of his generation in Scotland. The son of a miner, he grew up in the west central part of the country, an area of industrial poverty that never recovered from the depression of the 1930s. Former writer-in-residence at the University of Aberdeen, he once presented a book program on Scottish television and wrote a column for the *Sunday Standard.*

Jack Laidlaw, Insp.....Scottish police inspector in Glasgow, Scotland
- ❏ ❏ 1 - **Laidlaw (1977) Silver Dagger winner ★ Edgar nominee** ☆
- ❏ ❏ 2 - **The Papers of Tony Veitch (1983) Silver Dagger winner ★ Edgar nominee** ☆
- ❏ ❏ 3 - The Big Man (1985)
- ❏ ❏ 4 - Strange Loyalties (1991)

■ MCINERNY, Ralph

Ralph McInerny has written more than 40 mysteries, including 17 featuring Fox River parish priest, Father Roger Dowling, 5 with Indiana attorney Andrew Broom and 9 under the pseudonym Monica Quill. He recently launched a new series set on the University of Notre Dame campus where he has taught philosophy for more than 40 years. Starting with *On This Rockne* (1997), a visiting philosophy professor and his private eye brother find themselves in the midst of a $10-million battle to memorialize the legendary football coach. An authority on St. Thomas Aquinas, McInerny teaches philosophy and medieval studies. In addition to his mysteries, he has written at least 17 volumes of philosophy, ethics and religion and served as founder, publisher and editor of several Catholic magazines. Recipient of a Lifetime Achievement Anthony Award in 1993, he lives in South Bend (IN).

Andrew Broom...attorney in Wyler, Indiana
- ❏ ❏ 1 - Cause and Effect (1987)
- ❏ ❏ 2 - Body and Soil (1989)
- ❏ ❏ 3 - Frigor Mortis (1989)
- ❏ ❏ 4 - Savings and Loam (1990)
- ❏ ❏ 5 - Mom and Dead (1994)
- ❏ ❏ 6 - Law and Ardor (1995)

Roger Dowling, Father...St. Hilary's parish priest in Fox River, Illinois
- ❏ ❏ 1 - Her Death of Cold (1977)
- ❏ ❏ 2 - The Seventh Station (1977)
- ❏ ❏ 3 - Bishop as Pawn (1978)
- ❏ ❏ 4 - Lying Three (1979)
- ❏ ❏ 5 - Second Vespers (1980)
- ❏ ❏ 6 - Thicker than Water (1981)
- ❏ ❏ 7 - A Loss of Patients (1982)
- ❏ ❏ 8 - The Grass Widow (1983)
- ❏ ❏ 9 - Getting a Way with Murder (1984)
- ❏ ❏ 10 - Rest in Pieces (1985)
- ❏ ❏ 11 - The Basket Case (1987)
- ❏ ❏ nn - Four on the Floor [4 novellas] (1989)

      ❏ ❏ 12 - Abracadaver (1989) Brit.-Slight of Body
      ❏ ❏ 13 - Judas Priest (1991)
      ❏ ❏ 14 - Desert Sinner (1992)
      ❏ ❏ 15 - Seed of Doubt (1993)
      ❏ ❏ 16 - A Cardinal Offense (1994)
      ❏ ❏ 17 - The Tears of Things (1996)

■ MELVILLE, James [P]

James Melville is the pen name of (Roy) Peter Martin for 13 books featuring Supt. Tetsuo Otani who heads the third largest police force in Japan where he commands nearly 9,000 officers starting with *The Wages of Zen* (1979). Otani's supporting cast includes his beloved wife Hanae and his right and left hand—the debonair Insp. Jiro Kimura and the sinister Insp. "Ninja" Noguchi. While Kimura (who has a fondness for Western secretaries) is in charge of foreign residents, Noguchi handles drug control. As Hampton Charles, Melville has written 3 books in the Miss Seeton series about a retired art teacher who consults with Scotland Yard. As James Melville he is the author of 2 titles featuring British Council official Ben Lazenby. The author's own diplomatic experience includes postings to Indonesia, Japan and Hungary. He was awarded the Order of the British Empire in 1970.

Ben Lazenby...British Council official in England
      ❏ ❏ 1 - Diplomatic Baggage [Hungary] (1995)
      ❏ ❏ 2 - The Reluctant Spy (1995)

Tetsuo Otani...Japanese police superintendent in Kobe, Japan
      ❏ ❏ 1 - The Wages of Zen (1979)
      ❏ ❏ 2 - The Chrysanthemum Chain (1980)
      ❏ ❏ 3 - A Sort of Samurai (1981)
      ❏ ❏ 4 - The Ninth Netsuke (1982)
      ❏ ❏ 5 - Sayonara, Sweet Amaryllis (1983)
      ❏ ❏ 6 - Death of a Daimyo (1984)
      ❏ ❏ 7 - The Death Ceremony (1985)
      ❏ ❏ 8 - Go Gently, Gaijin (1986)
      ❏ ❏ 9 - Kimono for a Corpse (1987)
      ❏ ❏ 10 - The Reluctant Ronin (1988)
      ❏ ❏ 11 - A Haiku for Hanae (1989)
      ❏ ❏ 12 - The Bogus Buddha (1990)
      ❏ ❏ 13 - The Body Wore Brocade (1992)

■ MEYER, Charles

Charles Meyer is the creator of the Reverend Lucas Holt mysteries featuring a 40-something prison chaplain turned parish pastor with an Episcopal church in downtown Austin (TX). First seen in *The Saints of God Murders* (1995), Holt's parish is troubled by a serial killer who chooses his victims based on the church hymn "Saints of God." In book 2, parishioners who have put their parents in nursing homes are being murdered. Pastor Holt's supporting cast includes righthand man Nikky Dorati and several other reformed ex-cons known collectively as The God Squad; church secretary Maxine Blackwell, a former madam who was Holt's inmate secretary at the prison; and Lt. Susan Gregory of the Austin police department, an old friend and on-again/off-again romantic interest. The author is director of pastoral care and patient relations at a hospital in Austin (TX).

Lucas Holt, Rev....Episcopal church pastor in Austin, Texas
      ❏ ❏ 1 - The Saints of God Murders (1995)
      ❏ ❏ 2 - Blessed are the Merciless (1996)

■ MEYERS, Martin

Native New Yorker Martin Meyers is the author of 5 Patrick Hardy private eye novels published during the mid-'70s, starting with *Kiss and Tell* (1975). These days he is better known as Maan Meyers, a pseudonym he shares with wife Annette Meyers for their Dutchman series of historical novels set in Manhattan. The first 5 books in the series follow the Tonneman family from 1664 New Amsterdam to 1808 New York. In book 6, *The Lucifer Contract: A Civil War Thriller* (1998), it's 1864 and a 20-something Peter Tonneman is a correspondent for the *New York Evening Post*. After hearing rumors that Morgan's Raiders are hiding nearby with plans to burn the City, he joins forces with a barmaid to save the Union. Meyers' acting credits include *Zorba* on Broadway and Stan Perlo on *One Life to Live*. He has written song lyrics for the TV program *Captain Kangaroo* and a film novelization of *Suspect* (1987).

Patrick Hardy...private eye in New York, New York
- ❑ ❑ 1 - Kiss and Tell (1975)
- ❑ ❑ 2 - Spy and Die (1976)
- ❑ ❑ 3 - Red is for Murder (1976)
- ❑ ❑ 4 - Hung Up to Die (1976)
- ❑ ❑ 5 - Reunion for Death (1976)

■ MICHAELS, Grant [P]

Grant Michaels is the pseudonym of Michael Mesrobian for his series featuring gay Boston hairdresser and amateur sleuth Stan Kraychik, seen first in *A Body to Dye For* (1990). In book 3, *Dead on Your Feet* (1993), Stan's love interest, Nureyev-like choreographer Rafik Panossian, is working on a new ballet for a controversial director who ends up dead. Because he's on a first-name basis with members of the ballet company, Stan is given the go-ahead by Lt. Vito Branco (his former nemesis at the Boston PD) to investigate. Stan's next case, book 6, *Dead as a Doornail* (1998), finds him rehabbing the last unrenovated brownstone in Boston's chic South End. During a freak April snowstorm, the body of a contractor who looks suspiciously like Stan turns up dead in the brownstone and Lt. Branco thinks Stan was the target. The author lives in Boston (MA).

Stan Kraychik...gay hairdresser in Boston, Massachusetts
- ❑ ❑ 1 - A Body to Dye For (1990)
- ❑ ❑ 2 - Love You to Death (1992)
- ❑ ❑ 3 - Dead on Your Feet (1993)
- ❑ ❑ 4 - Mask for a Diva (1994)
- ❑ ❑ 5 - Time to Check Out (1996)

■ MILAN, Borto [P]

Borto Milan is the pseudonym of Jeff Collignon for a new series featuring motorcycle drifter Edward Ryan, starting with *In the Drift* (1995). Having left his Gulf Coast Florida home years earlier to escape an abusive, alcoholic family, Eddie must piece together the truth of his life when his younger brother is killed violently. In *Riding Toward Home* (1996) Eddie ends up in a small-town Kentucky jail where he meets a 17-year-old in trouble and agrees to drive her home to Michigan. What he finds there is scandal, unsolved murder, greed and corruption. Collignon's first novel, *Her Monster* (1992), is "a darkly modern version of Beauty and the Beast." Beauty is an orange-haired California girl; Beast is a reclusive science fiction writer who believes he is too hideously deformed to be seen. Kirkus called it an "intriguing debut" from a purported recluse and drifter.

Edward Ryan...motorcycle drifter in Southeast United States
- ❑ ❑ 1 - In the Drift (1995)
- ❑ ❑ 2 - Riding Toward Home (1996)

■ MILES, John [P]

John Miles is a pseudonym used by Oklahoma newspaper editor and journalism professor Jack Bickham for two series featuring women protagonists—one a small-town Colorado sheriff and the other a graduate student in social work. Johnelle "Johnnie" Baker is the Tenoclock (CO) sheriff appearing in two recent titles, while Laura Michaels rides herd on a group of geriatric detectives at the Timberlake (OK) Retirement Center. Author of more than 60 books, including westerns, mysteries and comedy, Bickham says he'd always wanted to write cozies, hence the two new series as John Miles (Bickham's middle name). For many years he taught journalism at the University of Oklahoma and was a guiding force behind the school's Professional Writing Program. A licensed private pilot, he has retired from teaching and moved to Alaska.

Johnelle Baker...Choctaw sheriff in Tenoclock, Colorado
- ❏ ❏ 1 - Missing at Tenoclock (1994)
- ❏ ❏ 2 - Tenoclock Scholar (1995)

Laura Michaels...retirement center social worker in Timberlake, Oklahoma
- ❏ ❏ 1 - Permanent Retirement (1993)
- ❏ ❏ 2 - Murder in Retirement (1994)
- ❏ ❏ 3 - Most Deadly Retirement (1995)

■ MILES, Keith

Keith Miles began writing golf mysteries during the late 1980s. A novelist and playwright with a lifelong interest in theater, he also began writing his Edgar-nominated mystery series featuring the stage manager for an Elizabethan theater troupe. These 16th century mysteries, as well as an 11th century series featuring a pair of land claims investigators for William the Conqueror, are written under the name Edward Marston. Born and raised in South Wales, Miles was educated at Oxford University and later lectured in history. In addition to his 20 mysteries, he has written over 40 plays for radio, television and theatre, as well as 20 children's books, 8 other novels and literary criticism. His latest mystery, *Murder in Perspective* (1997), launches a new series with a young Welsh architect who comes to Arizona in the '20s, hoping to work with Frank Lloyd Wright.

Alan Saxon...professional golfer
- ❏ ❏ 1 - Bullet Hole (1986)
- ❏ ❏ 2 - Double Eagle (1987)
- ❏ ❏ 3 - Green Murder (1990)
- ❏ ❏ 4 - Flagstick (1991)

Merlin Richards...1920s young Welsh architect in Phoenix, Arizona
- ❏ ❏ 1 - Murder in Perspective (1997)

■ MILLER, Rex

Rex Miller has written a 5-book series of Onyx paperback originals featuring Chicago police detective Jack Eichord, who is first seen in *Slob* (1987). The Chicago detective was also featured in *Frenzy* (1988), *Stone Shadow* (1989), *Slice* (1990) and *Iceman* (1990). Also introduced in Eichord's first case was Daniel Edward Flowers "Chaingang" Bunkowski, a 500-lb. execution machine with a genius I.Q., a mastery of explosives and the ability to use bad breath as a martial art. Starting with *Chaingang* (1992), which *Publishers Weekly* called "cheerfully malevolent," this character gets his own series, continuing with *Savant* (1994) and *Butcher* (1994). In *Savant*, Chaingang goes head to head with a mass murdering sniper who utters a line later stolen by Cyrus the Virus in the movie *Con Air*, according to an online review for *Savant* posted on amazon.com.

Jack Eichord...police detective in Chicago, Illinois
- ❏ ❏ 1 - Slob (1987)
- ❏ ❏ 2 - Frenzy (1988)
- ❏ ❏ 3 - Stone Shadow (1989)
- ❏ ❏ 4 - Slice (1990)
- ❏ ❏ 5 - Iceman (1990)

■ MILLER, Victor B.

Victor B. Miller wrote 9 books featuring NYPD Lt. Theo Kojak, novelizations of the popular CBS television series which ran from 1973 to 1978. According to William DeAndrea's *Encyclopedia Mysteriosa*, the bald-headed Greek-American detective, played by Telly Savalas, first appeared in the Abby Mann-scripted movie, *The Marcus-Nelson Murders*, based on a famous 1963 New York murder (the Wylie-Hoffert case). CBS aired reunion movies for the Kojak series in 1985 (*Kojak: The Belarus File*) and again in 1987 (*Kojak: The Price of Justice*). In 1989-90 ABC revived Kojak for its mystery wheel series but Savalas was the only surviving cast member. Now an inspector, Kojak was assisted by a young black detective named Blake played by Andre Braugher who later joined the cast of ABC's *Homicide*.

Theo Kojak...NYPD cop in New York, New York
- ❑ ❑ 1 - Siege (1974)
- ❑ ❑ 2 - Requiem for a Cop (1974)
- ❑ ❑ 3 - A Very Deadly Game (1975)
- ❑ ❑ 4 - Therapy in Dynamite (1975)
- ❑ ❑ 5 - The Trade-Off (1975)
- ❑ ❑ 6 - Take-Over (1975)
- ❑ ❑ 7 - Gun Business (1975)
- ❑ ❑ 8 - Girl in the River (1975)
- ❑ ❑ 9 - Death is Not a Passing Grade (1975)
      Brit.-Marked for Murder

■ MILLER, Wade [P]

Wade Miller was the shared pseudonym of Robert Wade and Bill Miller (1920-1961) who began their collaboration while still in school where they edited the *East San Diego Press* and wrote radio plays. In 1988 they were honored with a Lifetime Achievement award from Private Eye Writers of America. The Max Thursday private eye series, set in San Diego, starts with *Guilty Bystander* (1947), the writing team's second novel. In book 1 Max is a house detective in a cheap downtown hotel, but after the kidnapping of his son he salvages his career and becomes a successful P.I., despite a hot temper and bursts of violence he later regrets. The Wade Miller collaboration, one of the most successful in the history of crime fiction, turned out 33 novels, 2 screenplays, 200 radio scripts and countless novelettes and short stories. They also wrote together as Will Deamer, Whit Masterson and Dale Wilmer.

Max Thursday...private eye in San Diego, California
- ❑ ❑ 1 - Guilty Bystander (1947)
- ❑ ❑ 2 - Fatal Step (1948)
- ❑ ❑ 3 - Uneasy Street (1948)
- ❑ ❑ 4 - Calamity Fair (1950)
- ❑ ❑ 5 - Murder Charge (1950)
- ❑ ❑ 6 - Shoot to Kill (1951)

■ MILNE, John

British author John Milne is the creator of Jimmy Jenner, a pensioned-off cop with a wooden leg, who dislikes the French, is tormented by his ex-wife and communicates with the world largely by means of his telephone answering machine. The locale for his action is the Inner London suburb of Stoke Newington, an area undergoing urban gentrification, although still suitably seedy for our Columbo style P.I. In book 2, in the midst of tracking a missing man from London to Paris and back, Jenner meets the lovely Esmerelda Potts. Milne has also written 3 non-crime novels, *Tyro* (1982), *London Fields* (1983) and *Out of the Blue* (1985), along with numerous television plays for *The Bill*, *Bergerac*, *Boon*, *Perfect Scoundrel* and *East Enders* series. After earning a B.A. (with honors) in fine painting from Ravensbourne School of Art in London, Milne worked as a delivery driver, factory hand and policeman. He lives in France.

Jimmy Jenner...English private eye in England
- ❏ ❏ 1 - Dead Birds (1986)
- ❏ ❏ 2 - Shadow Play (1987)
        U.S.-The Moody Man
- ❏ ❏ 3 - Daddy's Girl (1988)

■ MITCHELL, Kirk

Author of more than a dozen books and film novelizations, Kirk Mitchell is the creator of Bureau of Land Management ranger Dee Laguerre, referred to by her detractors as "that skinny Basque bitch." Dee's rookie year is spent in the middle of Nevada's Owens Valley Water War, a 75-year-old struggle between outlying rural communities and the Los Angeles Dept. of Water and Power, which is being played out in actual events. Mitchell's personal experience as a Deputy Sheriff in Owens Valley included investigating sabotage for the Los Angeles aqueduct. In book 2, he has Dee working with an ATF explosives investigator trying to avert the arrival of LAPD swat teams when the city's water supply is severely threatened by sabotage. Mitchell's film novelizations include *Mississippi Burning*, *Backdraft* and *Blown Away*. A one-time tungsten miner, he lives in the Sierra Nevada Mountains.

Dee Laguerre...Bureau of Land Management ranger in Nevada
- ❏ ❏ 1 - **High Desert Malice (1995) Edgar nominee** ☆
- ❏ ❏ 2 - Deep Valley Malice (1996)

■ MOODY, Bill

Jazz musician and historian Bill Moody is the author of a new mystery series featuring jazz pianist Evan Horne, introduced in *Solo Hand* (1994) where a car accident leaves him with an injured left hand and no music career. As one fan put it, Evan's no prissy tickler of the ivories. He's someone who uses the discipline and preseverance that made him a musician to make him a detective. Drawn into cases by his record-collector buddy Ace, a Las Vegas professor, Horne solves murders involving famous names in jazz history. In book 3, lost tapes of long-dead trumpet player Clifford Brown turn up in Las Vegas and a collector is murdered for them. Musician, jazz DJ and college writing instructor, Moody has toured and recorded with Maynard Ferguson, Earl Fatha Hines and Jon Hendricks. A jazz drummer who grew up in Southern California, he lives in Las Vegas (NV) where he also writes for several jazz and mystery magazines.

Evan Horne...jazz pianist in Nevada
- ❏ ❏ 1 - Solo Hand (1994)
- ❏ ❏ 2 - Death of a Tenor Man (1995)
- ❏ ❏ 3 - Sound of the Trumpet (1997)

■ MOORE, Richard A.

American author Richard A. Moore has written two mysteries featuring Atlanta, Georgia newspaper reporter Bob Whitfield, introduced in *Death in the* Past (1981). According to Allen J. Hubin's *Crime Fiction II*, the author is a journalist who later worked as a press secretary to a United States senator. The fictional reporter's second appearance was titled *Death of a Source* (1982).

Bob Whitfield...newspaper reporter in Atlanta, Georgia
- ❏ ❏ 1 - Death in the Past (1981)
- ❏ ❏ 2 - Death of a Source (1982)

■ MORSE, L. A.

Edgar award winner L(arry) A(lan) Morse has written a pair of novels featuring Los Angeles P.I. Sam Hunter, introduced in *The Big Enchilada* (1982), assumed to be a parody. Hunter is a man of "such Neanderthal sentiments and ugly excesses that he makes Mike Hammer look cerebral," said Baker and Nietzel in *101 Knights* (1985), noting Hunter has sex 3 times with 3 different women in the first 53 pages of *The Big Enchilada*—against a wall on page 10, on the floor on page 30 and in the shower on page 53. Morse's Edgar-winning earlier novel *The Old Dick* (1981) featured a 78-year-old retired cop named Jake Spanner. The book also received a Shamus nomination. Under the name Runa Fairleigh he is the author of *An Old-Fashioned Mystery* (1983). Born in Fort Wayne (IN), Morse earned a B.A. from Berkeley and an M.A. from San Francisco State University. He lives in Toronto where he has worked in Canadian educational television.

Sam Hunter...private eye in Los Angeles, California
- ❏ ❏   1 - The Big Enchilada (1982)
- ❏ ❏   2 - Sleaze (1985)

■ MORSON, Ian

First-time novelist Ian Morson has introduced a new historical series featuring 13th century Oxford University regent William Falconer, a man of science and rationality in an age typically thought of as unenlightened. In book 1, *Falconer's Crusade* (1994), the year is 1264 and the regent master has his hands full when a young servant girl is savagely murdered as Simon de Montfort plots to overthrow King Henry III. Political and ecclesiastical chaos reign in book 2, *Falconer's Judgement* (1995), as Pope Alexander lies dying in Rome and the pitched battle for his successor is underway. While scouring the back alleys of Oxford in search of an alchemist in book 3, *Falconer and the Face of God* (1996), the regent master witnesses a murder among the ranks of a troupe of entertainers. His next appearance promises to be *A Psalm for Falconer* (1997).

William Falconer...13th century university regent master in Oxford, England
- ❏ ❏   1 - Falconer's Crusade (1994)
- ❏ ❏   2 - Falconer's Judgement (1995)
- ❏ ❏   3 - Falconer and the Face of God (1996)

■ MOSLEY, Walter

Before 1990 Walter Mosley was a relatively unknown mystery writer. Now he counts among his fans (and friends) President Clinton. An author who didn't start writing until his mid-30s, Mosley no longer has to get up at 5 AM to write before going to his real job as a computer programmer. His first published novel, *Devil in a Blue Dress* (1990), was an Edgar nominee and winner of Creasey and Shamus awards for best first novel. Since then the series has earned another Edgar nomination, as well as Anthony and Hammet nominations. Set in 1948, book 1 introduces Ezekial "Easy" Rawlins and his short-tempered sidekick Mouse. Mosley has said he envisions about 9 books in the series, bringing the narrative up to the 1980s. He has also written the mainstream novel *R.L.'s Dream* (1996) and the non-mystery *Gone Fishin'* (1997) which tells how Easy and Mouse met. In 1997 a new Mosley character debuts with a collection of short stories titled *Always Outnumbered, Always Outgunned*. Born in Los Angeles, Mosley lives in New York City.

Easy Rawlins...school maintenance supervisor in Watts
- ❏ ❏   **1 - Devil in a Blue Dress (1990) Creasey & Shamus winner ★★ Edgar nominee ☆**
- ❏ ❏   2 - A Red Death (1991)
- ❏ ❏   **3 - White Butterfly (1993) Edgar & Hammett nominee ☆☆**
- ❏ ❏   **4 - Black Betty (1994) Anthony nominee ☆**
- ❏ ❏   5 - A Little Yellow Dog (1996)
- ❏ ❏   6 - Gone Fishin' [prequel] (1997)
- ❏ ❏   7 - Bad Boy Bobby Brown (1998)

Socrates Fortlow...philosophical ex-con in California
❏ ❏ ss - Always Outnumbered, Always Outgunned
[short stories] (1997)

■ **MOST, Bruce W.**

Bruce Most is one of three Colorado writers who launched a mystery series in 1996 featuring a Denver bail bondsmen. What's different about the Most series is that his bondsman is a woman—fifty-something redhead Ruby Dark. Having inherited the business from her murdered husband, she operates Ruby's Bail Bonds with her law student nephew David. She chooses her clients from among the rich and famous; drives a red Lamborghini; owns a black Persian cat and an Old English mastiff named Collateral. A graduate of the University of Iowa, Most worked as a newspaper reporter before turning to freelance writing. He has ghosted one book and works primarily as a public relations writer in the area of personal finance. His first Ruby Dark novel is not the first he's written but it is the first published. He lives in Denver with his family and a cat named Claypool.

Ruby Dark...bail bondswoman in Denver, Colorado
❏ ❏ 1 - Bonded for Murder (1996)
❏ ❏ 2 - Missing Bonds (1997)

■ **MULLEN, Jack**

Early in his career as a San Diego (CA) cop, Jack Mullen started stuffing notes in a desk drawer, keeping track of colorful moments. After 15 years he had three drawers full and the beginnings of a manuscript. A three-generation law enforcement officer, he is the grandson of a New York City cop and the son of a 40-year Customs agent. His series opener, *In the Line of Duty* (1995), introduces Vincent Dowling, a man headed for success as a homicide detective until his wife commites suicide. Dowling returns in *Behind the Shield* (1996) with a brutal rapist on the loose. "Writing crime is a catharsis for all the years it was necessary to keep my emotions in check," he says. Dowling and other characters are composites of friends, associates and family members. Retired from the SDPD, Mullen is working on another Dowling story and a nonfiction baseball book. He lives in Oregon.

Vincent Dowling, Sgt.....police sergeant in San Diego, California
❏ ❏ 1 - Lost Honor (1995)
❏ ❏ 2 - Behind the Shield (1996)

■ **MURPHY, Dallas**

Edgar nominee Dallas Murphy is the creator of a trio of mysteries featuring Artie Deemer and his dog Jellyroll, the spokesdog for R-r-ruff Dog Food and a film star whose first big break was playing Seeing Eye dog for a blind detective. Thanks to Jellyroll, Artie has plenty of time to play pool, listen to jazz and investigate. And these two take their jazz seriously. Often they can be found in Artie's acoustically perfect living room where the only furniture is Artie's Morris chair and Jellyroll's Adirondack Spruce Bough Bed. Murphy's most recent book is *The Fast Forward M.B.A. in Marketing* (1997), part of the Portable M.B.A. series from John Wiley & Sons. A serious sailor, Murphy grew up in Florida but now lives in New York City where he works as a freelance writer specializing in business topics and cruising articles. He also teaches a course in mystery writing. A former playwright, Murphy holds an M.A. from the University of Massachusetts.

Artie Deemer...owner of celebrity spokesdog in New York, New York
❏ ❏ 1 - **Lover Man (1987) Edgar nominee** ☆
❏ ❏ 2 - Lush Life (1993)
❏ ❏ 3 - Don't Explain (1995)

■ MURPHY, Haughton [P]

Haughton Murphy is a pseudonym of James Duffy, creator of retired Wall Street attorney Reuben Frost, introduced in *Murder for Lunch* (1986). Married to Cynthia, a former ballerina, Frost is chairman of the National Ballet Company which figures prominently in book 2, *Murder Takes a Partner* (1987). The artistic director is killed in what was made to look like a street mugging. Cynthia helps sort out the suspects. When the host of the Frosts' literary discussion group is poisoned in book 5, *Murder Times Two* (1990), everybody's a suspect, including Cynthia. Frost is called back to his old firm in book 6, *Murder Saves Face* (1991), when a woman associate is found strangled on a bottom shelf of the law library. Frost finds clues in a computer file and a fax transmission. "Spiffy as a Venice-on-a-zillion-dollars-a-day-guide," said *Kirkus* of book 7, *A Very Venetian Murder* (1992). Murphy says all the restaurants and hotels are real.

Reuben Frost...retired Wall Street attorney in New York, New York
- ❏ ❏ 1 - Murder for Lunch (1986)
- ❏ ❏ 2 - Murder Takes a Partner (1987)
- ❏ ❏ 3 - Murder and Acquisitions (1988)
- ❏ ❏ 4 - Murder Keeps a Secret (1989)
- ❏ ❏ 5 - Murder Times Two (1990)
- ❏ ❏ 6 - Murder Saves Face (1991)
- ❏ ❏ 7 - A Very Venetian Murder (1992)

■ MURPHY, Warren B.

Edgar and Shamus winner Warren B. Murphy has written more than 150 novels and screenplays—cops, private eyes, action thrillers, humor and dark suspense, comic detectives, sword and sorcery spies and more. William DeAndrea called him the Alexander Dumas of mysteries—able to write prolifically to a standard of excellence in a wide variety of forms with a distinctive voice. Murphy says, "My apparent versatility is really based upon a character flaw: I have the attention span of melting ice cream." While secretary to the mayor of Jersey City, Murphy and City Hall reporter Richard Sapir (1936-1987) wrote their first Destroyer novel. With over 40 million copies of more than 108 titles in print, this series was the first to feature a brash young Westerner trained in martial arts by an inscrutable Oriental master. Writing with wife Molly Cochran, Murphy is co-author of the 1985 Edgar winner *Grandmaster* and several other titles including *The Broken Sword* (1997). They also write together as Dev Stryker in *Deathright* (1993) and *End Game* (1998).

Devlin Tracy...freelance insurance investigator in Las Vegas, Nevada
- ❏ ❏ 1 - **Trace (1983) Edgar & Shamus nominee** ☆☆
- ❏ ❏ 2 - **Trace and 47 Miles of Rope (1984) Shamus nominee** ☆
- ❏ ❏ 3 - When Elephants Forget (1984)
- ❏ ❏ 4 - **Pigs Get Fat (1985) Edgar winner ★ Shamus nominee** ☆
- ❏ ❏ 5 - Once a Mutt (1985)
- ❏ ❏ 6 - **Too Old a Cat [incl Razoni & Jackson] (1986) Shamus nominee** ☆
- ❏ ❏ 7 - Getting Up with Fleas (1987)

Ed Razoni & William Jackson...police detectives in New York, New York
- ❏ ❏ 1 - One Night Stand (1973)
- ❏ ❏ 2 - Dead End Street (1973)
- ❏ ❏ 3 - City in Heat (1973)
- ❏ ❏ 4 - Down and Dirty (1974)
- ❏ ❏ 5 - Lynch Town (1974)
- ❏ ❏ 6 - On the Dead Run (1975)

Julian "Digger" Burroughs...freelance insurance investigator in Las Vegas, Nevada
- ❏ ❏ 1 - **Smoked Out (1982) Shamus nominee** ☆
- ❏ ❏ 2 - Fool's Flight (1982)
- ❏ ❏ 3 - Dead Letter (1982)
- ❏ ❏ 4 - Lucifer's Weekend [with Robert J. Randisi] (1982)

Remo Williams aka The Destroyer...ex-cop turned government enforcer in New York, New York

❑ ❑ 1 - Created: The Destroyer (with Sapir) (1971)
❑ ❑ 2 - Death Check (with Sapir) (1971)
❑ ❑ 3 - The Chinese Puzzle (with Sapir) (1972)
❑ ❑ 4 - Mafia Fix (with Sapir) (1972)
❑ ❑ 5 - Dr. Quake (with Sapir) (1972)
❑ ❑ 6 - Death Therapy (with Sapir) (1972)
❑ ❑ 7 - Union Bust (with Sapir) (1973)
❑ ❑ 8 - Summit Chase (with Sapir) (1973)
❑ ❑ 9 - Murder's Shield (with Sapir) (1973)
❑ ❑ 10 - Terror Squad (with Sapir) (1973)
❑ ❑ 11 - Kill or Cure (with Sapir) (1973)
❑ ❑ 12 - Slave Safari (with Sapir) (1973)
❑ ❑ 13 - Acid Rock (with Sapir) (1973)
❑ ❑ 14 - Judgment Day (with Sapir) (1974)
❑ ❑ 15 - Murder Ward (with Sapir) (1974)
❑ ❑ 16 - Oil Slick (with Sapir) (1974)
❑ ❑ 17 - Last War Dance (with Sapir) (1974)
❑ ❑ 18 - Funny Money (with Sapir) (1975)
❑ ❑ 19 - Holy Terror (with Sapir) (1975)
❑ ❑ 20 - Assassins Play-Off (with Sapir) (1975)
❑ ❑ 21 - Deadly Seeds (with Sapir) (1975)
❑ ❑ 22 - Brain Drain (with Sapir) (1976)
❑ ❑ 23 - Child's Play (with Sapir) (1976)
❑ ❑ 24 - King's Curse (with Sapir) (1976)
❑ ❑ 25 - Sweet Dreams (w/Richard S. Meyers) (1976)
❑ ❑ 26 - In Enemy Hands (with Sapir) (1977)
❑ ❑ 27 - The Last Temple (w/Richard S. Meyers) (1977)
❑ ❑ 28 - Ship of Death (with Sapir) (1977)
❑ ❑ 29 - The Final Death (w/Richard S. Meyers) (1977)
❑ ❑ 30 - Mugger Blood (with Sapir) (1977)
❑ ❑ 31 - The Head Men (with Sapir) (1977)
❑ ❑ 32 - Killer Chromosomes (with Sapir) (1978)
❑ ❑ 33 - Voodoo Die (with Sapir) (1978)
❑ ❑ 34 - Chained Reaction (with Sapir) (1978)
❑ ❑ 35 - Last Call (1978)
❑ ❑ 36 - Power Play (1979)
❑ ❑ 37 - Bottom Line (1979)
❑ ❑ 38 - Bay City Blast (1979)
❑ ❑ 39 - Missing Link (1980)
❑ ❑ 40 - Dangerous Games (1980)
❑ ❑ 41 - Firing Line (1980)
❑ ❑ 42 - Timber Line (1980)
❑ ❑ 43 - Midnight Man (1981)
❑ ❑ 44 - The Balance of Power (1981)
❑ ❑ 45 - Spoils of War (1981)
❑ ❑ 46 - Next of Kin (1981)
❑ ❑ 47 - Dying Space (1982)
❑ ❑ 48 - Profit Motive (with Sapir) (1982)
❑ ❑ 49 - Skin Deep (1982)
❑ ❑ 50 - Killing Time (1982)
❑ ❑ 51 - Shock Value (1983)
❑ ❑ 52 - Fool's Gold (with Sapir) (1983)
❑ ❑ 53 - Time Trial (1983)
❑ ❑ 54 - Last Drop (1983)

❑ ❑ 55 - Master's Challenge (1984)
❑ ❑ 56 - Encounter Group (1984)
❑ ❑ 57 - Date With Death (1984)
❑ ❑ 58 - Total Recall (with Randisi) (1984)
❑ ❑ 59 - The Arms of Kali (1985)
❑ ❑ 60 - The End of the Game (1985)
❑ ❑ 61 - The Lords of the Earth (1985)
❑ ❑ 62 - The Seventh Stone (1985)
❑ ❑ 63 - The Sky is Falling (by Sapir) (1985)
❑ ❑ 64 - The Last Alchemist (by Sapir) (1986)
❑ ❑ 65 - Lost Yesterday (by Sapir) (1986)
❑ ❑ 66 - Sue Me (by Sapir) (1986)
❑ ❑ 67 - Look Into My Eyes (by Sapir) (1986)
❑ ❑ 68 - An Old-Fashioned War (by Sapir) (1987)
❑ ❑ 69 - Blood Ties (1987)
❑ ❑ 70 - The Eleventh Hour (1987)
❑ ❑ 71 - Return Engagement (1988)
❑ ❑ 72 - Sole Survivor (1988)
❑ ❑ 73 - Line of Succession (1988)
❑ ❑ 74 - Walking Wounded (1988)
❑ ❑ 75 - Rain of Terror (1988)
❑ ❑ 76 - The Final Crusade (1989)
❑ ❑ 77 - Coin of the Realm (1989)
❑ ❑ 78 - Blue Smoke and Mirrors (1989)
❑ ❑ 79 - Shooting Schedule (1990)
❑ ❑ 80 - Death Sentence (1990)

■ MURRAY, Stephen

British author Stephen Murray is the creator of Detective Inspector Alec Stainton, first seen in *A Cool Killing* (1987) where a missing doctor's body turns up in the morgue refrigerator. Stainton is vacationing at a seaside village when the body of a murdered young woman is found in *Salty Waters* (1988). The headmaster of an upperclass school is found hanging from a meat hook in his apartment in *The Noose of Time* (1989) while a book researcher is gunned down at an abandoned airfield when he gets too close to a story about a group of South African pilots stationed in England during World War II. This series was first published in England by HarperCollins and later in the U.S. by St. Martin's Press. Born in London and educated at Cambridge University, the author is a chartered surveyor turned writer according to Hubin's *Crime Fiction II*.

Alec Stainton, Det. Insp.... British police inspector in England
❑ ❑ 1 - A Cool Killing (1987)
❑ ❑ 2 - Salty Waters (1988)
❑ ❑ 3 - The Noose of Time (1989)
❑ ❑ 4 - Fetch Out No Shroud (1990)
❑ ❑ 5 - Fatal Opinions (1991)

■ MURRAY, William

William Murray caught horse fever as a preppy Park Avenue teenager. Since then he has been an owner, bettor, winner, loser and consummate fan of the sport of kings. Author of more than 20 books, he is the creator of a mystery series featuring Shifty Lou Anderson, professional magician and horse player at the

Santa Anita Racetrack, last seen in *A Fine Italian Hand* (1996) where Shifty is attending the International Brotherhood of Magicians conference in Milan. Murray is also the author of *The Right Horse: Winning More, Losing Less, and Having a Great Time at the Racetrack* (1997), sequel to *The Wrong Horse: An Odyssey Through the American Racing Scene* (1992). *New Yorker* staff writer and author of that magazine's "Letters from Italy," Murray was educated at Phillips Exeter Academy and Harvard University. He divides his time between southern California and Rome.

Shifty Lou Anderson...professional magician and horseplayer in Southern California
- ❏ ❏ 1 - Tip on a Dead Crab (1984)
- ❏ ❏ 2 - The Hardknocker's Luck (1985)
- ❏ ❏ 3 - When the Fat Man Sings (1987)
- ❏ ❏ 4 - The King of the Nightcap (1989)
- ❏ ❏ 5 - The Getaway Blues (1990)
- ❏ ❏ 6 - I'm Getting Killed Right Here (1991)
- ❏ ❏ 7 - We're Off to See the Killer (1993)
- ❏ ❏ 8 - Now You See Her, Now You Don't (1994)
- ❏ ❏ 9 - A Fine Italian Hand (1996)

■ MYLES, Simon [P]

Simon Myles is an early pseudonym of British thriller writer Ken Follett who became one of the world's youngest millionaire authors when he wrote his first bestseller before the age of 30. The Edgar-award winning title, *Eye of the Needle* (1978), reportedly sold 10 million copies in its first 10 years in print. Worldwide sales of all his titles have since surpassed 40 million copies. His earliest fiction was published pseudonymously, with the first books under his own name not appearing until 1975. The first Follett titles featured industrial spy Piers Roper, the James Bond of the board room. By Follet's own estimation, the Roper novels mark a place "half way between bad and good" in his development as a writer. His earlier work, including two titles published as Simon Myles, he describes as "crudely sensational, full of sex, violence and conspicuous consumption, all more or less gratuitous."

"Apples" Carstairs...private eye in England
- ❏ ❏ 1 - The Big Needle (1974)
        U.S.-The Big Apple
- ❏ ❏ 2 - The Big Black (1974)

■ NATHAN, Paul

Edgar award winner Paul Nathan is a contributing editor for *Publishers Weekly*, where as *Rights* columnist he reports on which agents broker what kind of deals for how much money. These newsy columns often recap the rights history of a work getting new attention and disclose who's scheduled to star in, direct, or produce film or TV adaptations of print media. Nathan's own books include fiction, nonfiction and a collection of Russian plays which he translated. His mystery fiction features divorced dad Bert Swain, a public relations expert in the medical research field, anxious to return to New York in book 1, to be closer to his 11-year-old daughter Paula. Nathan's other writing includes his Edgar-award-winning off-Broadway play *Ricochet* (1980) and *Texas Collects* (1988), his chronicle of remarkable private collectors in Texas and their amazing art collections.

Bert Swain...PR chief at a medical research center in New York, New York
- ❏ ❏ 1 - Protocol for Murder (1994)
- ❏ ❏ 2 - No Good Deed (1995)
- ❏ ❏ 3 - Count Your Enemies (1997)

■ NAVA, Michael

Four-time Lambda award winner for best gay men's mystery is Michael Nava, creator of a 6-book series of lawyer-detective myseries starring Henry Rios. A gay Latino ex-alcoholic criminal defense attorney in his hometown of Los Robles (CA), Rios is introduced in *The Little Death* (1986). He describes himself as "a magnet for the desperate, frightened and reviled, who somehow or other had heard about the fag lawyer who was a sap for a sad story." An attorney himself, Nava lives in San Francisco (CA). With historian Robert Davidoff, he has written *Created Equal: Why Gay Rights Matter to America* (1995). He also edited a collection of mystery and suspense short stories (*Finale*, 1997) including his own story "*Street People*".

Henry Rios...gay Latino ex-alcoholic criminal defense attorney in Los Robles, California
- ❏ ❏ 1 - The Little Death (1986)
- ❏ ❏ 2 - **Goldenboy (1988) Lambda winner** ★
- ❏ ❏ 3 - **How Town (1990) Lambda winner** ★
- ❏ ❏ 4 - **The Hidden Law (1992) Lambda winner** ★
- ❏ ❏ 5 - **The Death of Friends (1996) Lambda winner** ★
- ❏ ❏ 6 - The Burning Plain (1998)

■ NEVINS, Francis M., Jr.

Two-time Edgar award winner Francis M. Nevins Jr. has written 5 books in two St. Louis (MO) mystery series. The earlier series features a law school professor like Nevins himself who teaches at St. Louis University. In book 3, the fictional professor is on sabbatical at NYU when he gets a phone call from an old girlfriend who vanished 23 years earlier. Now she needs his help. Nevins' second series features a con man P.I. first seen in *The 120-Hour Clock* (1986) which includes an appearance by Prof. Mensing. In addition to his Edgar-award-winning biographies of Ellery Queen (1974) and Cornell Woolrich (1988), Nevins is working on a biography of Anthony Boucher, which will include 5 years of monthly articles and weekly review columns (covering mystery, fantasy and science fiction) written for the *San Francisco Chronicle* between 1942 and 1947.

Loren Mensing...law school professor in St. Louis, Missouri
- ❏ ❏ 1 - Publish and Perish (1975)
- ❏ ❏ 2 - Corrupt and Ensnare (1978)
- ❏ ❏ 3 - Into the Same River Twice (1996)

Milo Turner...con man private eye in St. Louis, Missouri
- ❏ ❏ 1 - The 120-Hour Clock [incl Loren Mensing] (1986)
- ❏ ❏ 2 - The Ninety Million Dollar Mouse (1987)

■ NEWMAN, Christopher

Edgar-nominee Christopher Newman is the creator of NYPD homicide detective Lt. Joe Dante, a cop from Brooklyn with a half-finished doctoral dissertation. With equal aplomb Dante socializes with glitterati and arrests killers. After spending most of book 8 bleeding his way to Miami (FL) in pursuit of the shooter who wounded him in a drug-related revenge hit, Dante is back on the streets of New York in book 9. This time a billion-dollar stock deal is the motive for murder. When Diana Webster's brother Bill is run down on New Year's Eve, it sets off a chain of financial killings (literally). A San Francisco native, Newman has worked as a merchant seaman, carpenter and beach bum. He attended UC-Santa Cruz (CA) and Birmingham University in England. An avid rose gardener and accomplished cook, he lives in New York City.

Joe Dante...maverick cop in New York, New York
- ❏ ❏ 1 - Midtown South (1986)
- ❏ ❏ 2 - The Sixth Precinct (1987)
- ❏ ❏ 3 - Knock-Off (1989)

❏ ❏   4 - **Midtown North (1991) Edgar nominee** ☆
❏ ❏   5 - Nineteenth Precinct (1992)
❏ ❏   6 - Precinct Command (1993)
❏ ❏   7 - Dead End Game (1994)
❏ ❏   8 - Killer (1997)
❏ ❏   9 - Hit and Run (1997)

■ NEWMAN, G. F.

English author Gordon F. Newman has written several stage, screen and television plays, in addition to more than 20 books, including 3 mysteries featuring a bent cop, Inspector Terry Sneed, introduced in *Sir, You Bastard* (1970). When this series opener was published in the U.S. in 1973 as *Rogue Cop* it was nominated for an Edgar award for best first novel. According to Donald C. Wall (*St. James Guide*, 4th edition), much of the suspense in this series comes from watching the power-hungry Sneed, who is actually an excellent detective, trying to extricate himself from one difficult situation after another. When last seen in *The Price* (1974), Sneed is up against a mob-connected American accountant who has grown tired of making hush payments to the British inspector. Newman lives in Hereford, England.

Terry Sneed, Insp.....bent police inspector in England
❏ ❏   1 - **Sir, You Bastard (1970) Edgar nominee** ☆
      APA-Rogue Cop
❏ ❏   2 - You Nice Bastard (1972)
❏ ❏   3 - The Price (1974)

■ NEWTON, Michael

Michael Newton has written more than 140 books during the past 20 years, mostly action-adventure and true crime. His series work includes 2 books with an LAPD homicide detective and 9 with a pair of FBI agents assigned to the Violent Criminal Apprehension Program (VICAP). His 70 books for the Executioner series include some of his earliest which were ghost-written for Don Pendleton. As Paul Malone he has written 3 novels featuring a DEA agent. For Writer's Digest Books he has written *Armed and Dangerous: A Writer's Guide to Weapons* (1990) and *How To Write Action Adventure Novels* (1989). During his school-teaching days in Las Vegas, he once spent a summer working as an armed guard at the home of Merle Haggard. The first time he drew his gun was on Merle—he didn't recognize him. A native of Bakersfield (CA), he currently lives in Nashville (IN).

Jonathan Steele...LAPD homicide detective in Los Angeles, California
❏ ❏   1 - The Ripper [as by Mike Newton] (1978)
❏ ❏   2 - The Satan Ring [as by Mike Newton] (1978)

Joseph Flynn & Martin Tanner...FBI agents with VICAP in Los Angeles, California
❏ ❏   1 - Blood Sport (1990)
❏ ❏   2 - Slay Ride (1990)
❏ ❏   3 - The Necro File (1991)
❏ ❏   4 - Head Games (1991)
❏ ❏   5 - Road Kills (1991)
❏ ❏   6 - Black Lace (1991)
❏ ❏   7 - Wet Work (1992)
❏ ❏   8 - Jigsaw (1992)
❏ ❏   9 - Dead Heat (1992)

■ NIGHBERT, David F.

David F. Nighbert is the creator of a 3-book series featuring ex-big league pitcher Bull Cochran, introduced in *Strikezone* (1988) which *Kirkus Reviews* called "Superior stuff...a sassy-mouthed, hard-boiled story of mayhem and revenge." When last seen in *Shutout* (1995) Bull was visting the old-money Knoxville (TN) home of his girlfriend Molly, where blackmail, shooting and nervous breakdowns were all part of the lineup. In addition to his mysteries, Nighbert has written a pair of science fiction titles featuring reformed cyborg assassin, Anton Stryker, and his mad scientist assistant, Albert. With "inventiveness, exuberance and wit" (*Kirkus*), they make their debut in *Timelapse* (1988) and return in *The Clouds of Magellan* (1991). After growing up in Tennessee, Nighbert now lives in New York City.

Bull Cochran...ex-big league pitcher in Knoxville, Tennessee
- ❏ ❏ 1 - Strikezone (1988)
- ❏ ❏ 2 - Squeezeplay (1992)
- ❏ ❏ 3 - Shutout (1995)

■ NOGUCHI, Thomas T. with Arthur Lyons

Former Los Angeles County (CA) Medical Examiner Thomas T. Noguchi has co-written a pair of forensic pathology mysteries with Arthur Lyons, author of his own Jacob Asch mysteries. Noguchi's fictional alter ego Dr. Eric Parker appears in *Physical Evidence* (1980) and *Unnatural Causes* (1988). The Japanese-born M.D. arrived in the U.S. at the age of 25 and gained notoriety 10 years later when he performed the 1962 autopsy on Marilyn Monroe. When LA County opened its first Forensic Science Center in 1972, Noguchi was among the first big-city medical examiners to assemble a staff of specially-trained crime scene experts. But by the time another 10 years had passed, Noguchi was the victim of Proposition 13 funding shortages and was forced to quite his office in 1982. He is currently teaching and writing.

Eric Parker, Dr.....forensic pathologist in Los Angeles, California
- ❏ ❏ 1 - Physical Evidence (1980)
- ❏ ❏ 2 - Unnatural Causes (1988)

■ NOLAN, William F.

William F. Nolan has written everything from suspense, horror and science fiction to poetry, biographies and essays. In addition to his international best-seller *Logan's Run* (MGM movie and CBS-TV series), he is the author of more than 60 books, 40 film or TV scripts and 700 articles, essays and reviews. At least 135 of his short stories have appeared in more than 250 anthologies, many of which he edited himself, including the *Bradbury Chronicles* (1991). With *The Black Mask Murders* (1994) he launches a series featuring America's best known private eye novelists—Dashiell Hammett, Raymond Chandler and Erle Stanley Gardner—who alternately narrate stories of murder and intrigue in 1930s Hollywood. The Boys make a return appearance in *The Marble Orchard* (1996). Born in Kansas City (MO), Nolan lives in the San Fernando Valley (CA) with his wife, writer Cameron Nolan, four cats and 10,000 books.

Bart Challis...hard-boiled private eye in Los Angeles, California
- ❏ ❏ 1 - Death is for Losers (1968)
- o o 2 - The White Cad Cross-Up (1969)

Black Mask Boys...1930s detective heroes in California
- ❏ ❏ 1 - The Black Mask Murders (1994)
- ❏ ❏ 2 - The Marble Orchard (1996)

Sam Space...private eye on Mars
- ❏ ❏ 1 - **Space for Hire (1971) Edgar nominee** ☆
- ❏ ❏ 2 - Look Out for Space (1985)

■ **NORDAN, Robert**

Robert Nordan has written 3 books featuring a Southern little old lady sleuth named Mavis Lashley, introduced in *All Dressed Up To Die* (1989). A reissue edition of book 2, *Death Beneath the Christmas Tree* (1991) is still in print for holiday mystery mavens. Mavis the Sunday School teacher saves the Season when she uncovers corruption and scandalous behaviour among some of the church's most highly-esteemed members. According to *Death on Wheels* (1993), Nordan was born in Raleigh (NC) and attended Duke University before completing his graduate studies at the University of Chicago. Having once written advertising copy in New York City, he now works as a clinical child psychologist at a Chicago hospital. He is also author of the nonseries novel *Rituals* (1989).

Mavis Lashley...little old lady Sunday School teacher in the Southern U.S.
- ❑ ❑ 1 - All Dressed Up to Die (1989)
- ❑ ❑ 2 - Death Beneath the Christmas Tree (1991)
- ❑ ❑ 3 - Death on Wheels (1993)

■ **NORTH, Gil [P]**

Gil North is the pseudonym used by Geoffrey Horne for an 11-book series featuring Sgt. Caleb Cluff of Yorkshire, introduced in 1960. North also produced 20 episodes for the TV series *Cluff*. Although more than one American reviewer found the Yorkshire dialect tough-going, others likened Cluff to a Yorkshire Maigret. The author's fondness for the letter "C" extended to Cluff's housekeeper Annie Croft and his constant canine companion Clive. Along with B.A. and M.A. degrees from Christ's College, Cambridge, the Yorkshire-born author earned a diploma in social anthropology. From the late '30s to the mid '50s he was a Colonial Service officer in what was then South-East Nigeria and Cameroons. His nonseries novel set in Africa features Supt. Katt in *A Corpse for Kofi Katt* (1978) where Katt's seaport jurisdiction is under attack by drug traders.

Caleb Cluff....Gunnarshaw police sergeant in Yorkshire, England
- ❑ ❑ 1 - Sergeant Cluff Stands Firm (1960)
- ❑ ❑ 2 - The Methods of Sergeant Cluff (1961)
- ❑ ❑ 3 - Sergeant Cluff Goes Fishing (1962)
- ❑ ❑ 4 - More Deaths for Sergeant Cluff (1963)
- ❑ ❑ 5 - Sergeant Cluff and the Madmen (1964)
- ❑ ❑ 6 - Sergeant Cluff and the Price of Pity (1965)
- ❑ ❑ 7 - The Confounding of Sergeant Cluff (1966)
- ❑ ❑ 8 - Sergeant Cluff and the Day of Reckoning (1967)
- ❑ ❑ 9 - The Procrastination of Sergeant Cluff (1969)
- ❑ ❑ 10 - No Choice for Sergeant Cluff (1971)
- ❑ ❑ 11 - Sergeant Cluff Rings True (1972)

■ **O'CONNELL, Jack**

When Jack O'Connell won the first Mysterious Discovery Contest, his Quinsigamond series opener, *Box Nine* (1992), was guaranteed publication by Mysterious Press. The book introduced an unusual cast of small-town New England characters, definitely not your Norman Rockwell America. In book 1, a woman police lieutenant working undercover faces her own addiction when a new psychedelic drug called Lingo hits the street. Another woman detective from Quinsigamond goes up against evil in book 2. This time a demented former FBI agent named Speer is responsible for the death of an activist priest who dies inside his own church. The third novel finds a young Mafia-connected filmmaker and an inquisitive photographer named Sylvia drawn into a world of porno houses, dwarfs and television evangelism.

Quinsigamond...decaying New England factory town in Massachuttes
- ❑ ❑ 1 - Box Nine (1992)
- ❑ ❑ 2 - Wireless (1993)
- ❑ ❑ 3 - Skin Palace (1995)

■ O'DONNELL, Peter

Peter O'Donnell is the creator of Modesty Blaise, who's been fighting crime with her knife-throwing sidekick Willie Garvin for 35 years in comics, movies, books and short stories. O'Donnell created the strip characters in 1962, wrote the screenplay for the original movie, and then launched the book series in 1965. Plenty of flashbacks are provided to explain everything from Modesty's orphaned past in refugee camps to how she got her amazing skills. "For colorful writing and nonstop action, the books about Modesty Blaise are hard to beat," according to Bill Crider (*1001 Midnights*), who recommends the short stories as a good starting point. Other O'Donnell cartoon series include *Garth* ('53-'66), *Tug Transom* ('54-'66) and *Romeo Brown* ('56-'62). Under the name Madeline Brent, he also wrote 9 non-crime novels. The London-born author lives in Brighton (England).

Modesty Blaise...gorgeous crime fighter for British Intelligence in London, England
- ❑ ❑ 1 - Modesty Blaise (1965)
- ❑ ❑ 2 - Sabre-Tooth (1966)
- ❑ ❑ 3 - I, Lucifer (1967)
- ❑ ❑ 4 - A Taste for Death (1969)
- ❑ ❑ 5 - The Impossible Virgin (1971)
- ❑ ❑ ss - Pieces of Modesty [short stories] (1972)
- ❑ ❑ 6 - The Silver Mistress (1973)
- ❑ ❑ 7 - Last Day in Limbo (1976)
- ❑ ❑ 8 - Dragon's Claw (1978)
- ❑ ❑ 9 - The Xanadu Talisman (1981)
- ❑ ❑ 10 - The Night of Morningstar (1982)
- ❑ ❑ 11 - Dead Man's Handle (1985)
- ❑ ❑ nn - Cobra Trap [5 novellas] (1996)

■ OLIVER, Steve

Steve Oliver is the creator of Scott Moody, a cab-driving ex-mental patient from Spokane (WA) who wants to be a private investigator. In *Moody Gets the Blues* (1996) he's hired by an ex-college girlfriend whose husband is missing. Set in the late '70s, this series opener shows Scott has a sense of humor about his condition and considerable knowledge about clinical depression. The unusual P.I. and single father is scheduled to make a return appearance in *Moody Becomes Eternal* (1997). Also from Scott Oliver is *Clueless in Seattle* (1995), an outrageous presentation of all sorts of personalties we've known (and been) in male-female relationships. An online reviewer called Oliver "a truly twisted technogeek with a sense of humor," suggesting that *Clueless* is a comic antidote to the ultrasweetness of Tom Hanks' 1993 movie *Sleepless in Seattle*.

Scott Moody...ex-mental patient turned P.I. in Spokane, Washington
- ❑ ❑ 1 - Moody Gets the Blues (1996)
- ❑ ❑ 2 - Moody Becomes Eternal (1997)

■ ORENSTEIN, Frank

Former Madison Avenue advertising executive Frank Orenstein says he always wanted to write but didn't get serious until it became too treacherous getting in and out of his steep driveway with his rear-wheel-drive car. He also claims he took early retirement to fulfill a lifelong dream of writing mysteries so he could eliminate a schoolmate who had beat him up and called him waffle ears when he was 8 and she was 10. His first series character was advertising executive Ev Franklin, introduced in *Murder on Madison Avenue* (1983). Ev appeared the following year in *The Man in the Gray Flannel Shroud* (1984) which introduced Orenstein's second detective, small town New York cop Hugh Morrison. Both Ev and Hugh appeared in two more titles each, for a total of 6 mysteries. Orenstein lives in New York State.

Ev Franklin...advertising executive in New York, New York
- ❏ ❏ 1 - Murder on Madison Avenue (1983)
- ❏ ❏ 2 - A Candidate for Murder (1987)
- ❏ ❏ 3 - Paradise of Death (1988)

Hugh Morrison...small-town cop in New York
- ❏ ❏ 1 - The Man in the Gray Flannel Shroud [incl Ev Franklin] (1984)
- ❏ ❏ 2 - A Killing in Real Estate (1988)
- ❏ ❏ 3 - A Vintage Year for Dying (1992)

■ **ORMEROD, Roger**

Roger Ormerod has written at least 40 books, including more than 25 in his two long-running crime series. Starting with *Time to Kill* (1974), introducing private investigator David Mallin, Ormerod produced 15 books with an easy-going first-person narrative. He later introduced Inspector Richard Patton, who was three days short of retirement in the series opener. Retitled *The Hanging Doll Murder* when it was published in the U.S., book 1 has the out-of-favor Insp. Patton falling in love with the wife of a missing man. Before starting his fiction-writing career, Ormerod spent 35 years as a court officer and Social Security executive, providing lots of authentic background for his crime novels. This one-time postman, who also worked as a shop loader in an engineering factory, lives in Staffordshire (England).

David Mallin...private eye in England
- ❏ ❏ 1 - Time to Kill (1974)
- ❏ ❏ 2 - The Silence of the Night (1974)
- ❏ ❏ 3 - Full Fury (1975)
- ❏ ❏ 4 - A Spoonful of Luger (1975)
- ❏ ❏ 5 - Sealed with a Loving Kill (1976)
- ❏ ❏ 6 - The Colour of Fear (1976)
- ❏ ❏ 7 - A Glimpse of Death (1976)
- ❏ ❏ 8 - Too Late for the Funeral (1977)
- ❏ ❏ 9 - A Dip into Murder (1978)
- ❏ ❏ 10 - The Weight of Evidence (1978)
- ❏ ❏ 11 - The Bright Face of Danger (1979)
- ❏ ❏ 12 - The Amnesia Trap (1979)
- ❏ ❏ 13 - Cart Before the Hearse (1979)
- ❏ ❏ 14 - More Dead Than Alive (1980)
- ❏ ❏ 15 - One Breathless Hour (1981)

Richard Patton, Insp....British police inspector in England
- ❏ ❏ 1 - Face Value (1983) U.S.-The Hanging Doll Murder
- ❏ ❏ 2 - Still Life with Pistol (1986)
- ❏ ❏ 3 - An Alibi Too Soon (1987)
- ❏ ❏ 4 - An Open Window (1988)
- ❏ ❏ 5 - Guilt on the Lily (1989)
- ❏ ❏ 6 - Death of an Innocent (1989)
- ❏ ❏ 7 - No Sign of Life (1990)
- ❏ ❏ 8 - When the Old Man Died (1991)
- ❏ ❏ 9 - Shame the Devil (1993)
- ❏ ❏ 10 - Mask of Innocence (1994)
- ❏ ❏ 11 - Stone Cold Dead (1995)

■ **ORVIS, Kenneth [P]**

Kenneth Orvis is the pseudonym used by Canadian author Kenneth Lemieux, a former professional hockey player turned newspaper writer. His faux James Bond character first appears in *Night Without Darkness* (1965), where an American scientist who knows the secret formula for a deadly paralysis mist is kidnapped by Communists. The action takes place in Bulgaria. The handsome Adam Breck, often mistaken for a professional tennis player, is out to save the world again in *The Doomsday List* (1974). Nonseries titles from this author include *The Damned and the Destroyed* (1962), *Cry Hallelujah!* (1970), *Into a Dark Mirror* (1971) set in France, and *The Disinherited* (1974) set in New York City.

Adam Breck...faux James Bond in London, England
- ❑ ❑ 1 - Night Without Darkness (1965)
- ❑ ❑ 2 - The Doomsday List (1974)

■ **OSBORN, David**

David D. Osborn has written 3 books featuring Margaret Barlow, a 50-something freelance journalist, introduced in *Murder on Martha's Vineyard* (1989). Margaret makes return appearances in *Murder on the Chesapeake* (1992) and *Murder in Napa Valley* (1993). Along with his screenwriter wife Elisabeth Charles-Williams, he adapted his nonseries novel *Open Season* (1974) for Columbia Pictures. His other screen credits include *Follow the Boys* (1963) for MGM, *Deadlier Than the Male* (1967) and *Chase a Crooked Shadow*. A former U.S. Marine test pilot, Osborn attended Columbia University and previously worked as a television camera operator and director, and a public relations representative. He lives in Maryland.

Margaret Barlow...50-something freelance journalist in the United States
- ❑ ❑ 1 - Murder on Martha's Vineyard (1989)
- ❑ ❑ 2 - Murder on the Chesapeake (1992)
- ❑ ❑ 3 - Murder in the Napa Valley (1993)

■ **OSTER, Jerry**

Jerry Oster has written more than a dozen novels, including 7 books in a pair of New York police series. Although his books have been published only in Germany since 1992, he expects book 3 in the Cullen series and a new cop novel featuring two women officers to be available on the Worldwide Web. A former reporter for United Press International, Reuters and the *New York Daily News*, Oster is currently a development writer at the Kenan-Flagler Business School at the University of North Carolina at Chapel Hill. Every day he writes fiction for 30 minutes or one page, whichever comes first, standing at his kitchen counter sipping coffee and typing on his laptop from 5:15 to 5:45 AM. Born in New Mexico, he grew up in New York and earned a B.A. in English literature from Columbia University.

Jacob "Jake" Neuman...police lieutenant in New York, New York
- ❑ ❑ 1 - Sweet Justice (1985)
- ❑ ❑ 2 - Nowhere Man (1987)
- ❑ ❑ 3 - Club Dead (1988)

Joe Cullen...Internal Affairs police sergeant in New York, New York
- ❑ ❑ 1 - Internal Affairs (1990)
- ❑ ❑ 2 - Violent Love (1991)
- ❑ ❑ 3 - Fixin' to Die (1992)
- ❑ ❑ 4 - When the Night Comes (1993)

■ **OWENS, Louis**

Louis Owens shares Chocktaw, Cherokee and Irish bloodlines with his protagonist, Cole McCurtain. And like McCurtain, Owens is a college professor. While the author teaches English at the University of New Mexico, the fictional professor teaches Indian Studies at the University of California at Santa Cruz. In a review of book 3 of this series from the University of Oklahoma Press, *Publishers Weekly* noted that "Owens expertly mixes genres and blends in generous amounts of Native American history. To his credit, he also leavens his grim but gripping tale with substantial humor." Owens has also written *Other Destinies: Understanding the American Indian Novel* (1994) and *The Grapes of Wrath: Trouble in the Promised Land* (1989). With Tom Colonnese he wrote *American Indian Novelists: An Annotated Critical Bibliography* (1985).

Cole McCurtain...Choctaw-Cherokee-Irish-Cajun college professor in Santa Cruz, California
- ❑ ❑ 1 - Wolfsong (1991)
- ❑ ❑ 2 - The Sharpest Sight (1992)
- ❑ ❑ 3 - Bone Game (1994)
- ❑ ❑ 4 - Nightland (1996)

■ **PAGE, Jake**

Jake Page has written 5 mysteries featuring blind wildlife sculptor Mo Bowdre, great nephew of Charles Bowdre, one of Billy The Kid's cronies in the Lincoln County War. Mo and his half-Hopi, half-Anglo girlfriend Connie are involved with everything from stolen sacred artifacts (inspired by a real situation) to research scientists dying in the desert, and the predatory art scene of modern Santa Fe. In addition to his work as an editor at *Natural History* and *Smithsonian* magazines, and columnist for *Science* magazine ("Jake's Page"), he has written more than 20 nonfiction books on wildlife, environmental issues, and Indian lore. His latest fiction includes two novels of alternative history, *Operation: Shatterhand* (1996) and *Apacheria* (1998). Born in Boston and raised in New York and New England, Page has worked as a ranchhand, and miner at the Climax Molybdenum mine (CO). He lives in New Mexico.

T. Moore "Mo" Bowdre...blind redneck sculptor in Santa Fe, NM
- ❑ ❑ 1 - The Stolen Gods (1993)
- ❑ ❑ 2 - The Deadly Canyon (1994)
- ❑ ❑ 3 - The Knotted Strings (1995)
- ❑ ❑ 4 - The Lethal Partner (1996)
- ❑ ❑ 5 - A Certain Malice (1998)

■ **PAIRO, Preston, III**

Preston Pairo III (pronounced PARE-oh) writes two Maryland mystery series—one featuring a sometime lawyer and motel owner in Ocean City; the other an ex-cop turned investigator for the Baltimore City Attorney's office. The surf and sun-loving Dallas Henry is ably assisted by Herbie the dropout genius and Susan the brainy lawyer. In series 2, the stylish, handsome 6'1" Jimmy Griffin is on the trail of a serial killer he thought he'd put away while still on the force. A practicing criminal defense attorney in Howard County (MD) and a lifelong Maryland resident, Pairo is the 10th consecutive lawyer in his family. A graduate of the University of Baltimore School of Law, he has written and sold over 200 short stories under various pen names. His nonseries mysteries include *Breach of Trust* (1995), *Midnight Razz* (1991), *Haitian Red* (1989), *Razor Moon* (1988) and *Winner's Cut* (1986).

Dallas Henry...sometime-lawyer and motel owner in Ocean City, Maryland
- ❑ ❑ 1 - Beach Money (1991)
- ❑ ❑ 2 - One Dead Judge (1993)

Jimmy "Griff" Griffin...ex-cop investigator for the city attorney in Baltimore, Maryland
- ❑ ❑ 1 - Bright Eyes (1996)
- ❑ ❑ 2 - The Angel's Crime (1998)

■ PALMER, Frank

Former reporter Frank Palmer is the author of a hard-boiled police series featuring "Jacko" Jackson, a detective inspector of the East Midlands Combined Constabulary centered in Leicester. When it was first published in the U.S., *Publishers Weekly* gave the series opener a starred review, praising its "taut suspense, solid characterization, [and] vivid sense of place." Fans of New York police stories will enjoy book 3, which starts in the Lincolnshire hamlet of New York, but ends up in Manhattan. When "Jacko" comes up against the beautiful secret lover of an accused hitman, he learns new respect for the word "temptation." A Fleet Street reporter for 25 years, Palmer was a member of the *Daily Mirror* news team that won the British Press Award for Reporter of the Year in 1978. Born in Lincoln, he lives near Nottingham (England).

"Jacko" Jackson...detective inspector in Leicester, England
- ❏ ❏ 1 - Testimony (1992)
- ❏ ❏ 2 - Unfit to Plead (1992)
- ❏ ❏ 3 - Bent Grasses (1993)
- ❏ ❏ 4 - Blood Brother (1993)
- ❏ ❏ 5 - Night Watch (1994)
- ❏ ❏ 6 - China Hand (1994)
- ❏ ❏ 7 - Double Exposure (1995)
- ❏ ❏ 8 - Dead Man's Handle (1995)

■ PALMER, William J.

William J. Palmer says his mystery series is based on newly-discovered secret journals of Wilkie Collins, bequeathed to the University of North Anglia by a great-grandson of Collins' life-long solicitor. As Charles Dickens' protege and closest friend, Collins played an active role in the murder cases of Dickens' friend, Insp. William Field of the Metropolitan Protectives. In book 3, one of the richest, most-powerful women in England (another friend of Dickens) is in trouble. Her family's bank is robbed, a member of the Women's Emancipation Society is dead, and a young actress with whom Dickens has fallen in love is suspect. The author shares his name with England's most notorious poisoner, Dr. William Palmer, hanged for his crimes in 1856. The doctor's effigy stands in the Hall of Murderers in Madame Tussaud's Wax Museum. The living Dr. Palmer teaches English at Purdue University (IN).

Wilkie Collins & Charles Dickens...19th century literary celebrities in London, England
- ❏ ❏ 1 - The Detective and Mr. Dickens (1990)
- ❏ ❏ 2 - The Highwayman and Mr. Dickens (1992)
- ❏ ❏ 3 - The Hoydens and Mr. Dickens (1997)

■ PARKER, Robert B.

Edgar-award winner and 4-time Shamus nominee Robert B. Parker is the creator of Spenser, the Boston private eye immortalized for American television by Robert Urich. Spenser's 25th appearance in print will mark the series' 25th anniversary with *Sudden Mischief* (1998). No doubt Spenser will be joined by his long-suffering girlfriend Susan and his enforcer Hawk. Parker wrote his doctoral dissertation on Hammett, Chandler and Macdonald and was later selected by the Chandler estate to complete the unfinished *Poodle Springs* (1989). He then wrote a sequel to Chandler's *The Big Sleep*, titled *Perchance to Dream* (1991). A new Parker series features an alcoholic LA homicide cop turned small town police chief in *Night Passage* (1997), which comes with a third person point of view, a bully sidekick, an ex-wife, a new girlfriend and a local conspiracy fueled by the whitepower militia.

Philip Marlowe...private eye in Los Angeles, California
- ❏ ❏ 1 - Poodle Springs [with Chandler] (1989)
- ❏ ❏ 2 - Perchance to Dream (1991)

Spenser...ex-boxer, ex-state cop turned P.I. in Boston, Massachusetts
- ❑ ❑ 1 - The Godwulf Manuscript (1973)
- ❑ ❑ 2 - God Save the Child (1974)
- ❑ ❑ 3 - Mortal Stakes (1975)
- ❑ ❑ 4 - **Promised Land (1976) Edgar winner ★**
- ❑ ❑ 5 - The Judas Goat (1978)
- ❑ ❑ 6 - Looking for Rachel Wallace (1980)
- ❑ ❑ 7 - **Early Autumn (1981) Shamus nominee ☆**
- ❑ ❑ 8 - A Savage Place (1981)
- ❑ ❑ 9 - **Ceremony (1982) Shamus nominee ☆**
- ❑ ❑ 10 - **The Widening Gyre (1983) Shamus nominee ☆**
- ❑ ❑ 11 - Valediction (1984)
- ❑ ❑ 12 - **A Catskill Eagle (1985) Shamus nominee ☆**
- ❑ ❑ 13 - Taming a Sea-Horse (1986)
- ❑ ❑ 14 - Pale Kings and Princes (1987)
- ❑ ❑ 15 - Crimson Joy (1988)
- ❑ ❑ 16 - Playmates (1989)
- ❑ ❑ 17 - Stardust (1990)
- ❑ ❑ 18 - Pastime (1991)
- ❑ ❑ 19 - Double Deuce (1992)
- ❑ ❑ 20 - Paper Doll (1993)
- ❑ ❑ 21 - Walking Shadow (1994)
- ❑ ❑ 22 - Thin Air (1995)
- ❑ ❑ 23 - Chance (1996)
- ❑ ❑ 24 - Small Vices (1997)

■ PARRISH, Frank [P]

Frank Parrish is one of the pseudonyms of Roger Erskine Longrigg who writes horror as Domini Taylor, general fiction as Longrigg and mysteries as Ivor Drummond and Frank Parrish. The Edgar-nominated series written under the Parrish name features a poacher and petty thief who lives with his arthritic mother outside the village of Medwell Fratorum. When she needs a hip replacement in *Fly in the Cobweb* (1986), he decides to steal the silver from Medwell Court. According to George Kelley writing in *St. James Guide* (4th edition), the chase scenes in book 6 are the best in the series. Author of more than 40 books, Longrigg has a degree in modern history from Oxford. During the '70s he also published 4 nonfiction books on the history of horse racing, foxhunting and the sport of English squires.

Dan Mallett...ex-London bank clerk turned handyman-poacher in Medwell Frtrm, England
- ❑ ❑ 1 - **A Fire in the Barley (1977) Edgar nominee ☆**
- ❑ ❑ 2 - Sting of the Honeybee (1978)
- ❑ ❑ 3 - Snare in the Dark (1982)
- ❑ ❑ 4 - Bait on the Hook (1983)
- ❑ ❑ 5 - Face at the Window (1984)
  U.S.-Death in the Rain
- ❑ ❑ 6 - Fly in the Cobweb (1986)
- ❑ ❑ 7 - Caught in the Birdlime (1987)
  U.S.-Bird in the Net
- ❑ ❑ 8 - Voices from the Dark (1993)

■ PARRISH, Richard

Brooklyn-born Richard Parrish, who has been both a prosecutor and a defense attorney, is the author of the Joshua Rabb courtroom mysteries featuring a 1940s attorney. Last seen in *Wind and Lies* (1996), a long-time friend of Rabb's is accused of murder. In this 1947 case, Rabb and his colleague/client get in the way of a fundamentalist Mormon splinter group trying to convert the local Papago Indians. Rabb's first contemporary legal thriller is *Abandoned Heart* (1996). Parrish spent 2 years as acting Jewish chaplain at the U.S. Military Chapel in the Palace of Justice at Nuremberg (Germany) and a year as articled law clerk in the Israeli Attorney General's Office in Jerusalem. He is currently in private practice in Tucson (AZ) where he founded and became the first director of the Economic Crime/Organized Crime unit of the Pima County Attorney's Office in 1977.

Joshua Rabb...1940s attorney in Tucson, Arizona
- ❑ ❑ 1 - The Dividing Line (1993)
- ❑ ❑ 2 - Versions of the Truth (1994)
- ❑ ❑ 3 - Nothing But the Truth (1995)
- ❑ ❑ 4 - Wind and Lies (1996)

■ PATTERSON, James

Edgar-award winner and best-selling author James Patterson is the creator of black psychiatrist and homicide cop Alex Cross, introduced in *Along Came a Spider* (1993). The Washington DC detective made his big screen debut in 1997 with Morgan Freeman and Ashley Judd starring in *Kiss the Girls* (book 2). Although many assume the author is black like Cross, this is not the case. Former New York creative director for J. Walter Thompson, Patterson is currently Chairman of JWT North America, one of the world's premier advertising agencies. Author of 9 novels, including his best-first-novel Edgar winner, *The Thomas Berryman Number* (1977), he has also written a non-fiction bestseller with Peter Kim, *The Day America Told the Truth: What People Really Believe About Everything That Matters* (1991).

Alex Cross...black psychiatrist and homicide cop in Washington, D.C.
- ❑ ❑ 1 - Along Came a Spider (1993)
- ❑ ❑ 2 - Kiss the Girls (1995)
- ❑ ❑ 3 - Jack and Jill (1996)
- ❑ ❑ 4 - Cat and Mouse (1997)

■ PATTERSON, Richard North

Edgar-award winner and former Watergate prosecutor Richard North Patterson has written 8 novels, including 3 featuring Christopher Kenyon Paget, a lawyer in the Special Investigations Section of the Washington Economic Crimes Commission. Paget debuts in *The Lasko Tangent* (1979), which earned Patterson a best-first-novel Edgar award. His most recent fiction is *Silent Witness* (1997). A practicing attorney until 1993, Patterson says his next novel will be about abortion politics in a presidential campaign, with the all the action taking place during 7 days in California. Born in Berkeley (CA), Patterson earned degrees at Ohio Wesleyan and Case Western Reserve universities, and later spent 15 years with the Securities and Exchange Commission office in San Francisco.

Christopher Paget...economic crimes special investigator in Washington, D.C.
- ❑ ❑ 1 - **The Lasko Tangent (1979) Edgar winner ★**
- ❑ ❑ 2 - Degree of Guilt (1992)
- ❑ ❑ 3 - Eyes of a Child (1994)

■ **PAUL, William**

William Paul is the author of a police series featuring Det. Chief Insp. David Fyfe of Edinburgh, Scotland. Introduced in *Sleeping Dogs* (1994), the DCI takes a case of petty theft as a favor to his chief constable, only to discover it may be linked to an old drug case. In book 2 he's faced with an unusual murder-suicide in the local village. But Fyfe's big weakness is women. He just can't seem to stay away from them. In book 3 he's living with his ex-wife but strongly attracted to a woman he met at a party when he receives an intriguing message from an old flame. *Booklist* called Fyfe an "oddly engaging antihero." An Edinburgh journalist, Paul is also the author of *Dance of Death* (1992), which has Mikhail Gorbachev attending a performance of the Bolshoi Ballet during the 50th Anniversary of the International Edinburg Festival. There's a killer masquerading as one of his protectors.

David Fyfe, D.C.I.....detective chief inspector in Edinburgh, Scotland
- ❏ ❏ 1 - Sleeping Dogs (1994)
- ❏ ❏ 2 - Sleeping Pretty (1995)
- ❏ ❏ 3 - Sleeping Partner (1996)

■ **PAWSON, Stuart**

Stuart Pawson is the creator of Detective Inspector Charlie Priest, an art school graduate turned Yorkshire detective. First seen in *The Picasso Scam* (1995), Charlie has gone from being the youngest-ever inspector to the longest-serving inspector, thanks to his unorthodox methods. But he's so compulsive about solving crime that he's built up 6 months' unused leave. His fifth case is *Deadly Friends* (1998). After working 32 years as an electrician in the coalmining industry, Pawson started volunteering with the probation service, where he acted as a mediator between offenders and their victims. Two books into his writing career, Pawson discovered he felt a conflict of interest coming home to write about crime after talking with victims all day. He resigned from the probation service with regret and now writes full time.

Charlie Priest, Det. Insp.....art school graduate turned police detective in Yorkshire, England
- ❏ ❏ 1 - The Picasso Scam (1995)
- ❏ ❏ 2 - The Mushroom Man (1995)
- ❏ ❏ 3 - The Judas Sheep (1996)
- ❏ ❏ 4 - Last Reminder (1997)

■ **PAYNE, Laurence**

Laurence Payne is a London-born actor and drama teacher who wrote his first cop novel after playing one too many "clever-dick" private eyes. He says he was tired of seeing the police in films "pipped at the post." His first novel, featuring Chief Insp. Sam Birkett (*The Nose on My Face*, 1962), was adapted for film as *Girl in the Headlines* and re-released as *The Model Murder Case*. After appearing in at least 28 Shakespearean plays as a member of the Stratford-upon-Avon and Old Vic companies, he later worked mostly in television and movies. His burning desire is to write a book about Beethoven (the man, not the musician) and he cites Beethoven and Shakespeare as his two gods. After 2 novels with a petty thief turned reluctant spy-hero, Payne wrote 5 books featuring an actor turned private eye. His hobbies are portrait painting, opera and riding.

John Tibbett...petty thief turned reluctant hero in London, England
- ❏ ❏ 1 - Spy For Sale (1969)
- ❏ ❏ 2 - Even My Foot's Asleep (1971)

Mark Savage...movie star turned private eye in the United States
- ❏ ❏ 1 - Take the Money and Run (1982)
- ❏ ❏ 2 - Malice in Camera (1983)
- ❏ ❏ 3 - Vienna Blood (1984)
- ❏ ❏ 4 - Dead for a Ducat [incl Birkett] (1986)
- ❏ ❏ 5 - Late Knight (1987) U.S.-Knight Fall

Sam Birkett, Chief Insp.....humorous Scotland Yard inspector in London, England
- ❑ ❑ 1 - The Nose on My Face (1962) APA-The First Body
- ❑ ❑ 2 - Too Small for His Shoes (1962)
- ❑ ❑ 3 - Deep and Crisp and Even (1964)

■ PEARCE, Michael

Last Laugh Award winner Michael Pearce is the creator of the Mamur Zapt (Capt. Garth Owen), British head of Cairo's Political CID. The series opens in 1908 as the long period of indirect British rule is coming to an end. Terrorist threats are mounting in preparation for Cairo's main religious festival, the Return of the Holy Carpet from Mecca. Think your favorite cop has political headaches? The Mamur Zapt has to deal with 3 primary languages and 4 competing legal systems in a city of multiple nationalities. Pearce grew up in what was then Anglo-Egyptian Sudan. He returned there later to teach, after which he followed what he describes as the standard academic rake's progress from teaching and writing to editing and administration. His new historical series, set in Tsarist Russia, opens with *Dmitri and the Milk Drinkers* (1997), featuring a young Scottish Russian magistrate.

Garth Owen, Capt.....British head of the secret police in Cairo, Egypt
- ❑ ❑ 1 - The Mamur Zapt and the Return of the Carpet (1988)
- ❑ ❑ 2 - The Mamur Zapt and the Night of the Dog (1989)
- ❑ ❑ 3 - The Mamur Zapt and the Donkey-Vous (1990)
- ❑ ❑ 4 - The Mamur Zapt and the Men Behind (1991)
- ❑ ❑ 5 - The Mamur Zapt and the Girl in the Nile (1992)
- ❑ ❑ 6 - **The Mamur Zapt and the Spoils of Egypt (1993) Last Laugh winner ★**
- ❑ ❑ 7 - The Mamur Zapt and the Camel of Destruction (1993)
- ❑ ❑ 8 - The Mamur Zapt & the Snake Catcher's Daughter (1994)
- ❑ ❑ 9 - The Mingrelian Conspiracy (1995)
- ❑ ❑ 10 - The Mamur Zapt and the Fig Tree Murder (1996)

■ PEARS, Iain

Iain Pears is the creator of British art dealer Jonathan Argyll and his lover Flavia di Stefano, assistant to General Taddeo Bottando, head of Rome's elite Art Theft Squad. *Booklist* praised the author's masterful juggling of plot elements while "providing delightful diversion in the contrasting manners of [his] English and Italian characters." Pears' most recent work of fiction is *An Instance of the Fingerpost* (1997), released in the U.S. in 1998. This 800-page historical novel presents 4 diverse first-person accounts of the murder of an Oxford academic in 1660, just after the English Civil War. This book with the tongue-twisting title, taken from a quote by Sir Francis Bacon, has drawn raves on both sides of the Atlantic, including a starred review from *Publishers Weekly*. Appearing in incidental roles are real personages of the time, such as John Locke, Sir Christopher Wren and King Charles II.

Jonathan Argyll...Bristish art dealer in England
- ❑ ❑ 1 - The Raphael Affair (1991)
- ❑ ❑ 2 - The Titian Committee (1992)
- ❑ ❑ 3 - The Bernini Bust (1993)
- ❑ ❑ 4 - The Last Judgment (1994)
- ❑ ❑ 5 - Giotto's Hand (1995)
- ❑ ❑ 6 - Death and Restoration (1996)

■ **PEARSON, Ridley**

In 1990 Ridley Pearson became the first American to be awarded the Raymond Chandler Fulbright Fellowship in detective fiction in association with Oxford University, where he researched and outlined his second and third police thrillers featuring Lou Boldt and Daphne Matthews. This series has been optioned by HBO for a three-film deal to star Jamie Lee Curtis. While writing songs for a touring bar band in the '70s, Pearson worked as a dishwasher and a housekeeper in a hospital surgery suite. He also wrote the orchestral score for the international award-winning documentary film *Cattle Drive*. A former Seattle resident, Pearson now lives in a high mountain valley in Idaho. He plays bass guitar for the Rock Bottom Remainders—a literary garage band with Dave Barry, Amy Tan and Stephen King.

Lou Boldt & Daphne Matthews...detective and police psychologist in Seattle, Washington
- ❑ ❑ 1 - Undercurrents (1988)
- ❑ ❑ 2 - The Angel Maker (1993)
- ❑ ❑ 3 - No Witnesses (1994)
- ❑ ❑ 4 - Beyond Recognition (1997)

■ **PELECANOS, George P.**

George P. Pelecanos has written 4 books featuring '50s DC bartender Nick Stefanos, introduced in *A Firing Offense* (1992). Set in 1949, book 4 has been called a retro noir prequel, *"Once Upon a Time in America* meets *The Big Combo"* (*Kirkus*). *Booklist*, *Library Journal* and *Publishers Weekly* each gave it a starred review. His latest DC crime fiction is *King Suckerman* (1997) where two small-time bunko artists become unwilling players in a savage game of cross and double-cross staged during the Bicentennial celebration in the Nation's Capital. *Booklist* called it "a fictional homage to the blaxploitation films of the '70s." Pelecanos works for Circle Films where he recently produced his first feature film (*Undertow*) shown at the Sundance Film Festival. Instrumental in bringing the films of John Woo to the U.S., this native of Washington DC lives in Silver Spring MD.

Nick Stefanos...1950s bartender P.I. in Washington, D.C.
- ❑ ❑ 1 - A Firing Offense (1992)
- ❑ ❑ 2 - Nick's Trip (1993)
- ❑ ❑ 3 - Down by the River Where the Dead Men Go (1995)
- ❑ ❑ 4 - The Big Blow Down (1996)

■ **PERRY, Ritchie**

British author Ritchie Perry has written 2 series set partly in Brazil. The longer series features a small-time smuggler recruited by the secret British Intelligence agency SR(2). In book 2 the fledgling agent finds himself allied with the KGB in a race with the Americans and Israelis to eliminate a freelance agent named Schnellinger. Chosen as one of the best books of 1981 by the *New York Times Book Review*, book 11 has Philis escorting Idi Amin's former mistress across Europe, leaving more than a few dead bodies in their wake. Settings for this high-action series include Norway, Holland, France, Brazil and the Bahamas. Perry has written at least 10 novels for children, including the Fenella Fang and George H. Ghastly horror series. He holds a B.A. in history from Oxford and spent several years in Brazil working for the Bank of London and South America.

Frank MacAllister...swashbuckling private eye in Brazil
- ❑ ❑ 1 - MacAllister (1984)
- ❑ ❑ 2 - Presumed Dead (1987)

Philis...Brazilian smuggler turned British Intelligence agent in Brazil
- ❑ ❑ 1 - The Fall Guy (1972)
- ❑ ❑ 2 - Nowhere Man (1973) U.S.-A Hard Man to Kill
- ❑ ❑ 3 - Ticket to Ride (1973)
- ❑ ❑ 4 - Holiday with a Vengeance (1974)

❏ ❏ 5 - Your Money and Your Wife (1975)
❏ ❏ 6 - One Good Death Deserves Another (1976)
❏ ❏ 7 - Dead End (1977)
❏ ❏ 8 - Dutch Courage (1978)
❏ ❏ 9 - Bishop's Pawn (1979)
❏ ❏ 10 - Grand Slam (1980)
❏ ❏ 11 - Fool's Mate (1981)
❏ ❏ 12 - Foul Up (1982)
❏ ❏ 13 - Kolwezi (1985)
❏ ❏ 14 - Comeback (1991)

■ PERRY, Thomas

Edgar award-winner Thomas Perry is the creator of Jane Whitefield, a Seneca Indian guide who is half Irish and a martial arts expert. She is also a one-woman witness-relocation and protection program, who helps people in need of new identities create them. Perry's best-first-novel Edgar was for *Butcher's Boy* (1982), which featured a mob hitman seen again in *Sleeping Dogs* (1992). His other fiction includes *Metzger's Dog* (1983), *Big Fish* (1985) and *Island* (1988). Born in Tonawanda (NY), Perry earned a B.A. from Cornell University and a Ph.D. in English literature from the University of Rochester. His former jobs include laborer, commercial fisherman, weapons mechanic, university teacher and administrator, and television writer and producer. He lives with his scriptwriter wife and 2 children in southern California.

Jane Whitefield...Native American guide in Deganawida, New York
❏ ❏ 1 - Vanishing Act (1995)
❏ ❏ 2 - Dance for the Dead (1996)
❏ ❏ 3 - Shadow Woman (1997)
❏ ❏ 4 - The Face Changers (1998)

■ PETERSON, Keith [P]

Keith Peterson is a pseudonym used by two-time Edgar-award winner Andrew Klavan for his paperback originals featuring New York reporter John Wells, a man who uses an old manual typewriter in a newsroom filled with computer terminals. The 45-year-old divorced Wells describes himself as "too ugly for the love of women, and too mean for the company of friends." After its Edgar-nominated opening, this series won best paperback honors for book 3, *The Rain* (1989). As Andrew Klavan, his most recent crime novels are *True Crime* (1995), *Corruption* (1994) and *The Animal Hour* (1993). Scheduled for 1998 release is *The Uncanny*, which will feature a Hollywood producer of horror movies whose ghost-hunting trip to England sets off a chain of events that brings his first horror movie to life. With Laurence Klavan he wrote the Edgar-award winning *Mrs. White* (1983) under the name Margaret Tracy.

John Wells...newspaper reporter in New York, New York
❏ ❏ 1 - **The Trapdoor (1988) Edgar nominee** ☆
❏ ❏ 2 - There Fell a Shadow (1988)
❏ ❏ 3 - **The Rain (1989) Edgar winner** ★
❏ ❏ 4 - Rough Justice (1989)
❏ ❏ 5 - The Scarred Man (1990)

■ PETIEVICH, Gerald

Gerald Petievich spent 3 years in Army Intelligence before joining the U.S. Treasury Department in 1970 where he was a special agent of the Secret Service assigned to counterfeit investigations. His crime fiction includes an authentic 4-book series featuring a pair of cynical U.S. Treasury agents working out of the Los Angeles (CA) office. The action shifts partly to Washington DC in book 2 with a paper theft (the kind used to print money) from the Bureau of Printing and Engraving. According to John Lutz (*1001*

Midnights), book 2 is an even better read than book 1 thanks to Petievich's "hard-edged and street-wise" dialogue and "direct, uncompromising style." Petievich is best known for his novel *To Live and Die in L.A.* (1984) for which he also wrote the screenplay with William Friedkin. His other crime novels include *Paramour* (1991), *Earth Angels* (1989) and *Shakedown* (1988).

Charles Carr & Jack Kelly...US Treasury agents in Los Angeles, California
- ❏ ❏ 1 - Money Men (1981)
- ❏ ❏ 2 - One Shot Deal (1983)
- ❏ ❏ 3 - To Die in Beverly Hills (1983)
- ❏ ❏ 4 - The Quality of the Informant (1985)

■ PHILBIN, Tom

Tom Philbin is the author of a 9-book series of paperback originals featuring Joe Lawless, Felony Squad commander at Fort Siberia in the Bronx, New York's toughest precinct. These police novels feature an ensemble cast of detectives named Piccolo, Stein, Edmunton, Babalino and Benton, who last appeared in *Dart Man* (1994). Philbin, who is the son and grandson of cops, has also written *Copspeak: The Lingo of Law Enforcement and Crime* (1996). With more than 24 home improvement books to his credit, he is a recognized expert in home repair. His titles include *How to Hire a Home Improvement Contractor Without Getting Chiseled* (1997); *Painting, Staining and Finishing* (1997), *The Everything Home Improvement Book* (1997) and *Knock It Down, Break It Up: The Definitive Guide to In-Home Demolition* (1993). A Long Island resident, he also wrote the movie tie-ins for *Blink* (1994) and *Rookie* (1991).

Joe Lawless...Felony Squad commander in the Bronx, New York
- ❏ ❏ 1 - Precinct: Siberia (1985)
- ❏ ❏ 2 - Under Cover (1986)
- ❏ ❏ 3 - Cop Killer (1986)
- ❏ ❏ 4 - A Matter of Degree (1987)
- ❏ ❏ 5 - Jamaica Kill (1989)
- ❏ ❏ 6 - Street Killer (1989)
- ❏ ❏ 7 - Death Sentence (1990)
- ❏ ❏ 8 - The Prosecuter (1991)
- ❏ ❏ 9 - Dart Man (1994)

■ PHILBRICK, W. R.

Shamus award winner W. R(odman) Philbrick has written 2 mystery series—one featuring a wheelchair-bound mystery writer in Boston (MA), and the other a Key West (FL) private eye whose adventures were twice nominated for Shamus awards. Other Philbrick novels include the Shamus award-winner *Brothers and Sinners* (1994) and *Slow Dancer* (1984) about a woman golf pro who takes up P.I. work in a small New England town. His recent fiction includes the first volume of a werewolf trilogy (*Night Creature*, 1996) and a story for Grades 5-8 about two young brothers on the run (*The Fire Pony*, 1997). Philbrick also wrote *Freak the Mighty* (1993), which comes to the movie screen in early 1998 as *The Mighty*, starring Sharon Stone, Gillian Anderson and Harry Dean Stanton. He also wrote the movie tie-in (*The Mighty*, 1998). As William R. Dantz he is the author of *Pulse* (1990) and *The Seventh Sleeper* (1991).

J. D. Hawkins...wheelchair-bound mystery writer in Boston, Massachusetts
- ❏ ❏ 1 - Shadow Kill (1985) Brit.-Slow Grave
- ❏ ❏ 2 - Ice for the Eskimo (1986)
- ❏ ❏ 3 - Paint It Black (1989)
- ❏ ❏ 4 - Walk on the Water (1991)

T. D. Stash...unlicensed private eye in Key West, Florida
- ❏ ❏ 1 - The Neon Flamingo (1987)
- ❏ ❏ 2 - **The Crystal Blue Persuasion (1988) Shamus nominee** ☆
- ❏ ❏ 3 - **Tough Enough (1989) Shamus nominee** ☆

■ **PHILLIPS, Gary**

Gary Phillips is the creator of tough, black private eye Ivan Monk, who works the mean streets of Los Angeles like an avenging angel, starting with *Violent Spring* (1994), optioned for an HBO original movie. In anticipation of their hardcover 1998 release of book 3, Berkeley issued paperback reprints of the first 2 series titles in 1997. Short stories featuring the brainy, brawny Monk appear in *Spooks, Spies, and Private Eyes* (1995), *Blue Lightning* (1998) from John Harvey's Slow Dancer Press and *Death on the Mother Road* (1998), a collection of stories featuring Route 66. A Los Angeles native, Phillips grew up in South Central LA. His political and cultural commentaries have appeared in the *Miami Herald*, *Los Angeles Times*, the *L.A. View*, *San Francisco Examiner*, and *CrossRoads* and *Freestyle* magazines. His column "*Raisin' Sand*" is featured in the suburban Los Angeles *Compton Bulletin*.

Ivan Monk...black private eye in Los Angeles, California
- ❑ ❑ 1 - Violent Spring (1994)
- ❑ ❑ 2 - Perdition USA (1996)
- ❑ ❑ 3 - Bad Night is Falling (1998)

■ **PHILLIPS, Mike**

Silver Dagger award winner Mike Phillips is the creator of Sam Dean, a street-smart London reporter born in Jamaica, introduced in *Blood Rights* (1989). After picking up his Crime Writers' award for book 2, Phillips sent Sammy to New York in book 3 in search of the daughter of a dying friend. But he's back in London behind the cameras of a tabloid television show in book 4, which *Publishers Weekly* praised for its "subtle psychological complexities and deadpan ironies." While *Kirkus* has called the Anglo-Carib journalist "a testy, strong-arm hero, with as hard-boiled a mindset as any Chicago/LA private eye," *Booklist* likes the author's "ingenious pacing, bold realism, understated sensuality, and startling originality in both character and setting." Phillips also wrote the novelization of the movie *Boyz in the Hood* (1991). Born in Guyana, he lives in London.

Sam Dean...Jamaica-born black journalist in London, England
- ❑ ❑ 1 - Blood Rights (1989)
- ❑ ❑ 2 - **The Late Candidate (1990) Silver Dagger winner** ★
- ❑ ❑ 3 - Point of Darkness (1995)
- ❑ ❑ 4 - An Image to Die For (1997)

■ **PHILLIPS, T. J. [P]**

T. J. Phillips is the pseudonym used by Tom Savage for his Joe Wilder mysteries featuring a struggling 30-something novelist and playwright who grew up in St. Thomas but now lives in Greenwich Village. Joe is called home to St. Thomas in *Dance of the Mongoose* (1995) when his oldest friend is suspected of murdering his own father, a judge with serious political ambitions. In book 2 Joe is back in New York trying to solve another mystery and thinking about opening a detective agency. Like Joe Wilder, Tom Savage was raised in St. Thomas, Virgin Islands, but now lives in New York City. Under his own name he writes psychological thrillers, including *Precipice* (1994), set in the Caribbean, and *Valentine* (1997), a novel of terror set in Greenwich Village. He works at Murder Ink mystery bookstore in New York City.

Joe Wilder...struggling playwright and novelist in New York, New York
- ❑ ❑ 1 - Dance of the Mongoose (1995)
- ❑ ❑ 2 - Woman in the Dark (1997)

■ **PIERCE, David M.**

Canadian expat David M. Pierce has lived in Paris since leaving Hollywood in 1986 after starring in a musical comedy with his songwriting partner. During his year in L.A., Pierce also recorded an album and co-wrote songs for Chad & Jeremy. His crime fiction hero is Vic Daniel, an offbeat 6' 7¼" cut-rate private eye who wears loud Hawaiian shirts and drives a pink and blue Nash Metropolitan. This "relentlessly jokey stringbean" (*Kirkus*) makes his first appearance in *Down in the Valley* (1989), referring to the San Fernando Valley where Daniel lives, in a city that he hates. As Pierce told Brad Spurgeon in a 1997 *Fingerprints* interview, he puts his hero in a place he hates, so he's got a built-in attitude every time he sticks his head out the door. In book 7, Vic's dog is instrumental in keeping a porn theater out of the neighborhood—the author's revenge against cats solving mysteries.

Vic Daniel...offbeat 6' 7 1/4" cut-rate P.I. in Los Angeles, California
- ❑ ❑ 1 - Down in the Valley (1989)
- ❑ ❑ 2 - Hear the Wind Blow, Dear... (1989)
- ❑ ❑ 3 - Roses Love Sunshine (1989)
- ❑ ❑ 4 - Angels in Heaven (1991)
- ❑ ❑ 5 - Write Me a Letter (1992)
- ❑ ❑ 6 - Build Me a Castle (1994)
- ❑ ❑ 7 - As She Rides By (1996)

■ **POMIDOR, Bill**

Physician Bill Pomidor writes a medical mystery series featuring Calista and Plato Marley, a pair of married doctors turned sleuths in Cleveland (OH). Calista is a professor of anatomy, deputy coroner for the county and a practicing pathologist, while Plato (who flunked anatomy his first year in medical school) is a family practitioner specializing in geriatrics. Pomidor alternates the point of view between Cal and her husband and sometimes gives the reader information the Marleys don't yet have. Although married to a doctor, Pomidor is not the geriatrician in the family. His wife is. He's an instructor in medical education at Northeastern Ohio Universities College of Medicine and quick to point out that he did not flunk anatomy or any other course while in medical school. He's currently at work on a medical thriller and the next Cal and Plato book.

Calista & Plato Marley...forensic pathologist wife & family physician husband in Cleveland, Ohio
- ❑ ❑ 1 - Murder by Prescription (1995)
- ❑ ❑ 2 - The Anatomy of a Murder (1996)
- ❑ ❑ 3 - Skeletons in the Closet (1997)
- ❑ ❑ 4 - Ten Little Medicine Men (1998)

■ **POYER, David**

Annapolis graduate David Poyer is a sport diver, marine engineer, sailor and officer in the Navy Reserve. Author of 16 novels, he was a Distinguished Visiting Author at the U.S. Naval Academy (1996), where his books are required reading in a course titled Literature of the Sea. His mystery series features black sheep salvage diver Lyle "Tiller" Galloway whose workaday world involves the most psychologically challenging and physically dangerous "adventure sport" there is. Poyer's military sea fiction chronicles the Navy career of Dan Lenson in *The Med* (1988), *The Gulf* (1990), *The Circle* (1992), *The Passage* (1995) and *Tomahawk* (1998). Poyer has also written 3 titles in a Hemlock County (PA) cycle featuring recluse W. T. Halvorsen appearing in *Dead of Winter* (1988), *Winter in the Heart* (1993) and *All the Wolves Love Winter* (1996). Poyer lives on the Virginia shore.

Tiller Galloway...ex-Navy SEAL turned salvage diver in Cape Hatteras, North Carolina
- ❑ ❑ 1 - Hatteras Blue (1989)
- ❑ ❑ 2 - Bahamas Blue (1991)
- ❑ ❑ 3 - Louisiana Blue (1994)
- ❑ ❑ 4 - Down to a Sunless Sea (1996)

■ PRATHER, Richard

Richard S. Prather (pronounced PRAY-ther) enjoyed huge success in the '50s and '60s with his 6'2" ex-Marine P.I. Shell Scott, selling over 40 million copies of his 36 adventures. Spending as much time chasing dames as clues, this P.I. enjoys tropical fish, his robin's egg blue Cadillac and his best friend Phil, captain of LAPD's central homicide division. According to Art Scott (*1001 Midnights*), Shell is out of fashion and out of print, but fondly remembered and "still marvelously entertaining...a successful hybrid of tough-guy fiction and knockabout low comedy." In *Strip for Murder* (1955), the author's own favorite, Scott is hired to protect a wealthy woman who lives in a nudist colony. Our hero leads morning calisthenics au naturel and barely escapes in a hot-air balloon over downtown Los Angeles. Prather received a Lifetime Achievement Award from Private Eye Writers of America in 1986.

Shell Scott...6'2" ex-Marine crew-cut private eye in Los Angeles, California

❑ ❑   1 - The Case of the Vanishing Beauty (1950)
❑ ❑   2 - Bodies in Bedlam (1951)
❑ ❑   3 - Everybody Had a Gun (1951)
❑ ❑   4 - Find This Woman (1951)
❑ ❑   5 - Way of a Wanton (1952)
❑ ❑   6 - Pattern for Murder [as by David Knight] (1952)
         APA-The Scrambled Yeggs [as by David Knight]
❑ ❑   7 - Dagger of Flesh (1952)
❑ ❑   8 - Darling, It's Death (1952)
❑ ❑   9 - Ride a High Horse (1953)
❑ ❑ 10 - Always Leave 'em Dying (1954)
❑ ❑ 11 - Pattern for Panic (1954)
❑ ❑ 12 - Strip for Murder (1955)
❑ ❑ 13 - The Wailing Frail (1956)
❑ ❑ nn - Three's a Shroud [3 novellas] (1957)
❑ ❑ 14 - Slab Happy (1958)
❑ ❑ 15 - Take a Murder, Darling (1958)
❑ ❑ 16 - Over Her Dead Body (1959)
❑ ❑ 17 - Double in Trouble [w/Marlowe & Chester Drum] (1959)
❑ ❑ 18 - Dance With the Dead (1960)
❑ ❑ 19 - Dig That Crazy Grave (1961)
❑ ❑ ss - Shell Scott's Seven Slaughters [short stories] (1961)
❑ ❑ 20 - Kill the Clown (1962)
❑ ❑ 21 - Dead Heat (1963)
❑ ❑ 22 - Joker in the Deck (1964)
❑ ❑ 23 - The Cockeyed Corpse (1964)
❑ ❑ 24 - The Trojan Hearse (1964)
❑ ❑ 25 - Kill Him Twice (1965)
❑ ❑ 26 - Dead Man's Walk (1965)
❑ ❑ 27 - The Meandering Corpse (1965)
❑ ❑ 28 - The Kubla Khan Caper (1966)
❑ ❑ 29 - Gat Heat (1967)
❑ ❑ 30 - The Cheim Manuscript (1969)
❑ ❑ 31 - Kill Me Tomorrow (1969)
❑ ❑ ss - The Shell Scott Sampler [short stories] (1969)
❑ ❑ 32 - Dead-Bang (1971)
❑ ❑ 33 - The Sweet Ride (1972)
❑ ❑ 34 - The Sure Thing (1975)
❑ ❑ 35 - The Amber Effect (1986)
❑ ❑ 36 - Shell Shock (1987)

■ **PRICE, Anthony**

Long-time journalist Anthony Price is the author of 19 books featuring historian Dr. David Audley, a British Intelligence agent introduced in Silver Dagger winner, *The Labryinth Makers* (1970). The randomly-ordered books move back and forth in time from 1944 when Audley enters the war as a young man. Price says his aim with this series was to combine elements of the spy thriller with the detective mystery using a group of characters who would take turns playing the lead. The linking role in all the stories is Dr. Audley, described by H. R. F. Keating as "intellectual, subtle-minded, reticent...honorable, past-imbued upper-class product, wartime soldier, would-be historian and dyed-in-the-wool Intelligence man." During his more than 35 years with Westminster Press, Price served as editor of the *Oxford Times*. He holds an M.A. in history from Oxford, where he currently resides.

David Audley, Dr.....historian and spy in England
- ❏ ❏ 1 - **The Labyrinth Makers (1970) Silver Dagger winner ★**
- ❏ ❏ 2 - The Alamut Ambush (1971)
- ❏ ❏ 3 - Colonel Butler's Wolf (1972)
- ❏ ❏ 4 - October Men (1973)
- ❏ ❏ 5 - **Other Paths to Glory (1974) Gold Dagger winner ★**
- ❏ ❏ 6 - Our Man in Camelot (1975)
- ❏ ❏ 7 - War Game (1976)
- ❏ ❏ 8 - The '44 Vintage (1978)
- ❏ ❏ 9 - Tomorrow's Ghost (1979)
- ❏ ❏ 10 - The Hour of the Donkey (1980)
- ❏ ❏ 11 - Soldier No More (1981)
- ❏ ❏ 12 - The Old Vengeful (1982)
- ❏ ❏ 13 - Gunner Kelly (1983)
- ❏ ❏ 14 - Sion Crossing (1985)
- ❏ ❏ 15 - Here Be Monsters (1985)
- ❏ ❏ 16 - For the Good of the State (1986)
- ❏ ❏ 17 - A New Kind of War (1987)
- ❏ ❏ 18 - A Prospect of Vengeance (1988)
- ❏ ❏ 19 - The Memory Trap (1989)

■ **PRONZINI, Bill**

Five-time Edgar nominee Bill Pronzini has written westerns, science fiction, horror and mysteries. His publication list includes more than 50 novels, over 300 short stories and magazine articles, at least 60 anthologies where he was editor or co-editor and numerous works of scholarship, including the Edgar-nominated *1001 Midnights* with Marcia Muller and the hilarious *Gun In Cheek* (1982), an affectionate guide to the "worst" in mystery fiction. William DeAndrea called him mystery's Blood Type O for his ability to collaborate with many, including Barry Maltzberg, Marcia Muller, John Lutz, Collin Wilcox and columnist Jack Anderson (*The Cambodia File*, 1981), among others. The two-time Shamus-winner, Lifetime Achievement recipient (1987) and first president of Private Eye Writers of America once admitted his P.I. is nameless only because he and his editor couldn't think of a suitable one.

John Quincannon...19th century private eye in San Francisco, California
- ❏ ❏ 1 - Quincannon (1985)
- ❏ ❏ 2 - Beyond the Grave [with Marcia Muller andElena Oliverez] (1986)

Nameless...pulp collector P.I. with no name in San Francisco, California
- ❏ ❏ 1 - The Snatch (1971)
- ❏ ❏ 2 - The Vanished (1973)
- ❏ ❏ 3 - Undercurrents (1973)
- ❏ ❏ 4 - Blowback (1977)

❏ ❏   5 - Twospot [with Colin Wilcox and Lt. Hastings] (1978)
❏ ❏   6 - Labyrinth (1980)
❏ ❏   7 - **Hoodwink (1981) Shamus winner ★**
❏ ❏   8 - Scattershot (1982)
❏ ❏   9 - Dragonfire (1982)
❏ ❏ 10 - Bindlestiff (1983)
❏ ❏ ss - Casefile [short stories] (1983)
❏ ❏ 11 - Quicksilver (1984)
❏ ❏ 12 - Nightshades (1984)
❏ ❏ 13 - Double [w/Marcia Muller and Sharon McCone] (1984)
❏ ❏ 14 - **Bones (1985) Shamus nominee ☆**
❏ ❏ 15 - Deadfall (1986)
❏ ❏ 16 - Shackles (1988)
❏ ❏ 17 - Jackpot (1990)
❏ ❏ 18 - Breakdown (1991)
❏ ❏ 19 - Quarry (1992)
❏ ❏ 20 - Epitaphs (1992)
❏ ❏ 21 - Demons (1993)
❏ ❏ 22 - Hardcase (1995)
❏ ❏ 23 - **Sentinels (1996) Shamus nominee ☆**
❏ ❏ ss - Spadework [short stories] (1996)
❏ ❏ 24 - Illusions (1997)

■ PUCKETT, Andrew

Andrew Puckett is the creator of Tom Jones, unconventional Home Office health investigator, seen first in *Bloodstains* (1987) and *Terminus* (1990). In *The Ladies of the Vale* (1994) he hooks up with nursing sister Jo Farewell of Latchvale Hospital who suspects a serial killer in the Intensive Therapy Unit. Her boss and the police dismiss her concerns, but Tom is convinced the deaths are not random, and his investigation soon reveals a sinister plot involving organ donors. Before becoming a full-time writer, Puckett worked as a medical technician and scientific researcher in the field of microbiology. A resident of Taunton, England, he is also the author of *Desolation Point* (1992), *Bloodhound* (1991) and *Bed of Nails* (1989).

Tom Jones...health investigator in England
❏ ❏   1 - Bloodstains (1987)
❏ ❏   2 - Terminus (1990)
❏ ❏   3 - Ladies of the Vale (1994)

■ QUILL, Monica [P]

Monica Quill is the pen name (literally; think about it) used by Ralph McInerny for his series featuring Sister Mary Teresa Dempsey, a 5'2" 200-lb. powerhouse nicknamed "Attila the Nun." A character created on a dare, "Emtee...is...what Nero Wolfe might have been if he had taken the veil," says the author. Under his own name, McInerny has written 17 Father Dowling books and 5 with attorney Andrew Broom. Recipient of a Lifetime Achievement Anthony Award in 1993, he recently launched a series set on the University of Notre Dame campus where he has taught philosophy for more than 40 years. An authority on St. Thomas Aquinas, McInerny teaches philosophy and medieval studies and directs the Jacques Maritain Center. In addition to more than 40 mysteries, he has written at least 17 volumes of philosophy, ethics and religion and served as founder, publisher and editor of several Catholic magazines.

Mary Teresa Dempsey...5'2" 200-lb. nun in Chicago, Illinois
❏ ❏   1 - Not A Blessed Thing (1981)
❏ ❏   2 - Let Us Prey (1982)
❏ ❏   3 - And Then There Was Nun (1984)
❏ ❏   4 - Nun of the Above (1985)

❑ ❑ 5 - Sine Qua Nun (1986)
❑ ❑ 6 - Veil of Ignorance (1988)
❑ ❑ 7 - Sister Hood (1991)
❑ ❑ 8 - Nun Plussed (1993)
❑ ❑ 9 - Half Past Nun (1997)

■ RALEIGH, Michael

Michael Raleigh is the creator of hard-boiled Chicago private eye Paul Whelan who works out of a gritty Uptown neighborhood—a fascinating ethnic mix of black and Vietnamese. The 40-something black ex-cop turned P.I. is introduced in *Death in Uptown* (1991). With its vagrants, runaways, missing persons, alcoholics and felons, Uptown is "rendered with shocking clarity" says *Chicago* magazine, "unforgiving, brutal, yet not without its moments of unexpected warmth." Raleigh has "a thing for losers, characterizing them with compassionate care," said *The New York Times Book Review*. Whelan's fifth case, *The Riverview Murders* (1997), focuses on the now-abandoned Riverview Park, once the site of the city's amusement park. A 40-year-old unsolved murder reunites a group of youthful friends. A native of Chicago, Raleigh still lives in the city where he teaches at Truman College.

Paul Whelan...40-something black cop turned P.I. in Chicago, Illinois
❑ ❑ 1 - Death in Uptown (1990)
❑ ❑ 2 - A Body in Belmont Harbor (1993)
❑ ❑ 3 - The Maxwell Street Blues (1994)
❑ ❑ 4 - Killer on Argyle Street (1995)
❑ ❑ 5 - The Riverview Murders (1997)

■ RAMOS, Manuel

Manuel Ramos is the creator of the Luis Montez mysteries featuring a Denver attorney and former Chicano activist first seen in the *The Ballad of Rocky Ruiz* (1993). Nominated for a best-first-novel Edgar, Ramos' series opener was described by *Kirkus Reviews* as "a powerfully elegiac memoir of the heady early days of Chicano activism." Things are really looking up for Luis in book 3, until his last client turns up dead and Luis is arrested for murder. His investigation leads out of the Rockies across the Nevada desert to the seaside barrios of San Diego. When last seen in *Blues for the Buffalo* (1997), Luis meets a beautiful woman on the beaches of Mexico. When she disappears, so does her latest manuscript and Luis is caught in a web of literary intrigue. An attorney with the Denver Legal Aid Society, Ramos teaches Chicano literature at Metropolitan State College of Denver. He lives in Denver.

Luis Montez...attorney and former Chicano activist in Denver, Colorado
❑ ❑ **1 - The Ballad of Rocky Ruiz (1993) Edgar nominee** ☆
❑ ❑ 2 - The Ballad of Gato Guerrero (1994)
❑ ❑ 3 - The Last Client of Luis Montez (1996)
❑ ❑ 4 - Blues for the Buffalo (1997)

■ RANDISI, Robert J.

Robert J. Randisi has written mysteries, westerns, action-adventure, horror, fantasy, historical and spy novels—more than 400 books since his first novel, *The Disappearance of Penny* (1980). Most prolific as a writer of westerns (200 installments of *The Gunsmith* series written as J.R. Roberts), he says the private eye genre is his favorite. Founder of the Private Eye Writers of America and creator of the PWA Shamus awards, Randisi writes private eye fiction under his own name. His newest P.I. is NYPD detective Joe Keough who is still on the force in his native Brooklyn in *Alone With the Dead* (1995), the same path Randisi followed when he left his native Brooklyn, where he spent 8 years as an NYPD administrative aide, to move to St. Louis (MO). He is editor of *First Cases I* (1997) featuring first appearances of classic private eyes and *First Cases II* (1997) first appearances of classic amateur detectives.

Joe Keough...NYPD detective in New York, New York
❑ ❑ 1 - Alone with the Dead (1995)
❑ ❑ 2 - In the Shadow of the Arch (1997)

Miles Jacoby...boxer turned P.I. in New York, New York
- ❏ ❏ 1 - Eye in the Ring (1982)
- ❏ ❏ 2 - **The Steinway Collection (1983) Shamus nominee** ☆
- ❏ ❏ 3 - **Full Contact (1984) Shamus nominee** ☆
- ❏ ❏ 4 - Separate Cases (1990)
- ❏ ❏ 5 - Hard Look (1993)
- ❏ ❏ 6 - Stand-Up (1994)

Nick Delvecchio...private eye in Brooklyn, New York
- ❏ ❏ 1 - No Exit From Brooklyn (1987)
- ❏ ❏ 2 - The Dead of Brooklyn (1991)

■ **RANKIN, Ian**

Ian Rankin's crime novels have been called "top notch," "simply awesome" and "unlikely to be endorsed by the Scottish Tourist Board." He likes to imagine that his Edinburgh novels are modern reworkings of *Dr. Jekyll and Mr. Hyde* in a style he calls "tartan noir." Next up for the Scottish inspector is book 9, *The Hanging Garden* (1998). An ex-journalist and ardent film fan, Rankin writes thrillers as Jack Harvey, which happens to be his son's name. Under the Harvey byline are *Blood Hunt* (1995), *Bleeding Hearts* (1994) and *Witch Hunt* (1993). Winner of the 1992 Chandler/Fulbright Prize, Rankin spent a year doing research in Seattle. After earning a degree from the University of Edinbugh, he has worked as a grape-picker, swineherd, taxman, alcohol researcher, hi-fi journalist and punk musician. A two-time Dagger winner for best short story, he has recently returned from France to live in Edinburgh.

John Rebus...detective sergeant in Edinburgh, Scotland
- ❏ ❏ 1 - Knots and Crosses (1987)
- ❏ ❏ 2 - Hide and Seek (1991)
- ❏ ❏ 3 - Wolfman (1992)
      U.S.-Tooth & Nail
- ❏ ❏ 4 - Strip Jack (1992)
- ❏ ❏ ss - A Good Hanging and Other Stories (1992)
- ❏ ❏ 5 - The Black Book (1993)
- ❏ ❏ 6 - Mortal Causes (1994)
- ❏ ❏ 7 - Let It Bleed (1995)
- ❏ ❏ 8 - Black and Blue (1997)

■ **RAPHAEL, Lev**

Academia is the perfect setting for murder and satire, says Lev Raphael, "It's got the vanity of professional sports, the hypocrisy of politics, the cruelty of big business and the single-mindedness of organized crime." Gay professor Nick Hoffman teaches at the fictional State University of Michigan, a thinly-disguised Michigan State University, where Lev Raphael, PhD, once taught. Nick's partner Stefan first appeared in the non-mystery *Winter Eyes* (1992). Born and raised in New York City, a child of Holocaust survivors, Raphael tells his personal story in 13 essays titled *Journeys & Arrivals: On Being Gay and Jewish* (1996). His nonfiction work, coauthored with Gershen Kauffman, includes *Stick Up for Yourself* (1990), *Dynamics of Power: Fighting Shame and Building Self-Esteem* (1991) and *Coming Out of Shame* (1996). His short story collection *Dancing on Tisa B'av* won a 1990 Lambda Literary Award.

Nick Hoffman...gay college professor in Michiganapolis, Michigan
- ❏ ❏ 1 - Let's Get Criminal (1996)
- ❏ ❏ 2 - The Edith Wharton Murders (1997)

■ **REED, Barry**

Barry Reed is the creator of Boston trial attorney Dan Sheridan, first seen in *The Verdict* (1980), a bestselling novel about medical malpractice that became the 1982 Academy Award-winning movie starring Paul Newman. Sheridan's next case, *The Choice* (1991), involves a miracle drug for heart disease that's causing birth defects. *Kirkus* called this one "the best novel of legal infighting ever." In book 3 a prominent surgeon is indicted for murder (*The Indictment*) and an old friend in the DA's office warns Sheridan his phones are tapped. But nobody tells him his new legal secretary is an undercover FBI agent. Sheridan is back in book 4, *The Deception* (1997), when he sues a prestigious hospital on behalf of the parents of a young tennis star dead by suicide. A veteran trial attorney, Reed is Chairman of the Massachusetts Trial Lawyers Association. He lives in Boston (MA).

Dan Sheridan...attorney in Boston, Massachusetts
- ❏ ❏ 1 - The Verdict (1980)
- ❏ ❏ 2 - The Choice (1991)
- ❏ ❏ 3 - The Indictment (1994)

■ **REEVES, Robert**

Former Harvard University professor Robert Reeves is the author of two mysteries featuring Boston history professor Thomas Theron, introduced in *Doubting Thomas* (1985) which *Kirkus Reviews* called "a zesty, classy original." In book 2, *Peeping Thomas* (1990), the professor has sex on his mind, but when roused from a hangover by renowned feminist Emma Pierce, he finds himself enlisted in the antiporn movement. "When it comes to smut," one colleague confides, "Thomas is generally thought to be part of the problem, not part of the solution." On the trail of the Porno Bomber, Thomas is assisted by his acerbic ex-wife Elizabeth. A longtime Boston resident and professor of English at Harvard, Reeves now lives in New York City where he is working on the third book in the series, *Thomas Solves the Mystery of Life*.

Thomas Theron...history professor in Boston, Massachusetts
- ❏ ❏ 1 - Doubting Thomas (1985)
- ❏ ❏ 2 - Peeping Thomas (1990)

■ **REID, Robert Sims**

Robert Sims Reid is a Missoula, Montana police detective who has created two Montana detectives, each with a pair of mysteries thus far. Ray Bartell, first seen in *Big Sky Blues* (1988), works for the Rozette (MT) police department. In book 2, *Wild Animals* (1996), the president is coming to Rozette and Bartell is detailed to help the Secret Service keep tabs on local lunatics, including an alleged eco-terrorist ex-con. Reid's other Montana detective is Leo Banks, first seen in *Benediction* (1992) where Leo is incensed about the involvement of an L.A. record producer and local real estate developer in the drug overdose of a teenage starlet. In *The Red Corvette* (1993) Leo returns to a small town in Southern Illinois to investigate the death of an ex-lover's husband. A 50-year-old crime provides the key to naming the killer.

Ray Bartell...police detective in Rozette, Montana
- ❏ ❏ 1 - Big Sky Blues (1988)
- ❏ ❏ 2 - Wild Animals (1995)

■ RESNICOW, Herbert

Herbert Resnicow (1922-1996) changed careers at the age of 60 and saw his first novel win an Edgar nomination. A civil engineer by training and profession, he modeled his first series character after himself when he introduced construction engineering genius and puzzle maven Alexander Gold in *The Gold Solution* (1983). Next came his crossword series with retired attorney Giles Sullivan and faculty dean Isabel Macintosh, first seen in *Murder Across and Down* (1985). Ed and Warren Baer, his father and son detecting team, appeared only twice. Resnicow also coauthored 3 celebrity sports mysteries featuring sportswriter Marcus Aurelius Burr, including one each with Fran Tarkenton (*Murder at the Superbowl*), Tom Seaver (*Bean Ball*) and Pelé (*World Cup Murder*). Later with Edward I. Koch he wrote *Murder at City Hall* (1996). Born in New York, Resnicow graduated from the Polytechnic Institute of Brooklyn and served overseas with the Army Corps of Engineers in World War II.

Alexander Gold...construction engineer & puzzle maven in New York, New York
- ❑ ❑ 1 - **The Gold Solution (1983) Edgar nominee** ☆
- ❑ ❑ 2 - The Gold Deadline (1984)
- ❑ ❑ 3 - The Gold Frame (1984)
- ❑ ❑ 4 - The Gold Curse (1986)
- ❑ ❑ 5 - The Gold Gamble (1988)

Ed & Warren Baer...father & son sleuths in Long Island, New York
- ❑ ❑ 1 - The Dead Room (1987)
- ❑ ❑ 2 - The Hot Place (1990)

Giles Sullivan & Isabel Macintosh...crossword expert & faculty dean in Vermont
- ❑ ❑ 1 - Murder Across and Down (1985)
- ❑ ❑ 2 - The Seventh Crossword (1985)
- ❑ ❑ 3 - The Crossword Code (1986)
- ❑ ❑ 4 - The Crossword Legacy (1987)
- ❑ ❑ 5 - The Crossword Hunt (1987)

■ REYNOLDS, William J

William J. Reynolds is the creator of an Omaha, Nebraska private eye who's given up his detective agency to write the great American novel. He first appears in *The Nebraska Quotient* (1984), a best-first-novel Shamus nominee. Nebraska is medium-boiled with plenty of comic overtones. Because he never intended to write more than one Nebraska novel, Reynolds says the series doesn't really begin until the second book. That's when he starts unloading some of the baggage he saddled himself with in book 1, which he describes as just short of parody. Reynolds, who holds a B.A. in political science from Creighton University (NE), previously worked as managing editor of *The Ambassador* magazine and creative director of a Sioux Falls (SD) advertising agency. A native of Omaha (NE), he lives in Sioux Falls (SD).

Nebraska...part-time P.I. trying to write in Omaha, Nebraska
- ❑ ❑ 1 - **The Nebraska Quotient (1984) Shamus nominee** ☆
- ❑ ❑ 2 - Moving Targets (1986)
- ❑ ❑ 3 - Money Trouble (1988)
- ❑ ❑ 4 - Things Invisible (1989)
- ❑ ❑ 5 - The Naked Eye (1990)
- ❑ ❑ 6 - Drive-by (1995)

■ RHEA, Nicholas [P]

Nicholas Rhea is a frequently-used pseudonym of Peter N. Walker, past Chairman of the Crime Writers' Association and author of more than 90 books. Yorkshire born, he is a former police officer and lecturer at law and police training schools. Founder and former editor of *Police Box*, he is a frequent contributor to police publications, often under the name Nicholas Rhea. Author of the weekly column "Countryman's Diary," he is also a frequent contributor of articles on folklore and rural matters, again under the Rhea pen name. His Rhea mysteries, written as autobiographical tales starring 1960s police constable Nick Rhea, have been made into the TV hit series *Heartbeat*, for which he serves as consultant and writer. *Omens of Death* (1997) is the first in a new series featuring superstitious and eccentric D.I. Montague Pluke, scheduled to return in *Superstitious Death* (1998).

Nick Rhea...police constable father of four in Aidensfield, North Yorkshire, England
- ❑ ❑ 1 - Constable on the Hill (1979)
- ❑ ❑ 2 - Constable on the Prowl (1980)
- ❑ ❑ 3 - Constable Around the Village (1981)
- ❑ ❑ 4 - Constable Across the Moors (1982)
- ❑ ❑ 5 - Constable in the Dale (1983)
- ❑ ❑ 6 - Constable by the Sea (1985)
- ❑ ❑ 7 - Constable Along the Lane (1986)
- ❑ ❑ 8 - Constable Through the Meadow (1988)
- ❑ ❑ 9 - Constable at the Double (1989)
- ❑ ❑ 10 - Constable in Disguise (1989)
- ❑ ❑ 11 - Constable Among the Heather (1990)
- ❑ ❑ 12 - Constable Beside the Stream (1991)
- ❑ ❑ 13 - Constable Around the Green (1993)
- ❑ ❑ 14 - Constable Beneath the Trees (1994)
- ❑ ❑ 15 - Constable in the Shrubbery (1995)

■ RICHARDSON, Robert

Robert Richardson is the creator of journalist-turned-playwright Augustus Maltravers, first seen in the Creasey Award-winning title *The Latimer Mercy* (1985). While his sister is trying to resurrect an Arts Festival in the imaginary cathedral city of Vercaster, Maltravers and his actress partner get involved in the theft of a rare 16th century Bible and the murder of a friend. With a seeming affinity for old books, Maltravers learns (in book 3) of a recently-discovered Sherlock Holmes novella that may have been written by Conan Doyle himself. After closing his series with book 6, *The Lazarus Tree* (1992), Richardson began writing psychological thrillers at the advice of his agent. His first such effort, *The Hand of Strange Children* (1993) was shortlisted for the Gold Dagger but did not succeed in finding a U.S. publisher. Born in Manchester, Richardson lives in Hertfordshire where he was formerly editor of the *Herts Advertiser*.

Augustus Maltravers...journalist turned playwright and novelist in England
- ❑ ❑ 1 - **The Latimer Mercy (1985) Creasey winner** ★
- ❑ ❑ 2 - Bellringer Street (1988)
- ❑ ❑ 3 - The Book of the Dead (1989)
- ❑ ❑ 4 - The Dying of the Light (1990)
- ❑ ❑ 5 - Sleeping in the Blood (1991) U.S.-Murder in Waiting
- ❑ ❑ 6 - The Lazarus Tree (1992)

■ RIDER, J. W. [P]

J. W. Rider is a pseudonym of Shane Stevens, winner of the 1987 best-first-novel Shamus award for *Jersey Tomatoes* (1986). Other nominees for best first private eye novel that year were Larry Beinhart for *No One Rides For Free* and Carl Hiassen for *Tourist Season*. Rider's Shamus winner introduced Jersey City (NJ) private eye Ryder Malone who returned the following year in *Hot Tickets* (1987). Both titles were published by Arbor House.

Ryder Malone...private eye in Jersey City, New Jersey
- ❑ ❑ 1 - **Jersey Tomatoes (1986) Shamus winner** ★
- ❑ ❑ 2 - Hot Tickets (1987)

■ RIDGWAY, Jason [P]

Jason Ridgway is one of the pseudonyms of Stephen Marlowe who has written 60 books under several names, including Milton Lesser (his birth name), Andrew Frazer, C. H. Thames and Stephen Marlowe. As Ridgway he has written at least 4 books featuring a New York P.I. named Brian Guy, first seen in *Adam's Fall* (1960). Better known are the 19 Chester Drum private eye novels written as Stephen Marlowe, including the Drum Beat sequence from the mid-'60s. More recently Marlowe has written *The Lighthouse at the End of the World* (1995), an alternative biography of Edgar Allan Poe where the facts of his life are interwoven with imaginary events. Characters from Poe's novels come to life, the dead are resurrected and people are lost in parallel time and space. Former vice-president of the New York chapter of Mystery Writers of America, Marlowe lives in New York City.

Brian Guy...private eye in New York, New York
- ❏ ❏ 1 - Adam's Fall (1960)
- ❏ ❏ 2 - People in Glass Houses (1961)
- ❏ ❏ 3 - Hardly a Man is Now Alive (1962)
- ❏ ❏ 4 - The Treasure of the Cosa Nostra (1966)

■ RIGGS, John R

John R(aymond) Riggs has written a dozen mysteries featuring small-town newspaper editor Garth Ryland of Oakalla, Wisconsin, first seen in *The Last Laugh* (1984), when the town joker dies after an apparent heart attack on April Fool's Day. In addition to his newspaper duties, Garth is unofficial special deputy which sometimes means working two jobs. In book 9, *Cold Hearts and Gentle People* (1994), the sheriff takes off for a two-week training program and the official deputy, Eugene Yuill, cracks under pressure. *Kirkus* said this story "crackles with authentic small-town tension." Vintage car lovers will enjoy book 2, *Let Sleeping Dogs Lie* (1985), where Garth finds his dream car—a vintage '36 Cadillac convertible—hidden in an abandoned barn. All it needs is an overhaul, but someone is sabotaging Garth's mechanics with kidnapping and arson.

Garth Ryland...small-town newspaper editor in Oakalla, Wisonsin
- ❏ ❏ 1 - The Last Laugh (1984)
- ❏ ❏ 2 - Let Sleeping Dogs Lie (1985)
- ❏ ❏ 3 - The Glory Hound (1987)
- ❏ ❏ 4 - The Haunt of the Nightingale (1988)
- ❏ ❏ 5 - Wolf in Sheep's Clothing (1989)
- ❏ ❏ 6 - One Man's Poison (1991)
- ❏ ❏ 7 - Dead Letters (1992)
- ❏ ❏ 8 - A Dragon Lives Forever (1992)
- ❏ ❏ 9 - Cold Hearts and Gentle People (1994)
- ❏ ❏ 10 - Killing Frost (1995)
- ❏ ❏ 11 - Snow on the Roses (1996)
- ❏ ❏ 12 - He Who Waits (1997)

■ RING, Raymond H.

Raymond H. Ring received an award for distinguished investigative reporting from Investigative Reporters and Editors in 1982 for posing undercover as a convicted murderer in a maximum-security prison in Arizona. He has also been recognized for his reporting on mismanagement of western national forests and mine safety. So it's hardly surprising that Henry Dyer, Ring's fictional detective, is a fish and game agent turned P.I. and passionate about the environment. Dyer is introduced in *Telluride Smile* (1988) and makes a second appearance in *Peregrine Dream* (1990). Ring is also the author of *Arizona Kiss* (1991). A graduate of the University of Colorado, he has worked for the *Denver Post*, *Tucson Weekly News* and *Arizona Daily Star*. His column "Boondocks News" appeared in seven western newspapers. A native of Glendale (CA), he lives in Arizona.

Henry Dyer...fish and game agent turned P.I. in Colorado
- ❑ ❑ 1 - Telluride Smile (1988)
- ❑ ❑ 2 - Peregrine Dream (1990)

■ RIPLEY, Jack [P]

Mike Ripley wrote *Just Another Angel* (1988) as therapy after three years of work on a serious (and unpublished) thriller. The sequel, *Angel Touch* (1989), won the first of his two Last Laugh Awards for Britain's funniest crime novel. The trumpet-playing taxi driver's exploits are not so much whodunits as 'how-does-he-get-out-of-this?' adventures. While each book involves Angel and his cat Springsteen in a different world, Angel always looks out for his friends. As crime critic for the *Sunday Telegraph* Ripley reviews 4 or 5 novels a week. He has also written scripts for radio and TV, including the BBC's *Lovejoy* series. He once told *CADS* that he writes only on Sunday morning but "thinks all the time." For 20 years he has worked in the brewing industry, primarily as public relations officer for the Brewers' Society in London. An honors graduate of the University of East Anglia, he lives nearby in a converted farmhouse.

John George Davis...small-town constable in England
- ❑ ❑ 1 - Davis Doesn't Live Here Anymore (1971)
- ❑ ❑ 2 - The Pig That Got Up and Slowly Walked Away (1971)
- ❑ ❑ 3 - My Word You Should Have Seen Us (1972)
- ❑ ❑ 4 - My God How the Money Rolls In (1972)

■ RIPLEY, Mike

Mike Ripley wrote *Just Another Angel* (1988) as therapy after three years of work on a serious (and unpublished) thriller. The sequel, *Angel Touch* (1989), won the first of his two Last Laugh Awards for Britain's funniest crime novel. The trumpet-playing taxi driver's exploits are not so much whodunits as 'how-does-he-get-out-of-this?' adventures. While each book involves Angel and his cat Springsteen in a different world, Angel always looks out for his friends. As crime critic for the *Sunday Telegraph* Ripley reviews 4 or 5 novels a week. He has also written scripts for radio and TV, including the BBC's *Lovejoy* series. He once told *CADS* that he writes only on Sunday morning but "thinks all the time." For 20 years he has worked in the brewing industry, primarily as public relations officer for the Brewers' Society in London. An honors graduate of the University of East Anglia, he lives nearby in a converted farmhouse.

Fitzroy Maclean Angel...trumpet-playing taxi driver in London, England
- ❑ ❑ 1 - Just Another Angel (1988)
- ❑ ❑ 2 - **Angel Touch (1989) Last Laugh winner ★**
- ❑ ❑ 3 - Angel Hunt (1990)
- ❑ ❑ 4 - Angel Eyes (1990)
- ❑ ❑ 5 - Angel City (1991)
- ❑ ❑ 6 - **Angels in Arms (1991) Last Laugh winner ★**
- ❑ ❑ 7 - Angel Confidential (1995)
- ❑ ❑ 8 - Family of Angels (1996)

■ RIPLEY, W. L.

W. L. Ripley is the creator of former NFL star and reluctant detective Wyatt Storme, introduced in *Dreamsicle* (1993). While on a hunting vacation in the Missouri Ozarks, the Vietnam vet from Colorado stumbles into an underworld drug operation making plans to manufacture a highly addictive pharmaceutical code-named 'dreamsicle.' An enthusiastic fan who rated *Dreamsicle* a '10,' hailing Wyatt Storme as a 'Midwestern Travis McGee,' posted the following on amazon.com: "Not since James Lee Burke has an author captured the 'True Testosterone Essence' (his caps and quotes) with such humor, excitement and humanity."

Wyatt Storme…Vietnam vet ex-NFL star in N. Branson, Missouri
- ❏ ❏   1 - Dreamsicle (1993)
- ❏ ❏   2 - Storme Front (1995)
- ❏ ❏   3 - Electric Country Roulette (1996)

■ ROAT, Ronald Clair

Journalism professor Ronald Clair Roat has written 3 novels featuring Lansing, Michigan's own private eye, Stuart Mallory, introduced in *Close Softly the Doors* (1991). Mallory's most recent case, *High Walk* (1995), takes him across Lake Michigan on the historic ferry *S.S. Badger*, through Northern Wisconsin and into the Upper Peninsula of Michigan in search of a missing Vietnam buddy. A Michigan native who grew up in Ludington, Roat has worked as an investigative reporter at the *Lansing State Journal, Saginaw News* and *Dayton Daily News*, where he was also Consumer Advocate for the City of Dayton for nearly 5 years. He is currently coordinator of the journalism program at the University of Southern Indiana where he also teaches and supervises student publications. A graduate of Michigan State and Oregon State University, he lives in Evansville (IN).

Stuart Mallory…private eye in Lansing, Michigan
- ❏ ❏   1 - Close Softly the Doors (1991)
- ❏ ❏   2 - A Still and Icy Silence (1993)
- ❏ ❏   3 - High Walk (1995)

■ ROBERTS, John Maddox

Author of more than 40 books, John Maddox Roberts is primarily a science fiction and fantasy writer. His first mystery, *SPQR* (1990), introduces Decius Caecilius Metellus the Younger, detective and junior senator featured in seven sufficiently complex volumes to have spawned the *Official Strategy Guide SPQR* (1996) to provide a guide to the plot line and story elements. Roberts is also the creator of private eye Gabe Treloar, an ex-Los Angeles cop introduced in *A Typical American Town* (1994). Gabe's boss is Randall "Kit" Carson, the former LAPD officer who taught him everything he knows. Carson's high-tech agency is headquartered in Cleveland where Gabe is called in book 3, *Desperate Highways* (1997). Roberts has written at least 8 volumes in the Conan series and 5 volumes in the Stormlands series, several Dragonlance mysteries and other science fiction and fantasy titles. He lives in Virginia.

Gabe Treloar…ex-LA cop turned P.I. in Ohio
- ❏ ❏   1 - A Typical American Town (1994)
- ❏ ❏   2 - The Ghosts of Saigon (1996)

■ **ROBERTS, Les**

Two-time Shamus nominee Les Roberts became the first winner of the SMP/PWA Best First Private Eye Novel Contest in 1986. His winning entry, *An Infinite Number of Monkeys* (1987), was the debut of his Hollywood P.I., last seen in *The Lemon Chicken Jones* (1994). Saxon is featured in Milan Jacovich's next case, *A Shoot in Cleveland* (1998), when he comes to Ohio on a film project and Milan is hired to provide security. With more than 20 years' experience as a Hollywood writer and producer, Roberts' TV credits include over 2500 network and syndicated half-hour shows such as *Hollywood Squares* (where he was the original producer), *The Lucy Show*, *The Man from U.N.C.L.E.* and many more. A professional jazz musician, screenwriter and actor, he has taught at UCLA and Case Western Reserve and currently writes a monthly mystery review column for *The Plain Dealer*. A former restaurant critic, he is also a gourmet cook. Roberts lives in Cleveland (OH).

Milan Jacovich...blue-collar Slovenian P.I. with a master's degree in Cleveland, Ohio
- ❏ ❏ 1 - Pepper Pike (1988)
- ❏ ❏ 2 - Full Cleveland (1989)
- ❏ ❏ 3 - Deep Shaker (1991)
- ❏ ❏ 4 - The Cleveland Connection (1993)
- ❏ ❏ 5 - **The Lake Effect (1994) Shamus nominee** ☆
- ❏ ❏ 6 - The Duke of Cleveland (1995)
- ❏ ❏ 7 - Collision Bend (1996)
- ❏ ❏ 8 - The Cleveland Local (1997)
- ❏ ❏ 9 - A Shoot in Cleveland [with Saxon] (1998)

Saxon...actor private eye in Los Angeles, California
- ❏ ❏ 1 - **An Infinite Number of Monkeys (1987) SMP/PWA winner ★ Shamus nominee** ☆
- ❏ ❏ 2 - Not Enough Horses (1988)
- ❏ ❏ 3 - A Carrot for the Donkey (1989)
- ❏ ❏ 4 - Snake Oil (1990)
- ❏ ❏ 5 - Seeing the Elephant (1992)
- ❏ ❏ 6 - The Lemon Chicken Jones (1994)

■ **ROBINSON, Kevin**

Syndicated newspaper columnist Kevin Robinson is the creator of Stick Foster, a paraplegic newspaper reporter from Orlando, Florida, first seen in *Split Seconds* (1991), followed by *Mall Rats* (1992) and *A Matter of Perspective* (1993). A former FM radio personality, teacher and business owner, this Geneva College graduate runs a non-profit arts training organization called the Hephaistos Foundation, dedicated to building an arts training and conference center in Colorado. He also writes the twice-a-month syndicated column "Disabled in America." An accidental fall put him in a wheelchair at the age of 24, but as his readers know, he recently located his high school sweetheart after a 15-year search and has moved back to New York State, near where he grew up. This blues harp player is watching his karma change before his eyes and sharing the story with his readers. Stay tuned.

Stick Foster...paraplegic newspaper reporter in Orlando, Florida
- ❏ ❏ 1 - Split Seconds (1991)
- ❏ ❏ 2 - Mall Rats (1992)
- ❏ ❏ 3 - A Matter of Perspective (1993)

■ ROBINSON, Peter

Peter Robinson grew up in Yorkshire where he earned a B.A. at Leeds University. He then emigrated to Canada where he spent two years as writer-in-residence at the University of Windsor studying with Joyce Carol Oates and completing his M.A. in English. Then it was back to England for a Ph.D. in English literature from York University. While writing his doctoral dissertation, he took a break and created Yorkshire detective chief inspector Alan Banks, introduced in *Gallow's View* (1987), the only unsolicited manuscript accepted that year by Penguin. The book went on to earn nominations for both Creasey and Ellis awards for best first novel. The series has since picked up 7 award nominations a best-novel prize from Crime Writers of Canada. His short story "Innocence" won a Dagger award from Crime Writers' Association in 1991. A former English instructor at Seneca College, he lives in Toronto.

Alan Banks...Eastvale detective chief inspector in Yorkshire, England
- ❑ ❑ 1 - **Gallows View (1987) Creasey & Ellis nominee** ☆☆
- ❑ ❑ 2 - **A Dedicated Man (1988) Ellis nominee** ☆
- ❑ ❑ 3 - A Necessary End (1989)
- ❑ ❑ 4 - **The Hanging Valley (1989) Ellis nominee** ☆
- ❑ ❑ 5 - **Past Reason Hated (1991) Ellis winner** ★
- ❑ ❑ 6 - **Wednesday's Child (1992) Edgar & Ellis** ☆☆
- ❑ ❑ 7 - Final Account (1994)
- ❑ ❑ 8 - **Innocent Graves (1996) Hammett nominee** ☆
- ❑ ❑ 9 - Dead Right (1997)

■ RODERUS, Frank

American Spur Award winner Frank Roderus is the author of 6 western private eye novels published in 1984 and 1985, beginning with *The Oil Rig* (1984). All were Bantam paperback originals starring Carl Heller. In a recent on-line interview, Roderus stated he was particularly proud of his recent book, *Potter's Fields* (1996). The protagonist, a killer who hides behind a badge, grew out of an ugly encounter Roderus' wife had with a man who had been one of Lt. William Calley's soldiers at My Lai. Roderus said they wondered what came first, this man's cruel indifference or the killing of innocents. Joe Potter was his attempt to answer that question. The book is set after Wounded Knee. Although Roderus hated crawling inside Potter's head when he sat down to write, it was the first time in more than 20 years of writing that the story and the people went down on paper exactly as he had hoped they would.

Carl Heller...private eye in Wyoming
- ❑ ❑ 1 - The Oil Rig (1984)
- ❑ ❑ 2 - The Video Vandal (1984)
- ❑ ❑ 3 - The Rain Rustlers (1984)
- ❑ ❑ 4 - The Turn-Out Man (1984)
- ❑ ❑ 5 - The Coyote Crossing (1985)
- ❑ ❑ 6 - The Dead Heat (1985)

■ ROE, C. F.

C. F(rancis) Roe writes medical thrillers as Francis Roe and medical mysteries as C.F. Roe. His paperback mysteries feature Scottish general practictioner, Dr. Jean Montrose, a character based in part on his sister. The Montrose household, seen first in *A Nasty Bit of Murder* (1990), includes Jean's husband Steven and their teenage daughters Fiona and Lisbie. Among Roe's thrillers are *Under the Knife* (1998) and *Second Opinion* (1996). After completing his degree in medicine at Aberdeen University, he spent three years in the RAF surgical division where he trained as a pilot. He completed his surgical residency at Columbia Presbyterian Hospital in New York and later practiced vascular surgery at Yale. Author of more than 20 scientific papers and inventor of several pieces of medical equipment, he previously taught anatomy at Harvard Medical School. A native of Scotland, he lives in New Mexico.

Jean Montrose, Dr.....general practitioner in Scotland
- ❏ ❏   1 - A Nasty Bit of Murder (1990)
- ❏ ❏   2 - A Fiery Hint of Murder (1990)
- ❏ ❏   3 - A Classy Touch of Murder (1991) Brit.-Bad Blood
- ❏ ❏   4 - A Bonny Case of Murder (1991) Brit.-Deadly Partnership
- ❏ ❏   5 - A Torrid Piece of Murder (1992)
- ❏ ❏   6 - A Relative Act of Murder (1993) Brit.-Death in the Family
- ❏ ❏   7 - A Hidden Cause of Murder (1996)
- ❏ ❏   8 - A Tangled Knot of Murder (1996)

■ ROME, Anthony [P]

Anthony Rome was one of the many pseudonyms of Philadelphia-born Marvin H. Albert (1924-1996), who authored more than 100 westerns, mysteries, spy novels, film novelizations, biographies and works of history before his 1996 death in the south of France where he had lived for 20 years. A one-time magazine writer and editor, Albert went to Hollywood in 1965 to adapt some of his novels for film, including the first of his Tony Rome series featuring a Miami ex-cop and gambler. This sleazy storefront detective was made famous by Frank Sinatra's portrayal in the 1967 movie *Tony Rome* and its 1968 sequel *Lady in Cement*. Other Albert pseudonyms include Mike Barone, Al and Albert Conroy, Ian MacAlister, Nick Quarry and what may end up his best-known, J. D. Christilian, under which he wrote the best-seller *Scarlet Women* (1996).

Tony Rome...ex-cop gambler private eye in Miami, Florida
- ❏ ❏   1 - Miami Mayhem (1960)
- ❏ ❏   2 - Lady in Cement (1961)
- ❏ ❏   3 - My Kind of Game (1962)

■ ROOSEVELT, Elliott

Elliott Roosevelt (1910-1990), son of Franklin and Eleanor, was an advertising executive, radio broadcaster, pilot, military officer, politician, rancher, editor, author and mayor of Miami Beach (FL) from 1965 to 1969. He was aviation editor for Hearst newspapers and later president of Hearst Radio. Although his publisher says Roosevelt left behind a stack of manuscripts when he died, it has long been assumed (based on acknowledgments in the early books) they were ghost-written by William Harrington, author of the Columbo series. Clearly these mysteries are enjoyed by many readers who eagerly suspend their disbelief that Eleanor Roosevelt was one clever detective. The 17th case for the former First Lady is *Murder in the Map Room* (1998), where a 1943 White House visit by Madame Chiang Kai-shek brings the opium trade and a dead Chinese shoe salesman to 1600 Pennsylvania Avenue.

Eleanor Roosevelt...1940s First Lady in Washington, D.C.
- ❏ ❏   1 - Murder and the First Lady (1984)
- ❏ ❏   2 - The Hyde Park Murder (1985)
- ❏ ❏   3 - Murder at Hobcaw Barony (1986)
- ❏ ❏   4 - The White House Pantry Murder (1987)
- ❏ ❏   5 - Murder at the Palace (1988)
- ❏ ❏   6 - Murder in the Rose Garden (1989)
- ❏ ❏   7 - Murder in the Oval Office (1989)
- ❏ ❏   8 - Murder in the Blue Room (1990)
- ❏ ❏   9 - A First Class Murder (1991)
- ❏ ❏ 10 - Murder in the Red Room (1991)
- ❏ ❏ 11 - Murder in the West Wing (1992)
- ❏ ❏ 12 - Murder in the East Room (1993)
- ❏ ❏ 13 - Royal Murder (1994)
- ❏ ❏ 14 - Murder in the Executive Mansion (1995)
- ❏ ❏ 15 - Murder in the Chateau (1996)
- ❏ ❏ 16 - Murder at Midnight (1997)

■ ROSEN, Richard

Richard Rosen is the creator of ex-baseball player private eye Harvey Blissberg, introduced in the the Edgar award-winning first novel, *Strike Three You're Dead* (1984). Harvey plays centerfield for the Providence (RI) Jewels, an American League expansion team, but turns detective when his roommate is murdered in the series opener. The action shifts to basketball and Boston when Harvey quits baseball in book 2, while television is the focus in book 3. As a favor to his brother, Harvey heads to Chicago in book 4 when a buddy of Norm's ends up dead. A graduate of Harvard who also attended Brown University, Rosen has worked as a *Playboy* assistant editor, a Somerville (MA) restaurant chef, an expository writing instructor at Harvard and a staff writer and columnist ("Dining Out") at *Boston* magazine. A native of Chicago, he lives in Cambridge (MA).

Harvey Blissberg...ex-baseball player turned private eye in Boston, Masachusetts
- ❏ ❏ 1 - **Strike Three, You're Dead (1984) Edgar winner ★**
- ❏ ❏ 2 - Fadeaway (1986)
- ❏ ❏ 3 - Saturday Night Dead (1988)
- ❏ ❏ 4 - World of Hurt (1994)

■ ROSENBERG, Robert

After growing up in the suburbs of Boston, Robert Rosenberg spent 15 years as a journalist before writing *Crimes of the City* (1991), his first novel about Avram Cohen, once Jerusalem's top detective and police commander. "Wracked by true believers of every stripe, Israel has become an ideal setting for crime fiction," said *Booklist*, "and Cohen, the detective perpetually caught in the crossfire, makes a wonderfully resonant hero." Since 1995 Rosenberg has maintained his own website <www.ariga.com> where he has posted the first chapters of all 3 Cohen mysteries, along with the entire text of book 2. Having worked every job a restaurant can offer, from dishwasher to maitre d', he now writes 6 to 8 hours a day from his apartment study, about a block from the beach in Tel Aviv. He is co-author with Moshe Betser of *Secret Soldier: The True Life Story of Israel's Greatest Commando* (1996).

Avram Cohen...recently retired police officer in Jerusalem, Israel
- ❏ ❏ 1 - Crimes of the City (1991)
- ❏ ❏ 2 - The Cutting Room (1993)
- ❏ ❏ 3 - House of Guilt (1996)

■ ROSS, Jonathan [P]

Jonathan Ross is the pseudonym of John Rossiter, an ex-detective chief superintendent of Wiltshire Constabulary and creator of the pipe-smoking Detective Superintendent George Rogers. This long-running police series, launched with *The Blood Running Cold* (1968), is set in the fictitious industrial city of Abbotsburn in the north of England. Det. Supt. Rogers has few illusions about himself—he is impatient, often irascible and highly intelligent. As one *Mystery News* reviewer so aptly put it, "he's thorny, horny, and engaging." As noted in *St. James* Guide, sex and a generous helping of violence are usually a component in these novels, but rarely to the detriment of the plot-line. Plots are complex and switches in identity, false trails and suspects who lie their heads off abound. Under his own name the author has written an espionage series featuring a British agent with a police background.

George Rogers, Insp.....police inspector in Abbotsburn, England
- ❏ ❏ 1 - The Blood Running Cold (1968)'
- ❏ ❏ 2 - Diminished by Death (1968)
- ❏ ❏ 3 - Dead at First Hand (1969)
- ❏ ❏ 4 - The Deadest Thing You Ever Saw (1969)
- ❏ ❏ 5 - Here Lies Nancy Frail (1972)
- ❏ ❏ 6 - The Burning of Billy Toober (1974)
- ❏ ❏ 7 - I Know What It's Like to Die (1976)

❑ ❑   8 - A Rattling of Old Bones (1979)
❑ ❑   9 - Dark Blue and Dangerous (1981)
❑ ❑ 10 - Death's Head (1982)
❑ ❑ 11 - Dead Eye (1983)
❑ ❑ 12 - Drop Dead (1984)
❑ ❑ 13 - Burial Deferred (1985)
❑ ❑ 14 - Fate Accomplished (1987)
❑ ❑ 15 - Sudden Departures (1988)
❑ ❑ 16 - A Time for Dying (1989)
❑ ❑ 17 - Daphne Dead and Done For (1990)
❑ ❑ 18 - Murder Be Hanged (1992)
❑ ❑ 19 - The Body of a Woman (1994)
            U.S.-None the Worse for a Hanging
❑ ❑ 20 - Murder! Murder! Burning Bright (1996)

■ ROSS, Philip [P]

Philip Ross is the pseudonym of Philip R. Eck who has written two paperback originals featuring Boston private investigator James Marley, first seen in the Shamus-nominated *Blue Heron* (1985) and later in *White Flower* (1989). He is also the author of a pair of espionage novels published by Tor in hardcover. American CIA operative, Tom Talley goes to Czechoslovakia on a mission in *Hovey's Deception* (1986), while his second outing, *Talley's Truth* (1987), also takes place in Europe. A writer and college professor who attended Amherst and Yale Drama School, according to Allen J. Hubin's *Crime Fiction II* (1994), Eck has written a textbook on stage design. Writing as Philip Ross, he is also the author of *True Lies* (1994) about a man and woman who fall in love in London, only to end up being chased by killers.

James Marley...P.I. investigator in Boston, Massachusetts
❑ ❑ 1 - **Blue Heron (1985) Shamus nominee** ☆
❑ ❑ 2 - White Flower (1989)

Tom Talley...American CIA operative
❑ ❑ 1 - Hovey's Deception (1986)
❑ ❑ 2 - Tally's Truth (1987)

■ ROSSITER, John

John Rossiter, ex-detective chief superintendent of Wiltshire Constabulary, spent 30 years as a police officer. Writing as Jonathan Ross he has created a long-running police series featuring Detective Superintendent George Rogers, whose constabulary includes the fictitious northern industrial city of Abbotsburn. Under his own name, he wrote a series of suspense espionage novels during the mid-1970s featuring an intelligence agent with a police background. Roger Tallis is first seen in *The Murder Makers* (1970). Also published under the Rossiter name were *The Man Who Came Back* (1978) and *Dark Flight* (1981). Born in Devon and educated at military schools and Police College (Hampshire), Rossiter once wrote a column for the *Wiltshire Courier*. Immediately following his retirement in 1969, he lived in Spain for 8 years. He has since returned to England and lives in Wiltshire.

Roger Tallis...British agent with a police background in England
❑ ❑ 1 - The Murder Makers (1970)
❑ ❑ 2 - The Deadly Green (1970)
❑ ❑ 3 - The Victims (1971)
❑ ❑ 4 - A Rope for General Dietz (1972)
❑ ❑ 5 - The Manipulators (1973)
❑ ❑ 6 - The Villains (1974)
❑ ❑ 7 - The Golden Virgin (1975)

■ RUSSELL, Alan

At 6' 7" Alan Russell is probably the world's tallest mystery writer. If that's not enough to make him stand out, he married a woman who talks with gorillas. His first novel, *No Sign of Murder* (1990), about a missing deaf woman who taught sign language to gorillas, makes use of his wife's research with world-famous gorillas Koko and Michael. After two private eye novels he wrote a pair of laugh-out-loud mysteries featuring San Diego hotel detective, Am Caulfield. Clearly his 15 years' experience as general manager of a similar beachfront hotel was put to good use. Macavity and Anthony nominations for best novel last year went to *Multiple Wounds* (1996), his first book featuring homicide detective Orson Cheever. In 1998 he'll publish *Shame* (1998), a nonseries thriller about the son of a serial murderer who may be re-enacting the sins of his father. Russell hopes to follow that with book 2 in his Orson Cheever series.

Am Caulfield...hotel detective in San Diego, California
- ❏ ❏　1 - The Hotel Detective (1994)
- ❏ ❏　2 - The Fat Innkeeper (1995)

Orson Cheever...homicide detective in San Diego, California
- ❏ ❏　1 - **Multiple Wounds (1996) Anthony & Macavity nominee** ☆☆

Stuart Winter...private eye in San Francisco, California
- ❏ ❏　1 - No Sign of Murder (1990)
- ❏ ❏　2 - The Forest Prime Evil (1992)

■ RUSSELL, Martin

British journalist Martin (James) Russell is the author of more than 35 crime novels, including five from the early 1970s featuring newspaper editor Jim Larkin, introduced in *Deadline* (1971). The editor's arrival in a seaside English town coincides with the start of a series of brutal murders. Casual cynicisms of the newsroom and growing tensions of the community are described with economy and conviction, according to Martin Edwards in *St. James Guide*. Edwards also notes Russell's skill at confounding expectations. Often his victims turn out to have been pursuing Machiavellian designs of their own. After starting his journalism career as a reporter for the *Kentish Times*, Russell moved to the *Croydon Advertiser* where he was a reporter and sub-editor for 15 years. His recent crime novels include *Leisure Pursuit* (1993) and *Mystery Lady* (1992).

Jim Larkin...journalist in England
- ❏ ❏　1 - Deadline (1971)
- ❏ ❏　2 - Concrete Evidence (1972)
- ❏ ❏　3 - Crime Wave (1974)
- ❏ ❏　4 - Phantom Holiday (1974)
- ❏ ❏　5 - Murder by the Mile (1975)

■ SADLER, Mark [P]

Mark Sadler is one of the pseudonyms of Dennis Lynds, author of 5 crime and mystery series under 5 different names. The 6-book series written as Mark Sadler features ex-actor private eye Paul Shaw who is part of a large investigations firm with offices in New York and Los Angeles. According to Francis M. Nevins, writing in *1001 Midnights* (1986), "No private-eye novels capture the nightmare America of the Vietnam and Nixon years like...Mark Sadler in the early '70s." Nevins rates *The Falling Man* (1971) the best and concludes, "Sadler has no peers at integrating the foul underside of that period into the traditional P.I. novel." Past president of Private Eye Writers of America, this author was awarded the PWA Lifetime Achievement Award in 1988. Married to mystery writer Gayle Lynds, he lives in Santa Barbara (CA).

Paul Shaw...private eye in New York
- ❏ ❏　1 - The Falling Man (1970)
- ❏ ❏　2 - Here To Die (1971)
- ❏ ❏　3 - Mirror Image (1972)

❏ ❏ 4 - Circle of Fire (1973)
❏ ❏ 5 - Touch of Death (1981)
❏ ❏ 6 - Deadly Innocents (1986)

■ **SALLIS, James**

James Sallis is a renowned critic, poet, essayist, teacher and novelist. In addition to his mystery series featuring black New Orleans private eye Lew Griffin, Sallis has written science fiction and a critical book about Jim Thompson, David Goodis and Chester Himes titled *Difficult Lives* (1993). The Griffin series opener was nominated for a Shamus award and named one of the 10 best mystery novels of 1992 by the *Los Angeles Times*. Lew's next case is his fourth, *Eye of the Cricket* (1997). Also new from Sallis is *Death Will Have Your Eyes* (1997), described as John le Carré meets the Coen brothers moving like a bullet train. After nine years of uneventful retirement, a former spy now known as David gets a midnight call with news that the only other survivor of their elite unit has gone rogue and it's David's job to bring him in. Sallis lives in Phoenix (AZ) after many years in New Orleans.

Lew Griffin...black private eye in New Orleans, Louisiana
❏ ❏ 1 - **The Long-Legged Fly (1992) Shamus nominee** ☆
❏ ❏ 2 - **Moth (1993) Shamus nominee** ☆
❏ ❏ 3 - Black Hornet [prequel] (1994)

■ **SANDERS, Lawrence**

Lawrence Sanders assembled his first novel, the Edgar award-winning *The Anderson Tapes* (1970), purportedly from surveillance transcripts. He then transformed one of its minor characters into a leading man and the "Deadly Sins" series was born. In the 1980 movie of *The First Deadly Sin* (1973), Frank Sinatra played Capt. Delaney (demoted to Sgt. in the film) and David Dukes the serial killer. In the early '90s he launched a comic whodunit series featuring Archy McNally, the foppish but likable head of discreet inquiries at his father's tony Palm Beach law firm. "Imagine Lord Peter Wimsey as a Floridian," suggested one reviewer. Tooling around town in his fire-engine red Miata, Archy keeps tabs on the rich and famous. Formerly the editor of *Science and Mechanics* magazine, Sanders was born in Brooklyn (NY). His caper novel (*Caper*, 1980), set in a male brothel, was written as Lesley Andress.

Arch McNally...playboy private eye in Palm Beach, Florida
❏ ❏ 1 - McNally's Secret (1992)
❏ ❏ 2 - McNally's Luck (1992)
❏ ❏ 3 - McNally's Risk (1993)
❏ ❏ 4 - McNally's Caper (1994)
❏ ❏ 5 - McNally's Trial (1995)
❏ ❏ 6 - McNally's Puzzle (1996)
❏ ❏ 7 - McNally's Gamble (1997)

Edward X. "Iron Balls" Delaney...retired chief of detectives in New York, New York
❏ ❏ 1 - The First Deadly Sin (1973)
❏ ❏ 2 - The Second Deadly Sin (1977)
❏ ❏ 3 - The Third Deadly Sin (1981)
❏ ❏ 4 - The Fourth Deadly Sin (1985)

Peter Tangent...troubleshooter for American oil company in Africa
❏ ❏ 1 - The Tangent Objective (1976)
❏ ❏ 2 - The Tangent Factor (1978)

Timothy Cone...Wall Street financial detective in New York, New York
❏ ❏ 1 - The Timothy Files (1987)
❏ ❏ 2 - Timothy's Game (1988)

■ SANDERS, William

William Sanders is the creator of Cherokee writer and Tulsa private eye Taggart Roper, who sometimes takes on not-quite-legal odd jobs to pay the bills. This P.I.'s supporting cast includes his Cherokee lover Rita Ninekiller and Wiley Harmon, the crookedest cop on the Tulsa PD. First seen in *The Next Victim* (1993), Roper is hired by a Sarah Lawrence student to look into the death of a prostitute which leads straight to a rich televangelist. Book 2 finds Roper suspected of murder with a half million dollars of stolen drug money adding to the excitement. *Booklist* ("great dialogue and wonderful witty characters") and *Publishers Weekly* loved these looks at the modern-day Native American scene told by a member of the Cherokee tribe. Born in Arkansas, Sanders lives in Tahlequah (OK). His more than a dozen other novels include *The Wild Blue and the Gray* (1991) and *Journey to Fusang* (1988).

Taggart Roper...Cherokee writer and private eye in Tulsa, Oklahoma
- ❏ ❏   1 - The Next Victim (1993)
- ❏ ❏   2 - A Death on 66 (1994)
- ❏ ❏   3 - Blood Autumn (1995)

■ SANDFORD, John [P]

John Sandford is the pseudonym of Pulitzer prize-winning journalist John Camp for his hard-edged thrillers starring Lucas Davenport, computer game designer and Porsche-driving homicide detective. As deputy chief (starting in book 6) his job is to put away the worst criminals and keep the media off the chief's back. The two women in Davenport's life are a surgeon named Weather and his childhood friend who is now a nun. As his spiritual advisor and a professor of psychology, he calls her Nun the Wiser. During the 1970s Sandford worked alongside Carl Hiassen and Edna Buchanan at the *Miami Herald*, later transferring to the *St. Paul Pioneer Press* where he won a 1986 Pulitzer for his year-long series on a Minnesota farming family. His new series stars Anna Batory (pronounced ba-TOR-ee), seen first in *The Night Crew* (1997). Davenport's next case is *Secret Prey* (1998).

Anna Batory...TV news video freelancer in Los Angeles, California
- ❏ ❏   1 - The Night Crew (1997)

Kidd & Luellen...computer whiz and thief in Minnesota
- ❏ ❏   1 - The Fool's Run (1989)
- ❏ ❏   2 - The Empress File (1991)

Lucas Davenport...police detective and war games designer in Minneapolis, Minnesota
- ❏ ❏   1 - Rules of Prey (1989)
- ❏ ❏   2 - Shadow Prey (1990)
- ❏ ❏   3 - Eyes of Prey (1991)
- ❏ ❏   4 - Silent Prey (1992)
- ❏ ❏   5 - Winter Prey (1993)
- ❏ ❏   6 - Night Prey (1994)
- ❏ ❏   7 - Mind Prey (1995)
- ❏ ❏   8 - Sudden Prey (1996)

■ SARRANTONIO, Al

Al Sarrantonio is a former Doubleday editor known primarily for his dark fantasy. He has also written science fiction, westerns and mysteries, including a pair of novels with Jack Blaine, retired Yonkers cop with a P.I. license. Introduced in the Shamus-nominated *Cold Night* (1989), Blaine, who has a fondness for telescopes and stargazing, has left the force under a cloud, after being forced out by some crooked cops. In book 2, he's coming back from a tragic affair that ended with his lover's suicide, so he's susceptible to the woman whose cop husband (a buddy of Blaine's) has disappeared under strange circumstances. Sarrantonio has written entries in both the Babylon 5 (*Personal Agendas*, 1997) and Five World Sagas (*Journey*, 1997 and *Return*, 1998), as well as several novels of the West for M. Evans.

Jack Blaine...retired Yonkers cop with a P.I. license in New York, New York
- ❏ ❏ 1 - **Cold Night (1989) Shamus nominee** ☆
- ❏ ❏ 2 - Summer Cool (1993)

■ SATTERTHWAIT, Walter

Walter Satterthwait earned a best-first-P.I.-novel Shamus nomination for *Wall of Glass* (1989), featuring Santa Fe (NM) private eye Joshua Croft and his partner Rita Mondragon. In addition to his best-novel Agatha nomination for *Escapade* (1995), which introduced Houdini and Sir Arthur Conan Doyle, Satterthwait's French publisher, Le Masque, flew him to Paris for a black-tie dinner in his honor and awarded him the Prix du Roman d'Aventures. The brilliant pair of detectives returns in *Masquerade* (1998). A resident of Sante Fe (NM), Satterthwait has lived in New York City, Portland (OR), Philadelphia (PA), an island off the coast of Kenya, Thailand, Greece, the Netherlands, England and France, where he has worked variously as an encyclopedia salesman, proofreader, bartender, and restaurant manager. He is also the author of historical mysteries *Miss Lizzie* (1989) and *Wilde West* (1991).

Houdini & Conan Doyle...19th century escape artist and writer in London, England
- ❏ ❏ 1 - **Escapade (1995) Prix Roman winner ★ Agatha nominee** ☆
- ❏ ❏ 2 - Masquerade (1998)

Joshua Croft...wisecracking P.I. in Sante Fe, New Mexico
- ❏ ❏ 1 - **Wall of Glass (1989) Shamus nominee** ☆
- ❏ ❏ 2 - At Ease With the Dead (1991)
- ❏ ❏ 3 - A Flower in the Desert (1992)
- ❏ ❏ 4 - The Hanged Man (1993)
- ❏ ❏ 5 - Accustomed to the Dark (1996)

■ SAUTER, Eric

Eric Sauter has written a trilogy of private eye novels featuring Robert E. Lee Hunter, whose first appearance won an Edgar nomination for best paperback original. A grown up child of the '60s, Hunter is a journalist whose book earned enough from the film rights to buy an island in the Delaware River. Along with his dog Jules, he just wants to rebuild the porch on his Victorian house. In book 2, he's hunting art forgeries and dealing with "insane Russians carrying a 500-year-old grudge, a vicious millionaire and a handful of government geeks." Three blockbuster thrillers followed the Hunter series, including *Predators* (1987), *Skeletons* (1990) and *Backfire* (1992). Formerly a reporter for the *Trenton Times* (NJ), Sauter has worked as a Senate speechwriter and publications manager for Squibb Corporation. Born in Bay City (MI), he is a graduate of Mchigan State University.

Robert Lee Hunter...30-something wealthy P.I. in New Jersey
- ❏ ❏ 1 - **Hunter (1983) Edgar nominee** ☆
- ❏ ❏ 2 - Hunter and the Ikon (1984)
- ❏ ❏ 3 - Hunter and the Raven (1984)

■ SAYLOR, Steven

Steven Saylor is the author of the Roma Sub Rosa historical mysteries featuring Gordianus the Finder. The screenplay for book 2 has been written by Donald Westlake, with the movie rights sold to Brad Wyman and United Artists. *Arms of Nemesis* (1992) takes place during the Spartacus slave revolt when Gordianus must find a killer or Rome's richest citizen will slaughter every slave in the household as retribution. Saylor's latest project is a big novel (*Honor the Dead*) about an actual case of serial murder in 1885 Austin, predating Jack the Ripper. A young Will Porter (who later became O Henry) was living in Austin at the time and dubbed the killer "The Servant Girl Annihilator." A Texas native and graduate of the University of Texas, Saylor lives in Berkeley (CA) where he can sit on his deck and write on his Powerbook eight months of the year, entertained by his cat Hildegarde.

Gordianus the Finder...private eye circa 56 B.C. in Rome, Italy
- ❏ ❏ 1 - Roman Blood (1990)
- ❏ ❏ 2 - Arms of Nemesis (1992)
- ❏ ❏ 3 - **Catalina's Riddle (1993) Lambda winner ★ Hammett nominee** ☆
- ❏ ❏ 4 - The Venus Throw (1995)
- ❏ ❏ 5 - A Murder on the Appian Way (1996)
- ❏ ❏ 6 - House of the Vestals (1997)

■ SCHOLEFIELD, Alan

Alan Scholefield is the creator of a British police series featuring an old-fashioned detective superintendent and his rookie partner, the suave intellectual. In book 3 (*Publishers Weekly* starred review), *Never Die in January* (1992), the older man's personal life is in such a shambles that rumors are circulating that he might be a bent cop. His own partner is ordered to investigate him, only to learn the older man is marked for death in a devious plot of revenge. Scholefield's newest series character is Anne Vernon, a doctor in an all-male prison, seen first in *Burn Out* (1994). Author of more than 20 novels, he has also published under the names Lee Jordan and A.T. Scholefield. A former journalist, he once wrote short stories in Spain. Born and educated in South Africa, he lives with his wife, novelist Anthea Goddard, in Hampshire (England).

Anne Vernon...prison doctor in Kingstown, Sussex, England
- ❏ ❏ 1 - Burn Out (1994)
- ❏ ❏ 2 - Buried Treasure (1995)

George Macrae, Det. Supt. & Leopold Silver, Det. Sgt.....old-fashioned copper & intellectual rookie partner in London, England
- ❏ ❏ 1 - Dirty Weekend (1989)
- ❏ ❏ 2 - Thief Taker (1991)
- ❏ ❏ 3 - Never Die in January (1992)
- ❏ ❏ 4 - Threats and Menaces (1993)
- ❏ ❏ 5 - Burn Out (1994)
- ❏ ❏ 6 - Night Moves (1996)

■ **SCHOONOVER, Winston [P]**

Winston Schoonover is the pseudonym of Charles Sevilla who published his first John Wilkes novel pseudonymously, while the sequel appeared under his own name. Book 1, *Wilkes: His Life and Crimes* (1990), introduces hot-headed, arrogant John Wilkes, the American Rumpole who succeeds repeatedly in turning a courtroom into a circus. In *Wilkes on Trial* (1993), our comic hero gets in over his head when a judge he has harassed in court turns up dead. Published under the byline Charles M. Sevilla is *Disorder in the Court: Great Fractured Moments in Courtroom History* (1993), a collection of verbatim exchanges from America's courtrooms, including the case of a lawyer who claims he was advised by God not to go to court. The author is a San Diego attorney.

John Wilkes...defense attorney in New York, New York
- ❏ ❏ 1 - Wilkes: His Life and Crimes (1990)
- ❏ ❏ 2 - Wilkes on Trial [as by Charles Sevilla] (1993)

■ **SCHOPEN, Bernard**

Ross Macdonald scholar Bernard Schopen is the author of *Ross Macdonald (Twayne's United States Author Series, No. 557)* published in 1990. He is also the Shamus-nominated creator of Reno (NV) lawyer-private eye Jack Ross, cast in the image of Lew Archer. Schopen "understands what made Macdonald so good," said *Booklist* in their review of book 3, *The Iris Deception* (1996), "and he has translated that understanding into a beautifully crafted novel that deserves such comparisons." The first two books in the series were published in hardcover by Mysterious Press in 1989 and 1990 and then reprinted in paperback in 1994 and 1995 by the University of Nevada Press as part of their Western Literature Series. The Nevada press followed with book 3 in 1996. A native of South Dakota, Schopen has taught English at Saint Anselm College in New Hampshire.

Jack Ross...private eye in Reno, Nevada
- ❏ ❏ 1 - The Big Silence (1989)
- ❏ ❏ **2 - The Desert Look (1990) Shamus nominee** ☆

■ **SCHORR, Mark**

Edgar award-winner Mark Schorr is the creator of a crabby New York cabbie transformed into Red Diamond, super hero, after waking up (in a strange hotel) stunned from the shock of discovering his wife had sold his prized pulp collection. As George Kelley points out in *St. James Guide*, this is the Clark Kent/Superman, David Banner/Incredible Hulk model applied to private eye fiction. What makes it work, he says, is the sophistication and feeling Schorr gives his characters. Under the name Scott Ellis, he published *The Borzoi Control* (1986), along with several P.I./espionage novels as Schorr during the late '80s. A New York City native, he has worked as a newspaper reporter, television investigative news producer and journalism instructor, until he recently changed careers. After earning an M.A. in counseling psychology from Lewis and Clark College, he is now working as a psychotherapist.

Robert Stark...private investigator in the United States
- ❏ ❏ 1 - Overkill (1987)
- ❏ ❏ 2 - Seize the Dragon (1988)
- ❏ ❏ 3 - Gunpowder (1989)

Simon Jaffe aka Red Diamond...cab-driving pulp collector turned P.I. in New York, New York
- ❏ ❏ **1 - Red Diamond, Private Eye (1983) Edgar winner** ★
- ❏ ❏ 2 - Ace of Diamonds (1984)
- ❏ ❏ 3 - Diamond Rock (1985)

■ SCHUTZ, Benjamin

Shamus and Edgar award-winner Benjamin M. Schutz is the author of a hard-boiled private eye series featuring Washington, DC investigator Leo Haggerty, first seen in *Embrace the Wolf* (1985), a best-first-novel Shamus nominee. The series has since been twice nominated and took best-novel Shamus honors for *A Tax in Blood* (1987). When last seen in *Mexico is Forever* (1994), Leo rated two thumbs up from *Booklist* and *Kirkus Reviews*: "Fast, mean and twisty, with all the usual violence saved for dessert: a perfect case for Leo's manic style." Schutz's short story "Mary, Mary, Shut the Door" (*Deadly Allies*) won Edgar and Shamus awards for best short story in 1993. Specializing in child custody and child sexual abuse cases, Schutz is a clinical and forensic psychologist. He lives in Northern Virginia.

Leo Haggerty...rough and tough P.I. in Washington, D.C.
- ❑ ❑ 1 - **Embrace the Wolf (1985) Shamus nominee** ☆
- ❑ ❑ 2 - All the Old Bargains (1985)
- ❑ ❑ 3 - **A Tax in Blood (1987) Shamus winner** ★
- ❑ ❑ 4 - The Things We Do for Love (1989)
- ❑ ❑ 5 - **A Fistful of Empty (1991) Shamus nominee** ☆
- ❑ ❑ 6 - Mexico Is Forever (1994)

SCOTT, Justin

Justin Scott is the creator of Connecticut real estate agent and former Wall Street trader Ben Abbott, introduced in *HardScape* (1994) and seen later in *Stone Dust* (1995). Author of 16 novels, including his Edgar-nominated *Many Happy Returns* (1973), Scott was born into a family of professional writers. His father, Bradford Scott, wrote some 250 westerns, while his mother penned novels, romances and short stories. With a B.A. and M.A. in American history, he has traveled in Russia, China and Scotland doing research. When stalled on another project some years ago, Scott began a rewrite of *Treasure Island* as a writing exercise. In late 1994, 111 years after the original, Scott published his line by line rewrite of the Stevenson classic updated to the 1950s. *Kirkus* loved it. "An enjoyable enough novel on its own," they said, "especially delightful when read with a copy of Stevenson's version on hand for comparison."

Ben Abbott...ex-Wall Street financier turned realtor in Newbury, Connecticut
- ❑ ❑ 1 - HardScape (1994)
- ❑ ❑ 2 - Stone Dust (1995)

■ SELWYN, Francis [P]

Francis Selwyn is the pseudonym of Donald Thomas, author of 5 mysteries featuring Sgt. William Clarence Verity, a portly, plodding Victorian policeman, introduced in *Cracksman on Velvet* (1974), also published as *Sgt. Verity and the Cracksman* (1975). The prudish, moralizing opinions of the sergeant are representative of the public morality of London at the time. As Fred Dueren in *St. James Guide* points out, Selwyn uses crime fiction to portray history rather than using history as a background for crime." In book 2, *Sgt. Verity and the Imperial Diamond* (1975), the righteous policeman survives his exposure to the heathen society of a mutinous 1850s India. A native of Sussex, the author attended Oxford University and later worked as an adult education organizer and research assistant for the BBC in London. Since 1971 he has worked as freelance translator and regular contributor to *Penthouse* (London).

William Clarence Verity...portly Victorian police sergeant in London, England
- ❑ ❑ 1 - Cracksman on Velvet (1974)
  - APA-Sgt. Verity and the Cracksman
- ❑ ❑ 2 - Sgt. Verity and the Imperial Diamond (1975)
- ❑ ❑ 3 - Sgt. Verity Presents His Compliments (1977)
- ❑ ❑ 4 - Sgt. Verity and the Blood Royal (1979)
- ❑ ❑ 5 - Sgt. Verity and the Swell Mob (1980)

■ **SERAFIN, David [P]**

David Serafin is the pseudonym of Oxford Spanish professor and medievalist Ian Michael for his series featuring Madrid police superintendent Luis Bernal, introduced in the Creasey Award-winning *Saturday of Glory* (1979). Book 2, *Madrid Underground* (1982), opens in May 1977 as Spain prepares for its first post-Franco general election. The book is "full of historical and political observations, plus some tidbits for tourists, including the correct term for draft beer (una caña)," says Nina King (*Crimes of the Scene*). In book 3 (published 2nd in the U.S.), Serafin uses the ecclesiastical calendar as an organizing device and the colors of traditional vestments provide clues for the liturgically-informed. "If a fuller flavor of Spain is required, no one could be a better guide than the hearty Bernal," says Ian Mechan (*St. James Guide*). Food lovers will be especially happy.

Luis Bernal....Spanish police superintendent in Spain
- ❏ ❏ 1 - **Saturday of Glory (1979) Creasey winner ★**
- ❏ ❏ 2 - Madrid Underground (1982)
- ❏ ❏ 3 - Christmas Rising (1982)
- ❏ ❏ 4 - The Body in Cadiz Bay (1985)
- ❏ ❏ 5 - Port of Light (1987)
- ❏ ❏ 6 - The Angel of Torremolinos (1988)

■ **SHATNER, William**

After his days as Captain James T. Kirk of the *Starship Enterprise* and *T.J. Hooker*, Shatner has reinvented himself as a novelist with the best-selling Tek series featuring Jake Cardigan, the greatest private detective of the 22nd century. Working through the Cosmos Detective Agency, ex-cop Cardigan and his partner Sid Gomez take on their next evil force in book 9, *Tek Net* (1997). According to *Publishers Weekly*, the Tek books have spawned a comic book series, a set of trading cards, four TV movies and a cable television series. Shatner has had two other careers in between acting and writing. He became a director (*Star Trek V: The Final Frontier*) and a horse breeder (Arabians). In addition to the Tek series he has written a nonseries novel (*Man O'War*, 1996) about an aging diplomat of the near future who's called on by the not-so-nice Earth government to convince a Martian colony to see it "our way."

Jack Cardigan...22nd century ex-cop private eye in Los Angeles, California
- ❏ ❏ 1 - Tekwar (1989)
- ❏ ❏ 2 - Teklords (1990)
- ❏ ❏ 3 - Tek Vengeance (1991)
- ❏ ❏ 4 - Teklab (1992)
- ❏ ❏ 5 - Tek Secret (1993)
- ❏ ❏ 6 - Tek Power (1994)
- ❏ ❏ 7 - Tek Money (1995)
- ❏ ❏ 8 - Tek Kill (1996)

■ **SHAW, Simon**

Simon Shaw is a professional actor who has "all but cornered the market in laugh-aloud surreal crime farce" according to *The Times* of London. Winner of two Last Laugh Daggers from the British Crime Writers' Association, Shaw is the creator of anti-hero Philip Fletcher, a supremely self-centered actor and murderer at work in the London theatre world. Introduced in *Murder Out of Tune* (1988), Fletcher's next performance with be his 5th, *Act of Darkness*, scheduled for 1997 release in England. One of Shaw's two Daggers for best comic mystery was for his nonseries *Killer Cinderella* (1990), the other was for Fletcher's 4th escapade, *The Villain of the Earth* (1994). Book 3, *Dead for a Ducat* appeared in British editions in 1992 but was not published in the U.S. until 1996.

Philip Fletcher...British thespian and killer in London, England
- ❏ ❏ 1 - Murder Out of Tune (1990)
- ❏ ❏ 2 - Bloody Instructions (1992)
- ❏ ❏ 3 - Dead for a Ducat (1992)
- ❏ ❏ 4 - **The Villain of the Earth (1994) Last Laugh winner ★**

■ SHERBURNE, James

James Sherburne's series mysteries feature an 1890s sportswriter named Paddy Moretti who was always on the hunt for the next big story in the world of sports. In the series opener, *Death's Pale Horse* (1980), he heads for Saratoga Springs, which was then in its heyday, to cover a great match race. In book 2 the story is a prize fight in Kansas, while book 3 centers on a New York political boss. And then it's off to Chicago to cover the American Derby, which in its time was as important as the Kentucky Derby is today. Book 5, *Death's Bright Arrow* (1989), takes Paddy to Kentucky again, this time to interview a well-known breeder. Shockingly, Paddy finds the man's horses have been attacked and his wife killed. But Paddy uses his sources about the track riffraff to find out what happened.

Paddy Moretti...1890s sportswriter in the United States
- ❏ ❏ 1 - Death's Pale Horse (1980)
- ❏ ❏ 2 - Death's Gray Angel (1981)
- ❏ ❏ 3 - Death's Clenched Fist (1982)
- ❏ ❏ 4 - Death's White City (1988)
- ❏ ❏ 5 - Death's Bright Arrow (1989)

■ SHERER, Michael W.

Michael W. Sherer has written four mysteries featuring freelance writer Emerson Ward, first seen in *An Option on Death* (1988). In book 2, *Little Use for Death* (1992), a student at a small college in upstate New York is found hanging from a tree and new teacher Emerson Ward investigates what seems to be a suicide. In book 3, *Death Came Dressed in White* (1993), Emerson's phone is tapped, his lover leaves him, one of his friends is reported missing and another is hospitalized after a brutal beating. Time to investigate. After book 1 was published in hardcover, the later books were released as paperback originals. Until 1994 Sherer operated his own business as a marketing communications consultant and freelance writer. He is currently vice-president and account supervisor for a marketing communications group in Seattle (WA).

Emerson Ward...freelance writer in Chicago, Illinois
- ❏ ❏ 1 - An Option on Death (1988)
- ❏ ❏ 2 - Little Use for Death (1992)
- ❏ ❏ 3 - Death Came Dressed in White (1993)
- ❏ ❏ 4 - A Forever Death (1994)

■ SHOEMAKER, Bill

Retired jockey Bill Shoemaker writes about the world of horse racing in a series in and around the tracks and track facilities in Kentucky, Maryland and New York that host the races of Triple Crown (Kentucky Derby, Preakness and Belmont Stakes). Shoemaker's jockey is Coley Killebrew who in book 3, *Dark Horse* (1996), is banned from racing for life as the result of the death of a horse and the injury of another jockey in a race. Falsely accused, he opens a restaurant (The Horse's Neck) and tries to convince himself he doesn't miss riding. This is a series with a sporting hero and an inside look at the high-stakes world of racing and breeding thoroughbred horses. According to *Deadly Pleasures* #10, "it is rumored this series is ghost-written by the talented Dick Lochte."

Coley Killebrew...ex-jockey turned restaurant owner in Lexington, Kentucky
- ❏ ❏ 1 - Stalking Horse (1994)
- ❏ ❏ 2 - Fire Horse (1995)
- ❏ ❏ 3 - Dark Horse (1996)

■ **SIMON, Roger L.**

Screenwriter and director Roger L(ichtenberg) Simon is the creator of the Moses Wine private eye series, starting with *The Big Fix* (1972), winner of the John Creasey Award. Originally published by Straight Arrow Books (owned by *Rolling Stone* magazine), the book was made into a 1975 film of the same name starring Richard Dreyfuss. After a 9-year hiatus Moses has returned in *The Lost Coast* (1997), where his son is on the run from the FBI, accused of killing a logger. Having given up his radical image for a lucrative corporate investigations practice, Moses and his ex-wife have to outrun and outsmart eco-crazies, feds and nasty business types. A graduate of Dartmouth College, Simon earned an M.F.A. from Yale Drama School. Among his screenplays is *Bustin' Loose*, the 1981 film starring Richard Pryor. *Dead Meet* (1988) is a reprint of his first published novel, *Heir* (1968).

Moses Wine...ex-hippie Jewish private eye in Los Angeles, California
- ❑ ❑ 1 - **The Big Fix (1972) Creasey winner ★**
- ❑ ❑ 2 - Wild Turkey (1975)
- ❑ ❑ 3 - Peking Duck (1979)
- ❑ ❑ 4 - California Roll (1985)
- ❑ ❑ 5 - **The Straight Man (1986) Edgar nominee ☆**
- ❑ ❑ 6 - Raising the Dead (1988)
- ❑ ❑ 7 - The Lost Coast (1997)

■ **SKLEPOWICH, Edward**

Edward Sklepowich is the creator of Urbino Macintyre, an American expatriate and biographer in Venice, Italy, first seen in *Death in a Serene City* (1990). The corpse of a thousand-year-old virgin saint is stolen and Macintyre investigates. When last seen in *Death in the Palazzo* (1997), he has accompanied the beautiful Contessa da Capo-Zendrini (Barbara Alvise) to a party marking the reunion of two grand families long divided. When a November squall cuts off communication with the outside world, a classic locked-room mystery unfolds in the Caravaggio Room, locked since 1938. The cast includes Venetian nobility, a British widow, an art historian, and our American dilletante-sleuth. Sklepowich has been a Fulbright scholar in Egypt and Algeria and a teacher in Italy. He divides his time between Venice and New York City.

Urbino Macintyre...American expatriate and biographer in Venice, Italy
- ❑ ❑ 1 - Death in a Serene City (1990)
- ❑ ❑ 2 - Farewell to the Flesh (1991)
- ❑ ❑ 3 - Liquid Desires (1993)
- ❑ ❑ 4 - Black Bridge (1995)
- ❑ ❑ 5 - Death in the Palazzo (1997)

■ **SLUSHER, William S.**

William S. Slusher is the author of the Lewis Cody mysteries, featuring the sheriff of Hunter County (VA), first seen in *Shepherd of the Wolves* (1995). Cody is a 6' 2" white male born the year of the atomic bomb; his gods all died in Vietnam and his politics lean gently to the right. He loves women, well-raised children, cold Norweigan beer and the Mother Blue Ridge, not necessarily in that order. The first two books include arson, gunfights, car crashes and horse slayings—in addition to murder. There's plenty of violence, rough language and sex because Hunter County is no country manor. Born in Virginia and raised in Tennessee, he lives on a small West Virginia horse farm. As a police officer and pilot for the Fairfax County PD, he flew thousands of hours of police and Medivac misions. Since retiring, he rides a horse named Shiloh and chases Welsh Corgi puppies.

Lewis Cody...sheriff in Hunter County, Virginia
- ❑ ❑ 1 - Shepherd of the Wolves (1995)
- ❑ ❑ 2 - Butcher of the Noble (1996)
- ❑ ❑ 3 - Cave of the Innocent (1997)

■ SMITH, Frank A.

Frank A. Smith is the author of *Corpse in Handcuffs* (1969), introducing Toronto's police Supt. Ian Pepper who later appears in *Defectors are Dead Men* (1971). His new police series features Shropshire DCI Neil Paget, introduced in *Fatal Flaw* (1996), nominated for a best-novel Ellis award. The crotchety Paget returns in *Stone Dead* (1998), when he and his more cheerful assistant Sgt. John Tregalles are baffled by an unidentified corpse found at the bottom of a stone well. *Booklist* called it a bewildering case and a rousing success: "all his characters lie through their teeth." A native of Regina, Saskatchewan, Smith left Canada at the age of 7 for England, where he received most of his formal education. Returning at the age of 21, he went to work for the Alberta Government. After living in Edmonton for many years, he is now a resident of British Columbia.

Ian Pepper...Canadian police superintendent in Toronto, Ontario
- ❏ ❏ 1 - Corpse in Handcuffs (1969)
- ❏ ❏ 2 - Defectors are Dead Men (1971)

■ SMITH, Martin Cruz

Martin Cruz Smith, writing as Martin Smith, won a best-first-novel Edgar for *Gypsy in Amber* (1971), introducing New York City Gypsy art dealer Roman Grey. The book was adapted for *The Art of Crime* (1975), an NBC-TV movie starring Ron Leibman as Grey. Eight years of research went into *Gorky Park* (1981), Smith's first novel featuring Arkady Renko, chief homicide investigator for the Moscow prosecutor's office. His novel *Rose* (1996) was awarded the 1997 Hammett Prize by the North American Chapter of the IACW. Under the name Simon Quinn he wrote 6 paperback originals in The Inquisitor series featuring a lay brother of the Vatican's Militia Christi (*His Eminence, Death*, 1974). As Jake Logan, he wrote a pair of novels for Playboy Press. Born in Reading (PA), Smith earned a B.A. from the University of Pennsylvania and worked as a journalist for 5 years after college.

Arkady Renko...Russian police officer in Moscow, Russia
- ❏ ❏ **1 - Gorky Park (1981) Gold Dagger winner ★**
- ❏ ❏ 2 - Polar Star (1989)
- ❏ ❏ 3 - Red Square (1992)

Roman Grey...Gypsy art dealer in New York, New York
- ❏ ❏ **1 - Gypsy in Amber (1971) Edgar winner ★**
- ❏ ❏ **2 - Canto for a Gypsy (1972) Edgar nominee ☆**

■ SOLOMITA, Stephen

Stephen Solomita was driving a cab, working 12-hours shifts in midtown Manhattan, when he started his first novel in 1983. He hadn't been near a typewriter, much less a computer terminal, in 15 years but the nightmare of New York City traffic drove him to finish the book. The result was *A Twist of the Knife* (1988), first in the Stanley Moodrow series featuring a 60-something NYPD detective turned private. The Hammett-nominated book 6, *Damaged Goods* (1996), was hailed by *Booklist* as "one helluva ride." Among Solomita's standalone thrillers are *A Good Day to Die* (1993) and *Last Chance for Glory* (1994). Published under the name David Cray is *Keeplock* (1995), featuring a career criminal about to be paroled from New York's toughest prison. At 38 he's ready to give up crime for good, but his prison buddy and two strong-arm cops think not.

Stanley Moodrow...cop turned private eye in New York, New York
- ❏ ❏ 1 - A Twist of the Knife (1988)
- ❏ ❏ 2 - Force of Nature (1989)
- ❏ ❏ 3 - Forced Entry (1990)
- ❏ ❏ 4 - Bad to the Bone (1991)
- ❏ ❏ 5 - Piece of the Action (1993)
- ❏ ❏ **6 - Damaged Goods (1996) Hammett nominee ☆**

■ **SOOS, Troy**

Troy Soos is the author of historical baseball mysteries featuring utility infielder Mickey Rawlings, first seen in *Murder at Fenway Park* (1994). Up next in book 6, Rawlings will be playing for the 1922 St. Louis Browns. After graduating from professional umpire school in 1976, Soos worked as an umpire for two years before earning degrees in physics from Rutgers and M.I.T. Before turning to full-time writing, he spent 10 years as a research physicist. Born in New Jersey two weeks after the Dodgers left Brooklyn, he is a member of the Society for American Baseball Research (SABR) and author of *Before the Curse* (1997), a history of early New England baseball. He says he plays the acoustic guitar badly, likes silent movies (especially Buster Keaton and Douglas Fairbanks) and the novels of Mark Twain and Charles Dickens. He lives in Florida.

Mickey Rawlings...1910s journeyman second baseman in the United States
- ❏ ❏ 1 - Murder at Fenway Park (1994)
- ❏ ❏ 2 - Murder at Ebbets Field (1995)
- ❏ ❏ 3 - Murder at Wrigley Field (1996)
- ❏ ❏ 4 - Hunting a Detroit Tiger (1997)
- ❏ ❏ 5 - The Cincinnati Red Stalkings (1998)

■ **SPENCER, John B.**

John B. Spencer is a British novelist whose first two Charley Case novels were set in 1997 but published in England in the mid-'80s. In 1997 comes book 3, *Quake City*, the first to be published in the United States. After the long-anticipated earthquake, the "Big One in '97", Los Angeles ends up an island. While Japan has been reduced to cinders and Europe is war-torn, the streets of Los Angeles are still mean. *Publishers Weekly* called it a "spicy amalgam of hardboiled mystery and science fiction." Spencer has also written a pair of noir thrillers for the Bloodlines series from Do Not Press, including *Perhaps She'll Die* (1997) and *Tooth & Nail* (1998), his sixth novel. In addition to his crime fiction, Spencer is a songwriter and musician and has released a number of CDs. He lives in West London.

Charley Case...private eye of the "1997" future in Los Angeles, California
- ❏ ❏ 1 - A Case for Charley (1984)
- ❏ ❏ 2 - Charley Gets the Picture (1985)
- ❏ ❏ 3 - Quake City (1997)

■ **SPENCER, Ross H.**

Ross H(arrison) Spencer is the author of 5 books featuring Chicago private eye Chance Perdue, first seen in *The DADA Caper* (1978), where he battles the diabolical organization Destroy America Destory America. Called the Groucho Marx of detective fiction, Spencer writes the Purdue novels without any punctuation except periods and question marks. Each paragraph has only one sentence, with lots of one-liners and nutty characters. Baker and Nietzel (*101 Knights*) call him a cross between Rodney Dangerfield and Mel Brooks: lots of jokes, sports humor, satire, farce and outrageous action. "It only takes an hour or so to read one of the Purdue capers, and a lot less to forget one," they say, "but if you read one, you're going to laugh." Born in West Virginia, Spencer has worked as a truck driver, steel and aircraft worker and railroad man.

Chance Purdue...private investigator in Chicago, Illinois
- ❏ ❏ 1 - The DADA Caper (1978)
- ❏ ❏ 2 - The Reggis Arms Caper (1979)
- ❏ ❏ 3 - The Stranger City Caper (1979)
- ❏ ❏ 4 - The Abu Wahab Caper (1980)
- ❏ ❏ 5 - The Radish River Caper (1981)

■ SPICER, Michael

Michael Spicer is the creator of sexy British secret agent Lady Jane Hildreth and her semi-retired partner Patricia Harrington, introduced in *Cotswold Manners* (1988). "He pulls off this improbable mystery with aplomb by means of a dryly witty, highly readable style," said *Publishers Weekly* of the series opener. When last seen in *Cotswold Moles* (1993), the duo is off to Australia at the request of their boss, the Chief. The caretaker-butler for a reclusive and mysterious woman turns up dead soon after the death of his mistress. During their investigation, Lady Jane and Patricia learn a few things about the mysterious Chief. A member of Parliament and former Thatcher cabinet insider, Spicer lives with his wife and children in an ancient house in the Cotswolds. He was born in Bath.

Jane Hildreth, Lady & Patricia Huntington...sexy British secret agent and partner in Cotswolds, England
- ❏ ❏ 1 - Cotswold Manners (1988)
- ❏ ❏ 2 - Cotswold Murders (1990)
- ❏ ❏ 3 - Cotswold Mistress (1992)
- ❏ ❏ 4 - Cotswold Moles (1993)

■ SPILLANE, Mickey

Mickey Spillane is the acknowledged living master of the hard-boiled mystery. With more than 200 million books sold (through 1995), he can lay claim to 7 of the 10 all-time best-selling fiction (not just mystery) best sellers, according to Max Allan Collins (*St. James Guide*). He wrote scripts for comics in the 1940s, including *Captain Marvel* and *Captain America*, and turned an unsold comic book, "Mike Danger," into *I, the Jury* (1947) in just 9 days. It became the first of 13 Mike Hammer private eye novels and Spillane's first best seller. Author of more than 30 books, he received the life achievement award from Private Eye Writers of America in 1983 and was named Grand Master by MWA in 1995. In Collins' opinion, Spillane's best work is his nonseries novel, *The Last Cop Out* (1973), written in third person with shifting points of view. Born in Brooklyn, Spillane is a former trampoline artist with Ringling Brothers Barnum and Bailey Circus.

Mike Hammer...super-patriot private investigator in New York, New York
- ❏ ❏ 1 - I, the Jury (1947)
- ❏ ❏ 2 - My Gun is Quick (1950)
- ❏ ❏ 3 - Vengeance is Mine! (1950)
- ❏ ❏ 4 - The Big Kill (1951)
- ❏ ❏ 5 - One Lonely Night (1951)
- ❏ ❏ 6 - Kiss Me, Deadly (1952)
- ❏ ❏ 7 - The Girl Hunters (1962)
- ❏ ❏ 8 - The Snake (1964)
- ❏ ❏ 9 - The Twisted Thing (1966)
- ❏ ❏ 10 - The Body Lovers (1967)
- ❏ ❏ 11 - Survival...Zero! (1971)
- ❏ ❏ 12 - **The Killing Man (1989) Shamus nominee** ☆
- ❏ ❏ 13 - Black Alley (1996)

Tiger Mann...freelance spy for a private right-wing group in New York, New York
- ❏ ❏ 1 - Day of the Guns (1964)
- ❏ ❏ 2 - Bloody Sunrise (1965)
- ❏ ❏ 3 - The Death Dealers (1965)
- ❏ ❏ 4 - The By-Pass Control (1966)
- ❏ ❏ 5 - Day of the Guns (1966)

■ **STANDIFORD, Les**

Les Standiford is the creator of Miami building contractor and amateur detective John Deal, introduced in *Done Deal* (1993). In book 2, *Raw Deal* (1994), the contractor and his small construction firm are helping rebuild Miami after Hurricane Andrew. Things are looking up until an arsonist destroys his house and almost kills his wife, locking Deal into deadly combat with a wealthy Cuban emigré who has his own plans for the city. Bibliomystery fans will be especially interested in book 4, *Deal on Ice* (1997), where Deal's long-time friend, independent bookseller Arch Dolan, is killed. The plight-of-the-small-bookstore subplot is something being played out around the country, so far without the suspicious death of any bookstore owners. Director of the creative writing program at Florida International University, Standiford lives in Miami.

John Deal...building contractor in Miami, Florida
- ❏ ❏ 1 - Done Deal (1993)
- ❏ ❏ 2 - Raw Deal (1994)
- ❏ ❏ 3 - Deal to Die For (1995)
- ❏ ❏ 4 - Deal on Ice (1997)

■ **STARK, Richard [P]**

Writing as Richard Stark, Grand Master Donald E. Westlake launched his Parker series in 1962 with *The Hunter*, adapted for film as *Point Blank* (1967) starring Lee Marvin, scheduled to be remade by actor-director Mel Gibson. A professional thief, shot and left for dead by his wife and associates, Parker is walking across the George Washington Bridge plotting his revenge at the opening of book 1. According to *Encyclopedia Mysteriosa* (1994), a walk across that same bridge on a winter night after his car had broken down is what 'hatched' the Parker character in Westlake's imagination. After a 23-year hiatus, everybody's favorite thief returned last year in the aptly-titled *Comeback* (1997), book 17 in the Edgar-nominated series. "In a world of warped values, an honest crook like Parker is a true treasure," says Marilyn Stasio of *The New York Times Book Review*.

Alan Grofield...actor and part-time bank robber in New York, New York
- ❏ ❏ 1 - The Damsel (1967)
- ❏ ❏ 2 - The Dame (1969)
- ❏ ❏ 3 - The Blackbird (1969)
- ❏ ❏ 4 - Lemons Never Lie (1971)

Parker...cold-blooded professional thief in New York, New York
- ❏ ❏ 1 - The Hunter (1962) Brit.-Point Blank
- ❏ ❏ 2 - The Man With the Getaway Face (1963) Brit.-The Steel Hit
- ❏ ❏ 3 - The Outfit (1963)
- ❏ ❏ 4 - The Mourner (1963)
- ❏ ❏ 5 - The Score [incl Grofield] (1964)
- ❏ ❏ 6 - The Jugger (1965)
- ❏ ❏ 7 - The Seventh (1966)
- ❏ ❏ 8 - The Handle [incl Grofield] (1966)
- ❏ ❏ 9 - The Rare Coin Score (1967)
- ❏ ❏ 10 - The Green Eagle Score (1967)
- ❏ ❏ 11 - The Black Ice Score (1968)
- ❏ ❏ **12 - The Sour Lemon Score (1969) Edgar nominee** ☆
- ❏ ❏ 13 - Deadly Edge (1971)
- ❏ ❏ 14 - Slayground (1971)
- ❏ ❏ 15 - Plunder Squad (1972)
- ❏ ❏ 16 - Butcher's Moon [incl Grofield] (1974)
- ❏ ❏ 17 - Comeback (1997)

■ **STEED, Neville**

Neville Steed is the creator of 1930s private detective Johnny Black and toyshop owner and antique toy collector Peter Marklin. While Black appeared only twice, in *Black Eye* (1989) and *Black Mail* (1990), there are 5 books in the toy-collecting series, starting with the Creasey Award winner *Tinplate* (1986). Specializing in metal toys of the '20s and '30s, Marklin heads up a wonderful cast of characters, including his stylish girlfriend Arabella Donna Trench, researcher for the TV series *Crime Busters*; his old sparring partner and fellow toy collector, Inspector Blake of Scotland Yard; and his best friend, eccentric retired fisherman Gus Tribble. Born in the West Country of England, Steed returned there after reading Law at Oxford and enjoying a successful advertising career in London where he wrote and directed television commercials.

Johnny Black...1930s private detective in England
- ❏ ❏ 1 - Black Eye (1989)
- ❏ ❏ 2 - Black Mail (1990)

Peter Marklin...toyshop owner and antique toy collector in Dorset, England
- ❏ ❏ 1 - **Tinplate (1986) Creasey winner ★**
- ❏ ❏ 2 - Die-Cast (1987)
- ❏ ❏ 3 - Chipped (1988)
- ❏ ❏ 4 - Clockwork (1989)
- ❏ ❏ 5 - Wind Up (1990)

■ **STEPHENS, Reed [P]**

Reed Stephens is the pseudonym of Stephen R. Donaldson, best-selling author of Tolkienesque fantasy novels (the Unbeliever series, the Gap series and others). His pseudonymous mysteries feature unlicensed California private eye Mick "Brew" Axbrewder, starting with *The Man Who Killed His Brother* (1980). When Mick intervened in what he thought was a bank robbery, he accidentally shot the cop chasing the robber—his brother Rick. Mick's been a drunk ever since. He's also the reclamation project of his partner Ginny Fistoulari of Fistoulari Investigations. Teetering on the edge of sobriety, Mick finally wakes up when Rick's daughter disappears. "This is grim stuff, full of harrowing circumstances and events," says Marcia Muller (*1001 Midnights*). She calls the series opener a riveting read, recommended for those who like their private eye fiction hard-boiled.

Mick "Brew" Axbrewder...unlicensed private eye in Puerta del Sol, CA
- ❏ ❏ 1 - The Man Who Killed His Brother (1980)
- ❏ ❏ 2 - **The Man Who Risked His Partner (1984) Shamus nominee ☆**
- ❏ ❏ 3 - The Man Who Tried to Get Away (1990)

■ **STEVENSON, Richard [P]**

Richard Stevenson is the pseudonym of journalist Richard Lipez for his Donald Strachey (pronounced STRAY-chee) mysteries about a gay private eye in Albany (NY). The satirical series begins with *Death Trick* (1981), introducing Strachey's love interest, the Jesuit-educated Timothy Callahan, their friends Dot and Edith and plenty of Albany dirty politics. In the early '60s Lipez went to Ethiopia as a Peace Corps volunteer and later worked as a program evaluator in Washington DC and anti-poverty program staffer in western Massachusetts. For 30 years he has lived in Pittsfield (MA) where he is an editorial writer for *The Berkshire Eagle* and mystery columnist for *The Washington Post Book World*. Like Strachey's, his travel destinations are exotic, and his experience with both Africa and mysteries is apparent in his chapter on Africa written for *Crimes of the Scene* (1997).

Donald Strachey...gay private eye in Albany, New York
- ❏ ❏ 1 - Death Trick (1981)
- ❏ ❏ 2 - On the Other Hand (1984)
- ❏ ❏ 3 - Ice Blues (1986)

❑ ❑ 4 - Third Man Out (1992)
❑ ❑ 5 - A Shock to the System (1995)
❑ ❑ 6 - Chain of Fools (1996)

■ STINSON, Jim

James Emerson Stinson writing as Jim Stinson is the author of four Los Angeles mysteries featuring a low-budget film maker named Stoney Winston, introduced in *Double Exposure* (1985). Also part of the series were *Low Angles* (1986), *Truck Shot* (1989) and *TV Safe* (1991). All four were originally published in hardcover by Scribner.

Stoney Winston...low-budget film maker in Los Angeles, California
❑ ❑ 1 - Double Exposure (1985)
❑ ❑ 2 - Low Angles (1986)
❑ ❑ 3 - Truck Shot (1989)
❑ ❑ 4 - TV Safe (1991)

■ STOCKLEY, Grif

Lawyer-turned-author Grif Stockley is the creator of the Gideon Page legal mysteries, beginning with *Expert Testimony* (1992). Page the public defender is assigned to represent a schizophrenic accused of murdering a senator. To complicate matters, the defendant is a patient of the dead man's wife, Dr. Carolyn Anderson. Still struggling with own his wife's death, Page is on the edge of a serious depression. When last seen in *Blind Judgment* (1997), he has returned to the Arkansas Delta where he grew up, to defend a black factory worker accused of murdering his Chinese-American employer. In the midst of escalating racial tension, the social-worker-turned-attorney must confront the ugly memories of his father's suicide and the desire to exact revenge from the rich family he holds responsible for his family's pain.

Gideon Page...defense attorney in Arkansas
❑ ❑ 1 - Expert Testimony (1992)
❑ ❑ 2 - Probable Cause (1993)
❑ ❑ 3 - Religious Conviction (1994)
❑ ❑ 4 - Illegal Motion (1995)
❑ ❑ 5 - Blind Judgment (1997)

■ STONE, Michael

Michael Stone is the creator of a Denver P.I. and bounty hunter named Streeter, first seen in *The Low End of Nowhere* (1996), a Shamus nominee for best first novel. As an employee of Dazzler's Bail Bonds, he lives in a converted church nicknamed Fort God. The ex-linebacker, ex-accountant, ex-bouncer has racked up 4 failed marriages and 3 broken engagements, but he's still on the field. And he's serious about fitness: five sets of 50 pushups are what he does to warm up for his workout. A Milwaukee (WI) native who has lived in Colorado since 1978, Stone has worked as a newspaper reporter and correspondent for UPI, the *Rocky Mountain News* and *Newsday*. Since 1985 he has owned his own detective agency where he works almost exclusively with attorneys specializing in criminal defense work. His all-time favorite job he says was County Stadium beer vendor for Brewers and Packers games in 1973.

Streeter...P.I. bounty hunter in Denver, Colorado
❑ ❑ 1 - **The Low End of Nowhere (1996) Shamus nominee** ☆
❑ ❑ 2 - A Long Reach (1997)
❑ ❑ 3 - Token of Remorse (1998)

■ STONE, Thomas H. [P]

Thomas H. Stone is a pseudonym of Terry Williams Harknett, author of more than 150 published novels by the time was 50, including a series of '70s paperbacks with Los Angeles mulatto detective Chester Fortune. Appearing only in England, these novels describe an alternate L.A. where the streets have kerbs, the cars have tyres and the populace includes coloured folk, according to Steve Lewis writing in *Deadly Pleasures #4*. "Stone is not a word stylist," he says, "but the story is forceful and compelling." According to *Hawk's Authors' Pseudonyms* (1995), Harknett has written as Frank Chandler (ghosted *A Fistful of Dollars*, 1972), David Ford, George G. Gilman, Peter Haining, Adam Hardy, Jane Harman, Joseph Hedges (12 Sphere novels), William M. James, Alex Peters, Charles R. Pike, William Pine, James Russell, Thomas H. Stone, Thomas P. Stone and William Terry.

Chester Fortune...mulatto detective in Los Angeles, California
- ❑ ❑ 1 - Dead Set (1972)
- ❑ ❑ 2 - One Horse Race (1972)
- ❑ ❑ 3 - Stopover for Murder (1973)
- ❑ ❑ 4 - Black Death (1973)

■ STRALEY, John

Alaska private detective John Straley has a statewide practice that takes him to crime scenes all over the North, working for defense attorneys and the State public defender's office. Too much time alone in places with nothing to do prompted him to write his first Cecil Younger novel, featuring a backsliding nice guy P.I. introduced in *The Woman Who Married a Bear* (1992), a Shamus best first novel winner. After growing up north of Seattle, Straley worked summers wrangling and shoeing horses before going to farrier's college in New Mexico. When he moved to Sitka (horse population: 3) with his marine biologist wife, he found there wasn't much work for a farrier. The Russian capital of America until the 1867 sale of Alaska to the U.S., Sitka is a place reachable only by boat or plane, with 12 miles of drivable road. Sounds like the perfect place for a working P.I. to write novels.

Cecil Younger...alcoholic private eye in Sitka, Alaska
- ❑ ❑ **1 - The Woman Who Married a Bear (1992) Shamus winner ★**
- ❑ ❑ 2 - The Curious Eat Themselves (1994)
- ❑ ❑ 3 - The Music of What Happens (1996)
- ❑ ❑ 4 - Death and the Language of Happiness (1997)
- ❑ ❑ 5 - Angels Will Not Care (1998)

■ STRUNK, Frank C.

Frank C. Strunk has written a pair of Depression-era Kentucky mysteries featuring Buxton roadhouse operator Berkley Jordon, introduced in *Jordon's Wager* (1991). In book 2, *Jordon's Showdown* (1993), the bar owner is forced into a dangerous race to prevent another killing in the already-devastated coal town. In *Throwback* (1996), Strunk returns to Stanton County, scene of his earlier Depression mysteries, with a story set in the "gaudy present" as *Kirkus* described it. The throwback is Cole Clayfield, a college-educated mountain man who makes furniture in his spare time. Haunted by memories of his wife's tragic death, he's content to commune with his dogs, until his beloved granddaughter is kidnapped by a sociopath named Darnell. Her other granddfather, a rich lawyer and political wheeler-dealer, has different ideas about how to get her back. The chase is on.

Berkley Jordon...1930s roadhouse operator in Buxton, Kentucky
- ❑ ❑ 1 - Jordon's Wager (1991)
- ❑ ❑ 2 - Jordon's Showdown (1993)

■ **SUBLETT, Jesse**

Jesse Sublett is the creator of Austin skip tracer and blues bass-player Martin Fender, introduced in *Rock Critic Murders* (1989), a Shamus nominee for best first private eye novel. When last seen in *Boiled in Concrete* (1992), our hero is broke and living in a Los Angeles ghetto, so he jumps at the chance to play in a midnight recording session that promises to prove music legend Richard James didn't die in a plane crash back in the '70s. When Cyclone Davis is killed, Martin must solve a mystery involving backwoods drug casualties. *Kirkus* called Martin an "appealing character" and praised Sublett's "excellent riff on the blues, club musicians, sound systems and chord changes." A musician and songwriter born in Austin (TX), Sublett lives in Los Angeles (CA).

Martin Fender...skip tracer in Austin, Texas
- ❑ ❑ 1 - **Rock Critic Murders (1989) Shamus nominee** ☆
- ❑ ❑ 2 - Tough Baby (1990)
- ❑ ❑ 3 - Boiled In Concrete (1992)

■ **SWAN, Thomas**

Thomas Swan is the creator of Scotland Yard art forgery investigator Jack Oxby, first seen in *The DaVinci Deception* (1990), a Bantam paperback original. In *The Cézanne Chase* (1997), a Newmarket Press hardcover, Oxby tracks a villain to Aix-en-Provence where a Céjzanne show is at risk, thanks to a psychopath intent on using his pharmaceutical skills to destroy Cézanne's self-portraits. "Some pretty nifty insights into the nitty-gritty of buying, selling, preserving—and destroying—great works of art," says Amazon's mystery editor. A former marketing director for Mobil Oil and American Express Card Division, Swan worked as an advertising copywriter, TV producer and account executive before starting his own agency. Author of two musicals, he once studied playwriting in the M.F.A. program at what is now Carnegie Mellon University. He lives in New Jersey.

Jack Oxby...Scotland Yard art forgery investigator in London, England
- ❑ ❑ 1 - The DaVinci Deception (1990)
- ❑ ❑ 2 - The Cezanne Chase (1997)
- ❑ ❑ 3 - The Faberge Factor (1998)

■ **SWANSON, Doug J.**

Doug J. Swanson won the John Creasey Award for his first novel featuring recovering no-account, mostly honest private eye Jack Flippo in *Big Town* (1994), nominated for Edgar and Anthony best-first honors the same year. Jack was on the fast track at the Dallas DA's office until he unwittingly slept with the wife of a drug kingpin. By the time he realized his mistake, he was out of a job, divorced, depressed and broke. *Booklist* called the series opener "wonderfully offbeat, darkly sinister, terrifically funny and oddly touching." Swanson's publisher called it the beginning of a new genre, chicken-fried noir. In *96 Tears* (1996), Jack is hired to stalk a stalker and soon discovers he's being stalked himself, by a wonderfully stupid thug named Teddy Tunstra II, a guy Jack once put in prison. Swanson has worked as a reporter for the *Dallas Morning News*.

Jack Flippo...recovering deadbeat P.I. in Dallas, Texas
- ❑ ❑ 1 - **Big Town (1994) Creasey winner** ★ **Anthony & Edgar nominee** ☆☆
- ❑ ❑ 2 - Dreamboat (1995)
- ❑ ❑ 3 - 96 Tears (1996)

■ TAIBO, Paco Ignacio, II

Mexican historian and writer, Paco Ignacio Taibo II, has won at least 7 international fiction prizes, including the Mortiz-Planeta Award for his crime and historical novels as well as mainstream fiction. The first book in his private eye series was originally published in 1977 but not translated from Spanish to English until 1990. Taibo's newest book is a biography of Che Guevara (*Guevara Also Known As Che*, 1997) which solves the mystery of the revolutionary's death and last days and the "missing year" he spent in the Congo. Taibo quotes extensively from a previously unknown manuscript of Guevara's, with text set in a different type interwoven with the author's voice, neatly providing two narrators for the story. Born in Spain, Taibo lives in Mexico City but travels frequently to the U.S.

Hector Belascoaran Shayne...correspondence-school-certified P.I. in Mexico City, Mexico
- ❏ ❏ 1 - An Easy Thing (1990)
- ❏ ❏ 2 - Calling All Heroes (1991)
- ❏ ❏ 3 - Some Clouds (1992)
- ❏ ❏ 4 - No Happy Ending (1993)
- ❏ ❏ 5 - Return to the Same City (1996)

■ TANENBAUM, Robert K.

Legal expert Robert K. Tanenbaum is the creator of a pair of 1970s New York prosecutors linked romantically in book one after she is injured by a letter bomb intended for him. The beautiful Marlene is described as "St. Theresa by Bernini except for the glass eye and two missing fingers." This wonderful crew of crime fighters recently made their 9th appearance. Former Asst. District Attorney and Manhattan Homicide Bureau Chief, Tanenbaum was Deputy Chief Counsel to the Congressional committees investigating the assasinations of JFK and Martin Luther King, Jr. Appearing regularly on CNN and KCAL-TV in Los Angeles, he was an expert commentator during the O.J. Simpson trial. His nonfiction titles include *Badge of the Assassin* (1994) and *The Piano Teacher* (1994) written with Peter S. Greenburg. Tanenbaum practices law in Beverly Hills (CA) where he was formerly Mayor.

Roger "Butch" Karp & Marlene Ciampi...1970s Criminal Courts Bureau chief & assistant DA New York
- ❏ ❏ 1 - No Lesser Plea (1987)
- ❏ ❏ 2 - Depraved Indifference (1989)
- ❏ ❏ 3 - Immoral Certainty (1991)
- ❏ ❏ 4 - Reversible Error (1992)
- ❏ ❏ 5 - Material Witness (1993)
- ❏ ❏ 6 - Justice Denied (1994)
- ❏ ❏ 7 - Corruption of Blood (1995)
- ❏ ❏ 8 - Falsely Accused (1996)
- ❏ ❏ 9 - Invisible Impulse (1997)

■ TAPPLY, William G.

William G. Tapply is the creator of Brady Coyne, a Boston lawyer who loves to fish, especially for trout. Showing a strong preference for clients who are old, smart, eccentric and rich, Brady debuts in *Death at Charity's Point* (1984), winner of Scribner's Crime Novel Award that year. Tapply is a contributing editor to *Field & Stream* magazine and shares Brady's passion for fishing. He also writes extensively on gardening, sports and nature for a variety of magazines, including *Outdoor Life*, *Sports Illustrated* and *Better Homes and Gardens.* Born in eastern Massachusetts, where his father was an outdoor writer, Tapply has written several nonfiction books including his latest, *A Fly-Fishing Life* (1997). After earning degrees from Amherst and Harvard, he did further graduate work at Tufts University, where he taught economics and directed the economic education program.

Brady Coyne...lawyer to the rich who loves to fish in Boston, Massachusetts
- ❏ ❏ 1 - Death at Charity's Point (1984)
- ❏ ❏ 2 - The Dutch Blue Error (1984)
- ❏ ❏ 3 - Follow the Sharks (1985)
- ❏ ❏ 4 - The Marine Corpse (1986) Brit.-A Rodent of Doubt
- ❏ ❏ 5 - Dead Meat (1987)
- ❏ ❏ 6 - The Vulgar Boatman (1987)
- ❏ ❏ 7 - A Void in Hearts (1988)
- ❏ ❏ 8 - Dead Winter (1989)
- ❏ ❏ 9 - Client Privilege (1990)
- ❏ ❏ 10 - The Spotted Cats (1991)
- ❏ ❏ 11 - Tight Lines (1992)
- ❏ ❏ 13 - The Snake Eater (1993)
- ❏ ❏ 14 - The Seventh Enemy (1995)
- ❏ ❏ 15 - Close to the Bone (1996)

■ **TAYLOR, Andrew**

Andrew Taylor has written more than 20 books since the early '80s, including 8 in the series featuring William Dougal, a detective who occasionally commits murders as well as solves them. The series opener won the Creasey Award, was nominated for an Edgar and reached a peak audience of 4 million when it was serialized on BBC Radio. His Blaines trilogy (*The Second Midnight, Blacklist* and *Toyshop*) features a British spy first appearing in book 3 of the Dougal series. Narrated by DI Richard Thornhill, the Lydmouth series is set during the '50s in the Lower Wye Valley on the Anglo-Welsh border. Taylor is currently writing the Roth trilogy beginning with *The Last Four Things* (1997) narrated by a woman training for the Anglican priesthood. Educated at the universities of Cambridge and London, he has worked as a boatbuilder, librarian and freelance publisher's editor. At least 2 of his juvenile titles appear under the name John Robert Taylor. He lives in the Forest of Dean on the Anglo-Welsh border.

Richard Thornhill, Det. Insp.....1950s detective inspector in Lydmouth, England
- ❏ ❏ 1 - An Air That Kills (1994)
- ❏ ❏ 2 - The Mortal Sickness (1995)
- ❏ ❏ 3 - The Lover of the Grave (1997)

William Dougal...post-grad student and security firm employee in England
- ❏ ❏ 1 - **Caroline Minuscule (1982) Creasey winner ★ Edgar nominee** ☆
- ❏ ❏ 2 - Waiting for the End of the World (1984)
- ❏ ❏ 3 - **Our Fathers' Lies (1985) Dagger nominee** ☆
- ❏ ❏ 4 - An Old School Tie (1986)
- ❏ ❏ 5 - Freelance Death (1987)
- ❏ ❏ 6 - Blood Relation (1990)
- ❏ ❏ 7 - The Sleeping Policeman (1992)
- ❏ ❏ 8 - Odd Man Out (1993)

■ TAYLOR, H. Baldwin [P]

H. Baldwin Taylor is one of the pseudonyms of Grand Master Hillary Waugh, who has written more than 45 novels including *Last Seen Wearing...* (1952), one of Julian Symons' picks for the 100 greatest crime novels every written. Under the Taylor pseudonym he wrote 3 books featuring David Halliday, Connecticut newspaper owner and editor, introduced in *The Duplicate* (1964). Halliday makes two return engagements in *The Triumvirate* (1966) and *The Trouble With Tycoons* (1967) published in London the same year as *The Missing Tycoon*. Under his own name, Waugh wrote 11 books in the Chief Fred Fellows police series, 3 books with Manhattan homicide detective Frank Sessions, 3 with New York private eye Sheridan Wesley and another 6 with New York P.I. Simon Kaye. He also wrote 5 books as Elissa Grandower which were published under his own name in England.

David Halliday...newspaper owner and editor in Connecticut
- ❏ ❏ 1 - The Duplicate (1964)
- ❏ ❏ 2 - The Triumvirate (1966)
- ❏ ❏ 3 - The Trouble with Tycoons (1967)

■ THOMSON, Maynard F.

Maynard F. Thomson has written a pair of mysteries featuring Boston private eye Nason "Nase" Nichols, whose first appearance in *Trade Secrets* (1994), finds him racing across New England in the company of a woman scientist, caught in a web of computer-chip intrigue. In *Breaking Faith* (1996), starred by Kirkus Reviews, Nase is driving a cab in Roxbury, working undercover for a mayoral commission investigating the murder of a high school hero and charges of police brutality. Born and raised in Cleveland (OH), where he lives currently, Thomson worked in Boston for 20 years as a trial attorney. His checkered academic past includes a B.A. in history from Boston University, M.A. from the University of Sussex in England, J.D. from Case Western Reserve and M.P.A. from Harvard. He has recently completed a figure-skating romance set in Japan during the Olympics.

Nason "Nase" Nichols...private eye in New York, New York
- ❏ ❏ 1 - Trade Secrets (1994)
- ❏ ❏ 2 - Breaking Faith (1996)

■ THURSTON, Robert

Science fiction writer Robert Thurston has written 3 mystery thrillers featuring Byron "Rugger" O'Toole, a detective of the future first appearing in *For the Silvership* (1985) set in Central America. Rugger later returns with *In Justice's Prison* (1985) and *Between Two Evils* (1986). With Glen A. Larson, Thurston wrote the novelization of the film script *Battlestar Gallactica* (1978), followed by 4 more books in the best-selling Gallactica series. His short stories are represented in numerous science fiction and fantasy anthologies. Before launching his science fiction writing career, Thurston worked as a bookstore manager, newspaper reporter and English professor. With bachelor's and master's degrees from the State University of New York at Buffalo, he currently lives in New York City.

Byron "Rugger" O'Toole...detective of the future in Central America
- ❏ ❏ 1 - For the Silvership (1985)
- ❏ ❏ 2 - In Justice's Prison (1985)
- ❏ ❏ 3 - Between Two Evils (1986)

■ TIERNEY, Ronald

Ronald Tierney's first mystery featuring Deets Shanahan was a runner-up for the SMP/PWA best first P.I. novel competition and later earned a Shamus nomination for best first novel. The series opener *Stone Veil* (1990) finds the 70-something Indianapolis P.I. semi-retired and estranged from his wife and son when his dog Casey discovers the body of William B. Stone, the disappearing husband Deets had been asked to find. In *Eclipse of the Heart* (1993) Tierney introduces Zachary Grayson, a middle-aged gay food writer whose life is turned upside down when he takes a trip to Puerto Vallarta. Tierney was previously the editor of an alternative weekly newspaper in Indianapolis. He currently lives in San Francisco where he is working on the 5th Shanahan novel, *Nickel Plated Steel*, and finishing a nonseries mystery.

"Deets" Shanahan...70-something private eye in Indianapolis, Indiana
- ❑ ❑ 1 - **The Stone Veil (1990) Shamus nominee** ☆
- ❑ ❑ 2 - The Steel Web (1991)
- ❑ ❑ 3 - The Iron Glove (1992)
- ❑ ❑ 4 - The Concrete Pillow (1995)

Zachary Grayson...gay author of trendy cookbooks in San Francisco, California
- ❑ ❑ 1 - Eclipse of the Heart (1993)

■ **TIMLIN, Mark**

British crime writer Mark Timlin has written more than a dozen books featuring South London ex-cop and private eye Nick Sharman, introduced in *A Good Year for the Roses* (1988) which tells the story of his departure from the force. Sharman drives an E-type Jag, has an ex-wife remarried to a dentist in Scotland and a young daughter named Judith whom he adores. According to a UK *Crimetime* magazine reviewer, "The Sharman books tend to divide people between those who think they're sleazy, bad taste, male chauvanist, violent, gun happy, fast action reads and those who don't like them." *The Sunday Times* calls the series "witty, sexy and tough." Sharman's next appearance in British editions is *A Street that Rhymed at 3 AM* (1997). British television star Clive Owen plays Nick Sharman in the Sharman ITV series loosely based on Timlin's character. The author served as a story consultant.

Nick Sharman...hard-living ex-cop private eye in London, England
- ❑ ❑ 1 - A Good Year for the Roses (1988)
- ❑ ❑ 2 - Romeo's Tune (1990)
- ❑ ❑ 3 - Gun Street Girl (1990)
- ❑ ❑ 4 - Take the A-Train (1991)
- ❑ ❑ 5 - The Turnaround (1992)
- ❑ ❑ 6 - Zip Gun Boogie (1992)
- ❑ ❑ 7 - Hearts of Stone (1992)
- ❑ ❑ 8 - Falls of the Shadow (1993)
- ❑ ❑ 9 - Ashes by Now (1993)
- ❑ ❑ 10 - Pretend We're Dead (1994)
- ❑ ❑ 11 - Paint It Black (1995)
- ❑ ❑ 12 - Find My Way Home (1996)
- ❑ ❑ ss - Sharman and Other Filth [short stories] (1996)

■ **TOPOR, Tom**

Journalist and playwright Tom Topor wrote a pair of private eye novels featuring New Yorker Kevin Fitzgerald who first appeared in *Bloodstar* (1978) and later in *Coda* (1984). He is best known currently for the novel *Codicil* (1995) where Detective Adam Bruno must find a dead man's son before his other heirs eliminate the potential $50-million drain on their inheritance. Topor's Broadway play *Nuts* was first produced in 1980 and he later wrote the screenplay which became the 1987 movie starring Barbra Streisand and Richard Dreyfuss. Among Topor's other screenwriting credits are the 1988 film *The Accused* for which Jodie Foster won Best Actress honors. Born in Vienna, Austria, Topor attended Brooklyn College and later worked for the New York Daily News, New York Times and New York Post.

Kevin Fitzgerald...private eye in New York, New York
- ❑ ❑ 1 - Bloodstar (1978)
- ❑ ❑ 2 - Coda (1984)

■ TOURNEY, Leonard

American author Leonard Tourney is the creator of an 8-book series featuring 17th century town constable and clothing merchant Matthew Stock of Chelmsford, 20 miles outside London. Matthew and Joan Stock, an Elizabethan *MacMillan and Wife*, are introduced in *The Player's Boy Is Dead* (1980). In book 5, *Old Saxon Blood* (1988), Elizabeth I has a major role and Tourney gives her some great speeches. In the Stock's 8th adventure, the story reaches into the past, involving an Eskimo brought back from Greenland by Sir Martin Frobisher 20 years earlier. A frequent lecturer and workshop leader on writing mystery novels, Tourney has taught English at Western Illinois, the University of Tulsa and UC, Santa Barbara where he earned his PhD. He lives in Santa Barbara where he continues to teach.

Matthew Stock...17th century town constable and clothier in Chelmsford, England
- ❏ ❏ 1 - The Players' Boy is Dead (1980)
- ❏ ❏ 2 - Low Treason (1983)
- ❏ ❏ 3 - Familiar Spirits (1985)
- ❏ ❏ 4 - The Bartholomew Fair Murders (1986)
- ❏ ❏ 5 - Old Saxon Blood (1988)
- ❏ ❏ 6 - Knaves Templar (1991)
- ❏ ❏ 7 - Witness of Bones (1992)
- ❏ ❏ 8 - Frobisher's Savage (1994)

■ TOWNEND, Peter

Peter R(obert) G(ascoigne) Townend is the creator of 3 mysteries featuring amateur detective Philip Quest, a photographer in Spain and Sardinia, first appearing in *Out of Focus* (1971). Peter returns in *Zoom!* (1972) and is back again in *Triple Exposure* (1977). According to Hubin, the author is a graduate of Cambridge University who has worked as a magazine publisher, photographer and magazine travel correspondent. He is the author of the nonseries novel *Fisheye* (1976) and the nonfiction titles *East Coast Pacifics at Work* and *Top Shed: A Pictorial History of Kings Cross Locomotive Depot*. Under the pseudonym Peter Gascoigne he wrote *Zero Always Wins* (1961).

Philip Quest...photographer in Sardinia
- ❏ ❏ 1 - Out of Focus (1971)
- ❏ ❏ 2 - Zoom! (1972)
- ❏ ❏ 3 - Triple Exposure (1977)

■ TRAINOR, J. F.

Mystery and romance writer J. F. Trainor is Joseph F. Trainor, author of more than 20 novels, including 5 in the Angela Biwaban series featuring an Anishinabe (Ah-NISH-ih-nah-bay means people) princess with an embezzlement conviction and an MBA. After spending 3 years in a South Dakota women's prison, Angie faces a year of weekly check-ins with her handsome probation officer Paul Holbrook, who is determined to keep her on the straight and narrow. From family powwows in Utah to friends in need in Michigan and undercover environmental assignments in Washington, Angie seems to be everywhere but South Dakota. While the first 3 books were paperback originals, the series is now in hardcover. A resident of Rhode Island, Trainor teaches mystery writing in the adult education program at Brown University.

Angela Biwaban...ex-embezzler Anishinabe princess in Minnesota
- ❏ ❏ 1 - Target for Murder (1993)
- ❏ ❏ 2 - Dynamite Pass (1993)
- ❏ ❏ 3 - Whiskey Jack (1994)
- ❏ ❏ 4 - Corona Blue (1994)
- ❏ ❏ 5 - High Country Murder (1995)

■ **TREMAYNE, Peter [P]**

Peter Tremayne is the pseudonym used by Peter Berresford Ellis for his Irish historical mysteries featuring 7th century Celtic legal advocate Sister Fidelma, who first appears in *Absolution by Murder* (1994). As Peter Tremayne, he has published more than 30 novels and 60 short stories for British and American magazines and journals. In addition to eight novels written as Peter MacAlan, he has also written more than 25 books under his own name, including works of history, biography and Irish and Celtic mythology. Most recent are *Celtic Women: Women in Celtic Society and Literature* (1996) and *Celt and Greek: Celts in the Hellenic World* (1997). Sister Fidelma returns in British editions of *Spider's Web* (1997), with at least three more titles to follow. A native of Coventry, England, the author has written a monthly column (*Here and There*) for the *Irish Democrat* since 1987.

Sister Fidelma...7th century Celtic sister & legal advocate in Kildaire, Ireland
- ❑ ❑ 1 - Absolution by Murder (1994)
- ❑ ❑ 2 - Shroud for the Archbishop (1995)
- ❑ ❑ 3 - Suffer Little Children (1995)
- ❑ ❑ 4 - The Subtle Serpent (1996)

■ **TRENCH, John**

Advertising executive John Trench is the creator of Martin Coterell, erudite British archaeologist, who first appears in *Docken Dead* (1953) which features a lost Arthurian manuscript. Described by B.A. Pike, writing in *St. James Guide* (4th edition), Coterell is "tough, lean, exuberant, inquisitive, well-connected, one-handed, and chronically untidy." In book 2 a dig unearths a recent corpse in a Dorset quarrying community, while book 3 views a brutal teenage gang both as terrorists and victims. Past chairman of the Buckinghamshire Archaeological Society, Trench has written *Archaeology Without a Spade* (1960), *History for Postmen* (1961) and *The Bones of Britain* (1962). Born in Sussex and educated at Wellington College and the Royal Military Academy, he served in the Royal Signals in Africa and Europe from 1939 to 1946.

Martin Coterell...erudite British archaeologist in England
- ❑ ❑ 1 - Docken Dead (1953)
- ❑ ❑ 2 - Dishonoured Bones (1954)
- ❑ ❑ 3 - What Rough Beast (1957)

■ **TRENHAILE, John**

Ex-barrister John Trenhaile wrote two espionage series totaling 6 books during the 1980s. The earlier books feature a Russian general named Povin, head of Soviet Intelligence, who later ends up deposed and imprisoned. The second series moves to Hong Kong, where British Intelligence officer Simon Young and his family are caught in a power struggle between the KGB and Chinese Central Intelligence. In the '90s Trenhaile turned to international thrillers, with paperback originals such as *Krysalis* (1992); *Blood Rules* (1993), a tale of terrorism with Shi'ite Muslims and Mossad agents; The *Tiger of Desire* (1994) and *A Means to Evil* (1995) where a southern California hunt for a perverse killer involves the Chinese American woman who heads the police psychological unit. Trenhaile earned B.A. (with honors) and M.A. degrees from Magdalen College, Oxford. Since 1995 he has served as editor of *Free China Review* in Taipei, Taiwan.

Povin, General...Soviet spy in Hong Kong, China
- ❑ ❑ 1 - Kyril (1981) APA-The Man Called Kyril
- ❑ ❑ 2 - A View from the Square (1983)
- ❑ ❑ 3 - Nocturne for the General (1985)

Simon Young...British Intelligence officer in Hong Kong, China
- ❑ ❑ 1 - The Mahjong Spies (1986)
- ❑ ❑ 2 - The Scroll of Benevolence (1988)
- ❑ ❑ 3 - The Gates of Exquisite View (1988)

■ TRIPP, Miles

Past chairman of the Crime Writers' Association (1968-69), Miles (Barton) Tripp is the author of at least 35 novels, including 12 in the series featuring British private investigator John Samson. Book 5 in the Samson series, *High Heels* (1980), is said to be among his best, but for the most part, critics think his nonseries work is his most important. Writing for *St. James Guide* (4th ed.), Don Cole identifies Tripp's best books (the author himself supposedly agrees) as *Kilo Forty* (1963), *A Man Without Friends* (1970), *Woman at Risk* (1974) and *High Heels*. Cole goes on to suggest that Tripp is such a master of psychological suspense he could have been a regular contributor to Alfred Hitchcock movies. A trained solicitor, Tripp spent 30 years as a member of the legal staff of London's Charity Commission. He has also written as Michael Brett and John Michael Brett.

John Samson...private investigator in England
- ❏ ❏ 1 - Obsession (1973)
- ❏ ❏ 2 - The Once a Year Man (1977)
- ❏ ❏ 3 - The Wife-Smuggler (1978)
- ❏ ❏ 4 - Cruel Victim (1979)
- ❏ ❏ 5 - High Heels (1980)
- ❏ ❏ 6 - One Lover Too Many (1983)
- ❏ ❏ 7 - Some Predators Are Male (1985)
- ❏ ❏ 8 - Death of a Man-Tamer (1987)
- ❏ ❏ 9 - The Frightened Wife (1987)
- ❏ ❏ 10 - The Cords of Vanity (1989)
- ❏ ❏ 11 - Video Vengeance (1990)
- ❏ ❏ 12 - Samson and the Greek Delilah (1995)

■ TROW, M. J.

M. J. Trow (rhymes with crow) is Meirion James Trow, creator of Inspector Lestrade, a 19th century Scotland Yard inspector who recently appeared in his 16th case. Trow says he was inspired to write these stories because he was so annoyed with the arrogance of Basil Rathbone's Sherlock Holmes portrayal in the 1940's films. More recently he has written two titles in a humorous series featuring widowed history teacher Peter Maxwell. A history teacher himself, Trow has been both actor and producer of community theater productions on the Isle of Wight. Passionate about the British cavalry and an accomplished artist on military subjects, he collects officers' uniforms and lectures to history societies and other groups. He earned an honors degree from King's College, London and a postgraduate education certificate from Jesus College, Cambridge.

Peter Maxwell...widowed teacher and golden-hearted cynic in England
- ❏ ❏ 1 - Maxwell's House (1994)
- ❏ ❏ **2 - Maxwell's Flame (1995) Last Laugh nominee** ☆

Sholto Joseph Lestrade, Insp.....19th century Scotland Yard inspector in London, England
- ❏ ❏ 1 - The Adventures of Inspector Lestrade (1985) U.S.-The Supreme Adventure of Insp. Lestrade
- ❏ ❏ 2 - Brigade (1986)
- ❏ ❏ 3 - Lestrade and the Hallowed House (1987)
- ❏ ❏ 4 - Lestrade and the Leviathan (1987)
- ❏ ❏ 5 - Lestrade and the Brother of Death (1988)
- ❏ ❏ 6 - Lestrade and the Ripper (1988)
- ❏ ❏ 7 - Lestrade and the Guardian Angel (1990)
- ❏ ❏ 8 - Lestrade and the Deadly Game (1990)
- ❏ ❏ 9 - Lestrade and the Gift of the Prince (1991)
- ❏ ❏ 10 - Lestrade and the Magpie (1991)
- ❏ ❏ 11 - Lestrade and the Dead Man's Hand (1992)

❑ ❑ 12 - Lestrade and the Sign of Nine (1992)
❑ ❑ 13 - Lestrade and the Sawdust Ring (1993)
❑ ❑ 14 - Lestrade and the Mirror of Murder (1993)
❑ ❑ 15 - Lestrade and the Kiss of Horus (1995)
❑ ❑ 16 - Lestrade and the Devil's Own (1996)

■ TURNBULL, Peter

Peter Turnbull is the creator of the P Division series set in a fictional police station in the center of Glasgow. Likened to Ed McBain's 87th Precinct series gone Glaswegian, these books are fixed in time where nobody gets older. More recently Turnbull has launched a new series with DC Carmen Pharaoh, a young woman transferred from London to the York CID in *Embracing Skeletons* (1996). In addition to his police series, Turnbull has written a thriller titled *The Claws of the Gryphon* (1986) and the novelization of a popular television series set in Glasgow—*The Justice Game: The Lady from Rome* (1990). Born in Yorkshire, he earned a diploma in social work from Cardiff University (Wales) and has worked as a steelworker, crematorium assistant and social worker in Sheffield, London and Glasgow. Under an exchange program, Turnbull has also done social work in Brooklyn, New York.

Carmen Pharaoh...young woman police detective in York, England
❑ ❑ 1 - Embracing Skeletons (1996)

P Division...police detectives in Glasgow, Scotland
❑ ❑ 1 - Deep and Crisp and Even (1981)
❑ ❑ 2 - Dead Knock (1982)
❑ ❑ 3 - Fair Friday (1983)
❑ ❑ 4 - Big Money (1984)
❑ ❑ 5 - Two Way Cut (1988)
❑ ❑ 6 - Condition Purple (1989)
❑ ❑ 7 - And Did Murder Him (1991)
❑ ❑ 8 - Long Day Monday (1993)
❑ ❑ 9 - The Killing Floor (1995)

■ VACHSS, Andrew H.

Andrew Vachss (rhymes with fax) is a well-known children's rights attorney and advocate for abused children. He's also the creator of an unlicensed private detective and outlaw soldier-of-fortune named Burke, whose supporting cast includes a transsexual hooker working as Burke's secretary to save money for a sex change operation; a deaf martial arts expert named Max the Silent; a techno-geek named Mole who freelances for the Mossad; and Pansy, the 175-lb. killer mastiff. These novels have been described as grim, dark and icy cold. A former social worker and director of a maximum-security juvenile detention facility, Vachss uses his 6-figure book advances to help finance the representation of kids who cannot afford legal help. He once told an interviewer that writing is a way of preaching his own particular gospel to a wider audience. "I'm always looking for a bigger jury than I'd find in a courtroom," he said.

Burke...outlaw soldier-of-fortune investigator in New York, New York
❑ ❑ 1 - **Flood (1985) Shamus nominee** ☆
❑ ❑ 2 - Strega (1987)
❑ ❑ 3 - Blue Belle (1988)
❑ ❑ 4 - Hard Candy (1989)
❑ ❑ 5 - Blossom (1990)
❑ ❑ 6 - Sacrifice (1991)
❑ ❑ 7 - Down in the Zero (1994)
❑ ❑ 8 - Footsteps of the Hawk (1995)
❑ ❑ 9 - False Allegations (1996)

■ VALIN, Jonathan

Shamus award winner Jonathan Valin is the creator of Cincinnati (OH) private eye Harry Stoner, introduced in *The Lime Pit* (1980). A big man with a face like a broken statue, Harry drives a Pinto and listens to radio music on his Zenith Globemaster almost constantly. One of his more unusual cases takes him to California (*Natural Causes*) in search of the killer of a soap opera's head writer. According to Robert J. Randisi writing in *1001 Midnights*, Valin's vivid depiction of the predatory world of big-time soap operas comes from his year spent as a story consultant on a popular daytime soap. Valin earned an M.A. degree from the University of Chicago and did several years of graduate study at Washington University in St. Louis where he was a lecturer in English and a student of mainstream writer Stanley Elkin.

Harry Stoner...private eye in Cincinnati, Ohio
- ❑ ❑ 1 - The Lime Pit (1980)
- ❑ ❑ 2 - Final Notice (1980)
- ❑ ❑ 3 - Dead Letter (1981)
- ❑ ❑ 4 - Day of Wrath (1982)
- ❑ ❑ 5 - Natural Causes (1984)
- ❑ ❑ 6 - Life's Work (1986)
- ❑ ❑ 7 - Fire Lake (1987)
- ❑ ❑ 8 - **Extenuating Circumstances (1989) Shamus winner ★**
- ❑ ❑ 9 - **Second Chance (1991) Shamus nominee ☆**
- ❑ ❑ 10 - The Music Lovers (1993)
- ❑ ❑ 11 - Missing (1995)

■ VAN DE WETERING, Janwillem

Himself a former cop in Amsterdam, Janwillem (yon-WILL-em) van de Wetering (von de VET-ering) is the creator of a pair of Dutch police detectives whose adventures are published in 15 languages. Now retired from the force, Gripstra (KIP-stra) and de Gier (de HEER) were once the subject of Holland's second most popular movie (after Star Wars). In book 14, *The Perfidious Parrot* (1997), they head to Key West in search of a hijacked oil tanker destined for Cuba. With de Gier retired to an island in Maine and Grijpstra a private detective, van de Wetering says there will only be another book or two before the series freezes in time. In a 1996 *CBS Sunday Morning* interview, he listed his primary interests these days as continuing his study of nihilism, keeping his lobster boat afloat and getting older. Since his year and a half in a Kyoto monastery during the '50s, van de Wetering has remained a practicing Buddhist. After living on 6 continents, he now resides on the coast of Maine.

Grijpstra and de Gier...Dutch police detectives in Amsterdam, Netherlands
- ❑ ❑ 1 - Outsider in Amsterdam (1975)
- ❑ ❑ 2 - Tumbleweed (1976)
- ❑ ❑ 3 - The Corpse on the Dike (1976)
- ❑ ❑ 4 - Death of a Hawker (1977)
- ❑ ❑ 5 - The Japanese Corpse (1977)
- ❑ ❑ 6 - The Blond Baboon (1978)
- ❑ ❑ 7 - The Maine Massacre (1979)
- ❑ ❑ 8 - The Mind-Murders (1981)
- ❑ ❑ 9 - The Streetbird (1983)
- ❑ ❑ 10 - The Rattle-Rat (1985)
- ❑ ❑ 11 - Hard Rain (1986)
- ❑ ❑ ss - The Sergeant's Cat and Other Stories [short stories] (1987)
- ❑ ❑ 12 - **Just a Corpse at Twilight (1994) Anthony nominee ☆**
- ❑ ❑ 13 - The Hollow-Eyed Angel (1996)

■ VANCE, Jack

Jack Vance's more than 60 books of science fiction, fantastic adventure and mystery have earned him Hugo, Nebula, Jupiter and Edgar awards, in addition to a Lifetime Achievement award from the World Fantasy Convention in 1984. His tale of intrigue and smuggling in Tangiers won him a best-first-mystery Edgar for *The Man in the Cage* (1960). Much of his science fiction includes a strong crime element such as the Keith Gersen series, beginning with *The Star King* (1964), where a man hunts five disguised nonhumans who murdered his parents. Published under the name John Holbrook Vance, his pair of mysteries featuring Sheriff Joe Bain is set in a fictitious county south of San Jose, much like the area where Vance grew up. Other mysteries from this author were published under the names Alan Wade and Peter Held. Born in San Francisco, he holds a B.A. from the University of California, Berkeley and lives in Oakland (CA).

Keith Gersen...hunter of nonhuman killers in the United States
- ❑ ❑ 1 - The Star King (1964)
- ❑ ❑ 2 - The Killing Machine (1964)
- ❑ ❑ 3 - The Palace of Love (1967)
- ❑ ❑ 4 - The Face (1979)
- ❑ ❑ 5 - The Book of Dreams (1981)

■ VANCE, John Holbrook

Author of more than 60 books, John Holbrook Vance is one of the bylines of Jack Vance. His novels of science fiction, fantastic adventure and mystery have earned him Hugo, Nebula, Jupiter and Edgar awards, in addition to a Lifetime Achievement award from the World Fantasy Convention in 1984. Published as John Holbrook Vance, his pair of mysteries featuring Sheriff Joe Bain is set in a fictitious county south of San Jose, much like the area where Vance grew up. Anthony Boucher said the setting is "wonderfully real, and so is Sheriff Bain." Other mysteries from this author were published under the names Alan Wade (*Isle of Peril*, 1957) and Peter Held (*Take My Face*, 1957). They were later re-released as by Jack Vance. Born in San Francisco, he holds a B.A. from the University of California, Berkeley and lives in Oakland (CA).

Joe Bain...sheriff in San Rodrigo County, California
- ❑ ❑ 1 - The Fox Valley Murders (1966)
- ❑ ❑ 2 - The Pleasant Grove Murders (1967)

■ VINCENT, Lawrence M.

Lawrence M. Vincent has written a pair of medical mysteries featuring radiologist Dr. Townsend Reeves of Kansas City (MO) and his ballerina girlfriend, Leslie Rosenthal, who later becomes his wife. In book 2 Dr. Reeves accidentally becomes a sperm donor while covering for a friend at a fertility clinic. Like his fictional creation, Vincent is a radiologist with professional ties to the dance world. Married to a former member of the Martha Graham Dance Company, Vincent himself danced with the Kansas City Ballet Company. A former editor of the *Harvard Lampoon*, he also wrote *Dancers and the Pursuit of the Ideal Body Form* (1979), *Competing With the Sylph* (1981), *The Dancer's Book of Health* (1988) and *The Quest for the Perfect Dance Body* (1989). A former academic radiologist, he is currently in private practice near Seattle.

Townsend Reeves, Dr.....radiologist with a ballerina girlfriend in Kansas City, Misouri
- ❑ ❑ 1 - Final Dictation (1989)
- ❑ ❑ 2 - Pas de Death (1994)

■ WADDELL, Martin

Belfast-born author Martin Waddell has written more than 120 children's mysteries, picture books, slapstick comedies, soccer stories and ghost tales under his own name and as Catherine Sefton. During the 1960s he created a series of satirical spy thrillers featuring amateur adventurer Gerald Otley, first seen in *Otley* (1966), adapted for film with Romy Schneider and Tom Courtenay in the lead roles. In 1972 Waddell was nearly killed by a bomb blast in a local church and was unable to write for at least 6 years. When his writing abilities returned, he began turning out children's books at a furious pace, including the Napper series which uses his goalkeeping experience to tell the stories. In 1996 he told Contemporary Authors he considered picture books for the very young to be his most challenging work at present.

Gerald Otley...amateur adventurer and part-time spy in London, England
- ❑ ❑ 1 - Otley (1966)
- ❑ ❑ 2 - Otley Pursued (1967)
- ❑ ❑ 3 - Otley Forever (1968)
- ❑ ❑ 4 - Otley Victorious (1969)

■ WAINRIGHT, John

John Wainright spent more than 20 years as a police officer in Yorkshire and began writing academic pieces for legal journals after earning his law degree. Since 1965 he has published more than 100 novels under his own name, several as Jack Ripley, some radio plays and four nonfiction titles including his war memoirs, *Tail-end Charlie* (1978), and *Wainright's Beat* (1987). His police series characters are numerous, and they frequently move in and out of each other's cases, most of which take place in Yorkshire. While critics agree his stories are stark, brutal, and ultrarealistic, it's been said his plotting is surprisingly stylish. Inspector Lyle's first case, *Brainwash* (1979), was bought by the French and turned into a film they called *Garde a vue*. It was called *The Inquisitor* in Britain and *Under Suspicion* in the U.S. When asked during the mid '80s if he had a favorite of his series characters, he told Contemporary Authors it was Superintendent Ripley.

Charles Ripley, Chief Supt.....head of the uniform branch in Yorkshire, England
- ❑ ❑ 1 - Evil Intent (1966)
- ❑ ❑ 2 - The Worms Must Wait (1967)
- ❑ ❑ 3 - The Darkening Glass (1968)
- ❑ ❑ 4 - Freeze Thy Blood Less Coldly (1970)
- ❑ ❑ 5 - A Touch of Malice (1973)
- ❑ ❑ 6 - The Hard Hit (1974)
- ❑ ❑ 7 - Death of a Big Man (1975)
- ❑ ❑ 8 - Portrait in Shadows (1986)

Gilliant, Chief Constable...chief constable in Yorkshire, England
- ❑ ❑ 1 - The Crystallised Carbon Pig (1966)
- ❑ ❑ 2 - Requiem for a Loser (1972)
- ❑ ❑ 3 - High-Class Kill (1973)
- ❑ ❑ 4 - A Ripple of Murders (1978)

Lennox, D.C.I.....detective chief inspector in Yorkshire, England
- ❑ ❑ 1 - The Evidence I Shall Give (1974)
- ❑ ❑ 2 - Square Dance (1975)
- ❑ ❑ 3 - Landscape with Violence [incl Supt. Blayde] (1975)
- ❑ ❑ 4 - Pool of Tears (1977)
- ❑ ❑ 5 - The Day of the Peppercorn Kill (1977)
- ❑ ❑ 6 - Take Murder... (1979)
- ❑ ❑ 7 - Spiral Staircase (1983)

❏ ❏ 8 - The Tenth Interview (1986)
❏ ❏ 9 - A Very Parochial Murder (1988)
❏ ❏ 10 - The Man Who Wasn't There (1089)

Lyle, Det. Insp.....detective inspector in Yorkshire, England
❏ ❏ 1 - Brainwash (1979)
❏ ❏ 2 - Duty Elsewhere [incl Blayde & Lennox] (1979)
❏ ❏ 3 - Dominoes [incl Blayde & Lennox] (1980)
❏ ❏ 4 - A Very Parochial Murder (1988)
❏ ❏ 5 - The Man Who Wasn't There (1989)
❏ ❏ 6 - Hangman's Lane (1992)

Ralph Flensing, D.C.S. & David Hoyle, D.C.I.....Lessford police ensemble in Yorkshire, England
❏ ❏ 1 - Their Evil Ways (1983)
❏ ❏ 2 - The Ride (1984)

Robert Blayde, Supt.....police superintendent in Yorkshire, England
❏ ❏ 1 - Landscape with Violence [incl Lennox] (1975)
❏ ❏ 2 - All on a Summer's Day (1981)
❏ ❏ 3 - An Urge for Justice (1981)
❏ ❏ 4 - Blayde R.I.P. (1982)

■ **WALKER, David J.**

David J. Walker spent 11 years as a parish priest and later worked for the Chicago Police Department investigating shootings and allegations of police brutality. His private eye Malachy (pronounced MAL-a-key) Foley, who rides a BMW motorcycle and plays jazz in a piano bar, is an attorney suspended for refusing to break a client confidence. Mal's first case as a P.I., *Fixed in His Folly* (1995), was nominated for a best first novel Edgar. His next and third case, *Applaud the Hollow Ghost* (1998), finds Mal trying to clear the name of a childhood classmate accused of assaulting a teenage girl. Walker's new series, starting with *Candle's Ticket* (1998), introduces a husband and wife detection team where he's a personal injury lawyer and she's a private eye. Walker is himself an attorney whose part-time Chicago area practice is defending attorneys charged with illegal or unethical conduct.

Malachy P. Foley...jazz piano-playing P.I. in Chicago, Illinois
❏ ❏ **1 - Fixed in His Folly (1995) Edgar Nominee** ☆
❏ ❏ 2 - Half the Truth (1996)

■ **WALKER, Peter N.**

Past Chairman of the Crime Writers' Association, Peter N. Walker is the author of more than 90 books, the majority of which are crime fiction, written under his own name and the pseudonyms Andrew Arncliffe, Christopher Coram, James Ferguson, Tom Ferris and Nicholas Rhea. Yorkshire born, he is a former police officer and lecturer at law and police training schools. His Panda One series features Jock Patterson, introduced in *Panda One on Duty* (1971), followed by 3 later installments. Founder and former editor of *Police Box*, he is a frequent contributor to police publications, often under the name Nicholas Rhea. Author of the weekly column "Countryman's Diary," he is also a frequent contributor of articles on folklore and rural matters, again under the Rhea pen name.

Jock Patterson, Constable...British constable in England
❏ ❏ 1 - Panda One on Duty (1971)
❏ ❏ 2 - Panda One Investigates (1973)
❏ ❏ 3 - Witchcraft for Panda One (1978)
❏ ❏ 4 - Siege for Panda One (1981)

■ WALKER, Robert W.

Robert W. Walker has written more than 20 adult novels, typically involving forensic investigations. His books are cast with a male and female lead who may or may not fall in love along the way. The Instinct series features FBI medical examiner Dr. Jessica Coran who makes her 6th appearance in *Extreme Instinct* (1998). In 1997 he launched a new series featuring police officer Lucas Stonecoat and psychiatrist Meredyth Sanger, first seen in *Cutting Edge*. As Geoffrey Caine he has written 3 books featuring an ex-Chicago cop turned archaeologist who relies on his psychic abilities. He has also written under the names Stephen Robertson and Glenn Hale. A Mississippi native, Walker earned both his B.A. and M.A. degrees from Northwestern University. He currently lives in Florida where he teaches English and creative writing at Daytona Beach Community College.

Jessica Coran, Dr.....FBI medical examiner in Washington, D.C.
- ❏ ❏ 1 - Killer Instinct (1992)
- ❏ ❏ 2 - Fatal Instinct (1993)
- ❏ ❏ 3 - Primal Instinct (1994)
- ❏ ❏ 4 - Pure Instinct (1995)
- ❏ ❏ 5 - Darkest Instinct (1996)

■ WALLACE, Robert [P]

Robert Wallace is the pseudonym of mystery writer Robin Wallace-Crabbe, creator of aging adventurer Essington Holt, whose interests include art forgery and sexual politics (at which he's a dud). Essington's travels regulary take him from Sydney and Melbourne to London, Paris, Amsterdam and Italy. In fact, the series opener is set in France, which is also part of the scenery for books 4 and 5. Essington's first short story appearance is in *Love Lies Bleeding, Crimes for a Summer Christmas #5* (1995). Wallace's other books, *Flood Rain* and *Art Rat*, feature characters less well mannered and more psychopathically inclinced than Essington Holt according to Wallace. Having grazed cattle on various runs in Australia's southest corner, he now lives on the Southern Tablelands, where he says he paints beautiful pictures and sits around in the sun doing nothing.

Essington Holt...aging adventurer with an interest in art forgery in Sydney, Australia
- ❏ ❏ 1 - To Catch a Forger [France] (1988)
- ❏ ❏ 2 - An Axe to Grind (1989)
- ❏ ❏ 3 - Payday [Melbourne] (1989)
- ❏ ❏ 4 - Paint Out [Paris & Amsterdam] (1990)
- ❏ ❏ 5 - Finger Play [France, Italy & London] (1991)

■ WARGA, Wayne

Los Angeles reporter and television writer Wayne Warga (1937-1994) won a Best First Novel Shamus for his creation of an ex-CIA courier-journalist turned rare book dealer. Jeffrey Dean first appeared in *Hard Cover* (1985) where he discovers a suspicious signature at a London book fair and begins the search to uncover the forger. Warga himself was once a *Life* magazine correspondent in Cuba and Central America and an accomplished book collector. Head writer during the earliest days of *Entertainment Tonight*, he cowrote at least 2 celebrity bios. With Buzz Aldrin he penned *Return to Earth* (1973) and with Lana Wood, *Natalie: A Memoir by Her Sister* (1984). Born in Los Angeles and educated at the University of Southern California, Warga was a frequent contributor to periodicals such as *TV Guide*, *Cosmopolitan* and *McCall's*.

Jeffrey Dean...ex-CIA courier-journalist turned rare book dealer in Los Angeles, California
- ❏ ❏ **1 - Hardcover (1985) Shamus winner ★**
- ❏ ❏ 2 - Fatal Impressions (1989)
- ❏ ❏ 3 - Singapore Transfer (1991)

■ WASHBURN, Stan

Stan Washburn is the creator of a quietly heroic San Francisco (CA) cop named Toby Parkman, who has appeared in two novels beginning with *Intent to Harm* (1995). Both the author's parents were academics, and at least 3 generations of authors have preceded him. A painter by training, Washburn paints for several weeks at a time and then writes, working in a corner of his studio, with paintings in progress against the walls. He often finds the answer to a writing problem in a painting and vice versa. Also a printmaker, he was once described as California's foremost 16th century artist. Included in many public and private collections, Washburn's work is represented by the North Point Gallery in San Franciso. He lives in Berkeley (CA) where he continues to paint and work on the third Toby Parkman novel.

Toby Parkman...quietly heroic cop in San Francisco, California
- ❑ ❑ 1 - Intent to Harm (1995)
- ❑ ❑ 2 - Into Thin Air (1996)

■ WAUGH, Hillary

Grand Master Hillary Waugh has written more than 45 novels including *Last Seen Wearing...* (1952), one of Julian Symons' picks for the 100 greatest crime novels ever written. Waugh's best-known series features Chief Fred Fellows of small-town Stockford (CT), a folksy, tobacco-chewing fellow first seen in *Sleep Long, My Love* (1959), which became the 1962 film *Jigsaw*. Fellows brings his intelligence to bear on 10 more cases. Waugh also wrote 3 books featuring a Manhattan homicide detective and two New York private eye series totalling 9 books. Under the pseudonyms Elissa Grandower and H. Baldwin Taylor, he wrote another 7 novels. For Writer's Digest Books, he wrote *Hillary Waugh's Guide to Mysteries and Mystery Writing* (1991). Among his earlier occupations were freelance cartoonist and song writer, high school math and physics teacher, weekly newspaper editor and Connecticut town selectman.

Frank Sessions. Lt.....Manhattan North homicide detective in New York, New York
- ❑ ❑ 1 - "30" Manhattan East (1968)
- ❑ ❑ 2 - The Young Prey (1969)
- ❑ ❑ 3 - Finish Me Off (1970)

Fred Fellows, Chief...small-town police chief in Stockford, Connecticut
- ❑ ❑ 1 - Sleep Long, My Love (1959)
  APA-Jigsaw
- ❑ ❑ 2 - Road Block (1959)
- ❑ ❑ 3 - That Night it Rained (1961)
- ❑ ❑ 4 - The Late Mrs. D (1962)
- ❑ ❑ 5 - Born Victim (1962)
- ❑ ❑ 6 - Death and Circumstance (1963)
- ❑ ❑ 7 - Prisoner's Plea (1963)
- ❑ ❑ 8 - The Missing Man (1964)
- ❑ ❑ 9 - End of a Party (1965)
- ❑ ❑ 10 - Pure Poison (1966)
- ❑ ❑ 11 - The Con Game (1968)

Sheridan Wesley...private investigator in New York, New York
- ❑ ❑ 1 - Madam Will Not Dine Tonight (1947)
  APA-If I Live to Dine
- ❑ ❑ 2 - Hope to Die (1948)
- ❑ ❑ 3 - The Odds Run Out (1949)

Simon Kaye...private eye in New York, New York
- ❏ ❏ 1 - The Glenna Powers Case (1980)
- ❏ ❏ 2 - The Doria Rafe Case (1980)
- ❏ ❏ 3 - The Billy Cantrell Case (1981)
- ❏ ❏ 4 - The Nerissa Claire Case (1983)
- ❏ ❏ 5 - The Veronica Dean Case (1984)
- ❏ ❏ 6 - The Priscilla Copperwaite Case (1986)

■ WEBB, Jack

Jack Webb wrote 9 mysteries during the '50s with a Jewish Los Angeles police detective (Sammy Golden) and a Catholic priest (Father Joseph Shanley) who first appeared in *The Big Sin* (1952). Despite the LAPD connection, this is not the Jack Webb (1920-1982) of TV Dragnet fame, who immortalized the words, "Just the facts, maam." According to Bill Crider (*1001 Midnights*), the mystery-writing Jack Webb also wrote two entertaining thrillers—*One for My Dame* (1961), which Crider says should have been a Hitchcock film, and *Make My Bed Soon* (1963). For best-of-the-Golden-series, Crider picks *Big Sin*, *Brass Halo* and *Deadly Sex*. Webb also wrote 4 novels under the name John Farr, two of which have wonderful zoo backgrounds, *Don't Feed the Animals* (1955) and *The Lady and the Snake* (1957). Webb's love of animals is also evident in the pet shop setting of *One for My Dame*.

Sammy Golden, Det. Sgt. & Joseph Shanley, Fr.....Jewish police detective & Catholic priest in Los Angeles
- ❏ ❏ 1 - The Big Sin (1952)
- ❏ ❏ 2 - The Naked Angel (1953)
      Brit.-Such Women Are Dangerous
- ❏ ❏ 3 - The Damned Lovely (1954)
- ❏ ❏ 4 - The Broken Doll (1955)
- ❏ ❏ 5 - The Bad Blonde (1956)
- ❏ ❏ 6 - The Brass Halo (1957)
- ❏ ❏ 7 - The Deadly Sex (1959)
- ❏ ❏ 8 - The Delicate Darling (1959)
- ❏ ❏ 9 - The Gilded Witch (1963)

■ WELCOME, John

John Welcome has written 6 books featuring English gentleman and sometimes British Intelligence agent Richard Graham, introduced in *Run for Cover* (1958). More recently he wrote *A Call to Arms* (1985), set in Ireland and Kenya during World War II. Involved all his life with fox-hunting, racing and horses, Welcome has served as senior steward of the Irish National Hunt Steeplechase Committee and written extensively on horse racing, including *Infamous Occasions* (1980) and *Great Racing Disasters* (1985). He has written at least 10 nonseries novels and 10 nonfiction books, including *Cheating at Cards: The Cases in Court* (1963). He has served as editor for a dozen short story collections, including *Great Racing Stories* (1989), co-edited with Dick Francis. Principal solicitor in a Wexford (Ireland) firm, Welcome has lived in England, Ireland, Kenya and several European cities.

Richard Graham...English gentleman secret agent in England
- ❏ ❏ 1 - Run for Cover (1958)
- ❏ ❏ 2 - Hard to Handle (1964)
- ❏ ❏ 3 - Wanted for Killing (1965)
- ❏ ❏ 4 - Hell is Where You Find It (1968)
- ❏ ❏ 5 - On the Stretch (1969)
- ❏ ❏ 6 - Go for Broke (1972)

■ **WEST, Christopher**

Christopher West travelled alone throughout China in the mid '80s and '90s where he met a vast range of people from senior Party officials to poor peasants. He says he heard many stories that needed telling. *Journey to the Middle Kingdom* (1991) and West's Insp. Wang mysteries are the results. Although raised as a Party member, the Insp. has not been the same since witnessing the massacre at Tiananmen Square. In the series opener he must deal with a murder at the Beijing Opera that culminates in a dramatic climax in the Tang dynasty cave-temples of Huashan. Book 2 takes the Insp. and his new wife to the village of his birth where a local Party official is murdered. Coming next in Britain is *Death of a Red Mandarin* (1997). West holds a degree in philosophy and once earned his living playing drums in a travelling band. He frequently writes about travel for the *Independent on Sunday*.

Wang Anzhuang, Insp.....Public Security Bureau inspector in Beijing, China
- ❏ ❏ 1 - **Death of a Blue Lantern (1994) Anthony nominee** ☆
- ❏ ❏ 2 - Death on a Black Dragon River (1995)

■ **WESTERMANN, John**

John Westermann spent 20 years as a Long Island (Nassau County) street cop, retiring in 1992. His first police novel, *High Crimes* (1988), features a pair of goof-off college-boy detectives suddenly caught up in mayhem and murder. Tough Long Island street cop Orin Boyd, introduced in *Exit Wounds* (1990), returns in *The Honor Farm* (1996) where he goes undercover as the commish's mole to investigate deaths at a prison for dirty cops. The ex-Marine, ex-drunk Boyd has enough mistakes in his past to fit in just fine with the rogues on the Farm. Westermann's next novel is a standalone thriller, *Ladies of the Night* (1998), about three women who disappear on Long Island. Would the Nassau County political machine stoop to kidnapping and murder just to keep a few women quiet?

Orin Boyd...Nassau County uniformed cop in Long Island, New York
- ❏ ❏ 1 - Exit Wounds (1990)
- ❏ ❏ 2 - The Honor Farm (1996)

■ **WESTLAKE, Donald E.**

Grand Master Donald E. Westlake is a 4-time Edgar winner who has written more than 40 novels under his own name and dozens more under the names Richard Stark, Tucker Coe, Timothy J. Culver and Curt Clark. After launching his writing career with *The Mercenaries* (1960), he wrote more than 15 books before the 1970 debut of perhaps his most popular creation, John Dortmunder and his merry band of inept accomplices, introduced in the Edgar best-novel-nominee *The Hot Rock*. Westlake has seen many of his books made into films, including his first Parker novel, *The Hunter* (1962), released in '67 as *Point Blank* starring Lee Marvin. The novel was later re-released as *Point Blank* and may yet be remade as a Mel Gibson movie. One of Westlake's lesser known pseudonymous titles is the 1961 biography *Elizabeth Taylor: A Fascinating Story of America's Most Talented Actress and the World's Most Beautiful Woman*.

John Dortmunder...comic thief in New York, New York
- ❏ ❏ 1 - **The Hot Rock (1970) Edgar nominee** ☆
- ❏ ❏ 2 - Bank Shot (1972)
- ❏ ❏ 3 - Jimmy the Kid (1974)
- ❏ ❏ 4 - Nobody's Perfect (1977)
- ❏ ❏ 5 - Why Me? (1983)
- ❏ ❏ 6 - Good Behavior (1986)
- ❏ ❏ 7 - Drowned Hopes (1990)
- ❏ ❏ 8 - Don't Ask (1993)
- ❏ ❏ 9 - What's the Worst That Could Happen? (1996)

■ WHITE, Randy Wayne

Randy Wayne White is the creator of Doc Ford, ex-operative turned marine biologist, who's been called a modern-day Thoreau. From his house-on-stilts in Dinkin's Bay marina, Ford runs a mail-order business supplying marine specimens to schools and research programs. During the 1980s as Randy Striker and Carl Ramm, White produced 18 paperback thrillers he says are best forgotten. His *Out There* columns which he continues to write for *Outside* magazine are collected in *Batfishing in the Rainforest* (1991). A veteran fishing guide who hosts a fishing show on PBS, White lives in a 1910 house built on an Indian mound on the Florida Gulf coast. He plays senior league baseball for the Fort Meyers Bombers where he is starting catcher and sometimes pitcher. "This is the real game," he says, "with stealing and spitting, where players wear helmets for a reason."

Doc Ford...ex-operative marine biologist in Sanibel Island, Florida
- ❏ ❏   1 - Sanibel Flats (1990)
- ❏ ❏   2 - The Heat Islands (1992)
- ❏ ❏   3 - The Man Who Invented Florida (1994)
- ❏ ❏   4 - Captiva (1996)
- ❏ ❏   5 - North of Havana (1997)

■ WHITE, Stephen

Stephen White is the creator of Alan Gregory and Lauren Crowder, practicing psychologist and attorney duo in Boulder (CO), last seen in *Remote Control* (1997), when the pair are caught up in computer crime and celebrity stalking after Lauren shoots a stalker while protecting a friend from kidnapping. In practice for 15 years before writing his first novel, White is a trained clinical psychologist. Former staff psychologist at Children's Hospital in Denver, he earned his Ph.D. at the University of Colorado, after starting his academic career at the University of California. During the past few years White has written more than a dozen Barney books for children. Among his 5 new titles in 1997 are *Barney's Christmas Wishes* and *Barney's Trick or Treat*. White says he has really enjoyed prowling the audiences at live Barney concerts watching kids and their parents enjoy his work. He lives in Boulder (CO).

Alan Gregory & Lauren Crowder...practicing psychologist & attorney in Boulder, Colorado
- ❏ ❏   1 - Privileged Information (1991)
- ❏ ❏   2 - Private Practices (1994)
- ❏ ❏   3 - Higher Authority (1994)
- ❏ ❏   4 - Harm's Way (1996)
- ❏ ❏   5 - Remote Control (1997)

■ WILCOX, Collin

Collin Wilcox (1924-1996) will be best remembered for his two longest-running San Francisco mystery series—one with ex-Detroit Lion and homicide detective Lt. Frank Hastings (20 books); the other actor-director private eye Alan Bernhardt (5 books). He also wrote 2 featuring psychic reporter Stephen Drake, 2 with Marshall McCloud, and 2 suspense thrillers under the name Carter Wick (*The Faceless Man*, 1975 and *Dark House, Dark Road*, 1982). After earning a pilot's license at age 55, he became largely responsible for Marcia Muller learning to fly. He threatened to stop giving her flying tips for her McCone books, if she didn't take lessons herself. Muller took that first lesson, after Wilcox signed her up with an instructor, and later earned her license. A former copywriter and art teacher, he once owned a custom lamp-making shop. An Antioch College (OH) graduate, he was born in Detroit but lived in San Francisco for more than 45 years.

Alan Bernhardt...actor-director private eye in San Francisco, California
- ❏ ❏   1 - Bernhardt's Edge (1988)
- ❏ ❏   2 - Silent Witness (1990)
- ❏ ❏   3 - Except for the Bones (1991)
- ❏ ❏   4 - Find Her a Grave (1993)
- ❏ ❏   5 - Full Circle (1994)

Frank Hastings, Lt.....co-commander SFPD homicide in San Francisco, California
- ❏ ❏ 1 - The Lonely Hunter (1969)
- ❏ ❏ 2 - The Disappearance (1970)
- ❏ ❏ 3 - Dead Aim (1971)
- ❏ ❏ 4 - Hiding Place (1973)
- ❏ ❏ 5 - Long Way Down (1974)
- ❏ ❏ 6 - Aftershock (1975)
- ❏ ❏ 7 - Doctor, Lawyer... (1976)
- ❏ ❏ 8 - The Third Victim (1976)
- ❏ ❏ 9 - Twospot [with Bill Pronzini & Nameless] (1978)
- ❏ ❏ 10 - Power Plays (1979)
- ❏ ❏ 11 - Mankiller (1980)
- ❏ ❏ 12 - Stalking Horse (1982)
- ❏ ❏ 13 - Victims (1985)
- ❏ ❏ 14 - Nightgames (1986)
- ❏ ❏ 15 - The Pariah (1988)
- ❏ ❏ 16 - A Death Before Dying (1990)
- ❏ ❏ 17 - Hire a Hangman (1991)
- ❏ ❏ 18 - Dead Center (1992)
- ❏ ❏ 19 - Switchback (1993)
- ❏ ❏ 20 - Calculated Risk (1995)

McCloud...New Mexico marshall in New York, New York
- ❏ ❏ 1 - McCloud (1973)
- ❏ ❏ 2 - The New Mexico Connection (1974)

Stephen Drake...newspaper reporter with ESP in San Francisco, California
- ❏ ❏ 1 - The Black Door (1967)
- ❏ ❏ 2 - The Third Figure (1967)

■ WILLIAMS, Alan

Newspaper correspondent Alan Williams wrote 11 crime novels during the '60s and '70s, with international settings ranging from the Caribbean to Switzerland, Vietnam, Russia and North Africa. His 3-book series featuring Charles Pol has the bandit-adventurer stealing U.S. government gold in book 1 and being hired by the Shah to kill the Shah in book 2. Pol owns a lingerie shop located behind the Gare St. Lazare in Paris. Williams also penned a pair of spy stories featuring swashbuckling Englishman Rupert Quinn, whose first appearance takes him to Morocco in *Long Run South* (1962), Williams's first novel. The cowardly hero returns in *Barbouze* (1964), published in the U.S. as *The False Beards*. The author is the son of actor-playwright Emlyn Williams (1905-1987), who wrote several crime-related plays and novels during his long career.

Charles Pol...Marxist bandit and lingerie shop owner in Paris, France
- ❏ ❏ 1 - The Tale of the Lazy Dog (1970)
- ❏ ❏ 2 - Shah-Mak (1976)
  - APA-A Bullet for the Shah
- ❏ ❏ 3 - Holy of Holies (1981)

Rupert Quinn...swashbuckling English courier in North Africa
- ❏ ❏ 1 - Long Run South (1962)
- ❏ ❏ 2 - Barbouze (1964)
  - U.S.-The false Beards

■ **WILLIAMS, David**

Welshman David Williams saw his first novel published at the age of 50, while still chairman of his own London advertising agency. Since the introduction of merchant banker Mark Treasure in *Unholy Writ* (1976), Williams has produced almost a book a year, adding 16 novels to his first series and 4 more in a newer group featuring two Welsh police detectives. The Mark Treasure banking mysteries have twice been shortlisted for the CWA Gold Dagger. In book 17, the banker sleuth is on the case when Sir Ray Bims is found dead, just as he is about to be charged in a Caribbean money laundering scheme. Among the colorful suspects are a concert pianist, a religious pest controller and a football team manager. Next for the Cardiff detectives is book 4, *A Terminal Case* (1997). Williams, who lives in Surrey, holds an Oxford degree in history.

Mark Treasure...merchant banker in London, England
- ❏ ❏ 1 - Unholy Writ (1976)
- ❏ ❏ 2 - Treasure by Degrees (1977)
- ❏ ❏ 3 - Treasure Up in Smoke (1978)
- ❏ ❏ 4 - Murder for Treasure (1980)
- ❏ ❏ 5 - Copper, Gold and Treasure (1982)
- ❏ ❏ 6 - Treasure Preserved (1983)
- ❏ ❏ 7 - Advertise for Treasure (1984)
- ❏ ❏ 8 - Wedding Treasure (1985)
- ❏ ❏ 9 - Murder in Advent (1985)
- ❏ ❏ 10 - Treasure in Roubles (1987)
- ❏ ❏ 11 - Divided Treasure (1987)
- ❏ ❏ 12 - Treasure in Oxford (1988)
- ❏ ❏ 13 - Holy Treasure! (1989)
- ❏ ❏ 14 - Prescription for Murder (1990)
- ❏ ❏ 15 - Treasure by Post (1991)
- ❏ ❏ 16 - Planning on Murder (1992)
- ❏ ❏ 17 - Banking on Murder (1993)

Merlin Parry, D.C.I. & Gomer Lloyd, D.S.....detective chief inspector & detective sergeant in Cardiff, Wales
- ❏ ❏ 1 - Last Seen Breathing (1994)
- ❏ ❏ 2 - Death of a Prodigal (1995)
- ❏ ❏ 3 - Dead in the Market (1996)

■ **WILSON, Derek**

Historian Derek Wilson, known primarily for his books about Tudor England, is the creator of a series of art world mysteries featuring ex-SAS officer Tim Lacey, owner of a security firm specializing in stolen art recoveries. The series opener deals with a lost Raphael canvas and book 6 with a chalice that belonged to Pope Alexander VI, who used it to poison his enemies. Shortly after Lacey buys the chalice for a client, 4 people drink from it and die within the hour. Wilson has written more than 40 books, including biographies of the Rothschilds, Astors, and Holbein. A graduate of Cambridge University, he has worked as a teacher, housemaster, antiques dealer and magazine editor. Shortly after its independence, Wilson spent 6 years in Kenya, where he was a radio broadcaster with Voice of Kenya from 1965-71. He has also written several books on African history.

Tim Lacey...ex-SAS officer and security firm owner in London, England
- ❏ ❏ 1 - The Triarchs (1994)
- ❏ ❏ 2 - The Dresden Text (1994)
- ❏ ❏ 3 - The Hellfire Papers (1995)
- ❏ ❏ 4 - The Camargue Brotherhood (1995)
- ❏ ❏ 5 - The Borgia Chalice (1996)
- ❏ ❏ 6 - Cumberland's Cradle (1996)

■ **WILTSE, David**

Playwright and novelist David Wiltse has written at least 10 novels, including 6 John Becker thrillers, and numerous plays for stage, screen and television. First produced at Lincoln Center in 1972, *Suggs* earned him a Drama Desk award for most promising playwright, while his teleplay for *Revenge of the Stepford Wives* won him an Edgar in 1981. New York FBI agent John Becker is forced to deal with a mad bomber named Spring in book 6, *Blown Away* (1996). While one madman is blowing up bridges and tunnels in and out of Manhattan, Becker is dealing with more than the usual number of losers, lunatics and hoods. A former contributing editor to Tennis magazine, Wiltse served as editor of *It Only Hurts When I Serve* (1980) and contributed to *Best Sports Stories* (1980). A graduate of the University of Nebraska, he lives in Connecticut.

John Becker...FBI agent in New York, New York
- ❏ ❏ 1 - Prayer for the Dead (1991)
- ❏ ❏ 2 - Close to the Bone (1992)
- ❏ ❏ 3 - The Edge of Sleep (1993)
- ❏ ❏ 4 - Into the Fire (1994)
- ❏ ❏ 5 - Bone Deep (1995)
- ❏ ❏ 6 - Blown Away (1996)

■ **WINGFIELD, R. D.**

R. D. Wingfield is Rodney D. Wingfield, a prolific writer of British radio plays and comedy scripts, in addition to his police novels featuring Detective Inspector Jack Frost of Denton Division. The series opener, *Frost at Christmas*, was published first in 1984 under the name Rodney D. Wingfield and re-released 5 years later as by R. D. Wingfield. Brought to life on British television by David Jason, D.I. Frost is an unkempt, unruly, rather crude fellow who is not liked by his superiors. As much as they'd like to get rid of him, it's Frost who always manages to save the day. In book 7 all he's looking for is cigarettes (filched from his commander), when he ends up doing emergency duty. Starting with a car crash involving tipsy high-ranking cops, it's Guy Fawkes night and mischief, perversion and mayhem abound. Wingfield lives in Essex, England.

Jack Frost, Det. Insp.....Denton Division detective inspector in England
- ❏ ❏ 1 - Frost at Christmas (1984)
- ❏ ❏ 2 - A Touch of Frost (1988)
- ❏ ❏ 3 - Night Frost (1992)
- ❏ ❏ 4 - **Hard Frost (1995) Edgar nominee** ☆

■ **WINSLOW, Don**

Don Winslow is the creator of Neal Carey, a youthful New York pickpocket turned private eye whose adventures are under development for a Fox-TV series. Book 1 was nominated for Edgar and Shamus awards for best first novel. Under the pseudonym MacDonald Lloyd, Winslow is also the author of *A Winter Spy* (1997). Son of a career Navy man, he was born in New York City on Halloween. Having worked as a movie theater manager, a documentary production assistant and a private investigator, he now consults with corporations on issues involving criminal litigation. After earning a B.A. in African history from the University of Nebraska, he later completed an M.A. in military history while working as a New York City private eye. He should not be confused with another Don Winslow who writes paperback erotic fiction published by Masquerade Books and Blue Moon.

Neal Carey...youthful pickpocket turned P.I. in New York, New York
- ❏ ❏ 1 - **A Cool Breeze on the Underground (1991) Edgar & Shamus nominee** ☆☆
- ❏ ❏ 2 - The Trail to Buddha's Mirror (1993)
- ❏ ❏ 3 - Way Down on the High Lonely (1994)
- ❏ ❏ 4 - A Long Walk Up the Waterslide (1995)
- ❏ ❏ 5 - While Drowning in the Desert (1996)

■ WOMACK, Steven

Three-time Shamus nominee and Edgar award winner Steven Womack writes 2 series—one with Nashville reporter turned private eye, Harry James Denton, and the other with New Orleans problem-solver and PR man, Jack Lynch. Optioned for both film and television, the Denton series continues with book 5 in early 1998, followed by at least one other installment. Womack's varied background includes work as a UPI reporter, city editor, news bureau photographer, graphic artist, typographer, screenwriting instructor and senior partner in a property tax management firm. His movie and television credits include the 1997 ABC-TV movie *Fire on the Mountain* and *The Days and Nights of Molly Dodd* which finished in the top 5 at the Houston International Film Festival in 1988. An honors graduate of Tulane, Womack lives in Nashville (TN) with his psychologist wife.

Harry James Denton...ex-newspaper reporter turned P.I. in Nashville, Tennessee
- ❑ ❑ 1 - **Dead Folk's Blues (1993) Edgar winner** ★
- ❑ ❑ 2 - **Torch Town Boogie (1993) Shamus nominee** ☆
- ❑ ❑ 3 - **Way Past Dead (1995) Shamus nominee** ☆
- ❑ ❑ 4 - **Chain of Fools (1996) Anthony & Shamus nominee** ☆☆

Jack Lynch...PR man and problem solver in New Orleans, Louisiana
- ❑ ❑ 1 - Murphy's Fault (1990)
- ❑ ❑ 2 - Smash Cut (1991)
- ❑ ❑ 3 - The Software Bomb (1993)

■ WOOD, Ted

Ted Wood is Edward John Wood, former Toronto police officer and author of a police series set in the fictional resort town of Murphy's Harbor, Toronto's cottage country. Wood's continuing characters are Reid Bennett and his German Shepherd partner Sam. Bennett is a former Toronto cop who resigned from the force after killing two bikers and seriously injuring a third while stopping the gang rape of a young girl. After being arrested by his own department and abandoned by his wife, Bennett decides to move away from the city and look for work in a small town. The author was born in England and emigrated to Canada in his early 20s after serving 3 years in the Royal Air Force. Following a short police career, he spent more than 15 years in advertising before turning to full-time writing in 1974. He lives in Whitbey, Ontario where he owns and operates a bed and breakfast.

Reid Bennett & Sam...small-town police chief & German Sheperd partner in Murphy's Harbor, Ontario
- ❑ ❑ 1 - Dead in the Water (1983)
- ❑ ❑ 2 - Murder on Ice (1984) Brit.-The Killing Cold
- ❑ ❑ 3 - Live Bait (1985) Brit.-Dead Centre
- ❑ ❑ 4 - Fool's Gold (1986)
- ❑ ❑ 5 - Corkscrew (1987)
- ❑ ❑ 6 - When the Killing Starts (1989)
- ❑ ❑ 7 - On the Inside (1990)
- ❑ ❑ 8 - Flashback (1992)
- ❑ ❑ 9 - Snowjob (1993)
- ❑ ❑ 10 - A Clean Kill (1995)

■ WOODRELL, Daniel

Hammett prize nominee Daniel Woodrell has written 3 books featuring Rene Shade, bayou town cop in St. Bruno, Louisiana. Book 1, *Under the Bright Lights* (1986), caused James Ellroy to remark, "Daniel Woodrell is stone brilliant, a bayou Dutch Leonard." "I flat out loved this novel and wished it had been twice as long," said James Crumley after reading book 3, *The Ones You Do* (1992). Woodrell, who grew up in a Mississippi River town and currently lives in the Ozarks, says he considers the St. Bruno series complete. He is also the author of *Woe To Live On* (1987), a Civil War novel set in the border states of Kansas and Missouri, optioned last year for film, and most recently, *Give Us a Kiss* (1996), which he calls a country noir. E. Annie Proulx called it a celebration of "blood kin, home country and hot sex...a rich, funky, headshakingly original novel."

Rene Shade...cop in a bayou town in St. Bruno, Louisiana
- ❏ ❏ 1 - Under the Bright Lights (1986)
- ❏ ❏ 2 - Muscle for the Wing (1988)
- ❏ ❏ 3 - **The Ones You Do (1988) Hammett nominee** ☆

■ **WOODS, Stuart**

Edgar award winner Stuart Woods has written 20 books including 3 in the series featuring suave ex-cop attorney-investigator Stone Barrington. In his most recent adventure, *Dead in the Water* (1997), Barrington is vacationing in Antigua when he gets involved with a young woman convicted in the disappearance of her wealthy husband. Former advertising creative director, Woods wrote his first book *Blue Water, Green Skipper* (1977) about sailing in the 1976 *Observer* Single-Handed Transatlantic Race (OSTAR), recounting how he built his own boat and learned to sail in 18 months. His best-first-novel Edgar was awarded for *Chiefs* (1980). A past contributing editor and restaurant critic for *Atlanta* magazine, he is the author of at least 4 books in the Romantic Guide series, including *A Romantic's Guide to the Country Inns of France*. A long-time resident of Atlanta, Woods lives in Santa Fe (NM).

Stone Barrington...suave ex-cop attorney in New York, New York
- ❏ ❏ 1 - New York Dead (1991)
- ❏ ❏ 2 - Dirt (1996)
- ❏ ❏ 3 - Dead in the Water (1997)

■ **WRIGHT, Eric**

London-born Eric Wright emigrated to Canada at the age of 22. A long-time teacher of English, he won both the Ellis and Creasey awards for his first novel, introducing 40-something Toronto police inspector Charlie Salter in *The Night the Gods Smiled* (1983). Wright won the best-novel Ellis for book 3 in which he deals with his love-hate relationship with the land of his birth. During '96-'97 he has introduced two new series concepts, one with a retired cop who first appeared in book 7, and more recently, a part-time Toronto librarian who inherits a detective agency in *Death of a Sunday Writer* (1997). Amazingly, Wright says he writes at home with a pencil because he can't write anywhere else and he can't write on any kind of a machine. In a *Contemporary Authors* interview he said the best compliment he ever received was from a woman who reported naming her dog Salter.

Charlie Salter, Insp.....police inspector in Toronto, Ontario
- ❏ ❏ 1 - **The Night the Gods Smiled (1983) Creasey & Ellis winner** ★★
- ❏ ❏ 2 - Smoke Detector (1984)
- ❏ ❏ 3 - **Death in the Old Country (1985) Ellis winner** ★
- ❏ ❏ 4 - The Man Who Changed His Name (1986) Brit.-Single Death
- ❏ ❏ 5 - A Body Surrounded by Water (1987)
- ❏ ❏ 6 - A Question of Murder (1988)
- ❏ ❏ 7 - A Sensitive Case [incl Mel Pickett] (1990)
- ❏ ❏ 8 - Final Cut (1991)
- ❏ ❏ 9 - A Fine Italian Hand (1992)
- ❏ ❏ 10 - Death by Degrees (1993)

Mel Pickett...60-something retired Toronto cop in Larch River, Ontario
- ❏ ❏ 1 - Buried in Stone (1996)

■ WYRICK, E. L.

E. L. Wyrick is Edward L. Wyrick, a lifelong Southener with a doctorate in counselling, who works as both a high-school counselor and college professor. He is also the creator of legal aid attorney Tammi Randall, introduced in *A Strange and Bitter Crop* (1994), where she defends a black teenager accused of murder while dealing with a real murderer out for revenge. Book 2, *Power in the Blood* (1996), finds her investigating the death of a Hollywood star who planned to buy the small Georgia town of Warrendale. Tammi signs on to defend the local delinquent, and before the case is over she travels to the fleshpots of Los Angeles and New Orleans in search of the killer. She learns there is a lot more danger in Warrendale, Georgia. Born in New Orleans, Wyrick lives in Athens (GA) with his wife and three daughters.

Tammi Randall...small-town lawyer in Patsboro, Georgia
- ❑ ❑   1 - A Strange and Bitter Crop (1994)
- ❑ ❑   2 - Power in the Blood (1996)

■ YAFFE, James

At the age of 15, James Yaffe saw his first detective story published in *Ellery Queen's Mystery Magazine*. The year was 1942. The magazine editor was Frederic Dannay, who with his cousin Manfred Lee, had created the legendary Queen for a writing contest in the late 1920s. Yaffe's 1942 story was the first of six featuring Paul Dawn, a New York police detective and head of the Department of Impossible Crimes. It wasn't until 8 years later that Yaffe wrote his first Mom story. This Jewish mother genius of armchair detection later starred in four novels and a short story collection. Mom could outwit the pros without ever visiting a crime scene. A former professor of literature, Yaffee was a Phi Beta Kappa at Yale University and once earned his living writing television scripts, plays (including one produced on Broadway) and several nonfiction books. A native of Chicago, he lives in Colorado.

Dave & Mom...ex-cop investigator for public defender & his mother in Mesa Grande, Colorado
- ❑ ❑   1 - A Nice Murder for Mom (1988)
- ❑ ❑   2 - Mom Meets Her Maker (1990)
- ❑ ❑   3 - Mom Doth Murder Sleep (1991)
- ❑ ❑   4 - Mom Among the Liars (1992)
- ❑ ❑   ss - My Mother, The Detective [short stories] (1997)

■ YORK, Andrew [P]

Andrew York is one of the many pseudonyms used by the prolific Christopher (Robin) Nicole who has written over 100 books, including historical romances, thrillers, mysteries, adventure novels, children's books and nonfiction on West Indian history and cricket. Son of a British Guiana (now Guyana) police officer, York grew up in the setting he uses for his Grand Flamingo series featuring cricket star turned police commissioner, Col. James Munroe Tallant. York has created a history, politics and a prime minister for the Flamingos, pronounced by *Crimes of the Scene* (1997) as "both instructive and very funny." His nine spy novels featuring Jonas Wilde are quite different. Wilde is The Eliminator, the most dangerous man in the world. But no guns for Wilde. He kills with a karate blow. York's most recent novels appear under the names Caroline Gray, Max Marlowe and Christopher Nicole.

James Munroe Tallant, Col.....cricket star turned police commissioner in Grand Flamingo, West Indies
- ❑ ❑   1 - Tallant for Trouble (1977)
- ❑ ❑   2 - Tallant for Disaster (1978)
- ❑ ❑   3 - Tallant for Democracy (1993)
- ❑ ❑   4 - Tallant for Terror (1995)

Jonas Wilde...British secret agent in England
- ❑ ❑   1 - The Eliminator (1966)
- ❑ ❑   2 - The Co-Ordinator (1967)
- ❑ ❑   3 - The Predator (1968)

❑ ❑   4 - The Deviator (1969)
❑ ❑   5 - The Dominator (1969)
❑ ❑   6 - The Infiltrator (1971)
❑ ❑   7 - The Expurgator (1973)
❑ ❑   8 - The Captivator (1974)
❑ ❑   9 - The Fascinator (1975)

■ YOUNG, Scott

Scott Young is a writer, broadcaster and journalist whose daily column has appeared in the *Toronto Globe and Mail* for more than 20 years. He is the author of 40 books, including a mystery series featuring full-blooded Inuit Mateesie Kitologitak, a Royal Canadian Mounted Police Inspector in the Northwest Territories. In book 2 Matt investigates a double murder in a small Arctic village and comes face to face with a native holy man. Young is the father of rock singer Neil Young and has written what was called by one Toronto reviewer "the least sordid rock biography ever written," *Neil and Me: The Neil Young Story* (1984), reissued in paperback in 1997. Young's first novel, *Red Shield in Action* (1948), was published by the Salvation Army. A former sports editor, he hosted intermission broadcasts on Hockey Night in Canada during the '60s.

Mateesie Kitologitak, Insp.....Inuit RCMP inspector in Northwest Territories, Canada
❑ ❑   1 - Murder in a Cold Climate (1990)
❑ ❑   2 - The Shaman's Knife (1993)\

■ ZIGAL, Thomas

Thomas Zigal (rhymes with wiggle) is the creator of a new series featuring Aspen (CO) sheriff Kurt Muller who's got his hands full in book two dealing with his 6-year-old son Lennon, a fallen-apart marriage, a band of environmental activists called the Green Briars and a right-wing group known as the Free West Rebellion. Just an average day in Glamour Gultch. A graduate of the University of Texas at Austin, Zigal earned his M.A. from Standford University where Scott Turow and April Smith were two of his classmates in the writing program. Born in Galveston, Zigal now lives in Austin (TX) where he works as a speech writer for the University of Texas president. During their three year stay in Aspen, Zigal's wife was the executive director of the Aspen Art Museum. They return for visits whenever they can and he continues to work on the third Kurt Muller novel.

Kurt Muller...ex-hippie single-father sheriff in Aspen, Colorado
❑ ❑   1 - Into Thin Air (1995)
❑ ❑   2 - Hardrock Stiff (1996)

■ ZIMMERMAN, Bruce

A former student at San Francisco State University, Bruce Zimmerman is well-acquainted with Quinn Parker's Bay Area turf. Introduced in the Edgar-nominated *Blood Under the Bridge* (1989), the phobia therapist has made three return appearances, most recently in *Crimson Green* (1994) when a famous golf pro is killed by a sniper in front of millions of viewers on the final hole of the U.S. Open at Pebble Beach. Quinn remembers his old friend had received a death threat and he sets out to track the murderer, aided by his sidekick Hank Wilkie the stand-up comic. Zimmerman grew up in an Air Force family and lived in various U.S. and overseas locations. Recently he has lived in Sacramento, Los Angeles, Costa Rica and Mexico where he worked as a journalist in San Miguel de Allende.

Quinn Parker...phobia therapist in San Francisco, California
❑ ❑   **1 - Blood Under the Bridge (1989) Edgar nominee** ☆
❑ ❑   2 - Thicker Than Water (1992)
❑ ❑   3 - Full-Bodied Red (1993)
❑ ❑   4 - Crimson Green (1994)

■ ZIMMERMAN, R. D.

Robert Dingwall Zimmerman is the creator of an award-winning series featuring gay TV news reporter Todd Mills whose third adventure is *Hostage* (1997). His earlier series is one of hypnotic detection, with distinguished psychologist Maddy Phillips who is blind and paraplegic. After quadrupling her sizable insurance settlement from the bus accident that put her in a wheelchair, she bought an island in northern Michigan and adapted it for her use. Maddy's wonderful house, complete with the rope-pulled elevator, is based on one built by R.D.'s great-grandfather which the family enjoyed on Lake Geneva (WI) for nearly a century. A graduate of Michigan State University, Zimmerman worked in Russia for the U.S. Information Agency and has written children's books under the pseudonym Alexander von Wacker. One of his Dingwall ancestors was a successful Broadway producer at the turn of the century who was killed by one of his chorus girls.

Alex & Maddy Phillips...brother and blind forensic psychiatrist sister in Upper Peninsula, Michigan
- ❑ ❑ 1 - Death Trance (1992)
- ❑ ❑ 2 - Blood Trance (1993)
- ❑ ❑ 3 - Red Trance (1995)

Todd Mills...gay TV news reporter in Minneapolis, Minnesota
- ❑ ❑ 1 - **Closet (1995) Lambda winner ★ Anthony nominee ☆**
- ❑ ❑ 2 - **Tribe (1996) Edgar nominee ☆**

■ ZUBRO, Mark

Lambda award-winning mystery writer Mark Richard Zubro writes two series featuring gay protagonists. The longer series features high school teacher Tom Mason whose partner Scott Carpenter is a professional baseball player accused of the murder of a small town sheriff in *Rust on the Razor* (1996). "The school politics are dead on and Tom and Scott...the sort of interesting couple one might like to have over for dinner," said a *Kirkus* reviewer. Zubro's second Chicago series stars gay police detective Paul Turner, the father of two sons, currently appearing in *The Truth Can Get You Killed* (1997). Zubro himself is an openly gay high school English teacher in suburban Chicago, where he is president of his local teacher's union. He speaks often about his writing and the struggles involved in being an educator and a gay novelist.

Paul Turner...gay Chicago cop & father of two teenage sons in Chicago, Illinois
- ❑ ❑ 1 - Sorry Now (1991)
- ❑ ❑ 2 - Political Poison (1993)
- ❑ ❑ 3 - Another Dead Teenager (1995)
- ❑ ❑ 4 - The Truth Can Get You Killed (1997)

Tom Mason & Scott Carpenter...high school teacher & pro baseball player in Chicago, Illinois
- ❑ ❑ 1 - **A Simple Suburban Murder (1989) Lambda winner ★**
- ❑ ❑ 2 - Why Isn't Becky Twitchell Dead? (1990)
- ❑ ❑ 3 - The Only Good Priest (1991)
- ❑ ❑ 4 - The Principal Cause of Death (1992)
- ❑ ❑ 5 - An Echo of Death (1994)
- ❑ ❑ 6 - Rust on the Razor (1996)

MYSTERY TYPES 2

Author	1 - #	Series Character	Occupation	Setting
Police Procedurals				
Adcock, Thomas	'89 - 6	Neil Hockaday	NYPD street crimes detective	New York, NY
Adler, Warren	'81 - 6	Fiona Fitzgerald	homicide detective	Washington, DC
Alding, Peter	'67 - 14	Kerr, Constable & Fusil	young police detective & his superior	Fortrow, England
Alexander, Bruce	'94 - 3	John Fielding	blind magistrate & founder of first police force	London, England
Alexander, Gary	'88 - 6	Bamsan Kiet, Supt.	police supt. in an imaginary country	Far East
Alexander, L.	'86 - 3	Teddy Roosevelt	1890s police commissioner	New York, NY
Allyn, Doug	'89 - 2	Lupe Garcia	tough Latino cop	Detroit, MI
Armistead, John	'94 - 3	Grover Bramlett	small-town sheriff	Sheffield, MS
Ashford, Jeffrey	'61 - 2	Don Kerry	British detective inspector	England
Barnard, Robert	'81 - 5	Perry Trethowan	Scotland Yard inspector	London, England
Barnard, Robert	'89 - 4	Charlie Peace	young black Scotland Yard detective	London, England
Barnes, Trevor	'89 - 2	Blanche Hampton	Scotland Yard detective superintendent	London, England
Barnett, James	'78 - 6	Owen Smith	chief superintendent	England
Baxt, George	'66 - 5	Pharoah Love	gay black NYPD detective	New York, NY
Baxt, George	'67 - 3	Sylvia Plotkin & Max Van Larsen	author-teacher & police detective	New York, NY
Bayer, William	'81 - 4	Frank Janek	NYPD homicide detective	New York, NY
Bean, Gregory	'95 - 3	Harry Starbranch	burned-out Denver cop turned small-town police chief	Victory, WY
Bishop, Paul	'88 - 3	Calico Jack Walker & Tina Tamiko	ex-patrol cop & his former rookie partner	Los Angeles, CA
Bishop, Paul	'94 - 4	Fey Croaker	40-something homicide unit supervisor	Los Angeles, CA
Blatty, William P.	'71 - 2	Bill Kinderman	police lieutenant	Washington, DC
Brady, John	'88 - 5	Matt Minogue	Irish police detective	Dublin, Ireland
Brett, John M.	'63 - 3	Hugo Baron	British adventurer	England
Bruno, Anthony	'97 - 1	Loretta Kovacs & Frank Marvelli	parole officer & partner	NJ
Bruno, Anthony	'88 - 6	Bert Gibbons & Mike Tozzi	FBI agents undercover with the Mob	New York, NY
Burke, James Lee	'87 - 9	Dave Robicheaux	deputy sheriff	LA
Burley, W. J.	'68 - 20	Charles Wycliffe, Supt.	area CID superintendent	West Country, England
Burns, Rex	'75 - 11	Gabe Wager	homicide detective	Denver, CO
Busby, Roger	'85 - 3	Tony Rowley, Det. Insp.	Scotland Yard inspector	London, England
Busby, Roger	'69 - 5	Leric, Det. Insp.	Scotland Yard inspector	London, England
Casley, Dennis	'94 - 3	James Odhiambo	chief inspector	Kenya
Charyn, Jerome	'75 - 9	Isaac Sidel	former police commissioner	New York, NY
Clark, Douglas	'69 - 27	George Masters, Chief Supt. & Bill Green, Chief Insp.	Scotland Yard detective team	London, England
Cleary, Jon	'66 - 13	Scobie Malone	family-man police inspector	Sydney, Australia
Coburn, Andrew	'92 - 2	James Morgan	chief of police	Boston Suburb, MA
Collins, Max A., Jr.	'87 - 4	Eliot Ness	1930s public safety officer	Cleveland, OH

Author	1 - #	Series Character	Occupation	Setting
Police Procedurals...cont.				
Connelly, Michael	'92 - 5	Harry Bosch	homicide detective	Los Angeles, CA
Constantine, K. C.	'72 - 13	Mario Balzic	small-town police chief	Rocksburg, PA
Cook, Stephen	'93 - 2	Judy Best	weight-lifting police officer	England
Cooper, Brian	'91 - 4	John Spencer Lubbock	retired World War II D.C.I.	Norfolk, England
Cork, Barry	'88 - 4	Angus Struan, Insp.	golfing police inspector	Scotland
Corris, Peter	'85 - 7	Ray Crawley	Federal Security Agency director	Sydney, Australia
Corris, Peter	'92 - 2	Luke Dunlop	ex-cop working witness protection	Sydney, Australia
Craig, Philip	'89 - 8	Jefferson "J. W." Jackson	30-something ex-Boston cop	Martha's Vineyard, MA
Crider, Bill	'86 - 9	Dan Rhodes	laid-back sheriff with a motley crew of deputies	Blacklin County, TX
Cunningham, E. V.	'67 - 7	Masao Masuto, Sgt.	Japanese-American police detective	Beverly Hills, CA
Cunningham, E. V.	'65 - 2	John Comaday & Larry Cohen	commissioner & DA's 1st assistant	New York, NY
Cunningham, E. V.	'64 - 2	Harvey Krim	NYPD detective	New York, NY
DeAndrea, William	'95 - 2	Lobo Blacke & Quinn Booker	crippled ex-frontier lawman & his biographer	Le Four, WY
Deaver, Jeffery	'97 - 1	Lincoln Rhyme & Amelia Sachs	disabled ex-head of NYPD forensics & rookie beat cop	New York, NY
Deaver, Jeffery	'89 - 3	Rune	NYPD detective	New York, NY
Dee, Ed	'94 - 3	Anthony Ryan & Joe Gregory	NYPD detective partners	New York, NY
DeMille, Nelson	'74 - 3	Joe Ryker, Det. Sgt.	NYPD homicide detective	New York, NY
DeMille, Nelson	'75 - 3	Joe Keller, Det. Sgt.	NYPD homicide detective	New York, NY
Dexter, Colin	'75 - 12	Morse, Chief Insp.	chief inspector	England
Dibdin, Michael	'88 - 5	Aurelio Zen, Insp.	Italian police inspector	Rome, Italy
Dickinson, Peter	'68 - 6	James Pibble, Supt.	Scotland Yard superintendent	London, England
Dold, Gaylord	'96 - 1	Grace Wu	undercover agent for the SFPD and DEA	San Francisco, CA
Doss, James D.	'94 - 4	Charlie Moon & Scott Parris	Ute police sergeant & Anglo colleague	Granite Creek, CO
Dunning, John	'92 - 2	Cliff Janeway	cop and rare book expert	Denver, CO
Eddenden, A. E.	'88 - 3	Albert V. Tretheway, Insp. & Jake Small, Constable	1940s Canadian police officers	Fort York, Ontario, Canada
Ellroy, James	'84 - 3	Lloyd Hopkins	detective sergeant in the Rampart Division	Los Angeles, CA
Emerson, Earl	'88 - 5	Mac Fontana	ex-firefighter and arson investigator	Staircase, WA
Estabrook, Barry	'91 - 2	Garwood Plunkett, Sheriff	veteran cop	Adirondack Mts, NY
Fliegel, Richard	'86 - 7	Shelly Lowenkopf, Sgt.	Allerton Avenue precinct cop	New York, NY
Fraser, James	'68 - 9	William Aveyard, Insp.	ambitious village police inspector	England
Freeling, Nicolas	'62 - 14	Van der Valk, Insp.	intellectual Dutch police inspector	Amsterdam, Netherlands
Freeling, Nicolas	'74 - 16	Henri Castang	French policeman	Brussels, Belgium
Fuller, Dean	'92 - 2	Alex Grismolet, Chief-Insp.	Chef-Insp. of the Sûrété	Paris, France
Gaitano, Nick	'95 - 2	Jake Phillips	homicide detective	Chicago, IL
Garfield, Brian	'72 - 2	Sam Watchman	part Navajo State trooper	AZ
Gibbs, Tony	'96 - 2	Neal Donahoe & Victoria "Tory" Lennox	harbor cop and Coast Guard Lt.	Santa Barbara, CA
Gilbert, Michael	'93 - 1	Patrick Petrella	Metropolitan Police inspector	London, England
Gilbert, Michael	'47 - 6	Hazelrigg, Insp.	British police inspector	London, England
Gill, Bartholomew	'77 - 12	Peter McGarr, Chief Insp.	Irish chief of detectives	Ireland
Goddard, Ken	'92 - 3	Henry Lightstone	National Fish and Wildlife investigator	OR
Gough, Laurence	'87 - 9	Jack Willows & Claire Parker	police detective partners	Vancouver, BC, Canada
Grady, James	'85 - 2	Devlin Rourke, Sgt.	police detective sergeant	Baltimore, MD
Granger, Bill	'80 - 4	Terry Flynn & Karen Kovac	Special Squad detectives	Chicago, IL
Grayson, Richard	'78 - 9	Jean-Paul Gautier, Insp.	fin-de-siècle French police inspector	Paris, France
Grayson, Richard	'55 - 4	John Bryant	British businessman	England
Hackler, Micah S.	'95 - 4	Cliff Lansing & Gabe Hanna	single-father part-time rancher-sheriff & his deputy	NM
Harknett, Terry	'74 - 3	John Crown.	chief superintendent	China
Harper, Richard	'86 - 2	Tom Ragnon	cop who lives in a trailer	AZ
Harrington, William	'93 - 6	Columbo, Lt.	rumpled police detective	Los Angeles, CA
Harrison, Ray	'83 - 14	Joseph Bragg & James Morton	Victorian police officers	England
Hart, Roy	'87 - 8	Douglas Roper	chief inspector	Dorset, England
Harvey, James Neal	'91 - 5	Ben Tolliver, Lt.	NYPD lieutenant	New York, NY
Harvey, John	'89 - 10	Charlie Resnick	40-something jazz fan police detective	Nottingham, England
Havill, Steven F.	'91 - 5	Bill Gastner	insomniac undersheriff	Posadas County, NM
Healy, R. Austin	'95 - 2	Mike Flint	ex-CIA and NYC cop	Saratoga, NY

Author	1 - #	Series Character	Occupation	Setting

Police Procedurals...cont.

Author	1 - #	Series Character	Occupation	Setting
Heffernan, William	'88 - 5	Paul Devlin	NYPD detective	New York, NY
Heller, Keith	'84 - 3	George Man	early 18th century parish watchman	London, England
Henderson, L.	'68 - 4	Arthur Milton	detective sergeant	England
Higgins, Jack	'65 - 2	Nick Miller	Central Division detective	London, England
Hill, John Spencer	'95 - 2	Carlo Arbati	policeman poet	Italy
Hill, Reginald	'70 - 15	Andrew Dalziel & Peter Pascoe	pair of police inspectors	Yorkshire, England
Hillerman, Tony	'80 - 9	Jim Chee	Navajo tribal police officer	AZ
Hillerman, Tony	'70 - 3	Joe Leaphorn	Navajo tribal police officer	AZ
Holton, Hugh	'94 - 4	Larry Cole	black police commander	Chicago, IL
Hornig, Doug	'87 - 2	Steven Kirk	burned-out government agent	Charlottesville, VA
Hunt, Richard	'93 - 4	Sidney Walsh	detective chief inspector	Cambridge, England
Hunter, Alan	'55 - 44	George Gently	chief superintendent of Scotland Yard	London, England
Hunter, Fred	'94 - 3	Jeremy Ransom & Emily Charters	homicide detective & his adopted grandmother	Chicago, IL
Jackson, Jon A.	'77 - 6	Fang Mulheisen	police detective sergeant	Detroit, MI
Jahn, Michael	'82 - 5	Bill Donovan.	chief of special investigations	New York, NY
James, Bill	'85 - 13	Colin Harpur & Desmond Iles	D.C.S. & detective constable	English seaport
Janes, J. Robert	'92 - 8	Jean-Louis St-Cyr & Hermann Kohler	1940s French police inspector & Gestapo agent	Paris, France
Jardine, Quintin	'93 - 5	Robert Skinner	high-ranking cop	Edinburgh, Scotland
Jecks, Michael	'95 - 5	Simon Puttock & Sir Baldwin Furnshill	medieval West County bailiff & ex-Templar Knight	Devon, England
Jeffers, H. Paul	'97 - 1	Arlene Flynn	chief investigator for the District Attorney	New York, NY
Jeffers, H. Paul	'95 - 3	John Bogdanovic	aide-de-camp to NYPD Chief of Detectives	New York, NY
Jeffries, Ian	'59 - 3	Sgt. Craig	police sergeant	England
Jeffries, Roderic	'74 - 20	Enrique Alvarez	Spanish police inspector	Mallorca, Spain
Johnson, E. Richard	'68 - 2	Tony Lonto	police detective	USA
Kaminsky, Stuart	'81 - 11	Porfiry Rostnikov	Russian police inspector	Moscow, Russia
Kaminsky, Stuart	'90 - 5	Abe Lieberman	60-something Jewish police detective	Chicago, IL
Keating, H. R. F.	'64 - 20	Ganesh Ghote	Indian police inspector	Bombay, India
Keegan, Alex	'93 - 4	Kathy "Caz" Flood	detective constable	Brighton, England
Kent, Bill	'89 - 3	Louis Monroe	Don Quixote-style cop	Atlantic City, NJ
Kenyon, Michael	'70 - 3	Supt. O'Malley	comic Irish cop	Ireland
Kenyon, Michael	'81 - 8	Henry Peckover	Scotland Yard's cockney poet	London, England
Kirton, Bill	'95 - 2	Carston	detective chief inspector	England
Knox, Bill	'57 - 21	Colin Thane & Phil Moss	Scottish Crime Squad officers	Glasgow, Scotland
Knox, Bill	'64 - 15	Webb Carrick	chief officer of the Scottish Fishery Protection Service	Scotland
Lake, M. D.	'89 - 9	Peggy O'Neill	university campus cop	MN
Lee, Christopher	'95 - 2	James Boswell Hodge Leonard	police inspector	Bath, England
Leonard, Elmore	'93 - 2	Raylan Givens	federal marshall	FL
Lescroart, John T.	'95 - 2	Abe Glitsky	black Jewish cop	San Francisco, CA
Lewin, Michael Z.	'76 - 3	Leroy Powder	cop friend of Albert Samson's	Indianapolis, IN
Lewis, Roy	'69 - 8	John Crow	British police inspector	England
Lindsay, Paul	'92 - 3	Mike Devlin	FBI agent	Detroit, MI
Lindsey, David L.	'83 - 5	Stuart Haydon	homicide detective	Houston, TX
Lovesey, Peter	'70 - 8	Richard Cribb & Edward Thackeray	Victorian policemen	London, England
Lovesey, Peter	'91 - 5	Peter Diamond	ex-cop	Bath, England
Luber, Philip	'94 - 2	Harry Kline & Veronica Pace	psychiatrist & FBI agent	Concord, MA
Lusby, Jim	'95 - 2	Carl McCadden	unconventional Irish police inspector	Waterford, Ireland
MacKenzie, Donald	'76 - 9	John Raven	unorthodox detective inspector	London, England
Mahoney, Dan	'93 - 3	Brian McKenna	police detective	New York, NY
Maitland, Barry	'94 - 3	Kathy Kolla & David Brock	young Scotland Yard detective & her mentor	London, , England
Malone, Paul	'91 - 3	Jack Fowler	DEA agent	USA
Marquis, Max	'91 - 3	Harry Timberlake	aloof detective inspector	London, England
Marshall, William	'75 - 14	Harry Feiffer	chief inspector of Yellowthread Street station	Hong Kong, Hong Kong
Marshall, William	'86 - 2	Felix Elizalde	detective of the Western District Bureau	Philippines
Marshall, William	'88 - 2	Tillman & Muldoon	turn-of-the-century policemen	New York, NY
Masters, J. D.	'89 - 6	Donovan Steele	police lieutenant	New York, NY
Mayor, Archer	'88 - 8	Joe Gunther	homicide detective	Brattleboro, VT
McBain, Ed	'56 - 47	87th Precinct	thinly-disguised NYPD cops	Isola, NY

Author	1 - #	Series Character	Occupation	Setting

Police Procedurals...cont.

Author	1 - #	Series Character	Occupation	Setting
McCall, Thomas	'93 - 2	Nora Callum	one-legged cop	Chicago, IL
McClure, James	'71 - 8	Tromp Kramer & Mickey Zondi	Afrikaner cop & Bantu detective assistant	South Africa
McCutchan, Philip	'74 - 11	Simon Shard	Scotland Yard supt. 2nd to the Foreign Office	London, England
McDonald, Gregory	'77 - 3	Francis Xavier Flynn	tenacious police inspector	Boston, MA
McEldowney, E.	'94 - 3	Cecil Megarry	hard-drinking Irish cop	Belfast, Ireland
McGarrity, Michael	'96 - 2	Kevin Kerney	ex-chief of detectives	Santa Fe, NM
McIlvanney, William	'77 - 4	Jack Laidlaw	Scottish police inspector	Glasgow, Scotland
Melville, James	'79 - 13	Tetsuo Otani	Japanese police superintendent	Kobe, Japan
Miles, John	'94 - 2	Johnelle Baker	Choctaw sheriff	Tenoclock, CO
Miller, Rex	'87 - 5	Jack Eichord	police detective	Chicago, IL
Miller, Victor B.	'74 - 9	Theo Kojak	NYPD cop	New York, NY
Mullen, Jack	'95 - 2	Vincent Dowling	police sergeant	San Diego, CA
Murphy, Warren B.	'73 - 6	Ed Razoni & William Jackson	police detectives	New York, NY
Murphy, Warren B.	'71 - 80	Remo Williams aka The Destroyer	ex-cop turned government enforcer	New York, NY
Murray, Stephen	'87 - 5	Alec Stainton	British police inspector	England
Newman, C.	'86 - 9	Joe Dante	maverick cop	New York, NY
Newman, G. F.	'70 - 3	Terry Sneed, Insp.	bent police inspector	England
Newton, Michael	'78 - 2	Jonathan Steele	LAPD homicide detective	Los Angeles, CA
Newton, Michael	'90 - 9	Joseph Flynn & Martin Tanner	FBI agents with VICAP	Los Angeles, CA
North, Gil	'60 - 11	Caleb Cluff	Gunnarshaw police sergeant	Yorkshire, England
O'Connell, Jack	'92 - 3	Quinsigamond	decaying New England factory town	Massachusetts
Orenstein, Frank	'84 - 3	Hugh Morrison	small-town cop	NY
Ormerod, Roger	'83 - 11	Richard Patton	British police inspector	England
Oster, Jerry	'85 - 3	Jacob "Jake" Neuman	police lieutenant	New York, NY
Oster, Jerry	'90 - 4	Joe Cullen	Internal Affairs police sergeant	New York, NY
Palmer, Frank	'92 - 8	"Jacko" Jackson	detective inspector	Leicester, England
Patterson, James	'93 - 4	Alex Cross	black psychiatrist and homicide cop	Washington, DC
Paul, William	'94 - 3	David Fyfe	detective chief inspector	Edinburgh, Scotland
Pawson, Stuart	'95 - 4	Charlie Priest	art school graduate turned police detective	Yorkshire, England
Payne, Laurence	'62 - 3	Sam Birkett	humorous Scotland Yard inspector	London, England
Pearce, Michael	'88 - 10	Garth Owen	British head of the secret police	Cairo, Egypt
Pearson, Ridley	'88 - 4	Lou Boldt & Daphne Matthews	detective & police psychologist	Seattle, WA
Petievich, Gerald	'81 - 4	Charles Carr & Jack Kelly	US Treasury agents	Los Angeles, CA
Philbin, Tom	'85 - 9	Joe Lawless	Felony Squad commander in the Bronx	New York, NY
Randisi, Robert J.	'95 - 2	Joe Keough	NYPD detective	New York, NY
Rankin, Ian	'87 - 8	John Rebus	detective sergeant	Edinburgh, Scotland
Reid, Robert Sims	'88 - 2	Ray Bartell	police detective	Rozette, MT
Rhea, Nicholas	'79 - 15	Nick Rhea	police constable father of four	Aidensfield, England
Ripley, Jack	'71 - 4	John George Davis	small-town constable	England
Robinson, Peter	'87 - 9	Alan Banks	Eastvale detective chief inspector	Yorkshire, England
Rosenberg, Robert	'91 - 3	Avram Cohen	recently-retired police officer	Jerusalem, Israel
Ross, Jonathan	'68 - 20	George Rogers	police inspector	Abbotsburn, England
Russell, Alan	'96 - 1	Orson Cheever	homicide detective	San Diego, CA
Sanders, Lawrence	'73 - 4	Edward X. "Iron Balls" Delaney	retired chief of detectives	New York, NY
Sandford, John	'89 - 8	Lucas Davenport	police detective and war games designer	Minneapolis, MN
Scholefield, Alan	'89 - 6	George Macrae & Leopold Silver	old-fashioned copper & intellectual rookie partner	London, England
Selwyn, Francis	'74 - 5	William Clarence Verity	portly Victorian police sergeant	London, England
Serafin, David	'79 - 6	Luis Bernal	Spanish police superintendent	Spain
Slusher, William S.	'95 - 3	Lewis Cody	sheriff	Hunter County, VA
Smith, Frank A.	'69 - 2	Supt. Pepper	Canadian police superintendent	Toronto, Ontario, Canada
Smith, Martin Cruz	'81 - 3	Arkady Renko	Russian police officer	Moscow, Russia
Swan, Thomas	'90 - 3	Jack Oxby	Scotland Yard art forgery investigator	London, England
Tanenbaum, R.	'87 - 9	Roger "Butch" Karp & Marlene Ciampi	1970s Criminal Courts Bureau chief & assistant DA	New York, NY
Taylor, Andrew	'94 - 3	Richard Thornhill	1950s detective inspector	Lydmouth, England
Tourney, Leonard	'80 - 8	Matthew Stock	17th century town constable and clothier	Chelmsford, England
Turnbull, Peter	'81 - 9	P Division	police detectives	Glasgow, Scotland
Turnbull, Peter	'96 - 1	Carmen Pharaoh	young woman police detective	York, England

Author	1 - #	Series Character	Occupation	Setting

Police Procedurals...cont.

Author	1 - #	Series Character	Occupation	Setting
Van de Wetering, J.	'75 - 13	Grijpstra and de Gier	Dutch police detectives	Amsterdam, Netherlands
Vance, John H.	'66 - 2	Joe Bain	sheriff	San Rodrigo Co, CA
Wainright, John	'66 - 8	Charles Ripley	head of the uniform branch	Yorkshire, England
Wainright, John	'79 - 6	Lyle	detective inspector	Yorkshire, England
Wainright, John	'74 - 10	Lennox	detective chief inspector	Yorkshire, England
Wainright, John	'66 - 4	Gilliant	chief constable	Yorkshire, England
Wainright, John	'75 - 4	Robert Blayde	police superintendent	Yorkshire, England
Wainright, John	'83 - 2	Ralph Flensing & David Hoyle	Lessford police ensemble	Yorkshire, England
Walker, Peter N.	'71 - 4	Jock Patterson	British constable	England
Walker, Robert W.	'92 - 5	Jessica Coran	FBI medical examiner	Washington, DC
Washburn, Stan	'95 - 2	Toby Parkman	quietly heroic cop	San Francisco, CA
Waugh, Hillary	'59 - 11	Fred Fellows	small-town police chief	Stockford, CT
Waugh, Hillary	'68 - 3	Frank Sessions. Lt.	Manhattan North homicide detective	New York, NY
Webb, Jack	'52 - 9	Sammy Golden & Joseph Shanley	Jewish police detective & Catholic priest	Los Angeles, CA
West, Christopher	'94 - 2	Wang Anzhuang, Insp.	Public Security Bureau inspector	Beijing, China
Westermann, John	'90 - 2	Orin Boyd	Nassau County uniformed cop	Long Island, NY
Wilcox, Collin	'69 - 20	Frank Hastings	co-commander SFPD homicide	San Francisco, CA
Wilcox, Collin	'73 - 2	McCloud	New Mexico marshall	New York, NY
Williams, David	'94 - 3	Merlin Parry & Gomer Lloyd	detective chief inspector & detective sergeant	Cardiff, Wales
Wiltse, David	'91 - 6	John Becker	FBI agent	New York, NY
Wingfield, R. D.	'84 - 4	Jack Frost	Denton Division detective inspector	England
Wood, Ted	'83 - 10	Reid Bennett & Sam	police chief and German Shepard	Murphy's Harbor, Ontario
Woodrell, Dan	'86 - 3	Rene Shade	cop in a bayou town	St. Bruno, LA
Wright, Eric	'83 - 10	Charlie Salter	police inspector	Toronto, Ontario, Canada
York, Andrew	'77 - 4	James Munroe Tallant	cricket star turned police commissioner	Grand Flamingo, West Indies
Young, Scott	'90 - 2	Mateesie Kitologitak	Inuit RCMP Inspector	NW Territories, Canada
Zigal, Thomas	'95 - 2	Kurt Muller	ex-hippie single-father sheriff	Aspen, CO
Zubro, Mark	'91 - 4	Paul Turner	gay Chicago cop & father of two teenage sons	Chicago, IL

Private Investigators

Author	1 - #	Series Character	Occupation	Setting
Albert, Marvin H.	'86 - 9	Pierre-Ange "Pete" Sawyer	French-speaking American P.I.	Paris, France
Albert, Neil	'91 - 6	Dave Garrett	disbarred lawyer turned private eye	Lancaster County, PA
Allegretto, Michael	'87 - 5	Jacob Lomax	ex-cop turned P.I.	Denver, CO
Anaya, Rudolfo	'95 - 2	Sonny Baca	part-time rodeo rider private eye	Albuquerque, NM
Avallone, Michael	'53 - 31	Ed Noon	movie-nut private eye	New York, NY
Ayres, E. C.	'94 - 3	Tony Lowell	photographer private eye	FL
Babula, William	'88 - 5	Jeremiah St. John	private investigator	San Francisco, CA
Baker, John	'95 - 2	Sam Turner	newly-sober private eye	York, England
Barnao, Jack	'87 - 3	John Locke	ex-Grenadier guard turned private security agent	Toronto, Ontario, Canada
Barre, Richard	'95 - 3	Wil Hardesty	Vietnam vet and greybeard surfer turned P.I.	Southern CA
Bass, Milton R.	'86 - 4	Benny Freedman	private eye	San Diego, CA
Bass, Milton R.	'93 - 2	Vinnie Altobelli	ex-cop coronary survivor P.I.	San Bernadino, CA
Bateson, David	'54 - 6	Larry Vernon	British private eye	England
Baxt, George	'84 - 12	Jacob Singer	1940s Hollywood private eye	Los Angeles, CA
Beinhart, Larry	'86 - 4	Tony Cassella	high-stakes private eye	New York, NY
Berlinski, David	'93 - 3	Aaron Asherfeld	cynical P.I. with 3 ex-wives	San Francisco, CA
Biggle, Lloyd, Jr.	'87 - 3	J. Pletcher & Raina Lambert	pair of private eyes	USA
Birkett, John	'88 - 2	Michael Rhineheart	private eye	Louisville, KY
Bishop, Paul	'91 - 2	Ian Chapel	one-eyed pro soccer goalie turned P.I.	Los Angeles, CA
Block, Lawrence	'76 - 13	Matt Scudder	unlicensed reformed alcoholic P.I.	New York, NY
Block, Lawrence	'70 - 4	Leo Haig	private investigator	New York, NY
Bogart, Stephen H.	'95 - 2	R. J. Brook	celebrity-son private eye	New York, NY
Brett, Michael	'66 - 10	Pete McGrath	wise-cracking private eye	New York, NY
Brewer, Steve	'94 - 4	Bubba Mabry	low-rent P.I.	Albuquerque, NM
Briody, Thomas G.	'95 - 2	Michael Carolina	former TV investigative reporter	Providence, RI
Burns, Rex	'87 - 4	Devlin Kirk	owner of industrial surveillance company	Denver, CO

Author	1 - #	Series Character	Occupation	Setting
Private Investigators...cont.				
Byrd, Max	'81 - 3	Mike Haller	P.I. specializing in missing persons	San Francisco, CA
Caine, Hamilton	'81 - 2	Ace Carpenter	private eye	Los Angeles, CA
Campbell, Harlen	'93 - 1	Rainbow Porter	Vietnam veteran turned detective	NM
Campbell, Robert	'86 - 4	Whistler	sentimental private eye	Hollywood, CA
Campbell, Robert	'88 - 2	Jake Hatch	railroad detective	Omaha, NE
Chambers, Peter	'61 - 36	Mark Preston	hard-nosed private eye	Monkton City, CA
Clarkson, John	'92 - 3	Jack Devlin	ex-Secret Service turned security firm investigator	USA
Coe, Tucker	'66 - 5	Mitch Tobin	ex-cop P.I.	Queens, NY
Collins, Max A., Jr.	'83 - 8	Nate Heller	1930s ex-cop turned private eye	Chicago, IL
Collins, Michael	'67 - 17	Dan Fortune	one-armed Polish-Lithuanian P. I.	New York, NY
Cook, Bruce	'88 - 4	Antonio "Chico" Cervantes	Mexican-American private eye	Los Angeles, CA
Cook, Glen	'87 - 8	Garrett	30-something fantasy private eye	GA
Cook, Thomas H.	'88 - 3	Frank Clemons	private eye	Atlanta, GA
Copper, Basil	'66 - 52	Mike Faraday	hard-boiled private eye who quotes Herrick	Los Angeles, CA
Cormany, Michael	'88 - 4	Dan Kruger	private investigator	Chicago, IL
Corris, Peter	'80 - 15	Cliff Hardy	Aussie private eye	Sydney, Australia
Corris, Peter	'87 - 8	Richard Browning	Aussie private eye with Hollywood ties	Sydney, Australia
Crais, Robert	'87 - 7	Elvis Cole & Joe Pike	pair of Hollywood private eyes	Los Angeles, CA
Crider, Bill	'91 - 4	Truman Smith	private eye	Galveston, TX
Crowe, John	'72 - 6	Lee Beckett	private eye	Buena Costa Co., CA
Crumley, James	'75 - 2	Milo Milodragovitch	ex-Army spy and hard-drinking P.I.	MT
Crumley, James	'78 - 3	C. W. Sughrue	ex-Army spy turned private investigator	MT
Cutler, Stan	'91 - 4	Rayford Goodman & Mark Bradley	jaded macho P. I. & gay writer of celebrity biographies	Hollywood, CA
Daniel, David	'94 - 2	Alex Rasmussen	private investigator	Lowell, MA,
Daniel, David & Chris Carpenter	'96 - 2	Frank Branco	ex-cop turned private eye	Boston, MA
Davis, J Madison	'90 - 2	Delbert "Dub" Greenert & Vonna Saucier	white & black investigator pair	New Orleans, LA
Davis, Kenn	'76 - 8	Carver Bascombe	suave black poet private eye	San Francisco, CA
Davis, Thomas D.	'91 - 3	Dave Strickland	private eye	Azalea, CA
DeAndrea, William	'79 - 3	Niccolo Benedetti	world-renowned criminologist professor	Sparta, NY
Dobyns, Stephen	'76 - 9	Charlie Bradshaw	ex-cop ex-stable security guard turned detective	Saratoga Springs, NY
Dold, Gaylord	'87 - 9	Mitch Roberts	1950s private eye	Wichita, KS
Downing, Warwick	'74 - 3	Joe Reddman	private investigator	Denver, CO
Duncan, W. Glenn	'87 - 6	Rafferty	ex-cop private eye	Dallas, TX
Dundee, Wayne	'88 - 3	Joe Hannibal	blue-collar P.I.	Rockford, IL
Ely, Ron	'94 - 2	Jake Sands	professional recoverer of lost things	Santa Barbara, CA
Emerson, Earl	'85 - 10	Thomas Black	bicycling enthusiast P.I.	Seattle, WA
Engel, Howard	'80 - 9	Benny Cooperman	small-town Jewish private eye	Grantham, Ontario
Engleman, Paul	'83 - 5	Mark Renzler	ex-baseball player private eye	Chicago, IL
Engleman, Paul	'93 - 2	Phil Moony	ex-firefighter private eye	Chicago, IL
Estleman, Loren D.	'80 - 11	Amos Walker	6' 1" Vietnam vet private eye	Detroit, MI
Estleman, Loren D.	'78 - 2	Sherlock Holmes	19th century consulting detective	London, England
Evers, Crabbe	'91 - 5	Duffy House	ex-sportswriter turned investigator	Chicago, IL
Everson, David H.	'87 - 7	Robert Miles	baseball minor leaguer turned P.I.	Springfield, IL
Eversz, Robert	'88 - 2	Paul Marston & Angel Cantini	private eye & female prize fighter	Los Angeles, CA
Faherty, Terence	'96 - 3	Scott Elliott	1940s failed actor turned private eye	Hollywood, CA
Finkelstein, Jay	'96 - 2	Leo Gold	30-something Jewish P.I.	New York, NY
Ford, G. M.	'95 - 4	Leo Waterman	wisecracking private eye	Seattle, WA
Francis, Dick	'65 - 3	Sid Halley	injured steeplechase jockey turned P. I.	England
Gat, Dimitri	'82 - 2	Yuri Nevsky	information specialist	Pittsburgh, PA
Goldberg, Lee	'95 - 2	Charlie Willis	ex-cop turned TV cop turned studio security agent	Los Angeles, CA
Gores, Joe	'72 - 5	Daniel Kearney Associates	auto repo & skip-tracing firm	San Francisco, CA
Gorman, Ed	'85 - 6	Jack Dwyer	ex-cop part-time actor and security guard	Cedar Rapids, IA
Gorman, Ed	'87 - 4	Leo Guild	1890s bounty hunter	Western US
Gorman, Ed	'91 - 1	Walsh	50-something private eye	Cedar Rapids, IA
Grady, James	'84 - 2	John Rankin	private investigator	Washington, DC

Author	1 - #	Series Character	Occupation	Setting
Private Investigators...cont.				
Grant, Maxwell	'64 - 8	The Shadow	P.I. of unknown identity	USA
Greenleaf, Stephen	'79 - 12	John Marshall Tanner	non-practicing attorney P.I.	San Francisco, CA
Greer, Robert O.	'96 - 3	C. J. Floyd	bail bondsman and bounty hunter	Denver, CO
Hall, James W.	'87 - 6	Thorn	eco-avenger P.I.	Key Largo, FL
Hall, Parnell	'87 - 13	Stanley Hastings	married actor and private eye	New York, NY
Hallinan, Timothy	'89 - 6	Simeon Grist	four-degreed P.I.	Los Angeles, CA
Hansen, Joseph	'70 - 11	Dave Brandstetter	gay death-claims investigator	Los Angeles, CA
Harknett, Terry	'62 - 9	Steve Wayne	private investigator	Far East
Harvey, John	'76 - 4	Scott Mitchell	private eye	England
Haywood, Gar A.	'88 - 5	Aaron Gunner	black wise-guy P.I.	Los Angeles, CA
Heald, Tim	'73 - 10	Simon Bognor	special investigator to the British Board of Trade	England
Healy, Jeremiah	'84 - 11	John Francis Cuddy	Army police lieutenant turned P.I.	Boston, MA
Hilary, Richard	'87 - 4	Ezell "Easy" Barnes	ex-prize fighter and cop turned P.I.	Newark, NJ
Hill, Reginald	'93 - 3	Joe Sixsmith	black private detective	England
Hoch, Edward D.	'71 - 3	Simon Ark	ancient hounder of Satan	New York, NY
Hornig, Doug	'84 - 4	Loren Swift	Vietnam vet private eye	Charlottesville, VA
Horwitz, Merle	'90 - 2	Harvey Ace	retired P. I. who plays the horses	Los Angeles, CA
Housewright, David	'95 - 2	Holland Taylor	ex-cop turned private investigator	St. Paul, MN
Hoyt, Richard	'80 - 7	John Denson	flaky private eye	Seattle, WA
Hoyt, Richard	'82 - 8	James Burlane	ex-CIA operative turned private	USA
Huebner, Frederick	'86 - 5	Matt Riordan	burned-out lawyer turned investigator	Seattle, WA
Irvine, Robert	'88 - 8	Moroni Traveler	non-Mormon ex-football player private eye	Salt Lake City, UT
Jaspersohn, William	'95 - 2	Peter Boone	ex-Red Sox pitcher turned P. I.	VT
Jeffers, H. Paul	'81 - 3	Harry MacNeil	1930s ex-cop private eye	New York, NY
Jenkins, Jerry	'79 - 13	Margo Franklin & Philip Spence	pair of private eyes	Chicago, IL
Kaminsky, Stuart	'77 - 20	Toby Peters	1940s Hollywood private investigator	Los Angeles, CA
Kaminsky, Stuart	'96 - 2	James Rockford	low-rent private eye	Los Angeles, CA
Kantner, Rob	'86 - 9	Ben Perkins	ex-union strike buster turned P.I.	Detroit, MI
Katz, Jon	'92 - 4	Kit DeLeeuw	Wall Street shark turned suburban detective	Rochambeau, NJ
Katz, Michael J.	'87 - 3	Murray Glick & Andy Sussman	P.I. & sportscaster buddy	Chicago, IL
Kavanagh, Dan	'80 - 4	Nick Duffy	bisexual ex-cop P.I.	London, England
Kemprecos, Paul	'91 - 7	Aristotle Plato Socarides	ex-cop part-time fisherman P.I.	Cape Cod, MA
Kennealy, Jerry	'87 - 10	Nick Polo	private eye	San Francisco, CA
Kerr, Philip	'89 - 3	Bernie Gunther	1930s German private eye	Berlin, Germany
Kilmer, Nicholas	'95 - 3	Fred Taylor	Vietnam veteran turned art hunter	Cambridge, MA
Knief, Charles	'96 - 2	John Caine	Navy SEAL turned P.I.	Pearl Harbor, HI
Knight, J. D.	'95 - 2	Virgil Proctor	bounty hunter P.I.	USA
Kuhlken, Ken	'91 - 3	Tom Hickey	1940s P.I. and restaurateur	San Diego, CA
Kurland, Michael	'79 - 2	James Moriarty	archenemy of Sherlock Holmes	London, England
Lehane, Dennis	'94 - 3	Patrick Kenzie & Angela Gennaro	private detectives	Boston, MA
Leslie, John	'94 - 3	Gideon Lowry	private eye	Key West, FL
Lewin, Michael Z.	'71 - 9	Albert Samson	middle-age low-key P.I.	Indianapolis, IN
Lewin, Michael Z.	'94 - 1	Lunghi family	3-generation private-eye family	Bath, England
Lipinski, Thomas	'94 - 3	Carroll Dorsey	ex-basketball star law-school dropout P.I.	Pittsburgh, PA
Livingston, Jack	'82 - 4	Joe Binney	hearing-impaired private eye	New York, NY
Lochte, Dick	'85 - 2	Serendipity Dahlquist & Leo Bloodworth	gum-snapping 15-yr-old girl & grumpy 50-something P.I.	Los Angeles, CA
Lochte, Dick	'92 - 2	Terry Manion	private eye	New Orleans, LA
Lupica, Mike	'95 - 1	DiMaggio	private eye in the sports world	New York, NY
Lupoff, Richard A.	'88 - 8	Hobart Lindsay & Marvia Plum	insurance claims adjuster & Berkeley detective	CA
Lutz, John	'76 - 10	Alo Nudger	antacid-chewing bad-luck P.I.	St. Louis, MO
Lutz, John	'86 - 10	Fred Carver	crippled ex-cop P.I.	Del Moray, FL
Lutz, John	'84 - 2	E. L. Oxman & Art Tobin	pair of investigators	USA
Lynch, Jack	'82 - 7	Peter Bragg	private eye	San Francisco, CA
Lyons, Arthur	'74 - 11	Jacob Asch	Jewish-Episcopal ex-reporter P.I.	Los Angeles, CA
MacLeod, Robert	'74 - 6	Andrew Laird	marine insurance claims investigator	international

Author	1 - #	Series Character	Occupation	Setting
Private Investigators...cont.				
MacLeod, Robert	'64 - 6	Talos Cord	United Nations troubleshooter	New York, NY
Maness, Larry	'95 - 2	Jake Eaton & Watson	P.I. & his superdog	Boston, MA
Margolis, Seth	'91 - 2	Joe DiGregorio	ex-Long Island cop turned Manhattan P. I.	New York, NY
Marlowe, Stephen	'55 - 19	Chester Drum	ex-FBI agent turned P.I.	Washington, DC
Martin, James E.	'89 - 4	Gil Disbro	teetotaler private eye	Cleveland , OH
Maxim, John	'89 - 4	Paul Bannerman	private investigations firm owner	Westport, CT
McCall, Wendell	'88 - 2	Chris Klick	6' 4" dropout-songwriter turned P.I.	ID
McConnell, Frank	'83 - 4	Harry Garnish & Bridget O'Toole	private investigators	Chicago, IL
Meyers, Martin	'75 - 5	Patrick Hardy	private eye	New York, NY
Miller, Wade	'47 - 6	Max Thursday	private eye	San Diego, CA
Milne, John	'86 - 3	Jimmy Jenner	English private eye	England
Morse, L. A.	'82 - 2	Sam Hunter	private eye	Los Angeles, CA
Mosley, Walter	'90 - 7	Easy Rawlins	school maintenance supervisor in Watts	Los Angeles, CA
Mosley, Walter	'97 - ss	Socrates Fortlow	philosophical ex-con	CA
Most, Bruce W.	'96 - 2	Ruby Dark	bail bondswoman	Denver, CO
Murphy, Warren B.	'82 - 4	Julian "Digger" Burroughs	freelance insurance investigator	Las Vegas, NV
Murphy, Warren B.	'83 - 7	Devlin Tracy	freelance insurance investigator	Las Vegas, NV
Myles, Simon	'74 - 2	"Apples" Carstairs	private eye	England
Nevins, Francis, Jr	'86 - 2	Milo Turner	con man private eye	St. Louis, MO
Nolan, William F.	'68 - 2	Bart Challis	hard-boiled private eye	Los Angeles, CA
Nolan, William F.	'71 - 2	Sam Space	private eye on Mars	Mars
Nolan, William F.	'94 - 2	Black Mask Boys	1930s detective heroes	CA
Oliver, Steve	'96 - 2	Scott Moody	ex-mental patient turned P.I.	Spokane, WA
Ormerod, Roger	'74 - 15	David Mallin	private eye	England
Pairo , Preston, III	'96 - 2	Jimmy "Griff" Griffin	ex-cop investigator for the city attorney	Baltimore, MD
Parker, Robert B.	'73 - 24	Spenser	ex-boxer, ex-state cop turned P.I.	Boston, MA
Parker, Robert B.	'89 - 2	Philip Marlowe	private eye	Los Angeles, CA
Payne, Laurence	'82 - 5	Mark Savage	movie star turned private eye	USA
Pelecanos, George	'92 - 4	Nick Stefanos	1950s bartender P.I.	Washington, DC
Perry, Ritchie	'84 - 2	Frank MacAllister	swashbuckling private eye	Brazil
Philbrick, W. R.	'87 - 3	T. D. Stash	unlicensed private eye	Key West, FL
Phillips, Gary	'94 - 3	Ivan Monk	black private eye	Los Angeles, CA
Pierce, David M.	'89 - 7	Vic Daniel	offbeat 6' 7-1/4" cut-rate P.I.	Los Angeles, CA
Prather, Richard	'50 - 36	Shell Scott	6' 2" ex-Marine crew-cut private eye	Los Angeles, CA
Pronzini, Bill	'71 - 24	Nameless	pulp collector P.I. with no name	San Francisco, CA
Pronzini, Bill	'85 - 2	John Quincannon	19th century private eye	San Francisco, CA
Raleigh, Michael	'90 - 2	Paul Whelan	40-something black cop turned P.I.	Chicago, IL
Randisi, Robert J.	'82 - 6	Miles Jacoby	boxer turned P.I.	New York, NY
Randisi, Robert J.	'87 - 2	Nick Delvecchio	private eye	Brooklyn, NY
Reynolds, William J.	'84 - 6	Nebraska	part-time P.I. trying to write	Omaha, NE
Rider, J. W.	'86 - 2	Ryder Malone	private eye	Jersey City, NJ
Ridgway, Jason	'60 - 4	Brian Guy	private eye	New York, NY
Ring, Raymond H.	'88 - 2	Henry Dyer	fish and game agent turned P.I.	CO
Ripley, W. L.	'93 - 3	Wyatt Storme	Vietnam vet ex-NFL star	N Branson, MO
Roat, Ronald Clair	'91 - 3	Stuart Mallory	private eye	Lansing, MI
Roberts, John	'94 - 2	Gabe Treloar	ex-LA cop turned P.I.	OH
Roberts, Les	'88 - 9	Milan Jacovich	blue-collar Slovenian P.I. with a master's degree	Cleveland, OH
Roberts, Les	'87 - 6	Saxon	actor private eye	Los Angeles, CA
Roderus, Frank	'84 - 6	Carl Heller	private eye	WY
Rome, Anthony	'60 - 3	Tony Rome	ex-cop gambler private eye	Miami, FL
Rosen, Richard	'84 - 4	Harvey Blissberg	ex-baseball player turned P. I.	Boston, MA
Ross, Philip	'85 - 2	James Marley	P.I. investigator	Boston, MA
Russell, Alan	'90 - 2	Stuart Winter	private eye	San Francisco, CA
Sadler, Mark	'70 - 6	Paul Shaw	private eye	NY
Sallis, James	'92 - 3	Lew Griffin	black private eye	New Orleans, LA
Sanders, Lawrence	'87 - 2	Timothy Cone	Wall Street financial detective	New York, NY
Sanders, Lawrence	'76 - 2	Peter Tangent	troubleshooter for American oil company	Africa
Sanders, Lawrence	'92 - 7	Arch McNally	playboy private eye	Palm Beach, FL
Sanders, William	'93 - 3	Taggart Roper	Cherokee writer and private eye	Tulsa, OK
Sarrantonio, Al	'89 - 2	Jack Blaine	retired Yonkers cop with a P.I. license	New York, NY

Author	1 - #	Series Character	Occupation	Setting

Private Investigators...cont.

Satterthwait, Walter	'89 - 5	Joshua Croft	wisecracking P.I.	Santa Fe, NM
Sauter, Eric	'83 - 3	Robert Lee Hunter	30-something wealthy P.I.	DE
Saylor, Steven	'90 - 6	Gordianus the Finder	private eye circa 56 B.C.	Rome, Italy
Schopen, Bernard	'89 - 2	Jack Ross	private eye	Reno, NV
Schorr, Mark	'83 - 3	Simon Jaffe aka Red Diamond	cab-driving pulp collector turned P.I.	New York, NY
Schorr, Mark	'88 - 3	Robert Stark	private investigator	USA
Schutz, Benjamin	'85 - 6	Leo Haggerty	rough and tough P.I.	Washington, DC
Shatner, William	'89 - 8	Jack Cardigan	22nd century ex-cop private eye	Los Angeles, CA
Simon, Roger L.	'73 - 8	Moses Wine	ex-hippie Jewish private eye	Los Angeles, CA
Solomita, Stephen	'88 - 6	Stanley Moodrow	cop turned private eye	New York, NY
Spencer, John	'84 - 3	Charley Case	private eye of the "1997" future	Los Angeles, CA
Spencer, Ross H.	'78 - 5	Chance Purdue	private investigator	Chicago, IL
Spillane, Mickey	'47 - 13	Mike Hammer	super-patriot private investigator	New York, NY
Spillane, Mickey	'64 - 5	Tiger Mann	freelance spy for a private right-wing group	New York, NY
Steed, Neville	'89 - 2	Johnny Black	1930s private detective	England
Stephens, Reed	'80 - 3	Mick "Brew" Axbrewder	unlicensed private eye	Puerta del Sol, CA
Stevenson, Richard	'81 - 6	Donald Strachey	gay private eye	Albany, NY
Stone, Michael	'96 - 2	Streeter	P.I. bounty hunter	Denver, CO
Stone, Thomas H.	'72 - 4	Chester Fortune	mulatto detective	Los Angeles, CA
Straley, John	'92 - 4	Cecil Younger	alcoholic private eye	Sitka, AK
Sublett, Jesse	'89 - 3	Martin Fender	skip tracer	Austin, TX
Swanson, Doug J.	'94 - 3	Jack Flippo	recovering deadbeat P.I.	Dallas, TX
Taibo, Paco I., II	'90 - 5	Hector Belascoaran Shayne	correspondence-school-certified P.I.	Mexico City, Mexico
Thomson, M.	'96 - 2	Nason "Nase" Nichols	private eye	New York, NY
Thurston, Robert	'85 - 3	Byron "Rugger" O'Toole	detective of the future	Central America
Tierney, Ronald	'90 - 4	"Deets" Shanahan	70-something private eye	Indianapolis, IN
Timlin, Mark	'88 - 12	Nick Sharman	hard-living ex-cop private eye	London, England
Topor, Tom	'78 - 2	Kevin Fitzgerald	private eye	New York, NY
Tripp, Miles	'73 - 12	John Samson	private investigator	England
Vachss, Andrew H.	'85 - 9	Burke	outlaw soldier-of-fortune investigator	New York, NY
Valin, Jonathan	'80 - 11	Harry Stoner	private eye	Cincinnati, OH
Vance, Jack	'64 - 5	Keith Gersen	hunter of nonhuman killers	USA
Walker, David J.	'95 - 2	Malachy P. Foley	jazz piano-playing P.I.	Chicago, IL
Waugh, Hillary	'47 - 3	Sheridan Wesley	private investigator	New York, NY
Waugh, Hillary	'80 - 6	Simon Kaye	private eye	New York, NY
Wilcox, Collin	'88 - 5	Alan Bernhardt	actor-director private eye	San Francisco, CA
Wilson, Derek	'94 - 6	Tim Lacey	ex-SAS officer and security firm owner	London, England
Winslow, Don	'91 - 5	Neal Carey	youthful pickpocket turned P.I.	New York, NY
Womack, Steven	'93 - 4	Harry James Denton	ex-newspaper reporter turned P.I.	Nashville, TN
Womack, Steven	'90 - 3	Jack Lynch	PR man and problem solver	New Orleans, LA
Wright, Eric	'96 - 1	Mel Pickett	60-something retired Toronto cop	Larch River, Ontario

Espionage

Allbeury, Ted	'74 - 3	Tad Anders	Polish-British agent	England
Ambler, Eric	'62 - 2	Arthur Abdel Simpson	comic rogue and petty crook	England
Arden, William	'68 - 5	Kane Jackson	industrial espionage specialist	NJ
Ardies, Tom	'71 - 3	Charlie Sparrow	handsome American spy	USA
Bickham, Jack	'89 - 6	Brad Smith	championship tennis player and part-time CIA agent	USA
Block, Lawrence	'66 - 7	Evan Tanner	government agent with permanent insomnia	USA
Bolton, Melvin	'84 - 3	Peter Lawson	British spy	England
Buckley, William F.	'76 - 11	Blackford "Blacky" Oakes	CIA agent recruited from Yale	Washington, DC
Butler, Richard	'75 - 2	Max Farne	luxury boat salesman and spy	Santa Margherita, Italy
Clancy, Tom	'84 - 8	Jack Ryan	CIA analyst	Washington, DC
Cleeve, Brian	'64 - 4	Sean Ryan	ex-Irish revolutionary turned British Intelligence	England
Cook, Bob	'85 - 3	Michael Wyman	philosophy professor and MI6 agent	London, England
Cory, Desmond	'51 - 16	Johnny Fedora	British agent	England
Cory, Desmond	'61 - 2	Mr. Dee	Englishman	England
Craig, David	'70 - 2	Stephen Bellecroix & Sheila Roath	British agents	England

Author	1 - #	Series Character	Occupation	Setting
Espionage...cont.				
Craig, David	'68 - 3	Roy Rickman	Home Office administrator	London, England
Cross, David	'86 - 3	John "Chant" Sinclair	renegade super ninja	New York, NY
DeAndrea, William	'84 - 4	Clifford Driscoll	no-name American spy	New York, NY
Deighton, Len	'83 - 9	Bernard Samson	middle-aged British spy	London, England
Deighton, Len	'62 - 7	Harry Palmer	lazy cynical British agent with no name	London, England
Doherty, P. C.	'86 - 10	Hugh Corbett	spy for King Edward I	England
Doherty, P. C.	'88 - 2	Matthew Jenkyn	15th century soldier, double-agent spy	England
Drummond, Ivor	'69 - 9	Jennifer Norrington, Alesandro Di Ganzarello & Coleridge Tucker, III	James Bond-like adventuring trio	London, England
Egleton, Clive	'70 - 3	David Garnett	resistance fighter	England
Egleton, Clive	'93 - 5	Peter Ashton	British spy	England
Fallon, Martin	'62 - 6	Paul Chavasse	globe-trotting British spy	London, England
Follett, Ken	'75 - 2	Piers Roper	industrial spy	London, England
Forbes, Colin	'82 - 9	Tweed	British Secret Service 2nd-in-command	London, England
Freemantle, Brian	'77 - 10	Charlie Muffin	working-class British agent	London, England
Freemantle, Brian	'92 - 2	William Cowley & Dimitri Danilov	FBI agent & Russian investigator	Washington, DC
Galway, Robert C.	'63 - 12	James Packard	British spy	London, England
Gardner, John	'81 - 14	James Bond	British agent	London, England
Gardner, John	'64 - 8	Boysie Oakes	cowardly British agent for Special Security	London, England
Gardner, John	'79 - 7	Herbie Kruger	British Intelligence senior operative	England
Gardner, John	'69 - 2	Derek Torry	British spy	England
Gilbert, Michael	'95 - 2	Joe Narrabone	WWI policeman turned British secret agent	London, England
Grady, James	'74 - 2	Richard Malcolm	CIA analyst and grad student	Washington, DC
Granger, Bill	'79 - 13	Devereaux aka November Man	field intelligence agent for R Section	New York, NY
Hamilton, Donald	'60 - 27	Matt Helm	American superspy	USA
Higgins, Jack	'75 - 4	Liam Devlin	1940s IRA hero	Ireland
Higgins, Jack	'92 - 6	Sean Dillon	IRA enforcer turned British special agent	Ireland
Hone, Joseph	'71 - 4	Peter Marlow	incompetent British spy	England
Jenkins, Geoffrey	'59 - 2	Geoffrey Peace	British naval commander	England
Le Carré, John	'61 - 8	George Smiley	British Intelligence agent and scholar	London, England
Lescroart, John T.	'86 - 2	Auguste Lupa	British Secret Service agent with U.S. passport	London, England
Mayo, J. K.	'85 - 6	Harry Seddall	British Intelligence officer	England
McCutchan, Philip	'60 - 22	Esmonde Shaw	Naval Intelligence turned anti-intelligence	London, England
O'Donnell, Peter	'65 - 11	Modesty Blaise	gorgeous crime fighter for British Intelligence	London, England
Orvis, Kenneth	'65 - 2	Adam Breck	faux James Bond	London, England
Payne, Laurence	'69 - 2	John Tibbett	petty thief turned reluctant hero	London, England
Perry, Ritchie	'72 - 14	Philis	Brazilian smuggler turned British Intelligence agent	Brazil
Price, Anthony	'70 - 19	David Audley	historian and spy	England
Ross, Philip	'86 - 2	Tom Talley	American CIA operative	Europe
Rossiter, John	'70 - 7	Roger Tallis	British agent with a police background	England
Spicer, Michael	'88 - 4	Jane Hildreth, Landy & Patricia Huntington	sexy British secret agent & friend	Cotswolds, England
Trenhaile, John	'86 - 3	Simon Young	British Intelligence officer	Hong Kong, Hong Kong
Trenhaile, John	'81 - 3	Povin, General	Soviet spy	Hong Kong, Hong Kong
Waddell, Martin	'66 - 4	Gerald Otley	amateur adventurer and part-time spy	London, England
Welcome, John	'58 - 5	Richard Graham	English gentleman secret agent	England
Williams, Alan	'62 - 2	Rupert Quinn	swashbuckling English courier	North Africa
York, Andrew	'66 - 9	Jonas Wilde	British secret agent	England

Author	1 - #	Series Character	Occupation	Setting

Background Type

Academic

Author	1 - #	Series Character	Occupation	Setting
Barnard, Robert	'90 - 1	Oddie	inner city schoolteacher	London, England
Bradberry, James	'94 - 3	Jamie Ramsgill, Prof.	architect and Princeton professor	Princeton, NJ
Chesbro, George	'77 - 13	Robert "Mongo" Frederickson	dwarf criminology prof and former circus gymnast	New York, NY
Cook, Bob	'85 - 3	Michael Wyman	philosophy professor and MI6 agent	London, England
Cory, Desmond	'91 - 3	John Dobie	math professor	Cardiff, Wales
Crider, Bill	'88 - 3	Carl Burns	college professor	TX
DeAndrea, William	'79 - 3	Niccolo Benedetti	world-renowned criminologist professor	Sparta, NY
Dowling, Gregory	'85 - 4	January Esposito	American teacher of English	Tuscany, Italy
Elkins, Aaron	'82 - 9	Gideon Oliver	anthropology professor	Port Angeles, WA
Fuller, Timothy	'36 - 5	Edmund "Jupiter" Jones	grad student in fine arts	MA
Jevons, Marshall	'78 - 3	Henry Spearman	Harvard professor	Cambridge, MA
Lake, M. D.	'89 - 9	Peggy O'Neill	university campus cop	MN
Lejeune, Anthony	'87 - 2	James Glowery	British professor	England
Morson, Ian	'94 - 3	William Falconer	13th century university regent master	Oxford, England
Nevins, Francis, Jr.	'75 - 3	Loren Mensing	law school professor	St. Louis, MO
Owens, Louis	'91 - 4	Cole McCurtain	Choctaw-Cherokee-Irish-Cajun college professor	Santa Cruz, CA
Price, Anthony	'70 - 19	David Audley	historian and spy	England
Raphael, Lev	'96 - 2	Nick Hoffman	gay college professor	Michiganapolis, MI
Reeves, Robert	'85 - 2	Thomas Theron	history professor	Boston, MA
Resnicow, Herbert	'85 - 5	Giles Sullivan & Isabel Macintosh	crossword expert & faculty dean	VT
Trow, M. J.	'94 - 2	Peter Maxwell	widowed teacher and golden-hearted cynic	England

Advertising & Public Relations

Author	1 - #	Series Character	Occupation	Setting
Box, Edgar	'52 - 3	Peter Cutler Sargeant II	public relations consultant	New York, NY
Murphy, Dallas	'87 - 3	Artie Deemer	owner of celebrity spokesdog	New York, NY
Nathan, Paul	'94 - 3	Bert Swain	PR chief at a medical research center	New York, NY
Orenstein, Frank	'83 - 3	Ev Franklin	advertising executive	New York, NY

Animals, cats

Author	1 - #	Series Character	Occupation	Setting
Adamson, Lydia	'90 - 15	Alice Nestleton	part-time actress and cat-sitter	New York, NY
Allen, Garrison	'94 - 3	Penelope Warren	ex-Marine mystery bookstore owner	Empty Creek, AZ

Animals, dogs

Author	1 - #	Series Character	Occupation	Setting
Hammond, Gerald	'89 - 8	John Cunningham	war hero and hunting dog trainer	Scotland
King, Frank	'88 - 2	Sally Tepper	unemployed actress with five dogs	New York, NY
Wood, Ted	'83 - 10	Reid Bennett & Sam	police chief & German Shepherd	Murphy's Harbor, Ontario

Animals, horses

Author	1 - #	Series Character	Occupation	Setting
Breen, Jon	'83 - 4	Jerry Brogan	track announcer at Surfside Meadows	CA
Dobyns, Stephen	'76 - 9	Charlie Bradshaw	ex-cop ex-stable security guard turned detective	Saratoga Springs, NY
Francis, Dick	'85 - 2	Kit Fielding	jockey	England
Francis, Dick	'65 - 3	Sid Halley	injured steeplechase jockey turned P. I.	England
Horwitz, Merle	'90 - 2	Harvey Ace	retired P. I. who plays the horses	Los Angeles, CA
Shoemaker, Bill	'94 - 3	Coley Killebrew	ex-jockey turned restaurant owner	Lexington, KY

Animals, other

Author	1 - #	Series Character	Occupation	Setting
Adamson, Lydia	'96 - 2	Lucy Wayles	ex-librarian birdwatcher	New York, NY

Architecture & Engineering

Author	1 - #	Series Character	Occupation	Setting
Bradberry, James	'94 - 3	Jamie Ramsgill	architect and Princeton professor	Princeton, NJ
Lewis, Roy	'82 - 11	Arnold Landon	medieval architecture expert & researcher	England
Miles, Keith	'97 - 1	Merlin Richards	1920s young Welsh architect	Phoenix, AZ
Resnicow, Herbert	'83 - 5	Alexander Gold	construction engineer & puzzle maven	New York, NY
Standiford, Les	'93 - 4	John Deal	building contractor	Miami, FL

Author	1 - #	Series Character	Occupation	Setting
Background Type...cont.				
Art & Antiques				
Ardin, William	'92 - 4	Charles Ramsay	Chelsea antiques dealer	London, England
Barrett, Neal, Jr.	'96 - 2	Wiley Moss	graphic artist for the Smithsonian	Washington, DC
Chesbro, George	'86 - 2	Veil Kendry	painter and adventurer	New York, NY
Conroy, Richard T.	'92 - 3	Henry Scruggs	40-something Smithsonian official	Washington, DC
Elkins, Aaron	'87 - 3	Chris Norgren	art museum curator	Seattle, WA
Gash, Jonathan	'77 - 19	Lovejoy	antiques expert and forger	East Anglia, England
Hanson, Rick	'94 - 4	Adam McCleet	ex-cop turned sculptor	Taos, NM
Kilmer, Nicholas	'95 - 3	Fred Taylor	Vietnam veteran turned art hunter	Cambridge, MA
Lewis, Roy H.	'80 - 5	Matthew Coll	antiquarian book dealer	England
Lupoff, Richard A.	'88 - 8	Hobart Lindsay & Marvia Plum	insurance claims adjuster & Berkeley detective	CA
Malcolm, John	'84 - 12	Tim Simpson	financial consultant turned art investment specialist	London, England
Page, Jake	'93 - 5	T. Moore "Mo" Bowdre	blind redneck sculptor	AZ
Pears, Iain	'91 - 6	Jonathan Argyll	British art dealer	England
Smith, Martin Cruz	'71 - 2	Roman Grey	Gypsy art dealer	New York, NY
Steed, Neville	'86 - 5	Peter Marklin	toyshop owner and antique toy collector	Dorset, England
Swan, Thomas	'90 - 3	Jack Oxby	Scotland Yard art forgery investigator	London, England
Wallace, Robert	'88 - 5	Essington Holt	aging adventurer with an interest in art forgery	Sydney, Australia
Warga, Wayne	'85 - 3	Jeffrey Dean	ex-CIA courier-journalist turned rare book dealer	Los Angeles, CA
Wilson, Derek	'94 - 6	Tim Lacey	ex-SAS officer and security firm owner	London, England
Assassins & Avengers				
Collins, Max A., Jr.	'76 - 5	Quarry	psychotic Vietnam vet and hired killer	IA
Estleman, Loren D.	'84 - 3	Peter Macklin	hit man for the mob	Detroit, MI
Garfield, Brian	'72 - 2	Paul Benjamin	vigilante murderer	AZ
Hall, James W.	'87 - 6	Thorn	eco-avenger P.I.	Key Largo, FL
Harvey, Clay	'96 - 2	Tyler Vance	ex-operative turned family man	NC
Hunter, Stephen	'93 - 2	Bob "the Nailer" Swagger	master sniper	USA
Shaw, Simon	'90 - 4	Philip Fletcher	British thespian and killer	London, England
Vachss, Andrew H.	'85 - 9	Burke	outlaw soldier-of-fortune investigator	New York, NY
Authors & Writers				
Ambler, Eric	'39 - 2	Charles Latimer	British university lecturer turned detective novelist	Turkey
Baxt, George	'67 - 3	Sylvia Plotkin & Max Van Larsen	author-teacher & police detective	New York, NY
Collins, Max A., Jr.	'83 - 5	Mallory	small-town student mystery writer	IA
Cutler, Stan	'91 - 4	Rayford Goodman & Mark Bradley	jaded macho P. I. & gay writer of celebrity biographies	Hollywood, CA
Davis, Kenn	'76 - 8	Carver Bascombe	suave black poet private eye	San Francisco, CA
Forrest, Richard	'75 - 8	Lyon & Bea Wentworth	children's book author & state senator	CT
Garfield, Henry	'95 - 2	Cyrus "Moondog" Nygerski	reclusive writer	Southern, CA
Graeme, Roderic	'52 - 20	Richard Verrel as Blackshirt	romantic thief and best-selling author	England
Handler, David	'88 - 8	Stewart "Hoagy" Hoag	celebrity ghostwriter	USA
Harriss, Will	'83 - 2	Cliff Dunbar	former English professor turned detective	Los Angeles, CA
Hemlin, Tim	'96 - 3	Neil Marshall	graduate student poet	Houston, TX
Hill, John Spencer	'95 - 2	Carlo Arbati	policeman poet	Italy
McGaughey, Neil	'94 - 4	Stokes Moran aka Kyle Malachi	syndicated mystery critic	Tipton, CT
Nolan, William F.	'94 - 2	Black Mask Boys	1930s detective heroes	CA
Palmer, William J.	'90 - 3	Wilkie Collins & Charles Dickens	19th century literary celebrities	London, England
Philbrick, W. R.	'85 - 4	J. D. Hawkins	wheelchair-bound mystery writer	Boston, MA
Phillips, T. J.	'95 - 2	Joe Wilder	struggling playwright and novelist	New York, NY
Reynolds, William	'84 - 6	Nebraska	part-time P.I. trying to write	Omaha, NE
Richardson, Robert	'85 - 5	Augustus Maltravers	journalist turned playwright and novelist	England
Satterthwait, Walter	'95 - 2	Houdini & Conan Doyle	19th century escape artist & writer	London, England
Sherer, Michael W.	'88 - 4	Emerson Ward	freelance writer	Chicago, IL
Sklepowich, Edward	'90 - 5	Urbino Macintyre	American expatriate and biographer	Venice, Italy

Author	1 - #	Series Character	Occupation	Setting

Background Type...cont.

Baseball [see Sports, baseball]

Bed & Breakfast [see Hotels & Inns]

Black Detectives

Author	1 - #	Series Character	Occupation	Setting
Barnard, Robert	'89 - 4	Charlie Peace	young black Scotland Yard detective	London, , England
Baxt, George	'66 - 5	Pharoah Love	gay black NYPD detective	New York, NY
Casley, Dennis	'94 - 3	James Odhiambo	chief inspector	Kenya
Davis, J Madison	'90 - 2	Delbert "Dub" Greenert & Vonna Saucier	white & black investigator pair	New Orleans, LA
Davis, Kenn	'76 - 8	Carver Bascombe	suave black poet private eye	San Francisco, CA
Greer, Robert O.	'96 - 3	C. J. Floyd	bail bondsman and bounty hunter	Denver, CO
Haywood, Gar A.	'88 - 5	Aaron Gunner	black wise-guy P.I.	Los Angeles, CA
Haywood, Gar A.	'94 - 2	Dottie & Joe Loudermilk	traveling retired black couple	USA
Hill, Reginald	'93 - 3	Joe Sixsmith	black private detective	England
Holton, Hugh	'94 - 4	Larry Cole	black police commander	Chicago, IL
Lescroart, John T.	'95 - 2	Abe Glitsky	black Jewish cop	San Francisco, CA
McClure, James	'71 - 8	Tromp Kramer & Mickey Zondi	Afrikaner cop & Bantu detective assistant	South Africa
Mosley, Walter	'90 - 7	Easy Rawlins	school maintenance supervisor in Watts	Los Angeles, CA
Mosley, Walter	'97 - ss	Socrates Fortlow	philosophical ex-con	CA
Patterson, James	'93 - 4	Alex Cross	black psychiatrist and homicide cop	Washington, DC
Phillips, Gary	'94 - 3	Ivan Monk	black private eye	Los Angeles, CA
Phillips, Mike	'89 - 4	Sam Dean	Jamaica-born black journalist	London, England
Raleigh, Michael	'90 - 5	Paul Whelan	40-something black cop turned P.I.	Chicago, IL
Sallis, James	'92 - 3	Lew Griffin	black private eye	New Orleans, LA
Stone, Thomas H.	'72 - 4	Chester Fortune	mulatto detective	Los Angeles, CA
York, Andrew	'77 - 4	James Munroe Tallant	cricket star turned police commissioner	Grand Flamingo, West Indies

Books & Libraries

Author	1 - #	Series Character	Occupation	Setting
Abbott, Jeff	'94 - 4	Jordan Poteet	small-town librarian	Mirabeau, TX
Allen, Garrison	'94 - 3	Penelope Warren	ex-Marine mystery bookstore owner	Empty Creek, AZ
Block, Lawrence	'77 - 8	Bernie Rhodenbarr	professional burglar and bibliophile	New York, NY
Breen, Jon	'84 - 2	Rachel Hennings	bookstore owner	Los Angeles, CA
Dunning, John	'92 - 2	Cliff Janeway	cop and rare book expert	Denver, CO
Gibbs, Tony	'92 - 2	Diana Speed	publishing company chief financial officer	New York, NY
Goodrum, Charles	'77 - 4	Edward George	retired Yale librarian	Washington, DC
Lewis, Roy H.	'80 - 5	Matthew Coll	antiquarian book dealer	England
Warga, Wayne	'85 - 3	Jeffrey Dean	ex-CIA courier-journalist turned rare book dealer	Los Angeles, CA

Botanical

Author	1 - #	Series Character	Occupation	Setting
Fraser, James	'68 - 9	William Aveyard	ambitious village police inspector	England

Business & Finance

Author	1 - #	Series Character	Occupation	Setting
Axler, Leo	'94 - 4	Bill Hawley	undertaker sleuth	Cleveland, OH
Bickham, Jack	'67 - 2	Charity Ross	1890s widowed frontier-ranch-owner	Oklahoma City, OK
Boland, John C.	'91 - 3	Donald McCarry	Wall Street stockbroker	New York, NY
Cluster, Dick	'88 - 2	Alex Glauberman	auto repair shop owner	Boston, MA
Follett, Ken	'75 - 2	Piers Roper	industrial spy	London, England
Foxx, Jack	'72 - 2	Dan Connell	freelance charter pilot	SE Asia
Gibbs, Tony	'92 - 2	Diana Speed	publishing company chief financial officer	New York, NY
Gores, Joe	'72 - 5	Daniel Kearney Associates	auto repo & skip-tracing firm	San Francisco, CA
Hansen, Joseph	'70 - 11	Dave Brandstetter	gay death-claims investigator	Los Angeles, CA
Janes, J. Robert	'91 - 1	Richard Hagen	1940s diamond dealer	Antwerp, Belgium
MacLeod, Robert	'70 - 10	Jonathan Gaunt	external auditor for the Queen	Edinburgh, Scotland
MacLeod, Robert	'74 - 6	Andrew Laird	marine insurance claims investigator	international
MacLeod, Robert	'64 - 6	Talos Cord	United Nations troubleshooter	New York, NY
Malcolm, John	'84 - 12	Tim Simpson	financial consultant turned art investment specialist	London, England
Mallett, Lyndon	'80 - 3	Taffin	fast-with-his-fists debt collector	Lasherham, Ireland

Author	1 - #	Series Character	Occupation	Setting

Background Type...cont.

Business & Finance...cont.

Author	1 - #	Series Character	Occupation	Setting
Michaels, Grant	'90 - 5	Stan Kraychik	gay hairdresser	Boston, MA
Petievich, Gerald	'81 - 4	Charles Carr & Jack Kelly	US Treasury agents	Los Angeles, CA
Resnicow, Herbert	'87 - 2	Ed & Warren Baer	father & son sleuths	Long Island, NY
Sanders, Lawrence	'87 - 2	Timothy Cone	Wall Street financial detective	New York, NY
Sanders, Lawrence	'76 - 2	Peter Tangent	troubleshooter for American oil co	Africa
Scott, Justin	'94 - 2	Ben Abbott	ex-Wall Street financier turned realtor	Newbury, CT
Strunk, Frank C.	'91 - 2	Berkley Jordon	roadhouse operator	Buxton, KY
Tourney, Leonard	'80 - 8	Matthew Stock	17th century town constable and clothier	Chelmsford, England
Williams, Alan	'70 - 3	Charles Pol	Marxist bandit and lingerie-shop owner	Paris, France
Williams, David	'76 - 17	Mark Treasure	merchant banker	London, England

Comic Mysteries [see Humor]

Computers & Technology

Author	1 - #	Series Character	Occupation	Setting
Sandford, John	'89 - 2	Kidd & Luellen	computer whiz & thief	MN

Criminals

Author	1 - #	Series Character	Occupation	Setting
Ambler, Eric	'62 - 2	Arthur Abdel Simpson	comic rogue and petty crook	England
Block, Lawrence	'77 - 8	Bernie Rhodenbarr	professional burglar and bibliophile	New York, NY
Brett, Simon	'86 - 5	Melita Pargeter	widow of a thief	England
Collins, Max A., Jr.	'73 - 7	Frank Nolan	aging thief	IA
Disher, Garry	'91 - 5	Wyatt	Aussie bank robber	Melbourne, Australia
Gash, Jonathan	'77 - 19	Lovejoy	antiques expert and forger	East Anglia, England
Graeme, Roderic	'52 - 20	Richard Verrel as Blackshirt	romantic thief and best-selling author	England
Kurland, Michael	'79 - 2	James Moriarty	archenemy of Sherlock Holmes	London, England
Sandford, John	'89 - 2	Kidd & Luellen	computer whiz & thief	MN
Stark, Richard	'62 - 17	Parker	cold-blooded professional thief	New York, NY
Stark, Richard	'67 - 4	Alan Grofield	actor and part-time bank robber	New York, NY
Westlake, Donald E.	'70 - 9	John Dortmunder	comic thief	New York, NY
Williams, Alan	'70 - 3	Charles Pol	Marxist bandit and lingerie-shop owner	Paris, France

Cross Genre

Author	1 - #	Series Character	Occupation	Setting
Bickham, Jack	'67 - 2	Charity Ross	1890s widowed frontier-ranch-owner	Oklahoma City, OK
Cook, Glen	'87 - 8	Garrett	30-something fantasy private eye	GA
Dukthas, Ann	'94 - 3	Nicholas Segalla	time-traveling scholar	England
Hoch, Edward D.	'71 - 3	Simon Ark	ancient hounder of Satan	New York, NY
Nolan, William F.	'71 - 2	Sam Space	private eye on Mars	Mars
Shatner, William	'89 - 8	Jack Cardigan	22nd century ex-cop private eye	Los Angeles, CA
Spencer, John	'84 - 3	Charley Case	private eye of the "1997" future	Los Angeles, CA
Thurston, Robert	'85 - 3	Byron "Rugger" O'Toole	detective of the future	Central America
Vance, Jack	'64 - 5	Keith Gersen	hunter of nonhuman killers	USA

Disabled Detectives

Author	1 - #	Series Character	Occupation	Setting
Alexander, Bruce	'94 - 3	John Fielding	blind magistrate & founder of first police force	London, England
Bishop, Paul	'91 - 2	Ian Chapel	one-eyed pro soccer goalie turned P.I.	Los Angeles, CA
Chesbro, George	'77 - 13	Robert "Mongo" Frederickson	dwarf criminology prof and former circus gymnast	New York, NY
Collins, Michael	'67 - 17	Dan Fortune	one-armed Polish-Lithuanian P. I.	New York, NY
DeAndrea, William	'95 - 2	Lobo Blacke & Quinn Booker	crippled ex-frontier lawman & his biographer	Le Four, WY
Deaver, Jeffery	'97 - 1	Lincoln Rhyme & Amelia Sachs	disabled ex-head of NYPD forensics & rookie beat cop	New York, NY
Francis, Dick	'65 - 3	Sid Halley	injured steeplechase jockey turned P. I.	England
Grissom, Ken	'88 - 3	John Rodrigue	one-eyed Creole salvager	Caribbean
Livingston, Jack	'82 - 4	Joe Binney	hearing-impaired private eye	New York, NY
Lutz, John	'86 - 10	Fred Carver	crippled ex-cop P.I.	Del Moray, FL
McCall, Thomas	'93 - 2	Nora Callum	one-legged cop	Chicago, IL
Page, Jake	'93 - 5	T. Moore "Mo" Bowdre	blind redneck sculptor	AZ
Philbrick, W. R.	'85 - 4	J. D. Hawkins	wheelchair-bound mystery writer	Boston, MA
Robinson, Kevin	'91 - 3	Stick Foster	paraplegic newspaper reporter	Orlando, FL

Author	1 - #	Series Character	Occupation	Setting

Background Type...cont.

Domestic & Family

Author	1 - #	Series Character	Occupation	Setting
Benison, C. C.	'96 - 3	Jane Bee	housemaid at Buckingham Palace	London, England
Hervey, Evelyn	'84 - 3	Harriet Unwin	19th century spinster governess	England
Katz, Jon	'92 - 4	Kit DeLeeuw	Wall Street shark turned suburban detective	Rochambeau, NJ
Lewin, Michael Z.	'94 - 1	Lunghi family	3-generation private-eye family	Bath, England

Ecclesiastical & Religious

Author	1 - #	Series Character	Occupation	Setting
Anthony, Michael	'90 - 2	Richard Harrison	Anglican church official	England
Clynes, Michael	'91 - 6	Roger Shallot	agent of Cardinal Wolsey	England
Feldmeyer, Dean	'94 - 2	Dan Thompson	small-town Methodist minister	Baird, KY
Greeley, Andrew M.	'85 - 8	John Blackwood "Blackie" Ryan	Catholic priest	Chicago, IL
Harding, Paul	'91 - 7	Athelstan, Brother & John Cranston	14th century Dominican monk & coroner	London, England
Kemelman, Harry	'64 - 11	David Small	rabbi sleuth	Barnard's Crossing, MA
Kienzle, William X.	'79 - 19	Robert Koesler	Catholic priest	Detroit, MI
McInerny, Ralph	'77 - 17	Roger Dowling, Father	St. Hilary's parish priest	Fox River, IL
Meyer, Charles	'95 - 2	Lucas Holt	Episcopal church pastor	Austin, TX
Quill, Monica	'81 - 9	Mary Teresa Dempsey, Sister	5' 2" 200-lb. nun	Chicago, IL
Tremayne, Peter	'94 - 4	Fidelma, Sister	7th century Celtic sister & legal advocate	Kildaire, Ireland
Webb, Jack	'52 - 9	Sammy Golden & Joseph Shanley	Jewish police detective & Catholic priest	Los Angeles, CA

Environment & Wilderness

Author	1 - #	Series Character	Occupation	Setting
Bowen, Peter	'94 - 4	Gabriel DuPre	Metis Indian cattle inspector and sometimes sheriff	MT
Cussler, Clive	'73 - 13	Dirk Pitt	special projs dir of nat'l underwater-marine agency	USA
Goddard, Ken	'92 - 3	Henry Lightstone	National Fish and Wildlife investigator	OR
Grissom, Ken	'88 - 3	John Rodrigue	one-eyed Creole salvager	Caribbean
Hall, James W.	'87 - 5	Thorn	eco-avenger P.I.	Key Largo, FL
Hoyt, Richard	'80 - 7	John Denson	flaky private eye	Seattle, WA
Knox, Bill	'64 - 15	Webb Carrick	chief officer of the Scottish Fishery Protection Service	Scotland
Leitz, David	'96 - 3	Max Addams	proprietor of trout-fishing lodge	Northern VT
Mitchell, Kirk	'95 - 2	Dee Laguerre	Bureau of Land Management ranger	NV
Ring, Raymond H.	'88 - 2	Henry Dyer	fish and game agent turned P.I.	CO
White, Randy W.	'90 - 5	Doc Ford	ex-operative marine biologist	Sanibel Island, FL

Ethnic & Native American

Author	1 - #	Series Character	Occupation	Setting
Alexander, Gary	'93 - 2	Luis Balam	ex-traffic cop turned tour operator	Yucatan, Mexico
Allyn, Doug	'89 - 2	Lupe Garcia	tough Latino cop	Detroit, MI
Anaya, Rudolfo	'95 - 2	Sonny Baca	part-time rodeo rider private eye	Albuquerque, NM
Bowen, Peter	'94 - 4	Gabriel DuPre	Metis Indian cattle inspector and sometimes sheriff	MT
Cook, Bruce	'88 - 4	Antonio "Chico" Cervantes	Mexican-American private eye	Los Angeles, CA
Cunningham, E. V.	'67 - 7	Masao Masuto	Japanese-American police detective	Beverly Hills, CA
Dold, Gaylord	'96 - 1	Grace Wu	undercover agent for the SFPD and DEA	San Francisco, CA
Furutani, Dale	'96 - 2	Ken Tanaka	Asian American computer programmer	Los Angeles, CA
Garfield, Brian	'72 - 2	Sam Watchman	part Navajo State trooper	AZ
Hackler, Micah S.	'95 - 4	Cliff Lansing & Gabe Hanna	single-father part-time rancher-sheriff & his deputy	NM
Hillerman, Tony	'80 - 9	Jim Chee	Navajo tribal police officer	AZ
Hillerman, Tony	'70 - 3	Joe Leaphorn	Navajo tribal police officer	AZ
Miles, John	'94 - 2	Johnelle Baker	Choctaw sheriff	Tenoclock, CO
Mitchell, Kirk	'95 - 2	Dee Laguerre	Bureau of Land Management ranger	NV
Nava, Michael	'86 - 6	Henry Rios	gay Latino ex-alcoholic defense attorney	Los Robles, CA

Author	1 - #	Series Character	Occupation	Setting
Background Type...cont.				
Ethnic & Native American...cont.				
Owens, Louis	'91 - 4	Cole McCurtain	Choctaw-Cherokee-Irish-Cajun college professor	Santa Cruz, CA
Page, Jake	'93 - 5	T. Moore "Mo" Bowdre	blind redneck sculptor	AZ
Perry, Thomas	'95 - 4	Jane Whitefield	Native American guide	Deganawida, NY
Ramos, Manuel	'93 - 4	Luis Montez	attorney and former Chicano activist	Denver, CO
Roberts, Les	'88 - 9	Milan Jacovich	blue-collar Slovenian P.I. with a master's degree	Cleveland, OH
Sanders, William	'93 - 3	Taggart Roper	Cherokee writer and private eye	Tulsa, OK
Smith, Martin Cruz	'71 - 2	Roman Grey	Gypsy art dealer	New York, NY
Trainor, J. F.	'93 - 5	Angela Biwaban	ex-embezzler Anishinabe princess	MN
Young, Scott	'90 - 2	Mateesie Kitologitak	Inuit RCMP Inspector	NW Territories, Canada
FBI [see Police Procedurals]				
Film Making [see Movies & Film Making]				
Gambling [see Toys & Games]				
Gardening [see Botanical]				
Gay & Lesbian Detectives				
Aldyne, Nathan	'80 - 4	Dan Valentine & Clarisse Lovelace	gay & straight bar owners	Boston, MA
Baxt, George	'66 - 5	Pharoah Love	gay black NYPD detective	New York, NY
Cutler, Stan	'91 - 4	Rayford Goodman & Mark Bradley	jaded macho P. I. & gay writer of celebrity biographies	Hollywood, CA
Hansen, Joseph	'70 - 11	Dave Brandstetter	gay death-claims investigator	Los Angeles, CA
Hunter, Fred W.	'97 - 2	Alex Reynolds	gay federal employee	Washington, DC
Kavanagh, Dan	'80 - 4	Nick Duffy	bisexual ex-cop P.I.	London, England
Lansdale, Joe R.	'90 - 4	Hap Collins & Leonard Pine	straight white & gay black good ol' boys	East, TX
Michaels, Grant	'90 - 5	Stan Kraychik	gay hairdresser	Boston, MA
Nava, Michael	'86 - 6	Henry Rios	gay Latino ex-alcoholic defense attorney	Los Robles, CA
Raphael, Lev	'96 - 2	Nick Hoffman	gay college professor	Michiganapolis, MI
Stevenson, Richard	'81 - 6	Donald Strachey	gay private eye	Albany, NY
Tierney, Ronald	'93 - 1	Zachary Grayson	gay author of trendy cookbooks	San Francisco, CA
Zimmerman, R. D.	'95 - 2	Todd Mills	gay TV news reporter	Minneapolis, MN
Zubro, Mark	'89 - 6	Tom Mason & Scott Carpenter	high school teacher & pro baseball player	Chicago, IL
Zubro, Mark	'91 - 4	Paul Turner	gay Chicago cop & father of two teenage sons	Chicago, IL
Gourmet & Food				
Aspler, Tony	'93 - 3	Ezra Brant	wine journalist	Toronto, Ontario, Canada
Bond, Michael	'83 - 8	Aristide Pamplemousse & Pommes Frites	gourmet test-eater & his bloodhound	La Douce, France
King, Peter	'96 - 3	Goodwin Harper	food consultant to Scotland Yard	London, England
Kuhlken, Ken	'91 - 3	Tom Hickey	1940s P.I. and restaurateur	San Diego, CA
Tierney, Ronald	'93 - 1	Zachary Grayson	gay author of trendy cookbooks	San Francisco, CA
Government & Politics				
Bowen, Michael	'90 - 4	Richard Michaelson	retired Foreign Service officer	Washington, DC
Campbell, Robert	'86 - 10	Jimmy Flannery	sewer inspector & Democratic precinct captain	Chicago, IL
Corris, Peter	'85 - 7	Ray Crawley	Federal Security Agency director	Sydney, Australia
Doolittle, Jerome	'90 - 6	Tom Bethany	political consultant and former wrestler	Cambridge, MA
Forrest, Richard	'75 - 8	Lyon & Bea Wentworth	children's book author & state senator	CT
Frost, Mark	'93 - 2	Conan Doyle & Jack Sparks	historical figure & special agent to the Queen	London, England
Grady, James	'74 - 2	Richard Malcolm	CIA analyst and grad student	Washington, DC
Heald, Tim	'73 - 10	Simon Bognor	special investigator to the British Board of Trade	England
Hensley, Joe L.	'71 - 10	Donald Robak	crusading defense attorney and state legislator	Bington, IN
Hunter, Fred W.	'97 - 2	Alex Reynolds	gay federal employee	Washington, DC

Author	1 - #	Series Character	Occupation	Setting
Background Type...cont.				
Government & Politics...cont.				
Lovesey, Peter	'87 - 3	Albert Edward	19th century heir to the British throne	London, England
Melville, James	'95 - 2	Ben Lazenby	British Council official	England
Roosevelt, Elliott	'84 - 16	Eleanor Roosevelt	1940s First Lady	Washington, DC
Historical, ancient				
Saylor, Steven	'90 - 6	Gordianus the Finder	private eye circa 56 B.C.	Rome, Italy
Historical, medieval				
Doherty, P. C.	'86 - 10	Hugh Corbett	spy for King Edward I	England
Doherty, P. C.	'94 - 4	Nicholas Chirke	young medieval lawyer	England
Harding, Paul	'91 - 7	Athelstan, Brother & John Cranston	14th century Dominican monk & coroner	London, England
Jecks, Michael	'95 - 5	Simon Puttock & Baldwin Furnshill	medieval West County bailiff & ex-Templar Knight	Devon, England
Tremayne, Peter	'94 - 4	Sister Fidelma	7th century Celtic sister & legal advocate	Kildaire, Ireland
Historical, 16th century				
Clynes, Michael	'91 - 6	Roger Shallot	agent of Cardinal Wolsey	England
Marston, Edward	'88 - 9	Nicholas Bracewell	stage manager for Elizabethan acting company	London, England
Historical, 17th century				
Tourney, Leonard	'80 - 8	Matthew Stock	17th century town constable and clothier	Chelmsford, England
Historical, 18th century				
Alexander, Bruce	'94 - 3	John Fielding	blind magistrate & founder of first police force	London, England
Burns, Ron	'93 - 2	Harrison Hull	18th century frontier Army captain	VA
Hall, Robert Lee	'88 - 6	Benjamin Franklin	18th century American inventor	London, England
Heller, Keith	'84 - 3	George Man	early 18th century parish watchman	London, England
Historical, 19th century				
Bastable, Bernard	'95 - 2	Wolfgang Mozart & Princess Victoria	19th century composer-teacher & British princess	London, England
Brewer, James D.	'94 - 4	Luke Williamson & Masey Baldridge	Yankee riverboat captain & Confederate veteran	Southern USA
DeAndrea, William	'95 - 2	Lobo Blacke & Quinn Booker	crippled ex-frontier lawman & his biographer	Le Four, WY
Estleman, Loren D.	'78 - 2	Sherlock Holmes	19th century consulting detective	London, England
Gardner, John	'74 - 2	James Moriarty	archenemy of Sherlock Holmes	London, England
Harrison, Ray	'83 - 14	Joseph Bragg & James Morton	Victorian police officers	England
Heck, Peter J.	'95 - 2	Mark Twain & Wentworth Cabot	19th century American author & his secretary	USA
Hervey, Evelyn	'84 - 3	Harriet Unwin	19th century spinster governess	England
Honig, Donald	'96 - 2	Thomas Maynard, Capt.	Civil War Army captain	Dakota Territory
Lovesey, Peter	'70 - 8	Richard Cribb & Edward Thackeray	Victorian policemen	London, England
Lovesey, Peter	'87 - 3	Albert Edward, Prince of Wales	19th century heir to the British throne	London, England
Palmer, William J.	'90 - 3	Wilkie Collins & Charles Dickens	19th century literary celebrities	London, England
Pronzini, Bill	'85 - 2	John Quincannon	19th century private eye	San Francisco, CA
Satterthwait, Walter	'95 - 2	Houdini & Conan Doyle	19th century escape artist & writer	London, England
Selwyn, Francis	'74 - 5	William Clarence Verity	portly Victorian police sergeant	London, England
Sherburne, James	'80 - 5	Paddy Moretti	1890s sportswriter	USA
Trow, M. J.	'85 - 16	Sholto Joseph Lestrade	19th century Scotland Yard inspector	London, England
Historical, 1920s				
Miles, Keith	'97 - 1	Merlin Richards	1920s young Welsh architect	Phoenix, AZ

Author	1 - #	Series Character	Occupation	Setting
Background Type...cont.				
Historical, 1930s				
Adams, Harold	'81 - 14	Carl Wilcox	Depression era sign-painter	Corden, SD
Collins, Max A., Jr.	'83 - 8	Nate Heller	1930s ex-cop turned private eye	Chicago, IL
Collins, Max A., Jr.	'87 - 4	Eliot Ness	1930s public safety officer	Cleveland, OH
Jeffers, H. Paul	'81 - 3	Harry MacNeil	1930s ex-cop private eye	New York, NY
Kerr, Philip	'89 - 3	Bernie Gunther	1930s German private eye	Berlin, Germany
Kurland, Michael	'97 - 1	Alexander Brass	1930s newspaper columnist	New York, NY
Nolan, William F.	'94 - 2	Black Mask Boys	1930s detective heroes	CA
Steed, Neville	'89 - 2	Johnny Black	1930s private detective	England
Historical, 1940s				
Baxt, George	'84 - 12	Jacob Singer	1940s Hollywood private eye	Los Angeles, CA
Cooper, Brian	'91 - 4	John Spencer Lubbock	retired World War II D.C.I.	Norfolk, England
Eddenden, A. E.	'88 - 3	Albert V. Tretheway & Jake Small	1940s Canadian police officers	Fort York, Ontario, Canada
Faherty, Terence	'96 - 3	Scott Elliott	1940s failed actor turned private eye	Hollywood, CA
Higgins, Jack	'75 - 4	Liam Devlin	1940s IRA hero	Ireland
Higgins, Jack	'86 - 2	Dougal Munro & Jack Carter	1940s brigadier & captain	Ireland
Janes, J. Robert	'92 - 8	Jean-Louis St-Cyr & Hermann Kohler	1940s French police inspector & Gestapo agent	Paris, France
Janes, J. Robert	'91 - 1	Richard Hagen	1940s diamond dealer	Antwerp, Belgium
Kaminsky, Stuart	'77 - 20	Toby Peters	1940s Hollywood private investigator	Los Angeles, CA
Kuhlken, Ken	'91 - 3	Tom Hickey	1940s P.I. and restaurateur	San Diego, CA
Parrish, Richard	'93 - 4	Joshua Rabb	1940s attorney	Tucson, AZ
Roosevelt, Elliott	'84 - 16	Eleanor Roosevelt	1940s First Lady	Washington, DC
Historical, 1950s				
Dold, Gaylord	'87 - 9	Mitch Roberts	1950s private eye	Wichita, KS
Pelecanos, George	'92 - 4	Nick Stefanos	1950s bartender P.I.	Washington, DC
Taylor, Andrew	'94 - 3	Richard Thornhill	1950s detective inspector	Lydmouth, England
Historical, 1960s				
Bowen, Michael	'89 - 3	Thomas & Sandrine Curry	1960s husband & wife detective team	New York, NY
Historical, 1970s				
Tanenbaum, R.	'87 - 9	Roger "Butch" Karp & Marlene Ciampi	1970s Criminal Courts Bureau chief & assistant DA	New York, NY
Hollywood [see Movies & Film Making]				
Hotels & Inns				
Leitz, David	'96 - 3	Max Addams	proprietor of trout-fishing lodge	Northern VT
Pairo , Preston, III	'91 - 2	Dallas Henry	sometime-lawyer and motel owner	Ocean City , MD
Russell, Alan	'94 - 2	Am Caulfield	hotel detective	San Diego, CA
Humor				
Aldyne, Nathan	'80 - 4	Dan Valentine & Clarisse Lovelace	gay & straight bar owners	Boston, MA
Ambler, Eric	'62 - 2	Arthur Abdel Simpson	comic rogue and petty crook	England
Barrett, Robert G.	'85 - 7	Les Norton	nightclub bouncer	Sydney, Australia
Barrett, Neal, Jr.	'96- 2	Wiley Moss	graphic artist for the Smithsonian	Washington DC
Block, Lawrence	'77 - 8	Bernie Rhodenbarr	professional burglar and bibliophile	New York, NY
Brett, Michael	'66 - 10	Pete McGrath	wise-cracking private eye	New York, NY
Brewer, Steve	'94 - 4	Bubba Mabry	low-rent P.I.	Albuquerque, NM
Conroy, Richard T.	'92 - 3	Henry Scruggs	40-something Smithsonian official	Washington DC
Cory, Desmond	'91 - 3	John Dobie	math professor	Cardiff, Wales
Cutler, Stan	'91 - 4	Rayford Goodman & Mark Bradley	jaded macho P.I. & gay writer of celebrity biographies	Hollywood, CA

Author	1 - #	Series Character	Occupation	Setting

Background Type...cont.

Humor...cont.

Author	1 - #	Series Character	Occupation	Setting
Ford, G. M.	'95 - 4	Leo Waterman	wisecracking private eye	Seattle, WA
Friedman, Kinky	'86 - 10	Kinky Friedman	country & western singer turned sleuth	New York, NY
Kenyon, Michael	'70 - 3	O'Malley	comic Irish cop	Ireland
Kenyon, Michael	'81 - 8	Henry Peckover	Scotland Yard's cockney poet	London, England
Kohler, Vince	'90 - 4	Eldon Larkin	small-town newspaper reporter	Port Jerome, OR
McDonald, Gregory	'74 - 11	Irwin M. Fletcher	reporter turned beach bum socialite	USA
McDonald, Gregory	'95 - 2	Skylar Whitfield	small-town good-ol'-boy	TN
Murphy, Dallas	'87 - 3	Artie Deemer	owner of celebrity spokesdog	New York, NY
Payne, Laurence	'62 - 3	Sam Birkett	humorous Scotland Yard inspector	London, England
Payne, Laurence	'69 - 2	John Tibbett	petty thief turned reluctant hero	London, England
Pearce, Michael	'88 - 10	Garth Owen	British head of the secret police	Cairo, Egypt
Ripley, Mike	'88 - 8	Fitzroy Maclean Angel	trumpet-playing taxi driver	London, England
Russell, Alan	'94 - 2	Am Caulfield	hotel detective	San Diego, CA
Shaw, Simon	'90 - 4	Philip Fletcher	British thespian and killer	London, England
Westlake, Donald E.	'70 - 9	John Dortmunder	comic thief	New York, NY
York, Andrew	'77 - 4	James Munroe Tallant	cricket star turned police commissioner	Grand Flamingo, West Indies

Journalism, magazine

Author	1 - #	Series Character	Occupation	Setting
Aspler, Tony	'93 - 3	Ezra Brant	wine journalist	Toronto, Ontario
Bourgeau, Art	'80 - 4	Claude "Snake" Kirlin & F. T. Zevich	magazine freelancer & sidekick	TN
DuBois, Brendan	'94 - 2	Lewis Cole	magazine writer	Tyler Beach, NH

Journalism, newspaper

Author	1 - #	Series Character	Occupation	Setting
Belsky, Dick	'85 - 2	Lucy Shannon	newspaper reporter	New York, NY
Berger, Bob	'95 - 2	James Denny aka Dr. Risk	risk theorist and newspaper columnist	New York, NY
Biderman, Bob	'85 - 4	Joseph Radkin	investigative journalist	San Francisco, CA
Boyle, Gerry	'93 - 4	Jack McMorrow	ex-NY Times reporter turned small town editor	Androscoggin, ME
DeAndrea, William	'95 - 2	Lobo Blacke & Quinn Booker	crippled ex-frontier lawman & his biographer	Le Four, WY
DeBrosse, Jim	'88 - 3	Rick Decker	investigative reporter	Cincinnati, OH
Flynn, Don	'83 - 5	Ed "Fitz" Fitzgerald	Daily Tribune reporter	New York, NY
Gorman, Ed	'87 - 2	Tobin	hot-tempered movie critic	New York, NY
Jenkins, Jerry	'83 - 6	Jennifer Grey	newspaper reporter and columnist	Chicago, IL
Kohler, Vince	'90 - 4	Eldon Larkin	small-town newspaper reporter	Port Jerome, OR
Kurland, Michael	'97 - 1	Alexander Brass	1930s newspaper columnist	New York, NY
Lejeune, Anthony	'61 - 3	Adam Gifford	crime reporter	London, England
Logue, John	'79 - 5	John Morris	Associated Press sportswriter	Atlanta, GA
Matthews, Lew	'92 - 3	Horatio T. Parker	crime reporter for a weekly newspaper	Hampstead, England
McGaughey, Neil	'94 - 4	Stokes Moran aka Kyle Malachi	syndicated mystery critic	Tipton, CT
Moore, Richard A.	'81 - 2	Bob Whitfield	newspaper reporter	Atlanta, GA
Osborn, David	'89 - 3	Margaret Barlow	50-something freelance journalist	USA
Peterson, Keith	'88 - 5	John Wells	newspaper reporter	New York, NY
Phillips, Mike	'89 - 4	Sam Dean	Jamaica-born black journalist	London, England
Riggs, John R	'84 - 12	Garth Ryland	small-town newspaper editor	Oakalla, WI
Robinson, Kevin	'91 - 3	Stick Foster	paraplegic newspaper reporter	Orlando, FL
Russell, Martin	'71 - 5	Jim Larkin	journalist	England
Sherburne, James	'80 - 5	Paddy Moretti	1890s sportswriter	USA
Taylor, H. Baldwin	'64 - 3	David Halliday	newspaper owner and editor	CT
Wilcox, Collin	'67 - 2	Stephen Drake	newspaper reporter with ESP	San Francisco, CA

Journalism, photography

Author	1 - #	Series Character	Occupation	Setting
Ayres, E. C.	'94 - 3	Tony Lowell	photographer private eye	FL
Douglas, John	'87 - 2	Jack Reese	photographer	Shawnee, WV
Townend, Peter	'71 - 3	Philip Quest	photographer	Sardinia

Author	1 - #	Series Character	Occupation	Setting

Background Type...cont.

Journalism, radio & television

Author	1 - #	Series Character	Occupation	Setting
Allen, Steve	'82 - 8	Steve Allen & Jane Meadows	celebrity crime-solving duo	Los Angeles, CA
Belsky, Dick	'89 - 4	Jenny McKay	TV news reporter	New York, NY
Briody, Thomas	'95 - 2	Michael Carolina	former TV investigative reporter	Providence, RI
DeAndrea, William	'78 - 8	Matt Cobb	network television executive	New York, NY
Faherty, Terence	'96 - 3	Scott Elliott	1940s failed actor turned private eye	Hollywood, CA
Fink, John	'91 - 2	Jimmy Gillespie	TV reporter and weekend anchor	Chicago, IL
Goldberg, Lee	'95 - 2	Charlie Willis	ex-cop turned TV cop turned studio security agent	Los Angeles, CA
Handberg, Ron	'92 - 3	TV newsroom series	newsroom crew	Minneapolis, MN
Irvine, Robert	'74 - 4	Robert Christopher	television reporter	Los Angeles, CA
Irvine, Robert	'94 - 1	Kevin Manwaring & Vicki Garcia	field producer & television reporter	Los Angeles, CA
Lupica, Mike	'86 - 3	Peter Finley	investigative TV reporter	New York, NY
Sandford, John	'97 - 1	Anna Batory	TV news video freelancer	Los Angeles, CA
Zimmerman, R. D.	'95 - 2	Todd Mills	gay TV news reporter	Minneapolis, MN

Legal, attorney

Author	1 - #	Series Character	Occupation	Setting
Batten, Jack	'87 - 4	Crang	lawyer and jazz buff	Toronto, Ontario
Bernhardt, William	'91 - 6	Ben Kincaid	attorney	Tulsa, OK
Champion, David	'95 - 2	Bomber Hanson	ace trial lawyer	Angleton, CA
Doherty, P. C.	'94 - 4	Nicholas Chirke	young medieval lawyer	England
Downing, Warwick	'90 - 3	Jack S. Bard	defense attorney	Denver, CO
Dunbar, Tony	'94 - 3	Tubby Dubonnet	bon vivant defense attorney	New Orleans, LA
Edwards, Martin	'91 - 5	Harry Devlin	solicitor	Liverpool, England
Gray, A. W.	'88 - 4	Bino Phillips	6' 6" attorney	Dallas, TX
Gregory, Sarah	'96 - 2	Sharon Hays	defense attorney	Dallas, TX
Hailey, J. P.	'88 - 5	Steve Winslow	courtroom attorney	New York, NY
Hensley, Joe L.	'71 - 10	Donald Robak	crusading defense attorney and state legislator	Bington, IN
Higgins, George V.	'80 - 4	Jerry Kennedy	criminal defense attorney	Boston, MA
Huebner, Frederick	'86 - 5	Matt Riordan	burned-out lawyer turned investigator	Seattle, WA
Jeffers, H. Paul	'97 - 1	Arlene Flynn	chief investigator for the District Attorney	New York, NY
Kahn, Michael A.	'88 - 5	Rachel Gold	defense attorney	St. Louis, MO
Kaufelt, David A.	'93 - 3	Wynsome "Wyn" Lewis	ex-Manhattan real estate attorney	Wagg's Neck Hrbr, NY
Kincaid, D.	'86 - 2	Harry Cain	unorthodox trial lawyer	Los Angeles, CA
Lashner, William	'95 - 2	Victor Carl	hard-boiled lawyer	Philadelphia, PA
Lescroart, John T.	'89 - 4	Dismas Hardy	ex-cop bartender and ex-ADA turned defense attorney	San Francisco, CA
Levine, Paul	'90 - 7	Jake Lassiter	ex-linebacker turned lawyer	Miami, FL
Levitsky, Ronald	'91 - 4	Nate Rosen	civil rights lawyer	Washington, DC
Lewis, Roy	'80 - 9	Eric Ward	policeman turned solicitor	England
Mann, Paul	'93 - 3	George Sansi	Anglo-Indian attorney	Goa, India
Marston, Edward	'93 - 5	Ralph Delchard & Gervase Bret	11th century soldier & lawyer	England
Martini, Steve	'92 - 4	Paul Madriani	defense attorney	CA
Masur, Harold Q.	'47 - 11	Scott Jordan	criminal defense attorney	New York, NY
McBain, Ed	'77 - 12	Matthew Hope	attorney	FL
McInerny, Ralph	'87 - 6	Andrew Broom	attorney	Wyler, IN
Murphy, Haughton	'86 - 7	Reuben Frost	retired Wall Street attorney	New York, NY
Nava, Michael	'86 - 6	Henry Rios	gay Latino ex-alcoholic criminal defense attorney	Los Robles, CA
Nevins, Francis, Jr	'75 - 3	Loren Mensing	law school professor	St. Louis, MO
Pairo, Preston, III	'91 - 2	Dallas Henry	sometime-lawyer and motel owner	Ocean City , MD
Pairo, Preston, III	'96 - 2	Jimmy "Griff" Griffin	ex-cop investigator for the city attorney	Baltimore, MD
Parrish, Richard	'93 - 3	Joshua Rabb	1940s attorney	Tucson, AZ
Patterson, Richard	'79 - 3	Christopher Paget	economic crimes special investigator	Washington, DC
Ramos, Manuel	'93 - 4	Luis Montez	attorney and former Chicano activist	Denver, CO
Reed, Barry	'80 - 3	Dan Sheridan	attorney	Boston, MA
Schoonover, W.	'90 - 2	John Wilkes	defense attorney	New York, NY
Stockley, Grif	'92 - 5	Gideon Page	defense attorney	AR
Tanenbaum, R.	'87 - 9	Roger "Butch" Karp & Marlene Ciampi	1970s Criminal Courts Bureau chief & assistant DA	New York, NY

Author	1 - #	Series Character	Occupation	Setting
Background Type...cont.				
Legal, attorney...cont.				
Tapply, William G.	'84 - 15	Brady Coyne	lawyer to the rich who loves to fish	Boston, MA
White, Stephen	'91 - 5	Alan Gregory & Lauren Crowder	practicing psychologist & attorney	Boulder, CO
Woods, Stuart	'91 - 3	Stone Barrington	suave ex-cop attorney	New York, NY
Wyrick, E. L.	'94 - 2	Tammi Randall	small-town lawyer	Patsboro, GA
Legal, judge				
Alexander, Bruce	'94 - 3	John Fielding	blind magistrate & founder of first police force	London, England
Legal, other				
Faherty, Terence	'91 - 5	Owen Keane	ex-seminarian and law firm researcher	Boston, MA
Leonard, Elmore	'76 - 2	Frank Ryan	process server	Detroit, MI
Legal, prosecutor [see Police Procedurals]				
Medical				
Bailey, Jo	'91 - 3	Jan Gallagher	hospital security guard	MN
Boyer, Rick	'82 - 8	Charlie "Doc" Adams	oral surgeon	Concord, MA
Clark, Douglas	'69 - 27	George Masters & Bill Green	Scotland Yard detective team poison expert	London, England
Donaldson, D. J.	'88 - 6	Kit Franklyn & Andy Broussard	criminal psychologist & medical examiner	New Orleans, LA
Gash, Jonathan	'97 - 1	Clare Burtonall, MD	hospital physician	England
Goldberg, Leonard	'92 - 4	Joanna Blalock & Jake Sinclair	forensic pathologist & police detective	Los Angeles, CA
Grace, C. L.	'93 - 4	Kathryn Swinbrooke	15th cent. physician, apothecary, death investigator	Canterbury, England
Harding, Paul	'91 - 7	Athelstan, Brother & John Cranston	14th century Dominican monk & coroner	London, England
Kellerman, J.	'85 - 12	Alex Delaware	child psychologist	Los Angeles, CA
Luber, Philip	'94 - 2	Harry Kline & Veronica Pace	psychiatrist & FBI agent	Concord, MA
Noguchi, Thomas T. w/Arthur Lyons	'80 - 2	Eric Parker	forensic pathologist	Los Angeles, CA
Patterson, James	'93 - 4	Alex Cross	black psychiatrist and homicide cop	Washington, DC
Pearson, Ridley	'88 - 4	Lou Boldt & Daphne Matthews	detective & police psychologist	Seattle, WA
Pomidor, Bill	'95 - 4	Calista & Plato Marley	forensic pathologist wife & family physician husband	Cleveland, OH
Puckett, Andrew	'87 - 3	Tom Jones	health investigator	England
Roe, C. F.	'90 - 8	Jean Montrose	general practitioner	Scotland
Scholefield, Alan	'94 - 2	Anne Vernon	prison doctor	Kingstown, England
Vincent, Lawrence	'89 - 2	Townsend Reeves	radiologist with a ballerina girlfriend	Kansas City, MO
Walker, Robert W.	'92 - 5	Jessica Coran	FBI medical examiner	Washington, DC
White, Stephen	'91 - 5	Alan Gregory & Lauren Crowder	practicing psychologist & attorney	Boulder, CO
Zimmerman, Bruce	'89 - 4	Quinn Parker	phobia therapist	San Francisco, CA
Zimmerman, R. D.	'92 - 3	Alex & Maddy Phillips	brother & blind forensic psychiatrist sister	Upper Peninsula, MI
Military				
Brewer, James D.	'94 - 4	Luke Williamson & Masey Baldridge	Yankee riverboat captain & Confederate veteran	Southern USA
Douglas, Arthur	'86 - 3	Jonathan Craythorne	British Army major	England
Higgins, Jack	'86 - 2	Dougal Munro & Jack Carter	1940s brigadier & captain	Ireland
Jenkins, Geoffrey	'59 - 2	Geoffrey Peace	British naval commander	England
Marston, Edward	'93 - 5	Ralph Delchard & Gervase Bret	11th century soldier & lawyer	England
Mayo, J. K.	'85 - 6	Harry Seddall	British Intelligence officer	England
Movies & Film Making				
Baxt, George	'84 - 12	Jacob Singer	1940s Hollywood private eye	Los Angeles, CA
Bogart, Stephen H.	'95 - 2	R. J. Brook	celebrity-son private eye	New York, NY
Kaminsky, Stuart	'77 - 20	Toby Peters	1940s Hollywood private investigator	Los Angeles, CA
Payne, Laurence	'82 - 5	Mark Savage	movie star turned private eye	USA
Stinson, Jim	'85 - 4	Stoney Winston	low-budget film maker	Los Angeles, CA

Author	1 - #	Series Character	Occupation	Setting
Background Type				
Music				
Bastable, Bernard	'95 - 2	Mozart & Princess Victoria	19th century composer & princess	London, England
Batten, Jack	'87 - 4	Crang	lawyer and jazz buff	Toronto, Ontario, Canada
Friedman, Kinky	'86 - 10	Kinky Friedman	country & western singer turned sleuth	New York, NY
Greeley, Andrew M.	'94 - 2	Nuala Ann McGrail	young Irish immigrant psychic and singer	Chicago, IL
Ripley, Mike	'88 - 8	Fitzroy Maclean Angel	trumpet-playing taxi driver	London, England
Walker, David J.	'95 - 2	Malachy P. Foley	jazz piano-playing P.I.	Chicago, IL
Psychological & Paranormal				
Chesbro, George	'86 - 2	Veil Kendry	painter and adventurer	New York, NY
Gorman, Ed	'94 - 2	Robert Payne	psychological profile investigator	New Hope, IA
Greeley, Andrew M.	'94 - 2	Nuala Ann McGrail	young Irish immigrant psychic and singer	Chicago, IL
Science Fiction & Fantasy [see Cross Genre]				
Secret Agents [see Espionage]				
Security & Protective Services				
Bailey, Jo	'91 - 3	Jan Gallagher	hospital security guard	MN
Barrett, Robert G.	'85 - 7	Les Norton	nightclub bouncer	Sydney, Australia
Taylor, Andrew	'82 - 8	William Dougal	post-grad student and security firm employee	England
Senior Sleuths				
Barth, Richard	'78 - 7	Margaret Binton	70-something little old lady	New York, NY
Brett, Simon	'86 - 5	Melita Pargeter	widow of a thief	England
DuBois, Brendan	'94 - 2	Lewis Cole	magazine writer	Tyler Beach, NH
Haywood, Gar A.	'94 - 2	Dottie & Joe Loudermilk	traveling retired black couple	USA
Kaminsky, Stuart	'90 - 5	Abe Lieberman	60-something Jewish police detective	Chicago, IL
Miles, John	'93 - 3	Laura Michaels	retirement center social worker	Timberlake, OK
Nordan, Robert	'89 - 3	Mavis Lashley	little old lady Sunday School teacher	Southern USA
Rosenberg, Robert	'91 - 3	Avram Cohen	recently-retired police officer	Jerusalem, Israel
Tierney, Ronald	'90 - 4	"Deets" Shanahan	70-something private eye	Indianapolis, IN
Wright, Eric	'96 - 1	Mel Pickett	60-something retired Toronto cop	Larch River, Ontario
Yaffe, James	'88 - 4	Dave & Mom	ex-cop investigator for public defender & his mother	Mesa Grande, CO
Small Town				
Abbott, Jeff	'94 - 4	Jordan Poteet	small-town librarian	Mirabeau, TX
Boyle, Gerry	'93 - 4	Jack McMorrow	ex-NY Times reporter turned small town editor	Androscoggin, ME
Collins, Max A. Jr.	'83 - 5	Mallory	small-town student mystery writer	IA
Constantine, K. C.	'72 - 13	Mario Balzic	small-town police chief	Rocksburg, PA
Engel, Howard	'80 - 9	Benny Cooperman	small-town Jewish private eye	Grantham, Ontario
Feldmeyer, Dean	'94 - 2	Dan Thompson	small-town Methodist minister	Baird, KY
Hautman, Pete	'94 - 3	Joe Crow, Sam O'Gara, Axel Speeter & Tommy Fabian	small-town professional gamblers	MN
Kohler, Vince	'90 - 4	Eldon Larkin	small-town newspaper reporter	Port Jerome, OR
McDonald, Gregory	'95 - 2	Skylar Whitfield	small-town good-ol'-boy	TN
Parrish, Frank	'77 - 8	Dan Mallett	ex-London bank clerk turned handyman-poacher	Medwell Frtrm, England
Riggs, John R.	'84 - 12	Garth Ryland	small-town newspaper editor	Oakalla, WI
Ripley, Jack	'71 - 4	John George Davis	small-town constable	England
Wood, Ted	'83 - 10	Reid Bennett & Sam	police chief & German Shepherd	Murphy's Hrbr, Ontario
Wyrick, E. L.	'94 - 2	Tammi Randall	small-town lawyer	Patsboro, GA
Sports, agents & writers				
Coben, Harlan	'95 - 4	Myron Bolitar	injured basketball player turned sports agent	New York, NY
Granger, Bill	'91 - 3	Jimmy Drover	ex-sportswriter	Chicago, IL
Logue, John	'79 - 5	John Morris	Associated Press sportswriter	Atlanta, GA
Sherburne, James	'80 - 5	Paddy Moretti	1890s sportswriter	USA

Author	1 - #	Series Character	Occupation	Setting
Background Type				
Sports, auto racing				
Judd, Bob	'89 - 5	Forrest Evers	former race car driver	international
Sports, baseball				
Evers, Crabbe	'91 - 5	Duffy House	ex-sportswriter turned investigator	Chicago, IL
Nighbert, David F.	'88 - 3	Bull Cochran	ex-big league pitcher	Knoxville, TN
Rosen, Richard	'84 - 4	Harvey Blissberg	ex-baseball player turned P.I.	Boston, MA
Soos, Troy	'94 - 5	Mickey Rawlings	1910s journeyman second baseman	USA
Sports, diving				
Allyn, Doug	'95 - 3	Michelle Mitchell	single mother and dive shop owner	Huron Harbor, MI
Poyer, David	'89 - 4	Tiller Galloway	ex-Navy SEAL turned salvage diver	Cape Hatteras, NC
Sports, fishing & hunting				
Leitz, David	'96 - 3	Max Addams	proprietor of trout-fishing lodge	Northern, VT
Sports, football				
Ripley, W. L.	'93 - 3	Wyatt Storme	Vietnam vet ex-NFL star	N Branson, MO
Sports, golf				
Cork, Barry	'88 - 4	Angus Struan	golfing police inspector	Scotland
Daly, Conor	'95 - 3	Kieran Lanahan	lawyer turned country club golf pro	Westcehster County, NY
Logue, John	'79 - 5	John Morris	Associated Press sportswriter	Atlanta, GA
Miles, Keith	'86 - 4	Alan Saxon	professional golfer	international
Zimmerman, Bruce	'89 - 4	Quinn Parker	phobia therapist	San Francisco, CA
Sports, horse racing				
Breen, Jon	'83 - 4	Jerry Brogan	track announcer at Surfside Meadows	CA
Francis, Dick	'85 - 2	Kit Fielding	jockey	England
Francis, Dick	'65 - 3	Sid Halley	injured steeplechase jockey turned P.I.	England
Horwitz, Merle	'90 - 2	Harvey Ace	retired P.I. who plays the horses	Los Angeles, CA
Murray, William	'84 - 9	Shifty Lou Anderson	professional magician and horse-player	Southern, CA
Sports, sailing & yachting				
Butler, Richard	'75 - 2	Max Farne	luxury boat salesman and spy	Santa Margherita, Italy
Gibbs, Tony	'96 - 2	Neal Donahoe & Victoria "Tory" Lennox	harbor cop and Coast Guard Lt.	Santa Barbara, CA
Gibbs, Tony	'88 - 3	Gillian Verdean, Jeremy Barr & Patrick O'Mara	yacht owner, skipper & mate	Long Island, NY
Sports, soccer				
Bishop, Paul	'91 - 2	Ian Chapel	one-eyed pro soccer goalie turned P.I.	Los Angeles, CA
Sports, tennis				
Bickham, Jack	'89 - 6	Brad Smith	championship tennis player and part-time CIA agent	USA
Suburban				
Andrus, Jeff	'94 - 2	John Tracer	family-man sleuth	Monterey, CA
Katz, Jon	'92 - 4	Kit DeLeeuw	Wall Street shark turned suburban detective	Rochambeau, NJ
Theatre & Performing Arts				
Adamson, Lydia	'90 - 15	Alice Nestleton	part-time actress and cat-sitter	New York, NY
Brett, Simon	'75 - 17	Charles Paris	charming alcoholic actor	England
Kelley, Patrick A.	'85 - 5	Harry Colderwood	professional magician	PA
King, Frank	'88 - 2	Sally Tepper	unemployed actress with five dogs	New York, NY
Marston, Edward	'88 - 9	Nicholas Bracewell	stage manager for Elizabethan acting company	London, England

Author	1 - #	Series Character	Occupation	Setting
Background Type				
Theatre & Performing Arts...cont.				
Moody, Bill	'94 - 3	Evan Horne	jazz pianist	NV
Murray, William	'84 - 9	Shifty Lou Anderson	professional magician and horse-player	Southern, CA
Satterthwait, Walter	'95 - 2	Houdini & Conan Doyle	19th century escape artist & writer	London, England
Shaw, Simon	'90 - 4	Philip Fletcher	British thespian and killer	London, England
Stark, Richard	'67 - 4	Alan Grofield	actor and part-time bank robber	New York, NY
Vincent, Lawrence	'89 - 2	Townsend Reeves	radiologist with a ballerina girlfriend	Kansas, KS
Wilcox, Collin	'88 - 5	Alan Bernhardt	actor-director private eye	San Francisco, CA
Toys & Games				
Hautman, Pete	'94 - 3	Joe Crow, Sam O'Gara, Axel Speeter & Tommy Fabian	small-town professional gamblers	MN
Kelley, Patrick A.	'85 - 5	Harry Colderwood	professional magician	PA
Lewis, Ted	'70 - 3	Jack Carter	employee of rackets organization	London, England
Murray, William	'84 - 9	Shifty Lou Anderson	professional magician and horse-player	Southern CA
Steed, Neville	'86 - 5	Peter Marklin	toyshop owner and antique toy collector	Dorset, England
Travel				
Bickham, Jack	'89 - 6	Brad Smith	championship tennis player and part-time CIA agent	USA
Drummond, Ivor	'69 - 9	Jennifer Norrington, Alesandro Di Ganzarello & Coleridge Tucker, III	James Bond-like adventuring trio	London, England
Elkins, Aaron	'87 - 3	Chris Norgren	art museum curator	Seattle, WA
Haywood, Gar A.	'94 - 2	Dottie & Joe Loudermilk	traveling retired black couple	USA
MacLeod, Robert	'70 - 10	Jonathan Gaunt	external auditor for the Queen	Edinburgh, Scotland
MacLeod, Robert	'74 - 6	Andrew Laird	marine insurance claims investigator	international
MacLeod, Robert	'64 - 6	Talos Cord	United Nations troubleshooter	New York, NY
Milan, Borto	'95 - 2	Edward Ryan	motorcycle drifter	Southeast USA
Western [see Cross Genre]				

SERIES 3 CHARACTERS

Series Character	Author	1 - #	Occupation	Setting
Character's First Name				
87th Precinct	McBain, Ed	'56 - 4	thinly-disguised NYPD cops	Isola, NY
A				
Aaron Asherfeld	Berlinski, David	'93 - 3	cynical P.I. with 3 ex-wives	San Francisco, CA
Aaron Gunner	Haywood, Gar A.	'88 - 5	black wise-guy P.I.	Los Angeles, CA
Abe Glitsky	Lescroart, John T.	'95 - 2	black Jewish cop	San Francisco, CA
Abe Lieberman	Kaminsky, Stuart	'90 - 5	60-something Jewish police detective	Chicago, IL
Ace Carpenter	Caine, Hamilton	'81 - 2	private eye	Los Angeles, CA
Adam Breck	Orvis, Kenneth	'65 - 2	faux James Bond	London, England
Adam Gifford	Lejeune, Anthony	'61 - 3	crime reporter	London, England
Adam McCleet	Hanson, Rick	'94 - 4	ex-cop turned sculptor	Taos, NM
Alan Banks	Robinson, Peter	'87 - 9	Eastvale detective chief inspector	Yorkshire, England
Alan Bernhardt	Wilcox, Collin	'88 - 5	actor-director private eye	San Francisco, CA
Alan Gregory & Lauren Crowder	White, Stephen	'91 - 5	practicing psychologist & attorney	Boulder, CO
Alan Grofield	Stark, Richard	'67 - 4	actor and part-time bank robber	New York, NY
Alan Saxon	Miles, Keith	'86 - 4	professional golfer	international
Albert Edward	Lovesey, Peter	'87 - 3	19th century heir to the British throne	London, England
Albert Samson	Lewin, Michael Z.	'71 - 9	middle-age low-key P.I.	Indianapolis, IN
Albert V. Tretheway & Jake Small	Eddenden, A. E.	'88 - 3	1940s Canadian police officers	Fort York, Ontario, Canada
Alec Stainton	Murray, Stephen	'87 - 5	British police inspector	England
Alesandro Di Ganzarello, Jennifer Norrington & Coleridge Tucker, III	Drummond, Ivor	'69 - 9	James Bond-like adventuring trio	London, England
Alex Cross	Patterson, James	'93 - 4	black psychiatrist and homicide cop	Washington, DC
Alex Delaware	Kellerman, J.	'85 -12	child psychologist	Los Angeles, CA
Alex Glauberman	Cluster, Dick	'88 - 2	auto repair shop owner	Boston, MA
Alex Grismolet	Fuller, Dean	'92 - 2	Chef-Insp. of the Sûréte	Paris, France
Alex & Maddy Phillips	Zimmerman, R. D.	'92 - 3	brother & blind forensic psychiatrist sister	Upper Peninsula, MI
Alex Rasmussen	Daniel, David	'94 - 2	private investigator	Lowell, MA
Alex Reynolds	Hunter, Fred W.	'97 - 2	gay federal employee	Washington, DC
Alexander Brass	Kurland, Michael	'97 - 1	1930s newspaper columnist	New York, NY
Alexander Gold	Resnicow, Herbert	'83 - 5	construction engineer & puzzle maven	New York, NY
Alice Nestleton	Adamson, Lydia	'90 -15	part-time actress and cat-sitter	New York, NY
Alo Nudger	Lutz, John	'76 -10	antacid-chewing bad-luck P.I.	St. Louis, MO
Am Caulfield	Russell, Alan	'94 - 2	hotel detective	San Diego, CA
Amelia Sachs & Lincoln Rhyme	Deaver, Jeffery	'97 - 1	disabled ex-head of NYPD forensics & rookie beat cop	New York, NY
Amos Walker	Estleman, Loren D.	'80 -11	6' 1" Vietnam vet private eye	Detroit, MI

Series Character	Author	1 - #	Occupation	Setting
First Name...cont.				
A...B				
Andrew Broom	McInerny, Ralph	'87 - 6	attorney	Wyler, IN
Andrew Dalziel & Peter Pascoe	Hill, Reginald	'70 -15	pair of police inspectors	Yorkshire, England
Andrew Laird	MacLeod, Robert	'74 - 6	marine insurance claims investigator	international
Andy Broussard & Kit Franklyn	Donaldson, D. J.	'88 - 6	criminal psychologist & medical examiner	New Orleans, LA
Andy Sussman & Murray Glick	Katz, Michael J.	'87 - 3	P.I. & sportscaster buddy	Chicago, IL
Angel Cantini & Paul Marston	Eversz, Robert	'88 - 2	private eye & female prize fighter	Los Angeles, CA
Angela Biwaban	Trainor, J. F.	'93 - 5	ex-embezzler Anishinabe princess	MN
Angela Gennaro & Patrick Kenzie	Lehane, Dennis	'94 - 3	private detectives	Boston, MA
Angus Struan	Cork, Barry	'88 - 4	golfing police inspector	Scotland
Anna Batory	Sandford, John	'97 - 1	TV news video freelancer	Los Angeles, CA
Anne Vernon	Scholefield, Alan	'94 - 2	prison doctor	Kingstown, England
Anthony Ryan & Joe Gregory	Dee, Ed	'94 - 3	NYPD detective partners	New York, NY
Antonio "Chico" Cervantes	Cook, Bruce	'88 - 4	Mexican-American private eye	Los Angeles, CA
"Apples" Carstairs	Myles, Simon	'74 - 2	private eye	England
Arch McNally	Sanders, Lawrence	'92 - 7	playboy private eye	Palm Beach, FL
Aristide Pamplemousse & Pommes Frites	Bond, Michael	'83 - 8	gourmet test-eater & his bloodhound	La Douce, France
Aristotle Plato Socarides	Kemprecos, Paul	'91 - 7	ex-cop part-time fisherman P.I.	Cape Cod, MA
Arkady Renko	Smith, Martin Cruz	'81 - 3	Russian police officer	Moscow, Russia
Arlene Flynn	Jeffers, H. Paul	'97 - 1	chief investigator for the District Attorney	New York, NY
Arnold Landon	Lewis, Roy	'82 -11	medieval architecture expert & researcher	England
Art Tobin & E. L. Oxman	Lutz, John	'84 - 2	pair of investigators	USA
Arthur Abdel Simpson	Ambler, Eric	'62 - 2	comic rogue and petty crook	England
Arthur Milton	Henderson, L.	'68 - 4	detective sergeant	England
Artie Deemer	Murphy, Dallas	'87 - 3	owner of celebrity spokesdog	New York, NY
Athelstan, Brother & John Cranston	Harding, Paul	'91 - 7	14th century Dominican monk & coroner	London, England
Auguste Lupa	Lescroart, John T.	'86 - 2	British Secret Service agent with U.S. passport	London, England
Augustus Maltravers	Richardson, Robert	'85 - 5	journalist turned playwright and novelist	England
Aurelio Zen	Dibdin, Michael	'88 - 5	Italian police inspector	Rome, Italy
Avram Cohen	Rosenberg, Robert	'91 - 3	recently-retired police officer	Jerusalem, Israel
Axel Speeter, Tommy Fabian, Joe Crow, & Sam O'Gara	Hautman, Pete	'94 - 3	small-town professional gamblers	MN
B				
Baldwin Furnshill & Simon Puttock	Jecks, Michael	'95 - 5	medieval West County bailiff & ex-Templar Knight	Devon, England
Bamsan Kiet	Alexander, Gary	'88 - 6	police supt. in an imaginary country	Far East
Bart Challis	Nolan, William F.	'68 - 2	hard-boiled private eye	Los Angeles, CA
Bea & Lynn Wentworth	Forrest, Richard	'75 - 8	children's book author & state senator	CT
Ben Abbott	Scott, Justin	'94 - 2	ex-Wall Street financier turned realtor	Newbury, CT
Ben Kincaid	Bernhardt, William	'91 - 6	attorney	Tulsa, OK
Ben Lazenby	Melville, James	'95 - 2	British Council official	England
Ben Perkins	Kantner, Rob	'86 - 9	ex-union strike buster turned P.I.	Detroit, MI
Ben Tolliver	Harvey, James Neal	'91 - 5	NYPD lieutenant	New York, NY
Benjamin Franklin	Hall, Robert Lee	'88 - 6	18th century American inventor	London, England
Benny Cooperman	Engel, Howard	'80 - 9	small-town Jewish private eye	Grantham, Ontario, Canada
Benny Freedman	Bass, Milton R.	'86 - 4	private eye	San Diego, CA
Berkley Jordon	Strunk, Frank C.	'91 - 2	roadhouse operator	Buxton, KY
Bernard Samson	Deighton, Len	'83 - 9	middle-aged British spy	London, England
Bernie Gunther	Kerr, Philip	'89 - 3	1930s German private eye	Berlin, Germany

Series Character	Author	1 - #	Occupation	Setting
First Name...cont.				
B...C				
Bernie Rhodenbarr	Block, Lawrence	'77 - 8	professional burglar and bibliophile	New York, NY
Bert Gibbons & Mike Tozzi	Bruno, Anthony	'88 - 6	FBI agents undercover with the Mob	New York, NY
Bert Swain	Nathan, Paul	'94 - 3	PR chief at a medical research center	New York, NY
Bill Donovan	Jahn, Michael	'82 - 5	chief of special investigations	New York, NY
Bill Gastner	Havill, Steven F.	'91 - 5	insomniac undersheriff	Posadas County, NM
Bill Green & George Masters	Clark, Douglas	'69 -27	Scotland Yard detective team	London, England
Bill Hawley	Axler, Leo	'94 - 4	undertaker sleuth	Cleveland, OH
Bill Kinderman	Blatty, William Peter	'71 - 2	police lieutenant	Washington, DC
Bino Phillips	Gray, A. W.	'88 - 4	6' 6" attorney	Dallas, TX
Black Mask Boys	Nolan, William F.	'94 - 2	1930s detective heroes	CA
Blackford "Blacky" Oakes	Buckley, William F.	'76 -11	CIA agent recruited from Yale	Washington , DC
Blanche Hampton	Barnes, Trevor	'89 - 2	Scotland Yard detective superintendent	London, England
Bob "the Nailer" Swagger	Hunter, Stephen	'93 - 2	master sniper	USA
Bob Whitfield	Moore, Richard A.	'81 - 2	newspaper reporter	Atlanta, GA
Bomber Hanson	Champion, David	'95 - 2	ace trial lawyer in California	Angleton, CA
Boysie Oakes	Gardner, John	'64 - 8	cowardly British agent for Special Security	London, England
Brad Smith	Bickham, Jack	'89 - 6	championship tennis player and part-time CIA agent	USA
Brady Coyne	Tapply, William G.	'84 -15	lawyer to the rich who loves to fish	Boston, MA
Brian Guy	Ridgway, Jason	'60 - 4	private eye	New York, NY
Brian McKenna	Mahoney, Dan	'93 - 3	police detective	New York, NY
Bridget O'Toole & Harry Garnish	McConnell, Frank	'83 - 4	private investigators	Chicago, IL
Bubba Mabry	Brewer, Steve	'94 - 4	low-rent P.I.	Albuquerque, NM
Bull Cochran	Nighbert, David F.	'88 - 3	ex-big league pitcher	Knoxville, TN
Burke	Vachss, Andrew H.	'85 - 9	outlaw soldier-of-fortune investigator	New York, NY
Byron "Rugger" O'Toole	Thurston, Robert	'85 - 3	detective of the future	Central America
C				
C. J. Floyd	Greer, Robert O.	'96 - 3	bail bondsman and bounty hunter	Denver, CO
C. W. Sughrue	Crumley, James	'78 - 3	ex-Army spy turned P.I.	MT
Caleb Cluff	North, Gil	'60 -11	Gunnarshaw police sergeant	Yorkshire, England
Calico Jack Walker & Tina Tamiko	Bishop, Paul	'88 - 3	ex-patrol cop & his former rookie partner	Los Angeles, CA
Calista & Plato Marley	Pomidor, Bill	'95 - 4	forensic pathologist wife & family physician husband	Cleveland, OH
Carl Burns	Crider, Bill	'88 - 3	college professor	TX
Carl Heller	Roderus, Frank	'84 - 6	private eye	WY
Carl McCadden	Lusby, Jim	'95 - 2	unconventional Irish police inspector	Waterford, Ireland
Carl Wilcox	Adams, Harold	'81 -14	Depression era sign-painter	Corden, SD
Carlo Arbati	Hill, John Spencer	'95 - 2	policeman poet	Italy
Carmen Pharaoh	Turnbull, Peter	'96 - 1	young woman police detective	York, England
Carroll Dorsey	Lipinski, Thomas	'94 - 3	ex-basketball star law-school dropout P.I.	Pittsburgh, PA
Carston	Kirton, Bill	'95 - 2	detective chief inspector	England
Carver Bascombe	Davis, Kenn	'76 - 8	suave black poet private eye	San Francisco, CA
Cecil Megarry	McEldowney, Eugene	'94 - 3	hard-drinking Irish cop	Belfast, Ireland
Cecil Younger	Straley, John	'92 - 4	alcoholic private eye	Sitka, AK
Chance Purdue	Spencer, Ross H.	'78 - 5	private investigator	Chicago, IL
Charity Ross	Bickham, Jack	'67 - 2	1890s widowed frontier-ranch-owner	Oklahoma City, OK
Charles Carr & Jack Kelly	Petievich, Gerald	'81 - 4	US Treasury agents	Los Angeles, CA
Charles Dickens & Wilkie Collins	Palmer, William J.	'90 - 3	19th century literary celebrities	London, England
Charles Latimer	Ambler, Eric	'39 - 2	British university lecturer turned detective novelist	Turkey
Charles Paris	Brett, Simon	'75 -17	charming alcoholic actor	England
Charles Pol	Williams, Alan	'70 - 3	Marxist bandit and lingerie-shop owner	Paris, France

Series Character	Author	1 - #	Occupation	Setting
First Name...cont.				
C...D				
Charles Ramsay	Ardin, William	'92 - 4	Chelsea antiques dealer	London, England
Charles Ripley	Wainright, John	'66 - 8	head of the uniform branch	Yorkshire, England
Charles Wycliffe	Burley, W. J.	'68 -20	area CID superintendent	West Country, England
Charley Case	Spencer, John	'84 - 3	private eye of the "1997" future	Los Angeles, CA
Charlie Bradshaw	Dobyns, Stephen	'76 - 9	ex-cop ex-stable security guard turned detective	Saratoga Springs, NY
Charlie "Doc" Adams	Boyer, Rick	'82 - 8	oral surgeon	Concord, MA
Charlie Moon & Scott Parris	Doss, James D.	'94 - 4	Ute police sergeant & Anglo colleague	Granite Creek, CO
Charlie Muffin	Freemantle, Brian	'77 -10	working-class British agent	London, England
Charlie Peace	Barnard, Robert	'89 - 4	young black Scotland Yard detective	London, England
Charlie Priest	Pawson, Stuart	'95 - 4	art school graduate turned police detective	Yorkshire, England
Charlie Resnick	Harvey, John	'89 -10	40-something jazz fan police detective	Nottingham, England
Charlie Salter	Wright, Eric	'83 -10	police inspector	Toronto, Ontario
Charlie Sparrow	Ardies, Tom	'71 - 3	handsome American spy	USA
Charlie Willis	Goldberg, Lee	'95 - 2	ex-cop turned TV cop turned studio security agent	Los Angeles, CA
Chester Drum	Marlowe, Stephen	'55 -19	ex-FBI agent turned P.I.	Washington, DC
Chester Fortune	Stone, Thomas H.	'72 - 4	mulatto detective	Los Angeles, CA
Chris Klick	McCall, Wendell	'88 - 2	6' 4" dropout-songwriter turned P.I.	ID
Chris Norgren	Elkins, Aaron	'87 - 3	art museum curator	Seattle, WA
Christopher Paget	Patterson, Richard	'79 - 3	economic crimes special investigator	Washington, DC
Claire Parker & Jack Willows	Gough, Laurence	'87 - 9	police detective partners	Vancouver, Canada
Clare Burtonall, MD	Gash, Jonathan	'97 - 1	hospital physician	England
Clarisse Lovelace & Dan Valentine	Aldyne, Nathan	'80 - 4	gay & straight bar owners	Boston, MA
Claude "Snake" Kirlin & F. T. Zevich	Bourgeau, Art	'80 - 4	magazine freelancer & sidekick	TN
Cliff Dunbar	Harriss, Will	'83 - 2	former English professor turned detective	Los Angeles, CA
Cliff Hardy	Corris, Peter	'80 -15	Aussie private eye	Sydney, Australia
Cliff Janeway	Dunning, John	'92 - 2	cop and rare book expert	Denver, CO
Cliff Lansing & Gabe Hanna	Hackler, Micah S.	'95 - 4	single-father part-time rancher-sheriff & his deputy	NM
Clifford Driscoll	DeAndrea, William	'84 - 4	no-name American spy	New York, NY
Cole McCurtain	Owens, Louis	'91 - 4	Choctaw-Cherokee-Irish-Cajun college professor	Santa Cruz, CA
Coleridge Tucker, III, Jennifer Norrington & Alesandro Di Ganzarello	Drummond, Ivor	'69 - 9	James Bond-like adventuring trio	London, England
Coley Killebrew	Shoemaker, Bill	'94 - 3	ex-jockey turned restaurant owner	Lexington, KY
Colin Harpur & Desmond Iles	James, Bill	'85 -13	detective chief superintendent & detective constable	English seaport
Colin Thane & Phil Moss	Knox, Bill	'57 -21	Scottish Crime Squad officers	Glasgow, Scotland
Columbo	Harrington, William	'93 - 6	rumpled police detective	Los Angeles, CA
Conan Doyle & Houdini	Satterthwait, Walter	'95 - 2	19th century escape artist & writer	London, England
Conan Doyle & Jack Sparks	Frost, Mark	'93 - 2	historical figure & special agent to the Queen	London, England
Craig	Jeffries, Ian	'59 - 3	police sergeant	England
Crang	Batten, Jack	'87 - 4	lawyer and jazz buff	Toronto, Ontario
Cyrus "Moondog" Nygerski	Garfield, Henry	'95 - 2	reclusive writer	Southern, CA
D				
Dallas Henry	Pairo , Preston, III	'91 - 2	sometime-lawyer and motel owner	Ocean City, MD
Dan Connell	Foxx, Jack	'72 - 2	freelance charter pilot	SE Asia
Dan Fortune	Collins, Michael	'67 -17	one-armed Polish-Lithuanian P.I.	New York, NY
Dan Kruger	Cormany, Michael	'88 - 4	private investigator	Chicago, IL
Dan Mallett	Parrish, Frank	'77 - 8	ex-London bank clerk turned handyman-poacher	Medwell Frtrm, England
Dan Rhodes	Crider, Bill	'86 - 9	laid-back sheriff with a motley crew of deputies	Blacklin County, TX
Dan Sheridan	Reed, Barry	'80 - 3	attorney	Boston, MA
Dan Thompson	Feldmeyer, Dean	'94 - 2	small-town Methodist minister	Baird, KY

Series Character	Author	1 - #	Occupation	Setting
First Name...cont.				
D...E				
Dan Valentine & Clarisse Lovelace	Aldyne, Nathan	'80 - 4	gay & straight bar owners	Boston, MA
Daniel Kearney Associates	Gores, Joe	'72 - 5	auto repo & skip-tracing firm	San Francisco, CA
Daphne Matthews & Lou Boldt	Pearson, Ridley	'88 - 4	detective & police psychologist	Seattle, WA
Dave Brandstetter	Hansen, Joseph	'70 -11	gay death-claims investigator	Los Angeles, CA
Dave Garrett	Albert, Neil	'91 - 6	disbarred lawyer turned private eye	Lancaster County, PA
Dave & Mom	Yaffe, James	'88 - 4	ex-cop investigator for public defender & his mother	Mesa Grande, CO
Dave Robicheaux	Burke, James Lee	'87 - 9	deputy sheriff	LA
Dave Strickland	Davis, Thomas D.	'91 - 3	private eye	Azalea, CA
David Audley	Price, Anthony	'70 -19	historian and spy	England
David Brock & Kathy Kolla	Maitland, Barry	'94 - 3	young Scotland Yard detective & her mentor	London, England
David Fyfe	Paul, William	'94 - 3	detective chief inspector	Edinburgh, Scotland
David Garnett	Egleton, Clive	'70 - 3	resistance fighter	England
David Halliday	Taylor, H. Baldwin	'64 - 3	newspaper owner and editor	CT
David Hoyle & Ralph Flensing	Wainright, John	'83 - 2	Lessford police ensemble	Yorkshire, England
David Mallin	Ormerod, Roger	'74 -15	private eye	England
David Small	Kemelman, Harry	'64 -11	rabbi sleuth	Barnard's Crossing, MA
de Gier and Grijpstra	van de Wetering, Janwillem	'75 -13	Dutch police detectives	Amsterdam, Netherlands
Dee Laguerre	Mitchell, Kirk	'95 - 2	Bureau of Land Management ranger	NV
"Deets" Shanahan	Tierney, Ronald	'90 - 4	70-something private eye	Indianapolis, IN
Deidre Nightingale	Adamson, Lydia	'94 - 7	young woman veterinarian	NY
Delbert "Dub" Greenert & Vonna Saucier	Davis, J Madison	'90 - 2	white & black investigator pair	New Orleans, LA
Derek Torry	Gardner, John	'69 - 2	British spy	England
Desmond Iles & Colin Harpur	James, Bill	'85 -13	detective chief superintendent & detective constable	English seaport
Devereaux aka November Man	Granger, Bill	'79 -13	field intelligence agent for R Section	New York, NY
Devlin Kirk	Burns, Rex	'87 - 4	owner of industrial surveillance company	Denver, CO
Devlin Rourke	Grady, James	'85 - 2	police detective sergeant	Baltimore, MD
Devlin Tracy	Murphy, Warren B.	'83 - 7	freelance insurance investigator	Las Vegas, NV
Diana Speed	Gibbs, Tony	'92 - 2	publishing company chief financial officer	New York, NY
DiMaggio	Lupica, Mike	'95 - 1	private eye in the sports world	New York, NY
Dimitri Danilov & William Cowley	Freemantle, Brian	'92 - 2	FBI agent & Russian investigator	Washington DC
Dirk Pitt	Cussler, Clive	'73 -13	special projs dir of nat'l underwater-marine agency	USA
Dismas Hardy	Lescroart, John T.	'89 - 4	ex-cop bartender and ex-ADA turned defense attorney	San Francisco, CA
Doc Ford	White, Randy W.	'90 - 5	ex-operative marine biologist	Sanibel Island, FL
Don Kerry	Ashford, Jeffrey	'61 - 2	British detective inspector	England
Donald McCarry	Boland, John C.	'91 - 3	Wall Street stockbroker	New York, NY
Donald Robak	Hensley, Joe L.	'71 -10	crusading defense attorney and state legislator	Bington, IN
Donald Strachey	Stevenson, Richard	'81 - 6	gay private eye	Albany, NY
Donovan Steele	Masters, J. D.	'89 - 6	police lieutenant	New York, NY
Dottie & Joe Loudermilk	Haywood, Gar A.	'94 - 2	traveling retired black couple	USA
Dougal Munro & Jack Carter	Higgins, Jack	'86 - 2	1940s brigadier & captain	Ireland
Douglas Roper	Hart, Roy	'87 - 8	chief inspector	Dorset, England
Duffy House	Evers, Crabbe	'91 - 5	ex-sportswriter turned investigator	Chicago, IL
E				
E. L. Oxman & Art Tobin	Lutz, John	'84 - 2	pair of investigators	USA
Easy Rawlins	Mosley, Walter	'90 - 7	school maintenance supervisor in Watts	Los Angeles, CA
Ed "Fitz" Fitzgerald	Flynn, Don	'83 - 5	Daily Tribune reporter	New York, NY

Series Character	Author	1 - #	Occupation	Setting
First Name...cont.				
E...F				
Ed Noon	Avallone, Michael	'53 -31	movie-nut private eye	New York, NY
Ed Razoni & William Jackson	Murphy, Warren B.	'73 - 6	police detectives	New York, NY
Ed & Warren Baer	Resnicow, Herbert	'87 - 2	father & son sleuths	Long Island, NY
Edmund "Jupiter" Jones	Fuller, Timothy	'36 - 5	grad student in fine arts	MA
Edward George	Goodrum, Charles	'77 - 4	retired Yale librarian	Washington, DC
Edward Ryan	Milan, Borto	'95 - 2	motorcycle drifter	SE USA
Edward Thackeray & Richard Cribb	Lovesey, Peter	'70 - 8	Victorian policemen	London, England
Edward X. "Iron Balls" Delaney	Sanders, Lawrence	'73 - 4	retired chief of detectives	New York, NY
Eldon Larkin	Kohler, Vince	'90 - 4	small-town newspaper reporter	Port Jerome, OR
Eleanor Roosevelt	Roosevelt, Elliott	'84 -16	1940s First Lady	Washington, DC
Eliot Ness	Collins, Max A., Jr.	'87 - 4	1930s public safety officer	Cleveland, OH
Elvis Cole & Joe Pike	Crais, Robert	'87 - 7	pair of Hollywood private eyes	Los Angeles, CA
Emerson Ward	Sherer, Michael W.	'88 - 4	freelance writer	Chicago, IL
Emily Charters & Jeremy Ransom	Hunter, Fred W.	'94 - 3	cop & his adopted grandmother	London, England
Enrique Alvarez	Jeffries, Roderic	'74 -20	Spanish police inspector	Mallorca, Spain
Eric Parker	Noguchi, Thomas T. w/Arthur Lyons	'80 - 2	forensic pathologist	Los Angeles, CA
Eric Ward	Lewis, Roy	'80 - 9	policeman turned solicitor	England
Esmonde Shaw	McCutchan, Philip	'60 -22	Naval Intelligence turned anti-intelligence	London, England
Essington Holt	Wallace, Robert	'88 - 5	aging adventurer with an interest in art forgery	Sydney, Australia
Ev Franklin	Orenstein, Frank	'83 - 3	advertising executive	New York, NY
Evan Horne	Moody, Bill	'94 - 3	jazz pianist	NV
Evan Tanner	Block, Lawrence	'66 - 7	government agent with permanent insomnia	USA
Ezell "Easy" Barnes	Hilary, Richard	'87 - 4	ex-prize fighter and cop turned P.I.	Newark, NJ
Ezra Brant	Aspler, Tony	'93 - 3	wine journalist	Toronto, Ontario, Canada
F				
F. T. Zevich & Claude "Snake" Kirlin	Bourgeau, Art	'80 - 4	magazine freelancer & sidekick	TN
Fang Mulheisen	Jackson, Jon A.	'77 - 6	police detective sergeant	Detroit, MI
Felix Elizalde	Marshall, William	'86 - 2	detective of the Western District Bureau	Philippines
Fey Croaker	Bishop, Paul	'94 - 4	40-something homicide unit supervisor	Los Angeles, CA
Fidelma	Tremayne, Peter	'94 - 4	7th century Celtic sister & legal advocate	Kildaire, Ireland
Fiona Fitzgerald	Adler, Warren	'81 - 6	homicide detective	Washington, DC
Fitzroy Maclean Angel	Ripley, Mike	'88 - 8	trumpet-playing taxi driver	London, England
Forrest Evers	Judd, Bob	'89 - 5	former race car driver	international
Francis Xavier Flynn	McDonald, Gregory	'77 - 3	tenacious police inspector	Boston, MA
Frank Branco	Daniel, David & Chris Carpenter	'96 - 2	ex-cop turned private eye	Boston, MA
Frank Clemons	Cook, Thomas H.	'88 - 3	private eye	Atlanta, GA
Frank Hastings	Wilcox, Collin	'69 -20	co-commander SFPD homicide	San Francisco, CA
Frank Janek	Bayer, William	'81 - 4	NYPD homicide detective	New York, NY
Frank MacAllister	Perry, Ritchie	'84 - 2	swashbuckling private eye	Brazil
Frank Marvelli & Loretta Kovacs	Bruno, Anthony	'97 - 1	parole officer & partner	NJ
Frank Nolan	Collins, Max A., Jr.	'73 - 7	aging thief	IA
Frank Ryan	Leonard, Elmore	'76 - 2	process server	Detroit, MI
Frank Sessions	Waugh, Hillary	'68 - 3	Manhattan North homicide detective	New York, NY
Fred Carver	Lutz, John	'86 -10	crippled ex-cop P.I.	Del Moray, FL
Fred Fellows	Waugh, Hillary	'59 -11	small-town police chief	Stockford, CT
Fred Taylor	Kilmer, Nicholas	'95 - 3	Vietnam veteran turned art hunter	Cambridge, MA
Fusil & Kerr	Alding, Peter	'67 -14	young police detective & his superior	Fortrow, England

Series Character	Author	1 - #	Occupation	Setting

First Name...cont.

G

Series Character	Author	1 - #	Occupation	Setting
Gabe Hanna & Cliff Lansing	Hackler, Micah S.	'95 -4	single-father part-time rancher-sheriff & his deputy	NM
Gabe Treloar	Roberts, John	'94 - 2	ex-LA cop turned P.I.	OH
Gabe Wagner	Burns, Rex	'75 -11	homicide detective	Denver, CO
Gabriel DuPre	Bowen, Peter	'94 - 4	Metis Indian cattle inspector and sometimes sheriff	MT
Ganesh Ghote	Keating, H. R. F.	'64 -20	Indian police inspector	Bombay, India
Garrett	Cook, Glen	'87 - 8	30-something fantasy private eye	GA
Garth Owen	Pearce, Michael	'88 -10	British head of the secret police	Cairo, Egypt
Garth Ryland	Riggs, John R	'84 -12	small-town newspaper editor	Oakalla, WI
Garwood Plunkett	Estabrook, Barry	'91 - 2	veteran cop	Adirondack Mts, NY
Geoffrey Peace	Jenkins, Geoffrey	'59 - 2	British naval commander	England
George Gently	Hunter, Alan	'55 -44	chief superintendent of Scotland Yard	London, England
George Macrae & Leopold Silver	Scholefield, Alan	'89 - 6	old-fashioned copper & intellectual rookie partner	London, England
George Man	Heller, Keith	'84 - 3	early 18th century parish watchman	London, England
George Masters & Bill Green	Clark, Douglas	'69 -27	Scotland Yard detective team	London, England
George Rogers	Ross, Jonathan	'68 -20	police inspector	Abbotsburn, England
George Sansi	Mann, Paul	'93 - 3	Anglo-Indian attorney	Goa, India
George Smiley	Le Carré, John	'61 - 8	British Intelligence agent and scholar	London, England
Gerald Otley	Waddell, Martin	'66 - 4	amateur adventurer and part-time spy	London, England
Gervase Bret & Ralph Delchard	Marston, Edward	'93 - 5	11th century soldier & lawyer	England
Gideon Lowry	Leslie, John	'94 - 3	private eye	Key West, FL
Gideon Oliver	Elkins, Aaron	'82 - 9	anthropology professor	Port Angeles, WA
Gideon Page	Stockley, Grif	'92 - 5	defense attorney	AR
Gil Disbro	Martin, James E.	'89 - 4	teetotaler private eye	Cleveland , OH
Giles Sullivan & Isabel Macintosh	Resnicow, Herbert	'85 - 5	crossword expert & faculty dean	VT
Gillian Verdean, Jeremy Barr & Patrick O'Mara	Gibbs, Tony	'88 - 3	yacht owner, skipper & mate	Long Island, NY
Gilliant	Wainright, John	'66 - 4	chief constable	Yorkshire, England
Gomer Lloyd & Merlin Parry	Williams, David	'94 - 3	detective chief inspector & detective sergeant	Cardiff, Wales
Goodwin Harper	King, Peter	'96 - 3	food consultant to Scotland Yard	London, England
Gordianus the Finder	Saylor, Steven	'90 - 6	private eye circa 56 B.C.	Rome, Italy
Grace Wu	Dold, Gaylord	'96 - 1	undercover agent for the SFPD and DEA	San Francisco, CA
Grijpstra and de Gier	van de Wetering, Janwillem	'75 -13	Dutch police detectives	Amsterdam, Netherlands
Grover Bramlett	Armistead, John	'94 - 3	small-town sheriff	Sheffield, MS

H

Series Character	Author	1 - #	Occupation	Setting
Hap Collins & Leonard Pine	Lansdale, Joe R.	'90 - 4	straight white & gay black good ol' boys	East TX
Harriet Unwin	Hervey, Evelyn	'84 - 3	19th century spinster governess	England
Harrison Hull	Burns, Ron	'93 - 2	18th century frontier Army captain	VA
Harry Barnett	Goddard, Robert	'90 - 2	middle-aged Englishman caretaker	Greece
Harry Bosch	Connelly, Michael	'92 - 5	homicide detective	Los Angeles, CA
Harry Cain	Kincaid, D.	'86 - 2	unorthodox trial lawyer	Los Angeles, CA
Harry Colderwood	Kelley, Patrick A.	'85 - 5	professional magician	PA
Harry Devlin	Edwards, Martin	'91 - 5	solicitor	Liverpool, England
Harry Feiffer	Marshall, William	'75 -14	chief inspector of Yellowthread Street station	Hong Kong, Hong Kong
Harry Garnish & Bridget O'Toole	McConnell, Frank	'83 - 4	private investigators	Chicago, IL
Harry James Denton	Womack, Steven	'93 - 4	ex-newspaper reporter turned P.I.	Nashville, TN
Harry Kline & Veronica Pace	Luber, Philip	'94 - 2	psychiatrist & FBI agent	Concord, MA
Harry MacNeil	Jeffers, H. Paul	'81 - 3	1930s ex-cop private eye	New York, NY
Harry Palmer	Deighton, Len	'62 - 7	lazy cynical British agent with no name	London, England
Harry Seddall	Mayo, J. K.	'85 - 6	British Intelligence officer	England

Series Character	Author	1 - #	Occupation	Setting
First Name...cont.				
H...I...J				
Harry Starbranch	Bean, Gregory	'95 - 3	burned-out Denver cop turned small-town police chief	Victory, WY
Harry Stoner	Valin, Jonathan	'80 -11	private eye	Cincinnati, OH
Harry Timberlake	Marquis, Max	'91 - 3	aloof detective inspector	London, England
Harvey Ace	Horwitz, Merle	'90 - 2	retired P.I. who plays the horses	Los Angeles, CA
Harvey Blissberg	Rosen, Richard	'84 - 4	ex-baseball player turned P.I.	Boston, MA,
Harvey Krim	Cunningham, E. V.	'64 - 2	NYPD detective	New York, NY
Hazelrigg	Gilbert, Michael	'47 - 6	British police inspector	London, England
Hector Belascoaran Shayne	Taibo, Paco Ignacio, II	'90 - 5	correspondence-school-certified P.I.	Mexico City, Mexico
Henri Castang	Freeling, Nicolas	'74 -16	French policeman	Brussels, Belgium
Henry Dyer	Ring, Raymond H.	'88 - 2	fish and game agent turned P.I.	CO
Henry Lightstone	Goddard, Ken	'92 - 3	National Fish and Wildlife investigator	OR
Henry Peckover	Kenyon, Michael	'81 - 8	Scotland Yard's cockney poet	London, England
Henry Rios	Nava, Michael	'86 - 6	gay Latino ex-alcoholic criminal defense attorney	Los Robles, CA
Henry Scruggs	Conroy, Richard T.	'92 - 3	40-something Smithsonian official	Washington, DC
Henry Spearman	Jevons, Marshall	'78 - 3	Harvard professor	Cambridge, MA
Herbie Kruger	Gardner, John	'79 - 7	British Intelligence senior operative	England
Hobart Lindsay & Marvia Plum	Lupoff, Richard A	'88 - 8	insurance claims adjuster & Berkeley detective	CA
Holland Taylor	Housewright, David	'95 - 2	ex-cop turned private investigator	St. Paul, MN
Horatio T. Parker	Matthews, Lew	'92 - 3	crime reporter for a weekly newspaper	Hampstead, England
Houdini & Conan Doyle	Satterthwait, Walter	'95 - 2	19th century escape artist & writer	London, England
Hugh Corbett	Doherty, P. C.	'86 -10	spy for King Edward I	England
Hugh Morrison	Orenstein, Frank	'84 - 3	small-town cop	NY
Hugo Baron	Brett, John Michael	'63 - 3	British adventurer	England
I				
Ian Chapel	Bishop, Paul	'91 - 2	one-eyed pro soccer goalie turned P.I.	Los Angeles, CA
Irwin M. Fletcher	McDonald, Gregory	'74 -11	reporter turned beach bum socialite	USA
Isaac Sidel	Charyn, Jerome	'75 - 9	former police commissioner	New York, NY
Isabel Macintosh & Giles Sullivan	Resnicow, Herbert	'85 - 5	crossword expert & faculty dean	VT
Ivan Monk	Phillips, Gary	'94 - 3	black private eye	Los Angeles, CA
J				
J. D. Hawkins	Philbrick, W. R.	'85 - 4	wheelchair-bound mystery writer	Boston, MA
J. Pletcher & Raina Lambert	Biggle, Lloyd, Jr.	'87 - 3	pair of private eyes	USA
Jack Blaine	Sarrantonio, Al	'89 - 2	retired Yonkers cop with a P.I. license	New York, NY
Jack Cardigan	Shatner, William	'89 - 8	22nd century ex-cop private eye	Los Angeles, CA
Jack Carter & Dougal Munro	Higgins, Jack	'86 - 2	1940s brigadier & captain	Ireland
Jack Carter	Lewis, Ted	'70 - 3	employee of rackets organization	London, England
Jack Devlin	Clarkson, John	'92 - 3	ex-Secret Service turned security firm investigator	USA
Jack Dwyer	Gorman, Ed	'85 - 6	ex-cop part-time actor and security guard	Cedar Rapids, IA
Jack Eichord	Miller, Rex	'87 - 5	police detective	Chicago, IL
Jack Flippo	Swanson, Doug J.	'94 - 3	recovering deadbeat P.I.	Dallas, TX
Jack Fowler	Malone, Paul	'91 - 3	DEA agent	USA
Jack Frost	Wingfield, R. D.	'84 - 4	Denton Division detective inspector	England
Jack Kelly & Charles Carr	Petievich, Gerald	'81 - 4	US Treasury agents	Los Angeles, CA
Jack Laidlaw	McIlvanney, William	'77 - 4	Scottish police inspector	Glasgow, Scotland
Jack Lynch	Womack, Steven	'90 - 3	PR man and problem solver	New Orleans, LA
Jack McMorrow	Boyle, Gerry	'93 - 4	ex-NY Times reporter turned small town editor	Androscoggin, ME
Jack Oxby	Swan, Thomas	'90 - 3	Scotland Yard art forgery investigator	London, England
Jack Reese	Douglas, John	'87 - 2	photographer	Shawnee, WV
Jack Ross	Schopen, Bernard	'89 - 2	private eye	Reno, NV
Jack Ryan	Clancy, Tom	'84 - 8	CIA analyst	Washington, DC
Jack S. Bard	Downing, Warwick	'90 - 3	defense attorney	Denver, CO
Jack Sparks & Conan Doyle	Frost, Mark	'93 - 2	historical figure & special agent to the Queen	London, England

Series Character	Author	1 - #	Occupation	Setting
First Name ...cont.				
J				
Jack Willows & Claire Parker	Gough, Laurence	'87 - 9	police detective partners	Vancouver, Canada
"Jacko" Jackson	Palmer, Frank	'92 - 8	detective inspector	Leicester, England
Jacob Asch	Lyons, Arthur	'74 -11	Jewish-Episcopal ex-reporter P.I.	Los Angeles, CA
Jacob "Jake" Neuman	Oster, Jerry	'85 - 3	police lieutenant	New York, NY
Jacob Lomax	Allegretto, Michael	'87 - 5	ex-cop turned P.I.	Denver, CO
Jacob Singer	Baxt, George	'84 -12	1940s Hollywood private eye	Los Angeles, CA
Jake Eaton & Watson	Maness, Larry	'95 - 2	P.I. & his superdog	Boston, MA
Jake Hatch	Campbell, Robert	'88 - 2	railroad detective in the USA	Omaha, NB
Jake Lassiter	Levine, Paul	'90 - 7	ex-linebacker turned lawyer	Miami, FL
Jake Phillips	Gaitano, Nick	'95 - 2	homicide detective	Chicago, IL
Jake Sands	Ely, Ron	'94 - 2	professional recoverer of lost things	Santa Barbara, CA
Jake Sinclair & Joanna Blalock	Goldberg, Leonard	'92 - 4	forensic pathologist & police detective	Los Angeles, CA
Jake Small & Albert V. Tretheway	Eddenden, A. E.	'88 - 3	1940s Canadian police officers	Fort York, Ontario, Canada
James Bond	Gardner, John	'81 -14	British agent	London, England
James Boswell Hodge Leonard	Lee, Christopher	'95 - 2	police inspector	Bath, England
James Burlane	Hoyt, Richard	'82 - 8	ex-CIA operative turned private	USA
James Denny aka Dr. Risk	Berger, Bob	'95 - 2	risk theorist and newspaper columnist	New York, NY
James Glowery	Lejeune, Anthony	'87 - 2	British professor	England
James Marley	Ross, Philip	'85 - 2	P.I. investigator	Boston, MA
James Morgan	Coburn, Andrew	'92 - 2	chief of police	Boston suburb, MA
James Moriarty	Gardner, John	'74 - 2	archenemy of Sherlock Holmes	London, England
James Moriarty	Kurland, Michael	'79 - 2	archenemy of Sherlock Holmes	London, England
James Morton & Joseph Bragg	Harrison, Ray	'83 -14	Victorian police officers	England
James Munroe Tallant	York, Andrew	'77 - 4	cricket star turned police commissioner	Grand Flamingo, West Indies
James Odhiambo	Casley, Dennis	'94 - 3	chief inspector	Kenya
James Packard	Galway, Robert C.	'63 -12	British spy	London, England
James Pibble	Dickinson, Peter	'68 - 6	Scotland Yard superintendent	London, England
James Rockford	Kaminsky, Stuart	'96 - 2	low-rent private eye	Los Angeles, CA
Jamie Ramsgill	Bradberry, James	'94 - 3	architect and Princeton professor	Princeton, NJ
Jan Gallagher	Bailey, Jo	'91 - 3	hospital security guard	MN
Jane Bee	Benison, C. C.	'96 - 3	housemaid at Buckingham Palace	London, England
Jane Hildreth & Patricia Huntington	Spicer, Michael	'88 - 4	sexy British secret agent & friend	Cotswolds, England
Jane Meadows & Steve Allen	Allen, Steve	'82 - 8	celebrity crime-solving duo	Los Angeles, CA
Jane Whitefield	Perry, Thomas	'95 - 4	Native American guide	Deganawida, NY
January Esposito	Dowling, Gregory	'85 - 4	American teacher of English	Tuscany, Italy
Jean Montrose	Roe, C. F.	'90 - 8	general practitioner	Scotland
Jean-Louis St-Cyr & Hermane Kohler	Janes, J. Robert	'92 - 8	1940s French police inspector & Gestapo agent	Paris, France
Jean-Paul Gautier	Grayson, Richard	'78 - 9	fin-de-siècle French police inspector	Paris, France
Jefferson "J. W." Jackson	Craig, Philip	'89 - 8	30-something ex-Boston cop	Martha's Vineyard, MA
Jeffrey Dean	Warga, Wayne	'85 - 3	ex-CIA courier-journalist turned rare book dealer	Los Angeles, CA
Jennifer Grey	Jenkins, Jerry	'83 - 6	newspaper reporter and columnist	Chicago, IL
Jennifer Norrington, Alesandro Di Ganzarello & Coleridge Tucker, III	Drummond, Ivor	'69 - 9	James Bond-like adventuring trio	London, England
Jenny McKay	Belsky, Dick	'89 - 4	TV news reporter	New York, NY
Jeremiah St. John	Babula, William	'88 - 5	private investigator	San Francisco, CA
Jeremy Barr, Gillian Verdean & Patrick O'Mara	Gibbs, Tony	'88 - 3	yacht owner, skipper & mate	Long Island, NY
Jeremy Ransom & Emily Charters	Hunter, Fred W.	'94 - 3	homicide detective & his adopted grandmother	Chicago, IL
Jerry Brogan	Breen, Jon	'83 - 4	track announcer at Surfside Meadows	CA
Jerry Kennedy	Higgins, George V.	'80 - 4	criminal defense attorney	Boston, MA

Series Character	Author	1 - #	Occupation	Setting

First Name...cont.

J

Series Character	Author	1 - #	Occupation	Setting
Jessica Coran	Walker, Robert W.	'92 - 5	FBI medical examiner	Washington, DC
Jim Chee	Hillerman, Tony	'80 - 9	Navajo tribal police officer	AZ
Jim Larkin	Russell, Martin	'71 - 5	journalist	England
Jimmy Drover	Granger, Bill	'91 - 3	ex-sportswriter	Chicago, IL
Jimmy Flannery	Campbell, Robert	'86 -10	sewer inspector & Democratic precinct	Chicago, IL
Jimmy Gillespie	Fink, John	'91 - 2	TV reporter and weekend anchor	Chicago, IL
Jimmy "Griff" Griffin	Pairo, Preston, III	'96 - 2	ex-cop investigator for the city attorney	Baltimore, MD
Jimmy Jenner	Milne, John	'86 - 3	English private eye	England
Joanna Blalock & Jake Sinclair	Goldberg, Leonard	'92 - 4	forensic pathologist & police detective	Los Angeles, CA
Jock Patterson	Walker, Peter N.	'71 - 4	British constable	England
Joe Bain	Vance, John H.	'66 - 2	sheriff	San Rodrigo Co, CA
Joe Binney	Livingston, Jack	'82 - 4	hearing-impaired private eye	New York, NY
Joe Crow, Sam O'Gara, Axel Speeter & Tommy Fabian	Hautman, Pete	'94 - 3	small-town professional gamblers	MN
Joe Cullen	Oster, Jerry	'90 - 4	Internal Affairs police sergeant	New York, NY
Joe Dante	Newman, C.	'86 - 9	maverick cop	New York, NY
Joe DiGregorio	Margolis, Seth	'91 - 2	ex-Long Island cop turned Manhattan P.I.	New York, NY
Joe Gregory & Anthony Ryan	Dee, Ed	'94 - 3	NYPD detective partners	New York, NY
Joe Gunther	Mayor, Archer	'88 - 8	homicide detective	Brattleboro, VT
Joe Hannibal	Dundee, Wayne	'88 - 3	blue-collar P.I.	Rockford, IL
Joe Keller	DeMille, Nelson	'75 - 3	NYPD homicide detective	New York, NY
Joe Keough	Randisi, Robert J.	'95 - 2	NYPD detective	New York, NY
Joe Lawless	Philbin, Tom	'85 - 9	Felony Squad commander in the Bronx	New York, NY
Joe Leaphorn	Hillerman, Tony	'70 - 3	Navajo tribal police officer	AZ
Joe & Dottie Loudermilk	Haywood, Gar A.	'94 - 2	traveling retired black couple	USA
Joe Narrabone	Gilbert, Michael	'95 - 2	WWI policeman turned British secret agent	London, England
Joe Pike & Elvis Cole	Crais, Robert	'87 - 7	pair of Hollywood private eyes	Los Angeles, CA
Joe Reddman	Downing, Warwick	'74 - 3	private investigator	Denver, CO
Joe Ryker	DeMille, Nelson	'74 - 3	NYPD homicide detective	New York, NY
Joe Sixsmith	Hill, Reginald	'93 - 3	black private detective	England
Joe Wilder	Phillips, T. J.	'95 - 2	struggling playwright and novelist	New York, NY
John Becker	Wiltse, David	'91 - 6	FBI agent	New York, NY
John Blackwood "Blackie" Ryan	Greeley, Andrew M.	'85 - 8	Catholic priest	Chicago, IL
John Bogdanovic	Jeffers, H. Paul	'95 - 3	aide-de-camp to NYPD Chief of Detectives	New York, NY
John Bryant	Grayson, Richard	'55 - 4	British businessman	England
John Caine	Knief, Charles	'96 - 2	Navy SEAL turned P.I.	Pearl Harbor, HI
John "Chant" Sinclair	Cross, David	'86 - 3	renegade super ninja	New York, NY
John Comaday & Larry Cohen	Cunningham, E. V.	'65 - 2	police commissioner & Manhattan DA's 1st assistant	New York, NY
John Cranston & Brother Athelstan	Harding, Paul	'91 - 7	14th century Dominican monk & coroner	London, England
John Crow	Lewis, Roy	'69 - 8	British police inspector	England
John Crown	Harknett, Terry	'74 - 3	chief superintendent	China
John Cunningham	Hammond, Gerald	'89 - 8	war hero and hunting dog trainer	Scotland
John Deal	Standiford, Les	'93 - 4	building contractor	Miami, FL
John Denson	Hoyt, Richard	'80 - 7	flaky private eye	Seattle, WA
John Dobie	Cory, Desmond	'91 - 3	math professor	Cardiff, Wales
John Dortmunder	Westlake, Donald E.	'70 - 9	comic thief	New York, NY
John Fielding	Alexander, Bruce	'94 - 3	blind magistrate & founder of first police force	London, England
John Francis Cuddy	Healy, Jeremiah	'84 -11	Army police lieutenant turned private investigator	Boston, MA
John George Davis	Ripley, Jack	'71 - 4	small-town constable	England
John Locke	Barnao, Jack	'87 - 3	ex-Grenadier guard turned private security agent	Toronto, Ontario, Canada
John Marshall Tanner	Greenleaf, Stephen	'79 -12	non-practicing attorney P.I.	San Francisco, CA

Series Character	Author	1 - #	Occupation	Setting

First Name...cont.

J...K

John Morris	Logue, John	'79 - 5	Associated Press sportswriter	Atlanta, GA,
John Quincannon	Pronzini, Bill	'85 - 2	19th century private eye	San Francisco, CA
John Rankin	Grady, James	'84 - 2	private investigator	Washington, DC
John Raven	MacKenzie, Donald	'76 - 9	unorthodox detective inspector	London, England
John Rebus	Rankin, Ian	'87 - 8	detective sergeant	Edinburgh, Scotland
John Rodrigue	Grissom, Ken	'88 - 3	one-eyed Creole salvager	Caribbean
John Samson	Tripp, Miles	'73 -12	private investigator	England
John Spencer Lubbock	Cooper, Brian	'91 - 4	retired World War II D.C.I.	Norfolk, England
John Tibbett	Payne, Laurence	'69 - 2	petty thief turned reluctant hero	London, England
John Tracer	Andrus, Jeff	'94 - 2	family-man sleuth	Monterey, CA
John Wells	Peterson, Keith	'88 - 5	newspaper reporter	New York, NY
John Wilkes	Schoonover, W.	'90 - 2	defense attorney	New York, NY
Johnelle Baker	Miles, John	'94 - 2	Choctaw sheriff	Tenoclock, CO
Johnny Black	Steed, Neville	'89 - 2	1930s private detective	England
Johnny Fedora	Cory, Desmond	'51 -16	British agent	England
Jonas Wilde	York, Andrew	'66 - 9	British secret agent	England
Jonathan Argyll	Pears, Iain	'91 - 6	British art dealer	England
Jonathan Craythorne	Douglas, Arthur	'86 - 3	British Army major	England
Jonathan Gaunt	MacLeod, Robert	'70 -10	external auditor for the Queen	Edinburgh, Scotland
Jonathan Steele	Newton, Michael	'78 - 2	LAPD homicide detective	Los Angeles, CA
Jordan Poteet	Abbott, Jeff	'94 - 4	small-town librarian	Mirabeau, TX
Joseph Bragg & James Morton	Harrison, Ray	'83 -14	Victorian police officers	England
Joseph Flynn & Martin Tanner	Newton, Michael	'90 - 9	FBI agents with VICAP	Los Angeles, CA
Joseph Radkin	Biderman, Bob	'85 - 4	investigative journalist	San Francisco, CA
Joseph Shanley & Sammy Golden	Webb, Jack	'52 - 9	Jewish police detective & Catholic priest	Los Angeles, CA
Joshua Croft	Satterthwait, Walter	'89 - 5	wisecracking P.I.	Santa Fe, NM
Joshua Rabb	Parrish, Richard	'93 - 4	1940s attorney	Tucson, AZ
Judy Best	Cook, Stephen	'93 - 2	weight-lifting police officer	England
Julian "Digger" Burroughs	Murphy, Warren B.	'82 - 4	freelance insurance investigator	Las Vegas, NV

K

Kane Jackson	Arden, William	'68 - 5	industrial espionage specialist	NJ
Karen Kovac & Terry Flynn	Granger, Bill	'80 - 4	Special Squad detectives	Chicago, IL
Kathryn Swinbrooke	Grace, C. L.	'93 - 4	15th cent. physician, apothecary, death investigator	Canterbury, England
Kathy "Caz" Flood	Keegan, Alex	'93 - 4	detective constable	Brighton, England
Kathy Kolla & David Brock	Maitland, Barry	'94 - 3	young Scotland Yard detective & her mentor	London, England
Keith Calder	Hammond, Gerald	'79 -23	gunsmith and sport shooter	Scotland
Keith Gersen	Vance, Jack	'64 - 5	hunter of nonhuman killers	USA
Ken Tanaka	Furutani, Dale	'96 - 2	Asian American computer programmer	Los Angeles, CA
Kerr & Fusil	Alding, Peter	'67 -14	young police detective & his superior	Fortrow, England
Kevin Fitzgerald	Topor, Tom	'78 - 2	private eye	New York, NY
Kevin Kerney	McGarrity, Michael	'96 - 2	ex-chief of detectives	Santa Fe, NM
Kevin Manwaring & Vicki Garcia	Irvine, Robert	'94 - 1	field producer & television reporter	Los Angeles, CA
Kidd & Luellen	Sandford, John	'89 - 2	computer whiz & thief	MN
Kieran Lanahan	Daly, Conor	'95 - 3	lawyer turned country club golf pro	Westcehster County, NY
Kinky Friedman	Friedman, Kinky	'86 -10	country & western singer turned sleuth	New York, NY
Kit DeLeeuw	Katz, Jon	'92 - 4	Wall Street shark turned suburban detective	Rochambeau, NJ
Kit Fielding	Francis, Dick	'85 - 2	jockey	England
Kit Franklyn & Andy Broussard	Donaldson, D. J.	'88 - 6	criminal psychologist & medical examiner	New Orleans, LA
Kurt Muller	Zigal, Thomas	'95 - 2	ex-hippie single-father sheriff	Aspen, CO

Series Character	Author	1 - #	Occupation	Setting

First Name...cont.

L

Series Character	Author	1 - #	Occupation	Setting
Larry Cohen & John Comaday	Cunningham, E. V.	'65 - 2	police commissioner & Manhattan DA's 1st assistant	New York, NY
Larry Cole	Holton, Hugh	'94 - 4	black police commander	Chicago, IL
Larry Vernon	Bateson, David	'54 - 6	British private eye	England
Laura Michaels	Miles, John	'93 - 3	retirement center social worker	Timberlake, OK
Lauren Crowder & Alan Gregory	White, Stephen	'91 - 5	practicing psychologist & attorney	Boulder, CO
Lee Beckett	Crowe, John	'72 - 6	private eye	Buena Costa Co., CA
Lennox	Wainright, John	'74 -10	detective chief inspector	Yorkshire, England
Leo Bloodworth & Serendipity Dahlquist	Lochte, Dick	'85 - 2	gum-snapping 15-yr-old girl & grumpy 50-something P.I.	Los Angeles, CA
Leo Gold	Finkelstein, Jay	'96 - 2	30-something Jewish P.I.	New York, NY
Leo Guild	Gorman, Ed	'87 - 4	1890s bounty hunter	Western USA
Leo Haggerty	Schutz, Benjamin	'85 - 6	rough and tough P.I.	Washington, DC
Leo Haig	Block, Lawrence	'70 - 4	private investigator	New York, NY
Leo Waterman	Ford, G. M.	'95 - 4	wisecracking private eye	Seattle, WA
Leonard Pine & Hap Collins	Lansdale, Joe R.	'90 - 4	straight white & gay black good ol' boys	East TX
Leopold Silver & George Macrae	Scholefield, Alan	'89 - 6	old-fashioned copper & intellectual rookie partner	London, England
Leric	Busby, Roger	'69 - 5	Scotland Yard inspector	London, England
Leroy Powder	Lewin, Michael Z.	'76 - 3	cop friend of Albert Samson's	Indianapolis, IN
Les Norton	Barrett, Robert G.	'85 - 7	nightclub bouncer	Sydney, Australia
Lew Griffin	Sallis, James	'92 - 3	black private eye	New Orleans, LA
Lewis Cody	Slusher, William S.	'95 - 3	sheriff	Hunter County, VA
Lewis Cole	DuBois, Brendan	'94 - 2	magazine writer	Tyler Beach, NH
Liam Devlin	Higgins, Jack	'75 - 4	1940s IRA hero	Ireland
Lincoln Rhyme & Amelia Sachs	Deaver, Jeffery	'97 - 1	disabled ex-head of NYPD forensics & rookie beat cop	New York, NY
Linda Grey	Cory, Desmond	'51 - 4	British female	England
Lloyd Hopkins	Ellroy, James	'84 - 3	detective sergeant in the Rampart Division	Los Angeles, CA
Lobo Blacke & Quinn Booker	DeAndrea, William	'95 - 2	crippled ex-frontier lawman & his biographer	Le Four, WY
Loren Mensing	Nevins, Francis, Jr	'75 - 3	law school professor	St. Louis, MO
Loren Swift	Hornig, Doug	'84 - 4	Vietnam vet private eye	Charlottesville, VA
Loretta Kovacs & Frank Marvelli	Bruno, Anthony	'97 - 1	parole officer & partner	NJ
Lou Boldt & Daphne Matthews	Pearson, Ridley	'88 - 4	detective & police psychologist	Seattle, WA
Louis Monroe	Kent, Bill	'89 - 3	Don Quixote-style cop	Atlantic City, NJ
Lovejoy	Gash, Jonathan	'77 -19	antiques expert and forger	East Anglia, England
Lucas Davenport	Sandford, John	'89 - 8	police detective and war games designer	Minneapolis, MN
Lucas Holt	Meyer, Charles	'95 - 2	Episcopal church pastor	Austin, TX
Lucy Beck	Conway, Peter	'72 - 3	female sleuth	England
Lucy Shannon	Belsky, Dick	'85 - 2	newspaper reporter	New York, NY
Lucy Wayles	Adamson, Lydia	'96 - 2	ex-librarian birdwatcher	New York, NY
Luellen & Kidd	Sandford, John	'89 - 2	computer whiz & thief	MN
Luis Balam	Alexander, Gary	'93 - 2	ex-traffic cop turned tour operator	Yucatan, Mexico
Luis Bernal	Serafin, David	'79 - 6	Spanish police superintendent	Spain
Luis Montez	Ramos, Manuel	'93 - 4	attorney and former Chicano activist	Denver, CO
Luke Dunlop	Corris, Peter	'92 - 2	ex-cop working witness protection	Sydney, Australia
Luke Williamson & Masey Baldridge	Brewer, James D.	'94 - 4	Yankee riverboat captain & Confederate veteran	Southern USA
Lunghi family	Lewin, Michael Z.	'94 - 1	3-generation private-eye family	Bath, England
Lupe Garcia	Allyn, Doug	'89 - 2	tough Latino cop	Detroit, MI
Lyle	Wainright, John	'79 - 6	detective inspector	Yorkshire, England
Lyon & Bea Wentworth	Forrest, Richard	'75 - 8	children's book author & state senator	CT

Series Character	Author	1 - #	Occupation	Setting

First Name...cont.

M

Series Character	Author	1 - #	Occupation	Setting
Mac Fontana	Emerson, Earl	'88 - 5	ex-firefighter and arson investigator	Staircase, WA
Maddy & Alex Phillips	Zimmerman, R. D.	'92 - 3	brother & blind forensic psychiatrist sister	Upper Peninsula, MI
Malachy P. Foley	Walker, David J.	'95 - 2	jazz piano-playing P.I.	Chicago, IL
Mallory	Collins, Max A. Jr.	'83 - 5	small-town student mystery writer	IA
Margaret Barlow	Osborn, David	'89 - 3	50-something freelance journalist	USA
Margaret Binton	Barth, Richard	'78 - 7	70-something little old lady	New York, NY
Margo Franklin & Philip Spence	Jenkins, Jerry	'79 -13	pair of private eyes	Chicago, IL
Mario Balzic	Constantine, K. C.	'72 -13	small-town police chief	Rocksburg, PA
Mark Bradley & Rayford Goodman	Cutler, Stan	'91 - 4	jaded macho P.I. & gay writer of celebrity biographies	Hollywood, CA
Mark Preston	Chambers, Peter	'61 -36	hard-nosed private eye	Monkton City, CA
Mark Renzler	Engleman, Paul	'83 - 5	ex-baseball player private eye	Chicago, IL
Mark Savage	Payne, Laurence	'82 - 5	movie star turned private eye	USA
Mark Treasure	Williams, David	'76 -17	merchant banker	London, England
Mark Twain & Wentworth Cabot	Heck, Peter J.	'95 - 2	19th century American author & his secretary	USA
Marlene Ciampi & Roger "Butch" Karp	Tanenbaum, R.	'87 - 9	1970s Criminal Courts Bureau chief & assistant DA	New York, NY
Martin Coterell	Trench, John	'53 - 3	erudite British archaeologist	England
Martin Fender	Sublett, Jesse	'89 - 3	skip tracer	Austin, TX
Martin Tanner & Joseph Flynn	Newton, Michael	'90 - 9	FBI agents with VICAP	Los Angeles, CA
Marvia Plum & Hobart Lindsay	Lupoff, Richard A	'88 - 8	insurance claims adjuster & Berkeley detective	CA
Mary Teresa Dempsey	Quill, Monica	'81 - 9	5' 2" 200-lb. nun	Chicago, IL
Masao Masuto	Cunningham, E. V.	'67 - 7	Japanese-American police detective	Beverly Hills, CA
Masey Baldridge & Luke Williamson	Brewer, James D.	'94 - 4	Yankee riverboat captain & Confederate veteran	Southern USA
Mateesie Kitologitak	Young, Scott	'90 - 2	Inuit RCMP Inspector	NW Territories, Canada
Matt Cobb	DeAndrea, William	'78 - 8	network television executive	New York, NY
Matt Helm	Hamilton, Donald	'60 -27	American superspy	USA
Matt Minogue	Brady, John	'88 - 5	Irish police detective	Dublin, Ireland
Matt Riordan	Huebner, Frederick	'86 - 5	burned-out lawyer turned investigator	Seattle, WA
Matt Scudder	Block, Lawrence	'76 -13	unlicensed reformed alcoholic P.I.	New York, NY
Matthew Coll	Lewis, Roy H.	'80 - 5	antiquarian book dealer	England
Matthew Hope	McBain, Ed	'77 -12	attorney	FL
Matthew Jenkyn	Doherty, P. C.	'88 - 2	15th century soldier, double-agent spy	England
Matthew Stock	Tourney, Leonard	'80 - 8	17th century town constable and clothier	Chelmsford, England
Mavis Lashley	Nordan, Robert	'89 - 3	little old lady Sunday School teacher	Southern USA
Max Addams	Leitz, David	'96 - 3	proprietor of trout-fishing lodge	Northern VT
Max Farne	Butler, Richard	'75 - 2	luxury boat salesman and spy	Santa Margherita, Italy
Max Thursday	Miller, Wade	'47 - 6	private eye	San Diego, CA
Max Van Larsen & Sylvia Plotkin	Baxt, George	'67 - 3	author-teacher & police detective	New York, NY
McCloud	Wilcox, Collin	'73 - 2	New Mexico marshall	New York, NY
Mel Pickett	Wright, Eric	'96 - 1	60-something retired Toronto cop	Larch River, Ontario, Canada
Melita Pargeter	Brett, Simon	'86 - 5	widow of a thief	England
Merlin Parry & Gomer Lloyd	Williams, David	'94 - 3	detective chief inspector & detective sergeant	Cardiff, Wales
Merlin Richards	Miles, Keith	'97 - 1	1920s young Welsh architect	Phoenix, AZ
Michael Carolina	Briody, Thomas G.	'95 - 2	former TV investigative reporter	Providence, RI
Michael Rhineheart	Birkett, John	'88 - 2	private eye	Louisville, KY
Michael Wyman	Cook, Bob	'85 - 3	philosophy professor and MI6 agent	London, England
Michelle Mitchell	Allyn, Doug	'95 - 3	single mother and dive shop owner	Huron Harbor, MI
Mick "Brew" Axbrewder	Stephens, Reed	'80 - 3	unlicensed private eye	Puerta del Sol, CA
Mickey Rawlings	Soos, Troy	'94 - 5	1910s journeyman second baseman	USA
Mickey Zondi & Tromp Kramer	McClure, James	'71 - 8	Afrikaner cop & Bantu detective assistant	South Africa
Mike Devlin	Lindsay, Paul	'92 - 3	FBI agent	Detroit, MI

Series Character	Author	1 - #	Occupation	Setting
First Name...cont.				
M...N				
Mike Faraday	Copper, Basil	'66 -52	hard-boiled private eye who quotes Herrick	Los Angeles, CA
Mike Flint	Healy, R. Austin	'95 - 2	ex-CIA and NYC cop	Saratoga, NY
Mike Haller	Byrd, Max	'81 - 3	P.I. specializing in missing persons	San Francisco, CA
Mike Hammer	Spillane, Mickey	'47 -13	super-patriot private investigator	New York, NY
Mike Tozzi & Bert Gibbons	Bruno, Anthony	'88 - 6	FBI agents undercover with the Mob	New York, NY
Milan Jacovich	Roberts, Les	'88 - 9	blue-collar Slovenian P.I. with a master's degree	Cleveland, OH
Miles Jacoby	Randisi, Robert J.	'82 - 6	boxer turned P.I.	New York, NY
Milo Milodragovitch	Crumley, James	'75 - 2	ex-Army spy and hard-drinking P.I.	MT
Milo Turner	Nevins, Francis, Jr	'86 - 2	con man private eye	St. Louis, MO
Mitch Roberts	Dold, Gaylord	'87 - 9	1950s private eye	Wichita, KS
Mitch Tobin	Coe, Tucker	'66 - 5	ex-cop P.I.	Queens, NY
Modesty Blaise	O'Donnell, Peter	'65 -11	gorgeous crime fighter for British Intelligence	London, England
Mom & Dave	Yaffe, James	'88 - 4	ex-cop investigator for public defender & his mother	Mesa Grande, CO
Moroni Traveler	Irvine, Robert	'88 - 8	non-Mormon ex-football player private eye	Salt Lake City, UT
Morse	Dexter, Colin	'75 -12	chief inspector	England
Moses Wine	Simon, Roger L.	'73 - 8	ex-hippie Jewish private eye	Los Angeles, CA
Mr. Dee	Cory, Desmond	'61 - 2	Englishman	England
Muldoon & Tillman	Marshall, William	'88 - 2	turn-of-the-century policemen	New York, NY
Murray Glick & Andy Sussman	Katz, Michael J.	'87 - 3	P.I. & sportscaster buddy	Chicago, IL
Myron Bolitar	Coben, Harlan	'95 - 4	injured basketball player turned sports agent	New York, NY
N				
Nameless	Pronzini, Bill	'71 -24	pulp collector P.I. with no name	San Francisco, CA
Nason "Nase" Nichols	Thomson, M.	'96 - 2	private eye	New York, NY
Nate Heller	Collins, Max A., Jr.	'83 - 8	1930s ex-cop turned private eye	Chicago, IL
Nate Rosen	Levitsky, Ronald	'91 - 4	civil rights lawyer	Washington, DC
Neal Carey	Winslow, Don	'91 - 5	youthful pickpocket turned P.I.	New York, NY
Neal Donahue & Victoria "Tory" Lennox	Gibbs, Tony	'96 - 1	harbor cop and Coast Guard Lt.	Santa Barbara, CA
Nebraska	Reynolds, William J	'84 - 6	part-time P.I. trying to write	Omaha, NE
Neil Hockaday	Adcock, Thomas	'89 - 6	NYPD street crimes detective	New York, NY
Neil Marshall	Hemlin, Tim	'96 - 3	graduate student poet	Houston, TX
Niccolo Benedetti	DeAndrea, William	'79 - 3	world-renowned criminologist-professor	Sparta, NY
Nicholas Bracewell	Marston, Edward	'88 - 9	stage manager for Elizabethan acting company	London, England
Nicholas Chirke	Doherty, P. C.	'94 - 4	young medieval lawyer	England
Nicholas Segalla	Dukthas, Ann	'94 - 3	time-traveling scholar	England
Nick Delvecchio	Randisi, Robert J.	'87 - 2	private eye	Brooklyn, NY
Nick Duffy	Kavanagh, Dan	'80 - 4	bisexual ex-cop P.I.	London, England
Nick Hoffman	Raphael, Lev	'96 - 2	gay college professor	Michiganapolis, MI
Nick Miller	Higgins, Jack	'65 - 2	Central Division detective	London, England
Nick Polo	Kennealy, Jerry	'87 -10	private eye	San Francisco, CA
Nick Rhea	Rhea, Nicholas	'79 -15	police constable father of four	Aidensfield, England
Nick Sharman	Timlin, Mark	'88 -12	hard-living ex-cop private eye	London, England
Nick Stefanos	Pelecanos, George	'92 - 5	1950s bartender P.I.	Washington, DC
Nora Callum	McCall, Thomas	'93 - 2	one-legged cop	Chicago, IL
Nuala Ann McGrail	Greeley, Andrew M.	'94 - 2	young Irish immigrant psychic and singer	Chicago, IL

Series Character	Author	1 - #	Occupation	Setting

First Name...cont.

O

Series Character	Author	1 - #	Occupation	Setting
O'Malley, Supt.	Kenyon, Michael	'70 - 3	comic Irish cop	Ireland
Oddie	Barnard, Robert	'90 - 1	inner city schoolteacher	London, England
Orin Boyd	Westermann, John	'90 - 2	Nassau County uniformed cop	Long Island, NY
Orson Cheever	Russell, Alan	'96 - 1	homicide detective	San Diego, CA
Owen Keane	Faherty, Terence	'91 - 5	ex-seminarian and law firm researcher	Boston, MA
Owen Smith	Barnett, James	'78 - 6	chief superintendent	England

P

Series Character	Author	1 - #	Occupation	Setting
P Division	Turnbull, Peter	'81 - 9	police detectives	Glasgow, Scotland
Paddy Moretti	Sherburne, James	'80 - 5	1890s sportswriter	USA
Parker	Stark, Richard	'62 -17	cold-blooded professional thief	New York, NY
Patricia Huntington & Jane Hildreth	Spicer, Michael	'88 - 4	sexy British secret agent & friend	Cotswolds, England
Patrick Hardy	Meyers, Martin	'75 - 5	private eye	New York, NY
Patrick Kenzie & Angela Gennaro	Lehane, Dennis	'94 - 3	private detectives	Boston, MA
Patrick O'Mara, Gillian Verdean, & Jeremy Barr	Gibbs, Tony	'88 - 3	yacht owner, skipper & mate	Long Island, NY
Patrick Petrella	Gilbert, Michael	'93 - 1	Metropolitan Police inspector	London, England
Paul Bannerman	Maxim, John	'89 - 4	private investigations firm owner	Westport, CT
Paul Benjamin	Garfield, Brian	'72 - 2	vigilante murderer	AZ
Paul Chavasse	Fallon, Martin	'62 - 6	globe-trotting British spy	London, England
Paul Devlin	Heffernan, William	'88 - 5	NYPD detective	New York, NY
Paul Madriani	Martini, Steve	'92 - 5	defense attorney	CA
Paul Marston & Angel Cantini	Eversz, Robert	'88 - 2	private eye & female prize fighter	Los Angeles, CA
Paul Shaw	Sadler, Mark	'70 - 6	private eye	NY
Paul Turner	Zubro, Mark	'91 - 4	gay Chicago cop & father of two teenage sons	Chicago, IL
Paul Whelan	Raleigh, Michael	'90 - 5	40-something black cop turned P.I.	Chicago, IL
Peggy O'Neill	Lake, M. D.	'89 - 9	university campus cop	MN
Penelope Warren	Allen, Garrison	'94 - 3	ex-Marine mystery bookstore owner	Empty Creek, AZ
Pepper	Smith, Frank A.	'69 - 2	Canadian police superintendent	Toronto, Ontario°
Perry Trethowan	Barnard, Robert	'81 - 5	Scotland Yard inspector	London, England
Pete McGrath	Brett, Michael	'66 -10	wise-cracking private eye	New York, NY
Peter Ashton	Egleton, Clive	'93 - 5	British spy	England
Peter Boone	Jaspersohn, William	'95 - 2	ex-Red Sox pitcher turned P.I.	VT
Peter Bragg	Lynch, Jack	'82 - 7	private eye	San Francisco, CA
Peter Cutler Sargeant II	Box, Edgar	'52 - 3	public relations consultant	New York, NY
Peter Diamond	Lovesey, Peter	'91 - 5	ex-cop	Bath, England
Peter Finley	Lupica, Mike	'86 - 3	investigative TV reporter	New York, NY
Peter Lawson	Bolton, Melvin	'84 - 3	British spy	England
Peter Macklin	Estleman, Loren D.	'84 - 3	hit man for the mob	Detroit, MI
Peter Marklin	Steed, Neville	'86 - 5	toyshop owner and antique toy collector	Dorset, England
Peter Marlow	Hone, Joseph	'71 - 4	incompetent British spy	England
Peter Maxwell	Trow, M. J.	'94 - 2	widowed teacher and golden-hearted cynic	England
Peter McGarr	Gill, Bartholomew	'77 -12	Irish chief of detectives	Ireland
Peter Pascoe & Andrew Dalziel	Hill, Reginald	'70 -15	pair of police inspectors	Yorkshire, England
Peter Tangent	Sanders, Lawrence	'76 - 2	troubleshooter for American oil co	Africa
Pharoah Love	Baxt, George	'66 - 5	gay black NYPD detective	New York, NY
Phil Moony	Engleman, Paul	'93 - 2	ex-firefighter private eye	Chicago, IL
Phil Moss & Colin Thane	Knox, Bill	'57 -21	Scottish Crime Squad officers	Glasgow, Scotland
Philip Fletcher	Shaw, Simon	'90 - 4	British thespian and killer	London, England
Philip Marlowe	Parker, Robert B.	'89 - 2	private eye	Los Angeles, CA
Philip Quest	Townend, Peter	'71 - 3	photographer	Sardinia
Philip Spence & Margo Franklin	Jenkins, Jerry	'79 -13	pair of private eyes	Chicago, IL
Philis	Perry, Ritchie	'72 -14	Brazilian smuggler turned British Intelligence agent	Brazil
Pierre-Ange "Pete" Sawyer	Albert, Marvin H.	'86 - 9	French-speaking American P.I.	Paris, France

Series Character	Author	1 - #	Occupation	Setting
First Name...cont.				
P...Q...R				
Piers Roper	Follett, Ken	'75 - 2	industrial spy	London, England
Plato & Calista Marley	Pomidor, Bill	'95 - 4	forensic pathologist wife & family physician husband	Cleveland, OH
Pommes Frites & Aristide Pamplemousse	Bond, Michael	'83 - 8	gourmet test-eater & his bloodhound	La Douce, France
Porfiry Rostnikov	Kaminsky, Stuart	'81 -11	Russian police inspector	Moscow, Russia
Povin, General	Trenhaile, John	'81 - 3	Soviet spy	Hong Kong, Hong Kong
Q				
Quarry	Collins, Max A., Jr.	'76 - 5	psychotic Vietnam vet and hired killer	IA
Quinn Booker & Lobo Blacke	DeAndrea, William	'95 - 2	crippled ex-frontier lawman & his biographer	Le Four, WY
Quinn Parker	Zimmerman, Bruce	'89 - 4	phobia therapist	San Francisco, CA
Quinsigamond	O'Connell, Jack	'92 - 3	decaying New England factory town	Massachusetts
R				
R. J. Brook	Bogart, Stephen H.	'95 - 2	celebrity-son private eye	New York, NY
Rachel Gold	Kahn, Michael A.	'88 - 5	defense attorney	St. Louis, MO
Rachel Hennings	Breen, Jon	'84 - 2	bookstore owner	Los Angeles, CA
Rafferty	Duncan, W. Glenn	'87 - 6	ex-cop private eye	Dallas, TX
Raina Lambert & J. Pletcher	Biggle, Lloyd, Jr.	'87 - 3	pair of private eyes	USA
Rainbow Porter	Campbell, Harlen	'93 - 1	Vietnam veteran turned detective	NM
Ralph Delchard & Gervase Bret	Marston, Edward	'93 - 5	11th century soldier & lawyer	England
Ralph Flensing & David Hoyle	Wainright, John	'83 - 2	Lessford police ensemble	Yorkshire, England
Ray Bartell	Reid, Robert Sims	'88 - 2	police detective	Rozette, MT
Ray Crawley	Corris, Peter	'85 - 7	Federal Security Agency director	Sydney, Australia
Rayford Goodman & Mark Bradley	Cutler, Stan	'91 - 4	jaded macho P.I. & gay writer of celebrity biographies	Hollywood, CA
Raylan Givens	Leonard, Elmore	'93 - 2	federal marshall	FL
Reid Bennett & Sam	Wood, Ted	'83 -10	police chief & German Shepherd	Murphy's Harbor, Ontario
Remo Williams aka The Destroyer	Murphy, Warren B.	'71 -80	ex-cop turned government enforcer	New York, NY
Rene Shade	Woodrell, Dan	'86 - 3	cop in a bayou town	St. Bruno, LA
Reuben Frost	Murphy, Haughton	'86 - 7	retired Wall Street attorney	New York, NY
Richard Browning	Corris, Peter	'87 - 8	Aussie private eye with Hollywood ties	Sydney, Australia
Richard Cribb & Edward Thackeray	Lovesey, Peter	'70 - 8	Victorian policemen	London, England
Richard Graham	Welcome, John	'58 - 5	English gentleman secret agent	England
Richard Hagen	Janes, J. Robert	'91 - 1	1940s diamond dealer	Antwerp, Belgium
Richard Harrison	Anthony, Michael	'90 - 2	Anglican church official	England
Richard Malcolm	Grady, James	'74 - 2	CIA analyst and grad student	Washington, DC
Richard Michaelson	Bowen, Michael	'90 - 4	retired Foreign Service officer	Washington, DC
Richard Patton, Insp.	Ormerod, Roger	'83 -11	British police inspector	England
Richard Thornhill	Taylor, Andrew	'94 - 3	1950s detective inspector	Lydmouth, England
Richard Verrel as Blackshirt	Graeme, Roderic	'52 -20	romantic thief and best-selling author	England
Rick Decker	DeBrosse, Jim	'88 - 3	investigative reporter	Cincinnati, OH
Robert Blayde	Wainright, John	'75 - 4	police superintendent	Yorkshire, England
Robert Christopher	Irvine, Robert	'74 - 4	television reporter	Los Angeles, CA
Robert Koesler	Kienzle, William X.	'79 -19	Catholic priest	Detroit, MI
Robert Lee Hunter	Sauter, Eric	'83 - 3	30-something wealthy P.I.	DE
Robert Miles	Everson, David H.	'87 - 7	baseball minor leaguer turned P.I.	Springfield, IL
Robert "Mongo" Frederickson	Chesbro, George	'77 -13	dwarf criminology prof and former circus gymnast	New York, NY
Robert Payne	Gorman, Ed	'94 - 2	psychological profile investigator	New Hope, IA
Robert Skinner	Jardine, Quintin	'93 - 5	high-ranking cop	Edinburgh, Scotland
Robert Stark	Schorr, Mark	'88 - 3	private investigator	USA
Roger "Butch" Karp & Marlene Ciampi	Tanenbaum, R.	'87 - 9	1970s Criminal Courts Bureau chief & assistant DA	New York, NY
Roger Dowling, Father	McInerny, Ralph	'77 -17	St. Hilary's parish priest	Fox River, IL
Roger Shallot	Clynes, Michael	'91 - 6	agent of Cardinal Wolsey	England
Roger Tallis	Rossiter, John	'70 - 7	British agent with a police background	England

Series Character	Author	1 - #	Occupation	Setting
First Name...cont.				
R...S				
Roman Grey	Smith, Martin Cruz	'71 - 2	Gypsy art dealer	New York, NY
Roy Rickman	Craig, David	'68 - 3	Home Office administrator	London, England
Ruby Dark	Most, Bruce W.	'96 - 2	bail bondswoman	Denver, CO
Rune	Deaver, Jeffery	'89 - 3	NYPD detective	New York, NY
Rupert Quinn	Williams, Alan	'62 - 2	swashbuckling English courier	North Africa
Ryder Malone	Rider, J. W.	'86 - 2	private eye	Jersey City, NJ
S				
Sally Tepper	King, Frank	'88 - 2	unemployed actress with five dogs	New York, NY
Sam & Reid Bennett	Wood, Ted	'83 -10	police chief & German Shepherd	Murphy's Harbor, Ontario
Sam Birkett	Payne, Laurence	'62 - 3	humorous Scotland Yard inspector	London, England
Sam Dean	Phillips, Mike	'89 - 4	Jamaica-born black journalist	London, England
Sam Hunter	Morse, L. A.	'82 - 2	private eye	Los Angeles, CA
Sam O'Gara, Axel Speeter, Joe Crow & Tommy Fabian	Hautman, Pete	'94 - 3	small-town professional gamblers	MN
Sam Space	Nolan, William F.	'71 - 2	private eye on Mars	Mars
Sam Turner	Baker, John	'95 - 2	newly-sober private eye	York, England
Sam Watchman	Garfield, Brian	'72 - 2	part Navajo State trooper	AZ
Sammy Golden & Joseph Shanley	Webb, Jack	'52 - 9	Jewish police detective & Catholic priest	Los Angeles, CA
Sandrine & Thomas Curry	Bowen, Michael	'89 - 3	1960s husband & wife detective team	New York, NY
Saxon	Roberts, Les	'87 - 6	actor private eye	Los Angeles, CA
Scobie Malone	Cleary, Jon	'66 -13	family-man police inspector	Sydney, Australia
Scott Carpenter & Tom Mason	Zubro, Mark	'89 - 6	high school teacher & pro baseball player	Chicago, IL
Scott Elliott	Faherty, Terence	'96 - 3	1940s failed actor turned private eye	Hollywood, CA
Scott Jordan	Masur, Harold Q.	'47 -11	criminal defense attorney	New York, NY
Scott Mitchell	Harvey, John	'76 - 4	private eye	England
Scott Moody	Oliver, Steve	'96 - 2	ex-mental patient turned P.I.	Spokane, WA
Scott Parris & Charlie Moon	Doss, James D.	'94 - 4	Ute police sergeant & Anglo colleague	Granite Creek, CO
Sean Dillon	Higgins, Jack	'92 - 6	IRA enforcer turned British special agent	Ireland
Sean Ryan	Cleeve, Brian	'64 - 4	ex-Irish revolutionary turned British Intelligence	England
Serendipity Dahlquist & Leo Bloodworth	Lochte, Dick	'85 - 2	gum-snapping 15-yr-old girl & grumpy 50-something P.I.	Los Angeles, CA
Sharon Hays	Gregory, Sarah	'96 - 2	defense attorney	Dallas, TX
Sheila Roath & Stephen Bellecroix	Craig, David	'70 - 2	British agents	England
Shell Scott	Prather, Richard	'50 -36	6' 2" ex-Marine crew-cut private eye	Los Angeles, CA
Shelly Lowenkopf	Fliegel, Richard	'88 - 7	Allerton Avenue precinct cop	New York, NY
Sheridan Wesley	Waugh, Hillary	'47 - 3	private investigator	New York, NY
Sherlock Holmes	Estleman, Loren D.	'78 - 2	19th century consulting detective	London, England
Shifty Lou Anderson	Murray, William	'84 - 9	professional magician and horse-player	Southern, CA
Sholto Joseph Lestrade	Trow, M. J.	'85 -16	19th century Scotland Yard inspector	London, England
Sid Halley	Francis, Dick	'65 - 3	injured steeplechase jockey turned P.I.	England
Sidney Walsh	Hunt, Richard	'93 - 4	detective chief inspector	Cambridge, England
Simeon Grist	Hallinan, Timothy	'89 - 6	four-degreed P.I.	Los Angeles, CA
Simon Ark	Hoch, Edward D.	'71 - 3	ancient hounder of Satan	New York, NY
Simon Bognor	Heald, Tim	'73 -10	special investigator to the British Board of Trade	England
Simon Jaffe aka Red Diamond	Schorr, Mark	'83 - 3	cab-driving pulp collector turned P.I.	New York, NY
Simon Kaye	Waugh, Hillary	'80 - 6	private eye	New York, NY
Simon Puttock & Baldwin Furnshill	Jecks, Michael	'95 - 5	medieval West County bailiff & ex-Templar Knight	Devon, England
Simon Shard	McCutchan, Philip	'74 -11	Scotland Yard supt. 2nd'd to the Foreign Office	London, England

Series Character	Author	1 - #	Occupation	Setting

First Name...cont.

S...T

Series Character	Author	1 - #	Occupation	Setting
Simon Young	Trenhaile, John	'86 - 3	British Intelligence officer	Hong Kong, Hong Kong
Skylar Whitfield	McDonald, Gregory	'95 - 2	small-town good-ol'-boy	TN
Socrates Fortlow	Mosley, Walter	'97 -ss	philosophical ex-con	CA
Sonny Baca	Anaya, Rudolfo	'95 - 2	part-time rodeo rider private eye	Albuquerque, NM
Spenser	Parker, Robert B.	'73 -24	ex-boxer, ex-state cop turned P.I.	Boston, MA
Stan Kraychik	Michaels, Grant	'90 - 5	gay hairdresser	Boston, MA
Stanley Hastings	Hall, Parnell	'87 -13	married actor and private eye	New York, NY
Stanley Moodrow	Solomita, Stephen	'88 - 6	cop turned private eye	New York, NY
Stephen Bellecroix & Sheila Roath	Craig, David	'70 - 2	British agents	England
Stephen Drake	Wilcox, Collin	'67 - 2	newspaper reporter with ESP	San Francisco, CA
Steve Allen & Jane Meadows	Allen, Steve	'82 - 8	celebrity crime-solving duo	Los Angeles, CA
Steve Wayne	Harknett, Terry	'62 - 9	private investigator	Far East
Steve Winslow	Hailey, J. P.	'88 - 5	courtroom attorney	New York, NY
Steven Kirk	Hornig, Doug	'87 - 2	burned-out government agent	Charlottesville, VA
Stewart "Hoagy" Hoag	Handler, David	'88 - 8	celebrity ghostwriter	USA
Stick Foster	Robinson, Kevin	'91 - 3	paraplegic newspaper reporter	Orlando, FL
Stokes Moran aka Kyle Malachi	McGaughey, Neil	'94 - 4	syndicated mystery critic	Tipton, CT
Stone Barrington	Woods, Stuart	'91 - 3	suave ex-cop attorney	New York, NY
Stoney Winston	Stinson, Jim	'85 - 4	low-budget film maker	Los Angeles, CA
Streeter	Stone, Michael	'96 - 2	P.I. bounty hunter	Denver, CO
Stuart Haydon	Lindsey, David L.	'83 - 5	homicide detective	Houston, TX
Stuart Mallory	Roat, Ronald Clair	'91 - 3	private eye	Lansing, MI
Stuart Winter	Russell, Alan	'90 - 2	private eye	San Francisco, CA
Sylvia Plotkin & Max Van Larsen	Baxt, George	'67 - 3	author-teacher & police detective	New York, NY

T

Series Character	Author	1 - #	Occupation	Setting
T. D. Stash	Philbrick, W. R.	'87 - 3	unlicensed private eye	Key West, FL
T. Moore "Mo" Bowdre	Page, Jake	'93 - 5	blind redneck sculptor	AZ
Tad Anders	Allbeury, Ted	'74 - 3	Polish-British agent	England
Taffin	Mallett, Lyndon	'80 - 3	fast-with-his-fists debt collector	Lasherham, Ireland
Taggart Roper	Sanders, William	'93 - 3	Cherokee writer and private eye	Tulsa, OK
Talos Cord	MacLeod, Robert	'64 - 6	United Nations troubleshooter	New York, NY
Tammi Randall	Wyrick, E. L.	'94 - 2	small-town lawyer	Patsboro, GA
Teddy Roosevelt	Alexander, L.	'86 - 3	1890s police commissioner	New York, NY
Terry Flynn & Karen Kovac	Granger, Bill	'80 - 4	Special Squad detectives	Chicago, IL
Terry Manion	Lochte, Dick	'92 - 2	private eye	New Orleans, LA
Terry Sneed	Newman, G. F.	'70 - 3	bent police inspector	England
Tetsuo Otani	Melville, James	'79 -13	Japanese police superintendent	Kobe, Japan
The Shadow	Grant, Maxwell	'64 - 8	P.I. of unknown identity	USA
Theo Kojak	Miller, Victor B.	'74 - 9	NYPD cop	New York, NY
Thomas Black	Emerson, Earl	'85 -10	bicycling enthusiast P.I.	Seattle, WA
Thomas Maynard	Honig, Donald	'96 - 2	Civil War Army captain	Dakota Territory
Thomas & Sandrine Curry	Bowen, Michael	'89 - 3	1960s husband & wife detective team	New York, NY
Thomas Theron	Reeves, Robert	'85 - 2	history professor	Boston, MA
Thorn	Hall, James W.	'87 - 6	eco-avenger P.I.	Key Largo, FL
Tiger Mann	Spillane, Mickey	'64 - 5	freelance spy for a private right-wing group	New York, NY
Tiller Galloway	Poyer, David	'89 - 4	ex-Navy SEAL turned salvage diver	Cape Hatteras, NC
Tillman & Muldoon	Marshall, William	'88 - 2	turn-of-the-century policemen	New York, NY
Tim Lacey	Wilson, Derek	'94 - 6	ex-SAS officer and security firm owner	London, England
Tim Simpson	Malcolm, John	'84 -12	financial consultant turned art investment specialist	London, England
Timothy Cone	Sanders, Lawrence	'87 - 2	Wall Street financial detective	New York, NY

Series Character	Author	1 - #	Occupation	Setting
First Name...cont.				
T...U...V...W				
Timothy Waverly	Kakonis, Tom	'88 - 3	would-be professor turned card sharp ex-con	Palm Beach, FL
Tina Tamiko & Calico Jack Walker	Bishop, Paul	'88 - 3	ex-patrol cop & his former rookie partner	Los Angeles, CA
Tobin	Gorman, Ed	'87 - 2	hot-tempered movie critic	New York, NY
Toby Parkman	Washburn, Stan	'95 - 2	quietly heroic cop	San Francisco, CA
Toby Peters	Kaminsky, Stuart	'77 -20	1940s Hollywood private investigator	Los Angeles, CA
Todd Mills	Zimmerman, R. D.	'95 - 2	gay TV news reporter	Minneapolis, MN
Tom Bethany	Doolittle, Jerome	'90 - 6	political consultant and former wrestler	Cambridge, MA
Tom Hickey	Kuhlken, Ken	'91 - 3	1940s P.I. and restaurateur	San Diego, CA
Tom Jones	Puckett, Andrew	'87 - 3	health investigator	England
Tom Mason & Scott Carpenter	Zubro, Mark	'89 - 6	high school teacher & pro baseball player	Chicago, IL
Tom Ragnon	Harper, Richard	'86 - 2	cop who lives in a trailer	AZ
Tom Talley	Ross, Philip	'86 - 2	American CIA operative	Europe
Tommy Fabian, Axel Speeter, Joe Crow & Sam O'Gara	Hautman, Pete	'94 - 3	small-town professional gamblers	MN
Tony Cassella	Beinhart, Larry	'86 - 3	high-stakes private eye	New York, NY
Tony Lonto	Johnson, E. Richard	'68 - 2	police detective	USA
Tony Lowell	Ayres, E. C.	'94 - 3	photographer private eye	FL
Tony Rome	Rome, Anthony	'60 - 3	ex-cop gambler private eye	Miami, FL
Tony Rowley	Busby, Roger	'85 - 3	Scotland Yard inspector	London, England
Townsend Reeves	Vincent, Lawrence M.	'89 - 2	radiologist with a ballerina girlfriend	Kansas City, MO
Tromp Kramer & Mickey Zondi	McClure, James	'71 - 8	Afrikaner cop & Bantu detective assistant	South Africa
Truman Smith	Crider, Bill	'91 - 4	private eye	Galveston, TX
Tubby Dubonnet	Dunbar, Tony	'94 - 3	bon vivant defense attorney	New Orleans, LA
TV newsroom series	Handberg, Ron	'92 - 3	newsroom crew	Minneapolis, MN
Tweed	Forbes, Colin	'82 - 9	British Secret Service 2nd-in-command	London, England
Tyler Vance	Harvey, Clay	'96 - 2	ex-operative turned family man	NC
U				
Urbino Macintyre	Sklepowich, Edward	'90 - 5	American expatriate and biographer	Venice, Italy
V				
Van der Valk	Freeling, Nicolas	'62 -14	intellectual Dutch police inspector	Amsterdam, Netherlands
Veil Kendry	Chesbro, George	'86 - 2	painter and adventurer	New York, NY
Veronica Pace & Harry Kline	Luber, Philip	'94 - 2	psychiatrist & FBI agent	Concord, MA
Vic Daniel	Pierce, David M.	'89 - 7	offbeat 6' 7-1/4" cut-rate P.I.	Los Angeles, CA
Vicki Garcia & Kevin Manwaring	Irvine, Robert	'94 - 1	field producer & television reporter	Los Angeles, CA
Victor Carl	Lashner, William	'95 - 2	hard-boiled lawyer	Philadelphia, PA
Victoria & Wolfgang Mozart	Bastable, Bernard	'95 - 2	19th century composer-teacher & British princess	London, England
Victoria "Tory" Lennox & Neal Donahoe	Gibbs, Tony	'96 - 1	harbor cop and Coast Guard Lt.	Santa Barbara, CA
Vincent Dowling	Mullen, Jack	'95 - 2	police sergeant	San Diego, CA
Vinnie Altobelli	Bass, Milton R.	'93 - 2	ex-cop coronary survivor P.I.	San Bernadino, CA
Virgil Proctor	Knight, J. D.	'95 - 2	bounty hunter P.I.	USA
Vonna Saucier & Delbert "Dub" Greenert	Davis, J Madison	'90 - 2	white & black investigator pair	New Orleans, LA
W				
Walsh	Gorman, Ed	'91 - 1	50-something private eye	Cedar Rapids, IA
Wang Anzhuang	West, Christopher	'94 - 2	Public Security Bureau inspector	Beijing, China
Warren & Ed Baer	Resnicow, Herbert	'87 - 2	father & son sleuths	Long Island, NY
Watson & Jake Eaton	Maness, Larry	'95 - 2	P.I. & his superdog	Boston, MA
Webb Carrick	Knox, Bill	'64 -15	chief officer of the Scottish Fishery Protection Service	Scotland

Series Character	Author	1 - #	Occupation	Setting
First Name...cont.				
W...Y...Z				
Wentworth Cabot & Mark Twain	Heck, Peter J.	'95 - 2	19th century American author & his secretary	USA
Whistler	Campbell, Robert	'86 - 4	sentimental private eye	Hollywood, CA
Wil Hardesty	Barre, Richard	'95 - 3	Vietnam vet and greybeard surfer turned P.I.	Southern, CA
Wiley Moss	Barrett, Jr., Neal	'96 - 2	graphic artist for the Smithsonian	Washington, DC
Wilkie Collins & Charles Dickens	Palmer, William J.	'90 - 3	19th century literary celebrities	London, England
William Aveyard	Fraser, James	'68 - 9	ambitious village police inspector	England
William Clarence Verity	Selwyn, Francis	'74 - 5	portly Victorian police sergeant	London, England
William Cowley & Dimitri Danilov	Freemantle, Brian	'92 - 2	FBI agent & Russian investigator	Washington, DC
William Dougal	Taylor, Andrew	'82 - 8	post-grad student and security firm employee	England
William Falconer	Morson, Ian	'94 - 3	13th century university regent master	Oxford, England
William Jackson & Ed Razoni	Murphy, Warren B.	'73 - 6	police detectives	New York, NY
Wolfgang Mozart & Victoria	Bastable, Bernard	'95 - 2	19th century composer-teacher & British princess	London, England
Wyatt	Disher, Garry	'91 - 5	Aussie bank robber	Melbourne, Australia
Wyatt Storme	Ripley, W. L.	'93 - 3	Vietnam vet ex-NFL star	N Branson, MO
Wynsome "Wyn" Lewis	Kaufelt, David A.	'93 - 3	ex-Manhattan real estate attorney	Wagg's Neck Hrb, NY
Y				
Yuri Nevsky	Gat, Dimitri	'82 - 2	information specialist	Pittsburgh, PA
Z				
Zachary Grayson	Tierney, Ronald	'93 - 1	gay author of trendy cookbooks	San Francisco, CA

SETTINGS 4

Setting	Author	1 - #	Series Character	Occupation
Africa *[see also Egypt and Kenya]*				
	Sanders, Lawrence	'72 - 2	Peter Tangent	troubleshooter for American oil company
North Africa	Williams, Alan	'62 - 2	Rupert Quinn	swashbuckling English courier
South Africa	McClure, James	'71 - 8	Tromp Kramer & Mickey Zondi	Africaner cop & Bantu detective assistant
Asia *[see also China, Hong Kong, Japan, and Philippines]*				
Far East	Alexander, Gary	'88 - 6	Bamsan Kiet	police supt. in an imaginary country
Far East	Harknett, Terry	'62 - 9	Steve Wayne	private investigator
Southeast Asia	Foxx, Jack	'72 - 2	Dan Connell	freelance charter pilot
Australia				
Melbourne	Disher, Garry	'91 - 5	Wyatt	Aussie bank robber
Sydney	Barrett, Robert G.	'85 - 7	Les Norton	nightclub bouncer
Sydney	Cleary, Jon	'66 -13	Scobie Malone	family-man police inspector
Sydney	Corris, Peter	'80 -15	Cliff Hardy	Aussie private eye
Sydney	Corris, Peter	'85 - 7	Ray Crawley	Federal Security Agency director
Sydney	Corris, Peter	'87 - 8	Richard Browning	Aussie private eye with Hollywood ties
Sydney	Corris, Peter	'92 - 2	Luke Dunlop	ex-cop working witness protection
Sydney	Wallace, Robert	'88 - 5	Essington Holt	aging adventurer with an interest in art forgery
Belgium				
Antwerp	Janes, J. Robert	'91 - 1	Richard Hagen	1940s diamond dealer
Brussels	Freeling, Nicolas	'74 -16	Henri Castang	French policeman
Brazil				
	Perry, Ritchie	'84 - 2	Frank MacAllister	swashbuckling private eye
	Perry, Ritchie	'72 -14	Philis	Brazilian smuggler turned British Intelligence agent
Canada				
British Columbia (BC)				
Vancouver	Gough, Laurence	'87 - 9	Jack Willows & Claire Parker	police detective partners
NW Territories (NWT)				
	Young, Scott	'90 - 2	Mateesie Kitologitak	Inuit RCMP Inspector

Setting	Author	1 - #	Series Character	Occupation

Canada...cont.

Ontario (ON)

Setting	Author	1 - #	Series Character	Occupation
Fort York	Eddenden, A. E.	'88 - 3	Albert V. Tretheway & Jake Small	1940s Canadian police officers
Grantham	Engel, Howard	'80 - 9	Benny Cooperman	small-town Jewish private eye
Larch River	Wright, Eric	'96 - 1	Mel Pickett	60-something retired Toronto cop
Murphy's Harbor	Wood, Ted	'83 -10	Reid Bennett & Sam	small-town police chief & German Shepherd
Toronto	Aspler, Tony	'93 - 3	Ezra Brant	wine journalist
Toronto	Barnao, Jack	'87 - 3	John Locke	ex-Grenadier guard turned private security agent
Toronto	Batten, Jack	'87 - 4	Crang	lawyer and jazz buff
Toronto	Smith, Frank A.	'69 - 2	Pepper, Supt.	Canadian police superintendent
Toronto	Wright, Eric	'83 -10	Charlie Salter	police inspector

Caribbean [see also West Indies]

Setting	Author	1 - #	Series Character	Occupation
	Grissom, Ken	'88 - 3	John Rodrigue	one-eyed Creole salvager
Grand Flamingo	York, Andrew	'77 - 4	James Munroe Tallant	cricket star turned police commissioner

Central America [see also Mexico]

Setting	Author	1 - #	Series Character	Occupation
	Thurston, Robert	'85 - 3	Byron "Rugger" O'Toole	detective of the future

China [see also Asia]

Setting	Author	1 - #	Series Character	Occupation
	Harknett, Terry	'74 - 3	John Crown	chief superintendent
Beijing	West, Christopher	'94 - 2	Wang Anzhuang	Public Security Bureau inspector

Egypt [see also Africa]

Setting	Author	1 - #	Series Character	Occupation
Cairo	Pearce, Michael	'88 -10	Garth Owen	British head of the secret police

England [see also Scotland and Wales]

Setting	Author	1 - #	Series Character	Occupation
	Allbeury, Ted	'74 - 3	Tad Anders	Polish-British agent
	Ambler, Eric	'62 - 2	Arthur Abdel Simpson	comic rogue and petty crook
	Anthony, Michael D.	'90 - 2	Richard Harrison	Anglican church official
	Ashford, Jeffrey	'61 - 2	Don Kerry	British detective inspector
	Barnett, James	'78 - 6	Owen Smith	chief superintendent
	Bateson, David	'54 - 6	Larry Vernon	British private eye
	Bolton, Melvin	'84 - 3	Peter Lawson	British spy
	Brett, John Michael	'63 - 3	Hugo Baron	British adventurer
	Brett, Simon	'75 -17	Charles Paris	charming alcoholic actor
	Brett, Simon	'86 - 5	Melita Pargeter	widow of a thief
	Cleeve, Brian	'64 - 4	Sean Ryan	ex-Irish revolutionary turned British Intelligence
	Clynes, Michael	'91 - 6	Roger Shallot	agent of Cardinal Wolsey
	Conway, Peter	'72 - 3	Lucy Beck	female sleuth
	Cook, Stephen	'93 - 2	Judy Best	weight-lifting police officer
	Cory, Desmond	'51 -16	Johnny Fedora	British agent
	Cory, Desmond	'51 - 4	Linda Grey	British female
	Cory, Desmond	'61 - 2	Mr. Dee	Englishman
	Craig, David	'70 - 2	Stephen Bellecroix & Sheila Roath	British agents
	Dexter, Colin	'75 -12	Chief Insp. Morse	chief inspector
	Doherty, P. C.	'86 -10	Hugh Corbett	spy for King Edward I
	Doherty, P. C.	'88 - 2	Matthew Jenkyn	15th century soldier, double-agent spy
	Doherty, P. C.	'94 - 4	Nicholas Chirke	young medieval lawyer
	Douglas, Arthur	'86 - 3	Jonathan Craythorne	British Army major
	Dukthas, Ann	'94 - 3	Nicholas Segalla	time-traveling scholar
	Egleton, Clive	'93 - 5	Peter Ashton	British spy
	Egleton, Clive	'70 - 3	David Garnett	resistance fighter
	Francis, Dick	'65 - 3	Sid Halley	injured steeplechase jockey turned P.I.
	Francis, Dick	'85 - 2	Kit Fielding	jockey
	Fraser, James	'68 - 9	William Aveyard	ambitious village police inspector
	Gardner, John	'69 - 2	Derek Torry	British spy

Setting	Author	1 - #	Series Character	Occupation
England...cont.				
	Gardner, John	'79 - 7	Herbie Kruger	British Intelligence senior operative
	Gash, Jonathan	'97 - 1	Clare Burtonall	hospital physician
	Graeme, Roderic	'52 -20	Richard Verrel as Blackshirt	romantic thief and best-selling author
	Grayson, Richard	'55 - 4	John Bryant	British businessman
	Harrison, Ray	'83 -14	Joseph Bragg & James Morton	Victorian police officers
	Harvey, John	'76 - 4	Scott Mitchell	private eye
	Heald, Tim	'73 -10	Simon Bognor	special investigator to the British Board of Trade
	Henderson, L.	'68 - 4	Arthur Milton	detective sergeant
	Hervey, Evelyn	'84 - 3	Harriet Unwin	19th century spinster governess
	Hill, Reginald	'93 - 3	Joe Sixsmith	black private detective
	Hone, Joseph	'71 - 4	Peter Marlow	incompetent British spy
	Jeffries, Ian	'59 - 3	Sgt. Craig	police sergeant
	Jenkins, Geoffrey	'59 - 2	Geoffrey Peace	British naval commander
	Kirton, Bill	'95 - 2	Carston	detective chief inspector
	Lejeune, Anthony	'87 - 2	James Glowery	British professor
	Lescroart, John T.	'86 - 2	Auguste Lupa	British Secret Service agent with U.S. passport
	Lewis, Roy	'69 - 8	John Crow	British police inspector
	Lewis, Roy	'80 - 9	Eric Ward	policeman turned solicitor
	Lewis, Roy	'82 -11	Arnold Landon	medieval architecture expert & researcher
	Lewis, Roy H.	'80 - 5	Matthew Coll	antiquarian book dealer
	Marston, Edward	'93 - 5	Ralph Delchard & Gervase Bret	11th century soldier & lawyer
	Mayo, J. K.	'85 - 6	Harry Seddall	British Intelligence officer
	Melville, James	'95 - 2	Ben Lazenby	British Council official
	Milne, John	'86 - 3	Jimmy Jenner	English private eye
	Murray, Stephen	'87 - 5	Alec Stainton	British police inspector
	Myles, Simon	'74 - 2	"Apples" Carstairs	private eye
	Newman, G. F.	'70 - 3	Terry Sneed	bent police inspector
	Ormerod, Roger	'74 -15	David Mallin	private eye
	Ormerod, Roger	'83 -11	Richard Patton	British police inspector
	Pears, Iain	'91 - 6	Jonathan Argyll	British art dealer
	Price, Anthony	'70 -19	David Audley	historian and spy
	Puckett, Andrew	'87 - 3	Tom Jones	health investigator
	Richardson, Robert	'85 - 5	Augustus Maltravers	journalist turned playwright and novelist
	Ripley, Jack	'71 - 4	John George Davis	small-town constable
	Rossiter, John	'70 - 7	Roger Tallis	British agent with a police background
	Russell, Martin	'71 - 5	Jim Larkin	journalist
	Steed, Neville	'89 - 2	Johnny Black	1930s private detective
	Taylor, Andrew	'82 - 8	William Dougal	post-grad student and security firm employee
	Trench, John	'53 - 3	Martin Coterell	erudite British archaeologist
	Tripp, Miles	'73 -12	John Samson	private investigator
	Trow, M. J.	'94 - 2	Peter Maxwell	widowed teacher and golden-hearted cynic
	Walker, Peter N.	'71 - 4	Jock Patterson	British constable
	Welcome, John	'58 - 5	Richard Graham	English gentleman secret agent
	Wingfield, R. D.	'84 - 4	Jack Frost	Denton Division detective inspector
	York, Andrew	'66 - 9	Jonas Wilde	British secret agent
Abbotsburn	Ross, Jonathan	'68 -20	George Rogers	police inspector
Bath	Lee, Christopher	'95 - 2	James Boswell Hodge Leonard	police inspector
Bath	Lewin, Michael Z.	'94 - 1	Lunghi family	3-generation private-eye family
Bath	Lovesey, Peter	'91 - 5	Peter Diamond	ex-cop
Brighton	Keegan, Alex	'93 - 4	Kathy "Caz" Flood	detective constable
Cambridge	Hunt, Richard	'93 - 4	Sidney Walsh	detective chief inspector
Canterbury	Grace, C. L.	'93 - 4	Kathryn Swinbrooke	15th cent. physician, apothecary, death investigator
Cotswolds	Spicer, Michael	'88 - 4	Jane Hildreth & Patricia Huntington	sexy British secret agent & friend
Devon	Jecks, Michael	'95 - 5	Simon Puttock & Baldwin Furnshill	medieval West County bailiff & ex-Templar Knight
Dorset	Hart, Roy	'87 - 8	Douglas Roper	chief inspector
Dorset	Steed, Neville	'86 - 5	Peter Marklin	toyshop owner and antique toy collector
East Anglia	Gash, Jonathan	'77 -19	Lovejoy	antiques expert and forger
Essex	Tourney, Leonard	'80 - 8	Matthew Stock	17th century town constable and clothier
Fortrow	Alding, Peter	'67 -14	Kerr & Fusil	young police detective & his superior

Setting	Author	1 - #	Series Character	Occupation
England...cont.				
Hampstead	Matthews, Lew	'92 - 3	Horatio T. Parker	crime reporter for a weekly newspaper
Leicester	Palmer, Frank	'92 - 8	"Jacko" Jackson	detective inspector
Liverpool	Edwards, Martin	'91 - 5	Harry Devlin	solicitor
London	Alexander, Bruce	'94 - 3	John Fielding	blind magistrate & founder of first police force
London	Ardin, William	'92 - 4	Charles Ramsay	Chelsea antiques dealer
London	Barnard, Robert	'81 - 5	Perry Trethowan	Scotland Yard inspector
London	Barnard, Robert	'89 - 4	Charlie Peace	young black Scotland Yard detective
London	Barnard, Robert	'90 - 1	Oddie	inner city schoolteacher
London	Barnes, Trevor	'89 - 2	Blanche Hampton	Scotland Yard detective superintendent
London	Bastable, Bernard	'95 - 2	Wolfgang Mozart & Princess Victoria	19th century composer-teacher & British princess
London	Benison, C. C.	'96 - 3	Jane Bee	housemaid at Buckingham Palace
London	Busby, Roger	'69 - 5	Leric	Scotland Yard inspector
London	Busby, Roger	'85 - 3	Tony Rowley	Scotland Yard inspector
London	Clark, Douglas	'69 -27	George Masters & Bill Green	Scotland Yard detective team
London	Cook, Bob	'85 - 3	Michael Wyman	philosophy professor and MI6 agent
London	Craig, David	'68 - 3	Roy Rickman	Home Office administrator
London	Deighton, Len	'62 - 7	Harry Palmer	lazy cynical British agent with no name
London	Deighton, Len	'83 - 9	Bernard Samson	middle-aged British spy
London	Dickinson, Peter	'68 - 6	James Pibble	Scotland Yard superintendent
London	Drummond, Ivor	'69 - 9	Jennifer Norrington, Alesandro Di Ganzarello & Coleridge Tucker, III	James Bond-like adventuring trio
London	Estleman, Loren D.	'78 - 2	Sherlock Holmes	19th century consulting detective
London	Fallon, Martin	'62 - 6	Paul Chavasse	globe-trotting British spy
London	Follett, Ken	'75 - 2	Piers Roper	industrial spy
London	Forbes, Colin	'82 - 9	Tweed	British Secret Service 2nd-in-command
London	Freemantle, Brian	'77 -10	Charlie Muffin	working-class British agent
London	Frost, Mark	'93 - 2	Conan Doyle & Jack Sparks	historical figure & special agent to the Queen
London	Galway, Robert C.	'63 -12	James Packard	British spy
London	Gardner, John	'64 - 8	Boysie Oakes	cowardly British agent for Special Security
London	Gardner, John	'74 - 2	James Moriarty	archenemy of Sherlock Holmes
London	Gardner, John	'81 -14	James Bond	British agent
London	Gilbert, Michael	'47 - 6	Insp. Hazelrigg	British police inspector
London	Gilbert, Michael	'93 - 1	Patrick Petrella	Metropolitan Police inspector
London	Gilbert, Michael	'95 - 2	Joe Narrabone	WWI policeman turned British secret agent
London	Hall, Robert Lee	'88 - 6	Benjamin Franklin	18th century American inventor
London	Harding, Paul	'91 - 7	Athelstan & John Cranston	14th century Dominican monk & coroner
London	Heller, Keith	'84 - 3	George Man	early 18th century parish watchman
London	Higgins, Jack	'65 - 2	Nick Miller	Central Division detective
London	Hunter, Alan	'55 -44	George Gently	chief superintendent of Scotland Yard
London	Kavanagh, Dan	'80 - 4	Nick Duffy	bisexual ex-cop P.I.
London	Kenyon, Michael	'81 - 8	Henry Peckover	Scotland Yard's cockney poet
London	King, Peter	'96 - 3	Goodwin Harper	food consultant to Scotland Yard
London	Kurland, Michael	'79 - 2	James Moriarty	archenemy of Sherlock Holmes
London	Le Carré, John	'61 - 8	George Smiley	British Intelligence agent and scholar
London	Lejeune, Anthony	'61 - 3	Adam Gifford	crime reporter
London	Lewis, Ted	'70 - 3	Jack Carter	employee of rackets organization
London	Lovesey, Peter	'70 - 8	Richard Cribb & Edward Thackeray	Victorian policemen
London	Lovesey, Peter	'87 - 3	Albert Edward	19th century heir to the British throne
London	MacKenzie, Donald	'76 - 9	John Raven	unorthodox detective inspector
London	Maitland, Barry	'94 - 3	Kathy Kolla & David Brock	young Scotland Yard detective & her mentor
London	Malcolm, John	'84 -12	Tim Simpson	financial consultant turned art investment specialist
London	Marquis, Max	'91 - 3	Harry Timberlake	aloof detective inspector
London	Marston, Edward	'88 - 9	Nicholas Bracewell	stage manager for Elizabethan acting company
London	McCutchan, Philip	'60 -22	Esmonde Shaw	Naval Intelligence turned anti-intelligence
London	McCutchan, Philip	'74 -11	Simon Shard	Scotland Yard supt. 2nd'd to the Foreign Office
London	O'Donnell, Peter	'65 -11	Modesty Blaise	gorgeous crime fighter for British Intelligence
London	Orvis, Kenneth	'65 - 2	Adam Breck	faux James Bond
London	Palmer, William J.	'90 - 3	Wilkie Collins & Charles Dickens	19th century literary celebrities
London	Payne, Laurence	'62 - 3	Sam Birkett	humorous Scotland Yard inspector

Setting	Author	1 - #	Series Character	Occupation

England...cont.

Setting	Author	1 - #	Series Character	Occupation
London	Payne, Laurence	'69 - 2	John Tibbett	petty thief turned reluctant hero
London	Phillips, Mike	'89 - 4	Sam Dean	Jamaica-born black journalist
London	Ripley, Mike	'88 - 8	Fitzroy Maclean Angel	trumpet-playing taxi driver
London	Satterthwait, Walter	'95 - 2	Houdini & Conan Doyle	19th century escape artist & writer
London	Scholefield, Alan	'89 - 6	George Macrae & Leopold Silver	old-fashioned copper & intellectual rookie partner
London	Selwyn, Francis	'74 - 5	William Clarence Verity	portly Victorian police sergeant
London	Shaw, Simon	'90 - 4	Philip Fletcher	British thespian and killer
London	Swan, Thomas	'90 - 3	Jack Oxby	Scotland Yard art forgery investigator
London	Timlin, Mark	'88 -12	Nick Sharman	hard-living ex-cop private eye
London	Trow, M. J.	'85 -16	Sholto Joseph Lestrade	19th century Scotland Yard inspector
London	Waddell, Martin	'66 - 4	Gerald Otley	amateur adventurer and part-time spy
London	Williams, David	'76 -17	Mark Treasure	merchant banker
London	Wilson, Derek	'94 - 6	Tim Lacey	ex-SAS officer and security firm owner
Lydmouth	Taylor, Andrew	'94 - 3	Richard Thornhill	'50s detective inspector
Medwell Frtrm	Parrish, Frank	'77 - 8	Dan Mallett	ex-London bank clerk turned handyman-poacher
Norfolk	Cooper, Brian	'91 - 4	John Spencer Lubbock	retired World War II D.C.I..
Nottingham	Harvey, John	'89 -10	Charlie Resnick	40-something jazz fan police detective
Oxford	Morson, Ian	'94 - 3	William Falconer	13th century university regent master
English seaport	James, Bill	'85 -13	Colin Harpur & Desmond Iles	detective chief superintendent & detective constable
Sussex	Scholefield, Alan	'94 - 2	Anne Vernon	Kingstown prison doctor
West Country	Burley, W. J.	'68 -20	Charles Wycliffe	area CID superintendent
York	Baker, John	'95 - 2	Sam Turner	newly-sober private eye
York	Turnbull, Peter	'96 - 1	Carmen Pharaoh	young woman police detective
Yorkshire	Hill, Reginald	'70 -15	Andrew Dalziel & Peter Pascoe	pair of police inspectors
Yorkshire	North, Gil	'60 -11	Caleb Cluff	Gunnarshaw police sergeant
Yorkshire	Pawson, Stuart	'95 - 4	Charlie Priest	art school graduate turned police detective
Yorkshire	Rhea, Nicholas	'79 -15	Nick Rhea	Aidensfield police constable father of four
Yorkshire	Robinson, Peter	'87 - 9	Alan Banks	Eastvale detective chief inspector
Yorkshire	Wainright, John	'66 - 8	Charles Ripley	head of the uniform branch
Yorkshire	Wainright, John	'66 - 4	Gilliant	chief constable
Yorkshire	Wainright, John	'83 - 2	Ralph Flensing & David Hoyle	Lessford police ensemble
Yorkshire	Wainright, John	'74 -10	Lennox	detective chief inspector
Yorkshire	Wainright, John	'75 - 4	Robert Blayde	police superintendent
Yorkshire	Wainright, John	'79 - 6	Lyle	detective inspector

France

Setting	Author	1 - #	Series Character	Occupation
La Douce	Bond, Michael	'83 - 8	Aristide Pamplemousse & Pommes Frites	gourmet test-eater & his bloodhound
Paris	Albert, Marvin H.	'86 - 9	Pierre-Ange "Pete" Sawyer	French-speaking American P.I.
Paris	Fuller, Dean	'92 - 2	Alex Grismolet	Chef-Insp. of the Sûréte
Paris	Grayson, Richard	'78 - 9	Jean-Paul Gautier	fin-de-siècle French police inspector
Paris	Janes, J. Robert	'92 - 8	Jean-Louis St-Cyr & Hermann Kohler	1940s French police inspector & Gestapo agent
Paris	Williams, Alan	'70 - 3	Charles Pol	Marxist bandit and lingerie-shop owner

Germany

Setting	Author	1 - #	Series Character	Occupation
Berlin	Kerr, Philip	'89 - 3	Bernie Gunther	1930s German private eye

Greece

Setting	Author	1 - #	Series Character	Occupation
	Goddard, Robert	'90 - 2	Harry Barnett	middle-aged Englishman caretaker

Hong Kong [see also Asia]

Setting	Author	1 - #	Series Character	Occupation
Hong Kong	Marshall, William	'75 -14	Harry Feiffer, Chief Insp.	chief inspector of Yellowthread Street station
Hong Kong	Trenhaile, John	'81 - 3	Povin, General	Soviet spy
Hong Kong	Trenhaile, John	'86 - 3	Simon Young	British Intelligence officer

India

Setting	Author	1 - #	Series Character	Occupation
Bombay	Keating, H. R. F.	'64 -20	Ganesh Ghote	Indian police inspector
Bombay	Mann, Paul	'93 - 3	George Sansi	Anglo-Indian attorney

Setting	Author	1 - #	Series Character	Occupation
Ireland				
	Gill, Bartholomew	'77 -12	Peter McGarr	Irish chief of detectives
	Higgins, Jack	'75 - 4	Liam Devlin	1940s IRA hero
	Higgins, Jack	'86 - 2	Dougal Munro & Jack Carter	1940s brigadier & captain
	Higgins, Jack	'92 - 6	Sean Dillon	IRA enforcer turned British special agent
	Kenyon, Michael	'70 - 3	Supt. O'Malley	comic Irish cop
Belfast	McEldowney, E.	'94 - 3	Cecil Megarry	hard-drinking Irish cop
Dublin	Brady, John	'88 - 5	Matt Minogue	Irish police detective
Kildaire	Tremayne, Peter	'94 - 4	Sister Fidelma	7th century Celtic sister & legal advocate
Lasherham	Mallett, Lyndon	'80 - 3	Taffin	fast-with-his-fists debt collector
Waterford	Lusby, Jim	'95 - 2	Carl McCadden	unconventional Irish police inspector
Israel				
Jerusalem	Rosenberg, Robert	'91 - 3	Avram Cohen	recently-retired police officer
Italy				
	Hill, John Spencer	'95 - 2	Carlo Arbati	policeman poet
Rome	Dibdin, Michael	'88 - 5	Aurelio Zen	Italian police inspector
Rome	Saylor, Steven	'90 - 6	Gordianus the Finder	private eye circa 56 B.C.
Santa Margherita	Butler, Richard	'75 - 2	Max Farne	luxury boat salesman and spy
Tuscany	Dowling, Gregory	'85 - 4	January Esposito	American teacher of English
Venice	Sklepowich, Edward	'90 - 5	Urbino Macintyre	American expatriate and biographer
Japan *[see also Asia]*				
Kobe	Melville, James	'79 -13	Tetsuo Otani	Japanese police superintendent
Kenya *[see also Africa]*				
	Casley, Dennis	'94 - 3	James Odhiambo	chief inspector
Mexico				
Mexico City	Taibo, Paco I., II	'90 - 5	Hector Belascoaran Shayne	correspondence-school-certified P.I.
Yucatan	Alexander, Gary	'93 - 2	Luis Balam	ex-traffic cop turned tour operator
Netherlands				
Amsterdam	Freeling, Nicolas	'62 -14	Van der Valk	intellectual Dutch police inspector
Amsterdam	Van de Wetering, J.	'75 -13	Grijpstra and de Gier	Dutch police detectives
Philippines *[see also Asia]*				
	Marshall, William	'86 - 2	Felix Elizalde	detective of the Western District Bureau
Russia				
Moscow	Kaminsky, Stuart M.	'81 -11	Porfiry Rostnikov	Russian police inspector
Moscow	Smith, Martin Cruz	'81 - 3	Arkady Renko	Russian police officer
Sardinia				
	Townend, Peter	'71 - 3	Philip Quest	photographer
Scotland				
	Cork, Barry	'88 - 4	Angus Struan	golfing police inspector
	Hammond, Gerald	'79 -23	Keith Calder	gunsmith and sport shooter
	Hammond, Gerald	'89 - 8	John Cunningham	war hero and hunting dog trainer
	Knox, Bill	'64 -15	Webb Carrick	chief officer of the Scottish Fishery Protection Service
	Roe, C. F.	'90 - 8	Jean Montrose	general practitioner
Edinburgh	Jardine, Quintin	'93 - 5	Robert Skinner	high-ranking cop
Edinburgh	MacLeod, Robert	'70 -10	Jonathan Gaunt	external auditor for the Queen
Edinburgh	Paul, William	'94 - 3	David Fyfe	detective chief inspector
Edinburgh	Rankin, Ian	'87 - 8	John Rebus	detective sergeant
Glasgow	Knox, Bill	'57 -21	Colin Thane & Phil Moss	Scottish Crime Squad officers

Setting	Author	1 - #	Series Character	Occupation
Scotland...cont.				
Glasgow	McIlvanney, William	'77 - 4	Jack Laidlaw	Scottish police inspector
Glasgow	Turnbull, Peter	'81 - 9	P Division	police detectives
Spain				
	Serafin, David	'79 - 6	Luis Bernal	Spanish police superintendent
Mallorca	Jeffries, Roderic	'74 -20	Enrique Alvarez	Spanish police inspector
Turkey				
	Ambler, Eric	'39 - 2	Charles Latimer	British university lecturer turned detective novelist
United States				
Alaska (AK)				
Sitka	Straley, John	'92 - 4	Cecil Younger	alcoholic private eye
Arkansas (AR)				
	Stockley, Grif	'92 - 5	Gideon Page	defense attorney
Arizona (AZ)				
	Garfield, Brian	'72 - 2	Paul Benjamin	vigilante murderer
	Garfield, Brian	'72 - 2	Sam Watchman	part Navajo State trooper
	Harper, Richard	'86 - 2	Tom Ragnon	cop who lives in a trailer
	Hillerman, Tony	'70 - 3	Joe Leaphorn	Navajo tribal police officer
	Hillerman, Tony	'80 - 9	Jim Chee	Navajo tribal police officer
	Page, Jake	'93 - 5	T. Moore "Mo" Bowdre	blind redneck sculptor
Empty Creek	Allen, Garrison	'94 - 3	Penelope Warren	ex-Marine mystery bookstore owner
Phoenix	Miles, Keith	'97 - 1	Merlin Richards	1920s young Welsh architect
Tucson	Parrish, Richard	'93 - 4	Joshua Rabb	1940s attorney
California (CA)				
	Breen, Jon	'83 - 4	Jerry Brogan	track announcer at Surfside Meadows
	Lupoff, Richard A.	'88 - 8	Hobart Lindsay & Marvia Plum	insurance claims adjuster & Berkeley detective
	Martini, Steve	'92 - 5	Paul Madriani	defense attorney
	Mosley, Walter	'97 -ss	Socrates Fortlow	philosophical ex-con
	Nolan, William F.	'94 - 2	Black Mask Boys	1930s detective heroes
Angleton	Champion, David	'95 - 2	Bomber Hanson	ace trial lawyer
Azalea	Davis, Thomas D.	'91 - 3	Dave Strickland	private eye
Beverly Hills	Cunningham, E. V.	'67 - 7	Masao Masuto	Japanese-American police detective
Buena Costa Co.	Crowe, John	'72 - 6	Lee Beckett	private eye
Hollywood	Campbell, Robert	'86 - 4	Whistler	sentimental private eye
Hollywood	Cutler, Stan	'91 - 4	Rayford Goodman & Mark Bradley	jaded macho P.I. & gay writer of celebrity biographies
Hollywood	Faherty, Terence	'96 - 3	Scott Elliott	1940s failed actor turned private eye
Los Angeles	Allen, Steve	'82 - 8	Steve Allen & Jane Meadows	crime-solving duo
Los Angeles	Baxt, George	'84 -12	Jacob Singer	1940s Hollywood private eye
Los Angeles	Bishop, Paul	'88 - 3	Calico Jack Walker & Tina Tamiko	ex-patrol cop & his former rookie partner
Los Angeles	Bishop, Paul	'91 - 2	Ian Chapel	one-eyed pro soccer goalie turned P.I.
Los Angeles	Bishop, Paul	'94 - 4	Fey Croaker	40-something homicide unit supervisor
Los Angeles	Breen, Jon	'84 - 2	Rachel Hennings	bookstore owner
Los Angeles	Caine, Hamilton	'81 - 2	Ace Carpenter	private eye
Los Angeles	Connelly, Michael	'92 - 5	Harry Bosch	homicide detective
Los Angeles	Cook, Bruce	'88 - 4	Antonio "Chico" Cervantes	Mexican-American private eye
Los Angeles	Copper, Basil	'66 -52	Mike Faraday	hard-boiled private eye who quotes Herrick
Los Angeles	Crais, Robert	'87 - 7	Elvis Cole & Joe Pike	pair of Hollywood private eyes
Los Angeles	Ellroy, James	'84 - 3	Lloyd Hopkins	detective sergeant in the Rampart Division
Los Angeles	Eversz, Robert	'88 - 2	Paul Marston & Angel Cantini	private eye & female prize fighter
Los Angeles	Furutani, Dale	'96 - 2	Ken Tanaka	Asian American computer programmer
Los Angeles	Goldberg, Lee	'95 - 2	Charlie Willis	ex-cop turned TV cop turned studio security agent
Los Angeles	Goldberg, Leonard	'92 - 4	Joanna Blalock & Jake Sinclair	forensic pathologist & police detective
Los Angeles	Hallinan, Timothy	'89 - 6	Simeon Grist	four-degreed P.I.
Los Angeles	Hansen, Joseph	'70 -11	Dave Brandstetter	gay death-claims investigator

Setting	Author	1 - #	Series Character	Occupation
United States...cont.				
California...cont.				
Los Angeles	Harrington, William	'93 - 6	Columbo, Lt.	rumpled police detective
Los Angeles	Harriss, Will	'83 - 2	Cliff Dunbar	former English professor turned detective
Los Angeles	Haywood, Gar A.	'88 - 5	Aaron Gunner	black wise-guy P.I.
Los Angeles	Horwitz, Merle	'90 - 2	Harvey Ace	retired P.I. who plays the horses
Los Angeles	Irvine, Robert	'74 - 4	Robert Christopher	television reporter
Los Angeles	Irvine, Robert	'94 - 1	Kevin Manwaring & Vicki Garcia	field producer & television reporter
Los Angeles	Kaminsky, Stuart	'77 -20	Toby Peters	1940s Hollywood private investigator
Los Angeles	Kaminsky, Stuart	'96 - 2	James Rockford	low-rent private eye
Los Angeles	Kellerman, J.	'85 -12	Alex Delaware	child psychologist
Los Angeles	Kincaid, D.	'86 - 2	Harry Cain	unorthodox trial lawyer
Los Angeles	Lochte, Dick	'85 - 2	Serendipity Dahlquist & Leo Bloodworth	gum-snapping 15-yr-old girl & grumpy 50-something P.I.
Los Angeles	Lyons, Arthur	'74 - 11	Jacob Asch	Jewish-Episcopal ex-reporter P.I.
Los Angeles	Morse, L. A.	'82 - 2	Sam Hunter	private eye
Los Angeles	Mosley, Walter	'90 - 7	Easy Rawlins	school maintenance supervisor in Watts
Los Angeles	Newton, Michael	'78 - 2	Jonathan Steele	LAPD homicide detective
Los Angeles	Newton, Michael	'90 - 9	Joseph Flynn & Martin Tanner	FBI agents with VICAP
Los Angeles	Noguchi, Thomas T. w/Arthur Lyons	'80 - 2	Eric Parker	forensic pathologist
Los Angeles	Nolan, William F.	'68 - 2	Bart Challis	hard-boiled private eye
Los Angeles	Parker, Robert B.	'89 - 2	Philip Marlowe	private eye
Los Angeles	Petievich, Gerald	'81 - 4	Charles Carr & Jack Kelly	US Treasury agents
Los Angeles	Phillips, Gary	'94 - 3	Ivan Monk	black private eye
Los Angeles	Pierce, David M.	'89 - 7	Vic Daniel	offbeat 6' 7-1/4" cut-rate P.I.
Los Angeles	Prather, Richard	'50 -36	Shell Scott	6' 2" ex-Marine crew-cut private eye
Los Angeles	Roberts, Les	'87 - 6	Saxon	actor private eye
Los Angeles	Sandford, John	'97 - 1	Anna Batory	TV news video freelancer
Los Angeles	Shatner, William	'89 - 8	Jack Cardigan	22nd century ex-cop private eye
Los Angeles	Simon, Roger L.	'73 - 8	Moses Wine	ex-hippie Jewish private eye
Los Angeles	Spencer, John	'84 - 3	Charley Case	private eye of the "'97" future
Los Angeles	Stinson, Jim	'85 - 4	Stoney Winston	low-budget film maker
Los Angeles	Stone, Thomas H.	'72 - 4	Chester Fortune	mulatto detective
Los Angeles	Warga, Wayne	'85 - 3	Jeffrey Dean	ex-CIA courier-journalist turned rare book dealer
Los Angeles	Webb, Jack	'52 - 9	Sammy Golden & Joseph Shanley	Jewish police detective & Catholic priest
Los Robles	Nava, Michael	'86 - 6	Henry Rios	gay Latino ex-alcoholic criminal defense attorney
Monkton City	Chambers, Peter	'61 -36	Mark Preston	hard-nosed private eye
Monterey	Andrus, Jeff	'94 - 2	John Tracer	family-man sleuth
San Bernadino	Bass, Milton R.	'93 - 2	Vinnie Altobelli	ex-cop coronary survivor P.I.
San Diego	Bass, Milton R.	'86 - 4	Benny Freedman	private eye
San Diego	Kuhlken, Ken	'91 - 3	Tom Hickey	1940s P.I. and restaurateur
San Diego	Miller, Wade	'47 - 6	Max Thursday	private eye
San Diego	Mullen, Jack	'95 - 2	Vincent Dowling	police sergeant
San Diego	Russell, Alan	'94 - 2	Am Caulfield	hotel detective
San Diego	Russell, Alan	'96 - 1	Orson Cheever	homicide detective
San Francisco	Babula, William	'88 - 5	Jeremiah St. John	private investigator
San Francisco	Berlinski, David	'93 - 3	Aaron Asherfeld	cynical P.I. with 3 ex-wives
San Francisco	Biderman, Bob	'85 - 4	Joseph Radkin	investigative journalist
San Francisco	Byrd, Max	'81 - 3	Mike Haller	P.I. specializing in missing persons
San Francisco	Davis, Kenn	'76 - 8	Carver Bascombe	suave black poet private eye
San Francisco	Dold, Gaylord	'96 - 1	Grace Wu	undercover agent for the SFPD and DEA
San Francisco	Gores, Joe	'72 - 5	Daniel Kearney Associates	auto repo & skip-tracing firm
San Francisco	Greenleaf, Stephen	'79 -12	John Marshall Tanner	non-practicing attorney P.I.
San Francisco	Kennealy, Jerry	'87 -10	Nick Polo	private eye
San Francisco	Lescroart, John T.	'89 - 4	Dismas Hardy	ex-cop bartender and ex-ADA turned defense attorney
San Francisco	Lescroart, John T.	'95 - 2	Abe Glitsky	black Jewish cop
San Francisco	Lynch, Jack	'82 - 7	Peter Bragg	private eye
San Francisco	Pronzini, Bill	'71 -24	Nameless	pulp collector P.I. with no name
San Francisco	Pronzini, Bill	'85 - 2	John Quincannon	19th century private eye
San Francisco	Russell, Alan	'90 - 2	Stuart Winter	private eye
San Francisco	Tierney, Ronald	'93 - 1	Zachary Grayson	gay author of trendy cookbooks
San Francisco	Washburn, Stan	'95 - 2	Toby Parkman	quietly heroic cop
San Francisco	Wilcox, Collin	'67 - 2	Stephen Drake	newspaper reporter with ESP

Setting	Author	1 - #	Series Character	Occupation
United States...cont.				
California...cont.				
San Francisco	Wilcox, Collin	'69 -20	Frank Hastings	co-commander SFPD homicide
San Francisco	Wilcox, Collin	'88 - 5	Alan Bernhardt	actor-director private eye
San Francisco	Zimmerman, Bruce	'89 - 4	Quinn Parker	phobia therapist
San Rodrigo Co.	Vance, John H.	66 - 2	Joe Bain	sheriff
Santa Barbara	Ely, Ron	'94 - 2	Jake Sands	professional recoverer of lost things
Santa Barbara	Gibbs, Tony	'96 - 2	Neal Donahoe & Victoria "Tory" Lennox	harbor cop and Coast Guard Lt.
Santa Cruz	Owens, Louis	'91 - 4	Cole McCurtain	Choctaw-Cherokee-Irish-Cajun college professor
Southern Cal.	Barre, Richard	'95 - 3	Wil Hardesty	Vietnam vet and greybeard surfer turned P.I.
Southern Cal.	Garfield, Henry	'95 - 2	Cyrus "Moondog" Nygerski	reclusive writer
Southern Cal.	Murray, William	'84 - 9	Shifty Lou Anderson	professional magician and horse-player
Colorado (CO)				
	Ring, Raymond H.	'88 - 2	Henry Dyer	fish and game agent turned P.I.
Aspen	Zigal, Thomas	'95 - 2	Kurt Muller	ex-hippie single-father sheriff
Boulder	White, Stephen	'91 - 5	Alan Gregory & Lauren Crowder	practicing psychologist & attorney
Denver	Allegretto, Michael	'87 - 5	Jacob Lomax	ex-cop turned P.I.
Denver	Burns, Rex	'75 -11	Gabe Wagner	homicide detective
Denver	Burns, Rex	'87 - 4	Devlin Kirk	owner of industrial surveillance company
Denver	Downing, Warwick	'74 - 3	Joe Reddman	private investigator
Denver	Downing, Warwick	'90 - 3	Jack S. Bard	defense attorney
Denver	Dunning, John	'92 - 2	Cliff Janeway	cop and rare book expert
Denver	Greer, Robert O.	'96 - 3	C. J. Floyd	bail bondsman and bounty hunter
Denver	Most, Bruce W.	'96 - 2	Ruby Dark	bail bondswoman
Denver	Ramos, Manuel	'93 - 4	Luis Montez	attorney and former Chicano activist
Denver	Stone, Michael	'96 - 2	Streeter	P.I. bounty hunter
Granite Creek	Doss, James D.	'94 - 4	Charlie Moon & Scott Parris	Ute police sergeant & Anglo colleague
Mesa Grande	Yaffe, James	'88 - 4	Dave & Mom	ex-cop investigator for public defender & his mother
Tenoclock	Miles, John	'94 - 2	Johnelle Baker	Choctaw sheriff
Connecticut (CT)				
	Forrest, Richard	'75 - 8	Lyon & Bea Wentworth	children's book author & state senator
	Taylor, H. Baldwin	'64 - 3	David Halliday	newspaper owner and editor
Newbury	Scott, Justin	'94 - 2	Ben Abbott	ex-Wall Street financier turned realtor
Stockford	Waugh, Hillary	'59 -11	Fred Fellows	small-town police chief
Tipton	McGaughey, Neil	'94 - 4	Stokes Moran aka Kyle Malachi	syndicated mystery critic
Westport	Maxim, John	'89 - 4	Paul Bannerman	private investigations firm owner
Dakota Territory				
	Honig, Donald	'96 - 2	Thomas Maynard	Civil War Army captain
District of Columbia (DC)				
Washington	Adler, Warren	'81 - 6	Fiona Fitzgerald	homicide detective
Washington	Barrett, Neal, Jr.	'96 - 2	Wiley Moss	graphic artist for the Smithsonian
Washington	Blatty, William Peter	'71 -12	Bill Kinderman	police lieutenant
Washington	Bowen, Michael	'90 - 4	Richard Michaelson	retired Foreign Service officer
Washington	Buckley, William F.	'76 -11	Blackford "Blacky" Oakes	CIA agent recruited from Yale
Washington	Clancy, Tom	'84 - 8	Jack Ryan	CIA analyst
Washington	Conroy, Richard T.	'92 - 3	Henry Scruggs	40-something Smithsonian official
Washington	Freemantle, Brian	'92 - 2	William Cowley & Dimitri Danilov	FBI agent & Russian investigator
Washington	Goodrum, Charles	'77 - 4	Edward George	retired Yale librarian
Washington	Grady, James	'74 - 2	Richard Malcolm	CIA analyst and grad student
Washington	Grady, James	'84 - 2	John Rankin	private investigator
Washington	Hunter, Fred W.	'97 - 2	Alex Reynolds	gay federal employee
Washington	Levitsky, Ronald	'91 - 4	Nate Rosen	civil rights lawyer
Washington	Marlowe, Stephen	'55 -19	Chester Drum	ex-FBI agent turned P.I.
Washington	Patterson, James	'95 - 4	Alex Cross	black psychiatrist and homicide cop

Setting	Author	1 - #	Series Character	Occupation
United States...cont.				
District of Columbia...cont.				
Washington	Patterson, Richard	79 - 3	Christopher Paget	economic crimes special investigator
Washington	Pelecanos, George	'92 - 4	Nick Stefanos	1950s bartender P.I.
Washington	Roosevelt, Elliott	'84 -16	Eleanor Roosevelt	1940s First Lady
Washington	Schutz, Benjamin	'85 - 6	Leo Haggerty	rough and tough P.I.
Washington	Walker, Robert W.	'92 - 5	Jessica Coran	FBI medical examiner
Delaware (DE)				
	Sauter, Eric	'83 - 3	Robert Lee Hunter	30-something wealthy P.I.
Florida (FL)				
	Ayres, E. C.	'94 - 3	Tony Lowell	photographer private eye
	Leonard, Elmore	'93 - 2	Raylan Givens	federal marshall
	McBain, Ed	'77 -12	Matthew Hope	attorney
Del Moray	Lutz, John	'86 -10	Fred Carver	crippled ex-cop P.I.
Key Largo	Hall, James W.	'87 - 6	Thorn	eco-avenger P.I.
Key West	Leslie, John	'94 - 3	Gideon Lowry	private eye
Key West	Philbrick, W. R.	'87 - 3	T. D. Stash	unlicensed private eye
Miami	Levine, Paul	'90 - 7	Jake Lassiter	ex-linebacker turned lawyer
Miami	Rome, Anthony	'60 - 3	Tony Rome	ex-cop gambler private eye
Miami	Standiford, Les	'93 - 4	John Deal	building contractor
Orlando	Robinson, Kevin	'91 - 3	Stick Foster	paraplegic newspaper reporter
Palm Beach	Kakonis, Tom	'88 - 3	Timothy Waverly	would-be professor turned card sharp ex-con
Palm Beach	Sanders, Lawrence	'92 - 7	Arch McNally	playboy private eye
Sanibel Island	White, Randy W.	'90 - 5	Doc Ford	ex-operative marine biologist
Georgia (GA)				
	Cook, Glen	'87 - 8	Garrett	30-something fantasy private eye
Atlanta	Cook, Thomas H.	'88 - 3	Frank Clemons	private eye
Atlanta	Logue, John	'79 - 5	John Morris	Associated Press sportswriter
Atlanta	Moore, Richard A.	'81 - 2	Bob Whitfield	newspaper reporter
Patsboro	Wyrick, E. L.	'94 - 2	Tammi Randall	small-town lawyer
Hawaii (HI)				
Pearl Harbor	Knief, Charles	'96 - 2	John Caine	Navy SEAL turned P.I.
Iowa (IA)				
	Collins, Max A., Jr.	'73 - 7	Frank Nolan	aging thief
	Collins, Max A., Jr.	'76 - 5	Quarry	psychotic Vietnam vet and hired killer
	Collins, Max A., Jr.	'83 - 5	Mallory	small-town student mystery writer
Cedar Rapids	Gorman, Ed	'85 - 6	Jack Dwyer	ex-cop part-time actor and security guard
Cedar Rapids	Gorman, Ed	'91 - 1	Walsh	50-something private eye
New Hope	Gorman, Ed	'94 - 2	Robert Payne	psychological profile investigator
Idaho (ID)				
	McCall, Wendell	'88 - 2	Chris Klick	6' 4" dropout-songwriter turned P.I.
Illinois (IL)				
Chicago	Campbell, Robert	'86 -10	Jimmy Flannery	sewer inspector & Democratic precinct captain
Chicago	Collins, Max A., Jr.	'83 - 8	Nate Heller	1930s ex-cop turned private eye
Chicago	Cormany, Michael	'88 - 4	Dan Kruger	private investigator
Chicago	Engleman, Paul	'83 - 5	Mark Renzler	ex-baseball player private eye
Chicago	Engleman, Paul	'93 - 2	Phil Moony	ex-firefighter private eye
Chicago	Evers, Crabbe	'91 - 5	Duffy House	ex-sportswriter turned investigator
Chicago	Fink, John	'91 - 2	Jimmy Gillespie	TV reporter and weekend anchor
Chicago	Gaitano, Nick	'95 - 2	Jake Phillips	homicide detective
Chicago	Granger, Bill	'80 - 4	Terry Flynn & Karen Kovac	Special Squad detectives
Chicago	Granger, Bill	'91 - 3	Jimmy Drover	ex-sportswriter

Setting	Author	1 - #	Series Character	Occupation

United States...cont.

California...cont.

Setting	Author	1 - #	Series Character	Occupation
Chicago	Greeley, Andrew M.	'85 - 8	John Blackwood "Blackie" Ryan	Catholic priest
Chicago	Greeley, Andrew M.	'94 - 2	Nuala Ann McGrail	young Irish immigrant psychic and singer
Chicago	Holton, Hugh	'94 - 4	Larry Cole	black police commander
Chicago	Hunter, Fred W.	'94 - 3	Jeremy Ransom & Emily Charters	homic°ide detective & adopted grandmother
Chicago	Jenkins, Jerry	'79 -13	Margo Franklin & Philip Spence	pair of private eyes
Chicago	Jenkins, Jerry	'83 - 6	Jennifer Grey	newspaper reporter and columnist
Chicago	Kaminsky, Stuart M.	'90 - 5	Abe Lieberman	60-something Jewish police detective
Chicago	Katz, Michael J.	'87 - 3	Murray Glick & Andy Sussman	P.I. & sportscaster buddy
Chicago	McCall, Thomas	'93 - 2	Nora Callum	one-legged cop
Chicago	McConnell, Frank	'83 - 4	Harry Garnish & Bridget O'Toole	private investigators
Chicago	Miller, Rex	'87 - 5	Jack Eichord	police detective
Chicago	Quill, Monica	'81 - 9	Mary Teresa Dempsey	5' 2" 200-lb. nun
Chicago	Raleigh, Michael	'90 - 5	Paul Whelan	40-something black cop turned P.I.
Chicago	Sherer, Michael W.	'88 - 4	Emerson Ward	freelance writer
Chicago	Spencer, Ross H.	'78 - 5	Chance Purdue	private investigator
Chicago	Walker, David J.	'95 - 2	Malachy P. Foley	jazz piano-playing P.I.
Chicago	Zubro, Mark	'89 - 6	Tom Mason & Scott Carpenter	high school teacher & pro baseball player
Chicago	Zubro, Mark	'91 - 4	Paul Turner	gay Chicago cop & father of two teenage sons
Fox River	McInerny, Ralph	'77 -17	Roger Dowling, Father	St. Hilary's parish priest
Rockford	Dundee, Wayne	'88 - 3	Joe Hannibal	blue-collar P.I.
Springfield	Everson, David H.	'87 - 7	Robert Miles	baseball minor leaguer turned P.I.

Indiana (IN)

Setting	Author	1 - #	Series Character	Occupation
Bington	Hensley, Joe L.	'71 -10	Donald Robak	crusading defense attorney and state legislator
Indianapolis	Lewin, Michael Z.	'71 - 9	Albert Samson	middle-age low-key P.I.
Indianapolis	Lewin, Michael Z.	'76 - 3	Leroy Powder	cop friend of Albert Samson's
Indianapolis	Tierney, Ronald	'90 - 4	"Deets" Shanahan	70-something private eye
Wyler	McInerny, Ralph	'87 - 6	Andrew Broom	attorney

Kansas (KS)

Setting	Author	1 - #	Series Character	Occupation
Wichita	Dold, Gaylord	'87 - 9	Mitch Roberts	1950s private eye

Kentucky (KY)

Setting	Author	1 - #	Series Character	Occupation
Baird	Feldmeyer, Dean	'94 - 2	Dan Thompson	small-town Methodist minister
Buxton	Strunk, Frank C.	'91 - 2	Berkley Jordon	roadhouse operator
Lexington	Shoemaker, Bill	'94 - 3	Coley Killebrew	ex-jockey turned restaurant owner
Louisville	Birkett, John	'88 - 2	Michael Rhineheart	private eye

Louisiana (LA)

Setting	Author	1 - #	Series Character	Occupation
	Burke, James Lee	'87 - 9	Dave Robicheaux	deputy sheriff
New Orleans	Davis, J. Madison	'90 - 2	Delbert "Dub" Greenert & Vonna Saucier	white & black investigator pair
New Orleans	Donaldson, D. J.	'88 - 6	Kit Franklyn & Andy Broussard	criminal psychologist & medical examiner
New Orleans	Dunbar, Tony	'94 - 3	Tubby Dubonnet	bon vivant defense attorney
New Orleans	Lochte, Dick	'92 - 2	Terry Manion	private eye
New Orleans	Sallis, James	'92 - 3	Lew Griffin	black private eye
New Orleans	Womack, Steven	'90 - 3	Jack Lynch	PR man and problem solver
St. Bruno	Woodrell, Dan	'86 - 3	Rene Shade	cop in a bayou town

Massachusetts (MA)

Setting	Author	1 - #	Series Character	Occupation
	Fuller, Timothy	'36 - 5	Edmund "Jupiter" Jones	grad student in fine arts
	O'Connell, Jack	'92 - 3	Quinsigamond	decaying New England factory town
Barnard's Cross.	Kemelman, Harry	'64 -11	David Small	rabbi sleuth
Boston	Aldyne, Nathan	'80 - 4	D. Valentine & C. Lovelace	gay & straight bar owners
Boston	Cluster, Dick	'88 - 2	Alex Glauberman	auto repair shop owner
Boston	Daniel, David & Chris Carpenter	'96 - 2	Frank Branco	ex-cop turned private eye

Setting	Author	1 - #	Series Character	Occupation
United States...cont.				
Massachusetts...cont.				
Boston	Faherty, Terence	'91 - 5	Owen Keane	ex-seminarian and law firm researcher
Boston	Healy, Jeremiah	'84 - 11	John Francis Cuddy	Arny police lieutenant turned private investigator
Boston	Higgins, George V.	'80 - 4	Jerry Kennedy	criminal defense attorney
Boston	Lehane, Dennis	'94 - 3	Patrick Kenzie & Angela Gennaro	private detectives
Boston	McDonald, Gregory	'77 - 3	Francis Xavier Flynn	tenacious police inspector
Boston	Michaels, Grant	'90 - 5	Stan Kraychik	gay hairdresser
Boston	Parker, Robert B.	'73 -24	Spenser	ex-boxer, ex-state cop turned P.I.
Boston	Philbrick, W. R.	'85 - 4	J. D. Hawkins	wheelchair-bound mystery writer
Boston	Reed, Barry	'80 - 3	Dan Sheridan	attorney
Boston	Reeves, Robert	'85 - 2	Thomas Theron	history professor
Boston	Rosen, Richard	'84 - 4	Harvey Blissberg	ex-baseball player turned P.I.
Boston	Ross, Philip	'85 - 2	James Marley	P.I. investigator
Boston	Tapply, William G.	'84 -15	Brady Coyne	lawyer to the rich who loves to fish
Boston suburb	Coburn, Andrew	'92 - 2	James Morgan	chief of police
Cambridge	Doolittle, Jerome	'90 - 6	Tom Bethany	political consultant and former wrestler
Cambridge	Jevons, Marshall	'78 - 3	Henry Spearman	Harvard professor
Cambridge	Kilmer, Nicholas	'95 - 3	Fred Taylor	Vietnam veteran turned art hunter
Cambridge	Maness, Larry	'95 - 2	Jake Eaton & Watson	P.I. & his superdog
Cape Cod	Kemprecos, Paul	'91 - 7	Aristotle Plato Socarides	ex-cop part-time fisherman P.I.
Concord	Boyer, Rick	'82 - 8	Charlie "Doc" Adams	oral surgeon
Concord	Luber, Philip	'94 - 2	Harry Kline & Veronica Pace	psychiatrist & FBI special agent
Lowell	Daniel, David	'94 - 2	Alex Rasmussen	private investigator
Martha's Vineyard	Craig, Philip	'89 - 8	Jefferson "J. W." Jackson	30-something ex-Boston cop
Maryland (MD)				
Baltimore	Grady, James	'85 - 2	Devlin Rourke	police detective sergeant
Baltimore	Pairo, Preston, III	'96 - 2	Jimmy "Griff" Griffin	ex-cop investigator for the city attorney
Ocean City	Pairo, Preston, III	'91 - 2	Dallas Henry	sometime-lawyer and motel owner
Maine (ME)				
Androscoggin	Boyle, Gerry	'93 - 4	Jack McMorrow	ex-NY Times reporter turned small town editor
Michigan (MI)				
Detroit	Allyn, Doug	'89 - 2	Lupe Garcia	tough Latino cop
Detroit	Estleman, Loren D.	'80 - 11	Amos Walker	6' 1" Vietnam vet private eye
Detroit	Estleman, Loren D.	'84 - 3	Peter Macklin	hit man for the mob
Detroit	Jackson, Jon A.	'77 - 6	Fang Mulheisen	police detective sergeant
Detroit	Kantner, Rob	'86 - 6	Ben Perkins	ex-union strike buster turned P.I.
Detroit	Kienzle, William X.	'79 - 19	Robert Koesler	Catholic priest
Detroit	Leonard, Elmore	'76 - 2	Frank Ryan	process server
Detroit	Lindsay, Paul	'92 - 3	Mike Devlin	FBI agent
Huron Harbor	Allyn, Doug	'95 - 3	Michelle Mitchell	single mother and dive shop owner
Lansing	Roat, Ronald Clair	'91 - 3	Stuart Mallory	private eye
Michiganapolis	Raphael, Lev	'96 - 2	Nick Hoffman	gay college professor
Upper Peninsula	Zimmerman, R. D.	'92 - 3	Alex & Maddy Phillips	brother & blind forensic psychiatrist sister
Minnesota (MN)				
	Bailey, Jo	'91 - 3	Jan Gallagher	hospital security guard
	Hautman, Pete	'94 - 3	Joe Crow, Sam O'Gara, Axel Speeter & Tommy Fabian	small-town professional gamblers
	Lake, M. D.	'89 - 9	Peggy O'Neill	university campus cop
	Sandford, John	'89 - 2	Kidd & Luellen	computer whiz & thief
	Trainor, J. F.	'93 - 5	Angela Biwaban	ex-embezzler Anishinabe princess
Minneapolis	Handberg, Ron	'92 - 3	TV newsroom series	newsroom crew
Minneapolis	Sandford, John	'89 - 8	Lucas Davenport	police detective and war games designer
Minneapolis	Zimmerman, R. D.	'95 - 2	Todd Mills	gay TV news reporter
St. Paul	Housewright, David	'95 - 2	Holland Taylor	ex-cop turned private investigator

Setting	Author	1 - #	Series Character	Occupation
United States...cont.				
Missouri (MO)				
Kansas City	Vincent, Lawrence	'89 - 2	Townsend Reeves	radiologist with a ballerina girlfriend
N Branson	Ripley, W. L.	'93 - 3	Wyatt Storme	Vietnam vet ex-NFL star
St. Louis	Kahn, Michael A.	'88 - 5	Rachel Gold	defense attorney
St. Louis	Lutz, John	'76 -10	Alo Nudger	anta-acid-chewing bad-luck P.I.
St. Louis	Nevins, Francis, Jr.	'75 - 3	Loren Mensing	law school professor
St. Louis	Nevins, Francis, Jr.	'86 - 2	Milo Turner	con man private eye
Mississippi (MS)				
Sheffield	Armistead, John	'94 - 3	Grover Bramlett	small-town sheriff
Montana (MT)				
	Bowen, Peter	'94 - 4	Gabriel DuPre	Metis Indian cattle inspector and sometimes sheriff
	Crumley, James	'75 - 2	Milo Milodragovitch	ex-Army spy and hard-drinking P.I.
	Crumley, James	'78 - 3	C. W. Sughrue	ex-Army spy turned private investigator
Rozette	Reid, Robert Sims	'88 - 2	Ray Bartell	police detective
Nebraska (NE)				
Omaha	Campbell, Robert	'88 - 2	Jake Hatch	railroad detective
Omaha	Reynolds, William J.	'84 - 6	Nebraska	part-time P.I. trying to write
New Hampshire (NH)				
Tyler Beach	DuBois, Brendan	'94 - 2	Lewis Cole	magazine writer
New Jersey (NJ)				
	Arden, William	'68 - 5	Kane Jackson	industrial espionage specialist
	Bruno, Anthony	'97 - 1	Loretta Kovacs & Frank Marvelli	parole officer & partner
Atlantic City	Kent, Bill	'89 - 3	Louis Monroe	Don Quixote-style cop
Jersey City	Rider, J. W.	'86 - 2	Ryder Malone	private eye
Newark	Hilary, Richard	'87 - 4	Ezell "Easy" Barnes	ex-prize fighter and cop turned P.I.
Princeton	Bradberry, James	'94 - 3	Jamie Ramsgill	architect and Princeton professor
Rochambeau	Katz, Jon	'92 - 4	Kit DeLeeuw	Wall Street shark turned surburban detective
New Mexico (NM)				
	Campbell, Harlen	'93 - 1	Rainbow Porter	Vietnam veteran turned detective
	Hackler, Micah S.	'95 - 4	Cliff Lansing & Gabe Hanna	single-father part-time rancher-sheriff & his deputy
Albuquerque	Anaya, Rudolfo	'95 - 2	Sonny Baca	part-time rodeo rider private eye
Albuquerque	Brewer, Steve	'94 - 4	Bubba Mabry	low-rent P.I.
Posadas County	Havill, Steven F.	'91 - 5	Bill Gastner	insomniac undersheriff
Santa Fe	McGarrity, Michael	'96 - 2	Kevin Kerney	ex-chief of detectives
Santa Fe	Satterthwait, Walter	'89 - 5	Joshua Croft	wisecracking P.I.
Taos	Hanson, Rick	'94 - 4	Adam McCleet	ex-cop turned sculptor
Nevada (NV)				
	Mitchell, Kirk	'95 - 2	Dee Laguerre	Bureau of Land Management ranger
	Moody, Bill	'94 - 3	Evan Horne	jazz pianist
Las Vegas	Murphy, Warren B.	'82 - 4	Julian "Digger" Burroughs	freelance insurance investigator
Las Vegas	Murphy, Warren B.	'83 - 7	Devlin Tracy	freelance insurance investigator
Reno	Schopen, Bernard	'89 - 2	Jack Ross	private eye
New York (NY)				
	Adamson, Lydia	'94 - 7	Deidre Nightingale	young woman veterinarian
	Orenstein, Frank	'84 - 3	Hugh Morrison	small-town cop
	Sadler, Mark	'70 - 6	Paul Shaw	private eye
Adirondack Mts	Estabrook, Barry	'91 - 2	Garwood Plunkett	veteran cop
Albany	Stevenson, Richard	'81 - 6	Donald Strachey	gay private eye
Brooklyn	Randisi, Robert J.	'87 - 2	Nick Delvecchio	private eye
Deganawida	Perry, Thomas	'95 - 4	Jane Whitefield	Native American guide
Isola	McBain, Ed	'56 -47	87th Precinct	thinly-disguised NYPD cops
Long Island	Gibbs, Tony	'88 - 3	G. Verdean, J. Barr & P. O'Mara	yacht owner, skipper & mate
Long Island	Resnicow, Herbert	'87 - 2	Ed & Warren Baer	father & son sleuths
Long Island	Westermann, John	'90 - 2	Orin Boyd	Nassau County uniformed cop

Setting	Author	1 - #	Series Character	Occupation
United States...cont.				
New York...cont.				
New York	Adamson, Lydia	'90 -15	Alice Nestleton	part-time actress and cat-sitter
New York	Adamson, Lydia	'96 - 2	Lucy Wayles	ex-librarian birdwatcher
New York	Adcock, Thomas	'89 - 6	Neil Hockaday	NYPD street crimes detective
New York	Alexander, L.	'86 -13	Teddy Roosevelt	1890s police commissioner
New York	Avallone, Michael	'53 -31	Ed Noon	movie-nut private eye
New York	Barth, Richard	'78 - 7	Margaret Binton	70-something little old lady
New York	Baxt, George	'66 - 5	Pharoah Love	gay black NYPD detective
New York	Baxt, George	'67 - 3	Sylvia Plotkin & Max Van Larsen	author-teacher & police detective
New York	Bayer, William	'81 - 4	Frank Janek	NYPD homicide detective
New York	Beinhart, Larry	'86 - 3	Tony Cassella	high-stakes private eye
New York	Belsky, Dick	'85 - 2	Lucy Shannon	newspaper reporter
New York	Belsky, Dick	'89 - 4	Jenny McKay	TV news reporter
New York	Berger, Bob	'95 - 2	James Denny aka Dr. Risk	risk theorist and newspaper columnist
New York	Block, Lawrence	'70 - 4	Leo Haig	private investigator
New York	Block, Lawrence	'76 -13	Matt Scudder	unlicensed reformed alcoholic P.I.
New York	Block, Lawrence	'77 - 8	Bernie Rhodenbarr	professional burglar and bibliophile
New York	Bogart, Stephen H.	'95 - 2	R. J. Brook	celebrity-son private eye
New York	Boland, John C.	'91 - 3	Donald McCarry	Wall Street stockbroker
New York	Bowen, Michael	'89 - 3	Thomas & Sandrine Curry	1960s husband & wife detective team
New York	Box, Edgar	'52 - 3	Peter Cutler Sargeant II	public relations consultant
New York	Brett, Michael	'66 -10	Pete McGrath	wise-cracking private eye
New York	Bruno, Anthony	'88 - 6	Bert Gibbons & Mike Tozzi	FBI agents undercover with the Mob
New York	Charyn, Jerome	'75 - 9	Isaac Sidel	former police commissioner
New York	Chesbro, George	'77 -13	Robert "Mongo" Frederickson	dwarf criminology prof and former circus gymnast
New York	Chesbro, George	'86 - 2	Veil Kendry	painter and adventurer
New York	Coben, Harlan	'95 - 4	Myron Bolitar	injured basketball player turned sports agent
New York	Collins, Michael	'67 -17	Dan Fortune	one-armed Polish-Lithuanian P.I.
New York	Cross, David	'86 - 3	John "Chant" Sinclair	renegade super ninja
New York	Cunningham, E. V.	'64 - 2	Harvey Krim	NYPD detective
New York	Cunningham, E. V.	'65 - 2	John Comaday & Larry Cohen	police commissioner & Manhattan DA's 1st assistant
New York	DeAndrea, William	'78 - 8	Matt Cobb	network television executive
New York	DeAndrea, William	'84 - 4	Clifford Driscoll	no-name American spy
New York	Deaver, Jeffery	'89 - 3	Rune	NYPD detective
New York	Deaver, Jeffery	'97 - 1	Lincoln Rhyme & Amelia Sachs	disabled ex-head of NYPD forensics & rookie beat cop
New York	Dee, Ed	'94 - 3	Anthony Ryan & Joe Gregory	NYPD detective partners
New York	DeMille, Nelson	'74 - 3	Joe Ryker	NYPD homicide detective
New York	DeMille, Nelson	'75 - 3	Joe Keller	NYPD homicide detective
New York	Finkelstein, Jay	'96 - 2	Leo Gold	30-something Jewish P.I.
New York	Fliegel, Richard	'88 - 7	Shelly Lowenkopf	Allerton Avenue precinct cop
New York	Flynn, Don	'83 - 5	Ed "Fitz" Fitzgerald	Daily Tribune reporter
New York	Friedman, Kinky	'86 -10	Kinky Friedman	country & western singer turned sleuth
New York	Gibbs, Tony	'92 - 2	Diana Speed	publishing company chief financial officer
New York	Gorman, Ed	'87 - 2	Tobin	hot-tempered movie critic
New York	Granger, Bill	'79 -13	Devereaux aka November Man	field intelligence agent for R section
New York	Hailey, J. P.	'88 - 5	Steve Winslow	courtroom attorney
New York	Hall, Parnell	'87 -13	Stanley Hastings	married actor and private eye
New York	Harvey, James Neal	'91 - 5	Ben Tolliver	NYPD lieutenant
New York	Heffernan, William	'88 - 5	Paul Devlin	NYPD detective
New York	Hoch, Edward D.	'71 - 3	Simon Ark	ancient hounder of Satan
New York	Jahn, Michael	'82 - 5	Bill Donovan	chief of special investigations
New York	Jeffers, H. Paul	'81 - 3	Harry MacNeil	1930s ex-cop private eye
New York	Jeffers, H. Paul	'95 - 3	John Bogdanovic	aide-de-camp to NYPD Chief of Detectives
New York	Jeffers, H. Paul	'97 - 1	Arlene Flynn	chief investigator for the District Attorney
New York	King, Frank	'88 - 2	Sally Tepper	unemployed actress with five dogs
New York	Kurland, Michael	'97 - 1	Alexander Brass	1930s newspaper columnist
New York	Livingston, Jack	'82 - 4	Joe Binney	hearing-impaired private eye
New York	Lupica, Mike	'95 - 1	DiMaggio	private eye in the sports world
New York	Lupica, Mike	'86 - 3	Peter Finley	investigative TV reporter
New York	MacLeod, Robert	'64 - 6	Talos Cord	United Nations troubleshooter
New York	Mahoney, Dan	'93 - 3	Brian McKenna	police detective

Setting	Author	1 - #	Series Character	Occupation
United States...cont.				
New York...cont.				
New York	Margolis, Seth	'91 - 2	Joe DiGregorio	ex-Long Island cop turned Manhattan P.I.
New York	Marshall, William	'88 - 2	Tillman & Muldoon	turn-of-the-century policemen
New York	Masters, J. D.	'89 - 6	Donovan Steele	police lieutenant
New York	Masur, Harold Q.	'47 - 11	Scott Jordan	criminal defense attorney
New York	Meyers, Martin	'75 - 5	Patrick Hardy	private eye
New York	Miller, Victor B.	'74 - 9	Theo Kojak	NYPD cop
New York	Murphy, Dallas	'87 - 3	Artie Deemer	owner of celebrity spokesdog
New York	Murphy, Haughton	'86 - 7	Reuben Frost	retired Wall Street attorney
New York	Murphy, Warren B.	'71 -80	Remo Williams	ex-cop turned government enforcer
New York	Murphy, Warren B.	'73 - 6	Ed Razoni & William Jackson	police detectives
New York	Nathan, Paul	'94 - 3	Bert Swain	PR chief at a medical research center
New York	Newman, C.	'86 - 9	Joe Dante	maverick cop
New York	Orenstein, Frank	'83 - 3	Ev Franklin	advertising executive
New York	Oster, Jerry	'85 - 3	Jacob "Jake" Neuman	police lieutenant
New York	Oster, Jerry	'90 - 4	Joe Cullen	Internal Affairs police sergeant
New York	Peterson, Keith	'88 - 5	John Wells	newspaper reporter
New York	Philbin, Tom	'85 - 9	Joe Lawless	Felony Squad commander in the Bronx
New York	Phillips, T. J.	'95 - 2	Joe Wilder	struggling playwright and novelist
New York	Randisi, Robert J.	'82 - 6	Miles Jacoby	boxer turned P.I.
New York	Randisi, Robert J.	'95 - 2	Joe Keough	NYPD detective
New York	Resnicow, Herbert	'83 - 5	Alexander Gold	construction engineer & puzzle maven
New York	Ridgway, Jason	'60 - 4	Brian Guy	private eye
New York	Sanders, Lawrence	'73 - 4	Edward X. "Iron Balls" Delaney	retired chief of detectives
New York	Sanders, Lawrence	'87 - 2	Timothy Cone	Wall Street financial detective
New York	Sarrantonio, Al	'89 - 2	Jack Blaine	retired Yonkers cop with a P.I. license
New York	Schoonover, W.	'90 - 2	John Wilkes	defense attorney
New York	Schorr, Mark	'83 - 3	Simon Jaffe aka Red Diamond	cab-driving pulp collector turned P.I.
New York	Smith, Martin Cruz	'71 - 2	Roman Grey	Gypsy art dealer
New York	Solomita, Stephen	'88 - 6	Stanley Moodrow	cop turned private eye
New York	Spillane, Mickey	'47 -13	Mike Hammer	super-patriot private investigator
New York	Spillane, Mickey	'64 - 5	Tiger Mann	freelance spy for a private right-wing group
New York	Stark, Richard	'62 -17	Parker	cold-blooded professional thief
New York	Stark, Richard	'67 - 4	Alan Grofield	actor and part-time bank robber
New York	Tanenbaum, R.	'87 - 9	"Butch" Karp & Marlene Ciampi	1970s Criminal Courts Bureau chief & assistant DA
New York	Thomson, M.	'96 - 2	Nason "Nase" Nichols	private eye
New York	Topor, Tom	'78 - 2	Kevin Fitzgerald	private eye
New York	Vachss, Andrew H.	'85 - 9	Burke	outlaw soldier-of-fortune investigator
New York	Waugh, Hillary	'47 - 3	Sheridan Wesley	private investigator
New York	Waugh, Hillary	'68 - 3	Frank Sessions	Manhattan North homicide detective
New York	Waugh, Hillary	'80 - 6	Simon Kaye	private eye
New York	Westlake, Donald E.	'70 - 9	John Dortmunder	comic thief
New York	Wilcox, Collin	'73 - 2	McCloud	New Mexico marshall
New York	Wiltse, David	'91 - 6	John Becker	FBI agent
New York	Winslow, Don	'91 - 5	Neal Carey	youthful pickpocket turned P.I.
New York	Woods, Stuart	'91 - 3	Stone Barrington	suave ex-cop attorney
Queens	Coe, Tucker	'66 - 5	Mitch Tobin	ex-cop P.I.
Saratoga	Healy, R. Austin	'95 - 2	Mike Flint	ex-CIA and NYC cop
Saratoga Springs	Dobyns, Stephen	'76 - 9	Charlie Bradshaw	ex-cop ex-stable security guard turned detective
Sparta	DeAndrea, William	'79 - 3	Niccolo Benedetti	world-renowned criminologist professor
Wagg's Neck Hrbr	Kaufelt, David A.	'93 - 3	Wynsome "Wyn" Lewis	ex-Manhattan real estate attorney
Westchester Co.	Daly, Conor	'95 - 3	Kieran Lanahan	lawyer turned country club golf pro
North Carolina (NC)				
	Harvey, Clay	'96 - 2	Tyler Vance	ex-operative turned family man
Cape Hatteras	Poyer, David	'89 - 4	Tiller Galloway	ex-Navy SEAL turned salvage diver

Setting	Author	1 - #	Series Character	Occupation

United States...cont.

Ohio (OH)

Setting	Author	1 - #	Series Character	Occupation
Cincinnati	Roberts, John M.	'94 - 2	Gabe Treloar	ex-LA cop turned P.I.
Cincinnati	DeBrosse, Jim	'88 - 3	Rick Decker	investigative reporter
Cincinnati	Valin, Jonathan	'80 - 11	Harry Stoner	private eye
Cleveland	Axler, Leo	'94 - 4	Bill Hawley	undertaker sleuth
Cleveland	Collins, Max A., Jr.	'87 - 4	Eliot Ness	1930s public safety officer
Cleveland	Martin, James E.	'89 - 4	Gil Disbro	teetotaler private eye
Cleveland	Pomidor, Bill	'95 - 4	Calista & Plato Marley	forensic pathologist wife & family physician husband
Cleveland	Roberts, Les	'88 - 9	Milan Jacovich	blue-collar Slovenian P.I. with a master's degree

Oklahoma (OK)

Setting	Author	1 - #	Series Character	Occupation
Oklahoma City	Bickham, Jack	'67 - 2	Charity Ross	1890s widowed frontier-ranch-owner
Timberlake	Miles, John	'93 - 3	Laura Michaels	retirement center social worker
Tulsa	Bernhardt, William	'91 - 6	Ben Kincaid	attorney
Tulsa	Sanders, William	'93 - 3	Taggart Roper	Cherokee writer and private eye

Oregon (OR)

Setting	Author	1 - #	Series Character	Occupation
	Goddard, Ken	'92 - 3	Henry Lightstone	National Fish and Wildlife investigator
Port Jerome	Kohler, Vince	'90 - 4	Eldon Larkin	small-town newspaper reporter

Pennsylvania (PA)

Setting	Author	1 - #	Series Character	Occupation
	Kelley, Patrick A.	'85 - 5	Harry Colderwood	professional magician
Lancaster County	Albert, Neil	'91 - 6	Dave Garrett	disbarred lawyer turned private eye
Philadelphia	Lashner, William	'95 - 2	Victor Carl	hard-boiled lawyer
Pittsburgh	Gat, Dimitri	'82 - 2	Yuri Nevsky	information specialist
Pittsburgh	Lipinski, Thomas	'94 - 3	Carroll Dorsey	ex-basketball star law-school dropout P.I.
Rocksburg	Constantine, K. C.	'72 -13	Mario Balzic	small-town police chief

Rhode Island (RI)

Setting	Author	1 - #	Series Character	Occupation
Providence	Briody, Thomas	'95 - 2	Michael Carolina	former TV investigative reporter

South Dakota (SD)

Setting	Author	1 - #	Series Character	Occupation
Corden	Adams, Harold	'81 -14	Carl Wilcox	Depression era sign-painter

Tennessee (TN)

Setting	Author	1 - #	Series Character	Occupation
	Bourgeau, Art	'80 - 4	Claude "Snake" Kirlin & F.T. Zevich	magazine freelancer & sidekick
	McDonald, Gregory	'95 - 2	Skylar Whitfield	small-town good-ol'-boy
Knoxville	Nighbert, David F.	'88 - 3	Bull Cochran	ex-big league pitcher
Nashville	Womack, Steven	'93 - 4	Harry James Denton	ex-newspaper reporter turned P.I.

Texas (TX)

Setting	Author	1 - #	Series Character	Occupation
	Crider, Bill	'88 - 3	Carl Burns	college professor
Austin	Meyer, Charles	'95 - 2	Lucas Holt	Episcopal church pastor
Austin	Sublett, Jesse	'89 - 3	Martin Fender	skip tracer
Blacklin County	Crider, Bill	'86 - 9	Dan Rhodes	laid-back sheriff with a motley crew of deputies
Dallas	Duncan, W. Glenn	'87 - 6	Rafferty	ex-cop private eye
Dallas	Gray, A. W.	'88 - 4	Bino Phillips	6' 6" attorney
Dallas	Gregory, Sarah	'96 - 2	Sharon Hays	defense attorney
Dallas	Swanson, Doug J.	'94 - 3	Jack Flippo	recovering deadbeat P.I.
East Texas	Lansdale, Joe R.	'90 - 4	Hap Collins & Leonard Pine	straight white & gay black good ol' boys
Galveston	Crider, Bill	'91 - 4	Truman Smith	private eye
Houston	Hemlin, Tim	'96 - 3	Neil Marshall	graduate student poet
Houston	Lindsey, David L.	'83 - 5	Stuart Haydon	homicide detective
Mirabeau	Abbott, Jeff	'94 - 4	Jordan Poteet	small-town librarian

Utah (UT)

Setting	Author	1 - #	Series Character	Occupation
Salt Lake City	Irvine, Robert	'88 - 8	Moroni Traveler	non-Mormon ex-football player private eye

Setting	Author	1 - #	Series Character	Occupation

United States...cont.

Virginia (VA)

Setting	Author	1 - #	Series Character	Occupation
Charlottesville	Burns, Ron	'93 - 2	Harrison Hull	18th century frontier Army captain
Charlottesville	Hornig, Doug	'84 - 4	Loren Swift	Vietnam vet private eye
Charlottesville	Hornig, Doug	'87 - 2	Steven Kirk	burned-out government agent
Hunter County	Slusher, William S.	'95 - 3	Lewis Cody	sheriff

Vermont (VT)

Setting	Author	1 - #	Series Character	Occupation
	Jaspersohn, William	'95 - 2	Peter Boone	ex-Red Sox pitcher turned P.I.
	Resnicow, Herbert	'85 - 5	Giles Sullivan & Isabel Macintosh	crossword expert & faculty dean
Brattleboro	Mayor, Archer	'88 - 8	Joe Gunther	homicide detective
Northern	Leitz, David	'96 - 3	Max Addams	proprietor of trout-fishing lodge

Washington (WA)

Setting	Author	1 - #	Series Character	Occupation
Port Angeles	Elkins, Aaron	'82 - 9	Gideon Oliver	anthropology professor
Seattle	Elkins, Aaron	'87 - 3	Chris Norgren	art museum curator
Seattle	Emerson, Earl	'85 -10	Thomas Black	bicycling enthusiast P.I.
Seattle	Ford, G. M.	'95 - 4	Leo Waterman	wisecracking private eye
Seattle	Hoyt, Richard	'80 - 7	John Denson	flaky private eye
Seattle	Huebner, Frederick	'86 - 5	Matt Riordan	burned-out lawyer turned investigator
Seattle	Pearson, Ridley	'88 - 4	Lou Boldt & Daphne Matthews	detective & police psychologist
Spokane	Oliver, Steve	'96 - 2	Scott Moody	ex-mental patient turned P.I.
Staircase	Emerson, Earl	'88 - 5	Mac Fontana	ex-firefighter and arson investigator

Wisconsin (WI)

Setting	Author	1 - #	Series Character	Occupation
Oakalla	Riggs, John R.	'84 -12	Garth Ryland	small-town newspaper editor

West Virginia (WV)

Setting	Author	1 - #	Series Character	Occupation
Shawnee	Douglas, John	'87 - 2	Jack Reese	photographer

Wyoming (WY)

Setting	Author	1 - #	Series Character	Occupation
Le Four	Roderus, Frank	'84 - 6	Carl Heller	private eye
	DeAndrea, William	'95 -12	Lobo Blacke & Quinn Booker	crippled ex-frontier lawman & his biographer
Victory	Bean, Gregory	'95 - 3	Harry Starbranch	burned-out Denver cop turned small-town police chief

Other U.S.

Setting	Author	1 - #	Series Character	Occupation
	Ardies, Tom	'71 - 3	Charlie Sparrow	handsome American spy
	Bickham, Jack	'89 - 6	Brad Smith	championship tennis player and part-time CIA agent
	Biggle, Lloyd, Jr.	'87 - 3	J. Pletcher & Raina Lambert	pair of private eyes
	Block, Lawrence	'66 - 7	Evan Tanner	government agent with permanent insomnia
	Clarkson, John	'92 - 3	Jack Devlin	ex-Secret Service turned security firm investigator
	Cussler, Clive	'73 -13	Dirk Pitt	special projs dir of nat'l underwater-marine agency
	Grant, Maxwell	'64 - 8	The Shadow	P.I. of unknown identity
	Hamilton, Donald	'60 -27	Matt Helm	American superspy
	Handler, David	'88 - 8	Stewart "Hoagy" Hoag	celebrity ghostwriter
	Haywood, Gar A.	'94 - 2	Dottie & Joe Loudermilk	traveling retired black couple
	Heck, Peter J.	'95 - 2	Mark Twain & Wentworth Cabot	19th century American author & his secretary
	Hoyt, Richard	'82 - 8	James Burlane	ex-CIA operative turned private
	Hunter, Stephen	'93 - 2	Bob "the Nailer" Swagger	master sniper
	Johnson, E. Richard	'68 - 2	Tony Lonto	police detective
	Knight, J. D.	'95 - 2	Virgil Proctor	bounty hunter P.I.
	Lutz, John	'84 - 2	E. L. Oxman & Art Tobin	pair of investigators
	Malone, Paul	'91 - 3	Jack Fowler	DEA agent
	McDonald, Gregory	'74 -11	Irwin M. Fletcher	reporter turned beach bum socialite
	Milan, Borto	'95 - 2	Edward Ryan	motorcycle drifter
	Osborn, David	'89 - 3	Margaret Barlow	50-something freelance journalist
	Payne, Laurence	'82 - 5	Mark Savage	movie star turned private eye
	Ross, Philip	'86 - 2	Tom Talley	American CIA operative
	Schorr, Mark	'88 - 3	Robert Stark	private investigator

Setting	Author	1 - #	Series Character	Occupation
United States...cont.				
Other U.S....cont.				
	Sherburne, James	'80 - 5	Paddy Moretti	1890s sportswriter
	Soos, Troy	'94 - 5	Mickey Rawlings	1910 journeyman second baseman
	Vance, Jack	'64 - 5	Keith Gersen	hunter of nonhuman killers
Western US	Gorman, Ed	'87 - 4	Leo Guild	1890s bounty hunter
Southern US	Brewer, James D.	'94 - 4	Luke Williamson & Masey Baldridge	Yankee riverboat captain & Confederate veteran
Southern US	Nordan, Robert	'89 - 3	Mavis Lashley	little old lady Sunday School teacher
Wales				
Cardiff	Cory, Desmond	'91 - 3	John Dobie	math professor
Cardiff	Williams, David	'94 - 3	Merlin Parry & Gomer Lloyd	detective chief inspector & detective sergeant
West Indies *[see also Caribbean]*				
	Grissom, Ken	'88 - 3	John Rodrigue	one-eyed Creole salvager
Grand Flamingo	York, Andrew	'77 - 4	James Munroe Tallant	cricket star turned police commissioner
International				
	Judd, Bob	'89 - 5	Forrest Evers	former race car driver
	MacLeod, Robert	'74 - 6	Andrew Laird	marine insurance claims investigator
	Miles, Keith	'86 - 4	Alan Saxon	professional golfer
	Vincent, Lawrence	'89 - 2	Townsend Reeves	radiologist with a ballerina girlfriend
Off-Planet				
Mars	Nolan, William F.	'71 - 2	Sam Space	private eye on Mars

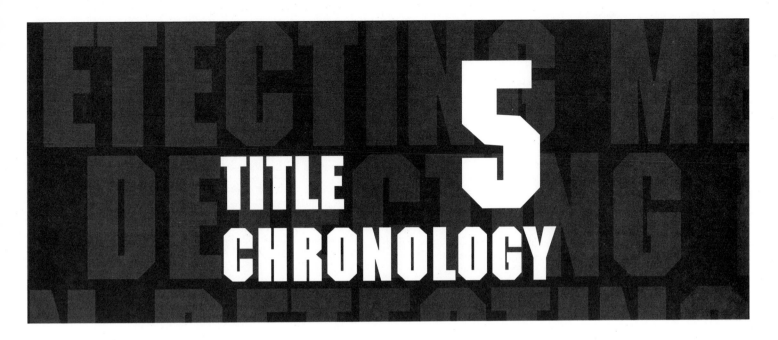

TITLE 5 CHRONOLOGY

1930s

| 1936 | 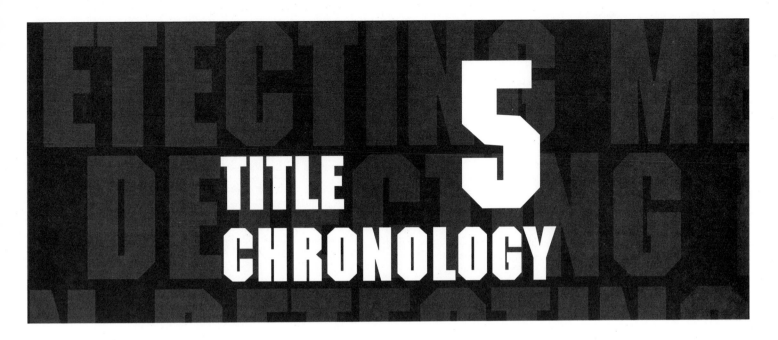 Harvard Has a Homicide [Brit.-J for Jupiter] (Fuller, Timothy) |
| 1939 | The Mask of Dimitrios [U.S.-A Coffin for Dimitrios] (Ambler, Eric) |

1940s

1941   Three Thirds of a Ghost (Fuller, Timothy)
1941   Reunion with Murder (Fuller, Timothy)

1943   This Is Murder, Mr. Jones (Fuller, Timothy)

1947   Close Quarters (Gilbert, Michael)
1947   Bury Me Deep (Masur, Harold Q.)
1947   Guilty Bystander (Miller, Wade)
1947   I, the Jury (Spillane, Mickey)
1947   Madam Will Not Dine Tonight [APA-If I Live to Dine] (Waugh, Hillary)

1948   They Never Looked Inside [U.S.-He Didn't Mind Danger] (Gilbert, Michael)
1948   Fatal Step (Miller, Wade)
1948   Uneasy Street (Miller, Wade)
1948   Hope To Die (Waugh, Hillary)
1949   The Doors Open (Gilbert, Michael)
1949   Suddenly a Corpse (Masur, Harold Q.)
1949   The Odds Run Out (Waugh, Hillary)

1950s

1950   Keep Cool, Mr. Jones (Fuller, Timothy)
1950   Smallbone Deceased (Gilbert, Michael)
1950   Calamity Fair (Miller, Wade)
1950   Murder Charge (Miller, Wade)
1950   The Case of the Vanishing Beauty (Prather, Richard)
1950   My Gun is Quick (Spillane, Mickey)
1950   Vengeance is Mine! (Spillane, Mickey)

1951   Secret Ministry (Cory, Desmond)
1951   Begin, Murderer! (Cory, Desmond)
1951   Death Has Deep Roots (Gilbert, Michael)
1951   You Can't Live Forever (Masur, Harold Q.)
1951   Shoot to Kill (Miller, Wade)
1951   Bodies in Bedlam (Prather, Richard)
1951   Everybody Had a Gun (Prather, Richard)
1951   Find This Woman (Prather, Richard)
1951   The Big Kill (Spillane, Mickey)
1951   One Lonely Night (Spillane, Mickey)

1952   Death in the Fifth Position (Box, Edgar)
1952   This Traitor, Death (Cory, Desmond)
1952   This is Jezebel (Cory, Desmond)
1952   Concerning Blackshirt (Graeme, Roderic)
1952   So Rich, So Lovely, and So Dead (Masur, Harold Q.)
1952   Way of a Wanton (Prather, Richard)
1952   Pattern for Murder [as by David Knight] [APA-The Scrambled Yeggs] (Prather, Richard)
1952   Dagger of Flesh (Prather, Richard)
1952   Darling, It's Death (Prather, Richard)
1952   Kiss Me, Deadly (Spillane, Mickey)
1952   The Big Sin (Webb, Jack)

1953   The Tall Dolores (Avallone, Michael)
1953   The Spitting Image (Avallone, Michael)
1953   Death Before Bedtime (Box, Edgar)
1953   Dead Man Falling (Cory, Desmond)
1953   Lady Lost (Cory, Desmond)
1953   Fear To Tread (Gilbert, Michael)
1953   Blackshirt Wins the Trick (Graeme, Roderic)
1953   Blackshirt Passes By (Graeme, Roderic)
1953   Ride a High Horse (Prather, Richard)
1953   Docken Dead (Trench, John)
1953   The Naked Angel [Brit.-Such Women Are Dangerous] (Webb, Jack)

1954   Dead Game (Avallone, Michael)
1954   It's Murder, Senorita (Bateson, David)
1954   Death Likes It Hot (Box, Edgar)
1954   Intrigue (Cory, Desmond)
1954   Salute to Blackshirt (Graeme, Roderic)
1954   The Big Money (Masur, Harold Q.)
1954   Always Leave 'em Dying (Prather, Richard)
1954   Pattern for Panic (Prather, Richard)
1954   Dishonoured Bones (Trench, John)
1954   The Damned Lovely (Webb, Jack)

1955   The Man from the Rock (Bateson, David)
1955   The Shaken Leaf (Cory, Desmond)
1955   Height of Day (Cory, Desmond)
1955   The Amazing Mr. Blackshirt (Graeme, Roderic)
1955   The Spiral Path (Grayson, Richard)
1955   Gently Does It (Hunter, Alan)
1955   The Second Longest Night (Marlowe, Stephen)
1955   Strip for Murder (Prather, Richard)
1955   The Broken Doll (Webb, Jack)

1956	Violence in Velvet (Avallone, Michael)
1956	The Big Tomorrow (Bateson, David)
1956	High Requiem (Cory, Desmond)
1956	Johnny Goes North (Cory, Desmond)
1956	Blackshirt Meets the Lady (Graeme, Roderic)
1956	Gently By the Shore (Hunter, Alan)
1956	Murder is My Dish (Marlowe, Stephen)
1956	Mecca for Murder (Marlowe, Stephen)
1956	Tall, Dark, and Deadly (Masur, Harold Q.)
1956 ∎	Cop Hater (McBain, Ed)
1956	The Mugger (McBain, Ed)
1956	The Pusher (McBain, Ed)
1956	The Wailing Frail (Prather, Richard)
1956	The Bad Blonde (Webb, Jack)

1957	The Case of the Bouncing Betty (Avallone, Michael)
1957	The Case of the Violent Virgin (Avallone, Michael)
1957	The Crazy Mixed Up Corpse (Avallone, Michael)
1957	The Voodoo Murders (Avallone, Michael)
1957	Paging Blackshirt (Graeme, Roderic)
1957	Death in Melting (Grayson, Richard)
1957	Gently Down the Stream (Hunter, Alan)
1957	Landed Gently (Hunter, Alan)
1957 ∎	Deadline for a Dream [U.S.-In at the Kill] (Knox, Bill)
1957	Trouble is My Name (Marlowe, Stephen)
1957	Killers are My Meat (Marlowe, Stephen)
1957	The Con Man (McBain, Ed)
1957	Killer's Choice (McBain, Ed)
1957	Three's a Shroud [3 novellas] (Prather, Richard)
1957	What Rough Beast (Trench, John)
1957	The Brass Halo (Webb, Jack)

1958	The Soho Jungle (Bateson, David)
1958	Johnny Goes East (Cory, Desmond)
1958	Blackshirt Helps Himself (Graeme, Roderic)
1958	Double for Blackshirt (Graeme, Roderic)
1958	Madman's Whisper (Grayson, Richard)
1958	Gently Through the Mill (Hunter, Alan)
1958	Violence is My Business (Marlowe, Stephen)
1958	Terror is My Trade (Marlowe, Stephen)
1958	The Last Gamble [Brit.-The Last Breath] (Masur, Harold Q.)
1958	Killer's Payoff (McBain, Ed)
1958	Killer's Wedge (McBain, Ed)
1958	Lady Killer (McBain, Ed)
1958	Slab Happy (Prather, Richard)
1958	Take a Murder, Darling (Prather, Richard)
1958 ∎	Run for Cover (Welcome, John)

1959	I'll Go Anywhere (Bateson, David)
1959	Johnny Goes West (Cory, Desmond)
1959	Johnny Goes South (Cory, Desmond)
1959	Blood and Judgment (Gilbert, Michael)
1959	Blackshirt Sets the Pace (Graeme, Roderic)
1959	Gently in the Sun (Hunter, Alan)
1959 ∎	Thirteen Days (Jeffries, Ian)
1959 ∎	A Twist of Sand (Jenkins, Geoffrey)
1959	Death Department (Knox, Bill)
1959	Homicide is My Game (Marlowe, Stephen)
1959	'Til Death (McBain, Ed)
1959	King's Ransom (McBain, Ed)
1959	Over Her Dead Body (Prather, Richard)
1959	Double in Trouble (Prather, Richard)
1959 ∎	Sleep Long, My Love [APA-Jigsaw] (Waugh, Hillary)
1959	Road Block (Waugh, Hillary)
1959	The Deadly Sex (Webb, Jack)
1959	The Delicate Darling (Webb, Jack)

1960s

1960	Meanwhile Back at the Morgue (Avallone, Michael)
1960	I'll Do Anything [Australia] (Bateson, David)
1960 ∎	The Head (Cory, Desmond)
1960	Blackshirt Sees It Through (Graeme, Roderic)
1960	Dead So Soon (Grayson, Richard)

1960 ∎	Death of a Citizen (Hamilton, Donald)
1960	The Wrecking Crew (Hamilton, Donald)
1960	Gently with the Painters (Hunter, Alan)
1960	Dignity and Purity (Jeffries, Ian)
1960	Leave it to the Hangman (Knox, Bill)
1960	Peril is My Pay (Marlowe, Stephen)
1960	Danger is My Line (Marlowe, Stephen)
1960	Death is My Comrade (Marlowe, Stephen)
1960	Send Another Hearse (Masur, Harold Q.)
1960	Give the Boys a Great Big Hand (McBain, Ed)
1960	The Heckler (McBain, Ed)
1960	See Them Die (McBain, Ed)
1960 ∎	Gibralter Road (McCutchan, Philip)
1960 ∎	Sergeant Cluff Stands Firm (North, Gil)
1960	Dance With the Dead (Prather, Richard)
1960 ∎	Adam's Fall (Ridgway, Jason)
1960 ∎	Miami Mayhem (Rome, Anthony)

1961 ∎	Investigations Are Proceeding [U.S.-The D. I.] (Ashford, Jeffrey)
1961	The Alarming Clock (Avallone, Michael)
1961 ∎	Murder is for Keeps (Chambers, Peter)
1961 ∎	Stranglehold (Cory, Desmond)
1961	Blackshirt Finds Trouble (Graeme, Roderic)
1961	The Removers (Hamilton, Donald)
1961	Gently to the Summit (Hunter, Alan)
1961	Gently Go Man (Hunter, Alan)
1961	It Wasn't Me! (Jeffries, Ian)
1961 ∎	Call for the Dead [APA-The Deadly Affair] (Le Carré, John) ★
1961 ∎	News of Murder (Lejeune, Anthony)
1961	Manhunt is My Mission (Marlowe, Stephen)
1961	Lady, Lady, I Did It! (McBain, Ed)
1961	Redcap (McCutchan, Philip)
1961	The Methods of Sergeant Cluff (North, Gil)
1961	Shell Scott's Seven Slaughters (Prather, Richard)
1961	Dig That Crazy Grave (Prather, Richard)
1961	People in Glass Houses (Ridgway, Jason)
1961	Lady in Cement (Rome, Anthony)
1961	That Night it Rained (Waugh, Hillary)

1962 ∎	The Light of Day [U.S.-Topkapi] (Ambler, Eric) ★★
1962	Wreath for a Redhead (Chambers, Peter)
1962	The Big Goodbye (Chambers, Peter)
1962	Undertow (Cory, Desmond)
1962 ∎	The Ipcress File (Deighton, Len)
1962 ∎	The Testament of Caspar Schultz (Fallon, Martin)
1962 ∎	Love in Amsterdam [U.S.-Death in Amsterdam] (Freeling, Nicolas)
1962	Blackshirt Takes the Trail (Graeme, Roderic)
1962	Murderer's Row (Hamilton, Donald)
1962	The Silencers (Hamilton, Donald)
1962 ∎	The Benevolent Blackmailer (Harknett, Terry)
1962	The Scratch on the Surface (Harknett, Terry)
1962	Gently Where the Roads Go (Hunter, Alan)
1962	Little Drops of Blood (Knox, Bill)
1962	Sanctuary Isle [U.S.-The Gray Sentinels] (Knox, Bill)
1962	A Murder of Quality (Le Carré, John)
1962	Duel in the Shadows (Lejeune, Anthony)
1962	Jeopardy is My Job (Marlowe, Stephen)
1962	The Name is Jordan (Masur, Harold Q.)
1962	The Empty Hours (McBain, Ed)
1962	Like Love (McBain, Ed)
1962	Bluebolt One (McCutchan, Philip)
1962	Sergeant Cluff Goes Fishing (North, Gil)
1962 ∎	The Nose on My Face [APA-The First Body] (Payne, Laurence)
1962	Too Small for His Shoes (Payne, Laurence)
1962	Kill the Clown (Prather, Richard)
1962	Hardly a Man is Now Alive (Ridgway, Jason)
1962	My Kind of Game (Rome, Anthony)
1962	The Girl Hunters (Spillane, Mickey)
1962 ∎	The Hunter [Brit.-Point Blank] (Stark, Richard)

1962		The Late Mrs. D (Waugh, Hillary)
1962		Born Victim (Waugh, Hillary)
1962	∎	Long Run South (Williams, Alan)

1963		The Bedroom Bolero [Brit.-The Bolero Murders] (Avallone, Michael)
1963		The Living Bomb (Avallone, Michael)
1963		There is Something About a Dame (Avallone, Michael)
1963	∎	Diecast (Brett, John Michael)
1963		Dames Can Be Deadly (Chambers, Peter)
1963		Down-Beat Kill (Chambers, Peter)
1963		Lady, This is Murder (Chambers, Peter)
1963		Hammerhead (Cory, Desmond)
1963		Horse Under Water (Deighton, Len)
1963		Year of the Tiger (Fallon, Martin)
1963		Because of the Cats (Freeling, Nicolas)
1963		Gun Before Butter [U.S.-Question of Loyalty] (Freeling, Nicolas) ★
1963	∎	The Timeless Sleep (Galway, Robert Conington)
1963		Assignment New York (Galway, Robert Conington)
1963		Assignment London (Galway, Robert Conington)
1963		Blackshirt on the Spot (Graeme, Roderic)
1963		Call for Blackshirt (Graeme, Roderic)
1963		The Ambushers (Hamilton, Donald)
1963		Invitation to a Funeral (Harknett, Terry)
1963		Dead Little Rich Girl (Harknett, Terry)
1963		Gently Floating (Hunter, Alan)
1963		The Man in the Bottle [U.S.-The Killing Game] (Knox, Bill)
1963		The Spy Who Came in From the Cold (Le Carré, John) ★★
1963		Francesca (Marlowe, Stephen)
1963		Ten Plus One (McBain, Ed)
1963		The Man from Moscow (McCutchan, Philip)
1963		Warmaster (McCutchan, Philip)
1963		More Deaths for Sergeant Cluff (North, Gil)
1963		Dead Heat (Prather, Richard)
1963		The Man With the Getaway Face [Brit.-The Steel Hit] (Stark, Richard)
1963		The Outfit (Stark, Richard)
1963		The Mourner (Stark, Richard)
1963		Death and Circumstance (Waugh, Hillary)
1963		Prisoner's Plea (Waugh, Hillary)
1963		The Gilded Witch (Webb, Jack)

1964		Enquiries Are Continuing [U.S.-The Superintendent's Room] (Ashford, Jeffrey)
1964		Lust is No Lady [Brit.-The Brutal Kook] (Avallone, Michael)
1964		This'll Kill You (Chambers, Peter)
1964		Nobody Lives Forever (Chambers, Peter)
1964	∎	Vote X for Treason [APA-Counterspy] (Cleeve, Brian)
1964		The Name of the Game (Cory, Desmond)
1964	∎	Lydia (Cunningham, E. V.)
1964		Funeral in Berlin (Deighton, Len) ☆
1964		Double-Barrel (Freeling, Nicolas)
1964	∎	The Liquidator (Gardner, John)
1964		Blackshirt Saves the Day (Graeme, Roderic)
1964	∎	The Shadow Strikes (Grant, Maxwell)
1964		The Shadowers (Hamilton, Donald)
1964		The Ravagers (Hamilton, Donald)
1964		The Evil Money (Harknett, Terry)
1964		The Man Who Did Not Die (Harknett, Terry)
1964		Gently Sahib (Hunter, Alan)
1964	∎	The Perfect Murder (Keating, H. R. F.) ★ ☆
1964	∎	Friday the Rabbi Slept Late (Kemelman, Harry) ★
1964	∎	The Scavengers (Knox, Bill)
1964	∎	Cave of Bats (MacLeod, Robert)
1964		Drum Beat—Berlin (Marlowe, Stephen)
1964		Make a Killing (Masur, Harold Q.)
1964		Ax (McBain, Ed)
1964		Moscow Coach (McCutchan, Philip)
1964		Sergeant Cluff and the Madmen (North, Gil)

1964		Deep and Crisp and Even (Payne, Laurence)
1964		Joker in the Deck (Prather, Richard)
1964		The Cockeyed Corpse (Prather, Richard)
1964		The Trojan Hearse (Prather, Richard)
1964	∎	Day of the Guns (Spillane, Mickey)
1964		The Snake (Spillane, Mickey)
1964		The Score (Stark, Richard)
1964	∎	The Duplicate (Taylor, H. Baldwin)
1964	∎	The Star King (Vance, Jack)
1964		The Killing Machine (Vance, Jack)
1964		The Missing Man (Waugh, Hillary)
1964		Hard to Handle (Welcome, John)
1964		Barbouze [U.S.-The False Beards] (Williams, Alan)

1965		A Plague of Dragons (Brett, John Michael)
1965		A Cargo of Spent Evil (Brett, John Michael)
1965		You're Better Off Dead (Chambers, Peter)
1965		Always Take the Big Ones (Chambers, Peter)
1965		Dark Blood, Dark Terror (Cleeve, Brian)
1965	∎	Penelope (Cunningham, E. V.)
1965		The Keys of Hell (Fallon, Martin)
1965	∎	Odds Against (Francis, Dick) ☆
1965		Criminal Conversation (Freeling, Nicolas)
1965		Assignment Andalusia (Galway, Robert Conington)
1965		The Understrike (Gardner, John)
1965		Danger for Blackshirt (Graeme, Roderic)
1965		Shadow Beware (Grant, Maxwell)
1965		Cry Shadow (Grant, Maxwell)
1965		The Shadow's Revenge (Grant, Maxwell)
1965		The Devastators (Hamilton, Donald)
1965	∎	The Graveyard Shift (Higgins, Jack)
1965		Gently with the Ladies (Hunter, Alan)
1965		The Taste of Proof (Knox, Bill)
1965		The Looking Glass War (Le Carré, John)
1965		The Dark Trade [U.S.-Death of a Pornographer] (Lejeune, Anthony)
1965		Drum Beat—Dominique (Marlowe, Stephen)
1965		He Who Hesitates (McBain, Ed)
1965		Doll (McBain, Ed)
1965		Sergeant Cluff and the Price of Pity (North, Gil)
1965	∎	Modesty Blaise (O'Donnell, Peter)
1965	∎	Night Without Darkness (Orvis, Kenneth)
1965		Kill Him Twice (Prather, Richard)
1965		Dead Man's Walk (Prather, Richard)
1965		The Meandering Corpse (Prather, Richard)
1965		Bloody Sunrise (Spillane, Mickey)
1965		The Death Dealers (Spillane, Mickey)
1965		The Jugger (Stark, Richard)
1965		End of a Party (Waugh, Hillary)

1966		The Fat Death (Avallone, Michael)
1966		The February Doll Murders (Avallone, Michael)
1966	∎	A Queer Kind of Death (Baxt, George)
1966	∎	The Thief Who Couldn't Sleep (Block, Lawrence)
1966		The Cancelled Czech (Block, Lawrence)
1966	∎	Kill Him Quickly, It's Raining (Brett, Michael)
1966		No Gold When You Go (Chambers, Peter)
1966		Don't Bother to Knock (Chambers, Peter)
1966	∎	The High Commissioner (Cleary, Jon)
1966		The Judas Goat [U.S.-Vice Isn't Private] (Cleeve, Brian)
1966	∎	Kinds of Love, Kinds of Death (Coe, Tucker)
1966	∎	The Dark Mirror (Copper, Basil)
1966		Night Frost (Copper, Basil)
1966		Feramontov (Cory, Desmond)
1966		Margie (Cunningham, E. V.)
1966		The Billion Dollar Brain (Deighton, Len)
1966		Midnight Never Comes (Fallon, Martin)
1966		The King of the Rainy Country (Freeling, Nicolas) ★
1966		The Dresden Green (Freeling, Nicolas)
1966		Assignment Malta (Galway, Robert Conington)
1966		Amber Nine (Gardner, John)
1966		Blackshirt at Large (Graeme, Roderic)
1966		Mark of the Shadow (Grant, Maxwell)
1966		Shadow—Go Mad! (Grant, Maxwell)

1966	The Night of the Shadow (Grant, Maxwell)
1966	The Betrayers (Hamilton, Donald)
1966	Hunter Killer (Jenkins, Geoffrey)
1966	Inspector Ghote's Good Crusade (Keating, H. R. F.)
1966	Saturday the Rabbi Went Hungry (Kemelman, Harry)
1966	Devilweed (Knox, Bill)
1966	The Deep Fall [U.S.-The Ghost Car] (Knox, Bill)
1966	Lake of Fury [U.S.-The Iron Sanctuary] (MacLeod, Robert)
1966	Drum Beat—Madrid (Marlowe, Stephen)
1966	Eighty Million Eyes (McBain, Ed)
1966	The Dead Line (McCutchan, Philip)
1966	Skyprobe (McCutchan, Philip)
1966	The Confounding of Sergeant Cluff (North, Gil)
1966	Sabre-Tooth (O'Donnell, Peter)
1966	The Kubla Khan Caper (Prather, Richard)
1966	The Treasure of the Cosa Nostra (Ridgway, Jason)
1966	The By-Pass Control (Spillane, Mickey)
1966	Day of the Guns (Spillane, Mickey)
1966	The Twisted Thing (Spillane, Mickey)
1966	The Seventh (Stark, Richard)
1966	The Handle [incl Grofield] (Stark, Richard)
1966	The Triumvirate (Taylor, H. Baldwin)
1966	❶ The Fox Valley Murders (Vance, John Holbrook)
1966	❶ Otley (Waddell, Martin)
1966	❶ Evil Intent (Wainright, John)
1966	❶ The Crystallised Carbon Pig (Wainright, John)
1966	Pure Poison (Waugh, Hillary)
1966	❶ The Eliminator (York, Andrew)

1967	❶ The C. I. D. Room [U.S.-All Leads Negative] (Alding, Peter)
1967	Dirty Story (Ambler, Eric)
1967	❶ A Parade of Cockeyed Creatures (Baxt, George) ☆
1967	❶ The War Against Charity Ross (Bickham, Jack)
1967	Tanner's Twelve Swingers (Block, Lawrence)
1967	Two for Tanner (Block, Lawrence)
1967	Another Day, Another Stiff (Brett, Michael)
1967	Dead, Upstairs in a Tub (Brett, Michael)
1967	An Ear for Murder (Brett, Michael)
1967	The Flight of the Stiff (Brett, Michael)
1967	Turn Blue, You Murderers (Brett, Michael)
1967	We the Killers (Brett, Michael)
1967	The Bad Die Young (Chambers, Peter)
1967	Violent Death of a Bitter Englishman (Cleeve, Brian)
1967	❶ Act of Fear (Collins, Michael) ★
1967	No Flowers for the General (Copper, Basil)
1967	Scratch on the Dark (Copper, Basil)
1967	Timelock (Cory, Desmond)
1967	❶ Samantha [APA-The Case of the Angry Actress] (Cunningham, E. V.)
1967	An Expensive Place to Die (Deighton, Len)
1967	Dark Side of the Street (Fallon, Martin)
1967	Strike Out Where Not Applicable (Freeling, Nicolas)
1967	Madrigal (Gardner, John)
1967	Blackshirt in Peril (Graeme, Roderic)
1967	The Shadow—Destination Moon (Grant, Maxwell)
1967	The Two-Way Frame (Harknett, Terry)
1967	Death of an Aunt (Harknett, Terry)
1967	Brought in Dead (Higgins, Jack)
1967	Gently North-West [U.S.-Gently in the Highlands] (Hunter, Alan)
1967	Gently Continental (Hunter, Alan)
1967	Inspector Ghote Caught in Meshes (Keating, H. R. F.)
1967	Blacklight (Knox, Bill)
1967	Justice on the Rocks (Knox, Bill)
1967	Isle of Dragons (MacLeod, Robert)
1967	Drum Beat—Erica (Marlowe, Stephen)
1967	The Legacy Lenders (Masur, Harold Q.)
1967	Sergeant Cluff and the Day of Reckoning (North, Gil)
1967	I, Lucifer (O'Donnell, Peter)
1967	Gat Heat (Prather, Richard)
1967	The Body Lovers (Spillane, Mickey)

1967	❶ The Damsel (Stark, Richard)
1967	The Rare Coin Score (Stark, Richard)
1967	The Green Eagle Score (Stark, Richard)
1967	❶ The Trouble with Tycoons (Taylor, H. Baldwin)
1967	The Palace of Love (Vance, Jack)
1967	The Pleasant Grove Murders (Vance, John Holbrook)
1967	Otley Pursued (Waddell, Martin)
1967	The Worms Must Wait (Wainright, John)
1967	❶ The Black Door (Wilcox, Collin)
1967	The Third Figure (Wilcox, Collin)
1967	The Co-Ordinator (York, Andrew)

1968	Circle of Danger (Alding, Peter)
1968	❶ A Dark Power (Arden, William)
1968	Assassins Don't Die in Bed (Avallone, Michael)
1968	The Horrible Man (Avallone, Michael)
1968	Topsy and Evil (Baxt, George)
1968	Target: Charity Ross (Bickham, Jack)
1968	Here Comes a Hero (Block, Lawrence)
1968	Tanner's Tiger (Block, Lawrence)
1968	Death of a Hippie (Brett, Michael)
1968	Lie a Little, Die a Little [APA-Cry Uncle!] (Brett, Michael)
1968	Slit My Throat, Gently (Brett, Michael)
1968	❶ Three-Toed Pussy (Burley, W. J.)
1968	The Blonde Wore Black (Chambers, Peter)
1968	No Peace for the Wicked (Chambers, Peter)
1968	Speak Ill of the Dead (Chambers, Peter)
1968	Murder Among Children (Coe, Tucker)
1968	Die Now, Live Later (Copper, Basil)
1968	Don't Bleed on Me (Copper, Basil)
1968	❶ The Alias Man (Craig, David)
1968	Cynthia (Cunningham, E. V.)
1968	❶ Skin Deep [U.S.-The Glass-Sided Ants' Nest] (Dickinson, Peter) ★
1968	❶ The Evergreen Death (Fraser, James)
1968	Assignment Gaolbreak (Galway, Robert Conington)
1968	The Menacers (Hamilton, Donald)
1968	❶ With Intent (Henderson, Laurence)
1968	❶ Silver Street [Brit.-The Silver Street Killer] (Johnson, E. Richard) ★
1968	Inspector Ghote Hunts the Peacock (Keating, H. R. F.)
1968	The Klondyker [U.S.-A Figurehead] (Knox, Bill)
1968	Drum Beat—Marianne (Marlowe, Stephen)
1968	Fuzz (McBain, Ed)
1968	The Screaming Dead Ballons (McCutchan, Philip)
1968	❶ Death is for Losers (Nolan, William F.)
1968	❶ The Blood Running Cold (Ross, Jonathan)
1968	Diminished by Death (Ross, Jonathan)
1968	The Black Ice Score (Stark, Richard)
1968	Otley Forever (Waddell, Martin)
1968	The Darkening Glass (Wainright, John)
1968	❶ "30" Manhattan East (Waugh, Hillary)
1968	The Con Game (Waugh, Hillary)
1968	Hell is Where You Find It (Welcome, John)
1968	The Predator (York, Andrew)

1969	Murder Among Thieves (Alding, Peter)
1969	The Intercom Conspiracy (Ambler, Eric)
1969	Deal in Violence (Arden, William)
1969	The Flower-Covered Corpse (Avallone, Michael)
1969	The Doomsday Bag [Brit.-Killer's Highway] (Avallone, Michael)
1969	"I!" Said the Demon (Baxt, George)
1969	❶ Robbery Blue (Busby, Roger)
1969	❶ Nobody's Perfect (Clark, Douglas)
1969	Death After Evensong (Clark, Douglas)
1969	The Brass Rainbow (Collins, Michael)
1969	The Marble Orchard (Copper, Basil)
1969	Message Ends (Craig, David)
1969	A Pride of Heroes [U.S.-The Old English Peep Show] (Dickinson, Peter) ★
1969	❶ The Man with the Tiny Head (Drummond, Ivor)
1969	A Fine Night for Dying (Fallon, Martin)

1969 A Cock-Pit of Roses (Fraser, James)
1969 Tsing-Boum [U.S.-Tsing-Boom!] (Freeling, Nicolas)
1969 Assignment Argentina (Galway, Robert Conington)
1969 Assignment Fenland (Galway, Robert Conington)
1969 Assignment Sea Bed (Galway, Robert Conington)
1969 **1** A Complete State of Death [U.S.-The Stone Killer] (Gardner, John)
1969 Founder Member (Gardner, John)
1969 Blackshirt Stirs Things Up (Graeme, Roderic)
1969 The Interlopers (Hamilton, Donald)
1969 Gently Coloured (Hunter, Alan)
1969 The Inside Man (Johnson, E. Richard)
1969 Inspector Ghote Plays a Joker (Keating, H. R. F.)
1969 Sunday the Rabbi Stayed Home (Kemelman, Harry)
1969 Blueback (Knox, Bill)
1969 **1** The Tallyman (Knox, Bill)
1969 **1** A Lover Too Many (Lewis, Roy)
1969 Place of Mists (MacLeod, Robert)
1969 Shotgun (McBain, Ed)
1969 The Bright Red Businessmen (McCutchan, Philip)
1969 The All-Purpose Bodies (McCutchan, Philip)
1969 The White Cad Cross-Up (Nolan, William F.)
1969 The Procrastination of Sergeant Cluff (North, Gil)
1969 A Taste for Death (O'Donnell, Peter)
1969 **1** Spy For Sale (Payne, Laurence)
1969 The Shell Scott Sampler (Prather, Richard)
1969 The Cheim Manuscript (Prather, Richard)
1969 Kill Me Tomorrow (Prather, Richard)
1969 Dead at First Hand (Ross, Jonathan)
1969 The Deadest Thing You Ever Saw (Ross, Jonathan)
1969 **1** Corpse in Handcuffs (Smith, Frank A.)
1969 The Dame (Stark, Richard)
1969 The Blackbird (Stark, Richard)
1969 The Sour Lemon Score (Stark, Richard) ☆
1969 Otley Victorious (Waddell, Martin)
1969 The Young Prey (Waugh, Hillary)
1969 On the Stretch (Welcome, John)
1969 **1** The Lonely Hunter (Wilcox, Collin)
1969 The Deviator (York, Andrew)
1969 The Dominator (York, Andrew)

1970s

1970 Guilt Without Proof (Alding, Peter)
1970 The Goliath Scheme (Arden, William)
1970 **1** No Score [as by Chip Harrison] (Block, Lawrence)
1970 Me Tanner, You Jane (Block, Lawrence)
1970 To Kill a Cat (Burley, W. J.)
1970 The Frighteners (Busby, Roger)
1970 Deadly Pattern (Clark, Douglas)
1970 Sweet Poison (Clark, Douglas)
1970 Helga's Web (Cleary, Jon)
1970 Wax Apple (Coe, Tucker)
1970 Night of the Toads (Collins, Michael)
1970 Dead File (Copper, Basil)
1970 **1** Young Men May Die (Craig, David)
1970 Contact Lost (Craig, David)
1970 The Seals [U.S.-The Sinful Stones] (Dickinson, Peter)
1970 The Priests of the Abomination (Drummond, Ivor)
1970 **1** A Piece of Resistance (Egleton, Clive)
1970 Deadly Nightshade (Fraser, James)
1970 Assignment Sydney (Galway, Robert Conington)
1970 Assignment Death Squad (Galway, Robert Conington)
1970 Traitor's Exit (Gardner, John)
1970 The Airline Pirates (Gardner, John)
1970 **1** Fadeout (Hansen, Joseph)
1970 Sitting Target (Henderson, Laurence)
1970 **1** A Clubbable Woman (Hill, Reginald)
1970 **1** The Blessing Way (Hillerman, Tony) ☆
1970 Gently with the Innocents (Hunter, Alan)
1970 Inspector Ghote Breaks an Egg (Keating, H. R. F.)
1970 **1** The 100,000 Welcomes (Kenyon, Michael)
1970 Seafire (Knox, Bill)

1970 **1** Children of the Mist [U.S.-Who Shot the Bull?] (Knox, Bill)
1970 **1** Jack's Return Home [APA-Get Carter] (Lewis, Ted)
1970 **1** Wobble to Death (Lovesey, Peter)
1970 **1** A Property in Cyprus [U.S.-A Flickering Death] (MacLeod, Robert)
1970 Jigsaw (McBain, Ed)
1970 Hartinger's Mouse (McCutchan, Philip)
1970 **1** Sir, You Bastard [APA-Rogue Cop] (Newman, G. F.) ☆
1970 **1** The Labyrinth Makers (Price, Anthony) ★
1970 **1** The Murder Makers (Rossiter, John)
1970 The Deadly Green (Rossiter, John)
1970 **1** The Falling Man (Sadler, Mark)
1970 Freeze Thy Blood Less Coldly (Wainright, John)
1970 Finish Me Off (Waugh, Hillary)
1970 **1** The Hot Rock (Westlake, Donald E.) ☆
1970 The Disappearance (Wilcox, Collin)
1970 **1** The Tale of the Lazy Dog (Williams, Alan)

1971 Despite the Evidence (Alding, Peter)
1971 **1** Their Man in the White House (Ardies, Tom)
1971 Death Dives Deep (Avallone, Michael)
1971 Little Miss Murder [Brit.-The Ultimate Client] (Avallone, Michael)
1971 **1** The Exorcist (Blaty, William Peter)
1971 Chip Harrison Scores Again [as by Chip Harrison] [APA-] (Block, Lawrence)
1971 Guilt Edged (Burley, W. J.)
1971 Deadlock (Busby, Roger)
1971 Sick to Death (Clark, Douglas)
1971 A Jade in Aries (Coe, Tucker)
1971 Walk a Black Wind (Collins, Michael)
1971 No Letters from the Grave (Copper, Basil)
1971 Sunburst (Cory, Desmond)
1971 A Walk at Night (Craig, David)
1971 Sleep and His Brother (Dickinson, Peter)
1971 Last Post for a Partisan (Egleton, Clive)
1971 Death in a Pheasant's Eye (Fraser, James)
1971 Over the High Side [U.S.-The Lovely Ladies] (Freeling, Nicolas)
1971 The Negative Man (Galway, Robert Conington)
1971 The Poisoners (Hamilton, Donald)
1971 The Softcover Kill (Harknett, Terry)
1971 **1** Deliver Us to Evil (Hensley, Joe L.)
1971 An Advancement of Learning (Hill, Reginald)
1971 **1** The Judges of Hades (Hoch, Edward D.)
1971 City of Brass (Hoch, Edward D.)
1971 **1** The Private Sector (Hone, Joseph)
1971 Gently at a Gallop (Hunter, Alan)
1971 Inspector Ghote Goes by Train (Keating, H. R. F.)
1971 To Kill a Witch (Knox, Bill)
1971 **1** Ask the Right Question (Lewin, Michael Z.) ☆
1971 Error of Judgement (Lewis, Roy)
1971 The Detective Wore Silk Drawers (Lovesey, Peter)
1971 Path of Ghosts (MacLeod, Robert)
1971 Hail, Hail, The Gang's All Here! (McBain, Ed)
1971 **1** The Steam Pig (McClure, James) ★
1971 This Drakotny (McCutchan, Philip)
1971 **1** Created: The Destroyer (Murphy, Warren B.)
1971 Death Check (Murphy, Warren B.)
1971 **1** Space for Hire (Nolan, William F.) ☆
1971 No Choice for Sergeant Cluff (North, Gil)
1971 The Impossible Virgin (O'Donnell, Peter)
1971 Even My Foot's Asleep (Payne, Laurence)
1971 Dead-Bang (Prather, Richard)
1971 The Alamut Ambush (Price, Anthony)
1971 **1** The Snatch (Pronzini, Bill)
1971 **1** Davis Doesn't Live Here Anymore (Ripley, Jack)
1971 The Pig That Got Up and Slowly Walked Away (Ripley, Jack)
1971 The Victims (Rossiter, John)
1971 **1** Deadline (Russell, Martin)
1971 Here To Die (Sadler, Mark)

1971		Defectors are Dead Men (Smith, Frank A.)
1971	❶	Gypsy in Amber (Smith, Martin Cruz) ★
1971		Survival...Zero! (Spillane, Mickey)
1971		Lemons Never Lie (Stark, Richard)
1971		Deadly Edge (Stark, Richard)
1971		Slayground (Stark, Richard)
1971	❶	Out of Focus (Townend, Peter)
1971	❶	Panda One on Duty (Walker, Peter N.)
1971		Dead Aim (Wilcox, Collin)
1971		The Infiltrator (York, Andrew)

1972		Call Back to Crime (Alding, Peter)
1972		Die to a Distant Drum [Brit.-Murder Underground] (Arden, William)
1972		This Suitcase is Going to Explode (Ardies, Tom)
1972		Shoot It Again, Sam (Avallone, Michael)
1972		The Girl in the Cockpit (Avallone, Michael)
1972		A Reasonable Man (Busby, Roger)
1972		Don't Lie to Me (Coe, Tucker)
1972		Shadow of a Tiger (Collins, Michael)
1972	❶	The Rocksburg Railroad Murders (Constantine, K. C.)
1972	❶	Motive for Revenge (Conway, Peter)
1972		The Big Chill (Copper, Basil)
1972		Strong-Arm (Copper, Basil)
1972	❶	Another Way to Die (Crowe, John)
1972		A Touch of Darkness (Crowe, John)
1972		The Lizard in the Cup (Dickinson, Peter)
1972		The Frog in the Moonflower (Drummond, Ivor)
1972		The Judas Mandate (Egleton, Clive)
1972	❶	The Jade Figurine (Foxx, Jack)
1972		Blood on a Widow's Cross (Fraser, James)
1972		A Long Silence [incl Arlette] [U.S.-Aupres de ma Blonde] (Freeling, Nicolas)
1972	❶	Relentless (Garfield, Brian)
1972	❶	Death Wish (Garfield, Brian)
1972	❶	Dead Skip (Gores, Joe)
1972		The Intriguers (Hamilton, Donald)
1972		Cage Until Tame (Henderson, Laurence)
1972		Legislative Body (Hensley, Joe L.)
1972		Vivienne: Gently Where She Lay (Hunter, Alan)
1972		Inspector Ghote Trusts the Heart (Keating, H. R. F.)
1972		Monday the Rabbi Took Off (Kemelman, Harry)
1972		The Shooting of Dan McGrew (Kenyon, Michael)
1972		Stormtide (Knox, Bill)
1972		A Secret Singing (Lewis, Roy)
1972		Abracadaver (Lovesey, Peter)
1972		A Killing in Malta (MacLeod, Robert)
1972		Sadie When She Died (McBain, Ed)
1972		Let's Hear It for the Deaf Man (McBain, Ed)
1972		The Caterpillar Cop (McClure, James)
1972		The Chinese Puzzle (Murphy, Warren B.)
1972		Mafia Fix (Murphy, Warren B.)
1972		Dr. Quake (Murphy, Warren B.)
1972		Death Therapy (Murphy, Warren B.)
1972		You Nice Bastard (Newman, G. F.)
1972		Sergeant Cluff Rings True (North, Gil)
1972		Pieces of Modesty (O'Donnell, Peter)
1972	❶	The Fall Guy (Perry, Ritchie)
1972		The Sweet Ride (Prather, Richard)
1972		Colonel Butler's Wolf (Price, Anthony)
1972		My Word You Should Have Seen Us (Ripley, Jack)
1972		My God How the Money Rolls In (Ripley, Jack)
1972		Here Lies Nancy Frail (Ross, Jonathan)
1972		A Rope for General Dietz (Rossiter, John)
1972		Concrete Evidence (Russell, Martin)
1972		Mirror Image (Sadler, Mark)
1972		Canto for a Gypsy (Smith, Martin Cruz) ☆
1972		Plunder Squad (Stark, Richard)
1972	❶	Dead Set (Stone, Thomas H.)
1972		One Horse Race (Stone, Thomas H.)
1972		Zoom! (Townend, Peter)
1972		Requiem for a Loser (Wainright, John)
1972		Go for Broke (Welcome, John)

1972		Bank Shot (Westlake, Donald E.)

1973		Field of Fire (Alding, Peter)
1973		Deadly Legacy (Arden, William)
1973		Pandemic (Ardies, Tom)
1973		Kill Her—You'll Like It (Avallone, Michael)
1973		The Hot Body (Avallone, Michael)
1973		Killer on the Keys (Avallone, Michael)
1973		The X-Rated Corpse (Avallone, Michael)
1973		Death in a Salubrious Place (Burley, W. J.)
1973		Pattern of Violence (Busby, Roger)
1973		They Call It Murder (Chambers, Peter)
1973		Ransom (Cleary, Jon)
1973	❶	Bait Money (Collins, Max Allan, Jr.)
1973		Blood Money (Collins, Max Allan, Jr.)
1973		The Silent Scream (Collins, Michael)
1973		The Man Who Liked to Look at Himself (Constantine, K. C.)
1973		The Padded Cell (Conway, Peter)
1973		A Great Year for Dying (Copper, Basil)
1973		Shock-Wave (Copper, Basil)
1973		The Breaking Point (Copper, Basil)
1973	❶	The Mediterranean Caper [Brit.-Mayday!] (Cussler, Clive) ☆
1973		The Jaws of the Watchdog (Drummond, Ivor)
1973		The Five-Leafed Clover (Fraser, James)
1973		Amateur in Violence (Gilbert, Michael)
1973		Final Notice (Gores, Joe)
1973		Death Claims (Hansen, Joseph)
1973	❶	Unbecoming Habits (Heald, Tim)
1973		Ruling Passion (Hill, Reginald)
1973		Dance Hall of the Dead (Hillerman, Tony) ★
1973		Gently French (Hunter, Alan)
1973		Draw Batons! (Knox, Bill)
1973		The Way We Die Now (Lewin, Michael Z.)
1973		Blood Money (Lewis, Roy)
1973		Mad Hatter's Holiday (Lovesey, Peter)
1973		A Burial in Portugal (MacLeod, Robert)
1973		Nest of Vultures (MacLeod, Robert)
1973		Hail to the Chief (McBain, Ed)
1973	❶	One Night Stand (Murphy, Warren B.)
1973		Dead End Street (Murphy, Warren B.)
1973		City in Heat (Murphy, Warren B.)
1973		Union Bust (Murphy, Warren B.)
1973		Summit Chase (Murphy, Warren B.)
1973		Murder's Shield (Murphy, Warren B.)
1973		Terror Squad (Murphy, Warren B.)
1973		Kill or Cure (Murphy, Warren B.)
1973		Slave Safari (Murphy, Warren B.)
1973		Acid Rock (Murphy, Warren B.)
1973		The Silver Mistress (O'Donnell, Peter)
1973	❶	The Godwulf Manuscript (Parker, Robert B.)
1973		Nowhere Man [U.S.-A Hard Man to Kill] (Perry, Ritchie)
1973		Ticket to Ride (Perry, Ritchie)
1973		October Men (Price, Anthony)
1973		The Vanished (Pronzini, Bill)
1973		Undercurrents (Pronzini, Bill)
1973		The Manipulators (Rossiter, John)
1973		Circle of Fire (Sadler, Mark)
1973	❶	The First Deadly Sin (Sanders, Lawrence)
1973	❶	The Big Fix (Simon, Roger L.) ★
1973		Stopover for Murder (Stone, Thomas H.)
1973		Black Death (Stone, Thomas H.)
1973	❶	Obsession (Tripp, Miles)
1973		High-Class Kill (Wainright, John)
1973		A Touch of Malice (Wainright, John)
1973		Panda One Investigates (Walker, Peter N.)
1973	❶	McCloud (Wilcox, Collin)
1973		Hiding Place (Wilcox, Collin)
1973		The Expurgator (York, Andrew)

1974		The Murder Line (Alding, Peter)
1974	❶	Snowball (Allbeury, Ted)
1974		Make Out With Murder [APA-Five Little Rich Girls] (Block, L.

1974		Death in Stanley Street (Burley, W. J.)
1974		The Blank Page (Constantine, K. C.)
1974		Escape to Danger (Conway, Peter)
1974		A Voice from the Dead (Copper, Basil)
1974		Feedback (Copper, Basil)
1974		Ricochet (Copper, Basil)
1974		Bloodwater (Crowe, John)
1974		Spy Story (Deighton, Len)
1974	■	The Sniper (DeMille, Nelson)
1974		The Hammer of God (DeMille, Nelson)
1974	■	The Player (Downing, Warwick)
1974		The Power of the Bug (Drummond, Ivor)
1974		A Wreath of Lords and Ladies (Fraser, James)
1974		Who Steals My Name? (Fraser, James)
1974	■	A Dressing of Diamond (Freeling, Nicolas)
1974	■	The Return of Moriarty [APA-Moriarty] (Gardner, John)
1974		The Corner Men (Gardner, John)
1974		The Threepersons Hunt (Garfield, Brian)
1974	■	Six Days of the Condor [APA-Three Days of the Condor] (Grady, James)
1974		The Intimidators (Hamilton, Donald)
1974	■	Crown: Macao Mayhem (Harknett, Terry)
1974		Crown: The Sweet and Sour Kill (Harknett, Terry)
1974		Blue Blood Will Out (Heald, Tim)
1974		Song of Corpus Juris (Hensley, Joe L.)
1974		Gently in Trees [U.S.-Gently Through the Woods] (Hunter, Alan)
1974	■	Jump Cut (Irvine, Robert) ☆
1974	■	Mistakenly in Mallorca (Jeffries, Roderic)
1974		Bats Fly Up for Inspector Ghote (Keating, H. R. F.)
1974		Tuesday the Rabbi Saw Red (Kemelman, Harry)
1974		A Sorry State (Kenyon, Michael)
1974		Whitewater (Knox, Bill)
1974		Tinker, Tailor, Solider, Spy (Le Carré, John)
1974		The Enemies Within (Lewin, Michael Z.)
1974		A Question of Degree (Lewis, Roy)
1974		Jack Carter's Law [APA-Jack Carter and the Law] (Lewis, Ted)
1974		Invitation to a Dynamite Party [U.S.-The Tick of Death] (Lovesey, Peter)
1974	■	The Dead Are Discreet (Lyons, Arthur)
1974	■	All Other Perils (MacLeod, Robert)
1974		Bread (McBain, Ed)
1974		The Gooseberry Fool (McClure, James)
1974	■	Call for Simon Shard (McCutchan, Philip)
1974	■	Fletch (McDonald, Gregory) ★
1974	■	Siege (Miller, Victor B.)
1974		Requiem for a Cop (Miller, Victor B.)
1974		Down and Dirty (Murphy, Warren B.)
1974		Lynch Town (Murphy, Warren B.)
1974		Judgment Day (Murphy, Warren B.)
1974		Murder Ward (Murphy, Warren B.)
1974		Oil Slick (Murphy, Warren B.)
1974		Last War Dance (Murphy, Warren B.)
1974	■	The Big Needle [U.S.-The Big Apple] (Myles, Simon)
1974		The Big Black (Myles, Simon)
1974		The Price (Newman, G. F.)
1974	■	Time to Kill (Ormerod, Roger)
1974		The Silence of the Night (Ormerod, Roger)
1974		The Doomsday List (Orvis, Kenneth)
1974		God Save the Child (Parker, Robert B.)
1974		Holiday with a Vengeance (Perry, Ritchie)
1974		Other Paths to Glory (Price, Anthony) ★
1974		The Burning of Billy Toober (Ross, Jonathan)
1974		The Villains (Rossiter, John)
1974		Crime Wave (Russell, Martin)
1974		Phantom Holiday (Russell, Martin)
1974	■	Cracksman on Velvet [APA-Sgt. Verity and the Cracksman] (Selwyn, Francis)
1974		Butcher's Moon (Stark, Richard)
1974	■	The Evidence I Shall Give (Wainright, John)
1974		The Hard Hit (Wainright, John)

1974		Jimmy the Kid (Westlake, Donald E.)
1974		The New Mexico Connection (Wilcox, Collin)
1974		Long Way Down (Wilcox, Collin)
1974		The Captivator (York, Andrew)
1975		Six Days to Death (Alding, Peter)
1975		The Topless Tulip Caper (Block, Lawrence)
1975	■	Cast, In Order of Disappearance (Brett, Simon)
1975		Wycliffe and the Pea-Green Boat (Burley, W. J.)
1975	■	The Alvarez Journal (Burns, Rex) ★
1975	■	Where All the Girls are Sweeter (Butler, Richard)
1975		Somebody Has to Lose (Chambers, Peter)
1975	■	Blue Eyes [Quartet] (Charyn, Jerome)
1975		Premedicated Murder (Clark, Douglas)
1975		Blue Death (Collins, Michael)
1975		A Fix Like This (Constantine, K. C.)
1975		The High Wall (Copper, Basil)
1975		Impact (Copper, Basil)
1975		A Good Place to Die (Copper, Basil)
1975		Crooked Shadows (Crowe, John)
1975	■	The Wrong Case (Crumley, James)
1975		Iceberg (Cussler, Clive)
1975	■	The Smack Man (DeMille, Nelson)
1975		The Cannibal (DeMille, Nelson)
1975		The Agent of Death (DeMille, Nelson)
1975		Night of the Phoenix (DeMille, Nelson)
1975	■	Last Bus to Woodstock (Dexter, Colin)
1975		The Mountains West of Town (Downing, Warwick)
1975	■	The Shakeout (Follett, Ken)
1975	■	A Child's Garden of Death (Forrest, Richard)
1975		Dead Run (Foxx, Jack)
1975		What Are the Bugles Blowing For? [U.S.-The Bugles Blowing] (Freeling, Nicolas)
1975		The Revenge of Moriarty (Gardner, John)
1975		A Killer for a Song (Gardner, John)
1975		Death Sentence (Garfield, Brian)
1975		Shadow of the Condor (Grady, James)
1975		The Terminators (Hamilton, Donald)
1975		Troublemaker (Hansen, Joseph)
1975		Crown: Bamboo Shoot-Out (Harknett, Terry)
1975		Deadline (Heald, Tim)
1975	■	The Eagle Has Landed (Higgins, Jack)
1975		An April Shroud (Hill, Reginald)
1975		The Sixth Directorate (Hone, Joseph)
1975		Gently With Love (Hunter, Alan)
1975		Rally to Kill (Knox, Bill)
1975		A Part of Virtue (Lewis, Roy)
1975		A Case of Spirits (Lovesey, Peter)
1975		All God's Children (Lyons, Arthur)
1975		A Witchdance in Bavaria (MacLeod, Robert)
1975	■	Yellowthread Street (Marshall, William)
1975		Blood Relatives (McBain, Ed)
1975		Snake (McClure, James)
1975		A Very Big Bang (McCutchan, Philip)
1975	■	Kiss and Tell (Meyers, Martin)
1975		A Very Deadly Game (Miller, Victor B.)
1975		Therapy in Dynamite (Miller, Victor B.)
1975		The Trade-Off (Miller, Victor B.)
1975		Take-Over (Miller, Victor B.)
1975		Gun Business (Miller, Victor B.)
1975		Girl in the River (Miller, Victor B.)
1975		Death is Not a Passing Grade [Brit.-Marked for Murder] (Miller, Victor B.)
1975		On the Dead Run (Murphy, Warren B.)
1975		Funny Money (Murphy, Warren B.)
1975		Holy Terror (Murphy, Warren B.)
1975		Assassins Play-Off (Murphy, Warren B.)
1975		Deadly Seeds (Murphy, Warren B.)
1975	■	Publish and Perish (Nevins, Francis M., Jr)
1975		Full Fury (Ormerod, Roger)
1975		A Spoonful of Luger (Ormerod, Roger)
1975		Mortal Stakes (Parker, Robert B.)
1975		Your Money and Your Wife (Perry, Ritchie)

1975	The Sure Thing (Prather, Richard)
1975	Our Man in Camelot (Price, Anthony)
1975	The Golden Virgin (Rossiter, John)
1975	Murder by the Mile (Russell, Martin)
1975	Sgt. Verity and the Imperial Diamond (Selwyn, Francis)
1975	Wild Turkey (Simon, Roger L.)
1975 ■	Outsider in Amsterdam (van de Wetering, Janwillem)
1975 ■	Landscape with Violence (Wainright, John)
1975	Square Dance (Wainright, John)
1975	Landscape with Violence (Wainright, John)
1975	Death of a Big Man (Wainright, John)
1975	Aftershock (Wilcox, Collin)
1975	The Fascinator (York, Andrew)
1976 ■	The Sins of the Fathers (Block, Lawrence)
1976	In the Midst of Death (Block, Lawrence)
1976	Time to Murder and Create (Block, Lawrence) ☆
1976	So Much Blood (Brett, Simon)
1976 ■	Saving the Queen (Buckley, William F.)
1976	Wycliffe and the Schoolgirls (Burley, W. J.)
1976	Italian Assets (Butler, Richard)
1976	Marilyn the Wild [Quartet] (Charyn, Jerome)
1976	The Education of Patrick Silver [Quartet] (Charyn, Jerome)
1976	Dread and Water (Clark, Douglas)
1976 ■	The Broker [APA-Quarry (1985)] (Collins, Max Allan, Jr.)
1976	The Broker's Wife [APA-Quarry's List (1985)] (Collins, Max Allan, Jr.)
1976	The Dealer [APA-Quarry's Deal (1986)] (Collins, Max Allan, Jr.)
1976	The Blood-Red Dream (Collins, Michael)
1976	The Lonely Place (Copper, Basil)
1976	Crack in the Sidewalk (Copper, Basil)
1976	Tight Corner (Copper, Basil)
1976	Raise the Titanic! (Cussler, Clive)
1976 ■	The Dark Side (Davis, Kenn w/ John Stanley) ☆
1976	Twinkle, Twinkle, Little Spy [U.S.-Catch a Falling Spy] (Deighton, Len)
1976	Last Seen Wearing (Dexter, Colin)
1976 ■	Saratoga Longshot (Dobyns, Stephen)
1976	The Gambler, the Minstrel, and the Dance Hall Queen (Downing, Warwick)
1976	A Tank of Sacred Eels (Drummond, Ivor)
1976	The Bear Raid (Follett, Ken)
1976	Lake Isle [U.S.-Sabine] (Freeling, Nicolas)
1976	The Retaliators (Hamilton, Donald) ☆
1976 ■	Amphetamines and Pearls (Harvey, John)
1976	The Geranium Kiss (Harvey, John)
1976	Let Sleeping Dogs Lie (Heald, Tim)
1976	Major Enquiry (Henderson, Laurence)
1976	Gently Where the Birds Are (Hunter, Alan)
1976	Freeze Frame (Irvine, Robert) ☆
1976	Two-Faced Death (Jeffries, Roderic)
1976	Filmi, Filmi, Inspector Ghote (Keating, H. R. F.)
1976	Wednesday the Rabbit Got Wet (Kemelman, Harry)
1976	Hellspout (Knox, Bill)
1976 ■	Swag [APA-Ryan's Rules] (Leonard, Elmore)
1976 ■	Night Cover (Lewin, Michael Z.)
1976	Swing, Swing Together (Lovesey, Peter)
1976 ■	Buyer Beware (Lutz, John)
1976	The Killing Floor (Lyons, Arthur)
1976 ■	Raven in Flight (MacKenzie, Donald)
1976	Dragonship (MacLeod, Robert)
1976	The Hatchet Man (Marshall, William)
1976	Gelignite (Marshall, William)
1976	So Long as You Both Shall Live (McBain, Ed)
1976	Blood Run East (McCutchan, Philip)
1976	Confess Fletch [incl Flynn] (McDonald, Gregory) ★
1976	Spy and Die (Meyers, Martin)
1976	Red is for Murder (Meyers, Martin)
1976	Hung Up to Die (Meyers, Martin)
1976	Reunion for Death (Meyers, Martin)

1976	Brain Drain (with Sapir) (Murphy, Warren B.)
1976	Child's Play (with Sapir) (Murphy, Warren B.)
1976	King's Curse (with Sapir) (Murphy, Warren B.)
1976	Sweet Dreams (w/Richard S. Meyers) (Murphy, Warren B.)
1976	Last Day in Limbo (O'Donnell, Peter)
1976	Sealed with a Loving Kill (Ormerod, Roger)
1976	The Colour of Fear (Ormerod, Roger)
1976	A Glimpse of Death (Ormerod, Roger)
1976	Promised Land (Parker, Robert B.) ★
1976	One Good Death Deserves Another (Perry, Ritchie)
1976	War Game (Price, Anthony)
1976	I Know What It's Like to Die (Ross, Jonathan)
1976 ■	The Tangent Objective (Sanders, Lawrence)
1976	Tumbleweed (van de Wetering, Janwillem)
1976	The Corpse on the Dike (van de Wetering, Janwillem)
1976	Doctor, Lawyer... (Wilcox, Collin)
1976	The Third Victim (Wilcox, Collin)
1976	Shah-Mak (Williams, Alan)
1976 ■	Unholy Writ (Williams, David)
1977	Murder is Suspected (Alding, Peter)
1977	The Big Stiffs (Avallone, Michael)
1977 ■	Burglars Can't Be Choosers (Block, Lawrence)
1977	Star Trap (Brett, Simon)
1977	The Farnsworth Score (Burns, Rex)
1977 ■	Shadow of a Broken Man (Chesbro, George)
1977	Table d'Hote (Clark, Douglas)
1977	The Gimmel Flask (Clark, Douglas)
1977	The Slasher [APA-Quarry's Cut (1986)] (Collins, Max Allan, Jr.)
1977	The Year of the Dragon (Copper, Basil)
1977	Death Squad (Copper, Basil)
1977	When They Kill Your Wife (Crowe, John)
1977	The Case of the One-Penny Orange (Cunningham, E. V.)
1977	The Silent World of Nicholas Quinn (Dexter, Colin)
1977	The Necklace of Skulls (Drummond, Ivor)
1977	The Wizard of Death (Forrest, Richard)
1977	Hearts Ease in Death (Fraser, James)
1977 ■	Charlie Muffin [U.S.-Charlie M] (Freemantle, Brian)
1977 ■	The Judas Pair (Gash, Jonathan) ★
1977	Petrella at Q (Gilbert, Michael)
1977 ■	McGarr and the Politician's Wife (Gill, Bartholomew)
1977	McGarr and the Sienese Conspiracy (Gill, Bartholomew)
1977 ■	Dewey Decimated (Goodrum, Charles A.) ☆
1977	The Terrorizers (Hamilton, Donald)
1977	Junkyard Angel (Harvey, John)
1977	Neon Madmen (Harvey, John)
1977	Just Desserts (Heald, Tim)
1977	Gently Instrumental (Hunter, Alan)
1977	The Diehard (Jackson, Jon A.)
1977	Troubled Deaths (Jeffries, Roderic)
1977 ■	Bullet for a Star (Kaminsky, Stuart M.)
1977	Witchrock (Knox, Bill)
1977	Pilot Error (Knox, Bill)
1977	The Honourable Schoolboy (Le Carré, John) ★
1977	Unknown Man No. 89 (Leonard, Elmore)
1977	Nothing but Foxes (Lewis, Roy)
1977	Jack Carter and the Mafia Pigeon (Lewis, Ted)
1977	Dead Ringer (Lyons, Arthur)
1977	Raven and the Ratcatcher (MacKenzie, Donald)
1977	Raven and the Kamikaze (MacKenzie, Donald)
1977	A Pay-Off in Switzerland (MacLeod, Robert)
1977	Thin Air (Marshall, William)
1977 ■	Goldilocks (McBain, Ed)
1977	Long Time No See (McBain, Ed)
1977	The Sunday Hangman (McClure, James)
1977	The Eros Affair (McCutchan, Philip)
1977 ■	Flynn (McDonald, Gregory)
1977 ■	Laidlaw (McIlvanney, William) ★ ☆
1977 ■	Her Death of Cold (McInerny, Ralph)
1977	The Seventh Station (McInerny, Ralph)
1977	In Enemy Hands (with Sapir) (Murphy, Warren B.)

1977	The Last Temple (w/Richard S. Meyers) (Murphy, Warren B.)	
1977	Ship of Death (with Sapir) (Murphy, Warren B.)	
1977	The Final Death (w/Richard S. Meyers) (Murphy, Warren B.)	
1977	Mugger Blood (with Sapir) (Murphy, Warren B.)	
1977	The Head Men (with Sapir) (Murphy, Warren B.)	
1977	Too Late for the Funeral (Ormerod, Roger)	
1977	■ A Fire in the Barley (Parrish, Frank) ☆	
1977	Dead End (Perry, Ritchie)	
1977	Blowback (Pronzini, Bill)	
1977	The Second Deadly Sin (Sanders, Lawrence)	
1977	Sgt. Verity Presents His Compliments (Selwyn, Francis)	
1977	Triple Exposure (Townend, Peter)	
1977	The Once a Year Man (Tripp, Miles)	
1977	Death of a Hawker (van de Wetering, Janwillem)	
1977	The Japanese Corpse (van de Wetering, Janwillem)	
1977	Pool of Tears (Wainright, John)	
1977	The Day of the Peppercorn Kill (Wainright, John)	
1977	Nobody's Perfect (Westlake, Donald E.)	
1977	Treasure by Degrees (Williams, David)	
1977	■ Tallant for Trouble (York, Andrew)	

1978	Dark on Monday (Avallone, Michael)	
1978	■ Head of the Force (Barnett, James)	
1978	■ The Rag Bag Clan (Barth, Richard)	
1978	The Burglar in the Closet (Block, Lawrence)	
1978	A Stab in the Dark (Block, Lawrence) ☆	
1978	An Amateur Corpse (Brett, Simon)	
1978	Stained Glass (Buckley, William F.)	
1978	Wycliffe and the Scapegoat (Burley, W. J.)	
1978	Speak for the Dead (Burns, Rex)	
1978	Secret Isaac [Quartet] (Charyn, Jerome)	
1978	City of Whispering Stone (Chesbro, George)	
1978	The Libertines (Clark, Douglas)	
1978	The Night Runners (Collins, Michael)	
1978	Murder One (Copper, Basil)	
1978	■ The Last Good Kiss (Crumley, James)	
1978	The Case of the Russian Diplomat (Cunningham, E. V.)	
1978	Vixen 03 (Cussler, Clive)	
1978	■ Killed in the Ratings (DeAndrea, William L.) ★	
1978	A Stench of Poppies (Drummond, Ivor)	
1978	■ Sherlock Holmes versus Dracula (Estleman, Loren D.)	
1978	Dr. Jekyll and Mr. Holmes (Estleman, Loren D.)	
1978	Death Through the Looking Glass (Forrest, Richard)	
1978	The Night Lords (Freeling, Nicolas)	
1978	Clap Hands, Here Comes Charlie [U.S.-Here Comes Charlie M] (Freemantle, Brian)	
1978	Gold from Gemini [U.S.-Gold by Gemini] (Gash, Jonathan)	
1978	McGarr on the Cliffs of Moher (Gill, Bartholomew)	
1978	Gone, No Forwarding (Gores, Joe)	
1978	■ The Murders at Impasse Louvain (Grayson, Richard)	
1978	The Man Everybody Was Afraid Of (Hansen, Joseph)	
1978	A Killing in Gold (Hensley, Joe L.)	
1978	A Pinch of Snuff (Hill, Reginald)	
1978	Listening Woman (Hillerman, Tony) ☆	
1978	Gently to a Sleep (Hunter, Alan)	
1978	Horizontal Hold (Irvine, Robert)	
1978	The Blind Pig (Jackson, Jon A.)	
1978	■ Murder at the Margin (Jevons, Marshall)	
1978	Murder on the Yellow Brick Road (Kaminsky, Stuart M.)	
1978	Thursday the Rabbi Walked Out (Kemelman, Harry)	
1978	Live Bait (Knox, Bill)	
1978	The Silent Salesman (Lewin, Michael Z.)	
1978	Waxwork (Lovesey, Peter) ★	
1978	Raven Settles a Score (MacKenzie, Donald)	
1978	Salvage Job (MacLeod, Robert)	
1978	Blackmail North (McCutchan, Philip)	
1978	Fletch's Fortune (McDonald, Gregory)	
1978	Bishop as Pawn (McInerny, Ralph)	
1978	Killer Chromosomes (Murphy, Warren B.)	
1978	Voodoo Die (Murphy, Warren B.)	

1978	Chained Reaction (Murphy, Warren B.)	
1978	Last Call (Murphy, Warren B.)	
1978	Corrupt and Ensnare (Nevins, Francis M., Jr)	
1978	■ The Ripper (Newton, Michael)	
1978	The Satan Ring (Newton, Michael)	
1978	Dragon's Claw (O'Donnell, Peter)	
1978	A Dip into Murder (Ormerod, Roger)	
1978	The Weight of Evidence (Ormerod, Roger)	
1978	The Judas Goat (Parker, Robert B.)	
1978	Sting of the Honeybee (Parrish, Frank)	
1978	Dutch Courage (Perry, Ritchie)	
1978	The '44 Vintage (Price, Anthony)	
1978	Twospot (Pronzini, Bill)	
1978	The Tangent Factor (Sanders, Lawrence)	
1978	■ The DADA Caper (Spencer, Ross H.)	
1978	■ Bloodstar (Topor, Tom)	
1978	The Wife-Smuggler (Tripp, Miles)	
1978	The Blond Baboon (van de Wetering, Janwillem)	
1978	A Ripple of Murders (Wainright, John)	
1978	Witchcraft for Panda One (Walker, Peter N.)	
1978	Twospot (Wilcox, Collin)	
1978	Treasure Up in Smoke (Williams, David)	
1978	Tallant for Disaster (York, Andrew)	

1979	Ransom Town (Alding, Peter)	
1979	Backfire is Hostile! (Barnett, James)	
1979	The Burglar Who Liked to Quote Kipling (Block, Lawrence) ★	
1979	A Comedian Dies (Brett, Simon)	
1979	Angle of Attack (Burns, Rex)	
1979	The Deadlier They Fall (Chambers, Peter)	
1979	Lady, You're Killing Me (Chambers, Peter)	
1979	The Day of the Big Dollar (Chambers, Peter)	
1979	An Affair of Sorcerors (Chesbro, George)	
1979	Heberden's Seat (Clark, Douglas)	
1979	A Quiet Room in Hell (Copper, Basil)	
1979	The Big Rip-Off (Copper, Basil)	
1979	Close to Death (Crowe, John)	
1979	The Case of the Poisoned Eclairs (Cunningham, E. V.)	
1979	The Forza Trap (Davis, Kenn)	
1979	■ The HOG Murders (DeAndrea, William)	
1979	Service of All the Dead (Dexter, Colin) ★	
1979	One Foot in the Grave (Dickinson, Peter)	
1979	The Death in the Willows (Forrest, Richard)	
1979	Whip Hand (Francis, Dick) ★★	
1979	The Widow (Freeling, Nicolas)	
1979	The Inscrutable Charlie Muffin (Freemantle, Brian)	
1979	■ The Nostradamus Traitor (Gardner, John)	
1979	The Grail Tree (Gash, Jonathan)	
1979	Carnage of the Realm [Brit.-Dead for a Penny] (Goodrum, Charles A.)	
1979	■ The November Man [Edinburg] (Granger, Bill)	
1979	■ Grave Error (Greenleaf, Stephen)	
1979	■ Dead Game (Hammond, Gerald)	
1979	Skinflick (Hansen, Joseph)	
1979	Minor Murders (Hensley, Joe L.)	
1979	Pascoe's Ghost (Hill, Reginald)	
1979	Murder Begets Murder (Jeffries, Roderic)	
1979	■ Margo [APA-The Woman at the Window] (Jenkins, Jerry)	
1979	You Bet Your Life (Kaminsky, Stuart M.)	
1979	The Howard Hughes Affair (Kaminsky, Stuart M.)	
1979	Inspector Ghote Draws a Line (Keating, H. R. F.)	
1979	■ The Rosary Murders (Kienzle, William X.)	
1979	■ The Infernal Device (Kurland, Michael) ☆	
1979	■ Follow the Leader [golf] (Logue, John) ☆	
1979	Raven Feathers His Nest [Brit.-Raven After Dark] (MacKenzie, Donald)	
1979	An Incident in Iceland (MacLeod, Robert)	
1979	Skulduggery (Marshall, William)	
1979	Calypso (McBain, Ed)	
1979	Sunstrike (McCutchan, Philip)	
1979	Lying Three (McInerny, Ralph)	
1979	■ The Wages of Zen (Melville, James)	

1979		Power Play (Murphy, Warren B.)
1979		Bottom Line (Murphy, Warren B.)
1979		Bay City Blast (Murphy, Warren B.)
1979		The Bright Face of Danger (Ormerod, Roger)
1979		The Amnesia Trap (Ormerod, Roger)
1979		Cart Before the Hearse (Ormerod, Roger)
1979	❶	The Lasko Tangent (Patterson, Richard North) ★
1979		Bishop's Pawn (Perry, Ritchie)
1979		Tomorrow's Ghost (Price, Anthony)
1979	❶	Constable on the Hill (Rhea, Nicholas)
1979		A Rattling of Old Bones (Ross, Jonathan)
1979		Sgt. Verity and the Blood Royal (Selwyn, Francis)
1979	❶	Saturday of Glory (Serafin, David) ★
1979		Peking Duck (Simon, Roger L.)
1979		The Stranger City Caper (Spencer, Ross H.)
1979		The Reggis Arms Caper (Spencer, Ross H.)
1979		Cruel Victim (Tripp, Miles)
1979		The Maine Massacre (van de Wetering, Janwillem)
1979		The Face (Vance, Jack)
1979	❶	Brainwash (Wainright, John)
1979		Duty Elsewhere (Wainright, John)
1979		Take Murder... (Wainright, John)
1979		Power Plays (Wilcox, Collin)

1980s

1980	❶	Vermilion (Aldyne, Nathan)
1980		Palmprint (Barnett, James)
1980	❶	A Lonely Way to Die (Bourgeau, Art)
1980		The Dead Side of the Mike (Brett, Simon)
1980		Who's on First (Buckley, William F.)
1980		Wycliffe in Paul's Court (Burley, W. J.)
1980		The Beautiful Golden Frame (Chambers, Peter)
1980		Nothing Personal (Chambers, Peter)
1980		The Deep Blue Cradle (Chambers, Peter)
1980		Poacher's Bag (Clark, Douglas)
1980		Golden Rain (Clark, Douglas)
1980		The Slasher (Collins, Michael)
1980		The Caligari Complex (Copper, Basil)
1980		Flip-Side (Copper, Basil)
1980	❶	The Dying Trade (Corris, Peter)
1980		The Diamonds of Loreta (Drummond, Ivor)
1980	❶	The Suicide Notice [U.S.-The Suicide Murders] (Engel, Howard)
1980	❶	Motor City Blue (Estleman, Loren D.)
1980		The Death at Yew Corner (Forrest, Richard)
1980		Castang's City (Freeling, Nicolas)
1980		Charlie Muffin's Uncle Sam [U.S.-Charlie Muffin USA] (Freemantle, Brian)
1980		The Garden of Weapons (Gardner, John)
1980		Spend Game (Gash, Jonathan)
1980		McGarr at the Dublin Horse Show (Gill, Bartholomew)
1980	❶	Public Murders (Granger, Bill) ★
1980		The Monterant Affair (Grayson, Richard)
1980		Death Bed (Greenleaf, Stephen)
1980		The Reward Game (Hammond, Gerald)
1980		Kennedy for the Defense (Higgins, George V.)
1980		A Killing Kindness (Hill, Reginald)
1980	❶	People of Darkness (Hillerman, Tony)
1980		The Flowers of the Forest [U.S.-The Oxford Gambit] (Hone, Joseph)
1980	❶	Decoys (Hoyt, Richard)
1980		The Honfleur Decision (Hunter, Alan)
1980		Just Desserts (Jeffries, Roderic)
1980		Hilary [APA-Murder Behind Bars] (Jenkins, Jerry)
1980		Karlyn [APA-The Daylight Intruder] (Jenkins, Jerry)
1980		Never Cross a Vampire (Kaminsky, Stuart M.)
1980	❶	Duffy (Kavanagh, Dan)
1980		Death Wears a Red Hat (Kienzle, William X.)
1980		Bombship (Knox, Bill)
1980		Smiley's People (Le Carré, John)
1980	❶	A Certain Blindness (Lewis, Roy)
1980	❶	A Cracking of Spines (Lewis, Roy H.)
1980		Castles Burning (Lyons, Arthur)

1980		Raven and the Paperhangers (MacKenzie, Donald)
1980		Raven's Revenge (MacKenzie, Donald)
1980		Cargo Risk (MacLeod, Robert)
1980	❶	Taffin (Mallett, Lyndon)
1980		Taffin's First Law (Mallett, Lyndon)
1980		Ghosts (McBain, Ed)
1980		The Blood of an Englishman (McClure, James)
1980		Corpse (McCutchan, Philip)
1980		Second Vespers (McInerny, Ralph)
1980		The Chrysanthemum Chain (Melville, James)
1980		Missing Link (Murphy, Warren B.)
1980		Dangerous Games (Murphy, Warren B.)
1980		Firing Line (Murphy, Warren B.)
1980		Timber Line (Murphy, Warren B.)
1980	❶	Physical Evidence (Noguchi, Thomas T. w/Arthur Lyons)
1980		More Dead Than Alive (Ormerod, Roger)
1980		Looking for Rachel Wallace (Parker, Robert B.)
1980		Grand Slam (Perry, Ritchie)
1980		The Hour of the Donkey (Price, Anthony)
1980		Labyrinth (Pronzini, Bill)
1980	❶	The Verdict (Reed, Barry)
1980		Constable on the Prowl (Rhea, Nicholas)
1980		Sgt. Verity and the Swell Mob (Selwyn, Francis)
1980	❶	Death's Pale Horse (Sherburne, James)
1980		The Abu Wahab Caper (Spencer, Ross H.)
1980	❶	The Man Who Killed His Brother (Stephens, Reed)
1980	❶	The Players' Boy is Dead (Tourney, Leonard)
1980		High Heels (Tripp, Miles)
1980	❶	The Lime Pit (Valin, Jonathan)
1980		Final Notice (Valin, Jonathan)
1980		Dominoes (Wainright, John)
1980	❶	The Glenna Powers Case (Waugh, Hillary)
1980		The Doria Rafe Case (Waugh, Hillary)
1980		Mankiller (Wilcox, Collin)
1980		Murder for Treasure (Williams, David)

1981	❶	Murder (Adams, Harold)
1981	❶	American Quartet (Adler, Warren)
1981		A Man Condemned (Alding, Peter)
1981	❶	Sheer Torture [U.S.-Death by Sheer Torture] (Barnard, Robert)
1981		The Firing Squad (Barnett, James)
1981		A Ragged Plot (Barth, Richard)
1981	❶	Peregrine (Bayer, William) ★
1981		The Burglar Who Studied Spinoza (Block, Lawrence)
1981		The Most Likely Suspects (Bourgeau, Art)
1981		Situation Tragedy (Brett, Simon)
1981	❶	California Thriller (Byrd, Max) ★
1981		Fly Away, Jill (Byrd, Max)
1981	❶	Carpenter, Detective (Caine, Hamilton) ☆
1981		A Long Time Dead (Chambers, Peter)
1981		The Lady Who Never Was (Chambers, Peter)
1981		Female—Handle With Care (Chambers, Peter)
1981		Roast Eggs (Clark, Douglas)
1981		The Longest Pleasure (Clark, Douglas)
1981		Fly Paper (Collins, Max Allan, Jr.)
1981		Hush Money (Collins, Max Allan, Jr.)
1981		Hard Cash (Collins, Max Allan, Jr.)
1981		The Long Rest (Copper, Basil)
1981		The Empty Silence (Copper, Basil)
1981		Dark Entry (Copper, Basil)
1981		White Meat (Corris, Peter)
1981		The Case of the Sliding Pool (Cunningham, E. V.)
1981		Night Probe! (Cussler, Clive)
1981		Killed in the Act (DeAndrea, William L.)
1981		The Dead of Jericho (Dexter, Colin) ★
1981		Saratoga Swimmer (Dobyns, Stephen)
1981		The Ransom Game (Engel, Howard)
1981		Angel Eyes (Estleman, Loren D.)
1981		One Damn Thing After Another [U.S.-Arlette] (Freeling, Nicolas)
1981		Madrigal for Charlie Muffin (Freemantle, Brian)
1981	❶	Licence Renewed (Gardner, John)

1981	The Vatican Rip (Gash, Jonathan)
1981	Schism [Florida] (Granger, Bill)
1981	The Death of the Abbe Didier (Grayson, Richard)
1981	The Revenge Game (Hammond, Gerald)
1981	Murder at Moose Jaw (Heald, Tim)
1981	Outcasts (Hensley, Joe L.)
1981	The Rat on Fire (Higgins, George V.)
1981	Gabrielle's Way [U.S.-The Scottish Decision] (Hunter, Alan)
1981	Fields of Heather [U.S.-Death on the Heath] (Hunter, Alan)
1981 ❶	The Rubout at the Onyx (Jeffers, H. Paul)
1981	Unseemly End (Jeffries, Roderic)
1981	Paige [APA-The Meeting at Midnight] (Jenkins, Jerry)
1981	Allyson [APA-The Silence is Broken] (Jenkins, Jerry)
1981 ❶	Death of a Dissident [Brit.-Rostnikov's Corpse] (Kaminsky, Stuart M.)
1981	High Midnight (Kaminsky, Stuart M.)
1981	Fiddle City (Kavanagh, Dan)
1981	Go West, Inspector Ghote (Keating, H. R. F.)
1981 ❶	Zigzag [U.S.-The Elgar Variation] (Kenyon, Michael)
1981	Mind Over Murder (Kienzle, William X.)
1981	A Killing in Antiques (Knox, Bill)
1981	Missing Woman (Lewin, Michael Z.)
1981	A Relative Distance (Lewis, Roy)
1981	The Manuscript Murders (Lewis, Roy H.)
1981	A Problem in Prague (MacLeod, Robert)
1981	Sci Fi (Marshall, William)
1981	Perfect End (Marshall, William)
1981	The Mourning After (Masur, Harold Q.)
1981	Rumplestiltskin (McBain, Ed)
1981	Heat (McBain, Ed)
1981	Shard Calls the Tune (McCutchan, Philip)
1981	The Buck Passes Flynn (McDonald, Gregory)
1981	Fletch and the Widow Bradley (McDonald, Gregory)
1981	Thicker than Water (McInerny, Ralph)
1981	A Sort of Samurai (Melville, James)
1981 ❶	Death in the Past (Moore, Richard A.)
1981	Midnight Man (Murphy, Warren B.)
1981	The Balance of Power (Murphy, Warren B.)
1981	Spoils of War (Murphy, Warren B.)
1981	Next of Kin (Murphy, Warren B.)
1981	The Xanadu Talisman (O'Donnell, Peter)
1981	One Breathless Hour (Ormerod, Roger)
1981	Early Autumn (Parker, Robert B.) ☆
1981	A Savage Place (Parker, Robert B.)
1981	Fool's Mate (Perry, Ritchie)
1981 ❶	Money Men (Petievich, Gerald)
1981	Soldier No More (Price, Anthony)
1981	Hoodwink (Pronzini, Bill) ★
1981 ❶	Not A Blessed Thing (Quill, Monica)
1981	Constable Around the Village (Rhea, Nicholas)
1981	Dark Blue and Dangerous (Ross, Jonathan)
1981	Touch of Death (Sadler, Mark)
1981	The Third Deadly Sin (Sanders, Lawrence)
1981	Death's Gray Angel (Sherburne, James)
1981 ❶	Gorky Park (Smith, Martin Cruz) ★
1981	The Radish River Caper (Spencer, Ross H.)
1981 ❶	Death Trick (Stevenson, Richard)
1981 ❶	Kyril [U.S.-The Man Called Kyril] (Trenhaile, John)
1981 ❶	Deep and Crisp and Even (Turnbull, Peter)
1981	Dead Letter (Valin, Jonathan)
1981	The Mind-Murders (van de Wetering, Janwillem)
1981	The Book of Dreams (Vance, Jack)
1981	All on a Summer's Day (Wainright, John)
1981	An Urge for Justice (Wainright, John)
1981	Siege for Panda One (Walker, Peter N.)
1981	The Billy Cantrell Case (Waugh, Hillary)
1981	Holy of Holies (Williams, Alan)

1982	Paint the Town Red (Adams, Harold)
1982	Betrayed by Death (Alding, Peter)
1982	Cobalt (Aldyne, Nathan)
1982 ❶	The Talk Show Murders (Allen, Steve)
1982	Death and the Princess (Barnard, Robert)
1982	Marked for Destruction (Barnett, James)
1982	One Dollar Death (Barth, Richard)
1982	Eight Million Ways to Die (Block, Lawrence) ★ ☆
1982 ❶	Billingsgate Shoal (Boyer, Rick) ★
1982	Murder Unprompted (Brett, Simon)
1982	Marco Polo, If You Can (Buckley, William F.)
1982	Wycliffe's Wild Goose Chase (Burley, W. J.)
1982	Murder Is Its Own Reward (Chambers, Peter)
1982	The Highly Explosive Case (Chambers, Peter)
1982	A Miniature Murder Mystery (Chambers, Peter)
1982	Shelf Life (Clark, Douglas)
1982	Doone Walk (Clark, Douglas)
1982	Scratch Fever (Collins, Max Allan, Jr.)
1982	The Man Who Liked Slow Tomatoes (Constantine, K. C.)
1982	Hang Loose (Copper, Basil)
1982	Shoot-Out (Copper, Basil)
1982	The Far Horizon (Copper, Basil)
1982	The Marvellous Boy (Corris, Peter)
1982	The Case of the Kidnapped Angel (Cunningham, E. V.)
1982 ❶	Fellowship of Fear (Elkins, Aaron)
1982	Murder on Location (Engel, Howard)
1982	The Midnight Man (Estleman, Loren D.)
1982 ❶	Double Jeopardy (Forbes, Colin)
1982	Wolfnight (Freeling, Nicolas)
1982	For Special Services (Gardner, John)
1982	The Quiet Dogs (Gardner, John)
1982	Firefly Gadroon (Gash, Jonathan)
1982 ❶	Nevsky's Return (Gat, Dimitri) ☆
1982	The Shattered Eye [France] (Granger, Bill)
1982	The Montmarte Murders (Grayson, Richard)
1982	State's Evidence (Greenleaf, Stephen)
1982	The Revengers (Hamilton, Donald)
1982	Fair Game (Hammond, Gerald)
1982	The Game (Hammond, Gerald)
1982	Gravedigger (Hansen, Joseph) ☆
1982	Masterstroke [U.S.-A Small Masterpiece] (Heald, Tim)
1982	Touch the Devil (Higgins, Jack)
1982	The Dark Wind (Hillerman, Tony)
1982	The Valley of the Fox (Hone, Joseph)
1982 ❶	Trotsky's Run (Hoyt, Richard)
1982	30 for a Harry (Hoyt, Richard) ☆
1982	Gently Between Tides (Hunter, Alan)
1982 ❶	Night Rituals (Jahn, Michael)
1982	Shannon [APA-Thank You, Good-Bye] (Jenkins, Jerry)
1982	Catch a Falling Clown (Kaminsky, Stuart M.)
1982	The God Squad Bod [U.S.-The Man at the Wheel] (Kenyon, Michael)
1982	Assault with Intent (Kienzle, William X.)
1982	Bloodtide (Knox, Bill)
1982	Death by Gaslight (Kurland, Michael)
1982	Hard Line (Lewin, Michael Z.)
1982 ❶	A Gathering of Ghosts (Lewis, Roy)
1982	Dwell in Danger (Lewis, Roy)
1982 ❶	A Piece of the Silence (Livingston, Jack) ☆
1982 ❶	Bragg's Hunch (Lynch, Jack)
1982	The Missing and the Dead (Lynch, Jack) ☆
1982	Pieces of Death (Lynch, Jack) ☆
1982	Hard Trade (Lyons, Arthur) ☆
1982	War Machine (Marshall, William)
1982	Werewolf (McCutchan, Philip)
1982	Fletch's Moxie (McDonald, Gregory)
1982	A Loss of Patients (McInerny, Ralph)
1982	The Ninth Netsuke (Melville, James)
1982	Death of a Source (Moore, Richard A.)
1982 ❶	The Big Enchilada (Morse, L. A.)
1982 ❶	Smoked Out (Murphy, Warren B.) ☆
1982	Fool's Flight (Murphy, Warren B.)

1982   Dead Letter (Murphy, Warren B.)
1982   Lucifer's Weekend (Murphy, Warren B.)
1982   Dying Space (Murphy, Warren B.)
1982   Profit Motive (Murphy, Warren B.)
1982   Skin Deep (Murphy, Warren B.)
1982   Killing Time (Murphy, Warren B.)
1982   The Night of Morningstar (O'Donnell, Peter)
1982   Ceremony (Parker, Robert B.) ☆
1982   Snare in the Dark (Parrish, Frank)
1982 ❶ Take the Money and Run (Payne, Laurence)
1982   Foul Up (Perry, Ritchie)
1982   The Old Vengeful (Price, Anthony)
1982   Scattershot (Pronzini, Bill)
1982   Dragonfire (Pronzini, Bill)
1982   Let Us Prey (Quill, Monica)
1982 ❶ Eye in the Ring (Randisi, Robert J.)
1982   Constable Across the Moors (Rhea, Nicholas)
1982   Death's Head (Ross, Jonathan)
1982   Madrid Underground (Serafin, David)
1982   Christmas Rising (Serafin, David)
1982   Death's Clenched Fist (Sherburne, James)
1982 ❶ Caroline Minuscule (Taylor, Andrew) ★ ☆
1982   Dead Knock (Turnbull, Peter)
1982   Day of Wrath (Valin, Jonathan)
1982   Blayde R. I. P. (Wainright, John)
1982   Stalking Horse (Wilcox, Collin)
1982   Copper, Gold and Treasure (Williams, David)

1983   The Missing Moon (Adams, Harold)
1983   American Sextet (Adler, Warren)
1983   One Man's Justice (Alding, Peter)
1983   The Missing Bronte [U.S.-The Case of the Missing Bronte] (Barnard, Robert)
1983   Legion (Blatty, William Peter)
1983   The Burglar Who Painted Like Mondrian (Block, Lawrence)
1983 ❶ Monsier Pamplemousse (Bond, Michael)
1983 ❶ Listen for the Click [Brit.-Vicar's Roses] (Breen, Jon)
1983   Murder in the Title (Brett, Simon)
1983   Wycliffe and the Beales (Burley, W. J.)
1983   The Avenging Angel (Burns, Rex)
1983   Finders Weepers (Byrd, Max) ☆
1983   Jail Bait (Chambers, Peter)
1983   Dragons Can Be Dangerous (Chambers, Peter)
1983   Vicious Circle (Clark, Douglas)
1983   The Monday Theory (Clark, Douglas)
1983 ❶ No Cure for Death (Collins, Max Allan, Jr.)
1983 ❶ True Detective (Collins, Max Allan, Jr.) ★
1983   The Baby Blue Rip-Off (Collins, Max Allan, Jr.)
1983   Freak (Collins, Michael)
1983   Always a Body to Trade (Constantine, K. C.)
1983   Trigger-Man (Copper, Basil)
1983   Pressure Point (Copper, Basil)
1983   Hard Contract (Copper, Basil)
1983   The Narrow Corner (Copper, Basil)
1983   The Empty Beach (Corris, Peter)
1983   Dancing Bear (Crumley, James) ☆
1983   Pacific Vortex! (Cussler, Clive)
1983   Killed with a Passion (DeAndrea, William L.)
1983 ❶ Berlin Game (Deighton, Len)
1983   The Riddle of the Third Mile (Dexter, Colin)
1983   The Dark Place (Elkins, Aaron)
1983 ❶ Dead in Centerfield (Engleman, Paul) ★
1983   The Glass Highway (Estleman, Loren D.) ☆
1983 ❶ Murder Isn't Enough (Flynn, Don)
1983   The Back of the North Wind (Freeling, Nicolas)
1983   Icebreaker (Gardner, John)
1983   The Sleepers of Erin (Gash, Jonathan)
1983   Nevsky's Demon (Gat, Dimitri)
1983   McGarr and the P.M. of Belgrave Square (Gill, Bartholomew)
1983   The British Cross (Granger, Bill)

1983   Crime Without Passion (Grayson, Richard)
1983   Fatal Obsession (Greenleaf, Stephen)
1983   The Annihilators (Hamilton, Donald)
1983 ❶ French Ordinary Murder [U.S.-Why Kill Arthur Potter?] (Harrison, Ray)
1983 ❶ The Bay Psalm Book Murder (Harriss, Will) ★
1983   Deadheads (Hill, Reginald)
1983   The Siskiyou Two-Step [APA-Siskiyou] (Hoyt, Richard)
1983   Amorous Leander [U.S.-Death on the Broadlands] (Hunter, Alan)
1983   The Unhung Man [U.S.-The Unhanged Man] (Hunter, Alan)
1983   Deadly Petard (Jeffries, Roderic)
1983 ❶ Gateway (Jenkins, Jerry)
1983   Heartbeat (Jenkins, Jerry)
1983   Three Days in Winter (Jenkins, Jerry)
1983   Courtney (Jenkins, Jerry)
1983   Erin [APA-Gold Medal Murder] (Jenkins, Jerry)
1983   Janell (Jenkins, Jerry)
1983   Lindsey [APA-Dying to Come Home] (Jenkins, Jerry)
1983   Megham (Jenkins, Jerry)
1983   Black Knight in Red Square (Kaminsky, Stuart M.) ☆
1983   He Done Her Wrong (Kaminsky, Stuart M.)
1983   A Free-Range Wife (Kenyon, Michael)
1983   Shadow of Death (Kienzle, William X.)
1983   The Hanging Tree (Knox, Bill)
1983   A Limited Vision (Lewis, Roy)
1983   A Pension for Death (Lewis, Roy H.)
1983 ❶ A Cold Mind (Lindsey, David L.)
1983   Replay: Murder (Logue, John)
1983   At the Hands of Another (Lyons, Arthur)
1983   Raven's Longest Night (MacKenzie, Donald)
1983   Mayday from Malaga (MacLeod, Robert)
1983   Beauty and the Beast (McBain, Ed)
1983   Ice (McBain, Ed)
1983 ❶ Murder Among Friends (McConnell, Frank)
1983   The Hoof (McCutchan, Philip)
1983   Fletch and the Man Who (McDonald, Gregory)
1983   The Papers of Tony Veitch (McIlvanney, William) ★ ☆
1983   The Grass Widow (McInerny, Ralph)
1983   Sayonara, Sweet Amaryllis (Melville, James)
1983 ❶ Trace (Murphy, Warren B.) ☆☆
1983   Shock Value (Murphy, Warren B.)
1983   Fool's Gold (Murphy, Warren B.)
1983   Time Trial (Murphy, Warren B.)
1983   Last Drop (Murphy, Warren B.)
1983 ❶ Murder on Madison Avenue (Orenstein, Frank)
1983 ❶ Face Value [U.S.-The Hanging Doll Murder] (Ormerod, Roger)
1983   The Widening Gyre (Parker, Robert B.) ☆
1983   Bait on the Hook (Parrish, Frank)
1983   Malice in Camera (Payne, Laurence)
1983   One Shot Deal (Petievich, Gerald)
1983   To Die in Beverly Hills (Petievich, Gerald)
1983   Gunner Kelly (Price, Anthony)
1983   Casefile (Pronzini, Bill)
1983   Bindlestiff (Pronzini, Bill)
1983   The Steinway Collection (Randisi, Robert J.) ☆
1983 ❶ The Gold Solution (Resnicow, Herbert) ☆
1983   Constable in the Dale (Rhea, Nicholas)
1983   Dead Eye (Ross, Jonathan)
1983 ❶ Hunter (Sauter, Eric) ☆
1983 ❶ Red Diamond, Private Eye (Schorr, Mark) ★
1983   Low Treason (Tourney, Leonard)
1983   A View from the Square (Trenhaile, John)
1983   One Lover Too Many (Tripp, Miles)
1983   Fair Friday (Turnbull, Peter)
1983   The Streetbird (van de Wetering, Janwillem)
1983 ❶ Their Evil Ways (Wainright, John)
1983   Spiral Staircase (Wainright, John)
1983   The Nerissa Claire Case (Waugh, Hillary)

1983		Why Me? (Westlake, Donald E.)
1983		Treasure Preserved (Williams, David)
1983	∎	Dead in the Water (Wood, Ted)
1983	∎	The Night the Gods Smiled (Wright, Eric) ★★
1984		Slate (Aldyne, Nathan)
1984		The Judas Factor (Allbeury, Ted)
1984		Diminished Responsibility (Barnett, James)
1984	∎	The Dorothy Parker Murder Case (Baxt, George)
1984		Switch (Bayer, William)
1984		Like a Lamb to the Slaughter (Block, Lawrence)
1984	∎	The Softener (Bolton, Melvin)
1984		Mr. Pamplemousse en Fete (Bond, Michael)
1984		The Penny Ferry (Boyer, Rick)
1984	∎	The Gathering Place (Breen, Jon)
1984		Not Dead, Only Resting (Brett, Simon)
1984		A Shock to the System (Brett, Simon) ☆
1984		The Story of Henri Tod (Buckley, William F.)
1984		Strip Search (Burns, Rex)
1984		Bomb-Scare Flight 147 (Chambers, Peter)
1984		The Moving Picture Writes (Chambers, Peter)
1984	∎	The Hunt for Red October (Clancy, Tom)
1984		Bouquet Garni (Clark, Douglas)
1984		Dead Letter (Clark, Douglas)
1984		True Crime (Collins, Max Allan, Jr.) ☆
1984		Kill Your Darlings (Collins, Max Allan, Jr.)
1984		The Hook (Copper, Basil)
1984		You Only Die Once (Copper, Basil)
1984		Heroin Annie (Corris, Peter)
1984		The Case of the Murdered Mackenzie (Cunningham, E. V.)
1984		Deep Six (Cussler, Clive)
1984		Words Can Kill (Davis, Kenn) ☆
1984	∎	Cronus (DeAndrea, William L.)
1984		Killed on the Ice (DeAndrea, William L.)
1984		Mexico Set (Deighton, Len)
1984	∎	Blood on the Moon (Ellroy, James)
1984		Because the Night (Ellroy, James)
1984		Murder Sees the Light (Engel, Howard) ★
1984	∎	Kill Zone (Estleman, Loren D.)
1984		Sugartown (Estleman, Loren D.) ★
1984		Terminal (Forbes, Colin)
1984		No Part in Your Death (Freeling, Nicolas)
1984		Role of Honour (Gardner, John)
1984		The Gondola Scam (Gash, Jonathan)
1984		McGarr and the Method of Descartes (Gill, Bartholomew)
1984	∎	Runner in the Street (Grady, James)
1984		Priestly Murders (Granger, Bill)
1984		The Zurich Numbers (Granger, Bill)
1984		The Infiltrators (Hamilton, Donald)
1984		Cousin Once Removed (Hammond, Gerald)
1984		Sauce for the Pigeon (Hammond, Gerald)
1984		Brandstetter and Others (Hansen, Joseph)
1984		Nightwork (Hansen, Joseph)
1984		Death of an Honourable Member (Harrison, Ray)
1984	∎	Blunt Darts (Healy, Jeremiah) ☆
1984	∎	Man's Illegal Life (Heller, Keith)
1984	∎	The Governess (Hervey, Evelyn)
1984		Exit Lines (Hill, Reginald)
1984		The Ghostway (Hillerman, Tony)
1984		The Quests of Simon Ark (Hoch, Edward D.)
1984	∎	Foul Shot (Hornig, Doug) ☆
1984		"Once a Prostitute" (Hunter, Alan)
1984		Murder on Mike (Jeffers, H. Paul)
1984		Three and One Make Five (Jeffries, Roderic)
1984		Too Late to Tell (Jenkins, Jerry)
1984		The Calling (Jenkins, Jerry)
1984		Lyssa (Jenkins, Jerry)
1984		Margo's Reunion (Jenkins, Jerry)
1984		The Fala Factor (Kaminsky, Stuart M.)
1984		The Sheriff of Bombay (Keating, H. R. F.)
1984		Kill and Tell (Kienzle, William X.)
1984		Out of Season, Out of Time [Brit.-Out of Time] (Lewin, Michael Z.)
1984		Most Cunning Workmen (Lewis, Roy)
1984		Once Dying, Twice Dead (Lewis, Roy)
1984		Heat From Another Sun (Lindsey, David L.)
1984		Die Again, Macready (Livingston, Jack) ☆
1984	∎	The Eye (Lutz, John)
1984		Sausalito (Lynch, Jack)
1984		San Quentin (Lynch, Jack) ☆
1984		Raven's Shadow (MacKenzie, Donald)
1984		A Legacy from Tenarife (MacLeod, Robert)
1984	∎	A Back Room in Somers Town (Malcolm, John)
1984		The Godwin Sideboard (Malcolm, John)
1984		The Far Away Man (Marshall, William)
1984		Jack and the Beanstalk (McBain, Ed)
1984		Lightning (McBain, Ed)
1984		The Artful Egg (McClure, James)
1984		Rollerball (McCutchan, Philip)
1984		Flynn's In (McDonald, Gregory)
1984		Carioca Fletch (McDonald, Gregory)
1984		Getting a Way with Murder (McInerny, Ralph)
1984		Death of a Daimyo (Melville, James)
1984		Trace and 47 Miles of Rope (Murphy, Warren B.) ☆
1984		When Elephants Forget (Murphy, Warren B.)
1984		Master's Challenge (Murphy, Warren B.)
1984		Encounter Group (Murphy, Warren B.)
1984		Date With Death (Murphy, Warren B.)
1984		Total Recall (Murphy, Warren B.)
1984	∎	Tip on a Dead Crab (Murray, William)
1984	∎	The Man in the Gray Flannel Shroud (Orenstein, Frank)
1984		Valediction (Parker, Robert B.)
1984		Face at the Window [U.S.-Death in the Rain] (Parrish, Frank)
1984		Vienna Blood (Payne, Laurence)
1984	∎	MacAllister (Perry, Ritchie)
1984		Quicksilver (Pronzini, Bill)
1984		Nightshades (Pronzini, Bill)
1984		Double (Pronzini, Bill)
1984		And Then There Was Nun (Quill, Monica)
1984		Full Contact (Randisi, Robert J.) ☆
1984		The Gold Deadline (Resnicow, Herbert)
1984		The Gold Frame (Resnicow, Herbert)
1984	∎	The Nebraska Quotient (Reynolds, William J) ☆
1984	∎	The Last Laugh (Riggs, John R.)
1984	∎	The Oil Rig (Roderus, Frank)
1984		The Video Vandal (Roderus, Frank)
1984		The Rain Rustlers (Roderus, Frank)
1984		The Turn-Out Man (Roderus, Frank)
1984	∎	Murder and the First Lady (Roosevelt, Elliott)
1984	∎	Strike Three, You're Dead (Rosen, Richard) ★
1984		Drop Dead (Ross, Jonathan)
1984		Hunter and the Ikon (Sauter, Eric)
1984		Hunter and the Raven (Sauter, Eric)
1984		Ace of Diamonds (Schorr, Mark)
1984	∎	A Case for Charley (Spencer, John)
1984		The Man Who Risked His Partner (Stephens, Reed) ☆
1984		On the Other Hand (Stevenson, John)
1984	∎	Death at Charity's Point (Tapply, William G.)
1984		The Dutch Blue Error (Tapply, William G.)
1984		Waiting for the End of the World (Taylor, Andrew)
1984		Coda (Topor, Tom)
1984		Big Money (Turnbull, Peter)
1984		Natural Causes (Valin, Jonathan)
1984		The Ride (Wainright, John)
1984		The Veroncia Dean Case (Waugh, Hillary)
1984		Advertise for Treasure (Williams, David)
1984	∎	Frost at Christmas (Wingfield, R. D.)
1984		Murder on Ice [Brit.-The Killing Cold] (Wood, Ted)
1984		Smoke Detector (Wright, Eric)
1985		The Naked Liar (Adams, Harold) ☆
1985	∎	You Wouldn't Be Dead for Quids (Barrett, Robert G.)
1985		The Condo Kill [Brit.-The Co-Op Kill] (Barth, Richard)
1985	∎	One For the Money (Belsky, Dick)
1985	∎	Strange Inheritance (Biderman, Bob)

1985   Mr. Pamplemousse and the Secret Mission
            (Bond, Michael)
1985   The Elvis Murders (Bourgeau, Art)
1985   Murder at the Cheatin' Heart Motel (Bourgeau, Art)
1985   Triple Crown (Breen, Jon)
1985   Dead Giveaway (Brett, Simon)
1985   Wycliffe and the Four Jacks (Burley, W. J.)
1985 ◼ The Hunter (Busby, Roger)
1985   The Vanishing Holes Murders (Chambers, Peter)
1985   The Beasts of Valhalla (Chesbro, George)
1985   Jewelled Eye (Clark, Douglas)
1985   Performance (Clark, Douglas)
1985   A Shroud for Aquarius (Collins, Max Allan, Jr.)
1985   Upon Some Midnights Clear (Constantine, K. C.)
1985 ◼ Disorderly Elements (Cook, Bob)
1985   Tuxedo Park (Copper, Basil)
1985   The Far Side of Fear (Copper, Basil)
1985   The Big Drop (Corris, Peter)
1985 ◼ Pokerface (Corris, Peter)
1985   Make Me Rich (Corris, Peter)
1985   Snark (DeAndrea, William L.)
1985   London Match (Deighton, Len)
1985   Saratoga Headhunter (Dobyns, Stephen)
1985 ◼ Double Take (Dowling, Gregory)
1985   Murder in the Queen's Armes (Elkins, Aaron)
1985 ◼ The Rainy City (Emerson, Earl) ☆
1985   Poverty Bay (Emerson, Earl) ★ ☆
1985   Nervous Laughter (Emerson, Earl)
1985   Roses Are Dead (Estleman, Loren D.)
1985   Murder on the Hudson (Flynn, Don)
1985   Cover Story (Forbes, Colin)
1985   Death Under the Lilacs (Forrest, Richard)
1985 ◼ Break-in (Francis, Dick)
1985   A City Solitary (Freeling, Nicolas)
1985   Charlie Muffin and the Russian Rose (Freemantle, Brian)
1985   Pearlhanger (Gash, Jonathan)
1985 ◼ Roughcut (Gorman, Ed)
1985   New, Improved Murder (Gorman, Ed) ☆
1985 ◼ Razor Game (Grady, James)
1985   Hard Bargains (Grady, James)
1985   Newspaper Murders (Granger, Bill)
1985 ◼ Happy Are the Meek (Greeley, Andrew M.)
1985   The Detonators (Hamilton, Donald)
1985   Pursuit of Arms (Hammond, Gerald)
1985   Death of a Dancing Lady (Harrison, Ray)
1985   Deathwatch (Harrison, Ray)
1985   Red Herrings (Heald, Tim)
1985   Man's Storm (Heller, Keith)
1985   Man's Loving Family (Heller, Keith)
1985   Robak's Cross (Hensley, Joe L.)
1985   The Man of Gold (Hervey, Evelyn)
1985   Penance for Jerry Kennedy (Higgins, George V.)
1985   Confessional (Higgins, Jack)
1985   Hardball (Hornig, Doug) ☆
1985   Head of State (Hoyt, Richard)
1985   Fish Story (Hoyt, Richard)
1985   The Chelsea Ghost (Hunter, Alan)
1985   Ratings are Murder (Irvine, Robert)
1985 ◼ You'd Better Believe It (James, Bill)
1985   Layers of Deceit (Jeffries, Roderic)
1985   Veiled Threat (Jenkins, Jerry)
1985   The Fatal Equilibrium (Jevons, Marshall)
1985   Red Chameleon (Kaminsky, Stuart M.)
1985   Down for the Count (Kaminsky, Stuart M.)
1985   Putting the Boot In (Kavanagh, Dan)
1985 ◼ When the Bough Breaks [Brit.-Shrunken Heads]
            (Kellerman, Jonathan) ★★
1985 ◼ Sleightly Murder (Kelley, Patrick A.)
1985   Someday the Rabbi Will Leave (Kemelman, Harry)
1985   Sudden Death (Kienzle, William X.)
1985   Wavecrest (Knox, Bill)
1985   Blurred Reality (Lewis, Roy)

1985 ◼ Sleeping Dog (Lochte, Dick) ★ ☆☆☆
1985   Nightlines (Lutz, John) ☆
1985   Seattle (Lynch, Jack)
1985   Monterey (Lynch, Jack)
1985   Three With a Bullet (Lyons, Arthur)
1985   The Gwen John Sculpture (Malcolm, John)
1985   Road Show (Marshall, William)
1985 ◼ The Hunting Season (Mayo, J. K.)
1985   Snow White and Rose Red (McBain, Ed)
1985   Eight Black Horses (McBain, Ed)
1985   Shard at Bay (McCutchan, Philip)
1985   Fletch Won (McDonald, Gregory)
1985   The Big Man (McIlvanney, William)
1985   Rest in Pieces (McInerny, Ralph)
1985   The Death Ceremony (Melville, James)
1985   Sleaze (Morse, L. A.)
1985   Pigs Get Fat (Murphy, Warren B.) ★ ☆
1985   Once a Mutt (Murphy, Warren B.)
1985   The Arms of Kali (Murphy, Warren B.)
1985   The End of the Game (Murphy, Warren B.)
1985   The Lords of the Earth (Murphy, Warren B.)
1985   The Seventh Stone (Murphy, Warren B.)
1985   The Sky is Falling (Murphy, Warren B.)
1985   The Hardknocker's Luck (Murray, William)
1985   Look Out for Space (Nolan, William F.)
1985   Dead Man's Handle (O'Donnell, Peter)
1985 ◼ Sweet Justice (Oster, Jerry)
1985   A Catskill Eagle (Parker, Robert B.) ☆
1985   Kolwezi (Perry, Ritchie)
1985   The Quality of the Informant (Petievich, Gerald)
1985 ◼ Precinct: Siberia (Philbin, Tom)
1985 ◼ Shadow Kill [Brit.-Slow Grave] (Philbrick, W. R.)
1985   Sion Crossing (Price, Anthony)
1985   Here Be Monsters (Price, Anthony)
1985 ◼ Quincannon (Pronzini, Bill)
1985   Bones (Pronzini, Bill) ☆
1985   Nun of the Above (Quill, Monica)
1985 ◼ Doubting Thomas (Reeves, Robert)
1985 ◼ Murder Across and Down (Resnicow, Herbert)
1985   The Seventh Crossword (Resnicow, Herbert)
1985   Constable by the Sea (Rhea, Nicholas)
1985 ◼ The Latimer Mercy (Richardson, Robert) ★
1985   Let Sleeping Dogs Lie (Riggs, John R.)
1985   The Coyote Crossing (Roderus, Frank)
1985   The Dead Heat (Roderus, Frank)
1985   The Hyde Park Murder (Roosevelt, Elliott)
1985   Burial Deferred (Ross, Jonathan)
1985 ◼ Blue Heron (Ross, Philip) ☆
1985   The Fiourth Deadly Sin (Sanders, Lawrence)
1985   Diamond Rock (Schorr, Mark)
1985 ◼ Embrace the Wolf (Schutz, Benjamin) ☆
1985   All the Old Bargains (Schutz, Benjamin)
1985   The Body in Cadiz Bay (Serafin, David)
1985   California Roll (Simon, Roger L.)
1985   Charley Gets the Picture (Spencer, John)
1985 ◼ Double Exposure (Stinson, Jim)
1985   Follow the Sharks (Tapply, William G.)
1985   Our Fathers' Lies (Taylor, Andrew) ☆
1985 ◼ For the Silvership (Thurston, Robert)
1985   In Justice's Prison (Thurston, Robert)
1985   Familiar Spirits (Tourney, Leonard)
1985   Nocturne for the General (Trenhaile, John)
1985   Some Predators Are Male (Tripp, Miles)
1985 ◼ The Adventures of Inspector Lestrade [U.S.-The Supreme
            Adventure of Insp. Lestrade] (Trow, M. J.)
1985 ◼ Flood (Vachss, Andrew H.) ☆
1985   The Rattle-Rat (van de Wetering, Janwillem)
1985 ◼ Hardcover (Warga, Wayne) ★
1985   Victims (Wilcox, Collin)
1985   Wedding Treasure (Williams, David)
1985   Murder in Advent (Williams, David)
1985   Live Bait [Brit.-Dead Centre] (Wood, Ted)

1985   Death in the Old Country (Wright, Eric) ★

1986   The Fourth Widow (Adams, Harold)
1986 **1** Stone Angel (Albert, Marvin H.) ☆
1986   Back in the Real World (Albert, Marvin H.)
1986   Canary (Aldyne, Nathan)
1986 **1** The Big Stick (Alexander, Lawrence)
1986   Bodies (Barnard, Robert)
1986   The Real Thing (Barrett, Robert G.)
1986 **1** The Moving Finger (Bass, Milton R.)
1986   Dirty Money (Bass, Milton R.)
1986   The Alfred Hitchcock Murder Case (Baxt, George)
1986 **1** No One Rides for Free (Beinhart, Larry) ★
1986   When the Sacred Ginmill Closes (Block, Lawrence) ☆
1986   Mr. Pamplemousse on the Spot (Bond, Michael)
1986   The Daisy Ducks (Boyer, Rick)
1986 **1** A Nice Class of Corpse (Brett, Simon)
1986   See You Later, Alligator (Buckley, William F.)
1986   High Jinx (Buckley, William F.)
1986   Wycliffe and the Quiet Virgin (Burley, W. J.)
1986   Ground Money (Burns, Rex)
1986   Hollywood Heroes (Caine, Hamilton)
1986 **1** The Junkyard Dog (Campbell, Robert) ★★
1986 **1** In La-La Land We Trust (Campbell, Robert) ☆
1986 **1** Veil (Chesbro, George)
1986   Two Songs This Archangel Sings (Chesbro, George)
1986   Storm Center (Clark, Douglas)
1986   The Big Grouse (Clark, Douglas)
1986   The Million Dollar Wound (Collins, Max Allan, Jr.) ☆
1986   Nice Weekend for a Murder (Collins, Max Allan, Jr.)
1986   Snow-Job (Copper, Basil)
1986   Jet-Lag (Copper, Basil)
1986   Blood on the Moon (Copper, Basil)
1986   Deal Me Out (Corris, Peter)
1986   The Greenwich Apartments (Corris, Peter)
1986 **1** Too Late to Die (Crider, Bill) ★
1986 **1** Chant (Cross, David)
1986   Silent Killer (Cross, David)
1986   Cyclops (Cussler, Clive)
1986   Melting Point (Davis, Kenn) ☆
1986   The Secret of Annexe 3 (Dexter, Colin)
1986   Saratoga Snapper (Dobyns, Stephen)
1986 **1** Satan in St. Mary's (Doherty, P. C.)
1986 **1** Last Rights (Douglas, Arthur)
1986   Suicide Hill (Ellroy, James)
1986   A City Called July (Engel, Howard)
1986   Catch a Fallen Angel [1969] (Engleman, Paul)
1986   Any Man's Death (Estleman, Loren D.)
1986   Every Brilliant Eye (Estleman, Loren D.)
1986   Bolt (Francis, Dick)
1986   Cold Iron (Freeling, Nicolas)
1986 **1** Greenwich Killing Time (Friedman, Kinky)
1986   Nobody Lives Forever (Gardner, John)
1986   The Tartan Ringers [U.S.-The Tartan Sell]
            (Gash, Jonathan)
1986   Moonspender (Gash, Jonathan)
1986   McGarr and the Legacy of a Woman Scorned
            (Gill, Bartholomew)
1986   Murder Straight Up (Gorman, Ed)
1986   Murder in the Wings (Gorman, Ed)
1986   Hemingway's Notebook (Granger, Bill)
1986   There Are No Spies (Granger, Bill)
1986   Death en Voyage (Grayson, Richard)
1986   Happy Are the Clean of Heart (Greeley, Andrew M.)
1986   Beyond Blame (Greenleaf, Stephen)
1986   The Vanishers (Hamilton, Donald)
1986   Silver City Scandal (Hammond, Gerald)
1986   The Executor (Hammond, Gerald)
1986   The Little Dog Laughed (Hansen, Joseph)
1986 **1** Death Raid (Harper, Richard)
1986   Timor Mortis (Harriss, Will)

1986   The Staked Goat [Brit.-Tethered Goat] (Healy, J.) ★
1986   Robak's Fire (Hensley, Joe L.)
1986   Into the Valley of Death (Hervey, Evelyn)
1986 **1** Night of the Fox (Higgins, Jack)
1986   The Dark Side (Hornig, Doug)
1986   The Dragon Portfolio (Hoyt, Richard)
1986 **1** The Joshua Sequence (Huebner, Frederick D.)
1986   Goodnight, Sweet Prince (Hunter, Alan)
1986   The Lolita Man (James, Bill)
1986   Almost Murder (Jeffries, Roderic)
1986   The Man Who Shot Lewis Vance (Kaminsky, Stuart M.)
1986 **1** The Back-Door Man (Kantner, Rob) ★
1986   Under a Monsoon Cloud (Keating, H. R. F.)
1986   Blood Test (Kellerman, Jonathan)
1986   Sleightly Lethal (Kelley, Patrick A.)
1986   A Healthy Way to Die (Kenyon, Michael)
1986   Deathbed (Kienzle, William X.)
1986 **1** The Sunset Bomber (Kincaid, D.)
1986   The Crossfire Killings (Knox, Bill) ★
1986 **1** Son of Holmes (Lescroart, John T.)
1986   Late Payments (Lewin, Michael Z.)
1986   A Trout in the Milk (Lewis, Roy)
1986   A Premium on Death (Lewis, Roy)
1986   Miracles Take a Little Longer (Lewis, Roy H.)
1986   Spiral (Lindsey, David L.)
1986   The Nightmare File (Livingston, Jack)
1986   Flawless Execution (Logue, John)
1986 **1** Dead Air (Lupica, Mike) ☆
1986 **1** Tropical Heat (Lutz, John)
1986   The Right to Sing the Blues (Lutz, John)
1986   Whistler in the Dark (Malcolm, John)
1986 **1** Manila Bay (Marshall, William)
1986   Head First (Marshall, William)
1986   Cinderella (McBain, Ed)
1986   The Executioners (McCutchan, Philip)
1986   Fletch, Too [prequel] (McDonald, Gregory)
1986   Go Gently, Gaijin (Melville, James)
1986 **1** Bullet Hole (Miles, Keith)
1986 **1** Dead Birds (Milne, John)
1986 **1** Murder for Lunch (Murphy, Haughton)
1986   Too Old a Cat (Murphy, Warren B.) ☆
1986   The Last Alchemist (Murphy, Warren B.)
1986   Lost Yesterday (Murphy, Warren B.)
1986   Sue Me (Murphy, Warren B.)
1986   Look Into My Eyes (Murphy, Warren B.)
1986 **1** The Little Death (Nava, Michael)
1986 **1** The 120-Hour Clock (Nevins, Francis M., Jr)
1986 **1** Midtown South (Newman, Christopher)
1986   Still Life with Pistol (Ormerod, Roger)
1986   Taming a Sea-Horse (Parker, Robert B.)
1986   Fly in the Cobweb (Parrish, Frank)
1986   Dead for a Ducat (Payne, Laurence)
1986   Cop Killer (Philbin, Tom)
1986   Under Cover (Philbin, Tom)
1986   Ice for the Eskimo (Philbrick, W. R.)
1986   The Amber Effect (Prather, Richard)
1986   For the Good of the State (Price, Anthony)
1986   Beyond the Grave (Pronzini, Bill)
1986   Deadfall (Pronzini, Bill)
1986   Sine Qua Nun (Quill, Monica)
1986   The Crossword Code (Resnicow, Herbert)
1986   The Gold Curse (Resnicow, Herbert)
1986   Moving Targets (Reynolds, William J)
1986   Constable Along the Lane (Rhea, Nicholas)
1986 **1** Jersey Tomatoes (Rider, J. W.) ★
1986   Murder at Hobcaw Barony (Roosevelt, Elliott)
1986   Fadeaway (Rosen, Richard)
1986 **1** Hovey's Deception (Ross, Philip)
1986   Deadly Innocents (Sadler, Mark)
1986   The Straight Man (Simon, Roger L.) ☆
1986 **1** Tinplate (Steed, Neville) ★

1986		Ice Blues (Stevenson, Richard)
1986		Low Angles (Stinson, Jim)
1986		The Marine Corpse [Brit.-A Rodent of Doubt] (Tapply, William G.)
1986		An Old School Tie (Taylor, Andrew)
1986		Between Two Evils (Thurston, Robert)
1986		The Bartholomew Fair Murders (Tourney, Leonard)
1986	∎	The Mahjong Spies (Trenhaile, John)
1986		Brigade (Trow, M. J.)
1986		Life's Work (Valin, Jonathan)
1986		Hard Rain (van de Wetering, Janwillem)
1986		Portrait in Shadows (Wainright, John)
1986		The Tenth Interview (Wainright, John)
1986		The Priscilla Copperwaite Case (Waugh, Hillary)
1986		Good Behavior (Westlake, Donald E.)
1986		Nightgames (Wilcox, Collin)
1986		Fool's Gold (Wood, Ted)
1986	∎	Under the Bright Lights (Woodrell, Dan)
1986		The Man Who Changed His Name [Brit.-Single Death] (Wright, Eric)

1987		The Barbed Wire Noose (Adams, Harold)
1987		Get Off at Babylon (Albert, Marvin H.)
1987		Long Teeth (Albert, Marvin H.)
1987		Speak Softly (Alexander, Lawrence)
1987	∎	Death on the Rocks (Allegretto, Michael) ★ ☆
1987	∎	Hammerlocke (Barnao, Jack)
1987		Death in Purple Prose [U.S.-The Cherry Blossom Corpse] (Barnard, Robert)
1987		The Boys from Binjiwunyawunya (Barrett, Robert G.)
1987		The Bandini Affair (Bass, Milton R.)
1987	∎	Crang Plays the Ace (Batten, Jack)
1987		Satan is a Woman (Baxt, George)
1987		The Tallulah Bankhead Murder Case (Baxt, George)
1987	∎	Interface for Murder (Biggle, Lloyd, Jr.)
1987		The Testing (Bolton, Melvin)
1987		Mr. Pamplemousse Takes the Cure (Bond, Michael)
1987		Moscow Metal (Boyer, Rick)
1987		What Bloody Man Is That? (Brett, Simon)
1987	∎	The Neon Rain (Burke, James Lee)
1987		Wycliffe and the Windsor Blue (Burley, W. J.)
1987	∎	Suicide Season (Burns, Rex)
1987		Snow Man (Busby, Roger) ★
1987		The 600-Pound Gorilla (Campbell, Robert)
1987		Alice in La-La Land (Campbell, Robert)
1987		Hip-Deep in Alligators (Campbell, Robert)
1987		Patriot Games (Clancy, Tom)
1987		Plain Sailing (Clark, Douglas)
1987		Dragons at the Party (Cleary, Jon)
1987	∎	The Dark City (Collins, Max Allan, Jr.)
1987		Primary Target (Collins, Max Allan, Jr.)
1987		Spree (Collins, Max Allan, Jr.)
1987		Minnesota Strip (Collins, Michael)
1987		Questions of Identity (Cook, Bob)
1987	∎	Sweet Silver Blues (Cook, Glen)
1987		Heavy Iron (Copper, Basil)
1987		Turn Down an Empty Glass (Copper, Basil)
1987		Bad Scene (Copper, Basil)
1987	∎	"Box Office" Browning (Corris, Peter)
1987		"Beverly Hills" Browning (Corris, Peter)
1987		The January Zone (Corris, Peter)
1987	∎	The Monkey's Raincoat (Crais, Robert) ★★★ ☆
1987		Shotgun Saturday Night (Crider, Bill)
1987		Code of Blood (Cross, David)
1987		Nijinsky is Dead (Davis, Kenn)
1987		As October Dies (Davis, Kenn)
1987		Azreal (DeAndrea, William L.)
1987	∎	Hot Summer, Cold Murder (Dold, Gaylord)
1987		Cold Cash (Dold, Gaylord)
1987		Snake Eyes (Dold, Gaylord) ☆
1987		A Very Wrong Number (Douglas, Arthur)
1987	∎	Shawnee Alley Fire (Douglas, John) ☆
1987	∎	Rafferty's Rules (Duncan, W. Glenn)

1987		Last Seen Alive (Duncan, W. Glenn)
1987	∎	A Deceptive Clarity (Elkins, Aaron)
1987		Old Bones (Elkins, Aaron) ★
1987		Fat Tuesday (Emerson, Earl)
1987		Murder-in-Law (Engleman, Paul)
1987		Lady Yesterday (Estleman, Loren D.) ☆
1987	∎	Recount (Everson, David H.) ☆
1987		Ordinary Murder (Flynn, Don)
1987		Charlie Muffin San [U.S.-See Charlie Run] (Freemantle, Brian)
1987		A Case of Lone Star (Friedman, Kinky)
1987		The Secret Houses (Gardner, John)
1987		No Deals Mr. Bond (Gardner, John)
1987		The Best Cellar (Goodrum, Charles A.)
1987	∎	Murder on the Aisle (Gorman, Ed)
1987	∎	Guild (Gorman, Ed)
1987		The Autumn Dead (Gorman, Ed) ☆
1987	∎	The Goldfish Bowl (Gough, Laurence) ★
1987		Just a Shot Away (Grady, James)
1987		The El Murders (Granger, Bill)
1987		The Infant of Prague (Granger, Bill)
1987		Happy Are Those Who Thirst for Justice (Greeley, Andrew M.)
1987		Toll Call (Greenleaf, Stephen)
1987	∎	Under Cover of Daylight (Hall, James W.)
1987	∎	Detective (Hall, Parnell) ☆☆
1987		The Demolishers (Hamilton, Donald)
1987		The Worried Widow (Hammond, Gerald)
1987		Adverse Report (Hammond, Gerald)
1987		Counterfeit of Murder (Harrison, Ray)
1987		A Season for Death (Harrison, Ray)
1987	∎	Seascape with Dead Figures (Hart, Roy)
1987		A Pretty Place for a Murder (Hart, Roy)
1987		So Like Sleep (Healy, Jeremiah)
1987		Robak's Firm (Hensley, Joe L.)
1987	∎	Snake in the Grasses (Hilary, Richard)
1987		Pieces of Cream (Hilary, Richard)
1987		Child's Play (Hill, Reginald)
1987		Skinwalkers (Hillerman, Tony) ★
1987	∎	Waterman (Hornig, Doug)
1987		Siege (Hoyt, Richard)
1987		The Black Rose (Huebner, Frederick D.)
1987		Strangling Man (Hunter, Alan)
1987		Death Games (Jahn, Michael)
1987		Halo Parade (James, Bill)
1987		The Ragdoll Murder (Jeffers, H. Paul)
1987		Relatively Dangerous (Jeffries, Roderic)
1987		A Fine Red Rain (Kaminsky, Stuart M.)
1987		Smart Moves (Kaminsky, Stuart M.)
1987		The Harder They Hit (Kantner, Rob)
1987	∎	Murder Off the Glass (Katz, Michael J.)
1987		Going to the Dogs (Kavanagh, Dan)
1987		The Body in the Billiard Room (Keating, H. R. F.)
1987		Over the Edge (Kellerman, Jonathan)
1987		Slightly Invisible (Kelley, Patrick A.)
1987		Slightly Deceived (Kelley, Patrick A.)
1987		One Fine Day the Rabbi Bought a Cross (Kemelman, Harry)
1987	∎	Polo Solo (Kennealy, Jerry)
1987		Deadline for a Critic (Kienzle, William X.)
1987		Dead Man's Mooring (Knox, Bill)
1987	∎	Professor in Peril (Lejeune, Anthony)
1987		Rasputin's Revenge (Lescroart, John T.)
1987		Men of Subtle Craft (Lewis, Roy)
1987	∎	Bertie and the Tinman (Lovesey, Peter)
1987		Scorcher (Lutz, John)
1987		Ride the Lightning (Lutz, John) ☆
1987		Fast Fade (Lyons, Arthur)
1987		The Money Mountain [U.S.-A Flight from Paris] (MacLeod, Robert)
1987		Gothic Pursuit (Malcolm, John)
1987		Frogmouth (Marshall, William)
1987		Wolf's Head (Mayo, J. K.)

1987		Puss in Boots (McBain, Ed)
1987		Poison (McBain, Ed)
1987		Tricks (McBain, Ed)
1987		Blood Lake (McConnell, Frank)
1987		Greenfly (McCutchan, Philip)
1987	❶	Cause and Effect (McInerny, Ralph)
1987		The Basket Case (McInerny, Ralph)
1987		Kimono for a Corpse (Melville, James)
1987		Double Eagle (Miles, Keith)
1987	❶	Slob (Miller, Rex)
1987		Shadow Play [U.S.-The Moody Man] (Milne, John)
1987		Lover Man (Murphy, Dallas) ☆
1987		Murder Takes a Partner (Murphy, Haughton)
1987		Getting Up with Fleas (Murphy, Warren B.)
1987		An Old-Fashioned War (Murphy, Warren B.)
1987		Blood Ties (Murphy, Warren B.)
1987		The Eleventh Hour (Murphy, Warren B.)
1987	❶	A Cool Killing (Murray, Stephen)
1987		When the Fat Man Sings (Murray, William)
1987		The Ninety Million Dollar Mouse (Nevins, Francis M., Jr.)
1987		The Sixth Precinct (Newman, Christopher)
1987		A Candidate for Murder (Orenstein, Frank)
1987		An Alibi Too Soon (Ormerod, Roger)
1987		Nowhere Man (Oster, Jerry)
1987		Pale Kings and Princes (Parker, Robert B.)
1987		Caught in the Birdlime [U.S.-Bird in the Net] (Parrish, Frank)
1987		Kate Knight (Payne, Laurence)
1987		Presumed Dead (Perry, Ritchie)
1987		A Matter of Degree (Philbin, Tom)
1987	❶	The Neon Flamingo (Philbrick, W. R.)
1987		Shell Shock (Prather, Richard)
1987		A New Kind of War (Price, Anthony)
1987	❶	Bloodstains (Puckett, Andrew)
1987	❶	No Exit From Brooklyn (Randisi, Robert J.)
1987	❶	Knots and Crosses (Rankin, Ian)
1987	❶	The Dead Room (Resnicow, Herbert)
1987		The Crossword Legacy (Resnicow, Herbert)
1987		The Crossword Hunt (Resnicow, Herbert)
1987		Hot Tickets (Rider, J. W.)
1987		The Glory Hound (Riggs, John R.)
1987	❶	An Infinite Number of Monkeys (Roberts, Les) ★ ☆
1987	❶	Gallows View (Robinson, Peter) ☆☆
1987		The White House Pantry Murder (Roosevelt, Elliott)
1987		Fate Accomplished (Ross, Jonathan)
1987		Tally's Truth (Ross, Philip)
1987	❶	The Timothy Files (Sanders, Lawrence)
1987		A Tax in Blood (Schutz, Benjamin) ★
1987		Port of Light (Serafin, David)
1987		Die-Cast (Steed, Neville)
1987	❶	No Lesser Plea (Tanenbaum, Robert K.)
1987		Dead Meat (Tapply, William G.)
1987		The Vulgar Boatman (Tapply, William G.)
1987		Freelance Death (Taylor, Andrew)
1987		Death of a Man-Tamer (Tripp, Miles)
1987		The Frightened Wife (Tripp, Miles)
1987		Lestrade and the Hallowed House (Trow, M. J.)
1987		Lestrade and the Leviathan (Trow, M. J.)
1987		Strega (Vachss, Andrew H.)
1987		Fire Lake (Valin, Jonathan)
1987		The Sergeant's Cat and Other Stories (van de Wetering, Janwillem)
1987		Treasure in Roubles (Williams, David)
1987		Divided Treasure (Williams, David)
1987		Corkscrew (Wood, Ted)
1987		A Body Surrounded by Water (Wright, Eric)
1988		The Man Who Met the Train (Adams, Harold)
1988		The Last Smile (Albert, Marvin H.)
1988	❶	Pigeon Blood (Alexander, Gary)
1988		Blood Stone (Allegretto, Michael)
1988		Murder in Hollywood (Allen, Steve)
1988		High Noon at Midnight (Avallone, Michael)

1988	❶	St. John's Baptism (Babula, William)
1988		Lockestep (Barnao, Jack)
1988		Deadly Climate (Barth, Richard)
1988		The Belfast Connection (Bass, Milton R.)
1988		You Get What You Pay For (Beinhart, Larry)
1988		The Genesis Files (Biderman, Bob)
1988	❶	The Last Private Eye (Birkett, John) ☆
1988	❶	Citadel Run (Bishop, Paul)
1988		The Offering (Bolton, Melvin)
1988		The Whale's Footprints (Boyer, Rick)
1988	❶	Stone of the Heart (Brady, John) ★
1988		Touch of the Past (Breen, Jon) ☆
1988		Mrs., Presumed Dead (Brett, Simon)
1988	❶	Bad Guys (Bruno, Anthony)
1988		Mongoose, R.I.P. (Buckley, William F.)
1988		Heaven's Prisoners (Burke, James Lee)
1988		Wycliffe and the Tangled Web (Burley, W. J.)
1988		The Killing Zone (Burns, Rex)
1988	❶	Plugged Nickle (Campbell, Robert)
1988		Thinning the Turkey Herd (Campbell, Robert)
1988		The Cat's Meow (Campbell, Robert)
1988		Jungle of Steel and Stone (Chesbro, George)
1988		The Cold Smell of Sacred Stone (Chesbro, George)
1988		The Cardinal of the Kremlin (Clancy, Tom)
1988		Now and Then, Amen (Cleary, Jon)
1988	❶	Return to Sender (Cluster, Dick)
1988		Butcher's Dozen (Collins, Max Allan, Jr.)
1988		Neon Mirage (Collins, Max Allan, Jr.) ☆
1988		Red Rosa (Collins, Michael)
1988		Joey's Case (Constantine, K. C.) ☆
1988		Faceless Mortals (Cook, Bob)
1988	❶	Mexican Standoff (Cook, Bruce)
1988		Cold Copper Tears (Cook, Glen)
1988		Bitter Gold Hearts (Cook, Glen)
1988	❶	Sacrificial Ground (Cook, Thomas H.) ☆
1988		House-Dick (Copper, Basil)
1988		Print-Out (Copper, Basil)
1988	❶	Deadball (Cork, Barry)
1988	❶	Lost Daughter (Cormany, Michael) ☆
1988		The Man in the Shadows (Corris, Peter)
1988		The Baltic Business (Corris, Peter)
1988		The Kimberly Killing (Corris, Peter)
1988	❶	One Dead Dean (Crider, Bill)
1988		Cursed to Death (Crider, Bill)
1988		Treasure (Cussler, Clive)
1988		Killed in Paradise (DeAndrea, William L.)
1988	❶	The Serpentine Wall (DeBrosse, Jim)
1988		Spy Hook (Deighton, Len)
1988	❶	Ratking (Dibdin, Michael) ★
1988		Saratoga Bestiary (Dobyns, Stephen)
1988	❶	The Whyte Hart (Doherty, P. C.)
1988		The Crown in Darkness (Doherty, P. C.)
1988		Spy in Chancery (Doherty, P. C.)
1988		Bone Pile (Dold, Gaylord) ☆
1988	❶	Cajun Nights (Donaldson, D. J.)
1988		A Worm Turns (Douglas, Arthur)
1988		Neapolitan Reel [U.S.-See Naples and Kill] (Dowling, Gregory)
1988		Poor Dead Cricket (Duncan, W. Glenn)
1988	❶	The Burning Season (Dundee, Wayne) ☆
1988	❶	A Good Year for Murder (Eddenden, A. E.)
1988	❶	Black Hearts and Slow Dancing (Emerson, Earl)
1988		Deviant Behavior (Emerson, Earl) ☆
1988		A Victim Must Be Found (Engel, Howard)
1988		General Murders (Estleman, Loren D.)
1988		Downriver (Estleman, Loren D.)
1988		Rebound (Everson, David H.) ☆
1988	❶	The Bottom Line is Murder (Eversz, Robert)
1988	❶	The Art of Death (Fliegel, Richard)
1988		Murder in A-Flat (Flynn, Don)
1988		The Janus Man (Forbes, Colin)
1988		Deadlock (Forbes, Colin)

1988		Lady Macbeth (Freeling, Nicolas)
1988		The Runaround (Freemantle, Brian)
1988		When the Cat's Away (Friedman, Kinky)
1988		Jade Woman (Gash, Jonathan)
1988	■	Dead Run (Gibbs, Tony)
1988		Young Petrella (Gilbert, Michael)
1988		Several Deaths Later (Gorman, Ed)
1988		Death Ground (Gorman, Ed)
1988		Death on a No. 8 Hook [U.S.-Silent Knives] (Gough, Laurence)
1988		Henry McGee Is Not Dead (Granger, Bill)
1988	■	Bino (Gray, A. W.)
1988		Death on the Cards (Grayson, Richard)
1988	■	Drop-Off (Grissom, Ken)
1988	■	The Baxter Trust (Hailey, J. P.)
1988		Murder (Hall, Parnell)
1988		Favor (Hall, Parnell)
1988	■	Benjamin Franklin Takes the Case (Hall, Robert Lee)
1988		Stray Shot (Hammond, Gerald)
1988	■	The Man Who Died Laughing (Handler, David)
1988		Obedience (Hansen, Joseph)
1988		Harvest of Death (Harrison, Ray)
1988		A Fox in the Night (Hart, Roy)
1988	■	Fear of the Dark (Haywood, Gar Anthony) ★★
1988		Brought to Book (Heald, Tim)
1988		Swan Dive (Healy, Jeremiah) ☆
1988	■	Ritual (Heffernan, William)
1988		Pillow of the Community (Hilary, Richard)
1988		Underworld (Hill, Reginald)
1988		A Thief of Time (Hillerman, Tony) ★ ☆
1988		Deep Dive (Hornig, Doug)
1988		Judgment by Fire (Huebner, Frederick D.) ☆
1988		Traitor's End (Hunter, Alan)
1988	■	Baptism for the Dead (Irvine, Robert)
1988		Protection [APA-Harpur and Iles] (James, Bill)
1988		Death Trick (Jeffries, Roderic)
1988	■	Canaan Legacy [APA-Grave Designs] (Kahn, Michael A.)
1988	■	Michigan Roll (Kakonis, Tom)
1988		A Cold Red Sunrise (Kaminsky, Stuart M.) ★
1988		Think Fast, Mr. Peters (Kaminsky, Stuart M.)
1988		Dirty Work (Kantner, Rob) ★
1988		Dead on Time (Keating, H. R. F.)
1988		Sleightly Guilty (Kelley, Patrick A.)
1988		Polo, Anyone? (Kennealy, Jerry)
1988		Polo's Ponies (Kennealy, Jerry)
1988		Peckover Holds the Baby (Kenyon, Michael)
1988		Marked for Murder (Kienzle, William X.)
1988	■	Sleeping Dogs Die (King, Frank)
1988		Key Without a Door (Lejeune, Anthony)
1988		And Baby Will Fall [Adele Buffington narrates] [Brit.-Child Proof] (Lewin, Michael Z.)
1988		The Salamander Chill (Lewis, Roy)
1988		In the Lake of the Moon (Lindsey, David L.) ☆
1988		Hell-Bent for Election [APA-Hell-Bent for Homicide] (Livingston, Jack)
1988		Laughing Dog (Lochte, Dick)
1988		Extra Credits (Lupica, Mike)
1988	■	The Comic Book Killer (Lupoff, Richard A.)
1988		Shadowtown (Lutz, John)
1988		Kiss (Lutz, John) ★
1988		Dancer's Debt (Lutz, John)
1988		Witchline (MacLeod, Robert)
1988		Mortal Ruin (Malcolm, John)
1988	■	Out of Nowhere (Marshall, William)
1988		Whisper (Marshall, William)
1988		Out of Nowhere (Marshall, William)
1988	■	The Queen's Head (Marston, Edward)
1988	■	Open Season (Mayor, Archer)
1988		The House That Jack Built (McBain, Ed)
1988	■	Dead Aim (McCall, Wendell)
1988		The Reluctant Ronin (Melville, James)
1988		Frenzy (Miller, Rex)

1988		Daddy's Girl (Milne, John)
1988		Murder and Acquisitions (Murphy, Haughton)
1988		Return Engagement (Murphy, Warren B.)
1988		Sole Survivor (Murphy, Warren B.)
1988		Line of Succession (Murphy, Warren B.)
1988		Walking Wounded (Murphy, Warren B.)
1988		Rain of Terror (Murphy, Warren B.)
1988		Salty Waters (Murray, Stephen)
1988		Goldenboy (Nava, Michael) ★
1988	■	Strikezone (Nighbert, David F.)
1988		Unnatural Causes (Noguchi, Thomas T. w/Arthur Lyons)
1988		A Killing in Real Estate (Orenstein, Frank)
1988		Paradise of Death (Orenstein, Frank)
1988		An Open Window (Ormerod, Roger)
1988		Club Dead (Oster, Jerry)
1988		Crimson Joy (Parker, Robert B.)
1988	■	The Mamur Zapt and the Return of the Carpet (Pearce, Michael)
1988	■	Undercurrents (Pearson, Ridley)
1988	■	The Trapdoor (Peterson, Keith) ☆
1988		There Fell a Shadow (Peterson, Keith)
1988		The Crystal Blue Persuasion (Philbrick, W. R.) ☆
1988		A Prospect of Vengeance (Price, Anthony)
1988		Shackles (Pronzini, Bill)
1988		Veil of Ignorance (Quill, Monica)
1988	■	Big Sky Blues (Reid, Robert Sims)
1988		The Gold Gamble (Resnicow, Herbert)
1988		Money Trouble (Reynolds, William J.)
1988		Constable Through the Meadow (Rhea, Nicholas)
1988		Bellringer Street (Richardson, Robert)
1988		The Haunt of the Nightingale (Riggs, John R.)
1988	■	Telluride Smile (Ring, Raymond H.)
1988	■	Just Another Angel (Ripley, Mike)
1988	■	Pepper Pike (Roberts, Les)
1988		Not Enough Horses (Roberts, Les)
1988		A Dedicated Man (Robinson, Peter) ☆
1988		Murder at the Palace (Roosevelt, Elliott)
1988		Saturday Night Dead (Rosen, Richard)
1988		Sudden Departures (Ross, Jonathan)
1988		Timothy's Game (Sanders, Lawrence)
1988	■	Overkill (Schorr, Mark)
1988		The Angel of Torremolinos (Serafin, David)
1988		Death's White City (Sherburne, James)
1988	■	An Option on Death (Sherer, Michael W.)
1988		Raising the Dead (Simon, Roger L.)
1988		Dead Meet (Simon, Roger L.)
1988	■	A Twist of the Knife (Solomita, Stephen)
1988	■	Cotswold Manners (Spicer, Michael)
1988		Chipped (Steed, Neville)
1988		A Void in Hearts (Tapply, William G.)
1988	■	A Good Year for the Roses (Timlin, Mark)
1988		Old Saxon Blood (Tourney, Leonard)
1988		The Scroll of Benevolence (Trenhaile, John)
1988		The Gates of Exquisite View (Trenhaile, John)
1988		Lestrade and the Brother of Death (Trow, M. J.)
1988		Lestrade and the Ripper (Trow, M. J.)
1988		Two Way Cut (Turnbull, Peter)
1988		Blue Belle (Vachss, Andrew H.)
1988		A Very Parochial Murder (Wainright, John)
1988		A Very Parochial Murder (Wainright, John)
1988	■	To Catch a Forger (Wallace, Robert)
1988	■	Bernhardt's Edge (Wilcox, Collin)
1988		The Pariah (Wilcox, Collin)
1988		Treasure in Oxford (Williams, David)
1988		A Touch of Frost (Wingfield, R. D.)
1988		Muscle for the Wing (Woodrell, Dan)
1988		The Ones You Do (Woodrell, Dan) ☆
1988		A Question of Murder (Wright, Eric)
1988	■	A Nice Murder for Mom (Yaffe, James)
1989		The Man Who Missed the Party (Adams, Harold)
1989	■	Sea of Green (Adcock, Thomas)

1989 The Midnight Sister (Albert, Marvin H.)
1989 Unfunny Money (Alexander, Gary)
1989 Kiet and the Golden Peacock (Alexander, Gary)
1989 The Dead of Winter (Allegretto, Michael)
1989 Murder on the Glitter Box (Allen, Steve)
1989 ❶ The Cheerio Killings (Allyn, Doug)
1989 According to St. John (Babula, William)
1989 ❶ Death and the Chaste Apprentice (Barnard, Robert)
1989 ❶ A Midsummer Night's Killing (Barnes, Trevor)
1989 The Godson (Barrett, Robert G.)
1989 Blood Doesn't Tell (Barth, Richard)
1989 Straight No Chaser (Batten, Jack)
1989 ❶ South Street Confidential [APA-Broadcast Clues] (Belsky, Dick)
1989 ❶ Tiebreaker (Bickham, Jack M.)
1989 Judgement of Death (Biderman, Bob)
1989 Out on the Cutting Edge (Block, Lawrence) ☆
1989 Mr. Pamplemousse Aloft (Bond, Michael)
1989 ❶ Badger Game (Bowen, Michael)
1989 Unholy Ground (Brady, John)
1989 A Series of Murders (Brett, Simon)
1989 Bad Blood (Bruno, Anthony)
1989 Black Cherry Blues (Burke, James Lee) ★
1989 Red Cent (Campbell, Robert)
1989 Nibbled to Death by Ducks (Campbell, Robert)
1989 Second Horseman Out of Eden (Chesbro, George)
1989 Clear and Present Danger (Clancy, Tom)
1989 Babylon South (Cleary, Jon)
1989 Repulse Monkey (Cluster, Dick)
1989 Bullet Proof (Collins, Max Allan, Jr.)
1989 Castrato (Collins, Michael)
1989 Old Tin Sorrows (Cook, Glen)
1989 Flesh and Blood (Cook, Thomas H.)
1989 Unnatural Hazard (Cork, Barry)
1989 Red Winter (Cormany, Michael)
1989 Browning Takes Off (Corris, Peter)
1989 O'Fear (Corris, Peter)
1989 ❶ A Beautiful Place to Die (Craig, Philip)
1989 Stalking the Angel (Crais, Robert)
1989 Dying Voices (Crider, Bill)
1989 Death on the Move (Crider, Bill)
1989 Acts of Homicide (Davis, Kenn)
1989 ❶ Manhattan is My Beat (Deaver, Jeffery)
1989 Spy Line (Deighton, Len)
1989 The Wench is Dead (Dexter, Colin) ★
1989 The Angel of Death (Doherty, P. C.)
1989 Muscle and Blood (Dold, Gaylord) ☆
1989 Wrong Place, Wrong Time (Duncan, W. Glenn)
1989 Curses! (Elkins, Aaron)
1989 Who Shot Longshot Sam? (Engleman, Paul)
1989 Silent Thunder (Estleman, Loren D.)
1989 Rematch (Everson, David H.)
1989 Instant Replay (Everson, David H.)
1989 The Next to Die (Fliegel, Richard)
1989 The Organ Grinder's Monkey (Fliegel, Richard)
1989 A Suitcase in Berlin (Flynn, Don)
1989 The Greek Key (Forbes, Colin)
1989 Death on the Mississippi (Forrest, Richard)
1989 Not as Far as Velma (Freeling, Nicolas)
1989 Sand Castles (Freeling, Nicolas)
1989 Comrade Charlie (Freemantle, Brian)
1989 Frequent Flyer (Friedman, Kinky)
1989 The Secret Families (Gardner, John)
1989 Win, Lose, or Die (Gardner, John)
1989 The Very Last Gambado (Gash, Jonathan)
1989 The Death of the Joyce Scholar (Gill, Bartholomew) ☆
1989 Blood Game (Gorman, Ed)
1989 Hot Shots (Gough, Laurence) ★
1989 The Man Who Heard Too Much (Granger, Bill)
1989 The Anonymous Client (Hailey, J. P.)
1989 Tropical Freeze [Brit.-Squall Line] (Hall, James W.)
1989 Strangler (Hall, Parnell)
1989 ❶ The Four Last Things (Hallinan, Timothy)

1989 The Frighteners (Hamilton, Donald)
1989 ❶ Dog in the Dark (Hammond, Gerald)
1989 Doghouse (Hammond, Gerald)
1989 A Brace of Skeet (Hammond, Gerald)
1989 The Man Who Lived By Night (Handler, David)
1989 Kinderkill (Harper, Richard)
1989 Tincture of Death (Harrison, Ray)
1989 Remains to be Seen (Hart, Roy)
1989 ❶ Lonely Hearts (Harvey, John)
1989 Business Unusual (Heald, Tim)
1989 Yesterday's News (Healy, Jeremiah)
1989 Behind the Fact (Hilary, Richard) ☆
1989 Talking God [incl Leaphorn] (Hillerman, Tony)
1989 Gently with the Millions (Hunter, Alan)
1989 The Angel's Share (Irvine, Robert)
1989 Come Clean (James, Bill)
1989 Dead Clever (Jeffries, Roderic)
1989 ❶ Formula One (Judd, Bob)
1989 Buried Caesars (Kaminsky, Stuart M.)
1989 Hell's Only Half Full (Kantner, Rob) H
1989 Last Dance in Redondo Beach (Katz, Michael J.)
1989 Inspector Ghote, His Life and Crimes (Keating, H. R. F.)
1989 Silent Partner (Kellerman, Jonathan)
1989 Polo in the Rough (Kenneally, Jerry)
1989 ❶ Under the Boardwalk (Kent, Bill)
1989 ❶ March Violets (Kerr, Philip)
1989 Eminence (Kienzle, William X.)
1989 The Interface Man (Knox, Bill)
1989 ❶ Amends for Murder (Lake, M. D.)
1989 ❶ Dead Irish (Lescroart, John T.) ☆
1989 The Devil is Dead (Lewis, Roy)
1989 A Necessary Dealing (Lewis, Roy)
1989 Death in Verona (Lewis, Roy H.)
1989 Time Exposure (Lutz, John)
1989 Other People's Money (Lyons, Arthur)
1989 Ask Taffin Nicely (Mallett, Lyndon)
1989 The Merry Devils (Marston, Edward)
1989 ❶ The Mercy Trap (Martin, James E.)
1989 ❶ Steele (Masters, J. D.)
1989 Cold Steele (Masters, J. D.)
1989 ❶ The Bannerman Solution [Brit.-Lesko's Ghost] (Maxim, John)
1989 Lullaby (McBain, Ed)
1989 The Boy Who Liked Monsters (McCutchan, Philip)
1989 Four on the Floor (McInerny, Ralph)
1989 Body and Soil (McInerny, Ralph)
1989 Frigor Mortis (McInerny, Ralph)
1989 Abracadaver [Brit.-Slight of Body] (McInerny, Ralph)
1989 A Haiku for Hanae (Melville, James)
1989 Stone Shadow (Miller, Rex)
1989 Murder Keeps a Secret (Murphy, Haughton)
1989 The Final Crusade (Murphy, Warren B.)
1989 Coin of the Realm (Murphy, Warren B.)
1989 Blue Smoke and Mirrors (Murphy, Warren B.)
1989 The Noose of Time (Murray, Stephen)
1989 The King of the Nightcap (Murray, William)
1989 Knock-Off (Newman, Christopher)
1989 ❶ All Dressed Up to Die (Nordan, Robert)
1989 Guilt on the Lily (Ormerod, Roger)
1989 Death of an Innocent (Ormerod, Roger)
1989 ❶ Murder on Martha's Vineyard (Osborn, David)
1989 ❶ Poodle Springs [with Chandler] (Parker, Robert B.)
1989 Playmates (Parker, Robert B.)
1989 The Mamur Zapt and the Night of the Dog (Pearce, Michael)
1989 The Rain (Peterson, Keith) ★
1989 Rough Justice (Peterson, Keith)
1989 Street Killer (Philbin, Tom)
1989 Jamaica Kill (Philbin, Tom)
1989 Tough Enough (Philbrick, W. R.) ☆
1989 Paint It Black (Philbrick, W. R.)
1989 ❶ Blood Rights (Phillips, Mike)

1989 ❶ Down in the Valley (Pierce, David M.)
1989 Hear the Wind Blow, Dear... (Pierce, David M.)
1989 Roses Love Sunshine (Pierce, David M.)
1989 ❶ Hatteras Blue (Poyer, David)
1989 The Memory Trap (Price, Anthony)
1989 Things Invisible (Reynolds, William J)
1989 Constable at the Double (Rhea, Nicholas)
1989 Constable in Disguise (Rhea, Nicholas)
1989 The Book of the Dead (Richardson, Robert)
1989 Wolf in Sheep's Clothing (Riggs, John R)
1989 Angel Touch (Ripley, Mike) ★
1989 Full Cleveland (Roberts, Les)
1989 A Carrot for the Donkey (Roberts, Les)
1989 A Necessary End (Robinson, Peter)
1989 The Hanging Valley (Robinson, Peter) ☆
1989 Murder in the Rose Garden (Roosevelt, Elliott)
1989 Murder in the Oval Office (Roosevelt, Elliott)
1989 A Time for Dying (Ross, Jonathan)
1989 White Flower (Ross, Philip)
1989 ❶ The Fool's Run (Sandford, John)
1989 ❶ Rules of Prey (Sandford, John)
1989 ❶ Cold Night (Sarrantonio, Al) ☆
1989 ❶ Wall of Glass (Satterthwait, Walter) ☆
1989 ❶ Dirty Weekend (Scholefield, Alan)
1989 ❶ The Big Silence (Schopen, Bernard)
1989 The Things We Do for Love (Schutz, Benjamin)
1989 ❶ Tekwar (Shatner, William)
1989 Death's Bright Arrow (Sherburne, James)
1989 Polar Star (Smith, Martin Cruz)
1989 Force of Nature (Solomita, Stephen)
1989 The Killing Man (Spillane, Mickey) ☆
1989 ❶ Black Eye (Steed, Neville)
1989 Clockwork (Steed, Neville)
1989 Truck Shot (Stinson, Jim)
1989 ❶ Rock Critic Murders (Sublett, Jesse) ☆
1989 Depraved Indifference (Tanenbaum, Robert K.)
1989 Dead Winter (Tapply, William G.)
1989 The Cords of Vanity (Tripp, Miles)
1989 Condition Purple (Turnbull, Peter)
1989 Hard Candy (Vachss, Andrew H.)
1989 Extenuating Circumstances (Valin, Jonathan) ★
1989 ❶ Final Dictation (Vincent, Lawrence M.)
1989 The Man Who Wasn't There (Wainright, John)
1989 An Axe to Grind (Wallace, Robert)
1989 Payday [Melbourne] (Wallace, Robert)
1989 Fatal Impressions (Warga, Wayne)
1989 Holy Treasure! (Williams, David)
1989 When the Killing Starts (Wood, Ted)
1989 ❶ Blood Under the Bridge (Zimmerman, Bruce) ☆
1989 1 A Simple Suburban Murder (Zubro, Mark) ★

1990

1990 ❶ A Cat in the Manger (Adamson, Lydia)
1990 A Cat of a Different Color (Adamson, Lydia)
1990 Bimbo Heaven (Albert, Marvin H.) ☆
1990 Kiet and the Opium War (Alexander, Gary)
1990 Murder in Manhattan (Allen, Steve)
1990 ❶ The Becket Factor (Anthony, Michael David)

1990 ❶ A City of Strangers (Barnard, Robert)
1990 Riviera Blues (Batten, Jack)
1990 The Talking Pictures Murder Case (Baxt, George)
1990 Dropshot (Bickham, Jack M.)
1990 Paper Cuts (Biderman, Bob)
1990 The Queen's Mare (Birkett, John) ☆
1990 Sand Against the Tide (Bishop, Paul)
1990 A Ticket to the Boneyard (Block, Lawrence) ☆
1990 Mr. Pamplemousse Investigates (Bond, Michael)
1990 ❶ Washington Deceased (Bowen, Michael)
1990 Gone to Earth (Boyer, Rick)
1990 Kaddish in Dublin (Brady, John)
1990 Loose Lips (Breen, Jon)
1990 Mrs. Pargeter's Package (Brett, Simon)
1990 Bad Luck (Bruno, Anthony)

1990 Tucker's Last Stand (Buckley, William F.)
1990 A Morning for Flamingoes (Burke, James Lee)
1990 Wycliffe and the Cycle of Death (Burley, W. J.)
1990 Parts Unknown (Burns, Rex)
1990 Crackshot (Busby, Roger)

1990 Sweet La-La Land (Campbell, Robert)
1990 The Gift Horse's Mouth (Campbell, Robert)
1990 The Good Policeman (Charyn, Jerome)
1990 In the House of Secret Enemies (Chesbro, George)
1990 The Language of Cannibals (Chesbro, George)
1990 Bitter Water (Clark, Douglas)
1990 Murder Song (Cleary, Jon)
1990 Chasing Eights (Collins, Michael)
1990 Sunshine Enemies (Constantine, K. C.)
1990 Rough Cut (Cook, Bruce)
1990 Dread Brass Shadows (Cook, Glen)
1990 Night Secrets (Cook, Thomas H.)
1990 Laid Dead (Cork, Barry)
1990 Rich or Dead (Cormany, Michael)
1990 The Cargo Club (Corris, Peter)
1990 Evil at the Root (Crider, Bill)
1990 Dragon (Cussler, Clive)

1990 ❶ White Rook (Davis, J Madison)
1990 Blood of Poets (Davis, Kenn)
1990 Atropos (DeAndrea, William L.)
1990 Killed on the Rocks (DeAndrea, William L.)
1990 Death of a Blue Movie Star (Deaver, Jeffery)
1990 Spy Sinker (Deighton, Len)
1990 Vendetta (Dibdin, Michael) ★
1990 Saratoga Hexameter (Dobyns, Stephen)
1990 The Serpent Among the Lilies (Doherty, P. C.)
1990 Disheveled City (Dold, Gaylord)
1990 ❶ Body Scissors (Doolittle, Jerome) ☆
1990 Haunts (Douglas, John)
1990 ❶ A Clear Case of Murder (Downing, Warwick)
1990 Cannon's Mouth (Duncan, W. Glenn)
1990 Fatal Sisters (Duncan, W. Glenn) ★
1990 The Skintight Shroud (Dundee, Wayne) ☆

1990 Icy Clutches (Elkins, Aaron)
1990 Help Wanted: Orphans Preferred (Emerson, Earl)
1990 Dead and Buried (Engel, Howard)
1990 Sweet Women Lie (Estleman, Loren D.)
1990 A Capital Killing (Everson, David H.)
1990 False Profit (Eversz, Robert)

1990 Time to Kill (Fliegel, Richard)
1990 Shockwave (Forbes, Colin)

1990 Brokenclaw (Gardner, John)
1990 The Great California Game (Gash, Jonathan)
1990 Running Fix (Gibbs, Tony)
1990 ❶ Into the Blue (Goddard, Robert)
1990 A Cry of Shadows (Gorman, Ed)
1990 Dark Trail (Gorman, Ed)
1990 Serious Crimes (Gough, Laurence)
1990 League of Terror (Granger, Bill)
1990 In Defense of Judges (Gray, A. W.)

1990 The Underground Man (Hailey, J. P.)
1990 The Naked Typist (Hailey, J. P.)
1990 Client (Hall, Parnell)
1990 Juror (Hall, Parnell)
1990 Benjamin Franklin and a Case of Christmas Murder (Hall, Robert Lee)
1990 Everything but the Squeal (Hallinan, Timothy)
1990 Whose Dog Are You? (Hammond, Gerald)
1990 Let Us Prey (Hammond, Gerald)
1990 Home to Roost (Hammond, Gerald)
1990 The Man Who Would Be F. Scott Fitzgerald (Handler, David) ★
1990 The Boy Who Was Buried This Morning (Hansen, Joseph)
1990 Sphere of Death (Harrison, Ray)
1990 Patently Murder (Harrison, Ray)
1990 Robbed Blind (Hart, Roy)

1990	Rough Treatment (Harvey, John) ☆
1990	Not Long for This World (Haywood, Gar Anthony)
1990	Robak's Run (Hensley, Joe L.)
1990	Cold Harbor (Higgins, Jack)
1990	Bones and Silence (Hill, Reginald) ★ ☆
1990	One Small Step (Hill, Reginald) ★ ☆
1990	Coyote Waits [incl Leaphorn] (Hillerman, Tony) ★
1990	Stinger (Hornig, Doug)
1990 **1**	Bloody Silks (Horwitz, Merle)
1990	Dead Heat (Horwitz, Merle)
1990	Picture Postcard (Huebner, Frederick D.)
1990	Gently Scandalous (Hunter, Alan)

1990	Gone to Glory (Irvine, Robert)

1990	Grootka (Jackson, Jon A.)
1990	Take (James, Bill)
1990	Too Clever by Half (Jeffries, Roderic)

1990 **1**	Lieberman's Folly (Kaminsky, Stuart M.)
1990	The Man Who Walked Like a Bear (Kaminsky, Stuart M.)
1990	Poor Butterfly (Kaminsky, Stuart M.) ☆
1990	Made in Detroit (Kantner, Rob) ☆
1990	The Iciest Sin (Keating, H. R. F.)
1990	Time Bomb (Kellerman, Jonathan)
1990	Polo's Wild Card (Kennealy, Jerry) ☆
1990	The Pale Criminal (Kerr, Philip)
1990	Masquerade (Kienzle, William X.)
1990	Take the D Train (King, Frank)
1990 **1**	Rainy North Woods (Kohler, Vince)

1990	Cold Comfort (Lake, M. D.)
1990 **1**	Savage Season (Lansdale, Joe R.)
1990	The Vig (Lescroart, John T.)
1990 **1**	To Speak for the Dead (Levine, Paul)
1990	Bertie and the Seven Bodies (Lovesey, Peter)
1990	Limited Partner (Lupica, Mike)
1990	Flame (Lutz, John)
1990	Diamond Eyes (Lutz, John)

1990	The Spanish Maze Game (MacLeod, Robert)
1990	The Wrong Impression (Malcolm, John)
1990	The Trip to Jerusalem (Marston, Edward)
1990	The Flip Side of Life (Martin, James E.)
1990	Jagged Steele (Masters, J. D.)
1990	Killer Steele (Masters, J. D.)
1990	Renegade Steele (Masters, J. D.)
1990	Target Steele (Masters, J. D.)
1990	The Bannerman Effect (Maxim, John)
1990	Cry Havoc (Mayo, J. K.)
1990	Borderlines (Mayor, Archer)
1990	Three Blind Mice (McBain, Ed)
1990	Vespers (McBain, Ed)
1990	Aim for the Heart (McCall, Wendell)
1990	The Frog King (McConnell, Frank)
1990	The Spatchcock Plan (McCutchan, Philip)
1990	Savings and Loam (McInerny, Ralph)
1990	The Bogus Buddha (Melville, James)
1990 **1**	A Body to Dye For (Michaels, Grant)
1990	Green Murder (Miles, Keith)
1990	Slice (Miller, Rex)
1990	Iceman (Miller, Rex)
1990 **1**	Devil in a Blue Dress (Mosley, Walter) ★★ ☆
1990	Murder Times Two (Murphy, Haughton)
1990	Shooting Schedule (Murphy, Warren B.)
1990	Death Sentence (Murphy, Warren B.)
1990	Fetch Out No Shroud (Murray, Stephen)
1990	The Getaway Blues (Murray, William)

1990	How Town (Nava, Michael) H
1990 **1**	Blood Sport (Newton, Michael)
1990	Slay Ride (Newton, Michael)

1990	No Sign of Life (Ormerod, Roger)
1990 **1**	Internal Affairs (Oster, Jerry)

1990 **1**	The Detective and Mr. Dickens (Palmer, William J.)
1990	Stardust (Parker, Robert B.)
1990	The Mamur Zapt and the Donkey-Vous (Pearce, Michael)
1990	The Scarred Man (Peterson, Keith)
1990	Death Sentence (Philbin, Tom)
1990	The Late Candidate (Phillips, Mike) ★
1990	Jackpot (Pronzini, Bill)
1990	Terminus (Puckett, Andrew)

1990 **1**	Death in Uptown (Raleigh, Michael)
1990	Separate Cases (Randisi, Robert J.)
1990	Peeping Thomas (Reeves, Robert)
1990	The Hot Place (Resnicow, Herbert)
1990	The Naked Eye (Reynolds, William J)
1990	Constable Among the Heather (Rhea, Nicholas)
1990	The Dying of the Light (Richardson, Robert)
1990	Peregrine Dream (Ring, Raymond H.)
1990	Angel Hunt (Ripley, Mike)
1990	Angel Eyes (Ripley, Mike)
1990	Snake Oil (Roberts, Les)
1990 **1**	A Nasty Bit of Murder (Roe, C. F.)
1990	A Fiery Hint of Murder (Roe, C. F.)
1990	Murder in the Blue Room (Roosevelt, Elliott)
1990	Daphne Dead and Done For (Ross, Jonathan)
1990 **1**	No Sign of Murder (Russell, Alan)

1990	Shadow Prey (Sandford, John)
1990 **1**	Roman Blood (Saylor, Steven)
1990 **1**	Wilkes: His Life and Crimes (Schoonover, Winston)
1990	The Desert Look (Schopen, Bernard) ☆
1990	Gunpower (Schorr, Mark)
1990	Seize the Dragon (Schorr, Mark)
1990	Teklords (Shatner, William)
1990 **1**	Murder Out of Tune (Shaw, Simon)
1990 **1**	Death in a Serene City (Sklepowich, Edward)
1990	Forced Entry (Solomita, Stephen)
1990	Cotswold Murders (Spicer, Michael)
1990	Black Mail (Steed, Neville)
1990	Wind Up (Steed, Neville)
1990	The Man Who Tried to Get Away (Stephens, Reed)
1990	Tough Baby (Sublett, Jesse)
1990 **1**	The DaVinci Deception (Swan, Thomas)

1990	An Easy Thing (Taibo, Paco Ignacio, II)
1990	Client Privilege (Tapply, William G.)
1990	Blood Relation (Taylor, Andrew)
1990 **1**	The Stone Veil (Tierney, Ronald) ☆
1990	Romeo's Tune (Timlin, Mark)
1990	Gun Street Girl (Timlin, Mark)
1990	Video Vengeance (Tripp, Miles)
1990	Lestrade and the Guardian Angel (Trow, M. J.)
1990	Lestrade and the Deadly Game (Trow, M. J.)

1990	Blossom (Vachss, Andrew H.)

1990	Paint Out (Wallace, Robert)
1990 **1**	Exit Wounds (Westermann, John)
1990	Drowned Hopes (Westlake, Donald E.)
1990 **1**	Sanibel Flats (White, Randy Wayne)
1990	Silent Witness (Wilcox, Collin)
1990	A Death Before Dying (Wilcox, Collin)
1990	Prescription for Murder (Williams, David)
1990 **1**	Murphy's Fault (Womack, Steven)
1990	On the Inside (Wood, Ted)
1990	A Sensitive Case (Wright, Eric)

1990	Mom Meets Her Maker (Yaffe, James)
1990 **1**	Murder in a Cold Climate (Young, Scott)

1990	Why Isn't Becky Twitchell Dead? (Zubro, Mark)

1991

1991	A Cat in Wolf's Clothing (Adamson, Lydia)
1991	Dark Maze (Adcock, Thomas) ★
1991	Immaculate Deception (Adler, Warren)
1991	Senator Love (Adler, Warren)

1991   The Zig-Zag Man (Albert, Marvin H.)
1991 ∎ The January Corpse (Albert, Neil) ☆
1991   Deadly Drought (Alexander, Gary)
1991   The Strenuous Life (Alexander, Lawrence)
1991   Murder in Vegas (Allen, Steve)

1991   St. John and the Seven Veils (Babula, William)
1991 ∎ Bagged (Bailey, Jo)
1991   Timelocke (Barnao, Jack)
1991   Between the Devlin and the Deep Blue Seas
        (Barrett, Robert G.)
1991   Blood Count (Batten, Jack)
1991   Wallflower (Bayer, William)
1991   Foreign Exchange (Beinhart, Larry)
1991 ∎ Primary Justice (Bernhardt, William)
1991   Overhead (Bickham, Jack M.)
1991   Breakfast at Wimbledon (Bickham, Jack M.)
1991   A Hazard of Losers (Biggle, Lloyd, Jr.)
1991 ∎ Chapel of the Ravens (Bishop, Paul)
1991   A Dance at the Slaughterhouse (Block, Lawrence) ★ ☆
1991 ∎ Brokered Death (Boland, John C.)
1991   Fielder's Choice (Bowen, Michael)
1991   Yellow Bird (Boyer, Rick)
1991   Hot Air (Breen, Jon)
1991   Corporate Bodies (Brett, Simon)
1991   Bad Business (Bruno, Anthony)
1991   Wycliffe and the Dead Flautist (Burley, W. J.)
1991   Body Guard (Burns, Rex)

1991   In a Pig's Eye (Campbell, Robert)
1991   The Fear in Yesterday's Rings (Chesbro, George)
1991   The Sum of All Fears (Clancy, Tom)
1991   Pride's Harvest (Cleary, Jon)
1991   Dark Summer (Cleary, Jon)
1991 ∎ The White Rose Murders (Clynes, Michael)
1991   Stolen Away (Collins, Max Allan, Jr.) ★
1991   The Irishman's Horse (Collins, Michael)
1991   Red Iron Nights (Cook, Glen)
1991 ∎ The Cross of San Vincente (Cooper, Brian)
1991   Winter Rules (Cork, Barry)
1991   Browning in Buckskin (Corris, Peter)
1991   The Azanian Action (Corris, Peter)
1991   Wet Graves (Corris, Peter)
1991   Aftershock (Corris, Peter)
1991 ∎ Strange Attractor [U.S.-The Catalyst] (Cory, Desmond)
1991   The Woman Who Walked into the Sea (Craig, Philip)
1991 ∎ Dead on the Island (Crider, Bill) ☆
1991 ∎ Best Performance by a Patsy (Cutler, Stan) ☆
1991   The Face on the Cutting Room Floor (Cutler, Stan)

1991 ∎ Suffer Little Children (Davis, Thomas D.) ★
1991   Hard News (Deaver, Jeffery)
1991   Hidden City (DeBrosse, Jim)
1991   The Jewel That Was Ours (Dexter, Colin)
1991 ∎ Kickback (Disher, Garry)
1991   A Penny for the Old Guy (Dold, Gaylord)
1991   Blood on the Bayou (Donaldson, D. J.)
1991   Strangle Hold (Doolittle, Jerome)
1991   Every Picture Tells a Story (Dowling, Gregory)

1991 ∎ All the Lonely People (Edwards, Martin)
1991   A Glancing Light (Elkins, Aaron)
1991   Make No Bones (Elkins, Aaron)
1991   Yellow Dog Party (Emerson, Earl)
1991 ∎ Bahama Heat (Estabrook, Barry)
1991 ∎ Murder in Wrigley Field (Evers, Crabbe)
1991   Murderer's Row (Evers, Crabbe)

1991 ∎ Deadstick (Faherty, Terence) ☆
1991 ∎ The Leaf Boats (Fink, John)
1991   A Semiprivate Doom (Fliegel, Richard)
1991   Whirlpool (Forbes, Colin)
1991   Musical Chairs (Friedman, Kinky)

1991   The Man from Barbarossa (Gardner, John)
1991   The Lies of Fair Ladies (Gash, Jonathan)
1991 ∎ The Night Remembers (Gorman, Ed)
1991   Accidental Deaths (Gough, Laurence)

1991 ∎ Drover (Granger, Bill)
1991   The Last Good German (Granger, Bill)
1991   Death off Stage (Grayson, Richard)
1991   Book Case (Greenleaf, Stephen)
1991   Big Fish (Grissom, Ken)

1991   Skin Deep (Hallinan, Timothy)
1991   In Camera (Hammond, Gerald)
1991   Snatch Crop (Hammond, Gerald)
1991   The Woman Who Fell From Grace (Handler, David)
1991   Country of Old Men (Hansen, Joseph) ★
1991 ∎ The Nightingale Gallery (Harding, Paul)
1991   Breach of Promise (Hart, Roy)
1991 ∎ By Reason of Insanity (Harvey, James Neal)
1991   Cutting Edge (Harvey, John)
1991 ∎ Heartshot (Havill, Steven F.)
1991   Right To Die (Healy, Jeremiah)
1991   Blood Rose (Heffernan, William)
1991   The Eagle Has Flown (Higgins, Jack)
1991   Whoo? (Hoyt, Richard)
1991   Gently to a Kill (Hunter, Alan)

1991   Called Home (Irvine, Robert)

1991   Club (James, Bill)
1991   Astride a Grave (James, Bill)
1991 ∎ The Alice Factor (Janes, J. Robert)
1991   A Fatal Fleece (Jeffries, Roderic)
1991   Murder's Long Memory (Jeffries, Roderic)
1991   Monza [APA-Curve] (Judd, Bob)

1991   Double Down (Kakonis, Tom)
1991   Rostnikov's Vacation (Kaminsky, Stuart M.)
1991   The Melting Clock (Kaminsky, Stuart M.)
1991   The Thousand-Yard Stare (Kantner, Rob) ☆
1991   The Big Freeze (Katz, Michael J.)
1991   Cheating Death (Keating, H.R.F.)
1991 ∎ The Cool Blue Tomb (Kemprecos, Paul) ★
1991   Neptune's Eye (Kemprecos, Paul)
1991   Green With Envy (Kennealy, Jerry)
1991   Kill the Butler (Kenyon, Michael)
1991   A German Requiem (Kerr, Philip)
1991   Cameleon (Kienzle, William X.)
1991   The Drowning Nets (Knox, Bill)
1991 ∎ The Loud Adios (Kuhlken, Ken) ★

1991   Poisoned Ivy (Lake, M. D.)
1991   A Gift for Murder (Lake, M. D.)
1991   The Secret Pilgrim (Le Carré, John)
1991 ∎ The Love That Kills (Levitsky, Ronald)
1991   Called by a Panther (Lewin, Michael Z.)
1991   A Wisp of Smoke (Lewis, Roy)
1991   A Kind of Transaction (Lewis, Roy)
1991 ∎ The Last Detective (Lovesey, Peter) ★
1991   Bloodfire (Lutz, John)

1991   Sheep, Goats and Soap (Malcolm, John)
1991 ∎ Trigger Pull (Malone, Paul)
1991   Pipeline (Malone, Paul)
1991 ∎ False Faces (Margolis, Seth)
1991 ∎ The Twelfth Man (Marquis, Max)
1991   Faces in the Crowd (Marshall, William)
1991   The Nine Giants (Marston, Edward)
1991   Bannerman's Law (Maxim, John)
1991   Widows (McBain, Ed)
1991   The Song Dog (McClure, James)
1991   The Logan File (McCutchan, Philip)
1991   Strange Loyalties (McIlvanney, James)
1991   Judas Priest (McInerny, Ralph)
1991   Flagstick (Miles, Keith)
1991   A Red Death (Mosley, Walter)
1991   Murder Saves Face (Murphy, Haughton)
1991   Fatal Opinions (Murray, Stephen)
1991   I'm Getting Killed Right Here (Murray, William)

1991   Midtown North (Newman, Christopher) ☆
1991   The Necro File (Newton, Michael)
1991   Head Games (Newton, Michael)

1991   Road Kills (Newton, Michael)
1991   Black Lace (Newton, Michael)
1991   Death Beneath the Christmas Tree (Nordan, Robert)

1991   When the Old Man Died (Ormerod, Roger)
1991   Violent Love (Oster, Jerry)
1991 **1** Wolfsong (Owens, Louis)

1991 **1** Beach Money (Pairo, Preston, III)
1991   Perchance to Dream (Parker, Robert B.)
1991   Pastime (Parker, Robert B.)
1991   The Mamur Zapt and the Men Behind (Pearce, Michael)
1991 **1** The Raphael Affair (Pears, Iain)
1991   Comeback (Perry, Ritchie)
1991   The Prosecutor (Philbin, Tom)
1991   Walk on the Water (Philbrick, W. R.)
1991   Angels in Heaven (Pierce, David M.)
1991   Bahamas Blue (Poyer, David)
1991   Breakdown (Pronzini, Bill)

1991   Sister Hood (Quill, Monica)

1991   The Dead of Brooklyn (Randisi, Robert J.)
1991   Hide and Seek (Rankin, Ian)
1991   The Choice (Reed, Barry)
1991   Constable Beside the Stream (Rhea, Nicholas)
1991   Sleeping In Blood (Richardson, Robert)
1991   One Man's Poison (Riggs, John R)
1991   Angel City (Ripley, Mike)
1991   Angels in Arms (Ripley, Mike) ★
1991 **1** Close Softly the Doors (Roat, Ronald Clair)
1991   Deep Shaker (Roberts, Les)
1991 **1** Split Seconds (Robinson, Kevin)
1991   Past Reason Hated (Robinson, Peter) ★
1991   A Classy Touch of Murder [Brit.-Bad Blood] (Roe, C. F.)
1991   A Bonny Case of Murder [Brit.-Deadly Partnership] (Roe, C. F.)
1991   A First-Class Murder (Roosevelt, Elliott)
1991   Murder in the Red Room (Roosevelt, Elliott)
1991   Crimes of the City (Rosenberg, Robert)

1991   The Empress File (Sandford, John)
1991   Eyes of Prey (Sandford, John)
1991   At Ease With the Dead (Satterthwait, Walter)
1991   Thief Taker (Scholefield, Alan)
1991   A Fistful of Empty (Schutz, Benjamin) ☆
1991   Tek Vengeance (Shatner, William)
1991   Farewell to the Flesh (Sklepowich, Edward)
1991   Bad to the Bone (Solomita, Stephen)
1991   TV Safe (Stinson, Jim)
1991 **1** Jordon's Wager (Strunk, Frank C.)

1991   Calling All Heroes (Taibo, Paco Ignacio, II)
1991   Immoral Certainty (Tanenbaum, Robert K.)
1991   The Spotted Cats (Tapply, William G.)
1991   The Steel Web (Tierney, Ronald)
1991   Take the A-Train (Timlin, Mark)
1991   Knaves Templar (Tourney, Leonard)
1991   Lestrade and the Gift of the Prince (Trow, M. J.)
1991   Lestrade and the Magpie (Trow, M. J.)
1991   And Did Murder Him (Turnbull, Peter)

1991   Sacrifice (Vachss, Andrew H.)
1991   Second Chance (Valin, Jonathan) ☆

1991   Finger Play (Wallace, Robert)
1991   Singapore Transfer (Warga, Wayne)
1991 **1** Privileged Information (White, Stephen)
1991   Except for the Bones (Wilcox, Collin)
1991   Hire a Hangman (Wilcox, Collin)
1991   Treasure by Post (Williams, David)
1991 **1** Prayer for the Dead (Wiltse, David)
1991 **1** A Cool Breeze on the Underground (Winslow, Don) ☆☆
1991   Smash Cut (Womack, Steven)
1991 **1** New York Dead (Woods, Stuart)
1991   Final Cut (Wright, Eric)

1991   Mom Doth Murder Sleep (Yaffe, James)

1991 **1** Sorry Now (Zubro, Mark)
1991   The Only Good Priest (Zubro, Mark)

1992

1992   The Man Who Was Taller Than God (Adams, Harold) ★
1992   A Cat in the Wings (Adamson, Lydia)
1992   A Cat by Any Other Name (Adamson, Lydia)
1992   The Witch of Watergate (Adler, Warren)
1992   The Riviera Contract (Albert, Marvin H.)
1992   The February Trouble (Albert, Neil)
1992   Kiet Goes West (Alexander, Gary)
1992   Blood Relative (Allegretto, Michael)
1992 **1** Plain Dealer (Ardin, William)

1992   A Fatal Attachment (Barnard, Robert)
1992   White Shoes, White Lines and Blackie (Barrett, Robert G.)
1992 **1** Pink Vodka Blues (Barrett, Jr., Neal)
1992   The Greta Garbo Murder Case (Baxt, George)
1992   The Noel Coward Murder Case (Baxt, George)
1992   Blind Justice (Bernhardt, William)
1992   A Walk Among the Tombstones (Block, Lawrence)
1992   Faithfully Executed (Bowen, Michael)
1992   Mrs. Pargeter's Pound of Flesh (Brett, Simon)
1992   Bad Moon (Bruno, Anthony)
1992   A Stained White Radiance (Burke, James Lee)
1992   Wycliffe and the Last Rites (Burley, W. J.)

1992   The Hot Money Caper (Chambers, Peter)
1992   Maria's Girls (Charyn, Jerome)
1992   Dark Chant in a Crimson Key (Chesbro, George)
1992 **1** And Justice for One (Clarkson, John)
1992   The Poisoned Chalice (Clynes, Michael)
1992 **1** No Way Home (Coburn, Andrew)
1992   Crime, Punishment and Resurrection (Collins, Michael)
1992   Cassandra in Red (Collins, Michael) ☆
1992 **1** The Black Echo (Connelly, Michael) ★
1992 **1** The India Exhibition (Conroy, Richard Timothy)
1992   Death as a Career Move (Cook, Bruce)
1992 **1** Set Up (Corris, Peter)
1992   Browning P. I. (Corris, Peter)
1992   The Japanese Job (Corris, Peter)
1992   Beware of the Dog (Corris, Peter)
1992   The Mask of Zeus (Cory, Desmond)
1992   The Double-Minded Men (Craig, Philip)
1992   Lullaby Town (Crais, Robert) ☆
1992   Gator Kill (Crider, Bill)
1992   Booked for a Hanging (Crider, Bill)
1992   Sahara (Cussler, Clive)

1992   Red Knight (Davis, J. Madison)
1992   The Werewolf Murders (DeAndrea, William)
1992   The Way Through the Woods (Dexter, Colin) ★
1992   Cabal (Dibdin, Michael)
1992   Paydirt (Disher, Garry)
1992   The Prince of Darkness (Doherty, P. C.)
1992   Murder Wears a Cowl (Doherty, P. C.)
1992   Rude Boys (Dold, Gaylord)
1992   No Mardi Gras for the Dead (Donaldson, D. J.)
1992   Bear Hug (Doolittle, Jerome)
1992   The Water Cure (Downing, Warwick)
1992   The Brutal Ballet (Dundee, Wayne) ☆
1992 **1** Booked to Die (Dunning, John) ★

1992   Murder on the Thirteenth (Eddenden, A. E.)
1992   Suspicious Minds (Edwards, Martin)
1992   Bleeding Dodger Blue (Evers, Crabbe)
1992   False Profits (Everson, David H.)

1992   Live to Regret (Faherty, Terence)
1992   The Pretty How Town [U.S.-The Flanders Sky] (Freeling, Nicolas)
1992 **1** The Button Man (Freemantle, Brian)
1992 **1** A Death in Paris (Fuller, Dean)

1992   Death is Forever (Gardner, John)
1992   Paid and Loving Eyes (Gash, Jonathan)
1992 **1** Shadow Queen (Gibbs, Tony)

1992 Land Fall (Gibbs, Tony)
1992 The Death of Love (Gill, Bartholomew)
1992 ▌ Prey (Goddard, Ken)
1992 ▌ Deadly Medicine (Goldberg, Leonard S.)
1992 A Slip of the Tong (Goodrum, Charles A.)
1992 32 Cadillacs (Gores, Joe) ☆
1992 Fall Down Easy (Gough, Laurence)
1992 Drover and the Zebras (Granger, Bill)
1992 Happy Are the Merciful (Greeley, Andrew M.)
1992 Blood Type (Greenleaf, Stephen)
1992 Drowned Man's Key (Grissom, Ken)

1992 The Wrong Gun (Hailey, J. P.)
1992 Shot (Hall, Parnell)
1992 Murder at Drury Lane (Hall, Robert Lee)
1992 Incinerator (Hallinan, Timothy)
1992 The Threateners (Hamilton, Donald)
1992 Give a Dog a Name (Hammond, Gerald)
1992 ▌ Savage Justice (Handberg, Ron)
1992 The House of the Red Slayer [U.S.-The Red Slayer]
       (Harding, Paul)
1992 Murder Most Holy (Harding, Paul)
1992 Akin to Murder (Harrison, Ray)
1992 Off Minor (Harvey, John)
1992 Bitter Recoil (Havill, Steven F.)
1992 Shallow Graves (Healy, Jeremiah) ☆
1992 Defending Billy Ryan (Higgins, George V.)
1992 ▌ Eye of the Storm (Higgins, Jack)
1992 Recalled to Life (Hill, Reginald)
1992 Marimba (Hoyt, Richard)
1992 Gently Tragic (Hunter, Alan)

1992 The Spoken Word (Irvine, Robert)

1992 City of God (Jahn, Michael)
1992 Gospel (James, Bill)
1992 ▌ Mayhem [U.S.-Mirage] (Janes, J. Robert)
1992 Carousel (Janes, J. Robert)
1992 Burn [Brit.-Phoenix] (Judd, Bob)
1992 Race (Judd, Bob)

1992 Death of a Russian Priest (Kaminsky, Stuart M.)
1992 The Quick and the Dead (Kantner, Rob)
1992 ▌ Death by Station Wagon (Katz, Jon)
1992 Private Eyes (Kellerman, Jonathan)
1992 The Day the Rabbi Resigned (Kemelman, Harry)
1992 Death in Deep Water (Kemprecos, Paul)
1992 Special Delivery (Kennealy, Jerry) ☆
1992 Body Count (Kienzle, William X.)
1992 The Lawyer's Tale (Kincaid, D.)
1992 Rising Dog (Kohler, Vince)

1992 Night Vision (Levine, Paul)
1992 The Wisdom of Serpents (Levitsky, Ronald)
1992 A Secret Dying (Lewis, Roy)
1992 ▌ Witness to the Truth (Lindsay, Paul)
1992 Body of Truth (Lindsey, David L.) ☆
1992 ▌ Blue Bayou (Lochte, Dick)
1992 Diamond Solitaire (Lovesey, Peter)
1992 The Classic Car Killer (Lupoff, Richard A.)
1992 Hot (Lutz, John)

1992 A Deceptive Appearance (Malcolm, John)
1992 Shakedown (Malone, Paul)
1992 The Mad Courtesan (Marston, Edward)
1992 The Silent Woman (Marston, Edward)
1992 And Then You Die (Martin, James E.)
1992 ▌ Compelling Evidence (Martini, Steve)
1992 ▌ Unseen Witness (Matthews, Lew)
1992 Scent of Evil (Mayor, Archer)
1992 Kiss (McBain, Ed)
1992 The Abbot of Stockbridge (McCutchan, Philip)
1992 Desert Sinner (McInerny, Ralph)
1992 The Body Wore Brocade (Melville, James)
1992 Love You to Death (Michaels, Grant)
1992 A Very Venetian Murder (Murphy, Haughton)

1992 The Hidden Law (Nava, Michael) ★
1992 Nineteenth Precinct (Newman, Christopher)
1992 Wet Work (Newton, Michael)
1992 Jigsaw (Newton, Michael)
1992 Dead Heat (Newton, Michael)
1992 Squeezeplay (Nighbert, David F.)

1992 ▌ Box Nine (O'Connell, Jack)
1992 A Vintage Year for Dying (Orenstein, Frank)
1992 Murder on the Chesapeake (Osborn, David)
1992 Fixin' to Die (Oster, Jerry)
1992 The Sharpest Sight (Owens, Louis)

1992 ▌ Testimony (Palmer, Frank)
1992 Unfit to Plead (Palmer, Frank)
1992 The Highwayman and Mr. Dickens (Palmer, William J.)
1992 Double Deuce (Parker, Robert B.)
1992 Degree of Guilt (Patterson, Richard North)
1992 The Mamur Zapt and the Girl in the Nile
       (Pearce, Michael)
1992 The Titian Committee (Pears, Iain)
1992 ▌ A Firing Offense (Pelecanos, George P.)
1992 Write Me a Letter (Pierce, David M.)
1992 Quarry (Pronzini, Bill)
1992 Epitaphs (Pronzini, Bill)

1992 A Good Hanging and Other Stories (Rankin, Ian)
1992 Wolfman [U.S.-Tooth & Nail] (Rankin, Ian)
1992 Strip Jack (Rankin, Ian)
1992 Dead Letters (Riggs, John R)
1992 A Dragon Lives Forever (Riggs, John R)
1992 Seeing the Elephant (Roberts, Les)
1992 Mall Rats (Robinson, Kevin)
1992 Wednesday's Child (Robinson, Peter) ☆☆
1992 A Torrid Piece of Murder (Roe, C. F.)
1992 Murder in the West Wing (Roosevelt, Elliott)
1992 Murder Be Hanged (Ross, Jonathan)
1992 The Forest Prime Evil (Russell, Alan)

1992 ▌ The Long-Legged Fly (Sallis, James) ☆
1992 ▌ McNally's Secret (Sanders, Lawrence)
1992 McNally's Luck (Sanders, Lawrence)
1992 Silent Prey (Sandford, John)
1992 A Flower in the Desert (Satterthwait, Walter)
1992 Arms of Nemesis (Saylor, Steven)
1992 Never Die in January (Scholefield, Alan)
1992 Teklab (Shatner, William)
1992 Bloody Instructions (Shaw, Simon)
1992 Dead for a Ducat (Shaw, Simon)
1992 Little Use for Death (Sherer, Michael W.)
1992 Red Square (Smith, Martin Cruz)
1992 Cotswold Mistress (Spicer, Michael)
1992 Third Man Out (Stevenson, Richard)
1992 ▌ Expert Testimony (Stockley, Grif)
1992 ▌ The Woman Who Married a Bear (Straley, John) ★
1992 ▌ Boiled in Concrete (Sublett, Jesse)

1992 Some Clouds (Taibo, Paco Ignacio, II)
1992 Reversible Error (Tanenbaum, Robert K.)
1992 Tight Lines (Tapply, William G.)
1992 The Sleeping Policeman (Taylor, Andrew)
1992 The Iron Glove (Tierney, Ronald)
1992 The Turnaround (Timlin, Mark)
1992 Zip Gun Boogie (Timlin, Mark)
1992 Hearts of Stone (Timlin, Mark)
1992 Witness of Bones (Tourney, Leonard)
1992 Lestrade and the Dead Man's Hand (Trow, M. J.)
1992 Lestrade and the Sign of Nine (Trow, M. J.)

1992 Hangman's Lane (Wainright, John)
1992 ▌ Killer Instinct (Walker, Robert W.)
1992 The Heat Islands (White, Randy Wayne)
1992 Dead Center (Wilcox, Collin)
1992 Planning on Murder (Williams, David)
1992 Close to the Bone (Wiltse, David)
1992 Night Frost (Wingfield, R. D.)
1992 Flashback (Wood, Ted)

1992		A Fine Italian Hand (Wright, Eric)
1992		Mom Among the Liars (Yaffe, James)
1992		Thicker Than Water (Zimmerman, Bruce)
1992	∎	Death Trance (Zimmerman, R. D.)
1992		The Principal Cause of Death (Zubro, Mark)

1993

1993		A Perfectly Proper Murder (Adams, Harold)
1993		A Cat with a Fiddle (Adamson, Lydia)
1993		A Cat in a Glass House (Adamson, Lydia)
1993	∎	Blood Sacrifice (Alexander, Gary)
1993		The Murder Game (Allen, Steve)
1993		Motown Underground (Allyn, Doug)
1993	∎	Blood Is Thicker Than Beaujolais (Aspler, Tony)
1993		Recycled (Bailey, Jo)
1993		A Hovering of Vultures (Barnard, Robert)
1993		A Pound of Flesh (Barnes, Trevor)
1993		Les Norton's Back In and de Fun Don't Done (Barrett, Robert G.)
1993		Deathics (Barth, Richard)
1993	∎	The Half-Hearted Detective (Bass, Milton R.) ☆
1993		The Marlene Dietrich Murder Case (Baxt, George)
1993		The Mae West Murder Case (Baxt, George)
1993		American Hero (Beinhart, Larry)
1993		Live from New York (Belsky, Dick)
1993	∎	A Clean Sweep (Berlinski, David)
1993		Deadly Justice (Bernhardt, William)
1993		Double Fault (Bickham, Jack M.)
1993		Sometimes You Get the Bear (Block, Lawrence)
1993		The Devil Knows You're Dead (Block, Lawrence) ★
1993		The Seventh Beaver (Boland, John C.)
1993		Mr. Pamplemousse Stands Firm (Bond, Michael)
1993		Act of Faith (Bowen, Michael)
1993	∎	Deadline (Boyle, Gerry)
1993		All Souls (Brady, John)
1993		A Reconstructed Corpse (Brett, Simon)
1993		In the Electric Mist with Confederate Dead (Burke, James Lee)
1993		Wycliffe and the Dunes Mystery (Burley, W. J.)
1993		Endangered Species (Burns, Rex)
1993	∎	The Mysterious Death of Meriwether Lewis (Burns, Ron)

1993	∎	Monkey on a Chain (Campbell, Harlen)
1993		Montezuma's Man (Charyn, Jerome)
1993		An Incident at Blood Tide (Chesbro, George)
1993		Without Remorse (Clancy, Tom)
1993		Bleak Spring (Cleary, Jon)
1993		The Grail Murders (Clynes, Michael)
1993		Murder by the Numbers (Collins, Max Allan, Jr.)
1993		The Black Ice (Connelly, Michael) ☆☆
1993		Mr. Smithson's Bones (Conroy, Richard Timothy)
1993		Bottom Liner Blues (Constantine, K. C.)
1993	∎	Dead Fit (Cook, Stephen)
1993		The Singing Stones (Cooper, Brian)
1993		Burn and Other Stories (Corris, Peter)
1993		Cross Off (Corris, Peter)
1993		Browning Battles On (Corris, Peter)
1993		Matrimonial Causes (Corris, Peter)
1993		The Dobie Paradox (Cory, Desmond)
1993		Cliff Hanger (Craig, Philip)
1993		Free Fall (Crais, Robert) ☆
1993		The Mexican Tree Duck (Crumley, James)
1993		Shot on Location (Cutler, Stan)

1993		Deathdeal (Disher, Garry)
1993		Saratoga Haunting (Dobyns, Stephen)
1993		The Assassin in the Greenwood (Doherty, P. C.)
1993		The World Beat (Dold, Gaylord)
1993		Head Lock (Doolittle, Jerome)
1993		A Lingering Doubt (Downing, Warwick)

1993		I Remember You (Edwards, Martin)
1993	∎	Hostile Intent (Egleton, Clive)

1993		Old Scores (Elkins, Aaron) ★ ☆
1993		Morons and Madmen (Emerson, Earl) ☆
1993		There Was an Old Woman (Engel, Howard)
1993	∎	The Man With My Name (Engleman, Paul)
1993		Fear in Fenway (Evers, Crabbe)

1993		The Lost Keats (Faherty, Terence)
1993		A Minyan for the Dead (Fliegel, Richard) ☆
1993		You Know Who (Freeling, Nicolas)
1993		Charlie's Apprentice (Freemantle, Brian)
1993		Elvis, Jesus & Coca Cola (Friedman, Kinky)
1993	∎	The List of 7 (Frost, Mark) ☆

1993		Maestro (Gardner, John)
1993		Never Send Flowers (Gardner, John)
1993		The Sin Within Her Smile (Gash, Jonathan)
1993	∎	Roller Coaster (Gilbert, Michael)
1993		Death on a Cold, Wild River (Gill, Bartholomew)
1993	∎	A Shrine of Murders (Grace, C. L.)
1993		Burning the Apostle (Granger, Bill)
1993		Killings (Gray, A. W.)
1993		Happy Are the Peacemakers (Greeley, Andrew M.)
1993		Southern Cross (Greenleaf, Stephen)

1993		Actor (Hall, Parnell)
1993		A Man With No Time (Hallinan, Timothy)
1993		The Damagers (Hamilton, Donald)
1993		The Curse of the Cockers (Hammond, Gerald)
1993		Thin Air (Hammond, Gerald)
1993		Cry Vengeance (Handberg, Ron)
1993		The Boy Who Never Grew Up (Handler, David)
1993		The Anger of God (Harding, Paul)
1993	∎	Columbo: The Grassy Knoll (Harrington, William)
1993		Murder in Petticoat Square (Harrison, Ray)
1993		Final Appointment (Hart, Roy)
1993		Wasted Years (Harvey, John)
1993		You Can Die Trying (Haywood, Gar Anthony)
1993		Foursome (Healy, Jeremiah) ☆
1993		Scarred (Heffernan, William)
1993		Thunder Point (Higgins, Jack)
1993	∎	Blood Sympathy (Hill, Reginald) ☆
1993		Sacred Clowns (Hillerman, Tony) ☆
1993		Bigfoot (Hoyt, Richard)
1993	∎	Death of a Merry Widow (Hunt, Richard)
1993		Gently in the Glens (Hunter, Alan)
1993	∎	Point of Impact (Hunter, Stephen)

1993		The Great Reminder (Irvine, Robert)

1993		Hit on the House (Jackson, Jon A.)
1993		Roses, Roses (James, Bill)
1993		Kaleidoscope (Janes, J. Robert)
1993	∎	Skinner's Rules (Jardine, Quintin) ☆
1993		Murder Confounded (Jeffries, Roderic)

1993		Death Benefits (Kahn, Michael A.)
1993		Shadow Counter (Kakonis, Tom)
1993		Lieberman's Choice (Kaminsky, Stuart M.)
1993		The Devil Met a Lady (Kaminsky, Stuart M.)
1993		The Red, White and Blues (Kantner, Rob)
1993	∎	The Fat Boy Murders (Kaufelt, David A.)
1993		Doing Wrong (Keating, H. R. F.)
1993	∎	Cuckoo (Keegan, Alex) ☆
1993		Devil's Waltz (Kellerman, Jonathan)
1993		Feeding Frenzy (Kemprecos, Paul)
1993		Vintage Polo (Kennealy, Jerry)
1993		Down by the Sea (Kent, Bill)
1993		Peckover Joins the Choir (Kenyon, Michael)
1993		Dead Wrong (Kienzle, William X.)
1993		The Venus Deal (Kuhlken, Ken)

1993		Murder by Mail (Lake, M. D.)
1993	∎	Pronto [Italy] (Leonard, Elmore)
1993		Hard Evidence (Lescroart, John T.)
1993		False Dawn (Levine, Paul)
1993		Stone Boy (Levitsky, Ronald)
1993		Bloodeagle (Lewis, Roy)

1993		Bertie and the Crime of Passion (Lovesey, Peter)
1993		Spark (Lutz, John)
1993		Thicker Than Blood (Lutz, John)
1993		False Pretenses (Lyons, Arthur)

1993	1	Detective First Grade (Mahoney, Dan)
1993		The Burning Ground (Malcolm, John)
1993	1	Season of the Monsoon (Mann, Paul)
1993		Vanishing Act (Margolis, Seth)
1993		Undignified Death (Marquis, Max)
1993	1	The Wolves of Savernake (Marston, Edward)
1993		Prime Witness (Martini, Steve)
1993		A Conviction of Guilt (Matthews, Lew)
1993		A Matter of Honor (Maxim, John)
1993		The Skeleton's Knee (Mayor, Archer)
1993		Mary, Mary (McBain, Ed)
1993		Mischief (McBain, Ed)
1993	1	A Wide and Capable Revenge (McCall, Thomas)
1993		Liar's Poker (McConnell, Frank)
1993		Son of Fletch (McDonald, Gregory)
1993		Seed of Doubt (McInerny, Ralph)
1993		Dead on Your Feet (Michaels, Grant)
1993	1	Permanent Retirement (Miles, John)
1993		White Butterfly (Mosley, Walter) ☆☆
1993		Lush Life (Murphy, Dallas)
1993		We're Off to See the Killer (Murray, William)

1993		Precinct Command (Newman, Christopher)
1993		Death on Wheels (Nordan, Robert)

1993		Wireless (O'Connell, Jack)
1993		Shame the Devil (Ormerod, Roger)
1993		Murder in the Napa Valley (Osborn, David)
1993		When the Night Comes (Oster, Jerry)

1993	1	The Stolen Gods (Page, Jake)
1993		One Dead Judge (Pairo, Preston, III)
1993		Bent Grasses (Palmer, Frank)
1993		Blood Brother (Palmer, Frank)
1993		Paper Doll (Parker, Robert B.)
1993		Voices from the Dark (Parrish, Frank)
1993	1	The Dividing Line (Parrish, Richard)
1993	1	Along Came a Spider (Patterson, James)
1993		The Mamur Zapt and the Spoils of Egypt (Pearce, Michael) ★
1993		The Mamur Zapt and the Camel of Destruction (Pearce, Michael)
1993		The Bernini Bust (Pears, Iain)
1993		The Angel Maker (Pearson, Ridley)
1993		Nick's Trip (Pelecanos, George P.)
1993		Demons (Pronzini, Bill)

1993		Nun Plussed (Quill, Monica)

1993		A Body in Belmont Harbor (Raleigh, Michael)
1993	1	The Ballad of Rocky Ruiz (Ramos, Manuel) ☆
1993		Hard Look (Randisi, Robert J.)
1993		The Black Book (Rankin, Ian)
1993		Constable Around the Green (Rhea, Nicholas)
1993	1	Dreamsicle (Ripley, W. L.)
1993		A Still and Icy Silence (Roat, Ronald Clair)
1993		The Cleveland Connection (Roberts, Les)
1993		A Matter of Perspective (Robinson, Kevin)
1993		A Relative Act of Murder [Brit.-Death in the Family] (Roe, C. F.)
1993		Murder in the East Room (Roosevelt, Elliott)
1993	1	The Cutting Room (Rosenberg, Robert)

1993		Moth (Sallis, James) ☆
1993		McNally's Risk (Sanders, Lawrence)
1993	1	The Next Victim (Sanders, William)
1993		Winter Prey (Sandford, John)
1993		Summer Cool (Sarrantonio, Al)
1993		The Hanged Man (Satterthwait, Walter)
1993		Catalina's Riddle (Saylor, Steven) ★☆
1993		Threats and Menaces (Scholefield, Alan)
1993		Wilkes on Trial (Schoonover, Winston)

1993		Tek Secret (Shatner, William)
1993		Death Came Dressed in White (Sherer, Michael W.)
1993		Liquid Desires (Sklepowich, Edward)
1993		Piece of the Action (Solomita, Stephen)
1993		Cotswold Moles (Spicer, Michael)
1993	1	Done Deal (Standiford, Les)
1993		Probable Cause (Stockley, Grif)
1993		Jordon's Showdown (Strunk, Frank C.)

1993		No Happy Ending (Taibo, Paco Ignacio, II)
1993		Material Witness (Tanenbaum, Robert K.)
1993		The Snake Eater (Tapply, William G.)
1993		Odd Man Out (Taylor, Andrew)
1993	1	Eclipse of the Heart (Tierney, Ronald)
1993		Falls of the Shadow (Timlin, Mark)
1993		Ashes by Now (Timlin, Mark)
1993	1	Dynamite Pass (Trainor, J. F.)
1993		Target for Murder (Trainor, J. F.)
1993		Lestrade and the Sawdust Ring (Trow, M. J.)
1993		Lestrade and the Mirror of Murder (Trow, M. J.)
1993		Long Day Monday (Turnbull, Peter)

1993		The Music Lovers (Valin, Jonathan)

1993		Fatal Instinct (Walker, Robert W.)
1993		Don't Ask (Westlake, Donald E.)
1993		Find Her a Grave (Wilcox, Collin)
1993		Switchback (Wilcox, Collin)
1993		Banking on Murder (Williams, David)
1993		The Edge of Sleep (Wiltse, David)
1993		The Trail to Buddha's Mirror (Winslow, Don)
1993	1	Dead Folk's Blues (Womack, Steven) ★
1993		Torch Town Boogie (Womack, Steven) ☆
1993		The Software Bomb (Womack, Steven)
1993		Snowjob (Wood, Ted)
1993		Death by Degrees (Wright, Eric)

1993		Tallant for Democracy (York, Andrew)
1993		The Shaman's Knife (Young, Scott)

1993		Full-Bodied Red (Zimmerman, Bruce)
1993		Blood Trance (Zimmerman, R. D.)
1993		Political Poison (Zubro, Mark)

1994

1994	1	Do Unto Others (Abbott, Jeff) ★★
1994		A Way With Widows (Adams, Harold)
1994	1	Dr. Nightingale Comes Home (Adamson, Lydia)
1994		Dr. Nightingale Rides the Elephant (Adamson, Lydia)
1994		A Cat with No Regrets (Adamson, Lydia)
1994		A Cat on the Cutting Edge (Adamson, Lydia)
1994		Drown All the Dogs (Adcock, Thomas)
1994		The Ties That Bind (Adler, Warren)
1994		Burning March (Albert, Neil)
1994	1	Blind Justice (Alexander, Bruce)
1994		Dead Dinosaurs (Alexander, Gary)
1994	1	Desert Cat (Allen, Garrison)
1994	1	Tracer, Inc. (Andrus, Jeff)
1994		Dark Provenance (Anthony, Michael David)
1994		Some Dark Antiquities (Ardin, William)
1994	1	A Legacy of Vengeance (Armistead, John)
1994	1	Final Viewing (Axler, Leo)
1994		Double Plot (Axler, Leo) ☆
1994	1	Hour of the Manatee (Ayres, E. C.) ★

1994		St. John's Bestiary (Babula, William)
1994		The Broken-Hearted Detective (Bass, Milton R.) ☆
1994		A Queer Kind of Love (Baxt, George)
1994		The Bette Davis Murder Case (Baxt, George)
1994		Mirror Maze (Bayer, William)
1994		The Mourning Show (Belsky, Dick)
1994		Less Than Meets the Eye (Berlinski, David)
1994		Perfect Justice (Bernhardt, William)
1994		The Davis Cup Conspiracy (Bickham, Jack M.)
1994		Where Dead Soldiers Walk (Biggle, Lloyd, Jr.)
1994	1	Kill Me Again (Bishop, Paul)

1994	The Burglar Who Traded Ted Williams (Block, Lawrence)
1994	A Long Line of Dead Men (Block, Lawrence) ☆☆
1994	Death in Jerusalem (Boland, John C.)
1994	Corruptly Procured (Bowen, Michael)
1994 ■	Coyote Wind (Bowen, Peter)
1994 ■	The Seventh Sacrament (Bradberry, James)
1994	The Good Life (Brady, John) ☆
1994 ■	No Bottom (Brewer, James D.)
1994 ■	Lonely Street (Brewer, Steve)
1994	Bad Apple (Bruno, Anthony)
1994	A Very Private Plot (Buckley, William F.)
1994	Dixie City Jam (Burke, James Lee) ☆
1994	Enslaved (Burns, Ron)

1994 ■	Death Underfoot (Casley, Dennis)
1994	Little Angel Street (Charyn, Jerome)
1994	Debt of Honor (Clancy, Tom)
1994	One Man's Law (Clarkson, John)
1994	Autumn Maze (Cleary, Jon)
1994	A Brood of Vipers (Clynes, Michael)
1994	Voices in the Dark (Coburn, Andrew)
1994	Carnal Hours (Collins, Max Allan, Jr.) ☆
1994	The Concrete Blonde (Connelly, Michael) ☆☆
1994	Old Ways in the New World (Conroy, Richard Timothy)
1994	The Sidewalk Hilton (Cook, Bruce)
1994	Deadly Quicksilver Lies (Cook, Glen)
1994	One Dead Tory (Cook, Stephen)
1994	Covenant with Death (Cooper, Brian)
1994	Browning Sahib (Corris, Peter)
1994	The Time Trap (Corris, Peter)
1994	Casino (Corris, Peter)
1994	Off Season (Craig, Philip)
1994	A Dangerous Thing (Crider, Bill)
1994	When Old Men Die (Crider, Bill)
1994	Murder Most Fowl (Crider, Bill)
1994	Inca Gold (Cussler, Clive)
1994	Rough Cut (Cutler, Stan)

1994 ■	The Heaven Stone (Daniel, David) ★ ☆
1994	Murdered Sleep (Davis, Thomas D.)
1994	The Manx Murders (DeAndrea, William)
1994	Southern Cross (DeBrosse, Jim)
1994 ■	14 Peck Slip (Dee, Ed)
1994	Faith (Deighton, Len)
1994	The Daughters of Cain (Dexter, Colin)
1994	Dead Lagoon (Dibdin, Michael)
1994	Crosskill (Disher, Garry)
1994	Saratoga Backtalk (Dobyns, Stephen)
1994 ■	An Ancient Evil (Doherty, P. C.)
1994	The Song of a Dark Angel (Doherty, P. C.)
1994	New Orleans Requiem (Donaldson, D. J.)
1994	Half Nelson (Doolittle, Jerome)
1994 ■	The Shaman Sings (Doss, James D.)
1994	A Nice Steady Job (Dowling, Gregory)
1994 ■	Dead Sand (DuBois, Brendan)
1994 ■	A Time for the Death of a King (Dukthas, Ann)
1994 ■	Crooked Man (Dunbar, Tony)

1994	Yesterday's Papers (Edwards, Martin)
1994	A Killing in Moscow (Egleton, Clive)
1994	Dead Men's Hearts (Elkins, Aaron)
1994 ■	Night Shadows (Ely, Ron)
1994	The Portland Laugher (Emerson, Earl)
1994	Tigers Burning (Evers, Crabbe)

1994	Die Dreaming (Faherty, Terence)
1994 ■	Viper Quarry (Feldmeyer, Dean) ☆
1994	The Man Who Murdered Himself (Fliegel, Richard)
1994	No Time for Heroes (Freemantle, Brian)
1994	Armadillos & Old Lace (Friedman, Kinky)

1994	Seafire (Gardner, John)
1994	Wildfire (Goddard, Ken)
1994	Deadly Practice (Goldberg, Leonard S.)
1994 ■	Blood Moon [Brit.-Blood Red Moon] (Gorman, Ed)
1994	Killers (Gough, Laurence)
1994	The Eye of God (Grace, C. L.)

1994	Drover and the Designated Hitter (Granger, Bill)
1994	Death au Gratin (Grayson, Richard)
1994 ■	Irish Gold (Greeley, Andrew M.)
1994	Happy Are the Poor in Spirit (Greeley, Andrew M.)
1994	False Conception (Greenleaf, Stephen)

1994	Mean High Tide (Hall, James W.)
1994	Blackmail (Hall, Parnell)
1994	A Case of Artful Murder (Hall, Robert Lee)
1994	Sting in the Tail (Hammond, Gerald)
1994	Hook or Crook (Hammond, Gerald)
1994 ■	Spare Parts (Hanson, Rick)
1994	By Murder's Bright Light (Harding, Paul)
1994	Columbo: The Helter Skelter Murders (Harrington, William)
1994	A Deadly Schedule (Hart, Roy)
1994	Painted Ladies (Harvey, James Neal)
1994	Flesh & Blood (Harvey, James Neal)
1994	Cold Light (Harvey, John)
1994 ■	Drawing Dead (Hautman, Pete)
1994	Twice Buried (Havill, Steven F.)
1994 ■	Going Nowhere Fast (Haywood, Gar Anthony)
1994	Act of God (Healy, Jeremiah)
1994	On Dangerous Ground (Higgins, Jack)
1994	Pictures of Perfection (Hill, Reginald) ☆
1994 ■	Presumed Dead (Holton, Hugh)
1994	Red Card (Hoyt, Richard)
1994	Methods of Execution (Huebner, Frederick D.)
1994	Deadlocked (Hunt, Richard)
1994	Bomber's Moon (Hunter, Alan)
1994 ■	Presence of Mind (Hunter, Fred W.)

| 1994 ■ | Barking Dogs (Irvine, Robert) |
| 1994 | Hosanna Shout (Irvine, Robert) |

1994	Deadman (Jackson, Jon A.)
1994	Murder at the Museum of Natural History (Jahn, Michael)
1994	In Good Hands (James, Bill)
1994	Mannequin (Janes, J. Robert)
1994	Salamander (Janes, J. Robert)
1994	Skinner's Festival (Jardine, Quintin)
1994	Skinner's Trail (Jardine, Quintin)
1994	Death Takes Time (Jeffries, Roderic)
1994	Spin (Judd, Bob)

1994	Firm Ambitions (Kahn, Michael A.)
1994	Concrete Hero (Kantner, Rob)
1994	The Family Stalker (Katz, Jon)
1994	The Winter Women Murders (Kaufelt, David A.)
1994	Vulture (Keegan, Alex)
1994	Bad Love (Kellerman, Jonathan)
1994	Beggars Choice (Kennealy, Jerry)
1994	Peckover and the Bog Man (Kenyon, Michael)
1994	Bishop as Pawn (Kienzle, William X.)
1994	Banjo Boy (Kohler, Vince)
1994	The Angel Gang (Kuhlken, Ken)

1994	Once Upon a Crime (Lake, M. D.)
1994	Mucho Mojo (Lansdale, Joe R.)
1994 ■	A Drink Before the War (Lehane, Dennis) ★★
1994	The 13th Juror (Lescroart, John T.) ☆
1994 ■	Killing Me Softly (Leslie, John)
1994	Mortal Sin (Levine, Paul)
1994	The Innocence That Kills (Levitsky, Ronald)
1994 ■	Family Business (Lewin, Michael Z.)
1994	Underdog (Lewin, Michael Z.)
1994	The Crossbearer (Lewis, Roy)
1994 ■	The Fall-Down Artist (Lipinski, Thomas) ☆
1994 ■	Forgive Us Our Sins (Luber, Philip)
1994	The Bessie Blue Killer (Lupoff, Richard A.)
1994	The Sepia Siren Killer (Lupoff, Richard A.)
1994	Torch (Lutz, John)

1994 ■	The Marx Sisters (Maitland, Barry) ☆
1994	Hung Over (Malcolm, John)
1994	Inches (Marshall, William)

1994   The Ravens of Blackwater (Marston, Edward)
1994   A Fine and Private Place (Martin, James E.)
1994   Undue Influence (Martini, Steve)
1994   Fruits of the Poisonous Tree (Mayor, Archer)
1994   There Was a Little Girl (McBain, Ed)
1994   Polecat Brennan (McCutchan, Philip)
1994   Fletch Reflected (McDonald, Gregory)
1994 ❶ A Kind of Homecoming (McEldowney, Eugene)
1994 ❶ Otherwise Known as Murder (McGaughey, Neil)
1994   A Cardinal Offense (McInerny, Ralph)
1994   Mom and Dead (McInerny, Ralph)
1994   Mask for a Diva (Michaels, Grant)
1994 ❶ Missing at Tenoclock (Miles, John)
1994   Murder in Retirement (Miles, John)
1994 ❶ Solo Hand (Moody, Bill)
1994 ❶ Falconer's Crusade (Morson, Ian)
1994   Black Betty (Mosley, Walter) ☆
1994   Now You See Her, Now You Don't (Murray, William)

1994 ❶ Protocol for Murder (Nathan, Paul)
1994   Dead End Game (Newman, Christopher)
1994 ❶ The Black Mask Murders (Nolan, William F.)

1994   Mask of Innocence (Ormerod, Roger)
1994   Bone Game (Owens, Louis)

1994   The Deadly Canyon (Page, Jake)
1994   Night Watch (Palmer, Frank)
1994   China Hand (Palmer, Frank)
1994   Walking Shadow (Parker, Robert B.)
1994   Versions of the Truth (Parrish, Richard)
1994   Eyes of a Child (Patterson, Richard North)
1994 ❶ Sleeping Dogs (Paul, William)
1994   The Mamur Zapt and the Snake Catcher's Daughter
        (Pearce, Michael)
1994   The Last Judgment (Pears, Iain)
1994   No Witnesses (Pearson, Ridley)
1994   Dart Man (Philbin, Tom)
1994 ❶ Violent Spring (Phillips, Gary)
1994   Build Me a Castle (Pierce, David M.)
1994   Louisiana Blue (Poyer, David)
1994   The Ladies of the Vale (Puckett, Andrew)

1994   The Maxwell Street Blues (Raleigh, Michael)
1994   The Ballad of Gato Guerrero (Ramos, Manuel)
1994   Stand-Up (Randisi, Robert J.)
1994   Mortal Causes (Rankin, Ian)
1994   The Indictment (Reed, Barry)
1994   Constable Beneath the Trees (Rhea, Nicholas)
1994   Cold Hearts and Gentle People (Riggs, John R)
1994 ❶ A Typical American Town (Roberts, John Maddox)
1994   The Lake Effect (Roberts, Les) ☆
1994   The Lemon Chicken Jones (Roberts, Les)
1994   Final Account (Robinson, Peter)
1994   Royal Murder (Roosevelt, Elliott)
1994   World of Hurt (Rosen, Richard)
1994   The Body of a Woman [U.S.-None the Worse for a
        Hanging] (Ross, Jonathan)
1994 ❶ The Hotel Detective (Russell, Alan)

1994   Black Hornet (Sallis, James)
1994   McNally's Caper (Sanders, Lawrence)
1994   A Death on 66 (Sanders, William)
1994   Night Prey (Sandford, John)
1994 ❶ Burn Out (Scholefield, Alan)
1994   Burn Out (Scholefield, Alan)
1994   Mexico Is Forever (Schutz, Benjamin)
1994 ❶ HardScape (Scott, Justin)
1994   Tek Power (Shatner, William)
1994   The Villain of the Earth (Shaw, Simon) ★
1994   A Forever Death (Sherer, Michael W.)
1994 ❶ Stalking Horse (Shoemaker, Bill)
1994 ❶ Murder at Fenway Park (Soos, Troy)
1994   Raw Deal (Standiford, Les)
1994   Religious Conviction (Stockley, Grif)

1994   The Curious Eat Themselves (Straley, John)
1994 ❶ Big Town (Swanson, Doug J.) ★ ☆☆

1994   Justice Denied (Tanenbaum, Robert K.)
1994 ❶ An Air That Kills (Taylor, Andrew)
1994   Pretend We're Dead (Timlin, Mark)
1994   Frobisher's Savage (Tourney, Leonard)
1994   Whiskey Jack (Trainor, J. F.)
1994   Corona Blue (Trainor, J. F.)
1994 ❶ Absolution by Murder (Tremayne, Peter)
1994 ❶ Maxwell's House (Trow, M. J.)

1994   Down in the Zero (Vachss, Andrew H.)
1994   Just a Corpse at Twilight (van de Wetering, Janwillem) ☆
1994   Pas de Death (Vincent, Lawrence M.)

1994   Primal Instinct (Walker, Robert W.)
1994 ❶ Death of a Blue Lantern (West, Christopher) ☆
1994   The Man Who Invented Florida (White, Randy Wayne)
1994   Private Practices (White, Stephen)
1994   Higher Authority (White, Stephen)
1994   Full Circle (Wilcox, Collin)
1994 ❶ Last Seen Breathing (Williams, David)
1994 ❶ The Triarchs (Wilson, Derek)
1994   The Dresden Text (Wilson, Derek)
1994   Into the Fire (Wiltse, David)
1994   Way Down on the High Lonely (Winslow, Don)
1994 ❶ A Strange and Bitter Crop (Wyrick, E. L.)

1994   Crimson Green (Zimmerman, Bruce)
1994   An Echo of Death (Zubro, Mark)

1995

1995   The Only Good Yankee (Abbott, Jeff)
1995   The Ditched Blond (Adams, Harold)
1995   Dr. Nightingale Goes to the Dogs (Adamson, Lydia)
1995   Dr. Nightingale Goes the Distance (Adamson, Lydia)
1995   A Cat on a Winning Streak (Adamson, Lydia)
1995   The Cat in Fine Style (Adamson, Lydia)
1995   Devil's Heaven (Adcock, Thomas)
1995   Cruel April (Albert, Neil)
1995   Murder in Grub Street (Alexander, Bruce)
1995   Grave Doubts (Allegretto, Michael)
1995   Royal Cat (Allen, Garrison)
1995   Murder on the Atlantic (Allen, Steve)
1995 ❶ Icewater Mansions (Allyn, Doug)
1995 ❶ Zia Summer (Anaya, Rudolfo)
1995   Light at Midnight (Ardin, William)
1995   A Homecoming for Murder (Armistead, John)
1995   Grave Matters (Axler, Leo)
1995   Eye of the Gator (Ayres, E. C.)

1995 ❶ Poet in the Gutter (Baker, John)
1995   The Bad Samaritan (Barnard, Robert)
1995 ❶ The Innocents (Barre, Richard) ★ ☆
1995 ❶ Dead, Mr. Mozart (Bastable, Bernard)
1995   Too Many Notes, Mr. Mozart (Bastable, Bernard)
1995   A Queer Kind of Umbrella (Baxt, George)
1995   The Humphrey Bogart Murder Case (Baxt, George)
1995 ❶ No Comfort in Victory (Bean, Gregory)
1995   Summertime News (Belsky, Dick)
1995 ❶ The Risk of Murder (Berger, Bob)
1995   The Burglar Who Thought He Was Bogart
        (Block, Lawrence)
1995 ❶ Play It Again (Bogart, Stephen Humphrey)
1995   Specimen Song (Bowen, Peter)
1995   Pirate Trade (Boyer, Rick)
1995   Bloodline (Boyle, Gerry)
1995   Sicken and So Die (Brett, Simon)
1995   No Virtue (Brewer, James D.)
1995   Baby Face (Brewer, Steve)
1995 ❶ Rogue's Isles (Briody, Thomas Gately)
1995   Brothers No More (Buckley, William F.)
1995   Burning Angel (Burke, James Lee)
1995   Wycliffe and the House of Fear (Burley, W. J.)
1995   Bloodline (Burns, Rex)

1995 The Wizard of La-La Land (Campbell, Robert)
1995 Sauce for the Goose (Campbell, Robert)
1995 Death Understates (Casley, Dennis)
1995 Death Undertow (Casley, Dennis)
1995 ■ The Mountain Massacres (Champion, David)
1995 Bleeding in the Eye of a Brainstorm (Chesbro, George)
1995 Winter Chill (Cleary, Jon)
1995 The Gallows Murders (Clynes, Michael)

1995 ■ Deal Breaker (Coben, Harlan) ★ ☆
1995 Blood and Thunder [Huey Long] (Collins, Max Allan, Jr.)
1995 The Last Coyote (Connelly, Michael) ☆☆☆
1995 Cranks and Shadows (Constantine, K. C.)
1995 Petty Pewter Gods (Cook, Glen)
1995 Shadows on the Sand (Cooper, Brian)
1995 Browning Without a Cause (Corris, Peter)
1995 A Case of Vineyard Poison (Craig, Philip)
1995 Vodoo River (Crais, Robert)

1995 ■ Local Knowledge (Daly, Conor)
1995 The Skelly Man (Daniel, David)
1995 ■ Written in Fire (DeAndrea, William L.)
1995 Killed in Fringe Time (DeAndrea, William L.)
1995 Bronx Angel (Dee, Ed)
1995 Hope (Deighton, Len)
1995 Port Villa Blues (Disher, Garry)
1995 Saratoga Fleshpot (Dobyns, Stephen)
1995 A Tapestry of Murders (Doherty, P. C.)
1995 Satan's Fire (Doherty, P. C.)
1995 Kill Story (Doolittle, Jerome)
1995 The Shaman Laughs (Doss, James D.)
1995 Black Tide (DuBois, Brendan)
1995 The Prince Lost to Time (Dukthas, Ann)
1995 City of Beads (Dunbar, Tony)
1995 Bookman's Wake (Dunning, John) ☆☆☆

1995 Death Throes (Egleton, Clive)
1995 A Lethal Involvement (Egleton, Clive)
1995 East Beach (Ely, Ron)
1995 The Vanishing Smile (Emerson, Earl) ☆
1995 Getting Away with Murder (Engel, Howard)
1995 Left for Dead (Engleman, Paul)
1995 Whirlpool (Estabrook, Barry)
1995 Suicide Squeeze (Everson, David H.)

1995 Pitchfork Hollow (Feldmeyer, Dean)
1995 Painted Leaves (Fink, John)
1995 ■ Who in Hell is Wanda Fuca? (Ford, G. M.) ☆☆
1995 Come to Grief (Francis, Dick) ★ ☆
1995 The Seacoast of Bohemia (Freeling, Nicolas)
1995 God Bless John Wayne (Friedman, Kinky)

1995 ■ Mr. X (Gaitano, Nick)
1995 Confessor (Gardner, John)
1995 Goldeneye (Gardner, John)
1995 ■ Moondog (Garfield, Henry)
1995 The Grace in Older Women (Gash, Jonathan)
1995 Capitol Offense (Gibbs, Tony)
1995 ■ Ring of Terror (Gilbert, Michael)
1995 Death of an Ardent Bibliophile (Gill, Bartholomew)
1995 ■ My Gun Has Bullets (Goldberg, Lee)
1995 Heartbreaker (Gough, Laurence)
1995 The Merchant of Death (Grace, C. L.)
1995 Bino's Blues (Gray, A. W.)
1995 Happy Are Those Who Mourn (Greeley, Andrew M.)

1995 ■ Legend of the Dead (Hackler, Micah S.)
1995 Gone Wild (Hall, James W.)
1995 Movie (Hall, Parnell) ☆
1995 Murder by the Waters (Hall, Robert Lee)
1995 The Bone Polisher (Hallinan, Timothy)
1995 Mad Dogs and Scotsmen (Hammond, Gerald)
1995 Carriage of Justice (Hammond, Gerald)
1995 The Man Who Cancelled Himself (Handler, David)
1995 Mortal Remains (Hanson, Rick)
1995 The House of Crows (Harding, Paul)

1995 Columbo: The Hoffa Connection (Harrington, William)
1995 Hallmark of Murder (Harrison, Ray)
1995 Living Proof (Harvey, John)
1995 Short Money (Hautman, Pete)
1995 Bad News Travels Fast (Haywood, Gar Anthony)
1995 Rescue (Healy, Jeremiah)
1995 ■ The Ninth Race (Healy, R. Austin)
1995 . ■ Death on the Mississippi (Heck, Peter J.)
1995 Tarnished Blue (Heffernan, William) ★
1995 Angel of Death (Higgins, Jack)
1995 ■ The Last Castrato (Hill, John Spencer)
1995 Born Guilty (Hill, Reginald)
1995 The Wood Beyond (Hill, Reginald)
1995 Windy City (Holton, Hugh)
1995 ■ Penance (Housewright, David) ★ ☆
1995 Japanese Game (Hoyt, Richard)
1995 Snake Eyes (Hoyt, Richard)
1995 Murder Benign (Hunt, Richard)
1995 Jackpot! (Hunter, Alan)
1995 Ransom for an Angel (Hunter, Fred W.)

1995 Pillar of Fire (Irvine, Robert)

1995 The Detective is Dead (James, Bill)
1995 Dollmaker (Janes, J. Robert)
1995 Stonekiller (Janes, J. Robert)
1995 Skinner's Round (Jardine, Quintin)
1995 ■ Native Angels (Jaspersohn, William) ★
1995 ■ The Last Templar (Jecks, Michael)
1995 The Merchant's Partner (Jecks, Michael)
1995 ■ A Grand Night for Murder (Jeffers, H. Paul)
1995 An Arcadian Death (Jeffries, Roderic)
1995 A Deadly Indifference (Jevons, Marshall)

1995 Due Diligence (Kahn, Michael A.)
1995 Lieberman's Day (Kaminsky, Stuart M.)
1995 Lieberman's Thief (Kaminsky, Stuart M.)
1995 Hard Currency (Kaminsky, Stuart M.)
1995 Tomorrow is Another Day (Kaminsky, Stuart M.)
1995 The Last Housewife (Katz, Jon)
1995 Kingfisher (Keegan, Alex)
1995 Self-Defense (Kellerman, Jonathan)
1995 The Mayflower Murder (Kemprecos, Paul)
1995 On a Blanket with my Baby (Kent, Bill)
1995 Call No Man Father (Kienzle, William X.)
1995 ■ Harmony in Flesh and Black (Kilmer, Nicholas)
1995 ■ Material Evidence (Kirton, Bill)
1995 ■ Zero Tolerance (Knight, J. D.) ☆

1995 Grave Choices (Lake, M. D.)
1995 The Two-Bear Mambo (Lansdale, Joe R.)
1995 ■ Hostile Witness (Lashner, William)
1995 ■ The Bath Detective (Lee, Christopher)
1995 Riding the Rap (Leonard, Elmore)
1995 ■ A Certain Justice (Lescroart, John T.)
1995 Night and Day (Leslie, John)
1995 Slashback (Levine, Paul)
1995 A Short Lived Ghost (Lewis, Roy)
1995 Angel of Death (Lewis, Roy)
1995 Codename: Gentkill (Lindsay, Paul)
1995 Neon Smile (Lochte, Dick) ☆
1995 The Summons (Lovesey, Peter) ☆★
1995 Jump (Lupica, Mike)
1995 The Cover Girl Killer (Lupoff, Richard A.)
1995 ■ Making the Cut (Lusby, Jim)
1995 Death By Jury (Lutz, John)
1995 Burn (Lutz, John)

1995 Edge of the City (Mahoney, Dan)
1995 The Malcontenta (Maitland, Barry) ★
1995 ■ Nantucket Revenge (Maness, Larry)
1995 The Ganja Coast (Mann, Paul)
1995 Written in Blood (Marquis, Max)
1995 The Dragons of Archenfield (Marston, Edward)
1995 The Roaring Boy (Marston, Edward) ☆

1995	The Judge (Martini, Steve)
1995	A Shred of Honour (Mayo, J. K.)
1995	The Masterless Men (Mayo, J. K.)
1995	The Dark Root (Mayor, Archer)
1995	Romance (McBain, Ed)
1995	Beyond Ice, Beyond Death (McCall, Thomas)
1995	Burn-Out (McCutchan, Philip)
1995 ■	Skylar (McDonald, Gregory)
1995	A Stone of the Heart (McEldowney, Eugene)
1995	The Strange Case of Harpo Higgins (McEldowney, Eugene)
1995	And Then There Were Ten (McGaughey, Neil)
1995	Law and Ardor (McInerny, Ralph)
1995 ■	Diplomatic Baggage (Melville, James)
1995	The Reluctant Spy (Melville, James)
1995 ■	The Saints of God Murders (Meyer, Charles)
1995 ■	In the Drift (Milan, Borto)
1995	Tenoclock Scholar (Miles, John)
1995	Most Deadly Retirement (Miles, John)
1995 ■	High Desert Malice (Mitchell, Kirk) ☆
1995	Death of a Tenor Man (Moody, Bill)
1995	Falconer's Judgement (Morson, Ian)
1995 ■	Lost Honor (Mullen, Jack)
1995	Don't Explain (Murphy, Dallas)

1995	No Good Deed (Nathan, Paul)
1995	Shutout (Nighbert, David F.)

1995	Skin Palace (O'Connell, Jack)
1995	Stone Cold Dead (Ormerod, Roger)

1995	The Knotted Strings (Page, Jake)
1995	Double Exposure (Palmer, Frank)
1995	Dead Man's Handle (Palmer, Frank)
1995	Thin Air (Parker, Robert B.)
1995	Nothing But the Truth (Parrish, Richard)
1995	Kiss the Girls (Patterson, James)
1995	Sleeping Pretty (Paul, William)
1995 ■	The Picasso Scam (Pawson, Stuart)
1995	The Mushroom Man (Pawson, Stuart)
1995	The Mingrelian Conspiracy (Pearce, Michael)
1995	Giotto's Hand (Pears, Iain)
1995	Down by the River Where the Dead Men Go (Pelecanos, George P.)
1995 ■	Vanishing Act (Perry, Thomas)
1995	Point of Darkness (Phillips, Mike)
1995 ■	Dance of the Mongoose (Phillips, T. J.)
1995 ■	Murder by Prescription (Pomidor, Bill)
1995	Hardcase (Pronzini, Bill)

1995	Killer on Argyle Street (Raleigh, Michael)
1995 ■	Alone with the Dead (Randisi, Robert J.)
1995	Let It Bleed (Rankin, Ian)
1995	Wild Animals (Reid, Robert Sims)
1995	Drive-by (Reynolds, William J)
1995	Constable in the Shrubbery (Rhea, Nicholas)
1995	Killing Frost (Riggs, John R)
1995	Angel Confidential (Ripley, Mike)
1995	Storm Front (Ripley, W. L.)
1995	High Walk (Roat, Ronald Clair)
1995	The Duke of Cleveland (Roberts, Les)
1995	Murder in the Executive Mansion (Roosevelt, Elliott)
1995	The Fat Innkeeper (Russell, Alan)

1995	McNally's Trial (Sanders, Lawrence)
1995	Blood Autumn (Sanders, William)
1995	Mind Prey (Sandford, John)
1995 ■	Escapade (Satterthwait, Walter) ★ ☆
1995	The Venus Throw (Saylor, Steven)
1995	Buried Treasure (Scholefield, Alan)
1995	Stone Dust (Scott, Justin)
1995	Tek Money (Shatner, William)
1995	Fire Horse (Shoemaker, Bill)
1995	Black Bridge (Sklepowich, Edward)
1995 ■	Shepherd of the Wolves (Slusher, William S.)

1995	Murder at Ebbets Field (Soos, Troy)
1995	Deal to Die For (Standiford, Les)
1995	A Shock to the System (Stevenson, Richard)
1995	Dreamboat (Swanson, Doug J.)

1995	Corruption of Blood (Tanenbaum, Robert K.)
1995	The Seventh Enemy (Tapply, William G.)
1995	The Mortal Sickness (Taylor, Andrew)
1995	The Concrete Pillow (Tierney, Ronald)
1995	Paint It Black (Timlin, Mark)
1995	High Country Murder (Trainor, J. F.)
1995	Shroud for the Archbishop (Tremayne, Peter)
1995	Suffer Little Children (Tremayne, Peter)
1995	Samson and the Greek Delilah (Tripp, Miles)
1995	Maxwell's Flame (Trow, M. J.) ☆
1995	Lestrade and the Kiss of Horus (Trow, M. J.)
1995	The Killing Floor (Turnbull, Peter)

1995	Footsteps of the Hawk (Vachss, Andrew H.)
1995	Missing (Valin, Jonathan)

1995 ■	Fixed in His Folly (Walker, David J.) ☆
1995	Pure Instinct (Walker, Robert W.)
1995 ■	Intent to Harm (Washburn, Stan)
1995	Death on a Black Dragon River (West, Christopher)
1995	Calculated Risk (Wilcox, Collin)
1995	Death of a Prodigal (Williams, David)
1995	The Hellfire Papers (Wilson, Derek)
1995	The Camargue Brotherhood (Wilson, Derek)
1995	Bone Deep (Wiltse, David)
1995	Hard Frost (Wingfield, R. D.) ☆
1995	A Long Walk Up the Waterslide (Winslow, Don)
1995	Way Past Dead (Womack, Steven) ☆
1995	A Clean Kill (Wood, Ted)

1995	Tallant for Terror (York, Andrew)

1995 ■	Into Thin Air (Zigal, Thomas)
1995 ■	Closet (Zimmerman, R. D.) ★ ☆
1995	Red Trance (Zimmerman, R. D.)
1995	Another Dead Teenager (Zubro, Mark)

1996

1996	Promises of Home (Abbott, Jeff)
1996	Distant Blood (Abbott, Jeff)
1996	Hatchet Job (Adams, Harold)
1996 ■	Beware the Tufted Duck (Adamson, Lydia)
1996	Dr. Nightingale Enters the Bear Cave (Adamson, Lydia)
1996	Dr. Nightingale Chases Three Little Pigs (Adamson, Lydia)
1996	A Cat in a Chorus Line (Adamson, Lydia)
1996	A Cat Under the Mistletoe (Adamson, Lydia)
1996	A Cat on a Couch (Adamson, Lydia)
1996	Thrown Away Child (Adcock, Thomas)
1996	An Appointment in May (Albert, Neil)
1996	Watery Grave (Alexander, Bruce)
1996	Stable Cat (Allen, Garrison)
1996	Wake Up to Murder (Allen, Steve)
1996	Black Water (Allyn, Doug)
1996	Rio Grande Fall (Anaya, Rudolfo)
1996	Neighborhood Watch (Andrus, Jeff)
1996	The Mary Medallion (Ardin, William)
1996	Cruel as the Grave (Armistead, John)
1996	The Beast of Barbaresco (Aspler, Tony)
1996	Separated at Death (Axler, Leo)

1996	Erased (Bailey, Jo)
1996	Death Minus Zero (Baker, John)
1996	Bearing Secrets (Barre, Richard)
1996	Skinny Annie Blues (Barrett, Jr., Neal)
1996	The William Powell and Myrna Loy Murder Case (Baxt, George)
1996	Long Shadows in Victory (Bean, Gregory)
1996 ■	Murder at Buckingham Palace (Benison, C. C.)
1996	Death at Sandringham House (Benison, C. C.)
1996	The Risk of Heaven (Berger, Bob)
1996	The Body Shop (Berlinski, David)
1996	Cruel Justice (Bernhardt, William)

1996	Twice Dead (Bishop, Paul)
1996	Worst Case Scenario (Bowen, Michael)
1996	Wolf, No Wolf (Bowen, Peter)
1996	Lifeline (Boyle, Gerry)
1996	Ruins of Civility (Bradberry, James)
1996	Mrs. Pargeter's Plot (Brett, Simon)
1996	No Justice (Brewer, James D.)
1996	Witchy Woman (Brewer, Steve)
1996	Rogue's Justice (Briody, Thomas Gately)
1996	Cadillac Jukebox (Burke, James Lee) ☆

1996	The Lion's Share (Campbell, Robert)
1996	Nobody Roots for Goliath (Champion, David)
1996	Dream of a Falling Eagle (Chesbro, George)
1996	Executive Orders (Clancy, Tom)
1996	One Way Out (Clarkson, John)
1996	Endpeace (Cleary, Jon)
1996	Relic Murders (Clynes, Michael)
1996	Dropshot (Coben, Harlan)
1996	Fade Away (Coben, Harlan) ★★☆
1996	Damned in Paradise [Clarence Darrow] (Collins, Max Allan, Jr.)
1996	Good Sons (Constantine, K. C.)
1996	Death on a Vineyard Beach (Craig, Philip)
1996	Sunset Express (Crais, Robert) ★
1996	The Prairie Chicken Kill (Crider, Bill)
1996	Winning Can Be Murder (Crider, Bill)
1996	Bordersnakes (Crumley, James)
1996	Shock Wave (Cussler, Clive)

1996	Buried Lies (Daly, Conor)
1996	❶ Murder at the Baseball Hall of Fame (Daniel, David & Chris Carpenter)
1996	Consuming Fire (Davis, Thomas D.)
1996	Killed in the Fog (DeAndrea, William L.)
1996	Charity (Deighton, Len)
1996	Death Is Now My Neighbor (Dexter, Colin) ☆
1996	Cosi Fan Tutti (Dibdin, Michael)
1996	A Tournament of Murders (Doherty, P. C.)
1996	The Devil's Hunt (Doherty, P. C.)
1996	❶ Schedule Two (Dold, Gaylord)
1996	Louisiana Fever (Donaldson, D. J.)
1996	The Shaman's Mistake (Doss, James D.)
1996	The Time of Murder at Mayerling (Dukthas, Ann)

1996	Murder at the Movies (Eddenden, A. E.)
1996	Eve of Destruction (Edwards, Martin)
1996	Warning Shot (Egleton, Clive)
1996	Going Crazy in Public (Emerson, Earl)
1996	The Million-Dollar Tattoo (Emerson, Earl)

1996	❶ Kill Me Again (Faherty, Terence)
1996	Prove the Nameless (Faherty, Terence)
1996	❶ See No Evil (Finkelstein, Jay)
1996	Precipice (Forbes, Colin)
1996	Cast in Stone (Ford, G. M.)
1996	A Dwarf Kingdom (Freeling, Nicolas)
1996	The Love Song of J. Edgar Hoover (Friedman, Kinky)
1996	The 6 Messiahs (Frost, Mark)
1996	Death of a Critic (Fuller, Dean)
1996	❶ Death in Little Tokyo (Furutani, Dale)

1996	Jaded (Gaitano, Nick)
1996	Cold Fall (Gardner, John)
1996	The Possessions of a Lady (Gash, Jonathan)
1996	❶ Shot in the Dark (Gibbs, Tony)
1996	Death of an Old Sea Wolf (Gill, Bartholomew)
1996	Out of the Sun (Goddard, Robert)
1996	Deadly Care (Goldberg, Leonard S.)
1996	Contract Null & Void (Gores, Joe)
1996	Hawk Moon (Gorman, Ed)
1996	Memory Lane (Gough, Laurance)
1996	The Book of Shadows (Grace, C. L.)
1996	Irish Lace (Greeley, Andrew M.)
1996	Happy Are the Oppressed (Greeley, Andrew M.)
1996	Flesh Wounds (Greenleaf, Stephen)

| 1996 | ❶ The Devil's Hatband (Greer, Robert O.) |
| 1996 | ❶ In Self Defense (Gregory, Sarah) |

1996	Coyote Returns (Hackler, Micah S.)
1996	Buzz Cut (Hall, James W.)
1996	Trial (Hall, Parnell)
1996	Bloodlines (Hammond, Gerald)
1996	Follow That Gun (Hammond, Gerald)
1996	The Girl Who Ran Off With Daddy (Handler, David)
1996	Still Life (Hanson, Rick)
1996	An Assassin's Riddle (Harding, Paul)
1996	Columbo: The Game Show Killer (Harrington, William)
1996	Murder by Design (Harrison, Ray)
1996	❶ A Flash of Red (Harvey, Clay)
1996	Mental Case (Harvey, James Neal)
1996	Easy Meat (Harvey, John)
1996	The Mortal Nuts (Hautman, Pete)
1996	Before She Dies (Havill, Steven F.)
1996	It's Not a Pretty Sight (Haywood, Gar Anthony)
1996	Invasion of Privacy (Healy, Jeremiah)
1996	Sweetfeed (Healy, R. Austin)
1996	A Connecticut Yankee in Criminal Court (Heck, Peter J.)
1996	❶ If Wishes Were Horses... (Hemlin, Tim)
1996	Drink with the Devil (Higgins, Jack)
1996	The Fallen Man (Hillerman, Tony)
1996	Chicago Blues (Holton, Hugh)
1996	❶ The Sword of General Englund (Honig, Donald)
1996	Tyger! Tyger! (Hoyt, Richard)
1996	The Man Trap (Hunt, Richard)
1996	Ransom for Our Sins (Hunter, Fred W.)
1996	Black Light (Hunter, Stephen)

1996	Dead Folks (Jackson, Jon A.)
1996	Top Banana (James, Bill)
1996	Sandman (Janes, J. Robert)
1996	Skinner's Ordeal (Jardine, Quintin)
1996	Lake Effect (Jaspersohn, William)
1996	A Moorland Hanging (Jecks, Michael)
1996	Reader's Guide to Murder (Jeffers, H. Paul)
1996	An Artistic Way to Go (Jeffries, Roderic)

1996	Sheer Gall (Kahn, Michael A.)
1996	❶ The Rockford Files: The Green Bottle (Kaminsky, Stuart M.)
1996	Lieberman's Law (Kaminsky, Stuart M.)
1996	Blood and Rubles (Kaminsky, Stuart M.)
1996	Dancing in the Dark (Kaminsky, Stuart M.)
1996	The Father's Club (Katz, Jon)
1996	Asking Questions (Keating, H. R. F.)
1996	Razorbill (Keegan, Alex)
1996	The Web (Kellerman, Jonathan)
1996	That Day the Rabbi Left Town (Kemelman, Harry)
1996	Rock Bottom (Kemprecos, Paul)
1996	Requiem for Moses (Kienzle, William X.)
1996	Man With a Squirrel (Kilmer, Nicholas)
1996	❶ The Gourmet Detective (King, Peter)
1996	Rough Justice (Kirton, Bill)
1996	❶ Diamond Head (Knief, Charles) ★
1996	The Counterfeit Killers (Knox, Bill)
1996	Raven's Widows (Kohler, Vince)
1996	Flirting with Death (Lake, M. D.)
1996	The Killing of Sally Keemer (Lee, Christopher)

1996	Darkness, Hold My Hand (Lehane, Dennis)
1996	❶ Casting in Dead Water (Leitz, David)
1996	Dying to Fly Fish (Leitz, David)
1996	Fool Me Twice (Levine, Paul)
1996	A Picture of Her Tombstone (Lipinski, Thomas)
1996	Murder on the Links (Logue, John)
1996	Bloodhounds (Lovesey, Peter) ★
1996	The Silver Chariot Killer (Lupoff, Richard A.)
1996	Flashback (Lusby, Jim)
1996	Lightning (Lutz, John)

| 1996 | All My Enemies (Maitland, Barry) |
| 1996 | Into the Vortex (Malcolm, John) |

1996	A Once Perfect Place (Maness, Larry)
1996	The Burning Ghats (Mann, Paul)
1996	The Lions of the North (Marston, Edward)
1996	The Serpents of Harbledown (Marston, Edward)
1996	The Laughing Hangman (Marston, Edward)
1996	A Picture of Innocence (Matthews, Lew)
1996	The Interloper (Mayo, J. K.)
1996	The Ragman's Memory (Mayor, Archer)
1996	Gladly the Cross-Eyed Bear (McBain, Ed)
1996 ■	Tularosa (McGarrity, Michael) ☆
1996	The Best Money Murder Can Buy (McGaughey, Neil)
1996	The Tears of Things (McInerny, Ralph)
1996	Blessed are the Merciless (Meyer, Charles)
1996	Time to Check Out (Michaels, Grant)
1996	Riding Toward Home (Milan, Borto)
1996	Deep Valley Malice (Mitchell, Kirk)
1996	Falconer and the Face of God (Morson, Ian)
1996	A Little Yellow Dog (Mosley, Walter)
1996 ■	Bonded for Murder (Most, Bruce W.)
1996	Behind the Shield (Mullen, Jack)
1996	A Fine Italian Hand (Murray, William)

1996	The Death of Friends (Nava, Michael) ★
1996	Into the Same River Twice (Nevins, Francis M., Jr)
1996	The Marble Orchard (Nolan, William)

1996	Cobra Trap (O'Donnell, Peter)
1996 ■	Moody Gets the Blues (Oliver, Steve)
1996	Nightland (Owens, Louis)

1996	The Lethal Partner (Page, Jake)
1996 ■	Bright Eyes (Pairo, Preston, III)
1996	Chance (Parker, Robert B.)
1996	Wind and Lies (Parrish, Richard)
1996	Jack and Jill (Patterson, James)
1996	Sleeping Partner (Paul, William)
1996	The Judas Sheep (Pawson, Stuart)
1996	The Mamur Zapt and the Fig Tree Murder (Pearce, Michael)
1996	Death and Restoration (Pears, Iain)
1996	The Big Blow Down (Pelecanos, George P.)
1996	Dance for the Dead (Perry, Thomas)
1996	Perdition USA (Phillips, Gary)
1996	As She Rides By (Pierce, David M.)
1996	The Anatomy of a Murder (Pomidor, Bill)
1996	Down to a Sunless Sea (Poyer, David)
1996	Spadework [short stories] (Pronzini, Bill)
1996	Sentinels (Pronzini, Bill)

1996	The Last Client of Luis Montez (Ramos, Manuel)
1996 ■	Let's Get Criminal (Raphael, Lev)
1996	Snow on the Roses (Riggs, John R.)
1996	Family of Angels (Ripley, Mike)
1996	Electric Country Roulette (Ripley, W. L.)
1996	The Ghosts of Saigon (Roberts, John Maddox)
1996	Collision Bend (Roberts, Les)
1996	Innocent Graves (Robinson, Peter)
1996	A Hidden Cause of Murder (Roe, C. F.)
1996	A Tangled Knot of Murder (Roe, C. F.)
1996	Murder in the Chateau (Roosevelt, Elliott)
1996	House of Guilt (Rosenberg, Robert)
1996	Murder! Murder! Burning Bright (Ross, Jonathan)
1996 ■	Multiple Wounds (Russell, Alan)

1996	McNally's Puzzle (Sanders, Lawrence)
1996	Sudden Prey (Sandford, John)
1996	Accustomed to the Dark (Satterthwait, Walter)
1996	A Murder on the Appian Way (Saylor, Steven)
1996	Night Moves (Scholefield, Alan)
1996	Tek Kill (Shatner, William)
1996	Dark Horse (Shoemaker, Bill)
1996	Butcher of the Noble (Slusher, William S.)
1996	Damaged Goods (Solomita, Stephen)
1996	Murder at Wrigley Field (Soos, Troy)
1996	Black Alley (Spillane, Mickey)

1996	Chain of Fools (Stevenson, Richard)
1996	Illegal Motion (Stockley, Grif)
1996 ■	The Low End of Nowhere (Stone, Michael)
1996	The Music of What Happens (Straley, John)
1996	96 Tears (Swanson, Doug J.)

1996 ■	Return to the Same City (Taibo, Paco Ignacio, II)
1996	Falsely Accused (Tanenbaum, Robert K.)
1996	Close to the Bone (Tapply, William G.)
1996 ■	Trade Secrets (Thomson, Maynard F.)
1996	Breaking Faith (Thomson, Maynard F.)
1996	Sharman and Other Filth (Timlin, Mark)
1996	Find My Way Home (Timlin, Mark)
1996	The Subtle Serpent (Tremayne, Peter)
1996	Lestrade and the Devil's Own (Trow, M. J.)
1996 ■	Embracing Skeletons (Turnbull, Peter)

1996	False Allegations (Vachss, Andrew H.)
1996	The Hollow-Eyed Angel (van de Wetering, Janwillem)

1996	Half the Truth (Walker, David J.)
1996	Darkest Instinct (Walker, Robert W.)
1996	Into Thin Air (Washburn, Stan)
1996	The Honor Farm (Westermann, John)
1996	What's the Worst That Could Happen? (Westlake, Donald E.)
1996	Captiva (White, Randy Wayne)
1996	Harm's Way (White, Stephen)
1996	Dead in the Market (Williams, David)
1996	The Borgia Chalice (Wilson, Derek)
1996	Cumberland's Cradle (Wilson, Derek)
1996	Blown Away (Wiltse, David)
1996	While Drowning in the Desert (Winslow, Don)
1996	Chain of Fools (Womack, Steven) ☆☆
1996	Dirt (Woods, Stuart)
1996 ■	Buried in Stone (Wright, Eric)
1996	Power in the Blood (Wyrick, E. L.)

1996	Hardrock Stiff (Zigal, Thomas)
1996	Tribe (Zimmerman, R. D.)
1996	Rust on the Razor (Zubro, Mark)

1997

1997	The Ice Pick Artist (Adams, Harold)
1997	Beware the Butcher (Adamson, Lydia)
1997	Dr. Nightingale Rides to the Hounds (Adamson, Lydia)
1997	A Cat on a Beach Blanket (Adamson, Lydia)
1997	Grief Street (Adock, Thomas)
1997	A Tangled June (Albert, Neil)
1997	Dance in Deep Water (Allyn, Doug))
1997	Death on the Douro (Aspler, Tony)

1997	Night of the Panther (Ayres, E. C.)

1997	St. John's Bread (Babula, William)
1997	The Ghosts of Morning (Barre, Richard)
1997	Bad Eye Blues (Barrett, Neal, Jr.)
1997	The Fred Astaire and Ginger Rogers Murder Case (Baxt, George)
1997	A Death in Victory (Bean, Gregory)
1997	Loverboy (Belsky, Dick)
1997	Death at Windsor Castle (Benison, C. C.)
1997	Naked Justice (Bernhardt, William)
1997	Tequila Mockingbird (Bishop, Paul)
1997	The Burglar in the Library (Block, Lawrence)
1997	Even the Wicked (Block, Lawrence)
1997	The Remake (Bogart, Stephen Humphrey)
1997	Notches (Bowen, Peter)
1997	Potshot (Boyle, Gerry)
1997	Eakins' Mistress (Bradberry, James)
1997	No Remorse (Brewer, James D.)
1997	Shaky Ground (Brewer, Steve)
1997 ■	Devil's Food (Bruno, Anthony)
1997	Body Slam (Burns, Rex)
1997	The Leaning Land (Burns, Rex)

1997	El Bronx (Charyn, Jerome)
1997	Backspin (Coben, Harlan)
1997	Trunk Music (Connelly, Michael)
1997	Family Values (Constantine, K. C.)
1997	The Washington Club (Corris, Peter)
1997	A Deadly Vineyard Holiday (Craig, Philip)
1997	Indigo Slam (Crais, Robert)
1997	Death by Accident (Crider, Bill)

1997	Outside Agency (Daly, Conor)
1997	Murder at the Tennis Hall of Fame (Daniel, David & Chris Carpenter)
1997	The Fatal Elixir (DeAndrea, William L.)
1997 ■	The Bone Collector (Deaver, Jeffery)
1997	Little Boy Blue (Dee, Ed)
1997	Ghostly Murders (Doherty, P. C.)
1997	Sleeping with the Crawfish (Donaldson, D. J.)
1997	The Shaman's Dream (Doss, James D.)
1997	Trick Question (Dunbar, Tony)

1997	Twenty Blue Devils (Elkins, Aaron)
1997	Dead Horse Paint Company (Emerson, Earl)
1997	Deception Pass (Emerson, Earl)
1997	The Man With My Cat (Engleman, Paul)
1997	Never Street (Estleman, Loren D.)

1997	Come Back Dead (Faherty, Terence)
1997	Idle Gossip (Finkelstein, Jay)
1997	The Bum's Rush (Ford, G. M.)
1997	The Pied Piper of Death (Forrest, Richard)
1997	Roadkill (Friedman, Kinky)
1997	The Toyotomi Blades (Furutani, Dale)

1997	Room 13 (Garfield, Henry)
1997 ■	Different Women Dancing (Gash, Jonathan)
1997	Into Battle (Gilbert, Michael)
1997	Fade to Black (Gibbs, Tony)
1997	Double Blind (Goddard, Ken)
1997	Beyond the Beyond (Goldberg, Lee)
1997	Deadly Harvest (Goldberg, Leonard S.)
1997	Past Tense (Greenleaf, Stephen)
1997	The Devil's Red Nickel (Greer, Robert O.)
1997	Public Trust (Gregory, Sarah)

1997	The Shadow Catcher (Hackler, Micah S.)
1997	The Dark Canyon (Hackler, Micah S.)
1997	Red Sky at Night (Hall, James W.)
1997	Scam (Hall, Parnell)
1997	London Blood (Hall, Robert Lee)
1997	Sink or Swim (Hammond, Gerald)
1997	Malice Intended (Handberg, Ron)
1997	The Man Who Loved Women to Death (Handler, David)
1997	Splitting Heirs (Hanson, Rick)
1997	Columbo: The Glitter Murder (Harrington, William)
1997	A Whisper of Black (Harvey, Clay)
1997	Dead Game (Harvey, James Neal)
1997	Still Water (Harvey, John)
1997	Privileged to Kill (Havill, Steven F.)
1997	Winter's Gold (Heffernan, William)
1997	A Whisper of Rage (Hemlin, Tim)
1997	People in Glass Houses (Hemlin, Tim)
1997	Robak's Witch (Hensley, Joe L.)
1997	The President's Daughter (Higgins, Jack)
1997	Ghirlandaio's Daughter (Hill, John Spencer)
1997	Killing the Lawyers (Hill, Reginald)
1997	Violent Crimes (Holton, Hugh)
1997	The Ghost of Major Pryor (Honig, Donald)
1997	Practice to Deceive (Housewright, David)
1997	The Love of Gods (Hunter, Alan)
1997 ■	Government Gay (Hunter, Fred W.)

1997	Murder on Theater Row (Jahn, Michael)
1997	The Crediton Killings (Jecks, Michael)
1997 ■	What Mommy Said (Jeffers, H. Paul)

| 1997 | Tarnished Icons (Kaminsky, Stuart M.) |
| 1997 | A Fatal Glass of Beer (Kaminsky, Stuart M.) |

1997	The Ruthless Realtor Murders (Kaufelt, David A.)
1997	The Clinic (Kellerman, Jonathan)
1997	Survival of the Fittest (Kellerman, Jonathan)
1997	Bluefin Blues (Kemprecos, Paul)
1997	All That Glitters (Kenneally, Jerry)
1997	The Man Who Loved God (Kienzle, William X.)
1997	O Sacred Head (Kilmer, Nicholas)
1997	Spiced to Death (King, Peter)
1997 ■	Too Soon Dead (Kurland, Michael)

1997	Midsummer Malice (Lake, M. D.)
1997	Bad Chili (Lansdale, Joe R.)
1997	Veritas (Lashner, William)
1997	Sacred (Lehane, Dennis)
1997	Fly Fishing Can Be Fatal (Leitz, David)
1997	Guilt (Lescroart, John T.)
1997	Love For Sale (Leslie, John)
1997	Flesh and Bones (Levine, Paul)
1997	Freedom to Kill (Lindsay, Paul)
1997	The Feathery Touch of Death [golf] (Logue, John)
1997	Upon a Dark Night (Lovesey, Peter)
1997	Deliver Us From Evil (Luber, Philip)
1997	The Radio Red Killer (Lupoff, Richard A.)
1997	Oops! (Lutz, John)

1997	Hyde (Mahoney, Dan)
1997	The Fair Maid of Bohemia (Marston, Edward)
1997	Bellows Falls (Mayor, Archer)
1997	Nocturne (McBain, Ed)
1997	Skylar in Yankeeland (McDonald, Gregory)
1997	Mexican Hat (McGarrity, Michael)
1997 ■	Murder in Perspective (Miles, Keith)
1997	Sound of the Trumpet (Moody, Bill)
1997	Always Outnumbered, Always Outgunned (Mosley, Walter)
1997	Gone Fishin' (Mosley, Walter)
1997	Missing Bonds (Most, Bruce W.)

1997	Count Your Enemies (Nathan, Paul)
1997	Killer (Newman, Christopher)
1997	Hit and Run (Newman, Christopher)

| 1997 | Moody Becomes Eternal (Oliver, Steve) |

1997	The Hoydens and Mr. Dickens (Palmer, William J.)
1997	Small Vices (Parker, Robert B.)
1997	Cat and Mouse (Patterson, James)
1997	Last Reminder (Pawson, Stuart)
1997	Beyond Recognition (Pearson, Ridley)
1997	Shadow Woman (Perry, Thomas)
1997	Bad Night is Falling (Phillips, Gary)
1997	An Image to Die For (Phillips, Mike)
1997	Woman in the Dark (Phillips, T. J.)
1997	Skeletons in the Closet (Pomidor, Bill)
1997	Illusions (Pronzini, Bill)

| 1997 | Half Past Nun (Quill, Monica) |

1997	The Riverview Murders (Raleigh, Michael)
1997	Blues for the Buffalo (Ramos, Manuel)
1997	In the Shadow of the Arch (Randisi, Robert J.)
1997	Black and Blue (Rankin, Ian)
1997	The Edith Wharton Murders (Raphael, Lev)
1997	He Who Waits (Riggs, John R.)
1997	The Cleveland Local (Roberts, Les)
1997	Dead Right [U.S.-Blood at the Root] (Robinson, Peter)
1997	Murder at Midnight (Roosevelt, Elliott)

1997	McNally's Gamble (Sanders, Lawrence)
1997 ■	The Night Crew (Sandford, John)
1997	House of the Vestals (Saylor, Steven)
1997	The Lost Coast (Simon, Roger L.)
1997	Death in the Palazzo (Sklepowich, Edward)
1997	Cave of the Innocent (Slusher, William S.)
1997	Hunting a Detroit Tiger (Soos, Troy)
1997	Quake City (Spencer, John)

1997   Deal on Ice (Standiford, Les)
1997   Comeback (Stark, Richard)
1997   Self-Incrimination (Stockley, Grif)
1997   A Long Reach (Stone, Michael)
1997   Death and the Language of Happiness (Straley, John)
1997   The Cezanne Chase (Swan, Thomas)

1997   Irresistable Impulse (Tanenbaum, Robert K.)
1997   The Lover of the Grave (Taylor, Andrew)

1997   North of Havana (White, Randy Wayne)
1997   Remote Control (White, Stephen)
1997   Dead in the Water (Woods, Stuart)

1997   My Mother, the Detective (Yaffe, James)

1997   The Truth Can Get You Killed (Zubro, Mark)

1998

1998   Criminal Tendencies (Bishop, Paul)
1998   Chalk Whispers (Bishop, Paul)
1988   Dark of the Heart (Bishop, Paul)

1998   Passage to Lisbon (Faherty, Terence)
1998   A Steak in the Action (Ford, G. M.)

1998   The Devil's Backbone (Greer, Robert O.)

1998   Suspense (Hall, Parnell)
1998   Columbo: The Hoover Files (Harrington, William)
1998   Last Rites (Harvey, John)
1998   When Last Seen Alive (Haywood, Gar Anthony)
1998   Federal Fag (Hunter, Fred W.)

1998   The Abbott's Gibbet (Jecks, Michael)
1998   Corpus Corpus (Jeffers, H. Paul)

1998   The Rockford Files: Devil on My Doorstep (Kaminsky, S.)
1998   Dying on the Vine (King, Peter)
1998   Sand Dollars (Knief, Charles)
1998   One-Way Ticket (Knight, J. D.)

1998   The Dust on God's Breath (Lipinski, Thomas)
1998   The Tinpan Tiger Killer (Lupoff, Richard A.)

1998   A Corpse By Any Other Name (McGaughey, Neil)
1998   Bad Boy Bobby Brown (Mosley, Walter)

1998   The Burning Plain (Nava, Michael)

1998   A Certain Malice (Page, Jake)
1998   The Angel's Crime (Pairo, Preston, III)
1998   The Face Changers (Perry, Thomas)
1998   Ten Little Medicine Men (Pomidor, Bill)

1998   A Shoot in Cleveland (Roberts, Les)

1998   Masquerade (Satterthwait, Walter)
1998   The Cincinnati Red Stalkings (Soos, Troy)
1998   The Faberge Factor (Swan, Thomas)

ALPHABETICAL LIST OF TITLES 6

■ 100,000 Welcomes [1970] (Kenyon, Michael)
■ 120-Hour Clock [1986] (Nevins, Francis M., Jr)
13th Juror [1994] (Lescroart, John T.) ☆
■ 14 Peck Slip [1994] (Dee, Ed)
30 for a Harry [1982] (Hoyt, Richard) ☆
■ "30" Manhattan East [1968] (Waugh, Hillary)
32 Cadillacs [1992] (Gores, Joe)☆
'44 Vintage [1978] (Price, Anthony)
6 Messiahs [1996] (Frost, Mark)
600-Pound Gorilla [1987] (Campbell, Robert)
96 Tears [1996] (Swanson, Doug J.)

A

Abbott's Gibbet [1998] (Jecks, Michael)
Abbot of Stockbridge [1992] (McCutchan, Philip)
Abracadaver [1972] (Lovesey, Peter)
■ Abracadaver [1989] (McInerny, Ralph)
■ Absolution by Murder [1994] (Tremayne, Peter)
Abu Wahab Caper [1980] (Spencer, Ross H.)
Accidental Deaths [1991] (Gough, Laurence)
According to St. John [1989] (Babula, William)
Accustomed to the Dark [1996] (Satterthwait, Walter)
Ace of Diamonds [1984] (Schorr, Mark)
■ Acid Rock (with Sapir) [1973] (Murphy, Warren B.)
Act of Faith [1993] (Bowen, Michael)
■ Act of Fear [1967] (Collins, Michael) ★
Act of God [1994] (Healy, Jeremiah)
Actor [1993] (Hall, Parnell)
Acts of Homicide [1989] (Davis, Kenn)
■ Adam's Fall [1960] (Ridgway, Jason)
Advancement of Learning [1971] (Hill, Reginald)
■ Adventures of Inspector Lestrade [1985] (Trow, M. J.)
■ Adverse Report [1987] (Hammond, Gerald)
Advertise for Treasure [1984] (Williams, David)
Affair of Sorcerors [1979] (Chesbro, George)
Aftershock [1991] (Corris, Peter)
Aftershock [1975] (Wilcox, Collin)
Agent of Death [1975] (DeMille, Nelson)
Aim for the Heart [1990] (McCall, Wendell)
■ Air That Kills [1994] (Taylor, Andrew)
Airline Pirates [1970] (Gardner, John)
Akin to Murder [1992] (Harrison, Ray)
Alamut Ambush [1971] (Price, Anthony)
Alarming Clock [1961] (Avallone, Michael)
Alfred Hitchcock Murder Case [1986] (Baxt, George)
■ Alias Man [1968] (Craig, David)
Alibi Too Soon [1987] (Ormerod, Roger)
■ Alice Factor [1991] (Janes, J. Robert)

Alice in La-La Land [1987] (Campbell, Robert)
■ All Dressed Up to Die [1989] (Nordan, Robert)
All God's Children [1975] (Lyons, Arthur)
■ All Leads Negative [U.S.] (Alding, Peter)
All My Enemies [1996] (Maitland, Barry)
All on a Summer's Day [1981] (Wainright, John)
■ All Other Perils [1974] (MacLeod, Robert)
All Souls [1993] (Brady, John)
All That Glitters [1997] (Kennealy, Jerry)
■ All the Lonely People [1991] (Edwards, Martin)
All the Old Bargains [1985] (Schutz, Benjamin)
All-Purpose Bodies [1969] (McCutchan, Philip)
Allyson [1981] (Jenkins, Jerry)
Almost Murder [1986] (Jeffries, Roderic)
■ Alone with the Dead [1995] (Randisi, Robert J.)
■ Along Came a Spider [1993] (Patterson, James)
■ Alvarez Journal [1975] (Burns, Rex) ★
Always a Body to Trade [1983] (Constantine, K. C.)
Always Leave 'em Dying [1954] (Prather, Richard)
Always Outnumbered, Always Outgunned [1997] (Mosley, Walter)
Always Take the Big Ones [1965] (Chambers, Peter)
Amateur Corpse [1978] (Brett, Simon)
Amateur in Violence [1973] (Gilbert, Michael)
Amazing Mr. Blackshirt [1955] (Graeme, Roderic)
Amber Effect [1986] (Prather, Richard)
Amber Nine [1966] (Gardner, John)
Ambushers [1963] (Hamilton, Donald)
■ Amends for Murder [1989] (Lake, M. D.)
American Hero [1993] (Beinhart, Larry)
■ American Quartet [1981] (Adler, Warren)
American Sextet [1983] (Adler, Warren)
■ Amnesia Trap [1979] (Ormerod, Roger)
Amorous Leander [1983] (Hunter, Alan)
■ Amphetamines and Pearls [1976] (Harvey, John)
Anatomy of a Murder [1996] (Pomidor, Bill)
■ Ancient Evil [1994] (Doherty, P. C.)
And Baby Will Fall [1988] (Lewin, Michael Z.)
And Did Murder Him [1991] (Turnbull, Peter)
■ And Justice for One [1992] (Clarkson, John)
And Then There Was Nun [1984] (Quill, Monica)
And Then There Were Ten [1995] (McGaughey, Neil)
And Then You Die [1992] (Martin, James E.)
Angel City [1991] (Ripley, Mike)
Angel Confidential [1995] (Ripley, Mike)
Angel Eyes [1981] (Estleman, Loren D.)
Angel Eyes [1990] (Ripley, Mike)

Angel Gang [1994] (Kuhlken, Ken)
Angel Hunt [1990] (Ripley, Mike)
Angel Maker [1993] (Pearson, Ridley)
Angel of Death [1989] (Doherty, P. C.)
Angel of Death [1995] (Higgins, Jack)
Angel of Death [1995] (Lewis, Roy)
Angel of Torremolinos [1988] (Serafin, David)
Angel Touch [1989] (Ripley, Mike) ★
Angel's Crime [1998] (Pairo, Preston, III)
Angel's Share [1989] (Irvine, Robert)
Angels in Arms [1991] (Ripley, Mike) ★
Angels in Heaven [1991] (Pierce, David M.)
Anger of God [1993] (Harding, Paul)
Angle of Attack [1979] (Burns, Rex)
Annihilators [1983] (Hamilton, Donald)
Anonymous Client [1989] (Hailey, J. P.)
Another Day, Another Stiff [1967] (Brett, Michael)
Another Dead Teenager [1995] (Zubro, Mark)
■ Another Way to Die [1972] (Crowe, John)
Any Man's Death [1986] (Estleman, Loren D.)
Appointment in May [1996] (Albert, Neil)
April Shroud [1975] (Hill, Reginald)
■ Arcadian Death [1995] (Jeffries, Roderic)
Arlette [U.S.] (Freeling, Nicolas)
Armadillos & Old Lace [1994] (Friedman, Kinky)
Arms of Kali [1985] (Murphy, Warren B.)
Arms of Nemesis [1992] (Saylor, Steven)
■ Art of Death [1988] (Fliegel, Richard)
Artful Egg [1984] (McClure, James)
Artistic Way to Go [1996] (Jeffries, Roderic)
As October Dies [1987] (Davis, Kenn)
As She Rides By [1996] (Pierce, David M.)
Ashes by Now [1993] (Timlin, Mark)
Ask Taffin Nicely [1989] (Mallett, Lyndon)
■ Ask the Right Question [1971] (Lewin, Michael Z.) ☆
■ Asking Questions [1996] (Keating, H. R. F.)
Assassin in the Greenwood [1993] (Doherty, P. C.)
■ Assassins Don't Die in Bed [1968] (Avallone, Michael)
Assassins Play-Off [1975] (Murphy, Warren B.)
Assassins's Riddle [1996] (Harding, Paul)
Assault with Intent [1982] (Kienzle, William X.)
Assignment Andalusia [1965] (Galway, Robert C.)
Assignment Argentina [1969] (Galway, Robert C.)
Assignment Death Squad [1970] (Galway, Robert C.)
Assignment Fenland [1969] (Galway, Robert C.)
Assignment Gaolbreak [1968] (Galway, Robert C.)
Assignment London [1963] (Galway, Robert C.)
Assignment Malta [1966] (Galway, Robert Conington)
Assignment New York [1963] (Galway, Robert C.)
Assignment Sea Bed [1969] (Galway, Robert C.)
Assignment Sydney [1970] (Galway, Robert C.)
Astride a Grave [1991] (James, Bill)
At Ease With the Dead [1991] (Satterthwait, Walter)
At the Hands of Another [1983] (Lyons, Arthur)
Atropos [1990] (DeAndrea, William L.)
Aupres de ma Blonde [U.S.] (Freeling, Nicolas)
Autumn Dead [1987] (Gorman, Ed) ☆
Autumn Maze [1994] (Cleary, Jon)
Avenging Angel [1983] (Burns, Rex)
■ Ax [1964] (McBain, Ed)
Axe to Grind [1989] (Wallace, Robert)
Azanian Action [1991] (Corris, Peter)
Azreal [1987] (DeAndrea, William L.)

B

Baby Blue Rip-Off [1983] (Collins, Max Allan, Jr.)
Baby Face [1995] (Brewer, Steve)
Babylon South [1989] (Cleary, Jon)
Back in the Real World [1986] (Albert, Marvin H.)
Back of the North Wind [1983] (Freeling, Nicolas)
■ Back Room in Somers Town [1984] (Malcolm, John)
■ Back-Door Man [1986] (Kantner, Rob) ★
Backfire is Hostile! [1979] (Barnett, James)

Backspin [1997] (Coben, Harlan)
Bad Apple [1994] (Bruno, Anthony)
Bad Blonde [1956] (Webb, Jack)
Bad Blood [1989] (Bruno, Anthony)
Bad Blood [Brit.] (Roe, C.F.)
Bad Boy Bobby Brown [1998] (Mosley, Walter)
Bad Business [1991] (Bruno, Anthony)
Bad Chili [1997] (Lansdale, Joe R.)
■ Bad Die Young [1967] (Chambers, Peter)
Bad Eye Blue [1997] (Barrett, Neal, Jr.)
■ Bad Guys [1988] (Bruno, Anthony)
Bad Love [1994] (Kellerman, Jonathan)
Bad Luck [1990] (Bruno, Anthony)
Bad Moon [1992] (Bruno, Anthony)
Bad News Travels Fast [1995] (Haywood, Gar Anthony)
Bad Night is Falling [1997] (Phillips, Gary)
Bad Samaritan [1995] (Barnard, Robert)
Bad Scene [1987] (Copper, Basil)
Bad to the Bone [1991] (Solomita, Stephen)
■ Badger Game [1989] (Bowen, Michael)
■ Bagged [1991] (Bailey, Jo)
■ Bahama Heat [1991] (Estabrook, Barry)
Bahamas Blue [1991] (Poyer, David)
■ Bait Money [1973] (Collins, Max Allan, Jr.)
Bait on the Hook [1983] (Parrish, Frank)
Balance of Power [1981] (Murphy, Warren B.)
Ballad of Gato Guerrero [1994] (Ramos, Manuel)
■ Ballad of Rocky Ruiz [1993] (Ramos, Manuel) ☆
Baltic Business [1988] (Corris, Peter)
Bandini Affair [1987] (Bass, Milton R.)
Banjo Boy [1994] (Kohler, Vince)
Bank Shot [1972] (Westlake, Donald E.)
■ Banking on Murder [1993] (Williams, David)
Bannerman Effect [1990] (Maxim, John)
■ Bannerman Solution [1989] (Maxim, John)
■ Bannerman's Law [1991] (Maxim, John)
■ Baptism for the Dead [1988] (Irvine, Robert)
Barbed Wire Noose [1987] (Adams, Harold)
Barbouze [1964] (Williams, Alan)
■ Barking Dogs [1994] (Irvine, Robert)
Bartholomew Fair Murders [1986] (Tourney, Leonard)
Basket Case [1987] (McInerny, Ralph)
■ Bath Detective [1995] (Lee, Christopher)
Bats Fly Up for Inspector Ghote [1974] (Keating, H. R. F.)
■ Baxter Trust [1988] (Hailey, J. P.)
Bay City Blast [1979] (Murphy, Warren B.)
■ Bay Psalm Book Murder [1983] (Harriss, Will) ★
■ Beach Money [1991] (Pairo, Preston, III)
Bear Hug [1992] (Doolittle, Jerome)
Bear Raid [1976] (Follett, Ken)
Bearing Secrets [1996] (Barre, Richard)
Beast of Barbaresco [1996] (Aspler, Tony)
Beasts of Valhalla [1985] (Chesbro, George)
Beautiful Golden Frame [1980] (Chambers, Peter)
■ Beautiful Place to Die [1989] (Craig, Philip)
Beauty and the Beast [1983] (McBain, Ed)
Because of the Cats [1963] (Freeling, Nicolas)
Because the Night [1984] (Ellroy, James)
■ Becket Factor [1990] (Anthony, Michael David)
Bedroom Bolero [1963] (Avallone, Michael)
Before She Dies [1996] (Havill, Steven F.)
Beggars Choice [1994] (Kennealy, Jerry)
■ Begin, Murderer! [1951] (Cory, Desmond)
Behind the Fact [1989] (Hilary, Richard)l
Behind the Shield [1996] (Mullen, Jack)
Belfast Connection [1988] (Bass, Milton R.)
Bellows Falls [1997] (Mayor, Archer)
Bellringer Street [1988] (Richardson, Robert)
■ Benevolent Blackmailer [1962] (Harknett, Terry)
Benjamin Franklin and a Case of Christmas Murder [1990]
   (Hall, Robert Lee)
■ Benjamin Franklin Takes the Case [1988] (Hall, Robert Lee)

Bent Grasses [1993] (Palmer, Frank)
■ Berlin Game [1983] (Deighton, Len)
■ Bernhardt's Edge [1988] (Wilcox, Collin)
Bernini Bust [1993] (Pears, Iain)
Bertie and the Crime of Passion [1993] (Lovesey, Peter)
Bertie and the Seven Bodies [1990] (Lovesey, Peter)
■ Bertie and the Tinman [1987] (Lovesey, Peter)
Bessie Blue Killer [1994] (Lupoff, Richard A.)
Best Cellar [1987] (Goodrum, Charles A.)
Best Money Murder Can Buy [1996] (McGaughey, Neil)
■ Best Performance by a Patsy [1991] (Cutler, Stan)☆
■ Betrayed by Death [1982] (Alding, Peter)
Betrayers [1966] (Hamilton, Donald)
Bette Davis Murder Case [1994] (Baxt, George)
Between the Devlin and the Deep Blue Seas [1991]
    (Barrett, Robert G.)
Between Two Evils [1986] (Thurston, Robert)
"Beverly Hills" Browning [1987] (Corris, Peter)
■ Beware of the Dog [1992] (Corris, Peter)
Beware the Butcher [1997] (Adamson, Lydia)
■ Beware the Tufted Duck [1996] (Adamson, Lydia)
Beyond Blame [1986] (Greenleaf, Stephen)
Beyond Ice, Beyond Death [1995] (McCall, Thomas)
Beyond Recognition [1997] (Pearson, Ridley)
Beyond the Beyond [1997] (Goldberg, Lee)
Beyond the Grave [1986] (Pronzini, Bill)
Big Black [1974] (Myles, Simon)
Big Blow Down [1996] (Pelecanos, George P.)
Big Chill [1972] (Copper, Basil)
Big Drop [short stories] [1985] (Corris, Peter)
■ Big Enchilada [1982] (Morse, L. A.)
Big Fish [1991] (Grissom, Ken)
■ Big Fix [1973] (Simon, Roger L.) ★
Big Freeze [1991] (Katz, Michael J.)
Big Goodbye [1962] (Chambers, Peter)
Big Grouse [1986] (Clark, Douglas)
Big Kill [1951] (Spillane, Mickey)
Big Man [1985] (McIlvanney, William)
Big Money [1954] (Masur, Harold Q.)
Big Money [1984] (Turnbull, Peter)
■ Big Needle [1974] (Myles, Simon)
Big Rip-Off [1979] (Copper, Basil)
■ Big Silence [1989] (Schopen, Bernard)
■ Big Sin [1952] (Webb, Jack)
■ Big Sky Blues [1988] (Reid, Robert Sims)
■ Big Stick [1986] (Alexander, Lawrence)
Big Stiffs [1977] (Avallone, Michael)
Big Tomorrow [1956] (Bateson, David)
■ Big Town [1994] (Swanson, Doug J.) ★ ☆☆
Bigfoot [1993] (Hoyt, Richard)
■ Billingsgate Shoal [1982] (Boyer, Rick) ★
Billion Dollar Brain [1966] (Deighton, Len)
Billy Cantrell Case [1981] (Waugh, Hillary)
Bimbo Heaven [1990] (Albert, Marvin H.) ☆
Bindlestiff [1983] (Pronzini, Bill)
■ Bino [1988] (Gray, A. W.)
Bino's Blues [1995] (Gray, A. W.)
Bird in the Net [U.S.] (Parrish Frank)
■ Bishop as Pawn [1994] (Kienzle, William X.)
Bishop as Pawn [1978] (McInerny, Ralph)
Bishop's Pawn [1979] (Perry, Ritchie)
Bitter Gold Hearts [1988] (Cook, Glen)
Bitter Recoil [1992] (Havill, Steven F.)
Bitter Water [1990] (Clark, Douglas)
■ Black Alley [1996] (Spillane, Mickey)
Black and Blue [1997] (Rankin, Ian)
Black Betty [1994] (Mosley, Walter) ☆
Black Book [1993] (Rankin, Ian)
Black Bridge [1995] (Sklepowich, Edward)
Black Cherry Blues [1989] (Burke, James Lee) ★
Black Death [1973] (Stone, Thomas H.)
■ Black Door [1967] (Wilcox, Collin)

■ Black Echo [1992] (Connelly, Michael) ★
■ Black Eye [1989] (Steed, Neville)
■ Black Hearts and Slow Dancing [1988] (Emerson, Earl)
Black Hornet [1994] (Sallis, James)
Black Ice [1993] (Connelly, Michael) ☆☆
Black Ice Score [1968] (Stark, Richard)
Black Knight in Red Square [1983] (Kaminsky, Stuart M.) ☆
Black Lace [1991] (Newton, Michael)
Black Light [1996] (Hunter, Stephen)
Black Mail [1990] (Steed, Neville)
■ Black Mask Murders [1994] (Nolan, William F.)
Black Rose [1987] (Huebner, Frederick D.)
Black Tide [1995] (DuBois, Brendan)
Black Water [1996] (Allyn, Doug)
Blackbird [1969] (Stark, Richard)
Blacklight [1967] (Knox, Bill)
Blackmail [1994] (Hall, Parnell)
Blackmail North [1978] (McCutchan, Philip)
■ Blackshirt at Large [1966] (Graeme, Roderic)
■ Blackshirt Finds Trouble [1961] (Graeme, Roderic)
Blackshirt Helps Himself [1958] (Graeme, Roderic)
■ Blackshirt in Peril [1967] (Graeme, Roderic)
Blackshirt Meets the Lady [1956] (Graeme, Roderic)
■ Blackshirt on the Spot [1963] (Graeme, Roderic)
Blackshirt Passes By [1953] (Graeme, Roderic)
■ Blackshirt Saves the Day [1964] (Graeme, Roderic)
Blackshirt Sees It Through [1960] (Graeme, Roderic)
Blackshirt Sets the Pace [1959] (Graeme, Roderic)
Blackshirt Stirs Things Up [1969] (Graeme, Roderic)
■ Blackshirt Takes the Trail [1962] (Graeme, Roderic)
Blackshirt Wins the Trick [1953] (Graeme, Roderic)
Blank Page [1974] (Constantine, K. C.)
Blayde R. I. P. [1982] (Wainright, John)
Bleak Spring [1993] (Cleary, Jon)
Bleeding Dodger Blue [1992] (Evers, Crabbe)
■ Bleeding in the Eye of a Brainstorm [1995] (Chesbro, George)
Blessed are the Merciless [1996] (Meyer, Charles)
■ Blessing Way [1970] (Hillerman, Tony) ☆
■ Blind Justice [1994] (Alexander, Bruce)
Blind Justice [1992] (Bernhardt, William)
Blind Pig [1978] (Jackson, Jon A.)
Blond Baboon [1978] (van de Wetering, Janwillem)
■ Blonde Wore Black [1968] (Chambers, Peter)
Blood and Judgment [1959] (Gilbert, Michael)
Blood and Rubles [1996] (Kaminsky, Stuart M.)
Blood and Thunder [Huey Long] [1995]
    (Collins, Max Allan, Jr.)
Blood at the Root [U.S.] (Robinson, Peter)
Blood Autumn [1995] (Sanders, William)
Blood Brother [1993] (Palmer, Frank)
Blood Count [1991] (Batten, Jack)
Blood Doesn't Tell [1989] (Barth, Richard)
Blood Game [1989] (Gorman, Ed)
■ Blood Is Thicker Than Beaujolais [1993] (Aspler, Tony)
Blood Lake [1987] (McConnell, Frank)
Blood Money [1973] (Collins, Max Allan, Jr.)
Blood Money [1973] (Lewis, Roy)
■ Blood Moon [1994] (Gorman, Ed)
Blood of an Englishman [1980] (McClure, James)
Blood of Poets [1990] (Davis, Kenn)
Blood on a Widow's Cross [1972] (Fraser, James)
Blood on the Bayou [1991] (Donaldson, D. J.)
Blood on the Moon [1986] (Copper, Basil)
■ Blood on the Moon [1984] (Ellroy, James)
Blood Red Moon [Brit.] (Gorman, Ed)
Blood Relation [1990] (Taylor, Andrew)
Blood Relative [1992] (Allegretto, Michael)
Blood Relatives [1975] (McBain, Ed)
■ Blood Rights [1989] (Phillips, Mike)
Blood Rose [1991] (Heffernan, William)
Blood Run East [1976] (McCutchan, Philip)

Burglar Who Painted Like Mondrian [1983] (Block, Lawrence)
Burglar Who Studied Spinoza [1981] (Block, Lawrence)
Burglar Who Thought He Was Bogart [1995] (Block, Lawrence)
Burglar Who Traded Ted Williams [1994] (Block, Lawrence)
■ Burglars Can't Be Choosers [1977] (Block, Lawrence)
■ Burial Deferred [1985] (Ross, Jonathan)
Burial in Portugal [1973] (MacLeod, Robert)
■ Buried Caesars [1989] (Kaminsky, Stuart M.)
■ Buried in Stone [1996] (Wright, Eric)
Buried Lies [1996] (Daly, Conor)
Buried Treasure [1995] (Scholefield, Alan)
Burn [1992] (Judd, Bob)
Burn [1995] (Lutz, John)
Burn and Other Stories [1993] (Corris, Peter)
■ Burn Out [1994] (Scholefield, Alan)
Burn-Out [1995] (McCutchan, Philip)
Burning Angel [1995] (Burke, James Lee)
Burning Ghats [1996] (Mann, Paul)
Burning Ground [1993] (Malcolm, John)
Burning March [1994] (Albert, Neil)
Burning of Billy Toober [1974] (Ross, Jonathan)
Burning Plain [1998] (Nara, Michael)
■ Burning Season [1988] (Dundee, Wayne) ☆
■ Burning the Apostle [1993] (Granger, Bill)
■ Bury Me Deep [1947] (Masur, Harold Q.)
Business Unusual [1989] (Heald, Tim)
Butcher of the Noble [1996] (Slusher, William S.)
Butcher's Dozen [1988] (Collins, Max Allan, Jr.)
■ Butcher's Moon [1974] (Stark, Richard)
■ Button Man [1992] (Freemantle, Brian)
■ Buyer Beware [1976] (Lutz, John)
Buzz Cut [1996] (Hall, James W.)
By Murder's Bright Light [1994] (Harding, Paul)
■ By Reason of Insanity [1991] (Harvey, James Neal)
By-Pass Control [1966] (Spillane, Mickey)

C

■ C. I. D. Room [1967] (Alding, Peter)
Cabal [1992] (Dibdin, Michael)
Cadillac Jukebox [1996] (Burke, James Lee) ☆
Cage Until Tame [1972] (Henderson, Laurence)
■ Cajun Nights [1988] (Donaldson, D. J.)
Calamity Fair [1950] (Miller, Wade)
Calculated Risk [1995] (Wilcox, Collin)
California Roll [1985] (Simon, Roger L.)
■ California Thriller [1981] (Byrd, Max) ★
Caligari Complex [1980] (Copper, Basil)
Call Back to Crime [1972] (Alding, Peter)
■ Call for Blackshirt [1963] (Graeme, Roderic)
■ Call for Simon Shard [1974] (McCutchan, Philip)
■ Call for the Dead [1961] (Le Carre, John) ★
■ Call No Man Father [1995] (Kienzle, William X.)
Called by a Panther [1991] (Lewin, Michael Z.)
Called Home [1991] (Irvine, Robert)
Calling [1984] (Jenkins, Jerry)
Calling all Heroes [1991] (Taibo, Paco Ignacio, II)
Calypso [1979] (McBain, Ed)
Camargue Brotherhood [1995] (Wilson, Derek)
■ Cameleon [1991] (Kienzle, William X.)
■ Canaan Legacy [1988] (Kahn, Michael A.)
Canary [1986] (Aldyne, Nathan)
Cancelled Czech [1966] (Block, Lawrence)
Candidate for Murder [1987] (Orenstein, Frank)
Cannibal [1975] (DeMille, Nelson)
Cannon's Mouth [1990] (Duncan, W. Glenn)
Canto for a Gypsy [1972] (Smith, Martin Cruz) ☆
Capital Killing [1990] (Everson, David H.)
Capitol Offense [1995] (Gibbs, Tony)
Captiva [1996] (White, Randy Wayne)
Captivator [1974] (York, Andrew)
Cardinal of the Kremlin [1988] (Clancy, Tom)
■ Cardinal Offense [1994] (McInerny, Ralph)
Cargo Club [1990] (Corris, Peter)
Cargo of Spent Evil [1965] (Brett, John Michael)

Cargo Risk [1980] (MacLeod, Robert)
Carioca Fletch [1984] (McDonald, Gregory)
Carnage of the Realm [1979] (Goodrum, Charles A.)
Carnal Hours [1994] (Collins, Max Allan, Jr.) ☆
■ Caroline Minuscule [1982] (Taylor, Andrew) ★ ☆
Carousel [1992] (Janes, J. Robert)
■ Carpenter, Detective [1981] (Caine, Hamilton) ☆
Carriage of Justice [1995] (Hammond, Gerald)
Carrot for the Donkey [1989] (Roberts, Les)
■ Cart Before the Hearse [1979] (Ormerod, Roger)
■ Case for Charley [1984] (Spencer, John)
Case of Artful Murder [1994] (Hall, Robert Lee)
Case of Lone Star [1987] (Friedman, Kinky)
Case of Spirits [1975] (Lovesey, Peter)
■ Case of the Angry Actress [APA] (Cunningham, E.V.)
Case of the Bouncing Betty [1957] (Avallone, Michael)
Case of the Kidnapped Angel [1982] (Cunningham, E. V.)
Case of the Missing Bronte [U.S.] (Barnard, Robert)
Case of the Murdered Mackenzie [1984] (Cunningham, E. V.)
Case of the One-Penny Orange [1977] (Cunningham, E. V.)
Case of the Poisoned Eclairs [1979] (Cunningham, E. V.)
Case of the Russian Diplomat [1978] (Cunningham, E. V.)
Case of the Sliding Pool [1981] (Cunningham, E. V.)
■ Case of the Vanishing Beauty [1950] (Prather, Richard)
Case of the Violent Virgin [1957] (Avallone, Michael)
Case of Vineyard Poison [1995] (Craig, Philip)
Casefile [1983] (Pronzini, Bill)
■ Casino [1994] (Corris, Peter)
■ Cassandra in Red [1992] (Collins, Michael) ☆
■ Cast, In Order of Disappearance [1975] (Brett, Simon)
Cast in Stone [1996] (Ford, G. M.)
Castang's City [1980] (Freeling, Nicolas)
■ Casting in Dead Water [1996] (Leitz, David)
Castles Burning [1980] (Lyons, Arthur)
■ Castrato [1989] (Collins, Michael)
Cat and Mouse [1997] (Patterson, James)
Cat by Any Other Name [1992] (Adamson, Lydia)
■ Cat in a Chorus Line [1996] (Adamson, Lydia)
Cat in a Glass House [1993] (Adamson, Lydia)
Cat in Fine Style [1995] (Adamson, Lydia)
■ Cat in the Manger [1990] (Adamson, Lydia)
Cat in the Wings [1992] (Adamson, Lydia)
Cat in Wolf's Clothing [1991] (Adamson, Lydia)
Cat of a Different Color [1990] (Adamson, Lydia)
■ Cat on a Beach Blanket [1997] (Adamson, Lydia)
■ Cat on a Couch [1996] (Adamson, Lydia)
Cat on a Winning Streak [1995] (Adamson, Lydia)
Cat on the Cutting Edge [1994] (Adamson, Lydia)
■ Cat Under the Mistletoe [1996] (Adamson, Lydia)
Cat with a Fiddle [1993] (Adamson, Lydia)
Cat with No Regrets [1994] (Adamson, Lydia)
Cat's Meow [1988] (Campbell, Robert)
Catalina's Riddle [1993] (Saylor, Steven) ★☆
Catch a Fallen Angel [1969] [1986] (Engleman, Paul)
Catch a Falling Clown [1982] (Kaminsky, Stuart M.)
Catch a Falling Spy [U.S.] (Deighton, Len)
Caterpillar Cop [1972] (McClure, James)
■ Catskill Eagle [1985] (Parker, Robert B.) ☆
Caught in the Birdlime [1987] (Parrish, Frank)
■ Cause and Effect [1987] (McInerny, Ralph)
■ Cave of Bats [1964] (MacLeod, Robert)
Cave of the Innocent [1997] (Slusher, William S.)
Ceremony [1982] (Parker, Robert B.) ☆
■ Certain Blindness [1980] (Lewis, Roy)
■ Certain Justice [1995] (Lescroart, John T.)
Certain Malice [1998] (Page, Jake)
Cezanne Chase [1997] (Swan, Thomas)
Chain of Fools [1996] (Stevenson, Richard)
Chain of Fools [1996] (Womack, Steven) ☆☆
Chained Reaction (with Sapir) [1978] (Murphy, Warren B.)
Chalk Whispers [1998] (Bishop, Paul)
Chance [1996] (Parker, Robert B.)
■ Chant [1986] (Cross, David)

■ Chapel of the Ravens [1991] (Bishop, Paul)
Charity [1996] (Deighton, Len)
Charley Gets the Picture [1985] (Spencer, John)
Charlie M [U.S.] (Freemantle, Brian)
■ Charlie Muffin [1977] (Freemantle, Brian)
Charlie Muffin and the Russian Rose [1985]
   (Freemantle, Brian)
Charlie Muffin San [1987] (Freemantle, Brian)
Charlie Muffin USA [U.S.] (Freemantle, Brian)
Charlie Muffin's Uncle Sam [1980] (Freemantle, Brian)
Charlie's Apprentice [1993] (Freemantle, Brian)
■ Chasing Eights [1990] (Collins, Michael)
Cheating Death [1991] (Keating, H.R.F.)
■ Cheerio Killings [1989] (Allyn, Doug)
Cheim Manuscript [1969] (Prather, Richard)
Chelsea Ghost [1985] (Hunter, Alan)
Cherry Blossom Corpse [U.S.] (Barnard, Robert)
Chicago Blues [1996] (Holton, Hugh)
Child Proof [Brit.] (Lewin. Michael Z.)
■ Child's Garden of Death [1975] (Forrest, Richard)
Child's Play [1987] (Hill, Reginald)
Children of the Mist [1970] (Knox, Bill)
China Hand [1994] (Palmer, Frank)
Chinese Puzzle [1972] (Murphy, Warren B.)
Chip Harrison Scores Again [1971] (Block, Lawrence)
Chipped [1988] (Steed, Neville)
Choice [1991] (Reed, Barry)
Christmas Rising [1982] (Serafin, David)
Chrysanthemum Chain [1980] (Melville, James)
Cincinnati Red Stalkings [1998] (Soos, Troy)
Cinderella [1986] (McBain, Ed)
Circle of Danger [1968] (Alding, Peter)
Circle of Fire [1973] (Sadler, Mark)
■ Citadel Run [1988] (Bishop, Paul)
City Called July [1986] (Engel, Howard)
City in Heat [1973] (Murphy, Warren B.)
City of Beads [1995] (Dunbar, Tony)
City of Brass [1971] (Hoch, Edward D.)
City of God [1992] (Jahn, Michael)
■ City of Strangers [1990] (Barnard, Robert)
City of Whispering Stone [1978] (Chesbro, George)
City Solitary [1985] (Freeling, Nicolas)
Clap Hands, Here Comes Charlie [1978] (Freemantle, Brian)
Classic Car Killer [1992] (Lupoff, Richard A.)
Classy Touch of Murder [1991] (Roe, C. F.)
Clean Kill [1995] (Wood, Ted)
■ Clean Sweep [1993] (Berlinski, David)
Clear and Present Danger [1989] (Clancy, Tom)
■ Clear Case of Murder [1990] (Downing, Warwick)
Cleveland Connection [1993] (Roberts, Les)
Cleveland Local [1997] (Roberts, Les)
Client [1990] (Hall, Parnell)
Client Privilege [1990] (Tapply, William G.)
Cliff Hanger [1993] (Craig, Philip)
Clinic [1997] (Kellerman, Jonathan)
Clockwork [1989] (Steed, Neville)
■ Close Quarters [1947] (Gilbert, Michael)
■ Close Softly the Doors [1991] (Roat, Ronald Clair)
Close to Death [1979] (Crowe, John)
■ Close to the Bone [1996] (Tapply, William G.)
Close to the Bone [1992] (Wiltse, David)
■ Closet [1995] (Zimmerman, R. D.) ★ ☆
Club [1991] (James, Bill)
Club Dead [1988] (Oster, Jerry)
■ Clubbable Woman [1970] (Hill, Reginald)
Co-Ordinator [1967] (York, Andrew)
Cobalt [1982] (Aldyne, Nathan)
Cobra Trap [1996] (O'Donnell, Peter)
Cock-Pit of Roses [1969] (Fraser, James)
Cockeyed Corpse [1964] (Prather, Richard)
Coda [1984] (Topor, Tom)
Code of Blood [1987] (Cross, David)
Codename: Gentkill [1995] (Lindsay, Paul)

■ Coffin for Dimitrios [U.S.] (Ambler, Eric)
Coin of the Realm [1989] (Murphy, Warren B.)
Cold Cash [1987] (Dold, Gaylord)
Cold Comfort [1990] (Lake, M. D.)
Cold Copper Tears [1988] (Cook, Glen)
■ Cold Fall [1996] (Gardner, John)
Cold Harbor [1990] (Higgins, Jack)
Cold Hearts and Gentle People [1994] (Riggs, John R.)
Cold Iron [1986] (Freeling, Nicolas)
Cold Light [1994] (Harvey, John)
■ Cold Mind [1983] (Lindsey, David L.)
■ Cold Night [1989] (Sarrantonio, Al) ☆
Cold Red Sunrise [1988] (Kaminsky, Stuart M.) ★
Cold Smell of Sacred Stone [1988] (Chesbro, George)
Cold Steele [1989] (Masters, J. D.)
Collision Bend [1996] (Roberts, Les)
Colonel Butler's Wolf [1972] (Price, Anthony)
Colour of Fear [1976] (Ormerod, Roger)
Columbo: The Game Show Killer [1996] (Harrington, William)
Columbo: The Glitter Murders [1997] (Harrington, William)
■ Columbo: The Grassy Knoll [1993] (Harrington, William)
Columbo: The Helter Skelter Murder [1994]
   (Harrington, William)
Columbo: The Hoffa Connection [1995] (Harrington, William)
Columbo: The Hoover Files [1998] (Harrington, William)
Come Back Dead [1997] (Faherty, Terence)
Come Clean [1989] (James, Bill)
Come to Grief [1995] (Francis, Dick) ★ ☆
■ Comeback [1991] (Perry, Ritchie)
■ Comeback [1997] (Stark, Richard)
Comedian Dies [1979] (Brett, Simon)
■ Comic Book Killer [1988] (Lupoff, Richard A.)
■ Compelling Evidence [1992] (Martini, Steve)
■ Complete State of Death [1969] (Gardner, John)
Comrade Charlie [1989] (Freemantle, Brian)
Con Game [1968] (Waugh, Hillary)
Con Man [1957] (McBain, Ed)
■ Concerning Blackshirt [1952] (Graeme, Roderic)
Concrete Blonde [1994] (Connelly, Michael) ☆ ☆
Concrete Evidence [1972] (Russell, Martin)
Concrete Hero [1994] (Kantner, Rob)
Concrete Pillow [1995] (Tierney, Ronald)
Condition Purple [1989] (Turnbull, Peter)
Condo Kill [1985] (Barth, Richard)
Confess Fletch [1976] (McDonald, Gregory) ★
Confessional [1985] (Higgins, Jack)
Confessor [1995] (Gardner, John)
Confounding of Sergeant Cluff [1966] (North, Gil)
Connecticut Yankee in Criminal Court [1996] (Heck, Peter J.)
Constable Across the Moors [1982] (Rhea, Nicholas)
Constable Along the Lane [1986] (Rhea, Nicholas)
Constable Among the Heather [1990] (Rhea, Nicholas)
■ Constable Around the Green [1993] (Rhea, Nicholas)
Constable Around the Village [1981] (Rhea, Nicholas)
Constable at the Double [1989] (Rhea, Nicholas)
■ Constable Beneath the Trees [1994] (Rhea, Nicholas)
■ Constable Beside the Stream [1991] (Rhea, Nicholas)
Constable by the Sea [1985] (Rhea, Nicholas)
Constable in Disguise [1989] (Rhea, Nicholas)
Constable in the Dale [1983] (Rhea, Nicholas)
■ Constable in the Shrubbery [1995] (Rhea, Nicholas)
■ Constable on the Hill [1979] (Rhea, Nicholas)
Constable on the Prowl [1980] (Rhea, Nicholas)
Constable Through the Meadow [1988] (Rhea, Nicholas)
Consuming Fire [1996] (Davis, Thomas D.)
Contact Lost [1970] (Craig, David)
Contract Null & Void [1996] (Gores, Joe)
Conviction of Guilt [1993] (Matthews, Lew)
■ Cool Blue Tomb [1991] (Kemprecos, Paul) ★
■ Cool Breeze on the Underground [1991] (Winslow, Don) ☆ ☆
■ Cool Killing [1987] (Murray, Stephen)
Co-Op Kill [Brit.] (Barth, Richard)

■ Cop Hater [1956] (McBain, Ed)
Cop Killer [1986] (Philbin, Tom)
Copper, Gold and Treasure [1982] (Williams, David)
Cords of Vanity [1989] (Tripp, Miles)
Corkscrew [1987] (Wood, Ted)
Corner Men [1974] (Gardner, John)
Corona Blue [1994] (Trainor, J. F.)
■ Corporate Bodies [1991] (Brett, Simon)
■ Corpse [1980] (McCutchan, Philip)
Corpse By Any Other Name [1998] (McGaughey, Neil)
■ Corpse in Handcuffs [1969] (Smith, Frank A.)
Corpse on the Dike [1976] (van de Wetering, Janwillem)
Corpus Corpus [1998] (Jeffers, H. Paul)
Corrupt and Ensnare [1978] (Nevins, Francis M., Jr)
Corruption of Blood [1995] (Tanenbaum, Robert K.)
Corruptly Procured [1994] (Bowen, Michael)
Cosi Fan Tutti [1996] (Dibdin, Michael)
■ Cotswold Manners [1988] (Spicer, Michael)
Cotswold Mistress [1992] (Spicer, Michael)
Cotswold Moles [1993] (Spicer, Michael)
Cotswold Murders [1990] (Spicer, Michael)
Count Your Enemies [1997] (Nathan, Paul)
Counterfeit Killers [1996] (Knox, Bill)
Counterfeit of Murder [1987] (Harrison, Ray)
■ Counterspy [APA] (Cleeve, Brian)
Country of Old Men [1991] (Hansen, Joseph) ★
Courtney [1983] (Jenkins, Jerry)
Cousin Once Removed [1984] (Hammond, Gerald)
Covenant with Death [1994] (Cooper, Brian)
Cover Girl Killer [1995] (Lupoff, Richard A.)
Cover Story [1985] (Forbes, Colin)
Coyote Crossing [1985] (Roderus, Frank)
Coyote Returns [1996] (Hackler, Micah S.)
Coyote Waits [1990] (Hillerman, Tony) ★
■ Coyote Wind [1994] (Bowen, Peter)
■ Crack in the Sidewalk [1976] (Copper, Basil)
■ Cracking of Spines [1980] (Lewis, Roy H.)
Crackshot [1990] (Busby, Roger)
■ Cracksman on Velvet [1974] (Selwyn, Francis)
■ Crang Plays the Ace [1987] (Batten, Jack)
Cranks and Shadows [1995] (Constantine, K. C.)
Crazy Mixed Up Corpse [1957] (Avallone, Michael)
■ Created: The Destroyer [1971] (Murphy, Warren B.)
Crediton Killings [1997] (Jecks, Michael)
Crime, Punishment and Resurrection [1992] (Collins, Michael)
Crime Wave [1974] (Russell, Martin)
Crime Without Passion [1983] (Grayson, Richard)
■ Crimes of the City [1991] (Rosenberg, Robert)
Criminal Conversation [1965] (Freeling, Nicolas)
Criminal Tendencies [1998] (Bishop, Paul)
Crimson Green [1994] (Zimmerman, Bruce)
■ Crimson Joy [1988] (Parker, Robert B.)
■ Cronus [1984] (DeAndrea, William L.)
■ Crooked Man [1994] (Dunbar, Tony)
Crooked Shadows [1975] (Crowe, John)
■ Cross of San Vincente [1991] (Cooper, Brian)
Cross Off [1993] (Corris, Peter)
Crossbearer [1994] (Lewis, Roy)
■ Crossfire Killings [1986] (Knox, Bill) ★
Crosskill [1994] (Disher, Garry)
Crossword Code [1986] (Resnicow, Herbert)
Crossword Hunt [1987] (Resnicow, Herbert)
Crossword Legacy [1987] (Resnicow, Herbert)
Crown: Bamboo Shoot-Out [1975] (Harknett, Terry)
Crown in Darkness [1988] (Doherty, P. C.)
■ Crown: Macao Mayhem [1974] (Harknett, Terry)
Crown: The Sweet and Sour Kill [1974] (Harknett, Terry)
Cruel April [1995] (Albert, Neil)
Cruel as the Grave [1996] (Armistead, John)
Cruel Justice [1996] (Bernhardt, William)
Cruel Victim [1979] (Tripp, Miles)
Cry Havoc [1990] (Mayo, J. K.)
Cry of Shadows [1990] (Gorman, Ed)
Cry Shadow [1965] (Grant, Maxwell)

Cry Uncle! [APA] (Brett, Michael)
Cry Vengeance [1993] (Handberg, Ron)
Crystal Blue Persuasion [1988] (Philbrick, W. R.)☆
■ Crystallised Carbon Pig [1966] (Wainright, John)
■ Cuckoo [1993] (Keegan, Alex) ☆
Cumberland's Cradle [1996] (Wilson, Derek)
Curious Eat Themselves [1994] (Straley, John)
Curse of the Cockers [1993] (Hammond, Gerald)
Cursed to Death [1988] (Crider, Bill)
Curses! [1989] (Elkins, Aaron)
Curve [APA] (Judd, Bob)
Cutting Edge [1991] (Harvey, John)
■ Cutting Room [1993] (Rosenberg, Robert)
Cyclops [1986] (Cussler, Clive)
Cynthia [1968] (Cunningham, E. V.)

D

■ DADA Caper [1978] (Spencer, Ross H.)
Daddy's Girl [1988] (Milne, John)
Dagger of Flesh [1952] (Prather, Richard)
Daisy Ducks [1986] (Boyer, Rick)
Damaged Goods [1996] (Solomita, Stephen)
Damagers [1993] (Hamilton, Donald)
Dame [1969] (Stark, Richard)
Dames Can Be Deadly [1963] (Chambers, Peter)
Damned in Paradise [Clarence Darrow] [1996]
    (Collins, Max Allan, Jr.)
Damned Lovely [1954] (Webb, Jack)
■ Damsel [1967] (Stark, Richard)
Dance at the Slaughterhouse [1991] (Block, Lawrence) ★ ☆
Dance for the Dead [1996] (Perry, Thomas)
Dance Hall of the Dead [1973] (Hillerman, Tony) ★
Dance in Deep Water [1997] (Allyn, Doug)
■ Dance of the Mongoose [1995] (Phillips, T. J.)
■ Dance With the Dead [1960] (Prather, Richard)
Dancer's Debt [1988] (Lutz, John)
Dancing Bear [1983] (Crumley, James) ☆
■ Dancing in the Dark [1996] (Kaminsky, Stuart M.)
■ Danger for Blackshirt [1965] (Graeme, Roderic)
Danger is My Line [1960] (Marlowe, Stephen)
Dangerous Games [1980] (Murphy, Warren B.)
Dangerous Thing [1994] (Crider, Bill)
■ Daphne Dead and Done For [1990] (Ross, Jonathan)
Dark Blood, Dark Terror [1965] (Cleeve, Brian)
Dark Blue and Dangerous [1981] (Ross, Jonathan)
Dark Canyon [1977] (Hackler, Micah S.)
Dark Chant in a Crimson Key [1992] (Chesbro, George)
■ Dark City [1987] (Collins, Max Allan, Jr.)
Dark Entry [1981] (Copper, Basil)
Dark Horse [1996] (Shoemaker, Bill)
Dark Maze [1991] (Adcock, Thomas) ★
■ Dark Mirror [1966] (Copper, Basil)
Dark of the Heart [1998] (Bishop, Paul)
Dark on Monday [1978] (Avallone, Michael)
Dark Place [1983] (Elkins, Aaron)
■ Dark Power [1968] (Arden, William)
Dark Provenance [1994] (Anthony, Michael David)
Dark Root [1995] (Mayor, Archer)
■ Dark Side [1976] (Davis, Kenn) [w/John Stanley] ☆
Dark Side [1986] (Hornig, Doug)
Dark Side of the Street [1967] (Fallon, Martin)
Dark Summer [1991] (Cleary, Jon)
Dark Trade [1965] (Lejeune, Anthony)
Dark Trail [1990] (Gorman, Ed)
Dark Wind [1982] (Hillerman, Tony)
Darkening Glass [1968] (Wainright, John)
Darkest Instinct [1996] (Walker, Robert W.)
Darkness, Hold My Hand [1996] (Lehane, Dennis)
Darling, It's Death [1952] (Prather, Richard)
Dart Man [1994] (Philbin, Tom)
Date With Death [1984] (Murphy, Warren B.)
Daughters of Cain [1994] (Dexter, Colin)
■ DaVinci Deception [1990] (Swan, Thomas)
Davis Cup Conspiracy [1994] (Bickham, Jack M.)

Death by Degrees [1993] (Wright, Eric)
Death by Gaslight [1982] (Kurland, Michael)
Death by Jury [1995] (Lutz, John)
■ Death by Sheer Torture [U.S.] (Barnard, Robert)
■ Death by Station Wagon [1992] (Katz, Jon)
Death Came Dressed in White [1993] (Sherer, Michael W.)
Death Ceremony [1985] (Melville, James)
Death Check [1971] (Murphy, Warren B.)
Death Claims [1973] (Hansen, Joseph)
Death Dealers [1965] (Spillane, Mickey)
Death Department [1959] (Knox, Bill)
Death Dives Deep [1971] (Avallone, Michael)
Death en Voyage [1986] (Grayson, Richard)
Death Games [1987] (Jahn, Michael)
Death Ground [1988] (Gorman, Ed)
Death Has Deep Roots [1951] (Gilbert, Michael)
■ Death in Amsterdam [U.S.] (Freeling, Nicolas)
Death in a Pheasant's Eye [1971] (Fraser, James)
Death in a Salubrious Place [1973] (Burley, W. J.)
■ Death in a Serene City [1990] (Sklepowich, Edward)
Death in Deep Water [1992] (Kemprecos, Paul)
Death in Jerusalem [1994] (Boland, John C.)
■ Death in Little Tokyo [1996] (Furutani, Dale)
Death in Melting [1957] (Grayson, Richard)
■ Death in Paris [1992] (Fuller, Dean)
Death in Purple Prose [1987] (Barnard, Robert)
Death in Stanley Street [1974] (Burley, W. J.)
Death in the Family [Brit.] (Roe, C.F.)
■ Death in the Fifth Position [1952] (Box, Edgar)
Death in the Old Country [1985] (Wright, Eric) ★
Death in the Palazzo [1997] (Sklepowich, Edward)
■ Death in the Past [1981] (Moore, Richard A.)
Death in the Rain [U.S.] (Parrish, Frank)
Death in the Willows [1979] (Forrest, Richard)
■ Death in Uptown [1990] (Raleigh, Michael)
Death in Verona [1989] (Lewis, Roy H.)
Death in Victory [1997] (Bean, Gregory)
■ Death is for Losers [1968] (Nolan, William F.)
Death is My Comrade [1960] (Marlowe, Stephen)
Death is Not a Passing Grade [1975] (Miller, Victor B.)
■ Death Is Now My Neighbor [1996] (Dexter, Colin)☆
Death Likes It Hot [1954] (Box, Edgar)
Death Minus Zero [1996] (Baker, John)
Death of a Big Man [1975] (Wainright, John)
■ Death of a Blue Lantern [1994] (West, Christopher) ☆
Death of a Blue Movie Star [1990] (Deaver, Jeffery)
■ Death of a Citizen [1960] (Hamilton, Donald)
Death of a Critic [1996] (Fuller, Dean)
Death of a Daimyo [1984] (Melville, James)
Death of a Dancing Lady [1985] (Harrison, Ray)
■ Death of a Dissident [1981] (Kaminsky, Stuart M.)
Death of a Hawker [1977] (van de Wetering, Janwillem)
Death of a Hippie [1968] (Brett, Michael)
Death of a Man-Tamer [1987] (Tripp, Miles)
■ Death of a Merry Widow [1993] (Hunt, Richard)
Death of a Pornographer [U.S.] (Lejeune, Anthony)
Death of a Prodigal [1995] (Williams, David)
Death of a Russian Priest [1992] (Kaminsky, Stuart M.)
Death of a Source [1982] (Moore, Richard A.)
Death of a Tenor Man [1995] (Moody, Bill)
Death of an Ardent Bibliophile [1995] (Gill, Bartholomew)
Death of an Aunt [1967] (Harknett, Terry)
Death of an Honourable Member [1984] (Harrison, Ray)
Death of an Innocent [1989] (Ormerod, Roger)
■ Death of an Old Sea Wolf [1996] (Gill, Bartholomew)
Death of Friends [1996] (Nava, Michael) ★
Death of Love [1992] (Gill, Bartholomew)
Death of the Abbe Didier [1981] (Grayson, Richard)
Death of the Joyce Scholar [1989] (Gill, Bartholomew) ☆
Death off Stage [1991] (Grayson, Richard)
Death on 66 [1994] (Sanders, William)
Death on a Black Dragon River [1995] (West, Christopher)
Death on a Cold, Wild River [1993] (Gill, Bartholomew)

Death on a No. 8 Hook [1988] (Gough, Laurence)
Death on a Vineyard Beach [1996] (Craig, Philip)
Death on the Broadlands [U.S.] (Hunter, Alan)
Death on the Cards [1988] (Grayson, Richard)
Death on the Douro [1997] (Aspler, Tony)
Death on the Heath [U.S.] (Hunter, Alan)
Death on the Mississippi [1989] (Forrest, Richard)
■ Death on the Mississippi [1995] (Heck, Peter J.)
Death on the Move [1989] (Crider, Bill)
■ Death on the Rocks [1987] (Allegretto, Michael) ★☆
Death on Wheels [1993] (Nordan, Robert)
■ Death Raid [1986] (Harper, Richard)
Death Sentence [1975] (Garfield, Brian)
Death Sentence [1990] (Murphy, Warren B.)
Death Sentence [1990] (Philbin, Tom)
Death Squad [1977] (Copper, Basil)
■ Death Takes Time [1994] (Jeffries, Roderic)
Death Therapy [1972] (Murphy, Warren B.)
Death Throes [1995] (Egleton, Clive)
Death Through the Looking Glass [1978] (Forrest, Richard)
■ Death Trance [1992] (Zimmerman, R. D.)
■ Death Trick [1988] (Jeffries, Roderic)
■ Death Trick [1981] (Stevenson, Richard)
Death Under the Lilacs [1985] (Forrest, Richard)
■ Death Underfoot [1994] (Casley, Dennis)
Death Understates [1995] (Casley, Dennis)
Death Undertow [1995] (Casley, Dennis)
Death Wears a Red Hat [1980] (Kienzle, William X.)
■ Death Wish [1972] (Garfield, Brian)
Death's Bright Arrow [1989] (Sherburne, James)
Death's Clenched Fist [1982] (Sherburne, James)
Death's Gray Angel [1981] (Sherburne, James)
Death's Head [1982] (Ross, Jonathan)
■ Death's Pale Horse [1980] (Sherburne, James)
Death's White City [1988] (Sherburne, James)
Deathbed [1986] (Kienzle, William X.)
Deathdeal [1993] (Disher, Garry)
Deathe is Forever [1992] (Gardner, John)
Deathics [1993] (Barth, Richard)
Deathwatch [1985] (Harrison, Ray)
Debt of Honor [1994] (Clancy, Tom)
Deception Pass [1997] (Emerson, Earl)
Deceptive Appearance [1992] (Malcolm, John)
■ Deceptive Clarity [1987] (Elkins, Aaron)
■ Decoys [1980] (Hoyt, Richard)
Dedicated Man [1988] (Robinson, Peter) ☆
Deep and Crisp and Even [1964] (Payne, Laurence)
■ Deep and Crisp and Even [1981] (Turnbull, Peter)
Deep Blue Cradle [1980] (Chambers, Peter)
Deep Dive [1988] (Hornig, Doug)
Deep Fall [1966] (Knox, Bill)
Deep Shaker [1991] (Roberts, Les)
Deep Six [1984] (Cussler, Clive)
Deep Valley Malice [1996] (Mitchell, Kirk)
Defectors are Dead Men [1971] (Smith, Frank A.)
■ Defending Billy Ryan [1992] (Higgins, George V.)
Degree of Guilt [1992] (Patterson, Richard North)
Delicate Darling [1959] (Webb, Jack)
Deliver Us From Evil [1997] (Luber, Philip)
■ Deliver Us to Evil [1971] (Hensley, Joe L.)
Demolishers [1987] (Hamilton, Donald)
Demons [1993] (Pronzini, Bill)
Depraved Indifference [1989] (Tanenbaum, Robert K.)
■ Desert Cat [1994] (Allen, Garrison)
Desert Look [1990] (Schopen, Bernard) ☆
■ Desert Sinner [1992] (Mclnerny, Ralph)
Despite the Evidence [1971] (Alding, Peter)
■ Detective [1987] (Hall, Parnell) ☆☆
■ Detective and Mr. Dickens [1990] (Palmer, William J.)
■ Detective First Grade [1993] (Mahoney, Dan)
■ Detective is Dead [1995] (James, Bill)
Detective Wore Silk Drawers [1971] (Lovesey, Peter)
Detonators [1985] (Hamilton, Donald)

Devastators [1965] (Hamilton, Donald)
Deviant Behavior [1988] (Emerson, Earl) ☆
Deviator [1969] (York, Andrew)
❶ Devil in a Blue Dress [1990] (Mosley, Walter) ★★ ☆
Devil is Dead [1989] (Lewis, Roy)
Devil Knows You're Dead [1993] (Block, Lawrence) ★
❶ Devil Met a Lady [1993] (Kaminsky, Stuart M.)
❶ Devil's Food [1997] (Bruno, Anthony)
❶ Devil's Hatband [1996] (Greer, Robert O.)
Devil's Heaven [1995] (Adcock, Thomas)
Devil's Hunt [1996] (Doherty, P. C.)
Devil's Backbone [1998] (Greer, Robert O.)
Devil's Red Nickel [1997] (Greer, Robert O.)
Devil's Waltz [1993] (Kellerman, Jonathan)
Devilweed [1966] (Knox, Bill)
❶ Dewey Decimated [1977] (Goodrum, Charles A.) ☆
❶ D.I. [U.S.] (Ashford, Jeffrey)
Diamond Eyes [1990] (Lutz, John)
❶ Diamond Head [1996] (Knief, Charles) ★
Diamond Rock [1985] (Schorr, Mark)
Diamond Solitaire [1992] (Lovesey, Peter)
Diamonds of Loreta [1980] (Drummond, Ivor)
Die Again, Macready [1984] (Livingston, Jack) ☆
Die Dreaming [1994] (Faherty, Terence)
Die Now, Live Later [1968] (Copper, Basil)
Die to a Distant Drum [1972] (Arden, William)
Die-Cast [1987] (Steed, Neville)
❶ Diecast [1963] (Brett, John Michael)
❶ Diehard [1977] (Jackson, Jon A.)
❶ Different Women Dancing [1997] (Gash, Jonathan)
❶ Dig That Crazy Grave [1961] (Prather, Richard)
Dignity and Purity [1960] (Jeffries, Ian)
Diminished by Death [1968] (Ross, Jonathan)
Diminished Responsibility [1984] (Barnett, James)
Dip into Murder [1978] (Ormerod, Roger)
❶ Diplomatic Baggage [1995] (Melville, James)
❶ Dirt [1996] (Woods, Stuart)
Dirty Money [1986] (Bass, Milton R.)
Dirty Story [1967] (Ambler, Eric)
❶ Dirty Weekend [1989] (Scholefield, Alan)
Dirty Work [1988] (Kantner, Rob) ★
Disappearance [1970] (Wilcox, Collin)
Disheveled City [1990] (Dold, Gaylord)
Dishonoured Bones [1954] (Trench, John)
❶ Disorderly Elements [1985] (Cook, Bob)
❶ Distant Blood [1996] (Abbott, Jeff)
Ditched Blond [1995] (Adams, Harold)
Divided Treasure [1987] (Williams, David)
❶ Dividing Line [1993] (Parrish, Richard)
❶ Dixie City Jam [1994] (Burke, James Lee) ☆
❶ Do Unto Others [1994] (Abbott, Jeff) ★★
❶ Dobie Paradox [1993] (Cory, Desmond)
❶ Docken Dead [1953] (Trench, John)
Doctor, Lawyer... [1976] (Wilcox, Collin)
❶ Dog in the Dark [1989] (Hammond, Gerald)
Doghouse [1989] (Hammond, Gerald)
❶ Doing Wrong [1993] (Keating, H. R. F.)
Doll [1965] (McBain, Ed)
Dollmaker [1995] (Janes, J. Robert)
Dominator [1969] (York, Andrew)
Dominoes [1980] (Wainright, John)
Don't Ask [1993] (Westlake, Donald E.)
Don't Bleed on Me [1968] (Copper, Basil)
❶ Don't Bother to Knock [1966] (Chambers, Peter)
Don't Explain [1995] (Murphy, Dallas)
Don't Lie to Me [1972] (Coe, Tucker)
❶ Done Deal [1993] (Standiford, Les)
Doomsday Bag [1969] (Avallone, Michael)
Doomsday List [1974] (Orvis, Kenneth)
❶ Doone Walk [1982] (Clark, Douglas)
Doors Open [1949] (Gilbert, Michael)
Doria Rafe Case [1980] (Waugh, Hillary)

❶ Dorothy Parker Murder Case [1984] (Baxt, George)
Double Blind [1997] (Goddard, Ken)
❶ Double Deuce [1992] (Parker, Robert B.)
Double Down [1991] (Kakonis, Tom)
Double Eagle [1987] (Miles, Keith)
Double Exposure [1995] (Palmer, Frank)
❶ Double Exposure [1985] (Stinson, Jim)
Double Fault [1993] (Bickham, Jack M.)
Double for Blackshirt [1958] (Graeme, Roderic)
❶ Double in Trouble [1959] (Prather, Richard)
❶ Double Jeopardy [1982] (Forbes, Colin)
Double Plot [1994] (Axler, Leo) ☆
❶ Double Take [1985] (Dowling, Gregory)
❶ Double [1984] (Pronzini, Bill)
Double-Barrel [1964] (Freeling, Nicolas)
Double-Minded Men [1992] (Craig, Philip)
❶ Doubting Thomas [1985] (Reeves, Robert)
Down and Dirty [1974] (Murphy, Warren B.)
Down by the River Where the Dead Men Go [1995] (Pelecanos, George P.)
Down by the Sea [1993] (Kent, Bill)
Down for the Count [1985] (Kaminsky, Stuart M.)
❶ Down in the Valley [1989] (Pierce, David M.)
Down in the Zero [1994] (Vachss, Andrew H.)
Down to a Sunless Sea [1996] (Poyer, David)
Down-Beat Kill [1963] (Chambers, Peter)
Downriver [1988] (Estleman, Loren D.)
Dr. Jekyll and Mr. Holmes [1978] (Estleman, Loren D.)
Dr. Nightingale Chases Three Little Pigs [1996] (Adamson, Lydia)
❶ Dr. Nightingale Comes Home [1994] (Adamson, Lydia)
Dr. Nightingale Enters the Bear Cave [1996] (Adamson, Lydia)
Dr. Nightingale Goes the Distance [1995] (Adamson, Lydia)
Dr. Nightingale Goes to the Dogs [1995] (Adamson, Lydia)
Dr. Nightingale Rides the Elephant [1994] (Adamson, Lydia)
Dr. Nightingale Rides to the Hounds [1997] (Adamson, Lydia)
Dr. Quake [1972] (Murphy, Warren B.)
Dragon [1990] (Cussler, Clive)
Dragon Lives Forever [1992] (Riggs, John R)
Dragon Portfolio [1986] (Hoyt, Richard)
Dragon's Claw [1978] (O'Donnell, Peter)
Dragonfire [1982] (Pronzini, Bill)
Dragons at the Party [1987] (Cleary, Jon)
Dragons Can Be Dangerous [1983] (Chambers, Peter)
Dragons of Archenfield [1995] (Marston, Edward)
Dragonship [1976] (MacLeod, Robert)
❶ Draw Batons! [1973] (Knox, Bill)
❶ Drawing Dead [1994] (Hautman, Pete)
Dread and Water [1976] (Clark, Douglas)
Dread Brass Shadows [1990] (Cook, Glen)
❶ Dream of a Falling Eagle [1996] (Chesbro, George)
Dreamboat [1995] (Swanson, Doug J.)
❶ Dreamsicle [1993] (Ripley, W. L.)
Dresden Green [1966] (Freeling, Nicolas)
Dresden Text [1994] (Wilson, Derek)
❶ Dressing of Diamond [1974] (Freeling, Nicolas)
❶ Drink Before the War [1994] (Lehane, Dennis) ★★
Drink with the Devil [1996] (Higgins, Jack)
Drive-by [1995] (Reynolds, William J.)
❶ Drop Dead [1984] (Ross, Jonathan)
❶ Drop-Off [1988] (Grissom, Ken)
Dropshot [1990] (Bickham, Jack M.)
Dropshot [1996] (Coben, Harlan)
❶ Drover [1991] (Granger, Bill)
Drover and the Designated Hitter [1994] (Granger, Bill)
Drover and the Zebras [1992] (Granger, Bill)
Drown All the Dogs [1994] (Adcock, Thomas)
Drowned Hopes [1990] (Westlake, Donald E.)
Drowned Man's Key [1992] (Grissom, Ken)
❶ Drowning Nets [1991] (Knox, Bill)
❶ Drum Beat—Berlin [1964] (Marlowe, Stephen)
❶ Drum Beat—Dominique [1965] (Marlowe, Stephen)

■ Drum Beat—Erica [1967] (Marlowe, Stephen)
■ Drum Beat—Madrid [1966] (Marlowe, Stephen)
■ Drum Beat—Marianne [1968] (Marlowe, Stephen)
Due Diligence [1995] (Kahn, Michael A.)
Duel in the Shadows [1962] (Lejeune, Anthony)
■ Duffy [1980] (Kavanagh, Dan)
Duke of Cleveland [1995] (Roberts, Les)
■ Duplicate [1964] (Taylor, H. Baldwin)
Dust on God's Breath [1998] (Lipinski, Thomas)
Dutch Blue Error [1984] (Tapply, William G.)
Dutch Courage [1978] (Perry, Ritchie)
Duty Elsewhere [1979] (Wainright, John)
■ Dwarf Kingdom [1996] (Freeling, Nicolas)
Dwell in Danger [1982] (Lewis, Roy)
Dying of the Light [1990] (Richardson, Robert)
Dying on the Vine [1998] (King, Peter)
Dying Space [1982] (Murphy, Warren B.)
Dying to Come Home [APA] (Jenkins, Jerry)
Dying to Fly Fish [1996] (Leitz, David)
■ Dying Trade [1980] (Corris, Peter)
Dying Voices [1989] (Crider, Bill)
■ Dynamite Pass [1993] (Trainor, J. F.)

E

Eagle Has Flown [1991] (Higgins, Jack)
■ Eagle Has Landed [1975] (Higgins, Jack)
Eakins' Mistress [1997] (Bradberry, James)
Ear for Murder [1967] (Brett, Michael)
Early Autumn [1981] (Parker, Robert B.) ☆
East Beach [1995] (Ely, Ron)
Easy Meat [1996] (Harvey, John)
Easy Thing [1990] (Taibo, Paco Ignacio, II)
■ Eclipse of the Heart [1993] (Tierney, Ronald)
Echo of Death [1994] (Zubro, Mark)
Edge of Sleep [1993] (Wiltse, David)
Edge of the City [1995] (Mahoney, Dan)
Edith Wharton Murders [1997] (Raphael, Lev)
Education of Patrick Silver [1976] (Charyn, Jerome)
Eight Black Horses [1985] (McBain, Ed)
Eight Million Ways to Die [1982] (Block, Lawrence) ★ ☆
Eighty Million Eyes [1966] (McBain, Ed)
El Bronx [1997] (Charyn, Jerome)
El Murders [1987] (Granger, Bill)
Electric Country Roulette [1996] (Ripley, W. L.)
Eleventh Hour [1987] (Murphy, Warren B.)
■ Elgar Variation [U.S.] (Kenyon, Michael)
■ Eliminator [1966] (York, Andrew)
Elvis, Jesus & Coca Cola [1993] (Friedman, Kinky)
Elvis Murders [1985] (Bourgeau, Art)
■ Embrace the Wolf [1985] (Schutz, Benjamin) ☆
■ Embracing Skeletons [1996] (Turnbull, Peter)
Eminence [1989] (Kienzle, William X.)
Empress File [1991] (Sandford, John)
Empty Beach [1983] (Corris, Peter)
■ Empty Hours [1962] (McBain, Ed)
Empty Silence [1981] (Copper, Basil)
Encounter Group [1984] (Murphy, Warren B.)
End of a Party [1965] (Waugh, Hillary)
End of the Game [1985] (Murphy, Warren B.)
Endangered Species [1993] (Burns, Rex)
■ Endpeace [1996] (Cleary, Jon)
Enemies Within [1974] (Lewin, Michael Z.)
Enquiries Are Continuing [1964] (Ashford, Jeffrey)
Enslaved [1994] (Burns, Ron)
Epitaphs [1992] (Pronzini, Bill)
Erased [1996] (Bailey, Jo)
Erin [1983] (Jenkins, Jerry)
Eros Affair [1977] (McCutchan, Philip)
Error of Judgement [1971] (Lewis, Roy)
■ Escapade [1995] (Satterthwait, Walter) ★ ☆
Escape to Danger [1974] (Conway, Peter)
Eve of Destruction [1996] (Edwards, Martin)
Even My Foot's Asleep [1971] (Payne, Laurence)
■ Even the Wicked [1997] (Block, Lawrence)

■ Evergreen Death [1968] (Fraser, James)
Every Brilliant Eye [1986] (Estleman, Loren D.)
Every Picture Tells a Story [1991] (Dowling, Gregory)
Everybody Had a Gun [1951] (Prather, Richard)
Everything but the Squeal [1990] (Hallinan, Timothy)
■ Evidence I Shall Give [1974] (Wainright, John)
■ Evil at the Root [1990] (Crider, Bill)
■ Evil Intent [1966] (Wainright, John)
Evil Money [1964] (Harknett, Terry)
■ Evil Ways [1983] (Wainright, John)
Except for the Bones [1991] (Wilcox, Collin)
Executioners [1986] (McCutchan, Philip)
Executive Orders [1996] (Clancy, Tom)
Executor [1986] (Hammond, Gerald)
Exit Lines [1984] (Hill, Reginald)
■ Exit Wounds [1990] (Westermann, John)
■ Exorcist [1971] (Blaty, William Peter)
Expensive Place to Die [1967] (Deighton, Len)
■ Expert Testimony [1992] (Stockley, Grif)
Expurgator [1973] (York, Andrew)
Extenuating Circumstances [1989] (Valin, Jonathan) ★
Extra Credits [1988] (Lupica, Mike)
■ Eye in the Ring [1982] (Randisi, Robert J.)
Eye of God [1994] (Grace, C. L.)
Eye of the Gator [1995] (Ayres, E. C.)
■ Eye of the Storm [1992] (Higgins, Jack)
■ Eye [1984] (Lutz, John)
Eyes of a Child [1994] (Patterson, Richard North)
Eyes of Prey [1991] (Sandford, John)

F

Faberge Factor [1998] (Swan, Thomas)
Face [1979] (Vance, Jack)
Face at the Window [1984] (Parrish, Frank)
Face Changers [1998] (Perry, Thomas)
Face on the Cutting Room Floor [1991] (Cutler, Stan)
■ Face Value [1983] (Ormerod, Roger)
Faceless Mortals [1988] (Cook, Bob)
Faces in the Crowd [1991] (Marshall, William)
Fade Away [1996] (Coben, Harlan) ★★☆
Fadeaway [1986] (Rosen, Richard)
■ Fadeout [1970] (Hansen, Joseph)
Fade to Black [1997] (Gibbs, Tony)
Fair Friday [1983] (Turnbull, Peter)
Fair Game [1982] (Hammond, Gerald)
Fair Maid of Bohemia [1997] (Marston, Edward)
Faith [1994] (Deighton, Len)
Faithfully Executed [1992] (Bowen, Michael)
Fala Factor [1984] (Kaminsky, Stuart M.)
Falconer and the Face of God [1996] (Morson, Ian)
■ Falconer's Crusade [1994] (Morson, Ian)
Falconer's Judgement [1995] (Morson, Ian)
Fall Down Easy [1992] (Gough, Laurence)
■ Fall Guy [1972] (Perry, Ritchie)
■ Fall-Down Artist [1994] (Lipinski, Thomas) ☆
Fallen Man [1996] (Hillerman, Tony)
■ Falling Man [1970] (Sadler, Mark)
Falls of the Shadow [1993] (Timlin, Mark)
False Allegations [1996] (Vachss, Andrew H.)
False Beards [U.S.] (Williams, Alan)
False Conception [1994] (Greenleaf, Stephen)
False Dawn [1993] (Levine, Paul)
■ False Faces [1991] (Margolis, Seth)
False Pretenses [1993] (Lyons, Arthur)
False Profit [1990] (Eversz, Robert)
False Profits [1992] (Everson, David H.)
Falsely Accused [1996] (Tanenbaum, Robert K.)
Familiar Spirits [1985] (Tourney, Leonard)
■ Family Business [1994] (Lewin, Michael Z.)
Family of Angels [1996] (Ripley, Mike)
Family Stalker [1994] (Katz, Jon)
■ Family Values [1997] (Constantine, K. C.)
Far Away Man [1984] (Marshall, William)

Far Horizon [1982] (Copper, Basil)
Far Side of Fear [1985] (Copper, Basil)
Farewell to the Flesh [1991] (Sklepowich, Edward)
Farnsworth Score [1977] (Burns, Rex)
Fascinator [1975] (York, Andrew)
Fast Fade [1987] (Lyons, Arthur)
∎ Fat Boy Murders [1993] (Kaufelt, David A.)
∎ Fat Death [1966] (Avallone, Michael)
Fat Innkeeper [1995] (Russell, Alan)
Fat Tuesday [1987] (Emerson, Earl)
Fatal Attachment [1992] (Barnard, Robert)
Fatal Elixir [1997] (DeAndrea, William L.)
Fatal Equilibrium [1985] (Jevons, Marshall)
∎ Fatal Fleece [1991] (Jeffries, Roderic)
Fatal Glass of Beer [1997] (Kaminsky, Stuart M.)
Fatal Impressions [1989] (Warga, Wayne)
Fatal Instinct [1993] (Walker, Robert W.)
Fatal Obsession [1983] (Greenleaf, Stephen)
Fatal Opinions [1991] (Murray, Stephen)
Fatal Sisters [1990] (Duncan, W. Glenn) ★
Fatal Step [1948] (Miller, Wade)
∎ Fate Accomplished [1987] (Ross, Jonathan)
Father's Club [1996] (Katz, Jon)
Favor [1988] (Hall, Parnell)
Fear in Fenway [1993] (Evers, Crabbe)
Fear in Yesterday's Rings [1991] (Chesbro, George)
∎ Fear of the Dark [1988] (Haywood, Gar Anthony) ★★
Fear To Tread [1953] (Gilbert, Michael)
Feathery Touch of Death [1997] (Logue, John)
∎ February Doll Murders [1966] (Avallone, Michael)
February Trouble [1992] (Albert, Neil)
Federal Fag [1998] (Hunter, Fred W.)
∎ Feedback [1974] (Copper, Basil)
Feeding Frenzy [1993] (Kemprecos, Paul)
∎ Fellowship of Fear [1982] (Elkins, Aaron)
Female—Handle With Care [1981] (Chambers, Peter)
∎ Feramontov [1966] (Cory, Desmond)
Fetch Out No Shroud [1990] (Murray, Stephen)
Fiddle City [1981] (Kavanagh, Dan)
Field of Fire [1973] (Alding, Peter)
Fielder's Choice [1991] (Bowen, Michael)
Fields of Heather [1981] (Hunter, Alan)
Fiery Hint of Murder [1990] (Roe, C. F.)
Figurehead [U.S.] (Knox, Bill)
Filmi, Filmi, Inspector Ghote [1976] (Keating, H. R. F.)
Final Account [1994] (Robinson, Peter)
Final Appointment [1993] (Hart, Roy)
Final Crusade [1989] (Murphy, Warren B.)
Final Cut [1991] (Wright, Eric)
Final Death [1977] (Murphy, Warren B.)
∎ Final Dictation [1989] (Vincent, Lawrence M.)
Final Notice [1973] (Gores, Joe)
Final Notice [1980] (Valin, Jonathan)
∎ Final Viewing [1994] (Axler, Leo)
Find Her a Grave [1993] (Wilcox, Collin)
∎ Find My Way Home [1996] (Timlin, Mark)
Find This Woman [1951] (Prather, Richard)
Finders Weepers [1983] (Byrd, Max)☆
Fine and Private Place [1994] (Martin, James E.)
Fine Italian Hand [1996] (Murray, William)
Fine Italian Hand [1992] (Wright, Eric)
Fine Night for Dying [1969] (Fallon, Martin)
Fine Red Rain [1987] (Kaminsky, Stuart M.)
Finger Play [1991] (Wallace, Robert)
Finish Me Off [1970] (Waugh, Hillary)
Fiourth Deadly Sin [1985] (Sanders, Lawrence)
Fire Horse [1995] (Shoemaker, Bill)
∎ Fire in the Barley [1977] (Parrish, Frank) ☆
Fire Lake [1987] (Valin, Jonathan)
Firefly Gadroon [1982] (Gash, Jonathan)
Firing Line [1980] (Murphy, Warren B.)
∎ Firing Offense [1992] (Pelecanos, George P.)

Firing Squad [1981] (Barnett, James)
Firm Ambitions [1994] (Kahn, Michael A.)
∎ First Body [APA] (Payne, Laurence)
First Class Murder [1991] (Roosevelt, Elliot)
∎ First Deadly Sin [1973] (Sanders, Lawrence)
Fish Story [1985] (Hoyt, Richard)
Fistful of Empty [1991] (Schutz, Benjamin) ☆
Five-Leafed Clover [1973] (Fraser, James)
∎ Five Little Rich Girls [APA] (Block, Lawrence)
Fix Like This [1975] (Constantine, K. C.)
∎ Fixed in His Folly [1995] (Walker, David J.) ☆
Fixin' to Die [1992] (Oster, Jerry)
Flagstick [1991] (Miles, Keith)
Flame [1990] (Lutz, John)
Flanders Sky [U.S.] (Freeling, Nicolas)
∎ Flash of Red [1996] (Harvey, Clay)
Flashback [1992] (Wood, Ted)
Flashback [1996] (Lusby, Jim)
Flawless Execution [1986] (Logue, John)
Flesh and Blood [1989] (Cook, Thomas H.)
Flesh and Bones [1997] (Levine, Paul)
Flesh & Blood [1994] (Harvey, James Neal)
Flesh Wounds [1996] (Greenleaf, Stephen)
∎ Fletch [1974] (McDonald, Gregory) ★
Fletch and the Man Who [1983] (McDonald, Gregory)
Fletch and the Widow Bradley [1981] (McDonald, Gregory)
Fletch Reflected [1994] (McDonald, Gregory)
Fletch, Too [1986] (McDonald, Gregory)
Fletch Won [1985] (McDonald, Gregory)
Fletch's Fortune [1978] (McDonald, Gregory)
Fletch's Moxie [1982] (McDonald, Gregory)
∎ Flickering Death [U.S.] (MacLeod, Robert)
Flight From Paris [U.S.] (MacLeod, Robert)
Flight of the Stiff [1967] (Brett, Michael)
Flip Side of Life [1990] (Martin, James E.)
Flip-Side [1980] (Copper, Basil)
Flirting with Death [1996] (Lake, M. D.)
∎ Flood [1985] (Vachss, Andrew H.) ☆
Flower in the Desert [1992] (Satterthwait, Walter)
∎ Flower-Covered Corpse [1969] (Avallone, Michael)
Flowers of the Forest [1980] (Hone, Joseph)
Fly Away, Jill [1981] (Byrd, Max)
Fly Fishing Can Be Fatal [1997] (Leitz, David)
Fly in the Cobweb [1986] (Parrish, Frank)
Fly Paper [1981] (Collins, Max Allan, Jr.)
∎ Flynn [1977] (McDonald, Gregory)
Flynn's In [1984] (McDonald, Gregory)
Follow That Gun [1996] (Hammond, Gerald)
∎ Follow the Leader [1979] (Logue, John) ☆
Follow the Sharks [1985] (Tapply, William G.)
Fool Me Twice [1996] (Levine, Paul)
Fool's Flight [1982] (Murphy, Warren B.)
Fool's Gold [1986] (Wood, Ted)
Fool's Gold [1983] (Murphy, Warren B.)
Fool's Mate [1981] (Perry, Ritchie)
∎ Fool's Run [1989] (Sandford, John)
Footsteps of the Hawk [1995] (Vachss, Andrew H.)
For Special Services [1982] (Gardner, John)
∎ For the Good of the State [1986] (Price, Anthony)
∎ For the Silvership [1985] (Thurston, Robert)
Force of Nature [1989] (Solomita, Stephen)
Forced Entry [1990] (Solomita, Stephen)
Foreign Exchange [1991] (Beinhart, Larry)
Forest Prime Evil [1992] (Russell, Alan)
Forever Death [1994] (Sherer, Michael W.)
∎ Forgive Us Our Sins [1994] (Luber, Philip)
∎ Formula One [1989] (Judd, Bob)
Forza Trap [1979] (Davis, Kenn)
∎ Foul Shot [1984] (Hornig, Doug) ☆
∎ Foul Up [1982] (Perry, Ritchie)
Founder Member [1969] (Gardner, John)
∎ Four Last Things [1989] (Hallinan, Timothy)

Four on the Floor [1989] (McInerny, Ralph)
Foursome [1993] (Healy, Jeremiah) ☆
Fourth Widow [1986] (Adams, Harold)
Fox in the Night [1988] (Hart, Roy)
■ Fox Valley Murders [1966] (Vance, John Holbrook)
■ Francesca [1963] (Marlowe, Stephen)
Freak [1983] (Collins, Michael)
■ Fred Astaire and Ginger Rogers Murder Case [1997]
   (Baxt, George)
Freedom to Kill [1997] (Lindsay, Paul)
Free Fall [1993] (Crais, Robert)☆
Free-Range Wife [1983] (Kenyon, Michael)
Freelance Death [1987] (Taylor, Andrew)
Freeze Frame [1976] (Irvine, Robert)☆
Freeze Thy Blood Less Coldly [1970] (Wainright, John)
■ French Ordinary Murder [1983] (Harrison, Ray)
Frenzy [1988] (Miller, Rex)
Frequent Flyer [1989] (Friedman, Kinky)
■ Friday the Rabbi Slept Late [1964] (Kemelman, Harry) ★
Frightened Wife [1987] (Tripp, Miles)
Frighteners [1970] (Busby, Roger)
Frighteners [1989] (Hamilton, Donald)
Frigor Mortis [1989] (McInerny, Ralph)
Frobisher's Savage [1994] (Tourney, Leonard)
Frog in the Moonflower [1972] (Drummond, Ivor)
Frog King [1990] (McConnell, Frank)
■ Frogmouth [1987] (Marshall, William)
■ Frost at Christmas [1984] (Wingfield, R. D.)
Fruits of the Poisonous Tree [1994] (Mayor, Archer)
Full Circle [1994] (Wilcox, Colin)
Full Cleveland [1989] (Roberts, Les)
Full Contact [1984] (Randisi, Robert J.) ☆
Full Fury [1975] (Ormerod, Roger)
Full-Bodied Red [1993] (Zimmerman, Bruce)
Funeral in Berlin [1964] (Deighton, Len) ☆
■ Funny Money [1975] (Murphy, Warren B.)
Fuzz [1968] (McBain, Ed)

G

Gabrielle's Way [1981] (Hunter, Alan)
Gallows Murders [1995] (Clynes, Michael)
■ Gallows View [1987] (Robinson, Peter) ☆☆
Gambler, the Minstrel, and the Dance Hall Queen [1976]
   (Downing, Warwick)
Game [1982] (Hammond, Gerald)
Ganja Coast [1995] (Mann, Paul)
Garden of Weapons [1980] (Gardner, John)
Gat Heat [1967] (Prather, Richard)
Gates of Exquisite View [1988] (Trenhaile, John)
■ Gateway [1983] (Jenkins, Jerry)
■ Gathering of Ghosts [1982] (Lewis, Roy)
■ Gathering Place [1984] (Breen, Jon)
Gator Kill [1992] (Crider, Bill)
Gelignite [1976] (Marshall, William)
General Murders [1988] (Estleman, Loren D.)
Genesis Files [1988] (Biderman, Bob)
■ Gently at a Gallop [1971] (Hunter, Alan)
Gently Between Tides [1982] (Hunter, Alan)
Gently By the Shore [1956] (Hunter, Alan)
■ Gently Coloured [1969] (Hunter, Alan)
■ Gently Continental [1967] (Hunter, Alan)
■ Gently Does It [1955] (Hunter, Alan)
Gently Down the Stream [1957] (Hunter, Alan)
Gently Floating [1963] (Hunter, Alan)
Gently French [1973] (Hunter, Alan)
Gently Go Man [1961] (Hunter, Alan)
Gently in the Glens [1993] (Hunter, Alan)
Gently in the Highlands [U.S] (Hunter, Alan)
Gently in the Sun [1959] (Hunter, Alan)
Gently in Trees [1974] (Hunter, Alan)
Gently Instrumental [1977] (Hunter, Alan)
■ Gently North-West [1967] (Hunter, Alan)

■ Gently Sahib [1964] (Hunter, Alan)
Gently Scandalous [1990] (Hunter, Alan)
Gently Through the Mill [1958] (Hunter, Alan)
Gently Through the Woods [U.S.] (Hunter, Alan)
Gently to a Kill [1991] (Hunter, Alan)
Gently to a Sleep [1978] (Hunter, Alan)
Gently to the Summit [1961] (Hunter, Alan)
Gently Tragic [1992] (Hunter, Alan)
Gently Where the Birds Are [1976] (Hunter, Alan)
Gently Where the Roads Go [1962] (Hunter, Alan)
Gently With Love [1975] (Hunter, Alan)
■ Gently with the Innocents [1970] (Hunter, Alan)
■ Gently with the Ladies [1965] (Hunter, Alan)
Gently with the Millions [1989] (Hunter, Alan)
Gently with the Painters [1960] (Hunter, Alan)
Geranium Kiss [1976] (Harvey, John)
German Requiem [1991] (Kerr, Philip)
■ Get Carter [APA] (Lewis, Ted)
Get Off at Babylon [1987] (Albert, Marvin H.)
Getaway Blues [1990] (Murray, William)
Getting a Way with Murder [1984] (McInerny, Ralph)
Getting Away with Murder [1995] (Engel, Howard)
Getting Up with Fleas [1987] (Murphy, Warren B.)
Ghirlandaio's Daughter [1997] (Hill, John Spencer)
Ghost Car [U.S.] (Knox, Bill)
Ghost of Major Pryor [1997] (Honig, Donald)
Ghostly Murders [1997] (Doherty, P. C.)
Ghosts [1980] (McBain, Ed)
Ghosts of Morning [1997] (Barre, Richard)
Ghosts of Saigon [1996] (Roberts, John Maddox)
Ghostway [1984] (Hillerman, Tony)
■ Gibralter Road [1960] (McCutchan, Philip)
Gift for Murder [1991] (Lake, M. D.)
Gift Horse's Mouth [1990] (Campbell, Robert)
Gilded Witch [1963] (Webb, Jack)
Gimmel Flask [1977] (Clark, Douglas)
Giotto's Hand [1995] (Pears, Iain)
Girl Hunters [1962] (Spillane, Mickey)
Girl in the Cockpit [1972] (Avallone, Michael)
Girl in the River [1975] (Miller, Victor B.)
Girl Who Ran Off With Daddy [1996] (Handler, David)
Give a Dog a Name [1992] (Hammond, Gerald)
Give the Boys a Great Big Hand [1960] (McBain, Ed)
■ Gladly the Cross-Eyed Bear [1996] (McBain, Ed)
Glancing Light [1991] (Elkins, Aaron)
Glass Highway [1983] (Estleman, Loren D.) ☆
■ Glass-Sided Ants' Nest [U.S.] (Dickinson, Peter) ★
■ Glenna Powers Case [1980] (Waugh, Hillary)
Glimpse of Death [1976] (Ormerod, Roger)
Glory Hound [1987] (Riggs, John R.)
Go for Broke [1972] (Welcome, John)
Go Gently, Gaijin [1986] (Melville, James)
■ Go West, Inspector Ghote [1981] (Keating, H. R. F.)
God Bless John Wayne [1995] (Friedman, Kinky)
God Save the Child [1974] (Parker, Robert B.)
God Squad Bod [1982] (Kenyon, Michael)
Godson [1989] (Barrett, Robert G.)
Godwin Sideboard [1984] (Malcolm, John)
■ Godwulf Manuscript [1973] (Parker, Robert B.)
Going Crazy in Public [1996] (Emerson, Earl)
■ Going Nowhere Fast [1994] (Haywood, Gar Anthony)
Going to the Dogs [1987] (Kavanagh, Dan)
Gold by Gemini [U.S.] (Gash, Jonathan)
Gold Curse [1986] (Resnicow, Herbert)
Gold Deadline [1984] (Resnicow, Herbert)
Gold Frame [1984] (Resnicow, Herbert)
Gold from Gemini [1978] (Gash, Jonathan)
Gold Gamble [1988] (Resnicow, Herbert)
Gold Medal Murder [APA] (Jenkins, Jerry)
■ Gold Solution [1983] (Resnicow, Herbert) ☆
■ Golden Rain [1980] (Clark, Douglas)
Golden Virgin [1975] (Rossiter, John)

◧ Goldenboy [1988] (Nava, Michael) ★
◧ Goldeneye [1995] (Gardner, John)
◧ Goldfish Bowl [1987] (Gough, Laurence) ★
◧ Goldilocks [1977] (McBain, Ed)
Goliath Scheme [1970] (Arden, William)
Gondola Scam [1984] (Gash, Jonathan)
Gone Fishin' [1997] (Mosley, Walter)
Gone, No Forwarding [1978] (Gores, Joe)
Gone to Earth [1990] (Boyer, Rick)
Gone to Glory [1990] (Irvine, Robert)
Gone Wild [1995] (Hall, James W.)
Good Behavior [1986] (Westlake, Donald E.)
Good Hanging and Other Stories [1992] (Rankin, Ian)
Good Life [1994] (Brady, John)☆
Good Place to Die [1975] (Copper, Basil)
Good Policeman [1990] (Charyn, Jerome)
◧ Good Sons [1996] (Constantine, K. C.)
◧ Good Year for Murder [1988] (Eddenden, A. E.)
◧ Good Year for the Roses [1988] (Timlin, Mark)
Goodnight, Sweet Prince [1986] (Hunter, Alan)
Gooseberry Fool [1974] (McClure, James)
◧ Gorky Park [1981] (Smith, Martin Cruz) ★
Gospel [1992] (James, Bill)
Gothic Pursuit [1987] (Malcolm, John)
◧ Gourmet Detective [1996] (King, Peter)
◧ Governess [1984] (Hervey, Evelyn)
◧ Government Gay [1997] (Hunter, Fred W.)
◧ Grace in Older Women [1995] (Gash, Jonathan)
Grail Murders [1993] (Clynes, Michael)
Grail Tree [1979] (Gash, Jonathan)
◧ Grand Night for Murder [1995] (Jeffers, H. Paul)
Grand Slam [1980] (Perry, Ritchie)
Grass Widow [1983] (McInerny, Ralph)
Grave Choices [1995] (Lake, M. D.)
◧ Grave Designs [APA] (Kahn, Michael)
Grave Doubts [1995] (Allegretto, Michael)
◧ Grave Error [1979] (Greenleaf, Stephen)
Grave Matters [1995] (Axler, Leo)
Gravedigger [1982] (Hansen, Joseph ☆
◧ Graveyard Shift [1965] (Higgins, Jack)
Gray Sentinels [U.S.] (Knox, Bill)
◧ Great California Game [1990] (Gash, Jonathan)
◧ Great Reminder [1993] (Irvine, Robert)
◧ Great Year for Dying [1973] (Copper, Basil)
Greek Key [1989] (Forbes, Colin)
Green Eagle Score [1967] (Stark, Richard)
Green Murder [1990] (Miles, Keith)
Green With Envy [1991] (Kennealy, Jerry)
◧ Greenfly [1987] (McCutchan, Philip)
Greenwich Apartments [1986] (Corris, Peter)
◧ Greenwich Killing Time [1986] (Friedman, Kinky)
Greta Garbo Murder Case [1992] (Baxt, George)
Grief Street [1997] (Adock, Thomas)
Grootka [1990] (Jackson, Jon A.)
Ground Money [1986] (Burns, Rex)
◧ Guild [1987] (Gorman, Ed)
Guilt [1997] (Lescroart, John T.)
Guilt Edged [1971] (Burley, W. J.)
Guilt on the Lily [1989] (Ormerod, Roger)
Guilt Without Proof [1970] (Alding, Peter)
◧ Guilty Bystander [1947] (Miller, Wade)
Gun Before Butter [1963] (Freeling, Nicolas) ★
Gun Business [1975] (Miller, Victor B.)
Gun Street Girl [1990] (Timlin, Mark)
◧ Gunner Kelly [1983] (Price, Anthony)
Gunpower [1990] (Schorr, Mark)
Gwen John Sculpture [1985] (Malcolm, John)
◧ Gypsy in Amber [1971] (Smith, Martin Cruz) ★

H

Haiku for Hanae [1989] (Melville, James)
Hail, Hail, The Gang's All Here! [1971] (McBain, Ed)
Hail to the Chief [1973] (McBain, Ed)
Half Nelson [1994] (Doolittle, Jerome)
Half Past Nun [1997] (Quill, Monica)
Half the Truth [1996] (Walker, David J.)
◧ Half-Hearted Detective [1993] (Bass, Milton R.) ☆
◧ Hallmark of Murder [1995] (Harrison, Ray)
Halo Parade [1987] (James, Bill)
Hammer of God [1974] (DeMille, Nelson)
◧ Hammerhead [1963] (Cory, Desmond)
◧ Hammerlocke [1987] (Barnao, Jack)
Handle [1966] (Stark, Richard)
Hang Loose [1982] (Copper, Basil)
Hanged Man [1993] (Satterthwait, Walter)
◧ Hanging Doll Murder [U.S.] (Ormerod, Roger)
◧ Hanging Tree [1983] (Knox, Bill)
Hanging Valley [1989] (Robinson, Peter) ☆
Hangman's Lane [1992] (Wainright, John)
Happy Are the Clean of Heart [1986] (Greeley, Andrew M.)
◧ Happy Are the Meek [1985] (Greeley, Andrew M.)
Happy Are the Merciful [1992] (Greeley, Andrew M.)
Happy Are the Oppressed [1996] (Greeley, Andrew M.)
Happy Are the Peacemakers [1993] (Greeley, Andrew M.)
Happy Are the Poor in Spirit [1994] (Greeley, Andrew M.)
Happy Are Those Who Mourn [1995] (Greeley, Andrew M.)
Happy Are Those Who Thirst for Justice [1987]
    (Greeley, Andrew M.)
Hard Bargains [1985] (Grady, James)
Hard Candy [1989] (Vachss, Andrew H.)
Hard Cash [1981] (Collins, Max Allan, Jr.)
Hard Contract [1983] (Copper, Basil)
◧ Hardcover [1985] (Warga, Wayne) ★
Hard Currency [1995] (Kaminsky, Stuart M.)
Hard Evidence [1993] (Lescroart, John T.)
Hard Frost [1995] (Wingfield, R. D.) ☆
Hard Hit [1974] (Wainright, John)
Hard Line [1982] (Lewin, Michael Z.)
Hard Look [1993] (Randisi, Robert J.)
Hard Man to Kill [U.S.] (Perry, Ritchie)
Hard News [1991] (Deaver, Jeffery)
Hard Rain [1986] (van de Wetering, Janwillem)
Hard to Handle [1964] (Welcome, John)
Hard Trade [1982] (Lyons, Arthur) ☆
Hardball [1985] (Hornig, Doug) ☆
Hardcase [1995] (Pronzini, Bill)
Harder They Hit [1987] (Kantner, Rob)
Hardknocker's Luck [1985] (Murray, William)
Hardly a Man is Now Alive [1962] (Ridgway, Jason)
Hardrock Stiff [1996] (Zigal, Thomas)
◧ HardScape [1994] (Scott, Justin)
Harm's Way [1996] (White, Stephen)
◧ Harmony in Flesh and Black [1995] (Kilmer, Nicholas)
Harpur and Iles [APA] (James, Bill)
◧ Hartinger's Mouse [1970] (McCutchan, Philip)
◧ Harvard Has a Homicide [1936] (Fuller, Timothy)
Harvest of Death [1988] (Harrison, Ray)
◧ Hatchet Job [1996] (Adams, Harold)
Hatchet Man [1976] (Marshall, William)
◧ Hatteras Blue [1989] (Poyer, David)
Haunt of the Nightingale [1988] (Riggs, John R)
Haunts [1990] (Douglas, John)
Hawk Moon [1996] (Gorman, Ed)
Hazard of Losers [1991] (Biggle, Lloyd, Jr.)
He Didn't Mind Danger [U.S.] (Gilbert, Michael)
He Done Her Wrong [1983] (Kaminsky, Stuart M.)
◧ He Who Hesitates [1965] (McBain, Ed)
◧ He Who Waits [1997] (Riggs, John R)
Head [1960] (Cory, Desmond)
Head First [1986] (Marshall, William)
Head Games [1991] (Newton, Michael)

Head Lock [1993] (Doolittle, Jerome)
Head Men [1977] (Murphy, Warren B.)
Head of State [1985] (Hoyt, Richard)
∎ Head of the Force [1978] (Barnett, James)
Healthy Way to Die [1986] (Kenyon, Michael)
Hear the Wind Blow, Dear... [1989] (Pierce, David M.)
Heartbeat [1983] (Jenkins, Jerry)
Heartbreaker [1995] (Gough, Laurence)
Hearts Ease in Death [1977] (Fraser, James)
Hearts of Stone [1992] (Timlin, Mark)
∎ Heartshot [1991] (Havill, Steven F.)
Heat [1981] (McBain, Ed)
Heat From Another Sun [1984] (Lindsey, David L.)
Heat Islands [1992] (White, Randy Wayne)
∎ Heaven Stone [1994] (Daniel, David) ★ ☆
Heaven's Prisoners [1988] (Burke, James Lee)
Heavy Iron [1987] (Copper, Basil)
Heberden's Seat [1979] (Clark, Douglas)
∎ Heckler [1960] (McBain, Ed)
Height of Day [1955] (Cory, Desmond)
Helga's Web [1970] (Cleary, Jon)
Hell Bent for Homicide [APA] (Livingston, Jack)
Hell is Where You Find It [1968] (Welcome, John)
Hell's Only Half Full [1989] (Kantner, Rob) ★
Hell-Bent for Election [1988] (Livingston, Jack)
Hellfire Papers [1995] (Wilson, Derek)
Hellspout [1976] (Knox, Bill)
Help Wanted: Orphans Preferred [1990] (Emerson, Earl)
Hemingway's Notebook [1986] (Granger, Bill)
Henry McGee Is Not Dead [1988] (Granger, Bill)
∎ Her Death of Cold [1977] (McInerny, Ralph)
∎ Here Be Monsters [1985] (Price, Anthony)
Here Comes a Hero [1968] (Block, Lawrence)
Here Comes Charlie M [U.S.] (Freemantle, Brian)
Here Lies Nancy Frail [1972] (Ross, Jonathan)
Here To Die [1971] (Sadler, Mark)
Heroin Annie [1984] (Corris, Peter)
Hidden Cause of Murder [1996] (Roe, C. F.)
Hidden City [1991] (DeBrosse, Jim)
Hidden Law [1992] (Nava, Michael) ★
Hide and Seek [1991] (Rankin, Ian)
Hiding Place [1973] (Wilcox, Collin)
∎ High Commissioner [1966] (Cleary, Jon)
High Country Murder [1995] (Trainor, J. F.)
∎ High Desert Malice [1995] (Mitchell, Kirk) ☆
High Heels [1980] (Tripp, Miles)
High Jinx [1986] (Buckley, William F.)
High Midnight [1981] (Kaminsky, Stuart M.)
High Noon at Midnight [1988] (Avallone, Michael)
High Requiem [1956] (Cory, Desmond)
High Walk [1995] (Roat, Ronald Clair)
∎ High Wall [1975] (Copper, Basil)
High-Class Kill [1973] (Wainright, John)
Higher Authority [1994] (White, Stephen)
Highly Explosive Case [1982] (Chambers, Peter)
Highwayman and Mr. Dickens [1992] (Palmer, William J.)
Hilary [1980] (Jenkins, Jerry)
Hip-Deep in Alligators [1987] (Campbell, Robert)
∎ Hire a Hangman [1991] (Wilcox, Collin)
Hit and Run [1998] (Newman, Christopher)
Hit on the House [1993] (Jackson, Jon A.)
∎ HOG Murders [1979] (DeAndrea, William)
Holiday with a Vengeance [1974] (Perry, Ritchie)
∎ Hollow-Eyed Angel [1996] (van de Wetering, Janwillem)
Hollywood Heroes [1986] (Caine, Hamilton)
Holy of Holies [1981] (Williams, Alan)
∎ Holy Terror [1975] (Murphy, Warren B.)
∎ Holy Treasure! [1989] (Williams, David)
∎ Home to Roost [1990] (Hammond, Gerald)
Homecoming for Murder [1995] (Armistead, John)
Homicide is My Game [1959] (Marlowe, Stephen)

Honfleur Decision [1980] (Hunter, Alan)
Honor Farm [1996] (Westermann, John)
Honourable Schoolboy [1977] (Le Carré, John) ★
Hoodwink [1981] (Pronzini, Bill) ★
Hoof [1983] (McCutchan, Philip)
Hook [1984] (Copper, Basil)
Hook or Crook [1994] (Hammond, Gerald)
Hope [1995] (Deighton, Len)
Hope To Die [1948] (Waugh, Hillary)
Horizontal Hold [1978] (Irvine, Robert)
∎ Horrible Man [1968] (Avallone, Michael)
Horse Under Water [1963] (Deighton, Len)
Hosanna Shout [1994] (Irvine, Robert)
∎ Hostile Intent [1993] (Egleton, Clive)
∎ Hostile Witness [1995] (Lashner, William)
Hot [1992] (Lutz, John)
Hot Air [1991] (Breen, Jon)
Hot Body [1973] (Avallone, Michael)
Hot Money Caper [1992] (Chambers, Peter)
Hot Place [1990] (Resnicow, Herbert)
∎ Hot Rock [1970] (Westlake, Donald E.) ☆
Hot Shots [1989] (Gough, Laurence) ★☆
Hot Summer, Cold Murder [1987] (Dold, Gaylord)
Hot Tickets [1987] (Rider, J. W.)
∎ Hotel Detective [1994] (Russell, Alan)
Hour of the Donkey [1980] (Price, Anthony)
∎ Hour of the Manatee [1994] (Ayres, E. C.) ★
House of Crows [1995] (Harding, Paul)
House of Guilt [1996] (Rosenberg, Robert)
House of the Red Slayer [1992] (Harding, Paul)
House of the Vestals [1997] (Saylor, Steven)
House That Jack Built [1988] (McBain, Ed)
House-Dick [1988] (Copper, Basil)
Hovering of Vultures [1993] (Barnard, Robert)
∎ Hovey's Deception [1986] (Ross, Philip)
How Town [1990] (Nava, Michael) ★
Howard Hughes Affair [1979] (Kaminsky, Stuart M.)
Hoydens and Mr. Dickens [1997] (Palmer, William J.)
Humphrey Bogart Murder Case [1995] (Baxt, George)
Hung Over [1994] (Malcolm, John)
Hung Up to Die [1976] (Meyers, Martin)
∎ Hunt for Red October [1984] (Clancy, Tom)
∎ Hunter [1985] (Busby, Roger)
∎ Hunter [1983] (Sauter, Eric)☆
∎ Hunter [1962] (Stark, Richard)
Hunter and the Ikon [1984] (Sauter, Eric)
Hunter and the Raven [1984] (Sauter, Eric)
Hunter Killer [1966] (Jenkins, Geoffrey)
Hunting a Detroit Tiger [1997] (Soos, Troy)
∎ Hunting Season [1985] (Mayo, J. K.)
Hush Money [1981] (Collins, Max Allan, Jr.)
Hyde [1997] (Mahoney, Dan)
Hyde Park Murder [1985] (Roosevelt, Elliott)

I

I Know What It's Like to Die [1976] (Ross, Jonathan)
I, Lucifer [1967] (O'Donnell, Peter)
I Remember You [1993] (Edwards, Martin)
"I!" Said the Demon [1969] (Baxt, George)
∎ I, the Jury [1947] (Spillane, Mickey)
I'll Do Anything [1960] (Bateson, David)
I'll Go Anywhere [1959] (Bateson, David)
I'm Getting Killed Right Here [1991] (Murray, William)
Ice [1983] (McBain, Ed)
Ice Blues [1986] (Stevenson, Richard)
Ice for the Eskimo [1986] (Philbrick, W. R.)
∎ Ice Pick Artist [1997] (Adams, Harold)
Iceberg [1975] (Cussler, Clive)
Icebreaker [1983] (Gardner, John)
Iceman [1990] (Miller, Rex)
∎ Icewater Mansions [1995] (Allyn, Doug)

🔢 Iciest Sin [1990] (Keating, H. R. F.)
Icy Clutches [1990] (Elkins, Aaron)
Idle Gossip [1997] (Finkelstein, Jay)
🔢 If I Live to Dine [APA] (Waugh, Hillary)
🔢 If Wishes Were Horses... [1996] (Hemlin, Tim)
Illegal Motion [1996] (Stockley, Grif)
Illusions [1997] (Pronzini, Bill)
Image to Die For [1997] (Phillips, Mike)
Immaculate Deception [1991] (Adler, Warren)
Immoral Certainty [1991] (Tanenbaum, Robert K.)
🔢 Impact [1975] (Copper, Basil)
Impossible Virgin [1971] (O'Donnell, Peter)
In a Pig's Eye [1991] (Campbell, Robert)
In at the Kill [U.S.] (Knox, Bill)
🔢 In Camera [1991] (Hammond, Gerald)
In Defense of Judges [1990] (Gray, A. W.)
In Enemy Hands [1977] (Murphy, Warren B.)
In Good Hands [1994] (James, Bill)
In Justice's Prison [1985] (Thurston, Robert)
🔢 In La-La Land We Trust [1986] (Campbell, Robert) ☆
🔢 In Self Defense [1996] (Gregory, Sarah)
🔢 In the Drift [1995] (Milan, Borto)
In the Electric Mist with Confederate Dead [1993]
    (Burke, James Lee)
In the House of Secret Enemies [1990] (Chesbro, George)
In the Lake of the Moon [1988] (Lindsey, David L.) ☆
In the Midst of Death [1976] (Block, Lawrence)
In the Shadow of the Arch [1997] (Randisi, Robert J.)
🔢 Inca Gold [1994] (Cussler, Clive)
🔢 Inches [1994] (Marshall, William)
Incident at Blood Tide [1993] (Chesbro, George)
Incident in Iceland [1979] (MacLeod, Robert)
Incinerator [1992] (Hallinan, Timothy)
🔢 India Exhibition [1992] (Conroy, Richard Timothy)
Indictment [1994] (Reed, Barry)
Indigo Slam [1997] (Crais, Robert)
Infant of Prague [1987] (Granger, Bill)
🔢 Infernal Device [1979] (Kurland, Michael) ☆
Infiltrator [1971] (York, Andrew)
Infiltrators [1984] (Hamilton, Donald)
🔢 Infinite Number of Monkeys [1987] (Roberts, Les) ★ ☆
Innocence That Kills [1994] (Levitsky, Ronald)
Innocent Graves [1996] (Robinson, Peter)
🔢 Innocents [1995] (Barre, Richard) ★ ☆
Inscrutable Charlie Muffin [1979] (Freemantle, Brian)
Inside Man [1969] (Johnson, E. Richard)
Inspector Ghote Breaks an Egg [1970] (Keating, H. R. F.)
Inspector Ghote Caught in Meshes [1967]
    (Keating, H. R. F.)
Inspector Ghote Draws a Line [1979] (Keating, H. R. F.)
Inspector Ghote Goes by Train [1971] (Keating, H. R. F.)
Inspector Ghote, His Life and Crimes [1989] (Keating, H. R. F.)
Inspector Ghote Hunts the Peacock [1968] (Keating, H. R. F.)
Inspector Ghote Plays a Joker [1969] (Keating, H. R. F.)
Inspector Ghote Trusts the Heart [1972] (Keating, H. R. F.)
Inspector Ghote's Good Crusade [1966] (Keating, H. R. F.)
Instant Replay [1989] (Everson, David H.)
🔢 Intent to Harm [1995] (Washburn, Stan)
Intercom Conspiracy [1969] (Ambler, Eric)
🔢 Interface for Murder [1987] (Biggle, Lloyd, Jr.)
Interface Man [1989] (Knox, Bill)
Interloper [1996] (Mayo, J. K.)
🔢 Interlopers [1969] (Hamilton, Donald)
🔢 Internal Affairs [1990] (Oster, Jerry)
🔢 Intimidators [1974] (Hamilton, Donald)
Into Battle [1997] (Gilbert, Michael)
🔢 Into the Blue [1990] (Goddard, Robert)
Into the Fire [1994] (Wiltse, David)
Into the Same River Twice [1996] (Nevins, Francis M., Jr.)
Into the Valley of Death [1986] (Hervey, Evelyn)
🔢 Into the Vortex [1996] (Malcolm, John)
Into Thin Air [1996] (Washburn, Stan)

🔢 Into Thin Air [1995] (Zigal, Thomas)
Intrigue [1954] (Cory, Desmond)
🔢 Intriguers [1972] (Hamilton, Donald)
Invasion of Privacy [1996] (Healy, Jeremiah)
🔢 Investigations Are Proceeding [1961] (Ashford, Jeffrey)
Invitation to a Dynamite Party [1974] (Lovesey, Peter)
Invitation to a Funeral [1963] (Harknett, Terry)
🔢 Ipcress File [1962] (Deighton, Len)
🔢 Irish Gold [1994] (Greeley, Andrew M.)
Irish Lace [1996] (Greeley, Andrew M.)
🔢 Irishman's Horse [1991] (Collins, Michael)
Iron Glove [1992] (Tierney, Ronald)
Iron Sanctuary [U.S.] (MacLeod, Robert)
Irresistible Impulse [1997] (Tannenbaum, Robert K.)
Isle of Dragons [1967] (MacLeod, Robert)
It Wasn't Me! [1961] (Jeffries, Ian)
🔢 It's Murder, Senorita [1954] (Bateson, David)
It's Not a Pretty Sight [1996] (Haywood, Gar Anthony)
Italian Assets [1976] (Butler, Richard)

J

🔢 J for Jupiter [Brit.] (Fuller, Timothy)
Jack and Jill [1996] (Patterson, James)
Jack and the Beanstalk [1984] (McBain, Ed)
Jack Carter and the Law [APA] (Lewis, Ted)
Jack Carter and the Mafia Pigeon [1977] (Lewis, Ted)
Jack Carter's Law [1974] (Lewis, Ted)
🔢 Jack's Return Home [1970] (Lewis, Ted)
Jackpot! [1995] (Hunter, Alan)
🔢 Jackpot [1990] (Pronzini, Bill)
🔢 Jade Figurine [1972] (Foxx, Jack)
Jade in Aries [1971] (Coe, Tucker)
🔢 Jade Woman [1988] (Gash, Jonathan)
Jaded [1996] (Gaitano, Nick)
Jagged Steele [1990] (Masters, J. D.)
Jail Bait [1983] (Chambers, Peter)
Jamaica Kill [1989] (Philbin, Tom)
Janell [1983] (Jenkins, Jerry)
🔢 January Corpse [1991] (Albert, Neil) ☆
January Zone [1987] (Corris, Peter)
Janus Man [1988] (Forbes, Colin)
Japanese Corpse [1977] (van de Wetering, Janwillem)
Japanese Game [1995] (Hoyt, Richard)
Japanese Job [1992] (Corris, Peter)
Jaws of the Watchdog [1973] (Drummond, Ivor)
🔢 Jeopardy is My Job [1962] (Marlowe, Stephen)
🔢 Jersey Tomatoes [1986] (Rider, J. W.) ★
Jet-Lag [1986] (Copper, Basil)
Jewel That Was Ours [1991] (Dexter, Colin)
Jewelled Eye [1985] (Clark, Douglas)
Jigsaw [1970] (McBain, Ed)
Jigsaw [1992] (Newton, Michael)
🔢 Jigsaw [APA] (Waugh, Hillary)
Jimmy the Kid [1974] (Westlake, Donald E.)
Joey's Case [1988] (Constantine, K. C.) ☆
Johnny Goes East [1958] (Cory, Desmond)
Johnny Goes North [1956] (Cory, Desmond)
Johnny Goes South [1959] (Cory, Desmond)
Johnny Goes West [1959] (Cory, Desmond)
Joker in the Deck [1964] (Prather, Richard)
Jordon's Showdown [1993] (Strunk, Frank C.)
🔢 Jordon's Wager [1991] (Strunk, Frank C.)
🔢 Joshua Sequence [1986] (Huebner, Frederick D.)
Judas Factor [1984] (Allbeury, Ted)
Judas Goat [1966] (Cleeve, Brian)
Judas Goat [1978] (Parker, Robert B.)
Judas Mandate [1972] (Egleton, Clive)
🔢 Judas Pair [1977] (Gash, Jonathan) ★
🔢 Judas Priest [1991] (McInerny, Ralph)
Judas Sheep [1996] (Pawson, Stuart)
Judge [1995] (Martini, Steve)
Judgement of Death [1989] (Biderman, Bob)

■ Judges of Hades [1971] (Hoch, Edward D.)
Judgment by Fire [1988] (Huebner, Frederick D.)☆
■ Judgment Day [1974] (Murphy, Warren B.)
Jugger [1965] (Stark, Richard)
■ Jump [1995] (Lupica, Mike)
■ Jump Cut [1974] (Irvine, Robert)☆
Jungle of Steel and Stone [1988] (Chesbro, George)
Junkyard Angel [1977] (Harvey, John)
■ Junkyard Dog [1986] (Campbell, Robert) ★★
Juror [1990] (Hall, Parnell)
■ Just a Corpse at Twilight [1994]
(van de Wetering, Janwillem) ☆
Just a Shot Away [1987] (Grady, James)
■ Just Another Angel [1988] (Ripley, Mike)
Just Desserts [1977] (Heald, Tim)
Just Desserts [1980] (Jeffries, Roderic)
Justice Denied [1994] (Tanenbaum, Robert K.)
Justice on the Rocks [1967] (Knox, Bill)

K

Kaddish in Dublin [1990] (Brady, John)
Kaleidoscope [1993] (Janes, J. Robert)
Karlyn [1980] (Jenkins, Jerry)
Keep Cool, Mr. Jones [1950] (Fuller, Timothy)
Kennedy for the Defense [1980] (Higgins, George V.)
Key Without a Door [1988] (Lejeune, Anthony)
Keys of Hell [1965] (Fallon, Martin)
■ Kickback [1991] (Disher, Garry)
Kiet and the Golden Peacock [1989] (Alexander, Gary)
Kiet and the Opium War [1990] (Alexander, Gary)
Kiet Goes West [1992] (Alexander, Gary)
Kill and Tell [1984] (Kienzle, William X.)
Kill Her—You'll Like It [1973] (Avallone, Michael)
■ Kill Him Quickly, It's Raining [1966] (Brett, Michael)
Kill Him Twice [1965] (Prather, Richard)
■ Kill Me Again [1994] (Bishop, Paul)
■ Kill Me Again [1996] (Faherty, Terence)
Kill Me Tomorrow [1969] (Prather, Richard)
Kill or Cure [1973] (Murphy, Warren B.)
Kill Story [1995] (Doolittle, Jerome)
Kill the Butler [1991] (Kenyon, Michael)
Kill the Clown [1962] (Prather, Richard)
Kill Your Darlings [1984] (Collins, Max Allan, Jr.)
■ Kill Zone [1984] (Estleman, Loren D.)
Killed in Fringe Time [1995] (DeAndrea, William L.)
Killed in Paradise [1988] (DeAndrea, William L.)
Killed in the Act [1981] (DeAndrea, William L.)
Killed in the Fog [1996] (DeAndrea, William L.)
■ Killed in the Ratings [1978] (DeAndrea, William L.) ★
Killed on the Ice [1984] (DeAndrea, William L.)
Killed on the Rocks [1990] (DeAndrea, William L.)
Killed with a Passion [1983] (DeAndrea, William L.)
Killer [1997] (Newman, Christopher)
Killer Chromosomes [1978] (Murphy, Warren B.)
Killer for a Song [1975] (Gardner, John)
■ Killer Instinct [1992] (Walker, Robert W.)
Killer on Argyle Street [1995] (Raleigh, Michael)
Killer on the Keys [1973] (Avallone, Michael)
Killer Steele [1990] (Masters, J. D.)
Killer's Choice [1957] (McBain, Ed)
Killer's Highway [Brit.] (Avallone, Michael)
Killer's Payoff [1958] (McBain, Ed)
Killer's Wedge [1958] (McBain, Ed)
Killers [1994] (Gough, Laurence)
Killers are My Meat [1957] (Marlowe, Stephen)
Killing Cold [Brit.] (Wood, Ted)
Killing Floor [1976] (Lyons, Arthur)
Killing Floor [1995] (Turnbull, Peter)
Killing Frost [1995] (Riggs, John R.)
Killing Game [U.S.] (Knox, Bill)
■ Killing in Antiques [1981] (Knox, Bill)
Killing in Gold [1978] (Hensley, Joe L.)

Killing in Malta [1972] (MacLeod, Robert)
Killing in Moscow [1994] (Egleton, Clive)
Killing in Real Estate [1988] (Orenstein, Frank)
Killing Kindness [1980] (Hill, Reginald)
Killing Machine [1964] (Vance, Jack)
■ Killing Man [1989] (Spillane, Mickey) ☆
■ Killing Me Softly [1994] (Leslie, John)
Killing of Sally Keemer [1996] (Lee, Christopher)
Killing the Lawyers [1997] (Hill, Reginald)
Killing Time [1982] (Murphy, Warren B.)
Killing Zone [1988] (Burns, Rex)
Killings [1993] (Gray, A. W.)
Kimberly Killing [1988] (Corris, Peter)
Kimono for a Corpse [1987] (Melville, James)
■ Kind of Homecoming [1994] (McEldowney, Eugene)
Kind of Transaction [1991] (Lewis, Roy)
Kinderkill [1989] (Harper, Richard)
■ Kinds of Love, Kinds of Death [1966] (Coe, Tucker)
King of the Nightcap [1989] (Murray, William)
King of the Rainy Country [1966] (Freeling, Nicolas) ★
King's Curse [1976] (Murphy, Warren B.)
King's Ransom [1959] (McBain, Ed)
Kingfisher [1995] (Keegan, Alex)
Kiss [1988] (Lutz, John) ★
Kiss [1992] (McBain, Ed)
■ Kiss and Tell [1975] (Meyers, Martin)
Kiss Me, Deadly [1952] (Spillane, Mickey)
Kiss the Girls [1995] (Patterson, James)
Klondyker [1968] (Knox, Bill)
Knaves Templar [1991] (Tourney, Leonard)
Knight Fall [U.S.] (Payne, Lawrence)
Knock-Off [1989] (Newman, Christopher)
■ Knots and Crosses [1987] (Rankin, Ian)
Knotted Strings [1995] (Page, Jake)
■ Kolwezi [1985] (Perry, Ritchie)
Kubla Khan Caper [1966] (Prather, Richard)
■ Kyril [1981] (Trenhaile, John)

L

Labyrinth [1980] (Pronzini, Bill)
■ Labyrinth Makers [1970] (Price, Anthony) ★
Ladies of the Vale [1994] (Puckett, Andrew)
Lady in Cement [1961] (Rome, Anthony)
Lady Killer [1958] (McBain, Ed)
■ Lady, Lady, I Did It! [1961] (McBain, Ed)
Lady Lost [1953] (Cory, Desmond)
Lady Macbeth [1988] (Freeling, Nicolas)
Lady, This is Murder [1963] (Chambers, Peter)
Lady Who Never Was [1981] (Chambers, Peter)
Lady Yesterday [1987] (Estleman, Loren D.) ☆
Lady, You're Killing Me [1979] (Chambers, Peter)
Laid Dead [1990] (Cork, Barry)
■ Laidlaw [1977] (McIlvanney, William) ★ ☆
Lake Effect [1996] (Jaspersohn, William)
Lake Effect [1994] (Roberts, Les) ☆
Lake Isle [1976] (Freeling, Nicolas)
Lake of Fury [1966] (MacLeod, Robert)
Land Fall [1992] (Gibbs, Tony)
Landed Gently [1957] (Hunter, Alan)
■ Landscape with Violence [1975] (Wainright, John)
Language of Cannibals [1990] (Chesbro, George)
■ Lasko Tangent [1979] (Patterson, Richard North) ★
Last Alchemist [1986] (Murphy, Warren B.)
Last Breath [Brit.] (Masur, Harold Q.)
■ Last Bus to Woodstock [1975] (Dexter, Colin)
Last Call [1978] (Murphy, Warren B.)
■ Last Castrato [1995] (Hill, John Spencer)
Last Client of Luis Montez [1996] (Ramos, Manuel)
Last Coyote [1995] (Connelly, Michael)☆☆☆
Last Dance in Redondo Beach [1989] (Katz, Michael J.)
Last Day in Limbo [1976] (O'Donnell, Peter)

■ Last Detective [1991] (Lovesey, Peter) ★
Last Drop [1983] (Murphy, Warren B.)
Last Gamble [1958] (Masur, Harold Q.)
■ Last Good German [1991] (Granger, Bill)
■ Last Good Kiss [1978] (Crumley, James)
Last Housewife [1995] (Katz, Jon)
Last Judgment [1994] (Pears, Iain)
■ Last Laugh [1984] (Riggs, John R)
Last Post for a Partisan [1971] (Egleton, Clive)
■ Last Private Eye [1988] (Birkett, John) ☆
Last Reminder [1997] (Pawson, Stuart)
■ Last Rights [1986] (Douglas, Arthur)
Last Rites [1998] (Harvey, John)
Last Seen Alive [1987] (Duncan, W. Glenn)
■ Last Seen Breathing [1994] (Williams, David)
Last Seen Wearing [1976] (Dexter, Colin)
Last Smile [1988] (Albert, Marvin H.)
■ Last Templar [1995] (Jecks, Michael)
Last Temple [1977] (Murphy, Warren B.)
■ Last War Dance [1974] (Murphy, Warren B.)
■ Late Candidate [1990] (Phillips, Mike) ★
Late Knight [1987] (Payne, Laurence)
Late Mrs. D [1962] (Waugh, Hillary)
Late Payments [1986] (Lewin, Michael Z.)
■ Latimer Mercy [1985] (Richardson, Robert) ★
Laughing Dog [1988] (Lochte, Dick)
Laughing Hangman [1996] (Marston, Edward)
Law and Ardor [1995] (McInerny, Ralph)
Lawyer's Tale [1992] (Kincaid, D.)
Layers of Deceit [1985] (Jeffries, Roderic)
■ Leaf Boats [1991] (Fink, John)
League of Terror [1990] (Granger, Bill)
Leaning Land [1997] (Burns, Rex)
Leave it to the Hangman [1960] (Knox, Bill)
Left for Dead [1972] [1995] (Engleman, Paul)
Legacy from Tenarife [1984] (MacLeod, Robert)
Legacy Lenders [1967] (Masur, Harold Q.)
■ Legacy of Vengeance [1994] (Armistead, John)
■ Legend of the Dead [1995] (Hackler, Micah S.)
Legion [1983] (Blatty, William Peter)
Legislative Body [1972] (Hensley, Joe L.)
Lemon Chicken Jones [1994] (Roberts, Les)
Lemons Never Lie [1971] (Stark, Richard)
Les Norton's Back In and de Fun Don't Done [1993]
    (Barrett, Robert G.)
■ Lesko's Ghost [Brit.] (Maxim, John)
Less Than Meets the Eye [1994] (Berlinski, David)
Lestrade and the Brother of Death [1988] (Trow, M. J.)
Lestrade and the Dead Man's Hand [1992] (Trow, M. J.)
Lestrade and the Deadly Game [1990] (Trow, M. J.)
■ Lestrade and the Devil's Own [1996] (Trow, M. J.)
Lestrade and the Gift of the Prince [1991] (Trow, M. J.)
Lestrade and the Guardian Angel [1990] (Trow, M. J.)
Lestrade and the Hallowed House [1987] (Trow, M. J.)
■ Lestrade and the Kiss of Horus [1995] (Trow, M. J.)
Lestrade and the Leviathan [1987] (Trow, M. J.)
Lestrade and the Magpie [1991] (Trow, M. J.)
■ Lestrade and the Mirror of Murder [1993] (Trow, M. J.)
Lestrade and the Ripper [1988] (Trow, M. J.)
■ Lestrade and the Sawdust Ring [1993] (Trow, M. J.)
■ Lestrade and the Sign of Nine [1992] (Trow, M. J.)
Let It Bleed [1995] (Rankin, Ian)
Let Sleeping Dogs Lie [1976] (Heald, Tim)
Let Sleeping Dogs Lie [1985] (Riggs, John R.)
■ Let Us Prey [1990] (Hammond, Gerald)
Let Us Prey [1982] (Quill, Monica)
■ Let's Get Criminal [1996] (Raphael, Lev)
Let's Hear It for the Deaf Man [1972] (McBain, Ed)
Lethal Involvement [1995] (Egleton, Clive)
Lethal Partner [1996] (Page, Jake)
Liar's Poker [1993] (McConnell, Frank)
Libertines [1978] (Clark, Douglas)
■ Licence Renewed [1981] (Gardner, John)

Lie a Little, Die a Little [1968] (Brett, Michael)
Lieberman's Choice [1993] (Kaminsky, Stuart M.)
Lieberman's Day [1995] (Kaminsky, Stuart M.)
■ Lieberman's Folly [1990] (Kaminsky, Stuart M.)
Lieberman's Law [1996] (Kaminsky, Stuart M.)
Lieberman's Thief [1995] (Kaminsky, Stuart M.)
■ Lies of Fair Ladies [1991] (Gash, Jonathan)
Life's Work [1986] (Valin, Jonathan)
Lifeline [1996] (Boyle, Gerry)
Light at Midnight [1995] (Ardin, William)
■ Light of Day [1962] (Ambler, Eric) ★★
Lightning [1996] (Lutz, John)
Lightning [1984] (McBain, Ed)
Like a Lamb to the Slaughter [1984] (Block, Lawrence)
■ Like Love [1962] (McBain, Ed)
■ Lime Pit [1980] (Valin, Jonathan)
Limited Partner [1990] (Lupica, Mike)
Limited Vision [1983] (Lewis, Roy)
Lion's Share [1996] (Campbell, Robert)
Lindsey [1983] (Jenkins, Jerry)
Line of Succession [1988] (Murphy, Warren B.)
Lingering Doubt [1993] (Downing, Warwick)
Lions of the North [1996] (Marston, Edward)
Liquid Desires [1993] (Sklepowich, Edward)
■ Liquidator [1964] (Gardner, John)
■ List of 7 [1993] (Frost, Mark) ☆
■ Listen for the Click [1983] (Breen, Jon)
Listening Woman [1978] (Hillerman, Tony) ☆
Little Angel Street [1994] (Charyn, Jerome)
Little Boy Blue [1997] (Dee, Ed)
■ Little Death [1986] (Nava, Michael)
Little Dog Laughed [1986] (Hansen, Joseph)
Little Drops of Blood [1962] (Knox, Bill)
Little Miss Murder [1971] (Avallone, Michael)
Little Use for Death [1992] (Sherer, Michael W.)
Little Yellow Dog [1996] (Mosley, Walter)
■ Live Bait [1978] (Knox, Bill)
Live Bait [1985] (Wood, Ted)
Live from New York [1993] (Belsky, Dick)
Live to Regret [1992] (Faherty, Terence)
■ Living Bomb [1963] (Avallone, Michael)
Living Proof [1995] (Harvey, John)
Lizard in the Cup [1972] (Dickinson, Peter)
■ Local Knowledge [1995] (Daly, Conor)
Lockestep [1988] (Barnao, Jack)
Logan File [1991] (McCutchan, Philip)
Lolita Man [1986] (James, Bill)
London Blood [1997] (Hall, Robert Lee)
London Match [1985] (Deighton, Len)
■ Lonely Hearts [1989] (Harvey, John)
■ Lonely Hunter [1969] (Wilcox, Collin)
Lonely Place [1976] (Copper, Basil)
■ Lonely Street [1994] (Brewer, Steve)
Lonely Way to Die [1980] (Bourgeau, Art)
Long Day Monday [1993] (Turnbull, Peter)
■ Long Line of Dead Men [1994] (Block, Lawrence) ☆☆
Long Reach [1997] (Stone, Michael)
Long Rest [1981] (Copper, Basil)
■ Long Run South [1962] (Williams, Alan)
Long Shadows in Victory [1996] (Bean, Gregory)
Long Silence [1972] (Freeling, Nicolas)
Long Teeth [1987] (Albert, Marvin H.)
Long Time Dead [1981] (Chambers, Peter)
Long Time No See [1977] (McBain, Ed)
Long Walk Up the Waterslide [1995] (Winslow, Don)
Long Way Down [1974] (Wilcox, Collin)
■ Long-Legged Fly [1992] (Sallis, James) ☆
■ Longest Pleasure [1981] (Clark, Douglas)
Look Into My Eyes [1986] (Murphy, Warren B.)
Look Out for Space [1985] (Nolan, William F.)
Looking for Rachel Wallace [1980] (Parker, Robert B.)
Looking Glass War [1965] (Le Carré, John)
Loose Lips [1990] (Breen, Jon)

Lords of the Earth [1985] (Murphy, Warren B.)
Loss of Patients [1982] (McInerny, Ralph)
Lost Coast [1997] (Simon, Roger L.)
■ Lost Daughter [1988] (Cormany, Michael) ☆
■ Lost Honor [1995] (Mullen, Jack)
Lost Keats [1993] (Faherty, Terence)
Lost Yesterday [1986] (Murphy, Warren B.)
■ Loud Adios [1991] (Kuhlken, Ken) ★
Louisiana Blue [1994] (Poyer, David)
Louisiana Fever [1996] (Donaldson, D. J.)
Love For Sale [1997] (Leslie, John)
■ Love in Amsterdam [1962] (Freeling, Nicolas)
Love of Gods [1997] (Hunter, Alan)
Love Song of J. Edgar Hoover [1996] (Friedman, Kinky)
■ Love That Kills [1991] (Levitsky, Ronald)
Love You to Death [1992] (Michaels, Grant)
Lovely Ladies [U.S.] (Freeling, Nicolas)
Lover of the Grave [1997] (Taylor, Andrew)
■ Lover Too Many [1969] (Lewis, Roy)
Loverboy [1997] (Belsky, Dick)
■ Lover Man [1987] (Murphy, Dallas) ☆
Low Angles [1986] (Stinson, Jim)
■ Low End of Nowhere [1996] (Stone, Michael)
Low Treason [1983] (Tourney, Leonard)
Lucifer's Weekend [1982] (Murphy, Warren B.)
Lullaby [1989] (McBain, Ed)
Lullaby Town [1992] (Crais, Robert) ☆
Lush Life [1993] (Murphy, Dallas)
■ Lust is No Lady [1964] (Avallone, Michael)
■ Lydia [1964] (Cunningham, E. V.)
Lying Three [1979] (McInerny, Ralph)
Lynch Town [1974] (Murphy, Warren B.)
■ Lyssa [1984] (Jenkins, Jerry)

M

■ MacAllister [1984] (Perry, Ritchie)
Mad Courtesan [1992] (Marston, Edward)
Mad Dogs and Scotsmen [1995] (Hammond, Gerald)
Mad Hatter's Holiday [1973] (Lovesey, Peter)
■ Madam Will Not Dine Tonight [1947] (Waugh, Hillary)
Made in Detroit [1990] (Kantner, Rob) ☆
Madman's Whisper [1958] (Grayson, Richard)
Madrid Underground [1982] (Serafin, David)
Madrigal [1967] (Gardner, John)
Madrigal for Charlie Muffin [1981] (Freemantle, Brian)
Mae West Murder Case [1993] (Baxt, George)
Maestro [1993] (Gardner, John)
Mafia Fix [1972] (Murphy, Warren B.)
■ Mahjong Spies [1986] (Trenhaile, John)
Maine Massacre [1979] (van de Wetering, Janwillem)
Major Enquiry [1976] (Henderson, Laurence)
Make a Killing [1964] (Masur, Harold Q.)
Make Me Rich [1985] (Corris, Peter)
Make No Bones [1991] (Elkins, Aaron)
Make Out With Murder [1974] (Block, Lawrence)
■ Making the Cut [1995] (Lusby, Jim)
Malcontenta [1995] (Maitland, Barry) ★
Malice in Camera [1983] (Payne, Laurence)
Malice Intended [1997] (Handberg, Ron)
Mall Rats [1992] (Robinson, Kevin)
Mamur Zapt and the Camel of Destruction [1993]
  (Pearce, Michael)
Mamur Zapt and the Donkey-Vous [1990] (Pearce, Michael)
Mamur Zapt and the Fig Tree Murder [1996] (Pearce, Michael)
Mamur Zapt and the Girl in the Nile [1992] (Pearce, Michael)
Mamur Zapt and the Men Behind [1991] (Pearce, Michael)
Mamur Zapt and the Night of the Dog [1989] (Pearce, Michael)
■ Mamur Zapt and the Return of the Carpet [1988]
  (Pearce, Michael)
Mamur Zapt and the Snake Catcher's Daughter [1994]
  (Pearce, Michael)
Mamur Zapt and the Spoils of Egypt [1993]
  (Pearce, Michael) ★

Man at the Wheel [U.S.] (Kenyon, Michael)
■ Man Called Kyril [U.S.] (Trenhaile, John)
■ Man Condemned [1981] (Alding, Peter)
Man Everybody Was Afraid Of [1978] (Hansen, Joseph)
Man from Barbarossa [1991] (Gardner, John)
Man from Moscow [1963] (McCutchan, Philip)
Man from the Rock [1955] (Bateson, David)
Man in the Bottle [1963] (Knox, Bill)
■ Man in the Gray Flannel Shroud [1984] (Orenstein, Frank)
Man in the Shadows [1988] (Corris, Peter)
Man of Gold [1985] (Hervey, Evelyn)
Man Trap [1996] (Hunt, Richard)
Man Who Cancelled Himself [1995] (Handler, David)
Man Who Changed His Name [1986] (Wright, Eric)
Man Who Did Not Die [1964] (Harknett, Terry)
■ Man Who Died Laughing [1988] (Handler, David)
Man Who Heard Too Much [1989] (Granger, Bill)
Man Who Invented Florida [1994] (White, Randy Wayne)
■ Man Who Killed His Brother [1980] (Stephens, Reed)
Man Who Liked Slow Tomatoes [1982] (Constantine, K. C.)
Man Who Liked to Look at Himself [1973] (Constantine, K. C.)
Man Who Lived By Night [1989] (Handler, David)
■ Man Who Loved God [1997] (Kienzle, William X.)
Man Who Loved Women to Death [1997] (Handler, David)
Man Who Met the Train [1988] (Adams, Harold)
Man Who Missed the Party [1989] (Adams, Harold)
Man Who Murdered Himself [1994] (Fliegel, Richard)
Man Who Risked His Partner [1984] (Stephens, Reed) ☆
Man Who Shot Lewis Vance [1986] (Kaminsky, Stuart M.)
Man Who Tried to Get Away [1990] (Stephens, Reed)
Man Who Walked Like a Bear [1990] (Kaminsky, Stuart M.)
Man Who Was Taller Than God [1992] (Adams, Harold) ★
Man Who Wasn't There [1989] (Wainright, John)
Man Who Would Be F. Scott Fitzgerald [1990]
  (Handler, David) ★
Man With a Squirrel [1996] (Kilmer, Nicholas)
Man With My Cat [1997] (Engleman, Paul)
Man With My Name [1993] (Engleman, Paul)
Man With No Time [1993] (Hallinan, Timothy)
Man With the Getaway Face [1963] (Stark, Richard)
■ Man With the Tiny Head [1969] (Drummond, Ivor)
■ Man's Illegal Life [1984] (Heller, Keith)
Man's Loving Family [1985] (Heller, Keith)
Man's Storm [1985] (Heller, Keith)
■ Manhattan is My Beat [1989] (Deaver, Jeffery) ☆
■ Manhunt is My Mission [1961] (Marlowe, Stephen)
■ Manila Bay [1986] (Marshall, William)
Manipulators [1973] (Rossiter, John)
Mankiller [1980] (Wilcox, Collin)
Mannequin [1994] (Janes, J. Robert)
Manuscript Murders [1981] (Lewis, Roy H.)
Manx Murders [1994] (DeAndrea, William)
Marble Orchard [1969] (Copper, Basil)
Marble Orchard [1996] (Nolan, William)
■ March Violets [1989] (Kerr, Philip)
Marco Polo, If You Can [1982] (Buckley, William F.)
Margie [1966] (Cunningham, E. V.)
■ Margo [1979] (Jenkins, Jerry)
■ Margo's Reunion [1984] (Jenkins, Jerry)
Maria's Girls [1992] (Charyn, Jerome)
Marilyn the Wild [1976] (Charyn, Jerome)
Marimba [1992] (Hoyt, Richard)
Marine Corpse [1986] (Tapply, William G.)
Mark of the Shadow [1966] (Grant, Maxwell)
Marked for Destruction [1982] (Barnett, James)
Marked for Murder [1988] (Kienzle, William X.)
Marked for Murder [Brit.] (Miller, Victor B.)
Marlene Dietrich Murder Case [1993] (Baxt, George)
Marvellous Boy [1982] (Corris, Peter)
■ Marx Sisters [1994] (Maitland, Barry) ☆
Mary, Mary [1993] (McBain, Ed)

Mary Medallion [1996] (Ardin, William)
Mask for a Diva [1994] (Michaels, Grant)
🔳 Mask of Dimitrios [1939] (Ambler, Eric)
Mask of Innocence [1994] (Ormerod, Roger)
Mask of Zeus [1992] (Cory, Desmond)
🔳 Masquerade [1990] (Kienzle, William X.)
Masquerade [1998] (Satterthwait, Walter)
Master's Challenge [1984] (Murphy, Warren B.)
Masterless Men [1995] (Mayo, J. K.)
Masterstroke [1982] (Heald, Tim)
🔳 Material Evidence [1995] (Kirton, Bill)
Material Witness [1993] (Tanenbaum, Robert K.)
🔳 Matrimonial Causes [1993] (Corris, Peter)
Matter of Degree [1987] (Philbin, Tom)
Matter of Honor [1993] (Maxim, Paul)
Matter of Perspective [1993] (Robinson, Kevin)
Maxwell Street Blues [1994] (Raleigh, Michael)
Maxwell's Flame [1995] (Trow, M. J.) ☆
🔳 Maxwell's House [1994] (Trow, M. J.)
🔳 Mayday! [Brit.] (Cussler, Clive)
Mayday from Malaga [1983] (MacLeod, Robert)
Mayflower Murder [1995] (Kemprecos, Paul)
🔳 Mayhem [1992] (Janes, J. Robert)
🔳 McCloud [1973] (Wilcox, Collin)
McGarr and the Legacy of a Woman Scorned [1986]
 (Gill, Bartholomew)
McGarr and the Method of Descartes [1984]
 (Gill, Bartholomew)
McGarr and the P.M. of Belgrave Square [1983]
 (Gill, Bartholomew)
🔳 McGarr and the Politician's Wife [1977]
 (Gill, Bartholomew)
McGarr and the Sienese Conspiracy [1977]
 (Gill, Bartholomew)
McGarr at the Dublin Horse Show [1980]
 (Gill, Bartholomew)
McGarr on the Cliffs of Moher [1978]
 (Gill, Bartholomew)
McNally's Caper [1994] (Sanders, Lawrence)
McNally's Gamble [1997] (Sanders, Lawrence)
McNally's Luck [1992] (Sanders, Lawrence)
McNally's Puzzle [1996] (Sanders, Lawrence)
McNally's Risk [1993] (Sanders, Lawrence)
🔳 McNally's Secret [1992] (Sanders, Lawrence)
McNally's Trial [1995] (Sanders, Lawrence)
Me Tanner, You Jane [1970] (Block, Lawrence)
Mean High Tide [1994] (Hall, James W.)
Meandering Corpse [1965] (Prather, Richard)
Meanwhile Back at the Morgue [1960] (Avallone, Michael)
Mecca for Murder [1956] (Marlowe, Stephen)
🔳 Mediterranean Caper [1973] (Cussler, Clive) ☆
Meeting at Midnight [APA] (Jenkins, Jerry)
Megham [1983] (Jenkins, Jerry)
🔳 Melting Clock [1991] (Kaminsky, Stuart M.)
Melting Point [1986] (Davis, Kenn) ☆
Memory Lane [1996] (Gough, Laurance)
🔳 Memory Trap [1989] (Price, Anthony)
Men of Subtle Craft [1987] (Lewis, Roy)
Menacers [1968] (Hamilton, Donald)
Mental Case [1996] (Harvey, James Neal)
Merchant of Death [1995] (Grace, C. L.)
Merchant's Partner [1995] (Jecks, Michael)
🔳 Mercy Trap [1989] (Martin, James E.)
Merry Devils [1989] (Marston, Edward)
Message Ends [1969] (Craig, David)
Methods of Execution [1994] (Huebner, Frederick D.)
Methods of Sergeant Cluff [1961] (North, Gil)
Mexican Hat [1997] (McGarrity, Michael)
🔳 Mexican Standoff [1988] (Cook, Bruce)
Mexican Tree Duck [1993] (Crumley, James)
Mexico Is Forever [1994] (Schutz, Benjamin)
Mexico Set [1984] (Deighton, Len)
🔳 Miami Mayhem [1960] (Rome, Anthony)

🔳 Michigan Roll [1988] (Kakonis, Tom)
Midnight Man [1982] (Estleman, Loren D.)
Midnight Man [1981] (Murphy, Warren B.)
Midnight Never Comes [1966] (Fallon, Martin)
Midnight Sister [1989] (Albert, Marvin H.)
Midsummer Malice [1997] (Lake, M. D.)
🔳 Midsummer Night's Killing [1989] (Barnes, Trevor)
Midtown North [1991] (Newman, Christopher) ☆
🔳 Midtown South [1986] (Newman, Christopher)
Million Dollar Wound [1986] (Collins, Max Allan, Jr.) ☆
Million-Dollar Tattoo [1996] (Emerson, Earl)
Mind Over Murder [1981] (Kienzle, William X.)
Mind Prey [1995] (Sandford, John)
Mind-Murders [1981] (van de Wetering, Janwillem)
Mingrelian Conspiracy [1995] (Pearce, Michael)
Miniature Murder Mystery [1982] (Chambers, Peter)
🔳 Minnesota Strip [1987] (Collins, Michael)
Minor Murders [1979] (Hensley, Joe L.)
Minyan for the Dead [1993] (Fliegel, Richard) ☆
Miracles Take a Little Longer [1986] (Lewis, Roy H.)
Mirror Image [1972] (Sadler, Mark)
Mirror Maze [1994] (Bayer, William)
Mischief [1993] (McBain, Ed)
Missing [1995] (Valin, Jonathan)
Missing and the Dead [1982] (Lynch, Jack) ☆
🔳 Missing at Tenoclock [1994] (Miles, John)
Missing Bonds [1997] (Most, Bruce W.)
Missing Bronte [1983] (Barnard, Robert)
Missing Link [1980] (Murphy, Warren B.)
Missing Man [1964] (Waugh, Hillary)
Missing Moon [1983] (Adams, Harold)
Missing Woman [1981] (Lewin, Michael Z.)
🔳 Mistakenly in Mallorca [1974] (Jeffries, Roderic)
🔳 Modesty Blaise [1965] (O'Donnell, Peter)
Mom Among the Liars [1992] (Yaffe, James)
Mom and Dead [1994] (McInerny, Ralph)
Mom Doth Murder Sleep [1991] (Yaffe, James)
Mom Meets Her Maker [1990] (Yaffe, James)
Monday the Rabbi Took Off [1972] (Kemelman, Harry)
🔳 Monday Theory [1983] (Clark, Douglas)
🔳 Money Men [1981] (Petievich, Gerald)
Money Mountain [1987] (MacLeod, Robert)
Money Trouble [1988] (Reynolds, William J.)
Mongoose, R.I.P. [1988] (Buckley, William F.)
🔳 Monkey on a Chain [1993] (Campbell, Harlen)
🔳 Monkey's Raincoat [1987] (Crais, Robert) ★★★ ☆
🔳 Monsier Pamplemousse [1983] (Bond, Michael)
Monterant Affair [1980] (Grayson, Richard)
Monterey [1985] (Lynch, Jack)
Montezuma's Man [1993] (Charyn, Jerome)
Montmarte Murders [1982] (Grayson, Richard)
Monza [1991] (Judd, Bob)
Moody Becomes Eternal [1997] (Oliver, Steve)
🔳 Moody Gets the Blues [1996] (Oliver, Steve)
Moody Man [U.S.] (Milne, John)
🔳 Moondog [1995] (Garfield, Henry)
Moonspender [1986] (Gash, Jonathan)
Moorland Hanging [1996] (Jecks, Michael)
More Dead Than Alive [1980] (Ormerod, Roger)
More Deaths for Sergeant Cluff [1963] (North, Gil)
🔳 Moriarty [APA] (Gardner, John)
Morning for Flamingoes [1990] (Burke, James Lee)
Morons and Madmen [1993] (Emerson, Earl) ☆
Mortal Causes [1994] (Rankin, Ian)
Mortal Nuts [1996] (Hautman, Pete)
Mortal Remains [1995] (Hanson, Rick)
Mortal Ruin [1988] (Malcolm, John)
Mortal Sickness [1995] (Taylor, Andrew)
Mortal Sin [1994] (Levine, Paul)
Mortal Stakes [1975] (Parker, Robert B.)
Moscow Coach [1964] (McCutchan, Philip)
Moscow Metal [1987] (Boyer, Rick)

Most Cunning Workmen [1984] (Lewis, Roy)
Most Deadly Retirement [1995] (Miles, John)
Most Likely Suspects [1981] (Bourgeau, Art)
Moth [1993] (Sallis, James) ☆
■ Motive for Revenge [1972] (Conway, Peter)
■ Motor City Blue [1980] (Estleman, Loren D.)
Motown Underground [1993] (Allyn, Doug)
■ Mountain Massacres [1995] (Champion, David)
Mountains West of Town [1975] (Downing, Warwick)
Mourner [1963] (Stark, Richard)
Mourning After [1981] (Masur, Harold Q.)
Mourning Show [1994] (Belsky, Dick)
Movie [1995] (Hall, Parnell) ☆
■ Moving Finger [1986] (Bass, Milton R.)
Moving Picture Writes [1984] (Chambers, Peter)
Moving Targets [1986] (Reynolds, William J.)
Mr. Pamplemousse Aloft [1989] (Bond, Michael)
Mr. Pamplemousse and the Secret Mission [1985]
    (Bond, Michael)
Mr. Pamplemousse en Fete [1984] (Bond, Michael)
Mr. Pamplemousse Investigates [1990] (Bond, Michael)
Mr. Pamplemousse on the Spot [1986] (Bond, Michael)
Mr. Pamplemousse Stands Firm [1993] (Bond, Michael)
Mr. Pamplemousse Takes the Cure [1987] (Bond, Michael)
Mr. Smithson's Bones [1993] (Conroy, Richard Timothy)
■ Mr. X [1995] (Gaitano, Nick)
Mrs. Pargeter's Package [1990] (Brett, Simon)
Mrs. Pargeter's Plot [1996] (Brett, Simon)
Mrs. Pargeter's Pound of Flesh [1992] (Brett, Simon)
Mrs., Presumed Dead [1988] (Brett, Simon)
Mucho Mojo [1994] (Lansdale, Joe R.)
Mugger [1956] (McBain, Ed)
Mugger Blood [1977] (Murphy, Warren B.)
■ Multiple Wounds [1996] (Russell, Alan)
■ Murder [1981] (Adams, Harold)
Murder [1988] (Hall, Parnell)
■ Murder Across and Down [1985] (Resnicow, Herbert)
■ Murder Among Children [1968] (Coe, Tucker)
■ Murder Among Friends [1983] (McConnell, Frank)
Murder Among Thieves [1969] (Alding, Peter)
Murder and Acquisitions [1988] (Murphy, Haughton)
■ Murder and the First Lady [1984] (Roosevelt, Elliott)
■ Murder at Buckingham Palace [1996] (Benison, C. C.)
Murder at Drury Lane [1992] (Hall, Robert Lee)
Murder at Ebbets Field [1995] (Soos, Troy)
■ Murder at Fenway Park [1994] (Soos, Troy)
Murder at Hobcaw Barony [1986] (Roosevelt, Elliott)
■ Murder at Midnight [1997] (Roosevelt, Elliott)
Murder at Moose Jaw [1981] (Heald, Tim)
■ Murder at the Baseball Hall of Fame [1996]
    (Daniel, David & Chris Carpenter)
Murder at the Cheatin' Heart Motel [1985] (Bourgeau, Art)
■ Murder at the Margin [1978] (Jevons, Marshall)
Murder at the Movies [1996] (Eddenden, A. E.)
Murder at the Museum of Natural History [1994]
    (Jahn, Michael)
Murder at the Palace [1988] (Roosevelt, Elliott)
Murder at the Tennis Hall of Fame [1997]
    (Daniel, David & Chris Carpenter)
Murder at Wrigley Field [1996] (Soos, Troy)
■ Murder Be Hanged [1992] (Ross, Jonathan)
Murder Begets Murder [1979] (Jeffries, Roderic)
Murder Behind Bars [APA] (Jenkins, Jerry)
Murder Benign [1995] (Hunt, Richard)
■ Murder by Design [1996] (Harrison, Ray)
Murder by Mail [1993] (Lake, M. D.)
■ Murder by Prescription [1995] (Pomidor, Bill)
Murder by the Mile [1975] (Russell, Martin)
Murder by the Numbers [1993] (Collins, Max Allan, Jr.)
Murder by the Waters [1995] (Hall, Robert Lee)
Murder Charge [1950] (Miller, Wade)
■ Murder Confounded [1993] (Jeffries, Roderic)

■ Murder for Lunch [1986] (Murphy, Haughton)
Murder for Treasure [1980] (Williams, David)
Murder Game [1993] (Allen, Steve)
■ Murder in a Cold Climate [1990] (Young, Scott)
Murder in A-Flat [1988] (Flynn, Don)
Murder in Advent [1985] (Williams, David)
Murder in Grub Street [1995] (Alexander, Bruce)
Murder in Hollywood [1988] (Allen, Steve)
Murder in Manhattan [1990] (Allen, Steve)
■ Murder in Perspective [1997] (Miles, Keith)
■ Murder in Petticoat Square [1993] (Harrison, Ray)
Murder in Retirement [1994] (Miles, John)
Murder in the Blue Room [1990] (Roosevelt, Elliott)
■ Murder in the Chateau [1996] (Roosevelt, Elliott)
■ Murder in the East Room [1993] (Roosevelt, Elliott)
■ Murder in the Executive Mansion [1995] (Roosevelt, Elliott)
Murder in the Napa Valley [1993] (Osborn, David)
Murder in the Oval Office [1989] (Roosevelt, Elliott)
Murder in the Queen's Arms [1985] (Elkins, Aaron)
Murder in the Red Room [1991] (Roosevelt, Elliott)
Murder in the Rose Garden [1989] (Roosevelt, Elliott)
Murder in the Title [1983] (Brett, Simon)
Murder in the West Wing [1992] (Roosevelt, Elliott)
Murder in the Wings [1986] (Gorman, Ed)
Murder in Vegas [1991] (Allen, Steve)
Murder in Waiting [U.S.] (Richardson, Robert)
■ Murder in Wrigley Field [1991] (Evers, Crabbe)
■ Murder is for Keeps [1961] (Chambers, Peter)
Murder Is Its Own Reward [1982] (Chambers, Peter)
Murder is My Dish [1956] (Marlowe, Stephen)
Murder is Suspected [1977] (Alding, Peter)
■ Murder Isn't Enough [1983] (Flynn, Don)
Murder Keeps a Secret [1989] (Murphy, Haughton)
Murder Line [1974] (Alding, Peter)
■ Murder Makers [1970] (Rossiter, John)
Murder Most Fowl [1994] (Crider, Bill)
Murder Most Holy [1992] (Harding, Paul)
Murder! Murder! Burning Bright [1996] (Ross, Jonathan)
Murder of Quality [1962] (Le Carré, John)
■ Murder Off the Glass [1987] (Katz, Michael J.)
Murder on Ice [1984] (Wood, Ted)
Murder on Location [1982] (Engel, Howard)
■ Murder on Madison Avenue [1983] (Orenstein, Frank)
■ Murder on Martha's Vineyard [1989] (Osborn, David)
Murder on Mike [1984] (Jeffers, H. Paul)
■ Murder on the Aisle [1987] (Gorman, Ed)
Murder on the Appian Way [1996] (Saylor, Steven)
Murder on the Atlantic [1995] (Allen, Steve)
Murder on the Chesapeake [1992] (Osborn, David)
Murder on the Glitter Box [1989] (Allen, Steve)
Murder on the Hudson [1985] (Flynn, Don)
Murder on the Links [1996] (Logue, John)
Murder on the Thirteenth [1992] (Eddenden, A. E.)
Murder on the Yellow Brick Road [1978] (Kaminsky, Stuart M.)
Murder on Theater Row [1997] (Jahn, Michael)
Murder One [1978] (Copper, Basil)
■ Murder Out of Tune [1990] (Shaw, Simon)
Murder Saves Face [1991] (Murphy, Haughton)
Murder Sees the Light [1984] (Engel, Howard) ★
Murder Song [1990] (Cleary, Jon)
Murder Straight Up [1986] (Gorman, Ed)
Murder Takes a Partner [1987] (Murphy, Haughton)
Murder Times Two [1990] (Murphy, Haughton)
Murder Underground [Brit.] (Arden, William)
Murder Unprompted [1982] (Brett, Simon)
■ Murder Ward [1974] (Murphy, Warren B.)
Murder Wears a Cowl [1992] (Doherty, P. C.)
■ Murder's Long Memory [1991] (Jeffries, Roderic)
Murder's Shield [1973] (Murphy, Warren B.)
Murder-in-Law [1987] (Engleman, Paul)
Murdered Sleep [1994] (Davis, Thomas D.)
Murderer's Row [1991] (Evers, Crabbe)

Murderer's Row [1962] (Hamilton, Donald)
■ Murders at Impasse Louvain [1978] (Grayson, Richard)
■ Murphy's Fault [1990] (Womack, Steven)
Muscle and Blood [1989] (Dold, Gaylord) ☆
Muscle for the Wing [1988] (Woodrell, Dan)
Mushroom Man [1995] (Pawson, Stuart)
Music Lovers [1993] (Valin, Jonathan)
Music of What Happens [1996] (Straley, John)
Musical Chairs [1991] (Friedman, Kinky)
My God How the Money Rolls In [1972] (Ripley, Jack)
■ My Gun Has Bullets [1995] (Goldberg, Lee)
My Gun is Quick [1950] (Spillane, Mickey)
My Kind of Game [1962] (Rome, Anthony)
My Mother, the Detective [1997] (Yaffe, James)
My Word You Should Have Seen Us [1972] (Ripley, Jack)
■ Mysterious Death of Meriwether Lewis [1993] (Burns, Ron)

N

Naked Angel [1953] (Webb, Jack)
Naked Eye [1990] (Reynolds, William J.)
Naked Justice [1997] (Bernhardt, William)
Naked Liar [1985] (Adams, Harold)☆
Naked Typist [1990] (Hailey, J. P.)
Name is Jordan [1962] (Masur, Harold Q.)
Name of the Game [1964] (Cory, Desmond)
■ Nantucket Revenge [1995] (Maness, Larry)
Narrow Corner [1983] (Copper, Basil)
■ Nasty Bit of Murder [1990] (Roe, C. F.)
■ Native Angels [1995] (Jaspersohn, William) ★
Natural Causes [1984] (Valin, Jonathan)
Neapolitan Reel [1988] (Dowling, Gregory)
■ Nebraska Quotient [1984] (Reynolds, William J) ☆
Necessary Dealing [1989] (Lewis, Roy)
Necessary End [1989] (Robinson, Peter)
Necklace of Skulls [1977] (Drummond, Ivor)
Necro File [1991] (Newton, Michael)
■ Negative Man [1971] (Galway, Robert Conington)
Neighborhood Watch [1996] (Andrus, Jeff)
■ Neon Flamingo [1987] (Philbrick, W. R.)
Neon Madmen [1977] (Harvey, John)
Neon Mirage [1988] (Collins, Max Allan, Jr.)☆
■ Neon Rain [1987] (Burke, James Lee)
Neon Smile [1995] (Lochte, Dick)☆
Neptune's Eye [1991] (Kemprecos, Paul)
Nerissa Claire Case [1983] (Waugh, Hillary)
Nervous Laughter [1985] (Emerson, Earl)
Nest of Vultures [1973] (MacLeod, Robert)
Never Cross a Vampire [1980] (Kaminsky, Stuart M.)
Never Die in January [1992] (Scholefield, Alan)
Never Send Flowers [1993] (Gardner, John)
Never Street [1997] (Estleman, Loren D.)
Nevsky's Demon [1983] (Gat, Dimitri)
■ Nevsky's Return [1982] (Gat, Dimitri)☆
New, Improved Murder [1985] (Gorman, Ed)☆
■ New Kind of War [1987] (Price, Anthony)
New Mexico Connection [1974] (Wilcox, Collin)
New Orleans Requiem [1994] (Donaldson, D. J.)
■ New York Dead [1991] (Woods, Stuart)
■ News of Murder [1961] (Lejeune, Anthony)
Newspaper Murders [as by Joe Gash] [1985] (Granger, Bill)
Next of Kin [1981] (Murphy, Warren B.)
■ Next to Die [1989] (Fliegel, Richard)
■ Next Victim [1993] (Sanders, William)
Nibbled to Death by Ducks [1989] (Campbell, Robert)
■ Nice Class of Corpse [1986] (Brett, Simon)
■ Nice Murder for Mom [1988] (Yaffe, James)
Nice Steady Job [1994] (Dowling, Gregory)
Nice Weekend for a Murder [1986] (Collins, Max Allan, Jr.)
Nick's Trip [1993] (Pelecanos, George P.)
Night and Day [1995] (Leslie, John)
■ Night Cover [1976] (Lewin, Michael Z.)
■ Night Crew [1997] (Sandford, John)

Night Frost [1966] (Copper, Basil)
Night Frost [1992] (Wingfield, R. D.)
Night Lords [1978] (Freeling, Nicolas)
Night Moves [1996] (Scholefield, Alan)
Night of Morningstar [1982] (O'Donnell, Peter)
■ Night of the Fox [1986] (Higgins, Jack)
Night of the Panther [1997] (Ayres, E. C.)
Night of the Phoenix [1975] (DeMille, Nelson)
Night of the Shadow [1966] (Grant, Maxwell)
Night of the Toads [1970] (Collins, Michael)
Night Prey [1994] (Sandford, John)
Night Probe! [1981] (Cussler, Clive)
■ Night Remembers [1991] (Gorman, Ed)
■ Night Rituals [1982] (Jahn, Michael)
Night Runners [1978] (Collins, Michael)
Night Secrets [1990] (Cook, Thomas H.)
■ Night Shadows [1994] (Ely, Ron)
■ Night the Gods Smiled [1983] (Wright, Eric) ★★
Night Vision [1992] (Levine, Paul)
Night Watch [1994] (Palmer, Frank)
■ Night Without Darkness [1965] (Orvis, Kenneth)
■ Nightgames [1986] (Wilcox, Collin)
■ Nightingale Gallery [1991] (Harding, Paul)
Nightland [1996] (Owens, Louis)
Nightlines [1985] (Lutz, John) ☆
Nightmare File [1986] (Livingston, Jack)
■ Nightshades [1984] (Pronzini, Bill)
Nightwork [1984] (Hansen, Joseph)
Nijinsky is Dead [1987] (Davis, Kenn)
Nine Giants [1991] (Marston, Edward)
Nineteenth Precinct [1992] (Newman, Christopher)
Ninety Million Dollar Mouse [1987] (Nevins, Francis M., Jr)
Ninth Netsuke [1982] (Melville, James)
■ Ninth Race [1995] (Healy, R. Austin)
■ No Bottom [1994] (Brewer, James D.)
No Choice for Sergeant Cluff [1971] (North, Gil)
■ No Comfort in Victory [1995] (Bean, Gregory)
■ No Cure for Death [1983] (Collins, Max Allan, Jr.)
No Deals Mr. Bond [1987] (Gardner, John)
■ No Exit From Brooklyn [1987] (Randisi, Robert J.)
No Flowers for the General [1967] (Copper, Basil)
No Gold When You Go [1966] (Chambers, Peter)
No Good Deed [1995] (Nathan, Paul)
No Happy Ending [1993] (Taibo, Paco Ignacio, II)
No Justice [1996] (Brewer, James D.)
■ No Lesser Plea [1987] (Tanenbaum, Robert K.)
No Letters from the Grave [1971] (Copper, Basil)
No Mardi Gras for the Dead [1992] (Donaldson, D. J.)
■ No One Rides for Free [1986] (Beinhart, Larry) ★
No Part in Your Death [1984] (Freeling, Nicolas)
■ No Peace for the Wicked [1968] (Chambers, Peter)
No Remorse [1997] (Brewer, James D.)
■ No Score [as by Chip Harrison] [1970] (Block, Lawrence)
■ No Sign of Life [1990] (Ormerod, Roger)
No Sign of Murder [1990] (Russell, Alan)
No Time for Heroes [1994] (Freemantle, Brian)
No Virtue [1995] (Brewer, James D.)
■ No Way Home [1992] (Coburn, Andrew)
No Witnesses [1994] (Pearson, Ridley)
Nobody Lives Forever [1964] (Chambers, Peter)
Nobody Lives Forever [1986] (Gardner, John)
Nobody Roots for Goliath [1996] (Champion, David)
■ Nobody's Perfect [1969] (Clark, Douglas)
Nobody's Perfect [1977] (Westlake, Donald E.)
Nocturne [1997] (McBain, Ed)
Nocturne for the General [1985] (Trenhaile, John)
Noel Coward Murder Case [1992] (Baxt, George)
None the Worse for a Hanging [U.S.] (Ross, Jonathan)
Noose of Time [1989] (Murray, Stephen)
North of Havana [1997] (White, Randy Wayne)
■ Nose on My Face [1962] (Payne, Laurence)
■ Nostradamus Traitor [1979] (Gardner, John)

■ Not A Blessed Thing [1981] (Quill, Monica)
■ Not as Far as Velma [1989] (Freeling, Nicolas)
Not Dead, Only Resting [1984] (Brett, Simon)
Not Enough Horses [1988] (Roberts, Les)
Not Long for This World [1990] (Haywood, Gar Anthony)
Notches [1997] (Bowen, Peter)
Nothing but Foxes [1977] (Lewis, Roy)
Nothing But the Truth [1995] (Parrish, Richard)
Nothing Personal [1980] (Chambers, Peter)
■ November Man [Edinburg] [1979] (Granger, Bill)
Now and Then, Amen [1988] (Cleary, Jon)
Now You See Her, Now You Don't [1994] (Murray, William)
Nowhere Man [1987] (Oster, Jerry)
Nowhere Man [1973] (Perry, Ritchie)
Nun of the Above [1985] (Quill, Monica)
Nun Plussed [1993] (Quill, Monica)

O

O Sacred Head [1997] (Kilmer, Nicholas)
O'Fear [1989] (Corris, Peter)
Obedience [1988] (Hansen, Joseph)
■ Obsession [1973] (Tripp, Miles)
October Men [1973] (Price, Anthony)
Odd Man Out [1993] (Taylor, Andrew)
■ Odds Against [1965] (Francis, Dick)☆
Odds Run Out [1949] (Waugh, Hillary)
Off Minor [1992] (Harvey, John)
Off Season [1994] (Craig, Philip)
Offering [1988] (Bolton, Melvin)
■ Oil Rig [1984] (Roderus, Frank)
■ Oil Slick [1974] (Murphy, Warren B.)
Old Bones [1987] (Elkins, Aaron) ★
Old English Peep Show [U.S.] (Dickinson, Peter) ★
Old Saxon Blood [1988] (Tourney, Leonard)
Old School Tie [1986] (Taylor, Andrew)
Old Scores [1993] (Elkins, Aaron) ★ ☆
Old Tin Sorrows [1989] (Cook, Glen)
■ Old Vengeful [1982] (Price, Anthony)
Old Ways in the New World [1994] (Conroy, Richard Timothy)
Old-Fashioned War [1987] (Murphy, Warren B.)
On a Blanket with my Baby [1995] (Kent, Bill)
On Dangerous Ground [1994] (Higgins, Jack)
On the Dead Run [1975] (Murphy, Warren B.)
On the Inside [1990] (Wood, Ted)
On the Other Hand [1984] (Stevenson, Richard)
On the Stretch [1969] (Welcome, John)
Once a Mutt [1985] (Murphy, Warren B.)
"Once a Prostitute" [1984] (Hunter, Alan)
Once a Year Man [1977] (Tripp, Miles)
Once Dying, Twice Dead [1984] (Lewis, Roy)
Once Perfect Place [1996] (Maness, Larry)
Once Upon a Crime [1994] (Lake, M. D.)
■ One Breathless Hour [1981] (Ormerod, Roger)
■ One Damn Thing After Another [1981] (Freeling, Nicolas)
■ One Dead Dean [1988] (Crider, Bill)
One Dead Judge [1993] (Pairo, Preston, III)
One Dead Tory [1994] (Cook, Stephen)
One Dollar Death [1982] (Barth, Richard)
One Fine Day the Rabbi Bought a Cross [1987]
   (Kemelman, Harry)
One Foot in the Grave [1979] (Dickinson, Peter)
■ One For the Money [1985] (Belsky, Dick)
One Good Death Deserves Another [1976] (Perry, Ritchie)
One Horse Race [1972] (Stone, Thomas H.)
One Lonely Night [1951] (Spillane, Mickey)
One Lover Too Many [1983] (Tripp, Miles)
■ One Man's Justice [1983] (Alding, Peter)
One Man's Law [1994] (Clarkson, John)
One Man's Poison [1991] (Riggs, John R)
■ One Night Stand [1973] (Murphy, Warren B.)
One Shot Deal [1983] (Petievich, Gerald)
■ One Small Step [1990] (Hill, Reginald)
One Way Out [1996] (Clarkson, John)

One-Way Ticket [1998] (Knight, J. D.)
Ones You Do [1988] (Woodrell, Dan) ☆
Only Good Priest [1991] (Zubro, Mark)
Only Good Yankee [1995] (Abbott, Jeff)
Oops! [1997] (Lutz, John)
■ Open Season [1988] (Mayor, Archer)
Open Window [1988] (Ormerod, Roger)
■ An Option on Death [1988] (Sherer, Michael W.)
Ordinary Murder [1987] (Flynn, Don)
Organ Grinder's Monkey [1989] (Fliegel, Richard)
Other Paths to Glory [1974] (Price, Anthony) ★
Other People's Money [1989] (Lyons, Arthur)
■ Otherwise Known as Murder [1994] (McGaughey, Neil)
■ Otley [1966] (Waddell, Martin)
Otley Forever [1968] (Waddell, Martin)
Otley Pursued [1967] (Waddell, Martin)
Otley Victorious [1969] (Waddell, Martin)
Our Fathers' Lies [1985] (Taylor, Andrew) ☆
Our Man in Camelot [1975] (Price, Anthony)
■ Out of Focus [1971] (Townend, Peter)
■ Out of Nowhere [1988] (Marshall, William)
Out of Season, Out of Time [1984] (Lewin, Michael Z.)
Out of the Sun [1996] (Goddard, Robert)
Out of Time [Brit.] (Lewin, Michael Z.)
Out on the Cutting Edge [1989] (Block, Lawrence) ☆
Outcasts [1981] (Hensley, Joe L.)
Outfit [1963] (Stark, Richard)
Outside Agency [1997] (Daly, Conor)
■ Outsider in Amsterdam [1975] (van de Wetering, Janwillem)
■ Over Her Dead Body [1959] (Prather, Richard)
Over the Edge [1987] (Kellerman, Jonathan)
Over the High Side [1971] (Freeling, Nicolas)
Overhead [1991] (Bickham, Jack M.)
■ Overkill [1988] (Schorr, Mark)
Oxford Gambit [U.S.] (Hone, Joseph)

P

Pacific Vortex! [1983] (Cussler, Clive)
Padded Cell [1973] (Conway, Peter)
Paging Blackshirt [1957] (Graeme, Roderic)
■ Paid and Loving Eyes [1992] (Gash, Jonathan)
Paige [1981] (Jenkins, Jerry)
Paint It Black [1989] (Philbrick, W. R.)
Paint It Black [1995] (Timlin, Mark)
Paint Out [1990] (Wallace, Robert)
Paint the Town Red [1982] (Adams, Harold)
Painted Ladies [1994] (Harvey, James Neal)
Painted Leaves [1995] (Fink, John)
Palace of Love [1967] (Vance, Jack)
Pale Criminal [1990] (Kerr, Philip)
■ Pale Kings and Princes [1987] (Parker, Robert B.)
Palmprint [1980] (Barnett, James)
Panda One Investigates [1973] (Walker, Peter N.)
■ Panda One on Duty [1971] (Walker, Peter N.)
Pandemic [1973] (Ardies, Tom)
Paper Cuts [1990] (Biderman, Bob)
Paper Doll [1993] (Parker, Robert B.)
Papers of Tony Veitch [1983] (McIlvanney, William) ★ ☆
■ Parade of Cockeyed Creatures [1967] (Baxt, George) ☆
Paradise of Death [1988] (Orenstein, Frank)
■ Pariah [1988] (Wilcox, Collin)
Part of Virtue [1975] (Lewis, Roy)
Parts Unknown [1990] (Burns, Rex)
Pas de Death [1994] (Vincent, Lawrence M.)
Pascoe's Ghost [1979] (Hill, Reginald)
Passage to Lisbon [1998] (Faherty, Terence)
Past Reason Hated [1991] (Robinson, Peter) ★
■ Past Tense [1997] (Greenleaf, Stephen)
■ Pastime [1991] (Parker, Robert B.)
Patently Murder [1990] (Harrison, Ray)
Path of Ghosts [1971] (MacLeod, Robert)
Patriot Games [1987] (Clancy, Tom)

Pattern for Murder [1952] (Prather, Richard)
Pattern for Panic [1954] (Prather, Richard)
Pattern of Violence [1973] (Busby, Roger)
Pay-Off in Switzerland [1977] (MacLeod, Robert)
Payday [1989] (Wallace, Robert)
Paydirt [1992] (Disher, Garry)
Pearlhanger [1985] (Gash, Jonathan)
Peckover and the Bog Man [1994] (Kenyon, Michael)
Peckover Holds the Baby [1988] (Kenyon, Michael)
Peckover Joins the Choir [1993] (Kenyon, Michael)
Peeping Thomas [1990] (Reeves, Robert)
Peking Duck [1979] (Simon, Roger L.)
■ Penance [1995] (Housewright, David) ★ ☆
Penance for Jerry Kennedy [1985] (Higgins, George V.)
■ Penelope [1965] (Cunningham, E. V.)
Penny Ferry [1984] (Boyer, Rick)
Penny for the Old Guy [1991] (Dold, Gaylord)
Pension for Death [1983] (Lewis, Roy H.)
People in Glass Houses [1997] (Hemlin, Tim)
People in Glass Houses [1961] (Ridgway, Jason)
■ People of Darkness [1980] (Hillerman, Tony)
■ Pepper Pike [1988] (Roberts, Les)
Perchance to Dream [1991] (Parker, Robert B.)
Perdition USA [1996] (Phillips, Gary)
■ Peregrine [1981] (Bayer, William) ★
Peregrine Dream [1990] (Ring, Raymond H.)
Perfect End [1981] (Marshall, William)
Perfect Justice [1994] (Bernhardt, William)
■ Perfect Murder [1964] (Keating, H. R. F.) ★ ☆
Perfectly Proper Murder [1993] (Adams, Harold)
Performance [1985] (Clark, Douglas)
Peril is My Pay [1960] (Marlowe, Stephen)
■ Permanent Retirement [1993] (Miles, John)
Petrella at Q [1977] (Gilbert, Michael)
Petty Pewter Gods [1995] (Cook, Glen)
Phantom Holiday [1974] (Russell, Martin)
Phoenix [Brit.] (Judd, Bob)
■ Physical Evidence [1980] (Noguchi, Thomas T. w/Arthur Lyons)
■ Picasso Scam [1995] (Pawson, Stuart)
Picture of Her Tombstone [1996] (Lipinski, Thomas)
Picture of Innocence [1996] (Matthews, Lew)
Picture Postcard [1990] (Huebner, Frederick D.)
■ Pictures of Perfection [1994] (Hill, Reginald) ☆
■ Piece of Resistance [1970] (Egleton, Clive)
Piece of the Action [1993] (Solomita, Stephen)
■ Piece of the Silence [1982] (Livingston, Jack) ☆
Pieces of Cream [1987] (Hilary, Richard)
Pieces of Death [1982] (Lynch, Jack) ☆
Pieces of Modesty [1972] (O'Donnell, Peter)
Pied Piper of Death [1997] (Forrest, Richard)
Pig That Got Up and Slowly Walked Away [1971] (Ripley, Jack)
■ Pigeon Blood [1988] (Alexander, Gary)
Pigs Get Fat [1985] (Murphy, Warren B.) ★ ☆
Pillar of Fire [1995] (Irvine, Robert)
Pillow of the Community [1988] (Hilary, Richard)
■ Pilot Error [1977] (Knox, Bill)
Pinch of Snuff [1978] (Hill, Reginald)
■ Pink Vodka Blues [1992] (Barrett, Neal, Jr.)
Pipeline [1991] (Malone, Paul)
Pirate Trade [1995] (Boyer, Rick)
Pitchfork Hollow [1995] (Feldmeyer, Dean)
Place of Mists [1969] (MacLeod, Robert)
Plague of Dragons [1965] (Brett, John Michael)
Plain Dealer [1992] (Ardin, William)
Plain Sailing [1987] (Clark, Douglas)
■ Planning on Murder [1992] (Williams, David)
■ Play It Again [1995] (Bogart, Stephen Humphrey)
■ Player [1974] (Downing, Warwick)
■ Players' Boy is Dead [1980] (Tourney, Leonard)
■ Playmates [1989] (Parker, Robert B.)
Pleasant Grove Murders [1967] (Vance, John Holbrook)
■ Plugged Nickle [1988] (Campbell, Robert)
■ Plunder Squad [1972] (Stark, Richard)

■ Poacher's Bag [1980] (Clark, Douglas)
■ Poet in the Gutter [1995] (Baker, John)
Point of Darkness [1995] (Phillips, Mike)
■ Point of Impact [1993] (Hunter, Stephen)
Poison [1987] (McBain, Ed)
Poisoned Chalice [1992] (Clynes, Michael)
Poisoned Ivy [1991] (Lake, M. D.)
■ Poisoners [1971] (Hamilton, Donald)
■ Pokerface [1985] (Corris, Peter)
Polar Star [1989] (Smith, Martin Cruz)
Polaroid Man [1991] (Cormany, Michael)
Polecat Brennan [1994] (McCutchan, Philip)
Political Poison [1993] (Zubro, Mark)
Polo, Anyone? [1988] (Kennealy, Jerry)
Polo in the Rough [1989] (Kennealy, Jerry)
■ Polo Solo [1987] (Kennealy, Jerry)
Polo's Ponies [1988] (Kennealy, Jerry)
Polo's Wild Card [1990] (Kennealy, Jerry) ☆
■ Poodle Springs [1989] (Parker, Robert B.)
Pool of Tears [1977] (Wainright, John)
■ Poor Butterfly [1990] (Kaminsky, Stuart M.) ☆
Poor Dead Cricket [1988] (Duncan, W. Glenn)
Port of Light [1987] (Serafin, David)
Port Villa Blues [1995] (Disher, Garry)
Portland Laugher [1994] (Emerson, Earl)
Portrait in Shadows [1986] (Wainright, John)
■ Possessions of a Lady [1996] (Gash, Jonathan)
Potshot [1997] (Boyle, Gerry)
Pound of Flesh [1993] (Barnes, Trevor)
Poverty Bay [1985] (Emerson, Earl) ★ ☆
Power in the Blood [1996] (Wyrick, E. L.)
Power of the Bug [1974] (Drummond, Ivor)
Power Play [1979] (Murphy, Warren B.)
Power Plays [1979] (Wilcox, Collin)
Practice to Deceive [1997] (Housewright, David)
Prairie Chicken Kill [1996] (Crider, Bill)
■ Prayer for the Dead [1991] (Wiltse, David)
Precinct Command [1993] (Newman, Christopher)
■ Precinct: Siberia [1985] (Philbin, Tom)
Precipice [1996] (Forbes, Colin)
Predator [1968] (York, Andrew)
Premedicated Murder [1975] (Clark, Douglas)
Premium on Death [1986] (Lewis, Roy)
■ Prescription for Murder [1990] (Williams, David)
■ Presence of Mind [1994] (Hunter, Fred W.)
President's Daughter [1997] (Higgins, Jack)
Pressure Point [1983] (Copper, Basil)
■ Presumed Dead [1994] (Holton, Hugh)
Presumed Dead [1987] (Perry, Ritchie)
Pretend We're Dead [1994] (Timlin, Mark)
■ Pretty How Town [1992] (Freeling, Nicolas)
Pretty Place for a Murder [1987] (Hart, Roy)
■ Prey [1992] (Goddard, Ken)
Price [1974] (Newman, G. F.)
Pride of Heroes [1969] (Dickinson, Peter) ★
Pride's Harvest [1991] (Cleary, Jon)
Priestly Murders [1984] (Granger, Bill)
Priests of the Abomination [1970] (Drummond, Ivor)
Primal Instinct [1994] (Walker, Robert W.)
■ Primary Justice [1991] (Bernhardt, William)
Primary Target [1987] (Collins, Max Allan, Jr.)
Prime Witness [1993] (Martini, Steve)
Prince Lost to Time [1995] (Dukthas, Ann)
Prince of Darkness [1992] (Doherty, P. C.)
Principal Cause of Death [1992] (Zubro, Mark)
Print-Out [1988] (Copper, Basil)
Priscilla Copperwaite Case [1986] (Waugh, Hillary)
Prisoner's Plea [1963] (Waugh, Hillary)
Private Eyes [1992] (Kellerman, Jonathan)
Private Practices [1994] (White, Stephen)
■ Private Sector [1971] (Hone, Joseph)
■ Privileged Information [1991] (White, Stephen)

Privileged to Kill [1997] (Havill, Steven F.)
Probable Cause [1993] (Stockley, Grif)
Problem in Prague [1981] (MacLeod, Robert)
Procrastination of Sergeant Cluff [1969] (North, Gil)
■ Professor in Peril [1987] (Lejeune, Anthony)
Profit Motive [1982] (Murphy, Warren B.)
Promised Land [1976] (Parker, Robert B.) ★
Promises of Home [1996] (Abbott, Jeff)
■ Pronto [1993] (Leonard, Elmore)
■ Property in Cyprus [1970] (MacLeod, Robert)
Prosecutor [1991] (Philbin, Tom)
■ Prospect of Vengeance [1988] (Price, Anthony)
Protection [1988] (James, Bill)
■ Protocol for Murder [1994] (Nathan, Paul)
Prove the Nameless [1996] (Faherty, Terence)
■ Public Murders [1980] (Granger, Bill)
Public Trust [1997] (Gregory, Sarah)
■ Publish and Perish [1975] (Nevins, Francis M., Jr)
Pure Instinct [1995] (Walker, Robert W.)
Pure Poison [1966] (Waugh, Hillary)
Pursuit of Arms [1985] (Hammond, Gerald)
Pusher [1956] (McBain, Ed)
Puss in Boots [1987] (McBain, Ed)
Putting the Boot In [1985] (Kavanagh, Dan)

Q

Quality of the Informant [1985] (Petievich, Gerald)
Quake City [1997] (Spencer, John)
■ Quarry [APA] (Collins, Max Allen, Jr.)
■ Quarry [1992] (Pronzini, Bill)
Quarry's Cut [APA] (Collins, Max Allen, Jr.)
Quarry's Deal [APA] (Collins, Max Allen, Jr.)
Quarry's List [APA] (Collins, Max Allen, Jr.)
■ Queen's Head [1988] (Marston, Edward)
Queen's Mare [1990] (Birkett, John)☆
■ Queer Kind of Death [1966] (Baxt, George)
Queer Kind of Love [1994] (Baxt, George)
Queer Kind of Umbrella [1995] (Baxt, George)
Question of Degree [1974] (Lewis, Roy)
Question of Loyalty [U.S.] (Freeling, Nicolas)
Question of Murder [1988] (Wright, Eric)
Questions of Identity [1987] (Cook, Bob)
Quests of Simon Ark [1984] (Hoch, Edward D.)
Quick and the Dead [1992] (Kantner, Rob)
Quicksilver [1984] (Pronzini, Bill)
Quiet Dogs [1982] (Gardner, John)
Quiet Room in Hell [1979] (Copper, Basil)
■ Quincannon [1985] (Pronzini, Bill)

R

Race [1992] (Judd, Bob)
Radio Red Killer [1997] (Lupoff, Richard A.)
Radish River Caper [1981] (Spencer, Ross H.)
■ Rafferty's Rules [1987] (Duncan, W. Glenn)
■ Rag Bag Clan [1978] (Barth, Richard)
Ragdoll Murder [1987] (Jeffers, H. Paul)
Ragged Plot [1981] (Barth, Richard)
Ragman's Memory [1996] (Mayor, Archer)
Rain [1989] (Peterson, Keith) ★
Rain of Terror [1988] (Murphy, Warren B.)
Rain Rustlers [1984] (Roderus, Frank)
■ Rainy City [1985] (Emerson, Earl)☆
■ Rainy North Woods [1990] (Kohler, Vince)
Raise the Titanic! [1976] (Cussler, Clive)
Raising the Dead [1988] (Simon, Roger L.)
■ Rally to Kill [1975] (Knox, Bill)
Ransom [1973] (Cleary, Jon)
Ransom for an Angel [1995] (Hunter, Fred W.)
Ransom for Our Sins [1996] (Hunter, Fred W.)
Ransom Game [1981] (Engel, Howard)
Ransom Town [1979] (Alding, Peter)
■ Raphael Affair [1991] (Pears, Iain)
Rare Coin Score [1967] (Stark, Richard)

Rasputin's Revenge [1916] [1987] (Lescroart, John T.)
Rat on Fire [1981] (Higgins, George V.)
Ratings are Murder [1985] (Irvine, Robert)
■ Ratking [1988] (Dibdin, Michael) ★
Rattle-Rat [1985] (van de Wetering, Janwillem)
Rattling of Old Bones [1979] (Ross, Jonathan)
Ravagers [1964] (Hamilton, Donald)
Raven After Dark [Brit.] (MacKenzie, Donald)
Raven and the Kamikaze [1977] (MacKenzie, Donald)
Raven and the Paperhangers [1980] (MacKenzie, Donald)
Raven and the Ratcatcher [1977] (MacKenzie, Donald)
Raven Feathers His Nest [1979] (MacKenzie, Donald)
■ Raven in Flight [1976] (MacKenzie, Donald)
Raven Settles a Score [1978] (MacKenzie, Donald)
Raven's Longest Night [1983] (MacKenzie, Donald)
Raven's Revenge [1980] (MacKenzie, Donald)
Raven's Shadow [1984] (MacKenzie, Donald)
Raven's Widows [1996] (Kohler, Vince)
Ravens of Blackwater [1994] (Marston, Edward)
Raw Deal [1994] (Standiford, Les)
■ Razor Game [1985] (Grady, James)
Razorbill [1996] (Keegan, Alex)
Reader's Guide to Murder [1996] (Jeffers, H. Paul)
Real Thing [1986] (Barrett, Robert G.)
Reasonable Man [1972] (Busby, Roger)
Rebound [1988] (Everson, David H.) ☆
■ Recalled to Life [1992] (Hill, Reginald)
■ Reconstructed Corpse [1993] (Brett, Simon)
■ Recount [1987] (Everson, David H.) ☆
Recycled [1993] (Bailey, Jo)
Red Card [1994] (Hoyt, Richard)
Red Cent [1989] (Campbell, Robert)
Red Chameleon [1985] (Kaminsky, Stuart M.)
Red Death [1991] (Mosley, Walter)
■ Red Diamond, Private Eye [1983] (Schorr, Mark) ★
Red Herrings [1985] (Heald, Tim)
Red Iron Nights [1991] (Cook, Glen)
Red is for Murder [1976] (Meyers, Martin)
Red Knight [1992] (Davis, J Madison)
■ Red Rosa [1988] (Collins, Michael)
Red Sky at Night [1997] (Hall, James W.)
Red Slayer [U.S.] (Harding, Paul)
Red Square [1992] (Smith, Martin Cruz)
Red Trance [1995] (Zimmerman, R. D.)
Red, White and Blues [1993] (Kantner, Rob)
Red Winter [1989] (Cormany, Michael)
Redcap [1961] (McCutchan, Philip)
Reggis Arms Caper [1979] (Spencer, Ross H.)
Relative Act of Murder [1993] (Roe, C. F.)
Relative Distance [1981] (Lewis, Roy)
Relatively Dangerous [1987] (Jeffries, Roderic)
■ Relentless [1972] (Garfield, Brian)
Relic Murders [1996] (Clynes, Michael)
Religious Conviction [1994] (Stockley, Grif)
Reluctant Ronin [1988] (Melville, James)
Reluctant Spy [1995] (Melville, James)
Remains to be Seen [1989] (Hart, Roy)
Remake [1997] (Bogart, Stephen Humphrey)
Rematch [1989] (Everson, David H.)
Remote Control [1997] (White, Stephen)
Removers [1961] (Hamilton, Donald)
Renegade Steele [1990] (Masters, J. D.)
Replay: Murder [1983] (Logue, John)
Repulse Monkey [1989] (Cluster, Dick)
Requiem for a Cop [1974] (Miller, Victor B.)
Requiem for a Loser [1972] (Wainright, John)
■ Requiem for Moses [1996] (Kienzle, William X.)
Rescue [1995] (Healy, Jeremiah)
Rest in Pieces [1985] (McInerny, Ralph)
Retaliators [1976] (Hamilton, Donald) ☆
Return Engagement [1988] (Murphy, Warren B.)
■ Return of Moriarty [1974] (Gardner, John)

■ Return to Sender [1988] (Cluster, Dick)
■ Return to the Same City [1996] (Taibo, Paco Ignacio, II)
Reunion for Death [1976] (Meyers, Martin)
Reunion with Murder [1941] (Fuller, Timothy)
Revenge Game [1981] (Hammond, Gerald)
Revenge of Moriarty [1975] (Gardner, John)
■ Revengers [1982] (Hamilton, Donald)
Reversible Error [1992] (Tanenbaum, Robert K.)
Reward Game [1980] (Hammond, Gerald)
Rich or Dead [1990] (Cormany, Michael)
■ Ricochet [1974] (Copper, Basil)
Riddle of the Third Mile [1983] (Dexter, Colin)
Ride [1984] (Wainright, John)
Ride a High Horse [1953] (Prather, Richard)
Ride the Lightning [1987] (Lutz, John) ☆
Riding the Rap [1995] (Leonard, Elmore)
Riding Toward Home [1996] (Milan, Borto)
Right To Die [1991] (Healy, Jeremiah)
Right to Sing the Blues [1986] (Lutz, John)
■ Ring of Terror [1995] (Gilbert, Michael)
Rio Grande Fall [1996] (Anaya, Rudolfo)
■ Ripper [1978] (Newton, Michael)
Ripple of Murders [1978] (Wainright, John)
Rising Dog [1992] (Kohler, Vince)
Risk of Heaven [1996] (Berger, Bob)
■ Risk of Murder [1995] (Berger, Bob)
■ Ritual [1988] (Heffernan, William)
Riverview Murders [1997] (Raleigh, Michael)
Riviera Blues [1990] (Batten, Jack)
Riviera Contract [1992] (Albert, Marvin H.)
Road Block [1959] (Waugh, Hillary)
Road Kills [1991] (Newton, Michael)
Road Show [1985] (Marshall, William)
Roadkill [1997] (Friedman, Kinky)
Roaring Boy [1995] (Marston, Edward) ☆
■ Roast Eggs [1981] (Clark, Douglas)
Robak's Cross [1985] (Hensley, Joe L.)
Robak's Fire [1986] (Hensley, Joe L.)
Robak's Firm [1987] (Hensley, Joe L.)
Robak's Run [1990] (Hensley, Joe L.)
Robak's Witch [1997] (Hensley, Joe L.)
Robbed Blind [1990] (Hart, Roy)
■ Robbery Blue [1969] (Busby, Roger)
Rock Bottom [1996] (Kemprecos, Paul)
■ Rock Critic Murders [1989] (Sublett, Jesse) ☆
Rockford Files: Devil on My Doorstep [1998] (Kaminsky, Stuart M.)
■ Rockford Files: The Green Bottle [1996] (Kaminsky, Stuart M.)
Rodent of Doubt [Brit] (Tapply, William G.)
■ Rogue Cop [APA] (Newman, G,F,) ☆
■ Rogue's Isles [1995] (Briody, Thomas Gately)
Rogue's Justice [1996] (Briody, Thomas Gately)
Role of Honour [1984] (Gardner, John)
■ Roller Coaster [1993] (Gilbert, Michael)
■ Rollerball [1984] (McCutchan, Philip)
■ Roman Blood [1990] (Saylor, Steven)
Romance [1995] (McBain, Ed)
Romeo's Tune [1990] (Timlin, Mark)
Room 13 [1997] (Garfield, Henry)
Rope for General Dietz [1972] (Rossiter, John)
■ Rosary Murders [1979] (Kienzle, William X.)
Roses Are Dead [1985] (Estleman, Loren D.)
Roses Love Sunshine [1989] (Pierce, David M.)
Roses, Roses [1993] (James, Bill)-
■ Rostnikov's Corpse [Brit.] (Kaminsky, Stuart M.)
Rostnikov's Vacation [1991] (Kaminsky, Stuart M.)
Rough Cut [1990] (Cook, Bruce)
Rough Cut [1994] (Cutler, Stan)
Rough Justice [1996] (Kirton, Bill)
Rough Justice [1989] (Peterson, Keith)
Rough Treatment [1990] (Harvey, John) ☆
■ Roughcut [1985] (Gorman, Ed)
Royal Cat [1995] (Allen, Garrison)

■ Royal Murder [1994] (Roosevelt, Elliott)
■ Rubout at the Onyx [1981] (Jeffers, H. Paul)
Rude Boys [1992] (Dold, Gaylord)
Ruins of Civility [1996] (Bradberry, James)
■ Rules of Prey [1989] (Sandford, John)
Ruling Passion [1973] (Hill, Reginald)
Rumplestiltskin [1981] (McBain, Ed)
■ Run for Cover [1958] (Welcome, John)
Runaround [1988] (Freemantle, Brian)
■ Runner in the Street [1984] (Grady, James)
Running Fix [1990] (Gibbs, Tony)
Rust on the Razor [1996] (Zubro, Mark)
Ruthless Realtor Murders [1997] (Kaufelt, David A.)
■ Ryan's Rules [APA] (Leonard, Elmore)

S

Sabine [U.S.] (Freeling, Nicolas)
Sabre-Tooth [1966] (O'Donnell, Peter)
Sacred [1997] (Lehane, Dennis)
Sacred Clowns [1993] (Hillerman, Tony)☆
Sacrifice [1991] (Vachss, Andrew H.)
■ Sacrificial Ground [1988] (Cook, Thomas H.) ☆
Sadie When She Died [1972] (McBain, Ed)
Sahara [1992] (Cussler, Clive)
■ Saints of God Murders [1995] (Meyer, Charles)
Salamander [1994] (Janes, J. Robert)
Salamander Chill [1988] (Lewis, Roy)
Salty Waters [1988] (Murray, Stephen)
Salute to Blackshirt [1954] (Graeme, Roderic)
Salvage Job [1978] (MacLeod, Robert)
■ Samantha [1967] (Cunningham, E. V.)
Same City [1996] (Taibo, Paco Ignacio, II)
■ Samson and the Greek Delilah [1995] (Tripp, Miles)
San Quentin [1984] (Lynch, Jack) ☆
Sanctuary Isle [1962] (Knox, Bill)
Sand Against the Tide [1990] (Bishop, Paul)
■ Sand Castles [1989] (Freeling, Nicolas)
Sand Dollars [1998] (Knief, Charles)
Sandman [1996] (Janes, J. Robert)
■ Sanibel Flats [1990] (White, Randy Wayne)
Saratoga Backtalk [1994] (Dobyns, Stephen)
Saratoga Bestiary [1988] (Dobyns, Stephen)
Saratoga Fleshpot [1995] (Dobyns, Stephen)
Saratoga Haunting [1993] (Dobyns, Stephen)
Saratoga Headhunter [1985] (Dobyns, Stephen)
Saratoga Hexameter [1990] (Dobyns, Stephen)
■ Saratoga Longshot [1976] (Dobyns, Stephen)
Saratoga Snapper [1986] (Dobyns, Stephen)
Saratoga Swimmer [1981] (Dobyns, Stephen)
■ Satan in St. Mary's [1986] (Doherty, P. C.)
Satan is a Woman [1987] (Baxt, George)
Satan Ring [1978] (Newton, Michael)
Satan's Fire [1995] (Doherty, P. C.)
Saturday Night Dead [1988] (Rosen, Richard)
■ Saturday of Glory [1979] (Serafin, David) ★
Saturday the Rabbi Went Hungry [1966] (Kemelman, Harry)
Sauce for the Goose [1995] (Campbell, Robert)
Sauce for the Pigeon [1984] (Hammond, Gerald)
Sausalito [1984] (Lynch, Jack)
■ Savage Justice [1992] (Handberg, Ron)
Savage Place [1981] (Parker, Robert B.)
■ Savage Season [1990] (Lansdale, Joe R.)
■ Saving the Queen [1976] (Buckley, William F.)
Savings and Loam [1990] (McInerny, Ralph)
Sayonara, Sweet Amaryllis [1983] (Melville, James)
■ Scam [1997] (Hall, Parnell)
Scarred [1993] (Heffernan, William)
Scarred Man [1990] (Peterson, Keith)
Scattershot [1982] (Pronzini, Bill)
■ Scavengers [1964] (Knox, Bill)
Scent of Evil [1992] (Mayor, Archer)
■ Schedule Two [1996] (Dold, Gaylord)
Schism [1981] (Granger, Bill)
Sci Fi [1981] (Marshall, William)

Scorcher [1987] (Lutz, John)
Score [1964] (Stark, Richard)
Scottish Decision [U.S.] (Hunter, Alan)
Scrambled Yeggs [APA] (Prather, Richard)
Scratch Fever [1982] (Collins, Max Allan, Jr.)
Scratch on the Dark [1967] (Copper, Basil)
Scratch on the Surface [1962] (Harknett, Terry)
Screaming Dead Ballons [1968] (McCutchan, Philip)
Scroll of Benevolence [1988] (Trenhaile, John)
∎ Sea of Green [1989] (Adcock, Thomas)
∎ Seacoast of Bohemia [1995] (Freeling, Nicolas)
∎ Seafire [1994] (Gardner, John)
Seafire [1970] (Knox, Bill)
Sealed with a Loving Kill [1976] (Ormerod, Roger)
Seals [1970] (Dickinson, Peter)
∎ Seascape with Dead Figures [1987] (Hart, Roy)
Season for Death [1987] (Harrison, Ray)
∎ Season of the Monsoon [1993] (Mann, Paul)
Seattle [1985] (Lynch, Jack)
Second Chance [1991] (Valin, Jonathan) ☆
Second Deadly Sin [1977] (Sanders, Lawrence)
Second Horseman Out of Eden [1989] (Chesbro, George)
∎ Second Longest Night [1955] (Marlowe, Stephen)
Second Vespers [1980] (McInerny, Ralph)
Secret Dying [1992] (Lewis, Roy)
Secret Families [1989] (Gardner, John)
Secret Houses [1987] (Gardner, John)
Secret Isaac [1978] (Charyn, Jerome)
∎ Secret Ministry [1951] (Cory, Desmond)
Secret of Annexe 3 [1986] (Dexter, Colin)
Secret Pilgrim [1991] (LeCarré, John)
Secret Singing [1972] (Lewis, Roy)
See Charlie Run [U.S.] (Freemantle, Brian)
See Naples and Kill [U.S.] (Dowling, Gregory)
∎ See No Evil [1996] (Finkelstein, Jay)
See Them Die [1960] (McBain, Ed)
See You Later, Alligator [1986] (Buckley, William F.)
∎ Seed of Doubt [1993] (McInerny, Ralph)
Seeing the Elephant [1992] (Roberts, Les)
Seize the Dragon [1990] (Schorr, Mark)
Self-Defense [1995] (Kellerman, Jonathan)
Self-Incrimination [1997] (Stockley, Grif)
Semiprivate Doom [1991] (Fliegel, Richard)
Senator Love [1991] (Adler, Warren)
Send Another Hearse [1960] (Masur, Harold Q.)
Sensitive Case [1990] (Wright, Eric)
Sentinels [1996] (Pronzini, Bill)
Separate Cases [1990] (Randisi, Robert J.)
Separated at Death [1996] (Axler, Leo)
Sepia Siren Killer [1994] (Lupoff, Richard A.)
Sergeant Cluff and the Day of Reckoning [1967] (North, Gil)
Sergeant Cluff and the Madmen [1964] (North, Gil)
Sergeant Cluff and the Price of Pity [1965] (North, Gil)
Sergeant Cluff Goes Fishing [1962] (North, Gil)
Sergeant Cluff Rings True [1972] (North, Gil)
∎ Sergeant Cluff Stands Firm [1960] (North, Gil)
Sergeant's Cat and Other Stories [1987]
  (van de Wetering, Janwillem)
∎ Series of Murders [1989] (Brett, Simon)
Serious Crimes [1990] (Gough, Laurence)
Serpent Among the Lilies [1990] (Doherty, P. C.)
∎ Serpentine Wall [1988] (DeBrosse, Jim)
Serpents of Harbledown [1996] (Marston, Edward)
Service of All the Dead [1979] (Dexter, Colin) ★
∎ Set Up [1992] (Corris, Peter)
Seventh [1966] (Stark, Richard)
Seventh Beaver [1993] (Boland, John C.)
Seventh Crossword [1985] (Resnicow, Herbert)
∎ Seventh Enemy [1995] (Tapply, William G.)
∎ Seventh Sacrament [1994] (Bradberry, James)
Seventh Station [1977] (McInerny, Ralph)
Seventh Stone [1985] (Murphy, Warren B.)

Several Deaths Later [1988] (Gorman, Ed)
Sgt. Verity and the Blood Royal [1979] (Selwyn, Francis)
Sgt. Verity and the Cracksman [APA] (Selwyn, Francis)
Sgt. Verity and the Imperial Diamond [1975] (Selwyn, Francis)
Sgt. Verity and the Swell Mob [1980] (Selwyn, Francis)
Sgt. Verity Presents His Compliments [1977] (Selwyn, Francis)
∎ Shackles [1988] (Pronzini, Bill)
Shadow Beware [1965] (Grant, Maxwell)
Shadow Catcher [1997] (Hackler, Micah S.)
Shadow Counter [1993] (Kakonis, Tom)
∎ Shadow Kill [1985] (Philbrick, W. R.)
∎ Shadow of a Broken Man [1977] (Chesbro, George)
Shadow of a Tiger [1972] (Collins, Michael)
Shadow of Death [1983] (Kienzle, William X.)
Shadow of the Condor [1975] (Grady, James)
Shadow Play [1987] (Milne, John)
Shadow Prey [1990] (Sandford, John)
∎ Shadow Queen [1992] (Gibbs, Tony)
∎ Shadow Strikes [1964] (Grant, Maxwell)
Shadow's Revenge [1965] (Grant, Maxwell)
Shadow Woman [1997] (Perry, Thomas)
Shadow—Destination Moon [1967] (Grant, Maxwell)
Shadow—Go Mad! [1966] (Grant, Maxwell)
Shadowers [1964] (Hamilton, Donald)
Shadows on the Sand [1995] (Cooper, Brian)
Shadowtown [1988] (Lutz, John)
Shah-Mak [1976] (Williams, Alan)
Shakedown [1992] (Malone, Paul)
Shaken Leaf [1955] (Cory, Desmond)
∎ Shakeout [1975] (Follett, Ken)
Shaky Ground [1997] (Brewer, Steve)
Shallow Graves [1992] (Healy, Jeremiah) ☆
Shaman Laughs [1995] (Doss, James D.)
∎ Shaman Sings [1994] (Doss, James D.)
Shaman's Dream [1997] (Doss, James D.)
Shaman's Knife [1993] (Young, Scott)
Shaman's Mistake [1996] (Doss, James D.)
Shame the Devil [1993] (Ormerod, Roger)
Shannon [1982] (Jenkins, Jerry)
Shard at Bay [1985] (McCutchan, Philip)
Shard Calls the Tune [1981] (McCutchan, Philip)
Sharman and Other Filth [1996] (Timlin, Mark)
Sharpest Sight [1992] (Owens, Louis)
Shattered Eye [1982] (Granger, Bill)
∎ Shawnee Alley Fire [1987] (Douglas, John) ☆
Sheep, Goats and Soap [1991] (Malcolm, John)
Sheer Gall [1996] (Kahn, Michael A.)
∎ Sheer Torture [1981] (Barnard, Robert)
∎ Shelf Life [1982] (Clark, Douglas)
Shell Scott Sampler [1969] (Prather, Richard)
Shell Scott's Seven Slaughters [1961] (Prather, Richard)
Shell Shock [1987] (Prather, Richard)
∎ Shepherd of the Wolves [1995] (Slusher, William S.)
∎ Sheriff of Bombay [1984] (Keating, H. R. F.)
∎ Sherlock Holmes versus Dracula [1978] (Estleman, Loren D.)
Ship of Death [1977] (Murphy, Warren B.)
Shock to the System [1984] (Brett, Simon) ☆
Shock to the System [1995] (Stevenson, Richard)
Shock Value [1983] (Murphy, Warren B.)
∎ Shock Wave [1996] (Cussler, Clive)
∎ Shock-Wave [1973] (Copper, Basil)
Shockwave [1990] (Forbes, Colin)
Shoot in Cleveland [1998] (Roberts, Les)
Shoot It Again, Sam [1972] (Avallone, Michael)
Shoot to Kill [1951] (Miller, Wade)
Shoot-Out [1982] (Copper, Basil)
Shooting of Dan McGrew [1972] (Kenyon, Michael)
Shooting Schedule [1990] (Murphy, Warren B.)
Short-Lived Ghost [1995] (Lewis, Roy)
Short Money [1995] (Hautman, Pete)
Shot [1992] (Hall, Parnell)
∎ Shot in the Dark [1996] (Gibbs, Tony)

Shot on Location [1993] (Cutler, Stan)
Shotgun [1969] (McBain, Ed)
Shotgun Saturday Night [1987] (Crider, Bill)
■ Shrine of Murders [1993] (Grace, C. L.)
Shroud for Aquarius [1985] (Collins, Max Allan, Jr.)
Shroud for the Archbishop [1995] (Tremayne, Peter)
■ Shrunken Heads [Brit.] (Kellerman, Jonathan) ★★
Shutout [1995] (Nighbert, David F.)
Sick to Death [1971] (Clark, Douglas)
■ Sicken and So Die [1995] (Brett, Simon)
Sidewalk Hilton [1994] (Cook, Bruce)
Siege [1987] (Hoyt, Richard)
■ Siege [1974] (Miller, Victor B.)
Siege for Panda One [1981] (Walker, Peter N.)
Silence is Broken [APA] (Jenkins, Jerry)
Silence of the Night [1974] (Ormerod, Roger)
Silencers [1962] (Hamilton, Donald)
Silent Killer [1986] (Cross, David)
Silent Knives [U.S.] (Gough, Lawrence)
Silent Partner [1989] (Kellerman, Jonathan)
Silent Prey [1992] (Sandford, John)
Silent Salesman [1978] (Lewin, Michael Z.)
Silent Scream [1973] (Collins, Michael)
Silent Thunder [1989] (Estleman, Loren D.)
Silent Witness [1990] (Wilcox, Collin)
Silent Woman [1992] (Marston, Edward)
Silent World of Nicholas Quinn [1977] (Dexter, Colin)
Silver Chariot Killer [1996] (Lupoff, Richard A.)
Silver City Scandal [1986] (Hammond, Gerald)
Silver Mistress [1973] (O'Donnell, Peter)
■ Silver Street [1968] (Johnson, E. Richard) ★
■ Silver Street Killer [Brit.] (Johnson, E. Richard) ★
■ Simple Suburban Murder [1989] (Zubro, Mark) ★
■ Sin Within Her Smile [1993] (Gash, Jonathan)
Sine Qua Nun [1986] (Quill, Monica)
Sinful Stones [U.S.] (Dickinson, Peter)
Singapore Transfer [1991] (Warga, Wayne)
Singing Stones [1993] (Cooper, Brian)
Single Death [Brit.] (Wright, Eric)
Sink or Swim [1997] (Hammond, Gerald)
■ Sins of the Fathers [1976] (Block, Lawrence)
■ Sion Crossing [1985] (Price, Anthony)
■ Sir, You Bastard [1970] (Newman, G. F.) ☆
Siskiyou [APA] (Hoyt, Richard)
Siskiyou Two-Step [1983] (Hoyt, Richard)
Sister Hood [1991] (Quill, Monica)
Sitting Target [1970] (Henderson, Laurence)
Situation Tragedy [1981] (Brett, Simon)
■ Six Days of the Condor [1974] (Grady, James)
Six Days to Death [1975] (Alding, Peter)
Sixth Directorate [1975] (Hone, Joseph)
Sixth Precinct [1987] (Newman, Christopher)
Skeleton's Knee [1993] (Mayor, Archer)
Skeletons in the Closet [1997] (Pomidor, Bill)
Skelly Man [1995] (Daniel, David)
■ Skin Deep [1968] (Dickinson, Peter) ★
Skin Deep [1991] (Hallinan, Timothy)
Skin Deep [1982] (Murphy, Warren B.)
Skin Palace [1995] (O'Connell, Jack)
Skinflick [1979] (Hansen, Joseph)
Skinner's Festival [1994] (Jardine, Quintin)
Skinner's Ordeal [1996] (Jardine, Quintin)
Skinner's Round [1995] (Jardine, Quintin)
■ Skinner's Rules [1993] (Jardine, Quintin) ☆
Skinner's Trail [1994] (Jardine, Quintin)
Skinny Annie Blues [1996] (Barrett, Neal, Jr.)
Skintight Shroud [1990] (Dundee, Wayne)☆
Skinwalkers [1987] (Hillerman, Tony) ★
Skulduggery [1979] (Marshall, William)
Sky is Falling [1985] (Murphy, Warren B.)
■ Skylar [1995] (McDonald, Gregory)

Skylar in Yankeeland [1997] (McDonald, Gregory)
Skyprobe [1966] (McCutchan, Philip)
■ Slab Happy [1958] (Prather, Richard)
Slashback [1995] (Levine, Paul)
Slasher [1977] (Collins, Max Allan, Jr.)
Slasher [1980] (Collins, Michael)
Slate [1984] (Aldyne, Nathan)
■ Slave Safari [1973] (Murphy, Warren B.)
Slay Ride [1990] (Newton, Michael)
■ Slayground [1971] (Stark, Richard)
Sleaze [1985] (Morse, L. A.)
Sleep and His Brother [1971] (Dickinson, Peter)
■ Sleep Long, My Love [1959] (Waugh, Hillary)
Sleepers of Erin [1983] (Gash, Jonathan)
■ Sleeping Dog [1985] (Lochte, Dick) ★ ☆☆☆
■ Sleeping Dogs [1994] (Paul, William)
■ Sleeping Dogs Die [1988] (King, Frank)
Sleeping in the Blood [1991] (Richardson, Robert)
Sleeping Partner [1996] (Paul, William)
Sleeping Policeman [1992] (Taylor, Andrew)
Sleeping Pretty [1995] (Paul, William)
Sleeping with the Crawfish [1997] (Donaldson, D. J.)
Sleightly Deceived [1987] (Kelley, Patrick A.)
Sleightly Guilty [1988] (Kelley, Patrick A.)
Sleightly Invisible [1987] (Kelley, Patrick A.)
Sleightly Lethal [1986] (Kelley, Patrick A.)
■ Sleightly Murder [1985] (Kelley, Patrick A.)
Slice [1990] (Miller, Rex)
Slight of Body [Brit] (McInerny, Ralph)
Slip of the Tong [1992] (Goodrum, Charles A.)
Slit My Throat, Gently [1968] (Brett, Michael)
■ Slob [1987] (Miller, Rex)
■ Slow Grave [Brit.] (Philbrick, W.R.)
■ Smack Man [1975] (DeMille, Nelson)
Small Masterpiece [U.S.] (Heald, Tim)
Small Vices [1997] (Parker, Robert B.)
Smallbone Deceased [1950] (Gilbert, Michael)
■ Smart Moves [1987] (Kaminsky, Stuart M.)
Smash Cut [1991] (Womack, Steven)
Smiley's People [1980] (Le Carré, John)
Smoke Detector [1984] (Wright, Eric)
■ Smoked Out [1982] (Murphy, Warren B.) ☆
Snake [1975] (McClure, James)
Snake [1964] (Spillane, Mickey)
■ Snake Eater [1993] (Tapply, William G.)
Snake Eyes [1987] (Dold, Gaylord)☆
Snake Eyes [1995] (Hoyt, Richard)
■ Snake in the Grasses [1987] (Hilary, Richard)
Snake Oil [1990] (Roberts, Les)
Snare in the Dark [1982] (Parrish, Frank)
Snark [1985] (DeAndrea, William L.)
■ Snatch [1971] (Pronzini, Bill)
■ Snatch Crop [1991] (Hammond, Gerald)
■ Sniper [1974] (DeMille, Nelson)
Snow Man [1987] (Busby, Roger) ★
Snow on the Roses [1996] (Riggs, John R)
Snow White and Rose Red [1985] (McBain, Ed)
Snow-Job [1986] (Copper, Basil)
■ Snowball [1974] (Allbeury, Ted)
Snowjob [1993] (Wood, Ted)
So Like Sleep [1987] (Healy, Jeremiah)
So Long as You Both Shall Live [1976] (McBain, Ed)
So Much Blood [1976] (Brett, Simon)
So Rich, So Lovely, and So Dead [1952] (Masur, Harold Q.)
Softcover Kill [1971] (Harknett, Terry)
■ Softener [1984] (Bolton, Melvin)
Software Bomb [1993] (Womack, Steven)
Soho Jungle [1958] (Bateson, David)
Soldier No More [1981] (Price, Anthony)
Sole Survivor [1988] (Murphy, Warren B.)
■ Solo Hand [1994] (Moody, Bill)
Some Clouds [1992] (Taibo, Paco Ignacio, II)

1 Some Dark Antiquities [1994] (Ardin, William)
Some Predators Are Male [1985] (Tripp, Miles)
1 Somebody Has to Lose [1975] (Chambers, Peter)
Someday the Rabbi Will Leave [1985] (Kemelman, Harry)
Sometimes You Get the Bear [1993] (Block, Lawrence)
Son of Fletch [1993] (McDonald, Gregory)
1 Son of Holmes [1986] (Lescroart, John T.)
Song Dog [1991] (McClure, James)
Song of a Dark Angel [1994] (Doherty, P. C.)
Song of Corpus Juris [1974] (Hensley, Joe L.)
1 Sorry Now [1991] (Zubro, Mark)
Sorry State [1974] (Kenyon, Michael)
Sort of Samurai [1981] (Melville, James)
Sound of the Trumpet [1997] (Moody, Bill)
1 Sour Lemon Score [1969] (Stark, Richard)☆
1 South Street Confidential [1989] (Belsky, Dick)
Southern Cross [1994] (DeBrosse, Jim)
Southern Cross [1993] (Greenleaf, Stephen)
1 Space for Hire [1971] (Nolan, William F.)☆
Spadework [1996] (Pronzini, Bill)
Spanish Maze Game [1990] (MacLeod, Robert)
1 Spare Parts [1994] (Hanson, Rick)
Spark [1993] (Lutz, John)
Spatchcock Plan [1990] (McCutchan, Philip)
Speak for the Dead [1978] (Burns, Rex)
1 Speak III of the Dead [1968] (Chambers, Peter)
Speak Softly [1987] (Alexander, Lawrence)
Special Delivery [1992] (Kennealy, Jerry) ☆
Specimen Song [1995] (Bowen, Peter)
Spend Game [1980] (Gash, Jonathan)
Sphere of Death [1990] (Harrison, Ray)
Spiced to Death [1997] (King, Peter)
Spin [1994] (Judd, Bob)
Spiral [1986] (Lindsey, David L.)
1 Spiral Path [1955] (Grayson, Richard)
Spiral Staircase [1983] (Wainright, John)
Spitting Image [1953] (Avallone, Michael)
1 Split Seconds [1991] (Robinson, Kevin)
Splitting Heirs [1997] (Hanson, Rick)
Spoils of War [1981] (Murphy, Warren B.)
Spoken Word [1992] (Irvine, Robert)
Spoonful of Luger [1975] (Ormerod, Roger)
Spotted Cats [1991] (Tapply, William G.)
Spree [1987] (Collins, Max Allan, Jr.)
Spy and Die [1976] (Meyers, Martin)
1 Spy For Sale [1969] (Payne, Laurence)
Spy Hook [1988] (Deighton, Len)
Spy in Chancery [1988] (Doherty, P. C.)
Spy Line [1989] (Deighton, Len)
Spy Sinker [1990] (Deighton, Len)
Spy Story [1974] (Deighton, Len)
Spy Who Came in from the Cold [1963] (Le Carré, John) ★★
Squall Line [Brit.] (Hall, James W.)
Square Dance [1975] (Wainright, John)
Squeezeplay [1992] (Nighbert, David F.)
St. John and the Seven Veils [1991] (Babula, William)
1 St. John's Baptism [1988] (Babula, William)
St. John's Bestiary [1994] (Babula, William)
St. John's Bread [1997] (Babula, William)
Stab in the Dark [1978] (Block, Lawrence) ☆
Stable Cat [1996] (Allen, Garrison)
Stained Glass [1978] (Buckley, William F.)
Stained White Radiance [1992] (Burke, James Lee)
Staked Goat [1986] (Healy, Jeremiah)
1 Stalking Horse [1994] (Shoemaker, Bill)
1 Stalking Horse [1982] (Wilcox, Collin)
Stalking the Angel [1989] (Crais, Robert)
Stand-Up [1994] (Randisi, Robert J.)
1 Star King [1964] (Vance, Jack)
Star Trap [1977] (Brett, Simon)
1 Stardust [1990] (Parker, Robert B.)
State's Evidence [1982] (Greenleaf, Stephen)

Steak in the Action [1998] (Ford, G. M.)
1 Steam Pig [1971] (McClure, James) ★
Steel Hit [Brit.] (Stark, Richard)
Steel Web [1991] (Tierney, Ronald)
1 Steele [1989] (Masters, J. D.)
Steinway Collection [1983] (Randisi, Robert J.) ☆
Stench of Poppies [1978] (Drummond, Ivor)
Still and Icy Silence [1993] (Roat, Ronald Clair)
Still Life [1996] (Hanson, Rick)
Still Life with Pistol [1986] (Ormerod, Roger)
Still Water [1997] (Harvey, John)
Sting in the Tail [1994] (Hammond, Gerald)
Sting of the Honeybee [1978] (Parrish, Frank)
Stinger [1990] (Hornig, Doug)
Stolen Away [1991] (Collins, Max Allan, Jr.) ★
1 Stolen Gods [1993] (Page, Jake)
1 Stone Angel [1986] (Albert, Marvin H.) ☆
Stone Boy [1993] (Levitsky, Ronald)
Stone Cold Dead [1995] (Ormerod, Roger)
Stone Dust [1995] (Scott, Justin)
1 Stone Killer [U.S.] (Gardner, John)
1 Stone of the Heart [1988] (Brady, John) ★
Stone of the Heart [1995] (McEldowney, Eugene)
Stone Shadow [1989] (Miller, Rex)
1 Stone Veil [1990] (Tierney, Ronald) ☆
Stonekiller [1995] (Janes, J. Robert)
Stopover for Murder [1973] (Stone, Thomas H.)
Storme Front [1995] (Ripley, W. L.)
Stormtide [1972] (Knox, Bill)
Storm Center [1986] (Clark, Douglas)
Story of Henri Tod [1984] (Buckley, William F.)
Straight Man [1986] (Simon, Roger L.)☆
Straight No Chaser [1989] (Batten, Jack)
1 Strange and Bitter Crop [1994] (Wyrick, E. L.)
1 Strange Attractor [1991] (Cory, Desmond)
Strange Case of Harpo Higgins [1995] (McEldowney, Eugene)
1 Strange Inheritance [1985] (Biderman, Bob)
Strange Loyalties [1991] (McIlvanney, William)
Stranger City Caper [1979] (Spencer, Ross H.)
Strangle Hold [1991] (Doolittle, Jerome)
1 Stranglehold [1961] (Cory, Desmond)
Strangler [1989] (Hall, Parnell)
Strangling Man [1987] (Hunter, Alan)
1 Stray Shot [1988] (Hammond, Gerald)
Street Killer [1989] (Philbin, Tom)
Streetbird [1983] (van de Wetering, Janwillem)
Strega [1987] (Vachss, Andrew H.)
Strenuous Life [1991] (Alexander, Lawrence)
Strike Out Where Not Applicable [1967] (Freeling, Nicolas)
1 Strike Three, You're Dead [1984] (Rosen, Richard) ★
1 Strikezone [1988] (Nighbert, David F.)
1 Strip for Murder [1955] (Prather, Richard)
Strip Jack [1992] (Rankin, Ian)
Strip Search [1984] (Burns, Rex)
Strong-Arm [1972] (Copper, Basil)
Subtle Serpent [1996] (Tremayne, Peter)
Such Women are Dangerous [Brit.] (Webb, Jack)
Sudden Death [1985] (Kienzle, William X.)
1 Sudden Departures [1988] (Ross, Jonathan)
Sudden Prey [1996] (Sandford, John)
Suddenly a Corpse [1949] (Masur, Harold Q.)
Sue Me (by Sapir) [1986] (Murphy, Warren B.)
1 Suffer Little Children [1991] (Davis, Thomas D.) ★
Suffer Little Children [1995] (Tremayne, Peter)
Sugartown [1984] (Estleman, Loren D.) ★
Suicide Hill [1986] (Ellroy, James)
1 Suicide Murders [U.S.] (Engel, Howard)
1 Suicide Notice [1980] (Engel, Howard)
1 Suicide Season [1987] (Burns, Rex)
Suicide Squeeze [1995] (Everson, David H.)
Suitcase in Berlin [1989] (Flynn, Don)
Sum of All Fears [1991] (Clancy, Tom)

Summer Cool [1993] (Sarrantonio, Al)
Summertime News [1995] (Belsky, Dick)
Summit Chase [1973] (Murphy, Warren B.)
Summons [1995] (Lovesey, Peter) ☆★
■ Sunburst [1971] (Cory, Desmond)
Sunday Hangman [1977] (McClure, James)
Sunday the Rabbi Stayed Home [1969] (Kemelman, Harry)
■ Sunset Bomber [1986] (Kincaid, D.)
Sunset Express [1996] (Crais, Robert) ★
Sunshine Enemies [1990] (Constantine, K. C.)
■ Sunstrike [1979] (McCutchan, Philip)
Superintendent's Room [U.S.] (Ashford, Jeffrey)
■ Supreme Adventure of Insp. Lestrade [U.S.] (Trow, M.J.)
Sure Thing [1975] (Prather, Richard)
Survival of the Fittest [1997] (Kellerman, Jonathan)
Survival...Zero! [1971] (Spillane, Mickey)
■ Suspense [1998] (Hall, Parnell)
Suspicious Minds [1992] (Edwards, Martin)
■ Swag [1976] (Leonard, Elmore)
Swan Dive [1988] (Healy, Jeremiah) ☆
Sweet Dreams [1976] (Murphy, Warren B.)
■ Sweet Justice [1985] (Oster, Jerry)
Sweet La-La Land [1990] (Campbell, Robert)
Sweet Poison [1970] (Clark, Douglas)
Sweet Ride [1972] (Prather, Richard)
■ Sweet Silver Blues [1987] (Cook, Glen)
Sweet Women Lie [1990] (Estleman, Loren D.)
Sweetfeed [1996] (Healy, R. Austin)
Swing Low, Sweet Harriett [1967] (Baxt, George)
Swing, Swing Together [1976] (Lovesey, Peter)
Switch [1984] (Bayer, William)
■ Switchback [1993] (Wilcox, Collin)
■ Sword of General Englund [1996] (Honig, Donald)

T

Table d'Hote [1977] (Clark, Douglas)
■ Taffin [1980] (Mallett, Lyndon)
Taffin's First Law [1980] (Mallett, Lyndon)
Take [1990] (James, Bill)
■ Take a Murder, Darling [1958] (Prather, Richard)
Take Murder... [1979] (Wainright, John)
Take the A-Train [1991] (Timlin, Mark)
Take the D Train [1990] (King, Frank)
■ Take the Money and Run [1982] (Payne, Laurence)
Take-Over [1975] (Miller, Victor B.)
■ Tale of the Lazy Dog [1970] (Williams, Alan)
■ Talk Show Murders [1982] (Allen, Steve)
Talking God [1989] (Hillerman, Tony)
Talking Pictures Murder Case [1990] (Baxt, George)
Tall, Dark, and Deadly [1956] (Masur, Harold Q.)
■ Tall Dolores [1953] (Avallone, Michael)
Tallant for Democracy [1993] (York, Andrew)
Tallant for Disaster [1978] (York, Andrew)
Tallant for Terror [1995] (York, Andrew)
■ Tallant for Trouble [1977] (York, Andrew)
Tallulah Bankhead Murder Case [1987] (Baxt, George)
Tally's Truth [1987] (Ross, Philip)
Tallyman [1969] (Knox, Bill)
■ Taming a Sea-Horse [1986] (Parker, Robert B.)
Tangent Factor [1978] (Sanders, Lawrence)
■ Tangent Objective [1976] (Sanders, Lawrence)
Tangled June [1997] (Albert, Neil)
Tangled Knot of Murder [1996] (Roe, C. F.)
Tank of Sacred Eels [1976] (Drummond, Ivor)
Tanner's Tiger [1968] (Block, Lawrence)
Tanner's Twelve Swingers [1967] (Block, Lawrence)
Tapestry of Murders [1995] (Doherty, P. C.)
Target: Charity Ross [1968] (Bickham, Jack)
Target for Murder [1993] (Trainor, J. F.)
Target Steele [1990] (Masters, J. D.)
Tarnished Blue [1995] (Heffernan, William) ★
Tarnished Icons [1997] (Kaminsky, Stuart M.)
Tartan Ringers [1986] (Gash, Jonathan)

Tartan Sell [U.S.] (Gash, Jonathan)
Taste for Death [1969] (O'Donnell, Peter)
Taste of Proof [1965] (Knox, Bill)
Tax in Blood [1987] (Schutz, Benjamin) ★
■ Tears of Things [1996] (McInerny, Ralph)
Tek Kill [1996] (Shatner, William)
Tek Money [1995] (Shatner, William)
Tek Power [1994] (Shatner, William)
Tek Secret [1993] (Shatner, William)
Tek Vengeance [1991] (Shatner, William)
Teklab [1992] (Shatner, William)
Teklords [1990] (Shatner, William)
■ Tekwar [1989] (Shatner, William)
■ Telluride Smile [1988] (Ring, Raymond H.)
Ten Little Medicine Men [1998] (Pomidor, Bill)
■ Ten Plus One [1963] (McBain, Ed)
Tenoclock Scholar [1995] (Miles, John)
Tenth Interview [1986] (Wainright, John)
Tequila Mockingbird [1997] (Bishop, Paul)
Terminal [1984] (Forbes, Colin)
■ Terminators [1975] (Hamilton, Donald)
Terminus [1990] (Puckett, Andrew)
Terror is My Trade [1958] (Marlowe, Stephen)
Terror Squad [1973] (Murphy, Warren B.)
■ Terrorizers [1977] (Hamilton, Donald)
■ Testament of Caspar Schultz [1962] (Fallon, Martin)
■ Testimony [1992] (Palmer, Frank)
Testing [1987] (Bolton, Melvin)
Tethered Goat [Brit.] (Healy, Jeremiah) ★
Thank You, Good-Bye [APA] (Jenkins, Jerry)
That Day the Rabbi Left Town [1996] (Kemelman, Harry) ★
That Night it Rained [1961] (Waugh, Hillary)
■ Their Man in the White House [1971] (Ardies, Tom)
Therapy in Dynamite [1975] (Miller, Victor B.)
There Are No Spies [1986] (Granger, Bill)
There Fell a Shadow [1988] (Peterson, Keith)
■ There is Something About a Dame [1963] (Avallone, Michael)
Tere Was a Little Girl [1994] (McBain, Ed)
There Was an Old Woman [1993] (Engel, Howard)
■ They Call It Murder [1973] (Chambers, Peter)
They Never Looked Inside [1948] (Gilbert, Michael)
Thicker than Blood [1993] (Lutz, John)
Thicker than Water [1981] (McInerny, Ralph)
Thicker Than Water [1992] (Zimmerman, Bruce)
Thief of Time [1988] (Hillerman, Tony) ★ ☆
Thief Taker [1991] (Scholefield, Alan)
Thief Who Couldn't Sleep [1966] (Block, Lawrence)
■ Thin Air [1993] (Hammond, Gerald)
Thin Air [1977] (Marshall, William)
Thin Air [1995] (Parker, Robert B.)
Things Invisible [1989] (Reynolds, William J.)
Things We Do for Love [1989] (Schutz, Benjamin)
■ Think Fast, Mr. Peters [1988] (Kaminsky, Stuart M.)
Thinning the Turkey Herd [1988] (Campbell, Robert)
Third Deadly Sin [1981] (Sanders, Lawrence)
Third Figure [1967] (Wilcox, Collin)
Third Man Out [1992] (Stevenson, Richard)
Third Victim [1976] (Wilcox, Collin)
■ Thirteen Days [1959] (Jeffries, Ian)
■ This Drakotny [1971] (McCutchan, Philip)
This is Jezebel [1952] (Cory, Desmond)
This Is Murder, Mr. Jones [1943] (Fuller, Timothy)
This Suitcase is Going to Explode [1972] (Ardies, Tom)
This Traitor, Death [1952] (Cory, Desmond)
This'll Kill You [1964] (Chambers, Peter)
Thousand-Yard Stare [1991] (Kantner, Rob) ☆
Threateners [1992] (Hamilton, Donald)
Threats and Menaces [1993] (Scholefield, Alan)
Three and One Make Five [1984] (Jeffries, Roderic)
Three Blind Mice [1990] (McBain, Ed)
Three Days in Winter [1983] (Jenkins, Jerry)
■ Three Days of the Condor [APA] (Grady, James)

Three Thirds of a Ghost [1941] (Fuller, Timothy)
Three With a Bullet [1985] (Lyons, Arthur)
Three's a Shroud [3 novellas] [1957] (Prather, Richard)
■ Three-Toed Pussy [1968] (Burley, W. J.)
Threepersons Hunt [1974] (Garfield, Brian)
Thrown Away Child [1996] (Adcock, Thomas)
Thunder Point [1993] (Higgins, Jack)
Thursday the Rabbi Walked Out [1978] (Kemelman, Harry)
Tick of Death [APA] (Lovesey, Peter)
Ticket to Ride [1973] (Perry, Ritchie)
Ticket to the Boneyard [1990] (Block, Lawrence) ☆
■ Tiebreaker [1989] (Bickham, Jack M.)
Ties That Bind [1994] (Adler, William)
Tigers Burning [1994] (Evers, Crabbe)
Tight Corner [1976] (Copper, Basil)
Tight Lines [1992] (Tapply, William G.)
'Til Death [1959] (McBain, Ed)
Timber Line [1980] (Murphy, Warren B.)
Time Bomb [1990] (Kellerman, Jonathan)
Time Exposure [1989] (Lutz, John)
■ Time for Dying [1989] (Ross, Jonathan)
■ Time for the Death of a King [1994] (Dukthas, Ann)
Timelocke [1991] (Barnao, Jack)
Time of Murder at Mayerling [1996] (Dukthas, Ann)
Time to Check Out [1996] (Michaels, Grant)
Time to Kill [1990] (Fliegel, Richard)
■ Time to Kill [1974] (Ormerod, Roger)
Time to Murder and Create [1976] (Block, Lawrence) ☆
Time Trap [1994] (Corris, Peter)
Time Trial [1983] (Murphy, Warren B.)
■ Timeless Sleep [1963] (Galway, Robert Conington)
■ Timelock [1967] (Cory, Desmond)
Timor Mortis [1986] (Harriss, Will)
■ Timothy Files [1987] (Sanders, Lawrence)
Timothy's Game [1988] (Sanders, Lawrence)
Tincture of Death [1989] (Harrison, Ray)
Tinker, Tailor, Solider, Spy [1974] (Le Carré, John)
Tinpan Tiger Killer [1998] (Lupoff, Richard A.)
■ Tinplate [1986] (Steed, Neville) ★
■ Tip on a Dead Crab [1984] (Murray, William)
Titian Committee [1992] (Pears, Iain)
■ To Catch a Forger [1988] (Wallace, Robert)
To Die in Beverly Hills [1983] (Petievich, Gerald)
To Kill a Cat [1970] (Burley, W. J.)
■ To Kill a Witch [1971] (Knox, Bill)
■ To Speak for the Dead [1990] (Levine, Paul)
Toll Call [1987] (Greenleaf, Stephen)
■ Tomorrow is Another Day [1995] (Kaminsky, Stuart M.)
Tomorrow's Ghost [1979] (Price, Anthony)
■ Too Clever by Half [1990] (Jeffries, Roderic)
Too Late for the Funeral [1977] (Ormerod, Roger)
■ Too Late to Die [1986] (Crider, Bill) ★
Too Late to Tell [1984] (Jenkins, Jerry)
Too Many Notes, Mr. Mozart [1995] (Bastable, Bernard)
Too Old a Cat [1986] (Murphy, Warren B.) ☆
Too Small for His Shoes [1962] (Payne, Laurence)
■ Too Soon Dead [1997] (Kurland, Michael)
■ Top Banana [1996] (James, Bill)
Tooth & Nail [U.S.] (Rankin, Ian)
■ Topkapi [U.S.] (Ambler, Eric) ★★
Topless Tulip Caper [1975] (Block, Lawrence)
Topsy and Evil [1968] (Baxt, George)
Torch [1994] (Lutz, John)
Torch Town Boogie [1993] (Womack, Steven) ☆
Torrid Piece of Murder [1992] (Roe, C. F.)
Total Recall [1984] (Murphy, Warren B.)
Touch of Darkness [1972] (Crowe, John)
Touch of Death [1981] (Sadler, Mark)
Touch of Frost [1988] (Wingfield, R. D.)
Touch of Malice [1973] (Wainright, John)
Touch of the Past [1988] (Breen, Jon) ☆

Touch the Devil [1982] (Higgins, Jack)
Tough Baby [1990] (Sublett, Jesse)
Tough Enough [1989] (Philbrick, W. R.) ☆
Tournament of Murders [1996] (Doherty, P. C.)
Toyotomi Blades [1997] (Furutani, Dale)
■ Trace [1983] (Murphy, Warren B.) ☆☆
Trace and 47 Miles of Rope [1984] (Murphy, Warren B.) ☆
■ Tracer, Inc. [1994] (Andrus, Jeff)
■ Trade Secrets [1996] (Thomson, Maynard F.)
Trade-Off [1975] (Miller, Victor B.)
Trail to Buddha's Mirror [1993] (Winslow, Don)
Traitor's End [1988] (Hunter, Alan)
Traitor's Exit [1970] (Gardner, John)
■ Trapdoor [1988] (Peterson, Keith) ☆
Treasure [1988] (Cussler, Clive)
Treasure by Degrees [1977] (Williams, David)
■ Treasure by Post [1991] (Williams, David)
■ Treasure in Oxford [1988] (Williams, David)
Treasure in Roubles [1987] (Williams, David)
Treasure of the Cosa Nostra [1966] (Ridgway, Jason)
Treasure Preserved [1983] (Williams, David)
Treasure Up in Smoke [1978] (Williams, David)
Trial [1996] (Hall, Parnell)
■ Triarchs [1994] (Wilson, Derek)
Tribe [1996] (Zimmerman, R. D.)
Trick Question [1997] (Dunbar, Tony)
Tricks [1987] (McBain, Ed)
■ Trigger Pull [1991] (Malone, Paul)
Trigger-Man [1983] (Copper, Basil)
Trip to Jerusalem [1990] (Marston, Edward)
Triple Crown [1985] (Breen, Jon)
Triple Exposure [1977] (Townend, Peter)
Triumvirate [1966] (Taylor, H. Baldwin)
Trojan Hearse [1964] (Prather, Richard)
Tropical Freeze [1989] (Hall, James W.)
■ Tropical Heat [1986] (Lutz, John)
■ Trotsky's Run [1982] (Hoyt, Richard)
Trouble is My Name [1957] (Marlowe, Stephen)
Trouble with Tycoons [1967] (Taylor, H. Baldwin)
Troubled Deaths [1977] (Jeffries, Roderic)
Troublemaker [1975] (Hansen, Joseph)
Trout in the Milk [1986] (Lewis, Roy)
Truck Shot [1989] (Stinson, Jim)
True Crime [1984] (Collins, Max Allan, Jr.) ☆
■ True Detective [1983] (Collins, Max Allan, Jr.) ★
Trunk Music [1997] (Connelly, Michael)
Truth Can Get You Killed [1997] (Zubro, Mark)
Tsing-Boom! [U.S.] (Freeling, Nicolas)
Tsing-Boum [1969] (Freeling, Nicolas)
Tucker's Last Stand [1990] (Buckley, William F.)
Tuesday the Rabbi Saw Red [1974] (Kemelman, Harry)
■ Tularosa [1996] (McGarrity, Michael) ☆
Tumbleweed [1976] (van de Wetering, Janwillem)
Turn Blue, You Murderers [1967] (Brett, Michael)
Turn Down an Empty Glass [1987] (Copper, Basil)
Turn-Out Man [1984] (Roderus, Frank)
Turnaround [1992] (Timlin, Mark)
Tuxedo Park [1985] (Copper, Basil)
TV Safe [1991] (Stinson, Jim)
■ Twelfth Man [1991] (Marquis, Max)
Twenty Blue Devils [1997] (Elkins, Aaron)
Twice Buried [1994] (Havill, Steven F.)
Twice Dead [1996] (Bishop, Paul)
Twinkle, Twinkle, Little Spy [1976] (Deighton, Len)
■ Twist of Sand [1959] (Jenkins, Geoffrey)
■ Twist of the Knife [1988] (Solomita, Stephen)
Twisted Thing [1966] (Spillane, Mickey)
Two for Tanner [1967] (Block, Lawrence)
Two Songs This Archangel Sings [1986] (Chesbro, George)
Two Way Cut [1988] (Turnbull, Peter)

Two-Bear Mambo [1995] (Lansdale, Joe R.)
Two-Faced Death [1976] (Jeffries, Roderic)
Two-Way Frame [1967] (Harknett, Terry)
Twospot [1978] (Wilcox, Collin)
Twospot [1978] (Pronzini, Bill)
Tyger! Tyger! [1996] (Hoyt, Richard)
∎ Typical American Town [1994] (Roberts, John Maddox)

U

Ultimate Client [Brit.] (Avallone, Michael)
∎ Unbecoming Habits [1973] (Heald, Tim)
∎ Under a Monsoon Cloud [1986] (Keating, H. R. F.)
Under Cover [1986] (Philbin, Tom)
∎ Under Cover of Daylight [1987] (Hall, James W.)
∎ Under the Boardwalk [1989] (Kent, Bill)
∎ Under the Bright Lights [1986] (Woodrell, Dan)
∎ Undercurrents [1988] (Pearson, Ridley)
Undercurrents [1973] (Pronzini, Bill)
Underdog [1994] (Lewin, Michael Z.)
Underground Man [1990] (Hailey, J. P.)
Understrike [1965] (Gardner, John)
∎ Undertow [1962] (Cory, Desmond)
Underworld [1988] (Hill, Reginald)
Undignified Death [1993] (Marquis, Max)
Undue Influence [1994] (Martini, Steve)
Uneasy Street [1948] (Miller, Wade)
Unfit to Plead [1992] (Palmer, Frank)
Unfunny Money [1989] (Alexander, Gary)
Unhanged Man [U.S.] (Hunter, Alan)
Unholy Ground [1989] (Brady, John)
∎ Unholy Writ [1976] (Williams, David)
Unhung Man [1983] (Hunter, Alan)
Union Bust [1973] (Murphy, Warren B.)
Unknown Man No. 89 [1977] (Leonard, Elmore)
Unnatural Causes [1988] (Noguchi, Thomas T. w/Arthur Lyons)
Unnatural Hazard [1989] (Cork, Barry)
Unseemly End [1981] (Jeffries, Roderic)
∎ Unseen Witness [1992] (Matthews, Lew)
Upon a Dark Night [1997] (Lovesey, Peter)
Upon Some Midnights Clear [1985] (Constantine, K. C.)
Urge for Justice [1981] (Wainright, John)

V

Valediction [1984] (Parker, Robert B.)
Valley of the Fox [1982] (Hone, Joseph)
Vanished [1973] (Pronzini, Bill)
Vanishers [1986] (Hamilton, Donald)
Vanishing Act [1993] (Margolis, Seth)
∎ Vanishing Act [1995] (Perry, Thomas)
Vanishing Holes Murders [1985] (Chambers, Peter)
Vanishing Smile [1995] (Emerson, Earl) ☆
Vatican Rip [1981] (Gash, Jonathan)
∎ Veil [1986] (Chesbro, George)
Veil of Ignorance [1988] (Quill, Monica)
Veiled Threat [1985] (Jenkins, Jerry)
Vendetta [1990] (Dibdin, Michael) ★
Vengeance is Mine! [1950] (Spillane, Mickey)
Venus Deal [1993] (Kuhlken, Ken)
Venus Throw [1995] (Saylor, Steven)
∎ Verdict [1980] (Reed, Barry)
Veritas [1997] (Lashner, William)
∎ Vermilion [1980] (Aldyne, Nathan)
Veroncia Dean Case [1984] (Waugh, Hillary)
Versions of the Truth [1994] (Parrish, Richard)
Very Big Bang [1975] (McCutchan, Philip)
Very Deadly Game [1975] (Miller, Victor B.)
∎ Very Last Gambado [1989] (Gash, Jonathan)
Very Parochial Murder [1988] (Wainright, John)
Very Parochial Murder [1988] (Wainright, John)
Very Private Plot [1994] (Buckley, William F.)
Very Venetian Murder [1992] (Murphy, Haughton)
Very Wrong Number [1987] (Douglas, Arthur)

Vespers [1990] (McBain, Ed)
∎ Vicar's Roses [Brit.] (Breen, Jon)
Vice Isn't Private [U.S.] (Cleeve, Brian)
∎ Vicous Circle [1983] (Clark, Douglas)
Victim Must Be Found [1988] (Engel, Howard)
Victims [1971] (Rossiter, John)
∎ Victims [1985] (Wilcox, Collin)
Video Vandal [1984] (Roderus, Frank)
Video Vengeance [1990] (Tripp, Miles)
Vienna Blood [1984] (Payne, Laurence)
View from the Square [1983] (Trenhaile, John)
Vig [1990] (Lescroart, John T.)
Villain of the Earth [1994] (Shaw, Simon) ★
Villains [1974] (Rossiter, John)
Vintage Polo [1993] (Kennealy, Jerry)
Vintage Year for Dying [1992] (Orenstein, Frank)
Violence in Velvet [1956] (Avallone, Michael)
Violence is My Business [1958] (Marlowe, Stephen)
Violent Crimes [1997] (Holton, Hugh)
Violent Death of a Bitter Englishman [1967] (Cleeve, Brian)
Violent Love [1991] (Oster, Jerry)
∎ Violent Spring [1994] (Phillips, Gary)
∎ Viper Quarry [1994] (Feldmeyer, Dean) ☆
∎ Vivienne: Gently Where She Lay [1972] (Hunter, Alan)
Vixen 03 [1978] (Cussler, Clive)
Vodoo River [1995] (Crais, Robert)
∎ Voice from the Dead [1974] (Copper, Basil)
Voices from the Dark [1993] (Parrish, Frank)
Voices in the Dark [1994] (Coburn, Andrew)
Void in Hearts [1988] (Tapply, William G.)
Voodoo Die [1978] (Murphy, Warren B.)
Voodoo Murders [1957] (Avallone, Michael)
∎ Vote X for Treason [1964] (Cleeve, Brian)
Vulgar Boatman [1987] (Tapply, William G.)
Vulture [1994] (Keegan, Alex)

W

∎ Wages of Zen [1979] (Melville, James)
∎ Wailing Frail [1956] (Prather, Richard)
Waiting for the End of the World [1984] (Taylor, Andrew)
Wake Up to Murder [1996] (Allen, Steve)
Walk a Black Wind [1971] (Collins, Michael)
Walk Among the Tombstones [1992] (Block, Lawrence)
Walk at Night [1971] (Craig, David)
Walk on the Water [1991] (Philbrick, W. R.)
Walking Shadow [1994] (Parker, Robert B.)
Walking Wounded [1988] (Murphy, Warren B.)
∎ Wall of Glass [1989] (Satterthwait, Walter) ☆
Wallflower [1991] (Bayer, William)
∎ War Against Charity Ross [1967] (Bickham, Jack)
War Game [1976] (Price, Anthony)
War Machine [1982] (Marshall, William)
Warmaster [1963] (McCutchan, Philip)
Warning Shot [1996] (Egleton, Clive)
∎ Washington Club [1997] (Corris, Peter)
∎ Washington Deceased [1990] (Bowen, Michael)
Wasted Years [1993] (Harvey, John)
Water Cure [1992] (Downing, Warwick)
∎ Waterman [1987] (Hornig, Doug)
Watery Grave [1996] (Alexander, Bruce)
∎ Wavecrest [1985] (Knox, Bill)
Wax Apple [1970] (Coe, Tucker)
Waxwork [1978] (Lovesey, Peter) ★
Way Down on the High Lonely [1994] (Winslow, Don)
Way of a Wanton [1952] (Prather, Richard)
Way Past Dead [1995] (Womack, Steven) ☆
Way Through the Woods [1992] (Dexter, Colin) ★
Way We Die Now [1973] (Lewin, Michael Z.)
Way With Widows [1994] (Adams, Harold)
We the Killers [1967] (Brett, Michael)
We're Off to See the Killer [1993] (Murray, William)

Web [1996] (Kellerman, Jonathan)
Wedding Treasure [1985] (Williams, David)
Wednesday the Rabbit Got Wet [1976] (Kemelman, Harry)
Wednesday's Child [1992] (Robinson, Peter) ☆☆
Weight of Evidence [1978] (Ormerod, Roger)
Wench is Dead [1989] (Dexter, Colin) ★
❶ Werewolf [1982] (McCutchan, Philip)
Werewolf Murders [1992] (DeAndrea, William)
Wet Graves [1991] (Corris, Peter)
Wet Work [1992] (Newton, Michael)
Whale's Footprints [1988] (Boyer, Rick)
What Are the Bugles Blowing For? [1975] (Freeling, Nicolas)
❶ What Bloody Man Is That? [1987] (Brett, Simon)
❶ What Mommy Said [1997] (Jeffers, H. Paul)
What Rough Beast [1957] (Trench, John)
What's the Worst That Could Happen? [1996]
 (Westlake, Donald E.)
When Elephants Forget [1984] (Murphy, Warren B.)
When Last Seen Alive [1998] (Haywood, Gar Anthony)
When Old Men Die [1994] (Crider, Bill)
❶ When the Bough Breaks [1985] (Kellerman, Jonathan) ★★
When the Cat's Away [1988] (Friedman, Kinky)
When the Fat Man Sings [1987] (Murray, William)
When the Killing Starts [1989] (Wood, Ted)
When the Night Comes [1993] (Oster, Jerry)
When the Old Man Died [1991] (Ormerod, Roger)
When the Sacred Ginmill Closes [1986] (Block, Lawrence)☆
When They Kill Your Wife [1977] (Crowe, John)
❶ Where All the Girls are Sweeter [1975] (Butler, Richard)
Where Dead Soldiers Walk [1994] (Biggle, Lloyd, Jr.)
While Drowning in the Desert [1996] (Winslow, Don)
Whip Hand [1979] (Francis, Dick) ★★
Whirlpool [1995] (Estabrook, Barry)
Whirlpool [1991] (Forbes, Colin)
Whiskey Jack [1994] (Trainor, J. F.)
Whisper [1988] (Marshall, William)
Whisper of Black [1997] (Harvey, Clay)
Whisper of Rage [1997] (Hemlin, Tim)
Whistler in the Dark [1986] (Malcolm, John)
White Butterfly [1993] (Mosley, Walter) ☆☆
White Cad Cross-Up [1969] (Nolan, William F.)
White Flower [1989] (Ross, Philip)
White House Pantry Murder [1987] (Roosevelt, Elliott)
White Meat [1981] (Corris, Peter)
❶ White Rook [1990] (Davis, J. Madison)
❶ White Rose Murders [1991] (Clynes, Michael)
White Shoes, White Lines and Blackie [1992]
 (Barrett, Robert G.)
Whitewater [1974] (Knox, Bill)
❶ Who in Hell is Wanda Fuca? [1995] (Ford, G. M.) ☆☆
Who Shot Longshot Sam? [1974] [1989] (Engleman, Paul)
❶ Who Shot the Bull? [U.S.] (Knox, Bill)
Who Steals My Name? [1974] (Fraser, James)
Who's on First [1980] (Buckley, William F.)
Whoo? [1991] (Hoyt, Richard)
Whose Dog Are You? [1990] (Hammond, Gerald)
Why Isn't Becky Twitchell Dead? [1990] (Zubro, Mark)
❶ Why Kill Arthur Potter? [U.S.] (Harrison, Ray)
Why Me? [1983] (Westlake, Donald E.)
❶ Whyte Hart [1988] (Doherty, P. C.)
❶ Wide and Capable Revenge [1993] (McCall, Thomas)
Widening Gyre [1983] (Parker, Robert B.) ☆
❶ Widow [1979] (Freeling, Nicolas)
Widows [1991] (McBain, Ed)
Wife-Smuggler [1978] (Tripp, Miles)
Wild Animals [1995] (Reid, Robert Sims)
Wild Turkey [1975] (Simon, Roger L.)
Wildfire [1994] (Goddard, Ken)
❶ Wilkes: His Life and Crimes [1990] (Schoonover, Winston)
Wilkes on Trial [as by Charles Sevilla] [1993]
 (Schoonover, Winston)
William Powell and Myrna Loy Murder Case [1996]

(Baxt, George)
Win, Lose, or Die [1989] (Gardner, John)
Wind and Lies [1996] (Parrish, Richard)
Wind Up [1990] (Steed, Neville)
Windy City [1995] (Holton, Hugh)
Winning Can Be Murder [1996] (Crider, Bill)
❶ Winter Chill [1995] (Cleary, Jon)
Winter Prey [1993] (Sandford, John)
Winter Rules [1991] (Cork, Barry)
Winter Women Murders [1994] (Kaufelt, David A.)
Winter's Gold [1997] (Heffernan, William)
Wireless [1993] (O'Connell, Jack)
Wisdom of Serpents [1992] (Levitsky, Ronald)
Wisp of Smoke [1991] (Lewis, Roy)
Witch of Watergate [1992] (Adler, Warren)
Witchcraft for Panda One [1978] (Walker, Peter N.)
Witchdance in Bavaria [1975] (MacLeod, Robert)
Witchline [1988] (MacLeod, Robert)
Witchrock [1977] (Knox, Bill)
Witchy Woman [1996] (Brewer, Steve)
❶ With Intent [1968] (Henderson, Laurence)
Without Remorse [1993] (Clancy, Tom)
Witness of Bones [1992] (Tourney, Leonard)
❶ Witness to the Truth [1992] (Lindsay, Paul)
Wizard of Death [1977] (Forrest, Richard)
Wizard of La-La Land [1995] (Campbell, Robert)
❶ Wobble to Death [1970] (Lovesey, Peter)
Wolf in Sheep's Clothing [1989] (Riggs, John R.)
Wolf, No Wolf [1996] (Bowen, Peter)
Wolf's Head [1987] (Mayo, J. K.)
Wolfman [1992] (Rankin, Ian)
Wolfnight [1982] (Freeling, Nicolas)
❶ Wolfsong [1991] (Owens, Louis)
❶ Wolves of Savernake [1993] (Marston, Edward)
❶ Woman at the Window [APA] (Jenkins, Jerry)
Woman in the Dark [1997] (Phillips, T. J.)
Woman Who Fell From Grace [1991] (Handler, David)
❶ Woman Who Married a Bear [1992] (Straley, John) ★
Woman Who Walked into the Sea [1991] (Craig, Philip)
❶ Wood Beyond [1995] (Hill, Reginald)
Words Can Kill [1984] (Davis, Kenn) ☆
World Beat [1993] (Dold, Gaylord)
World of Hurt [1994] (Rosen, Richard)
Worm Turns [1988] (Douglas, Arthur)
Worms Must Wait [1967] (Wainright, John)
Worried Widow [1987] (Hammond, Gerald)
Worst Case Scenario [1996] (Bowen, Michael)
Wreath for a Redhead [1962] (Chambers, Peter)
Wreath of Lords and Ladies [1974] (Fraser, James)
Wrecking Crew [1960] (Hamilton, Donald)
Write Me a Letter [1992] (Pierce, David M.)
Written in Blood [1995] (Marquis, Max)
❶ Written in Fire [1995] (DeAndrea, William L.)
❶ Wrong Case [1975] (Crumley, James)
Wrong Gun [1992] (Hailey, J. P.)
Wrong Impression [1990] (Malcolm, John)
Wrong Place, Wrong Time [1989] (Duncan, W. Glenn)
Wycliffe and the Beales [1983] (Burley, W. J.)
❶ Wycliffe and the Cycle of Death [1990] (Burley, W. J.)
❶ Wycliffe and the Dead Flautist [1991] (Burley, W. J.)
❶ Wycliffe and the Dunes Mystery [1993] (Burley, W. J.)
❶ Wycliffe and the Four Jacks [1985] (Burley, W. J.)
❶ Wycliffe and the House of Fear [1995] (Burley, W. J.)
❶ Wycliffe and the Last Rites [1992] (Burley, W. J.)
Wycliffe and the Pea-Green Boat [1975] (Burley, W. J.)
❶ Wycliffe and the Quiet Virgin [1986] (Burley, W. J.)
Wycliffe and the Scapegoat [1978] (Burley, W. J.)
Wycliffe and the Schoolgirls [1976] (Burley, W. J.)
❶ Wycliffe and the Tangled Web [1988] (Burley, W. J.)
❶ Wycliffe and the Windsor Blue [1987] (Burley, W. J.)
Wycliffe in Paul's Court [1980] (Burley, W. J.)
Wycliffe's Wild Goose Chase [1982] (Burley, W. J.)

X

X-Rated Corpse [1973] (Avallone, Michael)
Xanadu Talisman [1981] (O'Donnell, Peter)

Y

Year of the Dragon [1977] (Copper, Basil)
Year of the Tiger [1963] (Fallon, Martin)
Yellow Bird [1991] (Boyer, Rick)
Yellow Dog Party [1991] (Emerson, Earl)
■ Yellowthread Street [1975] (Marshall, William)
Yesterday's News [1989] (Healy, Jeremiah)
Yesterday's Papers [1994] (Edwards, Martin)
You Bet Your Life [1979] (Kaminsky, Stuart M.)
You Can Die Trying [1993] (Haywood, Gar Anthony)
You Can't Live Forever [1951] (Masur, Harold Q.)
You Get What You Pay For [1988] (Beinhart, Larry)
■ You Know Who [1993] (Freeling, Nicolas)
You Nice Bastard [1972] (Newman, G. F.)
You Only Die Once [1984] (Copper, Basil)
■ You Wouldn't Be Dead for Quids [1985] (Barrett, Robert G.)
■ You'd Better Believe It [1985] (James, Bill)
You're Better Off Dead [1965] (Chambers, Peter)
■ Young Men May Die [1970] (Craig, David)
Young Petrella [1988] (Gilbert, Michael)
Young Prey [1969] (Waugh, Hillary)
Your Money and Your Wife [1975] (Perry, Ritchie)

Z

■ Zero Tolerance [1995] (Knight, J. D.) ☆
■ Zia Summer [1995] (Anaya, Rudolfo)
■ Zigzag [incl O'Malley] [1981] (Kenyon, Michael)
Zig-Zag Man [1991] (Albert, Marvin H.)
Zip Gun Boogie [1992] (Timlin, Mark)
Zoom! [1972] (Townend, Peter)
Zurich Numbers [1984] (Granger, Bill)

Pseudonym literally means false name, from the Greek *pseudo* meaning false, pretended, or unreal. In the publishing world, pseudonyms are used to hide or protect an author's identity, often at the insistence of the publisher. Sometimes a pair of authors will choose a joint or shared pseudonym for the work they write together. For their private eye series featuring Easy Barnes, Richard Bodino and Hillary Connors became Richard Hillary. Robert Wade and Bill Miller, collaborating on Max Thursday, a '50s private eye series, wrote as Wade Miller. Sometimes a shared pseudonym is entirely different from either author's real name, such as Marshall Jevons, who turned out to be economics professors William Leo Breit and Kenneth Gerald Elzinga. When Michael McDowell and Dennis Schuetz launched their colorful Boston bar scene mysteries, it was as Nathan Aldyne. Although Schuetz is no longer living, McDowell will continue the series alone and the books will continue to appear under the Aldyne name.

A pseudonym might be used when an author's most recent work is a radical departure from earlier work and the publisher fears confusing the reader. It was reported not long ago that submitting his latest manuscript under a pseudonym netted a certain heretofore midlist author a million-dollar advance. In order to disguise an author's prolific output, his publisher might demand that books appear under a variety of names. Since the first Hugh Corbett novel was released in British editions in 1986, Oxford history scholar and headmaster P. C. Doherty has published at least 35 books in seven historical series ranging from the Medieval era to the 15th century. His series appear under the names Michael Clynes, P.C. Doherty, Ann Dukthas, C.L. Grace and Paul Harding. It is suspected that a new series published under the name Anna Apostolou (*Murder in Macedon*) is another from the prolific P. C. Doherty.

Writers who work in multiple genres frequently use pseudonyms at the insistence of their publishers. Mystery writer Andrew York is one of the many pseudonyms of British author Christopher (Robin) Nicole who has written historical romance, thrillers, adventure novels and books on West Indian history and cricket under as many as 15 names, both male and female. Dennis Lynds has written industrial espionage novels and mysteries for young adults as William Arden; The Shadow action/adventure series as Maxwell Grant; private eye series as Michael Collins, John Crowe, and Mark Sadler; as well as nonseries novels, short stories and novelizations of television plays under his own name.

Where it was once commonplace for publishers to use initials or androgynous names to hide a woman author's gender (E.X. Ferrars, for example), initials and female pseudonyms are now used by some male writers. When Father Dowling's creator Ralph McInerny writes about Sister Mary Teresa Dempsey, he becomes Monica Quill. And when Canadian journalist Douglas Whiteway's first novel (*Death at Buckingham Palace*) was released in early 1996, it was published under the name C.C. Benison. With a series featuring 20-something Canadian housemaid Jane Bee, in the service of the Queen, an author who was thought to be female seemed an obvious choice.

Lydia Adamson's light-hearted New York animal mysteries (now numbering three series with two dozen titles) faced a similar challenge. When the Alice Nestleton (New York actress and cat owner) series was launched in 1990, it was determined the books would have a larger audience if the author was thought to be a woman. In this case, the choice of Adamson also put the books at the beginning of the mystery section, assuming standard alphabetical shelving by author's last name. The Adamson debut was so successful that the publisher commissioned two additional series from the same author and now releases six Adamson books each year (two titles per series). More than one female reader has been disappointed to learn that the charming Mrs. Adamson is, in fact, Frank King.

The presentation of pseudonyms and pen names in this chapter takes two formats. Entries in the first list are sorted by pseudonym, whenever a pseudonym has been used for a mystery series written by a man who is part of the *Detecting Men* data base. If the author is not included in this book, you will not find pseudonym information for him. The second list (which is simply a re-sorting of the first) starts with the author's identity and links it to pseudonyms used for his mystery series. Both lists include the name of the series character written pseudonymously, date of the first book and number of books in the series, as well as additional pseudonyms used by the author. 'Other Pseudonyms' include work in other genres such as science fiction, westerns, fantasy or horror, non-series books and books for children.

If you know the pseudonym for a mystery series and are looking for the author's identity, start with the first list. If, on the other hand, you're looking for pseudonyms a particular author may have used, the second list will be more helpful. Because this information is tied to mystery series written by men using pseudonyms, you will not find an author listed unless series mysteries are part of the pseudonym equation. For example, R.D. Zimmerman used the pseudonym Alexander von Wacker for his children's mysteries, but that series is not part of the *Detecting Men* data base (which includes only adult fiction). Hence, there is no listing in this chapter for R.D. Zimmerman writing as Alexander von Wacker.

Throughout *Detecting Men* and *Detecting Men Pocket Guide*, the notation [P] is used to designate pseudonyms. You will not see a [P] when the author is simply using a byline. A byline is considered a variation of the author's name. For example, Jack Vance is a byline used by John Holbrook Vance. In certain cases the byline is a bit of a stretch, as with Jo Bailey, author of the Jan Gallagher series. Although it appears the author is a woman, we are told he is Joseph Bailey. In this case, Jo is apparently not the short form of Josephine, although we expect the publisher wants readers to think it is.

Pseudonym	Series Character	1 - #	Author Identity	Other Pseudonyms

List #1 - Pseudonyms Used for Mystery Series Written by Men...cont.

Pseudonym	Series Character	1 - #	Author Identity	Other Pseudonyms
Adamson, Lydia	Alice Nestleton	'90 –15	Frank King	
Adamson, Lydia	Deidre Nightingale	'94 –7	Frank King	
Adamson, Lydia	Lucy Wayles	'96 – 2	Frank King	
Alding, Peter	Kerr, Constable & Fusil	'67 –14	Roderic Jeffries	Jeffrey Ashford Roderic Graeme Graeme Hastings Julian Roberts
Aldyne, Nathan	Dan Valentine & Clarisse Lovelace	'80 – 4	Michael McDowell & Dennis Schuetz	
Alexander, Bruce	John Fielding	'94 – 3	Bruce Cook	
Allen, Garrison	Penelope Warren	'94 – 3	Gary Amo	
Arden, William	Kane Jackson	'68 – 5	Dennis Lynds	Nick Carter Michael Collins John Crowe Carl Dekker John Douglas Maxwell Grant Sheila McErlean Mark Sadler
Ashford, Jeffrey	Don Kerry	'61 – 2	Roderic G. Jeffries	Peter Alding Hastings Draper Roderic Graeme Graeme Hastings Julian Roberts
Axler, Leo	Bill Hawley	'94 – 4	Eugene Michael Lazuta	
Barnao, Jack	John Locke	'87 – 3	Ted (Edward John) Wood	
Bastable, Bernard	Wolfgang Mozart & Victoria	'95 – 2	Robert Barnard	
Benison, C. C.	Jane Bee	'96 – 3	Douglas Whiteway	
Box, Edgar	Peter Cutler Sargeant II	'52 – 3	Gore Vidal	
Brett, John Michael	Hugo Baron	'63 – 3	Miles Tripp	
Burns, Rex	Devlin Kirk	'87 – 4	Raoul Stephen Sehler	
Burns, Rex	Gabe Wager	'75 –11	Raoul Stephen Sehler	
Butler, Richard	Max Farne	'75 – 2	Ted Allbeury	Patrick Kelly
Caine, Hamilton	Ace Carpenter	'81 – 2	Stephen (Lee) Smoke	Wade Barker
Clynes, Michael	Roger Shallot	'91 – 6	P. C. Doherty	
Coe, Tucker	Mitch Tobin	'66 – 5	Donald E. Westlake	Curt Clark Timothy J. Culver Richard Stark
Collins, Michael	Dan Fortune	'67 –17	Dennis Lynds	William Arden Nick Carter John Crowe Carl Dekker John Douglas Maxwell Grant Sheila McErlean Mark Sadler
Constantine, K. C.	Mario Balzic	'72 –13	Carl Kosak	
Conway, Peter	Lucy Beck	'72 – 3	Peter Claudius Gautier-Smith	
Cory, Desmond	John Dobie	'91 – 3	Shaun Lloyd McCarthy	Theo Callas
Cory, Desmond	Johnny Fedora	'51 –16	Shaun Lloyd McCarthy	Theo Callas
Cory, Desmond	Linda Grey	'51 – 4	Shaun Lloyd McCarthy	Theo Callas
Cory, Desmond	Mr. Dee	'61 – 2	Shaun Lloyd McCarthy	Theo Callas
Craig, David	Roy Rickman	'68 – 3	Allan James Tucker	Bill James
Craig, David	Stephen Bellecroix & Sheila Roath	'70 – 2	Allan James Tucker	Bill James
Cross, David	John "Chant" Sinclair	'86 – 3	George Chesbro	

Pseudonym	Series Character	1 - #	Author Identity	Other Pseudonyms
List #1 - Pseudonyms Used for Mystery Series Written by Men...cont.				
Crowe, John	Lee Beckett	'72 – 6	Dennis Lynds	William Arden Nick Carter; Michael Collins Carl Dekker John Douglas Maxwell Grant Sheila McErlean Mark Sadler
Cunningham, E. V.	Harvey Krim	'64 – 2	Howard (Melvin) Fast	Walter Ericson
Cunningham, E. V.	John Comaday & Larry Cohen	'65 – 2	Howard (Melvin) Fast	Walter Ericson
Cunningham, E. V.	Masao Masuto	'67 – 7	Howard (Melvin) Fast	Walter Ericson
Douglas, Arthur	Jonathan Craythorne	'86 – 3	Gerald Hammond	Dalby Holden
Drummond, Ivor	Jennifer Norrington, Alesandro Di Ganzarello & Coleridge Tucker, III	'69 – 9	Roger Erskine Longrigg	Frank Parrish; Domini Taylor
Dukthas, Ann	Nicholas Segalla	'94 – 3	P. C. Doherty	
Evers, Crabbe	Duffy House	'91 – 5	William Brashler & Reinder Van Til	
Fallon, Martin	Paul Chavasse	'62 – 6	Harry Patterson	James Graham Jack Higgins Hugh Marlowe
Foxx, Jack	Dan Connell	'72 – 2	Bill Pronzini	Alex Saxon
Fraser, James	William Aveyard	'68 – 9	Alan White	Alan Whitney
Gaitano, Nick	Jake Phillips	'95 – 2	Eugene Izzi	
Galway, Robert C.	James Packard	'63 –12	Philip McCutchan	Duncan MacNeil T.I.G. Wigg
Gash, Jonathan	Clare Burtonall	'97 – 1	John Grant	Graham Gaunt
Gash, Jonathan	Lovejoy	'77 –19	John Grant	Graham Gaunt
Gill, Bartholomew	Peter McGarr	'77 –19	Mark McGarrity	
Grace, C. L.	Kathryn Swinbrooke	'93 – 4	P. C. Doherty	Michael Clynes P.C. Doherty Ann Dukthas
Graeme, Roderic	Richard Verrel as Blackshirt	'52 –20	Roderic Jeffries	Peter Alding Jeffrey Ashford Graeme Hastings Julian Roberts
Grant, Maxwell	The Shadow	'64 – 8	Dennis Lynds	William Arden Nick Carter Michael Collins John Crow Carl Dekker John Douglas Sheila McErlean Mark Sadler
Grayson, Richard	Jean-Paul Gautier	'78 – 9	Richard Grindal	
Grayson, Richard	John Bryant	'55 – 4	Richard Grindal	
Gregory, Sarah	Sharon Hays	'96 – 2	A. W. Gray	William Gray
Hailey, J. P.	Steve Winslow	'88 – 5	Parnell Hall	
Hervey, Evelyn	Harriet Unwin	'84 – 3	H. R. F. Keating	
Higgins, Jack	Dougal Munro & Jack Carter	'86 – 2	Harry Patterson	Martin Fallon James Graham Hugh Marlowe
Higgins, Jack	Liam Devlin	'75 – 4	Harry Patterson	Martin Fallon James Graham Hugh Marlowe
Higgins, Jack	Nick Miller	'65 – 2	Harry Patterson	Martin Fallon James Graham Hugh Marlowe
Higgins, Jack	Sean Dillon	'92 – 5	Harry Patterson	Martin Fallon James Graham Hugh Marlowe

Pseudonym	Series Character	1- #	Author Identity	Other Pseudonyms
List #1 - Pseudonyms Used for Mystery Series Written by Men...cont.				
Hilary, Richard	Ezell "Easy" Barnes	'87 – 4	Richard Bodino w/Hilary Connors	
James, Bill	Colin Harpur & Desmond Iles	'85 –13	(Allan) James Tucker	David Craig Bill James
Jeffries, Ian	Sgt. Craig	'59 – 3	Peter Hays	
Jevons, Marshall	Henry Spearman	'78 – 3	William Breit & Kenneth Elzinga	
Kavanagh, Dan	Nick Duffy	'80 – 4	Julian Barnes	
Kincaid, D.	Harry Cain	'86 – 2	Bert Fields	
Lake, M. D.	Peggy O'Neill	'89 – 9	J. Allen Simpson	
le Carré, John	George Smiley	'61 – 8	David John Moore Cornwell	
Lejeune, Anthony	Adam Gifford	'61 – 3	Edward Anthony Thompson	
Lejeune, Anthony	James Glowery	'87 – 2	Edward Anthony Thompson	
MacLeod, Robert	Andrew Laird	'74 – 6	Bill Knox	Michael Kirk Noah Webster
MacLeod, Robert	Jonathan Gaunt	'70 –10	Bill Knox	Michael Kirk Noah Webster
MacLeod, Robert	Talos Cord	'64 – 6	Bill Knox	Michael Kirk Noah Webster
Malcolm, John	Tim Simpson	'84 –12	John Malcolm Andrews	
Malone, Paul	Jack Fowler	'91 – 3	Michael Newton	
Marlowe, Stephen	Chester Drum	'55 –19	Milton Lesser	Andrew Frazer Jason Ridgway C. H. Thames
Marston, Edward	Nicholas Bracewell	'88 – 9	Keith Miles	
Marston, Edward	Ralph Delchard & Gervase Bret	'93 – 5	Keith Miles	
Matthews, Lew	Horatio T. Parker	'92 – 3	Matthew Z. Lewin	
McBain, Ed	87th Precinct	'56 –47	Evan Hunter	Curt Cannon Hunt Collins Ezra Hannon Richard Marston
McBain, Ed	Matthew Hope	'77 –12	Evan Hunter	Curt Cannon Hunt Collins Ezra Hannon Richard Marston
McCall, Wendell	Chris Klick	'88 – 2	Ridley Pearson	
Melville, James	Ben Lazenby	'95 – 2	(Roy) Peter Martin	Hampton Charles
Melville, James	Tetsuo Otani	'79 –13	(Roy) Peter Martin	Hampton Charles
Michaels, Grant	Stan Kraychik	'90 – 5	Michael Mesrobian	
Milan, Borto	Edward Ryan	'95 – 2	Jeff Collignon	
Miles, John	Johnelle Baker	'94 – 2	John Miles Bickham	
Miles, John	Laura Michaels	'93 – 3	John Miles Bickham	
Miller, Wade	Max Thursday	'47 – 6	Robert Wade & Bill Miller	Will Daemer; Whit Masterson Dale Wilmer
Murphy, Haughton	Reuben Frost	'86 – 7	James Duffy	
Myles, Simon	"Apples" Carstairs	'74 – 2	Ken Follett	Zachary Stone
North, Gil	Caleb Cluff	'60 –11	Geoffrey Horne	
Orvis, Kenneth	Adam Breck	'65 – 2	Kenneth Lemieux	
Parrish, Frank	Dan Mallett	'77 – 8	Roger Erskine Longrigg	Laura Black Ivor Drummond Domini Taylor
Peterson, Keith	John Wells	'88 – 5	Andrew Klavan	Margaret Tracy
Phillips, T. J.	Joe Wilder	'95 – 2	Tom Savage	
Quill, Monica	Mary Teresa Dempsey	'81 – 9	Ralph McInerny	Edward Mackin

Pseudonym	Series Character	1 - #	Author Identity	Other Pseudonyms
List #1 - Pseudonyms Used for Mystery Series Written by Men...cont.				
Rhea, Nicholas	Nick Rhea	'79 –15	Peter N. Walker	Anrew Arncliffe Christopher Coram Tom Ferris
Rider, J. W.	Ryder Malone	'86 – 2	Shane Stevens	
Ridgway, Jason	Brian Guy	'60 – 4	Stephen Marlowe	Andrew Frazer C. H. Thames
Ripley, Jack	John George Davis	'71 – 4	John Wainright	
Rome, Anthony	Tony Rome	'60 – 3	Marvin H. Albert	Mike Barone Al Conroy Albert Conroy Ian MacAlister Nick Quarry
Ross, Jonathan	George Rogers	'68 –20	John Rossiter	
Ross, Philip	James Marley	'85 – 2	Philip R. Eck	
Ross, Philip	Tom Talley	'86 – 2	Philip R. Eck	
Sadler, Mark	Paul Shaw	'70 – 6	Dennis Lynds	William Arden Nick Carter Michael Collins John Crowe Carl Dekker John Douglas Maxwell Grant Sheila McErlean
Sandford, John	Anna Batory	'97 – 1	John Camp	
Sandford, John	Kidd & Luellen	'89 – 2	John Camp	
Sandford, John	Lucas Davenport	'89 – 8	John Camp	
Schoonover, Winston	John Wilkes	'90 – 2	Charles Sevilla	
Stark, Richard	Alan Grofield	'67 – 4	Donald E. Westlake	Curt Clark Tucker Coe Timothy J. Culver
Stark, Richard	Parker	'62 –17	Donald E. Westlake	Curt Clark Tucker Coe Timothy J. Culver
Stephens, Reed	Mick "Brew" Axbrewder	'80 – 3	Stephen R. Donaldson	
Stevenson, Richard	Donald Strachey	'81 – 6	Richard Lipez	
Stone, Thomas H.	Chester Fortune	'72 – 4	Terry Harknett	Jane Harmon Joseph Hedges William Pine William Terry
Taylor, H. Baldwin	David Halliday	'64 – 3	Hillary Waugh	Elissa Grandower Harry Walker
Tremayne, Peter	Sister Fidelma	'94 – 4	Peter Beresford Ellis	Peter MacAlan
Wallace, Robert	Essington Holt	'88 – 5	Robin Wallace-Crabbe	
York, Andrew	James Munroe Tallant	'77 – 4	Christopher (Robin) Nicole	Daniel Adams Leslie Arden Robin Cade Peter Grange Nicholas Grant Carolyn Gray Mark Logan Simon McKay Christina Nicholson Robin Nicholson Alan Savage Alison York Andrew York Max Marlowe (w/wife Diana Bachmann)

Pseudonym	Series Character	1 - #	Author Identity	Other Pseudonyms

List #1 - Pseudonyms Used for Mystery Series Written by Men...cont.

Pseudonym	Series Character	1 - #	Author Identity	Other Pseudonyms
York, Andrew	Jonas Wilde	'66 – 9	Christopher (Robin) Nicole	Daniel Adams Leslie Arden Robin Cade Peter Grange Nicholas Grant Carolyn Gray Mark Logan Simon McKay Christina Nicholson Robin Nicholson Alan Savage Alison York Andrew York Max Marlowe (w/wife Diana Bachmann)

Author Identity	Pseudonym	Series Character	1 - #	Other Pseudonyms

List #2 - Male Authors Who Write Pseudonymous Mystery Series

Author Identity	Pseudonym	Series Character	1 - #	Other Pseudonyms
Albert, Marvin H.	Anthony Rome	Tony Rome	'60 – 3	Mike Barone Al Conroy Albert Conroy Ian MacAlister Nick Quarry
Allbeury, Ted	Richard Butler	Max Farne	'75 – 2	Patrick Kelly
Amo, Gary	Garrison Allen	Penelope Warren	'94 – 3	
Andrews, John Malcolm	John Malcolm	Tim Simpson	'84 – 12	
Barnard, Robert	Bernard Bastable	Wolfgang Mozart & Victoria	'95 – 2	
Barnes, Julian	Dan Kavanagh	Nick Duffy	'80 – 4	
Bickham, John Miles	John Miles	Johnelle Baker	'94 – 2	
Bickham, John Miles	John Miles	Laura Michaels	'93 – 3	
Bodino, Richard	Richard Hilary	Ezell "Easy" Barnes	'87 – 4	
Brashler, William	Crabbe Evers	Duffy House	'91 – 5	
Breit, William	Marshall Jevons	Henry Spearman	'78 – 3	
Camp, John	John Sandford	Anna Batory	'97 – 1	
Camp, John	John Sandford	Kidd & Luellen	'89 – 2	
Camp, John	John Sandford	Lucas Davenport	'89 – 8	
Chesbro, George	David Cross	John "Chant" Sinclair	'86 – 3	
Collignon, Jeff	Borto Milan	Edward Ryan	'95 – 2	
Cook, Bruce	Bruce Alexander	John Fielding	'94 – 3	
Cornwell, David John Moore	John le Carré	George Smiley	'61 – 8	
Doherty, P. C.	Paul Harding	Nicholas Chirke	'94 – 4	Michael Clynes Ann Dukthas C.L. Grace
Doherty, P. C.	Paul Harding	Hugh Corbett	'86 – 10	Michael Clynes Ann Dukthas C.L. Grace
Doherty, P. C.	Paul Harding	Matthew Jenkyn	'88 – 2	Michael Clynes Ann Dukthas C.L. Grace
Doherty, P. C.	Ann Dukthas	Nicholas Segalla	'94 – 3	Michael Clynes P.C. Doherty C.L. Grace
Doherty, P. C.	Michael Clynes	Roger Shallot	'91 – 6	P.C. Doherty Ann Dukthas C.L. Grace

Author Identity	Pseudonym	Series Character	1 - #	Other Pseudonyms
List #2 - Male Authors Who Write Pseudonymous Mystery Series...cont.				
Doherty, P. C.	C. L. Grace	Kathryn Swinbrooke	'93 – 4	Michael Clynes P.C. Doherty Ann Dukthas
Donaldson, Stephen R.	Reed Stephens	Mick "Brew" Axbrewder	'80 – 3	
Duffy, James	Haughton Murphy	Reuben Frost	'86 – 7	
Eck, Philip R. Eck, Philip R.	Philip Ross Philip Ross	James Marley Tom Talley	'85 – 2 '86 – 2	
Ellis, Peter Beresford	Peter Tremayne	Sister Fidelma	'94 – 4	Peter MacAlan
Fast, Howard (Melvin) Fast, Howard (Melvin) Fast, Howard (Melvin)	E. V. Cunningham E. V. Cunningham E. V. Cunningham	Harvey Krim John Comaday & Larry Cohen Masao Masuto	'64 – 2 '65 – 2 '67 – 7	Walter Ericson Walter Ericson Walter Ericson
Fields, Bert	D. Kincaid	Harry Cain	'86 – 2	
Follett, Ken	Simon Myles	"Apples" Carstairs	'74 – 2	Zachary Stone
Gautier-Smith, Peter Claudius	Peter Conway	Lucy Beck	'72 – 3	
Grant, John Grant, John	Jonathan Gash Jonathan Gash	Clare Burtonall, MD Lovejoy	'97 – 1 '77 – 19	Graham Gaunt Graham Gaunt
Gray, A. W.	Sarah Gregory	Sharon Hays	'96 – 2	William Gray
Grindal, Richard Grindal, Richard	Richard Grayson Richard Grayson	Jean-Paul Gautier John Bryant	'78 – 9 '55 – 4	
Hall, Parnell	J. P. Hailey	Steve Winslow	'88 – 5	
Hammond, Gerald	Arthur Douglas	Jonathan Craythorne	'86 – 3	Dalby Holden
Harknett, Terry	Thomas H. Stone	Chester Fortune	'72 – 4	Jane Harmon Joseph Hedges William Pine William Terry
Hays, Peter	Ian Jeffries	Craig, Sgt.	'59 – 3	
Horne, Geoffrey	Gil North	Caleb Cluff	'60 – 11	
Hunter, Evan	Ed McBain	87th Precinct	'56 – 47	Curt Cannon Hunt Collins Ezra Hannon Richard Marston
Hunter, Evan	Ed McBain	Matthew Hope	'77 – 12	Curt Cannon Hunt Collins Ezra Hannon Richard Marston
Izzi, Eugene	Nick Gaitano	Jake Phillips	'95 – 2	
Jeffries, Roderic	Jeffrey Ashford	Don Kerry	'61 – 2	Peter Alding Hastings Draper Roderic Graeme Graeme Hastings Julian Roberts
Jeffries, Roderic	Peter Alding	Kerr, Constable & Fusil	'67 – 14	Jeffrey Ashford Roderic Graeme Hastings Draper Graeme Hastings Julian Roberts
Jeffries, Roderic	Roderic Graeme	Richard Verrel as Blackshirt	'52 – 20	Peter Alding Jeffrey Ashford Hastings Draper Graeme Hastings Julian Roberts
Keating, H. R. F.	Evelyn Hervey	Harriet Unwin	'84 – 3	
King, Frank King, Frank King, Frank	Lydia Adamson Lydia Adamson Lydia Adamson	Alice Nestleton Deidre Nightingale Lucy Wayles	'90 – 15 '94 – 7 '96 – 2	

Author Identity	Pseudonym	Series Character	1 - #	Other Pseudonyms
List #2 - Male Authors Who Write Pseudonymous Mystery Series...cont.				
Klavan, Andrew	Keith Peterson	John Wells	'88 – 5	Margaret Tracy (w/Laurence Klavan)
Knox, Bill	Robert MacLeod	Andrew Laird	'74 – 6	Michael Kirk Noah Webster
Knox, Bill	Robert MacLeod	Jonathan Gaunt	'70 – 10	Michael Kirk Noah Webster
Knox, Bill	Robert MacLeod	Talos Cord	'64 – 6	Michael Kirk Noah Webster
Kosak, Carl	K. C. Constantine	Mario Balzic	'72 – 13	
Lazuta, Eugene Michael	Leo Axler	Bill Hawley	'94 – 4	
Lesser, Milton	Stephen Marlowe	Chester Drum	'55 – 19	Andrew Frazer Jason Ridgway C. H. Thames
Lemieux, Kenneth	Kenneth Orvis	Adam Breck	'65 – 2	
Lewin, Matthew Z.	Lew Matthews	Horatio T. Parker	'92 – 3	
Lipez, Richard	Richard Stevenson	Donald Strachey	'81 – 6	
Longrigg, Roger Erskine	Frank Parrish	Dan Mallett	'77 – 8	Laura Black Ivor Drummond Domini Taylor
Longrigg, Roger Erskine	Ivor Drummond	Jennifer Norrington, Alesandro Di Ganzarello & Coleridge Tucker, III	'69 – 9	Laura Black Frank Parrish Domini Taylor
Lynds, Dennis	Michael Collins	Dan Fortune	'67 – 17	William Arden Nick Carter Michael Collins John Crowe Carl Dekker John Douglas Sheila McErlean
Lynds, Dennis	William Arden	Kane Jackson	'68 – 5	William Arden Nick Carter Michael Collins John Crowe Carl Dekker John Douglas Sheila McErlean
Lynds, Dennis	John Crowe	Lee Beckett	'72 – 6	William Arden Nick Carter Michael Collins John Crowe Carl Dekker John Douglas Sheila McErlean
Lynds, Dennis	Mark Sadler	Paul Shaw	'70 – 6	William Arden Nick Carter Michael Collins John Crowe Carl Dekker John Douglas Sheila McErlean
Lynds, Dennis	Maxwell Grant	The Shadow	'64 – 8	William Arden Nick Carter Michael Collins John Crowe Carl Dekker John Douglas Sheila McErlean Mark Sadler

Author Identity	Pseudonym	Series Character	1 - #	Other Pseudonyms
List #2 - Male Authors Who Write Pseudonymous Mystery Series...cont.				
Marlowe, Stephen	Jason Ridgway	Brian Guy	'60 – 3	Andrew Frazer C. H. Thames
Martin, (Roy) Peter	James Melville	Ben Lazenby	'95 – 2	Hampton Charles
Martin, (Roy) Peter	James Melville	Tetsuo Otani	'79 – 13	Hampton Charles
McCarthy, Shaun Lloyd	Desmond Cory	John Dobie	'91 – 3	Theo Callas
McCarthy, Shaun Lloyd	Desmond Cory	Johnny Fedora	'51 – 16	Theo Callas
McCarthy, Shaun Lloyd	Desmond Cory	Linda Grey	'51 – 4	Theo Callas
McCarthy, Shaun Lloyd	Desmond Cory	Mr. Dee	'61 – 2	Theo Callas
McCutchan, Philip	Robert Conington Galway	James Packard	'63 – 12	Duncan MacNeil T.I.G. Wigg
McDowell, Michael	Nathan Aldyne	Dan Valentine & Clarisse Lovelace	'80 – 4	
McInerny, Ralph	Monica Quill	Mary Teresa Dempsey	'81 – 9	Edward Mackin
McGarrity, Mark	Bartholomew Gill	Peter McGarr	'77 – 12	
Mesrobian, Michael	Grant Michaels	Stan Kraychik	'90 – 5	
Miles, Keith	Edward Marston	Nicholas Bracewell	'88 – 9	
Miles, Keith	Edward Marston	Ralph Delchard & Gervase Bret	'93 – 5	
Newton, Michael	Paul Malone	Jack Fowler	'91 – 3	
Nicole, Christopher (Robin)	Andrew York	James Munroe Tallant	'77 – 4	Daniel Adams Leslie Arden Robin Cade Peter Grange Nicholas Grant Carolyn Gray Mark Logan Simon McKay Christina Nicholson Robin Nicholson Alan Savage Alison York Andrew York Max Marlowe (w/wife Diana Bachmann)
Nicole, Christopher (Robin)	Andrew York	Jonas Wilde	'66 – 9	Daniel Adams Leslie Arden Robin Cade Peter Grange Nicholas Grant Carolyn Gray Mark Logan Simon McKay Christina Nicholson Robin Nicholson Alan Savage Alison York Andrew York Max Marlowe (w/wife Diana Bachmann)
Patterson, Harry	Martin Fallon	Paul Chavasse	'62 – 6	James Graham Jack Higgins Hugh Marlowe
Patterson, Harry	Jack Higgins	Dougal Munro & Jack Carter	'86 – 2	Martin Fallon James Graham Hugh Marlowe
Patterson, Harry	Jack Higgins	Liam Devlin	'75 – 4	Martin Fallon James Graham Hugh Marlowe
Patterson, Harry	Jack Higgins	Nick Miller	'65 – 2	Martin Fallon James Graham Hugh Marlowe

Author Identity	Pseudonym	Series Character	1 - #	Other Pseudonyms
List #2 - Male Authors Who Write Pseudonymous Mystery Series...cont.				
Patterson, Harry	Jack Higgins	Sean Dillon	'92 – 5	Martin Fallon James Graham Hugh Marlowe
Pearson, Ridley	Wendell McCall	Chris Klick	'88 – 2	
Pronzini, Bill	Jack Foxx	Dan Connell	'72 – 2	Alex Saxon
Rossiter, John	Jonathan Ross	George Rogers	'68 – 20	
Savage, Tom	T. J. Phillips	Joe Wilder	'95 – 2	
Sehler, Raoul Stephen	Rex Burns	Devlin Kirk	'87 - 4	
Sehler, Raoul Stephen	Rex Burns	Gabe Wager	'75 - 11	
Sevilla, Charles	Winston Schoonover	John Wilkes	'90 - 2	
Simpson, J. Allen	M. D. Lake	Peggy O'Neill	'89 – 9	
Smoke, Stephen (Lee)	Hamilton Caine	Ace Carpenter	'81 – 2	Wade Barker
Stevens, Shane	J. W. Rider	Ryder Malone	'86 – 2	
Thompson, Edward Anthony	Anthony Lejeune	Adam Gifford	'61 – 3	
Thompson, Edward Anthony	Anthony Lejeune	James Glowery	'87 – 2	
Tripp, Miles	John Michael Brett	Hugo Baron	'63 – 3	John Michael Brett Michael Brett
Tucker, Allan James	Bill James	Colin Harpur & Desmond Iles	'85 – 13	David Craig Bill James
Tucker, Allan James	David Craig	Roy Rickman	'68 – 3	Bill James
Tucker, Allan James	David Craig	Stephen Bellecroix & Sheila Roath	'70 – 2	Bill James
Vidal, Gore	Edgar Box	Peter Cutler Sargeant II	'52 – 3	
Wainright, John	Jack Ripley	John George Davis	'71 – 4	
Walker, Peter N.	Nicholas Rhea	Nick Rhea	'79 – 15	Anrew Arncliffe Christopher Coram Tom Ferris
Wade, Robert	Wade Miller	Max Thursday	'47 – 6	Will Daemer Whit Masterson
Wallace-Crabbe, Robin	Robert Wallace	Essington Holt	'88 – 5	
Waugh, Hillary	H. Baldwin Taylor	David Halliday	'64 – 3	Elissa Grandower Harry Walker Dale Wilmer
Westlake, Donald E.	Tucker Coe	Mitch Tobin	'66 – 5	Curt Clark Timothy J. Culver Richard Stark
Westlake, Donald E.	Richard Stark	Alan Grofield	'67 – 4	Curt Clark Tucker Coe Timothy J. Culver
Westlake, Donald E.	Richard Stark	Parker	'62 – 17	Curt Clark Tucker Coe Timothy J. Culver
White, Alan	James Fraser	William Aveyard	'68 – 9	Alan Whitney
Whiteway, Douglas	C. C. Benison	Jane Bee	'96 – 3	
Wood, Ted (Edward John)	Jack Barnao	John Locke	'87 – 3	

8 MYSTERY BOOK AWARDS

Group	Name	Status	Category	Award	Pub	BOOK TITLE	Last, First

Awards List 1 – Winners and Nominees by Award Name

Includes ONLY series novels written by men

Group	Name	Status	Category	Award	Pub	BOOK TITLE	Last, First
Acad Fran	Prix Roman	Winner	Novel	1996	1995	Escapade	Satterthwait, Walter
B'con	Anthony	Nominee	First Novel	1997	1996	Death in Little Tokyo	Furutani, Dale
B'con	Anthony	Nominee	First Novel	1997	1996	Tularosa	McGarrity, Michael
B'con	Anthony	Nominee	First Novel	1996	1995	The Innocents	Barre, Richard
B'con	Anthony	Winner	First Novel	1995	1994	A Drink Before the War	Lehand, Dennis
B'con	Anthony	Nominee	First Novel	1995	1994	Big Town	Swanson, Doug J.
B'con	Anthony	Nominee	First Novel	1994	1993	Cuckoo	Keegan, Alex
B'con	Anthony	Nominee	First Novel	1987	1988	Death on the Rocks	Allegretto, Michael
B'con	Anthony	Winner	First Novel	1987	1986	Too Late to Die	Crider, Bill
B'con	Anthony	Winner	First Novel	1986	1985	When the Bough Breaks	Kellerman, Jonathan
B'con	Anthony	Nominee	First Novel	1986	1985	Sleeping Dog	Lochte, Dick
B'con	Anthony	Nominee	Novel	1997	1996	Multiple Wounds	Russell, Alan
B'con	Anthony	Nominee	Novel	1996	1995	The Last Coyote	Connelly, Michael
B'con	Anthony	Nominee	Novel	1996	1995	Who in Hell is Wanda Fuca?	Ford, G.M.
B'con	Anthony	Nominee	Novel	1995	1994	The Concrete Blonde	Connelly, Michael
B'con	Anthony	Nominee	Novel	1995	1994	Pictures of Perfection	Hill, Reginald
B'con	Anthony	Nominee	Novel	1995	1994	The 13th Juror	Lescroart, John T.
B'con	Anthony	Nominee	Novel	1995	1994	Black Betty	Mosley, Walter
B'con	Anthony	Nominee	Novel	1995	1994	Just a Corpse at Twilight	van de Wetering, J.
B'con	Anthony	Nominee	Novel	1995	1994	Death of a Blue Lantern	West, Christopher
B'con	Anthony	Nominee	Novel	1994	1993	Morons and Madmen	Emerson, Earl
B'con	Anthony	Nominee	Novel	1994	1993	Sacred Clowns	Hillerman, Tony
B'con	Anthony	Nominee	Novel	1993	1994	The Black Ice	Connelly, Michael
B'con	Anthony	Winner	Novel	1992	1991	The Last Detective	Lovesey, Peter
B'con	Anthony	Winner	Novel	1988	1987	Skinwalkers	Hillerman, Tony
B'con	Anthony	Nominee	PB Original	1997	1996	Chain of Fools	Womack, Steven
B'con	Anthony	Winner	PB Original	1997	1996	Fade Away	Coben, Harlan
B'con	Anthony	Winner	PB Original	1996	1995	Deal Breaker	Coben, Harlan
B'con	Anthony	Nominee	PB Original	1996	1995	Closet	Zimmerman, R.D.
B'con	Anthony	Winner	PB Original	1988	1987	The Monkey's Raincoat	Crais, Robert
B'con	Anthony	Winner	PB Original	1987	1986	The Junkyard Dog	Campbell, Robert
CWA	Creasey	Winner	First Novel	1995	1994	Big Town	Swanson, Doug J.
CWA	Creasey	Nominee	First Novel	1995	1994	The Marx Sisters	Maitland, Barry
CWA	Creasey	Nominee	First Novel	1994	1993	Skinner's Rules	Jardine, Quinn
CWA	Creasey	Winner	First Novel	1991	1990	Devil in a Blue Dress	Mosley, Walter
CWA	Creasey	Nominee	First Novel	1988	1987	Gallows View	Robinson, Peter
CWA	Creasey	Winner	First Novel	1987	1986	Tinplate	Steed, Neville
CWA	Creasey	Winner	First Novel	1983	1983	The Night the Gods Smiled	Wright, Eric
CWA	Creasey	Winner	First Novel	1982	1982	Caroline Minuscule	Taylor, Andrew
CWA	Creasey	Winner	First Novel	1980	1979	Saturday of Glory	Serafin, David
CWA	Creasey	Winner	First Novel	1978	1977	The Judas Pair	Gash, Jonathan
CWA	Creasey	Winner	First Novel	1974	1973	The Big Fix	Simon, Roger L.

Group	Name	Status	Category	Award	Pub	BOOK TITLE	Last, First

Awards List 1 – Winners and Nominees by Award Name

Includes ONLY series novels written by men

Group	Name	Status	Category	Award	Pub	BOOK TITLE	Last, First
CWA	Dagger	Nominee	Novel	1997	1996	Cadillac Jukebox	Burke, James Lee
CWA	Dagger	Nominee	Novel	1996	1996	Death is Now My Neighbor	Dexter, Colin
CWA	Silver Dagger	Winner	Novel	1996	1996	Bloodhounds	Lovesey, Peter
CWA	Dagger	Nominee	Novel	1995	1995	Bookman's Wake	Dunning, John
CWA	Silver Dagger	Winner	Novel	1995	1995	The Summons	Lovesey, Peter
CWA	Gold Dagger	Winner	Novel	1992	1992	The Way Through the Woods	Dexter, Colin
CWA	Dagger	Nominee	Novel	1990	1990	Rough Treatment	Harvey, John
CWA	Gold Dagger	Winner	Novel	1990	1990	Bones and Silence	Hill, Reginald
CWA	Silver Dagger	Winner	Novel	1990	1990	The Late Candidate	Phillips, Mike
CWA	Gold Dagger	Winner	Novel	1989	1989	The Wench is Dead	Dexter, Colin
CWA	Gold Dagger	Winner	Novel	1988	1988	Ratking	Dibdin, Michael
CWA	Dagger	Nominee	Novel	1988	1988	Touch of the Past	Breen, Jon
CWA	Dagger	Nominee	Novel	1985	1985	Our Father's Lies	Taylor, Andrew
CWA	Dagger	Nominee	Novel	1984	1984	Die Again, Macready	Livingston, Jack
CWA	Silver Dagger	Winner	Novel	1983	1983	The Papers of Tony Veitch	McIlvanney, William
CWA	Gold Dagger	Winner	Novel	1981	1981	Gorky Park	Smith, Martin Cruz
CWA	Silver Dagger	Winner	Novel	1981	1981	The Dead of Jericho	Dexter, Colin
CWA	Gold Dagger	Winner	Novel	1979	1979	Whip Hand	Francis, Dick
CWA	Silver Dagger	Winner	Novel	1979	1979	Service of All the Dead	Dexter, Colin
CWA	Silver Dagger	Winner	Novel	1978	1978	Waxwork	Lovesey, Peter
CWA	Gold Dagger	Winner	Novel	1977	1977	The Honorable Schoolboy	Le Carré, John
CWA	Silver Dagger	Winner	Novel	1977	1977	Laidlaw	McIlvanney, William
CWA	Gold Dagger	Winner	Novel	1974	1974	Other Paths to Glory	Price, Anthony
CWA	Gold Dagger	Winner	Novel	1971	1971	The Steam Pig	McClure, James
CWA	Silver Dagger	Winner	Novel	1970	1970	The Labyrinth Makers	Price, Anthony
CWA	Gold Dagger	Winner	Novel	1969	1969	A Pride of Heroes	Dickinson, Peter
CWA	Gold Dagger	Winner	Novel	1968	1968	Skin Deep	Dickinson, Peter
CWA	Gold Dagger	Winner	Novel	1964	1964	The Perfect Murder	Keating, H.R.F.
CWA	Gold Dagger	Winner	Novel	1963	1963	The Spy Who Came in from the Cold	Le Carré, John
CWA	Gold Dagger	Runnerup	Novel	1963	1963	Gun Before Butter	Freeling, Nicolas
CWA	Gold Dagger	Runnerup	Novel	1962	1962	The Light of Day	Ambler, Eric
CWA	Gold Dagger	Runnerup	Novel	1961	1961	Call for the Dead	Le Carre, John
CWA	CWA' 92	Winner	Novel-Europe	1990	1990	Vendetta	Dibdin, Michael
CWA	Last Laugh	Winner	Novel-Funniest	1995	1994	The Villian of the Earth	Shaw, Simon
CWA	Last Laugh	Nominee	Novel-Funniest	1995	1995	Maxwell's Flame	Trow, M. J.
CWA	Last Laugh	Winner	Novel-Funniest	1994	1993	The Mamur Zapt and the Spoils of Egypt	Pearce, Michael
CWA	Last Laugh	Nominee	Novel-Funniest	1993	1993	Blood Sympathy	Hill, Reginald
CWA	Last Laugh	Winner	Novel-Funniest	1992	1991	Angels in Arms	Ripley, Mike
CWA	Last Laugh	Winner	Novel-Funniest	1990	1989	Angel Touch	Ripley, Mike
CWA	Police Review	Winner	Novel-Police	1987	1987	Snow Man	Busby, Roger
CWA	Police Review	Winner	Novel-Police	1986	1986	The Crossfire Killings	Knox, Bill
CWAA	Ned Kelly	Winner	Novel	1996	1995	The Malcontenta	Maitland, Barry
CWC	Ellis	Winner	First Novel	1989	1988	Stone of the Heart	Brady, John
CWC	Ellis	Winner	First Novel	1988	1987	The Goldfish Bowl	Gough, Laurence
CWC	Ellis	Nominee	First Novel	1988	1987	Gallows View	Robinson, Peter
CWC	Ellis	Nominee	Novel	1995	1994	The Good Life	Brady, John
CWC	Ellis	Nominee	Novel	1993	1992	Wednesday's Child	Robinson, Peter
CWC	Ellis	Winner	Novel	1992	1991	Past Reason Hated	Robinson, Peter
CWC	Ellis	Winner	Novel	1990	1989	Hot Shots	Gough, Laurence
CWC	Ellis	Nominee	Novel	1990	1989	The Hanging Valley	Robinson, Peter
CWC	Ellis	Nominee	Novel	1989	1988	A Dedicated Man	Robinson, Peter
CWC	Ellis	Winner	Novel	1986	1985	Death in the Old Country	Wright, Eric
CWC	Ellis	Winner	Novel	1985	1984	Murder Sees the Light	Engel, Howard
CWC	Ellis	Winner	Novel	1984	1983	The Night the Gods Smiled	Wright, Eric
IACW	Hammett	Nominee	Novel	1997	1996	Buzz Cut	Hall, James W.
IACW	Hammett	Nominee	Novel	1997	1996	Innocent Graves	Robinson, Peter
IACW	Hammett	Nominee	Novel	1997	1996	Damaged Goods	Solmita, Stephen
IACW	Hammett	Nominee	Novel	1996	1995	The Last Coyote	Connelly, Michael
IACW	Hammett	Nominee	Novel	1995	1994	Dixie City Jam	Burke, James Lee
IACW	Hammett	Nominee	Novel	1995	1994	Catalina's Riddle	Saylor, Steven
IACW	Hammett	Winner	Novel	1994	1993	The Mexican Tree Duck	Crumley, James
IACW	Hammett	Nominee	Novel	1994	1993	The Black Ice	Connelly, Michael
IACW	Hammett	Nominee	Novel	1994	1993	White Butterfly	Mosley, Walter
IACW	Hammett	Nominee	Novel	1989	1988	The Ones You Do	Woodrell, Dan

Group	Name	Status	Category	Award	Pub	BOOK TITLE	Last, First
		A W A R D		**Y E A R**			**AUTHOR NAME**

Awards List 1 – Winners and Nominees by Award Name

Includes ONLY series novels written by men

Group	Name	Status	Category	Award	Pub	BOOK TITLE	Last, First
LBR	Lambda	Winner	Novel	1997	1996	Death of Friends	Nava, Michael
LBR	Lambda	Winner	Novel	1996	1995	Closet	Zimmerman, R.D.
LBR	Lambda	Winner	Novel	1994	1993	Catalina's Riddle	Saylor, Steven
LBR	Lambda	Winner	Novel	1993	1992	The Hidden Law	Nava, Michael
LBR	Lambda	Winner	Novel	1992	1991	Country of Old Men	Hansen, Joseph
LBR	Lambda	Winner	Novel	1991	1990	How Town	Nava, Michael
LBR	Lambda	Winner	Novel	1990	1989	A Simple Suburban Murder	Zubro, Mark
LBR	Lambda	Winner	Novel	1989	1988	Goldenboy	Nava, Michael
Malice	Agatha	Nominee	First Novel	1997	1996	Death in Little Tokyo	Furutani, Dale
Malice	Agatha	Winner	First Novel	1995	1994	Do Unto Others	Abbott, Jeff
Malice	Agatha	Nominee	Novel	1996	1995	Escapade	Satterthwait, Walter
Malice	Agatha	Nominee	Novel	1994	1993	Old Scores	Elkins, Aaron
MRI	Macavity	Nominee	First Novel	1997	1996	Death in Little Tokyo	Furutani, Dale
MRI	Macavity	Winner	First Novel	1995	1994	Do Unto Others	Abbott, Jeff
MRI	Macavity	Winner	First Novel	1988	1987	The Monkey's Raincoat	Crais, Robert
MRI	Macavity	Nominee	Novel	1997	1996	Bloodhounds	Lovesey, Peter
MRI	Macavity	Nominee	Novel	1997	1996	Multiple Wounds	Russell, Alan
MRI	Macavity	Nominee	Novel	1996	1995	The Last Coyote	Connelly, Michael
MRI	Macavity	Nominee	Novel	1996	1995	Bookman's Wake	Dunning, John
MRI	Macavity	Nominee	Novel	1995	1994	The Concrete Blonde	Connelly, Michael
MRI	Macavity	Winner	Novel	1989	1988	A Thief of Time	Hillerman, Tony
MWA	Edgar	Winner	First Novel	1996	1995	Penance	Housewright, David
MWA	Edgar	Nominee	First Novel	1996	1995	Fixed in His Folly	Walker, David J.
MWA	Edgar	Nominee	First Novel	1995	1994	Big Town	Swanson, Doug J.
MWA	Edgar	Nominee	First Novel	1994	1993	The List of 7	Frost, Mark
MWA	Edgar	Nominee	First Novel	1994	1993	The Ballad of Rocky Ruiz	Ramos, Manuel
MWA	Edgar	Winner	First Novel	1993	1992	The Black Echo	Connelly, Michael
MWA	Edgar	Nominee	First Novel	1992	1991	Deadstick	Faherty, Terence
MWA	Edgar	Nominee	First Novel	1992	1991	A Cool Breeze on the Underground	Winslow, Don
MWA	Edgar	Nominee	First Novel	1991	1990	Devil in a Blue Dress	Mosley, Walter
MWA	Edgar	Nominee	First Novel	1990	1989	Blood Under the Bridge	Zimmerman, Bruce
MWA	Edgar	Nominee	First Novel	1988	1987	Detective	Hall, Parnell
MWA	Edgar	Nominee	First Novel	1988	1987	Lover Man	Murphy, Dallas
MWA	Edgar	Winner	First Novel	1987	1986	No One Rides for Free	Beinhart, Larry
MWA	Edgar	Nominee	First Novel	1987	1986	Dead Air	Lupica, Mike
MWA	Edgar	Winner	First Novel	1986	1985	When the Bough Breaks	Kellerman, Jonathan
MWA	Edgar	Nominee	First Novel	1986	1985	Sleeping Dog	Lochte, Dick
MWA	Edgar	Winner	First Novel	1985	1984	Strike Three, You're Dead	Rosen, Richard
MWA	Edgar	Nominee	First Novel	1985	1984	Foul Shot	Hornig, Doug
MWA	Edgar	Winner	First Novel	1984	1983	The Bay Psalm Book Murder	Harriss, Will
MWA	Edgar	Winner	First Novel	1984	1983	Red Diamond, Private Eye	Schorr, Mark
MWA	Edgar	Nominee	First Novel	1984	1983	The Gold Solution	Resnicow, Herbert
MWA	Edgar	Nominee	First Novel	1983	1982	Caroline Minuscule	Taylor, Andrew
MWA	Edgar	Winner	First Novel	1980	1979	The Lasko Tangent	Patterson, Richard North
MWA	Edgar	Nominee	First Novel	1980	1979	Follow the Leader	Logue, John
MWA	Edgar	Winner	First Novel	1979	1978	Killed in the Ratings	DeAndrea, William L.
MWA	Edgar	Nominee	First Novel	1978	1977	Dewey Decimated	Goodrum, Charles A.
MWA	Edgar	Winner	First Novel	1977	1976	Confess Fletch	McDonald, Gregory
MWA	Edgar	Winner	First Novel	1976	1975	The Alvarez Journal	Burns, Rex
MWA	Edgar	Winner	First Novel	1975	1974	Fletch	McDonald, Gregory
MWA	Edgar	Winner	First Novel	1972	1971	Gypsy in Amber	Smith, Martin Cruz
MWA	Edgar	Nominee	First Novel	1972	1971	Ask the Right Question	Lewin, Michael Z.
MWA	Edgar	Nominee	First Novel	1971	1970	The Blessing Way	Hillerman, Tony
MWA	Edgar	Winner	First Novel	1969	1968	Silver Street	Johnson, E. Richard
MWA	Edgar	Winner	First Novel	1968	1967	Act of Fear	Collins, Michael
MWA	Edgar	Winner	First Novel	1965	1964	Friday the Rabbi Slept Late	Kemelman, Harry
MWA	Edgar	Nominee	First Novel	1965	1964	Funeral in Berlin	Deighton, Len
MWA	Edgar	Winner	Novel	1996	1995	Come to Grief	Francis, Dick
MWA	Edgar	Nominee	Novel	1996	1995	Bookman's Wake	Dunning, John
MWA	Edgar	Nominee	Novel	1996	1995	The Summons	Lovesey, Peter
MWA	Edgar	Nominee	Novel	1996	1995	The Roaring Boy	Marston, Edward
MWA	Edgar	Winner	Novel	1995	1994	A Long Line of Dead Men	Block, Lawrence

Group	Name	Status	Category	Award	Pub	BOOK TITLE	Last, First

AWARD / **YEAR** / **AUTHOR NAME**

Awards List 1 – Winners and Nominees by Award Name

Includes ONLY series novels written by men

Group	Name	Status	Category	Award	Pub	BOOK TITLE	Last, First
MWA	Edgar	Nominee	Novel	1994	1993	Free Fall	Crais, Robert
MWA	Edgar	Nominee	Novel	1994	1993	White Butterfly	Mosley, Walter
MWA	Edgar	Nominee	Novel	1993	1992	32 Cadilacs	Gores, Joe
MWA	Edgar	Nominee	Novel	1993	1992	Body of Truth	Lindsey, David L.
MWA	Edgar	Nominee	Novel	1993	1992	Wednesday's Child	Robinson, Peter
MWA	Edgar	Winner	Novel	1992	1991	A Dance at the Slaughterhouse	Block, Lawrence
MWA	Edgar	Nominee	Novel	1991	1990	Bones and Silence	Hill, Reginald
MWA	Edgar	Nominee	Novel	1991	1990	One Small Step	Hill, Reginald
MWA	Edgar	Winner	Novel	1990	1989	Black Cherry Blues	Burke, James Lee
MWA	Edgar	Nominee	Novel	1990	1989	The Death of the Joyce Scholar	Gill, Bartholomew
MWA	Edgar	Winner	Novel	1989	1988	A Cold Red Sunrise	Kaminsky, Stuart M.
MWA	Edgar	Nominee	Novel	1989	1988	Joey's Case	Constantine, K. C.
MWA	Edgar	Nominee	Novel	1989	1988	Sacrificial Ground	Cook, Thomas
MWA	Edgar	Nominee	Novel	1989	1988	A Thief of Time	Hillerman, Tony
MWA	Edgar	Nominee	Novel	1989	1988	In the Lake of the Moon	Lindsey, David L.
MWA	Edgar	Winner	Novel	1988	1987	Old Bones	Elkins, Aaron
MWA	Edgar	Nominee	Novel	1987	1986	The Straight Man	Simon, Roger L.
MWA	Edgar	Nominee	Novel	1985	1984	A Shock to the System	Brett, Simon
MWA	Edgar	Nominee	Novel	1984	1983	The Papers of Tony Veitch	McIlvanney, William
MWA	Edgar	Winner	Novel	1983	1982	Billingsgate Shoal	Boyer, Rick
MWA	Edgar	Nominee	Novel	1983	1982	Eight Million Ways to Die	Block, Lawrence
MWA	Edgar	Winner	Novel	1982	1981	Peregrine	Bayer, William
MWA	Edgar	Winner	Novel	1980	1979	Whip Hand	Francis, Dick
MWA	Edgar	Nominee	Novel	1979	1978	Listening Woman	Hillerman, Tony
MWA	Edgar	Nominee	Novel	1978	1977	Laidlaw	McIlvanney, William
MWA	Edgar	Nominee	Novel	1978	1977	A Fire in the Barley	Parrish, Frank
MWA	Edgar	Winner	Novel	1977	1976	Promised Land	Parker, Robert B.
MWA	Edgar	Winner	Novel	1974	1973	Dance Hall of the Dead	Hillerman, Tony
MWA	Edgar	Nominee	Novel	1973	1972	Canto for a Gypsy	Smitm, Martin Cruz
MWA	Edgar	Nominee	Novel	1971	1970	Sir, You Bastard	Newman, G.F.
MWA	Edgar	Nominee	Novel	1971	1970	The Hot Rock	Westlake, Donald E.
MWA	Edgar	Nominee	Novel	1968	1967	A Parade of Cockeyed Creatures	Baxt, George
MWA	Edgar	Winner	Novel	1967	1966	The King of the Rainy Country	Freeling, Nicolas
MWA	Edgar	Nominee	Novel	1966	1965	Odds Against	Francis, Dick
MWA	Edgar	Nominee	Novel	1965	1964	The Perfect Murder	Keating, H.R.F.
MWA	Edgar	Winner	Novel	1964	1963	The Spy Who Came in from the Cold	Le Carré, John
MWA	Edgar	Winner	Novel	1963	1962	The Light of Day	Ambler, Eric
MWA	Edgar	Winner	PB Original	1997	1996	Fade Away	Coben, Harlan
MWA	Edgar	Nominee	PB Original	1997	1996	Tribe	Zimmerman, R.D.
MWA	Edgar	Winner	PB Original	1996	1995	Tarnished Blue	Heffernan, William
MWA	Edgar	Nominee	PB Original	1996	1995	Deal Breaker	Coben, Harlan
MWA	Edgar	Nominee	PB Original	1996	1995	High Desert Malice	Mitchell, Kirk
MWA	Edgar	Nominee	PB Original	1996	1995	Hard Frost	Wingfield, R.D.
MWA	Edgar	Nominee	PB Original	1995	1994	The Broken-Hearted Detective	Bass, Milton R.
MWA	Edgar	Nominee	PB Original	1995	1994	Viper Quarry	Feldmeyer, Dean
MWA	Edgar	Winner	PB Original	1994	1993	Dead Folk's Blues	Womack, Steven
MWA	Edgar	Winner	PB Original	1992	1991	Dark Maze	Adcock, Thomas
MWA	Edgar	Winner	PB Original	1991	1990	The Man Who Would Be F. Scott Fitzgerald	Handler, David
MWA	Edgar	Winner	PB Original	1990	1989	The Rain	Peterson, Keith
MWA	Edgar	Nominee	PB Original	1990	1989	Manhattan is My Beat	Deaver, Jeffery
MWA	Edgar	Nominee	PB Original	1989	1988	Judgment by Fire	Huebner, Frederick D.
MWA	Edgar	Nominee	PB Original	1989	1988	The Trapdoor	Peterson, Keith
MWA	Edgar	Winner	PB Original	1988	1987	The Monkey's Raincoat	Crais, Robert
MWA	Edgar	Winner	PB Original	1987	1986	The Junkyard Dog	Campbell, Robert
MWA	Edgar	Winner	PB Original	1986	1985	Pigs Get Fat	Murphy, Warren B.
MWA	Edgar	Nominee	PB Original	1986	1985	Poverty Bay	Emerson, Earl
MWA	Edgar	Nominee	PB Original	1985	1984	Words Can Kill	Davis, Kenn
MWA	Edgar	Nominee	PB Original	1984	1983	Black Knight in Red Square	Kaminsky, Stuart M.
MWA	Edgar	Nominee	PB Original	1984	1983	Trace	Murphy, Warren B.
MWA	Edgar	Nominee	PB Original	1984	1983	Hunter	Sauter, Eric
MWA	Edgar	Nominee	PB Original	1983	1982	The Missing and the Dead	Lynch, Jack
MWA	Edgar	Winner	PB Original	1981	1980	Public Murders	Granger, Bill
MWA	Edgar	Winner	PB Original	1980	1979	The HOG Murders	DeAndrea, William L.

Group	Name	Status	Category	Award	Pub	BOOK TITLE	Last, First
		AWARD		YEAR			AUTHOR NAME

Awards List 1 – Winners and Nominees by Award Name

Includes ONLY series novels written by men

Group	Name	Status	Category	Award	Pub	BOOK TITLE	Last, First
MWA	Edgar	Nominee	PB Original	1980	1979	The Infernal Device	Kurland, Michael
MWA	Edgar	Nominee	PB Original	1978	1977	Time to Murder and Create	Block, Lawrence
MWA	Edgar	Nominee	PB Original	1977	1976	The Dark Side [w/John Stanley]	Davis, Kenn
MWA	Edgar	Nominee	PB Original	1977	1976	The Retaliators	Hamilton, Donald
MWA	Edgar	Nominee	PB Original	1977	1976	Freeze Frame	Irvine, Robert
MWA	Edgar	Nominee	PB Original	1975	1974	Jump Cut	Irvine, Robert
MWA	Edgar	Nominee	PB Original	1974	1973	The Mediterranean Caper	Cussler, Clive
MWA	Edgar	Nominee	PB Original	1972	1971	Space for Hire	Nolan, William F.
MWA	Edgar	Nominee	PB Original	1970	1969	The Sour Lemon Score	Stark, Richard
PWA	Shamus	Winner	First Novel	1996	1995	The Innocents	Barre, Richard
PWA	Shamus	Nominee	First Novel	1996	1995	Who in Hell is Wanda Fuca?	Ford, G.M.
PWA	Shamus	Nominee	First Novel	1996	1995	Penance	Housewright, David
PWA	Shamus	Winner	First Novel	1995	1994	A Drink Before the War	Lehand, Dennis
PWA	Shamus	Nominee	First Novel	1995	1994	The Heaven Stone	Daniel, David
PWA	Shamus	Nominee	First Novel	1995	1994	The Fall-Down Artist	Lipinski, Thomas
PWA	Shamus	Winner	First Novel	1993	1992	The Woman Who Married a Bear	Straley, John
PWA	Shamus	Nominee	First Novel	1993	1992	The Long-Legged Fly	Sallis, James
PWA	Shamus	Winner	First Novel	1992	1991	Suffer Little Children	Davis, Thomas D.
PWA	Shamus	Nominee	First Novel	1992	1991	The January Corpse	Albert, Neil
PWA	Shamus	Nominee	First Novel	1992	1991	Dead on the Island	Crider, Bill
PWA	Shamus	Nominee	First Novel	1992	1991	Best Performance by a Patsy	Cutler, Stan
PWA	Shamus	Nominee	First Novel	1992	1991	A Cool Breeze on the Underground	Winslow, Don
PWA	Shamus	Winner	First Novel	1991	1990	Devil in a Blue Dress	Mosley, Walter
PWA	Shamus	Nominee	First Novel	1991	1990	Body Scissors	Doolittle, Jerome
PWA	Shamus	Nominee	First Novel	1991	1990	The Stone Veil	Tierney, Ronald
PWA	Shamus	Nominee	First Novel	1990	1989	Cold Night	Sarrantonio, Al
PWA	Shamus	Nominee	First Novel	1990	1989	Wall of Glass	Satterthwait, Walter
PWA	Shamus	Nominee	First Novel	1990	1989	Rock Critic Murders	Sublett, Jesse
PWA	Shamus	Winner	First Novel	1989	1988	Fear of the Dark	Haywood, Gar Anthony
PWA	Shamus	Nominee	First Novel	1989	1988	Lost Daughter	Cormany, Michael
PWA	Shamus	Nominee	First Novel	1989	1988	The Burning Season	Dundee, Wayne
PWA	Shamus	Winner	First Novel	1988	1987	Death on the Rocks	Allegretto, Michael
PWA	Shamus	Nominee	First Novel	1988	1987	Shawnee Alley Fire	Douglas, John
PWA	Shamus	Nominee	First Novel	1988	1987	Detective	Hall, Parnell
PWA	Shamus	Nominee	First Novel	1988	1987	An Infinite Number of Monkeys	Roberts, Les
PWA	Shamus	Winner	First Novel	1987	1986	Jersey Tomatoes	Rider, J.W.
PWA	Shamus	Nominee	First Novel	1987	1986	No One Rides for Free	Beinhart, Larry
PWA	Shamus	Winner	First Novel	1986	1985	Hard Cover	Warga, Wayne
PWA	Shamus	Nominee	First Novel	1986	1985	New, Improved Murder	Gorman, Ed
PWA	Shamus	Nominee	First Novel	1986	1985	Sleeping Dog	Lochte, Dick
PWA	Shamus	Nominee	First Novel	1986	1985	Flood	Vachss, Andrew H.
PWA	Shamus	Nominee	First Novel	1985	1984	Blunt Darts	Healy, Jeremiah
PWA	Shamus	Nominee	First Novel	1985	1984	The Nebraska Quotient	Reynolds, William J.
PWA	Shamus	Nominee	Novel	1997	1996	Damned in Paradise	Collins, Max Allan, Jr
PWA	Shamus	Winner	Novel	1997	1996	Sunset Express	Crais, Robert
PWA	Shamus	Nominee	Novel	1997	1996	Flesh Wounds	Greenleaf, Stephen
PWA	Shamus	Nominee	Novel	1997	1996	Invasion of Privacy	Healy, Jeremiah
PWA	Shamus	Nominee	Novel	1997	1996	The Low End of Nowhere	Stone, Michael
PWA	Shamus	Nominee	Novel	1996	1995	The Vanishing Smile	Emerson, Earl
PWA	Shamus	Nominee	Novel	1996	1995	Come to Grief	Francis, Dick
PWA	Shamus	Nominee	Novel	1996	1995	Movie	Hall, Parnell
PWA	Shamus	Nominee	Novel	1996	1995	Neon Smile	Lochte, Dick
PWA	Shamus	Nominee	Novel	1996	1997	Sentinels	Pronzini, Bill
PWA	Shamus	Nominee	Novel	1995	1994	A Long Line of Dead Men	Block, Lawrence
PWA	Shamus	Nominee	Novel	1995	1994	Carnal Hours	Collins, Max Allan, Jr
PWA	Shamus	Nominee	Novel	1995	1994	The Lake Effect	Roberts, Les
PWA	Shamus	Winner	Novel	1994	1993	The Devil Knows You're Dead	Block, Lawrence
PWA	Shamus	Nominee	Novel	1994	1993	Foursome	Healy, Jeremiah
PWA	Shamus	Nominee	Novel	1994	1993	Moth	Sallis, James
PWA	Shamus	Winner	Novel	1993	1992	The Man Who Was Taller Than God	Adams, Harold
PWA	Shamus	Nominee	Novel	1993	1992	Cassandra in Red	Collins, Michael
PWA	Shamus	Nominee	Novel	1993	1992	Lullaby Town	Crais, Robert
PWA	Shamus	Nominee	Novel	1993	1992	Shallow Graves	Healy, Jeremiah
PWA	Shamus	Nominee	Novel	1993	1992	Special Delivery	Kennealy, Jerry

Group	Name	Status	Category	Award	Pub	BOOK TITLE	Last, First
		AWARD		YEAR			AUTHOR NAME

Awards List 1 – Winners and Nominees by Award Name

Includes ONLY series novels written by men

Group	Name	Status	Category	Award	Pub	BOOK TITLE	Last, First
PWA	Shamus	Winner	Novel	1992	1991	Stolen Away	Collins, Max Allan, Jr
PWA	Shamus	Nominee	Novel	1992	1991	A Dance at the Slaughterhouse	Block, Lawrence
PWA	Shamus	Nominee	Novel	1992	1991	A Fistful of Empty	Schutz, Benjamin
PWA	Shamus	Nominee	Novel	1992	1991	Second Chance	Valin, Jonathan
PWA	Shamus	Nominee	Novel	1991	1990	A Ticket to the Boneyard	Block, Lawrence
PWA	Shamus	Nominee	Novel	1991	1990	The Skintight Shroud	Dundee, Wayne
PWA	Shamus	Nominee	Novel	1991	1990	Poor Butterfly	Kaminsky, Stuart M.
PWA	Shamus	Nominee	Novel	1991	1990	Polo's Wild Card	Kennealy, Jerry
PWA	Shamus	Nominee	Novel	1991	1989	Dead Irish	Lescroart, John T.
PWA	Shamus	Nominee	Novel	1991	1990	The Desert Look	Schopen, Bernard
PWA	Shamus	Winner	Novel	1990	1989	Extenuating Circumstances	Valin, Jonathan
PWA	Shamus	Nominee	Novel	1990	1989	Out on the Cutting Edge	Block, Lawrence
PWA	Shamus	Nominee	Novel	1990	1989	The Killing Man	Spillane, Mickey
PWA	Shamus	Winner	Novel	1989	1988	Kiss	Lutz, John
PWA	Shamus	Nominee	Novel	1989	1988	Neon Mirage	Collins, Max Allan, Jr
PWA	Shamus	Nominee	Novel	1989	1988	Deviant Behavior	Emerson, Earl
PWA	Shamus	Nominee	Novel	1989	1988	Swan Dive	Healy, Jeremiah
PWA	Shamus	Winner	Novel	1988	1987	A Tax in Blood	Schutz, Benjamin
PWA	Shamus	Nominee	Novel	1988	1987	Lady Yesterday	Estleman, Loren D.
PWA	Shamus	Nominee	Novel	1988	1987	The Autumn Dead	Gorman, Ed
PWA	Shamus	Nominee	Novel	1988	1987	Ride the Lightning	Lutz, John
PWA	Shamus	Winner	Novel	1987	1986	The Staked Goat	Healy, Jeremiah
PWA	Shamus	Nominee	Novel	1987	1986	When the Sacred Ginmill Closes	Block, Lawrence
PWA	Shamus	Nominee	Novel	1987	1986	In La-La Land We Trust	Campbell, Robert
PWA	Shamus	Nominee	Novel	1987	1986	The Million Dollar Wound	Collins, Max Allan, Jr
PWA	Shamus	Nominee	Novel	1986	1985	The Naked Liar	Adams, Harold
PWA	Shamus	Nominee	Novel	1986	1985	Hardball	Hornig, Doug
PWA	Shamus	Nominee	Novel	1986	1985	Nightlines	Lutz, John
PWA	Shamus	Nominee	Novel	1986	1985	A Catskill Eagle	Parker, Robert B.
PWA	Shamus	Nominee	Novel	1986	1985	Bones	Pronzini, Bill
PWA	Shamus	Nominee	Novel	1986	1985	Embrace the Wolf	Schutz, Benjamin
PWA	Shamus	Winner	Novel	1985	1984	Sugartown	Estleman, Loren D.
PWA	Shamus	Nominee	Novel	1985	1984	True Crime	Collins, Max Allan, Jr
PWA	Shamus	Nominee	Novel	1985	1984	Die Again, Macready	Livingston, Jack
PWA	Shamus	Nominee	Novel	1985	1984	Full Contact	Randisi, Robert J.
PWA	Shamus	Winner	Novel	1984	1983	True Detective	Collins, Max Allan, Jr
PWA	Shamus	Nominee	Novel	1984	1983	Dancing Bear	Crumley, James
PWA	Shamus	Nominee	Novel	1984	1983	The Glass Highway	Estleman, Loren D.
PWA	Shamus	Nominee	Novel	1984	1983	The Widening Gyre	Parker, Robert B.
PWA	Shamus	Winner	Novel	1983	1982	Eight Million Ways to Die	Block, Lawrence
PWA	Shamus	Nominee	Novel	1983	1982	Gravedigger	Hansen, Joseph
PWA	Shamus	Nominee	Novel	1983	1982	30 for a Harry	Hoyt, Richard
PWA	Shamus	Nominee	Novel	1983	1982	A Piece of the Silence	Livingston, Jack
PWA	Shamus	Nominee	Novel	1983	1982	Hard Trade	Lyons, Arthur
PWA	Shamus	Nominee	Novel	1983	1982	Ceremony	Parker, Robert B.
PWA	Shamus	Winner	Novel	1982	1981	Hoodwink	Pronzini, Bill
PWA	Shamus	Nominee	Novel	1982	1981	Early Autumn	Parker, Robert B.
PWA	Shamus	Nominee	Novel	1979	1978	A Stab in the Dark	Block, Lawrence
PWA	Shamus	Nominee	PB Original	1997	1996	Fade Away	Coben, Harlan
PWA	Shamus	Nominee	PB Original	1997	1996	Chain of Fools	Womack, Steven
PWA	Shamus	Winner	PB Original	1996	1995	Native Angels	Jaspersohn, William
PWA	Shamus	Nominee	PB Original	1996	1995	Zero Tolerance	Knight, J.D.
PWA	Shamus	Nominee	PB Original	1996	1995	Way Past Dead	Womack, Steven
PWA	Shamus	Nominee	PB Original	1995	1994	Double Plot	Axler, Leo
PWA	Shamus	Nominee	PB Original	1994	1993	The Half-Hearted Detective	Bass; Milton R.
PWA	Shamus	Nominee	PB Original	1994	1993	A Minyan for the Dead	Fliegel, Richard
PWA	Shamus	Nominee	PB Original	1994	1993	Torch Town Boogie	Womack, Steven
PWA	Shamus	Nominee	PB Original	1993	1992	The Brutal Ballet	Dundee, Wayne
PWA	Shamus	Winner	PB Original	1992	1991	The Cool Blue Tomb	Kemprecos, Paul
PWA	Shamus	Nominee	PB Original	1992	1991	The Thousand-Yard Stare	Kantner, Rob
PWA	Shamus	Winner	PB Original	1991	1990	Fatal Sisters	Duncan, W. Glenn
PWA	Shamus	Nominee	PB Original	1991	1990	Bimbo Heaven	Albert, Marvin H.
PWA	Shamus	Nominee	PB Original	1991	1990	The Queen's Mare	Birkett, John
PWA	Shamus	Nominee	PB Original	1991	1990	Made in Detroit	Kantner, Rob
PWA	Shamus	Winner	PB Original	1990	1989	Hell's Only Half Full	Kantner, Rob

AWARD				YEAR			AUTHOR NAME
Group	Name	Status	Category	Award	Pub	BOOK TITLE	Last, First

Awards List 1 – Winners and Nominees by Award Name

Includes ONLY series novels written by men

Group	Name	Status	Category	Award	Pub	BOOK TITLE	Last, First
PWA	Shamus	Nominee	PB Original	1990	1989	Muscle and Blood	Dold, Gaylord
PWA	Shamus	Nominee	PB Original	1990	1989	Behind the Fact	Hilary, Richard
PWA	Shamus	Nominee	PB Original	1990	1989	Tough Enough	Philbrick, W.R.
PWA	Shamus	Winner	PB Original	1989	1988	Dirty Work	Kantner, Rob
PWA	Shamus	Nominee	PB Original	1989	1988	The Last Private Eye	Birkett, John
PWA	Shamus	Nominee	PB Original	1989	1988	Bone Pile	Dold, Gaylord
PWA	Shamus	Nominee	PB Original	1989	1988	Rebound	Everson, David H.
PWA	Shamus	Nominee	PB Original	1989	1988	The Crystal Blue Persuasion	Philbrick, W.R.
PWA	Shamus	Nominee	PB Original	1988	1987	The Monkey's Raincoat	Crais, Robert
PWA	Shamus	Nominee	PB Original	1988	1987	Snake Eyes	Dold, Gaylord
PWA	Shamus	Nominee	PB Original	1988	1987	Recount	Everson, David H.
PWA	Shamus	Winner	PB Original	1987	1986	The Back-Door Man	Kantner, Rob
PWA	Shamus	Nominee	PB Original	1987	1986	Stone Angel	Albert, Marvin H.
PWA	Shamus	Nominee	PB Original	1987	1986	Melting Point	Davis, Kenn
PWA	Shamus	Nominee	PB Original	1987	1986	Too Old a Cat	Murphy, Warren B.
PWA	Shamus	Winner	PB Original	1986	1985	Poverty Bay	Emerson, Earl
PWA	Shamus	Nominee	PB Original	1986	1985	The Rainy City	Emerson, Earl
PWA	Shamus	Nominee	PB Original	1986	1985	Pigs Get Fat	Murphy, Warren B.
PWA	Shamus	Nominee	PB Original	1986	1985	Blue Heron	Ross, Philip
PWA	Shamus	Nominee	PB Original	1985	1984	San Quentin	Lynch, Jack
PWA	Shamus	Nominee	PB Original	1985	1984	Trace and 47 Miles of Rope	Murphy, Warren B.
PWA	Shamus	Nominee	PB Original	1985	1984	The Man Who Risked His Partner	Stephens, Reed
PWA	Shamus	Winner	PB Original	1984	1983	Dead in Centerfield	Engleman, Paul
PWA	Shamus	Nominee	PB Original	1984	1983	Finders Weepers	Byrd, Max
PWA	Shamus	Nominee	PB Original	1984	1983	Trace	Murphy, Warren B.
PWA	Shamus	Nominee	PB Original	1984	1983	The Steinway Collection	Randisi, Robert J.
PWA	Shamus	Nominee	PB Original	1983	1982	Nevsky's Return	Gat, Dimitri
PWA	Shamus	Nominee	PB Original	1983	1982	Pieces of Death	Lynch, Jack
PWA	Shamus	Nominee	PB Original	1983	1982	Smoked Out	Murphy, Warren B.
PWA	Shamus	Winner	PB Original	1982	1981	California Thriller	Byrd, Max
SMP	SMP/PWA	Winner	First P.I. Novel	1995	1996	Diamond Head	Knief, Charles
SMP	SMP/PWA	Winner	First P.I. Novel	1993	1994	The Heaven Stone	Daniel, David
SMP	SMP/PWA	Winner	First P.I. Novel	1992	1994	Hour of the Manatee	Ayres, E.C.
SMP	SMP/PWA	Winner	First P.I. Novel	1990	1991	The Loud Adios	Kuhlken, Ken
SMP	SMP/PWA	Winner	First P.I. Novel	1986	1987	An Infinite Number of Monkeys	Roberts, Les
Wolfe Pack	Nero Wolfe	Winner	Novel	1994	1993	Old Scores	Elkins, Aaron
Wolfe Pack	Nero Wolfe	Winner	Novel	1993	1992	Booked to Die	Dunning, John
Wolfe Pack	Nero Wolfe	Winner	Novel	1991	1990	Coyote Waits	Hillerman, Tony
Wolfe Pack	Nero Wolfe	Winner	Novel	1986	1985	Sleeping Dog	Lochte, Dick
Wolfe Pack	Nero Wolfe	Winner	Novel	1980	1979	The Burglar Who Liked to Quote Kipling	Block, Lawrence

AWARD			YEAR				AUTHOR NAME
Category	Status	Name	Pub	Award	Conf'd by	BOOK TITLE	Last, First

Awards List 2 – Winners and Nominees by Award Category

Includes ONLY series novels written by men

Category	Status	Name	Pub	Award	Conf'd by	BOOK TITLE	Last, First
First Novel	Nominee	Anthony	1996	1997	B'con	Death in Little Tokyo	Furutani, Dale
First Novel	Nominee	Anthony	1996	1997	B'con	Tularosa	McGarrity, Michael
First Novel	Nominee	Agatha	1996	1997	Mal Dom	Death in Little Tokyo	Furutani, Dale
First Novel	Nominee	Macavity	1996	1997	MRI	Death in Little Tokyo	Furutani, Dale
First Novel	Winner	Edgar	1995	1996	MWA	Penance	Housewright, David
First Novel	Winner	Shamus	1995	1996	PWA	The Innocents	Barre, Richard
First Novel	Nominee	Anthony	1995	1996	B'con	The Innocents	Barre, Richard
First Novel	Nominee	Edgar	1995	1996	MWA	Fixed in His Folly	Walker, David J.
First Novel	Nominee	Shamus	1995	1996	PWA	Who in Hell is Wanda Fuca?	Ford, G.M.
First Novel	Nominee	Shamus	1995	1996	PWA	Penance	Housewright, David
First Novel	Winner	Anthony	1994	1995	B'con	A Drink Before the War	Lehane, Dennis
First Novel	Winner	Creasey	1994	1995	CWA	Big Town	Swanson, Doug J.
First Novel	Winner	Agatha	1994	1995	Mal Dom	Do Unto Others	Abbott, Jeff

AWARD			YEAR				AUTHOR NAME
Category	Status	Name	Pub	Award	Conf'd by	BOOK TITLE	Last, First

Awards List 2 – Winners and Nominees by Award Category

Includes ONLY series novels written by men

Category	Status	Name	Pub	Award	Conf'd by	BOOK TITLE	Last, First
First Novel	Winner	Macavity	1994	1995	MRI	Do Unto Others	Abbott, Jeff
First Novel	Winner	Shamus	1994	1995	PWA	A Drink Before the War	Lehand, Dennis
First Novel	Nominee	Anthony	1994	1995	B'con	Big Town	Swanson, Doug J.
First Novel	Nominee	Creasey	1994	1995	CWA	The Marx Sisters	Maitland, Barry
First Novel	Nominee	Edgar	1994	1995	MWA	Big Town	Swanson, Doug J.
First Novel	Nominee	Shamus	1994	1995	PWA	The Heaven Stone	Daniel, David
First Novel	Nominee	Shamus	1994	1995	PWA	The Fall-Down Artist	Lipinski, Thomas
First Novel	Nominee	Anthony	1993	1994	B'con	Cuckoo	Keegan, Alex
First Novel	Nominee	Creasey	1993	1994	CWA	Skinner's Rules	Jardine, Quinn
First Novel	Nominee	Edgar	1993	1994	MWA	The List of 7	Frost, Mark
First Novel	Nominee	Edgar	1993	1994	MWA	The Ballad of Rocky Ruiz	Ramos, Manuel
First Novel	Winner	Edgar	1992	1993	MWA	The Black Echo	Connelly, Michael
First Novel	Winner	Shamus	1992	1993	PWA	The Woman Who Married a Bear	Straley, John
First Novel	Nominee	Shamus	1992	1993	PWA	The Long-Legged Fly	Sallis, James
First Novel	Winner	Shamus	1991	1992	PWA	Suffer Little Children	Davis, Thomas D.
First Novel	Nominee	Edgar	1991	1992	MWA	Deadstick	Faherty, Terence
First Novel	Nominee	Edgar	1991	1992	MWA	A Cool Breeze on the Underground	Winslow, Don
First Novel	Nominee	Shamus	1991	1992	PWA	The January Corpse	Albert, Neil
First Novel	Nominee	Shamus	1991	1992	PWA	Dead on the Island	Crider, Bill
First Novel	Nominee	Shamus	1991	1992	PWA	Best Performance by a Patsy	Cutler, Stan
First Novel	Nominee	Shamus	1991	1992	PWA	A Cool Breeze on the Underground	Winslow, Don
First Novel	Winner	Creasey	1990	1991	CWA	Devil in a Blue Dress	Mosley, Walter
First Novel	Winner	Shamus	1990	1991	PWA	Devil in a Blue Dress	Mosley, Walter
First Novel	Nominee	Edgar	1990	1991	MWA	Devil in a Blue Dress	Mosley, Walter
First Novel	Nominee	Shamus	1990	1991	PWA	Body Scissors	Doolittle, Jerome
First Novel	Nominee	Shamus	1990	1991	PWA	The Stone Veil	Tierney, Ronald
First Novel	Nominee	Edgar	1989	1990	MWA	Blood Under the Bridge	Zimmerman, Bruce
First Novel	Nominee	Shamus	1989	1990	PWA	Cold Night	Sarrantonio, Al
First Novel	Nominee	Shamus	1989	1990	PWA	Wall of Glass	Satterthwait, Walter
First Novel	Nominee	Shamus	1989	1990	PWA	Rock Critic Murders	Sublett, Jesse
First Novel	Winner	Ellis	1988	1989	CWC	Stone of the Heart	Brady, John
First Novel	Winner	Shamus	1988	1989	PWA	Fear of the Dark	Haywood, Gar Anthony
First Novel	Nominee	Shamus	1988	1989	PWA	Lost Daughter	Cormany, Michael
First Novel	Nominee	Shamus	1988	1989	PWA	The Burning Season	Dundee, Wayne
First Novel	Winner	Ellis	1987	1988	CWC	The Goldfish Bowl	Gough, Laurence
First Novel	Winner	Macavity	1987	1988	MRI	The Monkey's Raincoat	Crais, Robert
First Novel	Winner	Shamus	1987	1988	PWA	Death on the Rocks	Allegretto, Michael
First Novel	Nominee	Anthony	1987	1988	B'con	Death on the Rocks	Allegretto, Michael
First Novel	Nominee	Creasey	1987	1988	CWA	Gallows View	Robinson, Peter
First Novel	Nominee	Ellis	1987	1988	CWC	Gallows View	Robinson, Peter
First Novel	Nominee	Edgar	1987	1988	MWA	Detective	Hall, Parnell
First Novel	Nominee	Edgar	1987	1988	MWA	Lover Man	Murphy, Dallas
First Novel	Nominee	Shamus	1987	1988	PWA	Shawnee Alley Fire	Douglas, John
First Novel	Nominee	Shamus	1987	1988	PWA	Detective	Hall, Parnell
First Novel	Nominee	Shamus	1987	1988	PWA	An Infinite Number of Monkeys	Roberts, Les
First Novel	Winner	Anthony	1986	1987	B'con	Too Late to Die	Crider, Bill
First Novel	Winner	Creasey	1986	1987	CWA	Tinplate	Steed, Neville
First Novel	Winner	Edgar	1986	1987	MWA	No One Rides for Free	Beinhart, Larry
First Novel	Winner	Shamus	1986	1987	PWA	Jersey Tomatoes	Rider, J.W.
First Novel	Nominee	Edgar	1986	1987	MWA	Dead Air	Lupica, Mike
First Novel	Nominee	Shamus	1986	1987	PWA	No One Rides for Free	Beinhart, Larry
First Novel	Winner	Anthony	1985	1986	B'con	When the Bough Breaks	Kellerman, Jonathan
First Novel	Winner	Edgar	1985	1986	MWA	When the Bough Breaks	Kellerman, Jonathan
First Novel	Winner	Shamus	1985	1986	PWA	Hard Cover	Warga, Wayne
First Novel	Nominee	Anthony	1985	1986	B'con	Sleeping Dog	Lochte, Dick
First Novel	Nominee	Edgar	1985	1986	MWA	Sleeping Dog	Lochte, Dick
First Novel	Nominee	Shamus	1985	1986	PWA	New, Improved Murder	Gorman, Ed
First Novel	Nominee	Shamus	1985	1986	PWA	Sleeping Dog	Lochte, Dick
First Novel	Nominee	Shamus	1985	1986	PWA	Flood	Vachss, Andrew H.
First Novel	Winner	Edgar	1984	1985	MWA	Strike Three, You're Dead	Rosen, Richard
First Novel	Nominee	Edgar	1984	1985	MWA	Foul Shot	Hornig, Doug

Category	Status	Name	Pub	Award	Conf'd by	BOOK TITLE	Last, First
AWARD			**YEAR**			**BOOK TITLE**	**AUTHOR NAME**

Awards List 2 – Winners and Nominees by Award Category

Includes ONLY series novels written by men

Category	Status	Name	Pub	Award	Conf'd by	BOOK TITLE	Last, First
First Novel	Nominee	Shamus	1984	1985	PWA	Blunt Darts	Healy, Jeremiah
First Novel	Nominee	Shamus	1984	1985	PWA	The Nebraska Quotient	Reynolds, William J.
First Novel	Winner	Edgar	1983	1984	MWA	The Bay Psalm Book Murder	Harriss, Will
First Novel	Winner	Edgar	1983	1984	MWA	Red Diamond, Private Eye	Schorr, Mark
First Novel	Nominee	Edgar	1983	1984	MWA	The Gold Solution	Resnicow, Herbert
First Novel	Winner	Creasey	1983	1983	CWA	The Night the Gods Smiled	Wright, Eric
First Novel	Nominee	Edgar	1982	1983	MWA	Caroline Minuscule	Taylor, Andrew
First Novel	Winner	Creasey	1982	1982	CWA	Caroline Minuscule	Taylor, Andrew
First Novel	Winner	Creasey	1979	1980	CWA	Saturday of Glory	Serafin, David
First Novel	Winner	Edgar	1979	1980	MWA	The Lasko Tangent	Patterson, Richard North
First Novel	Nominee	Edgar	1979	1980	MWA	Follow the Leader	Logue, John
First Novel	Winner	Edgar	1978	1979	MWA	Killed in the Ratings	DeAndrea, William L.
First Novel	Winner	Creasey	1977	1978	CWA	The Judas Pair	Gash, Jonathan
First Novel	Nominee	Edgar	1977	1978	MWA	Dewey Decimated	Goodrum, Charles A.
First Novel	Winner	Edgar	1976	1977	MWA	Confess Fletch	McDonald, Gregory
First Novel	Winner	Edgar	1975	1976	MWA	The Alvarez Journal	Burns, Rex
First Novel	Winner	Edgar	1974	1975	MWA	Fletch	McDonald, Gregory
First Novel	Winner	Creasey	1973	1974	CWA	The Big Fix	Simon, Roger L.
First Novel	Winner	Edgar	1971	1972	MWA	Gypsy in Amber	Smith, Martin Cruz
First Novel	Nominee	Edgar	1971	1972	MWA	Ask the Right Question	Lewin, Michael Z.
First Novel	Nominee	Edgar	1970	1971	MWA	The Blessing Way	Hillerman, Tony
First Novel	Winner	Edgar	1968	1969	MWA	Silver Street	Johnson, E. Richard
First Novel	Winner	Edgar	1967	1968	MWA	Act of Fear	Collins, Michael
First Novel	Winner	Edgar	1964	1965	MWA	Friday the Rabbi Slept Late	Kemelman, Harry
First Novel	Nominee	Edgar	1964	1965	MWA	Funeral in Berlin	Deighton, Len
First P.I. Novel	Winner	SMP/PWA	1996	1995	SMP	Diamond Head	Knief, Charles
First P.I. Novel	Winner	SMP/PWA	1994	1993	SMP	The Heaven Stone	Daniel, David
First P.I. Novel	Winner	SMP/PWA	1994	1992	SMP	Hour of the Manatee	Ayres, E.C.
First P.I. Novel	Winner	SMP/PWA	1991	1990	SMP	The Loud Adios	Kuhlken, Ken
First P.I. Nove.	Winner	SMP/PWA	1988	1987	SMP	Fear of the Dark	Haywood, Gar
First P.I. Novel	Winner	SMP/PWA	1987	1986	SMP	An Infinite Number of Monkeys	Roberts, Les
Novel	Winner	Lambda	1996	1997	LBR	Death of Friends	Nava, Michael
Novel	Nominee	Anthony	1996	1997	B'con	Multiple Wounds	Russell, Alan
Novel	Nominee	Dagger	1996	1997	CWA	Cadillac Jukebox	Burke, James Lee
Novel	Nominee	Hammett	1996	1997	IACW	Buzz Cut	Hall, James W.
Novel	Nominee	Hammett	1996	1997	IACW	Innocent Graves	Robinson, Peter
Novel	Nominee	Hammett	1996	1997	IACW	Damaged Goods	Solmita, Stephen
Novel	Nominee	Macavity	1996	1997	MRI	Bloodhounds	Lovesey, Peter
Novel	Nominee	Macavity	1996	1997	MRI	Multiple Wounds	Russell, Alan
Novel	Winner	Shamus	1996	1997	PWA	Sunset Express	Crais, Robert
Novel	Nominee	Shamus	1996	1997	PWA	Damned in Paradise	Collins, Max Allan, Jr
Novel	Nominee	Shamus	1996	1997	PWA	Flesh Wounds	Greenleaf, Stephen
Novel	Nominee	Shamus	1996	1997	PWA	Invasion of Privacy	Healy, Jeremiah
Novel	Nominee	Shamus	1996	1997	PWA	Sentinels	Pronzini, Bill
Novel	Nominee	Shamus	1996	1997	PWA	The Low End of Nowhere	Stone, Michael
Novel	Winner	Prix Roman	1995	1996	Acad Fran	Escapade	Satterthwait, Walter
Novel	Winner	Silver Dagger	1996	1996	CWA	Bloodhounds	Lovesey, Peter
Novel	Winner	Ned Kelly	1995	1996	CWAA	The Malcontenta	Maitland, Barry
Novel	Winner	Lambda	1995	1996	LBR	Closet	Zimmerman, R.D.
Novel	Winner	Edgar	1995	1996	MWA	Come to Grief	Francis, Dick
Novel	Nominee	Anthony	1995	1996	B'con	The Last Coyote	Connelly, Michael
Novel	Nominee	Anthony	1995	1996	B'con	Who in Hell is Wanda Fuca?	Ford, G.M.
Novel	Nominee	Dagger	1996	1996	CWA	Death is Now My Neighbor	Dexter, Colin
Novel	Nominee	Hammett	1995	1996	IACW	The Last Coyote	Connelly, Michael
Novel	Nominee	Agatha	1995	1996	Mal Dom	Escapade	Satterthwait, Walter
Novel	Nominee	Macavity	1995	1996	MRI	The Last Coyote	Connelly, Michael

AWARD			YEAR				AUTHOR NAME
Category	Status	Name	Pub	Award	Conf'd by	BOOK TITLE	Last, First

Awards List 2 – Winners and Nominees by Award Category

Includes ONLY series novels written by men

Category	Status	Name	Pub	Award	Conf'd by	BOOK TITLE	Last, First
Novel	Nominee	Macavity	1995	1996	MRI	Bookman's Wake	Dunning, John
Novel	Nominee	Edgar	1995	1996	MWA	Bookman's Wake	Dunning, John
Novel	Nominee	Edgar	1995	1996	MWA	The Summons	Lovesey, Peter
Novel	Nominee	Edgar	1995	1996	MWA	The Roaring Boy	Marston, Edward
Novel	Nominee	Shamus	1995	1996	PWA	The Vanishing Smile	Emerson, Earl
Novel	Nominee	Shamus	1995	1996	PWA	Come to Grief	Francis, Dick
Novel	Nominee	Shamus	1995	1996	PWA	Movie	Hall, Parnell
Novel	Nominee	Shamus	1995	1996	PWA	Neon Smile	Lochte, Dick
Novel	Winner	Silver Dagger	1995	1995	CWA	The Summons	Lovesey, Peter
Novel	Winner	Edgar	1994	1995	MWA	A Long Line of Dead Men	Block, Lawrence
Novel	Nominee	Anthony	1994	1995	B'con	The Concrete Blonde	Connelly, Michael
Novel	Nominee	Anthony	1994	1995	B'con	Pictures of Perfection	Hill, Reginald
Novel	Nominee	Anthony	1994	1995	B'con	The 13th Juror	Lescroart, John T.
Novel	Nominee	Anthony	1994	1995	B'con	Black Betty	Mosley, Walter
Novel	Nominee	Anthony	1994	1995	B'con	Just a Corpse at Twilight	van de Wetering, J.
Novel	Nominee	Anthony	1994	1995	B'con	Death of a Blue Lantern	West, Christopher
Novel	Nominee	Dagger	1995	1995	CWA	Bookman's Wake	Dunning, John
Novel	Nominee	Ellis	1994	1995	CWC	The Good Life	Brady, John
Novel	Nominee	Hammett	1994	1995	IACW	Dixie City Jam	Burke, James Lee
Novel	Nominee	Hammett	1994	1995	IACW	Catalina's Riddle	Saylor, Steven
Novel	Nominee	Macavity	1994	1995	MRI	The Concrete Blonde	Connelly, Michael
Novel	Nominee	Shamus	1994	1995	PWA	A Long Line of Dead Men	Block, Lawrence
Novel	Nominee	Shamus	1994	1995	PWA	Carnal Hours	Collins, Max Allan, Jr
Novel	Nominee	Shamus	1994	1995	PWA	The Lake Effect	Roberts, Les
Novel	Winner	Hammett	1993	1994	IACW	The Mexican Tree Duck	Crumley, James
Novel	Winner	Lambda	1993	1994	LBR	Catalina's Riddle	Saylor, Steven
Novel	Winner	Shamus	1993	1994	PWA	The Devil Knows You're Dead	Block, Lawrence
Novel	Winner	Nero Wolfe	1993	1994	Wolfe Pack	Old Scores	Elkins, Aaron
Novel	Nominee	Anthony	1993	1994	B'con	Morons and Madmen	Emerson, Earl
Novel	Nominee	Anthony	1993	1994	B'con	Sacred Clowns	Hillerman, Tony
Novel	Nominee	Hammett	1993	1994	IACW	The Black Ice	Connelly, Michael
Novel	Nominee	Hammett	1993	1994	B'con	The Black Ice	Connelly, Michael
Novel	Nominee	Hammett	1993	1994	IACW	White Butterfly	Mosley, Walter
Novel	Nominee	Agatha	1993	1994	Mal Dom	Old Scores	Elkins, Aaron
Novel	Nominee	Edgar	1993	1994	MWA	Free Fall	Crais, Robert
Novel	Nominee	Edgar	1993	1994	MWA	White Butterfly	Mosley, Walter
Novel	Nominee	Shamus	1993	1994	PWA	Foursome	Healy, Jeremiah
Novel	Nominee	Shamus	1993	1994	PWA	Moth	Sallis, James
Novel	Winner	Lambda	1992	1993	LBR	The Hidden Law	Nava, Michael
Novel	Winner	Shamus	1992	1993	PWA	The Man Who Was Taller Than God	Adams, Harold
Novel	Winner	Nero Wolfe	1992	1993	Wolfe Pack	Booked to Die	Dunning, John
Novel	Nominee	Ellis	1992	1993	CWC	Wednesday's Child	Robinson, Peter
Novel	Nominee	Edgar	1992	1993	MWA	32 Cadilacs	Gores, Joe
Novel	Nominee	Edgar	1992	1993	MWA	Body of Truth	Lindsey, David L.
Novel	Nominee	Edgar	1992	1993	MWA	Wednesday's Child	Robinson, Peter
Novel	Nominee	Shamus	1992	1993	PWA	Cassandra in Red	Collins, Michael
Novel	Nominee	Shamus	1992	1993	PWA	Lullaby Town	Crais, Robert
Novel	Nominee	Shamus	1992	1993	PWA	Shallow Graves	Healy, Jeremiah
Novel	Nominee	Shamus	1992	1993	PWA	Special Delivery	Kennealy, Jerry
Novel	Winner	Anthony	1991	1992	B'con	The Last Detective	Lovesey, Peter
Novel	Winner	Gold Dagger	1992	1992	CWA	The Way Through the Woods	Dexter, Colin
Novel	Winner	Ellis	1991	1992	CWC	Past Reason Hated	Robinson, Peter
Novel	Winner	Lambda	1991	1992	LBR	Country of Old Men	Hansen, Joseph
Novel	Winner	Edgar	1991	1992	MWA	A Dance at the Slaughterhouse	Block, Lawrence
Novel	Winner	Shamus	1991	1992	PWA	Stolen Away	Collins, Max Allan, Jr
Novel	Nominee	Shamus	1991	1992	PWA	A Dance at the Slaughterhouse	Block, Lawrence
Novel	Nominee	Shamus	1991	1992	PWA	A Fistful of Empty	Schutz, Benjamin
Novel	Nominee	Shamus	1991	1992	PWA	Second Chance	Valin, Jonathan
Novel	Winner	Lambda	1990	1991	LBR	How Town	Nava, Michael
Novel	Winner	Nero Wolfe	1990	1991	Wolfe Pack	Coyote Waits	Hillerman, Tony
Novel	Nominee	Edgar	1990	1991	MWA	Bones and Silence	Hill, Reginald
Novel	Nominee	Shamus	1990	1991	PWA	A Ticket to the Boneyard	Block, Lawrence

Category	Status	Name	Pub	Award	Conf'd by	BOOK TITLE	Last, First
		A W A R D		**Y E A R**			**AUTHOR NAME**

Awards List 2 – Winners and Nominees by Award Category

Includes ONLY series novels written by men

Category	Status	Name	Pub	Award	Conf'd by	BOOK TITLE	Last, First
Novel	Nominee	Shamus	1990	1991	PWA	The Skintight Shroud	Dundee, Wayne
Novel	Nominee	Shamus	1990	1991	PWA	Poor Butterfly	Kaminsky, Stuart M.
Novel	Nominee	Shamus	1990	1991	PWA	Polo's Wild Card	Kennealy, Jerry
Novel	Nominee	Shamus	1990	1991	PWA	The Desert Look	Schopen, Bernard
Novel	Winner	Gold Dagger	1990	1990	CWA	Bones and Silence	Hill, Reginald
Novel	Winner	Silver Dagger	1990	1990	CWA	The Late Candidate	Phillips, Mike
Novel	Nominee	Dagger	1990	1990	CWA	Rough Treatment	Harvey, John
Novel	Winner	Ellis	1989	1990	CWC	Hot Shots	Gough, Laurence
Novel	Winner	Lambda	1989	1990	LBR	A Simple Suburban Murder	Zubro, Mark
Novel	Winner	Edgar	1989	1990	MWA	Black Cherry Blues	Burke, James Lee
Novel	Winner	Shamus	1989	1990	PWA	Extenuating Circumstances	Valin, Jonathan
Novel	Nominee	Ellis	1989	1990	CWC	The Hanging Valley	Robinson, Peter
Novel	Nominee	Edgar	1989	1990	MWA	The Death of the Joyce Scholar	Gill, Bartholomew
Novel	Nominee	Shamus	1989	1990	PWA	Out on the Cutting Edge	Block, Lawrence
Novel	Nominee	Shamus	1989	1990	PWA	Dead Irish	Lescroart, John T.
Novel	Nominee	Shamus	1989	1990	PWA	The Killing Man	Spillane, Mickey
Novel	Winner	Gold Dagger	1989	1989	CWA	The Wench is Dead	Dexter, Colin
Novel	Winner	Lambda	1988	1989	LBR	Goldenboy	Nava, Michael
Novel	Winner	Macavity	1988	1989	MRI	A Thief of Time	Hillerman, Tony
Novel	Winner	Edgar	1988	1989	MWA	A Cold Red Sunrise	Kaminsky, Stuart M.
Novel	Winner	Shamus	1988	1989	PWA	Kiss	Lutz, John
Novel	Nominee	Ellis	1988	1989	CWC	A Dedicated Man	Robinson, Peter
Novel	Nominee	Hammett	1988	1989	IACW	The Ones You Do	Woodrell, Dan
Novel	Nominee	Edgar	1988	1989	MWA	Joey's Case	Constantine, K. C.
Novel	Nominee	Edgar	1988	1989	MWA	Sacrificial Ground	Cook, Thomas
Novel	Nominee	Edgar	1988	1989	MWA	A Thief of Time	Hillerman, Tony
Novel	Nominee	Edgar	1988	1989	MWA	In the Lake of the Moon	Lindsey, David L.
Novel	Nominee	Shamus	1988	1989	PWA	Neon Mirage	Collins, Max Allan, Jr
Novel	Nominee	Shamus	1988	1989	PWA	Deviant Behavior	Emerson, Earl
Novel	Nominee	Shamus	1988	1989	PWA	Swan Dive	Healy, Jeremiah
Novel	Winner	Anthony	1987	1988	B'con	Skinwalkers	Hillerman, Tony
Novel	Winner	Gold Dagger	1988	1988	CWA	Ratking	Dibdin, Michael
Novel	Winner	Edgar	1987	1988	MWA	Old Bones	Elkins, Aaron
Novel	Winner	Shamus	1987	1988	PWA	A Tax in Blood	Schutz, Benjamin
Novel	Nominee	Dagger	1988	1988	CWA	Touch of the Past	Breen, Jon
Novel	Nominee	Shamus	1987	1988	PWA	Lady Yesterday	Estleman, Loren D.
Novel	Nominee	Shamus	1987	1988	PWA	The Autumn Dead	Gorman, Ed
Novel	Nominee	Shamus	1987	1988	PWA	Ride the Lightning	Lutz, John
Novel	Winner	Shamus	1986	1987	PWA	The Staked Goat	Healy, Jeremiah
Novel	Nominee	Edgar	1986	1987	MWA	The Straight Man	Simon, Roger L.
Novel	Nominee	Shamus	1986	1987	PWA	When the Sacred Ginmill Closes	Block, Lawrence
Novel	Nominee	Shamus	1986	1987	PWA	In La-La Land We Trust	Campbell, Robert
Novel	Nominee	Shamus	1986	1987	PWA	The Million Dollar Wound	Collins, Max Allan, Jr
Novel	Winner	Ellis	1985	1986	CWC	Death in the Old Country	Wright, Eric
Novel	Winner	Nero Wolfe	1985	1986	Wolfe Pack	Sleeping Dog	Lochte, Dick
Novel	Nominee	Shamus	1985	1986	PWA	The Naked Liar	Adams, Harold
Novel	Nominee	Shamus	1985	1986	PWA	Hardball	Hornig, Doug
Novel	Nominee	Shamus	1985	1986	PWA	Nightlines	Lutz, John
Novel	Nominee	Shamus	1985	1986	PWA	A Catskill Eagle	Parker, Robert B.
Novel	Nominee	Shamus	1985	1986	PWA	Bones	Pronzini, Bill
Novel	Nominee	Shamus	1985	1986	PWA	Embrace the Wolf	Schutz, Benjamin
Novel	Winner	Ellis	1984	1985	CWC	Murder Sees the Light	Engel, Howard
Novel	Winner	Shamus	1984	1985	PWA	Sugartown	Estleman, Loren D.
Novel	Nominee	Dagger	1985	1985	CWA	Our Father's Lies	Taylor, Andrew
Novel	Nominee	Edgar	1984	1985	MWA	A Shock to the System	Brett, Simon
Novel	Nominee	Shamus	1984	1985	PWA	True Crime	Collins, Max Allan, Jr
Novel	Nominee	Shamus	1984	1985	PWA	Die Again, Macready	Livingston, Jack
Novel	Nominee	Shamus	1984	1985	PWA	Full Contact	Randisi, Robert J.
Novel	Winner	Ellis	1983	1984	CWC	The Night the Gods Smiled	Wright, Eric
Novel	Winner	Shamus	1983	1984	PWA	True Detective	Collins, Max Allan, Jr
Novel	Nominee	Dagger	1984	1984	CWA	Die Again, Macready	Livingston, Jack
Novel	Nominee	Edgar	1983	1984	MWA	The Papers of Tony Veitch	McIlvanney, William
Novel	Nominee	Shamus	1983	1984	PWA	Dancing Bear	Crumley, James

AWARD			YEAR			BOOK TITLE	AUTHOR NAME
Category	Status	Name	Pub	Award	Conf'd by		Last, First

Awards List 2 – Winners and Nominees by Award Category

Includes ONLY series novels written by men

Category	Status	Name	Pub	Award	Conf'd by	BOOK TITLE	Last, First
Novel	Nominee	Shamus	1983	1984	PWA	The Glass Highway	Estleman, Loren D.
Novel	Nominee	Shamus	1983	1984	PWA	The Widening Gyre	Parker, Robert B.
Novel	Winner	Silver Dagger	1983	1983	CWA	The Papers of Tony Veitch	McIlvanney, William
Novel	Winner	Edgar	1982	1983	MWA	Billingsgate Shoal	Boyer, Rick
Novel	Winner	Shamus	1982	1983	PWA	Eight Million Ways to Die	Block, Lawrence
Novel	Nominee	Edgar	1982	1983	MWA	Eight Million Ways to Die	Block, Lawrence
Novel	Nominee	Shamus	1982	1983	PWA	Gravedigger	Hansen, Joseph
Novel	Nominee	Shamus	1982	1983	PWA	30 for a Harry	Hoyt, Richard
Novel	Nominee	Shamus	1982	1983	PWA	A Piece of the Silence	Livingston, Jack
Novel	Nominee	Shamus	1982	1983	PWA	Hard Trade	Lyons, Arthur
Novel	Nominee	Shamus	1982	1983	PWA	Ceremony	Parker, Robert B.
Novel	Winner	Edgar	1981	1982	MWA	Peregrine	Bayer, William
Novel	Winner	Shamus	1981	1982	PWA	Hoodwink	Pronzini, Bill
Novel	Nominee	Shamus	1981	1982	PWA	Early Autumn	Parker, Robert B.
Novel	Winner	Gold Dagger	1981	1981	CWA	Gorky Park	Smith, Martin Cruz
Novel	Winner	Silver Dagger	1981	1981	CWA	The Dead of Jericho	Dexter, Colin
Novel	Winner	Edgar	1979	1980	MWA	Whip Hand	Francis, Dick
Novel	Winner	Nero Wolfe	1979	1980	Wolfe Pack	Burglar Who Liked to Quote Kipling	Block, Lawrence
Novel	Winner	Gold Dagger	1979	1979	CWA	Whip Hand	Francis, Dick
Novel	Winner	Silver Dagger	1979	1979	CWA	Service of All the Dead	Dexter, Colin
Novel	Nominee	Edgar	1978	1979	MWA	Listening Woman	Hillerman, Tony
Novel	Nominee	Shamus	1978	1979	PWA	A Stab in the Dark	Block, Lawrence
Novel	Winner	Silver Dagger	1978	1978	CWA	Waxwork	Lovesey, Peter
Novel	Nominee	Edgar	1977	1978	MWA	Laidlaw	McIlvanney, William
Novel	Nominee	Edgar	1977	1978	MWA	A Fire in the Barley	Parrish, Frank
Novel	Winner	Gold Dagger	1977	1977	CWA	The Honorable Schoolboy	Le Carré, John
Novel	Winner	Silver Dagger	1977	1977	CWA	Laidlaw	McIlvanney, William
Novel	Winner	Edgar	1976	1977	MWA	Promised Land	Parker, Robert B.
Novel	Winner	Gold Dagger	1974	1974	CWA	Other Paths to Glory	Price, Anthony
Novel	Winner	Edgar	1973	1974	MWA	Dance Hall of the Dead	Hillerman, Tony
Novel	Nominee	Edgar	1972	1973	MWA	Canto for a Gypsy	Smith, Martin Cruz
Novel	Winner	Gold Dagger	1971	1971	CWA	The Steam Pig	McClure, James
Novel	Nominee	Edgar	1970	1971	MWA	Sir, You Bastard	Newman, G.F.
Novel	Nominee	Edgar	1970	1971	MWA	The Hot Rock	Westlake, Donald E.
Novel	Winner	Silver Dagger	1970	1970	CWA	The Labyrinth Makers	Price, Anthony
Novel	Winner	Gold Dagger	1969	1969	CWA	A Pride of Heroes	Dickinson, Peter
Novel	Winner	Gold Dagger	1968	1968	CWA	Skin Deep	Dickinson, Peter
Novel	Nominee	Edgar	1967	1968	MWA	A Parade of Cockeyed Creatures	Baxt, George
Novel	Winner	Edgar	1966	1967	MWA	The King of the Rainy Country	Freeling, Nicolas
Novel	Nominee	Edgar	1965	1966	MWA	Odds Against	Francis, Dick
Novel	Nominee	Edgar	1964	1965	MWA	The Perfect Murder	Keating, H.R.F.
Novel	Winner	Gold Dagger	1964	1964	CWA	The Perfect Murder	Keating, H.R.F.
Novel	Winner	Edgar	1963	1964	MWA	The Spy Who Came in from the Cold	Le Carré, John
Novel	Winner	Gold Dagger	1963	1963	CWA	The Spy Who Came in from the Cold	Le Carré, John
Novel	Winner	Edgar	1962	1963	MWA	The Light of Day	Ambler, Eric
Novel	Runnerup	Gold Dagger	1963	1963	CWA	Gun Before Butter	Freeling, Nicolas
Novel	Runnerup	Gold Dagger	1962	1962	CWA	The Light of Day	Ambler, Eric
Novel	Runnerup	Gold Dagger	1961	1961	CWA	Call for the Dead	Le Carré, John
Novel-Europe	Winner	CWA '92	1990	1990	CWA	Vendetta	Dibdin, Michael
Novel-Funniest	Winner	Last Laugh	1994	1995	CWA	The Villian of the Earth	Shaw, Simon
Novel-Funniest	Nominee	Last Laugh	1995	1995	CWA	Maxwell's Flame	Trow, M. J.
Novel-Funniest	Winner	Last Laugh	1993	1994	CWA	The Mamur Zapt...Spoils of Egypt	Pearce, Michael
Novel-Funniest	Nominee	Last Laugh	1993	1993	CWA	Blood Sympathy	Hill, Reginald
Novel-Funniest	Winner	Last Laugh	1991	1992	CWA	Angels in Arms	Ripley, Mike
Novel-Funniest	Winner	Last Laugh	1989	1990	CWA	Angel Touch	Ripley, Mike
Novel-Police	Winner	Police Review	1987	1987	CWA	Snow Man	Busby, Roger
Novel-Police	Winner	Police Review	1986	1986	CWA	The Crossfire Killings	Knox, Bill
PB Original	Nominee	Anthony	1996	1997	B'con	Fade Away	Coben, Harlan
PB Original	Nominee	Anthony	1996	1997	B'con	Chain of Fools	Womack, Steven
PB Original	Winner	Shamus	1996	1997	PWA	Fade Away	Coben, Harlan
PB Original	Nominee	Shamus	1996	1997	PWA	Chain of Fools	Womack, Steven

Category	Status	Name	Pub	Award	Conf'd by	BOOK TITLE	Last, First
AWARD			**YEAR**				**AUTHOR NAME**

Awards List 2 – Winners and Nominees by Award Category

Includes ONLY series novels written by men

Category	Status	Name	Pub	Award	Conf'd by	BOOK TITLE	Last, First
PB Original	Winner	Anthony	1995	1996	B'con	Deal Breaker	Coben, Harlan
PB Original	Winner	Shamus	1995	1996	PWA	Native Angels	Jaspersohn, William
PB Original	Nominee	Anthony	1995	1996	B'con	Closet	Zimmerman, R.D.
PB Original	Nominee	Shamus	1995	1996	PWA	Zero Tolerance	Knight, J.D.
PB Original	Nominee	Shamus	1995	1996	PWA	Way Past Dead	Womack, Steven
PB Original	Nominee	Shamus	1994	1995	PWA	Double Plot	Axler, Leo
PB Original	Nominee	Shamus	1993	1994	PWA	The Half-Hearted Detective	Bass, Milton R.
PB Original	Nominee	Shamus	1993	1994	PWA	A Minyan for the Dead	Fliegel, Richard
PB Original	Nominee	Shamus	1993	1994	PWA	Torch Town Boogie	Womack, Steven
PB Original	Nominee	Shamus	1992	1993	PWA	The Brutal Ballet	Dundee, Wayne
PB Original	Winner	Shamus	1991	1992	PWA	The Cool Blue Tomb	Kemprecos, Paul
PB Original	Nominee	Shamus	1991	1992	PWA	The Thousand-Yard Stare	Kantner Rob
PB Original	Winner	Shamus	1990	1991	PWA	Fatal Sisters	Duncan, W. Glenn
PB Original	Nominee	Shamus	1990	1991	PWA	Bimbo Heaven	Albert , Marvin H.
PB Original	Nominee	Shamus	1990	1991	PWA	The Queen's Mare	Birkett, John
PB Original	Nominee	Shamus	1990	1991	PWA	Made in Detroit	Kantner, Rob
PB Original	Winner	Shamus	1989	1990	PWA	Hell's Only Half Full	Kantner, Rob
PB Original	Nominee	Shamus	1989	1990	PWA	Muscle and Blood	Dold, Gaylord
PB Original	Nominee	Shamus	1989	1990	PWA	Behind the Fact	Hilary, Richard
PB Original	Nominee	Shamus	1989	1990	PWA	Tough Enough	Philbrick, W.R.
PB Original	Winner	Shamus	1988	1989	PWA	Dirty Work	Kantner, Rob
PB Original	Nominee	Shamus	1988	1989	PWA	The Last Private Eye	Birkett, John
PB Original	Nominee	Shamus	1988	1989	PWA	Bone Pile	Dold, Gaylord
PB Original	Nominee	Shamus	1988	1989	PWA	Rebound	Everson, David H.
PB Original	Nominee	Shamus	1988	1989	PWA	The Crystal Blue Persuasion	Philbrick, W.R.
PB Original	Winner	Anthony	1987	1988	B'con	The Monkey's Raincoat	Crais, Robert
PB Original	Nominee	Shamus	1987	1988	PWA	The Monkey's Raincoat	Crais, Robert
PB Original	Nominee	Shamus	1987	1988	PWA	Snake Eyes	Dold, Gaylord
PB Original	Nominee	Shamus	1987	1988	PWA	Recount	Everson, David H.
PB Original	Winner	Anthony	1986	1987	B'con	The Junkyard Dog	Campbell, Robert
PB Original	Winner	Shamus	1986	1987	PWA	The Back-Door Man	Kantner, Rob
PB Original	Nominee	Shamus	1986	1987	PWA	Stone Angel	Albert, Marvin H.
PB Original	Nominee	Shamus	1986	1987	PWA	Melting Point	Davis, Kenn
PB Original	Nominee	Shamus	1986	1987	PWA	Too Old a Cat	Murphy, Warren B.
PB Original	Winner	Shamus	1985	1986	PWA	Poverty Bay	Emerson, Earl
PB Original	Nominee	Shamus	1985	1986	PWA	The Rainy City	Emerson, Earl
PB Original	Nominee	Shamus	1985	1986	PWA	Pigs Get Fat	Murphy, Warren B.
PB Original	Nominee	Shamus	1985	1986	PWA	Blue Heron	Ross, Philip
PB Original	Nominee	Edgar	1984	1985	MWA	Words Can Kill	Davis, Kenn
PB Original	Nominee	Shamus	1984	1985	PWA	San Quentin	Lynch, Jack
PB Original	Nominee	Shamus	1984	1985	PWA	Trace and 47 Miles of Rope	Murphy, Warren B.
PB Original	Nominee	Shamus	1984	1985	PWA	The Man Who Risked His Partner	Stephens, Reed
PB Original	Winner	Shamus	1983	1984	PWA	Dead in Centerfield	Engleman, Paul
PB Original	Nominee	Shamus	1983	1984	PWA	Finders Weepers	Byrd, Max
PB Original	Nominee	Shamus	1983	1984	PWA	Trace	Murphy, Warren B.
PB Original	Nominee	Shamus	1983	1984	PWA	The Steinway Collection	Randisi, Robert J.
PB Original	Nominee	Edgar	1982	1983	MWA	The Missing and the Dead	Lynch, Jack
PB Original	Nominee	Shamus	1982	1983	PWA	Nevsky's Return	Gat, Dimitri
PB Original	Nominee	Shamus	1982	1983	PWA	Pieces of Death	Lynch, Jack
PB Original	Nominee	Shamus	1982	1983	PWA	Smoked Out	Murphy, Warren B.
PB Original	Winner	Shamus	1981	1982	PWA	California Thriller	Byrd, Max
PB Original	Winner	Edgar	1996	1997	MWA	Fade Away	Coben, Harlan
PB Original	Nominee	Edgar	1996	1997	MWA	Tribe	Zimmerman, R.D.
PB Original	Winner	Edgar	1995	1996	MWA	Tarnished Blue	Heffernan, William
PB Original	Nominee	Edgar	1995	1996	MWA	Deal Breaker	Coben, Harlan
PB Original	Nominee	Edgar	1995	1996	MWA	High Desert Malice	Mitchell, Kirk
PB Original	Nominee	Edgar	1995	1996	MWA	Hard Frost	Wingfield, R.D.
PB Original	Nominee	Edgar	1994	1995	MWA	The Broken-Hearted Detective	Bass Milton R.
PB Original	Nominee	Edgar	1994	1995	MWA	Viper Quarry	Feldmeyer, Dean
PB Original	Winner	Edgar	1993	1994	MWA	Dead Folk's Blues	Womack, Steven
PB Original	Winner	Edgar	1991	1992	MWA	Dark Maze	Adcock, Thomas

AWARD			YEAR				AUTHOR NAME
Category	Status	Name	Pub	Award	Conf'd by	BOOK TITLE	Last, First

Awards List 2 – Winners and Nominees by Award Category

Includes ONLY series novels written by men

Category	Status	Name	Pub	Award	Conf'd by	BOOK TITLE	Last, First
PB Original	Winner	Edgar	1990	1991	MWA	The Man Who Would Be F. Scott Fitzgerald	Handler, David
PB Original	Winner	Edgar	1989	1990	MWA	The Rain	Peterson, Keith
PB Original	Nominee	Edgar	1989	1990	MWA	Manhattan is My Beat	Deaver, Jeffery
PB Original	Nominee	Edgar	1988	1989	MWA	Judgment by Fire	Huebner, Frederick D.
PB Original	Nominee	Edgar	1988	1989	MWA	The Trapdoor	Peterson, Keith
PB Original	Winner	Edgar	1987	1988	MWA	The Monkey's Raincoat	Crais, Robert
PB Original	Winner	Edgar	1986	1987	MWA	The Junkyard Dog	Campbell, Robert
PB Original	Winner	Edgar	1985	1986	MWA	Pigs Get Fat	Murphy, Warren B.
PB Original	Nominee	Edgar	1985	1986	MWA	Poverty Bay	Emerson, Earl
PB Original	Nominee	Edgar	1983	1984	MWA	Black Knight in Red Square	Kaminsky, Stuart M.
PB Original	Nominee	Edgar	1983	1984	MWA	Trace	Murphy, Warren B.
PB Original	Nominee	Edgar	1983	1984	MWA	Hunter	Sauter, Eric
PB Original	Winner	Edgar	1980	1981	MWA	Public Murders	Granger, Bill
PB Original	Winner	Edgar	1979	1980	MWA	The HOG Murders	DeAndrea, William L.
PB Original	Nominee	Edgar	1979	1980	MWA	The Infernal Device	Kurland, Michael
PB Original	Nominee	Edgar	1977	1978	MWA	Time to Murder and Create	Block, Lawrence
PB Original	Nominee	Edgar	1976	1977	MWA	The Dark Side [w/John Stanley]	Davis, Kenn
PB Original	Nominee	Edgar	1976	1977	MWA	The Retaliators	Hamilton, Donald
PB Original	Nominee	Edgar	1976	1977	MWA	Freeze Frame	Irvine, Robert
PB Original	Nominee	Edgar	1974	1975	MWA	Jump Cut	Irvine, Robert
PB Original	Nominee	Edgar	1973	1974	MWA	The Mediterranean Caper	Cussler, Clive
PB Original	Nominee	Edgar	1971	1972	MWA	Space for Hire	Nolan, William F.
PB Original	Nominee	Edgar	1969	1970	MWA	The Sour Lemon Score	Stark, Richard

AUTHOR NAME		YEAR			AWARD		
Last, First	BOOK TITLE	Pub	Award	Conf'd by	Name	Status	Category

Awards List 3 – Winners and Nominees by Author's Last Name

Includes ONLY series novels written by men

Last, First	BOOK TITLE	Pub	Award	Conf'd by	Name	Status	Category
Abbott, Jeff	Do Unto Others	1994	1995	Malice	Agatha	Winner	First Novel
Abbott, Jeff	Do Unto Others	1994	1995	MRI	Macavity	Winner	First Novel
Adams, Harold	The Man Who Was Taller Than God	1992	1993	PWA	Shamus	Winner	Novel
Adams, Harold	The Naked Liar	1985	1986	PWA	Shamus	Nominee	Novel
Adcock, Thomas	Dark Maze	1991	1992	MWA	Edgar	Winner	PB Original
Albert, Marvin H.	Bimbo Heaven	1990	1991	PWA	Shamus	Nominee	PB Original
Albert, Marvin H.	Stone Angel	1986	1987	PWA	Shamus	Nominee	PB Original
Albert, Neil	The January Corpse	1991	1992	PWA	Shamus	Nominee	First Novel
Allegretto, Michael	Death on the Rocks	1987	1988	PWA	Shamus	Winner	First Novel
Allegretto, Michael	Death on the Rocks	1987	1988	B'con	Anthony	Nominee	First Novel
Ambler, Eric	The Light of Day	1962	1962	CWA	Gold Dagger	Runnerup	Novel
Ambler, Eric	The Light of Day	1962	1963	MWA	Edgar	Winner	Novel
Axler, Leo	Double Plot	1994	1995	PWA	Shamus	Nominee	PB Original
Ayres, E.C.	Hour of the Manatee	1994	1992	SMP	SMP/PWA	Winner	First P.I. Novel
Barre, Richard	The Innocents	1995	1996	B'con	Anthony	Nominee	First Novel
Barre, Richard	The Innocents	1995	1996	PWA	Shamus	Winner	First Novel
Bass, Milton R.	The Broken-Hearted Detective	1994	1995	MWA	Edgar	Nominee	PB Original
Bass, Milton R.	The Half-Hearted Detective	1993	1994	PWA	Shamus	Nominee	PB Original
Baxt, George	A Parade of Cockeyed Creatures	1967	1968	MWA	Edgar	Nominee	Novel
Bayer, William	Peregrine	1981	1982	MWA	Edgar	Winner	Novel
Beinhart, Larry	No One Rides for Free	1986	1987	MWA	Edgar	Winner	First Novel
Beinhart, Larry	No One Rides for Free	1986	1987	PWA	Shamus	Nominee	First Novel
Birkett, John	The Queen's Mare	1990	1991	PWA	Shamus	Nominee	PB Original
Birkett, John	The Last Private Eye	1988	1989	PWA	Shamus	Nominee	PB Original
Block, Lawrence	A Long Line of Dead Men	1994	1995	MWA	Edgar	Winner	Novel
Block, Lawrence	A Long Line of Dead Men	1994	1995	PWA	Shamus	Nominee	Novel

AUTHOR NAME		YEAR		AWARD			
Last, First	BOOK TITLE	Pub	Award	Conf'd by	Name	Status	Category

Awards List 3 – Winners and Nominees by Author's Last Name

Includes ONLY series novels written by men

Block, Lawrence	The Devil Knows You're Dead	1993	1994	PWA	Shamus	Winner	Novel
Block, Lawrence	A Dance at the Slaughterhouse	1991	1992	MWA	Edgar	Winner	Novel
Block, Lawrence	A Dance at the Slaughterhouse	1991	1992	PWA	Shamus	Nominee	Novel
Block, Lawrence	A Ticket to the Boneyard	1990	1991	PWA	Shamus	Nominee	Novel
Block, Lawrence	Out on the Cutting Edge	1989	1990	PWA	Shamus	Nominee	Novel
Block, Lawrence	When the Sacred Ginmill Closes	1986	1987	PWA	Shamus	Nominee	Novel
Block, Lawrence	Eight Million Ways to Die	1982	1983	MWA	Edgar	Nominee	Novel
Block, Lawrence	Eight Million Ways to Die	1982	1983	PWA	Shamus	Winner	Novel
Block, Lawrence	The Burglar Who Liked to Quote Kipling	1979	1980	Wolfe Pack	Nero Wolfe	Winner	Novel
Block, Lawrence	A Stab in the Dark	1978	1979	PWA	Shamus	Nominee	Novel
Block, Lawrence	Time to Murder and Create	1977	1978	MWA	Edgar	Nominee	PB Original
Boyer, Rick	Billingsgate Shoal	1982	1983	MWA	Edgar	Winner	Novel
Brady, John	The Good Life	1994	1995	CWC	Ellis	Nominee	Novel
Brady, John	Stone of the Heart	1988	1989	CWC	Ellis	Winner	First Novel
Breen, Jon	Touch of the Past	1988	1988	CWA	Dagger	Nominee	Novel
Brett, Simon	A Shock to the System	1984	1985	MWA	Edgar	Nominee	Novel
Burke, James Lee	Cadillac Jukebox	1996	1997	CWA	Dagger	Nominee	Novel
Burke, James Lee	Dixie City Jam	1994	1995	IACW	Hammett	Nominee	Novel
Burke, James Lee	Black Cherry Blues	1989	1990	MWA	Edgar	Winner	Novel
Burns, Rex	The Alvarez Journal	1975	1976	MWA	Edgar	Winner	First Novel
Busby, Roger	Snow Man	1987	1987	CWA	Police Review	Winner	Novel-Police
Byrd, Max	Finders Weepers	1983	1984	PWA	Shamus	Nominee	PB Original
Byrd, Max	California Thriller	1981	1982	PWA	Shamus	Winner	PB Original
Campbell, Robert	The Junkyard Dog	1986	1987	B'con	Anthony	Winner	PB Original
Campbell, Robert	The Junkyard Dog	1986	1987	MWA	Edgar	Winner	PB Original
Campbell, Robert	In La-La Land We Trust	1986	1987	PWA	Shamus	Nominee	Novel
Coben, Harlan	Fade Away	1996	1997	B'con	Anthony	Nominee	PB Original
Coben, Harlan	Fade Away	1996	1997	MWA	Edgar	Winner	PB Original
Coben, Harlan	Fade Away	1996	1997	PWA	Shamus	Winner	PB Original
Coben, Harlan	Deal Breaker	1995	1996	B'con	Anthony	Winner	PB Original
Coben, Harlan	Deal Breaker	1995	1996	MWA	Edgar	Nominee	PB Original
Collins, Max Allan, Jr	Damned in Paradise	1996	1997	PWA	Shamus	Nominee	Novel
Collins, Max Allan, Jr	Carnal Hours	1994	1995	PWA	Shamus	Nominee	Novel
Collins, Max Allan, Jr	Stolen Away	1991	1992	PWA	Shamus	Winner	Novel
Collins, Max Allan, Jr	Neon Mirage	1988	1989	PWA	Shamus	Nominee	Novel
Collins, Max Allan, Jr	The Million Dollar Wound	1986	1987	PWA	Shamus	Nominee	Novel
Collins, Max Allan, Jr	True Crime	1984	1985	PWA	Shamus	Nominee	Novel
Collins, Max Allan, Jr	True Detective	1983	1984	PWA	Shamus	Winner	Novel
Collins, Michael	Cassandra in Red	1992	1993	PWA	Shamus	Nominee	Novel
Collins, Michael	Act of Fear	1967	1968	MWA	Edgar	Winner	First Novel
Connelly, Michael	The Last Coyote	1995	1996	B'con	Anthony	Nominee	Novel
Connelly, Michael	The Last Coyote	1995	1996	IACW	Hammett	Nominee	Novel
Connelly, Michael	The Last Coyote	1995	1996	MRI	Macavity	Nominee	Novel
Connelly, Michael	The Concrete Blonde	1994	1995	B'con	Anthony	Nominee	Novel
Connelly, Michael	The Concrete Blonde	1994	1995	MRI	Macavity	Nominee	Novel
Connelly, Michael	The Black Ice	1993	1994	IACW	Hammett	Nominee	Novel
Connelly, Michael	The Black Ice	1993	1994	B'com	Anthony	Nominee	Best Novel
Connelly, Michael	The Black Echo	1992	1993	MWA	Edgar	Winner	First Novel
Constantine, K. C.	Joey's Case	1988	1989	MWA	Edgar	Nominee	Novel
Cook, Thomas	Sacrificial Ground	1988	1989	MWA	Edgar	Nominee	Novel
Cormany, Michael	Lost Daughter	1988	1989	PWA	Shamus	Nominee	First Novel
Crais, Robert	Sunset Express	1996	1997	PWA	Shamus	Winner	Novel
Crais, Robert	Free Fall	1993	1994	MWA	Edgar	Nominee	Novel
Crais, Robert	Lullaby Town	1992	1993	PWA	Shamus	Nominee	Novel
Crais, Robert	The Monkey's Raincoat	1987	1988	B'con	Anthony	Winner	PB Original
Crais, Robert	The Monkey's Raincoat	1987	1988	MRI	Macavity	Winner	First Novel
Crais, Robert	The Monkey's Raincoat	1987	1988	MWA	Edgar	Winner	PB Original
Crais, Robert	The Monkey's Raincoat	1987	1988	PWA	Shamus	Nominee	PB Original

| AUTHOR NAME | | YEAR | | AWARD | | | |
Last, First	BOOK TITLE	Pub	Award	Conf'd by	Name	Status	Category

Awards List 3 – Winners and Nominees by Author's Last Name

Includes ONLY series novels written by men

Last, First	BOOK TITLE	Pub	Award	Conf'd by	Name	Status	Category
Crider, Bill	Dead on the Island	1991	1992	PWA	Shamus	Nominee	First Novel
Crider, Bill	Too Late to Die	1986	1987	B'con	Anthony	Winner	First Novel
Crumley, James	The Mexican Tree Duck	1993	1994	IACW	Hammett	Winner	Novel
Crumley, James	Dancing Bear	1983	1984	PWA	Shamus	Nominee	Novel
Cussler, Clive	The Mediterranean Caper	1973	1974	MWA	Edgar	Nominee	PB Original
Cutler, Stan	Best Performance by a Patsy	1991	1992	PWA	Shamus	Nominee	First Novel
Daniel, David	The Heaven Stone	1994	1995	PWA	Shamus	Nominee	First Novel
Daniel, David	The Heaven Stone	1994	1993	SMP	SMP/PWA	Winner	First P.I. Novel
Davis, Thomas D.	Suffer Little Children	1991	1992	PWA	Shamus	Winner	First Novel
Davis, Kenn	Melting Point	1986	1987	PWA	Shamus	Nominee	PB Original
Davis, Kenn	Words Can Kill	1984	1985	MWA	Edgar	Nominee	PB Original
Davis, Kenn	The Dark Side [w/John Stanley]	1976	1977	MWA	Edgar	Nominee	PB Original
DeAndrea, William L.	The HOG Murders	1979	1980	MWA	Edgar	Winner	PB Original
DeAndrea, William L.	Killed in the Ratings	1978	1979	MWA	Edgar	Winner	First Novel
Deaver, Jeffery	Manhattan is My Beat	1989	1990	MWA	Edgar	Nominee	PB Original
Deighton, Len	Funeral in Berlin	1964	1965	MWA	Edgar	Nominee	First Novel
Dexter, Colin	Death is Now My Neighbor	1996	1996	CWA	Dagger	Nominee	Novel
Dexter, Colin	The Way Through the Woods	1992	1992	CWA	Gold Dagger	Winner	Novel
Dexter, Colin	The Wench is Dead	1989	1989	CWA	Gold Dagger	Winner	Novel
Dexter, Colin	The Dead of Jericho	1981	1981	CWA	Silver Dagger	Winner	Novel
Dexter, Colin	Service of All the Dead	1979	1979	CWA	Silver Dagger	Winner	Novel
Dibdin, Michael	Vendetta	1990	1990	CWA	CWA' 92	Winner	Novel-Europe
Dibdin, Michael	Ratking	1988	1988	CWA	Gold Dagger	Winner	Novel
Dickinson, Peter	A Pride of Heroes	1969	1969	CWA	Gold Dagger	Winner	Novel
Dickinson, Peter	Skin Deep	1968	1968	CWA	Gold Dagger	Winner	Novel
Dold, Gaylord	Muscle and Blood	1989	1990	PWA	Shamus	Nominee	PB Original
Dold, Gaylord	Bone Pile	1988	1989	PWA	Shamus	Nominee	PB Original
Dold, Gaylord	Snake Eyes	1987	1988	PWA	Shamus	Nominee	PB Original
Doolittle, Jerome	Body Scissors	1990	1991	PWA	Shamus	Nominee	First Novel
Douglas, John	Shawnee Alley Fire	1987	1988	PWA	Shamus	Nominee	First Novel
Duncan, W. Glenn	Fatal Sisters	1990	1991	PWA	Shamus	Winner	PB Original
Dundee, Wayne	The Brutal Ballet	1992	1993	PWA	Shamus	Nominee	PB Original
Dundee, Wayne	The Skintight Shroud	1990	1991	PWA	Shamus	Nominee	Novel
Dundee, Wayne	The Burning Season	1988	1989	PWA	Shamus	Nominee	First Novel
Dunning, John	Bookman's Wake	1995	1995	CWA	Dagger	Nominee	Novel
Dunning, John	Bookman's Wake	1995	1996	MRI	Macavity	Nominee	Novel
Dunning, John	Bookman's Wake	1995	1996	MWA	Edgar	Nominee	Novel
Dunning, John	Booked to Die	1992	1993	Wolfe Pack	Nero Wolfe	Winner	Novel
Elkins, Aaron	Old Scores	1993	1994	Malice	Agatha	Nominee	Novel
Elkins, Aaron	Old Scores	1993	1994	Wolfe Pack	Nero Wolfe	Winner	Novel
Elkins, Aaron	Old Bones	1987	1988	MWA	Edgar	Winner	Novel
Emerson, Earl	The Vanishing Smile	1995	1996	PWA	Shamus	Nominee	Novel
Emerson, Earl	Morons and Madmen	1993	1994	B'con	Anthony	Nominee	Novel
Emerson, Earl	Deviant Behavior	1988	1989	PWA	Shamus	Nominee	Novel
Emerson, Earl	Poverty Bay	1985	1986	MWA	Edgar	Nominee	PB Original
Emerson, Earl	Poverty Bay	1985	1986	PWA	Shamus	Winner	PB Original
Emerson, Earl	The Rainy City	1985	1986	PWA	Shamus	Nominee	PB Original
Engel, Howard	Murder Sees the Light	1984	1985	CWC	Ellis	Winner	Novel
Engleman, Paul	Dead in Centerfield	1983	1984	PWA	Shamus	Winner	PB Original
Estleman, Loren D.	Lady Yesterday	1987	1988	PWA	Shamus	Nominee	Novel
Estleman, Loren D.	Sugartown	1984	1985	PWA	Shamus	Winner	Novel
Estleman, Loren D.	The Glass Highway	1983	1984	PWA	Shamus	Nominee	Novel
Everson, David H.	Rebound	1988	1989	PWA	Shamus	Nominee	PB Original
Everson, David H.	Recount	1987	1988	PWA	Shamus	Nominee	PB Original
Faherty, Terence	Deadstick	1991	1992	MWA	Edgar	Nominee	First Novel

AUTHOR NAME		YEAR		AWARD			
Last, First	BOOK TITLE	Pub	Award	Conf'd by	Name	Status	Category

Awards List 3 – Winners and Nominees by Author's Last Name

Includes ONLY series novels written by men

Last, First	BOOK TITLE	Pub	Award	Conf'd by	Name	Status	Category
Feldmeyer, Dean	Viper Quarry	1994	1995	MWA	Edgar	Nominee	PB Original
Fliegel, Richard	A Minyan for the Dead	1993	1994	PWA	Shamus	Nominee	PB Original
Ford, G.M.	Who in Hell is Wanda Fuca?	1995	1996	B'con	Anthony	Nominee	Novel
Ford, G.M.	Who in Hell is Wanda Fuca?	1995	1996	PWA	Shamus	Nominee	First Novel
Francis, Dick	Come to Grief	1995	1996	MWA	Edgar	Winner	Novel
Francis, Dick	Come to Grief	1995	1996	PWA	Shamus	Nominee	Novel
Francis, Dick	Whip Hand	1979	1979	CWA	Gold Dagger	Winner	Novel
Francis, Dick	Whip Hand	1979	1980	MWA	Edgar	Winner	Novel
Francis, Dick	Odds Against	1965	1966	MWA	Edgar	Nominee	Novel
Freeling, Nicolas	The King of the Rainy Country	1966	1967	MWA	Edgar	Winner	Novel
Freeling, Nicolas	Gun Before Butter	1963	1963	CWA	Gold Dagger	Runnerup	Novel
Frost, Mark	The List of 7	1993	1994	MWA	Edgar	Nominee	First Novel
Furutani, Dale	Death in Little Tokyo	1996	1997	B'con	Anthony	Winner	First Novel
Furutani, Dale	Death in Little Tokyo	1996	1997	Malice	Agatha	Nominee	First Novel
Furutani, Dale	Death in Little Tokyo	1996	1997	MRI	Macavity	Winner	First Novel
Gash, Jonathan	The Judas Pair	1977	1978	CWA	Creasey	Winner	First Novel
Gat, Dimitri	Nevsky's Return	1982	1983	PWA	Shamus	Nominee	PB Original
Gill, Bartholomew	The Death of the Joyce Scholar	1989	1990	MWA	Edgar	Nominee	Novel
Goodrum, Charles A.	Dewey Decimated	1977	1978	MWA	Edgar	Nominee	First Novel
Gores, Joe	32 Cadilacs	1992	1993	MWA	Edgar	Nominee	Novel
Gorman, Ed	The Autumn Dead	1987	1988	PWA	Shamus	Nominee	Novel
Gorman, Ed	New, Improved Murder	1985	1986	PWA	Shamus	Nominee	First Novel
Gough, Laurence	Hot Shots	1989	1990	CWC	Ellis	Winner	Novel
Gough, Laurence	The Goldfish Bowl	1987	1988	CWC	Ellis	Winner	First Novel
Granger, Bill	Public Murders	1980	1981	MWA	Edgar	Winner	PB Original
Greenleaf, Stephen	Flesh Wounds	1996	1997	PWA	Shamus	Nominee	Novel
Hall, James W.	Buzz Cut	1996	1997	IACW	Hammett	Nominee	Novel
Hall, Parnell	Movie	1995	1996	PWA	Shamus	Nominee	Novel
Hall, Parnell	Detective	1987	1988	MWA	Edgar	Nominee	First Novel
Hall, Parnell	Detective	1987	1988	PWA	Shamus	Nominee	First Novel
Hamilton, Donald	The Retaliators	1976	1977	MWA	Edgar	Nominee	PB Original
Handler, David	The Man Who Would Be F. Scott Fitzgerald	1990	1991	MWA	Edgar	Winner	PB Original
Hansen, Joseph	Country of Old Men	1991	1992	LBR	Lambda	Winner	Novel
Hansen, Joseph	Gravedigger	1982	1983	PWA	Shamus	Nominee	Novel
Harriss, Will	The Bay Psalm Book Murder	1983	1984	MWA	Edgar	Winner	First Novel
Harvey, John	Rough Treatment	1990	1990	CWA	Dagger	Nominee	Novel
Haywood, Gar Anthony	Fear of the Dark	1988	1989	PWA	Shamus	Winner	First Novel
Haywood, Gar Anthony	Fear of the Dark	1998	1989	SMP/PWA	SMP/PWA	Winner	First P.I. Novel
Healy, Jeremiah	Invasion of Privacy	1996	1997	PWA	Shamus	Nominee	Novel
Healy, Jeremiah	Foursome	1993	1994	PWA	Shamus	Nominee	Novel
Healy, Jeremiah	Shallow Graves	1992	1993	PWA	Shamus	Nominee	Novel
Healy, Jeremiah	Swan Dive	1988	1989	PWA	Shamus	Nominee	Novel
Healy, Jeremiah	The Staked Goat	1986	1987	PWA	Shamus	Winner	Novel
Healy, Jeremiah	Blunt Darts	1984	1985	PWA	Shamus	Nominee	First Novel
Heffernan, William	Tarnished Blue	1995	1996	MWA	Edgar	Winner	PB Original
Hilary, Richard	Behind the Fact	1989	1990	PWA	Shamus	Nominee	PB Original
Hill, Reginald	Pictures of Perfection	1994	1995	B'con	Anthony	Nominee	Novel
Hill, Reginald	Blood Sympathy	1993	1993	CWA	Last Laugh	Nominee	Novel-Funniest
Hill, Reginald	Bones and Silence	1990	1990	CWA	Gold Dagger	Winner	Novel
Hill, Reginald	Bones and Silence	1990	1991	MWA	Edgar	Nominee	Novel
Hillerman, Tony	Sacred Clowns	1993	1994	B'con	Anthony	Nominee	Novel
Hillerman, Tony	Coyote Waits	1990	1991	Wolfe Pack	Nero Wolfe	Winner	Novel

AUTHOR NAME		YEAR		AWARD			
Last, First	BOOK TITLE	Pub	Award	Conf'd by	Name	Status	Category

Awards List 3 – Winners and Nominees by Author's Last Name

Includes ONLY series novels written by men

Hillerman, Tony	A Thief of Time	1988	1989	MRI	Macavity	Winner	Novel
Hillerman, Tony	A Thief of Time	1988	1989	MWA	Edgar	Nominee	Novel
Hillerman, Tony	Skinwalkers	1987	1988	B'con	Anthony	Winner	Novel
Hillerman, Tony	Listening Woman	1978	1979	MWA	Edgar	Nominee	Novel
Hillerman, Tony	Dance Hall of the Dead	1973	1974	MWA	Edgar	Winner	Novel
Hillerman, Tony	The Blessing Way	1970	1971	MWA	Edgar	Nominee	First Novel
Hornig, Doug	Hardball	1985	1986	PWA	Shamus	Nominee	Novel
Hornig, Doug	Foul Shot	1984	1985	MWA	Edgar	Nominee	First Novel
Housewright, David	Penance	1995	1996	MWA	Edgar	Winner	First Novel
Housewright, David	Penance	1995	1996	PWA	Shamus	Nominee	First Novel
Hoyt, Richard	30 for a Harry	1982	1983	PWA	Shamus	Nominee	Novel
Huebner, Frederick D.	Judgment by Fire	1988	1989	MWA	Edgar	Nominee	PB Original
Irvine, Robert	Freeze Frame	1976	1977	MWA	Edgar	Nominee	PB Original
Irvine, Robert	Jump Cut	1974	1975	MWA	Edgar	Nominee	PB Original
Jardine, Quinn	Skinner's Rules	1993	1994	CWA	Creasey	Nominee	First Novel
Jaspersohn, William	Native Angels	1995	1996	PWA	Shamus	Winner	PB Original
Johnson, E. Richard	Silver Street	1968	1969	MWA	Edgar	Winner	First Novel
Kaminsky, Stuart M.	Poor Butterfly	1990	1991	PWA	Shamus	Nominee	Novel
Kaminsky, Stuart M.	A Cold Red Sunrise	1988	1989	MWA	Edgar	Winner	Novel
Kaminsky, Stuart M.	Black Knight in Red Square	1983	1984	MWA	Edgar	Nominee	PB Original
Kantner, Rob	The Thousand-Yard Stare	1991	1992	PWA	Shamus	Nominee	PB Original
Kantner, Rob	Made in Detroit	1990	1991	PWA	Shamus	Nominee	PB Original
Kantner, Rob	Hell's Only Half Full	1989	1990	PWA	Shamus	Winner	PB Original
Kantner, Rob	Dirty Work	1988	1989	PWA	Shamus	Winner	PB Original
Kantner, Rob	The Back-Door Man	1986	1987	PWA	Shamus	Winner	PB Original
Keating, H.R.F.	The Perfect Murder	1964	1964	CWA	Gold Dagger	Winner	Novel
Keating, H.R.F.	The Perfect Murder	1964	1965	MWA	Edgar	Nominee	Novel
Keegan, Alex	Cuckoo	1993	1994	B'con	Anthony	Nominee	First Novel
Kellerman, Jonathan	When the Bough Breaks	1985	1986	B'con	Anthony	Winner	First Novel
Kellerman, Jonathan	When the Bough Breaks	1985	1986	MWA	Edgar	Winner	First Novel
Kemelman, Harry	Friday the Rabbi Slept Late	1964	1965	MWA	Edgar	Winner	First Novel
Kemprecos, Paul	The Cool Blue Tomb	1991	1992	PWA	Shamus	Winner	PB Original
Kennealy, Jerry	Special Delivery	1992	1993	PWA	Shamus	Nominee	Novel
Kennealy, Jerry	Polo's Wild Card	1990	1991	PWA	Shamus	Nominee	Novel
Knief, Charles	Diamond Head	1996	1995	SMP	SMP/PWA	Winner	First P.I. Novel
Knight, J.D.	Zero Tolerance	1995	1996	PWA	Shamus	Nominee	PB Original
Knox, Bill	The Crossfire Killings	1986	1986	CWA	Police Review	Winner	Novel-Police
Kuhlken, Ken	The Loud Adios	1991	1990	SMP	SMP/PWA	Winner	First P.I. Novel
Kurland, Michael	The Infernal Device	1979	1980	MWA	Edgar	Nominee	PB Original
le Carré, John	The Honorable Schoolboy	1977	1977	CWA	Gold Dagger	Winner	Novel
le Carré, John	The Spy Who Came in from the Cold	1963	1963	CWA	Gold Dagger	Winner	Novel
le Carré, John	The Spy Who Came in from the Cold	1963	1964	MWA	Edgar	Winner	Novel
le Carré, John	Call for the Dead	1961	1961	CWA	Gold Dagger	Runnerup	Novel
Lehand, Dennis	A Drink Before the War	1994	1995	B'con	Anthony	Winner	First Novel
Lehand, Dennis	A Drink Before the War	1994	1995	PWA	Shamus	Winner	First Novel
Lescroart, John T.	The 13th Juror	1994	1995	B'con	Anthony	Nominee	Novel
Lescroart, John T.	Dead Irish	1989	1991	PWA	Shamus	Nominee	Novel
Lewin, Michael Z.	Ask the Right Question	1971	1972	MWA	Edgar	Nominee	First Novel
Lindsey, David L.	In the Lake of the Moon	1988	1989	MWA	Edgar	Nominee	Novel
Lipinski, Thomas	The Fall-Down Artist	1994	1995	PWA	Shamus	Nominee	First Novel
Livingston, Jack	Die Again, Macready	1984	1985	CWA	Dagger	Nominee	Novel
Livingston, Jack	Die Again, Macready	1984	1985	PWA	Shamus	Nominee	Novel
Livingston, Jack	A Piece of the Silence	1982	1983	PWA	Shamus	Nominee	Novel

| AUTHOR NAME | | YEAR | | | AWARD | | |
Last, First	BOOK TITLE	Pub	Award	Conf'd by	Name	Status	Category

Awards List 3 – Winners and Nominees by Author's Last Name

Includes ONLY series novels written by men

Last, First	BOOK TITLE	Pub	Award	Conf'd by	Name	Status	Category
Lochte, Dick	Neon Smile	1995	1996	PWA	Shamus	Nominee	Novel
Lochte, Dick	Sleeping Dog	1985	1986	B'con	Anthony	Nominee	First Novel
Lochte, Dick	Sleeping Dog	1985	1986	MWA	Edgar	Nominee	First Novel
Lochte, Dick	Sleeping Dog	1985	1986	PWA	Shamus	Nominee	First Novel
Lochte, Dick	Sleeping Dog	1985	1986	Wolfe Pack	Nero Wolfe	Winner	Novel
Logue, John	Follow the Leader	1979	1980	MWA	Edgar	Nominee	First Novel
Lovesey, Peter	Bloodhounds	1996	1996	CWA	Silver Dagger	Winner	Novel
Lovesey, Peter	Bloodhounds	1996	1997	MRI	Macavity	Nominee	Novel
Lovesey, Peter	The Summons	1995	1995	CWA	Silver Dagger	Winner	Novel
Lovesey, Peter	The Summons	1995	1996	MWA	Edgar	Nominee	Novel
Lovesey, Peter	The Last Detective	1991	1992	B'con	Anthony	Winner	Novel
Lovesey, Peter	Waxwork	1978	1978	CWA	Silver Dagger	Winner	Novel
Lupica, Mike	Dead Air	1986	1987	MWA	Edgar	Nominee	First Novel
Lutz, John	Kiss	1988	1989	PWA	Shamus	Winner	Novel
Lutz, John	Ride the Lightning	1987	1988	PWA	Shamus	Nominee	Novel
Lutz, John	Nightlines	1985	1986	PWA	Shamus	Nominee	Novel
Lynch, Jack	San Quentin	1984	1985	PWA	Shamus	Nominee	PB Original
Lynch, Jack	Pieces of Death	1982	1983	PWA	Shamus	Nominee	PB Original
Lynch, Jack	The Missing and the Dead	1982	1983	MWA	Edgar	Nominee	PB Original
Lyons, Arthur	Hard Trade	1982	1983	PWA	Shamus	Nominee	Novel
Maitland, Barry	The Malcontenta	1995	1996	CWAA	Ned Kelly	Winner	Novel
Maitland, Barry	The Marx Sisters	1994	1995	CWA	Creasey	Nominee	First Novel
Marston, Edward	The Roaring Boy	1995	1996	MWA	Edgar	Nominee	Novel
McClure, James	The Steam Pig	1971	1971	CWA	Gold Dagger	Winner	Novel
McDonald, Gregory	Confess Fletch	1976	1977	MWA	Edgar	Winner	First Novel
McDonald, Gregory	Fletch	1974	1975	MWA	Edgar	Winner	First Novel
McGarrity, Michael	Tularosa	1996	1997	B'con	Anthony	Nominee	First Novel
McIlvanney, William	The Papers of Tony Veitch	1983	1983	CWA	Silver Dagger	Winner	Novel
McIlvanney, William	The Papers of Tony Veitch	1983	1984	MWA	Edgar	Nominee	Novel
McIlvanney, William	Laidlaw	1977	1977	CWA	Silver Dagger	Winner	Novel
McIlvanney, William	Laidlaw	1977	1978	MWA	Edgar	Nominee	Novel
Mitchell, Kirk	High Desert Malice	1995	1996	MWA	Edgar	Nominee	PB Original
Mosley, Walter	Black Betty	1994	1995	B'con	Anthony	Nominee	Novel
Mosley, Walter	White Butterfly	1993	1994	IACW	Hammett	Nominee	Novel
Mosley, Walter	White Butterfly	1993	1994	MWA	Edgar	Nominee	Novel
Mosley, Walter	Devil in a Blue Dress	1990	1991	CWA	Creasey	Winner	First Novel
Mosley, Walter	Devil in a Blue Dress	1990	1991	MWA	Edgar	Nominee	First Novel
Mosley, Walter	Devil in a Blue Dress	1990	1991	PWA	Shamus	Winner	First Novel
Murphy, Dallas	Lover Man	1987	1988	MWA	Edgar	Nominee	First Novel
Murphy, Warren B.	Too Old a Cat	1986	1987	PWA	Shamus	Nominee	PB Original
Murphy, Warren B.	Pigs Get Fat	1985	1986	MWA	Edgar	Winner	PB Original
Murphy, Warren B.	Pigs Get Fat	1985	1986	PWA	Shamus	Nominee	PB Original
Murphy, Warren B.	Trace and 47 Miles of Rope	1984	1985	PWA	Shamus	Nominee	PB Original
Murphy, Warren B.	Trace	1983	1984	MWA	Edgar	Nominee	PB Original
Murphy, Warren B.	Trace	1983	1984	PWA	Shamus	Nominee	PB Original
Murphy, Warren B.	Smoked Out	1982	1983	PWA	Shamus	Nominee	PB Original
Nava, Michael	Death of Friends	1996	1997	LBR	Lambda	Winner	Novel
Nava, Michael	The Hidden Law	1992	1993	LBR	Lambda	Winner	Novel
Nava, Michael	How Town	1990	1991	LBR	Lambda	Winner	Novel
Nava, Michael	Goldenboy	1988	1989	LBR	Lambda	Winner	Novel
Newman, G.F.	Sir, You Bastard	1970	1971	MWA	Edgar	Nominee	Novel
Nolan, William F.	Space for Hire	1971	1972	MWA	Edgar	Nominee	PB Original
Parker, Robert B.	A Catskill Eagle	1985	1986	PWA	Shamus	Nominee	Novel
Parker, Robert B.	The Widening Gyre	1983	1984	PWA	Shamus	Nominee	Novel
Parker, Robert B.	Ceremony	1982	1983	PWA	Shamus	Nominee	Novel

AUTHOR NAME		YEAR		AWARD			
Last, First	BOOK TITLE	Pub	Award	Conf'd by	Name	Status	Category

Awards List 3 – Winners and Nominees by Author's Last Name

Includes ONLY series novels written by men

Last, First	BOOK TITLE	Pub	Award	Conf'd by	Name	Status	Category
Parker, Robert B.	Early Autumn	1981	1982	PWA	Shamus	Nominee	Novel
Parker, Robert B.	Promised Land	1976	1977	MWA	Edgar	Winner	Novel
Parrish, Frank	A Fire in the Barley	1977	1978	MWA	Edgar	Nominee	Novel
Patterson, Richard N.	The Lasko Tangent	1979	1980	MWA	Edgar	Winner	First Novel
Pearce, Michael	The Mamur Zapt and the Spoils of Egypt	1993	1994	CWA	Last Laugh	Winner	Novel-Funniest
Peterson, Keith	The Rain	1989	1990	MWA	Edgar	Winner	PB Original
Peterson, Keith	The Trapdoor	1988	1989	MWA	Edgar	Nominee	PB Original
Philbrick, W.R.	Tough Enough	1989	1990	PWA	Shamus	Nominee	PB Original
Philbrick, W.R.	The Crystal Blue Persuasion	1988	1989	PWA	Shamus	Nominee	PB Original
Phillips, Mike	The Late Candidate	1990	1990	CWA	Silver Dagger	Winner	Novel
Price, Anthony	Other Paths to Glory	1974	1974	CWA	Gold Dagger	Winner	Novel
Price, Anthony	The Labyrinth Makers	1970	1970	CWA	Silver Dagger	Winner	Novel
Pronzini, Bill	Sentinels	1996	1997	PWA	Shamus	Nominee	Novel
Pronzini, Bill	Bones	1985	1986	PWA	Shamus	Nominee	Novel
Pronzini, Bill	Hoodwink	1981	1982	PWA	Shamus	Winner	Novel
Ramos, Manuel	The Ballad of Rocky Ruiz	1993	1994	MWA	Edgar	Nominee	First Novel
Randisi, Robert J.	Full Contact	1984	1985	PWA	Shamus	Nominee	Novel
Randisi, Robert J.	The Steinway Collection	1983	1984	PWA	Shamus	Nominee	PB Original
Resnicow, Herbert	The Gold Solution	1983	1984	MWA	Edgar	Nominee	First Novel
Reynolds, William J.	The Nebraska Quotient	1984	1985	PWA	Shamus	Nominee	First Novel
Richardson, Robert	The Latimer Mercy	1985	1985	CWA	Creasey	Winner	First Novel
Rider, J.W.	Jersey Tomatoes	1986	1987	PWA	Shamus	Winner	First Novel
Ripley, Mike	Angels in Arms	1991	1992	CWA	Last Laugh	Winner	Novel-Funniest
Ripley, Mike	Angel Touch	1989	1990	CWA	Last Laugh	Winner	Novel-Funniest
Roberts, Les	The Lake Effect	1994	1995	PWA	Shamus	Nominee	Novel
Roberts, Les	An Infinite Number of Monkeys	1987	1988	PWA	Shamus	Nominee	First Novel
Roberts, Les	An Infinite Number of Monkeys	1987	1986	SMP	SMP/PWA	Winner	First P.I. Novel
Robinson, Peter	Innocent Graves	1996	1997	IACW	Hammett	Nominee	Novel
Robinson, Peter	Wednesday's Child	1992	1993	CWC	Ellis	Nominee	Novel
Robinson, Peter	Wednesday's Child	1992	1993	MWA	Edgar	Nominee	Novel
Robinson, Peter	Past Reason Hated	1991	1992	CWC	Ellis	Winner	Novel
Robinson, Peter	The Hanging Valley	1989	1990	CWC	Ellis	Nominee	Novel
Robinson, Peter	A Dedicated Man	1988	1989	CWC	Ellis	Nominee	Novel
Robinson, Peter	Gallows View	1987	1988	CWA	Creasey	Nominee	First Novel
Robinson, Peter	Gallows View	1987	1988	CWC	Ellis	Nominee	First Novel
Rosen, Richard	Strike Three, You're Dead	1984	1985	MWA	Edgar	Winner	First Novel
Ross, Philip	Blue Heron	1985	1986	PWA	Shamus	Nominee	PB Original
Russell, Alan	Multiple Wounds	1996	1997	B'con	Anthony	Nominee	Novel
Russell, Alan	Multiple Wounds	1996	1997	MRI	Macavity	Nominee	Novel
Sallis, James	Moth	1993	1994	PWA	Shamus	Nominee	Novel
Sallis, James	The Long-Legged Fly	1992	1993	PWA	Shamus	Nominee	First Novel
Sarrantonio, Al	Cold Night	1989	1990	PWA	Shamus	Nominee	First Novel
Satterthwait, Walter	Escapade	1995	1996	Acad Fran	Prix Roman	Winner	Novel
Satterthwait, Walter	Escapade	1995	1996	Malice	Agatha	Nominee	Novel
Satterthwait, Walter	Wall of Glass	1989	1990	PWA	Shamus	Nominee	First Novel
Sauter, Eric	Hunter	1983	1984	MWA	Edgar	Nominee	PB Original
Saylor, Steven	Catalina's Riddle	1994	1995	IACW	Hammett	Nominee	Novel
Saylor, Steven	Catalina's Riddle	1993	1994	LBR	Lambda	Winner	Novel
Schopen, Bernard	The Desert Look	1990	1991	PWA	Shamus	Nominee	Novel
Schorr, Mark	Red Diamond, Private Eye	1983	1984	MWA	Edgar	Winner	First Novel
Schutz, Benjamin	A Fistful of Empty	1991	1992	PWA	Shamus	Nominee	Novel
Schutz, Benjamin	A Tax in Blood	1987	1988	PWA	Shamus	Winner	Novel
Schutz, Benjamin	Embrace the Wolf	1985	1986	PWA	Shamus	Nominee	Novel

AUTHOR NAME		YEAR		AWARD			
Last, First	BOOK TITLE	Pub	Award	Conf'd by	Name	Status	Category

Awards List 3 – Winners and Nominees by Author's Last Name

Includes ONLY series novels written by men

Last, First	BOOK TITLE	Pub	Award	Conf'd by	Name	Status	Category
Serafin, David	Saturday of Glory	1979	1980	CWA	Creasey	Winner	First Novel
Shaw, Simon	The Villian of the Earth	1994	1995	CWA	Last Laugh	Winner	Novel-Funniest
Simon, Roger L.	The Straight Man	1986	1987	MWA	Edgar	Nominee	Novel
Simon, Roger L.	The Big Fix	1973	1974	CWA	Creasey	Winner	First Novel
Smith, Martin Cruz	Gorky Park	1981	1981	CWA	Gold Dagger	Winner	Novel
Smith, Martin Cruz	Gypsy in Amber	1971	1972	MWA	Edgar	Winner	First Novel
Smith, Martin Cruz	Canto for a Gypsy	1972	1973	MWA	Edgar	Nominee	Novel
Solmita, Stephen	Damaged Goods	1996	1997	IACW	Hammett	Nominee	Novel
Spillane, Mickey	The Killing Man	1989	1990	PWA	Shamus	Nominee	Novel
Stark, Richard	The Sour Lemon Score	1969	1970	MWA	Edgar	Nominee	PB Original
Steed, Neville	Tinplate	1986	1987	CWA	Creasey	Winner	First Novel
Stephens, Reed	The Man Who Risked His Partner	1984	1985	PWA	Shamus	Nominee	PB Original
Stone, Michael	The Low End of Nowhere	1996	1997	PWA	Shamus	Nominee	Novel
Straley, John	The Woman Who Married a Bear	1992	1993	PWA	Shamus	Winner	First Novel
Sublett, Jesse	Rock Critic Murders	1989	1990	PWA	Shamus	Nominee	First Novel
Swanson, Doug J.	Big Town	1994	1995	B'con	Anthony	Nominee	First Novel
Swanson, Doug J.	Big Town	1994	1995	CWA	Creasey	Winner	First Novel
Swanson, Doug J.	Big Town	1994	1995	MWA	Edgar	Nominee	First Novel
Taylor, Andrew	Our Father's Lies	1985	1985	CWA	Dagger	Nominee	Novel
Taylor, Andrew	Caroline Minuscule	1982	1982	CWA	Creasey	Winner	First Novel
Taylor, Andrew	Caroline Minuscule	1982	1983	MWA	Edgar	Nominee	First Novel
Tierney, Ronald	The Stone Veil	1990	1991	PWA	Shamus	Nominee	First Novel
Trow, M. J.	Maxwell's Flame	1995	1995	CWA	Last Laugh	Nominee	Novel-Funniest
Vachss, Andrew H.	Flood	1985	1986	PWA	Shamus	Nominee	First Novel
Valin, Jonathan	Second Chance	1991	1992	PWA	Shamus	Nominee	Novel
Valin, Jonathan	Extenuating Circumstances	1989	1990	PWA	Shamus	Winner	Novel
van de Wetering, J.	Just a Corpse at Twilight	1994	1995	B'con	Anthony	Nominee	Novel
Walker, David J.	Fixed in His Folly	1995	1996	MWA	Edgar	Nominee	First Novel
Warga, Wayne	Hard Cover	1985	1986	PWA	Shamus	Winner	First Novel
West, Christopher	Death of a Blue Lantern	1994	1995	B'con	Anthony	Nominee	Novel
Westlake, Donald E.	The Hot Rock	1970	1971	MWA	Edgar	Nominee	Novel
Wingfield, R.D.	Hard Frost	1995	1996	MWA	Edgar	Nominee	PB Original
Winslow, Don	A Cool Breeze on the Underground	1991	1992	MWA	Edgar	Nominee	First Novel
Winslow, Don	A Cool Breeze on the Underground	1991	1992	PWA	Shamus	Nominee	First Novel
Womack, Steven	Chain of Fools	1996	1997	B'con	Anthony	Nominee	PB Original
Womack, Steven	Chain of Fools	1996	1997	PWA	Shamus	Nominee	PB Original
Womack, Steven	Way Past Dead	1995	1996	PWA	Shamus	Nominee	PB Original
Womack, Steven	Dead Folk's Blues	1993	1994	MWA	Edgar	Winner	PB Original
Womack, Steven	Torch Town Boogie	1993	1994	PWA	Shamus	Nominee	PB Original
Woodrell, Dan	The Ones You Do	1988	1989	IACW	Hammett	Nominee	Novel
Wright, Eric	Death in the Old Country	1985	1986	CWC	Ellis	Winner	Novel
Wright, Eric	The Night the Gods Smiled	1983	1983	CWA	Creasey	Winner	First Novel
Wright, Eric	The Night the Gods Smiled	1983	1984	CWC	Ellis	Winner	Novel
Zimmerman, R.D.	Tribe	1996	1997	MWA	Edgar	Nominee	PB Original
Zimmerman, R.D.	Closet	1995	1996	B'con	Anthony	Nominee	PB Original
Zimmerman, R.D.	Closet	1995	1996	LBR	Lambda	Winner	Novel
Zimmerman, Bruce	Blood Under the Bridge	1989	1990	MWA	Edgar	Nominee	First Novel
Zubro, Mark	A Simple Suburban Murder	1989	1990	LBR	Lambda	Winner	Novel

Mystery Book Awards Glossary

The **Agatha Awards**, in honor of Dame Agatha Christie, are conferred by voters at Malice Domestic, the annual author and fan convention held in April or early May in Bethesda, Maryland. Dedicated to cozy and traditional mysteries, this award is in the form of a teapot. St. Martin's Press and Malice Domestic also sponsor a Best First Novel contest for cozy mysteries. The 1997 prize includes 1998 publication by St. Martin's Press and a $10,000 cash award.

Anthony Awards, voted each year by the membership of the World Mystery Convention, are presented annually at Bouchercon for work published during the prior year. Named in honor of Anthony Boucher (William Anthony Parker White), the prize categories change from year to year along with the convention organizing committee, the actual shape of the award and the convention location. 1997 categories included Best Novel, Best First Novel, Best Paperback Original, Best Short Story, Best Critical/Biographical and Best Fanzine.

Given by the Crime Writers of Canada since 1984, the **Arthur Ellis Awards** are named after the nom de travail of Canada's official hangman. Categories include Best Novel, Best First Novel, Best Short Story, Best True Crime, Best Juvenile and Best Play published by a Canadian author. The award statuette is a wooden gallows with its own rope and hanging puppet.

The British Crime Writers' Association (CWA), formed in 1953, was patterned after its US counterpart, the Mystery Writers of America. In 1955 CWA began awarding special honors to the best crime novel of the year. Originally named the Crossed Red Herrings Award, the prize later became known as the **Gold Dagger. A Silver Dagger** has been awarded to the runner-up since 1969. As of 1973 the association began conferring the **John Creasey Memorial Award** for best first novel, in honor of the famous British mystery writer (1908-1973) who produced almost 600 titles of mystery, crime, romance, western and suspense under 28 pseudonyms.

Sponsored by Cartier since 1986 is the **Diamond Dagger Award** for lifetime achievement. Since 1989 the **Last Laugh** award has gone to the funniest crime novel of the year. Hazel Wyn Jones created the **CWA '92** award (1990-1992) for best crime novel set partly or wholly in Europe. From 1985 to 1987, *The Police Review* sponsored an award for the crime novel that best portrayed police procedure. CWA awards are typically announced in December for books of the current year.

Each year since 1945, usually in April or May, Mystery Writers of America (MWA) confer the **Edgar Awards** (named for Edgar Allen Poe) in a variety of categories, including Best Novel, Best First Novel, Best Short Story, Best Original Paperback, Best Juvenile, Best Episode in a TV series, Best Fact Crime, Best TV Feature, Best Critical/Biographical, Best Motion Picture, and Best Young Adult.

Beginning with its selection of Agatha Christie in 1955, MWA began naming Grand Masters which now include 41 best-of-the-best:

1997	Ruth Rendell
1996	**Dick Francis**
1995	**Mickey Spillane**
1994	**Lawrence Block**
1993	**Donald Westlake**
1992	**Elmore Leonard**
1991	**Tony Hillerman**
1990	Helen McCloy
1989	**Hillary Waugh**
1988	Phyllis A. Whitney
1987	**Michael Gilbert**
1986	**Ed McBain**
1985	Dorothy Salisbury Davis
1984	**John le Carré**
1983	Margaret Millar
1982	**Julian Symons**
1981	**Stanley Ellin**
1980	**W.R. Burnett**
1979	**Aaron Marc Stein**
1978	Daphne du Maurier
	Dorothy B. Hughes
	Nagio Marsh

1977	*no award given*
1976	**Graham Greene**
1975	**Eric Ambler**
1974	**Ross Macdonald**
1973	**Judson Phillips**
	Alfred Hitchcock
1972	**John D. MacDonald**
1971	Mignon G. Eberhart
1970	**James M. Cain**
1969	**John Creasey**
1968	*no award given*
1967	**Baynard Kendrick**
1966	**Georges Simenon**
1965	*no award given*
1964	**George Harmon Coxe**
1963	**John Dickson Carr**
1962	**Erle Stanley Gardner**
1961	**Ellery Queen (Frederic Dannay and Manfred B. Lee)**
1960	*no award given*
1959	**Rex Stout**
1958	**Vincent Starrett**
1957	*no award given*
1956	*no award given*
1955	Agatha Christie

The International Association of Crime Writers (North American Branch), established in 1987, has presented the North American **Hammett Prize** annually since 1992 for the best work (fiction or nonfiction) of literary excellence in crime-writing by a US or Canadian author. The trophy is a bronze sculpture of a falcon-headed thin man symbolizing the literary spirit of Dashiell Hammett.

The Lambda Literary Awards, sponsored by the *Lambda Book Report* since 1989, are given annually to recognize excellence in gay and lesbian writing and publishing in the United States during the previous year. Including Best Lesbian Mystery and Best Gay Men's Mystery, Lambda awards are given in a total of 20 categories.

Mystery Readers International (MRI) has presented the **Macavity Awards** annually since 1987. Named for T.S. Eliot's mystery cat in **Old**

Possum's Book of Practical Cats, these awards are voted by MRI membership in four categories—Best Novel, Best First Novel, Best Non-Fiction and Best Short Story.

In 1996 Crime Writers' Association of Australia conferred its first **Ned Kelly Awards** named for the notorious 19th century Australian outlaw. Best Australian Crime Novel was shared by Barry Maitland (*The Malcontenta*) and Paul Thomas (*Inside Dope*), while John Dale (*Dark Angel*) won for Best First Australian Novel. Jon Cleary is the first recipient of the Lifetime Contribution Award.

Since 1979 the **Nero Wolfe Award** has been given to the novel that best captures the spirit and fair play of the work of Rex Stout, creator of Nero Wolfe, America's foremost armchair detective. This award is conferred by a group of Rex Stout aficionados known as the Wolfe Pack at their Black Orchid Dinner in New York each December.

The **Prix Roman d'Aventure** is an award given in France for best adventure novel. The 1996 award went to the French edition of *Escapade* by Walter Satterthwait who was flown to Paris for a black tie dinner in his honor.

The Private Eye Writers of America (PWA), founded by Robert J. Randisi in 1981, gave its first **Shamus Awards** (for works published in 1981) at Bouchercon XIII in San Francisco. Shamus award categories include Best Private Eye Novel, Best Private Eye Paperback Original, Best Private Eye Short Story (beginning in 1983), Best First Private Eye Novel (beginning in 1984) and The Eye Life Achievement Award. In recent years the private eye category has been expanded to include investigators who are paid for services rendered as part of their investigative work, such as news reporters and attorneys who do their own investigating.

In 1986 **St. Martin's Press and PWA (SMP/PWA)** launched a contest for Best First Private Eye Novel which has become an annual event. The award-winning PI novel is published simultaneously in the US by St. Martin's Press and in England by Macmillan.

Bibliography

The Armchair Detective, Vols. 27-30, Stine, Kate, editor-in-chief. New York: The Armchair Detective, Inc., 1994-1997.

The Armchair Detective Book of Lists. Revised Second Edition. Stine, Kate, editor. New York: Otto Penzler Books, 1995 by The Armchair Detective.

Bouchercon 25-28 Program Books, 1994-1997.

BuffCon '95 Program Book, 1995.

CADS, Crime and Detective Stories, Nos. 20-30, 1993-1997. Bradley, Geoff, editor, Essex, England.

Canadian Crime Fiction. An Annotated Comprehensive Bibliography of Canadian Crime Fiction from 1817 to 1996. Compiled by L. David St. C. Skene-Melvin. Shelburne, Ontario, Canada: The Battered Silicon Dispatch Box, 1996.

Cluefest, Dallas Mystery Readers Book Fair Program Books, 1996 and 1997.

Contemporary Authors, Volumes 1-157 and *Contemporary Authors New Revision Series*, Volumes 1-58. Gale Research, Detroit, Michigan.

Crime Fiction II, A Comprehensive Bibliography 1749-1990. Vols. 1-2. Hubin, Allen J. New York & London: Garland Publishing, Inc. 1994.

Crime In Store, London's Crime and Mystery Store Catalogues Nos. 2-6, 1996-1997.

Crimes of the Scene. A Mystery Novel Guide for the International Traveler. King, Nina with Robin Winks and other contributors, New York: St. Martin's Press, 1997.

The Crown Crime Companion, Compiled by Mickey Friedman. New York: Crown Publishers, 1995.

Deadly Pleasures, Nos. 1-17, 1993-1997. Easter, George A., editor.

Deadly Serious, References for Writers of Detective, Mystery and Crime Fiction. Villines, Sharon, editor, 1995.

Detectionary. A biographical dictionary of leading characters in mystery fiction. Compiled by Otto Penzler, Chris Steinbrunner, Marvin Lachman, Charles Shilbuk, Francis M. Nevins, Jr. Edited by Otto Penzler, Chris Steinbrunner, Marvin Lachman. Woodstock, NY: The Overlook Press, 1971.

Doubleday Crime Club Compendium, *1928-1991.* Nehr, Ellen, Martinez, CA: Offspring Press, 1992.

The Drood Review of Mystery, Nos. 133-148. Jim Huang, editor and publisher. Kalamazoo, Michigan: The Drood Review, 1994-1997.

Encyclopedia Mysteriosa, A Comprehensive Guide to the Art of Detection in Print, Film, Radio, and Television. DeAndrea, William L., New York: Prentice Hall General Reference, 1994.

EyeCon '95 Program Book, 1995.

Fine Art of Murder, The Mystery Reader's Indispensable Companion. Gorman, Ed, Martin H. Greenburg, Larry Segriff, editors with Jon L. Breen. New York: Carroll & Graf, 1993.

Genreflecting, A Guide to Reading Interests in Genre Fiction. Rosenberg, Betty and Diana Tixier Herald, editors, Third Edition, 1991. Englewood, Colorado: Libraries Unlimited, Inc.

Gun in Cheek, An Affectionate Guide to the "Worst" in Mystery Fiction. Pronzini, Bill, editor. New York: The Mysterious Press. 1982.

Hawk's Authors' Pseudonyms II. A comprehensive reference of Modern Authors' Pseudonyms. Compiled by Pat Hawk, Second Edition, Southlake, TX, 1995.

Left Coast Crime 6 and 7 Program Books,1996-1997.

Magna Cum Murder Program Books, 1995-1996. Ball State University, Muncie, Indiana.

Malice Domestic I-IX Program Books, 1989-1997.

Mid Atlantic Mystery Book Fair and Convention Program Books, 1995-1997.

Mostly Murder: Your Guide to Reading Mysteries. Setliff, Jay W.K., editor and publisher, 1994-1997. Dallas, Texas: Mostly Book Reviews, Inc.

Murder Ink, The Mystery Reader's Companion. Winn, Dilys, editor. New York: Workman Publishing, 1977.

Murderess Ink, The Better Half of Mystery. Winn, Dilys editor. New York: Workman Publishing, 1979.

Murderous Intent. A Magazine of Mystery & Suspense, 1995-1997. Power, Margo, editor. Vancouver WA: Madison Publishing Co.

Mystery News, 1994-96. Harriett Stay, editor, Port Townsend, WA.

Mystery News, 1997. Lynn Kaczmarek and Chris Aldrich, editors. Black Raven Press

Mystery & Detective Monthly, 1995-1997. Robert S. Napier, editor. Tacoma, WA: Snapbrim Press.

Mystery Readers Journal, The Journal of Mystery Readers International. Vols. 10-13, 1994-1997. Rudolph, Janet A., editor. Berkeley. CA.

The Mystery Review, A Quarterly Publication for Mystery Readers. Vols. 2-5, 1994-1997. Barbara Davey, editor. Colborne, Ontario, Canada.

Mystery Scene Magazine, Nos. 41-57, 1994-1997. Joe W. Gorman, editor. Cedar Rapids, IA: Mystery Enterprises.

Mystery Writers Market Place and Sourcebook. Collingwood, Donna, editor. Cincinnati: Writer's Digest Books, 1993.

Novel Verdicts: A Guide to Courtroom Fiction. Breen, Jon L., editor. Metuchen, NJ & London: The Scarecrow Press, Inc., 1984.

100 Great Detectives. Maxim Jakubowski, editor. New York: Carroll & Graf Publishers, Inc., 1991.

1001 Midnights, The Aficionado's Guide to Mystery and Detective Fiction. Bill Pronzini and Marcia Muller. New York: Arbor House, 1986.

Private Eyes: One Hundred and One Knights. A Survey of American Detective Fiction 1922-1984. Baker, Robert A. and Michael T. Nietzel. Bowling Green, OH: Bowling Green State University Popular Press, 1985.

Publishers Weekly, The International News Magazine of Book Publishing and Bookselling. 1995-1997. A Cahners/R.R. Bowker Publication.

The Purloined Letter, A monthly publication of The Rue Morgue Mystery Bookstore. Volumes 17 and 18, Boulder, CO, 1996-1997.

A Reader's Guide to the American Novel of Detection. Lachman, Marvin. New York: G. K. Hall & Co., 1993.

A Reader's Guide to the Classic British Mystery. Oleksiw, Susan. New York: Mysterious Press, 1989. Originally published by G.K. Hall & Co., Boston, 1988.

A Reader's Guide to the Police Procedural. Vicarel, Jo Ann, editor. New York: G.K. Hall & Co., 1995.

A Reader's Guide to The Private Eye Novel. Neibuhr, Gary Warren, New York: G.K. Hall & Co., 1993.

St. James Guide to Crime and Mystery Writes. Fourth Edition. Pederson, Jay P., editor. St. James Press, An Imprint of Gale, Detroit, 1996.

St. Martin's Press catalogues. Fall '93 through Fall '97.

The Shamus Awards 1982-1996. Compiled by Jan Grape and Dick Higgins. Private Eye Writers of America, 1996.

Spooks, Spies and Private Eyes: Black Mystery, Crime and Suspense Fiction. Woods, Paula, editor. Main Street Books, 1996.

The Subject is Murder. A Selective Subject Guide to Mystery Fiction. Menendez, Albert J., editor. New York &London: Garland Publishing, Inc., 1986.

Twentieth-Century Crime and Mystery Writers. Second Edition. Reilly, John M., editor. Chicago & London: St. James Press, 1985.

Twentieth-Century Crime and Mystery Writers. Third Edition. Henderson, Leslie, editor. London & Chicago: St. James Press, 1991.

The Ultimate Movie Thesaurus. A Henry Holt Reference Book. Case, Christopher. New York: Henry Holt and Company, 1996.

www.amazon.com, On-line catalogues and author interviews, 1997.

What About Murder? (1981-1991) A Guide to Books About Mystery and Detective Fiction. Breen, Jon L., editor. Metuchen, NJ & London: The Scarecrow Press, Inc., 1993.

What About Murder? A Guide to Books About Mystery and Detective Fiction. Breen, Jon L., editor. Metuchen, NJ & London: The Scarecrow Press, Inc., 1981.

What Do I Read Next? A Reader's Guide to Current Genre Fiction, 1990-1994. Detroit & London: Gale Research Inc.

Who Done It? A Guide to Detective Mystery and Suspense Fiction. Hagen, Ordean A. New York & London: R.R. Bowker Co., 1969.

Writing Mysteries. A Handbook By The Mystery Writers of America. Grafton, Sue, editor. Cincinnati OH: Writer's Digest Books, 1992.

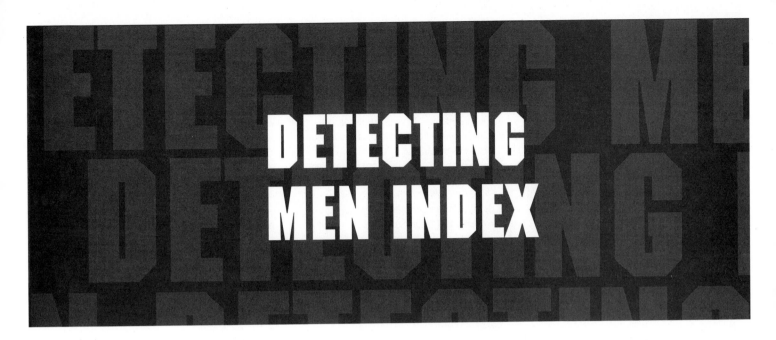

DETECTING MEN INDEX

■ *denotes authors in Master List*

■ *denotes authors in Master List*

■ *denotes authors in Master List*

H

■ *denotes authors in Master List*

Q

R

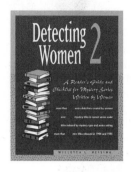

Winner of the 1997 Agatha, Anthony and Macavity Awards and 1997 Edgar nominee for Best Critical/Biographical ★★★☆

Mystery fans will wonder how they ever got along without this easy-to-use, fun-to-browse book which profiles over 500 women writers of series mysteries. Contains information on more than 3,500 titles in 650 mystery series, including over 500 new titles from 1994-95.

ISBN: 0-9644593-1-0
384 pages, 8-1/2 by 11 softcover, $24.95, c.1996

Don't miss the handy pocket guide checklist of all 3,500 titles in correct order by author and series. The perfect size to tuck in a book bag, briefcase or purse for trips to the bookstore or library, to keep track of what you've read and what book is next in your favorite series.

ISBN: 0-9644593-2-9
128 pages, 3-3/4 by 6-1/2-inch vinyl-covered paperback, $14.95, c.1996

Don't miss the Pocket Guide companion to the full-text edition of Detecting Men

122 ❧ DETECTING MEN

Timothy Cone
- ❏ ❏ 1 - The Timothy Files (1987)
- ❏ ❏ 2 - Timothy's Game (1988)

SANDERS, William
Taggart Roper
- ❏ ❏ 1 - The Next Victim (1993)
- ❏ ❏ 2 - A Death on 66 (1994)
- ❏ ❏ 3 - Blood Autumn (1995)

SANDFORD, John [P]
Anna Batory
- ❏ ❏ 1 - The Night Crew (1997)
Kidd & Luellen
- ❏ ❏ 1 - The Fool's Run (1989)
- ❏ ❏ 2 - The Empress File (1991)
Lucas Davenport
- ❏ ❏ 1 - Rules of Prey (1989)
- ❏ ❏ 2 - Shadow Prey (1990)
- ❏ ❏ 3 - Eyes of Prey (1991)
- ❏ ❏ 4 - Silent Prey (1992)
- ❏ ❏ 5 - Winter Prey (1993)
- ❏ ❏ 6 - Night Prey (1994)
- ❏ ❏ 7 - Mind Prey (1995)
- ❏ ❏ 8 - Sudden Prey (1996)

SARRANTONIO, AI
Jack Blaine
- ❏ ❏ 1 - Cold Night (1989) ☆
- ❏ ❏ 2 - Summer Cool (1993)

SATTERTHWAIT, Walter
Houdini & Conan Doyle
- ❏ ❏ 1 - Escapade (1995) ★ ☆
- ❏ ❏ 2 - Masquerade (1998)
Joshua Croft
- ❏ ❏ 1 - Wall of Glass (1989) ☆
- ❏ ❏ 2 - At Ease With the Dead (1991)
- ❏ ❏ 3 - A Flower in the Desert (1992)
- ❏ ❏ 4 - The Hanged Man (1993)
- ❏ ❏ 5 - Accustomed to the Dark (1996)

SAUTER, Eric
Robert Lee Hunter
- ❏ ❏ 1 - Hunter (1983) ☆
- ❏ ❏ 2 - Hunter and the Ikon (1984)
- ❏ ❏ 3 - Hunter and the Raven (1984)

SAYLOR, Steven
Gordianus the Finder
- ❏ ❏ 1 - Roman Blood (1990)
- ❏ ❏ 2 - Arms of Nemesis (1992)
- ❏ ❏ 3 - Catalina's Riddle (1994) ★
- ❏ ❏ 4 - The Venus Throw (1995)
- ❏ ❏ 5 - A Murder on the Appian Way (1996)
- ❏ ❏ 6 - House of the Vestals (1997)

SCHOLEFIELD, Alan
George Macrae, Det. Supt. & Leopold Silver, Det. Sgt.
- ❏ ❏ 1 - Dirty Weekend (1989)
- ❏ ❏ 2 - Thief Taker (1991)
- ❏ ❏ 3 - Never Die in January (1992)
- ❏ ❏ 4 - Threats and Menaces (1993)
- ❏ ❏ 5 - Burn Out (1994)
- ❏ ❏ 6 - Night Moves (1996)
Ann Vernon, Dr.
- ❏ ❏ 1 - Burn Out (1994)
- ❏ ❏ 2 - Buried Treasure (1995)

SCHOONOVER, Winston [P]
John Wilkes
- ❏ ❏ 1 - Wilkes: His Life and Crimes (1990)
- ❏ ❏ 2 - Wilkes on Trial [as by Charles Sevilla] (1993)

SCHOPEN, Bernard
Jack Ross
- ❏ ❏ 1 - The Big Silence (1989)
- ❏ ❏ 2 - The Desert Look (1990) ☆

SCHORR, Mark
Robert Stark
- ❏ ❏ 1 - Overkill (1988)
- ❏ ❏ 2 - Gunpower (1990)
- ❏ ❏ 3 - Seize the Dragon (1990)
Simon Jaffe aka Red Diamond
- ❏ ❏ 1 - Red Diamond, Private Eye (1983) ★
- ❏ ❏ 2 - Ace of Diamonds (1984)
- ❏ ❏ 3 - Diamond Rock (1985)

SCHUTZ, Benjamin
Leo Haggerty
- ❏ ❏ 1 - Embrace the Wolf (1985) ☆
- ❏ ❏ 2 - All the Old Bargains (1985)
- ❏ ❏ 3 - A Tax in Blood (1987) ★

pocket guide ➡ 123

sample pages

ISBN: 0-9644593-4-5   **144 pages, 4 by 7-inch vinyl-covered paperback, $16.95, c.1997**